Contents

Making Things Talk

Second Edition

Tom Igoe

O'REILLY®

BEIJING · CAMBRIDGE · FARNHAM · KÖLN · SEBASTOPOL · TOKYO

Making Things Talk

by Tom Igoe

Published by O'Reilly Media, Inc.
1005 Gravenstein Highway North, Sebastopol, CA 95472.

O'Reilly books may be purchased for educational, business, or sales promotional use.
For more information, contact our corporate/institutional sales department:
800-998-9938 or *corporate@oreilly.com*.

Print History	Editor: Brian Jepson
September 2007	Proofreader: Marlowe Shaeffer
First Edition	Cover Designer: Karen Montgomery
	Production Editor: Adam Zaremba
September 2011	Indexer: Lucie Haskins
Second Edition	Cover Photograph: Tom Igoe

ISBN: 978-1-449-39243-7
[TI]

Preface

A few years ago, Neil Gershenfeld wrote a smart book called *When Things Start to Think*. In it, he discussed a world in which everyday objects and devices are endowed with computational power: in other words, today. He talked about the implications of devices that exchange information about our identities, abilities, and actions. It's a good read, but I think he got the title wrong. I would have called it *When Things Start to Gossip*, because—let's face it—even the most exciting thoughts are worthwhile only once you start to talk to someone else about them. *Making Things Talk* teaches you how to make things that have computational power talk to each other, and about giving people the ability to use those things to communicate.

For a couple of decades now, computer scientists have used the term object-oriented programming to refer to a style of software development in which programs and sub-programs are thought of as objects. Like physical objects, they have properties and behaviors. They inherit these properties from the prototypes from which they descend. The canonical form of any object in software is the code that describes its type. Software objects make it easy to recombine objects in novel ways. You can reuse a software object if you know its interface—the collection of proper-ties and methods to which its creator allows you access (as well as the documents so that you know how to use them). It doesn't matter how a software object does what it does, as long as it does it consistently. Software objects are most effective when they're easy to understand and when they work well with other objects.

In the physical world, we're surrounded by all kinds of electronic objects: clock radios, toasters, mobile phones, music players, children's toys, and more. It can take a lot of work and a significant amount of knowledge to make a useful electronic gadget—it can take almost as much knowledge to make those gadgets talk to each other in useful ways. But that doesn't have to be the case. Electronic devices can be—and often are—built up from simple modules. As long as you understand the interfaces, you can make anything from them. Think of it as object-oriented hardware. Understanding the ways in which things talk to each other is central to making this work, regardless of whether the object is a toaster, an email program on your laptop, or a networked database. All of these objects can be connected if you can figure out how they communicate. This book is a guide to some of the tools for making those connections.

X

❝❝ Who This Book Is For

This book is written for people who want to make things talk to other things. Maybe you're a science teacher who wants to show your students how to monitor weather conditions at several locations around your school district simultaneously, or a sculptor who wants to make a whole room of choreographed mechanical sculptures. You might be an industrial designer who needs to be able to build quick mockups of new products, modeling both their forms and their functions. Maybe you're a cat owner, and you'd like to be able to play with your cat while you're away from home. This book is a primer for people with little technical training and a lot of interest. This book is for people who want to get projects done.

The main tools in this book are personal computers, web servers, and microcontrollers, the tiny computers inside everyday appliances. Over the past decade, microcontrollers and their programming tools have gone from being arcane items to common, easy-to-use tools. Elementary school students are using the tools that baffled graduate students only a decade ago. During that time, my colleagues and I have taught people from diverse backgrounds (few of them computer programmers) how to use these tools to increase the range of physical actions that computers can respond to, sense, and interpret.

In recent years, there's been a rising interest among people using microcontrollers to make their devices not only sense and control the physical world, but also talk to other things about what they're sensing and controlling. If you've built something with a Basic Stamp or a Lego Mindstorms kit, and want to make that thing communicate with things you or others have built, this book is for you. It is also useful for software programmers familiar with networking and web services who want an introduction to embedded network programming.

If you're the type of person who likes to get down to the very core of a technology, you may not find what you're looking for in this book. There aren't detailed code samples for Bluetooth or TCP/IP stacks, nor are there circuit diagrams for Ethernet controller chips. The

components used here strike a balance between simplicity, flexibility, and cost. They use object-oriented hardware, requiring relatively little wiring or code. They're designed to get you to the end goal of making things talk to each other as quickly as possible.
X

❝ What You Need to Know

In order to get the most from this book, you should have a basic knowledge of electronics and programming microcontrollers, some familiarity with the Internet, and access to both.

Many people whose programming experience begins with microcontrollers can do wonderful things with some sensors and a couple of servomotors, but they may not have done much to enable communication between the microcontroller and other programs on a personal computer. Similarly, many experienced network and multimedia programmers have never experimented with hardware of any sort, including microcontrollers. If you're either of these people, this book is for you. Because the audience of this book is diverse, you may find some of the introductory material a bit simple, depending on your background. If so, feel free to skip past the stuff you know to get to the meatier parts.

If you've never used a microcontroller, you'll need a little background before starting this book. I recommend you read my previous book, **Physical Computing: Sensing and Controlling the Physical World with Computers** (Thomson), co-authored with Dan O'Sullivan, which introduces the fundamentals of electronics, microcontrollers, and physical interaction design.

You should also have a basic understanding of computer programming before reading much further. If you've never done any programming, check out the Processing programming environment at www.processing.org. Processing is a simple language designed to teach nonprogrammers how to program, yet it's powerful enough to do a number of advanced tasks. It will be used throughout this book whenever graphic interface programming is needed.

This book includes code examples in a few different programming languages. They're all fairly simple examples, so if you don't want to work in the languages provided, you can use the comments in these examples to rewrite them in your favorite language.
X

❝ Contents of This Book

This book explains the concepts that underlie networked objects and then provides recipes to illustrate each set of concepts. Each chapter contains instructions for building working projects that make use of the new ideas introduced in that chapter.

In Chapter 1, you'll encounter the major programming tools in the book and get to "Hello World!" on each of them.

Chapter 2 introduces the most basic concepts needed to make things talk to each other. It covers the characteristics that need to be agreed upon in advance, and how keeping those things separate in your mind helps troubleshooting. You'll build a simple project that features one-to-one serial communication between a microcontroller and a personal computer using Bluetooth radios as an example of modem communication. You'll learn about data protocols, modem devices, and address schemes.

Chapter 3 introduces a more complex network: the Internet. It discusses the basic devices that hold it together, as well as the basic relationships among those devices. You'll see the messages that underlie some of the most common tasks you do on the Internet every day, and learn how to send those messages. You'll write your first set of programs to send data across the Net based on a physical activity in your home.

In Chapter 4, you'll build your first embedded device. You'll get more experience with command-line connections to the Net, and you'll connect a microcontroller to a web server without using a desktop or laptop computer as an intermediary.

Chapter 5 takes the Net connection a step further by explaining socket connections, which allow for longer interaction. You'll learn how to write your own server program that you can connect to anything connected to the Net. You'll connect to this server program from the command line and from a microcontroller, so that you can understand how different types of devices can connect to each other through the same server.

Chapter 6 introduces wireless communication. You'll learn some of the characteristics of wireless, along with its possibilities and limitations. Several short examples in this chapter enable you to say "Hello World!" over the air in a number of ways.

Chapter 7 offers a contrast to the socket connections of Chapter 5, by introducing message-based protocols like UDP on the Internet, and ZigBee and 802.15.4 for wireless networks. Instead of using the client-server model from earlier chapters, here you'll learn how to design conversations where each object in a network is equal to the others, exchanging information one message at a time.

Chapter 8 is about location. It introduces a few tools to help you locate things in physical space, and it offers some thoughts on the relationship between physical location and network relationships.

Chapter 9 deals with identification in physical space and network space. You'll learn a few techniques for generating unique network identities based on physical characteristics. You'll also learn a bit about how to determine a networked device's characteristics.

Chapter 10 introduces mobile telephony networks, covering many of the things that you can now do with phones and phone networks.

Chapter 11 provides a look back at the different types of protocols covered in this book, and gives you a framework to fit them all into for future reference.
X

🙶 On Buying Parts

You'll need a lot of parts for all of the projects in this book. As a result, you'll learn about a lot of vendors. Because there are no large electronics parts retailers in my city, I buy parts online all the time. If you're lucky enough to live in an area where you can buy from a brick-and-mortar store, good for you! If not, get to know some of these online vendors.

Jameco (http://jameco.com), Digi-Key (www.digikey.com), and Farnell (www.farnell.com) are general electronics parts retailers, and they sell many of the same things. Others, like Maker Shed (www.makershed.com), SparkFun (www.sparkfun.com), and Adafruit (http://adafruit.com) carry specialty components, kits, and bundles that make it easy to do popular projects. A full list of suppliers is included in the Appendix. Feel free to substitute parts for things with which you are familiar.

Because it's easy to order goods online, you might be tempted to communicate with vendors entirely through their websites. Don't be afraid to pick up the phone as well. Particularly when you're new to this type of project, it helps to talk to someone about what you're ordering and to ask questions. You're likely to find helpful people at the end of the phone line for most of the retailers listed here. I've listed phone numbers wherever possible—use them.
X

❝ Using Code Examples

This book is here to help you get your job done. In general, you may use the code in this book in your programs and documentation. You do not need to contact us for permission unless you're reproducing a significant portion of the code.

For example, writing a program that uses several chunks of code from this book does not require permission. Selling or distributing a CD-ROM of examples from O'Reilly books does require permission. Answering a question by citing this book and quoting example code does not require permission. Incorporating a significant amount of example code from this book into your product's documentation does require permission.

We appreciate attribution. An attribution usually includes the title, author, publisher, and ISBN. For example: "*Making Things Talk: Practical Methods for Connecting Physical Objects*, by Tom Igoe. Copyright 2011 O'Reilly Media, 978-1-4493-9243-7." If you feel that your use of code examples falls outside fair use or the permission given above, feel free to contact us at permissions@oreilly.com.

X

❝ Using Circuit Examples

In building the projects in this book, you're going to break things and void warranties. If you're averse to this, put this book down and walk away. This is not a book for those who are squeamish about taking things apart without knowing whether they'll go back together again.

Even though we want you to be adventurous, we also want you to be safe. Please don't take any unnecessary risks when building this book's projects. Every set of instructions is written with safety in mind; ignore the safety instructions at your own peril. Be sure you have the appropriate level of knowledge and experience to get the job done in a safe manner.

Please keep in mind that the projects and circuits shown in this book are for instructional purposes only. Details like power conditioning, automatic resets, RF shielding, and other things that make an electronic product certifiably ready for market are not included here. If you're designing real products to be used by people other than yourself, please do not rely on this information alone.

X

❝ Acknowledgments for the First Edition

This book is the product of many conversations and collaborations. It would not have been possible without the support and encouragement of my own network.

The Interactive Telecommunications Program in the Tisch School of the Arts at New York University has been my home for more than the past decade. It is a lively and warm place to work, crowded with many talented people. This book grew out of a class, Networked Objects, that I have taught there for several years. I hope that the ideas herein represent the spirit of the place and give you a sense of my enjoyment in working there.

Red Burns, the department's founder, has supported me since I first entered this field. She indulged my many flights of fancy and brought me firmly down to earth when needed. On every project, she challenges me to make sure that I use technology not for its own sake, but always so it empowers people.

Dan O'Sullivan, my colleague and now chair of the program, introduced me to physical computing and then generously allowed me to share in teaching it and shaping its role at ITP. He is a great advisor and collaborator, and offered constant feedback as I worked. Most of the chapters started with a rambling conversation with Dan. His fingerprints are all over this book, and it's a better book for it.

Clay Shirky, Daniel Rozin, and Dan Shiffman were also close advisors on this project. Clay watched indulgently as the pile of parts mounted in our office, and he graciously interrupted his own writing to give opinions on my ideas. Daniel Rozin offered valuable critical insight as well, and his ideas are heavily influential in this book. Dan Shiffman read many drafts and offered helpful feedback. He also contributed many great code samples and libraries.

Fellow faculty members Marianne Petit, Nancy Hechinger, and Jean-Marc Gauthier were supportive throughout this writing, offering encouragement and inspiration, covering departmental duties for me, and offering inspiration through their own work.

The rest of the faculty and staff at ITP also made this possible. George Agudow, Edward Gordon, Midori Yasuda, Megan Demarest, Nancy Lewis, Robert Ryan, John Duane, Marlon Evans, Tony Tseng, and Gloria Sed tolerated all kinds of insanity in the name of physical computing and networked objects, and made things possible for the other faculty and me, as well as the students. Research residents Carlyn Maw, Todd Holoubek, John Schimmel, Doria Fan, David Nolen, Peter Kerlin, and Michael Olson assisted faculty and students over the past few years to realize projects that influenced the ones you see in these chapters. Faculty members Patrick Dwyer, Michael Schneider, Greg Shakar, Scott Fitzgerald, Jamie Allen, Shawn Van Every, James Tu, and Raffi Krikorian have used the tools from this book in their classes, or have lent their own techniques to the projects described here.

The students of ITP have pushed the boundaries of possibility in this area, and their work is reflected in many of the projects. I cite specifics where they come up, but in general, I'd like to thank all the students who took my Networked Objects class—they helped me understand what this is all about. Those from the 2006 and 2007 classes were particularly influential, because they had to learn the stuff from early drafts of this book. They have caught several important mistakes in the manuscript.

A few people contributed significant amounts of code, ideas, or labor to this book. Geoff Smith gave me the original title for the course, Networked Objects, and introduced me to the idea of object-oriented hardware. John Schimmel showed me how to get a microcontroller to make HTTP calls. Dan O'Sullivan's server code was the root of all of my server code. All of my Processing code is more readable because of Dan Shiffman's coding style advice. Robert Faludi contributed many pieces of code, made the XBee examples in this book simpler to read, and corrected errors in many of them. Max Whitney helped me get Bluetooth exchanges working and get the cat bed finished (despite her allergies!). Dennis Crowley made the possibilities and limitations of 2D barcodes clear to me. Chris Heathcote heavily influenced my ideas on location. Durrell Bishop helped me think about identity. Mike Kuniavsky and the folks at the "Sketching in Hardware" workshops in 2006 and 2007 helped me see this work as part of a larger community, and introduced me to a lot of new tools. Noodles the cat put up with all manner of silliness in order to finish the cat bed and its photos. No animals were harmed in the making of this book, though one was bribed with catnip.

Casey Reas and Ben Fry made the software side of this book possible by creating Processing. Without Processing, the software side of networked objects was much more painful. Without Processing, there would be no simple, elegant programming interface for Arduino and Wiring. The originators of Arduino and Wiring made the hardware side of this book possible: Massimo Banzi, Gianluca Martino, David Cuartielles, and David Mellis on Arduino; Hernando Barragán on Wiring; and Nicholas Zambetti bridging the two. I have been lucky to work with them.

Though I've tried to use and cite many hardware vendors in this book, I must give a special mention to Nathan Seidle at Spark Fun. This book would not be what it is without him. While I've been talking about object-oriented hardware for years, Nathan and the folks at SparkFun have been quietly making it a reality.

Thanks also to the support team at Lantronix. Their products are good and their support is excellent. Garry Morris, Gary Marrs, and Jenny Eisenhauer answered my countless emails and phone calls helpfully and cheerfully.

In this book's projects, I drew ideas from many colleagues from around the world through conversations in workshops and visits. Thanks to the faculty and students I've worked with at the Royal College of Art's Interaction Design program, UCLA's Digital Media | Arts program, the Interaction Design program at the Oslo School of Architecture and Design, Interaction Design Institute Ivrea, and the Copenhagen Institute of Interaction Design.

Many networked object projects inspired this writing. Thanks to those whose work illustrates the chapters: Tuan Anh T. Nguyen, Joo Youn Paek, Doria Fan, Mauricio Melo, and Jason Kaufman; Tarikh Korula and Josh Rooke-Ley of Uncommon Projects; Jin-Yo Mok, Alex Beim, Andrew Schneider, Gilad Lotan and Angela Pablo; Mouna Andraos and Sonali Sridhar; Frank Lantz and Kevin Slavin of Area/Code; and Sarah Johansson.

Working for MAKE has been a great experience. Dale Dougherty encouraged of all of my ideas, dealt patiently with my delays, and indulged me when I wanted to try new things. He's never said no without offering an acceptable alternative (and often a better one). Brian Jepson has gone above and beyond the call of duty as an editor, building all of the projects, suggesting modifications, debugging code, helping with photography and illustrations, and being endlessly encouraging. It's an understatement to say that I couldn't have done this without him. I could not have asked for a better editor. Thanks to Nancy Kotary for her excellent copyedit of the manuscript. Katie Wilson made this book far better looking and readable than I could ever have hoped. Thanks also to Tim Lillis for the illustrations. Thanks to all of the MAKE team.

Thanks to my agents: Laura Lewin, who got the ball rolling; Neil Salkind, who picked it up from her; and the whole support team at Studio B. Thanks finally to my family and friends who listened to me rant enthusiastically or complain bitterly as this book progressed. Much love to you all.
X

We'd Like to Hear from You

Please address comments and questions concerning this book to the publisher:

O'Reilly Media, Inc.
1005 Gravenstein Highway North
Sebastopol, CA 95472
(800) 998-9938 (in the United States or Canada)
(707) 829-0515 (international or local)
(707) 829-0104 (fax)

We have a website for this book, where we list errata, examples, and any additional information. You can access this page at: www.makezine.com/go/MakingThingsTalk

To comment or ask technical questions about this book, send email to: bookquestions@oreilly.com

Maker Media is a division of O'Reilly Media devoted entirely to the growing community of resourceful people who believe that if you can imagine it, you can make it. Consisting of *MAKE Magazine*, *CRAFT Magazine*, Maker Faire, and the Hacks series of books, Maker Media encourages the Do-It-Yourself mentality by providing creative inspiration and instruction.

For more information about Maker Media, visit us online:
MAKE: www.makezine.com
CRAFT: www.craftzine.com
Maker Faire: www.makerfaire.com
Maker SHED: www.makershed.com

❝ Note on the Second Edition

Two general changes prompted the rewriting of this book: the emergence of an open source hardware movement, and the growth of participatory culture, particularly around making interactive things. The community surrounding Arduino, and the open source hardware movement more generally, has grown quickly. The effects of this are still being realized, but one thing is clear: object-oriented hardware and physical computing are becoming an everyday reality. Many more people are making things with electronics now than I could have imagined in 2005.

Before any technology is adopted in general use, there has to be a place for it in the popular imagination. People with no knowledge of the technology must have some idea what it is and for what it can be used. Prior to 2005, I spent a lot of time explaining to people what physical computing was and what I meant by "networked objects." Nowadays, everyone knows the Wii controller or the Kinect as an example of a device that expands the range of human physical expression available to computers. These days, it's difficult to find an electronic device that isn't networked.

While it's been great to see these ideas gain a general understanding, what's even more exciting is seeing them gain in use. People aren't just using their Kinects for gaming, they're building them into assistive interfaces for physically challenged clients. They're not just playing with the Wii, they're using it as a musical instrument controller. People have become accustomed to the idea that they can modify the use of their electronics—and they're doing it.

When I joined the project, my hope for Arduino was that it might fill a need for something more customizable than consumer electronic devices were at the time, yet be less difficult to learn than microcontroller systems. I thought the open source approach was a good way to go because it meant that hopefully the ideals of the platform would spread beyond the models we made. That hope has been realized in the scores of derivative boards, shields, spinoff products, and accessories that have popped up in the last several years. It's wonderful to see so many people not just making electronics for others to build on, but doing it in a way that doesn't demand professional expertise to get started.

The growth of Arduino shields and libraries has been big enough that I almost could have written this edition so that you wouldn't have to do any programming or circuit building. There's a shield or a library to do almost every project in this book. However, you can only learn so much by fitting premade pieces together, so I've tried to show some of the principles underlying electronic communications and physical interfaces. Where there is a simple hardware solution, I've indicated it but shown the circuit it encloses as well. The best code libraries and circuit designs practice what I think of as "glass-box enclosure"— they enclose the gory details and give you a convenient interface, but they let you look inside and see what's going on if you're interested. Furthermore, they're well-constructed so that the gory details don't seem that gory when you look closely at them. Hopefully, this edition will work in much the same way.

Software Reference

There have been a number of large changes made to the Arduino platform since I started this edition. The Arduino IDE was in beta development, but by the time this book comes out, version 1.0 will be available. If you're already familiar with Arduino, please make sure you've downloaded version 1.0beta1 or later of the IDE. This book was written using Arduino 1.0 beta1, which is available online at http://code.google.com/p/arduino/wiki/Arduino1. The final 1.0 version will be available on the Download page at www.arduino.cc. Check the Arduino site for the latest updates. The code for this book can be found online on my gitHub repository at https://github.com/tigoe/MakingThingsTalk2 and I'll write about any changes on the blog, www.makingthingstalk.com.

Hardware Reference

To keep the focus on communications between physical devices, I've chosen to use the Arduino Uno as the reference hardware design for this edition. Everything in this book will work on an Arduino Uno with the appropriate accessories or shields. A few projects were made with specialty Arduino models like the Arduino Ethernet or the Arduino LilyPad because their form factor was the most appropriate, but even those projects were tested on the Uno. Anything that is compatible with the Uno should be able to run this code and interface with these circuits.

Acknowledgments for the Second Edition

The network of people who make this book possible continues to grow.

The changes in this edition are due in no small part to the work of my partners on the Arduino team. Working with Massimo Banzi, David Cuartielles, Gianluca Martino, and David Mellis continues to be enjoyable, challenging, and full of surprises. I'm lucky to have them as collaborators.

The Interactive Telecommunications Program at NYU continues to support me in everything I do professionally. None of this would be possible without the engagement of my colleagues there. Dan O'Sullivan, as always, was a valued advisor on many of the projects that follow. Daniel Shiffman and Shawn Van Every provided assistance with desktop and Android versions of Processing. Marianne Petit, Nancy Hechinger, Clay Shirky, and Marina Zurkow offered critical and moral support. Red Burns, as ever, continues to inspire me on how to empower people by teaching them to understand the technologies that shape their lives.

The cast of resident researchers and adjunct professors at ITP is ever-changing and ever-helpful. During this edition, research residents Mustafa Bağdatlı, Caroline Brown, Jeremiah Johnson, Meredith Hasson, Liesje Hodgson, Craig Kapp, Adi Marom, Ariel Nevarez, Paul Rothman, Ithai Benjamin, Christian Cerrito, John Dimatos, Xiaoyang Feng, Kacie Kinzer, Zannah Marsh, Corey Menscher, Matt Parker, and Tymm Twillman helped with examples, tried projects, out, and kept things going at ITP when I was not available.

Adjunct faculty members Thomas Gerhardt, Scott Fitzgerald, Rory Nugent, and Dustyn Roberts were valued collaborators by teaching this material in the Introduction to Physical Computing course.

Rob Faludi remains my source on all things XBee- and Digi-related.

Thanks to Antoinette LaSorsa and Lille Troelstrup at the Adaptive Design Association for permission to use their tilt board design in Chapter 5.

Many people contributed to the development of Arduino through our developers mailing list and teachers list. In particular, Mikal Hart, Michael Margolis, Adrian McEwen, and Limor Fried influenced this book through their work on key communication libraries like SoftwareSerial, Ethernet, and TextFinder, and also through their personal advice and good nature in answering my many questions off-list. Michael Margolis' *Arduino Cookbook* (O'Reilly) was a reference for some of the code in this book as well. Thanks also to Ryan Mulligan and Alexander Brevig for their libraries, which I've used and adapted in this book.

Limor Fried and Phillip Torrone, owners of Adafruit, were constant advisors, critics, and cheerleaders throughout this book. Likewise, Nathan Seidle at SparkFun continues to be one of my key critics and advisors. Adafruit and SparkFun are my major sources of parts, because they make stuff that works well.

This edition looks better graphically thanks to Fritzing, an open source circuit drawing tool available at http://fritzing.org. Reto Wettach, André Knörig, and Jonathan Cohen created a great tool to make circuits and schematics more accessible. Thanks also to Ryan Owens at SparkFun for giving me advance access to some of its parts drawings. Thanks to Giorgio Olivero and Jody Culkin for additional drawings in this edition.

Thanks to David Boyhan, Jody Culkin, Zach Eveland, and Gabriela Gutiérrez for reading and offering feedback on sections of the manuscript.

Thanks to Keith Casey at Twilio; Bonifaz Kaufmann, creator of Amarino; Andreas Göransson for his help on Android; and Casey Reas and Ben Fry for creating Processing's Android mode, and for feedback on the Android section.

New projects have inspired the new work in this edition. Thanks to Benedetta Piantella and Justin Downs of Groundlab, and to Meredith Hasson, Ariel Nevarez, and Nahana Schelling, creators of SIMbalink. Thanks to Timo Arnall, Elnar Sneve Martinussen, and Jørn Knutsen at www.nearfield.org for their RFID inspiration and collaboration.Thanks to Daniel Hirschmann for reminding me how exciting lighting is and how easy DMX-512 can be. Thanks to Mustafa Bağdatlı for his advice on Poker Face, and thanks to Frances Gilbert and Jake for their role in the CatCam 2 project. Apologies to Anton Chekhov. Thanks to Tali Padan for the comedic inspiration.

Thanks to Giana Gonzalez, Younghui Kim, Jennifer Magnolfi, Jin-Yo Mok, Matt Parker, Andrew Schneider, Gilad Lotan, Angela Pablo, James Barnett, Morgan Noel, Noodles, and Monski for modeling projects in the chapters.

Thanks, as ever, to the MAKE team, especially my editor and collaborator Brian Jepson. His patience and persistence made another edition happen. Thanks to technical editor Scott Fitzgerald, who helped pull all the parts together as well. If you can find a part on the Web from this book, thank Scott. Thanks also to my agent Neil Salkind and everyone at Studio B.

In the final weeks of writing this edition, a group of close friends came to my assistance and made possible what I could not have done on my own. Zach Eveland, Denise Hand, Jennifer Magnolfi, Clive Thompson, and Max Whitney donated days and evenings to help cut, solder, wire, and assemble many of the final projects, and they also kept me company while I wrote. Joe Hobaica, giving up several days, provided production management to finish the book. He orchestrated the photo documentation of most of the new projects, organized my workflow, kept task lists, shopped for random parts, checked for continuity, and reminded me to eat and sleep. Together, they reminded me that making things talk is best done with friends.

X

1

The Tools

This book is a cookbook of sorts, and this chapter covers the key ingredients. The concepts and tools you'll use in every chapter are introduced here. There's enough information on each tool to get you to the point where you can make it say **"Hello World!"** Chances are you've used some of the tools in this chapter before—or ones just like them. Skip past the things you know and jump into learning the tools that are new to you. You may want to explore some of the less-familiar tools on your own to get a sense of what they can do. The projects in the following chapters only scratch the surface of what's possible for most of these tools. References for further investigation
are provided.

◀◀ **Happy Feedback Machine by Tuan Anh T. Nguyen**
The main pleasure of interacting with this piece comes from the feel of flipping the switches and turning the knobs. The lights and sounds produced as a result are secondary, and most people who play with it remember how it feels rather than its behavior.

❝ It Starts with the Stuff You Touch

All of the objects that you'll encounter in this book—tangible or intangible—will have certain behaviors. Software objects will send and receive messages, store data, or both. Physical objects will move, light up, or make noise. The first question to ask about any object is: what does it do? The second is: how do I make it do what it's supposed to do? Or, more simply, what is its interface?

An object's interface is made up of three elements. First, there's the physical interface. This is the stuff you touch—such as knobs, switches, keys, and other sensors—that react to your actions. The connectors that join objects are also part of the physical interface. Every network of objects begins and ends with a physical interface. Even though some objects in a network (such as software objects) have no physical interface, people construct mental models of how a system works based on the physical interface. A computer is much more than the keyboard, mouse, and screen, but that's what we think of it as, because that's what we see and touch. You can build all kinds of wonderful functions into your system, but if those functions aren't apparent in the things people see, hear, and touch, they will never be used. Remember the lesson of the VCR clock that constantly blinks 12:00 because no one can be bothered to learn how to set it? If the physical interface isn't good, the rest of the system suffers.

Second, there's the software interface—the commands that you send to the object to make it respond. In some projects, you'll invent your own software interface; in others, you'll rely on existing interfaces to do the work for you. The best software interfaces have simple, consistent functions that result in predictable outputs. Unfortunately,

not all software interfaces are as simple as you'd like them to be, so be prepared to experiment a little to get some software objects to do what you think they should do. When you're learning a new software interface, it helps to approach it mentally in the same way you approach a physical interface. Don't try to use all the functions at once; first, learn what each function does on its own. You don't learn to play the piano by starting with a Bach fugue—you start one note at a time. Likewise, you don't learn a software interface by writing a full application with it—you learn it one function at a time. There are many projects in this book; if you find any of their software functions confusing, write a simple program that demonstrates just that function, then return to the project.

Finally, there's the electrical interface—the pulses of electrical energy sent from one device to another to be interpreted as information. Unless you're designing new objects or the connections between them, you never have to deal with this interface. When you're designing new objects or the networks that connect them, however, you have to understand a few things about this interface, so that you know how to match up objects that might have slight differences in their electrical interfaces.

X

❝ It's About Pulses

In order to communicate with each other, objects use communications protocols. A protocol is a series of mutually agreed-upon standards for communication between two or more objects.

Serial protocols like RS-232, USB, and IEEE 1394 (also known as FireWire and i.Link) connect computers to printers, hard drives, keyboards, mice, and other peripheral devices. Network protocols like Ethernet and TCP/IP connect multiple computers through network hubs, routers, and switches. A communications protocol usually defines the rate at which messages are exchanged, the arrangement of data in the messages, and the grammar of the exchange. If it's a protocol for physical objects, it will also specify the electrical characteristics, and sometimes even the physical shape of the connectors. Protocols don't specify what happens between objects, however. The commands to make an object do something rely on protocols in the same way that clear instructions rely on good grammar—you can't give useful instructions if you can't form a good sentence.

One thing that all communications protocols have in common—from the simplest chip-to-chip message to the most complex network architecture—is this: it's all about pulses of energy. Digital devices exchange information by sending timed pulses of energy across a shared connection. The USB connection from your mouse to your computer uses two wires for transmission and reception, sending timed pulses of electrical energy across those wires. Likewise, wired network connections are made up of timed pulses of electrical energy sent down the wires. For longer distances and higher bandwidth, the electrical wires may be replaced with fiber optic cables , which carry timed pulses of light. In cases where a physical connection is inconvenient or impossible, the transmission can be sent using pulses of radio energy between radio transceivers (a transceiver is two-way radio, capable of transmitting and receiving). The meaning of data pulses is independent of the medium that's carrying them. You can use the same sequence of pulses whether you're sending them across wires, fiber optic cables, or radios. If you keep in mind that all of the communication you're dealing with starts with a series of pulses—and that somewhere there's a guide explaining the sequence of those pulses—you can work with any communication system you come across.
X

Computers of All Shapes and Sizes

You'll encounter at least four different types of computers in this book, grouped according to their physical interfaces. The most familiar of these is the personal computer. Whether it's a desktop or a laptop, it's got a keyboard, screen, and mouse, and you probably use it just about every working day. These three elements—the keyboard, the screen, and the mouse—make up its physical interface.

The second type of computer you'll encounter in this book, the microcontroller, has no physical interface that humans can interact with directly. It's just an electronic chip with input and output pins that can send or receive electrical pulses. Using a microcontroller is a three-step process:

1. You connect sensors to the inputs to convert physical energy like motion, heat, and sound into electrical energy.
2. You attach motors, speakers, and other devices to the outputs to convert electrical energy into physical action.
3. Finally, you write a program to determine how the input changes affect the outputs.

In other words, the microcontroller's physical interface is whatever you make of it.

The third type of computer in this book, the network server, is basically the same as a desktop computer—it may even have a keyboard, screen, and mouse. Even though it can do all the things you expect of a personal computer, its primary function is to send and receive data over a network. Most people don't think of servers as physical things because they only interact with them over a network, using their local computers as physical interfaces to the server. A server's most important interface for most users' purposes is its software interface.

The fourth group of computers is a mixed bag: mobile phones, music synthesizers, and motor controllers, to name a few. Some of them will have fully developed physical interfaces, some will have minimal physical interfaces but detailed software interfaces, and most will have a little of both. Even though you don't normally think of these devices as computers, they are. When you think of them as programmable objects with interfaces that you can manipulate, it's easier to figure out how they can all communicate, regardless of their end function.
X

66 Good Habits

Networking objects is a bit like love. The fundamental problem in both is that when you're sending a message, you never really know whether the receiver understands what you're saying, and there are a thousand ways for your message to get lost or garbled in transmission.

You may know how you feel but your partner doesn't. All he or she has to go on are the words you say and the actions you take. Likewise, you may know exactly what message your local computer is sending, how it's sending it, and what all the bits mean, but the remote computer has no idea what they mean unless you program it to understand them. All it has to go on are the bits it receives. If you want reliable, clear communications (in love or networking), there are a few simple things you have to do:

- Listen more than you speak.
- Never assume that what you said is what they heard.
- Agree on how you're going to say things in advance.
- Ask politely for clarification when messages aren't clear.

Listen More Than You Speak

The best way to make a good first impression, and to maintain a good relationship, is to be a good listener. Listening is more difficult than speaking. You can speak anytime you want, but since you never know when the other person is going to say something, you have to listen all the time. In networking terms, this means you should write your programs such that they're listening for new messages most of the time, and sending messages only when necessary. It's often easier to send out messages all the time rather than figure out when it's appropriate, but it can lead to all kinds of problems. It usually doesn't take a lot of work to limit your sending, and the benefits far outweigh the costs.

Never Assume

What you say is not always what the other person hears. Sometimes it's a matter of misinterpretation, and other times, you may not have been heard clearly. If you assume that the message got through and continue on obliviously, you're in for a world of hurt. Likewise, you may be inclined to first work out all the logic of your system—and all the steps of your messages before you start to connect things—then build it, and finally test it all at once. Avoid that temptation.

It's good to plan the whole system out in advance, but build it and test it in baby steps. Most of the errors that occur when building these projects happen in the communication between objects. Always send a quick "Hello World!" message from one object to the others, and make sure that the message got there intact before you proceed to the more complex details. Keep that "Hello World!" example on hand for testing when communication fails.

Getting the message wrong isn't the only misstep you can make. Most of the projects in this book involve building the physical, software, and electrical elements of the interface. One of the most common mistakes people make when developing hybrid projects like these is to assume that the problems are all in one place. Quite often, I've sweated over a bug in the software transmission of a message, only to find out later that the receiving device wasn't even connected, or wasn't ready to receive messages. Don't assume that communication errors are in the element of the system with which you're most familiar. They're most often in the element with which you're least familiar, and therefore, are avoiding. When you can't get a message through, think about every link in the chain from sender to receiver, and check every one. Then check the links you overlooked.

Agree on How You Say Things

In good relationships, you develop a shared language based on shared experience. You learn the best ways to say things so that your partner will be most receptive, and you develop shorthand for expressing things that you repeat all the time. Good data communications also rely on shared ways of saying things, or protocols. Sometimes you make up a protocol for all the objects in your system, and other times you have to rely on existing protocols. If you're working with a previously established protocol, make sure you understand all the parts before you start trying to interpret it. If you have the luxury of making up your own protocol, make sure you've considered the needs of both the sender and receiver when you define it. For example, you might decide to use a protocol that's easy to program on your web server, but that turns out to be impossible to handle on your microcontroller. A little thought to the strengths and weaknesses on both sides of the transmission, and a bit of compromise before you start to build, will make things flow much more smoothly.

Ask Politely for Clarification

Messages get garbled in countless ways. Perhaps you hear something that may not make much sense, but you act on it, only to find out that your partner said something entirely different from what you thought. It's always best to ask nicely for clarification to avoid making a stupid mistake. Likewise, in network communications, it's wise to check that any messages you receive make sense. When they don't, ask for a repeat transmission. It's also wise to check, rather than assume, that a message was sent. Saying nothing can be worse than saying something wrong. Minor problems can become major when no one speaks up to acknowledge that there's an issue. The same thing can occur in network communications. One device may wait forever for a message from the other side, not knowing, for example, that the remote device is unplugged. When you don't receive a response, send another message. Don't resend it too often, and give the other party time to reply. Acknowledging messages may seem like a luxury, but it can save a whole lot of time and energy when you're building a complex system.

X

❝ Tools

As you'll be working with the physical, software, and electrical interfaces of objects, you'll need physical tools, software, and (computer) hardware.

Physical Tools

If you've worked with electronics or microcontrollers before, chances are you have your own hand tools already. Figure 1-1 shows the ones used most frequently in this book. They're common tools that can be obtained from many vendors. A few are listed in Table 1-1.

In addition to hand tools, there are some common electronic components that you'll use all the time. They're listed as well, with part numbers from the retailers featured most frequently in this book. Not all retailers will carry all parts, so there are many gaps in the table.

NOTE: You'll find a number of component suppliers in this book. I buy from different vendors depending on who's got the best and the least expensive version of each part. Sometimes it's easier to buy from a vendor that you know carries what you need, rather than search through the massive catalog of a vendor who might carry it for less. Feel free to substitute your favorite vendors. A list of vendors can be found in the Appendix.

Figure 1-1. See the list below for number references.

Handy hand tools for networking objects.

1 Soldering iron Middle-of-the-line is best here. Cheap soldering irons die fast, but a mid-range iron like the Weller WLC-100 works great for small electronic work. Avoid the Cold Solder irons. They solder by creating a spark, and that spark can damage static-sensitive parts like microcontrollers. Jameco (http://jameco. com): 146595; Farnell (www.farnell.com): 1568159; RadioShack (http://radioshack. com): 640-2801 and 640-2078

2 Solder 21-23 AWG solder is best. Get lead-free solder if you can; it's healthier for you. Jameco: 668271; Farnell: 419266; RadioShack: 640-0013

3 Desoldering pump This helps when you mess up while soldering. Jameco: 305226; Spark Fun (www.SparkFun.com): TOL-00082; Farnell: 3125646

4 Wire stripper, Diagonal cutter, Needle-nose pliers Avoid the 3-in-1 versions of these tools. They'll only make you grumpy. These three tools are essential for working with wire, and you don't need expensive ones to have good ones. Wire stripper: Jameco: 159291; Farnell: 609195; Spark Fun: TOL-00089; RadioShack: 640-2129A

Diagonal cutter: Jameco: 161411; Farnell: 3125397; Spark Fun: TOL-00070; RadioShack: 640-2043
Needlenose pliers: Jameco: 35473; Farnell: 3127199; Spark Fun: TOL-00079; RadioShack: 640-2033

5 Mini-screwdriver Get one with both Phillips and slotted heads. You'll use it all the time. Jameco: 127271; Farnell: 4431212; RadioShack: 640-1963

6 Safety goggles Always a good idea when soldering, drilling, or other tasks. Spark Fun:SWG-09791; Farnell: 1696193

7 Helping hands These make soldering much easier. Jameco: 681002; Farnell: 1367049

8 Multimeter You don't need an expensive one. As long as it measures voltage, resistance, amperage, and continuity, it'll do the job. Jameco: 220812; Farnell: 7430566; Spark Fun: TOL-00078; RadioShack: 22-182

9 Oscilloscope Professional oscilloscopes are expensive, but the DSO Nano is only about $100 and a valuable aid when working on electronics. Spark Fun:

TOL-10244 (v2); Seeed Studio (www.seeed-studio.com): (TOL114C3M; Maker SHED (www.makershed.com): MKSEEED11

10 9–12V DC power supply You'll use this all the time, and you've probably got a spare from some dead electronic device. Make sure you know the polarity of the plug so you don't reverse polarity on a component and blow it up! Most of the devices shown in this book have a DC power jack that accepts a 2.1mm inner diameter/5.5mm outer diameter plug, so look for an adapter with the same dimensions. Jameco: 170245 (12V, 1000mA); Farnell: 1176248 (12V, 1000mA); Spark Fun: TOL-00298; RadioShack: 273-355 (9V 800mA)

11 Power connector, 2.1mm inside diameter/5.5mm outside diameter You'll need this to connect your microcontroller module or breadboard to a DC power supply. This size connector is the most common for the power supplies that will work with the circuits you'll be building here. Jameco: 159610; Digi-Key (www.digikey.com): CP-024A-ND; Farnell: 3648102

12 **9V Battery snap adapter and 9V battery** When you want to run a project off battery power, these adapters are a handy way to do it. Spark Fun: PRT-09518; Adafruit (http://adafruit.com): 80; Digi-Key: CP3-1000-ND and 84-4K-ND; Jameco: 28760 and 216452; Farnell: 1650675 and 1737256; RadioShack: 270-324 and 274-1569

13 **USB cables** You'll need both USB A-to-B (the most common USB cables) and USB A-to-mini-B (the kind that's common with digital cameras) for the projects in this book. Spark Fun: CAB-00512, CAB-00598; Farnell: 1838798, 1308878

14 **Alligator clip test leads** It's often hard to juggle the five or six things you have to hold when metering a circuit. Clip leads make this much easier. Jameco: 10444; RS (www.rs-online.com): 483-859; Spark Fun: CAB-00501; RadioShack: 278-016

15 **Serial-to-USB converter** This converter lets you speak TTL serial from a USB port. Breadboard serial-to-USB modules, like the FT232 modules shown here, are cheaper than the consumer models and easier to use in the projects in this book. Spark Fun: BOB-00718; Arduino Store (store.arduino.cc): A000014

16 **Microcontroller module** The microcontroller shown here is an Arduino Uno. Available from Spark Fun and Maker SHED (http://store.arduino.cc/ww/) in the U.S., and from multiple distributors internationally. See http://arduino.cc/en/Main/Buy for details about your region.

17 **Voltage regulator** Voltage regulators take a variable input voltage and output a constant (lower) voltage. The two most common you'll need for these projects are 5V and 3.3V. Be careful when using a regulator that you've never used before. Check the data sheet to make sure you have the pin connections correct. 3.3V: Digi-Key: 576-1134-ND; Jameco: 242115; Farnell: 1703357; RS: 534-3021 5V: Digi-Key: LM7805CT-ND; Jameco: 51262; Farnell: 1703357; RS: 298-8514

18 **TIP120 Transistor** Transistors act as digital switches, allowing you to control a circuit with high current or voltage from one with lower current and voltage. There are many types of transistors, the TIP120 is one used in a few projects in this book. Note that the TIP120 looks just like the voltage regulator next to it. Sometimes electronic components with different functions come in the same physical packages, so you need to check the part number written on the part. Digi-Key: TIP120-ND; Jameco: 32993; Farnell: 9804005

19 **Prototyping shields** These are add-on boards for the Arduino microcontroller module that have a bare grid of holes to which you can solder. You can build your own circuits on them by soldering, or you can use a tiny breadboard (also shown) to test circuits quickly. These are handy for projects where you need to prototype quickly, as well as a compact form to the electronics. Adafruit: 51; Arduino Store: A000024; Spark Fun: DEV-07914; Maker SHED: MSMS01
Breadboards for protoshields: Spark Fun: PRT-08802; Adafruit: included with board; Digi-Key: 923273-ND

20 **Solderless breadboard** Having a few around can be handy. I like the ones with two long rows on either side so that you can run power and ground on both sides. Jameco: 20723 (2 bus rows per side); Farnell: 4692810; Digi-Key: 438-1045-ND; Spark Fun: PRT-00137; RadioShack: 276-002

21 **Spare LEDs for tracing signals** LEDs are to the hardware developer what print statements are to the software developer. They let you see quickly whether there's voltage between two points, or whether a signal is going through. Keep spares on hand. Jameco: 3476; Farnell: 1057119; Digi-Key: 160-1144-ND; RadioShack: 278-016

22 **Resistors** You'll need resistors of various values for your projects. Common values are listed in Table 1-1.

23 **Header pins** You'll use these all the time. It's handy to have female ones around as well. Jameco: 103377; Digi-Key: A26509-20-ND; Farnell: 1593411

24 **Analog sensors (variable resistors)** There are countless varieties of variable resistors to measure all kinds of physical properties. They're the simplest of analog sensors, and they're very easy to build into test circuits. Flex sensors

and force-sensing resistors are handy for testing a circuit or a program. **Flex sensors:** Jameco: 150551; Images SI (www.imagesco.com): FLX-01
Force-sensing resistors: Parallax (www.parallax.com): 30056; Images SI: FSR-400, 402, 406, 408

25 **Pushbuttons** There are two types you'll find handy: the PCB-mount type, like the ones you find on Wiring and Arduino boards, used here mostly as reset buttons for breadboard projects; and panel-mount types used for interface controls for end users. But you can use just about any type you want. **PCB-mount type:** Digi-Key: SW400-ND; Jameco: 119011; Spark Fun: COM-00097 **Panel-mount type:** Digi-Key: GH1344-ND; Jameco: 164559PS

26 **Potentiometers** You'll need potentiometers to let people adjust settings in your project. Jameco: 29081; Spark Fun: COM-09939; RS: 91A1A-B28-B15L; RadioShack: 271-1715; Farnell: 1760793

27 **Ethernet cables** A couple of these will come in handy. Jameco: 522781; RadioShack: 55010852

28 **Black, red, blue, yellow wire** 22 AWG solid-core hook-up wire is best for making solderless breadboard connections. Get at least three colors, and always use red for voltage and black for ground. A little organization of your wires can go a long way.
Black: Jameco: 36792
Blue: Jameco: 36767
Green: Jameco: 36821
Red: Jameco: 36856; RadioShack: 278-1215
Yellow: Jameco: 36919
Mixed: RadioShack: 276-173

29 **Capacitors** You'll need capacitors of various values for your projects. Common values are listed in Table 1-1.

> ⚠ You're going to run across some hardware in the following chapters that was brand new when this edition was written, including the Arduino Ethernet board, the Arduino WiFi shield, wireless shield, RFID shield, USB-to-Serial adapter, and more. The distributors listed here didn't have part numbers for them as of this writing, so check for them by name. By the time you read this, distributors should have them in stock.

Table 1-1. Common components for electronic and microcontroller work.

D Digi-Key (http://digikey.com)   **R** RS (www.rs-online.com)
J Jameco (http://jameco.com)   **F** Farnell (www.farnell.com)

RESISTORS

100Ω .... **D** 100QBK-ND, **J** 690620, **F** 9337660, **R** 707-8625
220Ω .... **D** 220QBK-ND, **J** 690700, **F** 9337792, **R** 707-8842
470Ω .... **D** 470QBK-ND, **J** 690785, **F** 9337911, **R** 707-8659
1K .... **D** 1.0KQBK, **J** 29663, **F** 1735061, **R** 707-8669
10K .... **D** 10KQBK-ND, **J** 29911, **F** 9337687, **R** 707-8906
22K .... **D** 22KQBK-ND, **J** 30453, **F** 9337814, **R** 707-8729
100K .... **D** 100KQBK-ND, **J** 29997, **F** 9337695, **R** 707-8940
1M .... **D** 1.0MQBK-ND, **J** 29698, **F** 9337709, **R** 131-700

CAPACITORS

0.1μF ceramic .... **D** 399-4151-ND, **J** 15270, **F** 3322166, **R** 716-7135
1μF electrolytic .... **D** P10312-ND, **J** 94161, **F** 8126933, **R** 475-9009
10μF electrolytic .... **D** P11212-ND, **J** 29891, **F** 1144605, **R** 715-1638
100μF electrolytic .... **D** P10269-ND, **J** 158394, **F** 1144642, **R** 715-1657

VOLTAGE REGULATORS

3.3V .... **D** 576-1134-ND, **J** 242115, **F** 1703357, **R** 534-3021
5V .... **D** LM7805CT-ND, **J** 51262, **F** 1860277, **R** 298-8514

ANALOG SENSORS

Flex sensors .... **D** 905-1000-ND, **J** 150551, **R** 708-1277
FSRs .... **D** 1027-1000-ND, **J** 2128260

LED

T1, Green clear .... **D** 160-1144-ND, **J** 34761, **F** 1057119, **R** 247-1662
T1, Red, clear .... **D** 160-1665-ND, **J** 94511, **F** 1057129, **R** 826-830

TRANSISTORS

2N2222A .... **D** P2N2222AGOS-ND, **J** 38236, **F** 1611371, **R** 295-028
TIP120 .... **D** TIP120-ND, **J** 32993, **F** 9804005

DIODES

1N4004-R .... **D** 1N4004-E3, **J** 35992, **F** 9556109, **R** 628-9029
3.3V zener (1N5226) .. **D** 1N5226B-TPCT-ND, **J** 743488, **F** 1700785

PUSHBUTTONS

PCB .... **D** SW400-ND, **J** 119011, **F** 1555981
Panel Mount .... **D** GH1344-ND, **J** 164559PS, **F** 1634684, **R** 718-2213

SOLDERLESS BREADBOARDS

various .... **D** 438-1045-ND, **J** 20723, 20600, **F** 4692810

HOOKUP WIRE

red .... **D** C2117R-100-ND, **J** 36856, **F** 1662031
black .... **D** C2117B-100-ND, **J** 36792, **F** 1662027
blue .... **J** 36767, **F** 1662034
yellow .... **J** 36920, **F** 1662032

POTENTIOMETER

10K .... **D** 29081

HEADER PINS

straight .... **D** A26509-20-ND, **J** 103377, **S** PRT-00116
right angle .... **D** S1121E-36-ND, **S** PRT-00553

HEADERS

female .... **S** PRT-00115

BATTERY SNAP

9V .... **D** 2238K-ND, **J** 101470PS, **S** PRT-00091

Figure 1-2
The Processing editor window.

Software Tools

Processing

The multimedia programming environment used in this book is called Processing. Based on Java, it's made for designers, artists, and others who want to get something done without having to know all the gory details of programming. It's a useful tool for explaining programming ideas because it takes relatively little Processing code to make big things happen, such as opening a network connection, connecting to an external device through a serial port, or controlling a camera. It's a free, open source tool available at www.processing.org. Because it's based on Java, you can include Java classes and methods in your Processing programs. It runs on Mac OS X, Windows, and Linux, so you can run Processing on your favorite operating system. There's also Processing for Android phones and Processing for JavaScript, so you can use it in many ways. If you don't like working in Processing, you should be able to use this book's code samples and comments as pseudocode for whatever multimedia environment you prefer. Once you've downloaded and installed Processing on your computer, open the application. You'll get a screen that looks like Figure 1-2.

▶▶ Here's your first Processing program. Type this into the editor window, and then press the Run button on the top lefthand side of the toolbar.

```
println("Hello World!");
```

 It's not too flashy a program, but it's a classic. It should print Hello World! in the message box at the bottom of the editor window. It's that easy.

Programs in Processing are called sketches, and all the data for a sketch is saved in a folder with the sketch's name. The editor is very basic, without a lot of clutter to get in your way. The toolbar has buttons to run and stop a sketch, create a new file, open an existing sketch, save the current sketch, or export to a Java applet. You can also export your sketch as a standalone application from the File menu. Files are normally stored in a subdirectory of your **Documents** folder called **Processing**, but you can save them wherever you like.

▶▶ Here's a second program that's a bit more exciting. It illustrates some of the main programming structures in Processing.

> **NOTE:** All code examples in this book will have comments indicating the context in which they're to be used: Processing, Processing Android mode, Arduino, PHP, and so forth.

```
/*
    Triangle drawing program
    Context: Processing

    Draws a triangle whenever the mouse button is not pressed.
    Erases when the mouse button is pressed.

*/

// declare your variables:
float redValue = 0;     // variable to hold the red color
float greenValue = 0;   // variable to hold the green color
float blueValue = 0;    // variable to hold the blue color

// the setup() method runs once at the beginning of the program:

void setup() {
  size(320, 240);     // sets the size of the applet window
  background(0);      // sets the background of the window to black
  fill(0);            // sets the color to fill shapes with (0 = black)
  smooth();           // draw with antialiased edges
}

// the draw() method runs repeatedly, as long as the applet window
// is open.  It refreshes the window, and anything else you program
// it to do:

void draw() {

  // Pick random colors for red, green, and blue:
  redValue = random(255);
  greenValue = random(255);
  blueValue = random(255);

  // set the line color:
  stroke(redValue, greenValue, blueValue);

  // draw when the mouse is up (to hell with conventions):
  if (mousePressed == false) {
    // draw a triangle:
    triangle(mouseX, mouseY, width/2, height/2,pmouseX, pmouseY);
  }
  // erase when the mouse is down:
  else {
    background(0);
    fill(0);
  }
}
```

Every Processing program has two main routines, setup() and draw(). setup() happens once at the beginning of the program. It's where you set all your initial conditions, like the size of the applet window, initial states for variables, and so forth. draw() is the main loop of the program. It repeats continuously until you close the applet window.

In order to use variables in Processing, you have to declare the variable's data type. In the preceding program, the variables redValue, greenValue, and blueValue are all float types, meaning that they're floating decimal-point numbers. Other common variable types you'll use are ints (integers), booleans (true or false values), Strings of text, and bytes.

Like C, Java, and many other languages, Processing uses C-style syntax. All functions have a data type, just like variables (and many of them are the void type, meaning that they don't return any values). All lines end with a semicolon, and all blocks of code are wrapped in curly braces. Conditional statements (if-then statements), for-next loops, and comments all use the C syntax as well. The preceding code illustrates all of these except the for-next loop.

▶▶ Here's a typical for-next loop. Try this in a sketch of its own (to start a new sketch, select New from Processing's File menu).

```
for (int myCounter = 0; myCounter <=10; myCounter++) {
    println(myCounter);
}
```

BASIC users: If you've never used a C-style for-next loop, it can seem forbidding. What this bit of code does is establish a variable called myCounter. As long as a number is less than or equal to 10, it executes the instructions in the curly braces. myCounter++ tells the program to add one to myCounter each time through the loop. The equivalent BASIC code is:

```
for myCounter = 0 to 10
    Print myCounter
next
```

"Processing is a fun language to play with because you can make interactive graphics very quickly. It's also a simple introduction to Java for beginning programmers. If you're a Java programmer already, you can include Java directly in your Processing programs. Processing is expandable through code libraries. You'll be using two of the Processing code libraries frequently in this book: the serial library and the networking library.

For more on the syntax of Processing, see the language reference guide at www.processing.org. To learn more about programming in Processing, check out **Processing: A Programming Handbook for Visual Designers and Artists**, by Casey Reas and Ben Fry (MIT Press), the creators of Processing, or their shorter book, **Getting Started with Processing** (O'Reilly). Or, read Daniel Shiffman's excellent introduction, **Learning Processing** (Morgan Kaufmann). There are dozens of other Processing books on the market, so find one whose style you like best.

Remote-Access Applications

One of the most effective debugging tools you'll use when making the projects in this book is a command-line remote-access program, which gives you access to the command-line interface of a remote computer. If you've never used a command-line interface before, you'll find it a bit awkward at first, but you get used to it pretty quickly. This tool is especially important when you need to log into a web server, because you'll need the command line to work with PHP scripts that will be used in this book.

Most web hosting providers are based on Linux, BSD, Solaris, or some other Unix-like operating system. So, when you need to do some work on your web server, you may need to make a command-line connection to your web server.

NOTE: **If you already know how to create PHP and HTML documents and upload them to your web server, you can skip ahead to the "PHP" section.**

Although this is the most direct way to work with PHP, some people prefer to work more indirectly, by writing text files on their local computers and uploading them to the remote computer. Depending on how restrictive your web hosting service is, this may be your only option (however, there are many inexpensive hosting companies that offer full command-line access). Even if you prefer to work this way, there are times in this book when the command line is your only option, so it's worth getting to know a little bit about it now.

On Windows computers, there are a few remote access programs available, but the one that you'll use here is called PuTTY. You can download it from www.puttyssh.org. Download the Windows-style installer and run it. On Mac OS X and Linux, you can use OpenSSH, which is included with both operating systems, and can be run in the Terminal program with the command ssh.

Before you can run OpenSSH, you'll need to launch a terminal emulation program, which gives you access to your Linux or Mac OS X command line. On Mac OS X, the program is called Terminal, and you can find it in the **Utilities** subdirectory of the **Applications** directory. On Linux, look for a program called xterm, rxvt, Terminal, or Konsole.

NOTE: ssh **is a more modern cousin of a longtime Unix remote-access program called** telnet. ssh **is more secure; it scrambles all data sent from one computer to another before sending it, so it can't be snooped on en route.** telnet **sends all data from one computer to another with no encryption. You should use** ssh **to connect from one machine to another whenever you can. Where** telnet **is used in this book, it's because it's the only tool that will do what's needed for the examples in question. Think of** telnet **as an old friend: maybe he's not the coolest guy on the block, maybe he's a bit of a gossip, but he's stood by you forever, and you know you can trust him to do the job when everyone else lets you down. X**

▲ **Figure 1-3**
The main PuTTY window.

Making the SSH Connection

Mac OS X and Linux
Open your terminal program. These Terminal applications give you a plain-text window with a greeting like this:

```
Last login: Wed Feb 22 07:20:34 on ttyp1
ComputerName:~ username$
```

Type ssh username@myhost.com at the command line to connect to your web host. Replace username and myhost.com with your username and host address.

Windows
On Windows, you'll need to start up PuTTY (see Figure 1-3). To get started, type myhost.com (your web host's name) in the Host Name field, choose the SSH protocol, and then click Open.

The computer will try to connect to the remote host, asking for your password when it connects. Type it (you won't see what you type), followed by the Enter key.

" Using the Command Line

Once you've connected to the remote web server, you should see something like this:

```
Last login: Wed Feb 22 08:50:04 2006 from 216.157.45.215
[userid@myhost ~]$
```

Now you're at the command prompt of your web host's computer, and any command you give will be executed on that computer. Start off by learning what directory you're in. To do this, type:

```
pwd
```

which stands for "print working directory." It asks the computer to list the name and pathname of the directory in which you're currently working. (You'll see that many Unix commands are very terse, so you have to type less. The downside of this is that it makes them harder to remember.) The server will respond with a directory path, such as:

```
/home/igoe
```

This is the home directory for your account. On many web servers, this directory contains a subdirectory called **public_html** or **www**, which is where your web files belong. Files that you place in your home directory (that is, outside of **www** or **public_html**) can't be seen by web visitors.

NOTE: **You should check with your web host to learn how the files and directories in your home directory are set up.**

To find out what files are in a given directory, use the list (ls) command, like so:

```
ls -l .
```

NOTE: **The dot is shorthand for "the current working directory." Similarly, a double dot is shorthand for the directory (the** parent directory**) that contains the current directory.**

The -l means "list long." You'll get a response like this:

```
total 44
drwxr-xr-x  13 igoe users 4096 Apr 14 11:42 public_html
drwxr-xr-x   3 igoe users 4096 Nov 25  2005 share
```

This is a list of all the files and subdirectories of the current working directories, as well as their attributes. The first column lists who's got permissions to do what (read, modify, or execute/run a file). The second lists how many links there are to that file elsewhere on the system; most of the time, this is not something you'll have much need for. The third column tells you who owns it, and the fourth tells you the group (a collection of users) to which the file belongs. The fifth lists its size, and the sixth lists the date it was last modified. The final column lists the filename.

In a Unix environment, all files whose names begin with a dot are invisible. Some files, like access-control files that you'll see later in the book, need to be invisible. You can get a list of all the files, including the invisible ones, using the −a modifier for ls, this way:

```
ls -la
```

To move around from one directory to another, there's a "change directory" command, cd. To get into the **public_ html** directory, for example, type:

```
cd public_html
```

To go back up one level in the directory structure, type:

```
cd ..
```

To return to your home directory, use the ~ symbol, which is shorthand for your home directory:

```
cd ~
```

If you type cd on a line by itself, it also takes you to your home directory.

If you want to go into a subdirectory of a directory, for example the **cgi-bin** directory inside the **public_html** directory, you'd type cd public_html/cgi-bin. You can type the absolute path from the main directory of the server (called the root) by placing a **/** at the beginning of the file's pathname. Any other file pathname is called a relative path.

To make a new directory, type:

```
mkdir directoryname
```

This command will make a new directory in the current working directory. If you then use ls -l to see a list of files in the working directory, you'll see a new line with the new directory. If you then type cd directoryname to switch to the new directory and ls -la to see all of its contents, you'll see only two listings:

```
drwxr-xr-x  2 tqi6023 users 4096 Feb 17 10:19 .
drwxr-xr-x  4 tqi6023 users 4096 Feb 17 10:19 ..
```

The first file, . , is a reference to this directory itself. The second, .. , is a reference to the directory that contains it. Those two references will exist as long as the directory exists. You can't change them.

To remove a directory, type:

```
rmdir directoryname
```

You can remove only empty directories, so make sure that you've deleted all the files in a directory before you remove it. rmdir won't ask you if you're sure before it deletes your directory, so be careful. Don't remove any directories or files that you didn't make yourself.

Controlling Access to Files

Type ls −l to get a list of files in your current directory and to take a closer look at the permissions on the files. For example, a file marked drwx------ means that it's a directory, and that it's readable, writable, and executable by the system user who created the directory (also known as the owner of the file). Or, consider a file marked -rw-rw-rw. The - at the beginning means it's a regular file (not a directory) and that the owner, the group of users to which the file belongs (usually, the owner is a member of this group), and everyone else who accesses the system can read and write to this file. The first rw- refers to the owner, the second refers to the group, and the third refers to the rest of the world. If you're the owner of a file, you can change its permissions using the chmod command:

```
chmod go-w filename
```

The options following chmod refer to which users you want to affect. In the preceding example, you're removing write permission (-w) for the group (g) that the file belongs to, and for all others (o) besides the owner of the file. To restore write permissions for the group and others, and to also give them execute permission, you'd type:

```
chmod go +wx filename
```

A combination of u for user, g for group, and o for others, and a combination of + and - and r for read, w for write, and x for execute gives you the capability to change permissions on your files for anyone on the system. Be careful not to accidentally remove permissions from yourself (the user). Also, get in the habit of not leaving files accessible to the group and others unless you need to—on large hosting providers, it's not unusual for you to be sharing a server with hundreds of other users!

Creating, Viewing, and Deleting Files

Two other command-line programs you'll find useful are nano and less. nano is a text editor. It's very bare-bones, so you may prefer to edit your files using your favorite text editor on your own computer and then upload them to your server. But for quick changes right on the server, nano is great. To make a new file, type:

```
nano filename.txt
```

The nano editor will open up. Figure 1-4 shows how it looks like after I typed in some text.

All the commands to work in nano are keyboard commands you type using the Ctrl key. For example, to exit the program, type Ctrl-X. The editor will then ask whether you want to save, and prompt you for a filename. The most common commands are listed along the bottom of the screen.

While nano is for creating and editing files, less is for reading them. less takes any file and displays it to the screen one screenful at a time. To see the file you just created in nano, for example, type:

```
less filename.txt
```

You'll get a list of the file's contents, with a colon (:) prompt at the bottom of the screen. Press the space bar for the next screenful. When you've read enough, type q to quit. There's not much to less, but it's a handy way to read long files. You can even send other commands through less (or almost any command-line program) using the pipe (|) operator. For example, try this:

```
ls -la . | less
```

```
  ⊖ ⊖ ⊖              Terminal Window — nano — 80x24
 GNU nano 1.2.4                      File: test.txt

 Hello. This is a file written in nano.
 To close this file and save it, type control-x.

 The most common commands are at the bottom of the screen.
 The ^ character is shorthand for the control key.




                        [ Read 6 lines ]
^G Get Help  ^O WriteOut  ^R Read File  ^Y Prev Page  ^K Cut Text  ^C Cur Pos
^X Exit      ^J Justify   ^W Where Is   ^V Next Page  ^U UnCut Txt ^T To Spell
```

Figure 1-4
The nano text editor.

Once you've created a file, you can delete it using the rm command, like this:

```
rm filename
```

Like rmdir, rm won't ask whether you're sure before it deletes your file, so use it carefully.

There are many other commands available in the Unix command shell, but these will suffice to get you started. For more information, type help at the command prompt to get a list of commonly used commands. For any command, you can get its user manual by typing man commandname. When you're ready to close the connection to your server, type: logout. For more on getting around Unix and Linux systems using the command line, see **Learning the Unix Operating System** by Jerry Peek, Grace Todino-Gonguet, and John Strang (O'Reilly).

PHP

The server programs in this book are mostly in PHP. PHP is one of the most common scripting languages for applications that run on the web server (server-side scripts). Server-side scripts are programs that allow you to do more with a web server than just serve fixed pages of text or HTML. They allow you to access databases through a browser, save data from a web session to a text file, send mail from a browser, and more. You'll need a web hosting account with an Internet service provider for most of the projects in this book, and it's likely that your host already provides access to PHP.

To get started with PHP, you'll need to make a remote connection to your web hosting account using ssh as you did in the last section. Some of the more basic web hosts don't allow ssh connections, so check to see whether yours does (and if not, look around for an inexpensive hosting company that does; it will be well worth it for the flexibility of working from the command line). Once you're connected, type:

```
php -v
```

You should get a reply like this:

```
PHP 5.3.4 (cli) (built: Dec 15 2010 12:15:07)
Copyright (c) 1997-2010 The PHP Group
Zend Engine v2.3.0, Copyright (c) 1998-2010 Zend
Technologies
```

This tells what version of PHP is installed on your server. The code in this book was written using PHP5, so as long as you're running that version or later, you'll be fine. PHP makes it easy to write web pages that can display results from databases, send messages to other servers, send email, and more.

Most of the time, you won't be executing your PHP scripts directly from the command line. Instead, you'll be calling the web server application on your server—most likely a program called Apache—and asking it for a file (this is all accomplished simply by opening a web browser, typing in the address of a document on your web server, and pressing Enter—just like visiting any other web page). If

Figure 1-5
The results of your first PHP script,
in a browser.

the file you ask for is a PHP script, the web server application will look for your file and execute it. It'll then send a message back to you with the results.

For more on this, see Chapter 3. For now, let's get a simple PHP program or two working. Here's your first PHP program. Open your favorite text editor, type in the following code, and save it on the server with the name **hello. php** in your **public_html** directory (your web pages may be stored in a different directory, such as **www** or **web/public**):

```
<?php
echo "<html><head></head><body>\n";
echo "hello world!\n";
echo "</body></html>\n";
?>
```

Now, back at the command line, type the following to see the results:

```
php hello.php
```

You should get the following response:

```
<html><head></head><body>
hello world!
</body></html>
```

Now, try opening this file in a browser. To see this program in action, open a web browser and navigate to the file's address on your website. Because you saved it in **public_html**, the address is http://www.example.com/hello.php

> ⚠ **If you see the PHP source code instead of what's shown in Figure 1-5, you may have opened up the PHP script as a local file (make sure your web browser's location bar says** http:// **instead of** file://**).**

(replace example.com with your website and any additional path info needed to access your home files, such as http://tigoe.net/~tigoe/hello.php). You should get a web page like the one shown in Figure 1-5.

If it still doesn't work, your web server may not be configured for PHP. Another possibility is that your web server uses a different extension for php scripts, such as **.php4**. Consult with your web hosting provider for more information.

You may have noticed that the program is actually printing out HTML text. PHP was made to be combined with HTML. In fact, you can even embed PHP in HTML pages, by using the <? and ?> tags that start and end every PHP script. If you get an error when you try to open your PHP script in a browser, ask your system administrator whether there are any requirements as to which directories PHP scripts need to be in on your server, or on the file permissions for your PHP scripts.

Here's a slightly more complex PHP script. Save it to your server in the **public_html** directory as **time.php**:

```php
<?php
/*

   Date printer
   Context: PHP

   Prints the date and time in an HTML page.
*/
//    Get the date, and format it:
$date = date("Y-m-d h:i:s\t");

// print the beginning of an HTML page:
echo "<html><head></head><body>\n";
echo "hello world!<br>\n";
// Include the date:
echo "Today's date: $date<br>\n";
// finish the HTML:
echo "</body></html>\n";
?>
```

To see it in action, type http://www.example.com/time.php into your browser (replacing example.com as before). You should get the date and time. You can see this program uses a variable, $date, and calls a built-in PHP function, date(), to fill the variable. You don't have to declare the types of your variables in PHP. Any simple, or scalar, variable begins with a $ and can contain an integer, a floating-point number, or a string. PHP uses the same C-style syntax as Processing, so you'll see that if-then statements, repeat loops, and comments all look familiar.

Variables in PHP
PHP handles variables a little differently than Processing and Arduino. In the latter two, you give variables any name you like, as long as you don't use words that are commands in the language. You declare variables by putting the variable type before the name the first time you use it. In PHP, you don't need to declare a variable's type, but you do need to put a $ at the beginning of the name. You can see it in the PHP script above. $date is a variable, and you're putting a string into it using the date() command.

There are a number of commands for checking variables that you'll see in PHP. For example, isset() checks whether the variable's been given a value yet, or is_bool(), is_int(), and is_string() check to see whether the variable contains those particular data types (boolean, integer, and string, respectively).

In PHP, there are three important built-in variables, called environment variables, with which you should be familiar: $_REQUEST, $_GET, and $_POST. These give you the results of an HTTP request. Whether your PHP script was called by a HTML form or by a user entering a URL with a string of variables afterwards, these variables will give you the results. $_GET gives you the results if the PHP script was called using an HTTP GET request, $_POST gives the results of an HTTP POST request, and $_REQUEST gives you the results regardless of what type of request was made.

Since HTTP requests might contain a number of different pieces of information (think of all the fields you might fill out in a typical web form), these are all array variables. To get at a particular element, you can generally ask for it by name. For example, if the form you filled out had a field called Name, the name you fill in would end up in the $_REQUEST variable in an element called $_REQUEST['Name']. If the form made an HTTP POST request, you could also get the name from $_POST['Name']. There are other environment variables you'll learn about as well, but these three are the most useful for getting information from a client—whether it's a web browser or a microcontroller. You'll learn more about these, and see them in action, later in the book.

For more on PHP, check out www.php.net, the main source for PHP, where you'll find some good tutorials on how to use it. You can also read **Learning PHP 5** by David Sklar (O'Reilly) for a more in-depth treatment.

Serial Communication Tools
The remote-access programs in the earlier section were terminal emulation programs that gave you access to remote computers through the Internet, but that's not all a terminal emulation program can do. Before TCP/IP was ubiquitous as a way for computers to connect to networks, connectivity was handled through modems attached to the serial ports of computers. Back then, many users connected to bulletin boards (BBSes) and used menu-based systems to post messages on discussion boards, down-load files, and send mail to other users of the same BBS.

Nowadays, serial ports are used mainly to connect to some of your computer's peripheral devices. In microcontroller programming, they're used to exchange data between the computer and the microcontroller. For the projects in this book, you'll find that using a terminal program to connect to your serial ports is indispensable. There are several freeware and shareware terminal programs available. CoolTerm is an excellent piece of freeware by Roger Meier available from http://freeware.the-meiers.org. It works on Mac OS X and Windows, and it's my personal favorite these days. If you use it, do the right thing and make a donation because it's developed in the programmer's spare time. For Windows users, PuTTY is a decent alternative because it can open both serial and ssh terminals. PuTTY is also available for Linux. Alternatively, you can keep it simple and stick with a classic: the GNU screen program running in a terminal window. OS X users can use screen as well, though it's less full-featured than CoolTerm.

Windows serial communication

To get started, you'll need to know the serial port name. Click Start→Run (use the Search box on Windows 7), type devmgmt.msc, and press Enter to launch Device Manager. If you've got a serial device such as a Wiring or Arduino board attached, you'll see a listing for Ports (COM & LPT). Under that listing, you'll see all the available serial ports. Each new Wiring or Arduino board you connect will get a new name, such as COM5, COM6, COM7, and so forth.

Once you know the name of your serial port, open PuTTY. In the Session category, set the Connection Type to Serial, and enter the name of your port in the Serial Line box, as shown in Figure 1-6. Then click the Serial category at the end of the category list, and make sure that the serial line matches your port name. Configure the serial line for 9600 baud, 8 data bits, 1 stop bit, no parity, and no flow control. Then click the Open button, and a serial window will open. Anything you type in this window will be sent out the serial port, and any data that comes in the serial port will be displayed here as ASCII text.

NOTE: Unless your Arduino is running a program that communicates over the serial port (and you'll learn all about that shortly), you won't get any response yet.

Mac OS X serial communication

To get started, open CoolTerm and click the Options icon. In the Options tab, you'll see a pulldown menu for the port. In Mac OS X, the port names are similar to this: /dev/tty.usbmodem241241. To find your port for sure, check the list when your Arduino is unplugged, then plug it in and click Re-scan Serial Ports in the Options tab. The new port listed is your Arduino's serial connection. To open the serial port, click the Connect button in the main menu. To disconnect, click Disconnect.

 ## Who's Got the Port?

Serial ports aren't easily shared between applications. In fact, only one application can have control of a serial port at a time. If PuTTY, CoolTerm, or the screen program has the serial port open to an Arduino module, for example, the Arduino IDE can't download new code to the module. When an application tries to open a serial port, it requests exclusive control of it either by writing to a special file called a lock file, or by asking the operating system to lock the file on its behalf. When it closes the serial port, it releases the lock on the serial port. Sometimes when an application crashes while it's got a serial port open, it can forget to close the serial port, with the result that no other application can open the port. When this happens, the only thing you can do to fix it is to restart the operating system, which clears all the locks (alternatively, you could wait for the operating system to figure out that the lock should be released). To avoid this problem, make sure that you close the serial port whenever you switch from one application to another. Linux and Mac OS X users should get in the habit of closing down screen with Ctrl-A then Ctrl-\ every time, and Windows users should disconnect the connection in PuTTY. Otherwise, you may find yourself restarting your machine a lot.

Adventurous Mac OS X users can take advantage of the fact that it's Unix-based and follow the Linux instructions.

Linux serial communication

To get started with serial communication in Linux (or Mac OS X), open a terminal window and type:

```
ls /dev/tty.*    # Mac OS X
ls /dev/tty*     # Linux
```

This command will give you a list of available serial ports. The names of the serial ports in Mac OS X and Linux are more unique, but they're more cryptic than the COM1, COM2, and so on that Windows uses. Pick your serial port and type:

```
screen portname datarate.
```

Figure 1-6
Configuring a serial connection in PuTTY.

For example, to open the serial port on an Arduino board (discussed shortly) at 9600 bits per second, you might type screen /dev/tty.usbmodem241241 9600 on Mac OS X. On Linux, the command might be screen /dev/ttyUSB0 9600. The screen will be cleared, and any characters you type will be sent out the serial port you opened. They won't show up on the screen, however. Any bytes received in the serial port will be displayed in the window as characters. To close the serial port, type Ctrl-A followed by Ctrl-\.

In the next section, you'll use a serial communications program to communicate with a microcontroller.

Hardware

Arduino, Wiring, and Derivatives
The main microcontroller used in this book is the Arduino module. Arduino and Wiring, another microcontroller module, both came out of the Institute for Interaction Design in Ivrea, Italy, in 2005. They're based on the same microcontroller family, Atmel's ATmega series (www.atmel.com), and they're both programmed in C/C++. The "dialect" they speak is based on Processing, as is the software integrated development environments (IDEs) they use. You'll see that some Processing commands have made their way into Arduino and Wiring, such as the setup() and loop() methods (Processing's draw() method was originally called loop()), the map() function, and more.

When this book was first written, there was one Wiring board, four or five variants of Arduino, and almost no derivatives. Now, there are several Arduino models, two new Wiring models coming out shortly, and scores of Arduino-compatible derivatives, most of which are compatible enough that you can program them directly from the Arduino IDE. Others have their own IDEs and will work with some (but not all) of the code in this book. Still others are compatible in their physical design but are programmed with other languages. The derivatives cover a wide range of applications.

Figure 1-7
The CoolTerm serial terminal program.

The following projects have been tested extensively on Arduino boards and, when possible, on the classic Wiring board. Though you'll find some differences, code written for a Wiring board should work on an Arduino board, and vice versa. For Arduino derivatives, check with the manufacturer of your individual board. Many of them are very active in the Arduino forums and are happy to lend support.

You'll find that the editors for Arudino and Wiring look very similar. These free and open source programming environments are available through their respective websites: www.arduino.cc and www.wiring.org.co.

The hardware for both is also open source, and you can buy it from various online retailers, listed on the sites above. Or, if you're a hardcore hardware geek and like to make your own printed circuit boards, you can download the plans to do so. I recommend purchasing them online,

as it's much quicker (and more reliable, for most people). Figure 1-8 shows some of your options.

One of the best things about Wiring and Arduino is that they are cross-platform; they work well on Mac OS X, Windows, and Linux. This is a rarity in microcontroller development environments.

Another good thing about these environments is that, like Processing, they can be extended. Just as you can include Java classes and methods in your Processing programs, you can include C/C++ code, written in AVR-C, in your Wiring and Arduino programs. For more on how to do this, visit their respective websites.

For an excellent introduction to Arduino, see Massimo Banzi's book **Getting Started with Arduino** (O'Reilly). X

Figure 1-8. Varieties of Arduino, as well as a Wiring board: **1.** LilyPad Arduino **2.** Arduino Uno SMD **3.** Arduino Fio **4.** Arduino Pro Mini **5.** Arduino Mini **6.** Arduino Nano **7.** Arduino Mega 2560 **8.** Arduino Uno **9.** Wiring board **10.** Arduino Pro **11.** Arduino Ethernet **12.** Arduino Bluetooth **13.** Arduino Duemilanove.

Figure 1-9. A sampling of shields for Arduino: **1.** Arduino prototyping shield **2.** Adafruit prototyping shield **3.** Arduino Ethernet shield **4.** TinkerKit DMX shield **5.** Arduino wireless shield **6.** Oomlout Arduino/breadboard mount, manufactured by Adafruit **7.** Spark Fun microSD card shield **8.** Adafruit motor driver shield **9.** Spark Fun musical instrument shield.

Arduino Shields

One of the features that makes Arduino easy to work with are the add-on modules called shields, which allow you to add preassembled circuits to the main module. For most applications you can think of, there's a third-party company or individual making a shield to do it. Need a MIDI synthesizer? There's a shield for that. Need NTSC video output? There's a shield for that. Need WiFi or Ethernet? There's a shield for that, and you'll be using them extensively in this book.

The growth of shields has been a major factor in the spread of Arduino, and the well-designed and documented ones make it possible to build many projects with no electronic experience whatsoever. You'll be using some shields in this book, and for other projects, building the actual circuit yourself.

The shields you'll see most commonly in this book are the Ethernet shield, which gives you the ability to connect your controller to the Internet; the wireless shield, which lets you interface with Digi's XBee radios and other radios with the same footprint; and some prototyping shields, which make it easy to design a custom circuit for your project.

The shield footprint, like the board designs, is available online at www.arduino.cc. If you've got experience making printed circuit boards, try your hand at making your own shield—it's fun.

Until recently, shields for Arduino weren't physically compatible with Wiring boards. However, Rogue Robotics (www.roguerobotics.com) just started selling an adapter for the Wiring board that allows it to take shields for Arduino.

Beware! Not every shield is compatible with every board. Some derivative boards do not operate on the same voltage as the Arduino boards, so they may not be compatible with shields designed to operate at 5 volts. If you're using a different microcontroller board, check with the manufacturer of your board to be sure it works with your shields. X

Other Microcontrollers

Though the examples in this book focus on Arduino, there are many other microcontroller platforms that you can use to do the same work. Despite differences among the platforms, there are some principles that apply to them all. They're basically small computers. They communicate with the world by turning on or off the voltage on their output pins, or reading voltage changes on their input pins. Most microcontrollers can read variable voltage changes on a subset of their I/O pins. All microcontrollers can communicate with other computers using one or more forms of digital communication. Listed below are a few other microcontrollers on the market today.

8-bit controllers

The Atmel microcontrollers that are at the heart of both Arduino and Wiring are 8-bit controllers, meaning that they can process data and instructions in 8-bit chunks. 8-bit controllers are cheap and ubiquitous, and they can sense and control things in the physical world very effectively. They can sense simple physical characteristics at a resolution and speed that exceeds our senses. They show up in nearly every electronic device in your life, from your clock radio to your car to your refrigerator.

There are many other 8-bit controllers that are great for building physical devices. Parallax (www.parallax.com) Basic Stamp and Basic Stamp 2 (BS-2) are probably the most common microcontrollers in the hobbyist market. They are easy to use and include the same basic functions as Wiring and Arduino. However, the language they're programmed in, PBASIC, lacks the ability to pass parameters to functions, which makes programming many of the examples shown in this book more difficult. Revolution Education's PICAXE environment (www.rev-ed.co.uk) is very similar to the PBASIC of the Basic Stamp, but it's a less expensive way to get started than the Basic Stamp. Both the PICAXE and the Stamp are capable of doing the things shown in this book, but their limited programming language makes the doing a bit more tedious.

PIC and AVR

Microchip's PIC (www.microchip.com) and Atmel's AVR are excellent microcontrollers. You'll find the AVRs at the heart of Arduino and Wiring, and the PICs at the heart of the Basic Stamps and PICAXEs. The Basic Stamp, PICAXE, Wiring, and Arduino environments are essentially wrappers around these controllers, making them easier to work with. To use PICs or AVRs on their own, you need a hardware programmer that connects to your computer, and you need to install a programming environment and a compiler.

Though the microcontrollers themselves are cheap (between $1 and $10 apiece), getting all the tools set up for yourself can cost you some money. There's also a pretty significant time investment in getting set up, as the tools for programming these controllers from scratch assume a level of technical knowledge—both in software and hardware—that's higher than the other tools listed here.

32-bit controllers

Your personal computer is likely using a 64-bit processor, and your mobile phone is likely using a 32-bit processor. These processors are capable of more complex tasks, such as multitasking and media control and playback.

Initially, 32-bit processors were neither affordable nor easy to program, but that has been changing rapidly in the last couple of years, and there are now several 32-bit microcontroller platforms on the market. Texas Instruments' BeagleBoard (http://beagleboard.org) is a 32-bit processor board with almost everything you need to make a basic personal computer: HDMI video out, USB, SD card and connections for mass storage devices, and more. It can run a minimal version of the Linux operating system. Netduino (www.netduino.com) is a 32-bit processor designed to take Arduino shields, but it's programmed using an open source version of Microsoft's .NET programming framework. LeafLabs' Maple (http://leaflabs.com) is another 32-bit processor that uses the same footprint as the Arduino Uno, and is programmed in C/C++ like the Arduino and Wiring boards. In addition to these, there are several others coming on the market in the near future.

The increasing ease-of-use of 32-bit processors is bringing exciting changes for makers of physical interfaces, though not necessarily in basic input and output. 8-bit controllers can already sense simple physical

Other Microcontrollers (cont'd)

changes and control outputs at resolutions that exceed human perception. However, complex-sensing features— such as gesture recognition, multitasking, simpler memory management, and the ability to interface with devices using the same methods and libraries as personal computers—will make a big difference. 32-bit processors give physical interface makers the ability to use or convert code libraries and frameworks developed on servers and personal computers. There is where the real excitement of these processors lies.

These possibilities are just beginning to be realized and will easily fill another book, or several. However, basic sensing and networked communications are still well within the capabilities of 8-bit controllers, so I've chosen to keep the focus of this book on them.

Like all microcontrollers, the Arduino and Wiring modules are just small computers. Like every computer, they have inputs, outputs, a power supply, and a communications port to connect to other devices. You can power these modules either through a separate power supply or through the USB connection to your computer. For this introduction, you'll power the module from the USB connection. For many projects, you'll want to disconnect them from the computer once you've finished programming them. When you do, you'll power the board from the external power supply.

Figure 1-10 shows the inputs and outputs for the Arduino Uno. The other Arduino models and the Wiring module are similar. Each module has the same standard features as most microcontrollers: analog inputs, digital inputs and outputs, and power and ground connections. Some of the I/O pins can also be used for serial communication. Others can be used for pulse-width modulation (PWM), which is a way of creating a fake analog voltage by turning the pin on and off very fast. The Wiring and Arduino boards also have a USB connector that's connected to a USB-to-Serial controller, which allows the main controller to communicate with your computer serially over the USB port. They also have a programming header to allow you to reprogram the firmware (which you'll never do in this book) and a reset button. You'll see these diagrams repeated frequently, as they are the basis for all the microcontroller projects in the book.

Getting Started
Because the installation process for Wiring and Arduino is similar, I'll detail only the Arduino process here. Wiring users can follow along and do the same steps, substituting "Wiring" for "Arduino" in the instructions. Download the software from the appropriate site, then follow the instructions below. Check the sites for updates on these instructions.

Updates to the Arduino and Wiring software occur frequently. The notes in this book refer to Arduino version 1.0 and Wiring version 1.0. By the time you read this, the specifics may be slightly different, so check the Arduino and Wiring websites for the latest details.

Setup on Mac OS X
Double-click the downloaded file to unpack it, and you'll get a disk image that contains the Arduino application and an installer for FTDI USB-to-Serial drivers. Drag the application to your **Applications** directory. If you're using an Arduino Uno or newer board, you won't need the FTDI drivers, but if you're using a Duemilanove or older board, or a Wiring board, you'll need the drivers. Regardless of the board you have, there's no harm in installing them—even if you don't need them. Run the installer and follow the instructions to install the drivers.

Figure 1-10

Functional parts of an Arduino. Most microcontrollers have the same or similar parts: power connections, digital and analog inputs, and serial communications.

⌸ Document What You Make

You'll see a lot of circuit diagrams in this book, as well as flowcharts of programs, system diagrams, and more. The projects you'll make with this book are systems with many parts, and you'll find it helps to keep diagrams of what's involved, which parts talk to which, and what protocols they use to communicate. I used three drawing tools heavily in this book, all of which I recommend for documenting your work:

Adobe Illustrator (www.adobe.com/products/illustrator.html). You really can't beat it for drawing things, even though it's expensive and takes time to learn well. There are many libraries of electronic schematic symbols freely available on the Web.

Inkscape (www.inkscape.org). This is an open source tool for vector drawing. Though the GUI is not as well developed as Illustrator, it's pretty darn good. The majority of the schematics in this book were done in Illustrator and Inkscape.

Fritzing (www.fritzing.org). Fritzing is an open source tool for documenting, sharing, teaching, and designing interactive

electronic projects. It's a good tool for learning how to read schematics, because you can draw circuits as they physically look, and then have Fritzing generate a schematic of what you drew. Fritzing also has a good library of vector graphic electronics parts that can be used in other vector programs. This makes it easy to move from one program to another in order to take advantage of all three.

Figure 1-10 was cobbled together from all three tools, combining the work of Jody Culkin and Giorgio Olivero, with a few details from André Knörig and Jonathan Cohen's Fritzing drawings. You'll see it frequently throughout the book.

It's a good idea to keep notes on what you do as well, and share them publicly so others can learn from them. I rely on a combination of three note-taking tools: blogs powered by Wordpress (www.wordpress.org) at www.makingthingstalk.com, http://tigoe.net/blog, and http://tigoe.net/pcomp/code; a github repository (https://github.com/tigoe); and a stack of Maker's Notebooks (www.makershed.com, part no. 9780596519414).

⬆ **Figure 1-11**
Toolbars for Arduino version 0022, Arduino 1.0, and Wiring 1.0.

Once you're installed, open the Arduino application and you're ready to go.

Setup on Windows 7

Unzip the downloaded file. It can go anywhere on your system. The **Program Files** directory is a good place. Next, you'll need to install drivers, whether you have an Arduino Uno board or an older board, or a Wiring board.

Plug in your Arduino and wait for Windows to begin its driver installation process. If it's a Duemilanove or earlier, it will need the FTDI drivers. These should install automatically over the Internet when you plug your Duemilanove in; if not, there is a copy in the **drivers** directory of the Arduino application directory. If it's an Uno or newer, click on the Start Menu and open up the Control Panel. Open the "System and Security" tab. Next, click on System,

then open the Device Manager. Under Ports (COM & LPT), you should see a port named Arduino UNO (COMxx). Right-click on this port and choose the Update Driver Software option. Click the "Browse my computer for Driver software" option. Finally, navigate to and select the Uno's driver file, named **ArduinoUNO.inf**, located in the **drivers** directory. Windows will finish up the driver installation from there.

Setup on Linux

Arduino for Linux depends on the flavor of Linux you're using. See www.arduino.cc/playground/Learning/Linux for details on several Linux variants. For Ubuntu users, it's available from the Ubuntu Software Update tool.

Now you're ready to launch Arduino. Connect the module to your USB port and double-click the Arduino icon to launch the software. The editor looks like Figure 1-12.

The environment is based on Processing and has New, Open, and Save buttons on the main toolbar. In Arduino and Wiring, the Run function is called Verify, and there is

▶▶ **Figure 1-12**
The Arduino programming environment.
The Wiring environment looks similar,
except the color is different.

```
buttons | Arduino 1.0-beta1

buttons

void setup() {
  Serial.begin(9600);      // open serial communications
  pinMode(2, INPUT);       // make pin 2 an input
  pinMode(3, INPUT);       // make pin 3 an input
}

void loop() {
  int roundButton = digitalRead(2);    // read pin 2
  int squareButton = digitalRead(3);   // read pin 3
  Serial.print("round: ");             // print out:
  Serial.print(roundButton);               // pin 2
  Serial.print("   square: ");
  Serial.println(squareButton);            // pin 3
}

Done Saving.

13
```

an Upload button as well. Verify compiles your program
to check for any errors, and Upload both compiles
and uploads your code to the microcontroller module.
There's an additional button, Serial Monitor, that you can
use to receive serial data from the module while you're
debugging.

Changes to version 1.0

For Arduino users familiar with previous versions, you'll
see some changes in version 1.0. The toolbar has changed
a bit. Figure 1-11 compares the toolbars of Arduino version
0022 (pre-1.0), Arduino 1.0, and Wiring 1.0. Arduino 1.0
now saves files with the extension .ino instead of .pde, to
avoid conflict with Processing, which uses .pde. Wiring 1.0
still uses .pde. In addition, you can now upload sketches in
Arduino 1.0 using an external hardware programmer. The
Programmer submenu of the Tools menu lets you set your
programmer.
X

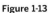

Figure 1-13
LED connected to pin 13 of an
Arduino board. Add 220-ohm cur-
rent-limiting resistor in series with
this if you plan to run it for more
than a few minutes.

Try It

Here's your first program.

```
/*  Blink
       Context: Arduino

       Blinks an LED attached to pin 13 every half second.

       Connections:
           Pin 13:  + leg of an LED (- leg goes to ground)
*/


int LEDPin = 13;


void setup() {
   pinMode(LEDPin, OUTPUT);      // set pin 13 to be an output
}


void loop() {
   digitalWrite(LEDPin, HIGH);      // turn the LED on pin 13 on
   delay(500);                      // wait half a second
   digitalWrite(LEDPin, LOW);       // turn the LED off
   delay(500);                      // wait half a second
}
```

" In order to see this run, you'll need to connect an LED from pin 13 of the board to ground (GND), as shown in Figure 1-13. The positive (long) end of the LED should go to 13, and the short end to ground.

Then type the code into the editor. Click on Tools→Board to choose your Arduino model, and then Tools→Serial Port to choose the serial port of the Arduino module. On the Mac or Linux, the serial port will have a name like this: /dev/tty.usbmodem241241. If it's an older board or a Wiring board, it will be more like this: /dev/tty.usbserial-1B1 (the letters and numbers after the dash will be slightly different each time you connect it). On Windows, it should be COMx, where x is some number (for example, COM5).

NOTE: On Windows, COM1–COM4 are generally reserved for built-in serial ports, regardless of whether your computer has them.

Once you've selected the port and model, click Verify to compile your code. When it's compiled, you'll get a message at the bottom of the window saying Done compiling. Then click Upload. This will take a few seconds. Once it's done, you'll get a message saying Done uploading, and a confirmation message in the serial monitor window that says:

Binary sketch size: 1010 bytes (of a 32256 byte maximum)

Once the sketch is uploaded, the LED you wired to the output pin will begin to blink. That's the microcontroller equivalent of "Hello World!"

NOTE: If it doesn't work, you might want to seek out some external help. The Arduino Learning section has many tutorials (www.arduino. cc/en/Tutorial). The Arduino (www.arduino.cc/forum) and Wiring (http://forum.wiring.co) forums are full of helpful people who love to hack these sort of things.

Serial communication

One of the most frequent tasks you'll use a microcontroller for in this book is to communicate serially with another device, either to send sensor readings over a network or to receive commands to control motors, lights, or other outputs from the microcontroller. Regardless of what device you're communicating with, the commands you'll use in your microcontroller program will be the same. First, you'll configure the serial connection for the right data rate. Then, you'll read bytes in, write bytes out, or both, depending on what device you're talking to and how the conversation is structured.

NOTE: If you've got experience with the Basic Stamp or PicBasic Pro, you will find Arduino serial communications a bit different than what you are used to. In PBasic and PicBasic Pro, the serial pins and the data rate are defined each time you send a message. In Wiring and Arduino, the serial pins are unchangeable, and the data rate is set at the beginning of the program. This way is a bit less flexible than the PBasic way, but there are some advantages, as you'll see shortly.

 Where's My Serial Port?

The USB serial port that's associated with the Arduino or Wiring module is actually a software driver that loads every time you plug in the module. When you unplug, the serial driver deactivates and the serial port will disappear from the list of available ports. You might also notice that the port name changes when you unplug and plug in the module. On Windows machines, you may get a new COM number. On Macs, you'll get a different alphanumeric code at the end of the port name.

Never unplug a USB serial device when you've got its serial port open; you must exit the Wiring or Arduino software environment before you unplug anything. Otherwise, you're sure to crash the application, and possibly the whole operating system, depending on how well behaved the software driver is.

Try It

This next Arduino program listens for incoming serial data. It adds one to whatever serial value it receives, and then sends the result back out. It also blinks an LED on pin regularly—on the same pin as the last example—to let you know that it's still working.

```
/*
    Simple Serial
    Context: Arduino
    Listens for an incoming serial byte, adds one to the byte
    and sends the result back out serially.
    Also blinks an LED on pin 13 every half second.
 */

int LEDPin = 13;             // you can use any digital I/O pin you want
int inByte = 0;              // variable to hold incoming serial data
long blinkTimer = 0;         // keeps track of how long since the LED
                             // was last turned off
int blinkInterval = 1000;    // a full second from on to off to on again

void setup() {
  pinMode(LEDPin, OUTPUT);   // set pin 13 to be an output
  Serial.begin(9600);        // configure the serial port for 9600 bps
                             // data rate.
}

void loop() {
  // if there are any incoming serial bytes available to read:
  if (Serial.available() > 0) {
    // then read the first available byte:
    inByte = Serial.read();
    // and add one to it, then send the result out:
```

»

```
Continued from previous page.

      Serial.write(inByte+1);
    }


    // Meanwhile, keep blinking the LED.
    // after a half of a second, turn the LED on:
    if (millis() - blinkTimer >= blinkInterval / 2) {
      digitalWrite(LEDPin, HIGH);        // turn the LED on pin 13 on
    }
    // after a half a second, turn the LED off and reset the timer:
    if (millis() - blinkTimer >= blinkInterval) {
      digitalWrite(LEDPin, LOW);         // turn the LED off
      blinkTimer = millis();             // reset the timer
    }
  }
}
```

To send bytes from the computer to the micro-controller module, first compile and upload this program. Then click the Serial Monitor icon (the rightmost icon on the toolbar). The screen will change to look like Figure 1-14. Set the serial rate to 9600 baud.

Type any letter in the text entry box and press Enter or click Send. The module will respond with the next letter in sequence. For every character you type, the module adds one to that character's ASCII value, and sends back the result.

Connecting Components to the Module

The Arduino and Wiring modules don't have many sockets for connections other than the I/O pins, so you'll need to keep a solderless breadboard handy to build subcircuits for your sensors and actuators (output devices). Figure 1-15 shows a standard setup for connections between the two.

Basic Circuits

There are two basic circuits that you'll use a lot in this book: digital input and analog input. If you're familiar with microcontroller development, you're already familiar with them. Any time you need to read a sensor value, you can start with one of these. Even if you're using a custom sensor in your final object, you can use these circuits as placeholders, just to see any changing sensor values.

Digital input

A digital input to a microcontroller is nothing more than a switch. The switch is connected to voltage and to a digital input pin of the microcontroller. A high-value resistor (10 kilohms is good) connects the input pin to ground. This is called a pull-down resistor. Other electronics tutorials may connect the switch to ground and the resistor to voltage. In that case, you'd call the resistor a pull-up resistor. Pull-up and pull-down resistors provide a reference to power (pull-up) and ground (pull-down) for digital input pins. When a switch is wired as shown in Figure 1-16, closing the switch sets the input pin high. Wired the other way, closing the switch sets the input pin low.

Analog input

The circuit in Figure 1-17 is called a voltage divider. The variable resistor and the fixed resistor divide the voltage between them. The ratio of the resistors' values deter-mines the voltage at this connection. If you connect the analog-to-digital converter of a microcontroller to this point, you'll see a changing voltage as the variable resistor changes. You can use any kind of variable resistor: pho-tocells, thermistors, force-sensing resistors, flex-sensing resistors, and more.

The potentiometer, shown in Figure 1-18, is a special type of variable resistor. It's a fixed resistor with a wiper that slides along its conductive surface. The resistance changes between the wiper and both ends of the resistor as you move the wiper. Basically, a potentiometer (pot for short) is two variable resistors in one package. If you connect the ends to voltage and ground, you can read a changing voltage at the wiper.

⬆ **Figure 1-14**

The Serial monitor in Arduino, running the previous sketch. The user typed BCDEFGH.

◀◀ **Figure 1-15**

Arduino connected to a breadboard. +5V and ground run from the module to the long rows of the board. This way, all sensors and actuators can share the +5V and ground connections of the board. Control or signal connections from each sensor or actuator run to the appropriate I/O pins. In this example, two pushbuttons are attached to digital pins 2 and 3 as digital inputs.

There are many other circuits you'll learn in the projects that follow, but these are the staples of all the projects in this book.

Specialty circuits and modules

You'll see a number of specialty circuits and modules throughout this book, like the Bluetooth Mate and the XBee radios. These are devices that allow you to send serial data wirelessly. You'll also build a few of your own circuits for specific projects. All of the circuits will be shown on a breadboard like these, but you can build them any way you like. If you're familiar with working on printed circuit boards and prefer to build your circuits that way, feel free to do so.

X

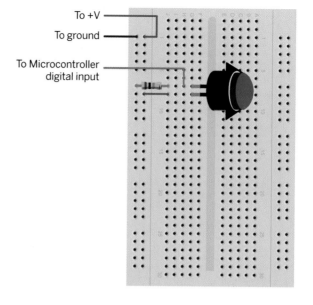

To +V
To ground
To Microcontroller digital input

⚠ You will encounter variations on many of the modules and components used in this book. For example, the Arduino module has several variations, as shown in Figure 1-8. The FTDI USB-to-Serial module used in later chapters has at least three variations. Even the voltage regulators used in this book have variations. Be sure to check the data sheet on whatever component or module you're using, as your version may vary from what is shown here.

Input voltage

To microcontroller digital input

Figure 1-16
Digital input to a microcontroller.
Top: breadboard view.
Bottom: schematic view.

Figure 1-17

Voltage divider used as analog input to a microcontroller.

Top: breadboard view.

Bottom: schematic view.

Figure 1-18

Potentiometer used as analog input to a microcontroller.

Top: breadboard view.

Bottom: schematic view.

❝ Using an Oscilloscope

Most of what you'll be building in this book involves computer circuits that read a changing voltage over time. Whether your microcontroller is reading a digital or analog input, controlling the speed of a motor, or sending data to a personal computer, it's either reading a voltage or generating a voltage that changes over time. The time intervals it works in are much faster than yours. For example, the serial communication you just saw involved an electrical pulse changing at about 10,000 times per second. You can't see anything that fast on a multimeter. This is when an oscilloscope is useful.

An oscilloscope is a tool for viewing the changes in an electrical signal over time. You can change the sensitivity of its voltage reading (in volts per division of the screen) and of the time interval (in seconds, milliseconds, or microseconds per division) at which it reads. You can also change how it displays the signal. You can show it in real time, starting or stopping it as you need, or you can capture it when a particular voltage threshold (called a trigger) is crossed.

Oscilloscopes were once beyond the budget of most hobbyists, but lately, a number of inexpensive ones have come on the market. The DSO Nano from Seeed Studio, shown in Figure 1-19, is a good example. At about $100, it's a really good value if you're a dedicated electronic hobbyist. It doesn't have all the features that a full professional 'scope has, but it does give you the ability to change the volts per division and seconds per division, and to set a voltage trigger for taking a snapshot. It can sample up to 1 million times a second, which is more than enough to measure most serial applications. The image you see in Figure 1-19 shows the output of an Arduino sending the message "Hello World!" Each block represents one bit of

Figure 1-19
DSO Nano oscilloscope reading a serial data stream.

data. The vertical axis is the voltage measurement, and the horizontal measurement is time. The Nano was sampling at 200 microseconds per division in this image, and 1 volt per division vertically. The 'scopes leads are attached to the ground pin of the Arduino and to digital pin 1, which is the serial transmit pin.

Besides inexpensive hardware 'scopes, there are also many software 'scopes available, both as freeware and as paid software. These typically use the audio input of your computer to sample the incoming voltage. The danger, of course, is that if you send in too much voltage you can damage your computer. For this reason, I prefer a hardware 'scope. But if you're interested in software 'scopes, a web search on software oscilloscope and your operating system will yield plenty of useful results.
X

❝ It Ends with the Stuff You Touch

Though most of this book is about the fascinating world of making things talk to each other, it's important to remember that you're most likely building your project for the enjoyment of someone who doesn't care about the technical details under the hood.

Even if you're building it only for yourself, you don't want to have to fix it all the time. All that matters to the person using your system are the parts that she can see, hear, and touch. All the inner details are irrelevant if the physical interface doesn't work. So don't spend all of your time focusing on the communication between devices and leave out the communication with people. In fact, it's best to think about the specifics of what the person does and sees first.

There are a number of details that are easy to overlook but are very important to humans. For example, many network communications can take several seconds or more. In a screen-based operating system, progress bars acknowledge a person's input and keep him informed as to the task's progress. Physical objects don't have progress bars, but they should incorporate some indicator as to what they're doing—perhaps as simple as playing a tune or pulsing an LED gently while the network transfer's happening.

Find your own solution, but make sure you give some physical indication as to the invisible activities of your objects.

Don't forget the basic elements, either. Build in a power switch or a reset button. Include a power indicator. Design the shape of the object so that it's clear which end is up. Make your physical controls clearly visible and easy to operate. Plan the sequence of actions you expect a person to take, and lay out the physical affordances for those actions sensibly. You can't tell people what to think about your object—you can only show them how to interact with it through its physical form. There may be times when you violate convention in the way you design your controls—perhaps in order to create a challenging game or to make the object seem more "magical"—but make sure you're doing it intentionally. Always think about the participant's expectations first.

By including the person's behavior in your system planning, you solve some problems that are computationally difficult but easy for human intelligence. Ultimately, the best reason to make things talk to each other is to give people more reasons to talk to each other.

X

2

The Simplest Network

The most basic network is a one-to-one connection between two objects. This chapter covers the details of two-way communication, beginning with the characteristics that have to be agreed upon in advance. You'll learn about some of the logistical elements of network communications: data protocols, flow control, and addressing. You'll practice all of this by building two examples using one-to-one serial communication between a microcontroller and a personal computer. You'll also learn about modem communications and how you can replace the cable connecting the two with Bluetooth radios.

◀◀ Joo Youn Paek's Zipper Orchestra (2006)
This is a musical installation that lets you control video and music using zippers. The zippers are wired to a micro-controller using conductive thread, and the microcontroller communicates serially with a multimedia computer that drives the playback of the zipper movies and sounds as you zip.
Photo courtesy of Joo Youn Paek.

◀⁞ Supplies for Chapter 2

DISTRIBUTOR KEY

- **A** Arduino Store (http://store.arduino.cc/ww/)
- **AF** Adafruit (http://adafruit.com)
- **D** Digi-Key (www.digikey.com)
- **F** Farnell (www.farnell.com)
- **J** Jameco (http://jameco.com)
- **MS** Maker SHED (www.makershed.com)
- **RS** RS (www.rs-online.com)
- **SF** Spark Fun (www.SparkFun.com)
- **SS** Seeed Studio (www.seeedstudio.com)

PROJECT 1: Type Brighter RGB LED Serial Control

» **1 Arduino module** Get something based on the Arduino Uno, but the project should work on other Arduino and Arduino-compatible boards.
D 1050-1019-ND, **J** 2121105, **SF** DEV-09950, **A** A000046, **AF** 50, **F** 1848687, **RS** 715-4081, **SS** ARD132D2P, **MS** MKSP4

» **1 RGB LED, common cathode** It's like three LEDs in one! This emits red, green, and blue on separate channels.
D 754-1492-ND, **J** 2125181, **SF** COM-00105, **F** 8738661, **RS** 713-4888

» **1 personal computer**

» **All necessary converters to communicate serially from microcontroller to computer** For the Arduino and Wiring modules, all you'll need is a USB cable. For other microcontrollers, you'll probably need a USB-to-serial converter and a connector to connect to your breadboard.

» **1 ping-pong ball** Get a white one from your local sports store.

Figure 2-1. New parts for this chapter: **1.** Project box **2.** Bluetooth Mate **3.** RGB LED **4.** Pushbuttons **5.** Flex sensors **6.** Prototyping shield, 7. 9V battery snap connector and female power plug. Don't forget plenty of male header pins for the breakout boards.

PROJECT 2: Monski Pong

» **1 Arduino module** An Arduino Uno or something based on the Arduino Uno, but the project should work on other Arduino and Arduino-compatible boards. **D** 1050-1019-ND, **J** 2121105, **SF** DEV-09950, **A** A000046,**AF** 50, **F** 1848687, **RS** 715-4081, **SS** ARD132D2P, **MS** MKSP4

» **2 flex sensor resistors D** 905-1000-ND, **J** 150551, **SF** SEN-10264, **AF** 182, **RS** 708-1277, **MS** JM150551

» **2 momentary switches** Available from any electronics retailer. Pick the one that makes you the happiest. **D** GH1344-ND, **J** 315432, **SF** COM-09337, **F** 1634684, **RS** 718-2213, **MS** JM315432

» **4 10-kilohm resistors D** 10KQBK-ND, **J** 29911, **F** 9337687, **RS** 707-8906

» **1 solderless breadboard D** 438-1045-ND, **J** 20723 or 20601, **SF** PRT-00137, **F** 4692810, **AF** 64, **SS** STR101C2M or STR102C2M, **MS** MKKN2

» **1 personal computer**

» **All necessary converters to communicate serially from microcontroller to computer** Just like the previous project.

» **1 small pink monkey** aka Monski. You may want a second one for a two-player game.

PROJECT 3: Wireless Monski Pong

» **1 completed Monski pong project** from project 2.

» **1 9V battery and snap connector D** 2238K-ND, **J** 101470, **SF** PRT-09518, **F** 1650675

» **Female power plug, 2.1mm ID, 5.5mm OD** If you got the Spark Fun battery connector, you don't need this part. **D** CP-024A-ND, **J** 159506, **F** 1737256

» **1 Bluetooth Mate module SF** WRL-09358 or WRL-10393

» **1 project box** to house the microcontroller, battery, and radio board.

PROJECT 4: Negotiating in Bluetooth

» **1 Bluetooth Mate module** the same one used in project 3. **SF** WRL-09358 or WRL-10393

» **1 FTDI-style USB-to-Serial adapter** Both the 5V or 3.3V versions will work; these come as cables or standalone modules. **SF** DEV-09718 or DEV-09716, **AF** 70 or 284, **A** A000059, **MS** MKAD22, **D** TTL-232R-3V3 or TTL-232R-5V

Figure 2-2

FTDI USB-to-TTL cable. This cable comes in handy for connecting to all sorts of serial devices. When plugged into a USB port, it can even provide power for the device with which it's communicating. The adapter boards shown here also act as USB-to-Serial adapters and can replace this cable. L to R: Arduino USB-to-Serial; Spark Fun FTDI Basic Breakout; Adafruit FTDI Friend. They require an additional USB-A-to-Mini-B cable (the kind that comes with most digital cameras), but have built-in LEDs attached to the transmit and receive lines. These LEDs flash when data's going through those lines, and they can be handy for troubleshooting serial problems.

The Arduino adapter, unlike the others, does not use the FTDI drivers. On Mac OS X and Linux, it needs no drivers. On Windows, it uses the same INF file as the Arduino Uno. *Photos courtesy of Spark Fun and Adafruit.*

" Layers of Agreement

Before you can get things to talk to each other, you have to lay some ground rules for the communication between them. These agreements can be broken down into five layers, each of which builds on the previous ones:

• Physical
How are the physical inputs and outputs of each device connected to the others? How many connections between the two devices do you need to get messages across?

• Electrical
What voltage levels will you send to represent the bits of your data?

• Logical
Does an increase in voltage level represent a 0 or a 1? When high voltage represents 1 and low voltage represents 0, it's called true logic. When it's reversed—high voltage represents 0 and low voltage represents 1—it's called inverted logic. You'll see examples of both in the pages that follow.

• Data
What's the timing of the bits? Are the bits read in groups of 8, 9, or 10? More? Are there bits at the beginning or end of each group to punctuate the groups?

• Application
How are the groups of bits arranged into messages? What is the order in which messages have to be exchanged for something to get done?

This is a simplified version of a common model for thinking about networking, called the Open Systems Interconnect (OSI) model. Networking issues are never really this neatly separated, but if you keep these elements distinct in your mind, troubleshooting any connection will be much easier. Thinking in layers like this gives you somewhere to start looking for the problem, and a way to eliminate parts of the system that are *not* the problem.

No matter how complex the network gets, never forget that the communication between electronic devices is all about pulses of energy. Serial communication involves changing the voltage of an electrical connection between the sender and receiver at a specific rate. Each interval of time represents one bit of information. The sender changes the voltage to send a value of 0 or 1 for the bit in question, and the receiver reads whether the voltage is high or low. There are two methods (see Figure 2-3) that the sender and receiver can use to agree on the rate at which bits are sent. In asynchronous serial communication, the rate is agreed upon mutually and clocked independently by sender and receiver. In synchronous serial communication, it's controlled by the sender, who pulses a separate connection high and low at a steady rate. Synchronous serial communication is used mostly for communication between integrated circuits (such as the communication between a computer processor and its memory chips). This chapter concentrates only on asynchronous serial communication, because that's the form of serial communication underlying the networks in the rest of the book.

X

Asynchronous Serial Communication

Sender

Receiver

RX ← Data goes this way — TX

TX — Data goes this way → RX

Ground ——————— Ground

◀◀ **Figure 2-3**
Types of serial communication.

Synchronous Serial Communication

Master

Slave

Chip Select ——————— CS

Master out, slave in — Data goes this way → MOSI

Master in, slave out ← Data goes this way — MISO

Clock — Clock signal goes this way → CLK

5V

Clock pulses

0V

⤓ **Figure 2-4**
Physical connections: USB,
RS-232 serial.

USB Type A

1 2 3 4

1 – +5V
2 – Data-
3 – Data+
4 – Ground

USB Type B

2 1

3 4

USB Type Mini B

1 2 3 4 5

1 – +5V
2 – Data-
3 – Data+
4 – ID
5 – Ground

RS-232

9 8 7 6

5 4 3 2 1

2 – PC Receive
3 – PC Transmit
5 – PC Ground

66 Making the Connection: The Lower Layers

You're already familiar with one example of serial communication, between a microcontroller and a personal computer. In Chapter 1, you connected an Arduino module to a personal computer through the computer's USB port. If you've worked with a different microcontroller, such as Parallax's Basic Stamp, you probably made the connection using a serial-to-USB converter or an older PC that still had a 9-pin RS-232 serial port. That simple connection involved two serial protocols.

First, there's the protocol that the microcontroller speaks, called TTL serial:

• Physical layer
What pins is the controller using to communicate? The Arduino module receives data on digital I/O pin 0, and sends it out on pin 1.

• Electrical layer
It uses pulses of 5 volts or 0 volts to represent bits. Some microcontrollers use 3.3 volts instead of 5 volts.

• Logical layer
A high-voltage (5 volt) signal represents the value 1, and a 0-volt signal represents the value 0.

• Data layer
Data is typically sent at 9600 bits per second. Each byte contains 8 bits, preceded by a start bit and followed by a stop bit (which you never have to bother with).

• Application layer
At this layer, you sent one byte from the PC to the Arduino and processed it, and the Arduino sent back one byte to the PC.

But wait, that's not all that's involved. The 5-volt and 0-volt pulses didn't go directly to the PC. First, they went to a serial-to-USB chip on the board that communicates using TTL serial on one side, and USB on the other.

Second, there's USB, the Universal Serial Bus protocol. It differs from TTL serial in many ways:

• Physical layer
USB sends data on two wires, Data+ and Data-. Every USB connector also has a 5-volt power supply line and a ground line.

• Electrical layer
The signal on Data − is always the polar opposite of what's on Data+, so the sum of their voltages is always zero. Because of this, a receiver can check for electrical errors by adding the two data voltages together. If the sum isn't zero, the receiver can disregard the signal at that point.

• Logical layer
A +5-volt signal (on Data+) or -5-volt signal (on Data-) represents the value 1, and a 0-volt signal represents the value 0.

• Data layer
The data layer of USB is more complex than TTL serial. Data can be sent at up to 480 megabits per second. Each byte contains 8 bits, preceded by a start bit and followed by a stop bit. Many USB devices can share the same pair of wires, sending signals at times dictated by the controlling PC. This arrangement is called a bus (the B in USB). As there can be many devices on the same bus, the operating system gives each one its own unique address, and sees to it that the bytes from each device on the bus go to the applications that need them.

• Application layer
At the application layer, the USB-to-Serial converter on the Arduino boards sends a few bytes to the operating system to identify itself. The operating system then associates the hardware with a library of driver software that other programs can use to access data from the device.

All that control is transparent to you because the computer's USB controller only passes you the bytes you need. The USB-to-Serial chip on your Arduino board presents itself to the operating system as a serial port, and it sends data through the USB connection at the rate you choose (9600 bits per second in the example in Chapter 1).

USB: An Endless Source of Serial Ports

One of the great things about microcontrollers is that, because they're cheap, you can use many of them. For example, in a project with many sensors, you can either write a complex program on the microcontroller to read them all, or you can give each sensor its own microcontroller. If you're trying to get all the information from those sensors into a personal computer, you might think it's easier to use one microcontroller because you've got a limited number of serial ports. Thanks to USB, however, that's not the case.

If your microcontroller speaks USB, or if you've got a USB-to-Serial adapter for it, you can just plug it in and it will show up in the operating system as another serial port.

For example, if you plug three Arduino modules into the same computer through a USB hub, you'll get three new serial ports, named something like this on Mac OS X:

```
/dev/tty.usbmodem241441
/dev/tty.usbmodem241461
/dev/tty.usbmodem241471
```

In Windows, you'd see something like COM8, COM9, COM10.

The Arduino boards come with their own USB-to-Serial adapter on board, but other microcontrollers and devices usually don't. You can buy a USB-to-Serial converter for about $15 to $40—Keyspan (www.keyspan.com) and IOGear (www.iogear.com) sell decent models. Most consumer models like these are USB-to-RS-232, because RS-232 was the standard serial connector for PCs before USB came along. USB-to-RS-232 adapters won't work directly with TTL serial devices.

FTDI makes a USB-to-TTL-Serial cable with a breadboard connector that's handy for interfacing to TTL serial devices. It's available from the Maker SHED, Spark Fun, Adafruit, and many other vendors. It comes in 5-volt and 3.3-volt versions. Arduino, Spark Fun, and Adafruit all make breakout boards with the same cable pin connections. Spark Fun's FTDI Basic Board has LEDs that flash when data is being transmitted. Adafruit's version is called the FTDI Friend. The Arduino USB-to-Serial adapter is based on a different chip but has the same pin connections. Any of these can be used for USB-to-Serial connections throughout this book. You can see them all at the beginning of this chapter. The pin connections are shown in Figure 2-6.

One more protocol: if you use a BASIC Stamp or another microcontroller with a non-USB serial interface, you probably have a 9-pin serial connector connecting your microcontroller to your PC or to a USB-to-Serial adapter. You can see it in Figure 2-4. This connector, called a DB-9 or D-sub-9, is a standard connector for another serial protocol, RS-232. RS-232 was the main serial protocol for computer serial connections before USB, and it's still seen on some older computer peripheral devices:

• **Physical layer**
A computer with an RS-232 serial port receives data on pin 2, and sends it out on pin 3. Pin 5 is the ground pin.

• **Electrical layer**
RS-232 sends data at two levels: 5 to 12 volts, and −5 to −12 volts.

• **Logical layer**
A 5- to 12- volt signal represents the value 0, and a −5 to −12 volt signal represents the value 1. This is inverted logic.

• **Data layer**
This is the same as TTL—8 bits per byte with a start and stop bit.

So why is it possible to connect some microcontrollers, like the BASIC Stamp or the BX-24, directly to RS-232 serial ports? It is because the voltage levels of TTL serial, 0 to 5 volts, are just barely enough to register in the higher RS-232 levels, and because you can invert the bits when sending or receiving from the microcontroller. RS-232 doesn't carry any of the addressing overhead of USB, so it's an easier protocol to deal with. Unfortunately, it's mostly obsolete, so USB-to-Serial converters are increasingly common tools for microcontroller programmers. Because the Arduino boards have an integrated USB-to-Serial converter, you can just plug them into a USB port.

When you're lucky, you never have to think about this kind of protocol mixing, and you can just use converters to do the job for you. You're not always lucky, though, so it's worth knowing a little about what's happening behind the

Figure 2-5
The MAX3232 chip. This circuit is really handy when you need to get any 3.3- to 5-volt TTL device to talk to a personal computer with an RS-232 serial port. This will also work for the MAX232.

scenes. For example, one of the most common problems in getting a serial device to communicate with a personal computer is converting the device's serial signals to USB or RS-232. A handy chip that does the TTL-to-RS-232 conversion for you is the MAX3232, available from Maxim Technologies (www.maxim-ic.com). It takes in RS-232 serial and spits out 3.3-V to 5-volt TTL serial, and vice versa. If you power it from a 3.3V source, you get 3.3V TTL serial output, and if you power it from 5V, you get 5V TTL serial output. Figure 2-5 shows the typical schematic for a MAX3232.

If you've done a lot of serial projects, you may know the MAX232, which preceded the MAX3232. In fact, the MAX232 was so common that the name became synonymous with all TTL-to-RS-232 converters, whether Maxim made them or not. The MAX232 worked only at 5 volts, but the MAX 3232 works at 3.3 to 5 volts. Because 3.3 volts is beginning to replace 5 volts as a standard supply voltage for electronic parts, it's handy to use a chip that can do both.

x

Figure 2-6
FTDI USB-to-TTL cable. In addition to the transmit, receive, voltage, and ground connections, it also has connections for hardware flow control, labeled Request to Send (RTS) and Clear to Send (CTS). Some devices use this to manage the flow of serial data.

FTDI
USB-to-TTL Serial Cable

Ground	GND	Black
Clear-to-send	CTS	Brown
Provides voltage output when plugged into USB port	Vcc	Red
To microcontroller RX	TX	Orange
To microcontroller TX	RX	Yellow
Request-to-send	RTS	Green

Using an Arduino As a USB-to-Serial Adapter

Arduino boards have a built-in USB-to-serial adapter so that the microcontroller can communicate with your personal computer serially. The USB-to-Serial adapter's transmit pin (TX) is attached to the microcontroller's receive pin (RX), and vice versa. This means you can bypass the microcontroller and use the Arduino board as a USB-to-Serial adapter. There are times when this is handy, like when you want to communicate directly with the Bluetooth radios you'll see later in this chapter. To do this, either remove the microcontroller carefully, or put a sketch on it that does nothing, like so:

```
void setup() {}
void loop() {}
```

Then connect the desired external serial device as follows:

External serial device's receive pin → Pin 0 of the Arduino board

External serial device's transmit pin → Pin 1 of the Arduino board

Now your serial device will communicate directly with the USB-to-Serial adapter on the Arduino, and the microcontroller will be bypassed. When you're ready to use the microcontroller again, just disconnect the external serial device and upload a new sketch.

66 Saying Something: The Application Layer

Now that you've got a sense of how to make the connections between devices, it's time to build a couple of projects to understand how to organize the data you send.

 Project 1

Type Brighter

In this example, you'll control the output of a microcontroller with keystrokes from your computer. It's a very simple example with minimal parts, so you can focus on the communication.

MATERIALS

» **1 RGB LED, common cathode**
» **1 Arduino microcontroller module**
» **1 personal computer**
» **All necessary converters to communicate serially from microcontroller to computer**
» **1 ping-pong ball**

Every application needs a communications protocol, no matter how simple it is. Even turning on a light requires that both the sender and receiver agree on how to say "turn on the light."

For this project, you'll make a tiny colored lamp. You'll be able to control the brightness and color of the lamp by sending it commands from your computer. The RGB LED at the heart of the lamp is actually three LEDs in one package: one red, one green, and one blue. They share a common cathode, or negative terminal. Connect the cathode, which is the longest leg, to the ground of your Arduino module, and connect the three other legs (called the anodes, one for each color) to pins 9, 10, and 11, as shown in Figure 2-7. Bend the cathode leg so it will fit, but make sure it's not touching the last leg, or it will create a short circuit.

When you've got the LED on the board, drill a small hole in the pong-pong ball, slightly larger than the LED. Fit the ball over the LED, as shown in Figure 2-10. It will act as a nice lampshade. If the LEDs form too harsh a spot on the ball, you can diffuse them slightly by sanding the top of the LED case.

The Protocol

Now that you've got the circuit wired up, you need to decide how you're going to communicate with the microcontroller to control the LEDs. You need a communications protocol. This one will be very simple:

- To choose a color of LED to control, send the first letter of the color, in lower-case (r, g, b).
- To set the brightness for that color, send a single digit, 0 through 9.

For example, to set red at 5, green at 3, and blue at (on a scale from 0 to 9), you'd send:

```
r5g3b7
```

Figure 2-7
RGB LED attached to pins 9, 10, 11, and ground. The ground leg is bent back so that it doesn't touch the leg connected to pin 11, which it crosses. In theory, this LED should have a resistor on each of the anodes to limit the current going through the LEDs. In practice, however, I've run this for several hours without the resistor with no damage to the Arduino or LED. When in doubt, be safe and add a 220-ohm resistor to each anode.

That's about as simple a protocol as you could imagine. However, you still need to write a program for the micro-controller to read the data one byte at a time, and then decide what to do based on the value of each byte.

The program flow is shown in Figure 2-8.

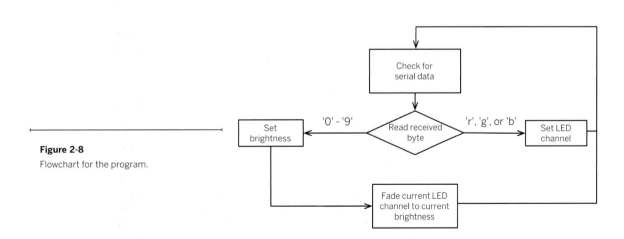

Figure 2-8
Flowchart for the program.

Try It

```
/*
  Serial RGB LED controller
  Context: Arduino

  Controls an RGB LED whose R, G and B legs are
  connected to pins 11, 9, and 10, respectively.
*/
```

▸ To start, you need to set up the constants to hold the pin numbers. You'll also need a variable to hold the number of the current pin to be faded, and one for the brightness.

```
// constants to hold the output pin numbers:
const int greenPin = 9;
const int bluePin = 10;
const int redPin = 11;

int currentPin = 0; // current pin to be faded
int brightness = 0; // current brightness level
```

▸ The setup() method opens serial communications and initializes the LED pins as outputs.

```
void setup() {
  // initiate serial communication:
  Serial.begin(9600);

  // initialize the LED pins as outputs:
  pinMode(redPin, OUTPUT);
  pinMode(greenPin, OUTPUT);
  pinMode(bluePin, OUTPUT);
}
```

▸ In the main loop, everything depends on whether you have incoming serial bytes to read.

```
void loop() {
  // if there's any serial data in the buffer, read a byte:
  if (Serial.available() > 0) {
    int inByte = Serial.read();

    // respond to the values 'r', 'g', 'b', or '0' through '9'.
```

▸ If you do have incoming data, there are only a few values you care about. When you get one of the values you want, use if statements to set the pin number and brightness value.

```
    // you don't care about any other value:
    if (inByte == 'r') {
      currentPin = redPin;
    }
    if (inByte == 'g') {
      currentPin = greenPin;
    }
    if (inByte == 'b') {
      currentPin = bluePin;
    }
```

▸ Finally, set the current pin to the current brightness level using the analogWrite() command.

```
    if (inByte >= '0' && inByte <= '9') {
      // map the incoming byte value to the range of
      // the analogRead() command:
      brightness = map(inByte, '0', '9', 0, 255);
      // set the current pin to the current brightness:
      analogWrite(currentPin, brightness);
    }
  }
}
```

Upload the sketch to your Arduino, then open the Serial Monitor by clicking on the icon at the top of the editor, as shown in Figure 2-9.

Once it's open, type:

r9

Then click send. You should see the ball light up red. Now try:

r2g7

The red will fade and the green will come up. Now try:

g0r0b8

The blue will come on. Voila, you've made a tiny serially controllable lamp!

If the colors don't correspond to the color you type, you probably bought an LED of a different model than the one specified above, so the pin numbers are different. You can fix this by changing the pin number constants in your sketch.

You don't have to control the lamp from the Serial Monitor. Any program that can control the serial port can send your protocol to the Arduino to control the lamp. Once you've finished the next project, try writing your own lamp controller in Processing.

X

Figure 2-9
Arduino toolbar, highlighting the Serial Monitor.

Figure 2-10
LED with a ping-pong ball on top to diffuse the light.

Notice in the program how the characters you type are in single quotes? That's because you're using the ASCII values for those characters. ASCII is a protocol that assigns numeric values to letters and numbers. For example, the ASCII value for the letter 'r' is 114. The ASCII value for '0' is 48. By putting the characters in single quotes, you're programming the Arduino to use the ASCII value for that character, not the character itself. For example, this line:

```
brightness = map(inByte, '0', '9', 0, 255);
```

could also be written like this:

```
brightness = map(inByte, 48, 57, 0, 255);
```

because in ASCII, the character '0' is represented by the value 48, and the character '9' is represented by the value 57. Using the character value in single quotes instead of the actual values isn't essential to make your program run, but it makes it easier to read. In the first version of the line above, you're using the ASCII characters to represent the values to map; in the second version, you're using the raw values themselves. You'll see examples in this book that use both approaches. For more on ASCII, see "What's ASCII?" on page 54.

Complex Conversations

In the previous project, you controlled the microcontroller from the computer using a very simple protocol. This time, the microcontroller will control an animation on the computer. The communications protocol is more complex as well.

Project 2

Monski Pong

In this example, you'll make a replacement for a mouse. If you think about the mouse as a data object, it looks like Figure 2-11.

MATERIALS

» **2 flex sensor resistors**
» **2 momentary switches**
» **4 10-kilohm resistors**
» **1 solderless breadboard**
» **1 Arduino microcontroller module**
» **1 personal computer**
» **All necessary converters to communicate serially from microcontroller to computer**
» **1 small pink monkey**

What the computer does with the mouse's data depends on the application. For this application, you'll make a small pink monkey play pong by waving his arms. He'll also have the capability to reset the game by pressing a button, and to serve the ball by pressing a second button.

Connect long wires to the flex sensors so that you can sew the sensors into the arms of the monkey without having the microcontroller in his lap. Use flexible wire; old telephone cable works well. A couple of feet should be fine for testing.

Connect long wires to the buttons as well, and mount them in a piece of scrap foam-core or cardboard until you've decided on a final housing for the electronics. Label the buttons "Reset" and "Serve." Wire the sensors to the microcontroller, as shown in Figure 2-12.

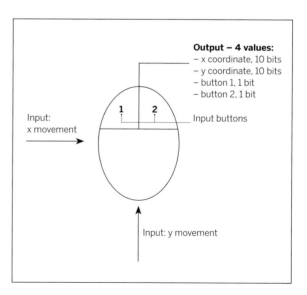

Figure 2-11
The mouse as a data object.

Figure 2-12
The Monski Pong circuit. Sensors are shown here with short wires so that the image is clear. You should attach longer wires to your sensors, though.

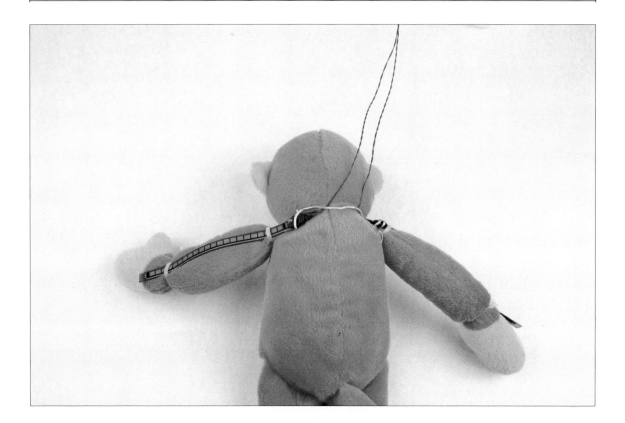

Cut a small slit in each of the monkey's armpits to insert the sensors. If you don't want to damage the monkey, you can use tie-wraps or tape to secure the sensors to the outsides of his arms, as shown in Figure 2-13. Position the sensors so that their movement is consistent. You should add some sort of support that keeps them in position relative to each other—a piece of flexible modeling wire will do the job nicely. Make sure that both sensors are facing the same direction, because flex sensors give different readings when flexed one direction than they do when flexed the other direction. Insulate the connections well, because the foam inside the monkey might generate considerable static electricity when he's moving. Hot glue will work well.

Make sure that the sensors and electrical connections are stable and secure before you start to work on code. Debugging is much harder if the electrical connections aren't consistent.

X

Figure 2-13

A stable support for the sensors is essential if you want good readings from them. Once you know your support works, move it inside the monkey and test it.

Test It   Now use the following code on the Arduino module to confirm that the sensors are working.

If you open the Serial Monitor in Arduino—or your preferred serial terminal application at 9600 bits per second, as you did in Chapter 1—you'll see a stream of results like this:

```
284,284,1,1,
285,283,1,1,
286,284,1,1,
289,283,1,1,
```

Just as you programmed it, each value is separated by a comma, and each set of readings is on a line by itself.

```
/*
  Sensor Reader
  Context: Arduino

  Reads two analog inputs and two digital inputs and outputs
  their values.

  Connections:
      analog sensors on analog input pins 0 and 1
      switches on digital I/O pins 2 and 3


 */

const int leftSensor = 0;    // analog input for the left arm
const int rightSensor = 1;   // analog input for tht right arm
const int resetButton = 2;   // digital input for the reset button
const int serveButton = 3;   // digital input for the serve button

int leftValue = 0;           // reading from the left arm
int rightValue = 0;          // reading from the right arm
int reset = 0;               // reading from the reset button
int serve = 0;               // reading from the serve button

void setup() {
  // configure the serial connection:
  Serial.begin(9600);
  // configure the digital inputs:
  pinMode(resetButton, INPUT);
  pinMode(serveButton, INPUT);
}

void loop() {
  // read the analog sensors:
  leftValue = analogRead(leftSensor);
  rightValue = analogRead(rightSensor);

  // read the digital sensors:
  reset = digitalRead(resetButton);
  serve = digitalRead(serveButton);

  // print the results:
  Serial.print(leftValue);
  Serial.print(",");
  Serial.print(rightValue);
  Serial.print(",");
  Serial.print(reset);
  Serial.print(",");
  // print the last sensor value with a println() so that
  // each set of four readings prints on a line by itself:
  Serial.println(serve);
}
```

▶▶ Try replacing the part of your code that prints the results with the code to the right.

When you view the results in the Serial Monitor or terminal, you'll get something that looks like this:

```
.,P,,
(,F,,
(,A,,
),I,,
```

```
// print the results:
Serial.write(leftValue);
Serial.write(44);
Serial.write(rightValue);
Serial.write(44);
Serial.write(reset);
Serial.write(44);
// print the last sensor value with a println() so that
// each set of four readings prints on a line by itself:
Serial.write(10);
Serial.write(13);
Serial.write(serve);
```

⚠ **Before you go to the next section, where you'll be writing some Processing code to interpret the output of this program, you must undo this change.**

What's going on? The original example uses the Serial.print() command, which displays the values of the sensors as their ASCII code values: this modification sends out the raw binary values using Serial.write(). The Serial Monitor and serial terminal applications assume that every byte they receive is an ASCII character, so they display the ASCII characters corresponding to the raw binary values in the second example. For example, the values 13 and 10 correspond to the ASCII return and newline characters, respectively. The value 44 corresponds to the ASCII comma character. Those are the bytes you're sending in between the sensor readings in the second example. The sensor variables (leftValue, rightValue, reset, and serve) are the source of the mystery characters. In the third line of the output, when the second sensor's value is 65, you see the character 'A' because the ASCII character 'A' has the value 65. For a complete list of the ASCII values corresponding to each character, see www.asciitable.com.

Which way should you format your sensor values: as raw binary or as ASCII? It depends on the capabilities of the system that's receiving the data, and of those that are passing it through. When you're writing software on a personal computer, it's often easier for your software to interpret raw values. However, many of the network

What's ASCII?

ASCII is the American Symbolic Code for Information Interchange. The scheme was created in 1967 by the American Standards Association (now ANSI) as a means for all computers, regardless of their operating systems, to be able to exchange text-based messages. In ASCII, each letter, numeral, or punctuation mark in the Roman alphabet is assigned a number. Anything an end user types is converted to a string of numbers, transmitted, and then reconverted on the other end. In addition to letters, numbers, and punctuation marks, certain page-formatting characters—like the linefeed and carriage return (ASCII 10 and 13, respectively)—have ASCII values. That way, not only the text of a the display format of the message could be transmitted along with the text. These are referred to as control characters, and they take up the first 32 values in the ASCII set (ASCII 0 31). All of the numbers, letters, punctuation, and control characters are covered by 128 possible values. However, ASCII is too limited to display non-English characters, and its few control characters don't offer enough control in the age of graphic user interfaces. Unicode—a more comprehensive code that's a superset of ASCII—has replaced ASCII as the standard for text interchange, and markup languages like PostScript and HTML have replaced ASCII's page formatting, but the original ASCII code still lingers on.

protocols you'll use in this book are ASCII-based. In addition, ASCII is readable by humans, so you may find it easier to send the data as ASCII. For Monski Pong, use the ASCII-formatted version (the first example); later in this chapter you'll see why it's the right choice.

If you haven't already done so, undo the changes you made on page 54 to the Sensor Reader program and make sure that it's working as it did originally. Once you've got the microcontroller sending the sensor values consistently to the terminal, it's time to send them to a program where you can use them to display a pong game. This program needs to run on a host computer that's connected to your Arduino board. Processing will do this well.

Try It   Open the Processing application and enter this code.

```
/*
 Serial String Reader
 Context: Processing

 */
import processing.serial.*;      // import the Processing serial library

Serial myPort;                   // The serial port
String resultString;             // string for the results

void setup() {
  size(480, 130);                // set the size of the applet window
  println(Serial.list());        // List all the available serial ports

  // get the name of your port from the serial list.
  // The first port in the serial list on my computer
  // is generally my Arduino module, so I open Serial.list()[0].
  // Change the 0 to the number of the serial port
  // to which your microcontroller is attached:
  String portName = Serial.list()[0];
  // open the serial port:
  myPort = new Serial(this, portName, 9600);

  // read bytes into a buffer until you get a linefeed (ASCII 10):
  myPort.bufferUntil('\n');
}

void draw() {
  // set the background and fill color for the applet window:
  background(#044f6f);
  fill(#ffffff);
  // show a string in the window:
  if (resultString != null) {
    text(resultString, 10, height/2);
  }
}

// serialEvent method is run automatically by the Processing sketch
// whenever the buffer reaches the byte value set in the bufferUntil()
// method in the setup():

void serialEvent(Serial myPort) {
  // read the serial buffer:
  String inputString = myPort.readStringUntil('\n');
```

»

Continued from previous page.

```
// trim the carrige return and linefeed from the input string:
inputString = trim(inputString);
// clear the resultString:
resultString = "";

// split the input string at the commas
// and convert the sections into integers:
int sensors[] = int(split(inputString, ','));

// add the values to the result string:
for (int sensorNum = 0; sensorNum < sensors.length; sensorNum++) {
  resultString += "Sensor " + sensorNum + ": ";
  resultString += sensors[sensorNum] + "\t";
}
// print the results to the console:
println(resultString);
}
```

Data Packets, Headers, Payloads, and Tails

Now that you've got data going from one device (the microcontroller attached to the monkey) to another (the computer running Processing), take a closer look at the sequence of bytes you're sending to exchange the data. Generally, it's formatted like this (with a comma, ASCII 44, between each field):

Left-arm sensor (0–1023)	Right-arm sensor (0–1023)	Reset button (0 or 1)	Serve button (0 or 1)	Return character, linefeed character
1–4 bytes	1–4 bytes	1 byte	1 byte	2 bytes

Each section of the sequence is separated by a single byte whose value is ASCII 44 (a comma). You've just made another data protocol. The bytes representing your sensor values and the commas that separate them are the payload, and the return and newline characters are the tail. The commas are the delimiters. This data protocol doesn't have a header, but many do.

A header is a sequence of bytes identifying what's to follow. It might also contain a description of the sequence to follow. On a network, where many possible devices could receive the same message, the header might contain the address of the sender, the receiver, or both. That way, any device can just read the header to decide whether it needs to read the rest of the message. Sometimes a header is as simple as a single byte of a constant value, identifying the beginning of

the message. In this example, where there is no header, the tail performs a similar function, separating one message from the next.

On a network, many messages like this are sent out all the time. Each discrete group of bytes is called a packet and includes a header, a payload, and usually a tail. Any given network has a maximum packet length. In this example, the packet length is determined by the size of the serial buffer on the personal computer. Processing can handle a buffer of a few thousand bytes, so this 16-byte packet is easy for it to handle. If you had a much longer message, you'd have to divide the message into several packets and reassemble them once they all arrived. In that case, the header might contain the packet number so the receiver knows the order in which the packets should be reassembled.

Let's take a break from writing code and test out the sketch. Make sure you've closed the Serial Monitor or serial port in your serial terminal application so that it releases the serial port. Then run this Processing application. You should see a list of the sensor values in the console and in the applet window, as shown on the right.

```
○ ○ ○              project2_serial_string_reader

Sensor 0: 497 Sensor 1: 452 Sensor 2: 0 Sensor 3: 1
```

▶▶ Next, it's time to use the data to play pong. First, add a few variables at the beginning of the Processing sketch before the setup() method, and change the setup() to set the window size and initialize some of the variables (the new lines are shown in blue).

NOTE: The variables relating to the paddle range in this example are floating-point numbers (floats), because when you divide integers, you get integer results only. For example, 480/400, gives 1, not 1.2, when both are integers. Likewise, 400/480 returns 0, not 0.8333. Using integers when you're dividing two numbers that are in the same order of magnitude produces useless results. Beware of this when using scaling functions like map().

```
float leftPaddle, rightPaddle;      // variables for the flex sensor values
int resetButton, serveButton;       // variables for the button values
int leftPaddleX, rightPaddleX;      // horizontal positions of the paddles
int paddleHeight = 50;              // vertical dimension of the paddles
int paddleWidth = 10;               // horizontal dimension of the paddles

float leftMinimum = 120;            // minimum value of the left flex sensor
float rightMinimum = 100;           // minimum value of the right flex sensor
float leftMaximum = 530;            // maximum value of the left flex sensor
float rightMaximum = 500;           // maximum value of the right flex sensor

void setup() {
  size(640, 480);                   // set the size of the applet window

    String portName = Serial.list()[0];
  // open the serial port:
  myPort = new Serial(this, portName, 9600);

  // read bytes into a buffer until you get a linefeed (ASCII 10):
  myPort.bufferUntil('\n');

  // initialize the sensor values:
  leftPaddle = height/2;
  rightPaddle = height/2;
  resetButton = 0;
  serveButton = 0;

  // initialize the paddle horizontal positions:
  leftPaddleX = 50;
  rightPaddleX = width - 50;

  // set no borders on drawn shapes:
  noStroke();
}
```

» Now, replace the serialEvent()
method with this version, which puts
the serial values into the sensor
variables.

```
void serialEvent(Serial myPort) {
  // read the serial buffer:
  String inputString = myPort.readStringUntil('\n');

  // trim the carriage return and linefeed from the input string:
  inputString = trim(inputString);
  // clear the resultString:
  resultString = "";

  // split the input string at the commas
  // and convert the sections into integers:
  int sensors[] = int(split(inputString, ','));
  // if you received all the sensor strings, use them:
  if (sensors.length == 4) {
    // scale the flex sensors' results to the paddles' range:
    leftPaddle = map(sensors[0], leftMinimum, leftMaximum, 0, height);
    rightPaddle = map(sensors[1], rightMinimum, rightMaximum, 0, height);

    // assign the switches' values to the button variables:
    resetButton = sensors[2];
    serveButton = sensors[3];

    // add the values to the result string:
    resultString += "left: "+ leftPaddle + "\tright: " + rightPaddle;
    resultString += "\treset: "+ resetButton + "\tserve: " + serveButton;
  }
}
```

» Finally, change the draw() method
to draw the paddles (new lines are
shown in blue).

```
void draw() {
  // set the background and fill color for the applet window:
  background(#044f6f);
  fill(#ffffff);

  // draw the left paddle:
  rect(leftPaddleX, leftPaddle, paddleWidth, paddleHeight);

  // draw the right paddle:
  rect(rightPaddleX, rightPaddle, paddleWidth, paddleHeight);
}
```

" You may not see the paddles until you flex the sensors. The range of your sensors will be different, depending on how they're physically attached to the monkey, and how far you can flex his arms. The map() function maps the sensors' ranges to the range of the paddle movement, but you need to determine what the sensors' range is. For this part, it's important that you have the sensors embedded in the monkey's arms, as you'll be fine-tuning the system, and you want the sensors in the locations where they'll actually get used.

Once you've set the sensors' positions in the monkey, run the Processing program again and watch the left and right sensor numbers as you flex the monkey's arms. Write down the maximum and minimum values on each arm. Then, fill them into the four variables, leftMinimum, leftMaximum, rightMinimum, and leftMaximum, in the setup() method. Once you've adjusted these variables, the paddles' movement should cover the screen height when you move the monkey's arms.

» Finally, it's time to add the ball. The ball will move from left to right diagonally. When it hits the top or bottom of the screen, it will bounce off and change vertical direction. When it reaches the left or right, it will reset to the center. If it touches either of the paddles, it will bounce off and change horizontal direction. To make all that happen, you'll need five new variables at the top of the program, just before the setup() method.

```
int ballSize = 10;      // the size of the ball
int xDirection = 1;     // the ball's horizontal direction.
                        // left is -1, right is 1.
int yDirection = 1;     // the ball's vertical direction.
                        // up is -1, down is 1.
int xPos, yPos;         // the ball's horizontal and vertical positions
```

» At the end of the setup() method, you need to give the ball an initial position in the middle of the window.

```
// initialize the ball in the center of the screen:
xPos = width/2;
yPos = height/2;
```

» Now, add two methods at the end of the program, one called animateBall() and another called resetBall(). You'll call these from the draw() method shortly.

```
void animateBall() {
  // if the ball is moving left:
  if (xDirection < 0) {
    // if the ball is to the left of the left paddle:
    if ((xPos <= leftPaddleX)) {
      // if the ball is in between the top and bottom
      // of the left paddle:
      if((leftPaddle - (paddleHeight/2) <= yPos) &&
        (yPos <= leftPaddle + (paddleHeight /2))) {
        // reverse the horizontal direction:
        xDirection =-xDirection;
      }
    }
  }
  // if the ball is moving right:
  else {
    // if the ball is to the right of the right paddle:
    if ((xPos >= ( rightPaddleX + ballSize/2))) {
      // if the ball is in between the top and bottom
      // of the right paddle:
      if((rightPaddle - (paddleHeight/2) <=yPos) &&
```

»

Continued from previous page.

```
        (yPos <= rightPaddle + (paddleHeight /2))) {

        // reverse the horizontal direction:
        xDirection =-xDirection;
      }
    }
  }

  // if the ball goes off the screen left:
  if (xPos < 0) {
    resetBall();
  }
  // if the ball goes off the screen right:
  if (xPos > width) {
    resetBall();
  }

  // stop the ball going off the top or the bottom of the screen:
  if ((yPos - ballSize/2 <= 0) || (yPos +ballSize/2 >=height)) {
    // reverse the y direction of the ball:
    yDirection = -yDirection;
  }
  // update the ball position:
  xPos = xPos + xDirection;
  yPos = yPos + yDirection;

  // Draw the ball:
  rect(xPos, yPos, ballSize, ballSize);
}

void resetBall() {
  // put the ball back in the center
  xPos = width/2;
  yPos = height/2;
}
```

▸ You're almost ready to set the ball in motion. But first, it's time to do something with the reset and serve buttons. Add another variable at the beginning of the code (just before the setup() method with all the other variable declarations) to keep track of whether the ball is in motion. Add two more variables to keep score.

```
boolean ballInMotion = false;   // whether the ball should be moving
int leftScore = 0;
int rightScore = 0;
```

▶▶ Now you're ready to animate the ball. It should move only if it's been served. This code goes at the end of the draw() method. The first if() statement starts the ball in motion when the serve button is pressed. The second moves it if it's in service. The third resets the ball to the center, and resets the score when the reset button is pressed.

```
// calculate the ball's position and draw it:
if (ballInMotion == true) {
  animateBall();
}

// if the serve button is pressed, start the ball moving:
if (serveButton == 1) {
  ballInMotion = true;
}

// if the reset button is pressed, reset the scores
// and start the ball moving:
if (resetButton == 1) {
  leftScore = 0;
  rightScore = 0;
  ballInMotion = true;
}
```

▶▶ Modify the animateBall() method so that when the ball goes off the screen left or right, the appropriate score is incremented (added lines are shown in blue).

```
// if the ball goes off the screen left:
if (xPos < 0) {
  rightScore++;
  resetBall();
}
// if the ball goes off the screen right:
if (xPos > width) {
  leftScore++;
  resetBall();
}
```

▶▶ To include the scoring display, add a new global variable before the setup() method.

```
int fontSize = 36;      // point size of the scoring font
```

▶▶ Then add two lines before the end of the setup() method to initialize the font.

```
// create a font with the third font available to the system:
PFont myFont = createFont(PFont.list()[2], fontSize);
textFont(myFont);
```

▶▶ Finally, add two lines before the end of the draw() method to display the scores.

```
// print the scores:
text(leftScore, fontSize, fontSize);
text(rightScore, width-fontSize, fontSize);
```

Now you can play Monski Pong! Figure 2-14 shows the game in action. For added excitement, get a second pink monkey and put one sensor in each monkey so you can play with a friend.

Figure 2-14
The completed Monski Pong Processing sketch.

❝ Flow Control

You may notice that the paddles don't always move as smoothly onscreen as Monski's arms move. Sometimes the paddles don't seem to move for a fraction of a second, and sometimes they seem to lag behind the actions you're taking. This is because the communication between the two devices is asynchronous.

Although the devices agree on the rate at which data is exchanged, it doesn't mean that the receiving computer's program has to use the bits as they're sent. Monitoring the incoming bits is actually handled by a dedicated hardware circuit, and the incoming bits are stored in a memory buffer, called the serial buffer, until the current program is ready to use them. Most personal computers allocate a buffer for each serial port that can hold a couple thousand bytes. The program using the bits (Processing, in the previous example) is juggling a number of other tasks, like redrawing the screen, handling the math that goes with it,

and sharing processor time with other programs through the operating system. It may get bytes from the buffer less than a hundred times a second—even though the bytes are coming in much faster.

There's another way to handle the communication between the two devices that can alleviate this problem. If Processing asks for data only when it needs it, and if the microcontroller only sends one packet of data when it gets a request for data, the two will be in tighter sync.

▸▸ To make this happen, first add the following lines to the startup() of the Arduino sketch. This makes the Arduino send out a serial message until it gets a response from Processin.:

```
while (Serial.available() <= 0) {
    Serial.println("hello");   // send a starting message
}
```

⏩ Next, wrap the whole of the loop() method in the Arduino program (the Sensor Reader program shown back in the beginning of the "Project #1: Monski Pong" section) in an if() statement like this (new lines are shown in blue).

In the next step, you'll add some code to the Monski Pong Processing sketch.

```
void loop() {
    // check to see whether there is a byte available
    // to read in the serial buffer:
    if (Serial.available() > 0)   {
        // read the serial buffer:
        // you don't care about the value of
        // the incoming byte, just that one was
        // sent:
        int inByte = Serial.read();
        // the rest of the existing main loop goes here
        // ...
    }
}
```

⏩ Add the following lines at the end of serialEvent() in the Processing sketch (new lines are shown in blue).

```
void serialEvent(Serial myPort) {
    // rest of the serialEvent goes here
    myPort.write('\r');        // send a carriage return
}
```

Now, the paddles should move much more smoothly. Here's what's happening: the microcontroller is programmed to send out a "hello" string until it receives any serial data. When it does, it goes into the main loop. There, it reads the byte just to clear the serial buffer, then sends out its data once, then waits for more data to arrive. Whenever it gets no bytes, it sends no bytes.

Processing, meanwhile, starts its program by waiting for incoming data. When it gets any string ending in a newline, serialEvent() is called, just as before. It reads the string, and if there are commas in it, it splits the string up and extracts the sensor values, like before. If there are no commas in the string (for example, if the string is "hello"), Processing doesn't do anything with it.

The change in the Processing sketch is at the end of the serialEvent(). There, it sends a byte back to the microcontroller, which, seeing a new byte coming in, sends out another packet of data, and the whole cycle repeats itself. This way, the serial buffer on Processing's side never fills up, and it's always got the freshest sensor readings.

The value of the byte that the microcontroller receives is irrelevant. It's used only as a signal from the Processing sketch to let the microcontroller know when it's ready for new data. Likewise, the "hello" that the controller sends is irrelevant—it's only there to trigger Processing to send an intial byte—so Processing discards it. This method of handling data flow control is sometimes referred to as a handshake method, or call-and-response. Whenever you're sending packets of data, call-and-response flow control can be a useful way to ensure consistent exchange.
X

Project 3

Wireless Monski Pong

Monski Pong is fun, but it would be more fun if Monski didn't have to be tethered to the computer through a USB cable. This project breaks the wired connection between the microcontroller and the personal computer, and introduces a few new networking concepts: the modem and the address.

MATERIALS

» **1 completed Monski Pong project**
» **1 9V battery and snap connector**
» **Female power plug, 2.1mm ID, 5.5mm OD**
» **1 Bluetooth Mate module**
» **1 project box**

NOTE: If your computer doesn't have built-in Bluetooth, you'll need a Bluetooth adapter. Most computer retailers carry USB-to-Bluetooth adapters.

Bluetooth: A Multilayer Network Protocol

The new piece of hardware in this project is the Bluetooth module. This module has two interfaces: two of its pins, marked RX and TX, are an asynchronous serial port that can communicate with a microcontroller. It also has a radio that communicates using the Bluetooth communications protocol. It acts as a modem, translating between the Bluetooth and regular asynchronous serial protocols.

NOTE: The first digital modems converted data signals to audio to send them across a telephone connection. They modulated the data on the audio connection, and demodulated the audio back into data. Now increasingly rare, their descendants are everywhere, from set-top boxes that modulate and demodulate between a cable TV signal and Internet connection, to the sonar modems that convert data into ultrasonic pings used in marine research.

Bluetooth is a multilayered communications protocol, designed to replace wired connections for a number of applications. As such, it's divided into a group of possible application protocols called profiles. The simplest Bluetooth devices are serial devices, like the module used in this project. These implement the Bluetooth Serial Port Profile (SPP). Other Bluetooth devices implement other protocols. Wireless headsets implement the audio Headset Profile. Wireless mice and keyboards implement the Human Interface Device (HID) Profile. Because there are a number of possible profiles a Bluetooth device might support, there is also a Service Discovery Protocol, by which radios exchange information about what they can do. Because the protocol is standardized, you get to skip over most of the details of making and maintaining the connection, letting you concentrate on exchanging data. It's a bit like how RS-232 and USB made it possible for you to ignore most of the electrical details necessary to connect your microcontroller to your personal computer, which let you focus on sending bytes in the last project.

Add the Bluetooth module to the Monski pong breadboard, as shown in Figure 2-16. Connect the module's ground and VCC to the breadboard ground and +5V, respectively. Connect Arduino's TX to the module's RX, and vice versa, Connect the battery, and the module will start up.

Pairing Your Computer with the Bluetooth Module

To make a wireless connection from your computer to the module, you have to pair them. To do this, open your computer's Bluetooth control panel to browse for new devices.

If you're using Mac OS X, choose the Apple menu→System Preferences, then click Bluetooth. Make sure Bluetooth is turned on and Discoverable, and click "Show Bluetooth status in the menu bar." At the bottom of the list of devices, click the + sign to launch the Bluetooth Setup Assistant. The computer will search for devices and find one called FireFly-XXX (Bluetooth Mate Gold) or RN42-XXX (Silver), where XXX is the Bluetooth module's serial number. If you have no other Bluetooth devices on, it will be the only one. Choose this device, and on the next screen, click Passkey Options. Choose "Use a Specific Passcode," and enter 1234. Click Continue. A connection will be established, as will a serial port. When you look for the serial port in CoolTerm, the Arduino serial port menu, or the Processing serial port list, it will be FireFly-XXX-SPP or RN42-XXX-SPP.

For Windows 7 users, there are different Bluetooth radios in different Windows-based PCs. If your PC doesn't have a built-in Bluetooth radio, any Bluetooth adapter that supports the Windows Bluetooth Stack will do. Most Bluetooth USB dongles on the market support it. Install the drivers according to your radio's instructions, and when it's done, click on the Show Hidden Icons icon in the taskbar (the small triangle in the lower-right-hand corner). When you do, you'll see the Bluetooth Devices icon, as shown in Figure 2-15. Click on this to add a new Bluetooth Device.

Figure 2-15
Where to find the Windows Bluetooth Devices icon (it's well hidden!). Click Customize... if you want to add it to your taskbar.

The system will search for new devices and present you with a list, which should include one called FireFly-XXX, where XXX is the serial number of your Bluetooth module. If you have no other Bluetooth devices nearby, it will be the only one. When prompted for the device's pairing code, enter 1234. This step will add a new serial port to your list of serial ports. Make note of the port name (mine is COM14) so you can use it later.

Ubuntu Linux's Bluetooth manager for version 1.0 is a bit limited, so it's easier to install BlueMan instead. Go to the Ubuntu Software center, search for BlueMan, and install it. When it's installed, open the System control panel and you'll see Bluetooth Manager, in addition to the default Bluetooth control panel. Open Bluetooth Manager, and it will scan for available devices and show them, including one called FireFly-XXX or RN42-XXX, where XXX is the serial number of your Bluetooth module. When prompted for the device's pairing code, enter 1234. Once it's added, click Setup, and you'll get a dialog asking you if you want to connect to a serial port. Click Forward, and it will tell you the name of the serial port for the Bluetooth module, **/dev/rfcomm0**.

Adjusting the Monski Pong Program
Once your computer has made contact with the Bluetooth module, you can connect to it like a serial port. Run the Monski Pong Processing sketch and check the list of serial ports. You should see the new port listed along with the others. Take note of which number it is, and change these lines in the setup() method:

```
String portName = Serial.list()[0];
// open the serial port:
myPort = new Serial(this, portName, 9600);
```

For example, if the Bluetooth port is the ninth port in your list, change the first line to open Serial.list[8]. Then change the data rate in the second line as follows:

```
myPort = new Serial(this, portName, 115200);
```

⚠ If you plug or unplug any serial devices after you do this, including the Arduino, you'll need to quit and restart the Processing program, as the count of serial ports will have changed.

Likewise, you'll need to change your Arduino sketch so that the Serial.begin() line reads as follows:

```
Serial.begin(115200);
```

Disconnect the Bluetooth module from the Arduino before you upload the modified sketch, as it will interfere with the upload. You can re-connect it once you've uploaded the new code. With no other changes in code, you should now be able to connect wirelessly. Monski is free to roam around the room as you play pong. When the Processing program makes a connection to the Bluetooth module, the green LED on the module will turn on.

If you haven't modified your Arduino and Processing code to match the call-and-response version of the Monski Pong program shown in the "Flow Control" section earlier, you might have a problem making a connection through the radio. If so, make the changes from that section first. Once you do, Monski Pong should operate as before, only now it's wireless.
X

Figure 2-16
Monski pong board, with Bluetooth module added. Once you've built the circuit for this, drill holes in the project box for the buttons and the wires leading to the flex sensors. Mount the breadboard, Arduino module, and battery in the project box.

Figure 2-17
If you didn't buy a battery snap with DC power adapter like the Spark Fun one, you'll need to solder the connector onto your battery snap, as shown here.

Finishing Touches: Tidy It Up, Box It Up

◀◀ **Figure 2-18.**
You might want to shrink Monski Pong so it's more compact. This figure shows the Monski Pong circuit on a breadboard shield. This is the same circuit as the one in Figure 2-16, it's just on a different breadboard so it can fit in a project box.

⏷ **Figure 2-19.**
Kitchen storage containers make excellent project boxes. Here's the Monski Pong controller with Monski attached.

Project 4

Negotiating in Bluetooth

The steps you went through to pair your Bluetooth module with your computer negotiated a series of exchanges that included discovering other radios, learning the services offered by those radios, and pairing to open a connection. It's very convenient to be able to do this from the graphical user interface, but it would be even better if the devices could negotiate this exchange themselves. In the section that follows, you'll negotiate some parts of that exchange directly, in order to understand how to program devices to handle that negotiation.

MATERIALS

» **1 Bluetooth Mate module**
» **1 FTDI USB-to-Serial converter**

The Bluetooth module is essentially a modem in that it converts from one communications medium (TTL serial carried over wires) to another (Bluetooth serial carried over radio). Modems are designed to open a connection to another modem, negotiate the terms of data exchange, carry on an exchange, and then disconnect. To do this, they must have two operating modes, usually referred to as command mode, in which you talk *to* the modem, and data mode, in which you talk *through* the modem. Bluetooth modems are no different in this respect.

Most Bluetooth modems (and many other communications devices) use a set of commands based on the those designed originally for telephone modems, known as the Hayes AT command protocol. All commands in the Hayes command protocol (and therefore in Bluetooth command protocols as well) are sent using ASCII characters. Devices

Figure 2-20

Bluetooth Mate module connected to an FT232RL USB-to-Serial converter. The Mate is designed to be a drop-in replacement for the FTDI cable, so it has the same pin configuration. As a result, you have to cross the transmit and receive connections to make the connection work.

using this protocol all have a command mode and a data mode. To switch from data mode to command mode in the Hayes protocol, send the string `+++`. There's a common structure to all the commands. Each command sent from the controlling device (like a microcontroller or personal computer) to the modem begins with the ASCII string AT, followed by a short string of letters and numbers representing the command, followed by any parameters of the

command, separated by commas. The command ends with an ASCII carriage return. The modem then responds to the command with the message OK, followed by any information it's expected to return.

The Bluetooth Mate doesn't use AT commands, but its protocol is similar. The commands are all ASCII-based.

There is a command mode and a data mode. In data mode, you send the string $$$ to switch to command mode.

The commands are all short strings, and the modem responds with the response AOK. To exit command mode, send the string ---\r (the \r is a carriage return, ASCII 13), and the Bluetooth modem switches back to data mode. In data mode, any bytes you send the modem are sent out over the radio, and any bytes received over the radio get sent out the serial connection.

Controlling the Bluetooth Module

Wire the Bluetooth module to the USB-to-Serial converter, as shown in Figure 2-20. Since the converter and the cable have identical pin configurations, you'll need to cross the TX and RX lines to make them connect. Connect the converter to a USB port on your computer.

For this project, you'll need a serial terminal program that can open two serial ports at the same time, so the Arduino Serial Monitor won't do. One serial port will be the wired connection to the Bluetooth module through the USB-to-serial adapter. The other will be the wireless connection via Bluetooth.

For Mac OS X and Windows users, CoolTerm will work well. For Ubuntu Linux users, GNU screen or PuTTY will do. Open a connection to the USB-to-Serial adapter at 115200 bits per second.

When you first power the Bluetooth Mate, it will be in data mode. To switch to command mode, send the string:

$$$

The module will respond like so:

CMD

You're now in command mode. Any time you want to check that the module is working and in command mode, type enter or return, and send it. It will respond with ?. To see a list of all possible commands, type H and then enter. There's a list of all the commands available for this module at www.SparkFun.com or www.rovingnetworks. com (the Bluetooth Mate Gold module uses the Roving

Networks RN-41 radio, if you're searching their site, and the Bluetooth Mate Silver uses the RN-42 radio). A few of the commands are covered here. Each Bluetooth modem manufacturer has its own set of commands; unfortunately, they're all different. But they all have the same basic structure as the one you see here.

Currently, the module is in command mode. One of the first things you'd like is to see its settings. Type D and hit return or enter. You'll get a list of the radio's settings, which looks like this:

```
***Settings***

BTA=000666112233
BTName=FireFly-7256
Baudrt(SW4)=115K
Parity=None
Mode=Slav
Authen=0
Encryp=0
PinCod=1234
Bonded=0
Rem=NONE SET
```

The first setting is the Bluetooth address. That's the part you need in order to make a connection to it. Manufacturers of Bluetooth devices agree on a standard addressing scheme so no two devices get the same address. The settings that follow give you information about the radio's configuration, such as the serial data rate (or baudrate), whether authentication's turned on, and what the passcode or PIN code is.

You may have noticed that you can't see what you type. That's because the keystrokes in a serial terminal program aren't echoed back to the screen—they're sent straight to the serial port. However, the Bluetooth Mate will echo your characters back to you if you type +\r. This turns Echo Mode on or off. It's useful to have on while issuing commands.

Now that you know something about your own module, you want it to give you a list of other Bluetooth-enabled devices in the area. Type I for inquiry. After several seconds, it will come back with a list like this:

```
?
Inquiry, COD=0
Found 9
0010C694AFBD,,1C010C
0023125C2DBE,tigoebook,3A010C
0017F29F7A67,screen1,102104
002241CE2E79,residents,380104
002241D70127,admints Mac mini,380104
0014519266B8,ERMac,102104
002241CE7839,VideoMac05,380104
E806889B12DD,,A041C
00236CBAC2F0,Fred Mac mini,302104
Inquiry Done
```

> ⚠️ You can't initiate a connection from the Bluetooth Mate to the computer unless you've previously paired with the Mate from the computer. This is because Bluetooth radios can't initiate a serial connection unless they've already made a pairing with the other device. You'll see more on these radios in Chapter 6.

This is a list of all the other Bluetooth devices it found. The first part of every string is the device's unique address. The second, when there is one, is the device's name; the third is the device class, or what type of device it is (you can probably pick out the device class number for Mac minis from the list above). Names don't have to be unique, but addresses do, which is why you always use the address to connect.

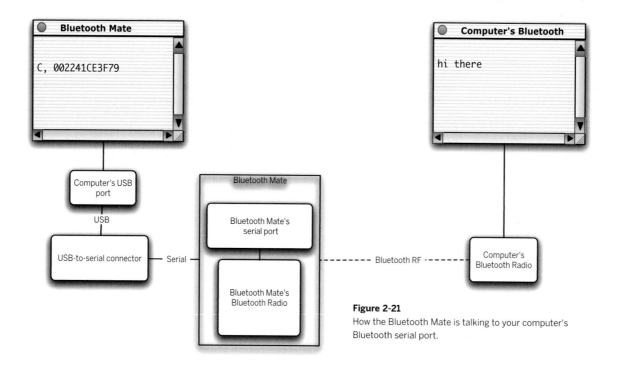

Figure 2-21
How the Bluetooth Mate is talking to your computer's Bluetooth serial port.

Now that you've got a list of connections, you're going to try to connect to the one that represents your computer. You must already be paired with the Bluetooth module for this to work, so if you aren't, go back to the previous project and do that now. Then, you need to open the serial port on your computer that's connected to its Bluetooth radio.

In Mac OS X, it's the Bluetooth PDA-Sync port. Open a second window in your terminal program, and connect to that serial port at 115200 bps.

For Windows 7 users, click on the Show Hidden Icons icon in the taskbar to get to the Bluetooth Devices. Click the Bluetooth Devices Icon and, from the menu, choose Open Settings. In the Settings window, choose the Options pane—and make sure that you've allowed other devices to find this computer, and that you've allowed them to connect as well. Then click the COM ports pane. If you've paired with your Bluetooth module before, there will be two ports indicated for it, one outgoing and one incoming. You're not using those, though, because Windows tries to initiate contact when you do. You want the Bluetooth modem to initiate contact. Add a new incoming port. Note the port number, then open that port in your serial terminal program at 115200 bps.

For Ubuntu Linux users, the Bluetooth Manager doesn't support binding a serial port to a discoverable Bluetooth serial port protocol (SPP) connection, so you'll need to make the connection outbound from Ubuntu, as described in the earlier section, "Pairing Your Computer with the Bluetooth Module." Once you're paired, however, the procedure to send and receive data, or to switch from command mode to data mode on the Bluetooth Mate, will be the same as for other platforms.

Once you've opened the serial port on your computer, go back to the window with the serial connection to the Bluetooth module, and send the following command:

```
C, address\r
```

where address is the Bluetooth address of your computer that you discovered earlier. When you get a good connection, the LED on the Mate will turn on, and you can type back and forth between the windows. This is more exciting if you have two computers and connect them via Bluetooth, but it works on one computer nonetheless.

You're now out of command mode and into data mode. You should be able to type directly from one window to the other.

To get out of data mode (to check the modem's status, for example), type (\r indicates that you should hit Enter or Return; don't type the \ or the r):

```
$$$\r
```

This will give you a CMD prompt again. You can now type any of the commands you want and get replies. To return to data mode, type:

```
---\r
```

Finally, when you're in command mode, you can type K,\r to disconnect. If you want to connect to another device, go into command mode and start over again.

Because these commands are just text strings, you can easily use them in microcontroller programs to control the module, make and break connections, and exchange data. Because all the commands are in ASCII, it's a good idea to exchange data in ASCII mode, too. So, the data string you set up earlier to send Monski's sensor readings in ASCII would work well over this modem.

X

❝ Conclusion

The projects in this chapter have covered a number of ideas that are central to all networked data communication. First, remember that data communication is based on a layered series of agreements, starting with the physical layer; then the electrical, the logical, the data layers; and finally, the application layer. Keep these layers in mind as you design and troubleshoot your projects, and you'll find it's easier to isolate problems.

Second, remember that serial data can be sent either as ASCII or as raw binary values, and which you choose to use depends both on the capabilities and limitations of all the connected devices. It might not be wise to send raw binary data, for example, if the modems or the software environments you program in are optimized for ASCII data transfer.

Third, when you think about your project, think about the messages that need to be exchanged, and come up with a data protocol that adequately describes all the information you need to send. This is your data packet. You might want to add header bytes, separators, or tail bytes to make reading the sequence easier.

Fourth, consider the flow of data, and look for ways to ensure a smooth flow with as little overflowing of buffers or waiting for data as possible. A simple call-and-response approach can make data flow much smoother.

Finally, get to know the modems and other devices that link the objects at the end of your connection. Understand their addressing schemes and any command protocols they use so that you can factor their strengths and limitations into your planning, and eliminate those parts that make your life more difficult. Whether you're connecting two objects or two hundred, these same principles will apply.
X

▸▸ The JitterBox by Gabriel Barcia-Colombo

The JitterBox is an interactive video Jukebox created from a vintage 1940s radio restored to working condition. It features a tiny video-projected dancer who shakes and shimmies to the music. The viewer can tune the radio and the dancer will move in time with the tunes. The JitterBox uses serial communication from an embedded potentiometer tuner—which is connected to an Arduino microcontroller—in order to select from a range of vintage 1940s songs. These songs are linked to video clips and played back out of a digital projector. The dancer trapped in the JitterBox is Ryan Myers.

3

A More Complex Network

Now that you've got the basics of network communications, it's time to tackle something more complex. The best place to start is with the most familiar data network: the Internet. It's not actually a single network, but a collection of networks owned by different network service providers and linked using some common protocols. This chapter describes the structure of the Internet, the devices that hold it together, and the shared protocols that make it possible. You'll get hands-on experience with what's going on behind the scenes when your web browser or email client is doing its job, and you'll use the same messages those tools use to connect your own objects to the Net.

◀︎◀︎ **Networked Flowers by Doria Fan, Mauricio Melo, and Jason Kaufman**
Networked Flowers is a personal communication device for sending someone digital blooms. Each bloom has a different lighting animation. The flower sculpture has a network connection. The flower is controlled from a website that sends commands to the flower when the web visitor chooses a lighting animation.

◀┊ Supplies for Chapter 3

DISTRIBUTOR KEY
- **A** Arduino Store (http://store.arduino.cc/ww)
- **AF** Adafruit (http://adafruit.com)
- **D** Digi-Key (www.digikey.com)
- **F** Farnell (www.farnell.com)
- **J** Jameco (http://jameco.com)
- **MS** Maker SHED (www.makershed.com)
- **RS** RS (www.rs-online.com)
- **RSH** RadioShack (www.radioshack.com)
- **SF** SparkFun (www.sparkfun.com)
- **SS** Seeed Studio (www.seeedstudio.com)

PROJECT 5: Networked Cat
» **Between 2 and 4 force sensing resistors, Interlink 400 series** (www.interlinkelec.com). The Interlink model 402 is shown in this project, but any of the 400 series will work well. **D** 1027-1000-ND, **J** 2128260, **SF** SEN-09673
» **One 1-Kilohm resistor** Any model will do. **D** 1.0KQBK-ND, **J** 29663, **F** 1735061, **RS** 707-8669

» **1 Arduino module** An Arduino Uno or something based on the Arduino Uno, but the project should work on other Arduino and Arduino-compatible boards. **D** 1050-1019-ND, **J** 2121105, **SF** DEV-09950, **A** A000046, **AF** 50, **F** 1848687, **RS** 715-4081, **SS** ARD132D2P, **MS** MKSP4
» **1 solderless breadboard D** 438-1045-ND, **J** 20723 or 20601, **SF** PRT-00137, **F** 4692810, **AF** 64, **SS** STR101C2M or STR102C2M, **MS** MKKN2
» **1 personal computer**
» **1 web camera**
» **1 cat** A dog will do if you have no cat.
» **1 cat mat**
» **2 thick pieces of wood or thick cardboard, about the size of the cat mat**
» **Wire-wrapping wire D** K445-ND, **J** 22577, **S** PRT-08031, **F** 150080
» **Wire-wrapping tool J** 242801, **F** 441089, **RSH** 276-1570, **S** TOL-00068
» **Male header pins D** A26509-20-ND, **J** 103377, **S** PRT-0011, **F** 1593411

Figure 3-1. New parts for this chapter: **1.** Interlink Series 402 force-sensing resistors (FSRs) **2.** 30AWG wire-wrapping wire **3.** Wire-wrapping pins (or long female headers) **4.** New tool: wire-wrapping tool. The wire stripper to the left of the tool lives inside the handle. Don't forget plenty of male header pins for the breakout boards.

❝ Network Maps and Addresses

In the previous chapter, it was easy to keep track of where messages went because there were only two points in the network you built: the sender and the receiver. In any network with more than two objects—from three to three billion—you need a map to keep track of which objects are connected to which. You also need an addressing scheme to know how a message gets to its destination.

Network Maps: How Things Are Connected

The arrangement of a network's physical connections depends on how you want to route its messages. The simplest way is to make a physical connection from each object in the network to every other object. That way, messages can get sent directly from one point to another. The problem with this approach, as you can see from the directly connected network in Figure 3-2, is that the number of connections gets large very fast, and the connections get tangled. A simpler alternative to this is to put a central controller in the middle and pass all messages through this hub, as seen in the star network shown in Figure 3-2. This way works great as long as the hub continues to function, but the more objects you add, the faster the hub must be to process all the messages. A third alternative is to daisy-chain the objects, connecting them together in a ring. This design makes for a small number of connections, and it means that any message has two possible paths, but it can take a long time for messages to get halfway around the ring to the most distant object.

In practice (such as on the Internet), a multitiered star model, like the one shown in Figure 3-3, works best. Each connector (symbolized by a light-colored circle) has a few objects connected to it, and each connector is linked to a more central connector. At the more central tier (the dark-colored circles in Figure 3-3), each connector may be linked to more than one other connector, so that enabling messages to pass from one endpoint to another via several different paths. This system takes advantage of the redundancy of multiple links between central connectors, but avoids the tangle caused by connecting every object to every other object.

If one of the central connectors isn't working, messages are routed around it. The connectors at the edges are the weakest points. If they aren't working, the objects that depend on them have no connection to the network. As

⤓ **Figure 3-2**

Three types of network: direct connections between all elements, a star network, and a ring network.

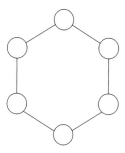

Directly connected network   Star network   Ring network

long as the number of objects connected to each of these is small, the effect on the whole network is minimal. It may not seem minimal when you're using the object whose connector fails, but the rest of the network remains stable, so it's easy to reconnect when your connector is working again.

If you're using the Internet as your network, you can take this model for granted. If you're building your own network, however, it's worth comparing all these models to see which is best for you. In simpler systems, one of the three networks shown in Figure 3-2 might do the job just fine, saving you some complications. As you get further into the book, you'll see some examples of these; for the rest of this chapter, you'll work with the multitiered model by relying on the Internet as your infrastructure.

X

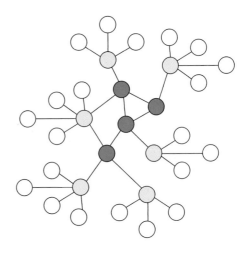

Multitiered network

▶▶ **Figure 3-3**
A complex, multitiered network.

Modems, Hubs, Switches, and Routers

The connectors in Figure 3-3 represent several different types of devices on the Internet. The most common among these are modems, hubs, switches, and routers. Depending on how your network is set up, you may be familiar with one or more of these. There's no need to go into detail as to the differences, but some basic definitions are in order:

A modem is a device that converts one type of signal into another, and connects one object to one other object. Your home cable or DSL modem is an example. It takes the digital data from your home computer or network, converts it to a signal that can be carried across the phone line or cable line, and connects to another modem on the other end of the line. That modem is connected to your Internet Service Provider's network. By this definition, the Bluetooth radios from Chapter 2 could be considered modems, as they convert electrical signals into radio signals and back.

A hub is a device that multiplexes data signals from several devices and passes them upstream to the rest of the net. It doesn't care about the recipients of the messages it's carrying—it just passes them through in both directions.

All the devices attached to a hub receive all the messages that pass through the hub, and each one is responsible for filtering out any messages that aren't addressed to it. Hubs are cheap and handy, but they don't really manage traffic.

A switch is like a hub, but it's more sophisticated. It keeps track of the addresses of the objects attached to it, and it passes along messages addressed to those objects only. Objects attached to a hub don't get to see messages that aren't addressed to them.

Modems, hubs, and switches generally don't actually have their own addresses on the network (though most cable and DSL modems do). A router, on the other hand, is visible to other objects on the network. It has an address of its own, and it can mask the objects attached to it from the rest of the net. It can give them private addresses, meaningful only to the other objects attached to the router, and pass on their messages as if they come from the router itself. It can also assign IP addresses to objects that don't have one when they're first connected to the router.

Figure 3-4
Network settings panels for Mac OS X and Windows.

Hardware Addresses and Network Addresses

Whether you're using a simple network model where all the objects are directly connected, a multitiered model, or anything in between, you need an addressing scheme to get messages from one point to another on the network. When you're making your own network from scratch, you have to create your own addressing scheme. For the projects you're making in this book, however, you're relying on existing network technologies, so you get to use the addressing schemes that come with them. For example, when you used the Bluetooth radios in Chapter 2, you used the Bluetooth protocol addressing scheme. When you connect Internet devices, you use the Internet Protocol (IP) addressing scheme. Because most of the devices you connect to the Internet also rely on a protocol called Ethernet, you also use the Ethernet address protocol. A device's IP address can change when it's moved from one network to another, but its hardware address, or Media Access Control (MAC) address, is burned into the device's memory and doesn't change. It's a unique ID number assigned by the manufacturer that differentiates that device from all the other Ethernet devices on the planet. WiFi adapters also have hardware addresses.

You're probably already familiar with your computer's IP address and maybe even its hardware address. In Mac OS X, click Apple Menu→Location→Network Preferences to open the Network control panel. Here you'll get a list of the possible network interfaces through which your computer can connect to the Internet. It's likely that you have at least a built-in Ethernet interface and an AirPort interface. The built-in Ethernet and AirPort interfaces both have hardware addresses, and if you select either, you can find out that interface's hardware address. In either interface, click on the Advanced button to get to both the Ethernet tab (where you can see the hardware address), and the TCP/IP tab (where you can see the machine's IP address if you're connected to a network).

In Windows 7, click the Start Menu→Control Panel, then double-click "Network and Internet". Each network interface has its own icon in this control panel. Click Local Area Connection for your built-in Ethernet connection, or Wireless Network Connection for your WiFi connection. Under the Support tab, click Details to see the IP settings and hardware address.

For Ubuntu Linux, click the System menu, then Preferences→Network Connections. You'll see a list of network interfaces. Click Edit to see their details.

Figure 3-4 shows the network connection settings for Mac OS X and Windows. No matter what platform you're on, the hardware address and the Internet address will take these forms:

- The hardware address is made up of six numbers written in hexadecimal notation, like this: 00:11:24:9b:f3:70
- The IP address is made up of four numbers written in decimal notation, like this: 192.168.1.20

You'll need to know the IP address to send and receive messages, and you'll need to know the hardware address in order to get an IP address on some networks. So, whenever you begin working on a new project, note both addresses for every device you're using.

Street, City, State, Country: How IP Addresses Are Structured

Geographic addresses can be broken down into layers of detail, starting with the most specific (the street address) and moving to the most general (the country). Internet Protocol (IP) addresses are also multilayered. The most specific part is the final number, which tells you the address of the computer itself. The numbers that precede this tell you the subnet that the computer is on. Your router shares the same subnet as your computer, and its number is usually identical except for the last number. The numbers of an IP address are called octets, and each octet is like a section of a geographic address. For example, imagine a machine with this number: 217.123.152.20. The router that this machine is attached to most likely has this address: 217.123.152.1.

Each octet can range from 0–255, and some numbers are reserved by convention for special purposes. For example, the router is often the address xxx.xxx.xxx.1. The subnet can be expressed as an address range, for example, 217.123.152.xxx. Sometimes a router manages a larger subnet or even a group of subnets, each with its own local router. The router that this router is connected to might have the address 217.123.1.1.

Each router controls access for a defined number of machines below it. The number of machines it controls is

encoded in its subnet mask. You may have encountered a subnet mask when configuring your personal computer. A typical subnet mask looks like this: 255.255.255.0.

You can read the number of machines in the subnet by reading the value of the last octets of the subnet mask. It's easiest if you think of the subnet in terms of bits. Four bytes is 32 bits. Each bit you subtract from the subnet increases the number of machines it can support. Basically, you "subtract" the subnet mask from its maximum value of 255.255.255.255 to get the number of machines. For example, if the subnet were 255.255.255.255, there could be only one machine in the subnet: the router itself. If the last octet is 0, as it is above, there can be up to 255 machines in the subnet in addition to the router. A subnet of 255.255.255.192 would support 63 machines and the router (255 − 192 = 64), and so forth. There are a few other reserved addresses, so the real numbers are a bit lower. Table 3-1 shows a few other representative values to give you an idea.

Table 3-1. The relationship between subnet mask and maximum number of machines on a network.

Subnet mask	Maximum number of machines on the subnet, including the router (accounting for reserved addresses)
255.255.255.255	1 (just the router)
255.255.255.192	62
255.255.255.0	254
255.255.252.0	1022
255.255.0.0	65,534

Knowing the way IP addresses are constructed helps you to manage the flow of messages you send and receive. Normally, all of this is handled for you by the software you use: browsers, email clients, and so forth. But when you're building your own networked objects, it's necessary to know at least this much about the IP addressing scheme so you can find your router and what's beyond it.

Numbers into Names

You're probably thinking this is ridiculous because you only know Internet addresses by their names, like www.makezine.com or www.archive.net. You never deal with numerical addresses, nor do you want to. There's a

Private and Public IP Addresses

Not every object on the Internet can be addressed by every other object. Sometimes, in order to support more objects, a router hides the addresses of the objects attached to it, sending all their outgoing messages to the rest of the net as if they came from the router itself. There are special ranges of addresses set aside in the IP addressing scheme for use as private addresses. For example, all addresses in the range 192.168.xxx.xxx (as well as 10.xxx.xxx.xxx, and 172.16.xxx.xxx–172.31.xxx.xxx) are to be used for private addressing only. This address range is used commonly in home routers, so if you have one, all the devices on your home network probably show up with addresses in this range. When they send messages to the outside world, though, those messages show up as if they came from your router's public IP address. Here's how it works:

My computer, with the address 192.168.1.45 on my home network, makes a request for a web page on a remote server. That request goes first to my home router. On my home network, the router's address is 192.168.1.1, but to the rest of the Internet, my router presents a public address, 66.187.145.75. The router passes on my message, sending it from its public address, and requesting that any replies come back to its public address. When it gets a reply, it sends the reply to my computer. Thanks to private addressing and subnet masks, multiple devices can share a single public IP address, which expands the total number of things that can be attached to the Internet.

separate protocol, the Domain Name System (DNS), for assigning names to the numbers. Machines on the network called nameservers keep track of which names are assigned to which numbers. In your computer's network configuration, you'll notice a slot where you can enter the DNS address. Most computers are configured to obtain this address from a router using the Dynamic Host Control Protocol (DHCP) , which also provides their IP address, so you don't have to worry about configuring DNS. In this chapter's project, you won't be going out to the Internet at large, so your devices won't have names, just numbers. When that happens, you'll need to know their numerical addresses.

Packet Switching: How Messages Travel the Net

So how does a message get from one machine to another? Imagine the process as akin to mailing a bicycle. The bike's too big to mail in one box, so first you break it into box-sized pieces. On the network, this is initially done at the Ethernet layer—also called the datalink layer—where each message is broken into chunks of more or less the same size, and given a header containing the packet number. Next, you'd put the address (and the return address) on the bike's boxes. This step is handled at the IP layer, where the sending and receiving addresses are attached to the message in another header. Finally, you send it. Your courier might want to break up the shipment among several trucks to make sure each truck is used

to its best capacity. On the Internet, this happens at the transport layer. This is the layer of the network responsible for making sure packets get to their destination. There are two main protocols used to handle transport of packets on the Internet: Transmission Control Protocol (TCP), and User Datagram Protocol (UDP). You'll learn more about these later. The main difference is that TCP provides more error-checking from origin to destination, but is slower than UDP. On the other hand, UDP trades off error-checking in favor of speed.

Each router sends off the packets one at a time to the routers to which it's connected. If it's attached to more than one other router, it sends the packets to whichever router is least busy. The packets may each take a different route to the receiver, and they may take several hops across several routers to get there. Once the packets reach their destination, the receiver strips off the headers and reassembles the message. This method of sending messages in chunks across multiple paths is called packet switching. It ensures that every path through the network is used most efficiently, but sometimes packets are dropped or lost. On the whole, though, the network is reliable enough that you can forget about dropped packets.

There's a command-line tool, ping, that can be useful in determining whether your messages are getting through.It sends a message to another object on the Net to say "Are you there?", and then waits for a reply.

To use it, open up the command-line application on your computer (Terminal on Mac OS X, the command prompt on Windows, and xterm or similar on Linux/Unix). On Mac OS X or Linux, type the following:

```
ping -c 10 127.0.0.1
```

On Windows, type this:

```
ping -n 10 127.0.0.1
```

This sends a message to address 127.0.0.1 and waits for a reply. Every time it gets a reply, it tells you how long it took, like this:

```
64 bytes from 127.0.0.1: icmp_seq=0 ttl=64 time=0.166 ms
64 bytes from 127.0.0.1: icmp_seq=1 ttl=64 time=0.157 ms
64 bytes from 127.0.0.1: icmp_seq=2 ttl=64 time=0.182 ms
```

After counting 10 packets (that's what the -c 10 on Mac and -n 10 on Windows means), it stops and gives you a summary, like this:

```
--- 127.0.0.1 ping statistics ---
10 packets transmitted, 10 packets received, 0% packet loss
round-trip min/avg/max/stddev = 0.143/0.164/0.206/0.015 ms
```

It gives you a good picture of not only how many packets got through, but also how long they took. It's a useful way to learn quickly whether a given device on the Internet is reachable or not, as well as how reliable the network is between you and that device. Later on, you'll be using devices that have no physical interface on which you can see activity, so *ping* is a handy way to check whether they're working.

NOTE: 127.0.0.1 is a special address called the loopback address or localhost address. Whenever you use it, the computer you're sending it from loops back and sends the message to itself. You can also use the name localhost in its place. You can test many network applications using this address, even when you don't have a network connection.
X

❝ Clients, Servers, and Message Protocols

Now you know how the Internet is organized, but how do things get done on the Net? For example, how does an email message get from you to your friend? Or how does a web page get to your computer when you type a URL into your browser or click on a link? It's all handled by sending messages back and forth between objects using the transport scheme just described. Once you know how that works, you can take it for granted and concentrate on the messages.

How Web Browsing Works

Figure 3-5 is a map of the routes web pages take to reach your computer. Your browser sends out a request for a page to a web server, and the server sends the page back. Which route the request and the reply take is irrelevant, as long as there is a route. The web server itself is just a program running on a computer somewhere else on the Internet. A server is a program that provides a service to other programs on the Net. The computer that a server runs on, also referred to as a server, is expected to be online and available at all times so that the service is not disrupted. In the case of a web server, the server provides access to a number of HTML files, images, sound files, and other elements of a website to clients from all over the Net. Clients are programs that take advantage of services. Your browser, a client, makes a connection to the server to request a page. The browser makes a connection to the server computer, the server program accepts the connection and delivers the files representing the page, and the exchange is made.

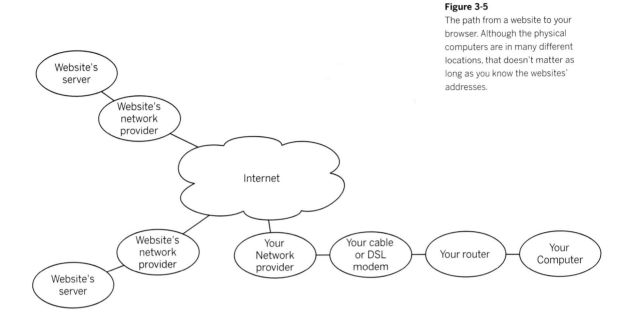

Figure 3-5
The path from a website to your browser. Although the physical computers are in many different locations, that doesn't matter as long as you know the websites' addresses.

The server computer shares its IP address with every server program running on it by assigning each program a port number. For example, every connection request for port 80 is passed to the web server program. Every request for port 25 is passed to the email server program. Any program can take control of an unused port, but only one program at a time can control a given port. In this way, network ports work much like serial ports. Many of the lower port numbers are assigned to common applications, such as mail, file transfer, telnet, and web browsing. Higher port numbers are either disabled or left open for custom applications (you'll write one of those soon). A specific request goes like this:

1. Type http://www.makezine.com/index.html into your browser.
2. The browser program contacts www.makezine.com on port 80.
3. The server program accepts the connection.

4. The browser program asks for a specific file name, **index.html**.
5. The server program looks up that file on its local file system, and prints the file out via the connection to the browser. Then, it closes the connection.
6. The browser reads the file, looks up any other files it needs (like images, movies, style sheets, and so forth), and repeats the connection request process, getting all the files it needs to display the page. When it has all the files, it strips out any header information and displays the page.

All the requests from browser to server, and all the responses from server to browser (except the images and movie files), are just strings of text. To see this process in action, you can duplicate the request process in the terminal window. Open up your terminal program again, just as you did for the *ping* example shown earlier (on Windows 7, use PuTTY).

Try It Type the code at right.

```
telnet www.google.com 80
```

The server will respond as follows (on Windows, use PuTTY and open a connection to www.google.com, port 80, Connection Type: Raw):

> The built-in Windows version of telnet is not very good. For example, you won't be able to see what you type without setting the localecho option, and the informative "Trying . . . Connected" prompts do not appear. Use PuTTY instead (http://www.chiark.greenend.org.uk/~sgtatham/putty).

```
Trying 64.233.161.147...
Connected to www.l.google.com.
Escape character is '^]'.
```

▶▶ Type the code to the right.

```
GET /index.html HTTP/1.1
Host: www.google.com
Connection: Close
```

Press the Return key twice after this last line. The server will then respond with something like this:

```
HTTP/1.1 200 OK
Date: Mon, 18 Jul 2011 00:04:06 GMT
Cache-Control: private, max-age=0
Content-Type: text/html; charset=ISO-8859-1
Server: gws
Connection: Close
```

NOTE: If telnet doesn't close on its own, you may need to press Ctrl-] to get to the telnet prompt, where you can type q followed by Enter to exit.

After the header, the next thing you'll see is a lot of HTML that looks nowhere near as simple as the normal Google web interface. This is the HTML of the index page of Google. This is how browsers and web servers talk to each other, using a text-based protocol called the Hypertext Transport Protocol (HTTP). The http:// at the beginning of every web address tells the browser to communicate using this protocol. The stuff that precedes the HTML is the HTTP header information. Browsers use it to learn the types of files that follow, how

the files are encoded, and more. The end user never needs this information, but it's very useful in managing the flow of data between client and server.

Remember the PHP time example from Chapter 1? It should still be sitting on your own web server, at www.example.com/time.php (replace www.example.com with the address of your server). Try getting this file from the command line.

Try It Modify the PHP program slightly, removing all the lines that print any HTML, like the code on the right.

Now, telnet into your web server on port 80 and request the file from the command line. Don't forget to specify the HOST in your request, as shown earlier in the request to Google.

You should get a much more abbreviated response.

```php
<?php
/* Date page
   Context: PHP
   Prints the date. */

// get the date, and format it:
$date = date("Y-m-d h:i:s\t");
// include the date:
echo "< $date >\n";

?>
```

" Even though the results of this approach aren't as pretty in a browser, it's very simple to extract the date from within a Processing program—or even a microcontroller program. Just look for the < character in the text received from the server, read everything until you get to the > character, and you've got it.

HTTP requests don't just request files. You can add parameters to your request. If the URL you're requesting is actually a program (like a PHP script), it can do something with those parameters. To add parameters to a request, add a question mark at the end of the request and parameters after that. Here's an example:

http://www.example.com/get-parameters.php?name=tom&age=14

In this case, you're sending two parameters, name and age. Their values are "tom" and "14", respectively. You can add as many parameters as you want, separating them with the ampersand (&).

There are predefined variables in PHP that give you access to these parameters and other aspects of the exchange between client and server. The variable $_REQUEST, used below, is an example that returns the parameters after the question mark in an HTTP request. Other predefined variables give you information about the client's browser and operating system, the server's operating system, any files the client's trying to upload, and much more.

Test It   Here's a PHP script that reads all the values sent in via a request and prints them out.

Save this script to your server as **get-parameters.php,** and view it in a browser using the URL shown earlier (you may need to modify the path to the file if you've put it in a subdirectory). You should get a page that says:

```
name: tom
age: 14
```

```php
<?php
/*
    Parameter reader
    Context: PHP

    Prints any parameters sent in using an HTTP GET command.
*/

// print out all the variables:
foreach ($_REQUEST as $key => $value)
    {
        echo "$key: $value<br>\n";
    }
?>
```

▶▶ You could also request it from telnet or PuTTY like you did earlier (be sure to include the ?name=tom&age=14 at the end of the argument to GET, as in GET /get-parameters.php?name=tom&age=14). You'd get something similar to the code at right, shown here with the HTTP header.

```
HTTP/1.1 200 OK
Date: Thu, 15 Mar 2007 15:10:51 GMT
Server: Apache
X-Powered-By: PHP/5.1.2
Vary: Accept-Encoding
Connection: close
Content-Type: text/html; charset=UTF-8


name: tom<br>
age: 14<br>
```

▸▸ Of course, because PHP is a programming language, you can do more than just print out the results. Try the script to the right.

Try requesting this script with the same parameter string as the last script, ?name=tom&age=14, and see what happens. Then change the age to a number greater than 21.

NOTE: **One great thing about PHP is that it automatically converts ASCII strings of numbers like "14" to their numerical values. Because all HTTP requests are ASCII-based, PHP is optimized for ASCII-based exchanges like this.**

```php
<?php
/*
   Age checker
   Context: PHP

   Expects two parameters from the HTTP request:
      name (a text string)
      age (an integer)
   Prints a personalized greeting based on the name and age.
*/

// read all the parameters and assign them to local variables:
foreach ($_REQUEST as $key => $value)
   {
      if ($key == "name") {
          $name = $value;
      }

      if ($key == "age") {
          $age = $value;
      }
   }

if ($age < 21) {
    echo "<p> $name, You're not old enough to drink.</p>\n";
} else {
    echo "<p> Hi $name. You're old enough to have a drink, ";
    echo "but do so responsibly.</p>\n";
}
?>
```

❝ HTTP GET and POST

The ability to respond to parameters sent in an HTTP request opens all kinds of possibilities. For example, you can write a script that lets you choose the address to which you send an email message, or what message to send. You'd just add parameters to the URL after the question mark, read them in PHP, and use them to set the various mail variables.

The method for sending variables in the URL after a question mark is called GET, and it's one of HTTP's four commands. Besides GET, you can also POST, PUT, and DELETE. Many browsers don't support PUT or DELETE, however, so stick to GET and POST for now.

POST is the method usually used to post data from a web form. Instead of adding the parameters on the end of the URL path as GET does, POST adds the parameters to the end of the whole HTTP request. There are a couple other parameters you need to add to a POST request too, like the content type and the content length. POST is a little more work to set up, but it's really useful for hiding the messy business of passing parameters, keeping your URLs tidy and easy to remember. Instead of the previous URL, all the user has to see is:

http://www.example.com/get-parameters.php

The rest can get delivered via POST.

Try It   Telnet into your web server on port 80 and request the file again from the command line. This time, type the POST request as shown here.

You'll get the same response as you did using GET, but now you can put all the parameters in one place, at the end.

```
POST /age_checker.php HTTP/1.0
Host: example.com
Connection: Close
Content-Type: application/x-www-form-urlencoded
Content-length: 16

name=tom&age=14
```

▶▶ The content length is the length of this string, plus a linefeed. If your name is longer than three letters, or your age is greater or fewer than two digits, change the content length to match.

▶▶ Now make a couple changes to the script. First, wrap the section that checks name and age in another if statement, like so (new lines are shown in blue).

```php
if (isset($name) && isset($age) ) {
    if ($age < 21) {
        echo "<p> $name, You're not old enough to drink.</p>\n";
    } else {
        echo "<p> Hi $name. You're old enough to have a drink, but do ";
        echo "so responsibly.</p>\n";
    }
}
?>
```

Add the following HTML to the **age_checker.php** file after the closing PHP tag.

When you reload this script in the browser, you will see a form as shown in Figure 3-6. The if statement you added makes sure the message about age doesn't show up unless you've entered values for name and age. And the HTML form calls the same script again when you submit your values, using an HTTP POST request.

```html
<html>
<body>

<form action="age_checker.php" method="post"
enctype="application/x-www-form-urlencoded">
Name: <input type="text" name="name" /><br>
Age: <input type="age" name="age" />
<input type="submit" value="Submit" />
</form>

</body>
</html>
```

Figure 3-6
The PHP age-checker form.

How Email Works

Transferring mail also uses a client-server model. It involves four applications: your email program and your friend's, and your email server (also called the mail host) and your friend's email server. Your email program adds a header to your message to say that this is a mail message, who the message is to and from, and what the subject is. Next, it contacts your mail server, which then sends the mail on to your friend's mail server. When your friend checks her mail, her mail program connects to her mail server and downloads any waiting messages. The mail servers are online all the time, waiting for new messages for all of their users.

The transport protocol for sending mail is called SMTP, the Simple Mail Transport Protocol. It's paired with two retrieval protocols: POP (Post Office Protocol) and IMAP (Internet Message Access Protocol). Just like HTTP, it's text-based. PHP has excellent functionality for sending and retrieving mail, and you can use it as an intermediary between any local application, like the Processing sketch that will follow, or some microcontroller applications you'll see later on.

Try It   Here's a PHP script that sends a mail to you. Save this script to your server as **mailer.php,** and view it in a browser as you did with the last script. You should get two results. In the browser, you'll get a page that says:

```
I mailed you@example.com
From: you@example.com
Hello world!

Hi there, how are you?
```

In your mail client, you'll get a message like this:

```
From:     You <you@example.com>
Subject:  Hello world!
Date:     May 8, 2013 2:57:42 PM EDT
To:       you <you@example.com>

Hi there, how are you?
```

```php
<?php
/*
    mailer
    Context: PHP

    sends an email.
*/

// set up your variables for mailing. Change to and from
// to your mail address:
$to = "you@example.com";
$subject = "Hello world!";
$from = "From: you@example.com";
$message = "Hi there, how are you?";

// send the mail:
mail($to, $subject, $message, $from);

// give notification in the browser:
echo "I mailed " . $to . "<br>";
echo $from . "<br>";
echo $subject. "<br><br>";
echo $message;
?>
```

Make sure your server is properly configured to send mail here. If you're using a web hosting service, the settings for mail will be part of your account settings. Also, make sure your from: address is one for which the mail server will relay mail. That typically means you can only send mail from your own domain. For example, if your domain name is example.com, then you can't send mail from cat@ohaikitteh.com.

As you can see, sending mail from PHP is very simple. So in addition to using it to serve web pages, you can use it to send messages via mail. As long as you have a device or program that can make a GET or POST, you can use PHP or other server-side programming languages to start a sequence of messages in many different applications across the Net. Now that you've got the basics of HTTP requests and mail sending, it's time to put them into action in a project.

Project 5

Networked Cat

Web browsing and email are all very simple for humans because we've developed computer interfaces that work well with our bodies. Keyboards work great with our fingers, and mice glide smoothly under our hands. It's not so easy for a cat to send email, though. This project attempts to remedy that while showing you how to build your first physical interface for the Internet.

MATERIALS

- » **Between 2 and 4 force-sensing resistors, Interlink 400 series**
- » **1 1-kilohm resistor**
- » **1 solderless breadboard**
- » **1 Arduino microcontroller module**
- » **1 personal computer**
- » **1 web camera**
- » **1 cat mat**
- » **1 cat**
- » **2 thin pieces of wood or thick cardboard, about the size of the cat mat**
- » **Wire-wrapping wire**
- » **Male header pins**

If you're a cat lover, you know how cute they can be when they curl up in their favorite spot for a nap. You might find it useful during stressful times at work to think of your cat, curled up and purring away. Wouldn't it be nice if the cat sent you an email when he lays down for a nap? It would be even better if you could then check in on the cat's website to see him at his cutest. This project makes that possible.

The system works like this: force-sensing resistors are mounted under the cat mat and attached to a micro-controller. The microcontroller is attached to a personal computer, as is a camera. When the cat lies down on the mat, his weight will cause a change in the sensor readings. The microcontroller then sends a signal to a program on the personal computer, which takes a picture with the camera and uploads it to a web server via a PHP script. Then the program calls another PHP script that sends you an email, letting you know that your cat is being particularly cute. Figure 3-7 shows the whole system.

You'll do this project in several parts:

1. Write an Arduino sketch to read sensors in the cat's mat and send the results serially to Processing.
2. Write a Processing sketch to read the serial data and when appropriate, call a PHP script that sends mail.
3. Write a PHP script to send mail.
4. Make a web page for the cat cam.
5. Write a second PHP script to accept new image uploads for the web page.
6. Modify the Processing sketch to take new images and upload them via the second PHP script.

Putting Sensors in the Cat Mat

First, you need a way to sense when the cat is on the mat. The simplest way to do this is to put force sensors under the mat and sense the difference in weight when he sits on it. How you do this depends on what kinds of force-sensing resistors you use. Interlink's 400 series FSRs work well for this project. Mount the sensors on something with a firm backing, like masonite, or another type of wood or firm cardboard.

There are some FSRs that are long and thin, like Interlink's 408 series. Long sensors aren't all that common, though, so you're more likely to have small round sensors like the 400 or 402 series. If you're using those or other smaller FSRs from another company like CUI or FlexiForce, you'll need to make a larger sensing pad. First, cut two pieces of wood or firm cardboard slightly smaller than the cat's mat. Don't use a really thick or hard piece of wood. You just need something firm enough to provide a relatively inflexible surface for the sensors. Attach the sensors to the corners of one of the pieces of wood or cardboard. Sandwich the sensors between the two boards. Tape the two boards together at the edges loosely, so that the weight of the cat can press down to affect the sensors. If you tape too tightly, the sensors will always be under force; too loose, and the boards will slide around too much and make the cat uncomfortable. If the sensors don't give enough of a reaction, get some little rubber feet—available at any electronics or hardware store—and position them on the

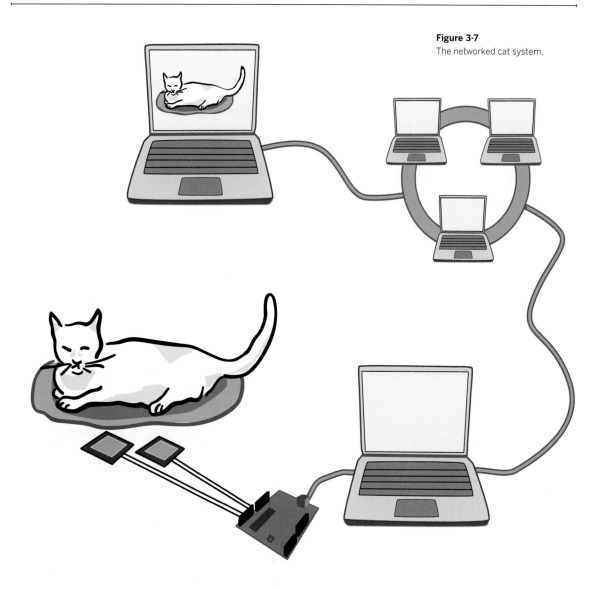

Figure 3-7
The networked cat system.

panel opposite the sensors so that they press down on the sensors. If the wood or cardboard panels have some flex in them, position an extra rubber foot or two at the center of the panel to reduce the flex. Figures 3-8, 3-9, and 3-10 show a working version of the sensor board.

Next, attach long wires to the force-sensing resistors to reach from the mat to the nearest possible place to put the microcontroller module.

You're using multiple sensors so you can sense a large area under the mat, but it doesn't matter much which one gets triggered. Connect the sensors to an analog input of the microcontroller in parallel with each other, using the voltage divider circuit shown in Figure 3-10. This circuit combines the input from all four into one input.

X

↟ Figure 3-8

Because the force-sensing resistors melt easily, I used 30AWG wire wrap instead of solder. Wire-wrapping tools are inexpensive and easy to use, but make a secure connection. After wire wrapping, I insulated the connections with heat shrink. (Heat shrink not shown.)

↠ Figure 3-9

The cat-sensing panel. The four FSRs are wired in parallel. Note the rubber feet that press down more precisely on the sensors. Make sure to insulate the connections before taping the panels together. The connector is just a pair of female wire-wrap headers.

Figure 3-10
The cat-sensing circuit. Because all of the force-sensing resistors are wired in parallel, there are only two connections for all of them. This circuit is simple enough that you can just solder a resistor to a header pin to make the connection to ground.

⚠ You may need a higher value depending on the resistance range of your force-sensing resistors and the weight of your cat. If a 1K resistor doesn't give you good values, try a 4.7K or a 10K resistor. The photo here shows a 10K resistor.

Test It   Once you've got the sensor panel together and connected to the microcontroller, run this code on the Arduino board to test the sensors.

To see the results, open the Serial Monitor at 9600 bits per second. Now, position the cat on the panel and note the number change. This can be tricky, as cats are difficult to command. You may want to put some cat treats or catnip on the pad to encourage the cat to stay there. When you're satisfied that the system works and that you can see a significant change in the value when the cat sits on the panel, you're ready to move on to the next step.

```
/*
   Analog sensor reader
   Context: Arduino

   Reads an analog input on Analog in 0, prints the result
   as an ASCII-formatted  decimal value.

   Connections:
      FSR analog sensors on Analog in 0
*/
void setup()
{
  // start serial port at 9600 bps:
  Serial.begin(9600);
}

void loop()
{
  // read analog input:
  int sensorValue = analogRead(A0);

  // send analog value out in ASCII decimal format:
  Serial.println(sensorValue, DEC);
}
```

Connect It   Next, send the sensor readings serially to Processing, which will send an email and trigger the camera to take a picture when the cat is on the mat. This sketch will look familiar to you because it's similar to the one you used to read the sensor values for Monski Pong in Chapter 2.

```
/*
   Serial String Reader
   Context: Processing

   Reads in a string of characters until it gets a linefeed (ASCII 10).
   Then converts the string into a number.
*/
import processing.serial.*;

Serial myPort;           // the serial port
float sensorValue = 0;   // the value from the sensor
float xPos = 0;          // horizontal position of the graph

void setup() {
  size(400,300);
  // list all the available serial ports
  println(Serial.list());

  // I know that the first port in the serial list on my Mac is always my
  // Arduino, so I open Serial.list()[0]. Open whatever port you're using
  // (the output of Serial.list() can help; they are listed in order
  // starting with the one that corresponds to [0]).
  myPort = new Serial(this, Serial.list()[0], 9600);

  // read bytes into a buffer until you get a newline (ASCII 10):
```

»

You don't want Processing sending a message constantly, because you'd get several thousand emails every time the cat sits on the mat. Instead, you want to recognize when the cat's there, send an email, and don't send again until he's left and returned to the mat. If he jumps on and off and on again in a minute or less, you don't want another email.

What does that look like in sensor terms? To find out, you need to do one of two things: get the cat to jump on and off the mat on cue (difficult to do without substantial bribery, using treats or a favorite toy), or weigh the cat and use a stand-in of the same weight. The advantage to using the cat is that you can see what happens when he's shifting his weight, preparing the bed by kneading it with his claws, and so forth. The advantage of the stand-in weight is that you don't have to herd cats to finish the project.

Continued from previous page.

```
  myPort.bufferUntil('\n');

  // set initial background and smooth drawing:
  background(#543174);
  smooth();
}

void draw () {
  // nothing happens here
}

void serialEvent (Serial myPort) {
  // get the ASCII string:
  String inString = myPort.readStringUntil('\n');

  if (inString != null) {
    // trim off any whitespace:
    inString = trim(inString);
    // convert to an int and map to the screen height:
    sensorValue = float(inString);
    sensorValue = map(sensorValue, 0, 1023, 0, height);
    println(sensorValue);
  }
}
```

Refine It   If your system is working correctly, you should notice a difference of several points in the sensor readings when the cat gets on the mat. It helps to graph the results so you can see clearly what the difference looks like. To do that, add a few extra variables to the variable list at the beginning of your Processing program.

```
float prevSensorValue = 0;   // previous value from the sensor
float lastXPos = 0;          // previous horizontal position
```

 Next, add a new method called drawGraph().

```
void drawGraph(float prevValue, float currentValue) {
  // subtract the values from the window height
  // so that higher numbers get drawn higher
  // on the screen:
  float yPos = height - currentValue;
  float lastYPos = height - prevValue;

  // draw the line in a pretty color:
  stroke(#C7AFDE);
  line(lastXPos, lastYPos, xPos, yPos);

  // at the edge of the screen, go back to the beginning:
  if (xPos >= width) {
```

NOTE: Once you've got the serial connection between the microcontroller and the
computer working, you might want to add in
the Bluetooth radio from the Monski Pong
project in Chapter 2. It will make your life
easier if your computer doesn't have to be
tethered to the cat mat in order to program.

```
    xPos = 0;
    lastXPos = 0;
    background(#543174);
  }
  else {
    // increment the horizontal position:
    xPos++;
    // save the current graph position
    // for next time:
    lastXPos = xPos;
  }
}
```

Finally, add the following to the
serialEvent() method, right after
you print the sensor value (new lines
are shown in blue).

```
    println(sensorValue);
    sensorValue = map(sensorValue, 0, 1023, 0, height);
    drawGraph(prevSensorValue, sensorValue);
    // save the current value for the next time:
    prevSensorValue = sensorValue;
  }
}
```

When you run the program, you'll see a graph
of the sensor values, as shown in Figure 3-11.
When the cat jumps on the mat, you should
see a sudden increase, and when he jumps off, you'll see
the graph decrease. You'll also see any small changes,
which you might need to filter out. If the changes are
small relative to the difference between the two states
you're looking for, you can ignore them. Using the sensor
values, you have enough knowledge to start defining the
cat's presence on the mat as an event. The event you care
about is when the sensor reading increases significantly,
because that's when the cat sat on the mat. To do this,
pick a threshold number in between the two states. When
the sensor reading changes from being less than threshold
to greater than or equal to it, that's your first event. When
the sensor value goes below the threshold, the cat has left
the mat. That's your second event.

Figure 3-11
Output of the sensor-graphing program.

You don't just want to respond to events, though. You might have a fickle cat who jumps on and off the mat a lot. Once you've sent a message, you don't want to send another one right away, even if the cat gets off the mat and back on. Decide on an appropriate interval, wait that long, and don't respond to any input during that time. Once the interval's over, start looking for input again.

▸▸ Add the following new variable to the beginning of your program. Determine the threshold value by watching the sensor value without the cat on the mat, and picking a number that's higher.

```
int threshold = 250;       // above this number, the cat is on the mat.
```

▸▸ Then put this code in your serialEvent() method, right after drawGraph() (new lines are shown in blue). Remove or comment out the line in the serialEvent() method that prints the sensor value.

```
drawGraph(prevSensorValue, sensorValue);

if (sensorValue > threshold ) {
  // if the last reading was less than the threshold,
  // then the cat just got on the mat.
  if (prevSensorValue <= threshold) {
    println("cat on mat");
    sendMail();
  }
}
else {
  // if the sensor value is less than the threshold,
  // and the previous value was greater, then the cat
  // just left the mat
  if (prevSensorValue > threshold) {
    println("cat not on mat");
  }
}
```

▸▸ Finally, add a method that sends mail. For now, it will just print a placeholder to the message window. After the next section, you'll write code to make it send mail for real. Add this method to the end of your program.

```
void sendMail() {
  println("This is where you'd send a mail.");
}
```

When you run the program, you should see messages in the console area saying when the cat jumps on or off the mat, and when a mail would be sent. Your cat may be fickle or may take his time settling on the mat, which can result in several mail messages as he gets comfortable. To avoid this, you want to change the sketch so that once it sends a message, it doesn't send any others for an acceptable period. You can do this by modifying the sendMail() method to keep track of when the last message was sent. Here's how to do it.

Tame It Every time the program sends a mail message, it should take note of the time. Add a few new variables at the beginning of the program.

```
int currentTime = 0;    // the current time as a single number
int lastMailTime = 0;   // last time you sent a mail
int mailInterval = 60;  // minimum seconds between mails
String mailUrl = "http://www.example.com/cat-script.php";
```

▸▸ Add one line at the beginning of the draw() method to update current-Time continuously.

```
void draw() {
  currentTime = hour() * 3600 + minute() * 60 + second();
```

▸▸ Now, modify the sendMail() method as shown in the code at right.

Once you're sure it works, adjust mail-Interval to an appropriate minimum number of seconds between emails.

```
void sendMail() {
  // how long has passed since the last mail:
  int timeDifference = currentTime - lastMailTime;

  if ( timeDifference > mailInterval) {
    String[] mailScript = loadStrings(mailUrl);
    println("results from mail script:");
    println(mailScript);

    // save the current minute for next time:
    lastMailTime = currentTime;
  }
}
```

When you run the sketch this time, you'll see an error message like this when you cross the threshold:

```
cat on mat
```

```
results from mail script:The file "http://www.example.com/cat-script.php" is missing or inaccessible, make sure the URL is
valid or that the file has been added to your sketch and is readable.
```

The sketch is now making an HTTP GET request to call a PHP script that's not there. In the next section, you'll write that script.

❝ Sending Mail from the Cat

Processing doesn't have any libraries for sending and receiving email, so you can call a PHP script to do the job. Processing has a simple command to make HTTP GET requests: loadStrings(). The same technique can be used to call other PHP scripts or web URLs from Processing. POST requests are a little more complicated; you'll see how to do that later.

Save the following PHP script to your server with the name **cat-script.php**. Test it from a browser. When you call it, you should get an email in your inbox. Some mail servers may require that you send mail only from your proper account name. If that's the case, replace cat@ example.com with the email address for your account name on the server on which the script is running.

Once you've confirmed that this script is running, go back to the Processing sketch. Double-check that the mailUrl variable is the URL of the script, and run the sketch. When the cat sits on the mat now, the sketch will call the mailer script and you should get an email from the cat. The console output will look like this:

```
cat on mat
results from mail script:
[0] "TO: you@example.com"
[1] "FROM: cat@example.com"
[2] "SUBJECT:the cat"
[3] ""
[4] "The cat is on the mat at http://www.example.com/
catcam."
[5] ""
```

```php
<?php
/*
    Mail sender
    Context: PHP

    Sends an email if sensorValue is above a threshold value.
*/
    // form the message:
    $to = "you@example.com";
    $subject = "the cat";
    $message = "The cat is on the mat at http://www.example.com/catcam.";
    $from = "cat@example.com";

    // send the mail:
    mail($to, $subject, $message, "From: $from");
    // reply to processing:
    echo "TO: " .$to;
    echo "\nFROM: " .$from;
    echo "\nSUBJECT:" .$subject;
    echo "\n\n" .$message . "\n\n";
?>
```

▸▸ **You'll need to change these email addresses.**

⚠ Now that you're sending emails from a program, you need to be very careful about how often it happens. You really don't want 10,000 messages in your inbox because you accidentally called the mail command in a repeating loop.

Now you're getting somewhere! You're able to send mail triggered by a physical event—the cat sitting on the mat. This is a good moment to stop and celebrate your achievement and pet the cat. In the next section, you're going to use a webcam to make your cat Internet-famous.

X

Making a Web Page for the Cat Cam

▸▸ Next, you need a web page for the cat cam. Take a picture of your cat and upload the image to the directory containing your script with the filename **catcam.jpg**. Once you know the image is there and visible, frame it with a web page in the directory, called **index.html**. Here is a bare-bones page that will automatically refresh itself in the user's browser every five seconds, as indicated by the meta tag in the head of the document. Feel free to make the page as detailed as you want, but keep the meta tag in place.

```html
<html>
<head>
    <title>Cat Cam</title>
    <meta http-equiv="refresh" content="5">
</head>
<body>
    <center>
        <h2>Cat Cam</h2>
            <img src="catcam.jpg">
    </center>
</body>
</html>
```

Refine It The previous page is really simple, but as you can see, it reloads the entire page each time. However, if you want only the image to reload, you can do something fancier with some CSS DIV tags and a little JavaScript.

This page is a bit more complex. Only the image reloads in this page. The other elements stay stable.

Once you've made the Cat Cam page to your liking, it's time to automate the process of taking the picture and uploading it. First, you'll make an uploader PHP script. Then you'll modify the Processing sketch to take a picture and upload it via the PHP script. Figure 3-12 shows the image uploaded to the Cat Cam page.
X

```html
<html>
<head>
    <title>Cat Cam</title>
    <script type="text/javascript">
        function refresh() {
            var refreshTime = 5 * 1000;      // 5000 ms
            var thisImage = "catcam.jpg";    // the image location
            var today = new Date();          // the current time
            // add the time to the end of the image string
            //to make a unique URL:
            document.images["pic"].src=thisImage+"?"+today;
            // reload if the images are loaded:
            if(document.images) {
                window.onload=refresh;
            }
            // if the time is up reload the image
            t=setTimeout('refresh()',refreshTime);
        }
    </script>
</head>
<body onload="refresh()">
    <center>
        <h2>Cat Cam</h2>
<img src="catcam.jpg" id="pic">
    </center>
</body>
</html>
```

Figure 3-12
Regardless of which option you use, the Cat Cam page will look like this.

Uploading Files to a Server Using PHP

Next, you're going to write a script that uploads images to the server. PHP has a predefined variable, $_FILES, that allows you to get information about any files the user attempts to upload via HTTP. Like $_REQUEST, which you saw earlier, $_FILES is an array, and each of the array elements is a property of the file. You can get the name of the file, the size of the file, and the file type, which will be useful when you write a script that takes only JPEG files below a certain size.

Try It

Here's a PHP script with an HTML form that uploads a file. The PHP script doesn't do anything much so far—it just shows you the results of the HTTP request. Save this to your server as **save2web.php**.

View this in a browser, and you'll get a simple form with a file chooser button and an upload button. Choose a JPEG image file and upload, and you'll get a response that looks like this:

```
Array ( [file] => Array ( [name] =>
catcam.jpg [type] => image/jpeg [tmp_
name] => /tmp/phpoZT3BS [error] => 0
[size] => 45745 ) )
```

This is the $_FILES variable printed out for you.

```php
<?php
if (isset($_FILES)) {
    print_r($_FILES);
}
?>

<html>
<body>

<form action="save2web.php" method="post"
enctype="multipart/form-data">
<label for="file">Filename:</label>
<input type="file" name="file" id="file" />
<br />
<input type="submit" name="submit" value="Upload" />
</form>

</body>
</html>
```

Replace the PHP part of this script (the part between <?php and ?>) with the following. This script checks to see that the uploaded file is a JPEG file with fewer than 100 kilobytes, and it saves it in the same directory as the script.

```php
<?php
if (isset($_FILES)) {
    // put the file parameters in variables:
    $fileName = $_FILES['file']['name'];
    $fileTempName = $_FILES['file']['tmp_name'];
    $fileType = $_FILES['file']['type'];
    $fileSize = $_FILES['file']['size'];
    $fileError = $_FILES['file']['error'];

    // if the file is a JPEG and under 100K, proceed:
    if (($fileType == "image/jpeg") && ($fileSize < 100000)){
        // if there's a file error, print it:
        if ( $fileError > 0){
            echo "Return Code: " . $fileError . "<br />";
        }
```

»

▶▶ Now when you load this script in a browser and upload a file, you'll be able to see the file in the directory afterwards. Try uploading a new JPEG of the cat, then reload the browser window of the **index.html** page you made earlier. You should see the same page with the new image.

```
Continued from previous page.
    // if there's no file error, print some HTML about the file:
    else {
        echo "Upload: " . $fileName . "<br />";
        echo "Type: " . $fileType . "<br />";
        echo "Size: " . ($fileSize / 1024) . " Kb<br />";
        echo "Temp file: " . $fileTempName . "<br />";

        // if the file already exists,
        // delete the previous version:
        if (file_exists($fileName)) {
            unlink($fileName);
        }
        // move the file from the temp location to
        // this directory:
        move_uploaded_file($fileTempName, $fileName);
        echo "Uploaded file stored as: ".$fileName;
    }
}
// if the file's not a JPEG or too big, say so:
else {
    echo "File is not a JPEG or too big.";
}
}
?>
```

❝ Capturing an Image and Uploading It Using Processing

Now that you've got an uploader script on the server, you need a program on your local computer to capture a picture of the cat and to call the script. There are several automated webcam applications on the market, but it's fun to do it on your own. This section will describe how you can do it in Processing using two external libraries: the Processing video library and the Processing net library.

Before you get going, there are a few things you'll need to do. First, make sure your webcam can be read by both your computer and by Processing.

If you're using Mac OS X, you're all set. The Processing video library works with QuickTime, which comes with your computer. Open a video applicatio,n like Photo Booth, just to make sure it's working, then you're ready to program.

For Windows 7 users, you'll need to install QuickTime, if you don't have it already. Download it from http://www.apple.com/quicktime and follow the installer directions. You'll also need a VDIG, which is a software library that allows Processing to connect to the webcam through QuickTime. You can download WinVDIG from http://www.eden.net.nz/7/20071008/. Use version 1.0.1, as it's the most stable as of this writing. Finally, you'll need to change the Compatibility settings for Processing. Open the Processing application directory, right-click on the Processing application icon, and choose Properties. In the application's Properties window, choose the Compatibility tab. In that tab, click the checkbox marked "Run this program in compatibility mode for:", and from the associated drop-down menu, choose "Windows XP (service pack 3)". Then click Apply, and you're ready to move on. The Processing team hopes to change this soon, so it may be much simpler by the time you read this.

For Ubuntu Linux users, you're out of luck this time. The Processing video library is not currently supported under Linux, though the developers welcome patches for this.

Try It Here's a sketch that uses the video library to paint a live image from the webcam to the screen. Run it and you'll see yourself (or your cat).

```
/**
 Image capture and upload
 Context: Processing
 */
import processing.video.*;     // import the video library
Capture myCam;                 // the camera

void setup() {
  size(640, 480);  // set the size of the window

  // For a list of cameras on your computer, use this line:
  println(Capture.list());

  // use the default camera for capture at 30 fps:
  myCam = new Capture(this, width, height, 30);
}

void draw() {
  // if there's data from the camera:
  if (myCam.available()) {
    myCam.read();       // read the camera image
    set(0, 0, myCam);  // draw the camera image to the screen
  }
}
```

» Add these lines after the set() command in the draw() method to draw a timestamp on the screen (new lines are shown in blue).

```
void draw() {
  // if there's data from the camera:
  if (myCam.available()) {
    myCam.read();       // read the camera image
    set(0, 0, myCam);  // draw the camera image to the screen

    // get the time as a string:
    String timeStamp = nf(hour(), 2) + ":" + nf(minute(), 2)
      + ":" + nf(second(), 2) + " " + nf(day(), 2) + "-"
        + nf(month(), 2) + "-" +  nf(year(), 4);

    // draw a dropshadow for the time text:
    fill(15);
    text(timeStamp, 11, height - 19);
    // draw the main time text:
    fill(255);
    text(timeStamp, 10, height - 20);
  }
}
```

» Now add a global variable at the top of your sketch for a filename, and add a method at the end of the sketch to save the window image to a JPEG file when you hit any key (new lines are shown in blue).

Save this sketch before you run it. When you run it, hit any key. Then check the sketch folder, and you should see a JPEG image generated by the sketch, like Figure 3-13.

```
import processing.video.*;    // import the video library
Capture myCam;                // the camera
String fileName = "catcam.jpg";

// setup and draw methods go here

void keyReleased() {
  PImage img = get();
  img.save(fileName);
}
```

Figure 3-13
The output of the Cat Cam Processing sketch.

» Next, it's time to add a method that can make an HTTP POST request. For that, you'll need the Processing network library. Like the serial library, it adds some functions to the core of Processing. The serial library allowed you to access the serial ports; the network library allows you to make network connections and a few more global variables. Add these before the setup() method.

```
import processing.net.*;

String pictureScriptUrl = "/save2web.php";
String boundary = "----H4rkNrF";
Client thisClient;
```

▶▶ Now you need a method to formulate and send the actual POST request. To do this, open a new Client connection to the server, then send the request. In this method, the content of the request is broken into three parts: everything that comes before the file itself; the actual file, which is loaded into a byte array; and the end of the request that comes after the file. Add this method at the end of your sketch.

```
void postPicture() {
  // load the saved image into an array of bytes:
  byte[] thisFile =loadBytes(fileName);

  // open a new connection to the server:
  thisClient = new Client(this, "www.example.com", 80);
  // make an HTTP POST request:
  thisClient.write("POST " + pictureScriptUrl + " HTTP/1.1\n");
  thisClient.write("Host: www.example.com\n");
  // tell the server you're sending the POST in multiple parts,
  // and send a unique string that will delineate the parts:
  thisClient.write("Content-Type: multipart/form-data; boundary=");
  thisClient.write(boundary + "\n");

  // form the beginning of the request:
  String requestHead ="\n--" + boundary + "\n";
  requestHead +="Content-Disposition: form-data; name=\"file\"; ";
  requestHead += "filename=\"" + fileName + "\"\n";
  requestHead +="Content-Type: image/jpeg\n\n";

  // form the end of the request:
  String tail ="\n--" + boundary + "--\n\n";
```

▶▶ Once you've got the three pieces of the request, calculate the total number of bytes by adding the length of the two strings and the byte array. Next, send the content length, and then the content itself. Finally, you close the connection by stopping the client.

```
  // calculate and send the length of the total request,
  // including the head of the request, the file, and the tail:
  int contentLength = requestHead.length() + thisFile.length + tail.length();
  thisClient.write("Content-Length: " + contentLength + "\n\n");

  // send the header of the request, the file, and the tail:
  thisClient.write(requestHead);
  thisClient.write(thisFile);
  thisClient.write(tail);

  // close the client:
  thisClient.stop();
}
```

▶▶ Finally, add a call to this new method in the keyReleased() method (new lines are shown in blue).

```
void keyReleased() {
  PImage img = get();
  img.save(fileName);
  postPicture();
}
```

Save the sketch and run it. Now when you type any key, the sketch will not only save the image locally, but also upload it to the **catcam** directory on your sever, via the **save2web.php** script.

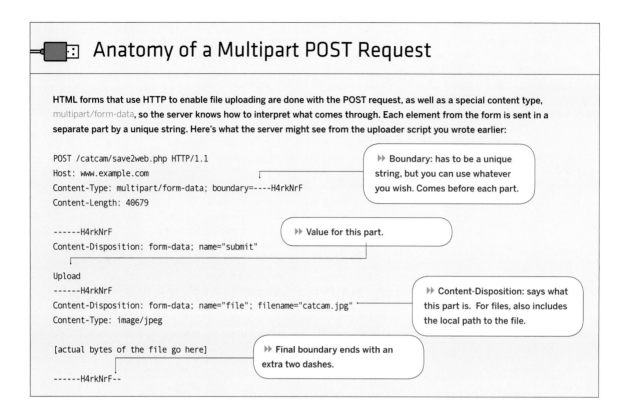

Anatomy of a Multipart POST Request

HTML forms that use HTTP to enable file uploading are done with the POST request, as well as a special content type, multipart/form-data, so the server knows how to interpret what comes through. Each element from the form is sent in a separate part by a unique string. Here's what the server might see from the uploader script you wrote earlier:

```
POST /catcam/save2web.php HTTP/1.1
Host: www.example.com
Content-Type: multipart/form-data; boundary=----H4rkNrF
Content-Length: 40679

------H4rkNrF
Content-Disposition: form-data; name="submit"

Upload
------H4rkNrF
Content-Disposition: form-data; name="file"; filename="catcam.jpg"
Content-Type: image/jpeg

[actual bytes of the file go here]

------H4rkNrF--
```

▶▶ Boundary: has to be a unique string, but you can use whatever you wish. Comes before each part.

▶▶ Value for this part.

▶▶ Content-Disposition: says what this part is. For files, also includes the local path to the file.

▶▶ Final boundary ends with an extra two dashes.

❝ Putting It All Together

Finally, it's time to combine the Processing sketch, which reads the serial port and calls the mailer script, with the one that takes the image and calls the image uploader script. The final sketch will work as shown in Figure 3-14. All the action is driven by the serial input of sensor data. If the received value is over the threshold, there's a cat there, so the sketch takes a picture. If it's been an appropriate time since the last picture, the picture is uploaded. If the sensor value has just changed from below the threshold to above, and enough time has passed since the last mail, the sketch sends you mail that the cat just jumped on the mat.

Figure 3-14
The flowchart of the Cat Cam sketch.

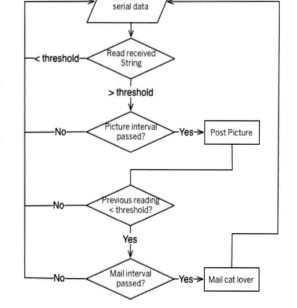

Try It Start by combining the list of global variables from both sketches. Here's what it should look like.

```
/*
Cat webcam uploader/emailer
Context: Processing

takes a webcam image continually, uploads it, and
mails you when it receives a serial string above a given value
*/

// import the libraries you need:  Network, serial, video:
import processing.serial.*;
import processing.video.*;
import processing.net.*;

Serial myPort;              // the serial port
float sensorValue = 0;      // the value from the sensor
float prevSensorValue = 0;  // previous value from the sensor
int threshold = 250;        // above this number, the cat is on the mat.

int currentTime = 0;        // the current time as a single number
int lastMailTime = 0;       // last minute you sent a mail
int mailInterval = 60;      // minimum seconds between mails
String mailUrl = "http://www.example.com/cat-script.php";
int lastPictureTime = 0;    // last minute you sent a picture
int pictureInterval = 10;   // minimum seconds between pictures

Capture myCam;                  // camera capture library instance
String fileName = "catcam.jpg"; // file name for the picture

// location on your server for the picture script:
String pictureScriptUrl = "/save2web.php";
String boundary = "----H4rkNrF"; // string boundary for the POST request

Client thisClient;          // instance of the net library
```

▶▶ Now combine the setup() methods like so.

```
void setup() {
  size(400,300);
  // list all the available serial ports
  println(Serial.list());

  // I know that the first port in the serial list on my Mac is always my
  // Arduino, so I open Serial.list()[0]. Open whatever port you're using
  // (the output of Serial.list() can help; they are listed in order
  // starting with the one that corresponds to [0]).
  myPort = new Serial(this, Serial.list()[0], 9600);

  // read bytes into a buffer until you get a newline (ASCII 10):
  myPort.bufferUntil('\n');
```

»

```
Continued from previous page.
// set initial background and smooth drawing:
background(#543174);
smooth();

// For a list of cameras on your computer, use this line:
println(Capture.list());

// use the default camera for capture at 30 fps:
myCam = new Capture(this, width, height, 30);
}
```

» The draw() method paints the camera image to the screen and adds a timestamp.

```
void draw () {
// make a single number from the current hour, minute, and second:
currentTime = hour() * 3600 + minute() * 60 + second();

if (myCam.available() == true) {
// draw the camera image to the screen:
myCam.read();
set(0, 0, myCam);

// get the time as a string:
String timeStamp = nf(hour(), 2) + ":" + nf(minute(), 2)
  + ":" + nf(second(), 2) + " " + nf(day(), 2) + "-"
    + nf(month(), 2) + "-" +  nf(year(), 4);

// draw a dropshadow for the time text:
fill(15);
text(timeStamp, 11, height - 19);
// draw the main time text:
fill(255);
text(timeStamp, 10, height - 20);
  }
}
```

» The main action happens in the serialEvent(), just as shown in the flowchart in Figure 3-14. If the sensor reading is greater than the threshold, the sketch takes a picture. Every five seconds, it uploads the picture. If the sensor reading just changed, it calls the sendMail() method.

```
void serialEvent (Serial myPort) {
// get the ASCII string:
String inString = myPort.readStringUntil('\n');

if (inString != null) {
// trim off any whitespace:
inString = trim(inString);
// convert to an int and map to the screen height:
sensorValue = float(inString);
sensorValue = map(sensorValue, 0, 1023, 0, height);

if (sensorValue > threshold ) {
  if (currentTime - lastPictureTime > pictureInterval) {
```

»

```
Continued from previous page.
        PImage thisFrame = get();
        thisFrame.save(fileName);
        postPicture();
        lastPictureTime = currentTime;
      }

      // if the last reading was less than the threshold,
      // then the cat just got on the mat.
      if (prevSensorValue <= threshold) {
        println("cat on mat");
        sendMail();
      }
    }
    else {
      // if the sensor value is less than the threshold,
      // and the previous value was greater, then the cat
      // just left the mat
      if (prevSensorValue > threshold) {
        println("cat not on mat");
      }
    }
    // save the current value for the next time:
    prevSensorValue = sensorValue;
  }
}
```

The sendMail() method checks to see whether enough time has passed since the last mail before it sends. Then it calls the **cat-mail.php** script using the loadStrings() function to make an HTTP GET request.

```
void sendMail() {
  // how long has passed since the last mail:
  int timeDifference = currentTime - lastMailTime;

  if ( timeDifference > mailInterval) {
    String[] mailScript = loadStrings(mailUrl);
    println("results from mail script:");
    println(mailScript);

    // save the current minute for next time:
    lastMailTime = currentTime;
  }
}
```

▸▸ Finally, the postPicture() method takes the last image saved. The method uploads it by calling the **save2web.php** script using an HTTP POST request.

```
void postPicture() {
  // load the saved image into an array of bytes:
  byte[] thisFile =loadBytes(fileName);

  // open a new connection to the server:
  thisClient = new Client(this, "www.example.com", 80);
  // make an HTTP POST request:
  thisClient.write("POST " + pictureScriptUrl + " HTTP/1.1\n");
  thisClient.write("Host: www.example.com\n");
  // tell the server you're sending the POST in multiple parts,
  // and send a unique string that will delineate the parts:
  thisClient.write("Content-Type: multipart/form-data; boundary=");
  thisClient.write(boundary + "\n");

  // form the beginning of the request:
  String requestHead ="\n--" + boundary + "\n";
  requestHead +="Content-Disposition: form-data; name=\"file\"; ";
  requestHead += "filename=\"" + fileName + "\"\n";
  requestHead +="Content-Type: image/jpeg\n\n";

  // form the end of the request:
  String tail ="\n\n--" + boundary + "--\n\n";

  // calculate and send the length of the total request,
  // including the head of the request, the file, and the tail:
  int contentLength = requestHead.length() + thisFile.length
      + tail.length();
  thisClient.write("Content-Length: " + contentLength + "\n\n");

  // send the header of the request, the file, and the tail:
  thisClient.write(requestHead);
  thisClient.write(thisFile);
  thisClient.write(tail);
}
```

" One Final Test

To test this code, open the browser to the Cat Cam page, and then run the sketch. On startup, it should take a picture and upload it. A few seconds later, the Cat Cam page will refresh itself, and you'll see that image. Then get the cat to jump on the mat. The sketch will take another image and upload it, and will then send you an email. Check your mail to see whether there's a new message from the cat.

As long as the cat stays on the mat, the sketch will upload a new image every five seconds. Watch for a minute or so to see the image change a few times, and then remove the cat from the mat. You should get another message in the console from the call to the mailer script. See whether the image changes once the cat is off the mat. It shouldn't; the image that remains should be the last one of the cat—that is, until the cat jumps on the mat again. The timestamp in that image will give you an idea when the cat was last on the mat.

When all that works, take a breath and admire your work. Figure 3-15 shows the finished cat bed. Congratulations! You've just made your first Internet-connected project. You and your cat can now be in constant contact.

X

Figure 3-15

The finished cat bed (at right) and a
detail of the sensor pad, which sits
under the cat bed itself. A bamboo
jewelry box houses the electronics—and
matches the furniture. The USB cable
runs to the computer. Make sure to
secure the wires thoroughly, or the cat
may try to chew on them.

❝❝ Conclusion

Now you have an understanding of the structure of the Internet, and how networked applications do their business.

The Internet is actually a network of networks, built up in multiple layers. Successful network transactions rely on there being at least one dependable route through the Internet from client to server. Client and server applications swap strings of text messages about the files they want to exchange, transferring their files and messages over network ports. To communicate with any given server, you need to know its message protocols. When you do, it's often possible to test the exchange between client and server using a telnet session and typing in the appropriate messages. Likewise, it's possible to write programs for a personal computer or microcontroller to send those same messages, as you saw in the cat bed project. Now that you understand how simple those messages can be, you'll soon get the chance to do it without a personal computer. In the next chapter, you'll connect a microcontroller to the Internet directly using an Ethernet interface for the microcontroller itself.

X

4

Look, Ma, No Computer! Microcontrollers on the Internet

The first response that comes to many people's minds after building a project like the networked cat bed in Chapter 3 is: "Great, but how can I do this without needing to connect to my computer?" It's cumbersome to have to attach the microcontroller to a laptop or desktop computer just to enable it to connect to the Internet. After all, as you saw in Chapter 3, Internet message protocols are just text strings, and microcontrollers are good at sending short text strings. So, in this chapter, you'll learn how to connect a microcontroller to the Internet through a device that's not much more complex than the Bluetooth radio modem you used in Chapter 2.

◀◀ **Uncommon Projects' YBox** (http://uncommonprojects.com/site/play/ybox-2) puts RSS feeds on your TV using an XPort serial-to-Ethernet module and a Propeller microchip. *Image courtesy of Uncommon Projects.*

In the past few years, a wide array of commercial appliances has come on the market that can connect directly to the Internet without the aid of a personal computer. Companies like D-Link, Sony, Axis, and others make security cameras with network interfaces, both Ethernet and WiFi. Ceiva, eStarling, and others make picture frames with WiFi connections to which you can upload images from the Net. Ambient Devices makes lamps and displays of various sorts that connect to the Net and change their appearance based on changes in information, such as stock market data, weather, and other scalar quantities. Cable television set-top boxes are computers in a small box, capable of routing streams of audio, video, and data all at the same time. In fact, the operating system in your set-top box might even be a variation of the same Linux operating system that's running on your network provider's web hosting machine. Home alarm systems are made up of networks of microcontrollers that talk among themselves, with one that can communicate with a central server, usually over phone lines using a modem.

All of these appliances engage in networked communication. The simplest handle only one transaction at a time, requesting information from a server and then waiting for a response, or sending a single message in response to some physical event. Others manage multiple streams of communication at once, allowing you to surf the Web while watching television. The more processing power a given device has, the more it can handle. For many applications, however, you don't need a lot of processing power, because the device you're making has only one or two functions.

X

Figure 4-1. New parts for this chapter: **1.** Arduino Ethernet shield—this one has a Power over Ethernet module on board **2.** Photocells **3.** Red, green, and blue lighting filter gels **4.** Voltmeter. You can use an off-the-shelf one, but it's better if you can find one that's antique. Don't forget plenty of male header pins for the breakout boards.

◀᠄ Supplies for Chapter 4

DISTRIBUTOR KEY
- **A** Arduino Store (http://store.arduino.cc/ww)
- **AF** Adafruit (http://adafruit.com)
- **D** Digi-Key (www.digikey.com)
- **F** Farnell (www.farnell.com)
- **J** Jameco (http://jameco.com)
- **MS** Maker SHED (www.makershed.com)
- **RS** RS (www.rs-online.com)
- **SF** SparkFun (www.sparkfun.com)
- **SS** Seeed Studio (www.seeedstudio.com)

PROJECT 6: Hello Internet! Daylight Color Web Server

» **1 Arduino Ethernet board A** A000050
Alternatively, an Uno-compatible board (see Chapter 2) with an Ethernet shield will work.
SF DEV-09026, **J** 2124242, **A** A000056, **AF** 201, **F** 1848680

» **1 Ethernet connection to the Internet** Your home router most likely has Ethernet jacks in the back. If you've hooked up your computer to the Internet using Ethernet, you know where the ports are.

» **3 10-kilohm resistors D** 10KQBK-ND, **J** 29911, **F** 9337687, **RS** 707-8906

» **3 photocells (light-dependent resistors) D** PDV-P9200-ND, **J** 202403, **SF** SEN-09088, **F** 7482280, **RS** 234-1050

» **1 solderless breadboard D** 438-1045-ND, **J** 20723 or 20601, **SF** PRT-00137, **F** 4692810, **AF** 64, **SS** STR101C2M or STR102C2M, **MS** MKKN2

» **3 lighting filters** One primary red, one primary green, and one primary blue. Available from your local lighting- or photo-equipment supplier.

PROJECT 7: Networked Air-Quality Meter

» **1 Arduino Ethernet board A** A000050
Alternatively, an Uno-compatible board (see Chapter 2) with an Ethernet shield will work.
SF DEV-09026, **J** 2124242, **A** A000056, **AF** 201, **F** 1848680

» **1 Ethernet connection to the Internet** Your home router most likely has Ethernet jacks in the back. If you've hooked up your computer to the Internet using Ethernet, you know where the ports are.

» **1 solderless breadboard D** 438-1045-ND, **J** 20723 or 20601, **SF** PRT-00137, **F** 4692810, **AF** 64, **SS** STR101C2M or STR102C2M, **MS** MKKN2

» **1 voltmeter** Get a nice-looking antique one if you can. Ideally, you want a meter that reads a range from 0–5V, or 0–10V at most.
SF TOL-10285, **F** 4692810, **RS** 244-890

» **4 LEDs D** 160-1144-ND or 160-1665-ND, **J** 34761 or 94511, **F** 1015878, **RS** 247-1662 or 826-830, **SF** COM-09592 or COM-09590

» **4 220-ohm resistors D** 220QBK-ND, **J** 690700, **F** 9337792, **RS** 707-8842

❝❝ Introducing Network Modules

It's possible to write a program for a microcontroller that can manage all the steps of network communication, from the physical and data connections to the network address management to the negotiation of protocols like SMTP and HTTP. A code library that encompasses all the layers needed for network connections is called a network stack, or TCP/IP stack. However, it's much easier to use a network interface module to do the job.

There are many such modules on the market, with varying prices and features. Just as you can choose how technical you want to get when you pick a microcontroller platform, you can also choose your technical level when you select a network controller. Some modules—like Rabbit Semiconductor's RabbitCore processors—come with all the source code for a TCP/IP stack, and expect you to modify it for your needs and program the device yourself. Others, like the Beagle Board, are a full network computer on a single circuit board. These are very powerful, and if you're an experienced network programmer, they present a very comfortable programming environment. However, they don't make it easy to add sensors and actuators, and for people not experienced with network programming, they present a steep learning curve. Others—like Lantronix'

modules, the XPort, XPort Direct, MatchPort, and WiPort—have a stack programmed into their firmware, and present you with a serial, telnet, or web-based interface. These are much simpler to use. The web interface gives you access from the browser of your personal computer; the telnet interface gives you access from a server or your personal computer; and the serial interface gives you access from a microcontroller. These are serial-to-Ethernet modems. They work much like the Bluetooth modems you used in Chapter 2, but they have a different serial protocol. These are a comfortable beginning place, and I used them extensively in the first edition of this book. For this edition, however, you'll learn about Ethernet modules that have a synchronous serial interface. These offer the ease-of-use of the Serial-to-Ethernet modules, but they don't take up

Figure 4-2
The Arduino Ethernet (left), an Arduino Ethernet shield (center), and an Ethernet shield with power-over-Ethernet module attached (right). You can use any of these for the Ethernet projects in this book.

an asynchronous serial port on your microcontroller. It means you can still use the serial port for debugging or communicating with other devices.

There are two options for Ethernet connections to an Arduino. One is the Arduino Ethernet board, which is an Arduino board that has an Ethernet module on the board itself. The Ethernet connector replaces the USB connector found on the standard Arduinos. To program this board, you also need an FTDI-style USB-to-Serial adapter. The other option is an add-on board for regular Arduino modules, called an Ethernet shield. There are a few versions of it on the market. The Arduino Ethernet shield uses an Ethernet chip from WizNet, the W5100. This shield has a built-in SD memory card slot as well, like the Arduino Ethernet board. The Adafruit Ethernet shield also uses the W5100 chip, or it can use the Lantronix serial-to-Ethernet modules mentioned earlier. The projects in this chapter will work with the Arduino Ethernet, with the Arduino Ethernet shield, or with the Adafruit Ethernet shield with the W5100 module, which are shown in Figure 4-2. They will not work with the Lantronix module, however.
X

Introducing Serial Peripheral Interface (SPI)

The Ethernet shield and Arduino Ethernet communicate with their Ethernet controllers using a form of synchronous serial communication called Serial Peripheral Interface, or SPI. SPI, along with another synchronous serial protocol, Inter-Integrated Circuit or I2C (sometimes called Two-Wire Interface, or TWI), are two of the most common synchronous serial protocols you'll encounter.

Synchronous serial protocols all feature a controlling device that generates a regular pulse, or clock signal, on one pin while exchanging data on every clock pulse (see Chapter 2). The advantage of a synchronous serial protocol is that it's a bus: you can have several devices sharing the same physical connections to one master controller. Each protocol implements the bus in a different way.

SPI connections have three or four connections between the controlling device (or master device) and the peripheral device (or slave), as follows:

Clock: The pin that the master pulses regularly.
Master Out, Slave In (MOSI): The master device sends a bit of data to the slave on this line every clock pulse.
Master In, Slave Out (MISO): The slave device sends a bit of data to the master on this line every clock pulse.
Slave Select (SS) or Chip Select (CS): Because several slave devices can share the same bus, each has a unique connection to the master. The master sets this pin low to address this particular slave device. If the master's not talking to a given slave, it will set the slave's select pin high.

If the slave doesn't need to send any data to the master, there will be no MISO pin.

The Arduino SPI library uses pin 11 for MOSI, pin 12 for MISO, and pin 13 for Clock. Pin 10 is the default Chip Select pin, but you can use others, as you'll see. For example, the Arduino Ethernet and Ethernet shield have two slave devices on their SPI bus: the WizNet chip and the SD card. They are both connected to pins 11, 12, and 13 for MISO, MOSI, and Clock. The WizNet module uses pin 10 for its Chip Select, while the SD card uses pin 4 for its Chip Select.

Project 6

Hello Internet!

To use any network module, you first need to connect it to the network. That's the goal here. In this project, you'll make a very simple web server on your Arduino that serves a web page whose background color changes with the color of the light where the Arduino is located.

MATERIALS

» **1 Arduino Ethernet or**
» **1 Arduino Ethernet shield and 1 Arduino microcontroller module**
» **1 Ethernet connection to the Internet**
» **3 10-kilohm resistors**
» **3 photocells (light-dependent resistors)**
» **1 solderless breadboard**
» **3 lighting filters**

⤒ **Figure 4-3**
The connections between the Ethernet shield and the Arduino controller when they're stacked together.

Making the Connections

If you're using the Arduino Ethernet board, just plug it into a USB-to-Serial adapter and it will show up in the list of serial ports like a regular Arduino. The USB-to-Serial adapter will supply it with power like a normal USB cable. Programming it is the same as with any other Arduino, but in the Tools→Board menu, choose Arduino Uno or Arduino Ethernet.

The Ethernet shield, like many shields for the Arduino, is very easy to connect to your controller. Just plug it into the board. Both the Ethernet module and the shield use pins 10, 11, 12, and 13 for communication to the Ethernet controller, and pins 4, 11, 12, and 13 for communication to the SD card, so you can't use those pins for other inputs or outputs. Connect the Ethernet module to your router using an Ethernet cable. Figure 4-3 shows the Arduino Ethernet shield's connections to the microcontroller.

You can use the Arduino Ethernet or Ethernet ahield with a standard Arduino interchangeably, so from here on out, I'll just use "Ethernet module" to refer to either.

To read the color of the ambient light, use three photocells and cover each one with a different color of lighting filter: red, green, and blue. You can get these at many lighting-supply stores, photo supply-stores, or art stores, or you can use any translucent colored plastic you have around the house. You don't have to be scientific here. Figure 4-4 shows the connection between the Arduino Ethernet module and the three photocells.

How the Ethernet Library Works

To begin, you're going to try a couple simple programs using the Ethernet library for Arduino. This library lets you control the Ethernet module using methods similar to those you use for printing to a serial port. There are two types of software objects you'll make: servers and clients. A server waits for connections from remote devices on the Internet and allows them to connect to the Ethernet module, just like regular servers. A client initiates a connection to remote devices, makes requests, and delivers the replies, just like a regular client. Both servers and clients can be read from and written to, using the read(), write(), print(), and println() commands that you've already seen with the Serial library. There's also

an available() command, as in the Serial library, to see whether there's any new data available from the server or client in question. The client object also has a connected() command that tells you whether it's connected to a remote server. This will be useful later, when you're trying to connect to a remote server to get data. Here, you'll get started with a simple server sketch.

Figure 4-4
The RGB server circuit. The connections are the same for either the Arduino Ethernet or the Arduino and Ethernet shield combo. Note the three color filters over the photocells.

Before you can write your program, you need to establish some basic information about how your Ethernet module will connect to the Internet. Just as you did in Chapter 3, you'll need the device's Media Access Control (MAC) address. That's the hardware address of your Ethernet controller. The Arduino Ethernet modules have a six-byte address on the back, written in hexadecimal notation, that you can use. If the sticker's missing for any reason, you can make up your own MAC address, or use the generic one you find in the examples below. You'll also need to know the router's address (aka the gateway address because your router is the gateway to the rest of the Internet), as well as the address that your device will use on the router's subnet.

Your device's IP address will be similar to your router's address, probably using the same three numbers for the start of the address, but a different number for the last. For example, if your router's local address is 192.168.1.1, you can use an address like 192.168.1.20 for your

Ethernet module—as long as no other device connected to the router is using the same address.

When a router assigns addresses to its connected devices, it masks part of the address space so that those devices can use only addresses in the same subnet as the router itself. For example, if the router is going to assign only addresses in the range 192.168.1.2 through 192.168.1.254, it masks out the top three numbers (octets). This is called the netmask, or subnet mask. In your PC's network settings, you'll see it written as a full network address, like so: 255.255.255.0. With the Ethernet module, you'll assign it similarly.

Once you know your MAC address, your router's address, your IP address, and your subnet mask, you're ready to go. X

Try It   To get started, you need to include the SPI library and the Ethernet library to control the module. You also need to initialize a variable to hold a server instance. The server will run on port 80, just as most web servers do.

You also need four variables for the MAC address, IP address, gateway address, and subnet mask. These last four will be arrays of bytes, one byte for each byte in the respective addresses.

```
/*
  Web  Server
  Context: Arduino

  */

#include <SPI.h>
#include <Ethernet.h>

Server server(80);

byte mac[] = { 0x00, 0xAA, 0xBB, 0xCC, 0xDE, 0x01 };
IPAddress gateway(192,168,1,1);
IPAddress subnet(255,255,255,0);
IPAddress ip(192,168,1,20);
```

▶▶ **Change these to match your own device and network.**

▶▶ In the setup() method, you'll start the Ethernet module and the server. Open the serial connection as well, for debugging purposes.

```
void setup()
{
  // start the Ethernet connection and the server:
  Ethernet.begin(mac, ip, gateway, subnet);
  server.begin();
  Serial.begin(9600);
}
```

▶▶ In the main loop, you'll spend all your time listening for a connection from a remote client. When you get a connection, you'll wait for the client to make an HTTP request, like you saw in Chapter 3. This loop won't reply to the client, but it will show you what the client requests.

```
void loop()
{
  // listen for incoming clients
  Client client = server.available();
  if (client) {
     while (client.connected()) {
       if (client.available()) {
         char thisChar = client.read();
         Serial.write(thisChar);
       }
     }
     // close the connection:
     client.stop();
  }
}
```

❝ Run this sketch with the Ethernet module attached to your router and the Serial Monitor open. Then open a browser window and go to the Arduino's address. Using the example as shown, you'd go to http://192.168.1.20. You won't see anything in the browser, but you will see the HTTP request come through in the Serial Monitor. Now you're seeing what the server saw when you made HTTP requests in Chapter 3. A typical request will look like this:

```
GET / HTTP/1.1
Host: 192.168.1.1
Connection: keep-alive
Accept: application/xml,application/xhtml+xml,text/
html;q=0.9,text/plain;q=0.8,image/png,*/*;q=0.5
User-Agent: Mozilla/5.0 (Macintosh; U; Intel Mac OS X
10_6_5; en-US) AppleWebKit/534.10 (KHTML, like Gecko)
Chrome/8.0.552.215 Safari/534.10
Accept-Encoding: gzip,deflate,sdch
Accept-Language: en-US,en;q=0.8
Accept-Charset: ISO-8859-1,utf-8;q=0.7,*;q=0.3
```

You can ignore most of the HTTP parameters, but two pieces are useful: the first line, where you see what the client is requesting; and the end, where it sends a blank line to finish the request. In this case, the first line shows that the client is asking for the main index page at the root of the server, signified by the / in GET / . You're only going to have one result to return, but in the future, you will write a more complex server that looks at this part of the request and responds with different results depending on what's requested.

For now, you can keep it simple and just look for the end of the request, which will be a linefeed (\n or ASCII 10), followed by a carriage return (\r or ASCII 13), followed by another linefeed. Figure 4-5 shows what happens in the code that follows.

X

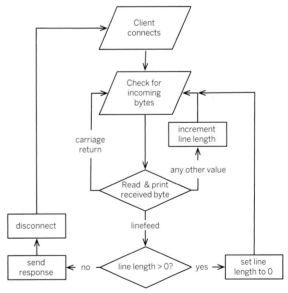

⬆ **Figure 4-5**
Logic flow for a simple server.

» Change your main loop as follows, adding the lines shown in blue after Serial.write(thisChar).

```
void loop()
{
  // listen for incoming clients
  Client client = server.available();
  if (client) {
    Serial.println("Got a client");
    String requestLine = "";

    while (client.connected()) {
      if (client.available()) {
        char thisChar = client.read();
        // if you get a linefeed and the request line is blank,
        // then the request is over:
        if (thisChar == '\n' && lineLength < 1) {
          // send a standard http response header
          makeResponse(client);
          break;
        }
        //if you get a newline or carriage return,
        // you're at the end of a line:
        if (thisChar == '\n' || thisChar == '\r') {
          lineLength = 0;
        }
        else {
          // for any other character, increment the line length:
          lineLength++;
        }
      }
    }
    // give the web browser time to receive the data
    delay(1);
    // close the connection:
    client.stop();
  }
}
```

» Before you can run this, you'll need to add a method , makeResponse(), at the end of your sketch to make a String to send the client. Here's a start.

```
void makeResponse(Client thisClient) {
  thisClient.print("HTTP/1.1 200 OK\n");
  thisClient.print("Content-Type: text/html\n\n");
  thisClient.print("Hello from Arduino</head><body>\n");
  thisClient.println("</body></html>\n");
}
```

"When you enter the Arduino's address in your browser now, you'll get a web page. There's not much there, but it's legitimate enough that your browser doesn't know the difference between your Arduino and any other web server. You can add anything you want in the HTML in the makeResponse() method—even links to images and content on other servers. Think of the Arduino as a portal to any other content you want the user to see, whether it's physical data from sensors or other web-based data. The complexity is really up to you. Once you start thinking creatively with the capabilities of the print() and println() statements, you get a wide range of ways to dynamically generate a web interface to your Arduino through the Ethernet shield.
X

How about printing the states of the analog inputs? Add the following to makeResponse() (new lines are shown in blue).

```
void makeResponse(Client thisClient) {
  thisClient.print("HTTP/1.1 200 OK\n");
  thisClient.print("Content-Type: text/html\n\n");
  thisClient.print("<html><head>");
  thisClient.print("<title>Hello from Arduino</title></head><body>\n");

  // output the value of each analog input pin
  for (int analogChannel = 0; analogChannel < 6; analogChannel++) {
    thisClient.print("analog input ");
    thisClient.print(analogChannel);
    thisClient.print(" is ");
    thisClient.print(analogRead(analogChannel));
    thisClient.print("<br />\n");
  }
  thisClient.println("</body></html>\n");
}
```

Reload the page, and you've got the states of the analog inputs. But how about updating them continually? You could use the methods you used for the Cat Cam in Chapter 3. Change the line in makeResponse() that prints the HTML head, like the code shown at right.

```
thisClient.print("Content-Type: text/html\n\n");
thisClient.print(
  "<html><head><meta http-equiv=\"refresh\" content=\"3\">");
```

You can do all sorts of things in the response. Now it's time to take advantage of those three photocells you attached to the analog inputs. This version of the makeResponse() method prints out a page that changes its background color with the values from the three photocells.

Now that you've got a light color server, look for colorful places to put it.

```
thisClient.print("Content-Type: text/html\n\n");
thisClient.print(
  "<html><head><meta http-equiv=\"refresh\" content=\"3\">");
thisClient.print("<title>Hello from Arduino</title></head>");
// set up the body background color tag:
thisClient.print("<body bgcolor=#");
// read the three analog sensors:
int red = analogRead(A0)/4;
int green = analogRead(A1)/4;
int blue = analogRead(A2)/4;
// print them as one hexadecimal string:
thisClient.print(red, HEX);
thisClient.print(green, HEX);
thisClient.print(blue, HEX);
// close the tag:
thisClient.print(">");
// now print the color in the body of the HTML page:
thisClient.print("The color of the light on the Arduino is #");
thisClient.print(red, HEX);
thisClient.print(green, HEX);
thisClient.println(blue, HEX);
// close the page:
thisClient.println("</body></html>\n");
}
```

Making a Private IP Device Visible to the Internet

Up until now, the Internet-related projects in this book either worked only on a local subnet, or have only sent data outbound and waited for a reply. This is the first project in which your device needs to be visible to the Internet at large. You can view it while you're on the same local network, but if it's connected to your home router and has a private IP address, it won't be visible to anyone outside your home. To get around this, you need to arrange for one of your router's ports to forward incoming messages and connection requests to your Ethernet shield.

To do this, open your router's administrator interface and look for controls for "port forwarding" or "port mapping." The interface will vary depending on the make and model of your router, but the settings generally go by one of these names. It's easiest if the forwarded port on the router is the same as the open port on the Ethernet module, so configure it so that port 80 on your router connects to port 80 on the Ethernet shield (if your router allows it). Once you've done this, any incoming requests to connect to your router's public IP address on that port will be forwarded to the Ethernet module's private IP address on the port that

you set. Note that the router reserves some ports for special purposes. For example, you may not be able to port forward port 80, because the router uses it for its own interface. That's why you might need to use a high number, like 8080.

Web browsers default to making their requests on port 80, but you can make a request on any port by adding the port number at the end of the server, address like so:

`http://www.myserver.com:8080/`

The new public address of your Ethernet module will follow this pattern, too. For example, if your home router's public address is 203.48.192.56, you'd access your new Arduino server at http://203.48.192.56:8080.

Figures 4-6 and 4-7 show the settings on an Apple AirPort Express router and a Linksys wireless router. On the Linksys router, you can find port forwarding under the Advanced tab.

Figure 4-6
Port mapping tab on an Apple AirPort Express router. Port mapping can be found under the Advanced tab.

Figure 4-7
Port forwarding on a Linksys wireless router.

🔊 An Embedded Network Client Application

Now that you've made your first server, it's time to make a client. This project is an embedded web scraper. It takes data from an existing website and uses it to affect a physical output. It's conceptually similar to devices made by Ambient Devices, Nabaztag, and others—but it's all yours.

 Project 7

Networked Air-Quality Meter

In this project, you'll make a networked air-quality meter. You'll need an analog panel meter, like the kind you find in speedometers and audio VU meters. I got mine at a yard sale, but you can often find them in electronics surplus stores or junk shops. The model recommended in the parts list is less picturesque than mine, but it will do for a placeholder until you find one you love.

Figure 4-8 shows how it works: the microcontroller makes a network connection to a PHP script through the Ethernet shield. The PHP script connects to another web page, reads a number from that page, and sends the number back to the microcontroller. The microcontroller uses that number to set the level of the meter. The web page in question is AIRNow, www.airnow.gov, the U.S. Environmental Protection Agency's site for reporting air quality. It reports hourly air quality status for many U.S. cities, listed by ZIP code. When you're done, you can set a meter from your home or office to see the current air quality in your city (assuming you live in the U.S.).

MATERIALS

» **1 Arduino Ethernet or**
» **1 Arduino Ethernet shield and 1 Arduino microcontroller module**
» **1 Ethernet connection to the Internet**
» **1 solderless breadboard**
» **1 voltmeter**
» **4 LEDs**
» **4 220-ohm resistors**

Control the Meter Using the Microcontroller

First, you need to generate a changing voltage from the microcontroller to control the meter. Microcontrollers can't output analog voltages, but they can generate a series of very rapid on-and-off pulses that can be filtered to give an average voltage. The higher the ratio of on-time to off-time in each pulse, the higher the average voltage. This technique is called pulse-width modulation (PWM). In order for a PWM signal to appear as an analog voltage, the circuit receiving the pulses has to react much more slowly than the rate of the pulses. For example, if you pulse-width modulate an LED, it will seem to be dimming because your eye can't detect the on-off transitions when they come faster than about 30 times per second. Analog voltmeters are very slow to react to changing voltages, so PWM works well as a way to control these meters. By connecting the positive terminal of the meter to an output pin of the microcontroller, and the negative pin to ground, and pulse-width modulating the output pin, you can easily control the position of the meter. Figure 4-9 shows the whole circuit for the project.

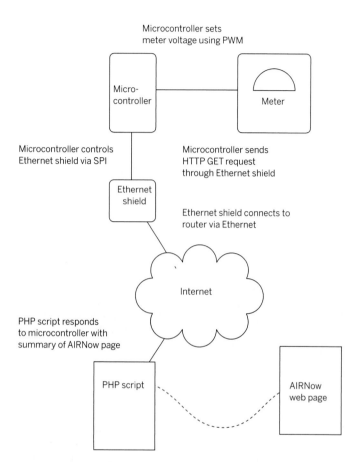

Microcontroller sets
meter voltage using PWM

Microcontroller controls
Ethernet shield via SPI

Microcontroller sends
HTTP GET request
through Ethernet shield

Ethernet shield connects to
router via Ethernet

PHP script responds
to microcontroller with
summary of AIRNow page

Figure 4-8
The networked air-quality meter.

Figure 4-9

The circuit for a networked meter. The Ethernet controller shown in the schematic is on the shield or the Arduino Ethernet board.

Test It The program to the right tests whether you can control the meter.

You will need to adjust the range of pwmValue depending on your meter's sensitivity. The meters used to design this project had different ranges. The meter in the parts list responds to a 0- to 5-volt range, so the preceding program moves it from its bottom to its top. The antique meter, on the other hand, responds to 0 to 3 volts, so it was necessary to limit the range of pwmValue to 0–165. When it was at 165, the meter reached its maximum. Note your meter's minimum and maximum values. You'll use them later to scale the air-quality reading to the meter's range.

```
/*
    Voltmeter Tester
    Uses analogWrite() to control a voltmeter.
    Context: Arduino
*/
const int meterPin = 9;

int pwmValue = 0;   // the value used to set the meter

void setup() {
  Serial.begin(9600);
}

void loop() {
  // move the meter from lowest to highest values:
  for (pwmValue = 0; pwmValue < 255; pwmValue ++) {
    analogWrite(meterPin, pwmValue);
    Serial.println(pwmValue);
    delay(10);
  }
  delay(1000);
  // reset the meter to zero and pause:
  analogWrite(meterPin, 0);
  delay(1000);
}
```

" Write a PHP Script to Read the Web Page

Next, you need to get the data from AIRNow's site in a form the microcontroller can read. The microcontroller can read in short strings serially, and converting those ASCII strings to a binary number is fairly simple. Using a microcontroller to parse through all the text of a web page is possible, but a bit complicated. However, it's the kind of task for which PHP was made. The program that follows reads the AIRNow page, extracts the current air-quality index (AQI) reading, and makes a simpler summary page that's easy to read with the microcontroller. The Ethernet controller is the microcontroller's gateway to the Internet, allowing it to open a TCP connection to your web host, where you will install this PHP script.

NOTE: You could also run this script on one of the computers on your local network. As long as the microcontroller is connected to the same network, you'll be able to connect to it and request the PHP page. For information on installing PHP or finding a web-hosting provider that supports PHP, see www.php.net/manual/en/tutorial.php#tutorial.requirements.

Figure 4-10 shows AIRNow's page for New York City (http://airnow.gov/?action=airnow.local_city&zipcode=10003&submit=Go). AIRNow's page is formatted well for extracting the data. The AQI number is clearly shown in text, and if you remove all the HTML tags, it appears on a line by itself, always following the line Current Conditions.

NOTE: One of the most difficult things about maintaining applications like this, which scrape data from an existing website, is the probability that the designers of the website could change the format of their page. If that happens, your application could stop working, and you'll need to rewrite your code. In fact, it happened between the first and second editions of this book. This is a case where it's useful to have the PHP script do the scraping of the remote site. It's more convenient to rewrite the PHP than it is to reprogram the microcontroller once it's in place.
X

Figure 4-10
AIRNow's page is nicely laid out for scraping. The PHP program used in this project ignores the ozone level.

Fetch It   This PHP script opens the AIRNow web page and prints it line by line. The fgetss() command reads a line of text and removes any HTML tags.

When you save this file on your web server and open it in a browser, you should get the text of the AIRNow page without any HTML markup or images. It's not very readable in the browser window, but if you view the source code (use the View Source option in your web browser), it looks a bit better. Scroll down and you'll find some lines like this:

```
Current Conditions
Air Quality Index (AQI)
observed at 17:00 EST
45
```

These are the only lines you care about.

```php
<?php
/*
    AIRNow Web Page Scraper
    Context: PHP
*/
    // Define variables:
    // url of the page with the air quality index data for New York City:
    $url =
        'http://airnow.gov/index.cfm?action=airnow.showlocal&cityid=164';

    // open the file at the URL for reading:
    $filePath = fopen ($url, "r");

    // as long as you haven't reached the end of the file:
    while (!feof($filePath))
    {
        // read one line at a time, and strip all HTML and
        // PHP tags from the line:
        $line = fgetss($filePath, 4096);
        echo $line;
    }
    // close the file at the URL, you're done:
    fclose($filePath);
?>
```

Scrape It   To extract the data you need from those lines, you'll need a couple more variables. Add this code before the fopen() command.

```
// whether you should check for a value
// on the line you're reading:
$checkForValue = false;

// value of the Air Quality reading:
$airQuality = -1;
```

▸▸ Replace the command echo $line; in the program with the block of code at right.

This block uses the preg_match() command to look for a string of text matching a pattern you give it. In this case, it looks for the pattern Current Conditions. When you see that line, you know the next line is the number you want. When the PHP script finds that line, it sets the variable $checkForValue to true.

```
// if the current line contains the substring "Current Conditions"
// then the next line with an integer is the air quality:
if (preg_match('/Current Conditions/', $line)) {
    $checkForValue = true;
}
```

▸▸ Now, add the following block of code after the one you just added. This code checks to see whether $check-ForValue is true, and whether the line contains an integer and nothing else. If so, the program reads the next line of text and converts it from a string to an integer value. It will only get a valid integer when it reaches the line with the AQI value.

```
if ($checkForValue == true && (int)$line > 0){
    $airQuality = (int)$line;
    $checkForValue = false;
}
```

▸▸ Finally, add the following lines at the end of the script, after the while loop. This prints out the air-quality reading and closes the connection to the remote site.

```
echo "Air Quality:". $airQuality;
// close the file at the URL, you're done:
fclose($filePath);
```

The result in your web browser should look like this:

```
Air Quality: 43
```

Now you've got a short string of text that your microcontroller can read. Even if the script got no result, the value -1 will tell you that there was no connection.

🎧 Read the PHP Script Using the Microcontroller

Next, it's time to connect to the PHP script through the Net using the Ethernet module. This time, you'll use the shield as a client, not a server. Before you start programming, plan the sequence of messages. Using the Ethernet module as a network client is very similar to using Processing as a network client. In both cases, you have to know the correct sequence of messages to send and how the responses will be formatted. You also have to write a program to manage the exchange of messages. Whether you're writing that program in Processing, in Arduino, or in another language on another microcontroller, the steps are still the same:

1. Open a connection to the web server.
2. Send an HTTP GET request.
3. Wait for a response.
4. Process the response.
5. Wait an appropriate interval and do it all again.

Figure 4-11

A flowchart of the Arduino program for making and processing an HTTP GET request.

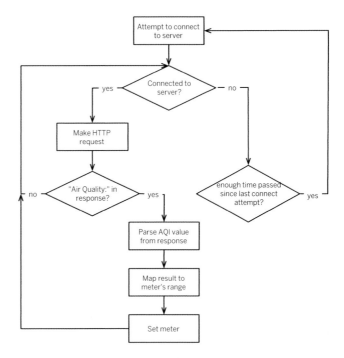

Figure 4-11 is a flowchart of what happens in the microcontroller program. The major decisions (if statements in your code) are marked by diamonds; the methods are marked by rectangles. Laying out the whole program in a flowchart like this will help you keep track of what's going on at any given point. It also helps you to see what methods depend on a particular condition being true or not.

The circuit for this project also uses LEDs to keep track of the state of the program. LEDs attached to I/O pins will indicate the state. There's an LED to indicate that it's connected, another to indicate that it's disconnected, a third to indicate if it got a valid reading, and a fourth to indicate that the microcontroller is resetting.

This program will check the PHP script every two minutes. If there's a new value for the air quality, it'll read it and set the meter. If it can't get a connection, it will try again two minutes later. Because it's a client and not a server, there's no web interface to the project, only the meter.

TextFinder Library

For this sketch, you're going to need Michael Margolis' TextFinder library for Arduino. Download it from www. arduino.cc/playground/Code/TextFinder, unzip it, and save the **TextFinder** folder to the **libraries** folder of your Arduino sketches directory (the default location is **Documents/ Arduino/libraries/** on OS X, **My Documents\Arduino\libraries** on Windows 7, and **~/Documents/Arduino/libraries/** on Ubuntu Linux. If the **libraries** directory doesn't exist, create it and put TextFinder inside. Restart Arduino, and the TextFinder library should show up in the Sketch→Import Library menu. TextFinder lets you find a substring of text from the incoming stream of bytes. It's useful for both Ethernet and serial applications, as you'll see.

TextFinder is under consideration for inclusion in version 1.0 of Arduino, in which case you would not need to install it. So check the Reference section of www.arduino.cc for the latest updates.

Connect It
The program starts out by including the SPI and Ethernet libraries, just as in the previous project. Then define the output pins, the minimum and maximum values for the meter that you determined earlier, and the time between HTTP requests using constant integers.

```
/*
  AirNow Web Scraper
  Context: Arduino
*/
#include <SPI.h>
#include <Ethernet.h>
#include <TextFinder.h>

const int connectedLED = 2;           // indicates a TCP connection
const int successLED = 3;             // indicates a successful read
const int resetLED = 4;               // indicates reset of Arduino
const int disconnectedLED = 5;        // indicates connection to server
const int meterPin = 9;               // controls VU meter
const int meterMin = 0;               // minimum level for the meter
const int meterMax = 200;             // maximum level for the meter
const int AQIMax = 200;               // maximum level for air quality
const int requestInterval = 10000;    // delay between updates to the server
```

Finding a Host's IP Address

This project uses numeric IP addresses rather than names. If you need to find a host's IP address, use the ping command mentioned in Chapter 3. For example, if you open a command prompt and type ping -c 1 www.oreillynet.com, (use -n instead of -c on Windows), you will get the following response, listing the IP address you need:

```
PING www.oreillynet.com (208.201.239.37): 56 data bytes
64 bytes from 208.201.239.37: icmp_seq=0 ttl=45 time=97.832 ms
```

If you can't use ping (some service providers block it, since it can be used for nefarious purposes), you can also use nslookup. For example, nslookup google.com will return the following:

```
Server:  8.8.8.8
Address: 8.8.8.8#53
```

▶▶ nslookup returns the Domain Name Server it used to do the lookup as well.

```
Non-authoritative answer:
Name:       google.com
Address:    173.194.33.104
```

Any one of the addresses listed will point to it's associated name, so you can use any of them.

» Next, initialize a few array variables with the network configuration for the module.

```
byte mac[] = { 0x00, 0xAA, 0xBB, 0xCC, 0xDE, 0x01 };
IPAddress ip(192,168,1,20);
IPAddress server(208,201,239,101 );
```

» **Change these to match your own device and server.**

» The last global variables you need to add are for the Client class, and a few variables relating to the transaction with the server.

```
// Initialize the Ethernet client library
Client client;

boolean requested;          // whether you've made a request
long lastAttemptTime = 0;    // last time you connected to the server
int airQuality = 0;          // AQI value
boolean meterIsSet = false;  // whether the meter is set
```

» setup() starts the serial and Ethernet connections, sets all the LED pins to be outputs, blinks the reset LED, and makes an initial attempt to connect to the server.

```
void setup() {
  // start the Ethernet connection:
  Ethernet.begin(mac, ip);
  // start the serial library:
  Serial.begin(9600);
  // set all status LED pins:
  pinMode(connectedLED, OUTPUT);
  pinMode(successLED, OUTPUT);
  pinMode(resetLED, OUTPUT);
  pinMode(disconnectedLED, OUTPUT);
  pinMode(meterPin, OUTPUT);

  // give the Ethernet shield a second to initialize:
  delay(1000);
  // blink the reset LED:
  blink(resetLED, 3);
  // attempt to connect:
  connectToServer();
}
```

» The blink() method called in the setup blinks the reset LED so you know the microcontroller's main loop is about to begin.

```
void blink(int thisPin, int howManyTimes) {
  //      Blink the reset LED:
  for (int blinks=0; blinks< howManyTimes; blinks++) {
    digitalWrite(thisPin, HIGH);
    delay(200);
    digitalWrite(thisPin, LOW);
    delay(200);
  }
}
```

▸ The loop() contains all the logic laid out in Figure 4-11. If the client is connected to the server, it makes an HTTP GET request. If it's made a request, it uses TextFinder to search the response for the air-quality string and then sets the meter. If the client isn't connected to the server, it waits another two minutes until the request interval's passed, and tries to connect again.

```
void loop()
{
  // if you're connected, save any incoming bytes
  // to the input string:
  if (client.connected()) {
    if (!requested) {
      requested = makeRequest();
    }
    else {
      // make an instance of TextFinder to search the response:
      TextFinder response(client);
      // see if the response from the server contains the AQI value:
      if(response.find("Air Quality:"))  {
        // convert the remaining part into an integer:
        airQuality = response.getValue();
        // set the meter:
        meterIsSet = setMeter(airQuality);
      }
    }
  }
  else if (millis() - lastAttemptTime > requestInterval) {
    // if you're not connected, and two minutes have passed since
    // your last connection, then attempt to connect again:
    client.stop();
    connectToServer();
  }

  // set the status LEDs:
  setLeds();
}
```

▸ Both setup() and loop() attempt to connect to the server using the connectToServer() method. If it gets a connection, it resets the requested variable so the main loop knows it can make a request.

```
void connectToServer() {
  // clear the state of the meter:
  meterIsSet = false;

  // attempt to connect, and wait a millisecond:
  Serial.println("connecting...");
  if (client.connect(server, 80)) {
    requested = false;
  }
  // note the time of this connect attempt:
  lastAttemptTime = millis();
}
```

▶▶ Once the client's connected, it sends an HTTP GET request. Here's the makeRequest() method. It returns a true value to set the requesting variable in the main loop, so the client doesn't request twice while it's connected.

The server replies to makeRequest() like so:

```
HTTP/1.1 200 OK
Date: Fri, 14 Nov 2010 21:31:37 GMT
Server: Apache/2.0.52 (Red Hat)
Content-Length: 10
Connection: close
Content-Type: text/html; charset=UTF-8

 Air Quality: 65
```

```
boolean makeRequest() {
  // make HTTP GET request and fill in the path to
  // the PHP script on your server:
  client.println("GET /~myaccount/scraper.php HTTP/1.1\n");
  // fill in your server's name:
  client.print("HOST:example.com\n\n");
  // update the state of the program:
  client.println();
  return true;
}
```

▶▶ Change these to match your own server name and path.

▶▶ Once the client's found the air-quality string and converted the bytes that follow into an integer, it calls setMeter() to set the meter with the result it obtained. You might want to adjust the AQIMax value to reflect the typical maximum for your geographic area.

```
boolean setMeter(int thisLevel) {
  Serial.println("setting meter...");
  boolean result = false;
  // map the result to a range the meter can use:
  int meterSetting = map(thisLevel, 0, AQIMax, meterMin, meterMax);
  // set the meter:
  analogWrite(meterPin, meterSetting);
  if (meterSetting > 0) {
    result = true;
  }
  return result;
}
```

▶▶ The last thing you need to do in the main loop is set the indicator LEDs so that you know where you are in the program. You can use the client.connected() status and the meterIsSet variable to set each of the LEDs.

That's the whole program. Once you've got this program working on the microcontroller, the controller will make the HTTP GET request once every ten minutes and set the meter accordingly.

```
void setLeds() {
  // connected LED and disconnected LED can just use
  // the client's connected() status:
  digitalWrite(connectedLED, client.connected());
  digitalWrite(disconnectedLED, !client.connected());
  // success LED depends on reading being successful:
  digitalWrite(successLED, meterIsSet);
}
```

The Finished Project

Figure 4-12
The completed networked air-quality meter.

DNS and DHCP

In Chapter 3 you learned that most Ethernet-connected devices obtain an IP address from their router using Dynamic Host Control Protocol (DHCP), and that IP-connected devices learn the name of other servers and clients using the Domain Name System (DNS). You can use DHCP and DNS with the Arduino Ethernet library as well. It's very simple—you just put the MAC address in the Ethernet.begin() method, like so:

```
byte mac[] = { 0xDE, 0xAD, 0xBE, 0xEF, 0xFE, 0xED};
Ethernet.begin(mac);
```

If the server grants an IP address, it returns true. If not, it returns false. The returned address is stored in Ethernet.localIP(). You may want a few other variables to use DHCP as well, including Ethernet.subnetMask(), Ethernet.gatewayIP(), and Ethernet. dnsServerIP().

Using DNS is just as simple. Instead of passing a numeric server to the client.connect() command, give it a text string, like so:

```
client.connect("www.example.com", 80);
```

The disadvantage of using DHCP and DNS is that they take a lot of RAM, so you may prefer to use the relevant numerical addresses (once you know them).

DNS and DHCP (cont'd)

The following example shows how to request an address using DHCP; it thenreports back the address obtained:

```
/* DHCP
 Context: Arduino
 */
#include <SPI.h>
#include <Ethernet.h>

byte mac[] = {
  0x00, 0xAA, 0xBB, 0xCC, 0xDE, 0x01};
IPAddress ip(192,168,1,20);              // an address to use if DHCP fails

void setup() {
  // start the serial library:
  Serial.begin(9600);
  // start the Ethernet connection:
  Serial.println("Asking for an IP address using DHCP...");
  if (!Ethernet.begin(mac)) {
    // if DHCP fails, set your own address:
    Ethernet.begin(mac, ip);
  }
  // print the bytes of the IP address, separated by dots:
  Serial.print("I got an IP address. It's ");
  Serial.println(Ethernet.localIP());
}

void loop() {
}
```

The begin() technique is useful in any Ethernet sketch because it uses DHCP if available, and sets an IP address manually if not. If you know you're going to set the address manually and want to save program memory, just comment out the if() line and the corresponding bracket, and leave the command inside it, like so:

```
//if (!Ethernet.begin(mac)) {
    // if DHCP fails, set your own address:
    Ethernet.begin(mac, ip);
// }
```

" Programming and Troubleshooting Tools for Embedded Modules

You may have hit a number of problems when making the connections in the last section. Probably the most challenging thing about troubleshooting them was that neither the Ethernet shield nor the microcontroller gave any indication that a problem occurred. This is the norm when you're working with embedded modules that you build yourself. This section covers a few things you should always check, and a few tools that will help you solve problems. These principles apply whether you're using the Ethernet modules or some other network or communications module. You'll use these methods over and over again in the rest of the book and beyond.

The Three Most Common Mistakes

Check Power and Ground

Always check whether you have made the power and ground connections correctly. This is less of an issue when you've got a nice plug-in module like the Ethernet shield that can connect only one way. But even with plug-in modules, you can get a pin misaligned and not notice. If you're lucky, the module you're using will have indicator LEDs that light up when it's working properly. Whether it does or not, check the voltage between power and ground with a meter to make sure you've got it powered correctly.

Check the Connections

When you're wiring a module to a microcontroller by hand, it's fairly common to get the wires wrong the first time. Make sure you know what each pin does, and double-check that the pin that one transmits on connects to the pin that the other receives on, and vice versa. If it's a synchronous serial connection, make sure the clock is connected.

Check the Configuration

If you're certain about the hardware connections, check the device's configuration to make sure it's all correct. Did you get the IP address correct? Is the router address correct? Is the netmask?

Diagnostic Tools and Methods

Once you know the device is working, you have to program the sequence of messages that constitutes your application. Depending on the application's needs, this sequence can get complex, so it's useful to have a few simple programs around to make sure things work as desired.

It's a good idea to test your module first using sample code—if it's provided. Every good communications module maker gives you a starting example. Use it, and keep it handy. When things go wrong, return to it to make sure that basic communications still work.

Physical Debugging Methods

Writing code makes things happen physically. It's easy to forget that when you're working on an exchange of information like the examples shown here. So, it's helpful to put in physical actions that you can trigger; this way, you can see that your code is working. In the last project, you saw LEDs turn on when the client connected or disconnected, when it made a successful request, and when it reset. Triggering an LED is the most basic and reliable thing you can do from a microcontroller—even more basic than sending a serial debugging message—so use LEDs liberally to help make sure each part of your code is working. You can always remove them later.

Serial Debugging Methods

Besides their physical form factor, the Ethernet shield and Arduino Ethernet make a number of things easy for you. For example, the fact that they use synchronous serial communication to talk to the Ethernet controller means you can still use the serial port to get messages about what's going on—as you saw in the previous example. Following are a few tips for effective serial debugging of networking code using serial messages.

It's important to keep in mind that serial communication takes time. When you have serial statements in your

code, they slow it down. The microcontroller has to save each bit of information received, which takes time away from your program. Even though the time is miniscule for each bit, it can add up. After a few hundred bytes, you might start to notice it. So, make sure to take out your serial transmission statements when you're done with them.

Debug It   One way to manage your debugging is to have a variable that changes the behavior of your program, like this. When every debugging statement is preceded by the if (DEBUG) conditional, you can easily turn them all off by setting DEBUG to false.

```
const boolean DEBUG = true;

void setup() {
  Serial.begin(9600);
}

void loop() {
  if (DEBUG) Serial.println("this is a debugging statement");
}
```

Announce It   In the Air-Quality Index client project, you had a lot of different methods in your code. It's not easy to tell whether every method is being called, so during troubleshooting, make it a habit to "announce" serially when every method is being called. To do so, put a serial print statement at the beginning of the method, like the code shown on the right.

```
void connectToServer() {
  if (DEBUG) Serial.print("running connectToServer()...");
  // rest of the method goes here
}

void makeRequest() {
  if (DEBUG) Serial.print("running makeRequest()...");
  // rest of the method goes here
}

boolean setMeter(int thisLevel) {
  if (DEBUG) Serial.print("running setMeter()...");
  // rest of the method goes here
}
```

Check Conditionals   It's common in a communications application like these to have multiple conditions that affect a particular result. As you're working, you can easily make mistakes that affect these nested if statements. As you work, check that they're still coming true when you think they are by announcing it, as shown here.

```
if (client.connected()) {
  if (DEBUG) Serial.print("connected");
  if (!requested) {
    if (DEBUG) Serial.print("connected, not requested.");
    requested = makeRequest();
  }
  else {
    if (DEBUG) Serial.print("not connected");
  }
}
```

Separate It Programmers like efficiency, so they will often combine several commands into one line of code. Sometimes the problem is in the combination. For example, this line attempts to connect using client.connect(), and then it checks the result in a conditional statement. It gave me all kinds of trouble until I separated the connection attempt from the check of the connection.

```
if (client.connect()) {
  // if you get a connection, report back via serial:
  Serial.println("connected");
}
else {
  // if you didn't get a connection to the server:
  Serial.println("connection failed");
}
```

Here's the less efficient code that solved the problem. Checking the connection immediately after connecting was apparently too soon. The delay stabilized the whole program.

```
client.connect();   // connect
delay(1);           // wait a millisecond
if (client.connected()) {
  // if you get a connection, report back via serial:
  Serial.println("connected");
}
else {
  // if you didn't get a connection to the server:
Serial.println("connection failed");
}
```

Just Watch It Sometimes it helps to step back from your complicated program and just watch what you're receiving from the other end. One technique I returned to again and again while developing this program was to simply print out what the Ethernet module was receiving. Several times it revealed the problem to me. Sometimes it was because I had logic problems in my code, and other times it was because I'd neglected some character that the server was sending as part of the protocol. Familiarity can blind you to what you need to see. So, remind yourself of what you are actually receiving, as opposed to what you think you are receiving.

```
// if you're connected, save any incoming bytes
// to the input string:
if (client.connected()) {
  if (client.available()) {
    char inChar = client.read();
    Serial.write(inChar);
  }
}
```

❝ Write a Test Client Program

It's easiest to work through the steps of the program if you can step through the sequence of events. More complex development environments allow you to step through a program one line at a time. Arduino doesn't give you that ability, but it can link to other environments. The following program simply passes anything that comes in the serial port to the Ethernet port, and vice versa. It turns your Arduino into a serial-to-Ethernet gateway. Using this code, you can connect to a serial terminal or to Processing—or to any other development environment that can communicate serially—to test the Ethernet connection.

Test It   The handy thing about this program is that you can test the exchange of messages manually, or by writing a program in a desktop environment. Once you know you have the sequence right, you can translate it into code for the Arduino module.

```
/*
  Serial To Ethernet
  Context: Arduino
*/

#include <SPI.h>
#include <Ethernet.h>

byte mac[] = { 0x00, 0xAA, 0xBB, 0xCC, 0xDE, 0x01 };
IPAddress ip(192,168,1,20);
IPAddress server(208,201,239,101 );

// Initialize the Ethernet client library
// with the IP address and port of the server
// that you want to connect to (port 80 is default for HTTP):
Client client;

void setup() {
  // start the serial library:
  Serial.begin(9600);
  // start the Ethernet connection:
  if (!Ethernet.begin(mac)) {
    Serial.println("DHCP failed, configuring manually.");
    // configure manually with your own IP address:
    Ethernet.begin(mac, ip);
  }
  // give the Ethernet shield a second to initialize:
  delay(1000);
  Serial.println("Ready to go.");
}

void loop() {
  if (client.connected()) {
    //if you're connected, pass bytes from client to serial:
    if (client.available()) {
      char netChar = client.read();
      Serial.write(netChar);
    }
    //pass bytes from serial to client:
    if (Serial.available()) {
      char serialChar = Serial.read();
```

▶▶ **Change these to match your own device and server.**

»

```
Continued from previous page.
      client.write(serialChar);
    }
  }
  else {
    // in case you were connected, stop the client:
    client.stop();
    // if you're not connected, and you get a serial C,
    // attempt to connect:
    if (Serial.available()) {
      char serialChar = Serial.read();
      if (serialChar == 'C') {
        connectToServer();
      }
    }
  }
}

void connectToServer() {
  // attempt to connect, and wait a millisecond:
  Serial.println("connecting...");
  if (client.connect(server, 80)) {
    // if you get a connection, report back via serial:
    Serial.println("connected");

  }
  else {
    // if you didn't get a connection to the server:
    Serial.println("connection failed");
    client.stop();
  }
}
```

Talk To It Here's a simple Processing sketch that will communicate serially with the preceding Arduino sketch to make an HTTP request. When you type a key the first time, it will send C to initiate a connection. The second keystroke will send the HTTP request.

```
/*
 Serial-to-ethernet HTTP request tester
 Context: Processing

 */
// include the serial library
import processing.serial.*;

Serial myPort;        // Serial object
int step = 0;         // which step in the process you're on
char linefeed = 10;   // ASCII linefeed character
```

```
Continued from previous page.
void setup()
{
  // get the list of serial ports:
  println(Serial.list());
  // open the serial port appropriate to your computer:
  myPort = new Serial(this, Serial.list()[0], 9600);
  // configure the serial object to buffer text until it receives a
  // linefeed character:
  myPort.bufferUntil(linefeed);
}

void draw()
{
  //no action in the draw loop
}

void serialEvent(Serial myPort) {
  // print any string that comes in serially to the monitor pane
  print(myPort.readString());
}

void keyReleased() {
  // if any key is pressed, take the next step:
  switch (step) {
  case 0:
    // open a connection to the server in question:
    myPort.write("C");
    // add one to step so that the next keystroke causes the next step:
    step++;
    break;
  case 1:
    // send an HTTP GET request
    myPort.write("GET /~myaccount/index.html HTTP/1.1\n");
    myPort.write("HOST:myserver.com\n\n");
    step++;
    break;
  }
}
```

▸▸ **Change these to match your own server.**

> Starting with this sketch as a base, you could work out the whole logic of the HTTP exchange in Processing, then convert your sketch into an Arduino sketch.

This approach allows you to work out the logical flow of an application in an environment with which you might be more familiar. It removes the complications of the microcontroller environment, allowing you to concentrate on the sequence of messages and the actions that trigger them.

Don't get too caught up in the technical details of your program when working this way. You're still going to have to deal with the details of the microcontroller program eventually. However, it often helps to see the similarities and differences between two languages when you're working on a problem. It helps you concentrate on the logic that underlies them.

X

Write a Test Server Program

The previous program allowed you to connect to a remote server and test the exchange of messages. The remote server was beyond your control, however, so you can't say for sure that the server ever received your messages. If you never made a connection, you have no way of knowing whether the module can connect to any server. To test this, write your own server program to which it can connect.

Here is a short Processing program that you can run on your PC. It listens for incoming connections, and prints out any messages sent over those connections. It sends an HTTP response and a simple web page.

To use this, first make sure your Ethernet module and your PC are on the same network. Then run this program, and connect to it from a browser, using the URL http://localhost:80.

When you know that works, write a client program for the Arduino that connects to your PC's IP address, port 80. You'll be able to see both sides of the communication, and determine where the problem lies. Once you've seen messages coming through to this program in the right sequence, just change the connect string in your microcontroller code to the address of the web server you want to connect to, and everything should work fine. If it doesn't, the problem is most likely with your web server. Contact your service provider for details on how to access any of their server diagnostic tools, especially any error logs for your server.

X

If this doesn't work for you, change to port 8080, which is a common alternative port for many web servers. If you're running a web server on your PC, you might have to change the port number inthis program.

```
/*
  Test Server Program
  Context: Processing

  Creates a server that listens for clients and prints
  what they say.  It also sends the last client anything that's
  typed on the keyboard.
*/

// include the net library:
import processing.net.*;

int port = 80;        // the port the server listens on
Server myServer;        // the server object
int counter = 0;
void setup()
{
  myServer = new Server(this, port); // Start the server
}


void draw()
{
  // get the next client that sends a message:
  Client thisClient = myServer.available();
  // if the message is not null, display what it sent:

  if (thisClient != null) {
    // read bytes incoming from the client:
    while(thisClient.available() > 0) {
      print(char(thisClient.read()));
    }
    // send an HTTP response:
    thisClient.write("HTTP/1.1 200 OK\r\n");
    thisClient.write("Content-Type: text/html\r\n\r\n");
    thisClient.write("<html><head><title>Hello</title></head>");
    thisClient.write("<body>Hello, Client! " + counter);
    thisClient.write("</body></html>\r\n\r\n");
    // disconnect:
    thisClient.stop();
    counter++;
  }
}
```

❝❝ Conclusion

The activities in this chapter show a model for networked objects that's very flexible and useful. The object is basically a browser or a server, requesting information from the Web and extracting the information it needs, or delivering information to a client. You can use these models in many different projects.

The advantage of these models is that they don't require a lot of work to repurpose existing web applications. At most, you need to write a variation of the PHP web scraper from earlier in this chapter to summarize the relevant information from an existing website. This flexibility makes it easier for microcontroller enthusiasts who aren't experienced in web development to collaborate with web programmers, and vice versa. It also makes it easy to reuse others' work if you can't find a willing collaborator.

The model has its limits, though, and in Chapter 5, you'll see some ways to get around those limits with a different model. Even if you're not using this model, don't forget the troubleshooting tools mentioned here. Making simple mock-ups of the programs on either end of a transaction can make your life much easier. This is because they let you see what should happen, and then modify what actually is happening to match that.

X

5

Communicating in (Near) Real Time

So far, most of the networked communications you've seen worked through a web browser. Your object made a request to a remote server, the server ran a program, and then it sent a response. This transaction worked by making a connection to the web server, exchanging some information, and then breaking the connection. In this chapter, you'll learn more about that connection, and you'll write a server program that allows you to maintain the connection in order to facilitate a faster and more consistent exchange between the server and client.

◀◀ **Musicbox by Jin-Yo Mok (2004)**

The music box is connected to a composition program over the Internet using a serial-to-Ethernet module. The composition program changes the lights on the music box and the sounds it will play. Real-time communication between the two gives the player feedback. *Photo courtesy of Jin-Yo Mok.*

🔊 Supplies for Chapter 5

DISTRIBUTOR KEY

- **A** Arduino Store (http://store.arduino.cc/ww)
- **AF** Adafruit (http://adafruit.com)
- **D** Digi-Key (www.digikey.com)
- **F** Farnell (www.farnell.com)
- **J** Jameco (http://jameco.com)
- **MS** Maker SHED (www.makershed.com)
- **P** Pololu (www.pololu.com)
- **RS** RS (www.rs-online.com)
- **SF** SparkFun (www.sparkfun.com)
- **SS** Seeed Studio (www.seeedstudio.com)

PROJECT 8: Networked Pong

NOTE: You'll see two devices you can build in this chapter. If you plan to build both, double the quantities on all parts except the joystick, the accelerometer, and the triple-wall cardboard.

» **1 Arduino Ethernet board A** A000050
Alternatively, an Uno-compatible board (see Chapter 2) with an Ethernet shield will work.
SF DEV-09026, **J** 2124242, **A** A000056, **AF** 201, **F** 1848680

» **1 Ethernet connection to the Internet** Your home router most likely has Ethernet jacks in the back. If you've hooked up your computer to the Internet using Ethernet, you know where the ports are.

» **1 100-ohm resistor D** 100QBK-ND, **J** 690620, **F** 9337660, **RS** 707-8625
» **3 220-ohm resistors D** 220QBK-ND, **J** 690700, **F** 9337792, **RS** 707-8842
» **1 2-axis joystick (for joystick client)** **J** 2082855, **SF** COM-09032, **AF** 245, **F** 1428461
» **1accelerometer (for tilt board client)** The circuit shown uses an ADXL330 accelerometer, but most any analog accelerometer should do the job.
J 28017, **SF** SEN-00692, **AF** 163, **RS** 726-3738, **P** 1247, **MS** MKPX7
» **1 perforated printed circuit board D** V2018-ND, **J** 616673, **SS** STR125C2B, **F** 4903213, **RS** 159-5420
» **4 LEDs** It's best to use at least two colors with established semantics: a big red one, a big green one, and two others of whatever color suits your fancy.
D 160-1144-ND or 160-1665-ND, **J** 34761 or 94511, **F** 1015878, **RS** 247-1662 or 826-830, **SF** COM-09592 or COM-09590
» **1 push button** Use one that's robust and can stand a good stomping.
» **1 project enclosure** Get creative with materials you have laying around the house.
» **1 sheet triple-wall cardboard (for tilt board client)**
» **1 tab of Velcro** Get any Velcro from your closest fabric or hardware store.

Figure 5-1. New parts for this chapter: **1.** Triple-wall cardboard **2.** 3-axis accelerometer **3.** 2-axis joystick **4.** Pushbutton **5.** Velcro **6.** Project enclosure, made from mat board **7.** 1/16" mat board template for project enclosure **8.** Perforated circuit board. Don't forget plenty of male header pins for the breakout boards.

❝❝ Interactive Systems and Feedback Loops

In every interactive system, there's a feedback loop: you take action, the system responds, you see the response—or a notification of it—and you take another action. In some systems, the timing of that loop can be very loose. In other applications, the timing must be tight.

For example, in the cat bed application in Chapter 3, there's no need for the system to respond in more than a few seconds, because your reaction is not very time-sensitive. As long as you get to see the cat while he's on the bed (which may be true for several minutes or hours), you're happy. Monski Pong in Chapter 2 relies on a reasonably tight feedback loop in order to be fun. If it took a half-second or longer for the paddles to move when you move Monski's arms, it would be no fun. The timing of the feedback loop depends on the shortest time that matters to the participant.

Any system that requires coordination between action and reaction needs a tight feedback loop. Consider remote control systems, for example. Perhaps you're building a robot that's operated over a network. In that case, you'd need not only a fast network for the control system, but also a fast response from the camera or sensors on the robot (or in its environment) that are giving you information about what's happening. You need to be able to both control it quickly and see the results quickly. Networked action games also need a fast network. It's no fun if your game console reacts slowly, allowing other players with a faster network connection to get the jump on you. For applications like this, an exchange protocol that's constantly opening and closing connections (like HTTP does) wouldn't be very effective.

When there's a one-to-one connection between two objects, it's easy to establish a tight feedback loop. When there are multiple objects involved, though, it gets harder. To begin with, you have to consider how the network of connections between all the objects will be configured. Will it be a star network, with all the participants connected through a central server? Will it be a ring network? Will it be a many-to-many network, where every object has a direct connection to every other object? Each of these configurations has different effects on the feedback loop timing. In a star network, the objects on the edge of the network aren't very busy, but the central one is. In a ring network, every object shares the load more or less equally, but it can take a long time for a message to reach objects on opposite sides of the ring. In a direct many-to-many network, the load is distributed equally, but each object needs to maintain a lot of connections.

In most cases where you have a limited number of objects in conversation, it's easiest to manage the exchange using a central server. The most common program example of this is a text-based chat server like IRC (Internet Relay Chat), or AOL's instant messenger servers (AIM). Server programs that accept incoming clients and manage text messages between them in real time are often referred to as chat servers. The Processing program you'll write in this chapter is a variation on a chat server. The server will listen for new connections and exchange messages with all the clients that connect to it. Because there's no guarantee how long messages take to pass through the Internet, the exchange of messages can't be instantaneous. But as long as you've got a fast network connection for both clients and server, the feedback loop will be faster than human reaction time.

X

❝❝ Transmission Control Protocol: Sockets & Sessions

Each time a client connects to a web server, the connection that's opened uses a protocol called Transmission Control Protocol, or TCP. TCP is a protocol that specifies how objects on the Internet open, maintain, and close a connection that will involve multiple exchanges of messages. The connection made between any two objects using TCP is called a socket. A socket is like a pipe joining the two objects. It allows data to flow back and forth between them as long as the connection is maintained. Both sides need to keep the connection open in order for it to work.

For example, think about the exchanges between a web client and server that you saw in the previous two chapters. The pipe is opened when the server acknowledges the client's contact, and it remains open until the server has finished sending the file. If there are multiple files needed for a web page, such as images and style sheets, then multiple socket connections are opened and closed.

There's a lot going on behind the scenes of a socket connection. The exchange of data over a TCP connection can range in size anywhere from a few bytes to a few terabytes or more. All that data is sent in discrete packets, and the packets are sent by the best route from one end to the other.

NOTE: "Best" is a deliberately vague term: network hardware calculates the optimal route is differently, which involves a variety of metrics (such as the number of hops between two points, as well as the available bandwidth and reliability of a given path).

The period between the opening of a socket and the successful close of the socket is called a session. During the session, the program that maintains the socket tracks the status of the connection (open or closed) and the port number; counts the number of packets sent and received; notes the order of the packets and sees to it that packets are presented in the right order, even if the later packets arrive first; and accounts for any missing packets by requesting that they be resent. All of that is taken care of for you when you use a TCP/IP stack like the Net library in Processing or the firmware on the Arduino Ethernet boards you first saw in Chapter 4.

The complexity of TCP is worthwhile when you're exchanging critical data. For example, in an email, every byte is a character in the message. If you drop a couple of bytes, you could lose crucial information. The error-checking of TCP does slow things down a little, though, and if you want to send messages to multiple receivers, you have to open a separate socket connection to each one.

There's a simpler type of transmission protocol that's also common on the Net: User Datagram Protocol (UDP). Where TCP communication is based on sockets and sessions, UDP is based only on the exchange of packets. You'll learn more about it in Chapter 7.
X

Project 8

Networked Pong

Networked games are a great way to learn about real-time connections. This project is a networked variation on Pong. In honor of everyone's favorite network status command, let's call it *ping* pong. The server will be a Processing program, and the clients will be physical interfaces that connect through Ethernet-enabled Arduinos. The clients and the server's screen have to be physically close so that everyone can see the screen. In this case, you're using a network for its flexibility in handling multiple connections, not for its ability to connect remote places.

From the Monski Pong project in Chapter 2, you're already aware of the methods needed to move the paddles and the ball, so some of the code will be familiar to you. As this is a more complex variation, it's important to start with a good description of the whole system. The system will work like this:

- The game has two teams of multiple players.
- Each player can move a paddle back and forth. The paddles are at the top and bottom of the screen, and the ball moves from top to bottom.
- Players connect to the game server through a TCP connection. Every time a player connects, another paddle is added to the screen. New connections alternate between the top and bottom teams. When a player connects, the server replies with the following string: hi, followed by a carriage return and a line feed (shown as \r\n).
- The client can send the following commands:
  - l (ASCII value 108): move left
  - r (ASCII value 114): move right
  - x (ASCII value 120): disconnect
- When the client sends x, the server replies with the following string, and then ends the socket connection:

      bye\r\n

That's the communications protocol for the whole game. Keep in mind that it doesn't define anything about the physical form of the client object. As long as the client can make a TCP connection to the server and can send and receive the appropriate ASCII messages, it can work with the server. You can attach any type of physical inputs to the client, or you can write a client that sends all these messages automatically, with no physical input from the world at all (though that would be boring). Later in this chapter, you'll see a few different clients, each of which can connect to the server and play the game.

A Test Chat Server

You need a server to get started. There's a lot of code to control the pong display that you don't need right now (you just want to confirm that the clients can connect), so the following is a simple server with all the basic elements to handle network communications. It will let you listen for new clients, and then send them messages by typing in the applet window that appears when you run the program. Run the server and open a telnet connection to it. Remember, it's listening on port 8080, so if your computer's IP address is, say, 192.168.1.45, you'd connect like so: telnet 192.168.1.45 8080. If you're telnetting in from the same machine, you can use: telnet localhost 8080 or telnet 127.0.0.1 8080.

Whatever you type in the telnet window will show up in the server's debugger pane, and whatever you type in the server's applet window will show up at the client's command line. However, you'll have to press Return after each character in order for the server to see it—unless you make a change after you connect.

On Mac OS X or Linux, press the telnet escape key combination (Ctrl-]), type the following, and then press Return:

    mode character

On Windows, telnet should not require any special configuration, but if you find otherwise, press Ctrl-], type the following, and press Return twice:

    set mode stream

Now every character you type will be sent to the server as soon as you type it.

X

Try It First, start with the variable declarations and definitions. The main variables are an instance of the Server class, a port number to serve on, and an ArrayList to keep track of the clients.

```
/*
 Test Server Program
 Context: Processing

 Creates a server that listens for clients and prints
 what they say.  It also sends the last client anything that's
 typed on the keyboard.
 */

// include the net library:
import processing.net.*;

int port = 8080;                    // the port the server listens on
Server myServer;                    // the server object
ArrayList clients = new ArrayList(); // list of clients
```

▶▶ This program uses a data type you may not have seen before: ArrayList. Think of it as a super-duper array. ArrayLists don't have a fixed number of elements to begin with, so you can add new elements as the program continues. It's useful when you don't know how many elements you'll have. In this case, you don't know how many clients you'll have, so you'll store them in an ArrayList, and add each new client to the list as it connects. ArrayLists include some other useful methods. There is an introduction to ArrayLists on the Processing website at www.processing.org.

▶▶ The setup() method starts the server.

```
void setup()
{
  myServer = new Server(this, port);
}
```

▶▶ The draw() method listens for new messages from clients and prints them. If a client says "exit," the server disconnects it and removes it from the list of clients.

```
void draw()
{
  // get the next client that sends a message:
  Client speakingClient = myServer.available();

  if (speakingClient !=null) {
    String message = trim(speakingClient.readString());
    // print who sent the message, and what they sent:
    println(speakingClient.ip() + "\t" + message);

    if (message.equals("exit")) {
      myServer.disconnect(speakingClient);
      clients.remove(speakingClient);
    }
  }
}
```

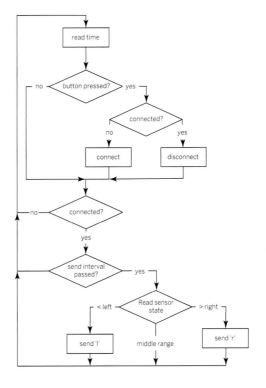

The serverEvent() message is generated by the server when a new client connects to it. serverEvent() announces new clients and adds them to the client list.

```
void serverEvent(Server myServer, Client thisClient) {
  println("We have a new client: " + thisClient.ip());
  clients.add(thisClient);
}
```

Finally, the keyReleased() method sends any keystrokes typed on the server to all connected clients.

```
void keyReleased() {
    myServer.write(key);
}
```

❝ The Clients

The pong client listens to local input and remote input. The local input is from you, the user. The remote input is from the server. The client is constantly listening to you, but it only listens to the server when it's connected.

To listen to you, the client needs:

- An input for sending a connect message. The same input can be used to send a disconnect message.
- An input for sending a left message.
- An input for sending a right message.

To let the user know what the client device is doing, add:

- An output to indicate whether the client is connected to the server.
- An output to indicate when the connect/disconnect button is pressed.
- An output to indicate when it's sending a left message.
- An output to indicate when it's sending a right message.

It's always a good idea to put outputs on the client to give local feedback when it receives input from the user. Even if there is no connection to the server, local feedback lets the user know that the client device is responding to her actions. For example, pressing the connect/disconnect button doesn't guarantee a connection, so it's important to separate the output that acknowledges a button push from the one that indicates successful connection. If there's a problem, this helps the user determine whether the problem is with the connection to the server, or with the client device itself.

Figure 5-2
Logic flowchart for the pong clients

Use outputs to indicate the client's status.In the following code, you can see that in addition to indicating when the sensors are triggered, you'll also indicate whether the client is connected or disconnected. If this client had a more complex set of states, you'd need more status indicators.

For this project, I built two clients. They have different methods of physical interaction and different input sensors, but they behave the same way to the server. You can build either, or both, or use the principles from them to build your own. Building both and comparing them will give you an idea of how the same protocol can result in very different behavior. One of these clients is much more responsive than the other, but the responsiveness has nothing to do with the communications protocol. It's all in the sensing and in the player's action. Both of the clients use logic shown in Figure 5-2.
x

" Client #1: A Joystick Client

The first client is a fairly traditional game controller, shown in Figure 5-3. It's got a joystick to control the left/right action, and a pushbutton to log in or out of the server. There are also four LEDs to indicate the controller's state. When it's logged in, the white LED is lit. When it's sending a left command, the red LED is lit. When it's sending a right command, the green LED is lit. When you're pressing the connect/disconnect button, the yellow LED lights up.

This client uses one axis of a two-axis joystick as its main input. The joystick contains two potentiometers: one for up/down movement and the other for left/right movement. You'll only need the output from the latter. Connect the pin marked L/R+ to +5V, the one marked GND to ground, and the one marked L/R to analog input 0 of your Arduino (the full circuit is shown in Figures 5-4 through 5-8). Then write a short program to read its output using analogRead(), just as you did with the Monski Pong sensors in Chapter 2 and the cat sensors in Chapter 3. Once you've got it working, note the values that indicate left and right, and save them for use in the client program.

You'll notice that the connection switch is wired differently from a normal switch. Instead of a 10-kilohm pulldown resistor, it's got a 100-ohm resistor and an LED connecting it to ground. This way, when you push the button, the LED lights up. There's no need to add any code to make this happen—the pushbutton will send current through the LED automatically, and you'll get local feedback on when the button is being pressed.

These two clients are laid out on printed circuit proto-typing boards (commonly known as perf boards). The perfboards make it possible for the circuits to be a little smaller and more physically robust. They're a bit harder to assemble than a solderless breadboard circuit, though.

MATERIALS FOR BOTH CLIENTS

» **1 Arduino Ethernet board or Arduino board with the Ethernet shield**
» **1 Ethernet connection to the Internet**
» **1 100-ohm resistor**
» **3 220-ohm resistors**
» **1 2-axis joystick (for joystick client)**
» **1 accelerometer (for tilt board client)**
» **1 perforated printed circuit board**
» **4 LEDs**
» **1 pushbutton**
» **1 project enclosure**
» **1 sheet extra-thick cardboard (for tilt board client)**

Both the perfboard and breadboard layouts are shown so you can choose whichever method you like.

You'll need an enclosure for the circuit. You can buy a project case from your favorite electronics retailer, but you can also get creative. For example, a pencil box from your friendly neighborhood stationery store will work well. Drill holes in the lid for the switch and the LEDs, cut a hole for the joystick, cut holes in the side for the Arduino and Ethernet jacks, and you're all set. If you're skilled with a mat knife, you can also make your own box from cardboard or mat board. Figure 5-7 shows the box I made, and Figure 5-9 shows the template from which I made it. If you're lucky enough to have access to a laser cutter, use it; if not, a mat knife and a steady hand can do the job.
x

◄◄ Figure 5-3

The joystick client, breadboard layout. Note the red and green LEDs to indicate left and right tilts. This client follows nautical tradition: port (left) is red and starboard (right) is green. Feel free to be less jaunty in your own choices, as long as they're clear.

◄ Figure 5-4

The joystick client schematic. The following page shows the layout for the circuit on a perforated circuit board.

⏶ Figure 5-5

The circuit as laid out on a perforated circuit board (perfboard). Note that male headers are only attached to the Arduino's analog input pins, power and ground pins, and digital pins 2 through 5. The rest aren't needed.

⏷ Figure 5-6

The circuit board layout showing where the solder joints are connected underneath the board.

⏶ Figure 5-7

The assembled joystick controller. The joystick circuit inside the housing was designed to be just tall enough so that the LEDs and joystick would stick through the top. Assemble the circuit first so you know how much space you need for the housing. A cable made from scrap stranded wire and male headers to connect the pushbutton makes it easier to open and close the box with the button mounted. The inner wires from a telephone cable work nicely for this.

⏷ Figure 5-8

Detail of the Arduino, Ethernet shield, and circuit board. Use female headers to mount the LEDs and the switch. For the LEDs, it makes the job of getting them to the right height much easier. You can trim them bit by bit until they are the right height, then stick them in the headers.

Figure 5-9

Template for the joystick housing. This template can be cut out of poster board or mat board and then folded to make a housing for the joystick controller. The dimensions will depend on how you assemble your circuit, so modify them as needed. Although they look precise here, they were measured with a caliper after the fact.

The first two prototypes were drawn by hand and cut out of paper, then scrap cardboard. I didn't move to a final version cut out of mat board until I had tested the fit of the sides with a paper version. Score the folds on the opposite side of the board so they fold better.

Try It First, start by importing the libraries you need and configuring your network connection for the client. This is similar to what you did for the Air-Quality Meter in Chapter 4, but the server address will be your computer's addesss.

```
/*
  Joystick client
  Context:  Arduino

  This program enables an Arduino to control one paddle
  in a networked Pong game.
*/

#include <SPI.h>
#include <Ethernet.h>

byte mac[] = { 0x00, 0xAA, 0xBB, 0xCC, 0xDE, 0x01 };
IPAddress ip(192,168,1,20);

// Enter the IP address of the computer on which
// you'll run the pong server:
IPAddress server(192,168,1,100);
```

> ▶▶ **Change these to match your own device and network.**

▶▶ You need a number of constants to keep track of the input and output pin numbers, the joystick's thresholds for left and right, and the minimum time between messages to the server. You'll need global variables for the connection Client, the previous state of the connect button, and the timestamp of the last message sent to the server.

You should update the left and right thresholds with the values you discovered earlier while testing the joystick.

```
const int connectButton = 2;    // the pushbutton for connecting/disconnecting
const int connectionLED = 3;    // this LED indicates whether you're connected
const int leftLED = 4;          // this LED indicates that you're moving left
const int rightLED = 5;         // this LED indicates that you're moving right
const int left = 200;           // threshold for the joystick to go left
const int right = 800;          // threshold for the joystick to go right
const int sendInterval = 20;    // minimum time between messages to the server
const int debounceInterval = 15;  // used to smooth out pushbutton readings

Client client;                  // instance of the Client class for connecting
int lastButtonState = 0;        // previous state of the pushbutton
long lastTimeSent = 0;          // timestamp of the last server message
```

▶▶ The setup() method just opens serial and Ethernet communications and initializes the digital I/O pins.

```
void setup()
{
  // initialize serial and Ethernet ports:
  Ethernet.begin(mac, ip);
  Serial.begin(9600);
  // initialize digital inputs and outputs:
  pinMode(connectButton, INPUT);
  pinMode(connectionLED, OUTPUT);
  pinMode(leftLED, OUTPUT);
  pinMode(rightLED, OUTPUT);

  delay(1000);       // give the Ethernet shield time to set up
  Serial.println("Starting");
}
```

▶▶ The main loop starts by updating the current time, which is used to keep track of how frequently you send to the server. Then, it checks to see whether the connect button has been pushed. If it has, and the client's already connected, the Arduino disconnects. If it's not connected, it tries to connect.

```
void loop()
{
  // note the current time in milliseconds:
  long currentTime = millis();
  // check to see if the pushbutton's pressed:
  boolean buttonPushed = buttonRead(connectButton);

  // if the button's just pressed:
  if (buttonPushed) {
    // if the client's connected, disconnect:
    if (client.connected()) {
      Serial.println("disconnecting");
      client.print("x");
      client.stop();
    } // if the client's disconnected, try to connect:
    else {
      Serial.println("connecting");
      client.connect(server, 8080);
    }
  }
```

▶▶ Next, check whether the client's connected to the server, and whether enough time has elapsed since the last time you sent to the server. If so, read the joystick and, if it's at one extreme or the other, send the message to the server and turn on the appropriate LED. If the joystick's in the middle, turn off the LEDs. Then save the current time as the most recent time you sent a message.

You may have to adjust your sendInterval value, depending on the responsiveness of your server and the sensitivity of your sensors. 20 milliseconds is a good place to start, but if you find the server slowing down with lots of clients, make it higher.

Finally, set the state of the connection LED using the state of the client itself.

```
  // if the client's connected, and the send interval has elapsed:
  if (client.connected() && (currentTime - lastTimeSent > sendInterval)) {
    // read the joystick and send messages as appropriate:
    int sensorValue = analogRead(A0);
    if (sensorValue < left) {    // moving left
      client.print("l");
      digitalWrite(leftLED, HIGH);
    }

    if (sensorValue > right) {    // moving right
      client.print("r");
      digitalWrite(rightLED, HIGH);
    }
    // if you're in the middle, turn off the LEDs:
    if (left < sensorValue && sensorValue < right) {
      digitalWrite(rightLED, LOW);
      digitalWrite(leftLED, LOW);
    }
    //save this moment as last time you sent a message:
    lastTimeSent = currentTime;
  }

  // set the connection LED based on the connection state:
  digitalWrite(connectionLED, client.connected());
}
```

▸▸ Finally, you can't just connect or disconnect every time the connect button is high. You want to send a message only when the button changes from low to high, indicating that the player just pressed it. This method checks for a low-to-high transition by comparing the state of the button with its previous state. It's called from the main loop.

This method also debounces the button, which means that it listens for a few extra milliseconds to see whether the button changes after the initial read. Sometimes a pushbutton can give several false readings for a few milliseconds, as the electrical contacts settle against one another. The cheaper the switch, the more common this is. If you find that your pushbutton gives multiple readings each time you push it, increase debounceInterval by a few milliseconds.

```
// this method reads the button to see if it's just changed
// from low to high, and debounces the button in case of
// electrical noise:

boolean buttonRead(int thisButton) {
  boolean result = false;
  // temporary state of the button:
  int currentState = digitalRead(thisButton);
  // final state of the button:
  int buttonState = lastButtonState;
  // get the current time to time the debounce interval:
  long lastDebounceTime = millis();

  while ((millis() - lastDebounceTime) < debounceInterval) {
    // read the state of the switch into a local variable:
    currentState = digitalRead(thisButton);

    // If the pushbutton changed due to noise:
    if (currentState != buttonState) {
      // reset the debouncing timer
      lastDebounceTime = millis();
    }

    // whatever the reading is at, it's been there for longer
    // than the debounce delay, so take it as the actual current state:
    buttonState = currentState;
  }
  // if the button's changed and it's high:
  if(buttonState != lastButtonState && buttonState == HIGH) {
    result = true;
  }

  // save the current state for next time:
  lastButtonState = buttonState;
  return result;
}
```

" Client #2: A Balance Board Client

Client #2 is a balance board. To control it, you stand on the board and tilt left or right. To stay in the middle, you have to balance the board. An accelerometer at the center of the board senses it tilt from side to side. The physical interaction for this controller is very different than the last. It requires more action from you, and it takes more physical agility to operate. However, the behavior of this client is identical to the previous one—from the server's point of view.

The balance board itself is based on a design by the Adaptive Design Association (http://adaptivedesign.org), a New York City-based organization that gets people involved—families and community volunteers—in making safe and affordable furniture and equipment for children with disabilities. A balance board is great for helping to strengthen your balance, and it's fun as well.

The physical construction for the balance board client case is similar to the joystick client—you can use the same template with the same LED setup. Just make the joystick hole smaller to hold the pushbutton, and don't cut a second hole.

To construct the board, you'll need heavy-duty triple-wall cardboard. Many packaging supply houses carry it. If you can't get triple-wall cardboard, you can laminate three sheets of regular cardboard together using white glue. When you're gluing layers together, make sure the grain of the corrugations for adjacent layers runs perpendicular to each other, for added stability.

Cut two circles approximately 15 inches in diameter from a sheet of triple-wall cardboard. In one of them, cut two slots, 12 inches long and as thick as your cardboard. In the board shown in Figure 5-12, the slots are roughly an inch thick. Each one is two inches from the center diameter of the circle, as shown in Figure 5-11. Glue the two circles together with their grains opposing each other.

Next, cut two arcs 12 inches across, as shown in Figure 5-10. Glue the arcs into the slots and let them dry. Make sure it's very solid before you try to balance on it.

The case for the balance board was adapted from the joystick client. The differences are that the connect/disconnect button took the place of the joystick, so the second large hole could be removed and the whole box made shorter. Mount the control box at the center of your balance board, as shown in Figure 5-12.

The code for the balance board client is also very similar to the joystick client. All you have to change is the values for the left and right thresholds. To discover them, do as you did with the joystick: put the accelerometer on the balance board, program the Arduino to print out the value of the analog input, and tilt it both ways to learn its extreme. Then fill those values in for left and right. Everything else stays the same. That's the beauty of using a clear, simple protocol: it doesn't matter what the physical input is, as long as you can map changes recorded by the sensors to a left-right movement, and program the microcontroller to send the appropriate messages.

It's worthwhile to try building both these clients, or one of your own, to look at how different physical affordances can affect the performance of different clients, even though it appears the same to the server.

X

⤓ Figure 5-10
The balance board rocker. Make two of these.
Design courtesy of the Adaptive Design Association.

12"

1"

cut along red lines

2"

15" diameter

2"

◄◄ Figure 5-11
The balance board base. Cut two circles this size, and cut the slots for the rockers in only one of them. Then, laminate the two circles together. *Design courtesy of the Adaptive Design Association.*

▶▶ Figure 5-12
The balance board in action. The two layers of triple-wall cardboard are laminated with the grain of their corrugations perpendicular to each other. This gives the board added stability. A couple of tabs of Velcro hold the controller box in place.

◀◀ **Figure 5-13**
The balance board client circuit, breadboard version. You can see it's identical to the joystick client, except for the accelerometer in place of the joystick.

⩔ **Figure 5-14**
The balance board client schematic.

◀◀ **Figure 5-15**
The balance board client circuit laid out on a perforated circuit board.

⤒ **Figure 5-16**
The circuit board layout showing where the solder joints are connected underneath the board.

❝ The Server

The server's tasks can be divided into two groups: those related to the game play, like animating the paddles and the ball and scoring; and those related to tracking new clients. To manage it all most effectively, you're going to use an object-oriented programming approach. If you've never done this before, there are a few basics you need to know in advance.

Anatomy of a Player Object

The most important thing to know is that all objects have properties and behaviors. You can think about an object's properties in much the same way as you think about physical properties. For example, a pong paddle has width and height, and it has a location, which you can express in terms of its horizontal and vertical positions. In your game, the paddles will have another important property: each paddle will be associated with a client. Of course, clients have properties as well, so each paddle will inherit an IP address from its client. You'll see all of these in the code that defines a paddle as an object.

A paddle also has a characteristic behavior: it moves left or right. That behavior will be encoded into the paddle as a method called movePaddle(). This behavior will update the properties of the paddle that define its location. A second behavior called showPaddle() will actually draw the paddle in its current location. You'll see later why these are kept separate.

Code It To define an object in Processing (or in Java for that matter), create a code block called a class. Here's the beginning of the class that defines a player in the pong server.

```
public class Player {
  // declare variables that belong to the object:
  float paddleH, paddleV;
  Client client;
```

cut along red lines
score and fold
along green lines

To Power Jack: 1.87"

To USB Jack: 1.84"

To Ethernet Jack: 1.07"

2.07"

0.79"

0.7"

2-1/4"

Ethernet
Jack
0.6" x 0.7"

USB
Jack
0.45" x 0.5"

power
Jack
0.43" x 0.36"

3-1/4"

3-1/4"

3-1/4"

1/4"   2-3/16"

2-3/16"   1/4"

2-1/4"

Hole centers:

2.64"

2.04"

1.79"

1.54"

0.94"

0.2" holes
for LEDs

0.6" diameter
for button

3-3/16"

1/4"

4"

1.6"

2.5"

Figure 5-17
Template for the balance board housing. As with the joystick client,
the template can be cut from 1/16" mat board. The dimensions
were changed to meet the needs of the smaller circuit.

As shown in the example, the variables declared at the beginning of the class are called instance variables. Every new instance of the class created makes its own copies of these variables. Every class has a constructor method, which gets called to bring the object into existence. You've already used constructors. When you made a new Serial port in Processing, you called the constructor method for the Serial class with something like, myPort = new Serial(this, portNum, dataRate).

▸▸ Here's the constructor for the Player class. It comes right after the instance variables in your code. As you can see, it just takes the values you give it when you call for a new Player, and assigns them to variables that belong to an instance (an individual player) of the class.

```
public Player (int hpos, int vpos, Client someClient) {
    // initialize the local instance variables:
    paddleH = hpos;
    paddleV = vpos;
    client = someClient;
}
```

▸▸ Next come the two other methods mentioned earlier, movePaddle() and showPaddle(). As you can see, they use the object's instance variables (paddleH, paddleV, and client) to store the location of the paddle and to draw it.

```
public void movePaddle(float howMuch) {
    float newPosition = paddleH + howMuch;
    // constrain the paddle's position to the width of the window:
    paddleH = constrain(newPosition, 0, width);
}

public void showPaddle() {
    rect(paddleH, paddleV, paddleWidth, paddleHeight);
    // display the address of this player near its paddle
    textSize(12);
    text(client.ip(), paddleH, paddleV - paddleWidth/8 );
}
}
```

▸▸ **This bracket closes the class.**

❝ That's all the code to define a Player. Put this code at the end of your program (shown next), just as if it were another method. To make a new Player object, write something like, Player newPlayer = new Player(xPosition, yPosition, thisClient).

When you do this, the new Player and all its instance variables and methods are accessible through the variable called newPlayer (the new Player is not actually stored in this variable; it's stuffed away in a portion of memory somewhere that you can get at through the newPlayer variable). Keep an eye out for this in the program.

The Main Pong Server Program

Before you write the code for the server as a whole, it's useful to make a flowchart of what happens. Figure 5-18 shows the main tasks and functions. A few details are left out for clarity's sake, but what's clear are the main relationships between the methods that run the program (setup(), draw(), and serverEvent()) and the Player objects. As with any program, the setup() method kicks things off, and then the draw() method takes over. The latter sees to it that the screen is updated and listens to any existing clients. If a new client connects, a server-Event() message is generated, which causes the method of that name to run. That method creates new Player objects. The draw() method takes advantage of the behaviors inside the Player objects to move and draw their paddles.

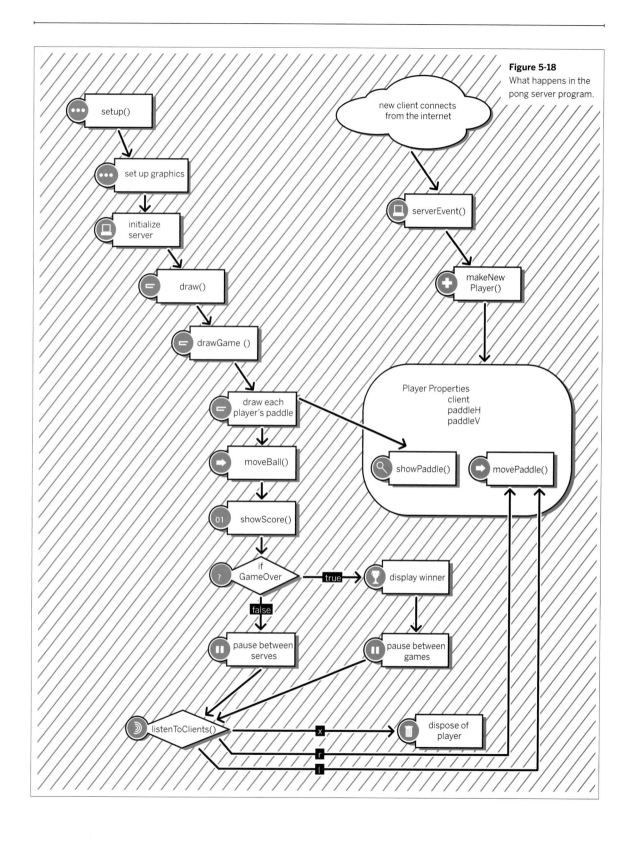

Figure 5-18
What happens in the pong server program.

The first thing to do in the server program is to define the variables. They're grouped here by those needed for keeping track of clients, versus those needed for managing the graphics of the game play.

```
// include the net library:
import processing.net.*;

// variables for keeping track of clients:
int port = 8080;                        // the port the server listens on
Server myServer;                        // the server object
ArrayList playerList = new ArrayList(); // list of clients

// variables for keeping track of the game play and graphics:
int ballSize = 10;                      // the size of the ball
int ballDirectionV = 2;                 // the ball's horizontal direction
                                        // left is negative, right is positive
int ballDirectionH = 2;                 // the ball's vertical direction
                                        // up is negative, down is positive
int ballPosV, ballPosH;                 // the ball's horizontal and vertical
                                        // positions
boolean ballInMotion = false;           // whether or not the ball should be moving

int topScore, bottomScore;              // scores for the top team and the bottom teams
int paddleHeight = 10;                  // vertical dimension of the paddles
int paddleWidth = 80;                   // horizontal dimension of the paddles
int nextTopPaddleV;                     // paddle positions for the next player
                                        // to be created
int nextBottomPaddleV;

boolean gameOver = false;               // whether or not a game is in progress
long delayCounter;                      // a counter for the delay after
                                        // a game is over
long gameOverDelay = 4000;              // pause after each game
long pointDelay = 2000;                 // pause after each point
```

▸▸ The setup() method sets all the initial conditions for the game, and then starts the server.

```
void setup() {
  // set the window size:
  size(480, 640);
  // set the frame rate:
  frameRate(90);
  // set the default font alignment:
  textAlign(CENTER);
  // set no borders on drawn shapes:
  noStroke();
  // set the rectMode so that all rectangle dimensions
  // are from the center of the rectangle (see Processing reference):
  rectMode(CENTER);

  // set up all the pong details:
  // initialize the delay counter:
  delayCounter = millis();
  // initialize paddle positions for the first player.
  // these will be incremented with each new player:
  nextTopPaddleV = 50;
  nextBottomPaddleV = height - 50;

  // initialize the ball in the center of the screen:
  ballPosV = height / 2;
  ballPosH = width / 2;

  // Start the server:
  myServer = new Server(this, port);
}
```

▸▸ The draw() method updates the screen using a method called drawGame(), and it listens for any messages from existing clients using the listenToClients() method.

```
void draw() {
  drawGame();
  listenToClients();
}
```

▶▶ When new clients connect to the server, the net library's serverEvent() method is called automatically; your Processing sketch has to have this method in order to respond to the event. It uses the new client to create a new Player object using a method called makeNewPlayer(). At right is the serverEvent() method.

```
// The ServerEvent message is generated when a new client
// connects to the server.
void serverEvent(Server thisServer, Client thisClient) {
  if (thisClient != null) {
    // iterate over the playerList:
    for (int p = 0; p < playerList.size(); p++) {
      // get the next object in the ArrayList and convert it
      // to a Player:
      Player newPlayer = (Player)playerList.get(p);

      // if thisPlayer's client matches the one that generated
      // the serverEvent, then this client is already a player, so quit
      // out of the method and return:
      if (newPlayer.client == thisClient) {
        return;
      }
    }

    // if the client isn't already a Player, then make a new Player
    // and add it to the playerList:
    makeNewPlayer(thisClient);
  }
}
```

▶▶ Now that you've seen the draw() and the serverEvent() methods, it's time to look at the methods they call. It's best to start with the creation of a new Player, so here's the makeNewPlayer() method.

A new Player is added to the bottom team if the last player is on the top, and vice versa.

The variables nextTopPaddleV and nextBottomPaddleV keep track of the positions for the next players on each team.

```
void makeNewPlayer(Client thisClient) {
  // paddle position for the new Player:
  int x = width/2;
  // if there are no players, add to the top:
  int y = nextTopPaddleV;

  /*
  Get the paddle position of the last player on the list.
   If it's on top, add the new player on the bottom, and vice versa.
   If there are  no other players, add the new player on the top.
   */
  // get the size of the list:
  int listSize = playerList.size() - 1;
  // if there are any other players:
  if  (listSize >= 0) {
    // get the last player on the list:
    Player lastPlayerAdded = (Player)playerList.get(listSize);
    // is the last player's on the top, add to the bottom:
    if (lastPlayerAdded.paddleV == nextTopPaddleV) {
      nextBottomPaddleV = nextBottomPaddleV - paddleHeight * 2;
      y = nextBottomPaddleV;
    }
    // is the last player's on the bottom, add to the top:
    else if (lastPlayerAdded.paddleV == nextBottomPaddleV) {
```

»

Continued from opposite page.

```
        nextTopPaddleV = nextTopPaddleV + paddleHeight * 2;
        y = nextTopPaddleV;
      }
    }

    // make a new Player object with the position you just calculated
    // and using the Client that generated the serverEvent:
    Player newPlayer = new Player(x, y, thisClient);
    // add the new Player to the playerList:
    playerList.add(newPlayer);
    // Announce the new Player:
    println("We have a new player: " + newPlayer.client.ip());
    newPlayer.client.write("hi\r\n");
  }
```

▶▶ Once a new Player has been created, you need to listen continuously for that Player's client to send any messages. The more often you check for messages, the tighter the interactive loop between sensor and action.

The listenToClients() method, called continuously from the draw() method, listens for messages from clients. If there's data available from any client, this method takes action. First, it iterates over the list of Players to see whether each one's client is speaking. Then, it checks to see whether the client sent any of the game messages (that is, l for left, r for right, or x for exit). If any of those messages was received, the program acts on the message appropriately.

```
void listenToClients() {
  // get the next client that sends a message:
  Client speakingClient = myServer.available();
  Player speakingPlayer = null;

  // iterate over the playerList to figure out whose
  // client sent the message:
  for (int p = 0; p < playerList.size(); p++) {
    // get the next object in the ArrayList and convert it
    // to a Player:
    Player thisPlayer = (Player)playerList.get(p);
    // compare the client of thisPlayer to the client that sent a message.
    // If they're the same, then this is the Player we want:
    if (thisPlayer.client == speakingClient) {
      speakingPlayer = thisPlayer;
      break;
    }
  }

  // read what the client sent:
  if (speakingPlayer != null) {
    int whatClientSaid = speakingPlayer.client.read();
    /*
  There are a number of things it might have said that we care about:
    x = exit
    l = move left
    r = move right
    */
    switch (whatClientSaid) {
      // If the client says "exit", disconnect it
      case 'x':
        // say goodbye to the client:
        speakingPlayer.client.write("bye\r\n");
```

»

Continued from previous page.

```
    // disconnect the client from the server:
    println(speakingPlayer.client.ip() + "\t logged out");
    myServer.disconnect(speakingPlayer.client);
    // remove the client's Player from the playerList:
    playerList.remove(speakingPlayer);
    break;
  case 'l':
    // if the client sends an "l", move the paddle left
    speakingPlayer.movePaddle(-10);
    break;
  case'r':
    // if the client sends an "r", move the paddle right
    speakingPlayer.movePaddle(10);
    break;
  }
 }
}
```

So far you've seen how the server receives new connections (using serverEvent()), creates new Players from the new clients (using make-NewPlayer()), and listens for messages (using listenTo-Clients()). That covers the interaction between the server and the clients. In addition, you've seen how the Player class defines all the properties and methods that are associated with each new player. Finally, it's time to look at the methods for controlling the drawing of the game.

drawGame(), called from the draw() method, is the main method for this. This method has four tasks:

- Iterate over the playerList and draw all the paddles at their most current positions.
- Draw the ball and the score.
- If the game is over, show a "Game Over" message and pause.
- Pause after each volley, then serve the ball again.

Show It   Here is the pongDraw() method.

You saw earlier that the listenToClients() method actually updates the positions of the paddles using the movePaddle() method from the Player object. That method doesn't actually draw the paddles, but this one does, using each Player's showPaddle() method. This is why the two methods are separated in the object.

```
void drawGame() {
  background(0);
  // draw all the paddles
  for (int p = 0; p < playerList.size(); p++) {
    Player thisPlayer = (Player)playerList.get(p);
    // show the paddle for this player:
    thisPlayer.showPaddle();
  }
```

Likewise, the moveBall() method, called here, checks to see whether the ball hit a paddle or a wall. It then calculates its new position from there, but it doesn't draw the ball itself because the ball needs to be drawn even if it's not in motion.

```
  // calculate ball's position:
  if (ballInMotion) {
    moveBall();
  }
  // draw the ball:
  rect(ballPosH, ballPosV, ballSize, ballSize);

  // show the score:
  showScore();
```

▶▶ If the game is over, the program stops the serving and displays the winner for four seconds.

Continued from previous page.

```
// if the game is over, show the winner:
if (gameOver) {
  textSize(24);
  gameOver = true;
  text("Game Over", width/2, height/2 - 30);
  if (topScore > bottomScore) {
    text("Top Team Wins!", width/2, height/2);
  }
  else {
    text("Bottom Team Wins!", width/2, height/2);
  }
}
// pause after each game:
if (gameOver && (millis() > delayCounter + gameOverDelay)) {
  gameOver = false;
  newGame();
}
```

▶▶ After each point is scored, the program takes a two-second pause. If there aren't at least two players after that pause, it doesn't serve another ball. This is to keep the game from running when there's no one playing.

That closes out the drawGame() method itself. It calls a few other methods: moveBall(), which calculates the ball's trajectory; showScore(), which shows the score; and newGame(), which resets the game. Those are shown next.

```
// pause after each point:
if (!gameOver && !ballInMotion && (millis() >
  delayCounter + pointDelay)) {

  // make sure there are at least two players:
  if (playerList.size() >=2) {
    ballInMotion = true;
  }
  else {
    ballInMotion = false;
    textSize(24);
    text("Waiting for two players", width/2, height/2 - 30);
    // reset the score:
    newGame();
  }
}
```

▶▶ First, moveBall() checks whether the position of the ball intersects any of the Players' paddles. To do this, it has to iterate over playerList, pull out each Player, and check to see whether the ball position is contained within the rectangle of the paddle. If the ball does intersect a paddle, its vertical direction is reversed.

```
void moveBall() {
  // Check to see if the ball contacts any paddles:
  for (int p = 0; p < playerList.size(); p++) {
    // get the player to check:
    Player thisPlayer = (Player)playerList.get(p);

    // calculate the horizontal edges of the paddle:
    float paddleRight = thisPlayer.paddleH + paddleWidth/2;
    float paddleLeft = thisPlayer.paddleH - paddleWidth/2;
    // check to see if the ball is in the horizontal range of the paddle:
    if ((ballPosH >= paddleLeft) && (ballPosH <= paddleRight)) {
```

»

Continued from previous page.

```
    // calculate the vertical edges of the paddle:
    float paddleTop = thisPlayer.paddleV - paddleHeight/2;
    float paddleBottom = thisPlayer.paddleV + paddleHeight/2;

    // check to see if the ball is in the
    // horizontal range of the paddle:
    if ((ballPosV >= paddleTop) && (ballPosV <= paddleBottom)) {
      // reverse the ball's vertical direction:
      ballDirectionV = -ballDirectionV;
    }
  }
}
```

» If the ball goes above the top of the screen or below the bottom, then one team has scored. If any team goes over five points, the game is over.

```
// if the ball goes off the screen top:
if (ballPosV < 0) {
  bottomScore++;
  ballDirectionV = int(random(2) + 1) * -1;
  resetBall();
}
// if the ball goes off the screen bottom:
if (ballPosV > height) {
  topScore++;
  ballDirectionV = int(random(2) + 1);
  resetBall();
}

// if any team goes over 5 points, the other team loses:
if ((topScore > 5) || (bottomScore > 5)) {
  delayCounter = millis();
  gameOver = true;
}
```

» Finally, moveBall() checks to see whether the ball hits one of the sides of the screen. If so, the horizontal direction is reversed.

```
// stop the ball going off the left or right of the screen:
if ((ballPosH - ballSize/2 <= 0) || (ballPosH +ballSize/2 >=width)) {
  // reverse the y direction of the ball:
  ballDirectionH = -ballDirectionH;
}
// update the ball position:
ballPosV = ballPosV + ballDirectionV;
ballPosH = ballPosH + ballDirectionH;
}
```

» The newGame() method just restarts the game play and resets the scores.

```
void newGame() {
  gameOver = false;
  topScore = 0;
  bottomScore = 0;
}
```

The showScore() method prints the scores on the screen.

```
public void showScore() {
  textSize(24);
  text(topScore, 20, 40);
  text(bottomScore, 20, height - 20);
}
```

 Finally, moveBall() calls a the resetBall() method, which resets the ball at the end of each point.

```
void resetBall() {
  // put the ball back in the center
  ballPosV = height/2;
  ballPosH = width/2;
  ballInMotion = false;
  delayCounter = millis();
}
```

❝ The beauty of this server is that it doesn't really care how many clients log into it; everyone gets to play *ping* pong. There's nothing in the server program that limits the response time for any client, either. The server attempts to satisfy everyone a soon as possible. This is a good habit to get in. If there's as need to limit the response time in any way, don't rely on the server of the network to do that. Whenever possible, let the network and the server remain dumb, fast, and reliable, and let the clients decide how fast they want to send data across. Figure 5-19 shows a screenshot of the server with two clients.

Once you've got the clients speaking with the server, try designing a new client of your own. Try to make the ultimate *ping* pong paddle.
X

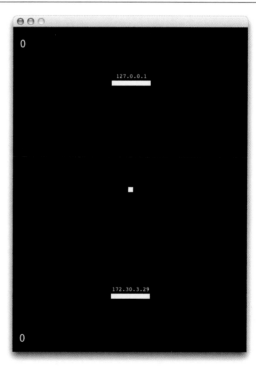

Figure 5-19
The output of the ping pong server sketch.

66 Conclusion

The basic structure of the clients and server in this chapter can be used any time you want to make a system that manages synchronous connections between several objects on the network. The server's main jobs are to listen for new clients, keep track of the existing clients, and make sure that the right messages reach the right clients. It must place a priority on listening at all times.

The client should also place a priority on listening, but it has to juggle listening to the server with listening to the physical inputs. It should always give a clear and immediate response to local input, and it should indicate the state of the network connection at all times.

The protocol that the objects in this system speak to each other should be as simple and as flexible as possible. Leave room for more commands, because you never know when you might decide to add something. Make sure to build in responses where appropriate, like the "hi" and "bye" responses from the server. Keep the messages unambiguous and, if possible, keep them short as well.

Finally, make sure you've got a reliable way to test the system. Simple tools like a telnet client and test server will save you much time in building every multiplayer server, and help you get to the fun sooner.

Now you've seen examples of both asynchronous client-server exchanges (the HTTP system in Chapter 4) and synchronous exchanges (the chat server on page 153). With those two tools, you can build almost any application in which there's a central server and a number of clients. For the next chapter, you'll step away from the Internet and take a look at various forms of wireless communication. X

◀◀ *At left*
Jin-Yo Mok's original sketches of the music box.

▶▶ *At right*
The music box composition interface.

6

Wireless Communication

If you're like most people interested in this area, you've been reading through the early chapters thinking, "but what about wireless?" Perhaps you're so eager that you just skipped straight to this chapter. If you did, go back and read the rest of the book! In particular, if you're not familiar with serial communication between computers and microcontrollers, you'll want to read Chapter 2 before reading this chapter. This chapter explains the basics of wireless communication between objects. In it, you'll learn about two types of wireless communication, and then build some working examples.

◀◀ **Alex Beim's Zygotes** (www.tangibleinteraction.com) are lightweight, inflatable rubber balls lit from within by LED lights. The balls change color in reaction to pressure on their surface, and they use ZigBee radios to communicate with a central computer. A network of zygotes at a concert allows the audience to have a direct effect not only on the balls themselves, but also on the music and video projections to which they are networked. *Photo courtesy of Alex Beim.*

◀ Supplies for Chapter 6

DISTRIBUTOR KEY

- **A** Arduino Store (http://store.arduino.cc/ww)
- **AF** Adafruit (http://adafruit.com)
- **D** Digi-Key (www.digikey.com)
- **F** Farnell (www.farnell.com)
- **J** Jameco (http://jameco.com)
- **MS** Maker SHED (www.makershed.com)
- **RS** RS (www.rs-online.com)
- **SF** SparkFun (www.sparkfun.com)
- **SS** Seeed Studio (www.seeedstudio.com)

PROJECT 9: Infrared Control of a Digital Camera

» **1 Arduino module** An Arduino Uno or something based on the Arduino Uno, but the project should work on other Arduino and Arduino-compatible boards. **D** 1050-1019-ND, **J** 2121105, **SF** DEV-09950, **A** A000046, **AF** 50, **F** 1848687, **RS** 715-4081, **SS** ARD132D2P, **MS** MKSP4

» **1 infrared LED J** 106526, **SF** COM-09469, **F** 1716710, **RS** 577-538, **SS** MTR102A2B

» **1 pushbutton** Any button will do. **D** GH1344-ND, **J** 315432, **SF** COM-10302, **F** 1634684, **RS** 718-2213

» **1 220-ohm resistor D** 220QBK-ND, **J** 690700, **F** 9337792, **RS** 707-8842

» **1 10-kilohm resistor D** 10KQBK-ND, **J** 29911, **F** 9337687, **RS** 707-8906

» **1 solderless breadboard D** 438-1045-ND, **J** 20723 or 20601, **SF** PRT-00137, **F** 4692810, **AF** 64, **SS** STR101C2M or STR102C2M, **MS** MKKN2

PROJECT 10: Duplex Radio Transmission

» **2 solderless breadboards D** 438-1045-ND, **J** 20723 or 20601, **SF** PRT-00137, **F** 4692810, **AF** 64, **SS** STR101C2M or STR102C2M

Figure 6-1. New parts for this chapter: **1.** Arduino wireless shield **2.** Spark Fun XBee breakout board **3.** 2mm female header pins **4.** Arduino WiFi shield **5.** Digi XBee 802.15.4 OEM module **6.** Adafruit XBee-to-USB adapter **7.** Spark Fun XBee Explorer **8.** Infrared LED **9.** Arduno Fio. Don't forget plenty of male header pins for the breakout boards.

» **2 Arduino modules** Arduino Fio models are a nice alternative designed to work with XBees, but any Uno-compatible board should work. **SF** DEV-10116

» **2 Digi XBee 802.15.4 RF modules** **J** 2113375, **SF** WRL-08664 , **AF** 128, **F** 1546394, **SS** WLS113A4M, **MS** MKAD14

» **2 Arduino wireless shields** You can opt to not use the shields and use the parts listed below instead. **A** A000064 or A000065. Alternative shields: **SF** WRL-09976, **AF** 126, **F** 1848697, **RS** 696-1670, **SS** WLS114A0P

» **2 potentiometers** **J** 29082, **SF** COM-09939, **F** 350072, **RS** 522-0625

» **1 USB-XBee adapter**
The following parts are only necessary if you are not using Wireless shields.
J 32400, **SF** WRL-08687, **AF** 247

» **2 3.3V regulators** **J** 242115, **D** 576-1134-ND, **SF** COM-00526, **F** 1703357, **RS** 534-3021

» **2 1µF capacitors** **J** 94161, **D** P10312-ND, **F** 8126933, **RS** 475-9009

» **2 10µF capacitors** **J** 29891, **D** P11212-ND, **F** 1144605, **RS** 715-1638

» **2 XBee breakout boards** **J** 32403**,** **SF** BOB-08276, **AF** 127

» **4 rows of 0.1-inch header pins** **J** 103377, **D** A26509-20ND, **SF** PRT-00116, **F** 1593411

» **4 2mm female header rows** **J** 2037747, **D** 3M9406-ND, **F** 1776193

» **6 LEDs** **D** 160-1144-ND or 160-1665-ND, **J** 34761 or 94511, **F** 1015878, **RS** 247-1662 or 826-830, **SF** COM-09592 or COM-09590

PROJECT 11: Bluetooth Transceivers

» **2 Arduino modules** Get something based on the Arduino Uno, but the project should work on other Arduino and Arduino-compatible boards. **D** 1050-1019-ND, **J** 2121105, **SF** DEV-09950, **A** A000046, **AF** 50, **F** 1848687, **RS** 715-4081, **SS** ARD132D2P, **MS** MKSP4

» **2 solderless breadboards** **D** 438-1045-ND, **J** 20723 or 20601, **SF** PRT-00137, **F** 4692810, **AF** 64, **SS** STR101C2M or STR102C2M

» **2 LEDs** **D** 160-1144-ND or 160-1665-ND, **J** 34761 or 94511, **F** 1015878, **RS** 247-1662 or 826-830, **SF** COM-09592 or COM-09590

» **2 potentiometers** Any analog sensor will work. **J** 29082, **SF** COM-09939, **F** 350072, **RS** 522-0625

» **2 pushbuttons** Any will do. **D** GH1344-ND, **J** 315432, **SF** COM-10302, **F** 1634684, **RS** 718-2213

» **2 220-ohm resistors** **D** 220QBK-ND, **J** 690700, **F** 9337792, **RS** 707-8842

» **2 10-kilohm resistors** **D** 10KQBK-ND, **J** 29911, **F** 9337687, **RS** 707-8906

» **1 FTDI USB-to-Serial adapter** Both the 5V or 3.3V versions will work; these come as cables or standalone modules. **SF** DEV-09718 or DEV-09716, **AF** 70, **A** A000059, **MS** MKAD22, **SS** PRO101D2P, **D** TTL-232R-3V3 or TTL-232R-5V

» **2 Bluetooth Mate modules** **SF** WRL-09358 or WRL-10393

PROJECT 12: Hello WiFi!

» **1 Arduino WiFi shield** **A** A000058

» **1 Arduino module** Get something based on the Arduino Uno, but the project should work on other Arduino and Arduino-compatible boards. **D** 1050-1019-ND, **J** 2121105, **SF** DEV-09950, **A** A000046, **AF** 50, **F** 1848687, **RS** 715-4081, **SS** ARD132D2P, **MS** MKSP4

» **1 WiFi Ethernet connection to the Internet**

» **3 10-kilohm resistors** **D** 10KQBK-ND, **J** 29911, **F** 9337687, **RS** 707-8906

» **3 photocells (light-dependent resistors)** **D** PDV-P9200-ND, **J** 202403, **SF** SEN-09088, **F** 7482280, **RS** 234-1050

» **1 solderless breadboard** **D** 438-1045-ND, **J** 20723 or 20601, **SF** PRT-00137, **F** 4692810, **AF** 64, **SS** STR101C2M or STR102C2M, **MS** MKKN2

» **3 lighting filters** One primary red, one primary green, and one primary blue. Available from your local lighting- or photo-equipment supplier.

The early part of this chapter covers how wireless works and what makes it stop working, giving you some background and starting places for troubleshooting. The second half of the chapter contains examples. The topic is so broad, even a survey of several different devices only covers the tip of the iceberg. For that reason, the exercises in this chapter will be less fully developed applications than the previous ones. Instead, you'll just get the basic "Hello World!" example for several forms of wireless device.

X

" Why Isn't Everything Wireless?

The advantage of wireless communication seems obvious: no wires! This makes physical design much simpler for any project where the devices have to move and talk to each other. Wearable sensor systems, digital musical instruments, and remote control vehicles are all simplified physically by wireless communication. However, there are some limits to this communication that you should consider before going wireless.

Wireless communication is never as reliable as wired communication

You have less control over the sources of interference. You can insulate and shield a wire carrying data communications, but you can never totally isolate a radio or infrared wireless link. There will always be some form of interference, so you must make sure that all the devices in your system know what to do if they get a garbled message, or no message at all, from their counterparts.

Wireless communication is never just one-to-one communication

The radio and infrared devices mentioned here broadcast their signals for all to hear. Sometimes that means they interfere with the communication between other devices. For example, Bluetooth, most WiFi radios (802.11b, g, and n), and ZigBee (802.15.4) radios all work in the same frequency range: 2.4 gigahertz (802.11n will also work at 5GHz). They're designed to not cause each other undue interference, but if you have a large number of ZigBee radios working in the same space as a busy WiFi network, for example, you'll get interference.

Wireless communication does not mean wireless power

You still have to provide power to your devices, and if they're moving, this means using battery power. Batteries add weight, and they don't last forever. The failure of a battery when you're testing a project can cause all kinds of errors that you might attribute to other causes. A classic example of this is the "mystery radio error." Many radios consume extra power when they're transmitting. This causes a slight dip in the voltage of the power source. If the radio isn't properly decoupled with a capacitor across its power and ground leads, the voltage can dip low enough to make the radio reset itself. The radio may appear to function normally when you're sending it serial messages, but it will never transmit, and you won't know why. When you start to develop wireless projects, it's good practice to first make sure that you have the communication working using a regulated, plugged-in power supply, and then create a stable battery supply.

Wireless communication generates electromagnetic radiation

This is easy to forget about, but every radio you use emits electromagnetic energy. The same energy that cooks your food in a microwave sends your mp3 files across the Internet. And while there are many studies indicating that it's safe at the low operating levels of the radios used here, why add to the general noise if you don't have to?

Make the wired version first

The radio and IR transceivers discussed here are replacements for the communications wires used in previous chapters. Before you decide to add wireless to any application, it's important to make sure you've got the basic exchange of messages between devices working over wires first.

X

" Two Flavors of Wireless: Infrared and Radio

There are two common types of wireless communication in most people's lives: infrared light communication and radio communication. The main difference between them, from a user's or developer's position, is their directionality.

Television remote controls typically use infrared (IR) communication. Unlike radio, it's dependent on the orientation between transmitter and receiver. There must be a clear line of sight between the two. Sometimes IR can work by bouncing the beam off another surface, but it's not as reliable. Ultimately, the receiver is an optical device, so it has to "see" the signal. Car door openers, mobile phones, garage door remote controls, and many other devices use radio. These work regardless of whether the transmitter and receiver are facing each other. They can even operate through walls, in some cases. In other words, their transmission is omnidirectional. Generally, IR is used for short-range line-of sight applications, and radio is used for everything else; Figure 6-2 illustrates this difference.

Figure 6-2
The signal from the LED at left radiates out in a beam from the LED, while the signal from a radio antenna like on the XBee radio at right radiates omnidirectionally.

Transmitters, Receivers, and Transceivers

There are three types of devices common to both IR and RF systems: transmitters, which send a signal but can't receive one; receivers, which receive a signal but can't send one; and transceivers, which can do both. You may wonder why everything isn't a transceiver, as it's the most flexible device. It's more complex to make a transceiver than it is to make the other two. In a transceiver, you have to make sure the receiver is not receiving its transmitter's transmission, or they'll interfere with each other and not listen to any other device. For many applications, it's cheaper to use a transmitter-receiver pair and handle any errors by just transmitting the message many times until the receiver gets it. That's how TV remote controls work, for example. It makes the components much cheaper.

It's increasingly common in radio applications to just make every device a transceiver, and incorporate a microcontroller to manage the transmitter-receiver filtering. All Bluetooth, ZigBee, and WiFi radios work this way. However, it's still possible to get transmitter-receiver pair radios, and they are still cheaper than their transceiver counterparts.

Keep in mind the distinction between transmitter-receiver pairs and transceivers when you plan your projects, and when you shop. Consider whether the communication in your project must be two-way, or whether it can be one-way only. If it's one-way, ask yourself what happens if the communication fails. Can the receiver operate without asking for clarification? Can the problem be solved by transmitting repeatedly until the message is received? If the answer is yes, you might be able to use a transmitter-receiver pair and save some money.

How Infrared Works

IR communication works by pulsing an IR LED at a set data rate, and receiving the pulses using an IR photodiode. It's simply serial communication transmitted using infrared light. Since there are many everyday sources of IR light (the sun, incandescent light bulbs, any heat source), it's necessary to differentiate the IR data signal from other IR energy. To do this, the serial output is sent to an oscillator before it's sent to the output LED. The wave created by the oscillator, called a carrier wave, is a regular pulse that's modulated by the pulses of the data signal. The receiver picks up all IR light but filters out anything that's not vibrating at the carrier frequency. Then it filters out the carrier frequency, so all that's left is the data signal. This method allows you to transmit data using infrared light without getting interference from other IR light sources—unless they happen to be oscillating at the same frequency as your carrier wave.

The directional nature of infrared makes it more limited, but cheaper than radio, and requires less power. As radios get cheaper, more power-efficient, and more robust, it's less common to see an IR port on a computer. However, it's still both cost-effective and power-efficient for line-of-sight remote control applications.

Data protocols for the IR remote controls of most home electronics vary from manufacturer to manufacturer. To decode them, you need to know both the carrier frequency and the message structure. Most commercial IR remote control devices operate using a carrier wave between 38 and 40 kHz. The carrier wave's frequency limits the rate at which you can send data on that wave, so IR transmission is usually done at a low data rate, typically between 500 and 2,000 bits per second. It's not great for high-bandwidth data transmission, but if you're only sending the values of a few pushbuttons on a remote, it's acceptable. Unlike the serial protocols you've seen so far in this book, IR protocols do not all use an 8-bit data format. For example, Sony's Control-S protocol has three formats: 12 bit, 15 bit, and 20 bit. Philips' RC5 format, common to many remotes, uses a 14-bit format.

If you have to send or receive remote control signals, you'll save a lot of time by looking for a specialty IR modulator chip to do the job, rather than trying to recreate the protocol yourself. Fortunately, there are many good sites on the Web that explain the various protocols. Reynolds Electronics (www.rentron.com) has many helpful tutorials, and sells a number of useful IR modulators and demodulators. EPanorama has a number of useful links describing many of the more common IR protocols at www.epanorama.net/links/irremote.html. There are also a number of libraries written for Arduino to help you send and receive IR signals for different protocols. Many

 ## Making Infrared Visible

There are two tools that are really helpful when you're working with IR transmitters and receivers: a camera and an oscilloscope.

Even though you can't see infrared light, cameras can. If you're not sure whether your IR LED is working, one quick way to check is to point the LED at a camera and look at the resulting image. If it's working, you'll see the LED light up. Figure 6-3 shows the IR LED in a home remote control, viewed through a webcam attached to a personal computer. You can even see this in the LCD viewfinder of a digital camera. If you try this with your IR LED, you may need to turn the lights down or close the curtains to see this effect. Some webcams have a built-in IR filter, so it's good to first check with an IR device that you know works, like a remote control, before you use it to detect whether your project is working.

⤒ **Figure 6-3.** Having a camera at hand is useful when troubleshooting IR projects.

of them are listed on the Arduino playground at http://arduino.cc/playground/Main/InterfacingWithHardware. You'll see one in action in the next project.

If you're building both the transmitter and receiver, your job is fairly straightforward. You just need an oscillator through which you can pass your serial data to an infrared LED, and a receiver that listens for the carrier wave and demodulates the data signal. It's possible to build your own IR modulator using a 555 timer IC, but there are a number of inexpensive modules you can buy to modulate or demodulate an IR signal as well.

X

Sniffing Infrared Signals

An oscilloscope is also useful when you're trying to decipher an IR signal (see Figure 6-4). You may not know the protocol for your receiver, but you can work it out by looking at the signal it sent. Connect an infrared phototransistor, a resistor, and a regular LED in series, as shown in Figure 6-5, and you should see the LED light up when you point your remote at the phototransistor.

To see the remote's signal on an oscilloscope, connect the scope probes to ground and to the phototransistor's emitter, and fire the remote at the phototransistor. Once you see activity, adjust the voltage and time divisions on

▲ **Figure 6-4**. An oscilloscope can help you see the pattern of an IR signal.

MATERIALS

» **1 solderless breadboard**
» **1 220-ohm resistor**
» **1 phototransistor** Digi-Key part no. 365-1068-ND.
» **1 LED**
» **1 battery or power source** 5V or less.
» **1 oscilloscope** DSO nano shown here.

the scope until you see readable activity. Most scopes will tell you the frequency of the signal automatically. Putting your scope in single-shot trigger mode will help you capture the actual signal. Once you can see the timing of each signal's pulse, you can work out how to duplicate it by generating your own pulses on an IR LED. For more on this, see many of the excellent blog posts on IR remote control using an Arduino. For example, read Ken Shirriff's very good explanation on his blog, at www.arcfn.com.

▲ **Figure 6-5**. An IR phototransistor and LED in series work well to test IR reception.

Project 9

Infrared Control of a Digital Camera

This example uses an infrared LED and an Arduino to control a digital camera. It's about the simplest IR control project you can do.

Most digital SLR cameras on the market today can be controlled remotely via infrared. Each brand uses a slightly different protocol, but they all tend to have the same basic commands: trigger the shutter, trigger after a delay, and auto-focus. Sebastian Setz has written an Arduino library that can send the signals for most common cameras. It's been tested with Canon, Nikon, Olympus, Pentax, and Sony. If you have an SLR from any of these brands, you should be able to control it with this library.

The circuit for this project is simple. Connect the push-button to pin 4 of the microcontoller (with a 10-kilohm pulldown resistor), and connect the infrared LED to pin 3 of the microcontroller, as shown in Figure 6-6.

Download the Multi Camera IR Control library from http://sebastian.setz.name/arduino/my-libraries/multi-camera-ir-control and copy it to the **libraries** directory of your Arduino sketch directory. If you've never installed a library before, you'll need to create this directory. One it's there, restart the Arduino application, and you should see a new library in the Sketch menu's Import Library submenu called MultiCameraIrControl. Now you're ready to get going.

X

MATERIALS

» **1 Arduino module**
» **1 infrared LED**
» **1 pushbutton**
» **1 220-ohm resistor**
» **1 10-kilohm resistor**
» **1 solderless breadboard or prototyping shield**

Figure 6-6
The microcontroller with an IR LED and pushbutton attached.

Try It To start your sketch, import the MultiCam-eralrControl library. Initialize the library to send signals on pin 3, to which the LED is connected. Then, set up a few variables to keep track of the state of the pushbutton.

```
/*
IR Camera control
Context: Arduino

This sketch controls a digital camera via an infrared LED.
*/

// include the library for camera control:
#include <multiCameraIrControl.h>

const int pushButtonPin = 4;
// set up pin 3 to control the IR LED.
// change this depending on the brand of your camera:
Nikon camera(3);

// Variables will change:
int buttonState = 0;        // current state of the button
int lastButtonState = 0;    // previous state of the button
```

▶ The setup method initializes the pushbutton as an input.

```
void setup(){
  // initialize the pushButton as input:
  pinMode(pushButtonPin, INPUT);
}
```

▶ The main loop listens for the pushbutton's state to change. Since you don't want the camera firing all the time, trigger the camera only when the pushbutton changes from OFF to ON. To do that, compare the button's state to its previous state by storing the current state as the previous state at the end of each loop.

That's the whole program. Now point the LED at your camera and start taking some pictures remotely. You may have to set your camera to remote control mode. Check the camera manual for how to do this, as it's different from camera to camera.

```
void loop(){
  // read the pushbutton input pin:
  buttonState = digitalRead(pushButtonPin);

  // compare the buttonState to its previous state
  // if it's changed, and it's high now, then the person
  // just punched the button:
  if (buttonState != lastButtonState && buttonState == HIGH) {
    // send the signal to open the shutter:
    camera.shutterNow();
  }
  // save the current state as the last state,
  //for next time through the loop
  lastButtonState = buttonState;
}
```

A. PIR sensor

Figure 6-7
This intervalometer was built using the same methods as shown above. An Arduino in the box senses a change from the PIR sensor and sends an IR signal to the camera to take a picture.

🌒 How Radio Works

Radio relies on the electrical property called induction. Any time you vary the electrical current in a wire, you generate a corresponding magnetic field that emanates from the wire. This changing magnetic field induces an electrical current in any other wires in the field. The frequency of the magnetic field is the same as the frequency of the current in the original wire. This means that if you want to send a signal without a wire, you can generate a changing current in one wire at a given frequency, and attach a circuit to the second wire to detect current changes at that frequency. That's how radio works.

The distance that you can transmit a radio signal depends on the signal strength, the sensitivity of the receiver, the nature of the antennas, and any obstacles that block the signal. The stronger the original current and the more sensitive the receiver, the farther apart the sender and receiver can be. The two wires act as antennas. Any conductor can be an antenna, but some work better than others. The length and shape of the antenna and the frequency of the signal all affect transmission. Antenna design is a whole field of study on its own, so I can't do it justice here, but a rough rule of thumb for a straight wire antenna is as follows:

Antenna length = 5,616 in. / frequency in MHz = 14,266.06 cm. / frequency in MHz

For more information, consult the technical specifications for the specific radios you're using. Instructions on making a good antenna are common in a radio's documentation.

Radio Transmission: Digital and Analog

As with everything else in the microcontroller world, it's important to distinguish between digital and analog radio transmission. Analog radios simply take an analog electrical signal, such as an audio signal, and superimpose it on the radio frequency in order to transmit it. The radio frequency acts as a carrier wave, carrying the audio signal. Digital radios superimpose digital signals on the carrier wave, so there must be a digital device on either end to encode or decode those signals. In other words, digital radios are basically modems, converting digital data to radio signals, and radio signals back into digital data.

Radio Interference

Though the antennas you'll use in this chapter are omni-directional, radio can be blocked by obstacles, particularly metal ones. A large metal sheet, for example, will reflect a radio signal rather than allowing it to pass through. This principle is used not only in designing antennas, but also in designing radio frequency (RF) shields. If you've ever cut open a computer cable and encountered a thin piece of foil wrapped around the inside wires, you've encountered an RF shield. Shields are used to prevent random radio signals from interfering with the data being transmitted down a wire. A shield doesn't have to be a solid sheet of metal, though. A mesh of conductive metal will block a radio signal as well—if the grid of the mesh is small enough. The effectiveness of a given mesh depends on the frequency it's designed to block. It's possible to block radio signals from a whole space by surrounding the space with an appropriate shield and grounding the shield. You'll hear this referred to as making a Faraday cage. The effect is named after the physicist Michael Faraday, who first demonstrated and documented it.

Sometimes radio transmission is blocked by unintentional shields. If you're having trouble getting radio signals through, look for metal that might be shielding the signal. Transmitting from inside a car can sometimes be tricky because the car body acts as a Faraday cage. Putting the antenna on the outside of the car improves reception. Bodies of water block RF effectively as well. This is true for just about every radio housing.

All kinds of electrical devices emit radio waves as side effects of their operation. Any alternating current can generate a radio signal, even the AC that powers your home or office. This is why you hear a hum when you lay speaker wires in parallel with a power cord. The AC signal is inducing a current in the speaker wires, and the speakers are reproducing the changes in current as sound. Likewise, it's why you may have trouble operating a wireless data network near a microwave oven. WiFi operates at frequencies in the gigahertz range, commonly called the microwave range, because the wavelength of

those signals is very short compared to lower frequency signals. To cook food, microwave ovens generate energy in this range to excite (heat up) the water molecules in food. Some of that energy leaks from the oven at low power, which is why you get all kinds of radio noise in the gigahertz range around a microwave.

Motors and generators are especially insidious sources of radio noise. A motor also operates by induction; specifi-cally, by spinning a pair of magnets around a shaft in the center of a coil of wire. By putting a current in the wire, you generate a magnetic field, which attracts or repulses the magnets, causing them to spin. Likewise, by using mechanical force to spin the magnets, you generate a current in the wire. So, a motor or a generator is essen-tially a little radio, generating noise at whatever frequency it's rotating.

Because there are so many sources of radio noise, there are many ways to interfere with a radio signal. It's important to keep these possible sources of noise in mind when you begin to work with radio devices. Knowledge of common interference sources, and knowing how to shield against them, is a valuable tool in radio troubleshooting.

Multiplexing and Protocols

When you're transmitting via radio, anyone with a com-patible receiver can receive your signal. There's no wire to contain the signal, so if two transmitters are sending at the same time, they will interfere with each other. This is the biggest weakness of radio: a given receiver has no way to know who sent the signal it's receiving. In contrast, consider a wired serial connection: you can be reasonably sure when you receive an electrical pulse on a serial cable that it came from the device on the other end of the wire. You have no such guarantee with radio. It's as if you were blindfolded at a cocktail party and everyone else there had the same voice. The only way you'd know who was talking to you was if each person clearly identified himself at the beginning and end of his conversation, and no one inter-rupted him during this time. In other words, it's all about protocols.

The first thing everyone at that cocktail party would have to do is agree on who speaks when. That way they could each have your attention for awhile. Sharing in radio com-munication is called multiplexing, and this form of sharing is called time-division multiplexing. Each transmitter gets a given time slot in which to transmit.

Of course, it depends on all the transmitters being in sync. When they're not, time-division multiplexing can still work reasonably well if all the transmitters speak much less than they listen (remember the first rule of love and networking from Chapter 1: listen more than you speak). If a given transmitter is sending for only a few milliseconds in each second, and if there's a limited number of transmitters, the chance that any two messages will overlap, or collide, is relatively low. This guideline, combined with a request for clarification from the receiver (rule number three), can ensure reasonably good RF communication.

Back to the cocktail party. If every person spoke in a different tone, you could distinguish each individual by her tone. In radio terms, this is called frequency-division multiplexing. It means that the receiver has to be able to receive on several frequencies simultaneously. But if there's a coordinator handing out frequencies to each pair of transmitters and receivers, it's reasonably effective.

Various combinations of time- and frequency-division multiplexing are used in every digital radio transmission system. The good news is that most of the time you never have to think about it becausethe radios handle it for you.

Multiplexing helps transmission by arranging for transmitters to take turns and to distinguish themselves based on frequency, but it doesn't concern itself with the content of what's being said. This is where data protocols come in. Just as you saw how data protocols made wired networking possible, you'll see them come into play here as well. To make sure the message is clear, it's common to use a data protocol on top of using multiplexing. For example, Bluetooth, ZigBee, and WiFi are nothing more than data networking protocols layered on top of a radio signal. All three of them could just as easily be implemented on a wired network (and, in a sense, WiFi is: it uses the same TCP/IP layer that Ethernet uses). The principles of these protocols are no different than those of wired networks, which makes it possible to understand wireless data transmission even if you're not a radio engineer. Remember the principles and troubleshooting methods you used when dealing with wired networks, because you'll use them again in wireless projects. The methods mentioned here are just new tools in your troubleshooting toolkit. You'll need them in the projects that follow.

Radio Transmitters, Receivers, and Transceivers

How do you know whether to choose a radio transmitter-receiver pair, or a pair of transceivers? The simplest answer is that if you need feedback from the device to which you're transmitting, then you need a transceiver. Most of the time, it's simplest to use transceivers. In fact, as transceivers have become cheaper to make (and therefore sell), transmit-receive pairs are getting harder to find.

There are many different kinds of data transceivers available. The simplest digital radio transceivers on the market connect directly to the serial transmit and receive pins of your microcontroller. Any serial data you send out the transmit line goes directly out as a radio signal. Any pulses received by the transceiver are sent into your microcontroller's receive line. They're simple to connect, but you have to manage the whole conversation yourself. If the receiving transceiver misses a bit of data, you'll get a garbled message. Any nearby radio device in the same frequency range can affect the quality of reception. As long as you're working with just two radios and no interference, transceivers like this do a decent job. However, this is seldom the case.

Nowadays, most transceivers on the market implement networking protocols, handling the conversation management for you. The Bluetooth modem in Chapter 2 ignored signals from other radios that it wasn't associated with, and handled error-checking for you. The XBee radios you'll use in the next project will do the same, and much more, which you'll see in Chapter 7. They require you to learn a bit more in terms of networking protocols, but the benefits you gain make them well worth that minor cost.

The biggest difference between networked radios and simple transceivers is that every device on a network has an address. That means you have to decide which other device you're speaking to, or whether you're speaking to all the other devices on the network.

Because of the complications of network management, all networked radios generally have two modes of operation: command and data modes (as described in Chapter 2). When looking at the communications protocol for a networked radio, one of the first things you'll learn is how to switch from command mode to data mode and back.

X

Project 10

Duplex Radio Transmission

In this example, you'll connect an RF transceiver and a potentiometer to the microcontroller. Each microcontroller will send a signal to the other when its potentiometer changes by more than 10 points. When either one receives a message, it will light up an LED to indicate that it got a message. Each device also has an LED for local feedback as well.

The RF transceivers used in this project implement the 802.15.4 wireless networking protocol on which ZigBee is based. In this example, you won't actually use any of the benefits of ZigBee, and few of the 802.15.4 benefits. 802.15.4 and ZigBee are designed to allow many different objects to communicate in a flexible networking scheme. Each radio has an address, and every time it sends a message, it has to specify the address to which to send. It can also send a broadcast message, addressed to every other radio in range—you'll see more of that in Chapter 7. For now, you'll give each of your two radios the other's address so they can pass messages back and forth.

There are many things that can go wrong with wireless transmission, and as radio transmissions are not detectable without a working radio, it can be difficult to troubleshoot. Because of that, you're going to build this project in stages. First, you'll communicate with the radio module itself serially, in order to set its local address and destination address. Then, you'll write a program to make the microcontroller send messages when the potentiometer changes, and to listen for the message to come through on a second radio attached to your personal computer. Finally, you'll make two microcontrollers talk to each other using the radios.

In this example, you won't actually use any of the features of ZigBee or the 802.15.4 protocol. Those protocols are designed to allow many different devices to communicate in a multitiered networking scheme. Each radio has an address, and every time it sends a message, it has to specify the address to which to send. It can also send a broadcast message, addressed to every other radio in range—you'll see how to send broadcast messages in Chapter 7. For now,

MATERIALS

» **2 solderless breadboards**
» **1 USB-to-XBee adapter**
» **2 Arduinos** Arduino Fio models are a nice alternative designed to work with XBees
» **2 Digi XBee 802.15.4 RF modules**
» **2 Arduino wireless shields**
   If you choose not to use wireless shields or Arduino Fios, you can use the parts below to connect the XBees to the Arduinos:
» **2 3.3V regulators**
» **2 1µF capacitors**
» **2 10µF capacitors**
» **2 XBee breakout boards**
» **4 rows of 0.1-inch header pins**
» **4 2mm female header rows**
» **6 LEDs**
» **2 potentiometers**

you'll give each of your two radios the other's address so they can pass messages back and forth.

⊙ Step 1: Configuring the XBee Modules Serially

The easiest way to connect an XBee to your personal computer is to use an XBee-to-USB serial adapter. Since this book's first edition was published, the popularity of XBees has grown exponentially, and multiple versions are now available (most hobbyist electronics vendors sell a version). They're all basically a USB-to-Serial adapter mounted on a board with pins spaced to fit an XBee radio. The first image in Figure 6-12 shows two options: Adafruit's XBee USB adapter board and Spark Fun's XBee Explorer. Both have LEDs mounted to indicate serial transmit and receive. Adafruit's model also has LEDs to indicate whether the radio is associated with a network or whether it's asleep. The sleep mode indicator LED is attached to pin 13, which goes low when the radio is in sleep mode, and high when it's active. The associate indicator LED is attached to pin 15. When the radio's associated, this LED will blink.

Plug your XBee into the adapter, connect it to your computer's USB port, and open your favorite serial terminal program.

Figure 6-8
XBee breakout board, in various stages. *Bottom:* bare board with necessary headers. *Top right:* finished board. *Top left:* finished board with XBee mounted.

Mounting the XBee Radios on a Breakout Board

The XBee radios have pins spaced 2mm apart, which is too narrow to fit on a breadboard. You can either solder wires to each pin to extend the legs, or you can mount the module on a breakout board. SparkFun has such a board: the Breakout Board for XBee Module (part number BOB-08276). Once you've got the breakout board, solder headers to the inner rows. These will plug into your breadboard. Next, attach the 2mm female headers. The XBee will plug into these, so you may find it useful to align them to the board by plugging them into the XBee first, then plugging it with the headers attached into the board.

The XBee command protocol is particular about how you terminate commands, expecting that each command is on a line terminated only with a carriage return (\r or ASCII 13). Most serial terminal programs allow you to control what is sent when you hit the Return key, however.

In CoolTerm for OS X and Windows, click the Options button and change the Enter Key Emulation to CR (see Figure 6-10). In PuTTY for Windows and Ubuntu Linux, choose the Terminal Configuration tab, and check "Implicit LF in every CR" (see Figure 6-11).

Once you've configured your serial terminal, open the port and type:

```
+++
```

Don't hit Return or any other key for at least one second afterward. The XBee should respond like so:

```
OK
```

This step is similar to the Bluetooth modem in Chapter 2, where you typed $$$ to enter command mode. The XBee is using an AT-style command set, and the +++ puts it into command mode. The one-second pause after this string is called the guard time. If you do nothing, the module will drop out of command mode after 10 seconds. So, if you're reading this while typing, you may need to type +++ again before the next step.

Choosing Which XBee Radios to Buy

Digi makes several variations on the XBee module, and picking the right one can be confusing. The point-to-multipoint modules are the most basic, featuring the ability to send directed messages or broadcast messages to any radio in the network. They form star networks, as described in Chapter 3, and are the easiest to set up. The mesh modules include the ability to form multi-tier mesh networks, but they are more complex to set up and operate. Robert Faludi's excellent book Building Wireless Sensor Networks (O'Reilly) covers the mesh network radios in depth. For most hobbyist projects, though, a mesh network is overkill, so point-to-multipoint radios are used in this book.

The basic model, the XBee 802.15.4 low-power modules, are the cheapest and have a nominal transmission range of about 300m. The XBee-PRO 802.15.4 extended range models have a longer range of about 1 mile (in practice, I've never gotten more than a quarter-mile), but they consume more power. Both the low-power and the PRO models can be used interchangeably for this book's projects.

The Digi radios have several antenna options. Only two options, the wire antenna or the chip antenna, require no extra parts, so I recommend them for these projects.

Their model numbers are:

Digi XBee 802.15.4 low-power module: XB24-AWI-001 or XB24-ACI-001

Digi XBee-PRO 802.15.4 extended range module: XBP24-AWI-001 or XBP24-ACI-001

Figure 6-9. XBee 802.15.4 modules. XBee low-power module with chip antenna on the left, and XBee-PRO extended range module with wire antenna on the right.
Pictures courtesy of Digi International.

Once you get the OK response, set the XBee's address. The XBee protocol uses either 16-bit or 64-bit long addresses, so there are two parts to the address: the high word and the low word (in computer memory, two or more bytes used for a single value are sometimes referred to as a word). For this project, you'll use 16-bit addressing and, therefore, get to choose your own address. You'll need only the low word of the address to do this. Type:

ATMY1234\r

(Remember that \r indicates you should press Enter or Return.) To confirm that you set it, type:

ATMY\r

The module should respond:

1234

Next, set the XBee's destination address (the address to which it will send messages). Make sure you're in command mode (+++), then type ATDL\r.

You'll likely get this:

0

The default destination address on these modules is 0. The destination address is two words long, so to see the high word, type:

ATDH\r

Figure 6-10
CoolTerm options menu. To use
CoolTerm to configure Digi radios (XBee
and otherwise), set Enter Key Emulation
to CR.

Figure 6-11
PuTTY Terminal Configuration menu.
To use PuTTY to configure Digi radios
(XBee and otherwise), choose "Implicit
LF in every CR."

This pair of commands can also be used to set the
destination address:

ATDL5678\r
ATDH0\r

These radios also have a group, or Personal Area Network
(PAN) ID. All radios with the same PAN ID can talk to each
other and ignore radios with a different PAN ID. Set the
PAN ID for your radio like so:

ATID1111\r

The XBee will respond to this command, like all
commands, with:

OK

Make sure to add WR after your last command, which
writes the parameters to the radio's memory. That way,
they'll remain the way you want them even after the radio
is powered off. For example:

ATID1111,WR\r

Choosing Which XBee Accessories to Buy

There are so many XBee accessories on the market now that picking the right parts can be confusing. There are basically three ways you'll use XBees in this book's projects:

XBee to computer via USB-to-XBee adapter. There are many of these available. Figure 6-12 shows two models, the SparkFun XBee Explorer in red, and the XBee USB adapter board—available from Adafruit and Parallax—in blue.

XBee to microcontroller. For this, you can either use a breakout board on which to mount the XBee, or a wireless shield for a regular Arduino. Or, you can use an Arduno Fio, which has an XBee mount built in.

XBee standalone. For this, XBee breakout boards work well, as does the XBee LilyPad board. The XBee LilyPad, the XBee Explorer Regulated (Spark Fun part no. WRL-09132) and the Adafruit XBee adapter kit (Adafruit part no. 126) all feature built-in voltage regulators, so you can use your XBee with a wider range of power supplies.

Figure 6-12. XBee accessories. Clockwise from top left: XBee USB adapter, XBee Explorer, Arduino Fio, Arduino wireless shield, XBee LilyPad.

Once you've configured one of your radios, disconnect your serial terminal program and unplug the board from your computer. Next, remove the XBee from the circuit, insert the second one, and configure it using the same procedure. Don't set a radio's destination address to the same value of its source address, or it will only talk to itself! You can use any 16-bit address for your radios. Here's a typical configuration for two radios that will talk to each other (don't forget to add the WR to the last command):

	ATMY	ATDL	ATDH	ATID
Radio 1	1234	5678	0	1111
Radio 2	5678	1234	0	1111

You can combine commands on the same line by separating them with commas. For example, to get both words of a module's source address, type:

```
ATDL, DH\r
```

The module will respond with both words at once. Likewise, to set both destination words and then make the module write them to its memory—so that it saves the address when it's turned off—type:

```
ATDL5678, DH0, WR\r
```

The module will respond to all three commands at once:

```
OK OK OK
X
```

Figure 6-13
To keep track of the radios, label them with a piece of tape. You'll be switching them between the USB-to-Serial adapter and the microcontroller a few times, and it's easy to lose track of which is which.

A. Serial Switch set to Micro (to the left)

Arduino Wireless Shield

Several companies now make wireless shields for Arduino that can work for this project. The original Arduino shield for XBees used in the first edition of this book has been substantially redesigned. Now called the Arduino wireless shield (because other radio devices with the same footprint can also work on this shield), it has a few nice features, such as a prototyping area, an optional microSD card slot (you'll see an SD card example later in the book), and a serial select switch to allow you to change the XBee's serial pin connections.

When the wireless shield's serial select switch is set to "Micro," the XBee will be connected to communicate with the ATMega328 microcontroller on the Arduino. When switched to "USB," it will be connected to communicate directly through the USB-to-Serial processor on the Arduino, bypassing the microcontroller. In this position, you can use the Arduino's USB-to-Serial connection to configure your XBees.

When you're programming the Arduino, it's a good idea to remove the XBee so that the radio's serial communications don't interfere with the program upload.

To configure the XBee radio on the shield using your Arduino board as a USB-to-Serial converter, program the Arduino with a blank sketch, just like this:

```
void setup() {
}
void loop() {
}
```

Then switch the serial select switch to USB. Open a serial terminal connection to the Arduino board's serial port, and send commands as shown in "Step 1: Configuring the XBee Modules Serially." Once you've configured the radio, unplug the XBee from the shield, set the serial select switch back to "Micro," and program your Arduino as usual.

→ Step 2: Programming the Microcontroller to Use the XBee Module

OK! Now you're ready to get two microcontrollers to talk to each other wirelessly via XBee radios. For now, you're going to leave one XBee connected to your computer via the USB adapter. Once you confirm that's working, you'll replace your computer with a second Arduino and XBee. Figure 6-14 shows a diagram of what's connected to what in this step. In Step 3, you'll remove the personal computer and replace it with a second Arduino.

Figure 6-15 shows an XBee module attached to a regular Arduino using the Arduino wireless shield. Figure 6-16 shows how you'd do it if you were using just an XBee breakout board instead of a shield. Note that the XBee is attached to a 3.3V regulator. The XBee's serial I/O connections are 5-volt tolerant, meaning they can accept 5-volt data signals, but the module operates at 3.3 volts. The Arduino Uno and newer models have a more robust 3.3V regulator that can power the XBee, but it doesn't hurt to add a dedicated one, as shown here.

Once your module is connected, it's time to program the microcontroller to send data through the XBee. In this program, the microcontroller will configure the XBee's destination address on startup, and then send an analog reading when the reading on analog pin 0 changes significantly.

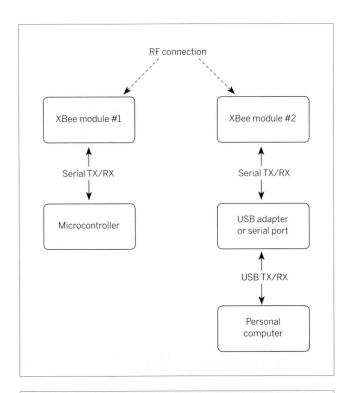

At right, above
Figure 6-14
XBee #1 is connected to the microcontroller. XBee #2 is connected via USB or serial to the PC. This enables a wireless link between the PC and the microcontroller.

At right, below
Figure 6-15
Arduino and wireless shield with potentiometer attached to analog pin 0. This circuit is the same as the one shown in Figure 6-16, but it's without the LED on pin 9. The LEDs attached to the XBee are built into the shield.

Figure 6-16

Top: XBee connected to an Arduino. If you don't want to use a shield, you can connect the two with just a breakout board. Note that this circuit assumes you have a bare breakout board with no voltage regulator. If you use Spark Fun's XBee Explorer Regulated (part no. WRL-09132) or Adafruit's XBee adapter kit (part no. 126), you won't need the voltage regulator because those two boards have built-in 3.3V regulators.

At left: Circuit diagram for Arduino-XBee connection.

Make It   First, give the I/O pins names, and set up some variables for tracking the change in the potentiometer.

```
const int sensorPin = A0;      // input sensor
const int analogLed = 3;       // LED that changes brightness w/incoming value
const int threshold = 10;      // threshold for sensor's change

int lastSensorReading = 0;     // previous state of the sensor

String inputString = "";
```

▶▶ Next, in the setup() method, configure serial transmission, set the modes on the I/O pin, and configure the XBee's destination address.

```
void setup() {
  // configure serial communications:
  Serial.begin(9600);

  // configure output pin:
  pinMode (analogLed, OUTPUT);

  // set XBee's destination address:
  setDestination();
  // blink the TX LED indicating that the main program's about to start:
  blink(analogLed, 3);
}
```

▶▶ The XBee configuration, handled by the setDestination() method, looks just like what you did earlier, only now you're instructing the microcontroller to do it.

```
void setDestination() {
  // put the radio in command mode:
  Serial.print("+++");
  // wait for the radio to respond with "OK\r"
  char thisByte = 0;
  while (thisByte != '\r') {
    if (Serial.available() > 0) {
      thisByte = Serial.read();
    }
  }

  // set the destination address, using 16-bit addressing.
  // if you're using two radios, one radio's destination
  // should be the other radio's MY address, and vice versa:
  Serial.print("ATDH0, DL5678\r");
  // set my address using 16-bit addressing:
  Serial.print("ATMY1234\r");
  // set the PAN ID. If you're working in a place where many people
  // are using XBees, you should set your own PAN ID distinct
  // from other projects.
  Serial.print("ATID1111\r");
  // put the radio in data mode:
  Serial.print("ATCN\r");
}
```

> ▶▶ Change the destination address to that of the radio you're attaching to your personal computer, not the one that's attached to your microcontroller.

▶▶ The blink() method is just like ones you've seen previously in this book. It blinks an LED to indicate that setup is over.

```
void blink(int thisPin, int howManyTimes) {
  //    Blink the LED:
  for (int blinks=0; blinks< howManyTimes; blinks++) {
    digitalWrite(thisPin, HIGH);
    delay(200);
    digitalWrite(thisPin, LOW);
    delay(200);
  }
}
```

▶▶ The main loop handles incoming serial data, reads the potentiometer, and sends out da if there's a sufficient change in the potentiometer's reading.

```
void loop() {
  // listen for incoming serial data:
  if (Serial.available() > 0) {
    handleSerial();
  }

  // listen to the potentiometer:
  int sensorValue = readSensor();

  // if there's something to send, send it:
  if (sensorValue > 0) {
    Serial.println(sensorValue, DEC);
  }
}
```

▶▶ Two other methods are called from the loop: handleSerial(), which listens for strings of ASCII numerals and converts them to bytes in order to set the brightness of the LED on the PWM output; and readSensor(), which reads the potentiometer and checks to see whether the change on it is high enough to send the new value out via radio. Here are those methods.

```
void handleSerial() {
  char inByte = Serial.read();

   // save only ASCII numeric characters (ASCII 0 - 9):
  if (isDigit(inByte)){
    inputString = inputString + inByte;
  }

  // if you get an ASCII newline:
  if (inByte == '\n') {
    // convert the string to a number:
    int brightness = inputString.toInt();
   // set the analog output LED:
    analogWrite(analogLed, brightness);
    // clear the input string for the
    // next value:
    inputString = "";
    Serial.print(brightness);
  }
}

int readSensor() {
  int result = analogRead(sensorPin);
```

»

Continued from previous page.

Continued from previous page.

NOTE: You should disconnect the XBee's receive and transmit connections to the microcontroller while programming (if you're using the Arduino wireless shield, use the serial select switch). The serial communications with the XBee can interfere with the serial communications with the programming computer. Once the microcontroller's programmed, you can re-connect the transmit and receive lines.

```
// look for a change from the last reading
// that's greater than the threshold:
if (abs(result - lastSensorReading) > threshold) {
  result = result/4;
  lastSensorReading = result;
} else {
 // if the change isn't significant, return 0:
 result = 0;
 }
 return result;
}
```

In the main loop, notice that you're not using any AT commands. That's because the XBee goes back into data mode (called idle mode in the XBee user's guide) automatically when you issue the ATCN command in the setDestination() method.

Remember, in data mode, any bytes sent to an AT-style modem go through as-is. The only exception to this rule is that if the string +++ is received, the modem switches to command mode. This behavior is the same as that of the Bluetooth module from Chapter 2, as well as almost any device that implements this kind of protocol. It's great because it means that once you're in data mode, you can send data with no extra commands, letting the radio itself handle all the error corrections for you.

Once you've programmed the microcontroller, set the des-tination address on the computer's XBee to the address of the microcontroller's radio. (If you did this in the earlier step, you shouldn't need to do it again.) Then, turn the potentiometer on the microcontroller. You should get a message like this in your serial terminal window:

120

The actual number will change as you turn the potenti-ometer. It might overwrite itself in the serial window— depending on your serial terminal application—because you're not sending a newline character. Congratulations! You've made your first wireless transceiver link. Keep turning the potentiometer until you're bored, then move on to Step 3.

X

→ Step 3: Two-Way Wireless Communication Between Microcontrollers

This step is simple. All you have to do is replace the computer in the previous step with a second micro-controller. Connect an Arduino to your second XBee module, as shown in Figure 6-16, or use a wireless shield. The program for both microcontrollers will be almost identical to each other; only the destination address of the XBee radio will be different. This program will both send and receive data over the modules. Turning the potentiometer causes it to send a number to the other microcontroller. When the microcontroller receives a number in the serial port, it uses it to set the brightness of an LED on pin 3.

First, connect the second XBee module to the second microcontroller. Then, program both microcontrollers with the previous program, making sure to set the destination addresses as noted in the program.

When you've programmed both modules, power them on and turn the potentiometer several times. As you turn the potenti-ometer, the LED on pin 3 of the other module should fade up and down. Now you've got the capability for duplex wireless communication between two microcontrollers. This opens up all kinds of possibilitiesfor interaction.

X

Wireless and Mobile

Now that you're able to communicate wirelessly, you might want to make your microcontroller mobile as well. To do this, all you have to do is power it from a battery. There's a simple way to do this for the standard Arduino boards, and there are a few models of Arduinos—and some derivative models—that are designed for mobile battery-powered use.

The simplest option is to connect a battery to the power input terminals, as shown in Figure 6-17. The Vin pin (Voltage input) can take from 6-15V input (the Arduino Uno will run off lower voltage—I've run one off 3.7V—but it's not always reliable). You can either plug into the ground and Vin pins, or make a plug adapter and plug into the power plug.

Figure 6-17
Arduino module powered by a 9V battery.

Figure 6-19
LilyPad Arduino Simple, with the LiPo battery connector. *Photo courtesy of Spark Fun.*

The Arduino Fio is great for XBee projects. It has a socket for an XBee and a battery connector for 3.7V Lithium Polymer batteries, as shown in Figure 6-18. The mini-USB jack on the Fio doesn't actually communicate with the microcontroller—it just charges the battery. To program the Fio, you either need an FTDI-style USB adapter, as described in Chapter 2, or you can program it wirelessly over the XBee. Programming the Fio wirelessly requires an understanding of XBees, so it's a good idea to program it using a wire first. For more on Fio programming, see http://arduino.cc/en/Main/ArduinoBoard-FioProgramming.

The LilyPad Arduinos are all made for use in clothing and soft goods. They're also programmed using an FTDI-style serial adapter. There are a couple LilyPad power adapters that take LiPo batteries. The LilyPad Arduino Simple has a jack so you can add a LiPo battery right to the board (see Figure 6-19).

It's a good idea to keep your microcontroller module connected to a power adapter or USB power while programming and debugging. When a battery starts to weaken, your module will operate inconsistently, which can make debugging impossible.

Figure 6-18
Detail of the Fio, showing battery connector and USB-to-Serial adapter connected for programming.

Project 11

Bluetooth Transceivers

In Chapter 2, you learned how to connect a microcontroller to your personal computer using a Bluetooth radio. This example shows you how to connect two microcontrollers using Bluetooth in a similar manner.

As mentioned in Chapter 2, Bluetooth was originally intended as a protocol for replacing the wire between two devices. As a result, it requires a tighter connection between devices than you saw in the preceding XBee project. In that project, a radio sent out a signal with no awareness of whether the receiver got the message, and it could send to a different receiver just by changing the destination address. In contrast, Bluetooth radios must establish a connection before sending data over a given channel, and they must break that connection before starting a conversation with a different radio over that channel. The advantage of Bluetooth is that it's built into many commercial devices today, so it's a convenient way to connect microcontroller projects to personal computers, phones, and more. For all its complications, it offers reliable data transmission.

The modules used here—the Bluetooth Mate radios from Spark Fun—use a radio from Roving Networks. The command set used here was defined by Roving Networks. Other Bluetooth modules from other manufacturers use command sets with a similar style, and they may execute similar functions, but their syntax is not the same. Unfortunately, Bluetooth radio manufacturers haven't set a standard syntax for their devices.

➲ Step 1: The Circuits

Instead of pairing a Bluetooth radio with your computer's Bluetooth radio as you did in Chapter 2, you're going to pair two radios attached to microcontrollers. When you're done, your computer won't be needed.

Because the Bluetooth connection process involves many steps, it's easiest to learn and understand it using a serial terminal program before you start to write code. Even when you are programming, the serial terminal program will be a useful diagnostic tool. You can use the

---

MATERIALS

- » **2 solderless breadboards**
- » **1 USB-to-TTL serial adapter**
- » **2 Arduino modules**
- » **2 Bluetooth Mate modules**
- » **2 potentiometers** or other analog sensors
- » **2 LEDs**
- » **2 220-ohm resistors**
- » **2 10-kilohm resistors**
- » **2 pushbuttons**

USB-to-serial modules shown for Project 4, Negotiating in Bluetooth in Chapter 2, but the goal of this project is to get two microcontrollers talking to each other over Bluetooth with no personal computer in the middle. So, instead of using the USB-to-Serial adapter, you can set up an Arduino board to pass the serial data from your computer to a Bluetooth radio. Then, when you're ready to remove the personal computer in Step 3, you'll just have to change the sketch and make a minor circuit change to remove the PC.

To set up an Arduino as a USB-to-Serial passthrough, first program the Arduino with a blank sketch. The BareMinimum sketch from the Basics examples will do fine. It looks like this:

```
void setup() {
}
void loop() {
}
```

When you upload this sketch, the microcontroller will do nothing, so you can use its connection to the USB-to-serial processor to communicate with the Bluetooth radio. Connect the radio as shown on the left (we'll call it Arduino #1 and radio #1) in Figure 6-20; then, connect it to your computer and using your serial terminal program, open a serial connection to it at 115200 bits per second.

For the moment, you'll use the second Arduino just to send a simple message so you can see things are working. Connect it to the second Bluetooth Mate using the circuit shown at right in Figure 6-20 (we'll call it Arduino #2 and radio #2). Eventually, they will both be wired this way.

Arduino #1: Bluetooth module is communicating with the PC through the USB-to-serial processor

Arduino #2: Bluetooth module is communicating with Arduino's processor

Figure 6-20
The Arduino module on the left is used as a USB-to-Serial adapter for a Bluetooth Mate module. Notice how RX is attached to RX and TX to TX. That's because the Bluetooth Mate is actually talking to the PC through the USB-to-Serial adapter, not the Arduino's main processor, so the serial connections are reversed. When you want the Bluetooth module to talk to the Arduino's main processor, you'll swap these two connections, as shown at right.

Program Arduino #2 using a basic serial sketch, as follows:

```
void setup() {
    Serial.begin(115200);
}

void loop() {
    Serial.println("Hello Bluetooth!");
}
```

When you open a Bluetooth connection to this radio, you'll see the following message over and over:

```
Hello Bluetooth!
Hello Bluetooth!
Hello Bluetooth!
```

→ Step 2: Getting to Know the Commands

The Bluetooth Mate radios use a serial command set for command and configuration, which has two modes—command mode and data mode—just like the XBee radios. When you first power up a Bluetooth Mate and connect to its serial interface (using Arduino #1 in Figure 6-20, for example), it's in data mode. To see that it's alive, type: $$$. It will respond:

```
CMD\r
```

All of the radio's responses will be followed by a carriage return, as shown here. All of your input commands should be followed by a carriage return (press Enter or Return).

Once you're in command mode, you can get some basic information about the radio by typing D, just as you did in Chapter 2. You'll get the radio's status, which includes its address:

```
***Settings***

BTA=000666112233
BTName=FireFly-7256
Baudrt(SW4)=115K
Parity=None
Mode  =Slav
Authen=0
Encryp=0
PinCod=1234
Bonded=0
Rem=NONE SET
```

The first line beginning with BTA= is the radio's address in hexadecimal notation. Write down this address or copy it to a text document—you'll need it in a moment. Next, check its connection status by typing GK\r. It will respond like so:

```
0
```

When it's connected and you do this, it will respond with 1 instead.

Now you want to see which other radios are available. Type the following (the capital letter i):

```
I\r
```

The radio will respond with a list of radios, as it did in Chapter 2:

```
Found 2
442A60F61837,Tom Igoe...s MacBook Air,38010C
000666481ADF,RN42-1FDF,1F00
Inquiry Done
```

You can see that each device has a different address, name, and device code. You can get a list of only the ones with a particular address code by typing:

```
IN 0,001F00\r
```

This is handy when you want only the other Bluetooth Mates in the area. As you might have guessed, the device code is 001F00. The IN command also eliminates the text names, so you can get just the addresses and device codes.

Now that you have the address of your other Bluetooth radio (which should have shown in the lists above, if you have it plugged into the other Arduino), you can connect to it like so:

```
C, 000666481ADF\r
```

Replace 000666481ADF with the address of the radio attached to Arduino #2. Radio #1 will respond:

```
TRYING
```

Once it makes a good connection, the green connect light on both Bluetooth Mates should come on, the radios will shift automatically to data mode, and you should see the message from Arduino #2 as follows:

```
Hello Bluetooth!
Hello Bluetooth!
Hello Bluetooth!
```

The connection goes both ways, of course. Anything you type in the serial terminal window gets sent to Arduino #2. It's not programmed to respond, though, so you won't see anything come back from it. When you're ready to close the connection, you first have to get back into command mode by typing:

```
$$$\r
```

The radio will give you a CMD again, after which you type:

```
K,
```

The connection will be broken, and you'll see:

```
KILL
```

There are other status commands as well, but these ones are most important at first.

X

Step 3: Connecting Two Bluetooth Radios

Now that you've gotthe basics of connecting and disconnecting, it's time to get the microcontrollers to do it. For this step, you'll connect via the same physical setup, adding in a few extra parts. You'll work on Arduino #2 instead of Arduino #1. For now, leave the latter wired up as a USB-to-Serial converter for the Bluetooth radio. Also leave the serial terminal to it open, so you can see what happens.

First, get the Bluetooth addresses for both of your radios. You already wrote down one. Replace it with the second radio in your Serial-to-USB circuit, and follow the same steps to get that radio's address as well. While you're getting the addresses, make one extra configuration on both radios, as follows:

SO,BT\r

This sets the status string to BT, so that when the radios connect or disconnect, they'll send a string to let you know, like this:

BTCONNECT\r

or:

BTDISCONNECT\r

Next, add a potentiometer and pushbutton, as shown in Figure 6-21. Just like the XBee example, it's got a potentiometer attached to the analog pin so that you can send its values. You can use any analog sensor on pin A0. The pushbutton will make or break the connection between the two radios. This is a big difference between the XBees and the Bluetooth radios—the latter have to be paired before they can communicate.

NOTE: It's a good idea to to remove your Bluetooth Mate while programming the Arduino boards, just as you've had to for other serial devices.

When the pushbutton is pressed for the first time, the following program connects to another Bluetooth Mate with a set address. When it connects, it sends its potentiometer value as an ASCII string, terminated by a carriage return.

Just like the XBee example, this program also looks for incoming ASCII strings and converts them to use as a PWM value to dim an LED on pin 3. It will take advantage of the TextFinder library that you saw in Chapter 4. If you haven't already installed it, do so now using the instructions from that chapter.

▸▸ First, here are the constants and variables for this program.

▸▸ Change this to the address of the other radio.

```
/*
  Bluetooth Analog Duplex sender
  Context: Arduino
 */
#include <TextFinder.h>

const int sensorPin = A0;         // analog input sensor
const int analogLed = 3;          // LED that changes brightness
const int threshold = 20;         // threshold for sensor's change
const int debounceInterval = 15;  // used to smooth out pushbutton readings
const int connectButton = 2;      // the pushbutton for connecting
int lastButtonState = 0;          // previous state of the pushbutton
int lastSensorReading = 0;        // previous state of the sensor
long lastReadingTime = 0;         // previous time you read the sensor

// address of the remote BT radio. Replace with the address
// of your remote radio
String remoteAddress = "112233445566";
String messageString = "";        // messages coming in serial port

boolean connected = false;        // whether you're connected or not
boolean commandMode = false;      // whether you're in command or data mode

TextFinder finder(Serial);        // for searching the serial input
```

Figure 6-21
Bluetooth Mate radio attached to
an Arduino. This circuit is similar
to the XBee microcontroller circuit
discussed earlier. The pushbutton will
connect or disconnect the two radios.

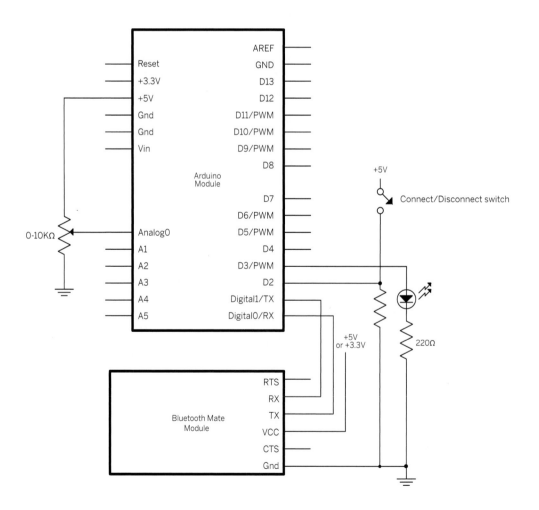

▶▶ The setup() method sets the states of the pins, initializes serial, and blinks an LED, as usual.

```
void setup() {
  // configure serial communications:
  Serial.begin(115200);

  // configure output pins:
  pinMode (analogLed, OUTPUT);

  // blink the TX LED indicating that
  // the main program's about to start:
  blink(analogLed, 3);
}
```

▶▶ The main loop listens for incoming serial data and checks to see whether the button's been pushed. If so, it connects or disconnects as appropriate. If the radios are connected, it reads the analog input and sends it out if there's been a significant change.

```
void loop() {
  // read incoming serial and parse it:
  handleSerial();

  // check to see if the pushbutton's pressed:
  boolean buttonPushed = buttonRead(connectButton);

  // if the button's just pressed:
  if (buttonPushed) {
    // if the client's connected, disconnect:
    if (connected) {
      BTDisconnect();
    } // if the client's disconnected, try to connect:
    else {
      BTConnect();
    }
  }
  // if connected, take sensor readings:
  if (connected) {
    // note the current time in milliseconds:
    long currentTime = millis();
    // if enough time has passed since the last reading:
    if (currentTime - lastReadingTime > debounceInterval) {
      // read the analog sensor, divide by 4 to get a 0-255 range:
      int sensorValue = analogRead(A0)/4;
      // if there's a significant difference between the
      // current sensor reading and the last, send it out:
      if (abs(sensorValue - lastSensorReading) > threshold) {
        Serial.println(sensorValue, DEC);
      }
      // update the last reading time
      // and last sensor reading:
      lastReadingTime = currentTime;
      lastSensorReading = sensorValue;
    }
  }
}
```

The blink() method is the same as
it was in the earlier XBee example.

```
void blink(int thisPin, int howManyTimes) {
  for (int i=0; i< howManyTimes; i++) {
    digitalWrite(thisPin, HIGH);
    delay(200);
    digitalWrite(thisPin, LOW);
    delay(200);
  }
}
```

The buttonRead() method will look
familiar, too,—it's the same one from
the pong clients in Chapter 5.

```
// this method reads the button to see if it's just changed
// from low to high, and debounces the button in case of
// electrical noise:

boolean buttonRead(int thisButton) {
  boolean result = false;
  // temporary state of the button:
  int currentState = digitalRead(thisButton);
  // final state of the button:
  int buttonState = lastButtonState;
  // get the current time to time the debounce interval:
  long lastDebounceTime = millis();

  while ((millis() - lastDebounceTime) < debounceInterval) {
    // read the state of the switch into a local variable:
    currentState = digitalRead(thisButton);

    // If the pushbutton changed due to noise:
    if (currentState != buttonState) {
      // reset the debouncing timer
      lastDebounceTime = millis();
    }

    // whatever the reading is at, it's been there for longer
    // than the debounce delay, so take it as the actual current state:
    buttonState = currentState;
  }
  // if the button's changed and it's high:
  if(buttonState != lastButtonState && buttonState == HIGH) {
    result = true;
  }

  // save the current state for next time:
  lastButtonState = buttonState;
  return result;
}
```

Because there's a dedicated connection between the two radios, you need to keep track of the connection status. When a new connection is made, the Bluetooth Mates send a serial message before dropping into data mode, thanks to your last configuration change. The serial message looks like this:

```
BTCONNECT\r
```

When the connection's broken, it sends this message and stays in command mode:

```
BTDISCONNECT\r
```

While trying to connect, the Mate sends:

```
TRYING\r
```

You can ignore the TRYING message because it'll always be followed by CONNECT or—if the Mate doesn't succeed in connecting—it sends:

```
CONNECT failed\r
```

Look for these to come in and use them to track the connection status. The Bluetooth Mates drop into data mode immediately after sending either of these two messages, so they're a handy way to keep track of the mode as well. The BTConnect(), BTDisconnect(), and handleSerial() methods use these strings to do their work, as follows.

BTConnect() checks the command/data mode status, then tries to make a connection. If the attempt fails, it stays in command mode.

```
void BTConnect() {
  // if in data mode, send $$$
  if (!commandMode) {
    Serial.print("$$$");
    // wait for a response:
    if (finder.find("CMD")) {
      commandMode = true;
    }
  }
  // once you're in command mode, send the connect command:
  if (commandMode) {
    Serial.print("C," + remoteAddress + "\r");
    // wait for a response:
    finder.find("CONNECT");
    // if the message is "CONNECT failed":
    if (finder.find("failed")) {
      connected = false;
    }
    else {
      connected = true;
      // radio automatically drops into data mode
      // when it connects:
      commandMode = false;
    }
  }
}
```

BTDisconnect() is similar to BTConnect(), but in reverse. It drops into command mode and sends the disconnect message you used earlier.

```
void BTDisconnect() {
  // if in data mode, send $$$
  if (!commandMode) {
    Serial.print("$$$");
    // wait for a response:
    if (finder.find("CMD")) {
      commandMode = true;
    }
  }
  // once you're in command mode,
  // send the disconnect command:
  if (commandMode) {
    // attempt to connect
    Serial.print("K,\r");
    // wait for a successful disconnect message:
    if (finder.find("BTDISCONNECT")) {
      connected = false;
      // radio automatically drops into data mode
      // when it disconnects:
      commandMode = false;
    }
  }
}
```

handleSerial() also looks for text messages, but it doesn't use TextFinder because it needs to be able to see one of three different options. TextFinder makes only one pass through the serial stream, so you can't check for a second string if it doesn't find the first string.

If a valid number is found, this method uses it to set the brightness of the LED on pin 3.

```
void handleSerial() {
  // look for message string
  // if it's BTCONNECT, connected = true;
  // if it's BTDISCONNECT, connected = false;
  // if it's CONNECT failed, connected = false;
  // if it's a number, set the LED
  char inByte = Serial.read();

  // add any ASCII alphanumeric characters
  // to the message string:
  if (isAscii(inByte)) {
    messageString = messageString + inByte;
  }

  // handle CONNECT and DISCONNECT messages:
  if (messageString == "BTDISCONNECT") {
    connected = false;
  }
  if (messageString == "BTCONNECT") {
    connected = true;
  }

  if (connected) {
    // convert the string to a number:
    int brightness = messageString.toInt();
    // set the analog output LED:
```

»

▶ Finally, handleSerial() looks for a carriage return; when it finds one, it clears the messageString in order to get the next message.

Continued from previous page.

```
    if (brightness > 0) {
      analogWrite(analogLed, brightness);
    }
  }

  // if you get an ASCII carriage return:
  if (inByte == '\r') {
    // clear the input string for the
    // next value:
    messageString = "";
  }
}
```

❝ That's the whole program. Run this on your microcontroller, filling in the address of the radio on Arduino #2 for the address in the remoteAddress array above. When you press the button on the first microcontroller, it will make a connection to the second and start sending sensor values through. In the serial terminal, your initial messages should look like this:

BTCONNECT
121
132
83

When you're connected, you can respond as if you were sending your own sensor values, and the microcontroller will fade the LED on pin 3 accordingly. Type:

```
12\r
120\r
255\r
1*
```

The LED should start dim, get brighter, then brightest, then get very dim. You should get four sensor readings in response. Then, when you press the button again, you should get:

BTDISCONNECT

When you've connected and disconnected a few times, you're ready for the final step.

➔ Step 4: Connecting Two Microcontrollers via Bluetooth

If you've been noticing the parallels between the XBee example and this one, you probably know what's coming. Build the same circuit for your second microcontroller, using the second radio by adding the switch and potentiometer, and swapping the serial TX and RX connections. Then change the Bluetooth address in the sketch above to be the address of the first radio, and program the second microcontroller. Then reset both microcontrollers. When you press the button on either one, it will attempt to connect to the other and begin exchanging data. When you press the button on either one a second time, they'll disconnect.

Now that you've got the basics down, you can modify this to handle a variety of situations with Bluetooth radios.
X

❝ Buying Radios

You've seen a few different kinds of wireless modules in this chapter. Though they do the job well, they're not the only options on the market. You should definitely shop around for modules that suit your needs. Here are a few things to consider when choosing your radios.

The wisest thing you can do when buying your radios is to buy them as a set. Matching a transmitter from one company to a receiver from another is asking for headaches. They may say that they operate in the same frequency range, but there's no guarantee. Likewise, trying to hack an analog radio—such as that from a baby monitor or a walkie-talkie—may seem like a cheap and easy solution, but in the end, it'll cost you time and eat your soul. When looking for radios, look for something that can take the serial output of your microcontroller. Most microcontrollers send serial data at TTL levels, with 0V for logic 0 and 3.3V or 5V for logic 1. Converting the output to RS-232 levels is also fairly simple, so radios that can take those signals are good for your purposes.

Consider the data rate you need for your application—more specifically, for the wireless part of it. You may not need high-speed wireless. One common use for wireless communication in the performance world is to get data off the bodies of performers, in order to control MIDI performance devices like samplers and lighting dimmers. You might think that you need your radios to work at MIDI data rates to do this, but you don't. You can send the sensor data from the performers wirelessly at a low data rate to a stationary microcontroller, then have the microcontroller send the data via MIDI at a higher data rate.

Consider the protocols of the devices that you already have at your disposal. For example, if you're building an object to speak to a mobile phone or a laptop computer, and there's only one object involved, consider Bluetooth. Most laptops and many mobile phones already have Bluetooth radios onboard, so you'll need only one radio to do the job. It may take some work to make your object compatible with the commands specific to your existing devices, but if you can concentrate on that instead of on getting the RF transmission consistent, you'll save a lot of time.
X

❝ What About WiFi?

So far, you've seen the most basic serial radios in action in the transmitter-receiver project, and more advanced radios at work in the transceiver projects. If you're thinking about networks of microcontrollers, you're probably wondering whether you can connect your projects to the Internet and to each other using WiFi. You can, but there are complications to consider.

Until recently, WiFi wasn't very common in microcontroller projects for a couple reasons: cost and power. Microcontroller-to-WiFi modules on the market are more expensive than equivalent transceivers implementing other protocols. That's starting to change. Many earlier WiFi modules were also power hungry, but that too is changing.

There are currently a few WiFi solutions on the market. Spark Fun makes the WiFly shield, and Digi just announced WiFi versions of their XBee modules. There's also a forthcoming Arduino WiFi shield, which is designed to be easy to incorporate into an existing Ethernet project with only minor code changes. A short introduction follows.
X

Project 12

Hello WiFi!

Remember the daylight color server you built in Project 6? In this project, you'll rebuild it using an Arduino WiFi shield. You'll see that most of the code and the circuit is exactly the same. It's only the physical communications layer that changes.

MATERIALS

» **1 Arduino WiFi shield**
» **1 Arduino microcontroller module**
» **1 WiFi Ethernet connection to the Internet**
» **3 10-kilohm resistors**
» **3 photocells (light-dependent resistors)**
» **1 solderless breadboard**
» **3 lighting filters**

Making the Connections

The WiFi shield communicates with the Arduino via SPI just like the Ethernet shield, so build the circuit just as you did in Figure 4-4, but replace the Ethernet shield with a WiFi shield.

To make the network connection, you'll need to know the name of the WiFi network you're connecting to (also called SSID), and what type of security it uses. This is the same information you use to connect other wireless devices to your WiFi router. The WiFi shield can connect to open networks or networks secured with WEP (both 40-bit and 128-bit), WPA, or WPA2 encryption. For WPA and WPA2, you'll need the password. For WEP, you'll need the key and the key index. A WEP key is a long string of hexadecimal digits that is used like a password. 40-bit WEP keys are 10 ASCII characters long, and 128-bit WEP keys are 26 characters long. WEP routers can store up to four keys,

NOTE: The WiFi shield can't work with the Arduino Ethernet or Ethernet shield because all three use the same SPI chip select pin.

so the key index indicates which one you're using. Most of the time, you'll use key index 0. Below are some typical examples of WEP and WPA combinations:

WPA network name: noodleNet
WPA password: m30ws3rs!

WEP network name: sandbox
WEP key index: 0
WEP 40-bit key: 1234567890

WEP network name: sandbox
WEP key index: 0
WEP 128-bit key: 1A2B3C4D5E6FDADADEEDFACE10

If you're using a home router, chances are you or a family member set up the wireless router so you know the information. If you're connecting to a school or institutional router, ask your network administrator for the details. Once you have this information, you're ready to start programming.

⚠️ The Arduino WiFi shield, shown in Figure 6-22, is a new product, so its programming interface is subject to change as it develops. For the latest updates on the WiFi shield, the WiFi library, and examples of how to use it, see the Hardware section at http://arduino.cc.

Figure 6-22
Arduino WiFi shield.

Configure It (WPA)

The first thing you need to do is take the network info as described above and put it into variables so you can connect. You'll still need the server and lineLength global variables from the previous RGB server sketch as well.

```
/*
  WiFi RGB Web  Server
  Context: Arduino
 */

#include <SPI.h>
#include <WiFi.h>

char ssid[] = "myNetwork";            // the name of your network
char password[] = "secretpassword"; // the password you're using to connect
int status = WL_IDLE_STATUS;         // the WiFi radio's status


Server server(80);
int lineLength = 0;     // length of the incoming text line
```

▶▶ **Change these to match your own network.**

Configure It (WEP)

If you're using WPA encryption, your configuration variables will look more like the code at right (changes are shown in blue).

```
char ssid[] = "myNetwork";       // the name of your network
char keyIndex = 0;               // WEP networks can have multiple keys.
// the 128-bit WEP key you're using to connect:
char key[] = "FACEDEEDDADA01234567890ABC";
int status = WL_IDLE_STATUS;     // the WiFi radio's status
```

▶▶ **Change these to match your own network. If your router has values for more than one key index, use key index 0.**

▶▶ The setup() looks different from the previous sketch because you're setting up a WiFi connection instead of a wired Ethernet connection. If you get a connection, print out the network name. If you don't, stop the program right there. The WiFi shield uses DHCP by default, so you don't need to do anything in your code to get an address via DHCP.

The remainder of the sketch is identical to the sketch in Project 6. You can copy the rest of the code from there. Because WiFi is also Ethernet, the Client and Server library interfaces are the same, so you can change between Ethernet and WiFi easily.

```
void setup() {
  // initialize serial:
  Serial.begin(9600);

  Serial.println("Attempting to connect to network...");
  // attempt to connect using WPA encryption:
  status = WiFi.begin(ssid, password);

  // or use this to attempt to connect using WEP 128-bit encryption:
  // status = WiFi.begin(ssid, keyIndex, key);

  Serial.print("SSID: ");
  Serial.println(ssid);

  // if you're not connected, stop here:
  if ( status != WL_CONNECTED) {
    Serial.println("Couldn't get a WiFi connection");
    while(true);
  }
}
```

" WiFi Diagnostics

The WiFi shield gives you the ability to make networked projects wireless, but it also gives you a few other useful features for diagnosing the health of your connection. Before you begin a WiFi project, run a few diagnostics to make sure you have a good connection. Like any wireless connection, it's invisible, and it's easy to get lost in trouble-shooting something else when the problem is just that you're not connected.

No matter what WiFi module you're working with, you're likely to run into some troubles when trying to connect your microcontroller. Here are a few common ones to look out for:

If you're working at a school or business where you don't control the WiFi routers, make sure you have all the configuration information in advance, and that it matches what your module can do. Enterprise protocols like WPA2 Enterprise are not available for microcontroller-based modules.

Some public networks use a captive portal, which is an open WiFi network, but you have to sign in through a web page before you can access the wider Internet. These are difficult to handle, because you have to program the microcontroller (not the WiFi module) to make an HTTP call to the captive portal with the login information first. If you can use a network that doesn't use a captive portal, you're better off.

Some WiFi modules, like the Arduino WiFi shield, can't see networks where the SSID is hidden. When possible, make sure your network is publicly visible—even when security is on.

Since you have no interface to get feedback on errors, compare your configuration with that of your laptop, mobile phone, or other device that you can connect successfully.

Here are two quick diagnostic code snippets for the Arduino WiFi shield that may be useful as well: scanning for available networks, and getting the signal strength of the network to which you're attached.

Here's how to scan for available networks:

```
// scan for nearby networks:
byte numSsid = WiFi.scanNetworks();

// print the list of networks seen:
Serial.print("SSID List:");
Serial.println(numSsid);
// print the network number and name
// for each network found:
for (int thisNet = 0; thisNet<numSsid; thisNet++) {
  Serial.print(thisNet);
  Serial.print(") Network: ");
  Serial.println(WiFi.SSID(thisNet));
}
```

Here's how to get the signal strength once you're attached to a network:

```
// print the received signal strength:
long rssi = WiFi.RSSI();
Serial.print("RSSI:");
Serial.println(rssi);
```

Both of these techniques are handy diagnostic tools. Depending on your environment and network setup, your wireless network may not be stable all the time. Likewise, you may want to wrap your whole main loop() in an if statement that checks whether you're still connected to the network, like so:

```
void loop() {
  if ( status == WL_CONNECTED) {
    // do everything here
  } else {
    // let the user know there's no connection
  }
}
X
```

❝❝ Conclusion

Wireless communication involves some significant differences from wired communication. Because of the complications, you can't count on the message getting through like you can with a wired connection, so you have to decide what you want to do about it.

If you opt for the least-expensive solutions, you can just implement a one-way wireless link with transmitter-receiver pairs and send the message again and again, hoping that it's eventually received. If you spend a little more money, you can implement a duplex connection, so that each side can query and acknowledge the other. Nowadays, a duplex connection is the standard, as the cost difference is minimal and the availability of transmitter-receiver pairs is waning. Regardless of which method you choose, you have to prepare for the inevitable noise that comes with a wireless connection. If you're using infrared, incandescent light and heat act as noise; if you're using radio, all kinds of electromagnetic sources act as noise, from microwave ovens to generators to cordless phones. You can write your own error-checking routines but, increasingly, wireless protocols like Bluetooth and ZigBee are making it possible for you to forget about that, because the modules that implement these protocols include their own error correction.

Just as you started learning about networks by working with the simplest one-to-one network in Chapter 2, you began with wireless connections by looking at simple pairs in this chapter. In the next chapter, you'll look at peer-to-peer networks, in which there is no central controller, and each object on the network can talk to any other object. You'll see both Ethernet and wireless examples.

X

▶▶ **Urban Sonar by Kate Hartman, Kati London, and Sai Sriskandarajah**
The jacket contains four ultrasonic sensors and two pulse sensors. A microcontroller in the jacket communicates via Bluetooth to your mobile phone. The personal space bubble, as measured by the sensors, and your changing heart rate, as a result of your changing personal space, paint a portrait of you that is sent over the phone to a visualizer on the Internet.

7

Sessionless Networks

So far, the network connections you've seen in this book have mostly been dedicated connections between two objects. Serial communications involve the control of a serial port; mail, web, and telnet connections involve a network port. In all these cases, there's a device that makes the port available (generally a server), and something that requests access to the port (a client). Project 8, Networked Pong, in Chapter 5 was a classic example of this—in that application, the server handled all the communications between the other devices. In this chapter, you'll learn how to make multiple devices on a network talk to each other directly, or talk to all the other devices at once.

◀◀ **Perform-o-shoes by Andrew Schneider**
The shoes exchange messages with a multimedia computer via XBee radio. When you moonwalk in the shoes, your pace and rhythm controls the playback of music from the computer.

◀⬱ Supplies for Chapter 7

DISTRIBUTOR KEY

- **A** Arduino Store (http://store.arduino.cc/ww)
- **AF** Adafruit (http://adafruit.com)
- **D** Digi-Key (www.digikey.com)
- **F** Farnell (www.farnell.com)
- **J** Jameco (http://jameco.com)
- **MS** Maker SHED (www.makershed.com)
- **P** Pololu (www.pololu.com)
- **PX** Parallax (www.parallax.com)
- **RS** RS (www.rs-online.com)
- **SF** SparkFun (www.sparkfun.com)
- **SS** Seeed Studio (www.seeedstudio.com)

BASIC XBEE BREADBOARD CIRCUIT

Several of the projects in this chapter use XBee radios. In each project, you have the option of using convenience modules like the Arduino wireless shield, Spark Fun's XBee Explorer Regulated, or the LilyPad XBee. If you choose not to use those parts, you can build a basic XBee breadboard circuit. Variations on this circuit are shown in Figures 7-5, 7-6, 7-8, and 7-14. The basic parts for it are listed below.

- » **1 solderless breadboard D** 438-1045-ND, **J** 20723 or 20601, **SF** PRT-00137, **F** 4692810, **AF** 64, **SS** STR101C2M or STR102C2M, **MS** MKKN2
- » **1 Digi XBee 802.15.4 RF module J** 2113375, **SF** WRL-08664, **AF** 128, **F** 1546394, **SS** WLS113A4M, **MS** MKAD14
- » **1 3.3V regulator J** 242115, **D** 576-1134-ND, **SF** COM-00526, **F** 1703357, **RS** 534-3021
- » **1 XBee breakout board J** 32403, **SF** BOB-08276, **AF** 127
- » **2 rows of 0.1-inch header pins J** 103377, **D** A26509-20ND, **SF** PRT-00116, **F** 1593411
- » **2 rows of 2mm female headers J** 2037747, **D** 3M9406-ND, **F** 1776193
- » **1 1µF capacitor J** 94161, **D** P10312-ND, **F** 8126933, **RS** 475-9009
- » **1 10µF capacitor J** 29891, **D** P11212-ND, **F** 1144605, **RS** 715-1638
- » **2 LEDs D** 160-1144-ND or 160-1665-ND, **J** 34761 or 94511, **F** 1015878, **RS** 247-1662 or 826-830, **SF** COM-09592 or COM-09590
- » **2 220-ohm resistors D** 220QBK-ND, **J** 690700, **F** 9337792, **RS** 707-8842

PROJECT 13: Reporting Toxic Chemicals in the Shop

- » **2 Basic XBee breadboard circuits** As described above.
- » **1 5V regulator J** 51262, **D** LM7805CT-ND, **SF** COM-00107, **F** 1860277, **RS** 298-8514
- » **1 9–12V DC power supply** Either a 9V battery or plug-in supply will do. **J** 170245, **SF** TOL-00298, **AF** 63, **F** 636363, **P** 1463
- » **1 Hanwei gas sensor** Hanwei makes a wide range of gas sensors, and many of the retailers in this book carry them. MQ-7 detects carbon monoxide; MQ-3 detects alcohol; MQ-6 detects propane and related gases; MG811 detects carbon dioxide. They all have similar operations, so pick one that you're most interested in. **SF** SEN-08880, SEN-09404, or SEN-09405, **P** 1480, 1634, 1633, 1481, 1482, or 1483, **PX** 605-00007, 605-00008, 605-00009, 605-00010, or 605-00011
- » **1 gas sensor breakout board** The Hanwei sensors have a pin layout that's not friendly to a breadboard, so these boards correct that. Pololu and Spark Fun both make a model. **SF** BOB-08891, **P** 1479 or 1639
- » **1 10-kilohm resistor D** 10KQBK-ND, **J** 29911, **F** 9337687, **RS** 707-8906
- » **1 Arduino Ethernet board A** A000050 Alternatively, an Uno-compatible board (see Chapter 2) with an Ethernet shield will work. **SF** DEV-09026, **J** 2124242, **A** 139, **AF** 201, **F** 1848680
- » **1 Arduino wireless shield** Alternatively, basic XBee breadboard circuit (see above) will work. **A** A000064 or A000065. Alternatives: **SF** WRL-09976, **AF** 126, **F** 1848697, **RS** 696-1670, **SS** WLS114A0P
- » **1 cymbal monkey** The one used here is a Charlie Chimp, ordered from the Aboyd Company (www.aboyd.com), part number ABC 40-1006.

NOTE: If your monkey uses a 3V power supply (such as two D batteries), you won't need the 3.3V regulator. Make sure that there's adequate amperage supplied for the radios. If you connect the circuit as shown and the radios behave erratically, the monkey's motor may be drawing all the power. If so, use a separate power supply for the radio circuit.

- » **1 potentiometer J** 29082, **SF** COM-09939, **F** 350072, **RS** 522-0625
- » **1 TIP120 Darlington NPN transistor D** TIP120-ND, **J** 32993, **F** 9804005
- » **1 1N4004 power diode D** 1N4004-E3 or 23GI-ND, **J** 35992, **F** 9556109, **RS** 628-9029
- » **1 1-kilohm resistor D** 1.0KQBK-ND, **J** 29663, **F** 1735061, **RS** 707-8669

» **1 100µF capacitor J** 158394, **D** P10269-ND,
F 1144642, **RS** 715-1657

PROJECT 14: Relaying Solar Cell Data Wirelessly
» **1 USB-XBee adapter J** 32400, **SF** WRL-08687, **AF** 247,
PX 32400
» **1 Basic XBee breadboard circuit** As described above.
This will be the base for the solar cell circuit
» **1 5V regulator J** 51262, **D** LM7805CT-ND, **SF** COM-
00107, **F** 1860277, **RS** 298-8514
» **3 4700µF electrolytic capacitors J** 199006, **D**
P10237-ND, **F** 1144683, **RS** 711-1526
» **1 MAX8212 voltage monitor** You can order free
samples from Maxim (www.maxim-ic.com).
D MAX8212CPA+-ND, **F** 1610130
» **1 10-kilohm resistor D** 10KQBK-ND, **J** 29911,
F 9337687, **RS** 707-8906
» **3 100-kilohm resistors D** 100KQBK-ND, **J** 29997,
F 9337695, **RS** 707-8940
» **1 4.7-kilohm resistor D** CF14JT4K70CT-ND, **J** 691024,
F 735033, **RS** 707-8693
» **1 1-kilohm resistor D** 1.0KQBK-ND, **J** 29663,
F 1735061, **RS** 707-8669

» **1 2N3906 PNP-type transistor J** 178618,
D 2N3906D26ZCT-ND, **SF** COM-00522, **F** 1459017,
RS 294-328
» **1 solar cell SF** PRT-07840, **P** 1691
» **1 Arduino Ethernet board A** A000050
Alternatively, an Uno-compatible board (see Chapter 2)
with an Ethernet shield will work.
SF DEV-09026, **J** 2124242, **A** 139, **AF** 201, **F** 1848680
» **1 Arduino wireless shield** Alternatively, basic XBee
breadboard circuit (see above) will work.
A A000064 or A000065. Alternatives: **SF** WRL-09976,
AF 126, **F** 1848697, **RS** 696-1670, **SS** WLS114A0P
» **1 9V battery clip D** 2238K-ND, **J** 101470, **SF** PRT-09518,
F 1650675
» **1 9V battery** You can use three or four AA batteries
instead—if you have a battery holder for them. Anything
in the 5–12V range should work.
» **XBee LilyPad** This will be the unit for the relay radio.
Alternatively, an XBee Explorer Regulated, or a Basic
XBee breadboard circuit, as described above, will work.
SF DEV-08937
» **1 XBee Explorer Regulated** This is an alternative to the
XBee LilyPad.
SF WRL-09132

Figure 7-1. New parts for this chapter: **1.** Charley Chimp **2.** 2N3906 transistor **3.** MAX8212 Voltage trigger **4.** Hanwei gas sensors **5.** Gas sensor breakout board **6.** Trimmer potentiometer **7.** Solar cell **8.** Don't forget plenty of male header pins for the breakout boards.

❝ Sessions vs. Messages

So far, most of the communication in this book has involved opening a dedicated connection between two points for the duration of the conversation. This is session-based communication. Sometimes you want to make a network in which objects can talk to each other more freely, switching conversational partners on the fly, or even addressing the whole group if the occasion warrants. For this, you need a more message-based protocol.

Sessions Versus Messages

In Chapter 5, you learned about the Transmission Control Protocol, TCP, which is used for much of the communication on the Internet. To use TCP, your device has to request a connection to another device. The other device opens a network port, and the connection is established. Once the connection is made, information is exchanged; then, the connection is closed. The whole request-connect-converse-disconnect sequence constitutes a session. If you want to talk to multiple devices, you have to open and maintain multiple sessions. Sessions characterize TCP communications.

Not all network communication is session-based. There's another protocol used on the Internet, called the User Datagram Protocol, or UDP. With UDP, you compose a message, give it an address, send it, and forget about it.

Unlike the session-based TCP, UDP communication is all about messages. UDP messages are called datagrams. Each datagram is given a destination address and is sent on its merry way. There is no two-way socket connection between the sender and receiver. It's the receiver's responsibility to decide what to do if some of the datagram packets don't arrive, or if they arrive in the wrong order.

Because UDP doesn't rely on a dedicated one-to-one connection between sender and receiver, it's possible to send a broadcast UDP message that goes to every other object on a given subnet. For example, if your address is 192.168.1.45, and you send a UDP message to 192.168.1.255, everybody on your subnet receives the message. Because this is such a handy thing to do, a special address is reserved for this purpose: 255.255.255.255. This is the limited broadcast address—it goes only to addresses on the same LAN, and does not require you to know your subnet address. This address is useful for tasks such as finding out who's on the subnet.

The advantage of UDP is that data moves faster because there's no error-checking. It's also easier to switch the end device that you're addressing on the fly. The disadvantage is that it's less reliable byte-for-byte, as dropped packets aren't resent. UDP is useful for streams of data where there's a lot of redundant information, like video or audio. If a packet is dropped in a video or audio stream, you may notice a blip, but you can still make sense of the image or sound.

The relationship between TCP and UDP is similar to the relationship between Bluetooth and 802.15.4. Bluetooth devices have to establish a session to each other to communicate, whereas 802.15.4 radios (like the XBee radios in Chapter 6) communicate simply by sending addressed messages out to the network without waiting for a result. Like TCP, Bluetooth is reliable for byte-critical applications, but it's less flexible in its pairings than 802.15.4.
X

🞂🞂 Who's Out There? Broadcast Messages

The first advantage to sessionless protocols like UDP and 802.15.4 is that they allow for broadcasting messages to everyone on the network at once. Although you don't want to do this all the time—because you'd flood the network with messages that not every device needs—it's a handy ability to have when you want to find out who else is on your network. You simply send out a broadcast message asking "Who's there?" and wait for replies.

Querying for Other Devices Using UDP

Arduino's Ethernet library includes the ability to send and receive UDP packets, so you can use it to write a simple sketch that listens for broadcast messages and responds to them. It's useful when you want to make a large number of networked devices all respond at once. You can use Processing to send your broadcast query.

There's no way to send UDP messages using the Processing Network library, but there's a good free UDP library

by Stephane Cousot available from the Processing. org's libraries page at http://processing.org/reference/libraries/#data_protocols. To use it, download it and make a new directory called **udp** in the **libraries** subdirectory of your Processing sketch directory. Then unzip the contents of the download and drop them in the directory you created. After that, restart Processing and you're ready to use the UDP library.

Any Arduino with an Ethernet shield connected to your network will do for this exercise. You don't need any extra hardware other than the shield.

Try It This Processing sketch sends out a broadcast UDP message on port 43770. This is an arbitrary number that's high enough that it's probably not used by other common applications.

It doesn't matter what the IP address or router of the machine running this sketch is, because it uses the special subnet broadcast address: 255.255.255.255.

Unlike session-based messaging, where you wrote and read bytes from a stream like serial communication, UDP messages are all sent with one discrete message, udp.send(), which includes the address and port for sending.

```
/*
  UDP broadcast query sender/receiver
  Context: Processing
 */
// import the UDP library:
import hypermedia.net.*;

UDP udp;        // initialize the UDP object

void setup() {
  udp = new UDP( this, 43770 );  // open a UDP port
  udp.listen( true );            // listen for incoming messages
}

void draw()
{
}

void keyPressed() {
  String ip = "255.255.255.255";   // the remote IP address
  int port = 43770;                // the destination port
  udp.send("Hello!\n", ip, port ); // the message to send
}
```

🞂🞂

The response is stored in an array called data[], and the receive() method in the UDP library prints it out one character at a time.

Continued from previous page.

```
void receive( byte[] data ) {
  // print the incoming data bytes as ASCII characters:
  for(int thisChar=0; thisChar < data.length; thisChar++) {
    print(char(data[thisChar]));
  }
  println();
}
```

Respond To It   Here's an Arduino sketch that listens for UDP messages on the same port and responds in kind. Load it onto an Arduino connected to your network with an Ethernet shield.

▶▶ **Change these to match your own device and network.**

```
/*
  UDP Query Responder
  Context: Arduino
*/

#include <SPI.h>
#include <Ethernet.h>
#include <Udp.h>

// Enter a MAC address and IP address for your controller below.
// The IP address will be dependent on your local network:
byte mac[] = {
  0x00, 0xAA, 0xBB, 0xCC, 0xDE, 0x01 };
IPAddress myIp(192,168,1,20);
unsigned int myPort = 43770;      // local port to listen on

// A UDP instance to send and receive packets over UDP
UDP query;

void setup() {
  // start the serial library:
  Serial.begin(9600);

  // start the Ethernet connection:
  Ethernet.begin(mac, myIp);
  // print your address:
  for (int thisByte = 0; thisByte < 4; thisByte++) {
    Serial.print(Ethernet.localIP()[thisByte], DEC);
    Serial.print(".");
  }
  Serial.println();

  query.begin(myPort);
  // give the Ethernet shield a second to initialize:
  delay(1000);
}
```

»

▶▶ The loop() just calls the listen() method, which listens for incoming UDP packets on the same port on which the Processing sketch broadcasts.

Receiving UDP packets is a bit different than receiving TCP packets. Each packet contains a header that tells you who sent it and from what port, kind of like an envelope. When you receive a packet, you have to parse out that data. The parsePacket() method in the Arduino UDP library does just that. You can see it in action here. First, you parsePacket() to separate the header elements from the message body. Then, you read the message body byte-by-byte, just like you've done already with TCP sockets and serial ports.

Continued from opposite page.

```
void loop()
{
  listen(query, myPort);
}

void listen(UDP thisUDP, unsigned int thisPort) {
  // check to see if there's an incoming packet, and
  // parse out the header:
  int messageSize = thisUDP.parsePacket();
  // if there's a payload, parse it all out:
  if (messageSize > 0) {
    Serial.print("message received from: ");
    // get remote address and port:
    IPAddress yourIp = thisUDP.remoteIP();
    unsigned int yourPort = thisUDP.remotePort();
    for (int thisByte = 0; thisByte < 4; thisByte++) {
      Serial.print(yourIp[thisByte], DEC);
      Serial.print(".");
    }
    Serial.println(" on port: " + String(thisPort));
    // send the payload out the serial port:
    while (thisUDP.available() > 0) {
      // read the packet into packetBufffer
      int udpByte = thisUDP.read();
      Serial.write(udpByte);
    }
    sendPacket(thisUDP, Ethernet.localIP(), yourIp, yourPort);
  }
}
```

▶▶ First, you parse the packet to get the header items.

▶▶ Then, you read the rest of the message body.

▶▶ The sendPacket() method sends a response packet to whatever address and port it receives a message from. It includes its IP address in the body of the message as an ASCII string.

You can see that UDP messaging is different than the socket-based messaging over TCP. Each message packet has to be started and ended. When you beginPacket(), the Ethernet controller starts saving bytes to send in its memory; when you endPacket(), it sends them out.

```
void sendPacket(UDP thisUDP, IPAddress thisAddress,
            IPAddress destAddress, unsigned int destPort) {
  // set up a packet to send:
  thisUDP.beginPacket(destAddress, destPort);
  for (int thisByte = 0; thisByte < 4; thisByte++) {
    // send the byte:
    thisUDP.print(thisAddress[thisByte], DEC);
    thisUDP.print(".");
  }
  thisUDP.println("Hi there!");
  thisUDP.endPacket();
}
```

When you've got the Arduino programmed, open a serial connection to it using the Serial Monitor. You should see a message like this in the Arduino Serial Monitor when the Arduino obtains an IP address:

```
192.168.1.20.
```

Next, run the Processing sketch and type any key. In the Arduino Serial Monitor, you should see:

```
message received from: 192.168.1.1. on port: 43770
Hello!
```

The address will be your computer's IP address. In the Processing monitor pane, you should see:

```
Hello!

192.168.1.20.Hi there!
```

The first Hello! is from Processing itself. When you send a broadcast message, it comes back to you as well! The second line is from the Arduino. If you have several Arduinos on your network all running this sketch, you'll get a response from each one of them. In fact, this exercise is most satisfying when you have multiple units responding.

This is a handy routine to add to any Ethernet-based project. You have to provide a separate UDP instance and port to listen on, but the sendPacket() method can work with other programs to get a response from your device when you send broadcast queries.
X

Querying for XBee Radios Using 802.15.4 Broadcast Messages

Just as you can query a subnet to discover devices using UDP, you can also query an XBee personal area net. The XBee radios have a command to query the air for any available radios. This is referred to as node discovery. When given the AT command ATND\r, the XBee radio sends out a broadcast message requesting that all other radios on the same personal area network (PAN) identify themselves. If a radio receives this message, it responds with its source address, serial number, received signal strength, and node identifier.

NOTE: To do node discovery, your radios must have version 10A1 or later of the XBee firmware. See the sidebar "Upgrading the Firmware on XBee Radios" for more details.

For the purposes of this exercise, you'll need at least two XBee radios connected to serial ports on your computer. The easiest way to do this is by using a USB-to-XBee Serial adapter like the XBee Explorer.

Once you've got the radios connected and working, open a serial terminal connection to one of them and issue the following command: +++. Then, wait for the radio to respond with OK. Then type (remember, \r means carriage return, so press Enter or Return instead of \r): ATND\r.

If there are other XBee radios on the same personal area network in range, the radio will respond after a few seconds with a string like this:

```
1234
13A200
400842A7
28
TIGOE1

5678
13A200
400842A9
1E
TIGOE3
```

Each grouping represents a different radio. The first number is the radio's source address (the number you get when you send it the command string ATMY). The second is the high word of the radio's serial number; the third is the low word. The fourth number is a measurement of the radio's received signal strength—in other words, it tells you how strong the radio signal of the query message was when it arrived at the receiving radio. The final line gives the radio's node identifier. This is a text string, up to 20 characters long, that you can enter to name the radio. You didn't use this function in Chapter 6, so your radios may not have node identifier strings. If you want to set the node identifier for further use, type: ATNI myname, WR\r

Replace myname with the name you want.

Broadcast messages are useful for many reasons. However, they should be used sparingly because they create more traffic than is necessary. In the next project, you'll use broadcast messages to reach all the other objects in a small, closed network.

Upgrading the Firmware on XBee Radios

To use the node discover, node identifier, and some of the other XBee AT commands covered in this chapter, your XBee radios need to be upgraded to at least version 10A1. To check the firmware version of your radios, send the following command: ATVR\r. The radio will respond: 10A2. If the number is 10A1 or above (remember, it's in hexadecimal),you're good to go. If not, go to http://www.digi.com/support/kbase/kbaseresultdetl.jsp?kb=125 and download the X-CTU software. Bad news, Mac OS X and Linux users: it only runs on Windows. You can run it under VirtualBox (free), Parallels ($80), VMWare ($80), or Windows using Bootcamp (Mac) or by dual booting (Linux).

Once you've installed the software, launch it. On the PC Settings tab, you'll be able to select the serial port to which your XBee radio is attached. Pick the port and leave the rest of the settings at their defaults. Click the Modem Configuration tab and you'll get to where you can update the firmware. Click the Read button to read the current firmware on your radio. You'll get a screenful of the settings of your radio, similar to that shown in Figure 7-2. The firmware version is shown in the upper-righthand corner. You can pull down that menu to see the latest versions available. Pick the latest one, then check the "Always update firmware" checkbox. Leave the Function Set menu choice set to XBEE 802.15.4. Then click the Write button. The software will download the new firmware to your radio, and you're ready

to go. The X-CTU software is useful to keep around, because it also lets you change and record your radio's settings without having to use the AT commands.

Figure 7-2. The X-CTU Modem Configuration tab.

Project 13

Reporting Toxic Chemicals in the Shop

If you've got a workshop, you'll appreciate this project. By attaching a volatile gas sensor to an XBee radio, you'll be able to sense the concentration of solvents in the air in your shop. When you're working in the shop by yourself, it's common to become insensitive to the fumes of the chemicals with which you're working. This project is an attempt to remedy that issue.

▸▸ **Figure 7-3**
The completed toxic sensor system: sensor, monkey, and network connection.

The sensor values are sent to two other radios. One is attached to an Arduino with an Ethernet shield, which is connected to the Internet as a web server. The other radio is attached to a cymbal-playing toy monkey, located elsewhere in the house, that makes an unholy racket when the organic solvent levels in the shop get high. That way, the rest of the family will know immediately if your shop is toxic. If you don't share my love of monkeys, this circuit can control anything that can be switched on from a transistor Figure 7-3 shows the completed elements of the project. Figure 7-4 shows this project's network.

⚠ This project is designed for demonstration purposes only. The sensor circuit hasn't been calibrated. It won't save your life; it'll just make you a bit more aware of the solvents in your environment. Don't rely on this circuit if you need an accurate measurement of the concentration of organic compounds. Check with your sensor manufacturer to learn how to build a properly calibrated sensor circuit.

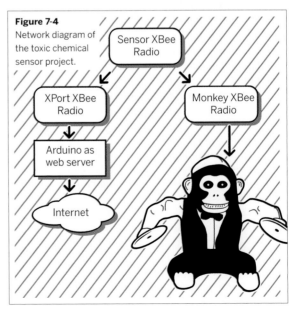

Figure 7-4
Network diagram of the toxic chemical sensor project.

Sensor XBee Radio

XPort XBee Radio

Monkey XBee Radio

Arduino as web server

Internet

MATERIALS

» **1 USB-to-XBee serial adapter**

Sensor Circuit
» **1 solderless breadboard**
» **1 Digi XBee OEM RF module**
» **1 5V regulator**
» **1 3.3V regulator**
» **1 9–12V DC power supply** Either a 9V battery or plug-in supply will do.
» **1 XBee breakout board**
» **2 rows of 0.1-inch header pins**
» **2 2mm female header rows**
» **1 1µF capacitor**
» **1 10µF capacitor**
» **1 Hanwei gas sensor**
» **1 gas sensor breakout board**
» **2 LEDs**
» **2 220-ohm resistors**
» **1 10-kilohm resistor**

Internet Connection Circuit
» **1 Arduino microcontroller module**
» **1 Arduino Ethernet shield**
» **1 Digi XBee OEM RF module**
» **1 Arduino wireless shield** If you use this, you won't need the rest of the parts listed below. They are all for connecting the XBee to your Arduino.
» **1 solderless breadboard**
» **1 3.3V regulator**
» **1 1µF capacitor**
» **1 10µF capacitor**
» **1 XBee breakout board**
» **2 rows of 0.1-inch header pins**
» **2 2mm female header rows**
» **2 LEDs**
» **2 220-ohm resistors**

Cymbal Monkey Circuit
» **1 solderless breadboard**
» **1 Digi XBee OEM RF module**
» **1 cymbal monkey**

NOTE: If your monkey uses a 3V power supply (such as two D batteries), you won't need the 3.3V regulator. Make sure that there's adequate amperage supplied for the radios. If you connect the circuit as shown and the radios behave erratically, the monkey's motor may be drawing all the power. If so, use a separate power supply for the radio circuit.

» **1 3.3V regulator**
» **1 XBee breakout board**
» **2 rows of 0.1-inch header pins**
» **2 2mm female header rows**
» **2 LEDs**
» **2 220-ohm resistors**
» **1 10K trimmer potentiometer**
» **1 TIP120 Darlington NPN transistor**.
» **1 1N4004 power diode**
» **1 1-kilohm resistor**
» **1 100µF capacitor**

You'll be building three separate circuits for this project, so the parts list is broken down for each one. Most of these items are available at retailers other than the ones listed here,.

Radio Settings

Connect one of the radios to the USB-to-XBee serial adapter. You'll use this for configuring the radios only. You've got three radios: the sensor's radio, the monkey's radio, and the Arduino's radio. In Chapter 6 you saw how to configure the radios' addresses, destination addresses, and Personal Area Network (PAN) IDs. In this project, you'll see how to configure some of their I/O pins' behavior. For example, you can configure the digital and analog I/O pins to operate as inputs, outputs, or to turn off. You can also set them to be digital or analog inputs, or digital or pulse-width modulation (PWM) outputs. You can even link an output pin's behavior to the signals it receives from another radio. (If you don't remember how to configure the XBee, see Step 1 in Project 10).

The sensor radio is the center of this project. You'll configure it to read an analog voltage on its first analog input (AD0, pin 20) and broadcast the value that it reads to all other radios on the same PAN. Its settings are as follows:

• ATMY01: Sets the sensor radio's source address.
• ATDLFFFF: Sets the destination address to broadcast to the whole PAN.
• ATID1111: Sets the PAN.
• ATD02: Sets I/O pin 0 (D0) to act as an analog input.
• ATIR64: Sets the analog input sample rate to 100 milliseconds (0x64 hex).
• ATIT5: Sets the radio to gather five samples before sending, so it will send every 500 milliseconds (5 samples x 100 milliseconds sample rate = 500 milliseconds.

The monkey radio will listen for messages on the PAN, and if any radio sends it a packet of data with an analog sensor reading formatted the way it expects, it will set the first pulse width modulation output (PWM0) to the value of the received data. In other words, the monkey radio's PWM0 output will be linked to the sensor radio's analog input. Its settings are as follows:

• ATMY02: Sets the monkey radio's source address.
• ATDL01: Sets the destination address to send only to the sensor radio (address 01). However, this doesn't really matter, as this radio won't be sending.

• ATID1111: Sets the PAN.
• ATP02: Sets PWM pin 0 (P0) to act as a PWM output.
• ATIU1: Sets the radio to send any I/O data packets out the serial port. This is used for debugging purposes only; you won't actually attach anything to this radio's serial port in the final project.
• ATIA01 or ATIAFFFF: Sets the radio to set its PWM outputs using any I/O data packets received from address 01 (the sensor radio's address). If you set this parameter to FFFF, the radio sets its PWM outputs using data received from any radio on the PAN.

The Arduino's radio listens for messages on the PAN and sends them out its serial port to the XBee. This radio's settings are the simplest, as it's doing the least. Its settings are as follows:

• ATMY03: Sets the radio's source address.
• ATDL01: Sets the destination address to send only to the sensor radio (address 01). It doesn't really matter, though,as this radio won't be sending.
• ATID1111: Sets the PAN.
• ATIU1: Sets the radio to send any I/O data packets out the serial port. This data will go to the attached Arduino.

NOTE: **If you want to reset your XBee radios to the factory default settings before configuring for this project, send them the command** ATRE\r.

Here's a summary of all the settings:

Sensor radio	Monkey radio	XPort radio
MY = 01	MY = 02	MY = 03
DL = FFFF	DL = 01	DL = 01
ID = 1111	ID = 1111	ID = 1111
DO = 2	PO = 2	IU = 1
IR = 64	IU = 1	
IT = 5	IA = 01 (or FFFF)	

Make sure to save the configuration to each radio's memory by finishing your commands with WR. You can set the whole configuration line by line or all at once. For example, to set the sensor radio, type:

+++

Then wait for the radio to respond with OK. Next, type the following (the 0 in D02 is the number 0):

```
ATMY1, DLFFFF\r
ATID1111, D02, IR64\r
ATIT5, WR\r
```

For the monkey radio, the configuration is:

```
ATMY2, DL1\r
ATID1111, P02\r
ATIU1, IA1, WR\r
```

And for the Arduino's radio, it's:

```
ATMY3, DL1\r
ATID1111, IU1, WR\r
```

The Circuits

Once you've got the radios configured, set up the circuits for the sensor, the monkey, and the Arduino. In all of these circuits, make sure to include the decoupling capacitors on either side of the voltage regulator—the XBee radios tend to be unreliable without them.

The sensor circuit

The gas sensor takes a 5V supply voltage, so you need a 5V regulator for it, a 3.3V regulator for the XBee, and a power supply that's at least 9V to supply voltage to the circuit. A 9V battery will do, or a 9–12V DC power adapter. Figure 7-5 shows the circuit. The gas sensor's output voltage should stay below 3.3V under the most likely shop conditions, but test it before connecting it to an XBee. Connect and power the circuit, but leave out the wire connecting the sensor's output to the XBee's analog input. Power up the circuit, and let it heat for a minute or two. The circuit takes time to warm up because there's a heater element in the sensor. Measure the voltage between the sensor's output and ground. You should get about 0.1 volt if the air is free of volatile organic compounds (VOCs). While still measuring the voltage, take a bottle of something that has an organic solvent (I used hand sanitizer, which has a lot of alcohol in it), and gently waft the fumes over the sensor. Be careful not to breathe it in yourself. You should get something considerably higher—up to 3 volts. If the voltage exceeds 3.3V, change the fixed resistor until you get results in a range below 3.3V, even when the solvent's fumes are high. Once you've got the sensor reading in an acceptable range, connect its output to the XBee's analog input pin, which is pin 20. Make sure to connect the XBee's voltage reference pin (pin 14) to 3.3 volts as well.

NOTE: Air out your workspace as soon as you've tested the sensor. You don't want to poison yourself making a poison sensor!

To test whether the XBee is reading the sensor correctly, connect its TX pin to the USB-to-XBee serial adapter's TX pin, its RX pin to the adapter's RX pin, and connect their ground lines together. Make sure there's no XBee in the socket when you do this. You're just using the adapter to connect to this circuit. Then plug the adapter into your computer and open a serial connection to it. Type +++ and wait for the OK. Then type ATIS\r. This command forces the XBee to read the analog inputs and return a series of values. You'll get a reply like this:

```
1
200
3FF
```

Don't worry about what the values yet; all that matters is that you're getting something. You'll see the actual values as the project develops later.

The monkey circuit

To control the monkey, disconnect the monkey's motor from its switch and connect the motor directly to the circuit shown in Figure 7-6. The monkey's battery pack supplies 3V, which is enough for the XBee radio, so you can power the whole radio circuit from the monkey. Connect leads from the battery pack's power and ground to the board. If your monkey runs on a different voltage, make sure to adapt the circuit accordingly so that your radio circuit is getting at least 3V. Figure 7-7 shows the modifications in the monkey's innards. I used an old telephone cord to wire the monkey to the board.

The cymbal monkey circuit takes the variable output that the radio received and turns it into an on-off switch. The PWM output from the XBee radio controls the base of a TIP120 transistor. The monkey itself has a motor built into it, which is controlled by a TIP120 Darlington transistor in this circuit. When the transistor's base goes high, the motor turns on. When it goes low, the motor turns off. The motor has physical inertia, however, so if the length of the pulse is short and the length of the pause between pulses is long, the motor doesn't turn. When the duty cycle (the ratio of the pulse and the pause) of the pulse width is high enough, the motor starts to turn.

To +9-12V DC supply

7805
+5V Voltage Reg

LD1117-33V
Voltage Reg

Hanwei
MQ-6
Gas Sensor

Xbee Radio

10μF   1μF

10KΩ

220Ω

220Ω

Vcc   AD0 / DIO0
TX   AD1 / DIO1
RX   AD2 / DIO2
DO8   AD3 / DIO3
RESET   RTS / AD6 / DIO6
PWM0 / RSSI   Ass't / AD5 / DIO5
PWM1   Vref
NC   SLP
DTR/DI8   CTS / DIO7
GND   AD4 / DIO4

Figure 7-5
XBee radio connected to a gas sensor. The MQ-6 is shown here, but the same circuit will work for many of the Hanwei sensors. You may have to change the 10K resistor to adjust the output voltage range, however.

The XBee shown on the bread-board below is mounted on a breakout board. The XBee's pins will not fit into a breadboard without the breakout board.

▶▶ Many of the projects in this chapter are made using the LD1117-33V 3.3V voltage regulator. The pins on this regulator are configured differently from the pins on the other regulators used in this book. Check the data sheet for your regulator to be sure you have the pins correct. You should make a habit of checking this because, otherwise, you will damage your regulator or other parts of your circuit.

Figure 7-6
XBee radio connected to a cymbal monkey.

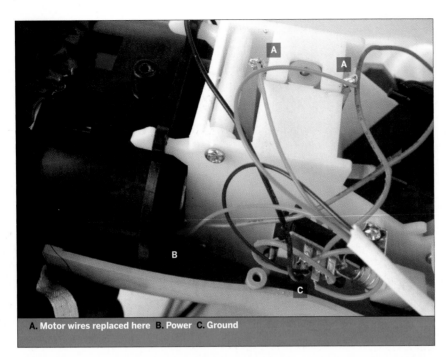

A. Motor wires replaced here   B. Power   C. Ground

Figure 7-7
The insides of the monkey, showing the wiring modifications. Solder the power to the breadboard to the positive terminal of the battery. Solder the ground wire to the ground terminal. Cut the existing motor leads, and add new ones that connect to the breadboard.

To test this circuit, make sure that the sensor radio is working, and turn it on. When the sensor's value is low, the motor should be turned off; when the sensor reads a high concentration of VOCs, the motor will turn on and the monkey will warn you by playing his cymbals. Use the potentiometer to affect the motor's activation threshold. Start with the potentiometer set very high, then slowly turn it down until the motor turns off. At that point, expose the sensor to some alcohol—the motor should turn on again. It should go off when the air around the sensor is clear. If you're unsure whether the motor circuit is working correctly, connect an LED and 220-ohm resistor in series from 3V to the collector of the transistor instead of the motor. The LED should grow brighter when the sensor reading is higher, and dimmer when the sensor reading is lower. The LED has no physical inertia like the motor does, and it consumes less current, so it turns on at a much lower duty cycle.

The Arduino circuit

If you're using an Arduino wireless shield, all you need to do for this project is stack that on top of an Ethernet shield or Arduino Ethernet board, and add them both to your microcontroller. If you're building the circuit yourself, it's shown in Figure 7-8.

The Arduino Ethernet and XBee circuit look a lot like the circuit you used for the duplex radio transmission project in Chapter 6. All you're doing differently is adding an Ethernet

shield. You don't need to connect the XBee's receive line to the Arduino's transmit line because the Arduino's never going to talk to the XBee—it will just listen. You also won't need the LED, or the potentiometer from that project.

When the Arduino receives the message from the gas sensor XBee, it will parse the message, extract the sensor value, and convert it to a voltage. It will act as a web server, so anyone who wants to know the sensor level can check on the Web. In order to make that happen, it's best to break the task into two parts: first, establish that you can read and parse the XBee's messages; then, add the web server component to your code.

Reading the XBee Protocol

So far, you've been able to rely on the XBee radios to do their work without having to understand their message protocol. Now it's time to interpret that protocol. The XBee radios format the readings from their analog-to-digital converters into a packet before they transmit. The format of the packet is explained in the Digi XBee 802.15.4 user's manual. It works like this:

- Byte 1: 0x7E, the start byte value.
- Byte 2–3: Packet size, a 2-byte value. This depends on your other settings.
- Byte 4: API identifier value, a code that says what this response is.

Figure 7-8
XBee radio connected to an Arduino with Ethernet shield.

- Byte 5–6: XBee sender's address.
- Byte 7: Received Signal Strength Indicator (RSSI).
- Byte 8: Broadcast options (not used here).
- Byte 9: Number of samples in the packet (you set it to 5 using the IT command shown earlier).
- Byte 10–11: Which I/O channels are currently being used. This example assumes only one analog channel, AD0, and no digital channels are in use.

- Byte 12–21: 10-bit values, each ADC sample from the sender. Each 10-bit sample represents a voltage from 0 to the XBee's maximum of 3.3V, so a value of 0 means 0 volts, and a value of 1023 means 3.3 volts. Each point of the sensor's value is then 3.3/1024, or 0.003 volts.

Because every packet starts with a constant value, 0x7E (that's decimal value 126), you can start by looking for that value.
X

Read It The following sketch reads bytes and puts them in an array until it sees the value 0x7E. Then, it parses the array to find the sensor's value. To start, you need the message length (or packet length), an array, and a counter to know where you are in the array. Then, you need to set up serial communications.

```
/*
  XBee message reader
  Context: Arduino
*/
const int packetLength = 22;    // XBee data messages will be 22 bytes long
int dataPacket[packetLength];   // array to hold the XBee data
int byteCounter = 0;            // counter for bytes received from the XBee

void setup() {
  // start serial communications:
  Serial.begin(9600);
}
```

The main loop doesn't do much in this sketch; it just calls a method, listenToSerial(), that goes through the bytes and does the work.

```
void loop() {
  // listen for incoming serial data:
  if (Serial.available() > 0) {
    listenToSerial();
  }
}
```

To start with, just read the bytes in and look for the value 0x7E. When you see it, print a linefeed. No matter what, print the byte values separated by a space.

```
void listenToSerial() {
  // read incoming byte:
  int inByte = Serial.read();
  // beginning of a new packet is 0x7E:
  if (inByte == 0x7E ) {
    Serial.println();
  }
  // print the bytes:
  Serial.print(inByte, DEC);
  Serial.print(" ");
}
```

NOTE: In this circuit, you didn't connect the Arduino's transmit pin to the XBee's receive pin on purpose. This way, you can use the serial connection both to receive from the XBee and to send debugging information to the Serial Monitor.

▶▶ When you run this sketch, you'll get a result like what's shown to the right.

Each line that starts with 126 (0x7E in hexadecimal) is a single XBee message. Most of the lines have 22 bytes, corresponding to the packet format described earlier. You may wonder why the first line of the output shown here didn't have a full complement of bytes. It's simply because there's no way to know what byte the XBee is sending when the Arduino first starts listening. That's OK, because the code below will filter out the incomplete packets.

```
201 1 201 1 200 1 197 91
126 0 18 131 0 1 43 0 5 2 0 1 197 1 196 1 198 1 198 1 197 106
126 0 18 131 0 1 43 0 5 2 0 1 197 1 193 1 193 1 192 1 192 125
126 0 18 131 0 1 44 0 5 2 0 1 194 1 194 1 193 1 190 1 190 130
126 0 18 131 0 1 43 0 5 2 0 1 189 1 189 1 191 1 190 1 190 143
126 0 18 131 0 1 43 0 5 2 0 1 190 1 186 1 186 1 186 1 188 156
126 0 18 131 0 1 43 0 5 2 0 1 187 1 187 1 186 1 183 1 183 166
126 0 18 131 0 1 43 0 5 2 0 1 182 1 182 1 184 1 183 1 183 178
126 0 18 131 0 1 43 0 5 2 0 1 181 1 180 1 179 1 179 1 182 191
126 0 18 131 0 1 43 0 5 2 0 1 181 1 181 1 180 1 178 1 177 195
126
```

Refine It

It would be handy to have each packet in its own array. That's how you'll use the global variables you set up before.

Next, change the listenToSerial() method, adding code to parse the dataPacket array; then, empty the array to prepare to receive new data. Replace everything in the if statement with the code shown in blue, and remove the two lines that printed the byte and the space.

This function calls another function, parseData(), that extracts and averages the sensor readings in bytes 12 to 21 of the packet.

```
void listenToSerial() {
  // read incoming byte:
  int inByte = Serial.read();
  // beginning of a new packet is 0x7E:
  if (inByte == 0x7E ) {
    // parse the last packet and get a reading:
    int thisReading = parseData();
    // print the reading:
    Serial.println(thisReading);
    // empty the data array:
    for (int thisByte = 0; thisByte < packetLength; thisByte++) {
      dataPacket[thisByte] = 0;
    }
    // reset the incoming byte counter:
    byteCounter = 0;
  }
  // if the byte counter is less than the data packet length,
  // add this byte to the data array:
  if (byteCounter < packetLength) {
    dataPacket[byteCounter] = inByte;
    // increment the byte counter:
    byteCounter++;
  }
}
```

Parse It This function goes through each complete message packet byte-by-byte, assembling the relevant values from the various bytes. When it's done, it returns the average of the five samples in the packet.

```
int parseData() {
  int adcStart = 11;                    // ADC reading starts at byte 12
  int numSamples = dataPacket[8];       // number of samples in packet
  int total = 0;                        // sum of all the ADC readings

  // read the address. It's a two-byte value, so you
  // add the two bytes as follows:
  int address = dataPacket[5] + dataPacket[4] * 256;

  // read <numSamples> 10-bit analog values, two at a time
  // because each reading is two bytes long:
  for (int thisByte = 0; thisByte < numSamples * 2;  thisByte=thisByte+2) {
    // 10-bit value = high byte * 256 + low byte:
    int thisSample = (dataPacket[thisByte + adcStart] * 256) +
      dataPacket[(thisByte + 1) + adcStart];
    // add the result to the total for averaging later:
    total = total + thisSample;
  }
  // average the result:
  int average = total / numSamples;
  return average;
}
```

When you run this sketch, you should get a value between 0 and 1023 every time you get a message from the sensor XBee radio. Make sure you're getting good values before you move on. If you're not, use the first version of the sketch that prints out the value of each byte to help diagnose the problem. Seeing every byte that you actually receive before you do anything with those bytes is the best way to get at the problem. There are a few common problems to look for:

- Are you getting anything at all? If not, is the sensor XBee transmitting?
- Does each radio have the correct settings? Connect them to a USB-to-XBee serial adapter and check in a serial terminal application.
- Is the receiving radio getting adequate power? Check the voltage between pins 1 and 10 of the receiving XBee. If you're using an older Arduino, and you're relying on the 3.3V output without a regulator, you may not be giving the radio enough power. The earlier Arduinos (before the Uno) didn't supply much amperage from the 3.3V output.

Also consider the advice in Figure 7-9 to make trouble-shooting easier. Once you know you're receiving properly, move on to adding the web server code.

Figure 7-9
Until you're finished troubleshooting, it's a good idea to label your XBee radios so you can tell them apart without having to check their configurations serially.

Serve It Now that you can read the XBee messages, add code to make a web server. The rest of this sketch is much like the RGB server from Chapter 4.

First, include the Ethernet and SPI libraries, and add a few more global variables at the top of your sketch to manage them. New lines are shown in blue.

```
// include SPI and Ethernet libraries:
#include <SPI.h>
#include <Ethernet.h>

// initialize a server instance:
Server server(80);

// Ethernet MAC address and IP address for server:
byte mac[] = {
  0x00, 0xAA, 0xBB, 0xCC, 0xDE, 0x01 };
IPAddress ip(192,168,1,20);

String requestLine = "";        // incoming HTTP request from client

const int packetLength = 22;   // XBee data messages will be 22 bytes long
int dataPacket[packetLength];  // array to hold the XBee data
int byteCounter = 0;           // counter for bytes received from the XBee

// variables for calculating a sensor average:
const int averageInterval = 10 * 1000;  // time between averages, in seconds
long sensorTotal = 0;                   // used for averaging sensor values
float averageVoltage = 0.0;             // the average value, in volts
long lastAverageTime = 0;               // when you last took an average
int readingCount = 0;                   // readings since last average
```

>> Change these to match your own device and network.

▶ Add some code to the main loop to listen for new clients and deal with them, and to average the values from the incoming XBee packets every 10 seconds. New lines are shown in blue.

```
void loop() {

  // listen for incoming serial data:
  if (Serial.available() > 0) {
    listenToSerial();
  }

  // listen for incoming clients:
  Client client = server.available();
  if (client) {
    listenToClient(client);
  }

  // calculate an average of readings after <averageInterval> seconds
  long now = millis();
  if (now - lastAverageTime > averageInterval) {
    averageVoltage = getAverageReading();
    Serial.println(averageVoltage);
  }
}
```

» Just as you had a method earlier to listen to serial data, now you're adding one to listen to incoming HTTP client requests. This method reads the bytes and saves them in a string until it gets a linefeed. It's not actually parsing the lines, except to look for linefeeds or carriage returns. Whenever it gets two linefeeds in a row, it knows the HTTP request is over, and it should respond by calling the makeResponse() routine.

```
// this method listens to requests from an HTTP client:
void listenToClient( Client thisClient) {
  while (thisClient.connected()) {
    if (thisClient.available()) {
      // read in a byte:
      char thisChar = thisClient.read();
      // for any other character, increment the line length:
      requestLine = requestLine + thisChar;
      // if you get a linefeed and the request line
      // has only a newline in it, then the request is over:
      if (thisChar == '\n' && requestLine.length() < 2) {
        // send an HTTP response:
        makeResponse(thisClient);
        break;
      }
      //if you get a newline or carriage return,
      // you're at the end of a line:
      if (thisChar == '\n' || thisChar == '\r') {
        // clear the last line:
        requestLine = "";
      }
    }
  }
  // give the web browser time to receive the data
  delay(1);
  // close the connection:
  thisClient.stop();
}
```

» The makeResponse() method sends an HTTP header and HTML response to the client, then closes the connection. It calls a method, getAverageReading(), which gets the average of all messages in the last 10 seconds and converts them to a voltage:

```
void makeResponse(Client thisClient) {
  // read the current average voltage:
  float thisVoltage = getAverageReading();

  // print the HTTP header:
  thisClient.print("HTTP/1.1 200 OK\n");
  thisClient.print("Content-Type: text/html\n\n");
  // print the HTML document:
  thisClient.print("<html><head><meta http-equiv=\"refresh\"
      content=\"3\">");
  thisClient.println("</head>");
  // if the reading is good, print it:
  if (thisVoltage > 0.0) {
    thisClient.print("<h1>reading = ");
    thisClient.print(thisVoltage);
    thisClient.print(" volts</h1>");
  } // if the reading is not good, print that:
  else {
    thisClient.print("<h1>No reading</h1>");
  }
  thisClient.println("</html>\n\n");
}
```

▶▶ The getAverageReading() is called every 10 seconds from the main loop, as well as every time a client makes a request. It takes the readings from a number of XBee messages and averages them all, as shown at right.

```
float getAverageReading() {
  int thisAverage = sensorTotal / readingCount;
  // convert to a voltage:
  float voltage = 3.3 * (thisAverage / 1024.0);
  // reset the reading count and totals for next time:
  readingCount = 0;
  sensorTotal = 0;
  // save the time you took this average:
  lastAverageTime = millis();
  // return the result:
  return voltage;
}
```

That's the whole sketch. Upload it to your Arduino, then open the Arduino's address in a browser, as shown in Figure 7-10.

Now when you're working in your shop, your family or friends have two ways to know whether the air is getting too foul for you to breathe. They can check the website or listen for the monkey to clang his cymbals.

NOTE: This code doesn't actually translate output voltage into concentration of gases. To do that calculation, you'll need to read the datasheet for the sensor you chose.

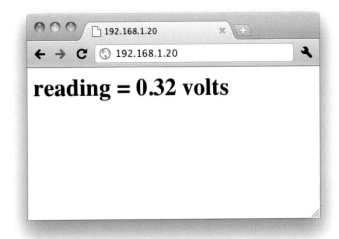

Figure 7-10
The results of the XBee gas server.

" What Happens in the Subnet Stays in the Subnet

You're probably thinking to yourself, "That's great, but how come I'm not sending these messages over the Internet via UDP? Isn't that the message-based protocol that's parallel to the message-based protocol of the XBee radios?" Yes, it is. However, it's wise to be careful with the use of UDP outside your own subnet. If you were to broadcast beyond your own subnet to the rest of the Net, you'd flood the whole network with unnecessary traffic. UDP and message-based protocols are used on the wider Net but, in general, they are used in a directed manner rather than as broadcast messages. For example, video and audio transmissions on the Internet are generally directed UDP streams. The client contacts the server first using an HTTP request, or a similar TCP-based request. The server tells the client to open a port on which to recieve UDP messages, the client opens the port, and the server starts a stream of UDP messages. That's a more polite use of UDP on the wider Internet.

In the next project, you'll use UDP-directed messages from one device to another, as well as XBee-directed messages. X

❝ Directed Messages

The more common way to use sessionless protocols is to send *directed messages* to the object to which you want to speak. You saw this in action already in Chapter 6, when you programmed your microcontrollers to speak to each other using XBee radios. Each radio had a source address (which you read and set using the *ATMY* command) and a destination address (which you read and set using the *ATDL* command). One radio's destination was another's source, and vice versa. Though there were only two radios in that example, you could have included many more radios, and decided which one to address by changing the destination address on the fly.

Sending Directed UDP Datagrams

In the example at the beginning of this chapter, you sent UDP datagrams between Processing and Arduino. The Processing sketch sent a broadcast packet, and the Arduinos sent a directed packet in response, by extracting the sender's address from the packet. As long as you know the address to which you want to send a datagram , it's really that simple.

If you've got more than one Ethernet-connected device (besides your personal computer), you can try this out with the following Processing sketch. It's an expansion on the broadcast sketch, allowing you to send both broadcast and directed messages. Using the same Arduino UDP query responder from before, try it on all the receiving Arduino Ethernet-connected devices. When you type a, all the receiving devices will respond. When you type b or c, only the one with that address will respond.

Send It This sketch, along with the Arduino UDP query responder sketch, is a useful way to test whether your network devices are all working. It's a good idea to do something simple like this to make sure the network connections are good before you try more complex sketches.

```
/*
  UDP directed or broadcast query sender/receiver
  Context: Processing
*/

// import the UDP library:
import hypermedia.net.*;

UDP udp;      // initialize the UDP object

void setup() {
  udp = new UDP( this, 43770 );  // open a UDP port
  udp.listen( true );            // listen for incoming messages
}

void draw()
{
}
```

»

Continued from previous page.

```
void keyPressed() {
  int port = 43770;                          // the destination port
  String message = ", I'm talking to YOU!";  // the message to send
  String ip = "255.255.255.255";             // the remote IP address

  // send to different addresses depending on which key is pressed:
  switch (key) {
  case 'a':                        // broadcast query
    message = "Calling all ducks!\n";
    break;
  case 'b':                        // directed query
    ip = "192.168.1.20";           // the remote IP address
    message =  ip + message;       // the message to send
    break;
  case 'c':                        // directed query
    ip = "192.168.1.30";           // the remote IP address
    message =  ip + message;       // the message to send
    break;
  }

  // send the message to the chosen address:
  udp.send(message, ip, port );
}


void receive( byte[] data ) {
  // print the incoming data bytes as ASCII characters:
  for(int thisChar=0; thisChar < data.length; thisChar++) {
    print(char(data[thisChar]));
  }
  println();
}
```

▶▶ You'll need to change these numbers.

Project 14

Relaying Solar Cell Data Wirelessly

In this project, you'll relay data from a solar cell via two XBee radios and an Arduino to a Processing sketch that graphs the result. This project is similar to the previous one in terms of hardware, but instead of using broadcast messages, you'll relay the data from the first to the second to the third using directed messages. In addition, the Arduino uses directed UDP datagrams to send messages to the Processing program.

This project comes from Gilad Lotan and Angela Pablo (as shown in Figure 7-11), former students at the Interactive Telecommunications Program (ITP) at New York University. The ITP is on the fourth floor of a 12-story building in Manhattan, and it maintains an 80-watt solar panel on the roof. The students wanted to watch how much useful energy the cell receives each day. Because it's used to charge a 12-volt battery, it's useful only when the output voltage is higher than 12V. In order to monitor the cell's output voltage on the fourth floor, Gilad and Angela (advised by a third student, Robert Faludi, who later wrote the book on XBee radios: **Building Wireless Sensor Networks** [O'Reilly]) arranged three XBee radios to relay the signal down the building's stairwell from the roof to the fourth floor. From there, the data went over the local network via an Ethernet processor and onto a SQL database. This example, based on their work, uses a smaller solar cell from Spark Fun, and a Processing program to graph the data instead of a SQL database.

There are three radios in this project: one attached to the solar cell, one relay radio standing on its own, and one attached to the Arduino. Figure 7-12 shows the network.

Radio Settings
The radio settings are similar to the settings from the previous project—the only difference is in the destination addresses. You won't be using broadcast addresses this time. Instead, the solar cell radio (address = 1) will send to the relay radio (address = 2), and that radio will send to the Arduino radio (address = 3). Instead of forming

Sensor radio	Relay radio	XPort radio
MY = 01	MY = 02	MY = 03
DL = 02	DL = 03	DL = 01
ID = 1111	ID = 1111	ID = 1111
DO = 2		
IR = 0x64		
IT = 5		

a broadcast network, they form a chain, extending the distance the message travels. Their settings are shown in the table above. Here are the command strings to set them. For the solar cell radio:

```
ATMY1, DL02\r
ATID1111, D02, IR64\r
ATIT5, WR\r
```

For the relay radio:

```
ATMY2, DL03, ID1111, WR\r
```

And for the Arduino radio:

```
ATMY3, DL01, ID1111, WR\r
```

The Circuits
The solar cell circuit runs off the solar cell itself, because the cell can produce the voltage and amperage in daylight needed to power the radio. The LD1117-33V regulator can take up to 15V input, and the solar panel's maximum output is 12V, so you're safe there. The MAX8212 IC is a voltage trigger. When the input voltage on its threshold pin goes above a level determined by the resistors attached to the circuit, the output pin switches from high to low. This change turns on the 2N3906 transistor. The transistor then allows voltage and current from the solar cell to power the regulator. When the solar cell isn't producing enough voltage, the radio will simply turn off. It's OK if the radio doesn't transmit when the cell is dark because there's nothing worth reporting then anyhow. The two resistors attached to the XBee's AD0 pin form a voltage divider that drops the voltage from the solar cell proportionally to something within the 3.3V range of the radio's analog-to-digital converter. The 4700µF capacitors store the charge from the solar cell like batteries, keeping the radio's supply constant. Figure 7-13 shows the circuit.

Mesh Networking

The XBee radios can be configured as a mesh network using the ZigBee protocol. In a mesh network, some radios function as routers, similar to how the relay radio works in this project. Routers can not only relay messages, they can also store and forward them when the radios at the end node are not on. This provides the whole network with net power saving, as the end nodes can be turned off most of the time. To do this, though, you need different radios: Digi's XBee or XBee-PRO ZigBee OEM modules. For details on how to use these, see Robert Faludi's book Building Wireless Sensor Networks (O'Reilly).

⬆ Figure 7-11
ITP students Gilad Lotan and Angela Pablo with the solar battery pack and XBee monitor radio.

◀◀ Figure 7-12
Network diagram for the solar project.

The Arduino radio circuit is identical to the one used in the previous project. Build it as shown in Figure 7-8.

The relay radio circuit is very simple. It's just a radio on a battery with its transmit pin and receive pin connected. This is how it will relay the messages. Any incoming messages will get sent out the serial transmit pin, then

MATERIALS

» **1 USB-to-XBee serial adapter**

Solar Cell Circuit
» **1 solderless breadboard**
» **1 Digi XBee OEM RF module**
» **1 3.3V regulator**
» **1 XBee breakout board**
» **2 rows of 0.1-inch header pins**
» **2 2mm female header rows**
» **1 1µF capacitor**
» **1 10µF capacitor**
» **3 4700µF electrolytic capacitors**
» **1 MAX8212 voltage monitor**
» **1 10-kilhom resistor**
» **3 100-kilhom resistors**
» **1 4.7-kilhom resistor**
» **1 1-kilhom resistor**
» **1 2N3906 PNP-type transistor**
» **2 LEDs**
» **2 220-ohm resistors**
» **1 solar cell**

Arduino Radio Circuit
This is identical to the Arduino radio circuit in the previous project.
» **1 Arduino microcontroller module**
» **1 Arduino Ethernet shield**
» **1 Digi XBee OEM RF module**
» **1 Arduino wireless shield** If you use this, you won't need the rest of the parts listed below. They are all for connecting the XBee to your Arduino.
» **1 solderless breadboard**
» **1 3.3V regulator**
» **1 1µF capacitor**
» **1 10µF capacitor**
» **1 XBee breakout board**
» **2 rows of 0.1-inch header pins**
» **2 2mm female header rows**
» **2 LEDs**
» **2 220Ω Resistors**

Relay Radio Circuit
This circuit is just an XBee radio by itself, powered by a battery. If you prefer, you can use the USB-to-XBee serial adapter instead of any of the three options below.
» **1 Digi XBee OEM RF module**
» **1 9V battery clip**
» **1 9V battery**

NOTE: If you use either of these, you won't need anything else but the XBee and the battery and a jumper wire to connect TX to RX.

Option 1:

» **1 XBee Explorer Regulated**

Option 2:

» **XBee LilyPad**

Option 3:

» **1 solderless breadboard**
» **1 3.3V regulator**
» **1 XBee breakout board**
» **2 rows of 0.1-inch header pins**
» **2 2mm female header rows**
» **2 LEDs**
» **2 220-ohm resistors**
» **1 10µF capacitor**
» **1 100µF capacitor**

12V solar cell

Figure 7-13
XBee radio attached to a solar cell. To reveal the components and wires beneath, the detail photos show the circuit without the 4700μF capacitors and without the XBee.

+9V battery

LM7833
Voltage Reg

Xbee Radio

In   Out

10µF   1µF

Vcc   AD0 / DIO0
TX   AD1 / DIO1
RX   AD2 / DIO2
DO8   AD3 / DIO3
RESET   RTS / AD6 / DIO6
PWM0 / RSSI   Ass't / AD5 / DIO5
PWM1   Vref
NC   SLP
DTR/DI8   CTS / DIO7
GND   AD4 / DIO4

220Ω

220Ω

◀◀ **Figure 7-14**
The XBee radio relay circuit.

⏷ **Figure 7-15**
Alternative to the relay
circuit: XBee LilyPad with
transmit pin attached to
receive pin.

XBee

back into the receive pin, where they will be sent out again as transmissions. Figure 7-14 shows the circuit. You could also use a LilyPad XBee, XBee Explorer Regulated, or any USB-to-XBee serial adapter. Just tie the transmit and receive pins together, and attach a battery to the voltage input of the regulator.

Once you've got the radios configured and working, you need to program the Arduino to read the incoming XBee packets and relay them to Processing. To do this, you'll use directed UDP datagrams.

Send It The Arduino sketch to read and send directed UDP datagrams is pretty simple. First, you need to include the relevant libraries and set up some global variables as usual. Notice that you're setting up a specific remote IP address and port—it should be the computer's address on which the Processing sketch will run.

▶▶ You'll need to change these numbers.

```
/*
  XBee to UDP
  Context: Arduino
 */

#include <SPI.h>
#include <Ethernet.h>
#include <Udp.h>

// Enter a MAC address and IP address for your controller below.
// The IP address will be dependent on your local network:
byte mac[] = {
  0x00, 0xAA, 0xBB, 0xCC, 0xDE, 0x02 };
IPAddress myIp(192,168,1,20);
IPAddress yourIp(192,168,1,21);

unsigned int myPort = 43770;      // local port to listen on
unsigned int yourPort = 43770;    // remote port to send to

// A UDP instance to send and receive packets over UDP
UDP udp;
```

▶▶ setup() starts the Ethernet connection, initializes serial communications, opens a UDP port, and starts an initial UDP packet for sending.

loop() just listens for serial input When it receives a byte of value 0x7E—indicating the beginning of a new XBee message—it sends the previous datagram using endPacket(), and begins a new packet. Finally, it adds any new byte to the current packet. That's it!

```
void setup() {
  // start the serial library:
  Serial.begin(9600);
  // start the Ethernet connection:
  Ethernet.begin(mac, myIp);
  // start UDP:
  udp.begin(myPort);
  // give the Ethernet shield a second to initialize:
  delay(1000);
  // set up a packet to send:
  udp.beginPacket(yourIp, yourPort);
}

void loop() {
  if (Serial.available()) {
    int serialByte = Serial.read();
    // if you get a 0x7E,
    // send the packet and begin a new one:
    if (serialByte == 0x7E) {
      udp.endPacket();
      // set up a packet to send:
      udp.beginPacket(yourIp, yourPort);
    }
    // send the byte:
    udp.write(serialByte);
  }
}
```

" Graphing the Results

Now that all the hardware is ready, it's time to write a Processing sketch to graph the data. This sketch will receive UDP packets from the Arduino, parse the XBee packets contained therein, and graph the results. You'll notice that the parsing routine looks very similar to the parsing routine you wrote for the Arduino in the previous project. It's useful to compare them to see how the same algorithm is implemented slightly differently in the two programming languages.

X

» First, you need to import the UDP library, initialize it, and write a method to listen for incoming datagrams.

This program will print out strings of numbers that look a lot like the initial ones from the Arduino sketch in the gas sensor project. That's because the datagrams the program is receiving are the same protocol—the XBee protocol for sending analog readings.

```
/*  XBee Packet Reader and Graphing Program
      Reads a packet from an XBee radio via UDP and parses it.
      Graphs the results over time.
     Context: Processing
 */


import hypermedia.net.*;
import processing.serial.*;

UDP udp;                             // define the UDP object
int queryPort = 43770;               // the port number for the device query

void setup() {
  // create a new connection to listen for
  // UDP datagrams on query port:
  udp = new UDP(this, queryPort);

  // listen for incoming packets:
  udp.listen( true );
}

void draw() {
    // nothing happens here.
}


/*
  listen for UDP responses
 */
void receive( byte[] data, String ip, int port ) {
  int[] inString = int(data);      // incoming data converted to string
  print(inString);
  println();
}
```

» Next, add a method to interpret the protocol. Not surprisingly, this looks a lot like the parsePacket() function from the Arduino sketch in the previous project. Add this method to the end of your program.

To call it, replace the print() and println() statements in the receive() method with this:

```
parseData(inString);
```

```
void parseData(int[] thisPacket) {
  // make sure the packet is 22 bytes long first:
  if (thisPacket.length >= 22) {
    int adcStart = 11;                         // ADC reading starts at byte 12
    int numSamples = thisPacket[8];            // number of samples in packet
    int[] adcValues = new int[numSamples];     // array to hold the 5 readings
    int total = 0;                             // sum of all the ADC readings

    // read the address. It's a two-byte value, so you
    // add the two bytes as follows:
    int address = thisPacket[5] + thisPacket[4] * 256;

    // read the received signal strength:
    int signalStrength = thisPacket[6];

    // read <numSamples> 10-bit analog values, two at a time
    // because each reading is two bytes long:
    for (int i = 0; i < numSamples * 2;  i=i+2) {
      // 10-bit value = high byte * 256 + low byte:
      int thisSample = (thisPacket[i + adcStart] * 256) +
        thisPacket[(i + 1) + adcStart];
      // put the result in one of 5 bytes:
      adcValues[i/2] = thisSample;
      // add the result to the total for averaging later:
      total = total + thisSample;
    }
    // average the result:
    int average = total / numSamples;
  }
}
```

» Now that you've got the average reading printing out, add some code to graph the result. For this, you'll need a new global variable before the setup() method that keeps track of where you are horizontally on the graph.

```
int hPos = 0;              // horizontal position on the graph
```

» You'll also need to add a line at the beginning of the setup() method to set the size of the window.

```
// set the window size:
size(400,300);
```

» Now, add a new method, drawGraph(), to the end of the program.

Call this from the parseData() method, replacing the println() statement that prints out the average, like so:

```
// draw a line on the graph:
drawGraph(average);
```

Now when you run the program, it should draw a graph of the sensor readings, updating every time it gets a new datagram.

```
void drawGraph(int thisValue) {
  // draw the line:
  stroke(#4F9FE1);
  // map the given value to the height of the window:
  float graphValue = map(thisValue, 0, 1023, 0, height);
  // determine the line height for the graph:
  float graphLineHeight = height - (graphValue);
  // draw the line:
  line(hPos, height, hPos, graphLineHeight);
  // at the edge of the screen, go back to the beginning:
  if (hPos >= width) {
    hPos = 0;
    //wipe the screen:
    background(0);
  }
  else {
    // increment the horizontal position to draw the next line:
    hPos++;
  }
}
```

» Next, add some code to add a time stamp. First, add a global variable to set the text line height.

```
int lineHeight = 14;        // a variable to set the line height
```

» Add a method to the end of the program, drawReadings() . This will display the date, time, voltage reading, and received signal strength.

Call this method from a few different places in the program; first, at the end of the setup() method:

```
// show the readings text:
drawReadings(0,0);
```

Next, to draw the latest readings, call it at the end of the parseData() method:

```
// draw a line on the graph,
// and the readings:
drawGraph(average);
drawReadings(average, signalStrength);
```

```
void drawReadings(int thisReading, int thisSignalStrength) {
  // set up an array to get the names of the months
  // from their numeric values:
  String[] months = {
    "Jan", "Feb", "Mar", "Apr", "May", "Jun", "Jul", "Aug",
    "Sep", "Oct", "Nov", "Dec"
  };

  // format the date string:
  String date = day() + " " + months[month() -1] + " " + year() ;

  // format the time string
  // all digits are number-formatted as two digits:
  String time = nf(hour(), 2) + ":" + nf(minute(), 2)  + ":" + nf(second(),
2);

  // calculate the voltage from the reading:
  float voltage = thisReading * 3.3 / 1024;

  // choose a position for the text:
  int xPos = 20;
  int yPos = 20;
```

»

» That's the whole program. When it's running, it should look like Figure 7-16.

Continued from previous page.

```
// erase the previous readings:
noStroke();
fill(0);
rect(xPos,yPos, 180, 80);
// change the fill color for the text:
fill(#4F9FE1);
// print the readings:
text(date, xPos, yPos + lineHeight);
text(time, xPos, yPos + (2 * lineHeight));
text("Voltage: " + voltage + "V", xPos, yPos + (3 * lineHeight));
text("Signal Strength: -" + thisSignalStrength + " dBm", xPos,
        yPos + (4 * lineHeight));
}
```

Figure 7-16
The output of the solar graph program. These sensor values were faked with a flashlight! Your actual values may differ.

❝❝ Conclusion

Sessionless networks can be really handy when you're just passing short messages around and don't need a lot of acknowledgment. They involve a lot less work because you don't have to maintain the connection. They also give you a lot more freedom in how many devices you want to address at once.

By comparing the two projects in this chapter, you can see there's not a lot of work to be done to switch from directed messages and broadcast messages when you're making a sessionless network. It's best to default to directed messages when you can, which reduces the traffic for those devices that don't need to get every message.

Now that you've got a good grasp of both session-based and sessionless networks, the next chapters switch direction slightly, covering two other activities of connecting networks to the physical world: location and identification.
X

⤒ **The solar energy display by Gilad Lotan and Angela Pablo**

**The solar panel powering the   ▸▸
display on the roof of NYU's
Tisch School of the Arts**

8

How to Locate (Almost) Anything

By now, you've got a pretty good sense of how to make things talk to each other over networks. You've learned about packets, sockets, datagrams, clients, servers, and all sorts of protocols. Now that you know how to talk, this chapter and the next deal with two common questions: "where am I?", and "who am I talking to?" Location and identification technologies share some important properties. As a result, it's not uncommon to confuse the two, and to think that a location technology can be used to identify a person or an object, and vice versa. These are two different tasks in the physical world, and often in the network environment as well. Systems for determining physical location aren't always very good at determining identity, and identification systems don't do a good job of determining precise location. Likewise, knowing who's talking on a network doesn't always help you to know where the speaker is. In the examples that follow, you'll see methods for determining location and identification in both physical and network environments.

◄◄ **Address 2007 by Mouna Andraos and Sonali Sridhar**

This necklace contains a GPS module. When activated, it displays the distance between the necklace and your home location. *Photo by J. Nordberg.*

Supplies for Chapter 8

This chapter is all about sensing location, so most of the new parts are sensors. You'll also reuse the radios from Chapters 6 and 7.

DISTRIBUTOR KEY
- **A** Arduino Store (http://store.arduino.cc/ww/)
- **AF** Adafruit (http://adafruit.com)
- **D** Digi-Key (www.digikey.com)
- **F** Farnell (http://farnell.com)
- **J** Jameco (http://jameco.com)
- **MS** Maker SHED (www.makershed.com)
- **P** Pololu (www.pololu.com)
- **PX** Parallax (www.parallax.com)
- **RS** RS (www.rs-online.com)
- **SF** Spark Fun (www.sparkfun.com)
- **SS** Seeed Studio (www.seeedstudio.com)

PROJECT 15: INFRARED DISTANCE-RANGER

» **1 Arduino module** An Arduino Uno or something based on the Arduino Uno, but the project should work on other Arduino and Arduino-compatible boards. **D** 1050-1019-ND, **J** 2121105, **SF** DEV-09950, **A** A000046, **AF** 50, **F** 1848687, **RS** 715-4081, **SS** ARD132D2P, **MS** MKSP4

» **1 Sharp GP2Y0A21 infrared ranger** This distance-ranging sensor operates on 5 volts, and outputs a 0–5V signal when it detects objects from 10 to 80cm away. It's one of a family of infrared-ranging sensors from Sharp. Available from many retailers, They are relatively inexpensive and very easy to use. **D** 425-2063-ND, **SF** SEN-00242, **RS** 666-6570, **P** 136

» **1 3-wire JST connector pigtail** This cable allows you to attach the sensor to your microcontroller easily. **SF** SEN-08733

» **1 10µF capacitor J** 29891, **D** P11212-ND, **F** 1144605, **RS** 715-1638

Figure 8-1. New parts for this chapter: **1.** Sharp GP20Y0A21 IR ranger **2.** JST pigtail for IR ranger **3.** Maxbotix LV-EZ1 ultrasonic ranger **4.** EM-406A GPS receiver **5.** Interface cable for EM-406A **6.** LMS303DLH digital compass **7.** LED tactile button **8.** Breakout board for button **9.** ADXL335 accelerometer. Don't forget plenty of male header pins for the breakout boards.

» **3 0.1-inch male header pins J** 103377, **D** A26509-20ND, **SF** PRT-00116, **F** 1593411

PROJECT 16: ULTRASONIC DISTANCE-RANGER

» **1 Arduino module** See description in Project 15. **D** 1050-1019-ND, **J** 2121105, **SF** DEV-09950, **A** A000046, **AF** 50, **F** 1848687, **RS** 715-4081, **SS** ARD132D2P, **MS** MKSP4

» **1 MaxBotix LV-EZ1 ultrasonic ranger** Another distance-ranging sensor, this one uses sonar and has a longer range; 0 to 6.4m. **SF** SEN-00639, **AF** 172, **P** 726, **SS** SEN136B5B

» **3 0.1-inch male header pins J** 103377, **D** A26509-20ND, **SF** PRT-00116, **F** 1593411

PROJECT 17: READING RECEIVED SIGNAL STRENGTH USING XBEE RADIOS

» **2 Digi XBee 802.15.4 RF modules J** 2113375, **SF** WRL-08664, **AF** 128, **F** 1546394, **SS** WLS113A4M, **MS** MKAD14

» **1 USB-XBee adapter J** 32400, **SF** WRL-08687, **AF** 247

» **XBee breakout board** Use the circuit you used for the XBee solar cell or gas monitor in Chapter 7. **J** 32403, **SF** BOB-08276, **AF** 127

PROJECT 18: READING RECEIVED STRENGTH USING BLUETOOTH RADIOS

» **1 Bluetooth Mate module** The same one used in Chapters 2 and 6. **SF** WRL-09358 or WRL-10393

» **1 USB-to-Serial adapter SF** DEV-09718 or DEV-09716, **AF** 70, **A** A000059, **M** MKAD22, **SS** PRO101D2P, **D** TTL-232R-3V3 or TTL-232R-5V

» **1 Bluetooth-enabled personal computer** If your laptop doesn't have a Bluetooth radio, use a USB Bluetooth adapter: **SF** WRL-09434, **F** 1814756

PROJECT 19: READING THE GPS SERIAL PROTOCOL

» **1 solderless breadboard** Just as you've used for previous projects. **D** 438-1045-ND, **J** 20723 or 20601, **SF** PRT-00137, **F** 4692810, **AF** 64, **SS** STR101C2M or STR102C2M, **MS** MKKN2

» **1 EM-406A GPS receiver module S** GPS-00465, **PX** 28146, **AF** 99

» **1 interface cable for GPS module S** GPS-09123, **PX** 805-00013

» **1 Bluetooth Mate module** The same one used in Chapters 2 and 6. **SF** WRL-09358 or WRL-10393

» **12 0.1-inch male header pins J** 103377, **D** A26509-20ND, **SF** PRT-00116, **F** 1593411

» **1 5V regulator J** 51262, **D** LM7805CT-ND, **SF** COM-00107, **F** 1860277, **RS** 298-8514

PROJECT 20: DETERMINING HEADING USING A DIGITAL COMPASS

» **1 solderless breadboard or prototyping shield** The same as used in previous projects. **D** 438-1045-ND, **J** 20723 or 20601, **SF** PRT-00137, **F** 4692810, **AF** 64, **SS** STR101C2M or STR102C2M, **MS** MKKN2

» **1 Arduino module** See description in Project 15. **D** 1050-1019-ND, **J** 2121105, **SF** DEV-09950, **A** A000046, **AF** 50, **F** 1848687, **RS** 715-4081, **SS** ARD132D2P, **MS** MKSP4

» **1 ST Microelectronics LSM303DLH digital compass** Both Pololu and Spark Fun carry a module with this compass. As of this writing, the Pololu model is operable at 5V with no external components, but the Spark Fun one is not. **SF** SEN-09810, **RS** 717-3723, **P** 1250

» **1 LED tactile button** This example uses an LED tactile button and breakout board from Spark Fun, which has a built-in LED, but you can use any pushbutton and LED. **SF** COM-10443 and **SF** BOB-10467

» **1 220-ohm resistor D** 220QBK-ND, **J** 690700, **F** 9337792, **RS** 707-8842

» **1 10-kilohm resistor D** 10KQBK-ND, **J** 29911, **F** 9337687, **RS** 707-8906

» **1 LED** Not needed if you are using the Spark Fun LED tactile button. **D** 160-1144-ND or 160-1665-ND, **J** 34761 or 94511, **F** 1015878, **RS** 247-1662 or 826-830, **SF** COM-09592 or COM-09590

» **13 0.1-inch male header pins J** 103377, **D** A26509-20ND, **SF** PRT-00116, **F** 1593411

PROJECT 21: DETERMINING ATTITUDE USING AN ACCELEROMETER

» **1 solderless breadboard or prototyping shield** The same as used in previous projects. **D** 438-1045-ND, **J** 20723 or 20601, **SF** PRT-00137, **F** 4692810, **AF** 64, **SS** STR101C2M or STR102C2M, **MS** MKKN2

» **1 Arduino module** See description in Project 15. **D** 1050-1019-ND, **J** 2121105, **SF** DEV-09950, **A** A000046, **AF** 50, **F** 1848687, **RS** 715-4081, **SS** ARD132D2P, **MS** MKSP4

» **1 Analog Devices ADXL320 accelerometer** This is a three-axis analog accelerometer, the same one as you used in the balance board client project in Chapter 5. You can also use the accelerometer on your LSM303DLH digital compass from the previous project. **J** 28017, **SF** SEN-00692, **AF** 163, **RS** 726-3738, **P** 1247, **MS** MKPX7

❝❝ Network Location and Physical Location

Locating things is one of the most common tasks people want to achieve with sensor systems. Once you understand the wide range of things that sensors can detect, it's natural to get excited about the freedom this affords. All of a sudden, you don't have to be confined to a chair to interact with computers. You're free to dance, run, jump—and it's still possible for a computer to read your action and respond in some way.

The downside of this freedom is the perception that in a networked world, you can be located anywhere. Ubiquitous surveillance cameras and systems like Wireless E911 (which locates mobile phones on a network), make it seem as though anyone or anything can be located anywhere and at any time—whether you want to be located or not. The reality of location technologies lies somewhere in between these extremes.

Locating things on a network is different than locating things in physical space. As soon as a device is connected to a network, you can get a general idea of its network location using a variety of means—from address lookup to measuring its signal strength—but that doesn't mean that you know its physical location. You just know its relationship to other nodes of the network. You might know that a cell phone is closest to a given cell transmitter tower, or that a computer is connected to a particular WiFi access point. You can use that information along with other data to form a picture of the person using the device. If you know that the cell transmitter tower is less than a mile from you, you'd know that the person with the cell phone is going to reach you soon, and you can act appropriately in response. For many network applications, you don't need to know physical location as much as you need to know relationship to other nodes in the network.

➲ Step 1: Ask a Person

People are really good at locating things. At the physical level, we have a variety of senses to throw at the problem as well as a brain that's wonderful at matching patterns of shapes and determining distances from different sensory clues. At the behavioral level, we've got thousands of patterns that make it easier to determine why you might be looking for something. Computer systems don't have these same advantages, so when you're designing an interactive system to locate things or people, the best tool you have to work with—and the first one you should consider—is the person for whom you're making your system.

Getting a good location starts with cultural and behavioral cues. If you want to know where you are, ask another person near you. In an instant, she's going to sum up all kinds of things—your appearance, your behavior, the setting you're both in, the things you're carrying, and more—in order to give you a reasonably accurate and contextually relevant answer. No amount of technology can do that, because the connection between where you are and why you want to know is seldom explicit in the question. As a result, the best thing you can do when you're designing a locating system is to harness the connection-making talents of the person who will be using that system. Providing him with cues as to where to position himself when he should take action, and what actions he can take, helps eliminate the need for a lot of technology. Asking him to tell your system where things are, or to position them so that the system can easily find them, makes for a more effective system.

For example, imagine you're making an interactive space that responds to the movements of its viewers. This is popular among interactive artists, who often begin by imagining a "body-as-cursor" project, in which the viewer is imagined as a body moving around in the space of the gallery. Some sort of tracking system is needed to determine his position and report it back in two dimensions, like the position of a cursor on a computer screen.

What's missing here is the reason why the viewer might be moving in the first place. If you start by defining what the viewer's doing, and give him cues as to what you expect him to do at each step, you can narrow down the space in which you need to track him. Perhaps you only need to know when he's approaching one of several sculptures in the space so that you can trigger the sculpture to move in response. If you think of the sculptures as nodes in a network, the task gets easier. Instead of tracking the viewer in an undefined two-dimensional space, now all you have to do is determine his proximity to one of several points in the room. Instead of building a tracking system, you can now just place a proximity sensor near each object, look up which he's near, and read how near he is to it. You're using a combination of spatial organization and technology to simplify the task. You can make your job even easier by giving him visual, auditory, and behavioral cues to interact appropriately. He's no longer passive; he's now an active participant in the work.

Or, take a different example: let's say you're designing a mobile phone city-guide application for tourists that relies on knowing the phone's position relative to nearby cell towers to determine the user's position. What do you do when you can't get a reliable signal from the cell towers? Perhaps you ask the tourist to input the address she's at, or the postal code she's in, or some other nearby cue. Then, your program can combine that data with the location based on the last reliable signal it received, and determine a better result. In these cases, and in all location-based systems, it's important to incorporate human talents in the system to make it better.

Step 2: Know the Environment

Before you can determine where you are, you need to determine your environment. For any location, there are several ways to describe it. For example, you could describe a street corner in terms of its address, its latitude and longitude, its postal code, or the businesses nearby. Which of these coordinates you choose depends in part on the technology you have on hand to determine it. If you're making the mobile city guide described earlier, you might use several different ones—the nearest cell transmitter ID, the street address, and the nearby businesses could all work to define the location. In this case, as in many, your job in designing the system is to figure out how to relate one system of coordinates to another in order to give some meaningful information.

Mapping places to coordinate systems is a lot of work, so most map databases are incomplete. Geocoding allows you to look up the latitude and longitude of most any U.S. street address. It doesn't work everywhere in the U.S., and it doesn't work most places outside the U.S. because the data hasn't been gathered and put in the public domain. Geocoding depends on having an accurate database of names mapped to locations. If you don't agree on the names, you're out of luck. The Virtual Terrain Project (www.vterrain.org) has a good list of geocoding resources for the U.S. and international locations at www.vterrain.org/Culture/geocoding.html. Geocoder.net offers a free U.S.-

based lookup at www.geocoder.us, and Worldkit offers an extended version that also looks up international cities: www.worldkit.org/geocoder.

Street addresses are the most common coordinates that are mapped to latitude and longitude, but there are other systems for which it would be useful to have physical coordinates as well. For example, mobile phone cell transmitters all have physical locations. It would be handy to have a database of physical coordinates for those towers. However, cell towers are privately owned by mobile telephone carriers, so detailed data about the tower locations is proprietary, and the data is not in the public domain. Projects such as OpenCellID (www.opencellid.org) attempt to map cell towers by using GPS-equipped mobile phones running custom software. As there are many different mobile phone operating systems, just developing the software to do the job is a huge challenge.

IP addresses don't map exactly to physical addresses because computers can move. Nevertheless, there are several geocoding databases for IP addresses. These work on the assumption that routers don't move a lot, so if you know the physical location of a router, then the devices gaining access to the Net through that router can't be too far away. The accuracy of IP geocoding is limited, but it can help you determine a general area of the world, and sometimes even a neighborhood or city block, where a device on the Internet is located. Of course, IP lookup doesn't work on private IP addresses. In the next chapter, you'll see an example that combines network identity and geocoding.

You can develop your own database relating physical locations to cultural or network locations if the amount of information you need is small, or if you have a large group of people to do the job. But, generally, it's better to rely on existing infrastructures when you can.

Step 3: Acquire and Refine

Once you know where you're going to look, there are two tasks that you have to do continually: acquire a new position, and refine the position's accuracy. Acquisition gives a rough position; it usually starts by identifying which device on a network is the center of activity. In the interactive installation example described earlier, you could acquire a new position by determining that the viewer tripped a sensor near one of the objects in the room. Once you know roughly where he is, you can refine the position by measuring his distance with the proximity sensor attached to the object.

Refining doesn't have to mean getting a more accurate physical position. Sometimes you refine what you know about the context or activity, not the position. When you have a rough idea of where something's happening, you need to know about the activity at that location in order to provide a response. In the interactive installation example, you may never need to know the viewer's physical coordinates in feet and inches (or meters and centimeters). When you know which object he's close to in the room—and whether he's close enough to relate to it—you can make that object respond. You might be changing the graphics on a display when he walks near, or activating an animatronic sculpture as he walks by. In both cases, you don't need to know the precise distance; you just need to know he's close enough to pay attention. Sometimes distance-ranging sensors are used as motion detectors to define general zones of activity rather than to measure distance.

Determining proximity doesn't always give you enough information to take action. Refining can also involve determining the orientation of one object relative to another. For example, if you're giving directions, you need to know which way you're oriented. It's also valuable information when two people or objects are close to each other. You don't want to activate the animatronic sculpture if the viewer has his back to the thing!

X

 # 35 Ways to Find Your Location

At the 2004 O'Reilly Emerging Technology Conference (ETech), interaction designer and writer Chris Heathcote gave an excellent presentation on cultural and technological solutions to finding things, entitled *35 Ways to Find Your Location*. He outlined a number of important factors to keep in mind before you choose tools to do the job. He pointed out that the best way to locate someone or something involves a combination of technological methods and interpretation of cultural and behavioral cues. His list is a handy tool for inspiring solutions when you need to develop a system to find locations. A few of the more popular techniques that Chris listed are:

- Assume: the Earth. Or a smaller domain, but assume that's the largest space you have to look in.
- Use the time.
- Ask someone.
- Association: who or what are you near?
- Proximity to phone boxes, public transport stops, and utility markings.
- Use a map.
- Which cell phone operators are available?
- Public phone operators?
- Phone number syntax?
- Newspapers available?
- Language being spoken?
- Post codes/ZIP codes.
- Street names.
- Street corners/intersections.
- Street numbers.
- Business names.
- Mobile phone location, through triangulation or trilateration.
- Triangulation and trilateration on other radio infrastructures, such as TV, radio, and public WiFi.
- GPS, assisted GPS, WAAS, and other GPS enhancements.
- Landmarks and "littlemarks."
- Dead reckoning.

❝ Determining Distance

Electronic locating systems—like GPS, mobile phone location, and sonar—seem magical at first because there's no visible evidence as to how they work. However, when you break the job down into its components, it becomes relatively straightforward. Most physical location systems are based on one of two methods: measuring the time of a signal's travel from a known location, or measuring its strength at the point of reception. Both methods combine measurements from multiple sources to determine a position in two or three dimensions using trilateration.

For example, a GPS receiver determines its position on the surface of the planet by measuring the time delay of received radio signals from several geosynchronous satellites. Mobile phone location systems function similarly, using the signal from nearby cell towers to determine the phone's position. Systems like Skyhook (www.skyhookwireless.com) use several different systems (WiFi, GPS, and cell tower location) to refine their positional accuracy. Sonar and infrared-ranging sensors work by sending out an acoustic signal (sonar) or an infrared signal (IR rangers), and then measuring the strength of that signal when it's reflected off the target.

Distance ranging techniques can be classified as active or passive. In active systems, the target has a radio, light, or acoustic source on it, and the receiver listens for the signal generated directly by the target. In passive systems, the target doesn't need to have any technology on board. The receiver emits a signal, then listens for the signal reflected back from the target. Mobile phone location is active because it relies on a two-way transmission between the phone and the cell tower. GPS is also active, even though the transmission is one-way, because the signal used to determine location is direct, not reflected. The target is a radio receiver. Sonar and infrared ranging are passive because the signal is reflected off the target, not generated by it.

Sometimes distance ranging is used for acquiring a position; other times, it's used for refining it. In the following examples, the passive distance rangers deliver a measurement of physical distance.

Passive Distance Ranging

Ultrasonic rangers like the MaxBotix LV-EZ1, and infrared rangers like the Sharp GP2Y0A21YK, shown in Figure 8-2, are examples of distance rangers. The MaxBotix sensor sends out an ultrasonic signal and listens for an echo. The Sharp sensor sends out an infrared light beam, and senses the reflection of that beam. These sensors work in a short range only. The Sharp sensor can read about 10cm to 80cm, and the MaxBotix sensor reads from about 0 to 7.5m. Passive sensors like these are handy when you want to measure the distance of a person in a limited space, and you don't want to put any hardware on the person. They're also useful when you're building moving objects that need to know their proximity to other objects in the same space as they move.

X

Project 15

Infrared Distance Ranger Example

The Sharp GP2*xx* series of infrared-rang-ing sensors give a decent measurement of short-range distance by bouncing an infrared light signal off the target, and then measuring the returned brightness. They're very simple to use. Figure 8-2 shows a circuit for a Sharp GP2YOA21 IR ranger, which can detect an object in front of it within about 10cm to 80cm. The sensor requires 5V power, and it outputs an analog voltage from 0 to 5V, depending on the distance to the nearest object in its sensing area.

MATERIALS

» **1 Arduino module**
» **1 Sharp GP2YOA21 IR ranger**
» **1 10µF capacitor**
» **3 male header pins**

The Sharp sensors' outputs are not linear, so if you want to get a linear range, you need to make a graph of the voltage over distance, and do some math. Fortunately, the good folks at Acroname Robotics have done the math for you. For the details, see www.acroname.com/robotics/info/articles/irlinear/irlinear.html. The sensor's datasheet at http://www.sharpsma.com/webfm_send/1208 includes a graph of voltage over the inverse of the distance. It shows a pretty linear relationship between the two from about 10 to 80cm, and the slope of that line is about 27V*cm. You can get a decent approximation of the distance using that.

▶▶ This sketch reads the sensor and converts the results to a voltage. Then, it uses the result explained above to convert the voltage to a distance measured in centimeters.

The conversion formula gives only an approximation, but it's accurate enough for general purposes.

For many applications, though, you don't need the absolute distance, but the relative distance. Is the person nearer or farther away? Has she passed a threshold that should trigger some other interaction? For such applications, you won't need this con-version. You can just use the output of the analogRead() command and choose a value for your threshold by experimentation.

```
/*
   Sharp GP2xx IR ranger reader
   Context: Arduino
*/
void setup() {
  // initialize serial communications at 9600 bps:
  Serial.begin(9600);
}


void loop() {
  int sensorValue = analogRead(A0);
  // convert to a voltage:
  float voltage = map(sensorValue, 0, 5, 0, 1023);

  // the sensor actually gives results that aren't linear.
  // This formula is derived from the datasheet's graph
  // of voltage over 1/distance. The slope of that line
  // is approximately 27:
  float distance = 27.0 /voltage;

  // print the sensor value
  Serial.print(distance);
  Serial.println(" cm");
  // wait 10 milliseconds before the next reading
  delay(10);
}
```

Figure 8-2
The Sharp GP2Y0A21YK IR ranger attached to a microcontroller. The capacitor attached to the body of the sensor smoothes out fluctuations due to the sensor's current load.

Project 16

Ultrasonic Distance Ranger Example

The MaxBotix (www.maxbotix.com) ultrasonic sensors measure distance using a similar method to the Sharp sensors, but theirs have a greater sensing range. Instead of infrared, they send out an ultrasonic signal and wait for the echo. Then they measure the distance based on the time required for the echo to return. These sensors require 5V power (the LV series can operate on 2.5–5V), and return their results via analog, pulse width, or asynchronous serial interface. They're available from MaxBotix, Spark Fun, Adafruit, Pololu, and many of the other retailers listed in this book.

MATERIALS

» 1 Arduino module
» 1 MaxBotix LV-EZ1 ultrasonic ranger
» 3 male header pins or 3 jumper wires

Distance rangers are great for measuring linear distance, but they have a limited conical field of sensitivity, so they're not great for determining location over a large two-dimensional area. The MaxBotix LV-EZ1 sensor, for example, has a cone-shaped field of sensitivity that's about 80-degrees wide (though the sensitivity drops off at the edges) and 6.4 meters from the sensor to the edge of the range. In order to use it to cover a room, you'd need to use several of them and arrange them creatively. Figure 8-3 shows one way to cover a 4m x 4m space using five of the rangers. In this case, you'd need to make sure that no two of the sensors were operating at the same instant, because their signals would interfere with each other. The sensors would have to be activated one after another in sequence. Because each one takes up to 5 milliseconds to return a result, you'd need up to 250 milliseconds to make a complete scan of the space.

Measuring distance top-to-bottom

Measuring distance side-to-side

⏩ This sketch is similar to the infrared ranging sketch in Project 15. It reads the sensor and converts the results to a voltage, then converts that to a distance measured in centimeters. The conversion formula again gives only an approximation.

The MaxBotix sensors can read only every 50 milliseconds, so you need a delay after each read to give the sensor time to stabilize before the next read.

```
/*
MaxBotix LV-EZ1 ultrasonic ranger reader
Context: Arduino
*/
void setup() {
  // initialize serial communications at 9600 bps:
  Serial.begin(9600);
}

void loop() {
  // read the sensor value and convert to a voltage:
  int sensorValue = analogRead(A0);
  float voltage = map(sensorValue, 0, 5, 0, 1023);

  // the sensor's output is about 9.8mV per inch,
  // so multiply by 2.54 to get it in centimeters:
  float distance = voltage * 2.54  / 0.0098;

  // print the sensor value
  Serial.print(distance);
  Serial.println(" cm");
  // wait 50 milliseconds before the next reading
  // so the sensor can stabilize:
  delay(50);
}
```

◀◀ **Figure 8-3**

at left, opposite page
Measuring distance in two dimensions using ultrasonic distance rangers. The square in each drawing is a 4m × 4m floor plan of a room. In order to cover the whole of a rectangular space, you need several sensors placed around the sides of the room.

◀◀ **Figure 8-4**

at right, opposite page
MaxBotix LV-EZ1 ultrasonic sensor connected to an Arduino module.

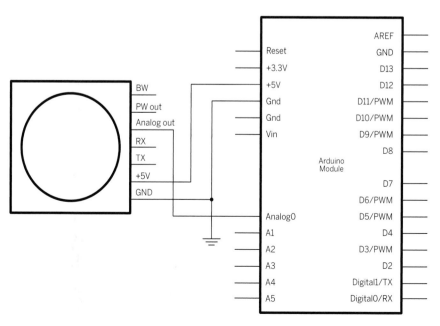

Figure 8-5
Schematic for MaxBotix LV-EZ1 ultrasonic sensor connected to an Arduino module.

❝❝ Active Distance Ranging

The ultrasonic and infrared rangers in the preceding sections are passive distance-sensing systems. Mobile phones and the Global Positioning System (GPS) measure longer distances by using ranging as well. These systems include a radio beacon (the cell tower or GPS satellite) and a radio receiver (the phone or GPS receiver). The receiver determines its distance from the beacon based on the received signal from the beacon. These systems can measure much greater distances on an urban or global scale. The disadvantage of active distance ranging is that you must have a powered device at both ends. You can't measure a person's distance from somewhere using active distance ranging unless you attach a receiver to the person.

GPS and cellular location systems don't actually give you the distance from their radio beacons, just the relative signal strength of the radio signal. Bluetooth, 802.15.4, ZigBee, and WiFi radios all provide data about signal strength as well. In order to relate this to distance, you need to be able to calculate that distance as a function of signal strength. The main function of a GPS receiver is to calculate distances to the GPS satellites based on signal strength, and then determine a position using those distances. The other radio systems mentioned here don't do those calculations for you.

In many applications, though, you don't need to know the distance—you just need to know how relatively near or far one person or object is to another. For example, if you're making a pet door lock that opens in response to the pet, you could imagine a Bluetooth beacon on the pet's collar and a receiver on the door lock. When the signal strength from the pet's collar is strong enough, the door lock opens. In this case, and in others like it, there's no need to know the actual distance.
X

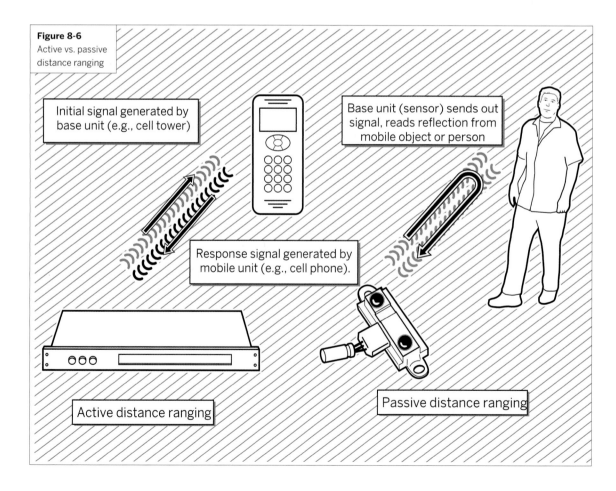

Figure 8-6
Active vs. passive distance ranging

Initial signal generated by base unit (e.g., cell tower)

Base unit (sensor) sends out signal, reads reflection from mobile object or person

Response signal generated by mobile unit (e.g., cell phone).

Active distance ranging

Passive distance ranging

Project 17

Reading Received Signal Strength Using XBee Radios

In the previous chapter, you saw the received signal strength, but you didn't do anything with it. The Processing code that read the solar cell's voltage output parsed the XBee packet for the received signal strength (RSSI). Here's a simpler variation on it that just reads the signal strength. To test it, you can use the same radio settings from Project 14, Relaying Solar Cell Data Wirelessly. Use a USB-to-XBee serial adapter for the receiving circuit, and see Figure 7-5 (the gas sensor circuit) or Figure 7-13 (the solar cell circuit) for circuits that work well as transmitters.

Run this Processing sketch to connect to the receiver radio via the USB-to-XBee serial adapter. When you run this program, you'll get a graphing bar like that shown in Figure 8-7.

```
/*
XBee Signal Strength Reader
Context: Processing

Reads a packet from an XBee radio and parses it.  The packet
should be 22 bytes long. It should be made up of the following:
byte 1:     0x7E, the start byte value
byte 2-3:   packet size, a 2-byte value  (not used here)
byte 4:     API identifier value, a code that says what this response
            is (not used here)
byte 5-6:   Sender's address
byte 7:     RSSI, Received Signal Strength Indicator (not used here)
byte 8:     Broadcast options (not used here)
byte 9:     Number of samples to follow
byte 10-11: Active channels indicator (not used here)
byte 12-21: 5 10-bit values, each ADC samples from the sender
*/
import processing.serial.*;
Serial XBee ;                  // input serial port from the XBee Radio
int[] packet = new int[22];    // with 5 samples, the XBee packet is
                               // 22 bytes long
int byteCounter;               // keeps track of where you are in
                               // the packet
int rssi = 0;                  // received signal strength
int address = 0;               // the sending XBee's address
int lastReading = 0;           // value of the previous incoming byte

void setup () {
  size(320, 480);        // window size

  // get a list of the serial ports:
  println(Serial.list());
  // open the serial port attached to your XBee radio:
  XBee = new Serial(this, Serial.list()[0], 9600);
}
```

»

```
Continued from previous page.

void draw() {
  // if you have new data and it's valid (>0), graph it:
  if ((rssi > 0 ) && (rssi != lastReading)) {
    // set the background:
    background(0);
    // set the bar height and width:
    int rectHeight = rssi;
    int rectWidth = 50;
    // draw the rect:
    stroke(23, 127, 255);
    fill (23, 127, 255);
    rect(width/2 - rectWidth, height-rectHeight, rectWidth, height);
    // write the number:
    text("XBee Radio Signal Strength test", 10, 20);
    text("Received from XBee with address: " + hex(address), 10, 40);

    text ("Received signal strength: -" + rssi + " dBm", 10, 60);
    // save the current byte for next read:
    lastReading = rssi;
  }
}

void serialEvent(Serial XBee ) {
  // read a byte from the port:
  int thisByte = XBee.read();
  // if the byte = 0x7E, the value of a start byte, you have
  // a new packet:
  if (thisByte == 0x7E) {   // start byte
    // parse the previous packet if there's data:
    if (packet[2] > 0) {
      rssi = parseData(packet);
    }
    // reset the byte counter:
    byteCounter = 0;
  }
  // put the current byte into the packet at the current position:
  packet[byteCounter] = thisByte;
  //  increment the byte counter:
  byteCounter++;
}

/*
 Once you've got a packet, you need to extract the useful data.
 This method gets the address of the sender and RSSI.
 */
int parseData(int[] thisPacket) {
  int result = -1;    // if you get no result, -1 will indicate that.

  // make sure you've got enough of a packet to read the data:
  if (thisPacket.length > 6) {
```

»

Continued from opposite page.

```
    // read the address. It's a two-byte value, so you
    // add the two bytes as follows:
    address = thisPacket[5] + thisPacket[4] * 256;
    // get RSSI:
    result = thisPacket[6];
  }
  return result;
}
```

Radio signal strength is measured in decibel-milliwatts (dBm). You might wonder why the signal reads -65dBm. How can the signal strength be negative? The relationship between milliwatts of power and dBm is logarithmic. To get the dBm, take the log of the milliwatts. So, for example, if you receive 1 milliwatt of signal strength, you've got log 1 dBm. Log 1 = 0, so 1 mW = 0 dBm. When the power drops below 1 mW, the dBm drops below 0, like so: 0.5 mW = (log 0.0005) dBm or -3.01 dBm. 0.25mW = (log 0.00025) dBm, or -6.02 dBm.

If logarithms confuse you, just remember that 0 dBm is the maximum transmission power, which means that signal strength is going to start at 0 dBm and go down from there. The minimum signal that the XBee radios you're using here can receive is -92 dBm. Bluetooth radios and WiFi radios typically have a similar range of sensitivity. In a perfect world, with no obstructions to create errors, the relationship between signal strength and distance would be a logarithmic curve.

Figure 8-7
Output of the XBee RSSI test program.

Project 18

Reading Received Signal Strength Using Bluetooth Radios

The Bluetooth modules used in Chapters 2 and 6 can also give you an RSSI reading. To see this, the radio needs to be connected to another Bluetooth radio. The simplest way is to pair your radio with your computer, as shown in Project #4.

Once you've done this, open a serial connection to the radio via Bluetooth. Once you're connected, drop out of data mode into command mode by typing the following:

```
$$$
```

You'll get a CMD prompt from the radio. Next, type L and hit Return. The radio will respond like so:

```
RSSI=ff,ff
RSSI=ff,ff
```

These are the signal strength values of the link, in hexadecimal. FF is the strongest possible value, and 00 is the weakest. The first of the two values is the current link quality; the second is the lowest recorded value so far. As you move the radio closer to or farther from your computer, the values will change just as it did in the XBee example in the preceding project. To turn this off and get back to sending data, type L and hit Return again. Then, type - - - and press Return to leave command mode.

❝❝ The Multipath Effect

The biggest source of error in distance ranging is what's called the multipath effect (see Figure 8-8). When electromagnetic waves radiate, they bounce off things. Your phone may receive multiple signals from a nearby cell tower if, for example, you're positioned near a large obstacle, such as a building. The reflected waves off the building create "phantom" signals that look as real to the receiver as the original signal. This issue makes it impossible for the receiver to calculate the distance from the beacon accurately, that causes degradation in the signal quality of mobile phone reception, as well as errors in locating the phones. For GPS receivers, multipath results in a much wider range of possible locations, as the error means that you can't calculate the position as accurately. It is possible to filter for the reflected signals, but not all radios incorporate such filtering.

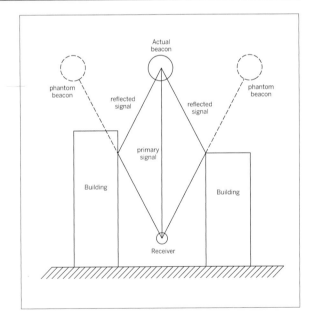

Figure 8-8
The multipath effect. Reflected radio waves create phantom beacons that the receiver can't tell from the real beacon, causing errors in calculating the distance based on signal strength.

" Determining Position Through Trilateration

Distance ranging tells you how far away an object is from your measuring point in one dimension, but it doesn't define the whole position. The distance between your position and the target object determines a circle around your position (or a sphere, if you're measuring in three dimensions). Your object could be anywhere on that circle.

In order to locate it within a two- or three-dimensional space, though, you need to know more than distance. The most common way to do this is by measuring the distance from at least three points. This method is called trilateration. If you measure the object's distance from two points, you get two possible places it could be on a plane, as shown in Figure 8-9. When you add a third circle, you have one distinct point on the plane where your object could be. A similar method, triangulation, uses two known points and calculates the position using the distance between these points; it then uses the angles of the triangle formed by those points and the position you want to know.

The Global Positioning System uses trilateration to determine an object's position. GPS uses a network of satellites circling the globe. The position of each satellite can be determined from its flight path and the current time. Each one is broadcasting its clock signal, and GPS receivers pick up that broadcast. When a receiver has at least three satellites, it can determine a rough position using the time difference between transmission and reception. Most receivers use at least six satellite signals to calculate their position, in order to correct any errors. Cell phone location systems like Wireless E911 calculate a phone's approximate position in a similar fashion, by measuring the distance from multiple cell towers based on the time difference of arrival (TDOA) of signals from those towers.

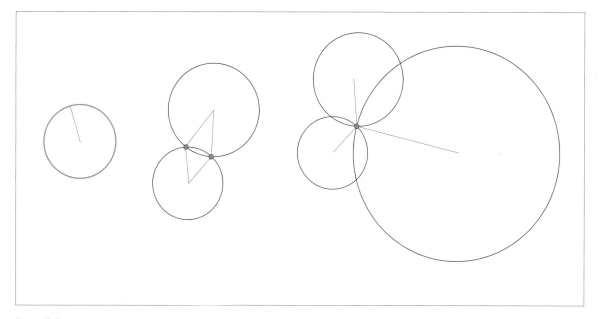

Figure 8-9
Trilateration on a two-dimensional plane. Knowing the distance from one point defines a circle of possible locations. Knowing the distance from two points narrows it to two possible points on the plane. Knowing the distance from three points determines a single point on the plane.

Project 19

Reading the GPS Serial Protocol

The good news is that if you're using GPS, you never have to do trilateration or triangulation calculations—GPS receivers do the work for you. They then give you the position in terms of latitude and longitude. There are several data protocols for GPS receivers, but the most common is the NMEA 0183 protocol established by the National Marine Electronics Association in the United States. Just about all receivers on the market output NMEA 0183, and usually one or two other protocols as well.

NMEA 0183 is a serial protocol that operates at 4800 bits per second, 8 data bits, no parity, and 1 stop bit (4800-8-N-1). Most receivers send this data using either RS-232 or TTL serial levels. The receiver used for this example, a US GlobalSat EM-406a receiver, sends NMEA data at 5V TTL levels.

You're going to connect the GPS receiver to a Bluetooth Mate for this project. Before you do, however, you need to match their data rates by resetting the Bluetooth Mate to 4800bps. To do this, connect your Mate to a USB-to-Serial adapter and open a connection to it in a serial terminal application (like CoolTerm or PuTTY) at 115200 bits per second (see Project 4 in Chapter 2 for more details). First, type: $$$. This command takes the radio out of data mode and puts it in command mode. The radio will respond: CMD

MATERIALS

» **1 solderless breadboard**
» **1 EM-406A GPS receiver**
» **1 interface cable for GPS receiver**
» **12 male header pins**
» **1 Bluetooth Mate**
» **1 5V voltage regulator**

Next, type:

SU,48\r

R,1\r

▸▸ This sets the radio to 9600 bps.

▸▸ This reboots the radio.

Your radio will save the new setting at 4800bps and reboot. Now you can connect it to the GPS module.

Figure 8-10 shows the module connected to a Bluetooth Mate radio. The GPS data will be sent over Bluetooth to a personal computer running Processing. If it's not already paired, you can pair the Bluetooth Mate to your personal computer using the instructions from Project 3 in Chapter 2. That will give you a Bluetooth serial port in your list of ports, as in that project. Open a connection to that port in a serial terminal application, and you should see data in the NMEA protocol, like what you see below.

```
$GPGGA,180226.000,4040.6559,N,07358.1789,W,1,04,6.6,75.4,M,-34.3,M,,0000*5B
$GPGSA,A,3,12,25,09,18,,,,,,,,6.7,6.6,1.0*36
$GPGSV,3,1,10,22,72,171,,14,67,338,,25,39,126,39,18,39,146,35*70
$GPGSV,3,2,10,31,35,228,20,12,35,073,37,09,15,047,29,11,09,302,20*7D
$GPGSV,3,3,10,32,04,314,17,27,02,049,15*73
$GPRMC,180226.000,A,4040.6559,N,07358.1789,W,0.29,290.90,220411,,*12
$GPGGA,180227.000,4040.6559,N,07358.1789,W,1,04,6.6,75.4,M,-34.3,M,,0000*5A
$GPGSA,A,3,12,25,09,18,,,,,,,,6.7,6.6,1.0*36
$GPRMC,180227.000,A,4040.6559,N,07358.1789,W,0.30,289.06,220411,,*1C
```

Figure 8-10
EM-406a GPS receiver attached to a Bluetooth radio. In order to get a real GPS signal, you'll have to go outside, so wireless data and a battery power source are handy.

NOTE: If your power is inconsistent, add in the decoupling capacitors on the input and output sides of the regulator, as seen in other projects using this regulator.

There are several types of sentences within the NMEA protocol, and each serves a different function. Some tell you your position, some tell you about the satellites in view of the receiver, some deliver information about your course heading, and so on. Each sentence begins with a dollar sign ($), followed by five letters that identify the type of sentence. After that come each of the parameters of the sentence, separated by commas. An asterisk comes after the parameters, then a checksum, then a carriage return and a linefeed.

Take a look at the $GPRMC sentence as an example:

`$GPRMC,155125.000,A,4043.8432,N,07359.7654,W,0.10,11.88,200407,,*20`

RMC stands for Recommended Minimum specifiC global navigation system satellite data. It gives the basic information almost any application might need. This sentence contains the information shown in the table.

Using the NMEA protocol in a program is just a matter of deciding which sentence gives you the information you need, reading the data in serially, and converting the data into values you can use. In most cases, the RMC sentence gives you all the data you need about position.

The Processing sketch shown next reads NMEA serial data in and parses out the time, date, latitude, longitude, and heading. It uses the $GPRMC sentence to get basic info, the $GPGSV sentence to get the satellites in view, and the $GPGGA sentence to get the number of satellites used to obtain a fix. It draws an arrow on the screen to indicate heading. The output looks like Figure 8-11. (Be sure to use the Bluetooth serial port when opening the serial port!)

NOTE: Extra credit. Figure out where I was when I wrote this chapter. Thanks to reader Derrick O'Brien who figured out from the first edition that there was an error in my calculations, and introduced me to Glen Murphy's excellent GPS processing example at http://bodytag.org/p5gps/p5gps.pde. With the changes in this edition, it will be easier to find me.

Message identifier	$GPRMC
Time	155125.000 or 15:51:25 GMT
Status of the data (valid or not valid)	A = valid data (V = not valid)
Latitude	4043.8432 or 40°43.8432'
North/South indicator	N = North (S = South)
Longitude	07359.7654 or 73°59.7654'
East/West indicator	W = West (E = East)
Speed over ground	0.10 knots
Course over ground	11.88° from north
Date	200407 or April 20, 2007
Magnetic variation	none
Mode	none
Checksum (there is no comma before the checksum; magnetic variation would appear to the left of that final comma, and mode would appear to the right)	*20

Figure 8-11
The output of the Processing GPS parser.

Find It First, set up your global variables as usual.

```
/*
GPS parser
Context: Processing

This program takes in NMEA 0183 serial data and parses
out the date, time, latitude, and longitude using the GPRMC sentence.
*/
// import the serial library:
import processing.serial.*;

Serial myPort;              // The serial port
float latitude = 0.0;       // the latitude reading in degrees
String northSouth = "N";    // north or south?
float longitude = 0.0;      // the longitude reading in degrees
String eastWest = "W";      // east or west?
float heading = 0.0;        // the heading in degrees

int hrs, mins, secs;        // time units
int currentDay, currentMonth, currentYear;

int satellitesInView = 0;   // satellites in view
int satellitesToFix = 0;    // satellites used to calculate fix

float textX = 50;           // position of the text on the screen
float textY = 30;
```

▸▸ The setup() method sets the window size, defines the drawing parameters, and opens the serial port.

```
void setup() {
  size(400, 400);           // window size

  // settings for drawing:
  noStroke();
  smooth();

  // List all the available serial ports
  println(Serial.list());

  // Open whatever port is the one you're using.
  // for a Bluetooth device, this may be further down your
  // serial port list:
  String portName = Serial.list()[6];
  myPort = new Serial(this, portName, 9600);

  // read bytes into a buffer until you get a carriage
  // return (ASCII 13):
  myPort.bufferUntil('\r');
}
```

▸▸ You will probably need to look at the output of Serial.list() and change this number to match the serial port that corresponds to your Bluetooth device.

The draw() method prints the readings in the window, and calls another method, drawArrow(), to draw the arrow and circle.

```
void draw() {
  // deep blue background:
  background(#0D1133);

  // pale slightly blue text:
  fill(#A3B5CF);

  // put all the text together in one big string:

  // display the date and time from the GPS sentence
  // as MM/DD/YYYY, HH:MM:SS GMT
  // all numbers are formatted using nf() to make them 2- or 4-digit:
  String displayString = nf(currentMonth, 2)+ "/"+ nf(currentDay, 2)
    + "/"+ nf(currentYear, 4) + ", " + nf(hrs, 2)+ ":"
    + nf(mins, 2)+ ":"+ nf(secs, 2) + " GMT\n";

  // display the position from the GPS sentence:
  displayString = displayString + latitude + " " + northSouth + ", "
    + longitude + " " + eastWest + "\n";

  // display the heading:
  displayString = displayString + "heading " + heading + " degrees\n";

  // show some info about the satellites used:
  displayString = displayString + "satellites in view: "
    + satellitesInView + "\n";
  displayString = displayString + "satellites used to calculate position: "
    + satellitesToFix;
  text(displayString, textX, textY);

  // draw an arrow using the heading:
  drawArrow(heading);
}
```

drawArrow() is called by the draw() method. It draws the arrow and the circle.

```
void drawArrow(float angle) {
  // move whatever you draw next so that (0,0) is centered on the screen:
  translate(width/2, height/2);

  // draw a circle in light blue:
  fill(80,200,230);
  ellipse(0,0,50,50);
  // make the arrow black:
  fill(0);
  // rotate using the heading:
  rotate(radians(angle));

  // draw the arrow.  center of the arrow is at (0,0):
  triangle(-10, 0, 0, -20, 10, 0);
  rect(-2,0, 4,20);
}
```

▶▶ The serialEvent() method gets any incoming data as usual, and passes it off to a method called parseString(). That method splits the incoming string into all the parts of the GPS sentence. It passes the incoming sentences to a few methods—getRMC(), getGGA(), and getGSV(), as appropriate—to handle them. If you were writing a more universal parser, you'd write similar methods for each type of sentence.

```
void serialEvent(Serial myPort) {
  // read the serial buffer:
  String myString = myPort.readStringUntil('\n');

  // if you got any bytes other than the linefeed, parse it:
  if (myString != null) {
    print(myString);
    parseString(myString);
  }
}

void parseString (String serialString) {
  // split the string at the commas:
  String items[] = (split(serialString, ','));

  // if the first item in the sentence is the identifier, parse the rest
  if (items[0].equals("$GPRMC")) {
    // $GPRMC gives time, date, position, course, and speed
    getRMC(items);
  }

  if (items[0].equals("$GPGGA")) {
    // $GPGGA gives time, date, position, satellites used
    getGGA(items);
  }

  if (items[0].equals("$GPGSV")) {
    // $GPGSV gives satellites in view
    satellitesInView = getGSV(items);
  }
}
```

▶▶ The getRMC() method converts the latitude, longitude, and other numerical parts of the sentence into numbers.

```
void getRMC(String[] data) {
  // move the items from the string into the variables:
  int time = int(data[1]);
  // first two digits of the time are hours:
  hrs = time/10000;
  // second two digits of the time are minutes:
  mins = (time % 10000)/100;
  // last two digits of the time are seconds:
  secs = (time%100);

  // if you have a valid reading, parse the rest of it:
  if (data[2].equals("A")) {
    latitude = minutesToDegrees(float(data[3]));

    northSouth = data[4];
    longitude = minutesToDegrees(float(data[5]));
    eastWest = data[6];
    heading = float(data[8]);
    int date = int(data[9]);
```

»

```
Continued from previous page.
    // last two digits of the date are year.  Add the century too:
    currentYear = date % 100 + 2000;
    // second two digits of the date are month:
    currentMonth =  (date % 10000)/100;
    // first two digits of the date are day:
    currentDay = date/10000;
  }
}
```

The getGGA() method parses out the parts of the $GPGGA sentence. Some of it is redundant with the $GPRMC sentence, but the number of satellites to fix a position is new.

```
void getGGA(String[] data) {
  // move the items from the string into the variables:
  int time = int(data[1]);
  // first two digits of the time are hours:
  hrs = time/10000;
  // second two digits of the time are minutes:
  mins = (time % 10000)/100;
  // last two digits of the time are seconds:
  secs = (time % 100);

  // if you have a valid reading, parse the rest of it:
  if (data[6].equals("1")) {
    latitude = minutesToDegrees(float(data[2]));
    northSouth = data[3];
    longitude = minutesToDegrees(float(data[4]));
    eastWest = data[5];
    satellitesToFix = int(data[7]);
  }
}
```

The getGSV() method parses out the parts of the $GPGSV sentence. It returns a single integer—the number of satellites in view.

```
int getGSV(String[] data) {
  int satellites = int(data[3]);
  return satellites;
}
```

Finally, the minutesToDegrees() method is used by both the getRMC() and getGGA() methods. The NMEA protocol sends latitude and longitude like this:

ddmm.mmmm

where dd is degrees, and mm.mmm is minutes. This method converts the minutes to a decimal fraction of the degrees.

```
float minutesToDegrees(float thisValue) {
  // get the integer portion of the degree measurement:
  int wholeNumber = (int)(thisValue / 100);
  // get the fraction portion, and convert minutes to a decimal fraction:
  float fraction = (thisValue - ( wholeNumber ) * 100) / 60;
  // combine the two and return it:
  float result = wholeNumber + fraction;
  return result;
}
```

When you run this sketch, it may take several minutes before you get a position. Different receivers take varying times to acquire an initial position when first started, or when moved to a new place on the planet. So, pick a spot with a clear view of the skies and be patient. Pay attention to the number of satellites in view as well. If that number is less than four, your receiver's not going to acquire a position too well. Satellites move, though, so if you don't get anything, wait a half-hour or so and try again.

Many mobile phones on the market these days feature a GPS receiver, and seem to have a signal most of the time, which may make you wonder why your receiver can't get a signal as fast. Remember, mobile phones tend to use both GPS and cellular location tracking together. So, even if they don't have enough satellite signals, they can generally determine their position relative to the nearest cell towers, and—using the known locations of those towers—approximate a fix.

NMEA 0183 is just one of many protocols used in mapping GPS data. You'll learn about a few more, as well as some tools for using them to map routes and locations, in Chapter 11. The great thing about NMEA, though, is that it's nearly ubiquitous among GPS receivers. No matter what other protocols they use, they all seem to have NMEA as an option. So it's a good one to know about no matter what GPS tools you're working with.
X

Choosing Which GPS Accessories to Buy

There are many GPS receiver modules on the market, and it can get confusing choosing the right tools for this job. Here are a few things to consider.

Most common GPS receivers communicate with the microcontroller via TTL serial, using the NMEA 0183 protocol. So when it comes to connecting them to your microcontroller, and reading their data, they're largely interchangeable. The big difference between them is how well they receive a GPS signal, which is influenced by how many channels they receive (generally more is better), what kind of antenna they have (generally larger is better), and how much power they consume. I prefer the EM-406a

receiver mentioned in this project because it gets good reception, acquires a fix fast, and has been the most reliable compared to others I've tested. There are other good ones, though. Spark Fun has a nice GPS receiver buying guide on their site.

To connect a GPS receiver, all you need is a serial transmit connection, power, and ground. There are some shields available that allow you to mount a receiver to your Arduino, but they're optional. You need only three wires.

Images courtesy of Spark Fun. Thanks to the students of 2011's Wildlife Tracking class for confirming my tests.
X

EM-406a GPS receiver. 20 channels, good reception, less expensive than other alternatives.

D2523T GPS receiver. 50 channels, great reception, but more expensive.

LS20126 receiver. Has a very small antenna, but works decently in open areas.

GPS MiniMod with GR10/ MN1010 receiver. Smallest I could find. Takes a long time to acquire a signal.

❝❝ Determining Orientation

People have an innate ability to determine their orientation relative to the world around them, but objects don't. So, orientation sensors are typically used for refining the position of objects rather than of people. In this section, you'll see two types of orientation sensors:

a digital compass for determining heading relative to Earth's magnetic field, and an accelerometer for determining orientation relative to Earth's gravitational field. Using these two sensors, you can determine which way is north and which way is up.

 Project 20

Determining Heading Using a Digital Compass

You can calculate heading using a compass if you are in a space that doesn't have a lot of magnetic interference. There are many digital compasses on the market. These acquire a heading by measuring the change in Earth's magnetic field along two axes, just as an analog compass does. Like analog compasses, they are subject to interference from other magnetic fields, including those generated by strong electrical induction.

This example uses a digital compass from ST Microelectronics, model LSM303DLH. Both Spark Fun and Pololu carry breakout boards for this compass. The Pololu version was used for this example because it has built-in voltage level shifters and works better at 5V. It measures magnetic field strength along three axes, and it has a three-axis accelerometer built in as well to help compensate for tilt. It reports the results via synchronous serial data sent over an I2C connection via the Wire library.

Figure 8-12 shows the compass connected to an Arduino. The compass requires calibration, so this project features a pushbutton to toggle between calibration mode and normal mode, and an LED to indicate when you're calibrating.

The compass operates on 5V. Its pins are as follows:

1. 1V8: 1.8V output. You won't use this pin.
2. 3V: 3-volt output. You won't use this pin.
3. Vin: 5-volt input. Connect to the microcontroller's 5V.
4. GND: ground. Connect to the microcontroller's ground.
5. SCL: Serial clock. Connect to microcontroller's SCL pin (analog pin 5).
6. SDA: Serial data. Connect to microcontroller's SDA pin (analog pin 4).
7. DRDY: Data ready indicator: outputs 1.8V when the compass is ready to be read. You won't use this pin.
8. INT1: interrupt 1. You won't use this pin.
9. INT2: interrupt 2. You won't use this pin.

MATERIALS

» **1 solderless breadboard or prototyping shield**
» **1 Arduino module**
» **1 digital compass, ST Microelectronics model LSM303DLH**
» **1 LED tactile pushbutton** This example uses an LED tactile button from Spark Fun, which has a built-in LED, but you can use any pushbutton and LED
» **1 220-ohm resistor**
» **1 10-kilohm resistor**
» **13 male header pins**

Figure 8-12
ST Microelectronics LSM303DLH compass connected to an Arduino.

NOTE: To calibrate the compass, rotate it slowly through 360 degrees on a flat, level surface while in calibration mode (see code). When calibrating the compass, you need to know the cardinal directions precisely. Get a magnetic needle compass and check properly. You should calibrate away from lots of electronic equipment and sources of magnetic energy (except the earth). For example, in my office, needle compasses tend to point west-southwest, so I calibrate outside, powering the whole Arduino circuit from a battery. To calibrate the accelerometer, rotate the module through every possible axis.

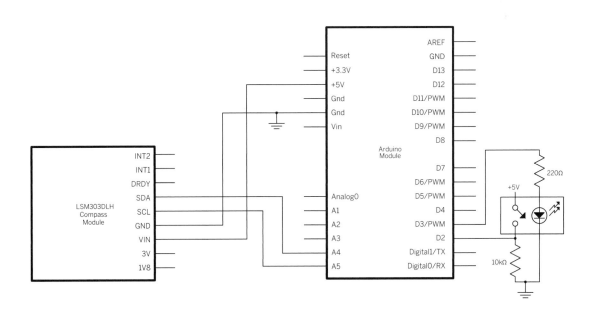

This sketch uses the Wire library to communicate via I2C with the compass. The Wire library is encapsulated in another library, the LSM303DLH library, originally written by Ryan Mulligan of Pololu. I've made a variation on it with a few extra functions, available at http://github.com/tigoe/LSM303DLH. Download version 1.1.0 (the latest as of this writing) and copy the **LSM303DLH** folder into the **libraries** directory of your Arduino sketch directory. Note that there is a folder called **LSM303DLH** *inside* the folder you download. It's the inner folder that you want.

This sketch also uses Alexander Brevig's Button library; the current Wiring version is at http://wiring.uniandes.edu.co/source/trunk/wiring/firmware/libraries/Button; the current Arduino version is at http://github.com/tigoe/Button. Download it to your **libraries** directory as well. Then, restart Arduino and you're ready to begin.

X

Try It There are no global variables, but before the setup() method, you have to include the library and define a couple of constants.

```
// include the necessary libraries:
#include <Wire.h>
#include <LSM303DLH.h>
#include <Button.h>

const int modeButton = 2;        // pushbutton for calibration mode
const int buttonLed = 3;         // LED for the button

// initialize the compass library
LSM303DLH compass;
// initialize a button on pin 2 :
Button button = Button(modeButton,BUTTON_PULLDOWN);
boolean calibrating = false;     // keep track of calibration state
```

The setup() method initializes the Wire and Serial libraries and enables the compass.

```
void setup() {
  // initialize serial:
  Serial.begin(9600);
    // set up the button LED:
  pinMode(buttonLed,OUTPUT);
  // start the Wire library and enable the compass:
  Wire.begin();
  compass.enable();
}
```

The main loop starts by checking the button. If the button is currently pressed and its state has changed since the last check, the sketch toggles between normal mode and calibrating mode. It also changes the LED state: on means you're calibrating, off means normal mode.

```
void loop() {
  // if the button changes state, change the calibration state
  // and the state of the LED:
  if(button.isPressed() && button.stateChanged()){
    calibrating = !calibrating;
    digitalWrite(buttonLed, calibrating);
  }
```

▶▶ If the sketch is in calibrating mode, it calls the compass calibrate() method continuously. If not, it reads the compass and reports the heading. Then it waits 100 milliseconds to let the compass stabilize before reading again.

When you run this sketch, open the Serial Monitor, and then put the compass in calibrating mode by pressing the button. Turn it around 360 degrees on a level surface for a second or two, then rotate it through all three axes for a few seconds. Next, press the button to put it in normal mode, and you'll see the heading values. Zero degrees should be due north, 180 degrees is due south, 90 degrees is east, and 270 degrees is west.

```
  // if you're in calibration mode, calibrate:
  if (calibrating) {
    compass.calibrate();
  }
  else {    // if in normal mode, read the heading:
    compass.read();
    int heading = compass.heading();
    Serial.println("Heading: " + String(heading) + " degrees");
  }
  delay(100);
}
```

Introducing the I2C Interface

The LSM303DLH compass uses a form of synchronous serial communication called Inter-Integrated Circuit, or I2C. Sometimes called Two-Wire Interface, or TWI, it's the other common synchronous serial protocol besides SPI, which you learned about in Chapter 4.

I2C is comparable to SPI, in that it uses a single clock on the master device to coordinate the devices that are communicating. Every I2C device uses two wires to send and receive data: a serial clock pin, called the SCL pin, that the microcontroller pulses at a regular interval; and a serial data pin, called the SDA pin, over which data is transmitted. For each serial clock pulse, a bit of data is sent or received. When the clock changes from low to high (known as the rising edge of the clock), a bit of data is transferred from the microcontroller to the I2C device. When the clock changes from high to low (known as the falling edge of the clock), a bit of data is transferred from the I2C device to the microcontroller.

Unlike SPI, I2C devices don't need a chip select pin. Each has a unique address, and the master device starts each exchange by sending the address of the device with which it wants to communicate.

I2C connections have just two connections between the controlling device (or master device) and the peripheral device (or slave), as follows:

Clock (SCK): The pin that the master pulses regularly.
Data (SDA): The pin that data is sent on, in both directions.

All devices on an I2C bus can share the same two lines.

The Arduino Wire library is the interface for I2C. On most Arduino boards, the SDA pin is analog input pin 4, and the SCL pin is on analog input pin 5. On the Arduino Mega, SDA is digital pin 20 and SCL is 21.

Project 21

Determining Attitude Using an Accelerometer

Compass heading is an excellent way to determine orientation if you're level with the earth. And if you've ever used an analog compass, you know how important it is to keep the compass level in order to get an accurate reading. In navigational terms, your tilt relative to the earth is called your attitude, and there are two major aspects to it: roll and pitch. Roll refers to how you're tilted side-to-side. Pitch refers to how you're tilted front-to-back.

Pitch and roll are only two of six navigational terms used to refer to movement. Pitch, roll, and yaw refer to angular motion around the X, Y, and Z axes. These are called rotations. Surge, sway, and heave refer to linear motion along those same axes. These are called translations. Figure 8-14 illustrates these six motions.

Measuring roll and pitch is relatively easy to do using an accelerometer. You used one of these already in Chapter 5, in the balance board ping-pong client. Accelerometers measure changing acceleration. At the center of an accelerometer is a tiny mass that's free to swing in one, two, or three dimensions. As the accelerometer tilts relative to the earth, the gravitational force exerted on the mass changes. Because force equals mass times acceleration, and because the mass of the accelerometer is constant, the change is read as a changing acceleration. In this project, you'll use an accelerometer to control the pitch and roll of a disk onscreen in Processing. The numeric values from the sensor are written on the disk as it tilts.

MATERIALS

- » **1 solderless breadboard or prototyping shield**
- » **1 Arduino module**
- » **1 Analog Devices ADXL320 accelerometer**
  You can also use the accelerometer on your LSM303DLH digital compass. An alternate sketch to do so is shown below.
- » **6 male header pins**

You can use the ADXL335 accelerometer module (the Adafruit version is shown in Figure 8-13) (or another analog accelerometer), or the accelerometer in the LSM303DLH compass module from the previous project.

Accelerometers come with various interfaces. The one on the compass module shares an I2C interface with the magnetometer. Others use a pulse-width interface. Many simply have analog outputs for each axis, like the ADXL accelerometers shown below. Accelerometers also come in a variety of resolutions. For many human activities, around 3–6g, or six times the acceleration due to gravity (9.8 meters per second, per second) will do. Most commercial products using accelerometers, like the Nintendo Wii or the majority of mobile phones, use an accelerometer in this range. The ADXL335 is a 3g accelerometer. Other activities require a much higher range. For example, a boxer's fist can decelerate at up to 100g when he hits!

If you're using the accelerometer on the LSM303DLH compass for this project, use the circuit as shown back in Figure 8-12, but without the LED and pushbutton. The first sketch below will work with any two- or three-axis analog accelerometer, and the second will work with the compass module's accelerometer. Both will communicate with the Processing sketch that follows them.
X

Figure 8-13

ADXL335 accelerometer connected to an Arduino. Shown here is an Adafruit breakout board for the ADXL335. This accelerometer operates on 3.3V, so its output range is also 0 to 3.3V. The microcontroller's analog reference pin is connected to 3.3V as well, so it knows that the maximum range of the analog inputs is from 0 to 3.3V.

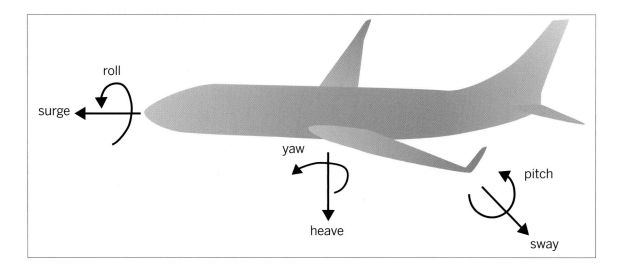

Figure 8-14
Rotations and translations of a body
in three dimensions.

" Determining Pitch and Roll from an Accelerometer

Three-axis accelerometers like the one you're using measure the linear acceleration of a body on each axis—in other words, the surge, sway, or heave of a body. They don't give you the roll, pitch, or yaw. However, you can calculate the roll and pitch when you know the acceleration along each axis. That calculation takes some tricky trigonometry. For a full explanation, see Freescale Semiconductor's application note on accelerometers at http://cache.freescale.com/files/sensors/doc/app_note/AN3461.pdf. Here are the highlights:

The force of gravity always acts perpendicular to the earth's surface. So when an object is tilted at an angle (called theta, or θ), part of that force acts along the X axis of the object, and part acts along the Y axis (see Figure 8-15). The X-axis acceleration and the Y-axis acceleration add up to the total force of gravity using the Pythagorean Theorem: $x^2 + y^2 = z^2$.

Since you know that, you can calculate the portions of the acceleration using sines and cosines. The X-axis portion of the acceleration is gravity * $\sin\theta$, and the Y-axis portion is gravity * $\cos\theta$ (remember, sine = opposite/hypotenuse, and cosine = adjacent/hypotenuse).

Figure 8-15
Calculating the portion of the force of gravity based on the angle of tilt.

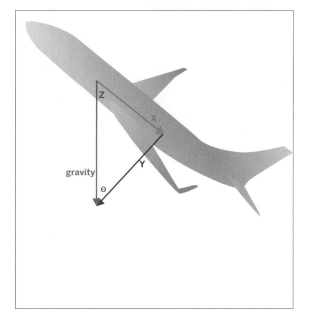

From there, you have to calculate the portions along all three axes at once. It turns out that:

```
roll = arctan (x-axis / √(y-axis² + z-axis²))
```

and:

```
pitch = arctan (y-axis / √(x-axis² + z-axis²))
```

In order to know the acceleration on each axis, though, you have to convert the reading you get from the analogRead() command. It's not too difficult. You already know that the accelerometer's range is from 0 volts to 3.3 volts (because the accelerometer operates on 3.3 volts), and that it gets converted to a range from 0 to 1023. So, you can say that:

```
voltage = analogRead(axis) * 3.3 / 1024;
```

Each axis has a zero acceleration point at half its range, or 1.65 volts. So subtract that from your reading, and any negative reading means tilt in the opposite direction.

From the accelerometer's data sheet, you can find out that the sensitivity of the accelerometer is 300 millivolts per g, where 1g is the amount of the acceleration due to gravity. When any axis is perpendicular to the ground, it experiences 1g of force, and should read about 300 mV, or 0.3V. So, the acceleration on each axis is the voltage reading divided by the sensitivity, or:

```
acceleration = voltage / 0.3;
```

Once you've got the acceleration for each axis, you can apply the earlier trigonometric formulas to get the pitch and roll.

The following sketch reads an analog accelerometer's X and Y axes, calculates pitch and roll as an angle from -90 degrees to 90 degrees, and sends the results out serially. If you want to use this sketch with an analog accelerometer other than the Adafruit ADXL335 module, rearrange the pins to match your accelerometer. If you're using a 5V accelerometer, change the voltage calculation as well.
X

Listen to It (Analog)

The setup() method initializes serial communications, and configures the analog-to-digital converter to take its reference from the external analog reference pin.

NOTE: Use this sketch with the Analog Devices ADXL320 accelerometer.

```
/*
 Accelerometer reader
 Context: Arduino
 Reads 2 axes of an accelerometer, calculates pitch and roll,
 and sends the values out the serial port
*/

void setup() {
  // initialize serial communication:
  Serial.begin(9600);
  // tell the microcontroller to read the external
  // analog reference voltage:
  analogReference(EXTERNAL);
}
```

» The loop() calls a method to convert the analog readings to acceleration values. Then it plugs those results into the trigonometric calculations described above, and prints the results.

```
void loop() {
  // read the accelerometer axes, and convert
  // the results to acceleration values:
  float xAxis = readAcceleration(analogRead(A0));
  delay(10);
  float yAxis= readAcceleration(analogRead(A1));
  delay(10);
  float zAxis = readAcceleration(analogRead(A2));

  // apply trigonometry to get the pitch and roll:
  float pitch = atan(xAxis/sqrt(pow(yAxis,2) + pow(zAxis,2)));
  float roll = atan(yAxis/sqrt(pow(xAxis,2) + pow(zAxis,2)));
  pitch = pitch * (180.0/PI);
  roll = roll * (180.0/PI) ;

  // print the results:
  Serial.print(pitch);
  Serial.print(",");
  Serial.println(roll);
}
```

» The readAcceleration() method takes an analog reading and converts it to an acceleration value from 0 to 1g.

```
float readAcceleration(int thisAxis) {
  // the accelerometer's zero reading is at half
  // its voltage range:
  float zeroPoint = 1.65;
  // convert the reading into a voltage:
  float voltage = (thisAxis * 3.3 / 1024.0) - zeroPoint;
  // divide by the accelerometer's sensitivity:
  float acceleration = voltage / 0.3;
  // return the acceleration in g's:
  return acceleration;
}
```

" Regardless of the accelerometer you're using, you'll find that the angle readings aren't always accurate, and that they can be quite noisy. The calculations explained above assume there are no forces acting on the accelerometer besides gravity, but that is seldom the case. As you move the accelerometer through space, your movement accelerates and decelerates, adding more force along all three axes to the calculation. Generally, accelerometer data is combined with data from gyrometers to help adjust for these forces.

If you're using the accelerometer on the LSM303DLH compass from the earlier project, you're in luck. The Arduino library for that accelerometer does the pitch and roll calculations for you, and simply returns the results as pitch and roll. The sketch below reads them and returns the values as angles from -90 degrees to 90 degrees, just like the analog accelerometer sketch above.
X

Listen to It (I2C)

This sketch reads the LSM303DLH accelerometer's X and Y axes and sends the results out serially. Like the previous project, it uses the LSM303DLH library, so make sure you have it installed.

NOTE: **This sketch uses the accelerometer on the LSM303DLH digital compass.**

```
/*
 I2C accelerometer
 Context: Arduino
 Reads an ST Microelectronics LSM303DLH compass and prints
 the X and Y axes accelerometer output.
 */

// include the necessary libraries:
#include <LSM303DLH.h>
#include <Wire.h>

// initialize the compass:
LSM303DLH compass;

void setup() {
  // initialize serial and Wire, and enable the compass:
  Serial.begin(9600);
  Wire.begin();
  compass.enable();

  // calibrate for the first five seconds after startup:
  while (millis() < 5000) {
    compass.calibrate();
  }
}

void loop() {
  // read the compass and print the accelerometer
  // X and Y readings:
  compass.read();
  Serial.print(compass.pitch());      // X axis angle
  Serial.print(",");
  Serial.println(compass.roll());     // Y axis angle
  delay(100);
}
```

Connect It This Processing sketch reads the incoming data from the microcontroller and uses it to change the attitude of a disc onscreen in three dimensions. It will work with either of the accelerometer sketches above, because they both output the same data in the same format. Make sure the serial port opened by the sketch matches the one to which your microcontroller is connected.

```
/*
Accelerometer Tilt
Context: Processing

Takes the values in serially from an accelerometer
attached to a microcontroller and uses them to set the
attitude of a disk on the screen.
*/
import processing.serial.*;       // import the serial lib

float pitch, roll;                // pitch and roll
float position;                   // position to translate to

Serial myPort;                    // the serial port
```

The setup() method initializes the window, the serial connection, and sets the graphics smoothing.

```
void setup() {
  // draw the window:
  size(400, 400, P3D);
  // calculate translate position for disc:
  position = width/2;

  // List all the available serial ports
  println(Serial.list());

  // Open whatever port is the one you're using.
  myPort = new Serial(this, Serial.list()[2], 9600);
  // only generate a serial event when you get a newline:
  myPort.bufferUntil('\n');
  // enable smoothing for 3D:
  hint(ENABLE_OPENGL_4X_SMOOTH);
}
```

▶▶ You will probably need to look at the output of Serial.list() and change this number to match the serial port that corresponds to your microcontroller.

The draw() method just refreshes the screen in the window, as usual. It calls a method, setAttitude(), to calculate the tilt of the plane. Then it calls a method, tilt(), to actually tilt the plane.

```
void draw () {
  // colors inspired by the Amazon rainforest:
  background(#20542E);
  fill(#79BF3D);
  // draw the disc:
  tilt();
}
```

» The 3D system in Processing works on rotations from zero to 2*PI. tilt() maps the accelerometer angles into that range. It uses Processing's translate() and rotate() methods to move and rotate the plane of the disc to correspond with the accelerometer's movement.

```
void tilt() {
  // translate from origin to center:
  translate(position, position, position);

  // X is front-to-back:
  rotateX(radians(roll + 90));
  // Y is left-to-right:
  rotateY(radians(pitch) );

  // set the disc fill color:
  fill(#79BF3D);
  // draw the disc:
  ellipse(0, 0, width/4, width/4);
  // set the text fill color:
  fill(#20542E);
  // Draw some text so you can tell front from back:
  text(pitch + "," + roll, -40, 10, 1);
}
```

» The serialEvent() method reads all the incoming serial bytes and parses them as comma-separated ASCII values, just as you did in Project 2, Monski pong in Chapter 2.

```
void serialEvent(Serial myPort) {
  // read the serial buffer:
  String myString = myPort.readStringUntil('\n');

  // if you got any bytes other than the linefeed:
  if (myString != null) {
    myString = trim(myString);
    // split the string at the commas
    String items[] = split(myString, ',');
    if (items.length > 1) {
      pitch = float(items[0]);
      roll = float(items[1]);
    }
  }
}
```

Figure 8-16
The output of the Processing accelerometer sketch.

Though it may seem like a lot of work to go from the raw output of an accelerometer to the visualization shown in Figure 8-16, it's useful to understand the process. You went from the translation of acclerations along three axes into analog voltages, then converted those voltages to digital values in the microcontroller's memory using analogRead(). From there, you converted the digital values into voltage readings, and then converted those to acceleration measurements relative to the acceleration due to gravity. Then, you used some trigonometry to convert the results to angles in degrees.

The advantage of having the results in degrees is that it's a known standard measurement, so you didn't have to do a lot of mapping when you sent the values to Processing. Instead, Processing could take the output from an accelerometer that gave it pitch and roll in degrees.

You don't always need this level of standardization. For many applications, all you care about is that the accelerometer readings are changing. However, if you want to convert those readings into a measurement of attitude relative to the ground, the process you went through is the process you'll use.
X

▸▸ **Address 2007 by Mouna Andraos and Sonali Sridhar**
Address shows that location technologies don't have to be purely utilitarian. *Photo by J. Nordberg.*

❝ Conclusion

When you start to develop projects that use location systems, you usually find that less is more. It's not unusual to start a project thinking you need to know position, distance, and orientation, then pare away systems as you develop the project. The physical limitations of the things you build and the spaces you build them in solve many problems for you.

This effect, combined with your users' innate ability to locate and orient themselves, makes your job much easier. Before you start to solve all problems in code or electronics, put yourself physically in the place for which you're building, and do what you intend for your users to do. You'll learn a lot about your project, and save yourself time, aggravation, and money.

The examples in this chapter are all focused on a solitary person or object. As soon as you introduce multiple participants, location and identification become more tightly connected. This is because you need to know whose signal is coming from a given location, or what location a given speaker is at. In the next chapter, you'll see methods crossing the line from physical identity to network identity. X

9

Identification

In the previous chapters, you assumed that identity equals address. Once you knew a device's address on the network, you started talking. Think about how disastrous this would be if you used this formula in everyday life: you pick up the phone, dial a number, and just start talking. What if you dialed the wrong number? What if someone other than the person you expected answers the phone?

Networked objects mark the boundaries of networks, but not of the communications that travel across them. We use these devices to send messages to other people. The network identity of the device and the physical identity of the person are two different things. Physical identity generally equates to presence (is it near me?) or address (where is it?), but network identity also takes into consideration network capabilities of the device and the state it's in when you contact it. In this chapter, you'll learn some methods for giving physical objects network identities. You'll also learn ways that devices on a network can learn each other's capabilities through the messages they send and the protocols they use.

◀◀ **Sniff, a toy for sight-impaired children, by Sara Johansson**
The dog's nose contains an RFID reader. When he detects RFID-tagged objects, he gives sound and tactile feedback—a unique response for each object. Designed by Sara Johansson, a student in the Tangible Interaction course at the Oslo School of Architecture and Design, under the instruction of tutors Timo Arnall and Mosse Sjaastad. *Photo courtesy of Sara Johansson.*

◀€ Supplies for Chapter 9

Cameras and RFID readers are your main new components in this chapter. You'll be using them to identify colors, faces, tags, and tokens.

Distributor KEY
- **A** Arduino Store (store.arduino.com)
- **AF** Adafruit (http://adafruit.com)
- **CR** CoreRFID (www.rfidshop.com)
- **D** Digi-Key (www.digikey.com)
- **F** Farnell (www.farnell.com)
- **J** Jameco (http://jameco.com)
- **MS** Maker SHED (www.makershed.com)
- **RSH** Radio Shack(www.radioshack.com)
- **RS** RS (www.rs-online.com)
- **SF** SparkFun (www.sparkfun.com)
- **SH** Smarthome (www.smarthome.com)
- **SS** Seeed Studio (www.seeedstudio.com)
- **ST** SamTec (www.samtec.com)

PROJECT 22: Color Recognition Using a Webcam
» **Personal computer with USB or FireWire port**
» **USB or FireWire webcam**
» **Colored objects**

PROJECT 23: Face Detection Using a Webcam
» **Personal computer with USB or FireWire port**
» **USB or FireWire webcam**
» **Face**

PROJECT 24: 2D Barcode Recognition Using Webcam
» **Personal computer with USB or FireWire port**
» **USB or FireWire webcam**
» **Printer**

PROJECT 25: Reading RFID Tags in Processing
» **RFID reader** The ID Innovations ID-12 or ID-20 can work in this project. The ID-20 has a slightly longer range than the ID-12, but otherwise their operation is identical. **CR** IDI003 or IDI004, **SF** SEN-08419
» **RFID breakout board** Works for either of the ID Innovations readers. **SF** SEN-08423

Figure 9-1. New parts for this chapter: **1.** Prototyping shield **2.** X10 interface module **3.** X10 lamp module or **4.** X10 appliance module **5.** Four-wire telephone (RJ-11) cable **6.** Perforated circuit board **7.** Eight-wire Ethernet cable **8.** EM4001 RFID tags **9.** Mifare RFID tags **10.** ID Innovations ID-12 or ID-20 125kHz RFID reader **11.** Spark Fun 13.56 MHz RFID board or **12.** TinkerKit RFID shield **13.** Antenna for SM130 RFID reader **14.** Extra-long female header pins **15.** 2x16 LCD screen. Don't forget plenty of male header pins for the breakout boards.

» **0.1-inch male header pins J** 103377, **D** A26509-20ND, **SF** PRT-00116, **F** 1593411

» **RFID tags** Get the tags that match your reader. All the retailers listed sell tags that match their readers in a variety of physical packages, so choose the ones you like best. The examples use EM4001 tags, which are interchangeable with EM4102 tags.
CR WON002, **SF** COM-10169

» **1 FTDI USB-to-Serial adapter** You could use the one you've been using throughout this book in conjunction with the RFID breakout board mentioned above. If you want a breakout that's designed specifically for your reader, you can use the RFID USB reader from Spark Fun, part SEN-09963.
SF DEV-09718 or DEV-09716, **AF** 70, **A** A000059, **M** MKAD22, **SS** PRO101D2P, **D** TTL-232R-3V3 or TTL-232R-5V

PROJECT 26: RFID Meets Home Automation

» **1 Arduino module** An Arduino Uno or something based on the Arduino Uno, but the project should work on other Arduino and Arduino-compatible boards.
D 1050-1019-ND, **J** 2121105, **SF** DEV-09950, **A** A000046, **AF** 50, **F** 1848687, **RS** 715-4081, **SS** ARD132D2P, **MS** MKSP4

» **1 prototyping shield J** 2124314, **SF** DEV-07914, **AF** 51, **F** 1848696, **SS** STR104B2P, **M** MSMS01

» **RFID reader** The ID Innovations ID-12 or ID-20 can work in this project. The ID-20 has a slightly longer range than the ID-12, but otherwise their operation is identical.
CR IDI003 or IDI004, **SF** SEN-08419

» **RFID reader breakout** Or use the parts below.
SF SEN-08423

» **Two 2mm 10 pin female header rows** Not necessary if using the breakout board. Samtec, like many part makers, supplies free samples of this part in small quantities.
ST MMS-110-01-L-SV, **J** 164822, **SF** PRT-08272, **F** 1109732

» **2 rows of 20 0.1-inch male header pins J** 103377, **D** A26509-20ND, **SF** PRT-00116, **F** 1593411

» **2mm 5-pin socket SF** PRT-10519

» **2mm 7-pin socket SF** PRT-10518

» **RFID tags** Get the tags that match your reader. All the retailers listed sell tags that match their readers in a variety of physical packages, so choose the ones you like best. The examples use EM4001 tags, which are interchangeable with EM4102 tags.
CR WON002, **SF** COM-10169

» **1 LED D** 160-1144-ND or 160-1665-ND, **J** 34761 or 94511, **F** 1015878, **RS** 247-1662 or 826-830, **SF** COM-09592 or COM-09590

» **1 220-ohm resistor D** 220QBK-ND, **J** 690700, **F** 9337792, **RS** 707-8842

» **Interface module: X10 One-Way Interface Module SH** 1134B

» **2 X10 modules** *Either:* 2 appliance modules from Smarthome, part number 2002; or 2 Powerhouse X10 lamp modules from Smarthome, part number 2000. You'll need two modules total. Choose one of each, or two of one as you see fit. If you're going to control incandescent lamps only, get lamp modules. For anything else, get appliance modules.

» **4-wire phone cable with RJ-11 connector** You can take this from any discarded phone, or get one at your local electronics shop.
D A1642R-07-ND, **J** 115617, **F** 1335141

PROJECT 27: Tweets from RFID

» **1 SonMicro SM130 RFID read/write module SF** SEN-10126

» **3 Mifare RFID read/write tags SF** SEN-10127

» **1 Arduino Ethernet board A** A000050
Alternatively, an Uno-compatible board (see Chapter 2) with an Ethernet shield will work.
SF DEV-09026, **J** 2124242, **A** A000056, **AF** 201, **F** 1848680

» **1 RFID shield SF** DEV-10406, **A** T040030 or T040031

» **13.56MHz antenna** Unless your reader incorporates an antenna, **A** C000027

» **2 potentiometers J** 29082, **SF** COM-09939, **F** 350072, **RS** 522-0625

» **1 perforated printed circuit board RSH** 276-150, **D** V2018-ND, **J** 616673, **SS** STR125C2B, **F** 4903213, **RS** 159-5420

» **1/16-inch Mat board**

» **16 pin female header rows ST** MMS-110-01-L-SV, **J** 164822, **SF** PRT-08272, **F** 1109732

» **6 pin stackable header SF** PRT-09280, **AF** 85

» **8-conductor wire** Ribbon cable or Ethernet cable will do.
D AE08A-5-ND , **F** 1301013

» **16x2 character LCD SF** LCD-00709

The parts for building the reader circuit without a shield are listed below, for those who prefer that option:

» **2 4.7-kilohm resistors J** 691024, **D** CF14JT4K70CT-ND, **F** 735033, **RS** 707-8693

» **1 solderless breadboard D** 438-1045-ND, **J** 20723 or 20601, **SF** PRT-00137, **F** 4692810, **AF** 64, **SS** STR101C2M or STR102C2M, **M** MKKN2

" Physical Identification

The process of identifying physical objects is such a fundamental part of our experience that we seldom think about how we do it. We use our senses, of course: we look at, feel, pick up, shake and listen to, smell, and taste objects until we have a reference—then we give them a label. The whole process relies on some pretty sophisticated work by our brains and bodies, and anyone who's ever dabbled in computer vision or artificial intelligence in general can tell you that teaching a computer to recognize physical objects is no small feat. Just as it's easier to determine location by having a human narrow it down for you, it's easier to distinguish objects computationally if you can limit the field—and if you can label the important objects.

Just as we identify things using information from our senses, so do computers. They can identify physical objects only by using information from their sensors. Two of the best-known digital identification techniques are optical recognition and radio frequency identification (RFID). Optical recognition can take many forms, from video color tracking and shape recognition to the ubiquitous barcode. Once an object has been recognized by a computer, the computer can give it an address on the network.

The network identity of a physical object can be centrally assigned and universally available, or it can be provisional. It can be used only by a small subset of devices on a larger network or used only for a short time. RFID is an interesting case in point. The RFID tag pasted on the side of a book may seem like a universal marker, but what it means depends on who reads it. The owner of a store may assign that tag's number a place in his inventory, but to the consumer who buys it, it means nothing unless she has a tool to read it and a database in which to categorize it. She has no way of knowing what the number meant to the store owner unless she has access to his database. Perhaps he linked that ID tag number to the book's title, or to the date on which it arrived in the store. Once it leaves the store, he may delete it from his database, so it loses all meaning to him. The consumer, on the other hand, may link it to entirely different data in her own database, or she may choose to ignore it, relying on other means to identify it. In other words, there is no central database linking RFID tags and the things to which they're attached or the people who possessed them.

Like locations, identities become more uniquely descriptive as the context they describe becomes larger. For example, knowing that my name is Tom doesn't give you much to go on. Knowing my last name narrows it down some more, but how effective that is depends on where you're looking. In the United States, there are dozens of Tom Igoes. In New York, there are at least three. When you need a unique identifier, you might choose a universal label, like using my Social Security number, or you might choose a provisional label, like calling me "Frank's son, Tom." Which you choose depends on your needs in a given situation. Likewise, you may choose to identify physical objects on a network using universal identifiers, or you might choose to use provisional labels in a given temporary situation.

The capabilities assigned to an identifier can be fluid as well. Considering the RFID example again: in the store, a given tag's number might be enough to set off alarms at the entrance gates, or to cause a cash register to add a price to your total purchase. In another store, that same tag might be assigned no capabilities at all, even if it's using the same protocol as other tags in the store. Confusion can set in when different contexts use similar identifiers. Have you ever left a store with a purchase and tripped the alarm, only to be waved on by the clerk who forgot to deactivate the tag on your purchase? Try walking into a Barnes & Noble bookstore with jeans you just bought at a Gap store. You're likely to trip the alarms because the two companies use the same RFID tags, but they don't always set their security systems to filter out tags that are not in their inventory.

Figure 9-2
Video color recognition in
Processing, using the code in
Project 22. This simple sketch
works well with vibrantly pink
monkeys.

Video Identification

All video identification relies on the same basic method:
the computer reads a camera's image and stores it as a
two-dimensional array of pixels. Each pixel has a characteristic brightness and color that can be measured
using any one of a number of palettes: red-green-blue is
a common scheme for video- and screen-based applications, as is hue-saturation-value. Cyan-magenta-yellow-
black is common in print applications. The properties of
the pixels, taken as a group, form patterns of color, brightness, and shape. When those patterns resemble other
patterns in the computer's memory, it can identify those
patterns as objects. Figure 9-2 shows an example, using a
bright pink monkey.

In the three projects below, you'll use a computer-vision
library called OpenCV to read an image from your personal
computer's camera or webcam, and then analyze the
image. The first, and simplest, will look for a color. The
second will look for something resembling a face. The third
will look for a 2D barcode called a QR (Quick Response)
code.

OpenCV is a computer-vision library originally developed
by Intel and released under an open source license. It's
been adapted for many programming environments,
including Processing. The Processing version can be found
linked off the Processing site at http://processing.org/
reference/libraries/. Follow the OpenCV link from that

page, then follow the directions to install OpenCV on your
platform. Download the Processing OpenCV library and
copy it to the **libraries** directory of your Processing sketch-
book directory (find it listed in Processing's preferences).
Now you're all set to build the examples below.

NOTE: **The current home of OpenCV for Processing as of this
writing is at** http://ubaa.net/shared/processing/opencv. **A new
version is in the works, so check the Processing site for the most
up-to-date link.**

Color Recognition

Recognizing objects by color is a relatively simple process,
if you know that the color you're looking for is unique in
the camera's image. This technique is used in film and
television production to make superheroes fly. The actor
is filmed against a screen of a unique color, usually green,
which isn't a natural color for human skin. Then, the pixels
of that color are removed, and the image is combined with
a background image.

Color identification can be an effective way to track
physi-cal objects in a controlled environment. Assuming
you've got a limited number of objects in the camera's view,
and each object's color is unique and doesn't change with
the lighting conditions, you can identify each object reasonably well. Even slight changes in lighting can change the
color of a pixel, however, so lighting conditions need to be
tightly controlled, as the following project illustrates.

x

Project 22

Color Recognition Using a Webcam

In this project, you'll get a firsthand look at how computer vision works. The Processing sketch shown here uses a video camera to generate a digital image, looks for pixels of a specific color, and then marks them on the copy of the image that it displays onscreen. The OpenCV library for Processing enables you to capture the image from a webcam attached to your computer and analyze the pixels.

The following Processing sketch is an example of color tracking using the OpenCV library. To use this, you'll need to have a camera attached to your computer, and also have the drivers installed. The camera you used in Chapter 3 for the cat camera should do the job fine. You'll also need some small colored objects—stickers or toy balls work well.

Before the setup(), set up a few global variables, including an instance of the OpenCV library, an array to hold the pixel color values, and a color variable for the color you want to track.

The setup() sets the initial conditions as usual, in this case, initializing OpenCV using the first camera available to your computer, sizing the window, and initializing smooth, antialised graphics.

NOTE: **Because the OpenCV application uses the first camera available, you may have problems if you have both a built-in camera on a laptop and an external webcam. One solution is to open the camera you don't want to use in another application, so only the one you want is available to OpenCV. It's a crude solution, but it works.**

```
/*
ColorTracking with openCV
Context: Processing
Based on an example by Daniel Shiffman
*/

// import the opencv library:
import hypermedia.video.*;

OpenCV opencv;          // opencv instance
int[] pixelArray;       // array to copy the pixel array to
color trackColor;       // the color you're looking for


void setup() {
  // initialize the window:
  size( 640, 480 );

  // initialize opencv
  opencv = new OpenCV( this );
  opencv.capture( width, height );
  // Start off tracking for red
  trackColor = color(255, 0, 0);
  // draw smooth edges:
  smooth();
}
```

➤ The draw() method begins by establishing a value for the closest matching color, a threshold for similarity, and X and Y positions of the closest matching pixel. Then it reads the camera and saves the resulting image in a pixel array.

```
void draw() {
  float closestMatch = 500;    // value representing the closest color match
  float colorThreshold = 10;   // the threshold of color similarity
  int closestX = 0;            // horizontal position of the closest color
  int closestY = 0;            // vertical position of the closest color

  // read the camera:
  opencv.read();
  // draw the camera image to the window:
  image(opencv.image(), 0, 0);
  // copy the camera pixel array:
  pixelArray = opencv.pixels();
```

➤ Next comes a pair of nested for loops that iterates over the rows and columns of pixels. This is a standard algorithm for examining all the pixels of an image. With each pixel, you determine its position in the array with the following formula (which you'll see frequently.)

arrayLocation = x + (y * width);

Once you have the pixel's position, you extract the red, green, and blue values, as well as the values for the color you wish to track.

```
  // Begin loop to walk through every pixel
  for (int x = 0; x < opencv.width; x++ ) {
    for (int y = 0; y < opencv.height; y++ ) {
      // calculate the pixel's position in the array
      // based on its width and height:
      int loc = x + y*opencv.width;
      // get the color of the current pixel:
      color currentColor = pixelArray[loc];
      float r1 = red(currentColor);
      float g1 = green(currentColor);
      float b1 = blue(currentColor);
      float r2 = red(trackColor);
      float g2 = green(trackColor);
      float b2 = blue(trackColor);
```

➤ Next, calculate the difference between the two colors. By treating the red, green, and blue values of each color as positions in 3-dimensional space, you can find the difference by calculating the Euclidean distance between them. Processing's dist() function is handy for this.

Once you know the difference, compare that to the closest match so far (which was set arbitrarily high for the first match). If the current difference is less than the closest match, the current pixel is the new closest match.

```
      // use the dist() function to figure the aggregate color
      // of the current pixel. This method treats the red, green, and blue
      // of the current pixel's color  and of the target color as
      // coordinates
      // in 3D space and calculates the difference between them
      // as Euclidean distance.
      // In this formula, closer distance = closer color similarity:
      float d = dist(r1, g1, b1, r2, g2, b2);

      // If current color is more similar to tracked color than
      // closest color, save current location and current difference
      if (d < closestMatch) {
        closestMatch = d;
        closestX = x;
        closestY = y;
      }
    }
  }
```

»

▸ Once you have the closest match, the nested for loops are over. All that remains in the draw() method is to see whether the closest match is less than the threshold you set as an acceptable match. If it is, draw a circle there.

Continued from previous page.

```
// Only consider the color found if its color distance is less than
// the color threshold. For greater color accuracy, make this lower.
// For more forgiving matching, make it higher:
if (closestMatch < colorThreshold) {
  // Draw a circle at the tracked pixel
  fill(trackColor);
  strokeWeight(2.0);
  stroke(0);
  ellipse(closestX, closestY, 16, 16);
}
}
```

▸ Now, add a handler for when the mouse is pressed. This changes the tracked color to whatever color is at the mouse location.

```
void mousePressed() {
  // Save color where the mouse is clicked in trackColor variable
  int loc = mouseX + mouseY*opencv.width;
  trackColor = pixelArray[loc];
}
```

❝ Lighting for Color Tracking

As you can see when you run this sketch, it's not the most robust color tracker! The closest match tends to jump around a lot. Changing the colorThreshold helps, but not a lot. You can get it to be more precise by controlling the image and the lighting very carefully. There are some lighting tricks you can use as well:

- DayGlo colors under ultraviolet fluorescent lighting tend to be the easiest to track, but they lock you into a very specific visual aesthetic.
- Objects that produce their own light are easier to track, especially if you put a filter on the camera to block out stray light. A black piece of 35mm film negative (if you can still find 35mm film!) works well as a visible light filter, blocking most everything but infrared light. Two polarizers, placed so that their polarizing axes are perpendicular, are also effective. Infrared LEDs track very well through this kind of filter, as do incandescent flashlight lamps.

- Regular LEDs don't work well as color-tracking objects unless they're relatively dim. Brighter LEDs tend to show up as white in a camera image because their brightness overwhelms the camera's sensor.
- Color recognition doesn't have to be done with a camera; color sensors can do the same job. Texas Advanced Optoelectronic Solutions (www.taosinc.com) makes a few different color sensors, including the TAOS TCS230. This sensor contains four photodiodes, three of which are covered with color filters; the fourth is not, so it can read red, green, blue, and white light. It outputs the intensity of all four channels as a changing pulse width. The cheaper TAOS TSL230R has no LEDs—it just detects ambient color. Other color sensors are available as well. Their shortcoming is that they are designed to detect color only relatively close (within a few centimeters), and they don't have the ability to see a coherent image. They are basically one-pixel camera sensors.

Challenges of Identifying Physical Tokens

Designer Durrell Bishop's marble telephone answering machine is an excellent example of the challenges of identifying physical tokens. With every new message the machine receives, it drops a marble into a tray on the front of the machine. The listener hears the messages played back by placing a marble on the machine's "play" tray. Messages are erased and the marbles are recycled when they are dropped back into the machine's hopper. Marbles become physical tokens representing the messages, making it very easy to tell at a glance how many messages there are.

Bishop tried many different methods to reliably identify and categorize physical tokens representing the messages:

> I first made a working version with a motor and large screw (like a vending machine delivery mechanism), with pieces of paper tickets hung on the screw, and had different color gray levels on the back. When it got a new message, the machine read the next gray before it rotated once and dropped the ticket. It was a bit painful, so I bought beads and stuffed resistors into the hole which was capped (soldered)

with sticky-backed copper tape. When I went to Apple and worked with Jonathan Cohen, we built a properly hacked version for the Mac with networked barcodes.

Later, again with Jonathan but this time at Interval Research, we used the Dallas ID chips.

Color by itself isn't enough to give you identity in most cases, but there are ways in which you can design a system to use color as a marker of physical identity. However, it has its limitations. In order to tell the marbles apart, Bishop could have used color recognition to read the marbles, but that would limit the design in at least two ways. First, there would be no way to tell the difference between multiple marbles of the same color. If, for example, he wanted to use color to identify the different people who received messages on the same answering machine, there would then be no way to tell the difference between multiple messages for each person. Second, the system would be limited by the number of colors between which the color recognition can reliably differentiate.

Shape and Pattern Recognition

Recognizing a color is relatively simple computationally; but recognizing a physical object is more challenging. To do this, you need to know the two-dimensional geometry of the object from every angle so that you can compare any view you get of the object.

A computer can't actually "see" in three dimensions using a single camera. The view it has of any object is just a two-dimensional shadow. Furthermore, it has no way of distinguishing one object from another in the camera view without some visual reference. The computer has no concept of a physical object. It can only compare and match patterns. It can rotate the view, stretch it, and do all kinds of mathematical transformations on the pixel array, but the computer doesn't understand an object as a discrete entity the same way a human does.

Face Detection

If you've used a digital camera developed in the past five years or so, chances are it's got a face-detection algorithm built in. It'll put a rectangle around each human face and attempt to focus on it. Face detection is a good example of visual pattern recognition. The camera looks for a pre-described pattern that describes, generically, a face. It has a particular proportion of height to width: there are two darker spots about one-third of the way from the top, a second darker spot about two-thirds of the way down, and so forth. Facial detection is not facial recognition—a face-detection algorithm generally isn't looking specifically enough at an image to tell you who the person is, just that they have something that more or less resembles a face.

OpenCV has patterns for facial detection that are very simple to use. The following project shows you how to detect faces.

X

Project 23

Face Detection Using a Webcam

Now that you've got a basic understanding of how optical detection works from the color-tracking project, it's time to try some simple pattern detection. In this project, you'll use OpenCV's facial-detection methods to look for faces in a camera image.

OpenCV's pattern detection uses pattern description files called cascades to describe the characteristics of a particular patern. A cascade describes the subregions of a given pattern, including their relative sizes, shapes, and contrast ratios. The patterns are designed to be general enough to allow for some variation, but specific enough to tell it from other patterns. The Processing OpenCV library comes with patterns for the following human features:

> **MATERIALS**
>
> » **Personal computer with USB or FireWire port**
> » **USB or FireWire webcam**
> » **Faces**

Frontal face view (four variations)
Profile face view
Full-body view
Lower-body view
Upper-body view

The sketch attempts basic facial recognition; see if you can fool it.

Before the setup(), set up the global variables as usual. These are almost identical to the last project, but you also need the Java Rectangle object. This is because the OpenCV detection method returns an array of Rectangles that it thinks contain faces.

The setup() is similar, but this time, you're going to have OpenCV look for detection pattern using the library's cascade() method. The available patterns are described on the Processing OpenCV site at http://ubaa.net/shared/processing/opencv/opencv_cascade.html.

Finally, the setup() sets the drawing conditions for ellipses, so you can draw circles over the faces.

```
/*
  Face detection using openCV
  Context: Processing
*/
// import the opencv and Rectangle libraries:
import hypermedia.video.*;
import java.awt.Rectangle;

OpenCV opencv;        // new instance of the openCV library


void setup() {
  // initialize the window:
  size( 320,240 );
  // initialize  opencv:
  opencv = new OpenCV( this );
  opencv.capture( width, height );
  // choose a detection description to use:
  opencv.cascade( OpenCV.CASCADE_FRONTALFACE_DEFAULT );
  // draw smooth edges:
  smooth();
  // set ellipses to draw from the upper left corner:
  ellipseMode(CORNER);
}
```

The draw() method is much simpler than the last project because you're not looking at every pixel. It uses the OpenCV detect() method to look for rectangles matching the pattern you chose, and delivers them in an array. Then it iterates over the array and draws ellipses over each face.

When you run this, point your face at it, and you'll get a nice fuchsia mask, as shown in Figure 9-3.

Try the program on different versions of faces and different conditions. Also try the other face-detection cascades mentioned on the OpenCV for Processing site.

```
void draw() {
  // grab a new frame:
  opencv.read();

  // Look for faces:
  Rectangle[] faces = opencv.detect();

  // display the image:
  image( opencv.image(), 0, 0 );

  // draw circles around the faces:
  fill(0xFF, 0x00, 0x84, 0x3F);   // a nice shade of fuchsia
  noStroke();                     // no border

  for ( int thisFace=0; thisFace<faces.length; thisFace++ ) {
    ellipse( faces[thisFace].x, faces[thisFace].y,
             faces[thisFace].width, faces[thisFace].height );
  }
}
```

Figure 9-3
The face detection finds me fairly well.

Turning sideways, I disappear.

It does well with a photo of people, even the abstracted face on my shirt. Facial hair and other markings make a person harder to detect.

Animals are not detected by this algorithm. Noodles is not detected (and not happy either).

" Barcode Recognition

A barcode is simply a pattern of dark and light lines or cells used to encode an alphanumeric string. A computer reads a barcode by scanning the image and interpreting the widths of the light and dark bands as zeroes or ones. This scanning can be done using a camera or a single photodiode, if the barcode can be passed over the photodiode at a constant speed. Many handheld barcode scanners work by having the user run a wand with an LED and a photodiode in the tip over the barcode, and reading the pattern of light and dark that the photodiode detects.

The best known barcode application is the Universal Product Code, or UPC, used by nearly every major manufacturer on the planet to label goods. There are many dozen different barcode symbologies, which are used for a wide range of applications. For example, the U.S. Postal Service uses POSTNET to automate mail sorting. European Article Numbering (EAN) and Japanese Article Numbering (JAN) are supersets of the UPC system developed to facilitate the international exchange of goods. Each symbology represents a different mapping of bars to characters. The symbologies are not interchangeable, so you can't properly interpret a POSTNET barcode if you're using an EAN interpreter. This means that either you have

Figure 9-4
A one-dimensional barcode. This is the ISBN bar code for this book.

9 781449 392437

to write a more comprehensive piece of software that can interpret several symbologies, or you have to know which one you're reading in advance. There are numerous software libraries for generating barcodes and several barcode fonts for printing the more popular symbologies.

Barcodes, such as the one shown in Figure 9-4, are called one-dimensional barcodes because the scanner or camera needs to read the image only along one axis. There are also two-dimensional barcodes that encode data in a two-dimensional matrix for more information density. As with one-dimensional barcodes, there are a variety of symbologies. Figure 9-5 shows a typical two-dimensional barcode. This type of code, the QR (Quick Response) code, was created in Japan and originally used for tracking vehicle parts, but it's since become popular for all kinds of product labeling. The inclusion of software to read these tags on many camera phones in Japan has made the tags more popular. The following project uses an open source Java library to read QR codes in Processing.

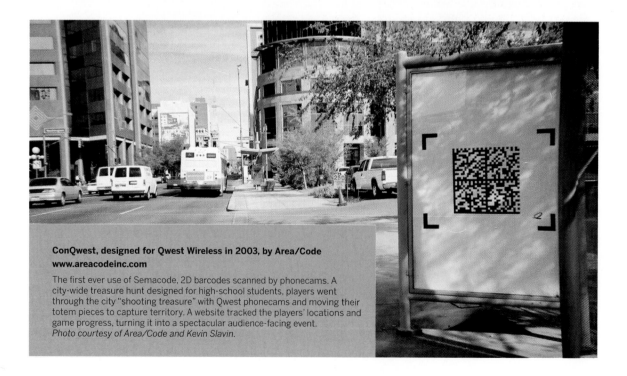

ConQwest, designed for Qwest Wireless in 2003, by Area/Code
www.areacodeinc.com
The first ever use of Semacode, 2D barcodes scanned by phonecams. A city-wide treasure hunt designed for high-school students, players went through the city "shooting treasure" with Qwest phonecams and moving their totem pieces to capture territory. A website tracked the players' locations and game progress, turning it into a spectacular audience-facing event.
Photo courtesy of Area/Code and Kevin Slavin.

Project 24

2D Barcode Recognition Using a Webcam

In this project, you'll generate some two-dimensional barcodes from text using an online QR code generator. Then you'll decode your tags using a camera and a computer. Once this works, try decoding the QR code illustrations in this book.

MATERIALS

» **Personal computer with USB or FireWire port**
» **Web Access**
» **USB or FireWire Webcam**
» **Printer**

This sketch reads QR codes using a camera attached to a personal computer. The video component is very similar to the color-tracking example earlier. Before you start on the sketch, though, you'll need some QR codes to read. Fortunately, there are a number of QR code generators available online. Just type the term into a search engine and see how many pop up. There's a good one at http://qrcode.kaywa.com, from which you can generate URLs, phone numbers, or plain text. The more text you enter, the larger the symbol. Generate a few codes and print them out for use later. Save them as **.png** files, because you'll need them for the sketch.

To run this sketch, you'll need to download the pqrcode library for Processing by Daniel Shiffman, It's based on the qrcode library from http://qrcode.sourceforge.jp. You can download the pqrcode library from www.shiffman.net/p5/pqrcode. Unzip it, and you'll get a directory called **pqrcode**. Drop it into the **libraries** subdirectory of your Processing application directory and restart Processing. Make a new sketch, and within the sketch's directory, make a subdirectory called **data**, and put in the **.jpg** or **.png** files of the QR codes that you generated earlier. Now you're ready to begin writing the sketch.

» In the setup() for this sketch, you'll import the pqrcode and OpenCV libraries, and initialize a few global variables.

```
/*
    QRCode reader
    Context: Processing
*/

import hypermedia.video.*;
import pqrcode.*;

OpenCV opencv;      // instance of the opencv library
Decoder decoder;    // instance of the pqrcode library

// a string to return messages:
String statusMsg = "Waiting for an image";

void setup() {
  // initialize the window:
  size(400, 320);

  // initialize opencv:
  opencv = new OpenCV( this );
  opencv.capture( width, height );

  // initialize the decoder:
  decoder = new Decoder(this);
}
```

» The draw() method draws the camera image and prints a status message to the screen. If the decoder library is in the middle of reading an image, it displays that image in the upper-lefthand corner, and changes the status message.

```
void draw() {
  // read the camera:
  opencv.read();
  // show the camera image:
  image( opencv.image(), 0, 0 );

  // Display status message:
  text(statusMsg, 10, height-4);

  // If you're currently decoding:
  if (decoder.decoding()) {
    // Display the image being decoded:
    PImage show = decoder.getImage();
    image(show, 0, 0, show.width/4, show.height/4);
    // update the status message:
    statusMsg = "Decoding image";
    // add a dot after every tenth frame:
    for (int dotCount = 0; dotCount < (frameCount) % 10; dotCount++) {
      statusMsg += ".";
    }
  }
}
```

» The pqrcode library has a method called decodeImage(). To use it, pass it an image in the keyReleased() method. A switch statement checks to see which key has been pressed. If you type f, it passes the decoder a file called **qrcode.png** from the **data** subdirectory. If you press the space bar, it passes the camera image. If you type s, it brings up a camera settings dialog box.

```
void keyReleased() {
  String code = "";
  // Depending on which key is hit, do different things:
  switch (key) {
  case ' ':          // space bar takes a picture and tests it:
    // Decode the image:
    decoder.decodeImage(opencv.image());
    break;
  case 'f':   // f runs a test on a file
    PImage preservedFrame = loadImage("qrcode.png");
    // Decode the file
    decoder.decodeImage(preservedFrame);
    break;
  }
}
```

» Once you've given the decoder an image, you wait. When it's decoded the image, it generates a decoder-Event(), and you can read the tag's ID using the getDecodedString() method.

```
// When the decoder object finishes
// this method will be invoked.
void decoderEvent(Decoder decoder) {
  statusMsg = decoder.getDecodedString();
}
```

" When you run this, notice how the **.jpg** or **.png** images scan much more reliably than the camera images. The distortion from the analog-to-digital conversion through the camera causes many errors. This error is made worse by poor optics or low-end camera imaging chips in mobile phones and webcams. Even with a good lens, if the code to be scanned isn't centered, the distortion at the edge of an image can throw off the pattern-recognition routine. You can improve the reliability of the scan by guiding the user to center the tag before taking an image. Even simple graphic hints like putting crop marks around the tag, as shown in Figure 9-5, can help. When you do this, users framing the image tend to frame to the crop marks, which ensures more space around the code and a better scan. Such methods help with any optical pattern recognition through a camera, whether it's one- or two-dimensional barcodes, or another type of pattern altogether.

Optical recognition forces one additional limitation besides those mentioned earlier: you have to be able to see the barcode. By now, most of the world is familiar with barcodes, because they decorate everything we buy or ship. This limitation is not only aesthetic. If you've ever turned a box over and over trying to get the barcode to scan, you know that it's also a functional limitation. A system that allowed for machine recognition of physical objects—but didn't rely on a line of sight to the identifying tag—would be an improvement. This is one of the main

Figure 9-5

A two-dimensional barcode (a QR code, to be specific) with crop marks around it. The image parsers won't read the crop marks, but they help users center the tag for image capture.

reasons that RFID is beginning to supersede bar codes in inventory control and other ID applications.

" Radio Frequency Identification (RFID)

Like barcode recognition, RFID relies on tagging objects in order to identify them. Unlike barcodes, however, RFID tags don't need to be visible to be read. An RFID reader sends out a short-range radio signal, which is picked up by an RFID tag. The tag then transmits back a short string of data. Depending on the size and sensitivity of the reader's antenna and the strength of the transmission, the tag can be several feet away from the reader, enclosed in a book, box, or item of clothing, and still be read. In fact, some clothing manufacturers are now sewing RFID tags into their merchandise, which customers remove after purchasing.

There are two types of RFID system: passive and active, just like distance-ranging systems. Passive RFID tags contain an integrated circuit that has a basic radio transceiver and a small amount of nonvolatile memory. They are powered by the current that the reader's signal induces in their antennas. The received energy is just enough to power the tag to transmit its data once, and the signal is relatively weak. Most passive readers can only read tags a few inches to a few feet away.

In an active RFID system, the tag has its own power supply and radio transceiver, and it transmits a signal in response to a received message from a reader. Active systems can transmit for a much longer range than passive systems, and they are less error-prone. They are also much more expensive. If you're a regular automobile commuter, and you pass through a toll gate during your commute, you're probably an active RFID user. Systems like E-ZPass use active RFID tags so that the reader can be placed several meters away from the tag.

Figure 9-6
The field of an RFID reader, by Timo Arnall. This stop-motion photo shows the effective range and shape of the RFID reader's field. The reader shown is an ID Innovations ID-20, which you'll see in the next project.

You might think that because RFID is radio-based, you could use it to do radio distance ranging as well, but that's not the case. Neither passive nor active RFID systems are typically designed to report the signal strength received from the tag. Without this information, it's impossible to use RFID systems to determine the actual location of a tag. All the reader can tell you is that the tag is within reading range. Although some high-end systems can report the tag signal strength, the vast majority of readers are not made for location as well as identification.

RFID systems vary widely in cost. Active systems can cost tens of thousands of dollars to purchase and install. Commercial passive systems can also be expensive. A typical passive reader that can read a tag a meter away from the antenna typically costs a few thousand dollars. At the low end, short-range passive readers can come as cheap as $30 or less. As of this writing, $30 to $100 gets you a reader that can read a few inches. Anything that can read a longer distance will be more expensive.

There are many different RFID protocols, just as with barcodes. Short-range passive readers come in at least three common frequencies: two low-frequency bands at 125 and 134.2kHz, and high-frequency readers at 13.56MHz. The higher-frequency readers allow for faster read rates and longer-range reading distances. In addition to different frequencies, there are also different protocols. For example, in the 13.56 band alone, there are the ISO 15693 and ISO 14443 and 14443-A standards. Within the ISO 15693 standard, there are different implementations by different manufacturers—Philips' I-Code, Texas Instruments' Tag-IT HF, Picotag—as well as implementations by Infineon, STMicroelectronics, and others. Within the ISO 14443 standard, there's Philips' Mifare and Mifare UL, ST's SR176, and others. So, you can't expect one reader to read every tag. You can't even count on one reader to read all the tags in a given frequency range. You have to match the tag to the reader.

There are a number of cheap and simple readers on the market now, covering the range of passive RFID frequencies and protocols. ID Innovations makes a range of small, inexpensive, and easy-to-use 125kHz readers with a serial output. The smallest of these is less than 1.5 inches on a side and is capable of reading the EM4001 protocol tags. Spark Fun and CoreRFID both sell these readers and matching tags. You'll use one of these in the next project.

Figure 9-7
RFID tags in all shapes and sizes. All of thes items have RFID tags in them. Photo by Timo Arnall. For more information on RFID design research by Arnall and his colleagues, see **www.nearfield.org**.

Parallax sells a 125kHz reader that can also read EM Micro-electronic tags, such as EM4001. It has a built-in antenna, and the whole module is about 2.5" x 3.5" on a flat circuit board. The ID Innovations readers and the Parallax readers can read the same tags. The EM4001 protocol isn't as common in everyday applications as the Mifare protocol, a variation on the ISO 14443 standard in the 13.56MHz range. Mifare shows up in many transit systems, like the London Tube. SonMicro makes a module that can both read from and write to these tags, which you'll see in the project after next.

As shown in Figure 9-7, RFID tags come in a number of different forms: sticker tags, coin discs, key fobs, credit cards, playing cards, even capsules designed for injection under the skin. The last are used for pet tracking and are not designed for human use, though there are some adventurous hackers who have inserted these tags under their own skin. Like any radio signal, RFID can be read through a number of materials, but it is blocked by any kind of RF shielding, such as wire mesh, conductive fabric lamé, metal foil, or adamantium skeletons. This feature means that you can embed it in all kinds of projects, as long as your reader has the signal strength to penetrate the materials.

Before picking a reader, think about the environment in which you plan to deploy it, and how that affects both the tags and the reading. Will the environment have a lot of RF noise? In what range? Then, consider a reader outside that range. Will you need a relatively long-range read? If so, look at the high-frequency readers. If you're planning to read existing tags rather than tags you purchase yourself,

research carefully in advance, because not all readers will read all tags. Pet tags can be some of the trickiest—many of them operate in the 134.2kHz range, in which there are fewer readers to choose from.

You also have to consider how it behaves when tags are in range. For example, even though the Parallax reader and the ID Innovations readers can read the same tags, they behave very differently when a tag is in range. The ID Innovations reader reports the tag ID only once. The Parallax reader reports it continually until the tag is out of range. The behavior of the reader can affect your project design, as you'll see later on.

The readers mentioned here have TTL serial interfaces, so they can be connected to a microcontroller or a USB-to-Serial module very easily. The ID Innovations and Parallax readers have a similar serial behavior, so you could swap one for the other with only a few code changes to your program.
X

> ⚠ Most RFID capsules are not sterilized for internal use in animals (humans included), and they're definitely not designed to be inserted without qualified medical supervision. Besides, insertion hurts. Don't RFID-enable yourself or your friends. Don't even do it to your pets—let your vet do it. If you're really gung-ho to be RFID-tagged, make yourself a nice set of RFID-tag earrings.

Project 25

Reading RFID Tags in Processing

In this project, you'll read some RFID tags to get a sense for how the readers behave. You'll see how far away from your reader a tag can be read. This is a handy test program to use any time you're adding RFID to a project.

MATERIALS

» **ID Innovations ID-12 or ID-20 RFID reader**
» **EM4001 RFID tags**
» **RFID breakout board**
» **Male header pins**
» **1 USB-to-TTL serial adapter**

The ID Innovations readers operate on 5 volts and have a TTL serial output, so the circuit is very simple.

There's also a buzzer pin, which goes high whenever a tag is read, so you know that the reader's working. An LED will work fine in place of the buzzer. Figure 9-8 shows the circuit for the ID Innovations reader connected to a USB-to-Serial adapter. The Parallax reader can work for this project too, though you'll have to modify the code to match its protocol.

All the ID Innovations readers use the same protocol. They operate at 9600bps. The serial sentence begins with a start-of-transmission (STX) byte (ASCII 02) and ends with an end-of-transmission (ETX) byte (ASCII 03). The STX is followed by the 10-byte tag ID. A checksum follows that, then a carriage return (ASCII 13) and linefeed (ASCII 10), then the ETX. The EM4001 tags format their tag IDs as ASCII-encoded hexadecimal values, so the string will never contain anything but the ASCII digits 0 through 9 and the letters A through F.

Try It   The Processing sketch shown here reads from an ID Innovations reader. The setup() should look very familiar to you by now—it's just opening the serial port and establishing a string for incoming data. Since the ID Innovations serial sentence ends with the value 03, you'll buffer any incoming serial until you see a byte of value 03.

```
/*
   ID Innovations RFID Reader
   Context: Processing

   Reads data serially from an ID Innovations ID-12 RFID reader.
*/
// import the serial library:
import processing.serial.*;

Serial myPort;      // the serial port you're using
String tagID = "";  // the string for the tag ID

void setup() {
  size(150,150);
  // list all the serial ports:
  println(Serial.list());

  // change the number below to match your port:
  String portnum = Serial.list()[2];
  // initialize the serial port:
  myPort = new Serial(this, portnum, 9600);
  // incoming string will end with 0x03:
  myPort.bufferUntil(0x03);
}
```

Figure 9-8
The ID Innovations ID-12 RFID reader attached to an FTDI USB-to-Serial adapter. The ID-12 has pins spaced 2mm apart. Spark Fun's breakout board breaks it out to standard breadboard spacing, however.

If you plan to use the ID Innovations readers a lot, you might consider replacing this circuit with Spark Fun's RFID USB reader (part no. SEN-09963), which combines the FTDI adapter and mount for the reader in one module.

>> The draw() method draws the tag ID to the screen.

```
void draw() {
  // clear the screen and choose
  // pleasant colors inspired by a seascape:
  background(#022E61);
  fill(#D9EADD);
  // print the string to the screen:
  text(tagID, width/4, height/2);
}
```

>> The real work happens in the serialEvent() method. It's called whenever a byte of value 03 comes in the serial port. It checks to see whether the string starts with a byte of value 02 and ends with 03. If so, it takes the first 10 bytes after the 02 as the tag ID.

Run this sketch with the ID Innovations reader attached, and wave some tags in front of it. With each tag, you should get a result like the screenshot in Figure 9-9.

```
void serialEvent(Serial myPort) {
  // get the serial input buffer in a string:
  String inputString = myPort.readString();

  // filter out the tag ID from the string:
  // first character of the input:
  char firstChar = inputString.charAt(0);
  // last character of the input:
  char lastChar = inputString.charAt(inputString.length() -1);

  // if the first char is STX (0x02) and the last char
  // is ETX (0x03), then put the next 10 bytes
  // into the tagID string:

  if ((firstChar == 0x02) && (lastChar == 0x03)) {
    tagID = inputString.substring(1, 11);
  }
}
```

10000CDFF7

Figure 9-9
Output of the ID Innovations Reader sketch.

When you have this sketch working, use it to test the range of your reader to see from how far away you can read a tag. You'll notice that the tag has to leave the reader's range before it can be read a second time. You may not be able to tell that from the screen output, but you'll notice that the LED goes off when the tag goes out of range, and it turns on again when it comes back in range. Many readers have a similar behavior. You should also see that the reader can't read more than one tag at a time—this is common among all the readers mentioned here.

X

Project 26

RFID Meets Home Automation

Between my officemate and me, we have dozens of devices drawing power in our office: several computers, two monitors, four or five lamps, a few hard drives, a soldering iron, Ethernet hubs, speakers, and so forth. Even when we're not in the office, the room is drawing a lot of power. The devices that are turned on at any given time depends largely on which of us is here, and what we're doing. This project is a system to reduce our power consumption, particularly when we're not there.

When we come into the office, all we have to do is touch our keys on a plate by the door, and the room turns on or off the devices we normally use. Each of us has a key ring with an RFID-tag key fob. The module behind the plate has an RFID reader in it, which reads the tags.

The reader is connected to a microcontroller module that communicates over the AC power lines using the X10 protocol. Each of the various power strips is plugged into an X10 appliance module. Depending on which tag is read, the microcontroller knows which modules to turn on or off. Figure 9-10 shows the system.

The Circuit

The X10 interface module connects to the microcontroller via a four-wire phone cable. Clip one end of the cable and solder headers onto the four wires. Then connect them to the microcontroller as shown in Figure 9-11. The schematic shows the phone jack (an RJ-11 jack) on the interface module as you're looking at it from the bottom. Make sure the wires at the header ends correspond with the pins on the jack from right to left.

NOTE: The colors for the four-wire cable shown in Figure 9-11 are typical for many four-wire phone cables in the U.S., but they do

---

MATERIALS

- » 1 solderless breadboard
- » 1 Arduino module
- » 1 ID Innovations ID-12 or ID-20 RFID reader
- » 2 EM4001 RFID tags
- » 1 RFID breakout board
- » Male header pins
- » Interface module: X10 One-Way Interface Module
- » 2 X10 modules
- » 4-wire phone cable with RJ-11 connector

---

not correspond to the colors used in other diagrams in this book, so be careful to connect the circuit exactly as shown.

The RFID reader's reset pin is connected to the microcontroller's reset pin so that whenever the latter is reset, the former will be as well.

The RFID reader is connected to the microcontroller a little differently than you might expect. Its serial transmit pin is connected to pin 7. You're going to use the SoftwareSerial library to add an extra serial connection to the Arduino this time. The SoftwareSerial library is included in the standard download for Arduino, so you won't need to download anything in order to use it.

To send X10 commands, use the X10 library for Arduino. You can download it from https://github.com/tigoe/x10. Unzip it and place the resulting directory in the **libraries** subdirectory of your Arduino sketch directory. Then restart the Arduino environment.

This project doesn't receive any X10 data, it only sends from the microcontroller to the modules. However, the circuit should be compatible with two-way interface modules. Likewise, the library—though not written to send both ways—could be adapted to send as well as receive. You'll need to add your own sending methods to the library, as the current ones are just stubs. The library should be compatible with both 50Hz and 60Hz AC systems as well. For experienced programmers, the stubs of receive methods can be found in the library's source code—feel free to adapt it as you see fit. For readers seeking a more advanced X10 library, see http://load-8-1.blogspot.com/2010_06_01_archive.html. Thanks to reader Tom Crites for the link.

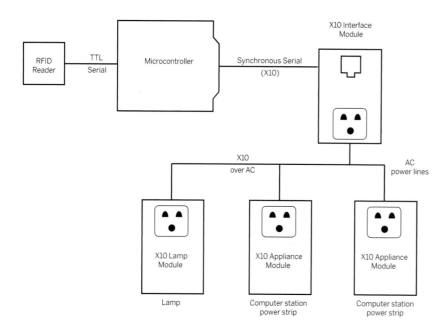

Figure 9-10
An RFID-controlled home (or office) automation system using X10.

What Is X10?

X10, a communications protocol that works over AC power lines, is designed for use in home automation. Companies such as Smarthome (www.smarthome.com) and X10.com (www.x10.com) sell various devices that communicate over power lines using X10: cameras, motion sensors, switch control panels, and more. It's a slow and limited protocol, but it has been popular with home automation enthusiasts for years because the equipment is relatively inexpensive and easy to obtain.

X10 is basically a synchronous serial protocol, like I2C and SPI. Instead of sending bits every time a master clock signal changes, X10 devices send a bit every time the AC power line crosses zero volts. This means that X10's maximum data rate is 120 bits per second in the U.S., as the AC signal crosses the zero point twice per cycle, and AC signals are 60Hz in the U.S. The protocol is tricky to program if you have to do it yourself, but many microcontroller-development systems include libraries to send X10 signals.

There are four devices that come in handy for developing X10 projects: an interface module, an appliance control module, a lamp control module, and a control panel module. You'll be building your own controllers, but the control panel

module is useful as a diagnostic tool because it already works. When you can't get the appliance or lamp modules to respond to your own projects, you can at least get them to respond to the control panel module—that way, you know whether the bits are passing over the power lines. Smarthome sells versions of all four of these:

- Interface module: X10 One-Way Interface Module, part number 1134B. You'll see two common versions of this: the PL513 and the TW523. They both work essentially the same way. The TW523 is a two-way module—it can send and receive X10 signals—while the PL513 can only send.

- Appliance control module: X10 Appliance Module 3-Pin, part number 2002. These can control anything you can plug into an AC socket, up to 15 Amps.

- Lamp control module: Powerhouse X10 Lamp Module, part number 2000. These can control incandescent (not fluorescent or neon) lamps only.

- Control panel module: X10 Mini Controller, part number 4030.

Figure 9-11
The circuit for the RFID-to-X10 project. The ID Innovations reader's reset is connected to the microcontroller's reset so that they will always reset together.

X10 device addresses have a two-tier structure. There are 16 house codes—labeled A through P—and within each house code you can have 16 individual units. These are assigned unit codes. Each X10 module has two click-wheels to set the house code and the unit code. For this project, get at least two appliance or lamp modules. Set the first module to house code A, unit 1, and the second module to house code A, unit 2.

Construction

The box for this project is similar to the ones for the Pong clients in Chapter 5. In fact, it's made from the same template, with the side heights and widths changed slightly. There's only a single LED hole, and there's no hole for the Ethernet jack (since there isn't one!). Instead, there's a hole for the X10 cable to go through. Figure 9-12 shows the finished prototype, and a commercially available version of an RFID door lock as well.

X

More Serial Ports: Software Serial

The Arduino's hardware serial connection (digital pins 0 and 1, labeled RX and TX) allow it to send and receive serial data reliably, no matter what your code is doing, because the processor has a dedicated UART (Universal Asynchronous Receiver-Transmitter) module that listens for serial all the time. What do you do when you need to attach more than one asynchronous serial device to your Arduino? The Arduino Mega 2560 has four UARTs, but you may not need all that a Mega has to offer just to get another serial port. This is where the SoftwareSerial library comes in handy. SoftwareSerial allows you to use two digital pins as a "fake" UART. The library can listen for incoming serial on those pins, and transmit as well. Because it's not a dedicated hardware UART, SoftwareSerial isn't as reliable as hardware serial at very high or very low speeds, though it does well from 4800bps through 57.6kbps. It can be very useful when you need an extra port, or when you want to use the hardware serial port for diagnostic purposes, as in this project.

Test the RFID The first thing you want to do is test both parts of your circuit. This sketch just reads from the RFID reader via a software serial port, and writes what it got to the hardware serial port. Open the Serial Monitor and wave a tag or two in front of the reader. You should see their tag numbers show up in the Serial Monitor. Write down your tags' IDs—you'll need them later.

```
/*
 RFID Reader
 Context: Arduino
*/
#include <SoftwareSerial.h>
SoftwareSerial rfid(7,8);        // 7 is rx, 8 is tx

void setup() {
  // begin serial:
  Serial.begin(9600);
  rfid.begin(9600);
}
void loop() {
  // read in from the reader and
  // write it out to the serial monitor:
  if (rfid.available()) {
    char thisChar = rfid.read();
    Serial.write(thisChar);
  }
}
```

Test the X10   Once you know
the RFID reader
works, it's time to test the X10 output.
This sketch turns on Unit 1 in house
A for half a second, then turns it off.
To test it, plug in your X10 interface
module to the wall, and plug in a lamp
module with a lamp connected and
turned on to the same circuit in your
house. When the sketch runs, the lamp
should blink.

```
/*
  X10 blink
  Context: Arduino
 */
#include <x10.h>

const int rxPin = 3;    // data receive pin
const int txPin = 4;    // data transmit pin
const int zcPin = 2;    // zero crossing pin

void setup() {
  // initialize serial and X10:
  Serial.begin(9600);
  x10.begin(rxPin, txPin, zcPin);
}

void loop() {
  // open transmission to house code A:
  x10.beginTransmission(A);
  Serial.println("Lights on:");
  // send a "lights on" command:
  x10.write(ON);

  delay(500);
  Serial.println("Lights off:");
  // send a "lights off" command:
  x10.write(OFF);
  x10.endTransmission();
  delay(500);
}
```

It's unlikely that this will work the first time. X10 is notorious for having synchronization problems while you're developing the hardware and firmware. For one thing, it doesn't work when the transmitter and receiver are on different circuits, so you need to know which circuits in your house's circuit-breaker panel control which outlets. Some surge protectors and power strips might filter out X10 as well, so make sure that the X10 units are plugged into the wall, not the surge protector. You can plug surge protectors into X10 appliance modules, but avoid plugging them into lamp modules unless everything plugged into the surge protector is an incandescent lamp.

X10 lamp modules allow you to dim incandescent lights, but they will control only resistive loads—that means no blow dryers, blenders, or anything with a motor. Compact fluorescent bulbs are generally not dimmable, and they are not designed for use on lamp modules either. If you're unsure, use an appliance module instead of a lamp module.

If your lights don't turn on correctly, first unplug everything, then set the addresses, then plug everything back in, then reset the Arduino. If that fails, make sure your units are on the same circuit, and eliminate surge protectors (if you're using them.) Try to turn the modules using a control panel module. Make sure the control panel isn't sending an ALL UNITS OFF signal at the same time as your Arduino. If needed, unplug the control panel once you know the lamp module is responding. Once you've got control over your modules, you can combine the RFID and X10 programs. **X**

Refine It This sketch reads incoming tags and checks them against a list of tags in memory. When it sees a tag it knows, it checks the status of an X10 lamp or appliance module that corresponds to that tag, and then changes the status.

The global variables are the X10 pin and SoftwareSerial pin numbers, the number of tags being used, and a bunch of arrays for the tag IDs, unit names, and unit states.

The setup() method initializes serial, software serial, and X10, then sends an ALL LIGHTS OFF code to reset all the remote X10 units.

```
/*
  RFID Tag checker
  Context: Arduino
*/
// include the X10  and softwareSerial library files:
#include <x10.h>
#include <SoftwareSerial.h>

const int x10ZeroCrossing = 2;  // x10 zero crossing pin
const int x10Tx = 3;            // x10 transmit pin
const int x10Rx = 4;            // x10 receive pin (not used)
const int rfidRx = 7;           // rfid receive pin
const int rfidTx = 8;           // rfid transmit pin (not used)
int numTags = 2;                // how many tags in your list

String currentTag;              // String to hold the tag you're reading
// lists of tags, unit names, and unit states:
String tag[] = {
  "10000CDFF7","0F00AD72B5"};
int unit[] = {
  UNIT_1, UNIT_2};
int unitState[] = {
  OFF, OFF};

SoftwareSerial rfid(rfidRx,rfidTx);

void setup() {
  // begin serial:
  Serial.begin(9600);
  rfid.begin(9600);
  // begin x10:
  x10.begin(x10Tx, x10Rx,x10ZeroCrossing);
  // Turn off all lights:
  x10.beginTransmission(A);
  x10.write(ALL_LIGHTS_OFF);
  x10.endTransmission();
}
```

» The loop() method just checks for new serial bytes from the RFID reader. The real work is left to a pair of other methods.

```
void loop() {
  // read in and parse serial data:
  if (rfid.available()) {
    readByte();
  }
}
```

➤ The readByte() method is called every time a new byte comes in from the RFID reader. If the incoming byte is 02, it starts a new current tag string. If the byte is 03, it checks the current tag against the list of known tags using a method called checkTags(). If it's any other byte, it checks to see whether the current tag string is long enough; if not, it adds the new byte to that string.

```
void readByte() {
  char thisChar = rfid.read();

  // depending on the byte's value,
  // take different actions:
  switch(thisChar) {
    // if the byte = 02, you're at the beginning
    // of a new tag:
  case 0x02:
    currentTag = "";
    break;
    // if the byte = 03, you're at the end of a tag:
  case 0x03:
    checkTags();
    break;
    // other bytes, if the current tag is less than
    // 10 bytes, you're still reading it:
  default:
    if (currentTag.length() < 10) {
      currentTag += thisChar;
    }
  }
}
```

➤ The checkTags() method checks the current tag string against the known list. When it finds the tag, it checks the state of the corresponding X10 unit from a list of unit states. Then it sends that unit a message to change its state from ON to OFF, or vice versa.

```
void checkTags() {
  // iterate over the list of tags:
  for (int thisTag = 0; thisTag < numTags; thisTag++) {
    // if the current tag matches the tag you're on:

    if (currentTag.equals(tag[thisTag])) {
      // unit number starts at 1, but list position starts at 0:
      Serial.print("unit " + String(thisTag +1));
      // start transmission to unit:
      x10.beginTransmission(A);
      x10.write(unit[thisTag]);
      // change the status of the corresponding unit:
      if (unitState[thisTag] == ON) {
        unitState[thisTag] = OFF;
        Serial.println(" turning OFF");
      }
      else {
        unitState[thisTag] = ON;
        Serial.println(" turning ON");
      }
      // send the new status:
      x10.write(unitState[thisTag]);
      // end transmission to unit:
      x10.endTransmission();
    }
  }
}
```

" When you run this code, you'll see that the RFID reader only reads when a new tag enters its field. The ID Innovations readers don't have the ability to read multiple tags if more than one tag is in the field. That's an important limitation. It means that you have to design the interaction so that the person using the system places only one tag at a time, and then removes it before placing the second one. In effect, it means that two people can't place their key tags on the reader at the same time. Users of the system need to take explicit action to make something happen. Presence isn't enough.

The simplest solution is to design the project physically so that the user has to remove the tag once he passes it by the reader, as shown in Figure 9-12. This is the most common commercial solution as well. For example, the front door of my apartment building uses an RFID lock.

The reader is vertical so I can't leave my keys on it, and the inside locks are regular keys, so I have incentive to remove the keyring once I open the front door if I want to open the inner door.

X

Figure 9-12

The finished RFID reader box, left, and a commmercially available RFID door lock on the front of an apartment building, right. Mounted by the door, it ensures that the user has to remove the tag. This works around the reader's limitation of being able to read only one tag at a time, To avoid a second wire, the prototype on the left is battery-powered.

Project 27

Tweets from RFID

You've seen RFID readers in action, but there are some RFID tags that can be written to as well. In the first part of this project, you'll use the popular Mifare standard RFID read/write tags and a SonMicro high-frequency reader to write Twitter handles to tags. In the second part, you'll build a microcontroller-based reader to read the data from those tags and display it on a 2x16-character LCD display. This links the physical identity of an RFID tag to your network identity on Twitter.

MATERIALS

» **1 SonMicro SM130 RFID read/write module**
» **3 Mifare RFID read/write tags**
» **Arduino Ethernet module**
» **1 RFID shield**
» **13.56MHz antenna** Unless your reader incorporates an antenna

The parts for building the reader circuit without a shield are listed below, for those who prefer that option:

» **2 4.7-kilohm resistors**
» **1 solderless breadboard**

RFID tags are often used for more than just the serial number stored on them. In some mass-transit systems, the customer's available balance is read from, decremented, and written to the card with each transaction. Some conferences use the RFID tag to store business card information, so attendees can exchange data digitally by tapping their cards to a reader. Near field communications (NFC) enhances this kind of exchange even further. NFC involves both passive and active exchange, where two devices communicate with each other over short distances. NFC accommodates a number of communications standards, including some of the RFID standards like ISO14443A and B, which includes Mifare. Because of this, NFC devices are often compatible with Mifare RFID readers and tags. It is starting to gain popularity in mobile phones and other portable devices, so look for many NFC and RFID applications in the near future. Projects like this one here may become relatively commonplace.

The Circuit

The SonMicro SM130 RFID reader operates on 5 volts, and it can communicate with a microcontroller using either asynchronous serial communication or synchronous serial via I2C. You'll see both in practice in this project. For the first part, you'll communicate with Processing directly using asynchronous serial. In the second part, you'll communicate with the microcontroller directly using I2C.

There are two Arduino shields available to connect the SM130 to an Arduino: the TinkerKit RFID shield and the Spark Fun RFID Evaluation shield 13.56MHz. Both allow you to connect to either the asynchronous serial or the I2C connections. The Spark Fun board uses solder jumpers, which let you choose whether to connect to digital pins 7 and 8 for a software serial connection. The TinkerKit shield has a switch that turns the serial connection hardware on or off. The Spark Fun comes with a built-in antenna. The TinkerKit shield has connections for an external antenna so you can place it where you wish, relative to the board.

To communicate with Processing, you could use a USB-to-Serial adapter, like you've done with many other projects, or you could use the Arduino as a USB-to-Serial adapter. For the Spark Fun board, you would need to include a sketch to pass the software serial data to the hardware serial, and vice versa. For the TinkerKit board, you would need to switch the serial switch to ON and put a blank sketch on the board. Both sketches are shown below.

There's only a difference between these two shields when you're communicating with the RFID reader via asynchronous serial, because they use differing pins for that. When you're communicating with the reader using I2C, as you will later in the project, they're functionally identical.

This project was built using the TinkerKit RFID shield. It's been tested on both, however.

If you're not using a shield, connect the SonMicro reader to a USB-to-Serial adapter, as shown in Figure 9-13. Then load the appropriate Arduino sketch below, and you're ready to try the Processing sketch on the following pages.
X

Bypass It (TinkerKit)

This sketch passes data from a SonMicro RFID reader on a TinkerKit RFID shield to the Arduino's USB-to-Serial adapter, bypassing the microcontroller. When your board is programmed this way, the Arduino acts as a USB-to-Serial adapter for the SonMicro reader.

```
/*
  TinkerKit RFID shield serial pass through
  Context: Arduino
*/

void setup() {
}

void loop() {
}
```

Bypass It (Spark Fun)

This sketch passes data from a SonMicro RFID reader on a Spark Fun RFID shield to the Arduino's hardware serial port, and vice versa. When your board is programmed this way, the Arduino acts as a USB-to-Serial adapter for the SonMicro reader.

```
/*
  Spark Fun RFID shield serial pass through
  Context: Arduino
*/

#include <SoftwareSerial.h>

// using pins 7 and 8 (7 is the Arduino's RX, 8 is TX)
SoftwareSerial rfid(7,8);

void setup() {
  rfid.begin(19200);     // set up software serial port
  Serial.begin(19200);   // set up serial port
}

void loop() {
  // pass any hardware serial to the software serial:
  if (Serial.available()) {
    rfid.write(Serial.read());
  }
  // pass any software serial to the hardware serial:
  if (rfid.available()) {
    Serial.write(rfid.read());
  }
}
```

◀◀ **Figure 9-13**
SonMicro RFID reader attached to a USB-to-Serial
adapter, exploded view. The reader and antenna
normally sit on the breadboard in the same
position as shown in the I2C breadboard view in
Figure 9-14.

� **Figure 9-14**
SonMicro RFID reader attached to an Arduino
via I2C, exploded view, showing the connections
under the module on the breadboard. The circuit
here is basically the same as both the TinkerKit
shield and the Spark Fun shield. The I2C connections need the two 4.7-kilohm pullup resistors.
You don't need this circuit if you're using an RFID
shield.

⬆ **Figure 9-15**
SonMicro RFID reader attached to an Arduino
via I2C, normal position on the breadboard. The
module sits in the same position on the board for
the USB-to-Serial adapter circuit as well.

▸▸ **Figure 9-16**
SonMicro RFID reader schematic. The I2C connections need pullup resistors. These resistors
are built into the TinkerKit shield and the Spark
Fun shield.

SonMicro Communications Protocol

The SonMicro readers use a binary communications protocol to communicate with other devices. The protocol is similar whether you're communicating over asynchronous serial or I2C. The I2C version looks like this:

Length	Command	Data	Checksum
1 byte	1 byte	N bytes	1 byte

The serial version just adds two extra header bytes. It looks like this:

Header	Reserved	Length	Command	Data	Checksum
1 byte	1 byte	1 byte	1 byte	N bytes	1 byte

The commands for the reader are single-byte values. The most common ones are shown below:

Byte value	Command
0x80	Reset
0x81	Get firmware version
0x82	Seek for tag
0x83	Select tag
0x85	Authenticate
0x86	Read memory block
0x89	Write memory block
0x90	Antenna power (turns on or off antenna)

The length byte indicates the length of the command, plus any data that goes with it. So, for example, a reset command—which has no data to follow the command— has a length of 1. A read command has one byte of data indicating the address you want to read from, so the length is 2.

The checksum is an error-checking value. To calculate the checksum, add together the command and data bytes; and if the value is greater than 255, take the lowest byte. For example, Here's the reset command's checksum:

```
0x01 (length) + 0x80 (command) = 0x81 (checksum)
```

If you were reading from memory address 04, the checksum would be as follows (note that these values are in hexadecimal):

```
0x02 (length) + 0x86 (command) + 0x04 (address) = 0x8C
(checksum)
```

For the asynchronous serial protocol, the header byte is always 0xFF, and the reserved byte is always 0. They're not added in the checksum, so you can use the same commands and calculations as you do for the I2C version, and just add 0xFF and 0x00 at the beginning. The replies sent back from the reader follow this same protocol.

There are both Processing and Arduino libraries to handle this protocol so you don't have to, but it's useful to know the basics. To start out, write a simple Processing sketch that sends the command to get the firmware version, and then reads the reply. Readers come with different firmware versions, and you might need to change the firmware on yours (see the sidebar on page 336), so you'll save a lot of troubleshooting time up front by knowing the firmware version.

When you run this sketch, you can see the responses in hexadecimal at the top, and in ASCII at the bottom (see Figure 9-17). The firmware command is the only one that returns any ASCII, because this is a binary protocol. The select tag command returns a binary string similar to the command protocol. It starts with the header and reserved byte (0xFF, 0x00), then the data length (0x06 if there's a tag, 0x02 if not), the command received (0x83), the tag type (0x02 means Mifare classic), four bytes representing the tag number (0x0A, 0xD4, 0xF0, 0x28, in my case), and the checksum (0x81). The ASCII representation, on the other hand, looks like garbage.

X

Talk to It   This Processing sketch sends commands to the SM130 module, and reads the result. The SM130's default data rate is 19200bps. Type s to select a tag in the field, and type any other key to read the firmware version.

```
/*
SonMicro Firmware version reader
Context: Processing
*/
import processing.serial.*;
Serial myPort;              // The serial port
String binaryString = "";
String asciiString = "";

void setup() {
  size(500, 200);          // window size
  // List all the available serial ports
  println(Serial.list());
  // Open whatever port is the one you're using.
  myPort = new Serial(this, Serial.list()[2], 19200);
}

void draw() {
  // Dystopian waterscape color scheme,
  // by arem114, http://kuler.adobe.com/
  background(#7B9B9D);
  fill(#59462E);
  // write the response, in hex and ASCII:
  text(binaryString, 10, height/3);
  text(asciiString, 10, 2*height/3);
}

void keyReleased() {
  int command = 0x81;    // read firmware command is the default
  int dataLength = 1;    // data length for both commands here is 1
  if (key == 's') {      // "select tag" command
    command = 0x83;
  }
  // send command:
  myPort.write(0xFF);
  myPort.write(0x00);
  myPort.write(dataLength);
  myPort.write(command);
  myPort.write(command + dataLength);
  // reset the response strings:
  binaryString = "";
  asciiString = "";
}

void serialEvent(Serial myPort) {
  // get the next incoming byte:
  char thisChar = (char)myPort.read();
  // add the byte to the response strings:
  binaryString += hex(thisChar, 2) + " ";
  asciiString += thisChar;
}
```

Figure 9-17
Screenshots of the Processing sketch to read SonMicro firmware, showing the results of the read firmware command (top) and the select tag command (bottom).

Writing to Mifare Tags

Now that you know a little about the SonMicro protocol, it's time to get on with writing data to the tags. To do this, you can use the Processing SonMicroReader library, which you can download from https://github.com/tigoe/SonMicroReader-for-Processing. Download the library, unzip it, copy the resulting folder to the **libraries** folder of your Processing sketch folder, and restart Processing. In the File → Examples menu, you should see a new entry for SonMicroReader under Contributed Libraries. The example called **SonMicroWriter0002.pde** follows.

This sketch has a graphical user interface with buttons for many of the common commands, and text responses in plain language as well as hexadecimal representations of the reader's responses. When you're working with a device that has a lot of functionality like this, sometimes it's worthwhile to write a tool to work all of its functions—or at least the most common ones.

When you run the sketch, you'll get the interface shown in Figure 9-18. Click the Firmware Version button to get the firmware version, just to make sure you've got good communication with the reader. Then try reading a few tags

with the Select Tag button. When there's no tag present, you get a response from the reader saying that. When you choose Seek Tag, however, you get an initial response that the command's in progress. Then, when you bring a tag in range, it reads automatically without you having to send another command.

In addition to their tag IDs, which can't change, Mifare tags have a small amount of RAM that you can read from and write to. Mifare standard tags have 1 kilobyte, Mifare classic tags have 4 kilobytes, and Mifare Ultralight tags have 512 bits. The former two use encrypted communication for reading and writing, and you have to authenticate a tag before you can read from or write to it. When you authenticate, you gain access to one 16-byte block of memory at a time.

The sequence for reading or writing to a block of memory is always:

- Select Tag
- Authenticate
- Read Block (or write block)

The code for this sketch follows.

Changing the Firmware on the SonMicro Readers

SonMicro SM130 readers come with different firmware versions, depending on which reader you buy. Different vendors carry different models, so it's good to check your firmware right away. All firmware versions can communicate serially, so the sketch shown above is a good way to check. Details of the firmware versions are available on SonMicro's site, www.sonmicro.com, under Products → 13.56 MHz RFID - MIFARE → OEM Modules & Readers. If your firmware version is UM 1.3 or UM 1.3c, you'll need to change the firmware in order to control the module using I2C. If your firmware version is I2C 2.8 or another I2C version, you can do both I2C and asynchronous serial and skip the rest of this sidebar.

If you have to upgrade your firmware, you'll need a Windows PC and the Firmware Upgrade tool called SM13X FU from SonMicro's site (it's downloadable from the 13.56 MHz RFID Mifare Support page, on the Software tab), and the SMRFID Mifare v1.2 diagnostic software. Download them both, then unzip and install them. You'll also need the I2C firmware—to get that, you have to email SonMicro. They are fast and friendly in response, though, and there's a technical inquiries link you can use to contact them from the Support page.

Connect your reader to your Windows PC using a USB-to-Serial adapter (the approach used for the Processing sketch above will work fine). Launch the SM13X FU application, click the "…" button, and browse to find the firmware file you want to upload. The file will be called i2c_28_b1.rme or something similar, depending on the version number. Then click Auto Upgrade. You should see messages at the bottom of the window ending with a successful upgrade.

But wait, you're not done yet. Close the firmware upgrader and open the SMRFID Mifare v1.2 application. Open the ComPort and choose Read I2C Address from the Hardware Commands menu. If the response is NOT 0x42, you should change it. Choose Set I2C Address and enter 42, then click OK. The reader's I2C address will be changed to 0x42, which is the default, and is what's used in the Arduino examples below.

You don't need to do any more with these applications to proceed with the project, but you may want to explore the SMRFID Mifare application. It's a useful tool for reading tags, writing to tags, and performing other diagnostic functions on the SM130 reader modules.

The SM Firmware Uploader (right) and a closeup of the SMRFID diagnostic application (below). When you've finished, you should see results in the SMRFID application like those shown here.

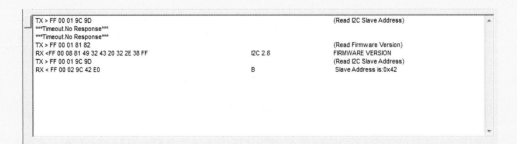

Figure 9-18
Screenshot of the Processing SonMicroWriter sketch, showing the response to a successful Read Block request.

Write to It   This Processing sketch lets you read from and write to the memory on a Mifare tag using the SM130 RFID reader. It uses the SonMicroReader library for Processing.

The global variables for this sketch are mostly properties of the last tag read. There is an ArrayList to keep track of the buttons onscreen, as well as a list of button names.

```
/*
 SonMicro RFID Writer example
 Context: Processing
 */

// import libraries:
import processing.serial.*;
import sonMicroReader.*;

String tagID = "";          // the string for the tag ID
Serial myPort;              // serial port instance
SonMicroReader myReader;    // SonMicroReader instance

int  lastCommand = 0;       // last command sent
int lastTagType = 0;        // last tag type received
int lastPacketLength = 0;   // last packet length received
String lastTag = null;      // last tag ID received
int lastErrorCode = 0;      // last error code received
int[] lastResponse = null;  // last response from the reader (raw data)
int lastAntennaPower = 0;   // last antenna power received
int lastChecksum = 0;       // last checksum received

int fontHeight = 14;        // font height for the text onscreen
String message = null;      // message read from tag
String outputString = "Hello world!";   // string to write to tag

// Color theme: Ghostly Music
// by banshee prime, http://kuler.adobe.com
color currentcolor = #CBD0D4;    // current button color
color highlight = #745370;
color buttoncolor = #968195;
color userText = #444929;
color buttonText = #ACB0B9;
```

»

Continued from previous page.

```
ArrayList buttons = new ArrayList();  // list of buttons
// the buttons themselves:
String[]  buttonNames = {
  "antenna power", "select tag", "authenticate", "read block", "seek Tag",
  "write block", "firmware version"
};
```

setup() initializes the serial connection and makes an instance of the SonMicroReader library. Then it makes fonts for drawing text on the screen, and calls the makeButtons() function to make the onscreen buttons. The button creation and control functions come later, at the end of the sketch.

```
void setup() {
  // set window size:
  size(600, 400);
  // list all the serial ports:
  println(Serial.list());

  // based on the list of serial ports printed from the
  // previous command, change the 0 to your port's number:
  String portnum = Serial.list()[0];
  // initialize the serial port. default data rate for
  // the SM130 reader is 19200:
  myPort = new Serial(this, portnum, 19200);
  // initialize the reader instance:
  myReader = new SonMicroReader(this, myPort);
  myReader.start();

  // create a font with the second font available to the system:
  PFont myFont = createFont(PFont.list()[2], fontHeight);
  textFont(myFont);
  // create the command buttons:
  makeButtons();
}
```

draw() draws text and buttons to the screen.

```
void draw() {
  background(currentcolor);
  // draw the command buttons:
  drawButtons();
  // draw the output fields:
  textAlign(LEFT);
  text("Command: " + hex(lastCommand, 2), 10, 30);
  text("Packet length: " +lastPacketLength, 10, 50);
  text("Antenna power: " + lastAntennaPower, 10, 70);
  text("Tag type: " + lastTagType, 10, 90);
  text("Tag string: " + lastTag, 10, 110);
  text("Error code: " + hex(lastErrorCode, 2), 10, 130);

  // print the hex values for all the bytes in the response:
```

»

Continued from opposite page.

```
String responseString = "";
if (lastResponse != null) {
  for (int b = 0; b < lastResponse.length; b++) {
    responseString += hex(lastResponse[b], 2);
    responseString += " ";
  }
  // wrap the full text so it doesn't overflow the buttons
  // and make the screen all messy:
  text("Full response:\n" + responseString, 10, 150, 300, 200);
}
// print any error messages from the reader:
text(myReader.getErrorMessage(), 10, 210);
// print the last message read from the tag:
text("last message read from tag:\n" + message, 10, 230);

// print the output message:
text("type your message to write to tag:\n", 10, 300);
fill(userText);
text(outputString, 10, 320);

// show the library version:
fill(0);
text("SonMicroReader version: " + myReader.version(),
width - 300, height - 30);
}
```

» TheSonMicroReader library uses the Serial library to communicate with the reader—like the Serial library—it generates an event when new data is available. sonMicroEvent() occurs whenever there's a response from the reader. In this sketch, you read all the parts of the response in the sonMicroEvent() method, including the tag number, tag type, any data returned from reading a memory block, the antenna status, and more.

```
/*
This function is called automatically whenever there's
a valid packet of data from the reader
*/
void sonMicroEvent(SonMicroReader myReader) {
  // get all the relevant data from the last data packet:
  lastCommand = myReader.getCommand();
  lastTagType = myReader.getTagType();
  lastPacketLength =  myReader.getPacketLength();
  lastTag = myReader.getTagString();
  lastErrorCode = myReader.getErrorCode();
  lastAntennaPower = myReader.getAntennaPower();
  lastResponse = myReader.getSonMicroReading();
  lastChecksum = myReader.getCheckSum();

  // if the last command sent was a read block command:
  if (lastCommand == 0x86) {
    int[] inputString = myReader.getPayload();
    message = "";
    for (int c = 0; c < inputString.length; c++) {
      message += char(inputString[c]);
    }
  }
```

» When you type something in
the sketch window, it's added
to a string. It's then sent to the RFID
tag when you command the SM130
to write to the tag. The keyTyped()
method attaches any keystrokes to the
output string.

```
}
/*
 If a key is typed, either add it to the output string
 or delete the string if it's a backspace:
*/
void keyTyped() {
  switch (key) {
  case BACKSPACE:  // delete
    outputString = "\0";
    break;
  default:

    if (outputString.length() < 16) {
      outputString += key;
    }
    else {
      outputString = "output string can't be more than 16 characters";
    }
  }
```

» The button functionality is handled
by a separate Java class in the sketch
called Button. There are also a few
methods for managing the list of
buttons, including makeButtons(),
which creates them initially, and draw-
Buttons(), which draws and updates
them.

```
}
/*
 initialize all the buttons
 */
void makeButtons() {
  // Define and create rectangle button
  for (int b = 0; b < buttonNames.length; b++) {
    // create a new button with the next name in the list:
    Button thisButton = new Button(400, 30 +b*30,
                                   150, 20,
                                   buttoncolor, highlight, buttonNames[b]);
    buttons.add(thisButton);
  }
}
/*
 draw all the buttons
 */
void drawButtons() {
  for (int b = 0; b < buttons.size(); b++) {
    // get this button from the Arraylist:
    Button thisButton = (Button)buttons.get(b);
    // update its pressed status:
    thisButton.update();
    // draw the button:
    thisButton.display();
  }
```

▶ mousePressed() checks to see whether one of the buttons is pressed. If so, it calls doButtonAction(), which sends the appropriate command for each button to the SM130.

```
}
void mousePressed() {
  // iterate over the buttons, activate the one pressed
  for (int b = 0; b < buttons.size(); b++) {
    Button thisButton = (Button)buttons.get(b);
    if (thisButton.containsMouse()) {
      doButtonAction(thisButton);
    }
  }
}

/*
  if one of the command buttons is pressed, figure out which one
 and take the appropriate action.
 */
void doButtonAction(Button thisButton) {
  // figure out which button this is in the ArrayList:
  int buttonNumber = buttons.indexOf(thisButton);

  // do the right thing:
  switch (buttonNumber) {
  case 0: //  set antenna power
    if (myReader.getAntennaPower() < 1) {
      myReader.setAntennaPower(0x01);
    }
    else {
      myReader.setAntennaPower(0x00);
    }
    break;
  case 1: // select tag
    myReader.selectTag();
    break;
  case 2:  // authenticate
    myReader.authenticate(0x04, 0xFF);
    break;
  case 3:   // read block
    myReader.readBlock(0x04);
    break;
  case 4:  // seek tag
    myReader.seekTag();
    break;
  case 5:  // write tag - must be 16 bytes or less
    myReader.writeBlock(0x04, outputString);
    outputString = "";
    break;
  case 6:  // get reader firmware version
    myReader.getFirmwareVersion();
    break;
  }
```

▶▶ Finally, the Button class defines the properties and behaviors of the buttons themselves.

This sketch doesn't include all the functionality of the SM130. For example, it only writes to block 4 of a Mifare tag's memory, and it only uses the default authentication scheme. However, it does give you the ability to read and write from tags, as well as the structure to understand how to use the SM130's functions.

```
}
class Button {
  int x, y, w, h;                        // positions of the buttons
  color basecolor, highlightcolor;       // color and highlight color
  color currentcolor;                    // current color of the button
  String name;

  // Constructor: sets all the initial values for
  // each instance of the Button class
  Button(int thisX, int thisY, int thisW, int thisH,
         color thisColor, color thisHighlight, String thisName) {
    x = thisX;
    y = thisY;
    h = thisH;
    w = thisW;
    basecolor = thisColor;
    highlightcolor = thisHighlight;
    currentcolor = basecolor;
    name = thisName;
  }

  // if the mouse is over the button, change the button's color:
  void update() {
    if (containsMouse()) {
      currentcolor = highlightcolor;
    }
    else {
      currentcolor = basecolor;
    }
  }

  // draw the button and its text:
  void display() {
    fill(currentcolor);
    rect(x, y, w, h);
    //put the name in the middle of the button:
    fill(0);
    textAlign(CENTER, CENTER);
    text(name, x+w/2, y+h/2);
  }

  // check to see if the mouse position is inside
  // the bounds of the rectangle:
  boolean containsMouse() {
    if (mouseX >= x && mouseX <= x+w &&
      mouseY >= y && mouseY <= y+h) {
      return true;
    }
    else {
      return false;
    }
  }
}
```

❝ Reading from Mifare Tags

To prepare for the next part of this project, use the previous Processing sketch to write Twitter handles to a few tags in this format:

@moleitau
@Kurt_Vonnegut
@pomeranian99

To do so, use the sequence mentioned at the beginning of this section:

- Put the tag in the reader's field
- Click Select Tag
- Click Authenticate
- Click Write Block

Then, to verify it:

- Put the tag in the reader's field
- Click Select Tag
- Click Authenticate
- Click Write Block

When you're sure you've got a couple tags with Twitter handles on them, you're ready to build the next part of the project: an Arduino tweet reader.

Circuit Additions

The circuit is the same as in Figures 9-14 and 9-15, but with an Ethernet connection and a 2x16 LCD attached. If you're already using an Arduino Ethernet, you're all set. If not, add an Ethernet shield. Either way, add the LCD as shown in Figure 9-19. To make sure your LCD works, test it with any of the LiquidCrystal library examples included in the Arduino software, just by changing the pin numbers to match your own. The pin numbers for these examples were chosen so as not to conflict with the pins that the Ethernet controller and SD card use.

The potentiometer on Analog input 1 will be used to control the speed of scrolling on the LCD. Pins A0 and A2 will be used as digital outputs, to act as voltage and ground for this pot. Below is a quick example to test the LCD.

Display It This sketch prints the number of seconds since the sketch started on a 2x16-LCD screen attached to an Arduino.

```
/*
  LCD Example
  Context: Arduino
  */
// include the library:
#include <LiquidCrystal.h>

// initialize the library with the numbers of the interface pins
LiquidCrystal lcd(9,8, 7, 6,5, 3);

void setup() {
  // set up the LCD's number of columns and rows:
  lcd.begin(16, 2);
  // Print a message to the LCD.
  lcd.print("I've been running for:");
}

void loop() {
  // set the cursor to column 0, line 1
  // (note: line 1 is the second row, since counting begins with 0):
  lcd.setCursor(0, 1);
  // print the number of seconds since reset:
  lcd.print(millis()/1000);
}
```

Figure 9-19

Connecting a 2x16 LCD to an Arduino. Breadboard view and schematic. The connection to the Ethernet shield and SM130 are not shown. Stack them on your Arduino and they will connect appropriately, as their pins are not used in the LCD circuit shown. The second potentiometer on pin A1 will be used to control scrolling speed.

> ⚠ If you're using the Ethernet shield rather than the Ethernet board, you might need to supply external power for this circuit. Together, the Ethernet shield, RFID shield, LCD display, and Arduino draw enough current that in the moment the RFID reader reads a tag, the circuit draws more current than USB can supply, causing the voltage to drop. In some cases, a 220µF capacitor across power and ground of the RFID shield will help, but if not, use an external power supply, a Power-over-Ethernet supply, or an Ethernet board instead of the Ethernet shield/Uno combination.

So far, you've only used the Arduino board as a serial pass-through, but for this phase of the project, you'll control the RFID reader using the I2C protocol. The Wire library that comes with Arduino lets you control I2C devices. For the main sketch, the Wire library commands will be wrapped inside another library that's specifically for the RFID reader. But to make sure things are working, and to see

I2C in action, try the sketch below. It sends a command to the reader to ask for the firmware revision, and prints the results to the Serial Monitor. You'll recognize some of the SonMicro communications protocol in this sketch.

Read the Firmware

This sketch reads the firmware of the SM130 module.

```
/*
  SM130 Firmware reader
  Context: Arduino
*/
#include <Wire.h>

void setup() {
  // initialize serial and I2C:
  Serial.begin(9600);
  Wire.begin();
  // give the reader time to reset:
  delay(2000);

  Serial.println("asking for firmware");
  // open the I2C connection,
  // the I2C address for the reader is 0x42:
  Wire.beginTransmission(0x42);
  Wire.write(0x01);      // length
  Wire.write(0x81);      // command
  Wire.write(0x82);      // checksum
  Wire.endTransmission();

  // reader needs 50ms in between responses:
  delay(50);
  Serial.print("getting reply: ");
  // wait for 10 bytes back via I2C:
  Wire.requestFrom(0x42,10);
  // don't do anything until new bytes arrive:
  while(!Wire.available()) {
    delay(50);
  }
  // when new bytes arrive on the I2C bus, read them:
  while(Wire.available()) {
    Serial.write(Wire.read());
  }
  // add a newline:
  Serial.println();
}

void loop() {
}
```

When you run the firmware reader sketch, you should get a response like this in the Serial Monitor:

```
asking for firmware
getting reply: I2C 2.8ÿ
```

That last byte is the checksum of the string of bytes that the reader sent in response. If you get a good response, you're ready to move on. If not, revisit the sidebar on page 344.

It would be convenient if, instead of having to remember the numeric values for each command, you could just call the commands by name, like you can with the Processing library above. The Arduino SonMicro library lets you do just that. In fact, most of its methods share the same names as the Processing library's methods. Download the latest version from https://github.com/tigoe/SonMicroReader-for-Arduino. Make a new directory called **SonMicroReader** in the **libraries** directory of your Arduino sketch directory, and copy the contents of the download package to it. Then restart the Arduino application. The new library should appear in the Examples submenu of the File menu as usual. Once that's done, move on to the sketch below.

This sketch looks for RFID tags and reads block 4 when it finds a tag. If it finds a Twitter handle there, it makes an HTTP call to Twitter's XML API to get the latest tweet from that Twitter user. Then it displays the result on an LCD screen.

Saving Program Memory

The sketch for this project is complex, and it takes a large chunk of the Arduino's program memory. You'll notice that the Serial print statements have a new syntax, like this:

```
Serial.println(F("Hello"));
```

The F() notation tells the print and println statements to store the text that follows in flash memory, not in program memory. Because the print statements are for debugging purposes only and are not going to change, this saves memory for your program.
X

Get the Tweet You'll be using a lot of libraries in this sketch. There are a few global variables associated with each one, starting with the current tag, the last tag read, and the address block from which to read on the tag.

The main loop() is a simple state machine. It does different things depending on what state it's in, so there's a variable to keep track of the state. There are four basic states:

- Looking for a tag
- Reading the tag you just got
- Making an HTTP request
- Waiting for the server's response

Regardless of what state the sketch is in, it should also update the LCD every time through the loop().

There are also the usual IP and Ethernet configuration variables.

```
/*
 Twitter RFID Web Client
 Context: Arduino
 */
#include <SPI.h>
#include <Ethernet.h>
#include <TextFinder.h>
#include <Wire.h>
#include <LiquidCrystal.h>
#include <SonMicroReader.h>

SonMicroReader Rfid;        // instance of the reader library
unsigned long tag = 0;      // address of the current tag
unsigned long lastTag = 0; // address of the previous tag
int addressBlock = 4;       // memory block on the tag to read

int state = 0;              // the state that the sketch is in

// Enter a MAC address and IP address for your controller below.
// The IP address will be dependent on your local network:
byte mac[] = { 0x00, 0xAA, 0xBB, 0xCC, 0xDE, 0x01 };
IPAddress ip(192,168,1,20);          // will only be used if DHCP fails
IPAddress server(199,59,149,200);    // Twitter's API address
Client client;                       // the client connection
```

▶▶ **Change these to match your own device and network.**

»

▶ There are also global variables to keep track of the tweeter, the tweet, when you last made an HTTP request, and how long to delay between requests.

Finally, there are global variables for the various characteristics of the LCD display and constants for the scroll-delay potentiometer.

```
Continued from opposite page.
String twitterHandle = "";        // the tweeter
String tweet = "";                // the tweet
int tweetBufferLength;            // the space to reserve for the tweet
int tweetLength = 0;              // the actual length of the tweet

long lastRequestTime = 0;         // last time you connected to the server
int requestDelay = 15 * 1000;     // time between HTTP requests


// initialize the library with the numbers of the interface pins
LiquidCrystal lcd(9,8, 7, 6,5, 3);
const int screenWidth = 16;       // width of the LCD in characters
long lastScrollTime = 0;          // last time you scrolled the LCD
int scrollDelay = 130;            // delay between LCD moves
int cursorPosition = 0;           // cursor position on the LCD

const int potVoltage = A0;        // voltage for the scroll delay pot
const int potGround = A2;         // ground for the scroll delay pot
const int potInput = A1;          // scroll delay pot
```

▶ setup() initializes communications: serial, Ethernet, communications to the RFID reader via I2C, and the LCD. It also sets A0 high as a digital output, and A2 low, to supply voltage and ground for the scroll-delay potentiometer.

```
void setup() {
  // initialize serial communications and the reader:
  Serial.begin(9600);
  // start the Ethernet connection:
  if (Ethernet.begin(mac) == 0) {
    Serial.println(F("Failed to configure Ethernet using DHCP"));
    Ethernet.begin(mac, ip);
  }
  // set pins A0 and A2 to digital out, and use them as
  // power and ground for the scroll speed potentiometer:
  pinMode(potGround, OUTPUT);
  pinMode(potVoltage, OUTPUT);
  digitalWrite(potGround, LOW);
  digitalWrite(potVoltage, HIGH);

  // reserve 140 * 2 screenWidths + 3 bytes extra for tweet:
  tweetBufferLength = 140 + 2*screenWidth + 3;
  tweet.reserve(tweetBufferLength);
  Rfid.begin();
  // set up the LCD's number of columns and rows:
  lcd.begin(screenWidth,2);
  lcd.clear();
  lcd.print(F("Ready"));
}
```

» loop() checks what state it's in using a switch statement. When it has finished what it needs to do in each state, it increments the state variable and moves to the next state on the next time through the loop(). If any of the later states don't succeed (for example, if it can't authenticate or read from the last tag it saw), it drops back to the first state, looking for a tag.

Once it has finished checking the state, loop() updates the LCD display. It prints the Twitter handle on the top line, and it scrolls the latest tweet on the bottom line, moving forward every scrollDelay milliseconds.

```
void loop() {
  switch(state) {
  case 0:     // get tag
    tag = Rfid.selectTag();
    if (tag != 0) {
      // you have a tag, so print it:
      Serial.println(tag, HEX);
      state++;    // go to the next state
    }
    break;
  case 1:     // read block
    if (Rfid.authenticate(addressBlock)) {
      Serial.print(F("authenticated "));
      // read the tag for the twitter handle:
      Rfid.readBlock(addressBlock);
      twitterHandle = Rfid.getString();
      // show the handle:
      lcd.clear();                 // clear previous stuff
      lcd.setCursor(0,0);          // move the cursor to the beginning
      lcd.print(twitterHandle); // tweet handle on the top line
      Serial.println(twitterHandle);
      state++;      // go to the next state
    }
    else state = 0;    // go back to first state
    break;
  case 2:     //connect to server
    // if this is a new tag, or if the request delay
    // has passed since the last time you made an HTTP request:
    if (tag != lastTag ||
      millis() - lastRequestTime > requestDelay) {
      // attempt to connect:
      if (connectToServer()) {
        state++;     // go to the next state
      }
      else state = 0;    // go back to first state
    }
    else state = 0;    // go back to first state
    lastTag = tag;
    break;
  case 3:     // read response
    tweetLength = readResponse();
    state = 0;    // go back to first state
    break;
  }

  // if you haven't moved the LCD recently:
  if (tweetLength > 0 && millis() - lastScrollTime > scrollDelay) {
    // advance the LCD:
    scrollLongString(cursorPosition);
    // increment the LCD cursor position:
    if (cursorPosition < tweetLength) {
      cursorPosition++;
```

»

Continued from opposite page.

```
      }
      else {
        cursorPosition = 0;
      }
      // note the last time you moved the LCD:
      lastScrollTime = millis();
    }
```

» Finally, it updates scrollDelay by mapping the input of the potentiometer on pin A1.

```
    // update the speed of scrolling from the second potentiometer:
    int sensorReading = analogRead(potInput);
    // map to a scrolling delay of 100 - 300 ms:
    scrollDelay = map(sensorReading, 0, 1023, 100, 300);
  }
```

» The scrollLongString() method takes a 16-character substring of the long tweet and displays it on the LCD display. It pads the beginning and end of the tweet with enough characters so that it scrolls all the way on and off the screen.

```
// this method takes a substring of the long
// tweet string to display on the screen
void scrollLongString(int startPos) {
  String shortString = "";             // the string to display on the screen
  // make sure there's enough of the long string left:
  if (startPos < tweetLength - screenWidth) {
    // take a 16-character substring:
    shortString = tweet.substring(startPos, startPos + screenWidth);
  }
  // refresh the LCD:
  lcd.clear();              // clear previous stuff
  lcd.setCursor(0,0);       // move the cursor to beginning of the top line
  lcd.print(twitterHandle); // tweet handle on the top line
  lcd.setCursor(0,1);       // move cursor to beginning of the bottom line
  lcd.print(shortString);   // tweet, scrolling, on the bottom
}
```

» The connectToServer() method is very similar to the connect method in the air-quality client in Chapter 4. It connects to the server and makes an HTTP GET request. In this case, it's not asking for an HTML page, but for an XML version of the tweet that you can get from http://api.twitter.com. Twitter, like many sites, makes it possible to get both a human-readable form of their site and a machine-readable one, delivered in XML.

```
// this method connects to the server
// and makes an HTTP request:
boolean connectToServer() {
  // note the time of this connect attempt:
  lastRequestTime = millis();
  // attempt to connect:
  Serial.println(F("connecting to server"));
  if (client.connect(server, 80)) {
    Serial.println(F("making HTTP request"));
    // make HTTP GET request:
    client.print(F("GET /1/statuses/user_timeline.xml?screen_name="));
    client.print(twitterHandle);
    client.println(F(" HTTP/1.1"));
    client.println(F("Host:api.twitter.com"));
    client.println();
    return true;
  }
```

»

Continued from previous page.

```
    else {
      Serial.print(F("failed to connect"));
      return false;
    }
  }
```

» The readResponse() method reads incoming bytes from the server after the HTTP request, and looks for the beginning and end of a tweet. The tweet is conveniently sandwiched between two tags: <tweet> and </tweet>. So, all you have to do is look for those and return what's between them. You can ignore the rest of the stream. If you want to see the whole XML feed, open the URL the sketch is using in a browser, and give it a Twitter handle at the end, like this:

http://api.twitter.com/1/statuses/user_timeline.xml?screen_name=halfpintingalls

```
int readResponse() {
  char tweetBuffer[141];    // 140 chars + 1 extra

  int result = 0;
  // if there are bytes available from the server:
  while (client.connected()) {
    if (client.available()) {
      // make an instance of TextFinder to search the response:
      TextFinder response(client);
      // see if the response from the server contains <text>:
      response.getString("<text>", "</text>", tweetBuffer, 141);
      // print the tweet string:
      Serial.println(tweetBuffer);
      // make a String with padding on both ends:
      tweet = "                " + String(tweetBuffer)
        + "               ";
      result = tweet.length();
      // you only care about the tweet:
      client.stop();
    }
  }
  return result;
}
```

" Troubleshooting

There are a lot of things that can go wrong in this sketch, so make sure you're clear on each of the parts, and have a plan for troubleshooting. Below are a few things to look for:

Is it reaching each of the four major states? If not, determine at which one it's stopping. Have the sketch print a message when it reaches each new state, as well as the results of the previous state.

Is it reading a tag? Can it read the tag's memory blocks? If not, try one of the example sketches that comes with the SonMicroReader library. In particular, the ReadBlock example was written to do a basic read of tags.

Can it reach the server? If not, try the HTTP test client in Chapter 4 with the URL that this sketch calls.

Can it read the user's tweets? Are you sure you didn't pick a Twitter user who protects her tweets? Or who hasn't tweeted yet? Put the URL in a browser and search for the <tweet> tags yourself. If they're not there, the sketch can't see them.

Is the LCD working? Separate this out using the Serial Monitor. This sketch contains a number of print statements to let you know what's happening. Use them when troubleshooting.

❝ Construction

This is a simple mat board box like the ones in Chapter 5, but the structure is different. The RFID antenna and the LCD screen are attached to the microcontroller by wires. You can use ribbon wire, or you can use an old Ethernet cable with the ends chopped off.

Make sure to test the circuit before you put it in the box!

Mount the LCD and the potentiometer that controls contrast on a separate perfboard, as shown in Figure 9-19. You can use a prototyping shield if you want, but it's not necessary; you can just attach headers to the wires and plug them directly into the board. You'll want to group the wires to make them easier to plug in, like so:

- Solder the wires for Arduino pins D8 and D9 to two headers.
- Solder the wires for pins D3 through D7 to a rwo of five headers, with an extra space for pin D4.
- Solder the wires for +5V and ground to a pair of headers.

Figure 9-20 shows the wires broken out of an Ethernet cable and attached to headers using this sequence.

Connect the scroll-speed potentiometer to pins A0 through A2 as shown in Figure 9-18 using any type of wire you have handy.

↥ Figure 9-21
The header pin connections for the cable to the perfboard.

↧ Figure 9-20
The LCD and potentiometer connections to a perfboard. The wire colors show which wires correspond to those in Figure 9-18.

Attach the RFID antenna to the top of the box with Velcro.
A set of extra long female headers provides enough length
to hold it above the wires of the LCD circuit. You can see
the inside of the box in Figure 9-22.

Mount the potentiometers to the top of the box, held in
place by their mounting nuts. Mount the LCD screen to
the top of the box using Velcro or double-stick tape on the
side of the screen itself. A tab of Velcro on the bottom of
Arduino holds it nicely in place on the bottom of the box
as well.

Once you're done, you've got a handy Twitter reader for
your desk, as shown in Figure 9-23. Write your favorite
Twitter users to a series of tags so you've got them handy
to check at a moment's notice. You've made a connection between tangible identification using the tags, and
network identification using the Twitter feed.
X

Figure 9-22
The inside of the box with the LCD
perfboard in the foreground.

Figure 9-23
The final box.

❝ Network Identification

So far, you've identified network devices computationally by their address. For devices on the Internet, you've seen both IP and MAC addresses. Bluetooth and 802.15.4 devices have standard addresses as well. However, the address of a device doesn't tell you anything about what the device is or what it does.

Recall the networked air-quality project in Chapter 4. The microcontroller made a request via HTTP and the PHP script sent back a response. Because you already knew the microcontroller's capabilities, you could send a response that was short enough for it to process efficiently, and format it in a way that made it easy to read. But what if that same PHP script had to respond to HTTP requests from an Arduino Ethernet, a desktop browser like Safari or Chrome, and a mobile phone browser? How would it know how to format the information?

Most Internet communications protocols include a basic exchange of information—as part of the initial header messages—about the sender's and receiver's identity and capabilities. You can use these to your advantage when designing network systems like the ones you've seen here. There's not space to discuss this concept comprehensively, but following are two examples that use HTTP and mail.

HTTP Environment Variables

When a server-side program, such as a PHP script, receives an HTTP request, it has access to a lot more information about the server, the client, and more than you've seen thus far.

▶▶ To see some of it, save the following PHP script to your web server, then open it in a browser. Name it **env.php**.

```php
<?php
/*
    Environment Variable Printer
    Context: PHP

    Prints out the environment variables
*/
    foreach ($_REQUEST as $key => $value)
    {
        echo "$key: $value<br>\n";
    }
    foreach ($_SERVER as $key => $value)
    {
        echo "$key: $value<br>\n";
    }
?>
```

You should get something like this in your browser:

```
#CGI __utmz: 152494652.1295382826.13.2.utmccn=(referral)
|utmcsr=itp.nyu.edu|utmcct=/physcomp/studio/Spring2011/
TomIgoe|utmcmd=referral
__utma: 152494652.402968136.1288069605.1308754712.130876886
1.29
PATH: /usr/local/bin:/usr/bin:/bin
REDIRECT_HANDLER: php-cgi
REDIRECT_STATUS: 200
UNIQUE_ID: Thtgla3sqiUAAFdwW-UAAAAP
SCRIPT_URL: /php/09_env.php
SCRIPT_URI: http://www.example.com/php/09_env.php
HTTP_HOST: www.example.com
HTTP_CONNECTION: keep-alive
HTTP_USER_AGENT: Mozilla/5.0 (Macintosh; Intel Mac
OS X 10_6_8) AppleWebKit/534.30 (KHTML, like Gecko)
Chrome/12.0.742.112 Safari/534.30
HTTP_ACCEPT: text/html,application/xhtml+xml,application/
xml;q=0.9,*/*;q=0.8
HTTP_ACCEPT_ENCODING: gzip,deflate,sdch
HTTP_ACCEPT_LANGUAGE: en-US,en;q=0.8
HTTP_ACCEPT_CHARSET: ISO-8859-1,utf-8;q=0.7,*;q=0.3
HTTP_COOKIE: __utmz=152494652.1295382826.13.2.utmccn=(refer
ral)|utmcsr=itp.nyu.edu|utmcct=/physcomp/studio/Spring2011/
TomIgoe|utmcmd=referral; __utma=152494652.402968136.12880696
05.1308754712.1308768861.29
SERVER_SIGNATURE:
SERVER_SOFTWARE: Apache
SERVER_NAME: www.example.com
SERVER_ADDR: 77.248.128.3
SERVER_PORT: 80
REMOTE_ADDR: 66.168.47.40
DOCUMENT_ROOT: /home/username/example.com
SERVER_ADMIN: webmaster@example.com
SCRIPT_FILENAME: /home/username/example.com/php/09_env.php
REMOTE_PORT: 52138
REDIRECT_URL: /php/09_env.php
GATEWAY_INTERFACE: CGI/1.1
SERVER_PROTOCOL: HTTP/1.1
REQUEST_METHOD: GET
QUERY_STRING:
REQUEST_URI: /php/09_env.php
SCRIPT_NAME: /php/09_env.php
ORIG_SCRIPT_FILENAME: /dh/cgi-system/php5.cgi
ORIG_PATH_INFO: /php/09_env.php
ORIG_PATH_TRANSLATED: /home/username/example.com/php/09_env.
php
ORIG_SCRIPT_NAME: /cgi-system/php5.cgi
PHP_SELF: /php/09_env.php
REQUEST_TIME: 1310417045
```

As you can see, there's a lot of information: the web server's IP address, the client's IP address, the browser type, the directory path to the script, and more. You probably never knew you were giving up so much information by making a simple HTTP request, and this is only a small part of it! This is very useful when you want to write server-side scripts that can respond to different clients in different ways.

For example, HTTP_USER_AGENT tells you the name of the software browser with which the client connected. From that, you can determine whether if it's a mobile phone, desktop, or something else, and serve appropriate content for each. HTTP_ACCEPT_LANGUAGE tells you the language in which the client would like the response. When you combine REMOTE_ADDR with the IP geocoding example to follow, you can even make a reasonable estimation as to where the client is, assuming its request did not come through a proxy.

Project 28

IP Geocoding

The next example uses the client's IP address to get its latitude and longitude. It gets this information from www.hostip.info, a community-based IP geocoding project. The data there is not always the most accurate, but it is free. This script also uses the HTTP user agent to determine whether the client is a desktop browser or an Ethernet module. It then formats its response appropriately for each device.

Locate It   Save this to your server as **ip_geocoder.php**.

```php
<?php
/*  IP geocoder
    Context: PHP

    Uses a client's IP address to get latitude and longitude.
    Uses the client's user agent to format the response.
*/
    // initialize variables:
    $lat = 0;
    $long = 0;
    $country = "unknown";

    // check to see what type of client this is:
    $userAgent  = getenv('HTTP_USER_AGENT');
    // get the client's IP address:
    $ipAddress = getenv('REMOTE_ADDR');
```

The website www.hostip.info will return the latitude and longitude from the IP address in a convenient XML format. The latitude and longitude are inside a tag called <gml:coordinates>. That's what you're looking for. First, format the HTTP request string and make the request. Then wait for the results in a while loop, and separate the results into the constituent parts.

```php
    // use http://www.hostIP.info to get the latitude and longitude
    // from the IP address.  First, format the HTTP request string:
    $IpLocatorUrl = "http://api.hostip.info/?&position=true&ip=";
    // add the IP address:
    $IpLocatorUrl .= $ipAddress;

    // make the HTTP request:
    $filePath = fopen ($IpLocatorUrl, "r");

    // as long as you haven't reached the end of the incoming text:
    while (!feof($filePath)) {
        // read one line at a time
        $line = fgets($filePath, 4096);
        // if the line contains the coordinates, then you want it:
        if (preg_match('/<gml:coordinates>/', $line)) {
            $position = strip_tags($line);       // strip the XML tags
            $position = trim($position);         // trim the whitespace
            $coordinates = explode(",",$position); // split on the comma
            $lat = $coordinates[0];
            $long = $coordinates[1];
        }
    }
```

»

Now that you've got the location, it's time to find out who you're sending the results to, and format your response appropriately. The information you want is in the HTTP user agent.

Continued from previous page.

```php
// close the connection:
fclose($filePath);

// decide on the output based on the client type:
switch ($userAgent) {
    case "arduino":
        // Arduino wants a nice short answer:
        echo "<$lat,$long,$country>\n";
        break;
    case "processing":
        // Processing does well with lines:
        echo "Latitude:$lat\nLongitude:$long\nCountry:$country\n\n";
        break;
    default:
        // other clients can take a long answer:
        echo <<<END
<html>
<head></head>

<body>
    <h2>Where You Are:</h2>
        Your country: $country<br>
        Your IP: $ipAddress<br>
        Latitude: $lat<br>
        Longitude: $long<br>
</body>
</html>
END;
    }
?>
```

> If you call this script from a browser, you'll get the HTML version. If you want to get the "processing" or "arduino" responses, you'll need to send a custom HTTP request. Try calling it from your terminal program, as follows.

First, connect to the server as you did before:

```
telnet example.com 80
```

Then send the following (press Enter one extra time after you type that last line):

```
GET /~yourAccount/ip_geocoder.php HTTP/1.1
HOST: example.com
USER-AGENT: arduino
```

You should get a response like this:

```
HTTP/1.1 200 OK
Date: Thu, 21 Jun 2007 14:44:11 GMT
Server: Apache/2.0.52 (Red Hat)
Content-Length: 38
Connection: close
Content-Type: text/html; charset=UTF-8


<40.6698,-73.9438,UNITED STATES (US)>
```

If you change the user agent from **arduino** to **processing**, you'll get:

```
HTTP/1.1 200 OK
Date: Thu, 21 Jun 2007 14:44:21 GMT
Server: Apache/2.0.52 (Red Hat)
Content-Length: 64
Connection: close
Content-Type: text/html; charset=UTF-8


Latitude:40.6698
Longitude:-73.9438
Country:UNITED STATES (US)
```

As you can see, this is a powerful feature. To use it, all you need to do is add one line to your HTTP requests from Processing or the microcontroller (see Chapter 3). Just add an extra print statement to send the user agent, and you're all set. In Processing or Arduino, the HTTP request would now look like this:

```
// Send the HTTP GET request:
String requestString = "/~yourAccount/ip_geocoder.php";
client.write("GET  " + requestString + " HTTP/1.0\r\n");
client.write("HOST: example.com\r\n");
client.write("USER-AGENT: processing\r\n\r\n");
```

Using the user agent variable like this can simplify your development a great deal. This is because it means that you can easily use a browser or the command line to debug programs that you're writing for any type of client.

Mail Environment Variables

Email affords a more flexible relationship between objects than you get with IP addresses, because it gives you the ability to structure complex conversations. An object can communicate not only who it is (the from: address), but to whom it would like you to reply (using the reply-to: field), and whom you should include in the conversation (cc: and bcc: fields). All of that information can be communicated without even using the subject or body of the message. PHP gives you simple tools to do the parsing. Because so many devices communicate via email (mobile phone text messaging can interface with email as well), it expands the range of possible devices you can add to a system.

Like HTTP, email protocols have environment variables that you can take advantage of as well. If you've ever viewed the full headers of an email in your favorite mail client, you've seen some of these. To look at mail in more depth, you can use PHP's IMAP mail functions. Internet Message Access Protocol is a mail protocol that lets you get mail from a server from multiple clients. The mail stays on the server until a client tells the server to delete a particular message. This allows you to use multiple mail clients for the same account, and keep mail coordinated across them.

Send It Put the following PHP script on your server.

```php
<?php
/*
    mail reader
    Context: PHP
*/

// keep your personal info in a separate file:
@include_once('pwds.php');

// open a connection to your gmail inbox on port 993
// using SSL, but no certificate to validate the connection:
$mailServer = '{imap.gmail.com:993/imap/ssl/novalidate-cert}INBOX';
$mbox = imap_open($mailServer, $user, $pass);

// get the message headers in the inbox:
$headers = imap_headers($mbox);

// if there are no messages, there is no mail:
if ($headers == false) {
    echo "Failed to get mail<br />\n";
} else {
    // print the number of messages
    echo "number of messages: ".imap_num_msg($mbox);
    echo "\n\n";
    // print the header of the first message:
echo imap_fetchheader($mbox,1);
}
// close the inbox:
imap_close($mbox);
?>
```

▸ Next, make a separate file called **pwds.php** on your server. This file contains your username and password. Keep it separate from the main PHP file so that you can protect it. Format it as shown at right:

```php
<?php
$user='username';        // your mail login
$pass='password';        // exactly as you normally type it
?>
```

As soon as you've saved the **pwds.php** file, change its permissions so that only the owner (you) can read and write from it. From the command line, type:

```
chmod go-rwx pwds.php
```

Figure 9-24
Permissions for the **pwds.php** file. Make sure that no one can read from and write to it—besides you.

NOTE: If you're using a graphic SFTP or FTP client, your settings for this file will look like Figure 9-24. This protection will deter anyone who doesn't have access to your account from getting your account info. It isn't an ideal security solution, but it serves for demonstration purposes and can be made more secure by changing your password frequently.

> You'll need to make sure you have at least one unread mail message on your server for that code to work. When you do, you should get something like this when you open the script in a browser:

```
number of messages: 85

Delivered-To: tom.igoe@gmail.com
Received: by 10.52.188.138 with SMTP id ga10cs129118vdc;
Sat, 28 May 2011
 12:32:30 -0700 (PDT)
Received: by 10.42.176.136 with SMTP id
be8mr4324248icb.15.1306611150331; Sat,
 28 May 2011 12:32:30 -0700 (PDT)
Return-Path: <tigoe@algenib.myhost.com>
Received: from myhost.com (crusty.g.myhost.
com [67.225.8.42]) by mx.google.com with ESMTP id
f8si10612848icy.106.2011.05.28.12.32.29; Sat,  28 May 2011
12:32:29 -0700 (PDT)
Received-SPF: pass (google.com: domain of tigoe@algenib.
myhost.com designates 67.225.8.42 as permitted sender)
client-ip=67.225.8.42;
Authentication-Results: mx.google.com; spf=pass (google.com:
domain of tigoe@algenib.myhost.com designates 67.225.8.42 as
permitted sender) smtp.mail=tigoe@algenib.myhost.com
Received: from algenib.myhost.com (algenib.myhost.com
[173.236.170.37]) by crusty.g.myhost.com (Postfix) with
ESMTP id 6EAC3BE813 for <tom.igoe@gmail.com>; Sat, 28 May
2011 12:31:15 -0700 (PDT)
Received: by algenib.myhost.com (Postfix, from userid
1774740) id 00AD1156BB6; Sat, 28 May 2011 12:32:09 -0700
(PDT)
To: tom.igoe@gmail.com
Subject: Hello world!
From: cat@catmail.com
Message-Id: <20110528193210.00AD1156BB6@algenib.myhost.com>
Date: Sat, 28 May 2011 12:32:10 -0700 (PDT)
```

There's a lot of useful information in this header. Though the mail says it's from cat@catmail.com, it's actually from a server that's run by myhost.com. It's common to put an alias on the from: address, to assign a different reply-to: address than the from: address, or both. It allows sending from a script such as the **cat** script in Chapter 3, yet the reply goes to a real person who can answer it. It's important to keep this in mind if you're writing scripts that reply to each other. If you're using email to communicate between networked devices, the program for each device must be able to tell the from: address from the reply-to: address—otherwise, they might not get each other's messages.

This particular message doesn't have a field called X-Mailer:, though many do. X-Mailer tells you which program sent the mail. For example, Apple Mail messages always show up with an X-mailer of Apple Mail, followed by a version number such as (2.752.3). Like the HTTP User Agent, the X-Mailer field can help you decide how to format mail messages. You could use it in a similar fashion, to tell something about the device that's mailing you, so you can format messages appropriately when mailing back.

❝ Conclusion

The boundary between physical identity and network identity always introduces the possibility for confusion and miscommunication. No system for moving information across that boundary is foolproof. Establishing identity, capability, and activity are all complex tasks, so the more human input you can incorporate into the situation, the better your results will be.

Security is essential when you're transmitting identifying characteristics because it maintains the trust of the people using what you make and keeps them safe. Once you're connected to the Internet, nothing's truly private and nothing's truly closed, so learning to work with the openness makes your life easier. In the end, keep in mind that clear, simple ways of marking identity are the most effective, whether they're universal or not. Both beginners and experienced network professionals often get caught on this point, because they feel that identity has to be absolute and clear to the whole world. Don't get caught up in how comprehensively you can identify things at first. It doesn't matter if you can identify someone or something to the whole world—it only matters that you can identify them for your own purposes. Once that's established, you've got a foundation on which to build.

When you start to develop projects that use location systems, you usually find that less is more. It's not unusual to start a project thinking you need to know position, distance, and orientation, then pare away systems as you develop the project. The physical limitations of the things you build and the spaces you build them in will solve many problems for you.

x

10

Mobile Phone Networks and the Physical World

Ethernet and WiFi are handy ways to talk to people and things on the Internet, but there's a great big chunk missing: the mobile telephone network. Nowadays, telephony and the Internet are so intertwined that it doesn't make sense to talk about them separately. It's getting increasingly easy to connect physical devices other than mobile phones through mobile phone networks. In this chapter, you'll learn how to connect these two networks, and when it's useful to do so.

◀◀ **ohai lion, how r u??? txt me l8r!!!**

This lion can send you an SMS. Groundlab, in conjunction with Living with Lions and Lion Guardians, developed this tracking collar that utilizes a GPS/GSM module to transmit lions' locations via SMS to researchers and Maasai herders. This open source system aims to help conservationists protect the last 2,000 lions living in the wild in Southern Kenya, and safeguard the Maasai herders' cattle, restoring Maasai land to a working ecosystem. *Photo courtesy of Groundlabs.*

◀⋮ Supplies for Chapter 10

There's not a lot that's brand new in this chapter. Many of the basic hardware parts will seem familiar. You will get the chance to work with 120V or 220V AC, though, and to work with conductive fabrics and threads. You'll also learn about reading and writing from an SD card.

DISTRIBUTOR KEY
- **A** Arduino Store (http://store.arduino.cc/ww/)
- **AF** Adafruit (http://adafruit.com)
- **D** Digi-Key (www.digikey.com)
- **F** Farnell (www.farnell.com)
- **J** Jameco (http://jameco.com)

- **L** Less EMF (www.lessemf.com)
- **MS** Maker SHED (www.makershed.com)
- **RS** RS (www.rs-online.com)
- **SF** Spark Fun (www.sparkfun.com)
- **SS** Seeed Studio (www.seeedstudio.com)

PROJECT 29: CatCam Redux
» **1 Arduino Ethernet board A** A000050
  Alternatively, an Uno-compatible board (see Chapter 2) with an Ethernet shield will work.
  SF DEV-09026, **J** 2124242 , **A** 139, **AF** 201, **F** 1848680
» **SD card reader that can read MicroSD** Ethernet shields and the Arduino Ethernet have one onboard.
» **MicroSD card** Available at most any electronics store.
» **IP-based camera** The examples use a D-Link DCS-930L.
» **Temperature sensor AF** 165, **D** TMP36GT9Z-ND, **F** 1438760, **RS** 427-351

Figure 10-1. New parts for this chapter: 1. IP-based camera 2. Hoodie 3. Conductive ribbon 4. Conductive thread 5. LilyPad Arduino Simple 6. Lithium Polymer battery charger 7. Shieldex conductive fabric 8. Embroidery thread 9. Lithium Polymer battery 10. Android device 11. TMP36 temperature sensors 12. MicroSD card 13. MicroSD card reader 14. Relay board 15. AC junction box and socket 16. AC cord.

» **Relay Control PCB** This is used to mount the rest of the components below. Alternately, you can use the Power Switch Tail below. **SF** COM-09096
» **1 Relay SF** COM-00101, **D** T9AV1D12-12-ND, **F** 1629059
» **2 1-kilohm resistors** Any model will do. **D** 1.0KQBK-ND, **J** 29663, **F** 1735061, **RS** 707-8669
» **1 10-kilohm resistor D** 10KQBK-ND, **J** 29911, **F** 9337687, **RS** 707-8906
» **1 1N4148 diode SF** COM-08588, **F** 1081177, **D** 1N4148TACT-ND, **RS** 544-3480
» **1 2N3906 PNP-type transistor J** 178618, **D** 2N3906D26ZCT-ND, **SF** COM-00522, **F** 1459017, **RS** 294-328
» **1 LED D** 160-1144-ND or 160-1665-ND, **J** 34761 or 94511, **F** 1015878, **RS** 247-1662 or 826-830, **SF** COM-09592 or COM-09590
» **1 2-pin Screw Terminal SF** PRT-08432, **D** 732-2030-ND, **F** 1792766, **RS** 189-5893
» **1 3-pin Screw Terminal SF** PRT-08235, **D** 732-2031-ND, **F** 1792767, **RS** 710-0166
» **1 Power Switch Tail** This is an alternative device to the relay board, relay, and support parts above. A 240V version is available from www.powerswitchtail.com. **SF** COM-09842, **AF** 268, **MS** MKPS01
» **Cat**
» **Air conditioner**
» **Country estate (optional)**

PROJECT 30: Phoning the Thermostat
» **Completed Project 27**
» **Twilio account**

PROJECT 31: Personal Mobile Datalogger
» **Android device** You'll need a device running version 2.1 or later. See http://wiki.processing.org/w/Android for details.
» **LilyPad Arduino SF** DEV-09266, **A** A000011,
» **1 Bluetooth Mate module SF** WRL-09358 or WRL-10393
» **Lithium Polymer Ion Battery SF** PRT-00341, **AF** 258, **RS** 615-2472, **F** 1848660
» **1 270-kilohm resistor J** 691446, **D** P270KBACT-ND, **RS** 163-921, **F** 1565367
» **Conductive ribbon SF** DEV-10172
» **Thick conductive thread SF** DEV-10120, **L** A304
» **Shieldit Super Conductive Fabric L** A1220-14
» **Velcro**
» **Hoodie MS** MKSWT
» **Embroidery thread** Available at most fabric or yarn shops.

❝❝ One Big Network

Before the Internet, there was the telephone network. All connections were analog electrical circuits, and all phone calls were circuit-switched, meaning that there had to be a dedicated circuit between callers. Then modems came along, which allowed computers to send bits over those same analog circuits. Gradually, switchboards were replaced with routers, and now telephone networks are mostly digital as well. Circuits are virtual, and what takes place behind the scenes of your phone calls is not that different from what occurs behind the scenes of your email or chat conversation: a session is established, bits are exchanged, and communication happens. The difference between a phone call and an email is now a matter of network protocols, not electrical circuits.

There are plenty of IP-based telephony tools that blur the line between phone call and Internet connection, including the open source telephony server Asterisk (www.asterisk.org), as well as telephony services from companies like Twilio (www.twilio.com), Google Voice (www.voice.google.com), and Skype (www.skype.com). These voice services are compatible with those offered by your phone company. What the phone company is giving you on top of the software service is a network of wires and routers that prioritizes voice services, so you are guaranteed a quality of service that you don't always get on IP-only telephony services.

Telephony services and Internet services meet on gateway servers and routers that run software to translate between protocols. For example, mobile phone carriers all offer SMS gateway services that allow you to send an email that becomes an SMS, or to send an SMS that emails the person you want to reach. Google Voice and many of the other online telephony services offer voicemail-to-text, in which an incoming call is recorded as a digital audio file, then run through voice-recognition software and turned into text, and finally emailed to you. The major task when building projects that use the telephony network is learning how to convert from one protocol to another.

A Computer in Your Pocket

Mobile phones are far more than just phones now. The typical smartphone—such as an Android phone, iPhone, Blackberry, or Windows Phone—is a computer capable of running a full operating system. The processing power is well beyond that of older desktop machines, and smartphones run operating systems that are slightly stripped down versions of what you find on a laptop, desktop, or tablet computer. Most smartphones also incorporate some basic sensors, such as a camera, accelerometer, light sensor, and sometimes GPS. And, of course, they are networked all the time. What they lack, however, is the capability for adding sensors, motors, and other actuators—the stuff for which microcontrollers are made. When you treat the phone as a multimedia computer and mobile network gateway, you open up a whole host of possibilities for interesting projects.

Interfacing phones and microcontrollers can be done in a number of ways, depending on the phone's capabilities. For the purposes of this chapter, I'll be talking about smartphones, so you can assume most or all of the following capabilities, many of which you'll use in the projects to come:

- Programmability
- Touchscreen or keyboard
- Mobile network access
- Bluetooth serial port
- USB connection
- Microphone, speaker
- Onboard accelerometer
- Onboard GPS

▶▶ **Figure 10-2**
Possible ways of linking microcontrollers and mobile phones.

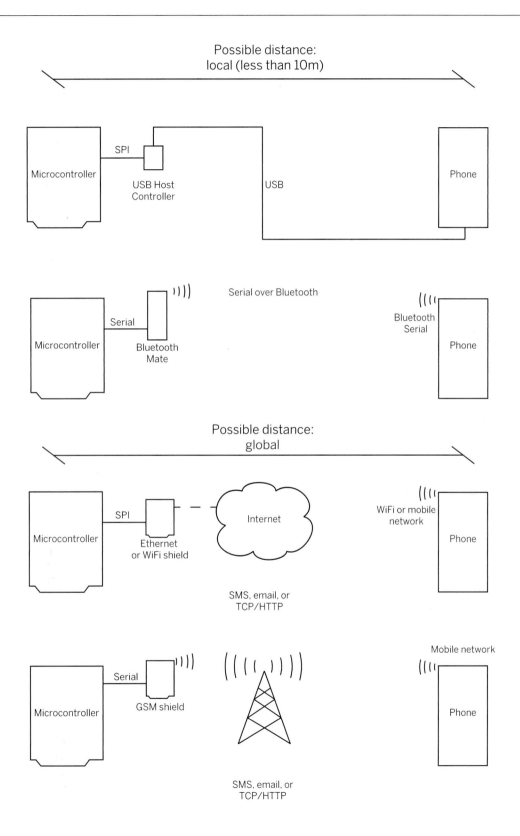

There are a few possible system arrangements afforded by these capabilities and the kinds of things you might want to make. Figure 10-2 shows the four most common arrangements.

Three of the four options shown use wireless links. Current mobile phones don't make it easy to make a wired serial link to external devices, though that is beginning to change. So, for most applications, a wireless link is the better option. It's not often that you'd prefer your phone be tethered to your project.

Start with What Happens

By now this should be a common theme to you: start with what you want people to do with the thing you're building, and design whatever makes that easiest to do. Are you making a system where your users have real-time interactive control over a nearby model helicopter or boat? Are they controlling a remote device like their home thermostat while on vacation? Consider how tight an interactive coupling you need. Do you need real-time interaction like you saw in Chapter 5, or will updates every few seconds or minutes be enough? And what about the distance between the devices—do you need to be able to communicate at long range, or will a local connection like Bluetooth or USB suffice? If it's a remote connection, how will your users know what happened on the other side? Can they see the result? Do they get an email or SMS message telling them about it? Evaluate whether you need a wired or wireless connection, based on how the people need to move and manipulate the devices involved. Consider what networks are available where you plan to use your system. Got WiFi? Got mobile networks? Got Ethernet? Can you create a local network between the two devices using Bluetooth or WiFi?

Browser Interfaces

If you want to control an existing networked device from a mobile phone, the easiest thing to do is to give the device an Internet connection and control it from your phone's browser. You don't have to learn anything specific to a particular phone operating system to do this—you just need to be able to make an HTTP connection between them. Make the microcontroller a simple server like you saw in Project 6, Hello Internet!, and you're done.

Native Application Interfaces

If you don't want to use the browser, you can build your own application on the phone to interact with the microcontroller via Bluetooth, network, SMS, or USB. You'll see an example of this using Processing for Android later in the chapter. The advantage of building a dedicated app is that you have complete control over what happens. The disadvantage is the challenge of learning a new programming environment, as well as the limitation of not being able to use your program on a phone with a different operating system. Because most phone operating systems don't allow the browser to access the communications hardware of the phone directly, you have to build an app if you plan to use local connections like Bluetooth or USB.

SMS and Email Interfaces

Not every project requires real-time interaction between your phone and the thing you're building. If you just want to get occasional updates from remote sensors, or you want to start a remote process that can then run by itself—like turning on a sprinkler or controlling your house lights via a remote timer—SMS or email might be useful. You can make a microcontroller application that can receive SMS messages using a GPRS modem, or you can write a networked server that checks email and sends messages to an Internet-connected microcontroller when it gets a particular email message. The advantage of this method is that you can control remote things using applications that are already on your phone, email, and SMS.

Voice Interfaces

Don't forget the phone's original purpose: two-way communication of sound over distance. Voice interfaces for networked devices can be simple and fun. Telephony gateways like Asterisk and Twilio allow you to use voice calls to generate networked actions.

Phone As Gateway

Not all applications in this area involve control of a remote device from the phone. Sometimes you just want to use the mobile phone as a network connection for sensors on your body or near you. In these cases, you'll make a local connection from the microcontroller to the phone, most likely over Bluetooth or USB, and then send the data from those sensors to a remote server. In these cases, you probably don't need to build a complex application—you just need to make the connection between the two devices, and between the phone and the network.

Project 29

CatCam Redux

If the phone has a web browser, you don't need to know how to program it to make a mobile application. In this project, you'll make a variation on the cat cam from Project 5. But this time, you'll use a micro-controller that serves files from an SD card and an IP-based camera that needs no computer to connect to the Internet.

My neighbor, let's call her Luba, has a cat named Gospodin Fuzzipantsovich. Luba has a country estate with cherry trees. She likes to summer there, at least on summer weekends, but she can't take Fuzzipantso-vich with her. Because the country estate has huge expenses (samovars and the like), Luba can't afford an air conditioner with a thermostat for her city place. So, I made her a web-based temperature monitor. It works as follows.

Luba opens a browser on her phone or laptop and logs into the thermostat's web interface. She sees the current temperature in her city apartment and the air conditioner's state, along with a camera view of Fuzzipantsovich. If it's too hot, she sets the trigger temperature lower. If it's too cool, she sets it higher. The interface updates the thermostat, and shows her the new trigger point.

Before you build this project, you should diagram the devices and protocols involved, and break the action into steps to understand what needs to happen. Figure 10-3 shows the system, and Figure 10-4 details the interaction.

There are several pieces of hardware involved and protocols to communicate between them. Many of them are familiar to you by now. The Ethernet control-ler on the Ethernet shield (or Arduino Ethernet)

MATERIALS

» **Arduino Ethernet or Arduino Uno and Ethernet shield**
» **SD card reader that can read MicroSD**
» **MicroSD card**
» **IP-based camera**
» **Temperature sensor**
» **Relay Control PCB**
» **Relay**
» **2 1-kilohm resistors**
» **1 10-kilohm resistor**
» **1 diode**
» **1 transistor**
» **1 LED**
» **1 2-pin Screw Terminal**
» **1 3-pin Screw Terminal**
» **Cat**
» **Air conditioner**
» **Country estate (optional)**

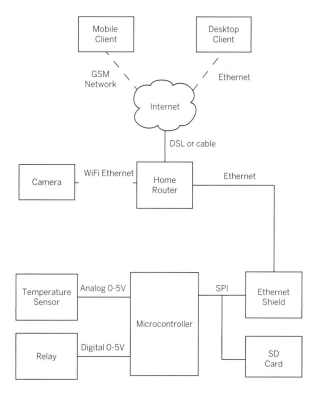

▸▸ Figure 10-3
The system diagram for the CatCam 2 and air conditioner controller.

communicates with the microcontroller via SPI, as does the SD card on the shield or board. The temperature sensor is an analog input, and the 120V relay to control the air conditioner is a digital output. The IP camera in this project is a consumer item that has a built-in server, so all you have to do is configure it to speak to your router. The clients are just web browsers on your smartphone, tablet, or personal computer.

Even though it seems simple enough, there are actually 10 steps to the interaction, which are listed below:

1. The client makes an HTTP GET request for the main interface page (**index.htm**).
2. The microcontroller server reads the page from the SD card.
3. The server reads the temperature…

4. … and the current thermostat trigger point.
5. The server sends the resulting page to the client.
6. Because the cat cam image is embedded in the page, the client requests it from the IP camera.
7. The IP camera sends the image to the client.
8. The client changes the trigger point via a form on the page, and submits it using HTTP POST.
9. The server reads the POST request and updates the thermostat.
10. The server sends back a response page.

Some of this, like getting the camera image and the resulting page, can be solved using HTML. You won't need to do any extra programming, because it will be taken care of by the browser when it interprets the HTML. The main programming challenge is to build a basic web server on the Arduino that serves files from the SD card.

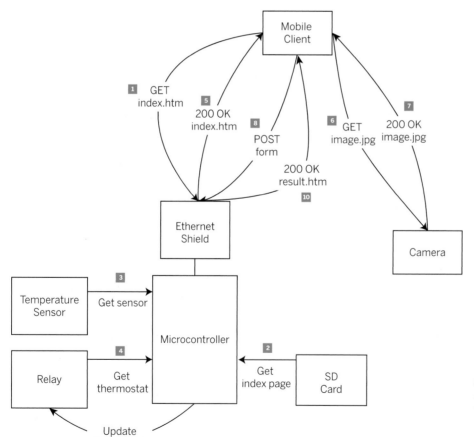

◀◀ **Figure 10-4**
The interaction diagram for the CatCam 2 and air conditioner controller.

Figure 10-5
The relay board is connected to an AC cord, which has been cut on one side to attach it to the relay.

Figure 10-6
An AC junction box with the relay inside, and the control lines from the relay connecting to an Arduino. This is the safer way to build this project.

Figure 10-7
The CatCam 2 and air conditioner circuit.

The Circuit

Once you've got a grasp on the plan and the system, you're ready to build it. The circuit is shown in Figure 10-7. Because the SD card is on the Ethernet module (Ethernet shield or Arduino Ethernet), you only need to add the temperature sensor and the relay.

The relay contains a coil wrapped around a thin switch. When the coil gets voltage, it forms a magnetic field through induction, pulling the two sides of the switch together. To use it, take an alternating current circuit (AC) and break one of the wires, as shown in Figures 10-5 through 10-7.

Working with AC can be dangerous, so make sure everything is connected properly before plugging it in. If you're uncomfortable building an AC circuit, the Power Switch Tail will allow you to control 120V AC. A 240V version was recently announced at www.powerswitchtail.com. It's available from Adafruit, Spark Fun, and the Maker SHED.

Spark Fun's AC relay board is a safe and less expensive option if you want to build your own circuit. Solder the relay to the relay board. Then take an AC cord, cut one of the two wires, and attach it to the relay board's LOAD connections. Figure 10-5 shows a close-up of a household AC cord attached to the relay. The relay's ground, control, and 5V connections connect to your microcontroller. To build a more robust version—such as the one shown in Figure 10-6—with a household electrical outlet junction box, see Nathan Seidle's excellent tutorial at www.sparkfun.com/tutorials/119.

To test the circuit safely *before you plug it in*, set your multimeter to measure continuity, and to measure between one of the plug's pins and the corresponding socket hole on the other end of the cord. One pin/hole pair should have continuity all the time. The other should not, unless you power the 5V and ground contacts of the relay and connect the control line to 5V. Then you'll get continuity. When you connect the control line to ground, you won't get continuity. When you're sure the circuit's working, test it by attaching the control line to a pin of your microcontroller and use the Blink sketch to turn the relay on and off.

Figure 10-8

The CatCam 2 and air conditioner schematic.

Make sure to install your circuit in an insulated box and add plenty of strain relief to the AC lines. If they accidentally disconnect, they can cause a short circuit—and AC shorts are not pleasant. An electronic project case is safest. You can add strain relief to the wires by using hot glue or rubber caulking, though some cases come with wire strain relief glands to hold the wire in place. Once you've done that, give the wires a tug to make sure they won't move. Take your time and get this part very secure before you proceed.

The Code

Since the sketch is complex, it's built up piece-by-piece below, as follows:

1. Read the temperature sensor (for more on this sensor, see Adafruit's tutorial at www.ladyada.net/learn/sensors/tmp36.html).
2. Control the relay.
3. Read from the SD card.
4. Write a web server. This one will be more full-featured than the one you wrote in Chapter 4.

Try It   Reading the temperature sensor is pretty simple. It outputs an analog voltage that's proportional to the temperature. The formula is:

Temp(°C) = (Vout (in mV) - 500) / 10

Since you'll need to do other things in the main loop, read the temperature and convert it to Celsius in a separate function. Return the result as a float.

Your reading will look like this:

Temperature: 26.17

The reading is in Celsius, but if you want to convert it to Fahrenheit, the formula is:

F = 9/5*C + 32

When you run the sketch at this point, you'll get a continual printout of the temperature in the Serial Monitor.

Next, it's time to add the relay control.

```
/*
TMP36 Temperature reader and relay control
Context:  Arduino
Reads a TMP36 temperature sensor
*/

void setup() {
  // initialize serial communication:
  Serial.begin(9600);
}

void loop() {
   Serial.print("Temperature: ");
   Serial.println( readSensor() );
}

// read the temperature sensor:
float readSensor() {
  // read the value from the sensor:
  int sensorValue = analogRead(A0);
  // convert the reading to volts:
  float voltage = (sensorValue *  5.0) / 1024.0;
  // convert the voltage to temperature  in Celsius
  // (100mv per degree - 500mV offset):
  float temperature = (voltage - 0.5) * 100;
  // return the temperature:
  return temperature;
}
```

Control It The relay should be switched only every few seconds at most, so when you add code to control it, wrap the check in an if statement that checks to see whether an appropriate delay has passed. There are some global variables and constants to add, as well as changes to setup() and loop(). New lines are shown in blue.

It would be useful to be able to store the thermostat value, even when the Arduino is not powered. Adding the EEPROM library will allow that. At the top of the sketch, you'll read from EEPROM to get the thermostat value. Later on, you'll store new values back to EEPROM.

Add a new method, checkThermostat(), at the end of your sketch. It checks the temperature and compares it to a set thermostat point. If the temperature is greater, it turns the relay on. If the temperature is less, the relay is turned off.

When you run the sketch at this point, you'll see the relay turn on or off depending on the thermostat value. The value read from the EEPROM will probably be 255, so the relay won't turn on. Try changing the thermostat value to something less than the temperature sensor's reading and uploading your code again to see what happens.

```
#include <EEPROM.h>
const int relayPin = 2;                    // pin that the relay is attached to
const long tempCheckInterval = 10000;  // time between checks (in ms)
const int thermostatAddress = 10;          // EEPROM address for thermostat
long now;                                  // last temperature check time
// trigger point for the thermostat:
int thermostat = EEPROM.read(thermostatAddress);

void setup() {
  // initialize serial communication:
  Serial.begin(9600);
  // initialize the relay output:
  pinMode(relayPin, OUTPUT);
}

void loop() {
  // periodically check the temperature to see if you should
  // turn on the thermostat:
  if (millis() - now > tempCheckInterval) {
    Serial.print("Temperature: ");
    Serial.println(readSensor());
    if (checkThermostat()) {
      Serial.println("Thermostat is on");
    }
    else {
      Serial.println("Thermostat is off");
    }
    now = millis();
  }
}

// NOTE: the readSensor() method shown earlier goes here.

// Check the temperature and control the relay accordingly:
boolean checkThermostat() {
  // assume the relay should be off:
  boolean relayState = LOW;
  // if the temperature's greater than the thermostat point,
  // the relay should be on:
  if(readSensor() > thermostat) {
    relayState = HIGH;
  }
  // set the relay on or off:
  digitalWrite(relayPin, relayState);
  return relayState;
}
```

Read It   Next, it's time to read from the SD card. To do this, you'll need to add the SD library. On the Arduino shields that have an SD card, the SD Chip Select pin is pin 4. It varies for other manufacturers' shields, though, so make sure to check if you're using a different company's SD shield.

First, check whether the card is present using SD.begin(). If it's not, there's not much point in continuing. If it is, you can read from it. Add a new method, sendFile(), which will take an array of characters as a filename. New lines are shown in blue.

This new code won't work until you have a properly formatted MicroSD card inserted in the shield with a file on it called **index.htm**. Put the bare bones of an HTML document in the file, like so:

```
<html>
   <head>
      <title>Hello!</title>
   </head>
   <body>
   Hello!
   </body>
</html>
```

When you run the sketch at this point, it will print out the **index.htm** file in the Serial Monitor at the beginning, then go into the temperature reading and relay control behavior from the previous page.

```
#include <EEPROM.h>
#include <SD.h>
const int sdChipSelect = 4;              // SD card chipSelect

// NOTE: the constants and global variables shown earlier must go here

void setup() {
  // initialize serial communication:
  Serial.begin(9600);
  // initialize the relay output:
  pinMode(relayPin, OUTPUT);
  if (!SD.begin(sdChipSelect)) {
    // if you can't read the SD card, don't go on:
    Serial.println(F("initialization failed!"));
  }
  else {
    Serial.println(F("initialization done."));
    sendFile("index.htm");
  }
}

// NOTE: the loop(), readSensor(), and checkThermostat() methods shown
// earlier go here.

// send the file that was requested:
void sendFile(char thisFile[]) {
  String outputString = "";      // a String to get each line of the file

  // open the file for reading:
  File myFile = SD.open(thisFile);
  if (myFile) {
    // read from the file until there's nothing else in it:
    while (myFile.available()) {
      // add the current char to the output string:
      char thisChar = myFile.read();
      outputString += thisChar;

      // when you get a newline, send out and clear outputString:
      if (thisChar == '\n') {
        Serial.print(outputString);
        outputString = "";
      }
    }
    // close the file:
    myFile.close();
  }
  else {
    // if the file didn't open:
    Serial.print("I couldn't open the file.");
  }
}
```

🍎🍎 Writing to an SD Card

Arduino's SD library makes it easy to write to an SD card, and there are several SD card-mount options available. All of them use the SPI synchronous serial protocol that the Arduino Ethernet shield and Ethernet board use to communicate with the Ethernet chip. As you saw in Chapter 4, this protocol can be used with a number of different devices, all attached to the same serial clock and data pins, but each device will need its own Chip Select pin. The Arduino communicates with all SPI devices through pin 11 for MOSI (Master Out, Slave In), Pin 12 for MISO (Master In, Slave Out), and pin 13 for Clock. The Arduino Ethernet shield and board use pin 10 for the Ethernet module's Chip Select, and pin 4 for the SD card's Chip Select. SD boards from other companies use other pins for chip select. Spark Fun's SD card shield uses pin 8, and Adafruit's SD card breakout board (shown in Figure 10-9) uses pin 10. Whenever you're using multiple SPI devices in a project, like the Ethernet and the SD card together, you need to check to see that they all have individual Chip Select pins.

SD cards operate on 3.3V only! So if you're using a socket that attaches your SD card directly to the pins of any microcontroller operating 5 volts, you need to make sure the input pins receive only 3.3V.

Figure 10-9

The Adafruit SD card shield connected to the Arduino using the SPI pins 11 (MOSI), 12 (MISO), and 13 (Clock). Different SPI card boards use different pins for the Chip Select pin, however. This one uses pin 10.

Good SD Card Practice

To get the most reliable results out of an SD card shield or an adapter with an Arduino, there are some habits you should develop.

Never insert or eject the card while the sketch is running. You'd never pull a card out of your computer while it's in use, and the same goes for the Arduino. Make sure the microcontroller's not using the card when you insert or remove it. The simplest way to do this is to hold the reset button of the Arduino whenever you're inserting or removing the card.

Format cards as FAT16 or FAT32. The SD card library works only with these two file formats. Fortunately, every operating system can format disks this way. Check your operating system's disk-utility application for how to format your card as FAT16 or FAT32.

Filenames have to be in 8.3 format. The SD library uses the old DOS file-naming convention that all filenames are a maximum of eight-characters long with a three-character exension. All file names are case-insensitive and spaces are not allowed. So, **datalog1.txt** and **mypage.htm** are OK, but **really long file name** or **someArbitraryWebPage.html** are not.

Writing to the card takes time. Normally, the file write(), print(), and println() operations saves data in a volatile buffer on the card, which is lost when the card is removed. Only the flush() or close() operations save to the card permanently, but they take time. To keep up with user interaction, use flush() and close() the way you would to save a file on a regular computer: do it frequently, but not too frequently, and preferably when the user or other devices aren't doing anything else.

Practice safe file management. The SD library gives you some helpful tools for managing your files. filename. exists() lets you check whether a file already exists. if (filename) lets you check whether the file can be accessed. filename.remove() lets you remove a file. size(), position(), seek(), and peek() let you see how big a file is, where you're at in the file, and to move around in the file. mkdir() and rmdir() let you make and remove whole directories. Use these methods, especially those that let you look without changing, like exists(), size(), and peek(), which keep track of what you're doing when you write more complex file-handling sketches.

Indicate when you're accessing the card, and when you can't. Using LEDs to indicate when the Arduino is accessing the card and when there's an error is a handy way to know what's going on when you can't see the output on a screen.

For this project, you'll only read from the card from the microcontroller. To write to the card, you'll need an SD card reader/writer that can handle MicroSD cards. Readers are cheap, and they are becoming more and more ubiqitous. If your computer is a recent model, it may even have one built in. Most microSD cards come with an adapter to allow you to fit them into a regular SD card slot. Some cards even come with their own readers.

Once you've formatted your card, make a text file called **index.htm** and save it to the card. Then insert it into your shield. When the sketch runs, it should print the file out once at the end of setup(), then proceed to read the temperature sensor and control the relay as it did before. When that's working, you're ready to write the server. This code can be added to the sketch you've already got in progress.

Serve It   At the beginning of the sketch, add the Ethernet library and the necessary constants and global variables to use it and to set up a server. New lines, as usual, shown in blue.

```
/*
 GET/POST Web server with SD card read
 Context:  Arduino
*/
#include <EEPROM.h>
#include <SD.h>
#include <SPI.h>
#include <Ethernet.h>
#include <TextFinder.h>

// configuration for the Ethernet connection:
byte mac[] = {
  0x00, 0xAA, 0xBB, 0xCC, 0xDE, 0x01 };
IPAddress gateway(192,168,1,1);
IPAddress subnet(255,255,255,0);
IPAddress ip(192,168,1,20);
// Initialize the Ethernet server library:
Server server(80);

const int inputLength = 16;              // length of the file requested
const int typeLength = 6;                // length of GET or POST
const int sdChipSelect = 4;              // SD card chipSelect
const long tempCheckInterval = 10000;    // time between checks (in ms)
const int thermostatAddress = 10;        // EEPROM address for thermostat

char inputString[inputLength];           // for input from the browser
char requestTypeString[typeLength];      // what type of request: GET or POST
int nextChar = 0;                        // index counter for requestTypeString
const int fileStringLength = 16;         // length of the file requested
char fileString[fileStringLength];       // for input from the browser
long now;                                // last temperature check time
```

▶▶ Change these to match your own device and router.

▶▶ These will be used to manage the incoming HTTP requests.

▶▶ In setup(), replace the call to sendFile() with this code to get an IP address and start the server. New lines are shown in blue.

```
void setup() {
  // initialize serial communication:
  Serial.begin(9600);
  // initialize the relay output:
  pinMode(relayPin, OUTPUT);

  //see if the SD card is there:
  Serial.print(F("Initializing SD card..."));
  if (!SD.begin(sdChipSelect)) {
    // if you can't read the SD card, print the error and go on:
    Serial.println(F("initialization failed!"));
  }
  else {
    Serial.println(F("initialization done."));
  }
  // give the Ethernet controller time to start:
  delay(1000);
  Serial.println(F("attempting to get address"));
  // Attempt to start via DHCP. If not, do it manually:
  if (!Ethernet.begin(mac)) {
    Ethernet.begin(mac, ip, gateway, subnet);
  }
  // print IP address and start the server:
  Serial.println(Ethernet.localIP());
  server.begin();
}
```

▶▶ The loop() will change quite a bit. Starting at the beginning, add the following local variables. The final one listens for new clients to connect. If you get a client, make an instance of the TextFinder library to look for text in the incoming stream from the client.

```
void loop() {
  String fileName = "";  // filename the client requests
  char inChar = 0;       // incoming character from client
  int requestType = 0;   // what type of request (GET or POST);
  int requestedFileLength = 0;  // length of the filename they asked for

  // listen for incoming clients:
  Client client = server.available();

  if (client) {
    // make an instance of TextFinder to look for stuff from the client:
    TextFinder finder(client );
```

Remember what a client GET or POST request looks like. Here's the GET request:

```
GET /index.htm HTTP/1.0
```

And here's a POST request that provides a variable:

```
POST /response.htm HTTP/1.0
thermostat=23
```

Put this while() block inside the if statement that checks to see whether the client exists. It checks to see whether the client is connected, and whether it has sent any bytes. If so, it looks for the GET or POST requests, and gets the file requested as well. If it gets a POST, it extracts the thermostat variable. Then it calls sendFile() to send the file to the client.

```
while (client.connected()) {
    if (client.available()) {
      // look for whatever comes before the /. It should be GET or POST:
      if(finder.getString("","/", requestTypeString,typeLength)){
        // Do something different for GET or POST:
        if(String(requestTypeString) == "GET " ) {
          requestType = 1;
        }
        else if(String(requestTypeString) == "POST ") {
          requestType = 2;
        }

        // gather what comes after the / into an array,
        // it's the filename the client wants:
        requestedFileLength = finder.getString("", " ",
            fileString, fileStringLength);

        // now you're done with the GET/POST line, process what you got:
        switch (requestType) {
        case 1:    // GET
          // do nothing with GET except send the file, below
          break;
        case 2:    //POST
          // skip the rest of the header,
          // which ends with newline and carriage return:
          finder.find("\n\r");
          // if the client sends a value for thermostat, take it:
          if (finder.find("thermostat")) {
            int newThermostat = finder.getValue('=');
            // if it's changed, save it:
            if (thermostat != newThermostat) {
              thermostat = newThermostat;
             // constrain it to a range from 20 to 40 degrees:
              thermostat = constrain(thermostat, 20, 40);
              // save it to EEPROM:
              EEPROM.write(thermostatAddress, thermostat);
            }
          }
          break;
        }

        // whether it's GET or POST, give them the string they asked for.
        // if there's nothing after the /,
        // then the client wants the index:
        if (requestedFileLength < 2) {
          sendFile(client, "index.htm");
        }
        // otherwise send whatever file they asked for:
        else  {
          sendFile(client, fileString);
        }
      }
```

>> Wait, this sendFile() call looks different from the one on page page 375! The change is coming up.

»

▸▸ After the while() block, the thermostat check block from the original sketch closes out the loop() method.

Continued from previous page.

```
        // give the client time to receive the data:
        delay(1);
        // close the connection:
        Serial.println(F("Closing the connection"));
        client.stop();
      }    // close of the if (client.available() block
    }      // close of the while (client.connected() block
  }        // close of the if (client) block
  // NOTE: the thermostat check (the body of the loop() method on
  // page 374) goes here.
}
```

▸▸ The sendFile() method needs to change so you can send to the client instead of printing it out. It also needs to send the HTTP headers that come before the file. If the file isn't available, you should tell the client that, too. And you might as well use the standard HTTP error codes to do it. So now sendFile() sends an HTTP 200 OK header if it can read the file, and an HTTP 404 File Not Found header if it can't. Changes are shown in blue.

```
// send the file that was requested:
void sendFile(Client thisClient, char thisFile[]) {
  String outputString = "";      // a String to get each line of the file

  // open the file for reading:
  File myFile = SD.open(thisFile);
  if (myFile) {
    // send an OK header:
    sendHttpHeader(thisClient, 200);
    // read from the file until there's nothing else in it:
    while (myFile.available()) {
      // add the current char to the output string:
      char thisChar = myFile.read();
      outputString += thisChar;

      // when you get a newline, send out and clear outputString:
      if (thisChar == '\n') {
        thisClient.print(outputString);
        outputString = "";
      }
    }
    // if the file does not end with a newline, send the last line:
    if (outputString != "") {
      thisClient.print(outputString);
    }

    // close the file:
    myFile.close();
  }
  else {
    // if the file didn't open:
    sendHttpHeader(thisClient, 404);
  }
}
```

>> The sendHttpHeader() method looks like this.

```
// send an HTTP header to the client:
void sendHttpHeader(Client thisClient, int errorCode) {
  thisClient.print(F("HTTP/1.1 "));
  switch(errorCode) {
  case 200:      // OK
    thisClient.println(F("200 OK"));
    thisClient.println(F("Content-Type: text/html"));
    break;
  case 404:      // file not found
    thisClient.println(F("404 Not Found"));
    break;
  }
  // response header ends with an extra linefeed:
  thisClient.println();
}
```

" If you run the code you've got so far, you should have a working web server. Whatever text files you put on the SD card should be accessible via the browser. You're not set up to serve anything other than HTML text documents (note that the sendHttpHeader() method only returns Content-Type: text/html), but you can do a lot with that. Try making a few pages that link to each other and put them on the SD card, then navigate through them with a browser. Try it on a mobile phone browser, too, since that's your original goal here. Resist the temptation to send the URL to all your friends just yet—there is more work to do.

Next, it's time to write the actual HTML interface pages. You need a page that can show the temperature and provide a form to enter a new thermostat setting. When the user submits the form, she should get feedback that her new setting has been received and stored, and the interface should reset itself. You also need a camera to get a picture of the room. Finally, it should look good on the small screen of a tablet or smartphone. All of this can be done in HTML.

Mark It Up   The main interface page will be called **index.htm**. You're using the three-letter extension rather than .html because the SD library only takes eight-letter, three-letter extension names.

The head of the document needs a little meta info. There's a link to a .css stylesheet—so you can set fonts and colors and such—and two meta tags allowing mobile browsers to format the page to suit their screens.

Finally, there's JavaScript that allows the image to refresh without changing the rest of the page.

```
<html>
  <head>
    <link rel="stylesheet" type="text/css" href="mystyle.css" />
    <meta name="HandheldFriendly" content="true" />
    <meta name="viewport"
        content="width=device-width, height=device-height" />

    <script type="text/javascript">
        function refresh() {
            var today=new Date();
            document.images["pic"].src=
"http://visitor:password!@yourname.dyndns.com/image/jpeg.cgi"+"?"+today;

            if(document.images) window.onload=refresh;
            t=setTimeout('refresh()',500);
        }
    </script>
  </head>
```

>>

▶▶ The body of the document has an image tag that links to an image on another server; more details on that below.

The form in the body is for setting the thermostat level. It calls a separate document, **response.htm**, using a POST request, to which the server has to respond. You already wrote the initial response in your sketch above, when the server looks for the "thermo-stat" value at the end of the POST request. Check out case 2 in the switch statement in the sketch above. You can see that the temperature is con-strained to a range from 20 degrees to 40 degrees, which is reasonable in Celsius.

Save this as **index.htm**, and then start a new document called **response.htm**.

```
Continued from previous page.
  <body onload="refresh()">
    <div class="header"><h1>Thermostat Control</h1></div>

    <div class="main">
      <img src="http://visitor:password!@yourname.dyndns.com/image/jpeg.
cgi" width="300" id="pic">
      <form name="tempSetting" action="response.htm" method="POST">
        <p>Current temperature:
        $temperature
        </p>
        Thermostat setting (&#176;C):
        <input name="thermostat" type="number"
          min="20"
          max="40"
          step="1"
          value=$thermostat>
        <input type="submit" value="submit">
      </form>
      Air conditioner is $status
    </div>
  </body>
</html>
```

▶▶ The server will need to replace these variables before serving the file. You'll see how to do this later in this chapter.

Give a Response

The response page, **response.htm**, is a lot simpler than the index page. All it does is report the temperature, the thermostat setting, and the status of the air conditioner attached to the relay. It uses the same CSS, and the same mobile phone meta tags, as well as a meta http-equiv tag that sends the browser back to the index after three seconds. You may recognize this technique from the cat cam page in Chapter 3.

Did you notice the variables in the HTTP documents that look like PHP variables, starting with dollar signs? These need to be replaced with data from the server before the page is served. You don't have PHP on the Arduino, but you can write code into your sketch to look for these strings and replace them.

Before that, though, you need to finish by writing a CSS document for the site.

```
<html>
  <head>
    <meta http-equiv="refresh" content="3; URL=index.htm" />
    <link rel="stylesheet" type="text/css" href="mystyle.css" />
    <meta name="HandheldFriendly" content="true" />
    <meta name="viewport" content="width=device-width, height=device-
height" />
  </head>
  <body>
    <div class="header"><h1>Thermostat Control</h1></div>

    <div class="main">
      <p>Current temperature:
      $temperature
      &#176;C
      </p>
      <p>
      Thermostat setting changed to $thermostat&#176;C
      </p>
      <p>Air conditioner is $status
      </p>
      <a href="index.htm">Return to controls</a>
    </div>
  </body>
</html>
```

▶▶ The server will need to replace these variables before serving the file.

Style It The final document is the stylesheet. Save this as **mystyle.css**, then copy this and the two preceding files to the SD card. Don't put them in a folder, but in the main directory (the root) of the SD card.

Feel free to change the colors and fonts for this document—they're purely cosmetic.

Once you have these files on the SD card, reinsert it into the Ethernet module, and then try to view them in a browser. You should get something like Figure 10-10. Your current version won't have values for the temperature, thermostat setting, and status, but read on.

```css
.main {
    background-color: #fefefe;
    color: #0a1840;
    font-family: "Lucida Grande", Verdana, Arial, sans-serif;
}

.header {
    background-color: #0a173E;
    color: #f1fffe;
    font-family: sans-serif, "Lucida Grande", Verdana, Arial;
}
```

" Making Your Server Public

Since your Ethernet module is running as a server, you need it to be publicly visible on the Internet if you plan to access it from outside your own network. If you can assign the module to a fixed address on your network, that helps, but if you're setting it up at home, that address is not likely to be visible outside your home network. You'll need to set up port forwarding on your router, as explained in the sidebar, "Making a Private IP Device Visible to the Internet," in Chapter 4. Using port forwarding, you can give devices that are attached to your home router a face on the public Internet. They will only appear as numeric addresses, because they don't have names assigned to them. However, that may be enough.

There are two solutions to giving your devices names you can remember through port forwarding. The simplest way is to embed the address of the module in a page on your public web page—you'll never need to remember the numeric address. For example, if your router's public address is 63.118.45.189, set up port forwarding so that port 80 of the router points to port 80 of the Ethernet module. Then restart your router. When you have a connection again, open a browser and go to http://63.118.45.189, and you should have access to the module. Put this link in a web page on a hosted web server with a real hostname, and you're all set.

The second solution is Dynamic DNS.

Dynamic DNS

If you definitely need a named URL for your module, you can use a Dynamic DNS (DDNS) host, such as www.dyndns.com. A DDNS host is simply a DNS host that continually updates the DNS record of your domain. Your router or device becomes a client, and when it connects to the DDNS host, it requests that the domain name you choose, such as yourserver.com, should point to the number from which the client is connecting. For example, your Ethernet module (local IP address 192.168.1.20) makes a DDNS request to dyndns.com. Because it goes through your router, which has IP address 63.118.45.189, dyndns.com links yourserver.com to 63.118.45.189. The numeric address is referred to as the CNAME, or Canonical Name record, of the name address. So when someone browses to yourserver.com, he's pointed to 63.118.45.189. And if you set up your router to have port forwarding turned on, pointing its public port 80 at 192.168.1.20 port 80, your Ethernet module appears to the public Internet as yourserver.com.

Dynamic DNS hosting does not have to be expensive. For a single domain that ends with a name the DDNS host owns, like fuzzipantsovich.dyndns.tv, it can be free. For custom names, or multiple names, it's usually a reasonable monthly fee that gives you a way to provide named hostnames for devices on your home network.

X

🙶 Network Cameras

Cameras that connect to the Internet have been available for several years now, and the prices on them, predictably, get cheaper and cheaper. For about $60, you can get a small camera that has a WiFi module onboard and that runs as its own server. The one used for this project, the D-Link DCS-930L, was purchased at an office-supply store for $70.

Setting up these cameras is very straightforward, and is explained in the documentation that comes with them. First, you need to connect to the camera through a wired Ethernet connection, and open its administrator page in a browser (just like you're building for the air conditioner—hey, how about that!). There, you configure the WiFi network you want to connect to, save it to the camera's memory, and restart the camera.

Since the camera is running a server, you need to know its address. You can use the same methods to make your camera public as you did for your Ethernet module. You may have to change the port that your camera serves images on, because you probably want port 80—the default HTTP port—to point to the Ethernet module. Port 8080 is usually a good second bet.

Once you've set up port forwarding for your camera, you can embed the address in a link in the Ethernet module's HTML. For example, if you're using the DCS-930L, the path to the image as a .jpg file is **/image/jpeg.cgi**. Let's imagine the public address of your home router is 63.118.45.189 (it isn't, so go look it up), and you set port forwarding on port 8080 to point to your camera's port 80. The link for the public page would then be <a href ="http://63.118.45.189:8080/image/jpeg.cgi">. However, the D-Link cameras, and many other brands, expect you to supply a password to access the camera. So, add a visitor user account that has view-only access to the image, and change the URL to <a href ="http://username :password@63.118.45.189:8080/image/jpeg.cgi"> (fill in the username and password that you set). This is highly insecure because anyone who views source on the page can see the password, so make sure the account has no privileges whatsoever to change or view settings!

Once you think you know the public URL of your camera's image, test it in a browser. It's a good idea to test away from your home network. When you're satisfied it works, embed the link in the **index.htm** page that you wrote previously, and try it out. You'll also need to make the change to the image's URL in the JavaScript in the document's head. Now your server is on the Internet for real!

There's one last stage of this project. You have to replace those placeholder variables for the temperature, thermostat setting, and air conditioner status. To do that, you need to add some more code to your sketch.

X

Figure 10-10

Screenshot of the final CatCam Thermostat control, taken on an Android phone.

Report It To change the variables in the HTML documents, the server needs to read those documents as it serves them. It does this inside the while() block in the sendFile() method. Add the following to that method. New lines are shown in blue.

When you run this, the server will read the file. Whenever it hits one of the named strings, $temperature, $thermostat, or $status, it will replace that string with the corresoponding variable's value.

Notice that the if() statement to change the temperature is different than the other two. There is no function to convert a float variable to a String, so you have to use print() or println() to do the job. That means you need to print the temperature variable directly to the client rather than just swapping out that part of the string before you print it.

```
while (myFile.available()) {
    // add the current char to the output string:
    char thisChar = myFile.read();
    outputString += thisChar;

    // check for temperature variable and replace
    // (floats can't be converted to Strings, so send it directly):
    if (outputString.endsWith("$temperature")) {
        outputString = "";
        // limit the result to 2 decimal places:
        thisClient.print(readSensor(),2);
    }

    // check for thermostat variable and replace:
    if (outputString.endsWith("$thermostat")) {
        outputString.replace("$thermostat", String(thermostat));
    }

    // check for relay status variable and replace:
    if (outputString.endsWith("$status")) {
        String relayStatus = "off";
        if (checkThermostat()) {
            relayStatus = "on";
        }
        outputString.replace("$status", relayStatus);
    }

    // when you get a newline, send out and clear outputString:
    if (thisChar == '\n') {
        thisClient.print(outputString);
        outputString = "";
    }
}
```

Once you've made this change and uploaded it, you're done. When you go to the Arduino's address in your browser, you'll get the temperature, the current thermostat setting, and the status of the air conditioner. If you change any of the settings, you'll change the temperature in your home as a result. With the change you made to the image tag and the JavaScript in the **index.htm** document to accommodate your camera, you'll have an image from home as well. In a browser, your final application should look like Figure 10-10.

The great thing about using the browser as your application interface for mobile applications is that you only have to write the app once for all platforms. Many of the popular mobile applications are developed by making a basic browser shell without any user interface, then developing the user interface in HTML5. When you click through the app's interfaces, you're just browsing pages on their site. Because so many mobile phone applications are mainly network applications, it makes sense to use this as your primary approach. By doing so, you avail yourself of all the protocols the Web has to offer.

The web approach to mobile apps means you get to take advantage of protocols that don't run in a browser, but still rely on HTTP. You'll see this in practice in the next project. **X**

Project 30

Phoning the Thermostat

You put a lot of work into the last project. Fortunately, you get to reuse it in this project. You're going to keep the hardware exactly the same, but change the software in order to build an interface that lets you call the thermostat on the phone, hear the temperature and status by voice, and set the thermostat with your phone keypad.

MATERIALS

» **Completed Project 27**
» **Twilio account**

Luba is a bit of a luddite when it comes to new technologies, and she's not really fond of the mobile web interface for the thermostat. "But it's a phone!", she complains. "Couldn't I just call someone and have them stop by to change the temperature?" It's a fair point: if you've got a phone, you should be able to make things happen with a phone call.

IP-based telephony has taken leaps and bounds in the last several years, to the point where the line between a phone call and a web page is very blurry. Server applications such as Google Voice and Asterisk are like virtual switchboards—they connect the public switched telephone network (PSTN), and the Internet. These servers use a protocol called Session Initiation Protocol, or SIP, to establish a connection between two clients and determine what services they are capable of sending and receiving. For example, a SIP client might be able to handle voice communications, text messages, route messages to other clients, and so forth. Sometimes a SIP server sets up the connection between the clients, then gets out of the way and lets them communicate directly. Other times it manages the traffic between them, translating the protocols of one into something that the other can understand. It's the 21st-century version of the old switchboard operators. When application designers have done their job right, you never need to know anything about SIP, because your phone or software just tells you what it can do, and provides you a way to address other people. The phone does this by presenting you with a dial tone and a keypad.

If you've called an automated help service in the last few years, chances are you were talking to a SIP server. When you spoke, it tried to recognize your words using speech-to-text software, or it directed you to touch numbers on your keypad using text-to-speech software. When you entered numbers or words, it translated your input into HTTP GET or POST requests to query a remote server or local database. When it got results, it read those back to you using text-to-speech again. If it couldn't understand what you were saying (perhaps you were screaming "Operator! Operator! Give me a human being!" as I often do), it rerouted your call to a number where a human would answer.

For this project, you're going to use a commercial SIP service from Twilio to make a voice interface to the thermostat you just built. Twilio provides a variety of Voice over IP (VoIP) services like voicemail, conference calling, and more. With their commercial accounts, you can buy phone numbers to which you attach these services, so your customers can call your service directly. They also have a free trial service. With the free service, you must use the phone number they assign to you, and you have to use a passcode to access your application once you've called in. For readers outside the U.S. and Canada, Twilio offers only U.S./Canada-based numbers at the time of this writing. Read on to get the general idea, then find an equivalent service that works in your country. Phone number exchange is unfortunately one place the PSTN lags considerably behind the Internet, mostly for commercial and political reasons. If you really want to get deep into VoIP and SIP, check out **Asterisk: The Future of Telephony** by Jim Van Meggelen, Jared Smith, and Leif Madsen (O'Reilly).
X

❝ What's the Standard?

Here's the bad news about SIP and VoIP applications: there's not a standard approach to them yet. They all offer slightly different services, though the basics of making calls, sending SMS messages, recording calls, and reading touchtones are available most everywhere. Each server and each commercial provider has a different approach to providing an application programming interface (API) for its service. The markup you learn here for Twilio won't apply when you're building an application using another service like Tropo, Google Voice, or any of the dozens of other providers out there.

There are four questions that can help you choose which tool to use for any project:

- Does it offer the features I need?
- Is it available in my area?
- Is it simple to use?
- Will it work with my existing tools?

For this application, I chose Twilio because its markup language, TwiML, is very simple. Also, Twilio's examples make it clear how to separate the markup language from another server-based language, like PHP or Ruby. Everything happens through GET or POST. Twilio has excellent PHP examples, but you don't need them to get started. Its debugger is useful, and its technical support is good as well. It lacks features that other services have—like the ability to get the audio level while recording, or speech-to-text conversion—but, on the whole, the benefits of its simplicity outweigh any of the missing features.

To complete this project, you'll need an account on www.twilio.com. You can build and run this project with a free account, or you can use a paid account. If you use the free account, you will have to enter a passcode in addition to the phone number every time you call, and you'll only be able to support one application at a time. For this introduction, that's enough.

You'll also need the URL of your Arduino server from the previous project. For example, if your server is at 63.118.45.189, the address for this project will be http://63.118.45.189/voice.xml. Log in to your Twilio account and go to the dashboard. There, you'll be given a sandbox phone number and passcode. The phone number will connect you to Twilio's gateway. The gateway will connect you to an HTTP server whose address you provide (give it the one above). Once you've done that, it's time to write an XML file for the server, and to modify the sketch so it will respond as needed. Figure 10-11 shows the dashboard panel.

A Brief Introduction to XML

XML, or eXtensible Markup Language, is a general markup language used by many web and database services. XML allows you to describe nearly anything in machine-readable form. XML is made up of tags that begin and end with < and >. Tags describe elements, which can be any concept you want to label. Elements can have subelements; for example, a <body> might have <paragraph> subelements, marked up like so:

```
<body>
    <p>This is the content of the paragraph</p>
</body>
```

▶▶ **Figure 10-11**
The Twilio dashboard. Enter the URL for your Arduino server in the Voice URL box.

DEVELOPER TOOLS

API Credentials

Account SID

Auth Token

Sandbox

Number   PIN

Voice URL   http://63.118.45.189/voice.xml

SMS URL   http://demo.twilio.com/welcome/sms

HTTP Method   POST ▾

Save

The stuff between the tags is the content of an element. It's usually the stuff that humans want to read, but that the machines don't care about.

Every element should have an opening and closing tag, though sometimes a tag can close itself, like this:

```
<Pause length="10" />
```

What's inside a tag other than the tag's name are its attributes. The length above is an attribute of a Pause, and this specific pause's length is 10 seconds. Attributes allow you to describe elements in great detail.

If you're thinking all of this looks like HTML, you're right. XML and HTML are related markup languages, but XML's syntax is much stricter. Because it's such a general language, though, it's possible to write XML-parsing programs that work from one schema to another.

TwiML

Twilio's markup schema, TwiML, is a description of the functions Twilio offers written in XML. It describes what you can do with Twilio. There are elements for handling a voice call, and elements for handling an SMS message. The list of elements is pretty short:

Voice elements:

```
<Say>
<Play>
<Gather>
<Record>
<Sms>
<Dial>
<Number>
<Conference>
<Hangup>
<Redirect>
<Reject>
<Pause>
```

SMS elements:

```
<Sms>
<Redirect>
```

They're all explained in depth on Twilio's documentation pages, but you can probably guess what most of them do.

For this project, you're going to describe a <Response>. Within that, you'll use <Gather> to collect keypresses from the caller. The <Gather> element is TwiML's version of an HTML form, so it has an action attribute and a method attribute that you'll use to tell it where and how to send its results. You'll also use the <Say> element to speak to the caller using text-to-speech.

X

Mark It Up There's only one TwiML document you need for this project. When a caller dials in, this document will be the initial response; when she enters keypresses, the document will call itself again to update the settings. Save it as **voice.xml** to the SD card from your previous project.

You can see the same variables from your previous project: $temperature, $thermostat, and $status. The server will replace them just like it does with the HTML documents. That part of your sketch won't need to change.

The changes that need to be made to the server sketch follow on the next page.

```xml
<?xml version="1.0" encoding="UTF-8"?>
<Response>
    <Gather action="voice.xml" method="POST">
        <Say>
            The current temperature is
            $temperature
            degrees Celsius.
            The thermostat is set to $thermostat degrees Celsius.
            The air conditioner is $status.
            If you would like to change the thermostat, please enter
            a new setting.
            If you are satisfied, please hang up.
        </Say>
    </Gather>
    <Say>
            You didn't give a new setting,
            so the thermostat will remain at $thermostat degrees. Goodbye!
    </Say>
</Response>
```

Modify the Server There are only a few changes you need to make to the server to get it to be a voice server. The first is in the loop(). When Twilio makes a POST request, it sends back the digits that the caller pressed on the phone keypad using a variable called Digits. So where you were looking for a variable called thermostat in the POST request, you'll now look for Digits. The new line is shown in blue.

```
case 2:    //POST
           // skip the rest of the header,
           // which ends with newline and carriage return:
           finder.find("\n\r");
           // if the client sends a value for thermostat, take it:
           if (finder.find("Digits")) {
             int newThermostat = finder.getValue('=');
```

▸▸ The Twilio gateway that acts as a client to your server is a bit more picky about what it expects than most browsers. It works best when you tell it in advance the length of the content you're going to send it. That means you need to make some changes to sendFile() and sendHttpHeader(). First, in sendFile(), you're going to get the size of the file you're sending, and identify whether the file you're sending is HTML or XML. Then you'll send the file size and type to the sendHttpHeader() method. The beginning of the sendFile() changes, as follows, are in blue.

```
// send the file that was requested:
void sendFile(Client thisClient, char thisFile[]) {
  String outputString = "";      // a String to get each line of the file

  // open the file for reading:
  File myFile = SD.open(thisFile);
  if (myFile) {
    // get the file size:
    int mySize = myFile.size();
    // determine whether the file is XML or HTML
    // based on the extension (but assume it's HTML):
    int fileType = 1;            // 1 = html, 2 = xml
    if (String(thisFile).endsWith("xml")) {
      fileType = 2;
    }

    // send an OK header:
    sendHttpHeader(thisClient, 200, mySize, fileType);
    // read from the file until there's nothing else in it:
    while (myFile.available()) {
```

▸▸ You also need to change the call to sendHttpHeader() for a 404 error, which occurs later in sendFile(), as follows.

```
else {
  // if the file didn't open:
  sendHttpHeader(thisClient, 404, 0, 1);
}
```

> NOTE: When developing this project, I benefited greatly by writing a test server—like the one described in Chapter 4—to simply read the whole request from Twilio before I wrote my final code. Twilio's online debugger also helped me find the problems.

>> The sendHttpHeader() method will now send a lot more information. Previously, you were sending the minimum amount needed to respond to most browsers, but the Twilio gateway client expects more. You've seen more detailed responses from the server—for example, in the air-quality project in Chapter 4. What you're sending here is similar. You're sending the name of the server application (Arduino), and then determining the content type based on what you learned in sendFile(). Then you're sending the content length, based on the file size. This tells the client how many bytes to expect before it closes the connection.

```
// send an HTTP header to the client:
void sendHttpHeader(Client thisClient, int errorCode,
                    int fileSize, int fileType) {
  thisClient.print(F("HTTP/1.1 "));
  switch(errorCode) {
  case 200:        // OK
    thisClient.println(F("200 OK"));
    break;
  case 404:      // file not found
    thisClient.println(F("404 Not Found"));
    break;
  }
  thisClient.println(F("Server: Arduino"));
  thisClient.print(F("Content-Type: text/"));
  if (fileType == 1) {
    thisClient.println(F("html"));
  }
  if (fileType == 2) {
    thisClient.println(F("xml"));
  }
  thisClient.print(F("Content-Length: "));
  thisClient.println(fileSize);
  // response header ends with an extra linefeed:
  thisClient.println();
}
```

> When you've made these changes and put the **voice.xml** file on your SD card, restart the server and call your Twilio sandbox number. Enter the PIN, and the phone will ring. If you did everything right, you'll hear the text of the document read out to you, and you'll be able to enter a new thermostat setting using your phone keypad. You can keep changing the thermostat setting for as long as you like; when you're done, hang up.

Getting the Content Length Right

The server can theoretically serve both the XML and HTML documents now, so you should be able to see the pages in a browser as well. However, your browser may have problems with the content length. If you paid close attention, you may have realized that the size of the file is not actually the number of bytes you're sending as content.

The file size is determined before you replaced the $temperature, $thermostat, and $status variables with their actual values. For example, when the temperature is 27.28 degrees Celsius, you're replacing "$temperature" with "27.28"—that's 5 characters instead of 12. The same

is true with $thermostat, which you're replacing with a two-digit number, and $status, which you're replacing with a two- or three-character string. To calculate the content length correctly, you have to account for this. There are two possible solutions.

The hack solution: Since most browsers don't care about the content length, don't print it if you're serving HTML. Put an if statement around the two lines that print the content length, like so:

```
if (fileType == 1) {
  thisClient.print(F("Content-Length: "));
  thisClient.println(fileSize);
}
```

The thorough solution: You know that the thermostat is a two-digit number because you constrained it. That's nine fewer characters than "$thermostat". You also know that the temperature is a five-character string because you limited it to two decimal places (and over 100°C is deadly). That's seven fewer than "$temperature". You know that the status string is two or three characters, which is five or four fewer than "$status". So, calculate the difference before you send the HTTP header. The total is 20 or 21 characters shorter than the original file, depending on the relay status, which you can determine by calling checkThermostat(). You can change the sendFile() to adjust for this right before it sends the OK header, like this:

```
if (checkThermostat()) {
  mySize = mySize - 21;
}
else {
  mySize = mySize - 20;
}
// send an OK header:
sendHttpHeader(thisClient, 200, mySize, fileType);
```

When you're changing the contents of a file dynamically before you serve it, you have to make adjustments like this all the time. So, it's good to know a few methods for doing it. On a server with plenty of memory, you might simply put the whole file in an array and get the size of the array. One of the valuable things you learn when working on microcontrollers with limited memory is how to do work-arounds like this.

I'll admit it: I went for the hack solution first.
X

HTML5 and Other Mobile Web Approaches

There's currently a lot of excitement among mobile application developers around HTML5, the next version of the HyperText Markup Language standard. HTML5 aims to make HTML able to support a greater amount of interaction and control over how web pages look and behave. In fact, what makes HTML5 interesting is not just the markup language itself, but the possibilities it offers when combined with JavaScript and CSS3, the Cascading Style Sheets standard.

So, how do HTML5, JavaScript, and CSS3 work together? Roughly, you could say that HTML gives you nouns, CSS gives you adjectives and adverbs, and JavaScript gives you the verbs to put them into action. HTML describes the basic page structure and the elements within it: forms, input elements, blocks of text, and so forth. CSS primarily describes the characteristics of the visual elements: the colors, fonts, spacing, etc. The scripting language JavaScript allows you to make connections between the elements of a page, between pages in a browser, and between the browser and remote servers. The grammar analogy isn't perfect, but the point is that the three tools give you a wide range of means to present information, listen to user input, generate interactive responses, and send and retrieve data to locations other than the browser—whether the data is on the user's hard drive or a remote server.

Previously, applications running within a web browser had very limited access to the hardware of the computer on which they were running. Operating system manufacturers felt that it was unsafe to allow an application that you downloaded from the Internet to access your hard drive, camera, microphone, or other computer hardware. Hackers might do evil things! Of course, now that nearly every application is downloaded from the Internet, that thinking seems dated. You could still download a program that does malicious things—but, by now, most people have a sense of what makes an online source more or less trustworthy, whether that source is delivering a web page or an application that's native to your operating system. At the same time, more of the data we need to access lives online today, whether on a social media site or a web data storage service like Google Docs or Dropbox. There's no need for a browser to access your hard drive if your files are online.

The blurring of the distinction between browser security and general security is good news if you like to build physical interfaces. HTML5 and JavaScript include methods to access some of the hardware of your computer or phone. For example, there are methods now that let you determine the device's orientation by reading an accelerometer, if you have one built in (and most smartphones do); reading the compass and GPS receiver, if they're available; and more.

The bad news is that not all of these new methods are universally agreed upon among the companies who make browsers. Not every browser gives you access to all of these features, and not every browser implements them the same way. For example, the Safari browser on Apple's iPhone and iPad gives you access to the accelerometer as of this writing, but the standard browser on Android does not. So, while it's easy to access devices external to your phone through the browser, getting access to the ones on your phone may take a bit more work.

PhoneGap

If you're interested in getting access to the sensors on your phone, and you're comfortable working in JavaScript, PhoneGap (www.phonegap.com) is a very promising option. PhoneGap is a platform that gives you access to all the phone's hardware sensors through HTML5 and JavaScript. Basically, PhoneGap embedded the phone's built-in browser engine (which implements all of HTML5's new standards), added a bunch of hooks into useful functionality (such as built-in sensors) and released it as a basic frame for you to develop in. You download the application framework, which is written in your phone's preferred programming language (Java on Android, Objective-C on

iOS). You don't need to do anything to that code—it's just there to act as a shell for your app. You write your own HTML5 and JavaScript documents, which form the core of your app. Then you compile it all and upload it to your phone. PhoneGap also offers an online compilation service: upload your HTML files and it compiles an application for you to download to your phone.

There are things you don't get with PhoneGap. For example, you can't open a connection to your phone's Bluetooth serial port, if it has one, nor can you access the phone's USB connection. Despite that, it's a promising start.

PhoneGap is not the only platform for developing mobile phone apps for multiple operating systems. MoSync (www.mosync.com) also offers application frameworks for multiple platforms, but you develop your own application in C++, not in HTML. You get access to more of the hardware with MoSync, but it definitely requires a greater familiarity with programming than anything you've seen in this book so far. Several other companies are offering cross-platform tools like this now, and more will certainly come along. If you're interested in developing applications for the phone that use built-in sensors, and you don't want to write an application native to each different phone operating system, PhoneGap is your best option until the browsers catch up.

X

" Text-Messaging Interfaces

Text messaging is fast becoming the most common use for mobile phones. Many people regard texts as less intrusive than voice calls in the flow of daily life. With a text message, you can get information across quickly and with no introduction. In addition, it's easy to send email to SMS, and vice versa; they're not platform-dependent—as long as you have a mobile phone or email account. For situations where you need an immediate, unobtrusive notification, or to give a single instruction, they work wonderfully.

SMS, or Short Messaging Service, began as a way of sending information over the mobile phone networks' signaling channel. The idea was to send bytes as part of the data sent to signal incoming calls, but to do so when there was no incoming call. These short messages could be used for diagnostic purposes, to notify the receiver of voicemail, or for other quick notifications. When SMS was rolled out as a commercial service option for customers, however, it became much more than that. SMS may be limited to 140 characters per message, but people have found many creative ways to pack a lot of info into those 140 characters.

Almost all mobile carriers provide an SMS-to-email gateway as part of their service, which means you can send an SMS from an email client and receive SMS messages in your inbox. To test this out, send a text message from your phone, but instead of sending it to a phone number, enter your email address as the destination. Depending on your carrier, it may be sent via MMS, or Multimedia Message Service, or it may simply go as an SMS. Check your inbox, and you'll see a message from yourself. Now you'll know the email address to use if you want to send yourself a text message via email as well. Most of the time it's simply your phone number @ your carrier's email address. Here are some common SMS-to-email servers for a few U.S., Canada, and European carriers:

AT&T: phonenumber@txt.att.net
T-Mobile: phonenumber@tmomail.net
Virgin Mobile: phonenumber@vmobl.com
Sprint: phonenumber@messaging.sprintpcs.com

Verizon: phonenumber@vtext.com
Bell Canada: phonenumber@txt.bellmobility.ca
Telenor Norway: phonenumber@mobilpost.no
Telia Denmark: phonenumber@gsm1800.telia.dk
Swisscom: phonenumber@bluewin.ch
T-Mobile Austria: phonenumber@sms.t-mobile.at
T-Mobile Germany: phonenumber@t-d1-sms.de
T-Mobile UK: phonenumber@t-mobile.uk.net

A longer list can be found at www.emailtextmessages.com (warning: I have not verified every one of these). With U.S. carriers, many expect a simple 10-digit phone number without the leading country code (which is +1 for the U.S.), but carriers in the U.S. and around the world tend to be idiosyncratic about this. Check with your carrier's customer support to find out how they handle it.

The PHP script on the next page creates a simple form that lets you send a text message to any of the carriers listed above, and a few others. Modified, it can be used as an SMS gateway script for a networked device.

Try It To send an SMS, just send mail to the 10-digit phone number at the recipient's carrier. Here's a PHP script to send yourself an SMS. Save this as **sms.php**.

⚠ Consider password-protecting this script, or removing it after you're done testing. It could become the target of abuse if it's found by a roving spambot with a pocket full of phone numbers.

```php
<?php
/*
    SMS messenger
    Context:  PHP
*/
    $phoneNumber = $_REQUEST["phoneNumber"];    // get the phone number
    $carrier    = $_REQUEST["carrier"];         // get the carrier
    $message    = $_REQUEST["message"];         // get the message
    $recipient  = $phoneNumber."@".$carrier;    // compose the recipient
    $subject = "Message for you";

    // if all the fields are filled in, send a message:
    if (isset($phoneNumber)&& isset($carrier) && isset($message)) {
        mail($recipient, $subject, $message);
    }
?>


<html>
<head></head>
<body>
    <h2>SMS Messenger</h2>
    <form name="txter" action="sms.php" method="post">

        Phone number: <input type="text" name="phoneNumber"
        size="15" maxlength="15"><br>
        Message:<br>
        <textarea name="message" rows="5" cols="30" maxlength="140">
Put your sms message here (140 characters max.)
        </textarea>
        </br>
        Carrier:
        <select name="carrier">
            <option value="txt.att.net">AT&T US</option>
            <option value="txt.bellmobility.ca">Bell Canada</option>
            <option value="messaging.nextel.com">Nextel US</option>
            <option value="messaging.sprintpcs.com US">Sprint</option>
            <option value="bluewin.ch">Swisscom</option>
            <option value="sms.t-mobile.at">T-Mobile Austria</option>
            <option value="t-d1-sms.de">T-Mobile Germany</option>
            <option value="t-mobile.uk.net">T-Mobile UK</option>
            <option value="tmomail.net">T-Mobile US</option>
            <option value="gsm1800.telia.dk">Telia Denmark</option>
            <option value="mobilpost.no">Telenor Norway</option>
            <option value="vtext.com">Verizon</option>
            <option value="vmobl.com">Virgin Mobile US</option>
        </select>

        <input type="submit" value="send message">
    </form>
</body>
</html>
```

GPRS for Microcontrollers

There are a handful of devices on the market that allow you to connect a microcontroller to mobile phone networks directly. Using one of these, your microcontroller connects to the Internet the same way that your mobile phone does. It has a phone number, and it can send and receive SMS messages, make HTTP calls, and do anything else you can do on the Internet. The trade-offs to using them are that they can get expensive—in terms of both power usage and connectivity costs.

Telit's modules are the high end of the GPRS module market, and there are a few evaluation boards and shields for Arduino based on these. They feature a TTL serial interface, an AT-style command set (meaning they operate as a modem, like the Bluetooth Mates, but with different commands). They have their own TCP/IP libraries on board, so you can make network connections, and some models feature GPS as well. One model even has a Python interpreter so you can run programs written in the Python programming language on it.

Spark Fun sells breakout boards for the Telit GE865 and GM862, as well as one for ADH Tech's ADH8066 module, These breakout boards give you all the pins of the module on 0.1-inch spacings, and usually a USB-to-Serial connection. They're not designed to be used with any particular microcontroller, so you'll have to start from the command set and the manufacturer's datasheet if you want to use these.

They also sell a GPRS shield for Arduino based on Spreadtrum Technologies' SM5100B module. This module isn't as feature-laden as the Telit modules, but it has an AT command set, and it can send and receive SMS messages and make network connections. John Boxall has a nice set of tutorials for using this shield at tronixstuff.wordpress.com/2011/01/19/tutorial-arduino-and-gsm-cellular-part-one.

Libelium (www.libelium.com) sells a number of different GPRS shields for Arduino through their Cooking Hacks site (www.cooking-hacks.com). They have dual-band and quad-band modules, meaning that some of their modules can operate in the U.S., Europe, Africa, and much of Asia, depending on the country and carrier.

Seeed Studio carries a quad-band GPRS shield as well, with built-in audio jacks for voice communications in case you want to build your own phone.

The two challenges to using any of these GPRS shields are power and price. The SM5100B shield, for example, can draw up to 2 amps when it's making a call. That's more than the Arduino's regulator can feed it, so the shield connects to the board's Vin pin. That means you need to supply the board with at least 2 amps just for the GPRS module. The board won't draw all that current the whole time, but if it can't get it when it needs it, you won't make the connection.

For any of these modules, you'll need a mobile subscription and working SIM card from your favorite mobile carrier. Unless you have a flat-rate data and text plan, you can spend a lot of money testing and debugging GPRS projects. A second alternative is a pay-as-you-go plan for your SIM card. Neither is an ideal choice, unfortunately, so do as much troubleshooting as you can offline to save money where possible.

Two ways to get GPRS to a microcontroller: the Telit GM862 evaluation board breaks out all the pins of the module to 0.1" spacing; the SM5100B shield breaks out the serial pins of its module to the Arduino's serial pins.

🙶 Native Applications for Mobile Phones

Even though web and SMS interfaces offer many possibilities, there are projects for which you really need access to a mobile phone's operating system. Web applications make it difficult—if not impossible—to access the phone's hardware or file system, for example. In these cases, you need to get to know your phone's operating system and the programming tools available for it. If you're aiming to make an application for all mobile phones, you need to become familiar with several operating systems.

The mobile phone industry is fast changing, as are its smartphone operating systems, and keeping up with it all can be exhausting. Google's Android OS, Blackberry, Palm's webOS, Windows Mobile, Symbian, and Apple's iOS (for iPad, iPhone, and iPod touch) are currently the largest players. Of those, Android, iOS, and Blackberry are the three largest at the moment, covering most of the market. Nokia's Symbian was one of the largest, but Nokia is no longer supporting it as its primary operating system. As of the last quarter of 2010, Android was the most popular of smartphone operating systems, taking 35% of the world market.

There's a lot of interest in programming for iOS because it's such an attractive environment, but Apple is notoriously controlling about iOS development. You have to register as a developer, and they've limited the available toolkits severely. In addition, you can't just distribute your app independently—you have to do it through the App Store. That's fine for commercial developers, but for hobbyists and home hackers, it can be quite forbidding. For more on iPhone programming, see Alasdair Allan's books, *Learning iPhone Programming* (O'Reilly) and *iOS Sensor Programming* (O'Reilly). Alasdair has done a great deal to make iPhone programming accessible.

Android, on the other hand, is somewhat more accessible to programmers. Applications can be installed on Android phones using the Android Market, or they can be installed over USB. Based on Linux and programmed in Java, it

offers an environment familiar to many experienced developers. For those less comfortable with code, Google offers a graphic programming environment called App Inventor (http://appinventor.googlelabs.com) that allows you to create applications by combining graphic objects. For the rest of this chapter, you'll learn to make Android apps using a familiar environment: Processing. As of version 1.5, Processing can compile and install sketches as Android apps.

Processing for Android

Processing for Android is a very exciting update to Processing, but as it is very new, it is still under development. The examples that follow were developed at the same time as the tools to make them possible—in some cases, they are the first real tests of the libraries they use. So be warned, you're sailing in uncharted waters now. As the Processing for Android wiki (http://wiki.processing.org/w/Android) explains: "Do not use this code while operating heavy equipment. Do not rely on this code for thesis or diploma work, as you will not graduate. Do not use this code if you're prone to whining about incomplete software that you download for free." The libraries used here are likely to change after the publication of this book, and they will hopefully become more stable and easier to use. So make sure to check the online documentation of anything mentioned here for updates.

Setting Up Processing for Android

Processing for Android has a slightly different workflow than standard Processing, so you'll need to install some new components and get used to some new tools. The first thing you'll need is Processing version 1.5.1 or later, which can be downloaded from the Processing site (www.processing.org/download). You'll also need the Android Software Developers' Kit (SDK), available at http://developer.android.com/sdk. Download and install both. Then open Processing. You'll see a new button in the main toolbar labeled Standard, as shown in Figure 10-12. Click it and choose Android. You'll get a dialog box asking you if the Android SDK is installed. Click Yes. Another dialog box will pop up asking you where it is. Navigate to the Android ADK folder that you just installed. The Processing editor color scheme will turn green, and you'll be in Android mode.

You now need to install some components of the Android SDK, so go to the new Android menu and choose Android SDK & AVD Manager. This will open the Android SDK Manager, where you can install new Android packages as new versions become available. Click Available Packages to install new packages. At minimum, you need to install three things.

Underneath Android Repository, check the boxes for "Android SDK Platform-tools" and "SDK Platform Android 2.1, API 7".

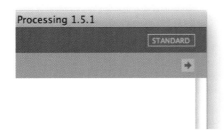

Figure 10-12
Processing's Mode button set to Standard mode.

Beneath "Third party Add-ons", expand the Google Inc. entry, and select "Google APIs by Google Inc., Android API 7".

You can install more recent packages if you want, depending on what version of Android your device is running, and what features you want to access (but you need at least these for Processing for Android to work).

To check your device's operating system version, go to the home sceeen, and from the menu, choose Settings. Scroll to the bottom and choose "About phone". In that menu, you'll see a listing of the Android version. Figure 10-13 shows the menu. If you have a later version than 2.1, you might want to install the latest that your phone can run. For example, I installed the SDK Platform Android 2.3.3, API 10, revision 1 to work with a Nexus S phone that was running version 2.3.4, and the Google APIs Android API 10, revision 2, as well.

Figure 10-13
The "About phone" menu, showing your Android version.

Where Does the App Run?

You have two choices as to where your app will run when you click the Run button: it can run in an emulator on your desktop, or it can run on your actual phone. The emulator is useful if you don't have an Android phone handy. The SDK Manager should install an emulator for you automatically, but if not, you can install one by clicking Virtual Devices in the SDK Manager. Emulators tend to be slow, though, and they're nowhere near as exciting as running the app on your actual phone.

To enable your Processing sketches to run directly on your Android device, first go to the device's Settings menu and choose Applications. From there, choose Development. Finally, click USB Debugging. This enables your device to install applications over USB, and to send debugging information back to Processing or any other development environment over USB as well.

Once you've enabled USB debugging, plug your phone into your computer with a USB cable, and open one of the Processing for Android example sketches (remember, examples are in the File menu, under Examples). The Accelerometer example in the **Sensors** folder is fun. While holding down the Shift key, click Run. This should change the title in the toolbar from "Run in Emulator" to "Run on Device" (see Figure 10-14). The sketch will compile, then install on your device and start running. Ta Dah! You're now an Android developer!

The handy thing about "Run on Device" is that you can get messages back from the sketch while it's running on your device. This is because you enabled USB debugging. Any print() or println() commands in your sketch will print to the debugger pane of Processing on your desktop just like always. This makes debugging your sketch so much easier. Make sure to remove your print() and println() statements when your sketch is done, though. When the device is not connected to your computer, those commands write to a log file on the device, and they will start to fill up its available storage space.

Differences to Watch Out For

There are a few big differences between Standard-mode Processing and Processing for Android.

Many libraries for Standard mode do not work in Android mode. This will likely change as library developers adapt the useful ones to Android mode, but for the moment, it's best not to assume.

Figure 10-14
To run a sketch directly on your phone, hold down Shift while clicking the Run button.

An Android mode sketch is an activity in Android Java terms. Activities have a few core methods: onCreate(), which is equivalent to Processing for Android's setup() method; and onPause() and onResume(), which are called by Processing's pause() and resume() methods. Activities (and therefore sketches) pause and resume frequently: whenever your device goes into idle mode, and every time you rotate the orientation, and every time you switch to another application. So, you should put in pause() and resume() methods to manage those transitions smoothly.

Interaction is different with a touchscreen. There's no mouse button, so the mouse button events don't work. mouseX and mouseY still work, and you've also got new variables—motionX, motionY, pMotionY, and motionPressure—that you can use to tell something about touch as well. mousePressed also still works.

Since an Android sketch takes over the whole screen, there's no point in setting size(), so it doesn't work in Android mode. You can get the screenWidth and screenHeight if you want them, though. You can also lock the orientation, like so:

```
orientation(PORTRAIT);
orientation(LANDSCAPE);
```

Fonts still work as before. To get a list of the system fonts, use this line of code:

```
println( PFont.list() );
```

You need to enable different permissions to get at different functions of the device. In the Android menu, you'll see a list of Sketch Permissions. You can set most of them from this menu. This menu writes to the **AndroidManifest.xml** file in the sketch directory.

Whenever possible, use the permissions menu rather than editing the manifest. For everything you need in this book, you can use the permissions menu and be safe. It's easy to mess things up by editing it wrong—remember, XML is not forgiving.

Since your sketch restarts every time you change orientation, you might want to use saveStrings() and loadStrings() to save and load variables that need to persist.

For more tips on the differences, see http://wiki.processing.org/w/Android for the latest information.

Now here's a quick sketch to get you started. It reads the mouse position and saves data when you pause and resume. You'll need to set the Sketch Permissions to enable WRITE_EXTERNAL_STORAGE.
X

Touch It This sketch will show you how mouseX, mouseY, and motionPressure work on Android. It will reorient itself, and save and reload data when you rotate the device.

```
/*
  Processing for Android test
 Context:  Processing
 */
float ballX, ballY;        // position of the ball
// file to save data for pause and resume:
String datafile = "sketchFile.dat";

void setup() {
  // create a font for the screen:
  String[]fontList = PFont.list();
  PFont androidFont = createFont(fontList[0], 24, true);
  textFont(androidFont, 24);
}

void draw() {
  // color theme: Sandy stone beach ocean diver by ps
  // http://kuler.adobe.com:
  background(#002F2F);
  fill(#EFECCA);
  // show the mouse X and Y and finger pressure:
  text("mouseX:" + mouseX, 10, 50);
  text("mouseY:" + mouseY, 10, 80);
  text("motionPressure:" + motionPressure, 10, 170);
  // move the ball if the person is pressing:
  if (mousePressed) {
    ballX = mouseX;
    ballY = mouseY;
  }
  // draw a nice blue ball where you touch:
  fill(#046380);
  ellipse(ballX, ballY, 50, 50);
}
```

The pause() and resume() methods use an external file saved to your device to save variables that persist when the sketch restarts. Each variable is a separate string, saved on its own line. A newline character (\n) separates each line. Figure 10-14 shows the results.

```
void pause() {
  // make a string of the ball position:
  String ballPos = ballX+ "\n" + ballY;
  /// put the string in an array and save to a file:
  String[] data = {
    ballPos
  };
  saveStrings(datafile, data);
}

void resume() {
  //load the data file:
  String[] data = loadStrings(datafile);
  // if there's a file there:
  if (data != null) {
    // and there are two strings, get them for X and Y:
    if (data.length > 1) {
      ballX = float(data[0]);
      ballY = float(data[1]);
    }
  }
}
```

"Play around with some of the Android examples that come with Processing as well. The Accelerometer and Compass sketches are good fun, and they show you how to get at those useful components on your phone. Once you're familiar with Processing for Android, you're ready to make your own datalogger on the phone.

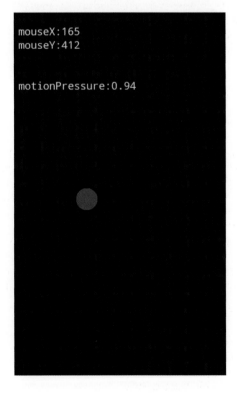

▶ **Figure 10-15**
The Processing for Android sketch that you just wrote.

Project 31

Personal Mobile Datalogger

One popular reason to develop native applications on a mobile phone is to use the phone's Bluetooth radio as a serial connection to other devices. In this way, your phone can become a mobile data-logger, or a conduit to send the data to a database on the Internet. In this project, you'll sense your Galvanic skin response using an Arduino, send the data via Bluetooth to your Android phone, and log the result to a file on the Internet.

> **MATERIALS**
>
> » **Android device**
> » **LilyPad Arduino Simple**
> » **Bluetooth Mate**
> » **Lithium Polymer Ion Battery**
> » **1 resistor, 270-kilohm**
> » **Conductive ribbon**
> » **Conductive thread**
> » **Shieldit Super 14" fabric**
> » **Velcro**
> » **Hoodie**
> » **Embroidery thread**

A growing number of personal data enthusiasts are gathering personal biometric data for many different purposes, from visualizing their activity patterns in order to improve exercise habits, to tracking sleep patterns in order to find solutions to insomnia. Quantified Self meetups (http://quantifiedself.com) are popping up around the world for people to share tips and tricks on how to do this, and devices like the FitBit (www.fitbit.com) and the Zeo (www.myzeo.com) have come on the market to make biometric tracking easier.

This project is based on the work of ITP alumnus Mustafa Bağdatlı, shown in Figure 10-15. Mustafa wanted to track his Galvanic skin response (GSR) and heart rate against his calendar, so he could see when his mood—as reflected in his heart rate and GSR—were affected by the events of the day. His project, Poker Face, tracked the two biometric characteristics on a LilyPad Arduino, transmitted them via Bluetooth to a mobile phone, and logged the result on the Web. You can find more on Poker Face at http://mustafabagdatli.com In this project, you'll build the same, but without the heart rate sensor to keep it simple.

Feel free to change the sensor for whatever you want to track yourself.

Figure 10-17 shows the system for this project. A micro-controller reads the analog voltage from the sensor and sends it serially to a Bluetooth Mate. The data is then transmitted over Bluetooth to a mobile phone using the Serial Port Profile, or SPP, that you used in other Bluetooth projects in this book. The phone then makes an HTTP GET request to a PHP script on a web server. The script saves the incoming data to a file. What you do with the data from there is up to you.

▸▸ Figure 10-16
Mustafa Bağdatlı wearing Poker Face, a biometric datalogger linked to a mobile phone. *Photo courtesy of Mustafa Bağdatlı.*

The Circuit

The circuit for this project is quite simple. To measure Galvanic skin response, all you need is a high-value resistor and your skin. As a test, take a multimeter and measure the resistance across your wrist. You'll find that the resistance is high, probably in the megohm range if your skin is cool and dry. Work up a sweat and measure it again. You'll see that the resistance has gone down. When you exercise, or when you're faced with stressful or arousing situations (good or bad), you perspire more, changing the conductance of your skin. That's what this project will measure.

The sensor is basically a voltage divider, with your skin as the variable resistor and a fixed resistor completing the circuit. A 270-kilohm resistor is used here (see Figure 10-19 and Figure 10-20), but feel free to change it to suit your skin. Generally, below 10 kilohm won't work.

Conductive fabric and conductive thread were used to make the sensor for this circuit, and to attach the LilyPad Arduino to the garment. Different conductive fabrics and threads have different material and electrical properties, so you might want to experiment with a few to find what works for you. Mustafa used stretchable conductive fabric sewn into wristbands for his cuffs, as you can see in Figure 10-18. For this project, I used Shieldit Super fabric with adhesive backing. For more information about conductive fabrics, see Leah Buechley's excellent introduction at http://web.media.mit.edu/~leah/grad_work/diy/diy.html; Syuzi Pakhchyan's book *Fashioning Technology: A DIY Intro to Smart Crafting* (O'Reilly); or Hannah Perner-Wilson's excellent online resource at web.media.mit.edu/~plusea.

> ⚠ **Test the whole circuit with the code below before sewing it into the garment. Hardware debugging after you sew it is difficult.**

The Construction

For this project, you'll use iron-on conductive fabric attached inside the pocket of a hoodie as your sensor contacts. When you reach in your pocket, you can touch the fabric contacts with the palm of your hand, and take a reading on your phone with the other hand. Or, you can let the mobile app run continually to take a reading every two minutes.

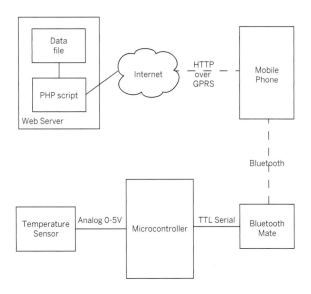

Figure 10-17
The system diagram for the mobile datalogger project.

Figure 10-18
Detail photo of the Poker Face GSR wristband. Here, the wristband is inside-out to show the conductive fabric contacts. *Photo courtesy of Mustafa Bağdatlı.*

⤒ **Figure 10-19**
The mobile datalogger circuit. The contacts for the sensor are conductive fabric.

◀◀ **Figure 10-20**
The mobile datalogger circuit schematic.

NOTE: When you're using Lithium Polymer batteries in your project, get a USB charger for them. Adafruit's USB LiIon/LiPoly charger (ID: 259) or Spark Fun's LiPo Charger Basic - Micro-USB (sku: PRT-10217) work well.

Conductive thread connects the fabric contacts on one side of the garment to a three-wire conductive ribbon on the other side of the garment. The microcontroller and battery will be sewn into the bottom band of the hoodie just below the pocket, and the conductive ribbon will connect them, sewn onto the inside lining of the hoodie. Figure 10-21 shows the layout on the inside of the garment.

Iron the conductive fabric contacts into the pocket. Space them so they cover about the width of the heel of your palm, and contact it comfortably when you put your hand in the pocket. Figure 10-22 shows you the inside of the pocket.

Split the ends of the three-wire conductive ribbon about an inch on either end with a pair of scissors. You need enough distance between the wires to span the space between the conductive fabric contacts on one end, and between two contacts of the LilyPad Arduino Simple on the other. Tin the tips of the outside wire ends to keep them from fraying. You're not using the middle wire, so cut it out, down to the end of each split. You can also embroider the two outside conductors with yarn that matches the hoodie to keep them from fraying, if you wish. Solder one pair of the conductive ribbon's leads to pins 11 and A0 of the LilyPad Arduino.

Cut a hole in one side of the bottom band just below the pocket to insert the microcontroller with the Bluetooth Mate and battery attached. You'll need to be able to get the battery in and out for charging, so finish the edges of the hole so they won't fray with repeated use. Iron-on fabric, or embroidery thread will do the job. Then add Velcro to the inside edges to provide a closure.

Cut another small slit in the band about six inches (10cm) away from the large hole so you can insert the ribbon through the bottom band. Figure 10-21 shows the two cuts.

Make sure the LilyPad Arduino Simple is programmed and the circuit is fully assembled before you sew it into the garment. The sketch is below.

Position the ends of the ribbon on the inner lining of the garment opposite the fabric contacts in the pocket. Sew the conductive ribbon to the contacts through the material with conductive thread. Use tight stitches for a good connection. Use a meter to check connectivity between the contacts and the opposite end of the ribbon when you've finished your sewing. This way, you know the signal makes it from the contacts through the garment to the end of the ribbon that will attach to the LilyPad.

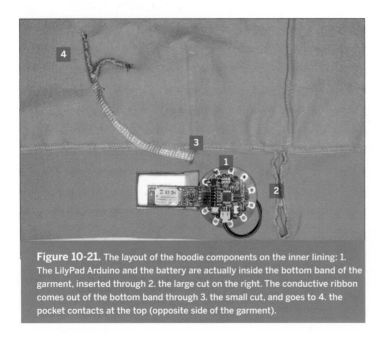

Figure 10-21. The layout of the hoodie components on the inner lining: 1. The LilyPad Arduino and the battery are actually inside the bottom band of the garment, inserted through 2. the large cut on the right. The conductive ribbon comes out of the bottom band through 3. the small cut, and goes to 4. the pocket contacts at the top (opposite side of the garment).

Figure 10-22. The conductive fabric contacts inside the hoodie pocket.

Tack the ribbon down to the garment's inner lining about every inch, so it's secure and won't fold over itself when worn. Don't sew the battery in—you'll need to remove it for recharging. You shouldn't need to sew the other components in either, but Velcro on the back of the LilyPad Arduino and in the lining of the band will secure it nicely.

At this point, the circuit should be fully functional. Test it with a wired connection before going Bluetooth. To test it, attach a USB-to-Serial connector to the LilyPad Arduino (which will take some creative cabling) and open the serial connection in the Serial Monitor or another serial terminal program at 115200bps. Put your hand on the contacts in the pocket. Then send any byte, and you should get back a sensor value. To see a change in the value, either work up a sweat or lick your hand and put it on the contacts again. When you know it works, remove the USB-to-Serial line, and connect the Bluetooth Mate and the battery and turn it on. Now connect from the Serial Monitor or a serial terminal program via the Mate's serial port. This will work like it did in Chapter 2 when you added the Bluetooth Mate to Monski Pong.

The Code
There are three pieces of code for this project: the PHP script, the Arduino sketch, and the Processing sketch. The first two are relatively simple, and having them done and tested makes the Processing sketch easier to understand.

The Arduino sketch listens for serial input and when a byte arrives, it takes a reading, maps it to a voltage range, and sends it out.

The PHP script accepts a request string and looks for one variable, called data. It appends everything from that variable into an existing text file called **datalog.txt**. It returns a basic HTML page with the data that the client sent.

The Processing sketch checks if it's connected to the Arduino's Bluetooth Mate. If it's connected, it asks for a reading once every 10 seconds. Once every two minutes, it sends the accumulated readings to the PHP script. There are also two buttons: one to get a reading and another to send the reading to the server.
X

Read It The Arduino sketch's global constants include the two pins to be used as voltage and ground for the sensor.

setup() initializes serial at 115200bps (the default rate for the Bluetooth Mate) and sets the voltage and ground pins for the sensor appropriately.

loop() checks to see whether there's been any serial input. When there is, it reads the byte just to clear the serial buffer, then takes a sensor reading, maps it, and returns it.

Notice that the mapping is to a range from 0 to 3.7V. That's because the Lithium Polymer battery supplies the microcontroller at 3.7V when fully charged.

```
/*
 Galvanic Skin Response reader
 Context: Arduino
 */
const int voltagePin = 11;    // use pin 11 as voltage
const int groundPin = A1;     // use pin A1 as ground

void setup() {
  // initialize serial:
  Serial.begin(115200);
  // set powerPin and groundPin as digital outputs:
  pinMode(voltagePin, OUTPUT);
  pinMode(groundPin, OUTPUT);
  // set them high and low respectively:
  digitalWrite(voltagePin, HIGH);
  digitalWrite(groundPin, LOW);
}

void loop() {
  // if serial available, send average
  if (Serial.available() > 0) {
    int inByte = Serial.read();
    int sensorReading = analogRead(A0);
    float voltage = map(sensorReading, 0, 1023, 0,3.7);
    Serial.println(voltage);
  }
}
```

Log It   The PHP script uses the $_REQUEST array variable to get the results of the HTTP request. Even though the Processing sketch is making a GET request, this script doesn't care—it will read GET or POST.

First, it checks to see whether the $_REQUEST array has a value set. If so, it looks for a variable within it called data.

Next, it checks to see whether the datalog file exists. If so, it opens it and puts its contents in a variable called $currentData. Then it appends the new data from the client to the end of that variable, and overwrites the file with the result.

The HTML following the script echoes back to the client what it sent. Putting it in HTML format is handy for checking it in a browser.

```php
<?php
/*
        Data logger
        Context:  PHP
*/

// name of the file on the server
// where you want to save stuff:
$dataFile = 'datalog.txt';

// see if the client uploaded a file:
if (isset($_REQUEST)) {
   $newData = $_REQUEST['data'];
   if (file_exists($dataFile)) {
      // Open the existing file to get existing content
      $currentData = file_get_contents($dataFile);
      // Add what you got from the client:
      $currentData .= $newData;
      // Write everything back to the existing file
      file_put_contents($dataFile, $currentData);
   }
}
?>

<html>
   <body>
         Here's what you sent:
      <?php echo $newData; ?>
   </body>
</html>
```

Figure 10-23
What the logger script returns in a browser.

To enable the PHP script to write to the datalog file, you'll first need to create the file on your server. Make a blank text file called **datalog.txt** in the same directory as the PHP script (in the Linux or Mac OS X Terminal, you can use the command touch datalog.txt). Change its permissions so that it's readable and writable by others. From the command line of a Linux or Mac OS X system, type:

```
chmod o+rw datalog.txt
```

If you're creating the file using a GUI-based program, get info on the file and set the permissions that way. Figure 10-24 shows the Get Info window from BBEdit, which is similar to many other programs. Once you've made this file, call it from the browser with a query string like this:

```
http://www.yourserver.com/logger.php?data=blahblahblah
```

You should get a page that looks like Figure 10-23. Open the **datalog.txt** file. You'll see something like this:

```
blahblahblah
blahblahblah
blahblahblah
```

If you do, you know everything is working and you're ready to write the Processing sketch.

X

Figure 10-24

Setting the read-write permissions for a file from a GUI-based program.

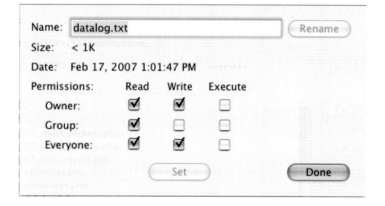

Bluetooth Serial Library

In order to use the Processing for Android sketch, you'll need the Bluetooth Serial (BtSerial) library. This library allows you to make serial connections over Bluetooth using similar commands to those you used with the serial library in Processing's Standard mode. You can download it from https://github.com/arduino/BtSerial. Click the Downloads link and pick the latest download package (0.1.6 as of this writing). Make sure to download the download package not the source. Unzip the file. You'll get a directory called btserial-0.1.6. Inside it is a directory called **btserial**. Place that in the libraries folder of your Processing sketch directory, as you've done with other libraries.

In Android mode in Processing version 1.5.1, libraries are not always imported into your sketch automatically. This will be fixed in future versions so that it works like the Standard mode. If when you try to run your sketch you get an error that says package cc.arduino.btserial does not exist, make a subdirectory, **code**, in the sketch's directory and copy the file **btserial.jar** from the **library** subdirectory of the **btserial** directory that you just installed into **code**. Then try running your sketch again.

This is not ideal, but it should be addressed by the time this book is in publication—the Processing team is very good with bug fixes.

X

Send It The global variables for this sketch include: values for the sensor reading interval, in seconds, and the interval for updating the server, in minutes; the times of the last read and send; the address of your server PHP script; the state of the connection; two buttons for reading and sending on demand; and the color scheme for the app.

▸▸ **Change this to match your PHP script's URL.**

```
/*
Datalogger
Receives data via Bluetooth every ten seconds
Uploads data via HTTP every two minutes
Context:  Processing, Android mode
*/
import cc.arduino.btserial.*;
// instance of the library:
BtSerial bt;

int readInterval = 10;      // in seconds
int sendInterval = 2;       // in minutes

int lastRead = second();    // the seconds last time you read
int lastSend = minute();    // the minutes last time you read
String lastSendTime;        // String timestamp of last  server update

// URL of your PHP Script:
String url = "http://www.yourserver.com/logger.php?data=";
String currentReadings = ""; // group of readings, with datestamps
String thisReading;          // most recent reading

String connectionState = ""; // connected to Bluetooth or not?

Button readButton;          // Button for prompting immediate read
Button sendButton;          // Button for prompting immediate send
boolean updateNow = false;  // flag to force an update
boolean sendNow = false;    // flag to force a send

// color scheme from http://kuler.adobe.com
// deep optimism by nicanore:
color bgColor = #2B0D15;
color textColor = #FFEB97;
color buttonColor = #565F63;
color buttonHighlightColor = #ACBD9B;
```

The setup() method sets the background and fill colors, and initializes the text parameters. Then, it makes a new instance of the BtSerial library and tries to connect to the Bluetooth Mate using the connect() method. Finally, it initializes the two onscreen buttons.

```
void setup() {
  // set color scheme:
  background(bgColor);
  fill(textColor);

  // Setup Fonts:
  String[] fontList = PFont.list();
  PFont androidFont = createFont(fontList[0], 24, true);
  textFont(androidFont, 24);

  // instantiate the library:
  bt = new BtSerial( this );
```

»

» Note that the button and text positions are all relative to the screenWidth and screenHeight variables. This is so that they stay in the same relation to each other and the screen if the device is rotated.

Continued from opposite page.

```
  // try to connect to Bluetooth:
  connectionState = connect();

  readButton = new Button(screenWidth/2 - 100, 2*screenHeight/3,
      200, 60, buttonColor, buttonHighlightColor, "Get Reading");
  sendButton = new Button(screenWidth/2 - 100, 2*screenHeight/3 + 80,
      200, 60, buttonColor, buttonHighlightColor, "Send Reading");
}
```

» The draw() method starts by drawing the text strings and buttons. Then it checks to see whether the sensor reading interval has passed, or whether the updateNow variable has been set (when you click the Read Now button, this variable is set to true). If either of these is true, the sketch takes a reading via Bluetooth using the getData() method, and adds it to a string of readings taken since the last time it updated the server.

Next, it checks whether the send interval or sendNow has been set by a click of the Send Now button. If either of these is true, it sends the current string of readings to the server using the sendData() method.

```
void draw() {
  // display data onscreen:
  background(bgColor);
  fill(textColor);
  textAlign(LEFT);
  text(connectionState, 10, screenHeight/4);
  text(getTime(), 10, screenHeight/4 + 60);
  text("latest reading (volts): " + thisReading, 10, screenHeight/4 + 90);
  text("Server updated at:\n" + lastSendTime, 10, screenHeight/4 + 120);

  // draw the buttons:
  readButton.display();
  sendButton.display();

  if (sendNow) {
    textAlign(LEFT);
    text("sending to server, please wait...", 10, screenHeight/4 - 60);
  }

  // if the update interval has passed,
  // or updateNow is true, update automatically:
  if (abs(second() - lastRead) >= readInterval || updateNow) {
    thisReading = getData();

    // if you got a valid reading, add a timestamp:
    if (thisReading != null) {
      currentReadings += getTime() +"," + thisReading;
      // take note of when you last updated:
      lastRead = second();
      // you've updated, no need to do it again until prompted:
      updateNow = false;
    }
  }

  // if the send interval has passed,
  // or sendNow is true, update automatically:
  if (abs(minute() - lastSend) >= sendInterval || sendNow ) {
    sendData(currentReadings);
    // get the time two ways:
```

»

Last, the draw() method reads the buttons, then sets their previous states once it's read them. This sketch uses a modified version of the Button class from the Processing RFID writer sketch in Chapter 9. Because the cursor on a touchscreen (namely, your finger) can disappear, there's no equivalent to the mousePressed and mouseReleased events, so you have to make one up. You're doing that in this case by having a method in the Button class called isPressed(), a variable called pressedLastTime, and two methods that let you get and set this variable. With these, you can check the current state of the button (isPressed()), save it when you're done (setLastState()), and get the state last time you checked it (getLastState()).

Continued from previous page.

```
    lastSendTime = getTime();    // a String to print on the screen
    lastSend = minute();         // an int for further comparison
}

// if the read button changed from not pressed to pressed,
// set updateNow, to force an update next time through the
// loop. Do the same for the send button and sendNow, right below:
if (readButton.isPressed() && !readButton.getLastState()) {
  updateNow = true;
}
//save the state of the button for next check:
readButton.setLastState(readButton.isPressed());

if (sendButton.isPressed() && !sendButton.getLastState()) {
  sendNow = true;
}
//save the state of the button for next check:
sendButton.setLastState(sendButton.isPressed());
}
```

When the sketch pauses, the pause() method is called. This method sends any current readings to the server, then disconnects the Bluetooth serial connection so you can open it again on resume. There is no resume() method, since setup() gets called by default every time an Android activity resumes (remember, a Processing sketch for Android is an activity).

```
void pause() {
  // if you have any readings, send them:
  if (!currentReadings.equals("")) {
    sendData(currentReadings);
  }
  // stop the Bluetooth connection so you can start it again:
  if (bt != null && bt.isConnected()) {
    bt.disconnect();
  }
}
```

The connect() method tries to make a Bluetooth connection. First, it makes sure there's a valid instance of the BtSerial library and that it's not already connected to the remote device (the Bluetooth Mate in this case). Then it gets a list of all paired devices on your phone and tries to connect to the first one.

Before you run the sketch, go to the Bluetooth Settings on your phone (under Settings→Wireless Settings), and pair with your Bluetooth Mate. If

```
String connect() {
  String result = "Bluetooth not initialized yet...";
  if (bt !=null) {
    // if you are connnected, get data:
    if (!bt.isConnected() ) {
      // get the list of paired devices:
      String[] pairedDevices = bt.list();

      if (pairedDevices.length > 0) {
        println(pairedDevices);
        // open a connection to the first one:
        bt.connect( pairedDevices[0] );
        result = "Connected to \n" + bt.getName();
      }
```

»

» you don't, the app can't see the
Bluetooth Mate. If your Bluetooth
Mate isn't the first item in the list of
devices, be sure to change the call to:

```
bt.connect( pairedDevices[0] );
```

to match the number of your Bluetooth
Mate in the list.

Continued from opposite page.

```
    }
    else {
      result = "Couldn't get any paired devices";
    }
  }
  return result;
}
```

» The getData() method checks
to see that there's a valid Bluetooth
connection. Then, it sends a byte
prompting the Arduino to send a
reading in return. It adds all the bytes it
gets in response to a result string.

Since the Bluetooth connection might
get broken, the method checks to see
that what it got ended with a newline,
which is the last byte that the Arduino
will send. If the method has a valid
reading string, it returns it. Otherwise,
it returns null.

If there isn't a valid connection,
getData() attempts to make one.

```
String getData() {
  String result = "";

  if (bt != null) {
    // if you are connnected, get data:
    if ( bt.isConnected() ) {
      // send data to get new data:
      bt.write("A");
      // wait for incoming data:
      while (bt.available () == 0);
      // if there are incoming bytes available, read them:
      while (bt.available () > 0) {
        // add the incoming bytes to the result string:
        result += char(bt.read());
      }
      // get the last character of the result string:
      char lastChar = result.charAt(result.length() - 1);
      // make sure it's a newline, or you don't have valid data:
      if (lastChar != '\n') {
        result = null;
      }
    } // if you're not connected, try to pair:
    else {
      connectionState = connect();
    }
  }
  return result;
}
```

▶▶ The sendData() method sends the current readings to the server using Processing's loadStrings() method. loadStrings() does a basic HTTP GET request, and returns whatever the server sends it.

```
void sendData(String thisData) {
  // if there's data to send
  if (thisData != null) {
    // URL-encode the data and URL:
    String sendString = formatData(url + thisData);
    //send the data via HTTP GET:
    String[] result = loadStrings(sendString);
    // clear currentReadings to get more:
    String currentReadings = "";
  }
}
```

▶▶ URL strings need to be formatted cleanly (no spaces, no newlines or carriage returns, and so forth), so sendData() calls formatData(), which converts spaces, newlines, and returns into their HTTP-safe equivalents.

```
String formatData(String thisString) {
  // convert newlines, carriage returns, and
  // spaces to HTML-safe equivalent:
  String result = thisString.replaceAll(" ", "%20");
  result = result.replaceAll("\n", "%0A");
  result = result.replaceAll("\r", "%0D");
  return result;
}
```

▶▶ The final method in the main sketch is getTime(), which just returns a formatted date/time string.

```
// get the date and time as a String:
String getTime() {
  Date currentDate = new Date();
  return currentDate.toString();
}
```

▶▶ The Button class for this sketch differs from the one for the RFID Writer sketch in Chapter 9, in that it has a variable and methods to track its pressed state the last time you checked it.

```
// The Button class defines the behavior and look
// of the onscreen buttons.  Their behavior is slightly
// different on a touchscreen than on a mouse-based
// screen, because there is no mouseClick handler.
class Button {
  int x, y, w, h;                        // positions of the buttons
  color basecolor, highlightcolor;       // color and highlight color
  color currentcolor;                    // current color of the button
  String name;                           // name on the button
  boolean pressedLastTime;               // if it was pressed last time

  // Constructor: sets all the initial values for
  // each instance of the Button class
  Button(int thisX, int thisY, int thisW, int thisH,
      color thisColor, color thisHighlight, String thisName) {
    x = thisX;
    y = thisY;
    h = thisH;
```

»

▶▶ The constructor for this Button
class is almost the same, except
for the new variable, pressedLastTime.

Continued from opposite page.

```
    w = thisW;
    basecolor = thisColor;
    highlightcolor = thisHighlight;
    currentcolor = basecolor;
    name = thisName;
    pressedLastTime = false;
  }
```

The display() method combines the
functions of update() and display()
from Chapter 9's RFID Writer example,
both changing the color as needed and
drawing the actual button.

```
  // draw the button and its text:
  void display() {
    // if pressed, change the color:
    if (isPressed()) {
      currentcolor = highlightcolor;
    }
    else {
      currentcolor = basecolor;
    }
    fill(currentcolor);
    rect(x, y, w, h);

    //put the name in the middle of the button:
    fill(textColor);
    textAlign(CENTER);
    text(name, x+w/2, y+h/2);
  }
```

isPressed() checks not only whether
the mouseX and mouseY are within
the button's bounds, but it also uses
mousePressed to indicate whether the
user is touching the screen at all.

```
  // check to see if the mouse position is inside
  // the bounds of the rectangle and sets its current state:
  boolean isPressed() {
    if (mouseX >= x && mouseX <= x+w &&
      mouseY >= y && mouseY <= y+h && mousePressed) {
      return true;
    }
    else {
      return false;
    }
  }
```

setLastState() and getLastState()
give you access to the last state of the
button from outside the class.

That's the end of the whole sketch; see
Figure 10-24 for an illustration.

```
  //this method is for setting the state of the button
  // last time it was checked, as opposed to its
  // current state:
  void setLastState(boolean state) {
    pressedLastTime = state;
  }
  boolean getLastState() {
    return pressedLastTime;
  }
}
```

When you run this sketch on an Android device, it will try to connect. When it succeeds in doing so, it will check for new readings every 10 seconds. It will then attempt to send those to the server every two minutes. It doesn't check that it got a valid response, however; that is left as an exercise for you.

Armed with this much, there's a lot you can do with Processing for Android. You've got the ability to contact the Internet and to contact local devices wirelessly. You can also contact the built-in sensors, of course. The phone is now your hub to connect a whole lot of things.

What About USB?

Android devices are normally USB end devices, not USB hosts. So, you can't plug an end device like a mouse, a keyboard, or an Arduino into them and have them work like they do on your computer. However, Google decided that you might want to develop USB accessories, so they recently announced the Google Accessory Development Kit, an open hardware platform for developing USB accessories for Android. The Accessory Development Kit is based on an Arduino Mega 2650 with a USB Host shield (originally designed by Oleg Mazurov of www.circuitsathome.com) built into it. Circuits@Home sells a few good variants on the USB Host shield: for the standard Arduino shield form and for the Mini Pro. The Arduino Store carries the Arduino Mega ADK, and a Processing for Android library is in development. Several others are in the works from different companies, so by the time you read this, you'll have lots of options.

X

Figure 10-25
The datalogger sketch.

Figure 10-26
The datalogger hoodie in action. How excited is he to be wearing it? Check his GSR readings online to find out!

❝❝ Conclusion

The connection between the Internet and mobile networks widens your options by offering a ubiquitous connection and a variety of communication methods. Taking advantage of it requires some creative thinking about how to hop across different interfaces, systems, and protocols.

These days, mobile phone networks cover almost the entire planet, more than any other form of network connection. The technology of mobile networks changes quickly, and many of the tools disappear almost as fast as they appeared. If you're making projects using mobile network technologies, it's best to take a broad view. Look for the things that seem simpler and stabler—like SMS and HTTP—and be prepared to shift your approach when the tools change. In Chapter 11, you'll review some of the protocols you've seen throughout the book in order to get a wide view of what's possible.

X

⤒ **SIMbaLink, by Meredith Hasson, Ariel Nevarez, and Nahana Schelling. The SIMbaLink team developed a device that remotely monitors the health of a solar home system and reports it back to the SIMbaLink client website via a GPRS modem. Working in conjunction with a solar company in Ethiopia, SIMbaLink remotely monitored solar home systems outside Awassa, Ethiopia. The systems consisted of a 10W solar panel, a battery, and four 1-watt LED lamps. This simple setup brings light to an otherwise dark and unpowered rural home.** *Photos courtesy of Meredith Hasson.*

Protocols Revisited

One of the most valuable skills you can develop is the ability to create graceful transitions between seemingly incompatible systems. An understanding of different protocols is central to that skill. You've used a number of communications protocols in this book, but by the time you read this, the protocols you learned may have changed or become obsolete. However, if you understand how to learn new ones, you'll do fine. This final chapter is a view from the high ground, looking over the landscape of protocols you've seen in this book to consider their similarities and differences, how they all fit together, and how to go about learning new ones in the future.

◀€ Supplies for Chapter 11

DISTRIBUTOR KEY

- **A** Arduino Store (http://store.arduino.cc/ww)
- **AF** Adafruit (www.adafruit.com)
- **D** Digi-Key (www.digikey.com)
- **F** Farnell (www.farnell.com)
- **J** Jameco (http://jameco.com)
- **MS** Maker SHED (www.makershed.com)
- **RS** RS (www.rs-online.com)
- **SF** Spark Fun (www.sparkfun.com)
- **SS** Seeed Studio (www.seeedstudio.com)

PROJECT 32: Fun with MIDI

» **1 Arduino module** An Arduino Uno or something based on the Arduino Uno, but the project should work on other Arduino and Arduino-compatible boards. **D** 1050-1019-ND, **J** 2121105, **SF** DEV-09950, **A** A000046, **AF** 50, **F** 1848687, **RS** 715-4081, **SS** ARD132D2P, **MS** MKSP4

» **1 Spark Fun Musical Instrument shield SF** DEV-10587

» **1 MaxBotix LV-EZ1 sensor SF** SEN-00639

» **100µF capacitors J** 158394, **D** P10269-ND, **F** 1144642, **RS** 715-1657

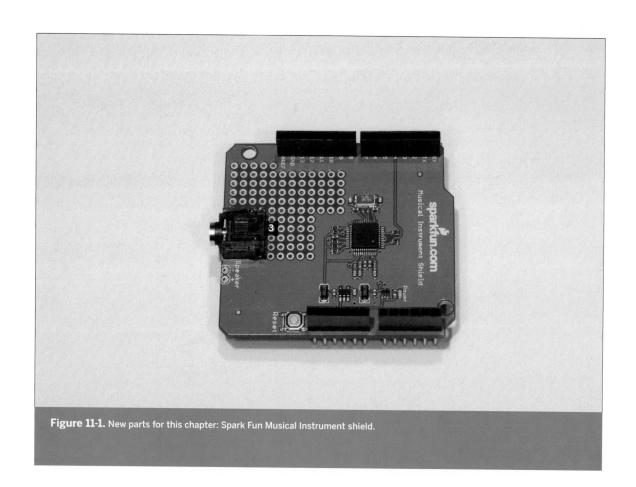

Figure 11-1. New parts for this chapter: Spark Fun Musical Instrument shield.

🔠 Make the Connections

Protocols are much easier to learn when you can relate them to ones you know already. Fortunately, you now know several. You can compare them at any of the levels discussed in Chapter 2. The three that will affect your project the most are the physical, the data, and the application. You can also consider the structures of the networks on which they communicate: direct one-to-one connections, networks with a central hub or controller, multitiered networks, rings, and buses. Once you know the structure of the system, you can consider the grammar and syntax of the communications protocols being used. Each of these things will help you translate from one device or system to another, and each aspect of the communication will tell you something about the other aspects.

For example, if you're dealing with a protocol that uses addresses, you can be sure that it's designed for communication between more than two things. If the address is broken into several pieces, like IP addresses, you can assume it's probably used on a multitiered network.

Know Your Options at the Physical Level

When you start to work with a new electronic device, get familiar with what protocols it speaks. By now you're

Figure 11-2
The Arduino's communications options. Asynchronous serial ports are referred to as Universal Asynchronous Receiver-Transmitters (UARTs) in technical documentation, so get familiar with the term.

familiar with the various protocols that the Arduino speaks. Figure 11-2 gives you an overview of them.

This figure tells you something about the physical layer (which pins are used for which modes of communication) and the data layer (which data protocols the device can speak). You know by now that if you're using a particular set of pins for its communications functions, you can't use it for other functions.

Most of the single-purpose devices you used in the book spoke only one protocol, but that's not always the case. For example, the ultrasonic ranger you used in Chapter 8 offers three different interfaces. It has an analog voltage output (0-5V, the one you used); an asynchronous RS-232 serial port (Tx and Rx) that sends data at 9600 bits per second; and a pulse-width output (PW), which outputs a pulse that goes from low to high to low again, changing the width of the pulse with the distance of the detected object. All of this is described in the ranger's datasheet, which you can find online at www.maxbotix.com. These multiple protocols are useful when you're interfacing the sensor to a microcontroller with no analog inputs; when you want to talk directly to a computer that has an RS-232 serial port; or when you're not using a computer at all, and want to control a simple circuit with a changing pulse width or voltage.

The SonMicro RFID reader you used in Chapter 9 also offered two different communications options: TTL serial

and I2C. The serial port was useful for communicating directly with your personal computer; the I2C option was useful when working with the microcontroller, because it left the microcontroller's serial port open for programming and debugging.

When you're planning a project, consider which of your devices' ports are used for configuring, programming, and debugging, and try to leave them free when possible. On the other hand, if the programming interface offers the fastest and most reliable means of communication, it may be worthwhile to deal with having to use it for both programming and its final application.

Picking a Serial Protocol

When planning a project, picking a serial protocol may seem confusing: synchronous or asynchronous? TTL serial or RS-232? I2C or SPI? USB? Most of the time, the choices are made for you because there's some component that you have to use—and it only speaks one protocol. But when you have a choice, here are a few things to consider.

What protocols are common to all the devices in your system? If all of your devices speak the same protocol, it's probably the obvious choice.

Do your devices need to be able to decide independently when they'll send information? If so, then any system that combines them in a master-slave relationship, like any of the synchronous serial protocols, won't work.

Do you need multiple devices to communicate over the same wires? If so, consider protocols that use a bus system. Synchronous serial protocols and some asynchronous ones, like USB and RS-485, use such a system. All of these require some form of addressing.

Is distance or speed a factor? Many protocols that need to be able to transmit over long distances use differential signaling, in which there's both a data+ and data- line. The same data is sent over both lines, always adding up to zero volts. This minimizes electrical noise. USB, RS-485, and Ethernet all use differential signaling. Differential signaling generally allows for faster data rates as well.

Figure 11-3
MaxBotix LV-EZ-1 communications options.

Pulse width out
(147µs per inch)

Analog Voltage out
(~9.8mV per inch)

RS-232 serial
(9600bps, 8-N-1, outputs
"Rxxx\r",
where xxx is 0-255)

Rx
Tx

This table shows a summary, and lists the characteristics, of a few serial protocols mentioned in the book.

Synchronous Serial Protocols	Asynchronous Serial Protocols	Asynchronous Serial Bus Protocols
• Master-slave relationship between devices • Several devices share the same data lines • Needs a clock line from the master to slaves • Distance: 1m or less • Various voltage ranges, commonly 5V or 3.3V	• No common clock, but agreement on data rate • Typically used for one-to-one communication, not networks	• No common clock, but agreement on data rate • Often used for longer distances or networks • Typically differential signaling • 3 to 4 wires: Data+, Data-, Ground, Voltage (optional)
I2C/TWI • 3 wires: Data, Clock, Ground • Each slave gets a unique address, sent first	**TTL Serial** • Various voltage ranges, commonly 5V or 3.3V • 3 wires: Transmit, Receive, Ground • Logic: +V = logic 1, 0V = logic 0 • Distance: typically 1m or less	**USB** • Voltage range: 0 to 5V • Distance: 10m or less
SPI • 4 + n wires: Master In Slave Out (MISO), Master Out Slave In (MOSI), Clock, Ground, 1 Chip Select for each slave device • Addressing is done using chip select lines	**RS-232** • Voltage range: ±3 to ±15V • Logic: -V = logic 1, +V = logic 0 • 0V has no logical meaning • Distance: 300m or less	**RS-485 (DMX-512)** • Voltage range: −7 to +12V • Distance: 1200m or less

Plan the Physical System and Information Flow Early

When you know your physical communications protocol options, you can plan how things communicate before you begin to program or configure anything. Doing so will save you a lot of time.

Consider the CatCam web server in Chapter 10. It involved several devices:

• Microcontroller
• Ethernet controller
• SD card
• Temperature sensor
• Relay control
• IP-based camera

To plan a project like that, you can (and should) diagram the flow of information between all the elements, as you saw in Figures 10-3 and 10-4, so you know what each one needs from the others. Consider what pins of your microcontroller are available for the various functions you need. Decide where images and web pages are best served from, and what links and permissions are required to make it all happen. Consider which way data flows, and who needs to know whose address. Decide where you'll place the server and the camera physically, and how you will house them. That way, you can reduce your actual production workload, and concentrate on building only what you need in code, in circuits, and in materials.

❝ Text or Binary?

One of the most confusing aspects of data communications is understanding the difference between a binary protocol and a text-encoded protocol. As you learned in Chapter 2, there is a common scheme for translating the data you send into alphanumeric characters. ASCII—and its more modern cousin, Unicode—allow you to convert any stream of text into binary information that a computer can read, and vice versa. Understanding the difference between a protocol that is text-based and one that's not, and why you'd make that choice, is essential to understanding how electronic things communicate.

Isn't All Data Binary?

Well, yes. After all, computers only operate on binary logic. So, even text-based protocols are, at their core, binary. However, it's often easier to write your messages in text and insist that the computers translate that text into bits themselves. For example, take the phrase "1-2-3, go". You can see it laid out in characters below, with the ASCII code for each character, and the bits that make up that code. It may seem like a lot of ones and zeroes for the computer to process, but when it's reading them at millions or billions of bits a second, it's no big deal. But what about when it's sending it to another computer? There are 80 bits there. Imagine you're sending it using TTL serial at 9600bps. If you add a stop bit and a start bit between each one—as TTL and RS-232 serial protocols do—that's 96 bits, meaning you could send this message in 1/100th of a second. That's still pretty fast.

Character	1	-	2	-	3	,		g	o	!
ASCII code	49	45	50	45	51	44	32	103	111	33
Binary	00110001	00101101	00110010	00101101	00110011	00101100	01000000	01100111	01101111	01000001

What about when the messages you have to send are not text-based? Imagine you're sending a string of RGB pixel values, each ranging from 0 to 255 like this:

102,198,255,127,127,212,255,155,127,

You know that each reading is eight bits, so in their most basic form, they take up three bytes per pixel. But if you're sending them in text form it's one byte per character, so the string above would be 36 bytes to send nine values. If you hadn't encoded it in text form, but just sent each value as a byte, you'd have only sent nine bytes. When you start to send millions of pixels, that's a big difference! In cases like this, where all the data you want to send is purely numeric (you don't need any text to describe the pixels because you know the first byte is always red, the second green, the third blue, and so on), sending data without encoding it as text makes sense. When you need to send text (for example, email or hypertext), encoding it as ASCII/Unicode makes sense. When the number of bytes you'd send is minimal, as with most of the sensor strings you've sent in this book, encoding it as ASCII/Unicode can help with debugging, because most serial or network terminal programs interpret all bytes that they receive as text, as you've seen. So:

- If there's a lot of data and it's all numeric, send as raw binary.
- If there's text, send as Unicode/ASCII.
- If it's a short data string, send as whichever makes you happy.

Interpreting a Binary Protocol

Since most of the protocols you've dealt with in this book have been text-based, you haven't had to do a lot of interpreting of the bits of a byte. Binary protocols often demand that you know which bit represents what, so it's useful to know a little about the architecture of a byte and how to manipulate it. Let's now talk for a bit about bits.

Binary protocols often show up in communications between chips in a complex device, particularly in synchronous serial protocols. Many SPI and I2C devices have small command sets. Their single-byte operational codes, or opcodes, are often combined with the parameters for the commands in the same byte. You saw this in action in Chapter 9 when you sent the opcode to read the firmware of the SM130 RFID reader.

These protocols are usually written out in hexadecimal notation, binary notation, or both. You've seen hexadecimal or base-16 notation already in this book. Just as hexadecimal numbers begin with 0x, binary numbers in Arduino—and by extension in C—begin with 0b, like so 0b10101010.

Which digit matters most in the number below?

$2,508

The 2, because it represents the largest amount, two thousands, or two groups of 10^3. It is the most significant digit. That number was in decimal, or base-10 notation. The same principle applies when you're writing in binary, or base-2. Which is the most significant bit:

0b10010110

The leftmost 1 is most significant because it represents 1 group of 128, or 2^7. Usually when you see bits written out, though, you care less about their decimal numeric values than their position in the byte. For example, in the project that follows, you're going to make music using MIDI, the Musical Instrument Digital Interface protocol. MIDI is a binary protocol in which all bytes with a 1 in the most significant bit are commands (verbs), and all bytes with a 0 in the most significant bit are data bytes (nouns, adjectives, or adverbs). A MIDI interpreter could look at the most significant bit (which happens to be the first to arrive serially) and know whether it's getting a command or not.

Bit Reading and Writing

Arduino offers you some commands for reading and writing the bits of a byte:

```
// to read the value of a bit:
myBit = bitRead(someByte, bitNumber);

// to write the value of a bit:
bitWrite(someByte, bitNumber, bitValue);
```

Giving a bit the value 1 is called setting the bit in general programming terms, and giving it the value 0 is known as clearing the bit. So you also have commands for these:

```
// to make a bit equal to 1:
bitSet(someByte, bitNumber);

// to make a bit equal to 0:
bitClear(someByte, bitNumber);
```

Bit Shifting

Sometimes it's easier to manipulate several bits at once. The shift left and shift right operators in Arduino, C, and Java allow you to just that. The shift left operator (<<) moves bits to the left in a byte, and the shift right operator (>>) moves them to the right:

```
0b00001111 << 2; // gives 0b00111100
0b10000000 >> 7; // gives 0b0000001
```

Bit shifting is useful when you need a particular value to be in a specific part of a byte, as you'll see shortly.

Bit Masking

The logical operators AND, OR, and XOR allow you to combine bits in some interesting ways.

AND (&): if the two bits are equal, the result is 1. Otherwise, it's 0:

```
1 & 1 = 1
0 & 0 = 1
1 & 0 = 0
0 & 1 = 0
```

OR (|): if either bit is 1, the result is 1. Otherwise, it's 0:

```
1 | 1 = 1
0 | 0 = 0
1 | 0 = 1
0 | 1 = 1
```

XOR (^): if the bits are not equal, the result is 1. Otherwise, it's 0:

```
1 ^ 1 = 0
0 ^ 0 = 0
1 ^ 0 = 1
0 ^ 1 = 1
```

Using the logical, or bitwise, operators, you can isolate one bit of a byte, like so:

```
// Check if bit 7 of someByte is 1:
if (someByte & 0b10000000) {}
```

In MIDI command bytes, for example, the command is the leftmost four bits, and the MIDI channel is the rightmost four bits. So, you could isolate the MIDI channel by using the AND operator:

```
channel = commandByte & 0b00001111;
```

Or, you could use bit shifting to get the command and lose the channel:

```
command = commandByte >> 4;
```

Combined, these bit-manipulation commands give you all the power you need to work with binary protocols.

Hex: What Is It Good For?

Since you can manipulate binary protocols bit by bit, you're probably wondering what hexadecimal notation is good for. Hex is useful when you're working in groups of 16, of course. For example, MIDI is grouped into banks of instruments, with 128 instruments per bank, and each instrument can play on up to 16 channels. So, those command bytes you were manipulating earlier could also be manipulated in hex. For example, 0x9n is a Note On command, where n is the channel number, from 0 to A in hex. 0x9A means note on, channel A (or 10 in decimal). Similarly, 0x8A means note off, channel A. Once you know that MIDI is organized in groups of 16, it makes a lot of sense to read and manipulate it in hexadecimal. In fact, many binary protocols can be grouped similarly, so knowing how to manipulate them in binary or hexadecimal is handy.

The next project puts these principles in action to control a MIDI synthesizer.
X

❝ MIDI

The Musical Instrument Digital Interface (MIDI) protocol enables real-time communication between digital musical instruments. It's the granddaddy of digital synthesizer protocols.

Most music synthesizers, sequencers, samplers, keyboards, and workstations on the market today speak MIDI. If you plan to make music using hardware, you're going to run across it. MIDI is a comprehensive specification covering serial communication, hardware, and even the arrangement of banks of sounds in a synthesizer's memory. Because it's so comprehensive, it's enabled composers and musicians to work across a wide range of MIDI synthesizers, samplers, and controllers for decades. The full protocol is detailed on the MIDI Manufacturers' Association page at www.midi.org.

MIDI is a music description protocol. MIDI messages don't actually play notes—they describe what notes to play to a synthesizer. In that sense, MIDI is to music as HTML is to web pages. MIDI relies on a synthesizer to render music, just as HTML relies on a browser to render your page.

MIDI devices are loosely grouped into controllers, or things that generate MIDI messages, and playback devices, which receive messages and do something with them. Keyboards and other input devices fall into the first category. Synthesizers, samplers, and many other devices fall into the latter.

The MIDI serial protocol runs at 31,250 bps. There's a standard MIDI connector, a DIN5, that you'll find on all MIDI gear. All the connectors on the gear are female plugs, and the cables all have male connectors on both ends. All MIDI inputs to a device are supposed to be opto-isolated, so there is no direct electrical connection from one device to the next. An opto-isolator is a component containing an LED and a phototransistor. The input turns on the LED, and the LED triggers the phototransistor, which turns on the output. Figure 11-4 shows how to build a MIDI input and output circuit if you plan to build your own. This circuit would allow you to connect your microcontroller to any MIDI synthesizer or controller. There are several MIDI shields on the market if you don't want to build your own.

Microcontrollers are more frequently used as MIDI controllers than as MIDI input devices. There are so many good synthesizers and samplers on the market that just need a controller to make music, and controllers are fun and easy to build. For the project that follows, you'll build a very basic controller and use Spark Fun's Musical Instrument shield as your MIDI input device, which is a general MIDI synthesizer on a shield. The same code will work if you want to connect the microcontroller to any general MIDI synth, because the general MIDI specification covers not only the messages, but how synthesizers organize their banks of sounds.

MIDI messages are divided into three or more bytes. The first byte, a command byte, is always 128 (0x80) or greater in value. Its value depends on the command. The bytes that follow it are called status bytes. All status bytes have values of 127 (0x7F) or less.

There are a number of different MIDI commands. The most basic, note on and note off messages, control the playing of notes on 16 different channels of a synthesizer. Each note on or note off command contains two status bytes, specifying the pitch in a range from 0–127 (a seven-bit range) and the velocity (how hard the note should be struck), which is also seven bits. Pitch value 0x45 is defined as A above middle C (A-440) by the general MIDI specification. This specification also covers the instruments that you're likely to find on each channel. For a full listing of the General MIDI instrument specification, see www.midi.org/techspecs/gm1sound.php.

For more information on MIDI, see Paul D. Lehrman and Tim Tully's book **MIDI for the Professional** (Amsco).

Figure 11-4

MIDI input and output from a microcontroller. When you have to build your own MIDI input or output, this is how you do it.

Project 32

Fun with MIDI

In this project, you'll see how a binary protocol is handled by running some basic MIDI exercises. Because of the wide range of MIDI controllers and input devices on the market, MIDI offers a very broad range of sonic possibilities. So, MIDI is a good protocol to be familiar with if you like sound projects.

The best way to get started with MIDI is to build a very simple controller, connect it to a synthesizer, and see what it can do. If you have your own synthesizer, you can use the circuit in Figure 11-4; if not, you can use the Musical Instrument shield as shown in Figure 11-5. It just stacks on top of an Arduino like other shields. The synth receives MIDI in from the Arduino's pin 3. To communicate with it, you'll use the SoftwareSerial library.

> **MATERIALS**
>
> » **1 Arduino**
> » **MIDI Musical Instrument shield**
> » **1 Sharp IR ranger**
> » **1 100µF capacitor**
> » **1 pair headphones or speakers**

The first sketch below is a test of the available instruments and channels. You'll notice that for each instrument, channel 10 is percussion—that's also part of the general MIDI instrument specification. This specification makes it possible for you to use a controller on the same channel and instrument with any MIDI synthesizer, and know more or less what kind of sound you'll get.

Play It Start by setting up your pins, as usual. MIDI out will be on pin 3, and the Music Instrument shield reset pin is on pin 4. If you're using an external synth and the circuit in Figure 11-4, you won't need the reset connection.

setup() starts the serial and MIDI connection, and resets the shield. Then it sends a MIDI Control Change command on channel 0 (0xB0) to perform a Bank Selection. This sets the bank of instruments you'll play.

This example is based on Nathan Seidle's example sketches for the Musical Instrument Shield, available at www.sparkfun.com/products/10587.

```
/*
  MIDI general instrument demo
  Context: Arduino

  Plays all the instruments in a General MIDI instrument bank
  */
#include <SoftwareSerial.h>
// set up a software serial port to send MIDI:
SoftwareSerial midi(2,3);

const byte resetMIDI = 4; // Midi synth chip reset line

void setup() {
  // initialize serial communications at 9600 bps:
  Serial.begin(9600);
  // initialize MIDI serial on the software serial pins:
  midi.begin(31250);

  //Reset the MIDI synth:
  pinMode(resetMIDI, OUTPUT);
  digitalWrite(resetMIDI, LOW);
  delay(20);
  digitalWrite(resetMIDI, HIGH);
  delay(20);
  // send a MIDI control change to change to the GM sound bank:
  sendMidi(0xB0, 0, 0);
}
```

loop() cycles through all the instruments in the bank. For each instrument, it performs a MIDI Program change to select the instrument; then, it cycles through each of the 16 channels. For each channel, it plays notes from 21 (A0, the lowest note on an 88-key piano) to 109 (C8, the highest note).

```
void loop() {
  //Cycle through all the instruments in the bank:
  for(int instrument = 0 ; instrument < 127 ; instrument++) {
    Serial.print(" Instrument: ");
    Serial.println(instrument + 1);
    // Program select. Has only one status byte:
    sendMidi(0xC0, instrument, 0);
    // change channels within the instrument:
    for (int thisChannel = 0; thisChannel < 16; thisChannel++) {
      Serial.print("Channel: ") ;
      Serial.println(thisChannel + 1);
      for (int thisNote = 21; thisNote < 109; thisNote++) {
        // note on
        noteOn(thisChannel, thisNote, 127);
        delay(30);

        // note off
        noteOff(thisChannel, thisNote, 0);
        delay(30);
      }
    }
  }
}
```

noteOn(), noteOff(), and sendMidi() are methods to send MIDI commands. The sendMidi() method just sends the three bytes you give it. The noteOn() and noteOff() methods use a bitwise OR operation to combine the command (0x80 or 0x90) with the channel into a single byte.

When you run this sketch, you should hear all the sounds your synth can make on the first bank of sounds.

```
//Send a MIDI note-on message.  Like pressing a piano key
//channel ranges from 0-15
void noteOn(byte channel, byte note, byte velocity) {
  sendMidi( (0x90 | channel), note, velocity);
}

//Send a MIDI note-off message.  Like releasing a piano key
void noteOff(byte channel, byte note, byte velocity) {
  sendMidi( (0x80 | channel), note, velocity);
}
void sendMidi(int cmd, int data1, int data2) {
  midi.write(cmd);
  midi.write(data1);
  midi.write(data2);
}
```

Wave at It Of course, you can't be a self-respecting MIDI enthusiast until you've built your first theremin. It's like calling yourself a writer before you've written your autobiography—it's just not done! Waving at a distance ranger to make notes is a rite of passage in MIDI-land. So, here's your first MIDI theremin program. This one's a bit different than most, as you'll see.

The global variables include a threshold setting for the infrared ranger, and a variable to hold the previous reading.

setup() opens communications and resets the shield.

```
/*
  Stinger player
  Context:  Arduino
*/

#include <SoftwareSerial.h>
// set up a software serial port to send MIDI:
SoftwareSerial midi(2, 3);

const int midiResetPin = 4;    // Musical instrument shield's reset pin
const int threshold = 100;     // sensor threshold
int lastReading = 0;           // last sensor reading

void setup() {
  // initialize hardware serial and MIDI serial:
  Serial.begin(9600);
  midi.begin(31250);

  // reset the musical instrument shield:
  resetMidi(midiResetPin);
}
```

Figure 11-5
Spark Fun Musical Instrument shield attached to an Arduino and an infrared ranger. The 100μF capacitor smoothes the sensor's readings a bit, but it's optional if your sensor gives reliable readings without it.

▶▶ The loop() reads the sensor, and when it crosses a threshold, it triggers a method called playStinger() that plays a sequence of notes.

```
void loop() {
  // read the sensor:
  int sensorReading = analogRead(A0);
  Serial.println(sensorReading);

  // if the sensor's higher than the threshold and
  // was lower than the threshold last time,
  // then play the stinger:
  if (sensorReading <= threshold
    && lastReading > threshold ) {
    playStinger();
  }
  // save the current reading for next time:
  lastReading = sensorReading;
}
```

▶▶ playStinger() plays a sequence of notes with a sequence of pauses in between. To do this, it calls notes from an array using noteOn() and noteOff(), and then pauses, according to the rest times given by an array.

noteon(), noteOff(), and sendMidi() are the same as in the previous example, and you can copy them from there.

```
void playStinger() {
  int note[] = {43, 41, 49};
  int rest[] = {70, 180, 750};

  // loop over the three notes:
  for (int thisNote = 0; thisNote < 3; thisNote++) {
    // Turn on note:
    noteOn(9, note[thisNote], 60);
    delay(rest[thisNote]);
    //Turn off the note:
    noteOff(9, note[thisNote], 60);
    // a little pause after the second note:
    if (thisNote == 1) {
      delay(50);
    }
  }
}
//NOTE: the noteOn(), noteOff() and sendMidi() methods from the previous
//example go here.
```

▶▶ resetMidi() takes the reset from the previous example out of setup() and puts it in its own method.

When you've uploaded this sketch, say the following:

"A guy walks into a bar and says 'OUCH!'"

Then wave your hand over the IR ranger. You're a comedian! And you've made your first MIDI instrument!

```
void resetMidi(int thisPin) {
  // Reset the Musical Instrument Shield:
  pinMode(thisPin, OUTPUT);
  digitalWrite(thisPin, LOW);
  delay(100);
  digitalWrite(thisPin, HIGH);
  delay(100);
}
```

" DMX512

DMX512 is another binary protocol worth knowing about. It's a real-time serial protocol for communicating between stage-lighting control systems and lighting dimmers. It has been the industry standard for stage lighting and show control equipment for a couple of decades now. It's also used to control special-effects machines, moving lights, projection systems, and more.

DMX512 uses the RS-485 serial protocol as its physical layer. RS-485 is a bus-style serial protocol, meaning you can have several devices sharing the same transmit and receive lines, as long as each has a unique address. It uses differential signaling so that signal wires can be very long—up to 1200m. DMX512 devices generally use an XLR-style connector, either three pin or five pin, though many devices now use an RJ-45 Ethernet-style connector.

At 250kbps, DMX512 is fast for a serial protocol; it's fast enough that you can't just send it as regular TTL serial data from a microcontroller. However, there is a DMX library for Arduino called Simple DMX, and there are a

few shields on the market that have DMX connectors on them. I've only tested two personally, both of which work well: the Tinker DMX shield is available from the Arduino Store at http://store.arduino.cc/ww/, and Daniel Hirschmann's Super DMX shield is available from http://www.hirschandmann.com/2011/super-dmx-shield-for-arduino/. The former lets you add your own connector; the latter has XLR, RJ-45 connectors, and terminals for you to add your own. Further notes can be found on the Arduino playground site at www.arduino.cc/playground/Learning/DMX. For more on DMX, see www.opendmx.net.

Like MIDI, DMX is an aging protocol. The lighting industry has started to develop its successor, Advanced Controller Network, or ACN, which can run over Ethernet. Over the next few years, you can expect to see it grow in prominence. For more on show control protocols in general, John Huntington's book **Control Systems for Live Entertainment** (Focal Press) can't be beat.
X

Figure 11-6
Tinker DMX shield, left, and Daniel Hirschmann's Super DMX shield, right. Both allow you to communicate with DMX512-based lighting and show control systems.

The Structure and Syntax of Text-Based Protocols

You've seen a number of text-based protocols throughout this book, and you've even written a few of your own. Protocols are basically ways of structuring data. Some protocols simply relay information, and others give commands—either explicitly or implicitly—through a request. It's worth reviewing some of their grammars so that when you run into similar ones, you'll know what to look for.

Simple Data Formats

The simplest was the comma-separated value string you wrote for Monski Pong. Comma-separated values (CSV) and tab-separated values (TSV) are ubiquitous, and it's common to end a CSV string with a newline, or a newline and carriage return. The NMEA-0183 protocol used by GPS receivers is a good example of CSV in practice.

You also saw a few examples of organizing data in name-value pairs. Any time you have a list of items, and each has a name associated with it, you've got a name-value pair. The environment variables in PHP—including $_GET, $_POST, $_REQUEST, and $_SERVER—give you name-value pairs. In programming languages, associative arrays are basically lists of name-value pairs.

You've also used a few Internet transfer protocols, like HyperText Transfer Protocol (HTTP) and Simple Mail Transfer Protocol (SMTP). They share a common format as well: they open with a command like GET or POST, and then follow with properties of the transfer, each on its own line. Each line starts with the description of the property, like the content-length, separated from the actual value by a colon. The header of the transfer is separated from the body of the message by two newlines, and the message is usually closed with two newlines as well. Any data coming from the client was sent as name-value pair arrays, separated by a colon for information about the transfer, or by an ampersand for data items in the content of the transfer. Take a second look at this HTTP POST request from Chapter 2 as an example:

```
POST /age_checker.php HTTP/1.1
Host: example.com
Connection:Close
Content-Type: application/x-www-form-urlencoded
Content-length: 16

name=tom&age=14
```

Everything in the header is a parameter of the request: who you're requesting from, the connection type, the type of content to be exchanged, the content length. Everything in the body is a parameter of the content: name and age. Having a clear separation between the header formatting and the content formatting makes it easier to separate them when writing a program, as you've already seen.

Structured Data Formats

When you've got data to exchange that's more complex than a list of name-value pairs, you need a structure for it. For example, imagine an array of sensors spread around your house:

Address	Location	Last read	Value
1	kitchen	12:30:00 PM	60
2	living room	05:40:00 AM	54
3	bathroom	01:15:00 AM	23
4	bedroom	09:25:00 AM	18
5	hallway	06:20:00 AM	3

You've got more than just a list of single items, and more than just a few name-value pairs. In fact, each line of the table is a list of name-value pairs. This is where a structured data format comes in handy. JavaScript Object Notation, or JSON, is a popular notation format for structured data like this.

JSON represents each cell of the table as a name-value pair. Each line is a comma-separated list of pairs, enclosed in curly braces. The whole table is a comma-separated list of lists, like so:

```
[{"Address":1,"Location":"kitchen","Last read":"12:30:00 PM","value":60},
{"Address":2,"Location":"living room","Last read":"05:40:00 AM","value":54},
{"Address":3,"Location":"bathroom","Last read":"01:15:00 AM","value":23},
{"Address":4,"Location":"bedroom","Last read":"09:25:00 AM","value":18},
{"Address":5,"Location":"hallway","Last read":"06:20:00 AM","value":3}]
```

This way of formatting data is relatively simple. The punctuation that separates each element is just a single character, so you can scan through it one character at a time and know when you're done with each element. Because it's text, it's human-readable as well as machine-readable. Spaces, newlines, and tabs aren't considered part of the structure of JSON, so you can reformat it for easier reading like so:

```
[
    {
      "Address":1,
      "Location":"kitchen",
      "Last read":"12:30:00 PM",
      "value":60
    },
    {
      "Address":2,
      "Location":"living room",
      "Last read":"05:40:00 AM",
      "value":54
    },
    {
      "Address":3,
      "Location":"bathroom",
      "Last read":"01:15:00 AM",
      "value":23
    },
    {
      "Address":4,
      "Location":"bedroom",
      "Last read":"09:25:00 AM",
      "value":18
    },
    {
      "Address":5,
      "Location":"hallway",
      "Last read":"06:20:00 AM",
      "value":3
    }
]
```

The advantage of a data interchange format like JSON is that it's lightweight, meaning there aren't a lot of extra bytes needed to structure the information you want to send. It gives you more power than a simple list but is still efficient to send from a server to a client. You can send JSON as the body of an HTTP request, and as long as there's a program on the client that can parse it, you've got a quick way to exchange complex data.

When you've got something more complex to represent, you need a markup language. Markup languages provide a way to describe the structure of a text document in detail. Markup languages divide data into the content and the markup, a series of descriptive tags for organizing the content. The content is what you want to present; the markup describes how to present the content, what to do with it—and in some cases—how to interpret it.

Markup tags are typically strings of text separated from the content by a special pair of punctuation marks. You've seen them frequently in HTML:

```
<title> this is the document title</title>
```

If a tag has any attributes, they go inside the tag brackets as well:

```
<a href="www.example.com>A link</a>
```

Strict markup languages like XML always expect that every opening tag has a closing tag. Markup languages are strict in their formatting because they're designed to be machine-readable. A computer program can't assume where you meant to put a closing tag, so it will just keep looking until it finds the next one. If it finds a second opening tag before it gets to a closing tag, it gets confused.

Markup languages describe the structure of the document and how it's to be presented, but they don't tell you anything about what's in the document. They are to text documents what MIDI is to music: it describes the parameters of how to play a note without telling you anything about the actual timbre of the note.

You may have noticed that none of the transfer protocols you saw used the characters < and >. That is one reason why HTML uses these for tag markup. In parsing an HTTP response, you can know that you've reached the main text when you hit the first < character. Similarly, wiki markup typically uses square brackets, [and], to enclose tags. This helps distinguish it from HTML or XML markup. That way, the same document can contain both types of markup without causing conflict.

The bytes that form a web page can pass through a lot of programs before they reach the end, each using a different protocol. When each protocol is designed to take the others into account—as you can see with HTTP, HTML, and wiki markup languages—it's easy for each program to parse the bytes that matter to it and leave the rest alone.

Most of the time, you don't need all the information you're given in a typical information transfer. Knowing the protocol's structure and syntax not only helps you understand what's said, it also helps you determine what to ignore. Having to evaluate every chunk of data you receive can tax your system (and your patience) quite a bit. But when you know what you can ignore, you win. For example, consider the HTTP POST request that Twilio sends in Chapter 10. There's a huge amount of data there, more than 500 bytes. The only part you cared about, though, was the Digits property, so your sketch just scanned through the incoming stream of text, not saving anything until it saw the string "Digits". That kind of scanning and ignoring is central to good data parsing.

Markup vs. Programming Languages

Markup languages are primarily descriptive languages, not always active ones. They are interpreted by the program that displays them. For example, consider HTML, or HyperText Markup Language. HTML describes what a page should look like, but it doesn't have verbs to tell the browser to initiate action. It might describe an element to be displayed, such as a movie or audio file, and specify that the element be played on loading. There aren't HTML commands to make anything happen once the page is loaded. Markup languages usually rely on an outside actor, like the user, to prompt action.

In contrast, programming languages initiate action based on their own internal logic. Programming languages are sets of commands that make things happen. Your job as a programmer is to structure a set of commands to make things happen they way you want them to.

Programming languages have variables and arrays to manage simple data, but they generally don't dictate how you format complex data. The assumption is that you'll come up with a data format or protocol, and then use the programming language to read it byte-by-byte and interpret it, or to assemble it byte-by-byte. Useful programming languages come with libraries that can read and write common data formats, which you've seen throughout this book. Most of the libraries you used were designed to read or write a given data format. HTML5 represents a good combination of a markup language (HTML and CSS) and a programming language (JavaScript) that allows designers and developers to create full applications in a browser.

By now you've noticed that programming languages can be somewhat unforgiving when you leave out a comma or a semicolon, or get the capitalization of a word wrong. This is because the text of the programming language you write is actually a sort of markup language for the compiler. The compiler reads your text and translates it into machine language, so the text you write has to be machine-readable, just as markup languages and data formats do. The challenge to designing a good programming language is similar to designing a good data protocol: you want it to be efficient for the machine to read and interpret, yet still readable by humans.

The key to interpreting any data protocol—from the most simple comma-separated list to the most complex programming or markup language—is to start by asking what it's designed to do, and then look closely at its structure to see how it's organized. As you can see, many different protocols and languages share similar elements of punctuation or structure, so knowing one helps you to learn others.

X

" Representational State Transfer

Underlying the HyperText Transfer Protocol (HTTP) is a principle known as Representational State Transfer, or REST. It's not a protocol—it's more of an architectural style for information exchange. Though it started with the Web, it has applications in other areas. Understanding a little about REST will not only help you understand other systems, it will design your own communications protocols as well. Once you know about it, you can never get enough REST in your life.

The basic idea of REST is this: there is a thing somewhere on a network. Maybe it's a database, or maybe it's a microcontroller controlling your household appliances, like you made in the previous chapter. You either want to know what state it's in, or you want to change its state. REST gives you a way to describe, or *represent*, the *state* of the thing on the Net, and to *transfer* that representation to a remote user. REST is an addressing scheme for any remote thing.

You've been using REST already—it's what HTTP is all about. You want to know about the thing, you make a request to GET that information or to POST changes to the thing. The thing responds to your request, either with a representation of the state of affairs (for example, the HTML page delivered by the air conditioner controller, which included representations of the temperature and the state of the thermostat), or by changing the state of affairs (for example, by updating the thermostat setting).

In RESTful thinking, URLs are nouns that describe things, and requests are the verbs that act on nouns. The properties of things are described in the URL, separated by slashes. For example, here's a RESTful description of one of an Arduino's pins:

`/pin/A0/`

If you want to know the state of that pin, you might say to the Arduino:

`GET /pin/A0/`

The Arduino would then reply with the state of pin A0, a number between 0 and 1023. Or, perhaps you want to change the state of a digital output pin. You might do this:

`POST /pin/D2/1/`

The Arduino would know that it should set digital pin 2 to be an output, and set it high (1 =HIGH). In this scenario, the Arduino is the server—serving you up representations of its state—and you're the client.

There are three important elements to this exchange:

1. The representation (called a resource) and its attributes are separated by slashes. You can think of the attributes like the properties of an object.
2. The verb is the request: whether you want to get some information or change the state of the thing, you start with the verb. The verbs are HTTP's verbs: GET, POST, PUT, and DELETE (the last two are used less often).
3. The description is technology-independent. There's no actual mention as to whether the resource is delivered to you as an HTML page or XML from a web server, or whether it's printed by a PHP or Ruby script on a server, a C/C++ program running on an Arduino, or black magic. It doesn't matter how the result is generated, you just want to know what the state of things is, and it's the server's job to do that.

The beauty of being technology-independent is that you can use REST for just about any control interface. For example, Open Sound Control, or OSC, a protocol for musical controllers that's designed to supersede MIDI, is RESTful. ACN, the Advanced Controller Networking protocol designed to replace DMX512, is also RESTful. It's also independent of the transport mechanism, and it can be sent over Ethernet, serial, or any other physical data transmission. REST provides a standard way of naming, or addressing, things so that you keep using that addressing scheme when you change environments, programming tools, or network technologies. It's simple enough that you can read it with a limited processor, and general enough to describe most anything you want information about or want to control.

There's another advantage to REST when designing websites: if you change the programming environment you use to run your site, you don't have to change the URLs. The client never sees the .php, .rb (Ruby), or .pl (Perl) file extension, so it doesn't know or care what programming environment powers your service. If you want to change languages, go ahead! The site structure can stay the same.

To design RESTfully on the Web, think of the site or device you're making in terms of its properties, and come up with an addressing scheme that gives clients access to view and change those properties appropriately. Practically, what it means is that all the URLs of your site end at the /. There's no index.html (or anything .html), and no GET query string. Query parameters are passed using POST, and they're generally the last item in the address, as you'll see below. Following are two examples: one is a traditional website and the other is a physical device on a network.

A Traditional Web Service

Perhaps you're making a social media site for runners to compare their daily runs. As part of it, each runner has a profile with various attributes for each day's run: the date (day, month, and year), the distance of the run, and the time of the run. For a run on 31 January 2012, the URLs to address those attributes might look like this.

To get the distance:

http://myrun.example.com/runnerName/31/1/2012/distance/

To set the distance to 12.56km:

http://myrun.example.com/runnerName/31/1/2012/distance/12.56

To set the time to 1 hour, 2 minutes, 34 seconds:

http://myrun.example.com/runnerName/31/1/2012/time/1:02:34

Notice how you can tell a call that gets the value of a parameter from one that sets the value: the former has nothing following the name of the parameter.

A Web-Based Device

Imagine you're building a device that controls the window blinds in your office. There are 12 windows, each with its own blind. The blinds can be positioned variably, in a range from 1 to 10. The client can get the state of any blind, or you can set it. The URLs to see the state of the windows might look like this.

To see them all at once:

http://mywindows.example.com/window/all

To see an individual window (window number 2):

http://mywindows.example.com/window/2

To set a window's blind halfway down:

http://mywindows.example.com/window/2/50

To close them all:

http://mywindows.example.com/window/all/0

If you don't like these particular addressing schemes, you could make your own, of course. Just follow the basic RESTful style of /object/attribute/newValue to get the value of a parameter, and /object/attribute/newValue to set it.

What the actual interface returned by the URL looks like is up to you. You might choose to make a graphic that shows images of the windows with blinds, or you might show the result in text only. RESTful architecture just determines where to find something, not what you'll find there.

RESTful addresses are designed to be easy for a computer to parse. All you have to do is to separate the incoming request into substrings on the slashes, look at each substring to see what it is, and act appropriately on the substrings that follow it. They're also easy for people to read. A URL like the ones above is much more comprehensible than the equivalent GET request:

http://myrun.example.com/?runnerName=George&day=31&month=1&year=2012&distance=12.56

The project that follows shows you how to set up a PHP-based server that can parse RESTful addresses.
X

Project 33

Fun with REST

If you've only done static HTML web design before, you're probably used to the idea that the slashes in a URL tell you in what directory on a server the final HTML file resides. However, it doesn't have to be that way. You can tell the server how to interpret the URL. In this project, you'll do just that.

Back in the "Network Identification" section of Chapter 9, you wrote a PHP script that printed out all of the environment variables returned by the server when you make an HTTP request. One of them was called REQUEST_URI. It gave you the string of text that follows the GET request from the client. That's the variable you want access to if you plan to build a RESTful web service. Each of the pieces of the request URI will be part of your interface, just like in the example URLs shown previously.

It's most likely that your web server is running the Apache web server program. If so, you can create a special file inside any directory called **.htaccess** that determines the behavior of the server with respect to that directory. You can hide files and subdirectrories, password protect the directory, and more.

For this project, you'll set up a base directory for the project, and change the **.htaccess** file so that the server redirects anything that looks like a subdirectory to the script you're writing. Then you'll use the REQUEST_URI variable to make your own RESTful interface.

NOTE: URI stands for Uniform Resource Indicator. It's a synonym for Uniform Resource Locator, or URL, the term commonly used for web addresses.

Change the Access Start by making a new directory on your web server. Call it **myservice**. Inside it, make a new file called **.htaccess**. Files that begin with a dot are invisible files on the Linux and Mac OS X operating systems. So it's best to make this file directly on the server, either through the command line or your favorite web-editing tool. Here's the text of the file.

This file tells the server to rewrite client HTTP requests starting with the name of this directory on your account. It takes any string after the directory name and replaces it with the index file, **index.php**.

```
RewriteEngine On
# put in the base path to your directory:
RewriteBase /~username/myservice
# redirect anything after the base directory to index.php:
RewriteCond %{REQUEST_FILENAME} -s [OR]
RewriteCond %{REQUEST_FILENAME} -l
RewriteRule ^.*$ - [NC,L]
RewriteRule ^.*$ index.php [NC,L]
```

 In order for this to work, your web host needs to be running Apache's MOD_REWRITE module on its server. It's a pretty common module, so it's likely that it is, but if you find that this script doesn't work as described, check with your system administrator to see whether MOD_REWRITE is enabled.

Read It Here's the **index.php** file. It takes the $_REQUEST_URI variable and splits it up into an array of strings, using the slash (/) as the points on which to split.

Once you've saved this to the server, try entering the following URL in a browser:

http://www.myserver.com/myservice/this/is/a/list/of/restful/parameters/

You should get a response in the browser like this:

```
Item:
Item: myservice
Item: this
Item: is
Item: a
Item: list
Item: of
Item: restful
Item: parameters
```

```php
<?php
/*
        RESTful reader
        Context: PHP
*/
// split the URI string into a list:
$parameters = explode("/", $_SERVER['REQUEST_URI']);

// print out each of the elements of the list:
 foreach($parameters as $item) {
        echo "Item: ";
        echo $item."<br>";
 }
?>
```

Now that you've got anything that comes in from the client in an array, you can do whatever you want with it. This is where things get interesting. From here, you can write a program to look for and act on different elements in the list. The following is a brief example that would pull out the distance and time parameters based on the runners' website example above.

Modify It Take out the foreach() block from the previous example and replace it as shown here. New lines are shown in blue.

Type the URL as follows into your browser (change the hostname and path as needed):

http://www.example.com/ myService/runnerName/31/1/2012/ distance/12.45/time/0:45:34

When you type this into the browser, you'll get back:

Your distance: 12.45
Your time: 0:45:34

```php
<?php
// split the URI string into a list:
$$parameters = explode("/", $_SERVER['REQUEST_URI']);

$position = array_search('distance', $parameters);
if ($position) {
    $distance = $parameters[$position+1];
    echo "Your distance: ".$distance."<br />";
}


$position = array_search('time', $parameters);
if ($position) {
    $time = $parameters[$position+1];
    echo "Your time: ".$time."<br />";
}
?>
```

> When you combine this approach with standard HTML forms using HTTP POST, you have two ways of passing in parameters, and your URLs reflect the state of the resource. It makes for a powerful and flexible way to build the architecture of a web service, resulting in URLs that are both machine-readable and easier for humans to understand.

Every server-side programming language has a variety of frameworks designed to make REST easier to implement. PHP frameworks like Cake and CodeIgniter, Ruby frameworks like Rails and Sinatra, and many others attempt to make it easier for you to build applications, and their application programming interfaces (APIs) are designed to encourage you to build in a RESTful way. With these, you can often build proxy applications that take data in a more complex format, and summarize it in a simpler format for the more limited devices in your system.

X

❝❝ Conclusion

By definition, networked devices don't stand alone. If you're connecting a device to the Internet, you should take advantage of the power it offers. The more tools and protocols you know, the easier and more fun that is. Consider advantages offered by servers that have public addresses—and plenty of computing horsepower to spare. Consider combinations of wired and wireless protocols to give the things you build maximum freedom to respond to their physical environments.

As you can see by now, the physical interfaces that are the most flexible are usually the ones that are the most ephemeral on the network. They get turned on and off, they connect through private networks, and they use limited processors to save size, weight, and power. They're not always capable of doing everything that a dedicated web server can do, nor are they available at all times. However, these are not limitations when such devices are used in conversation with dedicated servers.

As hubs of your projects, use public, persistent servers that have public addresses and are always on the Net. They can store messages for physical devices that aren't online and deliver them later. They can act as proxies to take care of things for which simpler devices aren't designed, like complex data management or authentication. Don't be afraid to use tools and protocols in ways not thought of by their original designers. Make the technology fit the person's needs.

Making things talk to each other always comes back to two questions. Who are you serving in making what you're making? What does that person need, and how can you best give it to her?

To design a flexible network of physical things that's really useful to humans, you have to think about the person's needs and actions first. Then, it's all about the rules of love and networking:

- Listen More Than You Speak
- Never Assume
- Agree on How You Say Things
- Ask Politely for Clarification

The Internet of Things is useless if those things don't improve the quality of our lives and the ways in which we communicate with each other.

Appendix

Where to Get Stuff

Many different hardware suppliers and software sources are mentioned in this book. This appendix provides a list of those parts and a summary of the vendors, along with a brief description of each. It's organized into three sections: Supplies, Hardware, and Software.

Supplies

Here's a shopping list of the parts used in this book. Each part lists the projects in which it's used.

If there are updates to this list, you'll find a link to them at http://oreilly.com/catalog/0636920010920.

DISTRIBUTOR KEY

- **A** Arduino Store (http://store.arduino.cc/ww/)
- **AF** Adafruit (www.adafruit.com)
- **CR** CoreRFID (www.rfidshop.com)
- **D** Digi-Key (www.digikey.com)
- **F** Farnell (www.farnell.com)
- **J** Jameco (http://jameco.com)
- **L** LessEMF (www.lessemf.com)
- **MS** Maker SHED (www.makershed.com)
- **P** Pololu (www.pololu.com)
- **RS** RS (www.rs-online.com)
- **SF** SparkFun (www.sparkfun.com)
- **SH** Smarthome (www.smarthome.com)
- **SS** Seeed Studio (www.seeedstudio.com)

Infrastructure

- » **Personal computer** Used in all projects.
- » **Ethernet connection to the Internet** Used in many projects.
- » **Project enclosure** Used in most projects.
- » **1/16-inch Mat board** Used in projects: 8, 26, 27 for project enclosures.
- » **1 Bluetooth-enabled personal computer** Used in projects: 3, 4, 11, 18, 19. If your laptop doesn't have a Bluetooth radio, use a USB Bluetooth adapter. **SF** WRL-09434, **F** 1814756
- » **Android device** Used in project: 31.

Microcontrollers, Shields, and Prototyping Boards

- » **Arduino Uno module** Used in projects: 1, 2, 3, 9, 10, 11, 15, 16, 20, 21, 26, 32.
  D 1050-1019-ND, **J** 2121105, **SF** DEV-09950, **A** A000046, **AF** 50, **F** 1848687, **RS** 715-4081, **SS** ARD132D2P, **MS** MKSP4
- » **Arduino Fio module** Used in project: 10.
  SF DEV-10116
- » **Arduino Ethernet board** Used in projects: 6, 7, 8, 13, 14, 27, 29. Alternatively, an Uno-compatible board (above) with an Ethernet shield will work.
  SF DEV-09026, **J** 2124242, **A** A000056, **AF** 201, **F** 1848680
- » **LilyPad Arduino** Used in project: 31.
  SF DEV-09266, **A** A000011
- » **Arduino WiFi shield** Used in project: 12, but it can be used in any of the Ethernet projects.
  A A000058
- » **Arduino wireless shield** Used in projects: 10, 13, 14.
  A A000064 or A000065. Alternative shields: **SF** WRL-09976, **AF** 126, **F** 1848697, **RS** 696-1670, **SS** WLS114A0P
- » **RFID shield** Used in project: 27.
  SF DEV-10406, **A** T040030 or T040031
- » **Spark Fun Musical Instrument shield** Used in project: 32.
  SF DEV-10587
- » **Solderless breadboard** Used in projects: 2, 3, 5, 6, 7, 9, 10, 11, 12, 19, 20, 21, 27. Alternatively, you can use prototyping shields for Arduino.
  D 438-1045-ND, **J** 20723 or 20601, **SF** PRT-00137, **F** 4692810, **AF** 64, **SS** STR101C2M or STR102C2M, **MS** MKKN2

- » **Prototyping shields for Arduino** Used in project: 26. Also an alternative to solderless breadboards in all projects, but you'll still need a tiny breadboard with them.
  AF 51, **A** A000024, **SF** DEV-07914, **MS** MSMS01
  Breadboards for protoshields:
  SF PRT-08802, **AF** included with board, **D** 923273-ND
- » **Perforated printed circuit board** Used in projects: 8, 27.
  D V2018-ND, **J** 616673, **SS** STR125C2B, **F** 4903213, **RS** 159-5420

Communications Modules

- » **FTDI-style USB-to-Serial adapter** Used in most projects.
  SF DEV-09718 or DEV-09716, **AF** 70 or 284, **A** A000059, **MS** MKAD22, **D** TTL-232R-3V3 or TTL-232R-5V
- » **Bluetooth Mate module** Used in projects: 3, 4, 11, 18, 19, 31.
  SF WRL-09358 or WRL-10393
- » **Digi XBee 802.15.4 RF modules** Used in projects: 10, 14, 17.
  J 2113375, **SF** WRL-08664, **AF** 128, **F** 1546394, **SS** WLS113A4M, **MS** MKAD14
- » **USB-XBee adapter** Used in projects: 10, 14, 17.
  J 32400, **SF** WRL-08687, **AF** 247
- » **Interface module: X10 One-Way Interface module** Used in project: 26.
  SH 1134B
- » **X10 modules** Used in project: 26.
  SH 2002 or 2000.
- » **RFID reader** Used in projects: 25, 26.
  CR IDI003 or IDI004, **SF** SEN-08419
- » **RFID tags** Used in projects: 25, 26.
  CR WON002, **SF** COM-10169
- » **1 SonMicro SM130 RFID read/write module** Used in project: 27.
  SF SEN-10126
- » **Mifare RFID read/write tags** Used in project: 27.
  SF SEN-10127

» **13.56MHz antenna** Used in project: 27.
A C000027

» **SD card reader that can read MicroSD** Available at any local electronics or office-supply store. Used in projects: 29, 30.
MicroSD card Used in projects: 29, 30.
IP-based camera Used in projects: 29, 30. D-Link DCS-930L

Breakout Boards and Connectors

» **LilyPad XBee** Used in project: 14.
SF DEV-08937

» **XBee Explorer Regulated** Used in project: 14.
SF WRL-09132

» **Gas sensor breakout board** Used in project: 13.
SF BOB-08891, **P** 1479 or 1639

» **3-wire JST connector pigtail** Used in project: 15.
SF SEN-08733

» **9V battery clip** Used in projects: 3, 14.
D 2238K-ND, **J** 101470, **SF** PRT-09518, **F** 1650675

» **Female power plug, 2.1mm ID, 5.5mm OD** Used in project: 3.
D CP-024A-ND, **J** 159506, **F** 1737256

» **Wire-wrapping wire** Used in project: 5.
D K445-ND, **J** 22577, **SF** PRT-08031, **F** 150080

» **Wire-wrapping tool** Used in project: 5.
J 242801, **F** 441089, **RSH** 276-1570, **S** TOL-00068

» **0.1-inch male header pins** Used in projects: 5, 10, 14, 15, 16, 19, 20, 25, 26, 27.
D A26509-20-ND, **J** 103377, **SF** PRT-0011, **F** 1593411

» **2mm female header rows** Used in projects: 10, 14.
J 2037747, **D** 3M9406-ND, **F** 1776193

» **2mm 5-pin socket** Used in projects: 25, 26.
SF PRT-10519

» **2mm 7-pin socket** Used in projects: 25, 26.
SF PRT-10518

» **6 pin stackable header** Used in project: 27.
SF PRT-09280, **AF** 85

» **8-conductor wire** Used in project: 27.
D AE08A-5-ND, **F** 1301013

» **Interface cable for GPS module** Used in project: 19.
SF GPS-00465, **P** 28146

» **RFID breakout board** Used in projects: 25, 26.
SF SEN-08423

» **4-wire phone cable with RJ-11 connector**
Used in project: 26.
D A1642R-07-ND, **J** 115617, **F** 1335141

» **2-pin Screw Terminal** Used in projects: 29, 30.
SF PRT-08432, **D** 732-2030-ND, **F** 1792766, **RS** 189-5893

» **3-pin Screw Terminal** Used in projects: 29, 30.
SF PRT-08235, **D** 732-2031-ND, **F** 1792767, **RS** 710-0166

Common Components

» **100-ohm resistor** Used in project: 8.
D 100QBK-ND, **J** 690620, **F** 9337660, **RS** 707-8625

» **220-ohm resistor** Used in projects: 5, 8, 9, 11, 20, 26.
D 220QBK-ND, **J** 690700, **F** 9337792, **RS** 707-8842

» **1-kilohm resistor** Used in projects: 5, 13, 14, 29, 30.
D 1.0KQBK-ND, **J** 29663, **F** 1735061, **RS** 707-8669

» **10-kilohm resistors** Used in projects: 2, 6, 9, 11, 12, 13, 14, 20.
D 10KQBK-ND, **J** 29911, **F** 9337687, **RS** 707-8906

» **4.7-kilohm resistor** Used in projects: 14, 27.
D CF14JT4K70CT-ND, **J** 691024, **F** 735033, **RS** 707-8693

» **10-kilohm potentiometers** Used in projects: 10, 11, 13, 14, 27, 29, 30.
J 29082, **SF** COM-09939, **F** 350072, **RS** 522-0625

» **100-kilohm resistors** Used in project: 14.
D 100KQBK-ND, **J** 29997, **F** 9337695, **RS** 707-8940

» **270-kilohm resistor** Used in project: 31.
J 691446, **D** P270KBACT-ND, **RS** 163-921, **F** 1565367

» **LEDs** Used in projects: 7, 8, 10, 11, 20, 26, 29, 30.
D 160-1144-ND or 160-1665-ND, **J** 34761 or 94511, **F** 1015878, **RS** 247-1662 or 826-830, **SF** COM-09592 or COM-09590

» **RGB LED, common cathode** Used in project: 1.
D 754-1492-ND, **J** 2125181, **SF** COM-00105, **F** 8738661, **RS** 713-4888

» **Infrared LED** Used in project: 9.
J 106526, **SF** COM-09469, **F** 1716710, **RS** 577-538, **SS** MTR102A2B

» **5V regulator** Used in project: 13, 14, 19.
J 51262, **D** LM7805CT-ND, **SF** COM-00107, **F** 1860277, **RS** 298-8514

» **3.3V regulator** Used in projects: 10, 14.
J 242115, **D** 576-1134-ND, **SF** COM-00526, **F** 1703357, **RS** 534-3021

» **1µF capacitor** Used in projects: 10, 14.
J 94161, **D** P10312-ND, **F** 8126933, **RS** 475-9009

» **10µF capacitor** Used in projects: 10, 14, 15.
J 29891, **D** P11212-ND, **F** 1144605, **RS** 715-1638

» **100µF capacitor** Used in projects: 13, 32.
J 158394, **D** P10269-ND, **F** 1144642, **RS** 715-1657

» **4700µF electrolytic capacitor**
Used in project: 14.
J 199006, **D** P10237-ND,
F 1144683, **RS** 711-1526
» **TIP120 Darlington NPN
transistor** Used in project: 13.
D TIP120-ND, **J** 32993, **F** 9804005
» **1N4004 power diode** Used in
project: 13.
D 1N4004-E3 or 23GI-ND, **J** 35992,
F 9556109, **RS** 628-9029
» **2N3906 PNP-type transistor**
Used in projects: 14, 29, 30.
J 178618, **D** 2N3906D26ZCT-
ND, **SF** COM-00522, **F** 1459017,
RS 294-328
» **9V battery** Used in projects: 3, 14.
» **9–12V DC power supply** Used in
project: 13.
J 170245, **SF** TOL-00298, **AF** 63,
F 636363, **P** 1463
» **Lithium Polymer ion battery**
Used in project: 31.
SF PRT-00341, **AF** 258, **RS** 615-
2472, **F** 1848660
» **USB LiPoly charger** Used in project:
31.
A 259, **SF** PRT-10217

Specialty Components

» **Voltmeter** Used in project: 7.
SF TOL-10285, **F** 4692810, **RS** 244-
890
» **MAX8212 voltage monitor** Used
in project: 14.
D MAX8212CPA+-ND, **F** 1610130
» **solar cell** Used in project: 14.
SF PRT-07840, **P** 1691
» **16x2 character LCD** Used in
project: 27.
SF LCD-00709
» **Relay Control PCB** Used in
projects: 29, 30.
SF COM-09096
» **Relay** Used in project: 29, 30.
SF COM-00101, **D** T9AV1D12-12-
ND, **F** 1629059

» **1N4148 diode** Used in projects:
29, 30.
SF COM-08588, **F** 1081177,
D 1N4148TACT-ND, **RS** 544-3480
» **PowerSwitch Tail** Alternative part
used in projects: 29, 30.
SF COM-09842, **AF** 268

Sensors

» **Flex Sensor resistors** Used in
project: 2.
D 905-1000-ND, **J** 150551,
SF SEN-10264, **AF** 182, **RS** 708-
1277, **MS** JM150551
» **Momentary switches or
pushbuttons** Used in projects: 2,
8, 9, 11.
D GH1344-ND, **J** 315432, **SF** COM-
09337, **F** 1634684,
RS 718-2213, **MS** JM315432
» **Force-sensing resistors, Interlink
400 series** Used in project: 5.
D 1027-1000-ND, **J** 2128260,
SF SEN-09673
» **web camera** Used in project: 5.
» **Photocells (light-dependent
resistors)** Used in projects: 6, 12.
D PDV-P9200-ND, **J** 202403,
SF SEN-09088, **F** 7482280, **RS**
234-1050
» **2-axis joystick** Used in project: 8.
J 2082855, **SF** COM-09032,
AF 245, **F** 1428461
» **Accelerometer** Used in projects:
8, 21.
J 28017, **SF** SEN-00692, **AF** 163,
RS 726-3738, **P** 1247, **MS** MKPX7
» **Hanwei gas sensor** Used in
project: 13.
SF SEN-08880, SEN-09404, or
SEN-09405, **P** 1480, 1634, 1633,
1481, 1482, or 1483
» **Sharp GP2Y0A21 infrared ranger**
Used in project: 15.
D 425-2063-ND, **SF** SEN-00242,
RS 666-6570, **P** 136
» **MaxBotix LV-EZ1 ultrasonic
ranger** Used in projects: 16, 32.
SF SEN-00639, **AF** 172, **P** 726,
SS SEN136B5B

» **EM-406A GPS receiver module**
Used in project: 19.
SF GPS-00465 **P** 28146 **AF** 99
» **ST Microelectronics LSM303DLH
digital compass** Used in project:
20.
SF SEN-09810, **RS** 717-3723,
P 1250
» **LED tactile button** Used in
project: 20.
SF COM-10443 and BOB-10467
» **Temperature sensor** Used in
projects: 29, 30.
AF 165, **D** TMP36GT9Z-ND,
F 1438760, **RS** 427-351

Miscellaneous

» **Ping-pong ball** Used in project: 1.
» **Small pink monkey** Used in
projects: 2, 3.
» **cat** Used in projects: 5, 29, 30.
» **cat mat** Used in project: 5.
» **thick pieces of wood or thick
cardboard, about the size of the
cat mat** Used in project: 5
» **Lighting filters** Used in projects:
6, 12.
» **Triple-wall cardboard** Used in
project: 8.
» **Velcro** Used in projects: 8, 31.
» **Cymbal monkey** Used in project:
13.
» **Conductive ribbon** Used in
project: 31.
SF DEV-10172
» **Conductive thread** Used in
project: 31.
SF DEV-10120, **L** A304
» **Shieldit Super Conductive Fabric**
Used in project: 31.
L A1220-14
» **Hoodie** Used in project: 31.
» **Embroidery thread** Used in
project: 31.

Hardware

This list includes all vendors for current and past editions.

KEY
≈ Phone / * Toll free
△ Fax
🐾 Mailing address

Abacom Technologies

Abacom sells a range of RF transmitters, receivers, and transceivers, and serial-to-Ethernet modules.
www.www.abacom-tech.com
email: abacom@abacom-tech.com
🐾 3210 Wharton Way
Mississauga ON L4X 2C1, Canada

Aboyd Company

The Aboyd Company sells art supplies, costumes, novelties, cardboard standups, home décor, and more. They're also a good source of Charley Chimp cymbal-playing monkeys.
www.aboyd.com
email: info@aboyd.com
≈ +1-888-458-2693
≈ +1-601-948-3477 International
△ +1-601-948-3479
🐾 P.O. Box 4568
   Jackson, MS 39296, USA

Acroname Robotics

Acroname sells a wide variety of sensors and actuators for robotics and electronics projects. They've got an excellent range of esoteric sensors like UV-flame sensors, cameras, and thermal-array sensors. They've got a lot of basic distance rangers as well. They also have a number of good tutorials on their site on how to use their parts.

www.acroname.com
email: info@acroname.com
≈ +1-720-564-0373
△ +1-720-564-0376.
   4822 Sterling Dr.
   Boulder, CO 80301-2350, USA

Adafruit Industries

Adafruit makes a number of useful open source DIY electronics kits, including an AVR programmer, an MP3 player, and more.
www.adafruit.com
email: sales@adafruit.com

Arduino Store

The Arduino Store sells Arduino microcontroller boards and shields, as well as TinkerKit parts and accessories for Arduino selected by the Arduino team. It includes some of the Arduino team's favorite third-party accessories.
http://store.arduino.cc/ww/
🐾 GHEO SA
via soldini, 22
CH-6830 Chiasso, Switzerland

Atmel

Atmel makes the AVR microcontrollers that are at the heart of the Arduino, Wiring, and BX-24 modules. They also make the ARM microcontroller that runs the Make controller.
www.atmel.com
≈ +1-408-441-0311
🐾 2325 Orchard Parkway
   San Jose, CA 95131, USA

CoreRFID

CoreRFID sells a variety of RFID readers, tags, and other RFID products.
www.rfidshop.com
e-mail: info@corerfid.com
≈ +44 (0) 845-071-0985
🐾 +44 (0) 845-071-0989
🐾 Dallam Court
Dallam Lane
Warrington, WA2 7LT, United Kingdom

D-Link

D-link makes a number of USB, Ethernet, and WiFi products, including the D-link IP-based WiFi camera used in Chapter 10.
www.dlink.com
e-mail: productinfo@dlink.com
≈ +1-800-326-1688

Devantech/Robot Electronics

Devantech makes ultrasonic ranger sensors, electronic compasses, LCD displays, motor drivers, relay controllers, and other useful add-ons for microcontroller projects.
http://robot-electronics.co.uk
e-mail: sales@robot-electronics.co.uk
≈ +44 (0)195-345-7387
△ +44 (0)195-345-9793
🐾 Maurice Gaymer Road
Attleborough
Norfolk, NR17 2QZ, England

Digi

Digi makes XBee radios, radio modems, and Ethernet bridges.
www.digi.com
≈ +1-877-912-3444
△ +1-952-912-4952
🐾 11001 Bren Road East
Minnetonka, MN 55343, USA

Digi-Key Electronics

Digi-Key is one of the U.S.'s largest retailers of electronics components. They're a staple source for things you use all the time—resistors, capacitors, connectors, some sensors, breadboards, wire, solder, and more.
www.digikey.com
≈ +1-800-344-4539 or
≈ +1-218-681-6674
△ +1-218-681-3380
🐾 701 Brooks Avenue South
   Thief River Falls, MN 56701, USA

ELFA

ELFA is one of Northern Europe's largest electronics components suppliers.
www.elfa.se
email: export@elfa.se
≈ +46 8-580-941-30
🐾 S-175 80 Järfälla, Sweden

Farnell

Farnell supplies electronics components for all of Europe. Their catalog part numbers are consistent with Newark in the U.S., so if you're working on both sides of the Atlantic, sourcing Farnell parts can be convenient.
http://uk.farnell.com
email: sales@farnell.co.uk
≈ +44-8701-200-200
△ +44-8701-200-201
🐾 Canal Road,
    Leeds, LS12 2TU, United Kingdom

Figaro USA, Inc.

Figaro Sensor sells a range of gas sensors, including volatile organic-compound sensors, carbon-monoxide sensors, oxygen sensors, and more.
www.figarosensor.com
email: figarousa@figarosensor.com
≈ +1-847-832-1701
△ +1-847-832-1705
🐾 3703 West Lake Ave., Suite 203
    Glenview, IL 60026, USA

Future Technology Devices International, Ltd. +(FTDI)

FTDI makes a range of USB-to-Serial adapter chips, including the FT232RL that's on many of the modules in this book.
www.ftdichip.com
email: admin1@ftdichip.com
≈ +44 (0) 141-429-2777
🐾 373 Scotland Street
    Glasgow, G5 8QB, United Kingdom

Glolab

Glolab makes a range of electronic kits and modules, including several useful RF and IR transmitters, receivers, and transceivers.
www.glolab.com
email: lab@glolab.com

Gridconnect

Gridconnect distributes networking products, including those from Lantronix and Digi.
www.gridconnect.com
email: sales@gridconnect.com
≈ +1 630-245-1445
△ +1 630-245-1717
≈* +1-800-975-GRID (4743)
🐾 1630 W. Diehl Road
    Naperville, IL 60563, USA

Images SI, Inc.

Images SI sells robotics and electronics parts. They carry a range of RFID parts, force-sensing resistors, stretch sensors, gas sensors, electronic kits, speech-recognition kits, solar energy parts, and microcontrollers.
www.imagesco.com
email: imagesco@verizon.net
≈ +1-718-966-3694
△ +1-718-966-3695
🐾 109 Woods of Arden Road
    Staten Island, NY 10312, USA

Interlink Electronics

Interlink makes force-sensing resistors, touchpads, and other input devices.
www.interlinkelectronics.com
email: specialty@interlink
          electronics.com
≈ +1-805-484-8855
△ +1-805-484-8989
🐾 546 Flynn Road
    Camarillo, CA 93012, USA

IOGear

IOGear make computer adapters. Their USB-to-Serial adapters are good, and they carry Powerline Ethernet products.
www.iogear.com
email: sales@iogear.com
≈* +1-866-946-4327
≈ +1-949-453-8782
△ +1-949-453-8785
🐾 23 Hubble Drive
    Irvine, CA 92618, USA

Jameco Electronics

Jameco carries bulk and individual electronics components, cables, breadboards, tools, and other staples for the electronics hobbyist or professional.
http://jameco.com

email: domestic@jameco.com
international@jameco.com
custservice@jameco.com
≈ +1-800-831-4242
    Toll-free 24-hour order line
≈ +1-650-592-8097
    International order line
△ +1-650-592-2503 *International*
△ +1-800-237-6948* *Toll-free fax*
△ +001-800-593-1449*
    Mexico toll-free fax
△ +1-803-015-237-6948*
    Indonesia toll-free fax
🐾 1355 Shoreway Road
    Belmont, CA 94002, USA

Keyspan

Keyspan makes computer adapters. Their USA-19xx series of USB-to-Serial adapters are very handy for microcontroller work.
www.keyspan.com
email: info@keyspan.com
≈ +1-510-222-0131 *Info/sales*
≈ +1-510-222-8802 *Support*
△ +1-510-222-0323
🐾 4118 Lakeside Dr
    Richmond, CA 94806, USA

Lantronix

Lantronix makes serial-to-Ethernet modules: the XPort, the WiPort, the WiMicro, the Micro, and many others.
www.lantronix.com
email: sales@lantronix.com
≈ +1-800-526-8766
≈ +1-949-453-3990
△ +1-949-450-7249
🐀 5353 Barranca Parkway
Irvine, CA 92618, USA

Libelium

Libelium makes an XBee-based product and other wireless products.
www.libelium.com
email: info@libelium.com
🐀 *Libelium Comunicaciones*
Distribuidas S.L.
Maria de Luna 11, Instalaciones
CEEIARAGON, C.P: 50018
Zaragoza, Spain

Linx Technologies

Linx makes a number of RF receivers, transmitters, and transceivers.
www.linxtechnologies.com
email: info@linxtechnologies.com
≈ +1-800-736-6677 *U.S.*
≈ +1-541-471-6256 *International*
△ +1-541-471-6251
🐀 159 Ort Lane
Merlin, OR 97532, USA

Low Power Radio Solutions

LPRS makes a number of RF receivers, transmitters, and transceivers.
www.lprs.co.uk
email: info@lprs.co.uk
≈ +44-1993-709418
△ +44-1993-708575
🐀 *Two Rivers Industrial Estate*
Station Lane, Witney
Oxon, OX28 4BH, United Kingdom

Maker SHED

Launched originally as a source for back issues of *MAKE Magazine*, the Maker SHED now has a variety of stuff for makers, crafters, and budding scientists.
www.makershed.com
email: help@makershed.com
≈+1-800-889-8969
🐀 1005 Gravenstein Hwy N
Sebastopol, CA 95472, USA

Making Things

Making Things makes the MAKE controller, and originated the now-discontinued Teleo controllers. They do custom hardware-engineering solutions.
www.makingthings.com
email: info@makingthings.com
△ +1-415-255-9513
🐀 1020 Mariposa Street, #2
San Francisco, CA 94110, USA

Maxim Integrated Products

Maxim makes sensors, communications chips, power-management chips, and more. They also own Dallas Semiconductor. Together, they're one of the major sources for chips related to serial communication, temperature sensors, LCD control, and much more.
www.maxim-ic.com
email: info2@maxim-ic.com
≈ +1-408-737-7600
△ +1-408-737-7194
🐀 120 San Gabriel Drive
Sunnyvale, CA 94086, USA

Microchip

Microchip makes the PIC family of microcontrollers. They have a very wide range of microcontrollers, for just about every conceivable purpose.
www.microchip.com
≈ +1-480-792-7200
🐀 2355 West Chandler Blvd.
Chandler, AZ, 85224-6199, USA

Mouser

Mouser is a large retailer of electronic components in the U.S. They stock most of the staple parts used in the projects in this book, such as resistors, capacitors, and some sensors. They also carry the FTDI USB-to-Serial cable.
www.mouser.com
email: help@mouser.com
🐀 1000 North Main Street
Mansfield, TX 76063, USA

NetMedia

NetMedia makes the BX-24 microcontroller module and the SitePlayer Ethernet module.
www.basicx.com
siteplayer.com
email: sales@netmedia.com
≈ +1-520-544-4567
△ +1-520-544-0800
🐀 10940 N. Stallard Place
Tucson, AZ 85737, USA

Newark In One Electronics

Newark supplies electronics components in the U.S. Their catalog part numbers are consistent with Farnell in Europe, so if you're working on both sides of the Atlantic, sourcing parts from Farnell and Newark can be convenient.
www.newark.com
email: somewhere@something.com
≈ +1-773-784-5100
△ +1-888-551-4801
🐀 4801 N. Ravenswood
Chicago, IL 60640-4496, USA

New Micros

New Micros sells a number of micro-controller modules. They also sell a USB-XBee dongle that allows you to connect Digi XBee radios to a computer really easily. Their dongles also have all the necessary pins connected for reflashing the XBee's firmware serially.
www.newmicros.com
email: nmisales@newmicros.com
≈ +1-214-339-2204

Parallax

Parallax makes the Basic Stamp family of microcontrollers. They also make the Propeller microcontroller, and a wide range of sensors, beginners' kits, robots, and other useful tools for people interested in electronics and microcontroller projects.
www.parallax.com
email: sales@parallax.com
≈* +1-888-512-1024 *Toll-free sales*
≈ +1-916-624-8333
     Office/international
Δ +1-916-624-8003
🐏 599 Menlo Drive
     Rocklin, California 95765, USA

Phidgets

Phidgets makes input and output modules that connect desktop and laptop computers to the physical world.
www.phidgets.com
email: sales@phidgets.com
≈ +1-403-282-7335
Δ +1-402-282-7332
🐏 2715A 16A NW
     Calgary, Alberta T2M3R7, Canada

Pololu

Pololu makes a variety of electronic components and breakout boards for robotics and other projects.
www.pololu.com
email: www@pololu.com
≈ +1-702-262-6648
≈ +1-877-776-5658 U.S. only
Δ + 1-702-262-6894
🐏 3095 E. Patrick Ln. #12
Las Vegas, NV 89120, USA

RadioShack

Hooray! RadioShack has begun to realizedthat the DIY electronics market in the U.S. never went away, and they're carrying more parts again. By the time you read this, maybe they'll be carrying Arduinos as well. Check the website for part numbers, and call your local store first to see whether they've got what you need. It'll save you time.
www.radioshack.com

Reynolds Electronics

Reynolds Electronics makes a number of small kits and modules for RF and infrared communications, IR remote control, and other useful add-on functions for microcontroller projects.
www.rentron.com
email: sales@rentron.com
≈ +1-772-589-8510
Δ +1-772-589-8620
🐏 12300 Highway A1A
     Vero Beach, Florida, 32963, USA

Roving Networks

Roving Networks makes and sells Bluetooth radio modules for electronics manufacturers. Their radios are at the heart of Spark Fun's Bluetooth Mate modules.
www.rovingnetworks.com
email: info@rovingnetworks.com
≈ +1-408-395-6539
Δ +1-603-843-7550
🐏 102 Cooper Court
Los Gatos, CA 95032, USA

RS Online

RS Online is one of Europe's largest electronics retailers. They sell worldwide.
www. rs-online.com
email: general@rs-components.com
≈ 0845-850-9900
Δ 01536-405678

Samtec

Samtec makes electronic connectors. They have a very wide range of connectors, so if you're looking for something odd, they probably make it.
www.samtec.com
email: info@samtec.com
≈ +1-800-SAMTEC-9

Seeed Studio

Seeed Studio makes a number of useful and inventive open source electronics parts.
www.seeedstudio.com
email: techsupport@seeedstudio.com
≈ +86-755-26407752
🐏 Room 0728, Bld 5,
Dong Hua Yuan,
NanHai Ave. NanShan dist.
Shenzhen 518054 China

SkyeTek

SkyeTek makes RFID readers, writers, and antennas.

www.skyetek.com

≈ +1-720-565-0441

△ +1-720-565-8989

🐎 11030 Circle Point Road, Suite 300
Westminster, CO 80020, USA

Smarthome

Smarthome makes a wide variety of home-automation devices, including cameras, appliance controllers, X10, and INSTEON.

www.smarthome.com

email: custsvc@smarthome.com

≈ 1-800-762-7846

≈ + 1-800-871-5719 *Canada*

≈ +1-949-221-9200 *International*

🐎 16542 Millikan Avenue
Irvine, CA 92606, USA

Spark Fun Electronics

Spark Fun makes it easier to use all kinds of electronic components. They make breakout boards for sensors, radios, and power regulators, and they sell a variety of microcontroller platforms.

www.sparkfun.com

email: spark@sparkfun.com

🐎 2500 Central Avenue, Suite Q
Boulder, CO 80301, USA

Symmetry Electronics

Symmetry sells ZigBee and Bluetooth radios, serial-to-Ethernet modules, WiFi modules, cellular modems, and other electronic communications devices.

www.semiconductorstore.com

≈ +1-877-466-9722

≈ +1-310-643-3470 *International*

△ +1-310-297-9719

🐎 5400 West Rosecrans Avenue
Hawthorne, CA 90250, USA

TI-RFID

TIRIS is Texas Instruments' RFID division. They make tags and readers for RFID in many bandwidths and protocols.

www.tiris.com

≈ +1-800-962-RFID (7343)

△ +1-214-567-RFID (7343)

🐎 *Radio Frequency
Identification Systems*
6550 Chase Oaks Blvd., MS 8470
Plano, TX 75023, USA

Trossen Robotics

Trossen Robotics sells a range of RFID supplies and robotics. They have a number of good sensors, including Interlink force-sensing resistors, linear actuators, Phidgets kits, RFID readers, and tags for most RFID ranges.

www.trossenrobotics.com

email: jenniej@trossenrobotics.com

≈ +1-877-898-1005

△ +1-708-531-1614

🐎 1 Westbrook Co. Center, Suite 910
Westchester, IL 60154, USA

Uncommon Projects

Uncommon Projects makes the YBox, a text-overlay device that puts text from web feeds on your TV.

www.uncommonprojects.com

ybox.tv

email: info@uncommonprojects.com

🐎 68 Jay Street #206
Brooklyn, NY 11201, USA

Software

Most of the software listed in this book is open source. In the following listings, anything that's not open source is noted explicitly as a commercial application. If there's no note, you can assume it's open.

Arduino

Arduino is a programming environment for AVR microcontrollers. It's based on Processing's programming interface. It runs on Mac OS X, Linux, and Windows operating systems.
www.arduino.cc

Asterisk

Asterisk is a software private branch exchange (PBX) manager for telephony. It runs on Linux and Unix operating systems.
www.asterisk.org

AVRlib

AVRlib is a library of C functions for a variety of tasks using AVR processors. It runs on Mac OS X, Linux, and Windows operating systems as a library for the avr-gcc compiler.
hubbard.engr.scu.edu/avr/avrlib

avr-gcc

The GNU avr-gcc is a C compiler and assembler for AVR microcontrollers. It runs on Mac OS X, Linux, and Windows operating systems.
www.avrfreaks.net/AVRGCC

CCS C

CCS C is a commercial C compiler for the PIC microcontroller. It runs on Windows and Linux operating systems.
www.ccsinfo.com

CoolTerm

CoolTerm is a freeware (though not open source) serial terminal application for Mac OS X and Windows written by Roger Meier.
http://freeware.the-meiers.org

Dave's Telnet

Dave's Telnet is a telnet application for Windows.
http://dtelnet.sourceforge.net

Eclipse

Eclipse is an integrated development environment (IDE) for programming in many different languages. It's extensible through a plug-in architecture, and there are compiler links to most major programming languages. It runs on Mac OS X, Linux, and Windows.
www.eclipse.org

Evocam

Evocam is a commercial webcam application for Mac OS X.
http://evological.com

Exemplar

Exemplar is a tool for authoring sensor applications through behavior rather than through programming. It runs on Mac OS X, Linux, and Windows operating systems as a plug-in for Eclipse.
http://hci.stanford.edu/research/exemplar

Fwink

Fwink is a webcam application for Windows.
www.lundie.ca/fwink

Girder

Girder is a commercial home automation application for Windows.
www.girder.nl

GitHub

GitHub is a host for git, a version-control tool for programming source code of any language. Git and github are great tools to share your code.
http://git-scm.com
https://github.com

Java

Java is a programming language. It runs on Mac OS X, Linux, and Windows operating systems, and many embedded systems as well.
http://java.sun.com

Macam

Macam is a webcam driver for Mac OS X.
http://webcam-osx.sourceforge.net/

Max/MSP

Max is a commercial graphic data-flow authoring tool. It allows you to program by connecting graphic objects rather than writing text. Connected with Max are MSP, a real-time audio-signal processing library, and Jitter, a real-time video-signal processing library. It runs on Mac OS X and Windows operating systems.
www.cycling74.com

PEAR

PEAR is the PHP Extension and Application Repository. It hosts extension libraries for PHP scripting.
http://pear.php.net

PHP

PHP is a scripting language that is especially suited for web development and can be embedded into HTML. It runs on Mac OS X, Linux, and Windows operating systems.
www.php.net

PicBasic Pro

PicBasic Pro is a commercial BASIC compiler for PIC microcontrollers. It runs on Windows.
http://melabs.com

Processing

Processing is a programming language and environment designed for the non-technical user who wants to program images, animation, and interaction. It runs on Mac OS X, Linux, and Windows.
www.processing.org

Puredata (PD)

Puredata (PD) is a graphic data-flow authoring tool. It allows you to program by connecting graphic objects rather than writing text. It's developed by one of the original developers of Max, Miller Puckette. It runs on Mac OS X, Linux, and Windows operating systems.
http://puredata.info

PuTTY SSH

PuTTY is a telnet/SSH/serial port client for Windows.
www.puttyssh.org

QR Code Library

QR Code Library is a set of libraries for encoding and decoding QR Code 2D barcodes. It runs on Mac OS X, Linux, and Windows as a library for Java.
http://qrcode.sourceforge.jp

Dan Shiffman's Processing Libraries

Dan Shiffman has written a number of useful libraries for Processing, including the pqrcode library used in this book (www.shiffman.net/p5/pqrcode). He's also got an SFTP library (www.shiffman.net/2007/06/04/sftp-with-java-processing) and a sudden-motion sensor library for Mac OS X (www.shiffman.net/2006/10/28/processingsms).

Sketchtools NADA

NADA is a proxy tool for connecting programming environments with hardware devices. Originally a commercial tool, it's since been open sourced.
code.google.com/p/nadamobile

TinkerProxy

TinkerProxy is a TCP-to-Serial proxy application.
code.google.com/p/tinkerit/wiki/TinkerProxy

Twilio

Twilio is a commercial IP telephony provider. They provide application programming interfaces that allow you to connect telephone calls to web applications.
www.twilio.com

UDP Library for Processing

Hypermedia's UDP library for Processing enables you to communicate via UDP from Processing. It runs on Mac OS X, Linux, and Windows as a library for Processing.
hypermedia.loeil.org/processing

Wiring

Wiring is a programming environment for AVR microcontrollers. It's based on Processing's programming interface. It runs on Mac OS X, Linux, and Windows operating systems.
www.wiring.org.co

Index

Four hot Arduino kits from the makers behind MAKE and Maker Faire!

Ultimate Microcontroller Pack

The Ultimate Microcontroller Pack includes everything you need to dive right into the world of microcontollers. The 100+ components allow you to complete nearly any online tutorial without having to source individual parts. Everyone from beginners to advanced users will appreciate all that the Ultimate Microcontroller Pack has to offer.

Mintronics: Survival Pack

You never know when you'll find yourself in a MacGyver moment. It can happen anywhere, at any time. Wouldn't it be easier to hack those electronics with some real components instead of a rubber band and a paper clip? The Mintronics: Survival Pack from the Maker Shed contains over 60 useful components for making, hacking, and modifying electronic circuits and repairs on the go.

MakerShield Kit

The ultimate open source prototyping shield for Arduino & compatible microcontrollers. Create your circuits the way you want, and easily changes without having to solder.

Arduino Uno

Arduino is a tool for making computers that can sense and control more of the physical world than your desktop computer!

Get even more for your money.

Join the O'Reilly Community, and register the O'Reilly books you own. It's free, and you'll get:

- $4.99 ebook upgrade offer
- 40% upgrade offer on O'Reilly print books
- Membership discounts on books and events
- Free lifetime updates to ebooks and videos
- Multiple ebook formats, DRM FREE
- Participation in the O'Reilly community
- Newsletters
- Account management
- 100% Satisfaction Guarantee

Signing up is easy:

1. **Go to: oreilly.com/go/register**
2. **Create an O'Reilly login.**
3. **Provide your address.**
4. **Register your books.**

Note: English-language books only

To order books online:

oreilly.com/store

For questions about products or an order:

orders@oreilly.com

To sign up to get topic-specific email announcements and/or news about upcoming books, conferences, special offers, and new technologies:

elists@oreilly.com

For technical questions about book content:

booktech@oreilly.com

To submit new book proposals to our editors:

proposals@oreilly.com

O'Reilly books are available in multiple DRM-free ebook formats. For more information:

oreilly.com/ebooks

O'REILLY®

Spreading the knowledge of innovators   oreilly.com

Have it your way.

LIBRARY, UNIVERSITY OF CHESTER

Students report that the labs are enjoyable to complete and enable them to see how the abstract concepts of cognitive psychology are tested. My students have reported that they not only have a better grasp of the cognitive concepts covered in class, but that they also have a better understanding of how psychological concepts in general can be empirically tested I am pleased that they are able to see how the information that they learned in statistics and research methods is used in the study of cognitive psychology.

– Lisa Bauer, Pepperdine University

I am a big fan of the Coglab on CD. The students experienced research first-hand, gained knowledge of the experience of being a subject, practiced reading and interpreting trends in data, and learned more about cognitive psychology than I did as an undergraduate.

– Darrell Rudmann, Indiana University—East

Available *CogLab* experiments

ATTENTION
Attentional Blink
Change Detection*
Simon Effect
Spatial Cueing
Stroop Effect

PERCEPTION
Apparent Motion
Garner Task: Integral*
Garner Task: Separable*
Müller-Lyer Illusion
Signal Detection
Visual Search

NEUROCOGNITION
Brain Asymmetry
Mapping the Blind Spot
Receptive Fields

SENSORY MEMORY
Metacontrast Masking
Modality Effect*
Partial Report
Suffix Effect

SHORT-TERM MEMORY
Brown-Peterson
Position Error*
Sternberg Search

WORKING MEMORY
Irrelevant Speech
Memory Span
Operation Span
Phonological Similarity*

MEMORY PROCESS
Encoding Specificity*
Levels of Processing*
Serial Position
Von Restorff Effect

METAMEMORY
False Memory
Forgot It All Along
Remember/Know

IMAGERY
Link Word*
Mental Rotation
Mental Scanning*

SPEECH & LANGUAGE
Categorical Perception: Identification
Categorical Perception: Discrimination
Lexical Decision
Word Superiority

CONCEPTS
Absolute Identification
Implicit Learning
Prototypes

JUDGMENT
Monty Hall
Risky Decisions
Typical Reasoning
Wason Selection*
Typical Reasoning

*New Experiments

Ordering Options:

CogLab™ Student Manual for 36 Experiments (with online access code): 0-534-57410-6
Packaged with the Sternberg's *Cognitive Psychology*, Fourth Edition: 0-495-06061-5

CogLab™ On A CD-ROM: 0-534-64067-2
Packaged with Sternberg's *Cognitive Psychology*, Fourth Edition: 0-495-06063-1

Also Available:
CogLab Reader by Aimée Surprenant, Gregory Francis, and Ian Neath: 0-534-64120-2
This reader includes 32 articles, each of which corresponds to a demonstration or set of demonstrations in **CogLab** while also offering an in-depth look into the historical and theoretical context for the experiments.

http://coglab.wadsworth.com

www.wadsworth.com

wadsworth.com is the World Wide Web site for Wadsworth and is your direct source to dozens of online resources.

At *wadsworth.com* you can find out about supplements, demonstration software, and student resources. You can also send email to many of our authors and preview new publications and exciting new technologies.

wadsworth.com
Changing the way the world learns®

EDITION 4

Cognitive Psychology

Robert J. Sternberg
Yale University

with contributions of the
Investigating Cognitive Psychology boxes by

Jeff Mio
California State University–Pomona

THOMSON

WADSWORTH

Australia • Brazil • Canada • Mexico • Singapore
Spain • United Kingdom • United States

THOMSON
™
WADSWORTH

Cognitive Psychology, **Fourth Edition**
Robert J. Sternberg

Psychology Editor: Marianne Taflinger
Publisher: Vicki Knight
Assistant Editor: Jennifer Keever
Editorial Assistant: Lucy Faridany
Technology Project Manager: Darin Derstine
Marketing Manager: Chris Caldeira
Marketing Assistant: Nicole Morinon
Marketing Communications Manager: Laurel Anderson
Project Manager, Editorial Production: Jennifer Klos
Creative Director: Rob Hugel
Art Director: Vernon Boes
Print Buyer: Barbara Britton

Permissions Editor: Joohee Lee
Production Service and Compositor: Graphic World Inc.
Photo Researcher: Kathleen Olson
Copy Editor: Graphic World Inc.
Cover Designer: Larry Didona
Cover Image: Clockwise from the top: IT Stock Free/ PictureQuest; Digital Vision/PictureQuest, Brand X Pictures/PictureQuest, Don Farrall/Photodisc/Getty Images
Cover Printer: Phoenix Color Corp
Printer: R.R. Donnelley/Crawfordsville

Library of Congress Control Number: 2005926690

Student Edition: ISBN 0-534-51421-9

International Student Edition: ISBN 0-495-00699-8
   (Not for sale in the United States)

Thomson Higher Education
10 Davis Drive
Belmont, CA 94002-3098
USA

For more information about our products, contact us at:
   Thomson Learning Academic Resource Center
   1-800-423-0563
For permission to use material from this text or product, submit a request online at
   http://www.thomsonrights.com.
Any additional questions about permissions can be submitted by e-mail to
   thomsonrights@thomson.com.

Contents in Brief

Contents

Contents in Brief

Contents

CHAPTER 4

Perception   110

CHAPTER 5

Memory: Models and Research Methods   156

CHAPTER 6

Memory Processes   193

CHAPTER 7

Representation and Manipulation of Knowledge in Memory: Images and Propositions 228

CHAPTER **8**

Representation and Organization of Knowledge in Memory: Concepts, Categories, Networks, and Schemas   274

CHAPTER **9**

Language: Nature and Acquisition   310

C H A P T E R **10**

Language in Context   346

CHAPTER 12

Decision Making and Reasoning   439

CHAPTER 13

Human and Artificial Intelligence   484

To the Instructor

Every year it was a gamble, and every year I lost: I had taught cognitive psychology a number of times during my 20 years at Yale, and I had never used the same textbook twice. For whatever reason, my students were never taken with any of the books I chose and neither was I. The book was too hard or too easy, too narrow or too broad, too dated or too trendy. They were decent books, just not the right books. Finally, I decided to stack the deck and write the book myself. In this preface, I describe my goals for both the 4th edition and for the original text in particular.

What's New in the 4th Edition

The 4th edition of *Cognitive Psychology* continues the tradition the book has established of providing a comprehensive grounding in the basics of cognitive psychology. What are the general and specific revisions?

General Revision Plan

The book differs in 12 key respects from the earlier editions:

1. *Complete rewriting at the sentence level.* In retrospect, the book was not as user-friendly as it could have been. In order to increase its user-friendliness, I have examined every individual sentence in the book and rewritten many of them to make them clearer and, in many cases, shorter. The main result is a much clearer text. A subsidiary result is a reduced reading level that will accommodate students at a greater diversity of reading levels. The goal was not to "pander" to students, but rather, to make the exposition clearer so they could invest their cognitive resources where they should be invested—in understanding the concepts of cognitive psychology rather than the way in which they are presented.

2. *Removal of cognitive development as a separate chapter.* Reviews indicated that relatively few instructors were using the cognitive-development chapter (Chapter 13 in previous editions). I therefore removed this chapter. Material such as Piaget's developmental theory is no longer included in the book, because it is usually covered (often multiple times) in other courses. However, material directly relevant to the substance of cognitive psychology, such as memory development, has been placed in the appropriate substantive chapters.

3. *Streamlining of the chapter about cognitive neuropsychology.* Reviewers generally felt that the material in Chapter 2 about cognitive neuropsychology on neurons and related topics was not necessary for a course in cognitive psychology and repeated what was learned in other courses, especially introductory psychology and biologically oriented courses in psychology. This material has therefore been removed.

4. *Enhancement of coverage of biological approaches to cognitive psychology in relevant chapters.* By removing material from Chapter 2, space opened up for increased coverage of biological and especially neuropsychological material in chapters on individual substantive topics.

5. *Addition of common themes section to each chapter.* Reviewers indicated that the themes suggested in Chapter 1 got lost in the subsequent text. In order to ensure that they could be found again, a separate section of common themes has been added at the end of each subsequent chapter, which shows how at least three of the seven themes could be applied to the concepts in the chapter. These themes are (1) nature versus nurture, (2) rationalism versus empiricism, (3) structure versus process, (4) domain generality versus domain specificity, (5) validity of causal inferences versus ecological validity, (6) basic versus applied research, and (7) biological versus behavioral research. It is made clear that the approaches under each theme are to a large extent complementary rather than contradictory.

6. *Shortening of annotated suggested readings.* Reviews suggest that instructors have not made great use of the annotated suggested readings. Therefore, just one key contemporary reading has been retained.

7. *General updating.* Because the field of cognitive psychology moves ahead so rapidly, each edition has been extensively updated, including the 4th.

8. *Topical updating.* New topics have been added to the chapters. These are discussed in the Specific Revision Plan for Cognitive Psychology, 4th ed.

9. *New In the Lab of. . . boxes.* In the Lab of. . . boxes have been updated. About one third of them are entirely new.

10. *New activities for readers.* An entirely new set of active-learning activities has been added to each chapter in this edition by Jeff Mio of California State University–Pomona. Each Investigating Cognitive Psychology box is focused on demonstrating a principle.

11. *Streamlining of historical material in chapters.* The amount of historical material in chapters has been streamlined.

12. *New emphasis on working memory distributed throughout chapters.* The role of working memory in different cognitive processes is highlighted, not just in the memory chapters, but throughout.

Specific Revision Plan

Chapter 1

- Added new figures.
- Deleted historical material that reviewers thought was too detailed.
- Themes at the end of the chapter are now discussed explicitly in all chapters.

Chapter 2

- Deleted material about the structure of nervous system, as requested by reviewers.
- Deleted material about the structure and function of neurons, as requested by reviewers.
- Added new figures.
- Deleted some of the historical material, as requested by reviewers.
- Elaborated further about lobes.
- Added a section on cognitive consequences of brain disorders: stroke, brain tumors, and head injuries.

Chapter 3

- Added material about Cheesman & Merikle's follow-up to Marcel's work on subliminal perception.
- Added material about blindsight based on Weiskrantz's work with D. B.
- Added material about airport security detection as a practical example of signal-detection theory.
- Added new figures.
- Added material about deterring terrorists as an example of vigilance.
- Added material about multimode theory.
- Added material about driving as an example of selective attention, with statistics on various causes of accidents due to inattention.
- Added material about simulated driving as a way of measuring selective attention.
- Added material about protocol analysis methodology.
- Added material about Wegner's and Wilson's work on conscious control of behavior.
- Added material about change blindness.
- Added material about attention deficit hyperactivity disorder.
- Added more information about visual neglect.

Chapter 4

- Added material about viewer-centered versus object-centered approaches to object perception.
- Added new figures.
- Added new figures showing Farah's theory of pattern perception, in particular as it pertains to face perception.
- Added new material about prosopagnosia and its relation to face perception in general.
- Added more material about how perception affects experience and experience affects perception.
- Added more material about how visual control of perception and of action are mediated by different cortical pathways.
- Added more material about other types of agnosias (auditory, apperceptive, associative).
- Added a new section about different types of color-blindness.
- Added a new section about akinetopsia.

Chapter 5

- Added material about Luck's work on the visual short-term store.
- Added material about Chun's follow-up of Luck's work.
- Increased coverage of the nature of working memory.
- Increased coverage of the measurement of working memory.
- Added new figures.
- Added material about Tulving's HERA (hemispheric encoding/retrieval asymmetry) model.
- Added material about disputes to connectionist claims.
- Added material about hypermnesia.
- Added material about the effects of Alzheimer's disease on memory.
- Added material about the role of the amygdala in emotional memory.
- Added material about sex differences in emotional memory.

Chapter 6

- Added material about eyewitness identification.
- Added material about how to make eyewitness identification more accurate.
- Added material about source monitoring (Johnson's research).
- Added material about memory development.

Chapter 7

- Changed title to more accurately reflect chapter content.
- Added material about faulty mental models.
- Added new figures.
- Added material about the development of visuospatial skills.

Chapter 8

- Changed title to more accurately reflect chapter content.
- Added material about natural kinds and artifact kinds.
- Added material about ad hoc categories.
- Added material about nominal kinds.
- Added material about theory-based view of meaning.
- Described Rips' research on theory-based view.
- Deleted material about compound cues, as suggested by reviewers.
- Added material about connectionist representation compared with semantic-network representation.
- Added more material about the theory-based view of meaning.
- Added new material about essentialism.

Chapter 9

- Added material about the relevance of animal language for understanding human cognition.
- Added material about the nature of animal language.
- Added more material about the advantage of infants over adults in being able to recognize different phonemes.

Chapter 10

- Added new material about dyslexia.
- Added new material about aphasias.
- Added new material about autism and its effects on language.
- Added a new section about Baron-Cohen's theory of autism.

Chapter 11

- Added new material about the importance of comprehension processes in problem solving.
- Added new material about the importance of working memory for problem solving as illustrated in the Tower of London problem.
- Added new material about the importance of knowledge in problem solving and how it interacts with coherence of text presenting problems.
- Added new material showing that to understand radio announcers of baseball games, knowledge about baseball is of paramount importance.
- Added new material about the importance of looking ahead in expert problem solving.
- Added new material about the importance of systematicity in expert problem solving.
- Added new material about the personality traits underlying creative problem solving.

Chapter 12

- Added new figures.
- Added new material about the role of working memory in reasoning.
- Added new material about the role of mood in deductive reasoning.
- Added new material about the fundamental and new riddles of induction.
- Added new material about Kim and Ahn's work on theory-based causal inference in clinical reasoning.
- Added material about the development of inductive reasoning.

Chapter 13

- Added new material about Ackerman's integrative approach to studying intelligence.
- Added new material about cultural approaches to intelligence.
- Added new material about Tomasello's work.
- Added material about the development of intelligence in adults.
- Moved the artificial intelligence section to the end of the chapter.
- Added new material about human-machine interactions.

The Original Goals of This Book

When I first undertook to write this textbook, I knew what I wanted in a textbook, and I knew what my students wanted; or at least I thought I did. We wanted a book that would achieve a number of objectives.

1. *Combine readability with integrity.* I have chosen books that were so chewy that only the strongest stomachs could digest their contents, and I have chosen ones that melted like cotton candy, with substance to match. I have tried to write a book that would give students something to chew on, but one that they could easily digest.

2. *Balance a clear presentation of the big questions of cognitive psychology with a respect for the important details of the field.* Perhaps in no course more than in cognitive psychology are both the forest and the trees important. The best and most lasting work in the field is driven by enduring and fundamental questions. However, that work also respects the details of methods and data analysis needed to produce meaningful results. In order to achieve the balance, I have opened each chapter with a preview of the big questions dealt with in that chapter and ended each chapter with a summary of what we have learned in the field that addresses each question. Within the chapters, the writing has been guided by the big questions, while conveying to students the kinds of details to which cognitive psychologists need to attend in both their theory and research.

3. *Balance the learning of subject matter with thinking about the subject matter.* An expert cognitive psychologist knows the discipline but can also use the knowledge. Knowledge without thought is useless, but thought without knowledge is empty. I have tried to balance a respect for subject matter with an equal respect for its use. Every chapter ends with diverse questions that emphasize comprehension of the subject matter, as well as analytical, creative, and practical thinking with that subject matter. Students using this book will learn not only the basic ideas and facts of cognitive psychology, but also how to think with them.

4. *Recognize both the traditional and emerging trends in the field.* This book has all the traditional topics found in the chapters of the large majority of textbooks, including the nature of cognitive psychology and how people think about issues in cognitive psychology (Chapter 1), attention and consciousness (Chapter 3), perception (Chapter 4), memory (Chapters 5 and 6), knowledge representation (Chapters 7 and 8), language (Chapters 9 and 10), problem solving and creativity (Chapter 11), and decision making and reasoning (Chapter 12). I have also included two chapters that are not typically included as chapters in other books.

Cognitive Neuroscience (Chapter 2) is included because the dividing line between cognitive psychology and psychobiology is becoming increasingly indistinct. A great deal of exciting work today is at the interface between the two fields, and so, whereas the cognitive psychologist of 20 years ago might have been able to get away without an understanding of biological foundations, I believe that today such a cognitive psychologist would be ill served.

Human and artificial intelligence (Chapter 13) are becoming increasingly important to the field of cognitive psychology. Twenty years ago, the field of human intelligence was dominated by psychometric (test-based) approaches. The field of artificial intelligence was dominated by programs that were functionally rather remote from human thought processes. Today, both fields of intelligence are much more heavily influenced by cognitive models of how people process information. I include both human- and computer-based models in the same chapter because I believe that their goals, ultimately, are the same—namely, to understand human cognition.

Although the book ends with the chapter on intelligence, intelligence also plays a major role in the beginning and the middle of the book, because it is the organizing framework within which cognitive psychology is presented. This framework is not in terms of a traditional psychometric model of intelligence, but rather in terms of intelligence as the fundamental organizing framework for all of human cognition.

I have tried to balance not only traditional and newer topics, but also older and more recent citations. Some books seem to suggest that almost nothing new has happened over the past decade, whereas others seem to suggest that cognitive psychology was invented in that decade. The goal of this book is to balance citation and description of classic studies with equal attention to recent exciting contributions to the field.

5. *Show the basic unity of cognitive psychology.* On the one hand, cognitive psychologists disagree about the extent to which the mechanisms of cognition are domain-specific versus domain-general. On the other hand, I believe that almost all cognitive psychologists believe that there is a fundamental functional unity to human cognition. This unity, I believe, is expressed through the concept of human intelligence.

The concept of intelligence can be seen as providing a unifying umbrella via which one can understand the adaptive nature of human cognition. Through this single concept, society, as well as psychological science, acknowledges that as diverse as cognition may be, it comes together in providing us with a functionally unified way of making sense of and adapting to the environment. Thus, the unity of human cognition, as expressed by the concept of intelligence, serves as an integrating message for this book.

6. *Balance various forms of learning and instruction.* Students learn best when they learn material in a variety of ways and from different vantage points. To this end, I have sought to achieve a balance among a traditional presentation of text, a variety of kinds of questions about the material (factual, analytical, creative, practical), demonstrations of key ideas in cognitive psychology, and annotated suggested readings that students can consult if they wish further information about a topic. A chapter outline at the beginning of each chapter also serves as an advance organizer for what is to come. The opening questions and closing answers help students appreciate the main questions in the field, as well as what progress we have made toward answering them. The text itself emphasizes how contemporary ideas have evolved from past ones and how these ideas address the key questions cognitive psychologists have sought to answer in their research.

Acknowledgments

I am grateful to a number of individuals who have contributed to the development of this book: Laura Da Costa, University of Illinois at Springfield; Susan Dutch, Westfield State College; Jocelyn Folk, Kent State University; Christina Frederick-Recascino, Embry-Riddle Aeronautical University; Andrew Herbert, Rochester Institute of Technology; Gretchen Kambe, University of Nevada, Las Vegas; Gary Klatsky, SUNY Oswego; Erica Kleinknecht, Pacific University; Padraig O'Seaghdha, Lehigh University; Takashi Yamauchi, Texas A & M University.

To the Student

Why do we remember people whom we met years ago but sometimes seem to forget what we learned in a course shortly after we take the final exam (or worse, sometimes right before)? How do we manage to carry on a conversation with one person at a party, and simultaneously eavesdrop on another, more interesting conversation taking place nearby? Why are people so often certain that they are correct in answering a question when in fact they are not? These are just three of the many questions that are addressed by the field of cognitive psychology.

Cognitive psychologists study how people perceive, learn, remember, and think. Although cognitive psychology is a unified field, it draws on many other fields, most notably neuroscience, computer science, linguistics, anthropology, and philosophy. Thus, you will find some of the thinking of all these fields represented in this book. Moreover, cognitive psychology interacts with other fields within psychology, such as psychobiology, developmental psychology, social psychology, and clinical psychology.

For example, it is difficult to be a clinical psychologist today without a solid knowledge of developments in cognitive psychology, because so much of the thinking in the clinical field draws on cognitive ideas, both in diagnosis and in therapy. Cognitive psychology has also provided a means for psychologists to investigate experimentally some of the exciting ideas that have emerged from clinical theory and practice, such as notions of unconscious thought.

Cognitive psychology will be important to you not only in its own right but also in helping you in all of your work. For example, knowledge of cognitive psychology can help you better understand things such as how best to study for tests, how to read effectively, and how to remember difficult-to-learn material. However, in order to best acquire this knowledge, you need to make use of the following pedagogical features of this book.

1. *Chapter outlines*, beginning each chapter, summarize the main topics covered in each chapter and thus give you an advance overview of what is to be covered in that chapter.

2. *Opening questions* emphasize the main questions each chapter addresses.

3. *Boldface terms*, indexed at ends of chapters and defined in the glossary, help you acquire the vocabulary of cognitive psychology.

4. *End-of-chapter summaries* return to the questions at the opening of each chapter and show our current state of knowledge with regard to these questions.

5. *End-of-chapter questions* help you ensure both that you have learned the basic material and that you can think in a variety of ways (analytical, creative, and practical) with this material.

6. *Annotated suggested readings* refer you to other sources you can consult for further information on the topics covered in each chapter.

7. *Investigating Cognitive Psychology* demonstrations, appearing throughout the chapters, help you see how cognitive psychology can be used to demonstrate various psychological phenomena.

8. *Practical Applications of Cognitive Psychology* demonstrations show you how you and others can apply cognitive psychology to your everyday life.

9. *"In the Lab of. . ." boxes* tell you about what it really is like to do research in cognitive psychology. Prominent researchers speak in their own words about their research—what research problems excite them most and what they are doing to address these problems.

10. *Active Learning Activities*. These activities are there to help you learn actively rather than merely passively.

11. *Key Themes*. The key themes section near the end of each chapter relates the content of the chapters to the key themes expressed in Chapter 1 of the book. This section will help you to see the continuity of the main ideas of cognitive psychology across its various subfields.

12. *CogLab*. The publisher of this textbook, Wadsworth, has an exciting series of laboratory demonstrations in cognitive psychology that are keyed to this text. You can actively participate in these demonstrations and thereby learn first-hand what it is like to be involved in cognitive-psychological research.

This book contains an overriding theme that unifies all the diverse topics found in the various chapters: Human cognition has evolved over time as a means of adapting to our environment, and we can call this ability to adapt to the environment *intelligence*. Through intelligence, we cope in an integrated and adaptive way with the many challenges with which the environment presents us.

Although cognitive psychologists disagree about many issues, there is one issue about which almost all of them agree; namely, that cognition enables us successfully to adapt to the environments in which we find ourselves. Thus, we need a construct such as that of *human intelligence*, if only to provide a shorthand way of expressing this fundamental unity of adaptive skill. We can see this unity at all levels in the study of cognitive psychology. For example, diverse measures of the psychophysiological functioning of the human brain show correlations with scores on a variety of tests of intelligence. Selective attention, the ability to tune in certain stimuli and tune out others, is also related to intelligence, and it has even been proposed that an intelligent person is one who knows what information to attend to and what information to ignore. Various language and problem-solving skills are also related to intelligence, pretty much without regard to how it is measured. In brief, then, human intelligence can be seen as an entity that unifies and provides direction to the workings of the human cognitive system.

I hope you enjoy this book, and I hope you see why I am enthusiastic about cognitive psychology and proud to be a cognitive psychologist.

About the Author

ROBERT J. STERNBERG

Robert J. Sternberg is IBM Professor of Psychology and Education and the Director of the Center for the Psychology of Abilities, Competencies, and Expertise at Yale University. The Center is dedicated to the encouragement of theory, research, practice, and policy advancing the notion of intelligence as developing expertise—as a construct that is modifiable and capable, to some extent, of development throughout the life span. The center seeks to have an impact on science, on education, and on society.

Sternberg received the Ph.D. from Stanford University in 1975 and the B.A. summa cum laude, Phi Beta Kappa, from Yale University in 1972. He also holds honorary doctorates from the Complutense University of Madrid, Spain; the University of Leuven, Belgium; the University of Cyprus; and the University of Paris V, France.

Sternberg is the author of more than 100 journal articles, book chapters, and books, and he has received more than $20 million in government and other grants and contracts for his research. The central focus of his research is on intelligence, creativity, and wisdom, and he also has studied love and close relationships as well as hate. This research has been conducted on five different continents.

Sternberg is past president of the American Psychological Association. He is also a fellow of the American Academy of Arts and Sciences, the American Association for the Advancement of Science, the American Psychological Association (in 15 divisions), the Society of Experimental Psychologists, and the American Psychological Society. He has won many awards from the American Psychological Association (APA), the American Educational Research Association (AERA), the American Psychological Society (APS), and other organizations. These awards include the Early Career Award, E. L. Thorndike Award for Career Achievement in Educational Psychology, and Boyd R. McCandless Award from APA; the Palmer O. Johnson, Research Review, Outstanding Book, and Sylvia Scribner Awards from AERA; the James McKeen Cattell Award from APS; the Distinguished Lifetime Contribution to Psychology Award from the Connecticut Psychological Association; the International Award of the Association of Portuguese Psychologists; the Cattell Award of the Society for Multivariate Experimental Psychology; the Award for Excellence of the Mensa Education and Research Foundation; the Distinction of Honor SEK from the Institucion SEK (Madrid); the Sidney Siegel Memorial Award of Stanford University; and the Wohlenberg Prize of Yale University. He has held a Guggenheim Fellowship and Yale University Senior and Junior Faculty Fellowships, as well as a National Science Foundation (NSF) Graduate Fellowship. He also has held the Honored Visitor Fellowship of the Taiwan National Science Council and the Sir Edward Youde Memorial Visiting Professorship of the City University of Hong Kong. He has been listed in the *Esquire* Register of outstanding men and women under 40 and was listed as one of 100 top young scientists by *Science Digest*. He has been president of the Divisions of General Psychology, Educational Psychology, Psychology and the Arts, and Theoretical and Philosophical Psychology of the APA, and has served as Editor of the *Psychological Bulletin* and was Editor of *Contemporary Psychology*. Sternberg is most well known for his theory of successful intelligence, his investment theory of creativity (developed with Todd Lubart), his theory of thinking styles as mental self-government, balance theory of wisdom, and his triangular theory of love and theory of love as a story.

Introduction to Cognitive Psychology

EXPLORING COGNITIVE PSYCHOLOGY

1. What is cognitive psychology?

2. How did psychology develop as a science?

3. How did cognitive psychology develop from psychology?

4. How have other disciplines contributed to the development of theory and research in cognitive psychology?

5. What methods do cognitive psychologists use to study how people think?

6. What are the current issues and various fields of study within cognitive psychology?

Cognitive Psychology Defined

What will you be studying in a textbook about cognitive psychology?

1. *Cognition:* People think.
2. *Cognitive psychology:* Scientists think about how people think.
3. *Students of cognitive psychology:* People think about how scientists think about how people think.
4. *Professors who profess to students about cognitive psychology:* You get the idea.

To be more specific, **cognitive psychology** is the study of how people perceive, learn, remember, and think about information. A cognitive psychologist might study how people perceive various shapes, why they remember some facts but forget others, or how they learn language. Consider some examples:

- Why do objects look farther away on foggy days than they really are? The discrepancy can be dangerous, even deceiving drivers into having car accidents.
- Why do many people remember a particular experience (e.g., a very happy moment or an embarrassment during childhood), yet they forget the names of people whom they have known for many years?
- Why are many people more afraid of traveling in planes than in automobiles? After all, the chances of injury or death are much higher in an automobile than in a plane.

These are some of the kinds of questions that we can answer through the study of cognitive psychology.

This chapter introduces the field of cognitive psychology. It describes some of the intellectual history of the study of human thinking. It particularly emphasizes some of the issues and concerns that arise when we think about how people think. Next is a brief overview of the major methods, issues, and content areas of cognitive psychology.

The ideas presented in this chapter will provide a foundation on which to build an understanding of the topics in cognitive psychology.

Why study the history of this field, or of any other field, for that matter? For one thing, if we know where we came from, we may have a better understanding of where we are heading. For another, we may learn from past mistakes. In this way, when we make mistakes they will be fresh, new mistakes and not the same, old ones. Our ways of addressing fundamental issues have changed. But some of the fundamental questions remain much the same. Ultimately, we may learn something about how people think by studying how people have thought about thinking.

The progression of ideas often involves a *dialectic*. A dialectic is a developmental process whereby ideas evolve over time through a pattern of transformation. What is this pattern? In a dialectic:

- A thesis is proposed. A *thesis* is a statement of belief. For example, some people believe that human nature governs many aspects of human behavior (e.g., intelligence or personality; Sternberg, 1999). After a while, however, certain individuals notice apparent flaws in the thesis.

- Eventually, or perhaps even quite soon, an antithesis emerges. An *antithesis* is a statement that counters a previous statement of belief. For example, an alternative view is that our nurture (the environmental contexts in which we are reared) almost entirely determines many aspects of human behavior.

- Sooner or later, the debate between the thesis and the antithesis leads to a synthesis. A *synthesis* integrates the most credible features of each of two (or more) views. For example, in the debate over nature versus nurture, the interaction between our innate (inborn) nature and environmental nurture may govern human nature. Indeed, the most widely accepted current view is that the "nature" and "nurture" views are both incomplete. Nature and nurture work together in our development.

If a synthesis seems to advance our understanding of a subject, it then serves as a new thesis. A new antithesis then follows it, then a new synthesis, and so on. Georg Hegel (1770–1831) observed this dialectical progression of ideas. He was a German philosopher who came to his ideas by his own dialectic. He synthesized some of the views of his intellectual predecessors and contemporaries.

Philosophical Antecedents of Psychology: Rationalism versus Empiricism

Where and when did the study of cognitive psychology begin? Historians of psychology usually trace the earliest roots of psychology to two different approaches to understanding the human mind:

Philosophy seeks to understand the general nature of many aspects of the world, primarily through *introspection,* the examination of inner ideas and experiences (from *intro-,* "inward, within," and *-spect,* "look").

Physiology seeks a scientific study of life-sustaining functions in living matter, primarily through *empirical* (observation-based) methods.

Two Greek philosophers, Plato (ca. 428–348 B.C.) and his student Aristotle (384–322 B.C.), have profoundly affected modern thinking in psychology and in many other fields. Plato and Aristotle disagreed regarding how to investigate ideas. Plato was a rationalist. A **rationalist** believes that the route to knowledge is through logical analysis. In contrast, Aristotle (a naturalist and biologist as well as a philosopher) was an empiricist. An **empiricist** believes that we acquire knowledge via empirical evidence—that is, we obtain evidence through experience and observation (Figure 1.1).

Aristotle's view, then, leads directly to empirical investigations of psychology. In contrast, Plato's view foreshadows the various uses of reasoning in theory development. Rationalist theories without any connection to observations may not be valid. But mountains of observational data without an organizing theoretical framework may not be meaningful. We might see Plato's rationalist view of the world as a thesis and Aristotle's empirical view as an antithesis. Most psychologists today seek a synthesis of the two. They base empirical observations on theory. In turn, they use these observations to revise their theories.

During the Middle Ages, much of cognitive psychology as it then existed was an attempt to elaborate on Aristotle's ideas (Kemp, 1996, 2000). Early attempts also were made to locate cognitive processes in the brain. By the seventeenth century, the contrasting ideas of rationalism and empiricism emerged again with the French rationalist René Descartes (1596–1650) and the British empiricist John Locke (1632–1704). Descartes agreed with Plato. He viewed the introspective, reflective method as being superior to empirical methods for finding truth. Locke, in contrast, shared Aristotle's enthusiasm for empirical observation (Leahey, 2000; Manent, 1998; Smith, 1997).

Locke believed that humans are born without knowledge and therefore must seek knowledge through empirical observation. Locke's term for this view was *tabula*

FIGURE 1.1

(a)   (b)

(a) According to the rationalist, the only route to truth is reasoned contemplation; (b) according to the empiricist, the only route to truth is meticulous observation. Cognitive psychology, like other sciences, depends on the work of both rationalists and empiricists.

rasa (meaning "blank slate" in Latin). The idea is that life and experience "write" knowledge on us. For Locke, then, the study of learning was the key to understanding the human mind. He believed that there are no innate ideas whatsoever. In the eighteenth century, German philosopher Immanuel Kant (1724–1804) dialectically synthesized the view of Descartes and Locke, arguing that both rationalism and empiricism have their place. Both must work together in the quest for truth. Most psychologists today accept Kant's synthesis.

Psychological Antecedents of Cognitive Psychology

Early Dialectics in the Psychology of Cognition

Structuralism

An early dialectic in the history of psychology is that between structuralism and functionalism (Leahey, 1997; Morawski, 2000). Structuralism was the first major school of thought in psychology. **Structuralism** seeks to understand the structure (configuration of elements) of the mind and its perceptions by analyzing those perceptions into their constituent components. Consider, for example, the perception of a flower. Structuralists would analyze this perception in terms of the constituent colors, geometric forms, size relations, and so on.

A German psychologist whose ideas later would contribute to the development of structuralism was Wilhelm Wundt (1832–1920). Wundt advocated the study of sensory experiences through introspection. **Introspection** is a looking inward at pieces of information passing through consciousness (Lyons, 2003). An example is the sensations experienced when looking at a flower. In effect, we analyze our own perceptions.

Wundt had many followers. One was an American student Edward Titchener (1867–1927). Titchener (1910) helped bring structuralism to the United States.

Wilhelm Wundt was no great success in school, failing time and again and frequently finding himself subject to the ridicule of others. However, Wundt later showed that school performance does not always predict career success because he is considered to be among the most influential psychologists of all time.

Other early psychologists criticized both the method (introspection) and the focus (elementary structures of sensation) of structuralism.

Functionalism: An Alternative to Structuralism

An alternative to structuralism suggested that psychologists should focus on the *processes* of thought rather than on its contents. **Functionalism** seeks to understand what people *do*, and *why* they do it. This principal question was in contrast to that of the structuralists, who had asked what the elementary contents (structures) of the human mind were. Functionalists held that the key to understanding the human mind and behavior was to study the processes of how and why the mind works as it does, rather than to study the structural contents and elements of the mind.

Functionalists were unified by the kinds of questions they asked but not necessarily by the answers they found or by the methods they used for finding those answers. Because functionalists believed in using whichever methods best answered a given researcher's questions, it seems natural for functionalism to have led to pragmatism. **Pragmatists** believe that knowledge is validated by its usefulness: What can you *do* with it? Pragmatists are concerned not only with knowing what people do, they want to know what we can do with our knowledge of what people do. For example, pragmatists believe in the importance of the psychology of learning and memory. Why? Because it can help us improve the performance of children in school.

A leader in guiding functionalism toward pragmatism was William James (1842–1910). His chief functional contribution to the field of psychology was a single book: his landmark *Principles of Psychology* (1890/1970). Even today, cognitive psychologists frequently point to the writings of James in discussions of core topics in the field, such as attention, consciousness, and perception. John Dewey (1859–1952) was another early pragmatist who profoundly influenced contemporary thinking in cognitive psychology. Dewey is remembered primarily for his pragmatic approach to thinking and schooling.

Archives of the History of American Psychology, University of Akron

Many cognitive psychologists continue to regard William James, a physician, philosopher, psychologist, and brother of author Henry James, as among the greatest psychologists ever, although James himself seems to have rejected psychology later in his life.

Take a moment right now to put the idea of pragmatism into use. Think about ways to make the information you are learning in this course more useful to you. Part of the work already has been done—notice that the chapter begins with questions that make the information more coherent and useful, and the chapter summary returns to those questions. Does the text successfully answer the questions posed at the beginning of the chapter? Come up with your own questions and try organizing your notes in the form of answers to your questions. Also, try relating this material to other courses or activities you participate in. For example, you may be called on to explain to a friend how to use a new computer program. A good way to start would be to ask that person if he or she has any questions. That way, the information you provide is more directly useful to your friend, rather than forcing this individual to search for the information he or she needs in a long, one-sided lecture.

PRACTICAL APPLICATIONS OF COGNITIVE PSYCHOLOGY

Associationism: An Integrative Synthesis

Associationism, like functionalism, was less a rigid school of psychology than an influential way of thinking. **Associationism** examines how events or ideas can become associated with one another in the mind to result in a form of learning. For example, associations may result from *contiguity* (associating things that tend to occur together at about the same time), *similarity* (associating things with similar features or properties), or *contrast* (associating things that seem to show polarities, such as hot/cold, light/dark, day/night).

In the late 1800s, associationist Hermann Ebbinghaus (1850–1909) was the first experimenter to apply associationist principles systematically. Specifically, Ebbinghaus studied and observed his own mental processes. He counted his errors and recorded his response times. Through his self-observations, Ebbinghaus studied how people learn and remember material through rehearsal. *Rehearsal* is the conscious repetition of to-be-learned material. Among other findings, he made a groundbreaking experimental discovery. He found that frequent repetition can fix mental associations more firmly in memory. Thus, repetition aids in learning (see Chapter 6).

Another influential associationist, Edward Lee Thorndike (1874–1949), held that the role of "satisfaction" is the key to forming associations. Thorndike termed this principle the *law of effect* (1905): A stimulus will tend to produce a certain response over time if an organism is rewarded for that response. Thorndike believed that an organism learns to respond in a given way (the *effect*) in a given situation if it is rewarded repeatedly for doing so (the *satisfaction*, which serves as a stimulus to future actions). Thus, a child given treats for solving arithmetic problems correctly learns to solve arithmetic problems accurately because he or she forms associations between valid solutions and treats.

From Associationism to Behaviorism

Other researchers who were contemporaries of Thorndike used animal experiments to probe stimulus-response relationships in ways that differed from those of Thorndike and his fellow associationists. These researchers straddled the line between associationism and the emerging field of behaviorism. **Behaviorism** is a theoretical outlook that psychology should focus only on the relation between observable behavior, on the one hand, and environmental events or stimuli, on the other. The idea was to make whatever others might have called "mental," physical (Lycan, 2003). Some of these researchers, like Thorndike and other associationists, studied responses that were voluntary (although perhaps lacking any conscious thought, as in Thorndike's work). Others studied responses that were involuntarily triggered, in response to what appear to be unrelated external events.

In Russia, Nobel Prize–winning physiologist Ivan Pavlov (1849–1936) studied involuntary learning behavior of this sort. He began with the observation that dogs salivated in response to the sight of the lab technician who fed them. This response occurred before the dogs even saw whether the technician had food. To Pavlov, this response indicated a form of learning, classically conditioned learning, over which the dogs had no conscious control. In the dogs' minds, some type of involuntary learning linked the technician to the food (Pavlov, 1955). Pavlov's landmark work paved the way for the development of behaviorism. Classical conditioning involves more than just an association based on temporal contiguity (e.g., the food and the conditioned stimulus occurring at about the same time; Rescorla, 1967). Effective conditioning requires *contingency* (e.g., the presentation of food being contingent on the presentation of the conditioned stimulus; Rescorla & Wagner, 1972; Wagner & Rescorla, 1972).

Behaviorism may be considered an extreme version of associationism. It focuses entirely on the association between the environment and an observable behavior. According to strict, extreme ("radical") behaviorists, any hypotheses about internal thoughts and ways of thinking are nothing more than speculation.

Proponents of Behaviorism

The "father" of radical behaviorism is John Watson (1878–1958). Watson had no use for internal mental contents or mechanisms. He believed that psychologists should concentrate only on the study of observable behavior (Doyle, 2000). He dismissed thinking as subvocalized speech. Behaviorism also differed from previous movements in psychology by shifting the emphasis of experimental research from human to animal participants. Historically, much behaviorist work has been conducted (and still is) with laboratory animals, such as rats, because these animals allow for much greater behavioral control of relationships between the environment and the behavior emitted in reaction to it. One problem with using animals, however, is determining whether the research can be *generalized* to humans (i.e., applied more generally to humans instead of just to the kinds of animals that were studied).

B. F. Skinner (1904–1990), a radical behaviorist, believed that virtually all forms of human behavior, not just learning, could be explained by behavior emitted in reaction to the environment. Skinner conducted research primarily with nonhuman animals. He rejected mental mechanisms. He believed instead that *operant conditioning*—involving the strengthening or weakening of behavior, contingent on the presence or absence of reinforcement (rewards) or punishments—could explain all forms of human behavior. Skinner applied his experimental analysis of behavior to many psychological phenomena, such as learning, language acquisition, and problem solving. Largely because of Skinner's towering presence, behaviorism dominated the discipline of psychology for several decades.

Behaviorists Daring to Peek into the Black Box

Some psychologists rejected radical behaviorism. They were curious about the contents of the mysterious box. For example, Edward Tolman (1886–1959) thought that understanding behavior required taking into account the purpose of, and the plan for, the behavior. Tolman (1932) believed that all behavior is directed toward some goal. For example, the goal of a rat in a maze may be to try to find food in that maze. Tolman is sometimes viewed as a forefather of modern cognitive psychology.

Another criticism of behaviorism (Bandura, 1977b) is that learning appears to result not merely from direct rewards for behavior. It also can be social, resulting from observations of the rewards or punishments given to others. This view emphasizes how we observe and model our own behavior after the behavior of others. We learn by example. This consideration of social learning opens the way to considering what is happening inside the mind of the individual.

Gestalt Psychology

Of the many critics of behaviorism, Gestalt psychologists may have been among the most avid. **Gestalt psychology** states that we best understand psychological phenomena when we view them as organized, structured wholes. According to this view, we cannot fully understand behavior when we only break phenomena down into smaller parts.

The maxim "the whole differs from the sum of its parts" aptly sums up the Gestalt perspective. To understand the perception of a flower, for example, we would have to take into account the whole of the experience. We could not understand such a perception merely in terms of a description of forms, colors, sizes, and so on. Similarly, we could not understand problem solving merely by looking at minute elements of observable behavior (Köhler, 1927, 1940; Wertheimer, 1945, 1959).

Emergence of Cognitive Psychology

A more recent approach is **cognitivism,** the belief that much of human behavior can be understood in terms of how people think.

Early Role of Psychobiology

Ironically, one of Watson's former students, Karl Spencer Lashley (1890–1958), brashly challenged the behaviorist view that the human brain is a passive organ merely responding to environmental contingencies outside the individual (Gardner, 1985). Instead, Lashley considered the brain to be an active, dynamic organizer of behavior. Lashley sought to understand how the macro-organization of the human brain made possible such complex, planned activities as musical performance, game playing, and using language. None of these were, in his view, readily explicable in terms of simple conditioning.

In the same vein but at a different level of analysis, Donald Hebb (1949) proposed the concept of cell assemblies as the basis for learning in the brain. Cell assemblies are coordinated neural structures that develop through frequent stimulation.

They develop over time as the ability of one neuron (nerve cell) to stimulate firing in a connected neuron increases. Behaviorists did not jump at the opportunity to agree with theorists like Lashley and Hebb. In fact, behaviorist B. F. Skinner (1957) wrote an entire book describing how language acquisition and usage could be explained purely in terms of environmental contingencies. This work stretched Skinner's framework too far, leaving Skinner open to attack. An attack was indeed forthcoming. Linguist Noam Chomsky (1959) wrote a scathing review of Skinner's ideas. In his article, Chomsky stressed both the biological basis and the creative potential of language. He pointed out the infinite numbers of sentences we can produce with ease. He thereby defied behaviorist notions that we learn language by reinforcement. Even young children continually are producing novel sentences for which they could not have been reinforced in the past. Chomsky argued that our understanding of language is constrained not so much by what we have heard, but rather, by an innate language acquisition device (LAD) that all humans possess. This device allows the infant to use what it hears to infer the grammar of its linguistic environment. In particular, the LAD actively limits the number of permissible grammatical constructions. Thus, it is the structure of the mind, rather than the structure of environmental contingencies, that guides our acquisition of language.

Add a Dash of Technology: Engineering and Computation

By the end of the 1950s some psychologists were intrigued by the tantalizing notion that machines could be programmed to demonstrate the intelligent processing of information (Rychlak & Struckman, 2000). Turing (1950) suggested that soon it would be hard to distinguish the communication of machines from that of humans. He suggested a test, now called the "Turing test," by which a computer program would be judged as successful to the extent that its output was indistinguishable, by humans, from the output of humans (Cummins & Cummins, 2000). In other words, suppose you communicated with a computer and you could not tell that it was a computer. The computer then passed the Turing test (Schonbein & Bechtel, 2003). By 1956 a new phrase had entered our vocabulary. **Artificial intelligence (AI)** is the attempt by humans to construct systems that show intelligence and, particularly, the intelligent processing of information (*Merriam-Webster's Collegiate Dictionary*, 1993). Chess-playing programs, which now can beat most humans, are examples of artificial intelligence.

By the early 1960s developments in psychobiology, linguistics, anthropology, and artificial intelligence, as well as the reactions against behaviorism by many mainstream psychologists, converged to create an atmosphere ripe for revolution. Early cognitivists argued (e.g., Miller, Galanter, & Pribram, 1960; Newell, Shaw, & Simon, 1957b) that traditional behaviorist accounts of behavior were inadequate precisely because they said nothing about how people think. Ulric Neisser's book *Cognitive Psychology* (Neisser, 1967) was especially critical in bringing cognitivism to prominence by informing undergraduates, graduate students, and academics about the newly developing field. Neisser defined *cognitive psychology* as the study of how people learn, structure, store, and use knowledge. Subsequently, Allen Newell and Herbert Simon (1972) proposed detailed models of human thinking and problem solving from the most basic levels to the most complex. By the 1970s cognitive psychology was recog-

Ulric Neisser is a professor of psychology at Cornell University. His book, Cognitive Psychology, *was instrumental in launching the cognitive revolution in psychology. He also has been a major proponent of an ecological approach to cognition and has shown the importance of studying cognitive processing in ecologically valid contexts*

nized widely as a major field of psychological study, with a distinctive set of research methods.

Research Methods in Cognitive Psychology

Goals of Research

To better understand the specific methods used by cognitive psychologists, one must first grasp the goals of research in cognitive psychology, some of which are highlighted here. Briefly, those goals include data gathering, data analysis, theory development, hypothesis formulation, hypothesis testing, and perhaps even application to settings outside the research environment. Often researchers simply seek to gather as much information as possible about a particular phenomenon. They may or may not have preconceived notions regarding what they may find while gathering the data. Their research focuses on describing particular cognitive phenomena, such as how people recognize faces or how they develop expertise.

Data gathering reflects an empirical aspect of the scientific enterprise. Once there are sufficient data on the cognitive phenomenon of interest, cognitive psychologists use various methods for drawing inferences from the data. Ideally, they use multiple converging types of evidence to support their hypotheses. Sometimes, just a quick glance at the data leads to intuitive inferences regarding patterns that emerge from those data. More commonly, however, researchers use various statistical means of analyzing the data.

Data gathering and statistical analysis aid researchers in describing cognitive phenomena. No scientific pursuit could get far without such descriptions. However, most cognitive psychologists want to understand more than the *what* of cognition; most also seek to understand the *how* and the *why* of thinking. That is, researchers seek ways to explain cognition as well as to describe it. To move beyond descriptions, cognitive psychologists must leap from what is observed directly to what can be inferred regarding observations.

Suppose that we wish to study one particular aspect of cognition. An example would be how people comprehend information in textbooks. We usually start with a theory. A **theory** is an organized body of general explanatory principles regarding a phenomenon. It generates **hypotheses,** tentative proposals regarding expected empirical consequences of the theory, such as the outcomes of research. Then we seek to test the theory and thereby to see whether it has the power to predict certain aspects of the phenomenon in question. In other words, our thought process is, "If our theory is correct, then whenever x occurs, outcome y should result."

Next, we test our hypotheses through experimentation. Even if particular findings appear to confirm a given hypothesis, the findings must be subjected to statistical analysis to determine their statistical significance. **Statistical significance** indicates the likelihood that a given set of results would be obtained if only chance factors were in operation.

Once our hypothetical predictions have been experimentally tested and statistically analyzed, the findings from those experiments may lead to further work. For

Herbert A. Simon was a professor of computer science and psychology at Carnegie-Mellon University. He is known for his pioneering work, with Allen Newell and others, on constructing and testing computer models that simulate human thought, and for his experimental tests of these models. He also was a major advocate of thinking-aloud protocols as a means of studying cognitive processing. Simon died in 2001.

example, the psychologist may engage in further data gathering, data analysis, theory development, hypothesis formulation, and hypothesis testing. In addition, many cognitive psychologists hope to use insights gained from research to help people use cognition in real-life situations. Some research in cognitive psychology is applied from the start. It seeks to help people improve their lives and the conditions under which they live their lives. Thus, basic research may lead to everyday applications. For each of these purposes, different research methods offer differing advantages and disadvantages.

IN THE LAB OF LUDY T. BENJAMIN, JR.

Courtesy of Dr. Ludy T. Benjamin, Jr.

Pop psychology—it's everywhere! The public loves it; psychologists hate it. It is the stuff of television, movies, books, plays, and magazines. It is pervasive in American life and has been so since the nineteenth century when phrenologists measured the bumps on people's heads to advise them about their career choices, physiognomists analyzed facial features (e.g., shape of the chin or nose) to help business executives decide who was to be hired or promoted, or graphologists studied handwriting samples to help individuals find compatible marriage partners. When scientific psychology arrived in American universities in the late nineteenth century, these new psychologists sought to displace the old psychology, attempting to convince the public of the validity of their approach and the absurdity of what they labeled pseudopsychologies.

In our research program we are examining the differences between these two psychologies, attempting to understand why the public has continued to embrace the claims of nonscientific psychology. Our program of research is historical, part of a growing scholarship in social history and the history of science, which includes the history of psychology. As historical research, our work is empirical but not experimental. We have studied popular psychology in several ways, including analyzing encyclopedia articles from the nineteenth and early twentieth centuries (Benjamin & associates, 1997) and examining the many surveys of the public's image of psychology

(Wood, Jones, & Benjamin, 1986). Currently we are focusing on the American popular psychology magazines (more than 50 different titles) that were published between 1900 and 1960. These magazines promoted the belief that their contents would help readers achieve health, happiness, and success (Benjamin & Bryant, 1997).

To date we have examined more than a thousand of these magazines, studying their articles and advertisements. We are trying to identify themes, such as marriage, childrearing, sex, and job satisfaction, that are constant across magazines of the same time period but that may change over time, and we are comparing those themes with what was being published in scientific psychology at the same time and with what were pervasive themes in American culture during those times. For example, the 1920s marked a turning point in American history regarding opportunities for women. The 19th amendment gave women the right to vote, and an economic boom boosted job opportunities for women. We have found that the popular psychology magazines spoke to the interests of these women; few psychologists or psychology journals showed any such interests. These differences certainly could be partly responsible for why the public has embraced the claims of popular psychology while rejecting the counterclaims of scientific psychology. This topic is inherently interesting in its own right, but discovering the reasons for popular psychology's appeal has greater importance. Such understanding is critical if the modern science and practice of psychology is ever to reach the public effectively.

Distinctive Research Methods

Cognitive psychologists use various methods to explore how humans think. These methods include (a) laboratory or other controlled experiments, (b) psychobiological research, (c) self-reports, (d) case studies, (e) naturalistic observation, and (f) computer simulations and artificial intelligence (see Table 1.1 for descriptions and examples of each method). As the table shows, each method offers distinctive advantages and disadvantages.

Experiments on Human Behavior

In controlled experimental designs, an experimenter conducts research, typically in a laboratory setting. The experimenter controls as many aspects of the experimental situation as possible. The experimenter then manipulates the independent variables. He or she controls for the effects of irrelevant variables and observes the effects on the dependent variables (outcomes).

In implementing the experimental method, the experimenter must use a representative sample of the population of interest. He or she must exert rigorous control over the experimental conditions. The experimenter also must randomly assign participants to the treatment and control conditions. If those requisites for the experimental method are fulfilled, the experimenter may be able to infer probable causality. This inference is of the effects of the independent variable or variables (the treatment) on the dependent variable (the outcome).

Suppose the outcomes in the treatment condition show a statistically significant difference from the outcomes in the control condition. The experimenter then can infer the likelihood of a causal link between the independent variable(s) and the dependent variable. Because the researcher can establish a likely causal link between the given independent variables and the dependent variables, controlled laboratory experiments offer an excellent means of testing hypotheses.

For example, suppose that we wanted to see whether loud, distracting noises influence the ability to perform well on a particular cognitive task (e.g., reading a passage from a textbook and responding to comprehension questions). Ideally, we first would select a random sample of participants from within our total population of interest. We then would randomly assign each participant to a treatment condition or a control condition. Then we would introduce some distracting loud noises to the participants in our treatment condition. The participants in our control condition would not receive this treatment. We would present the cognitive task to participants in both the treatment condition and the control condition. We then would measure their performance by some means (e.g., speed and accuracy of responses to comprehension questions). Finally, we would analyze our results statistically. We thereby would examine whether the difference between the two groups reached statistical significance. Suppose the participants in the treatment condition showed poorer performance at a statistically significant level than the participants in the control condition. We then might infer that loud distracting noises did, indeed, influence the ability to perform well on this particular cognitive task.

In cognitive-psychological research, the dependent variables may be quite diverse. But they often involve various outcome measures of accuracy (e.g., frequency of errors), of response times, or of both. Among the myriad possibilities for independent

TABLE 1.1 — Research Methods

Cognitive psychologists use controlled experiments, psychobiological research, self-reports, case studies, naturalistic observation, and computer simulations and artificial intelligence when studying cognitive phenomena.

Method	Controlled Laboratory Experiments	Psychobiological Research	Self-Reports, Such as Verbal Protocols, Self-Ratings, Diaries
Description of method	Obtain samples of performance at a particular time and place	Study animal brains and human brains, using postmortem studies and various psychobiological measures or imaging techniques (see Chapter 2)	Obtain participants' reports of own cognition in progress or as recollected
Validity of causal inferences: random assignment of subjects	Usually	Not usually	Not applicable
Validity of causal inferences: experimental control of independent variables	Usually	Varies widely, depending on the particular technique	Probably not
Samples: size	May be any size	Often small	Probably small
Samples: representativeness	May be representative	Often not representative	May be representative
Ecological validity	Not unlikely; depends on the task and the context to which it is being applied	Unlikely under some circumstances	Maybe; see strengths and weaknesses
Information about individual differences	Usually de-emphasized	Yes	Yes
Strengths	Ease of administration, of scoring, and of statistical analysis make it relatively easy to apply to representative samples of a population; relatively high probability of drawing valid causal inferences	Provides "hard" evidence of cognitive functions by relating them to physiological activity; offers an alternative view of cognitive processes unavailable by other means; may lead to possibilities for treating persons with serious cognitive deficits	Access to introspective insights from participants' point of view, which may be unavailable via other means
Weaknesses	Not always possible to generalize results beyond a specific place, time, and task setting; discrepancies between real-life behavior and behavior in the laboratory	Limited accessibility for most researchers; requires access both to appropriate subjects and to equipment that may be extremely expensive and difficult to obtain; small samples; many studies are based on studies of abnormal brains or of animal brains, so generalizability of findings to normal human populations may be troublesome	Inability to report on processes occurring outside conscious awareness **Verbal protocols & self-ratings:** Data gathering may influence cognitive process being reported. **Recollections:** Possible discrepancies between actual cognition and recollected cognitive processes and products
Examples	David Meyer and Roger Schvaneveldt (1971) developed a laboratory task in which they very briefly presented two strings of letters (either words or nonwords) to subjects, and then they asked the subjects to make a decision about each of the strings of letters, such as deciding whether the letters made a legitimate word or deciding whether a word belonged to a predesignated category	Elizabeth Warrington and Tim Shallice (1972; Shallice & Warrington, 1970) have observed that lesions (areas of injury) in the left parietal lobe of the brain are associated with serious deficits in short-term (brief, active) memory but no impairment of long-term memory, but persons with lesions in the medial (middle) temporal regions of the brain show relatively normal short-term memory but grave deficits in long-term memory (Shallice, 1979; Warrington, 1982)	In a study of mental imagery, Stephen Kosslyn and his colleagues (Kosslyn, Seger, Pani, & Hillger, 1990) asked students to keep a weeklong diary recording all of their mental images in each sensory modality

CASE STUDIES	NATURALISTIC OBSERVATIONS	COMPUTER SIMULATIONS AND ARTIFICIAL INTELLIGENCE (AI)
Engage in intensive study of single individuals, drawing general conclusions about behavior	Observe real-life situations, as in classrooms, work settings, or homes	**Simulations:** Attempt to make computers simulate human cognitive performance on various tasks **AI:** Attempt to make computers demonstrate intelligent cognitive performance, regardless of whether the process resembles human cognitive processing
Highly unlikely	Not applicable	Not applicable
Highly unlikely	No	Full control of variables of interest
Almost certain to be small	Probably small	Not applicable
Not likely to be representative	May be representative	Not applicable
High ecological validity for individual cases; lower generalizability to others	Yes	Not applicable
Yes; richly detailed information regarding individuals	Possible, but emphasis is on environmental distinctions, not on individual differences	Not applicable
Access to richly detailed information about individuals, including information about historical and current contexts, which may not be available via other means; may lead to specialized applications for groups of exceptional individuals (e.g., prodigies, persons with brain damage)	Access to rich contextual information, which may be unavailable via other means	Allows exploration of a wide range of possibilities for modeling cognitive processes; allows clear testing to see whether hypotheses accurately predicted outcomes; may lead to wide range of practical applications (e.g., robotics for performing dangerous tasks or for performing in hazardous environments)
Applicability to other persons; small sample size and nonrepresentativeness of sample generally limits generalizability to population	Lack of experimental control; possible influence on naturalistic behavior due to the presence of the observer	Limitations imposed by limits of the hardware (i.e., the computer software) and the hardware (the programs written by the researchers); distinctions between human intelligence and machine intelligence—even in simulations involving sophisticated modeling techniques, simulations may imperfectly model the way that the human brain thinks
Howard Gruber (1974/1981) conducted a case study of Charles Darwin, to explore in depth the psychological context for great intellectual creativity	Michael Cole (Cole, Gay, Glick, & Sharp, 1971) studied members of the Kpelle tribe in Africa, noting how the Kpelle's definitions of intelligence compared with traditional Western definitions of intelligence, as well as how cultural definitions of intelligence may govern intelligent behavior	**Simulations:** Through detailed computations, David Marr (1982) attempted to simulate human visual perception and proposed a theory of visual perception based on his computer models **AI:** Various AI programs have been written that can demonstrate expertise (e.g., playing chess), but they probably do so via different processes than those used by human experts

variables are characteristics of the situation, of the task, or of the participants. For example, characteristics of the situation may involve the presence versus the absence of particular stimuli or hints during a problem-solving task. Characteristics of the task may involve reading versus listening to a series of words and then responding to comprehension questions. Characteristics of the participants may include age differences, differences in educational status, or differences based on test scores.

On the one hand, characteristics of the situation or task may be manipulated through random assignment of participants to either the treatment or the control group. On the other hand, characteristics of the participant are not easily manipulated experimentally. For example, suppose the experimenter wants to study the effects of aging on speed and accuracy of problem solving. The researcher cannot randomly assign participants to various age groups because people's ages cannot be manipulated (although participants of various age groups can be assigned at random to various experimental conditions). In such situations researchers often use other kinds of studies. Examples are studies involving *correlation* (a statistical relationship between two or more attributes, such as characteristics of the participants or of a situation). Correlations are expressed as numbers on a scale that ranges from −1.00 (a negative correlation) to 0 (no correlation) to 1.00 (a positive correlation). For example, we may expect a negative correlation between fatigue and alertness. There probably would be no correlation between intelligence and length of ear lobe. And a positive correlation would be likely between vocabulary size and reading comprehension.

Findings of statistical relationships are highly informative. Their value should not be underrated. Also, because correlational studies do not require the random assignment of participants to treatment and control conditions, these methods may be applied flexibly. However, correlational studies generally do not permit unequivocal inferences regarding causality. As a result, many cognitive psychologists strongly prefer experimental data to correlational data.

Psychobiological Research

Through *psychobiological research*, investigators study the relationship between cognitive performance and cerebral events and structures. Chapter 2 describes various specific techniques used in psychobiological research. These techniques generally fall into three categories. The first category is that of techniques for studying an individual's brain *postmortem* (after the death of an individual), relating the individual's cognitive function prior to death to observable features of the brain. The second category is techniques for studying images showing structures of or activities in the brain of an individual who is known to have a particular cognitive deficit. The third is techniques for obtaining information about cerebral processes during the normal performance of a cognitive activity.

Postmortem studies offered some of the first insights into how specific *lesions* (areas of injury in the brain) may be associated with particular cognitive deficits. Such studies continue to provide useful insights into how the brain influences cognitive function. Recent technological developments also have increasingly enabled researchers to study individuals with known cognitive deficits *in vivo* (while the individual is alive). The study of individuals with abnormal cognitive functions linked to cerebral damage often enhances our understanding of normal cognitive functions.

In addition, psychobiological researchers study some aspects of normal cognitive functioning by studying cerebral activity in animal participants. Researchers often use animal participants for experiments involving neurosurgical procedures that cannot be performed on humans because such procedures would be difficult, unethical, or impractical. For example, studies mapping neural activity in the cortex have been conducted on cats and monkeys (e.g., psychobiological research on how the brain responds to visual stimuli; see Chapter 4).

Can cognitive and cerebral functioning of animals and of abnormal humans be generalized to apply to the cognitive and cerebral functioning of normal humans? Psychobiologists have responded to these questions in various ways. Most of them go beyond the scope of this chapter (see Chapter 2). As just one example, for some kinds of cognitive activity, the available technology permits researchers to study the dynamic cerebral activity of normal human participants during cognitive processing (see the brain-imaging techniques described in Chapter 2).

Self-Reports, Case Studies, and Naturalistic Observation

Individual experiments and psychobiological studies often focus on precise specification of discrete aspects of cognition across individuals. To obtain richly textured information about how particular individuals think in a broad range of contexts, researchers may use other methods. These methods include *self-reports* (an individual's own account of cognitive processes), case studies (in-depth studies of individuals), and *naturalistic observation* (detailed studies of cognitive performance in everyday situations and nonlaboratory contexts). On the one hand, experimental research is most useful for testing hypotheses. On the other hand, research based on self-reports, case studies, and naturalistic observation is often particularly useful for the formulation of hypotheses.

The reliability of data based on various kinds of self-reports depends on the candor of the participants providing the reports. Participants may be completely truthful in their reports. But reports involving recollected information (e.g., diaries, retrospective accounts, questionnaires, and surveys) are notably less reliable than reports provided during the cognitive processing under investigation. The reason is that participants sometimes forget what they did. In studying complex cognitive processes, such as problem solving or decision making, researchers often use a verbal protocol. In a *verbal protocol*, the participants describe aloud all of their thoughts and ideas during the performance of a given cognitive task (e.g., "I like the apartment with the swimming pool better, but I can't really afford it, so I might choose . . . .")

An alternative to a verbal protocol is for participants to report specific information regarding a particular aspect of their cognitive processing. Consider, for example, a study of insightful problem solving (see Chapter 11). Participants were asked at 15-second intervals to report numerical ratings indicating how close they felt they were to reaching a solution to a given problem. Unfortunately, even these methods of self-reporting have their limitations. As one example, cognitive processes may be altered by the act of giving the report (e.g., processes involving brief forms of memory; see Chapter 5). As another example, cognitive processes may occur outside of conscious awareness (e.g., processes that do not require conscious attention or that take place so rapidly that we fail to notice them; see Chapter 3). To get an idea of some of the difficulties with self-reports, carry out the following "Investigating Cognitive Psychology" tasks. Reflect on your experiences with self-reports.

INVESTIGATING COGNITIVE PSYCHOLOGY	1. Without looking at your shoes, try reporting aloud the various steps involved in tying your shoe. 2. Recall aloud what you did on your last birthday. 3. Now, actually tie your shoe (or something else, such as a string tied around a table leg), reporting aloud the steps you take. Do you notice any differences between Task 1 and Task 3? 4. Report aloud how you pulled into consciousness the steps involved in tying your shoe or your memories of your last birthday. Can you report exactly how you pulled the information into conscious awareness? Can you report which part of your brain was most active during each of these tasks?

Ask half of your friends individually one of the following series of questions and the other half the other series. Ask them to respond as quickly as they can:

Set 1:

What do silkworms weave?

What is a popular material for clothing that comes from silkworms?

What do cows drink?

Set 2:

What do bees make?

What grows in fields that is eventually made into material for clothing?

What do cows drink?

For many of your friends, when they get to question #3 in set 1, they will say "milk" when we all know that cows drink water. Most of your friends responding to set 2 will say "water" and not say "milk." You have just conducted an experiment. The experimental method divides people into two equal groups, changes one aspect between the two groups (in your case, you asked a series of questions before asking the critical question), then measures the difference between the two groups. The number of mistakes is what you are measuring, and it is likely that your friends in group 1 will make more mistakes than your friends in group 2.

Case studies (e.g., the study of exceptionally gifted individuals) and naturalistic observations (e.g., the observation of individuals operating in nuclear power plants) may be used to complement findings from laboratory experiments. The former two methods of cognitive research offer high **ecological validity,** the degree to which particular findings in one environmental context may be considered relevant outside of that context. As you probably know, *ecology* is the study of the interactive relationship between an organism (or organisms) and its environment. Many cognitive psychologists seek to understand the interactive relationship between human thought processes and the environments in which humans are thinking. Sometimes, cognitive processes that commonly are observed in one setting (e.g., in a laboratory) are not identical to those observed in another setting (e.g., in an air-traffic control tower or a classroom).

Computer Simulations and Artificial Intelligence

Digital computers played a fundamental role in the emergence of the study of cognitive psychology. One kind of influence is indirect—through models of human cognition based on models of how computers process information. Another kind is direct—through computer simulations and artificial intelligence.

In *computer simulations*, researchers program computers to imitate a given human function or process. Examples are performance on particular cognitive tasks (e.g., manipulating objects within three-dimensional space) and performance of particular cognitive processes (e.g., pattern recognition). Some researchers even have attempted to create computer models of the entire cognitive architecture of the human mind. Their models have stimulated heated discussions regarding how the human mind may function as a whole (see Chapter 8). Sometimes the distinction between simulation and artificial intelligence is blurred. An example would be certain programs that are designed to simulate human performance and to maximize functioning simultaneously.

Putting It All Together

Cognitive psychologists often broaden and deepen their understanding of cognition through research in cognitive science. **Cognitive science** is a cross-disciplinary field that uses ideas and methods from cognitive psychology, psychobiology, artificial intelligence, philosophy, linguistics, and anthropology (Nickerson, 2003; Von Eckardt, 2003). Cognitive scientists use these ideas and methods to focus on the study of how humans acquire and use knowledge. Cognitive psychologists also profit from collaborations with other kinds of psychologists. Examples are social psychologists (e.g., in the cross-disciplinary field of social cognition), psychologists who study motivation and emotion, and engineering psychologists (i.e., psychologists who study human-machine interactions).

Key Issues and Fields within Cognitive Psychology

Throughout this chapter, we have alluded to some of the key themes that arise in the study of cognitive psychology. Because these themes appear again and again in the various chapters of this textbook, a summary of these themes follows. Some of these questions go to the very core of the nature of the human mind.

Underlying Themes in the Study of Cognitive Psychology

If we review the major ideas in this chapter, we discover some of the major themes that underlie all of cognitive psychology. What are some of these themes? Here are seven of them:

1. *Nature versus nurture:* Which is more influential in human cognition—nature or nurture? If we believe that innate characteristics of human cognition are more important, we might focus our research on studying innate characteristics of cognition. If we believe that the environment plays an important role in cognition, we might conduct research exploring how distinctive characteristics of the environment seem to influence cognition. Today most scholars believe that nature and nurture interact in almost all we do.

2. *Rationalism versus empiricism:* How should we discover the truth about ourselves and about the world around us? Should we do so by trying to reason logically, based on what we already know? Or should we do so by observing and testing our observations of what we can perceive through our senses?

3. *Structures versus processes:* Should we study the structures (contents, attributes, and products) of the human mind? Or should we focus on the processes of human thinking?

4. *Domain generality versus domain specificity:* Are the processes we observe limited to single domains, or are they general across a variety of domains? Do observations in one domain apply also to all domains, or do they apply only to the specific domains observed?

5. *Validity of causal inferences versus ecological validity:* Should we study cognition by using highly controlled experiments that increase the probability of valid inferences regarding causality? Or should we use more naturalistic techniques, which increase the likelihood of obtaining ecologically valid findings but possibly at the expense of experimental control?

6. *Applied versus basic research:* Should we conduct research into fundamental cognitive processes? Or should we study ways in which to help people use cognition effectively in practical situations? Can the two kinds of research be combined dialectically, so that basic research leads to applied research, which leads to further basic research, and so on?

7. *Biological versus behavioral methods:* Should we study the brain and its functioning directly, perhaps even scanning the brain while people are performing cognitive tasks? Or should we study people's behavior in cognitive tasks, looking at measures such as percentage correct and reaction time?

Although many of these questions are posed in "either-or" form, remember that often a synthesis of views or methods proves more useful than one extreme position or another. For example, our nature may provide an inherited framework for our distinctive characteristics and patterns of thinking and acting. But our nurture may shape the specific ways in which we flesh out that framework. We may use empirical methods for gathering data and for testing hypotheses. But we may use rationalist methods for interpreting data, constructing theories, and formulating hypotheses based on theories. Our understanding of cognition deepens when we consider both basic research into fundamental cognitive processes and applied research regarding effective uses of cognition in real-world settings. Syntheses constantly are evolving. What today may be viewed as a synthesis may tomorrow be viewed as an extreme position or vice versa.

Key Ideas in Cognitive Psychology

Certain key ideas seem to keep emerging in cognitive psychology, regardless of the particular phenomenon one studies. Here are what might be considered five major ideas.

1. *Data in cognitive psychology can be fully understood only in the context of an explanatory theory, but theories are empty without empirical data.*

   Science is not merely a collection of empirically collected facts. Rather, it comprises such facts that are explained and organized by scientific theories. Theories give meaning to data. For example, suppose that we know that people's ability to recognize information that they have seen is better than their ability to recall such information. As an example, they are better at recognizing whether they heard a word said on a list than they are at recalling the word without the word's being given. This is an interesting empirical generalization. But science requires us not only to be able to make the generalization but also to understand why memory works this way. For one thing, an important goal of science is explanation. An empirical generalization does not, in the absence of an underlying theory, provide *explanation*. For another thing, theory helps us understand the limitations of empirical generalizations and when and why they occur. For example, a theory proposed by Tulving and Thomson (1973) suggested that, in fact, recognition should not always be better than recall. An important goal of science is also *prediction*. Tulving and Thomson's theory led them to predict the circumstances under which recall should be better than recognition. Subsequent data collection proved them to be right. Under some circumstances, recall is indeed better than recognition. Theory therefore suggested under which circumstances, among the many circumstances one might examine, limitations to the generalization should occur. Theory thus assists both in explanation and prediction.

   At the same time, theory without data is empty. Almost anyone can sit in an armchair and propose a theory—even a plausible sounding one. Science, however, requires empirical testing of such theories. Without such testing, theories remain merely speculative. Thus, theories and data depend on each other. Theories generate data collections, which help correct theories, which then lead to further data collections, and so forth. It is through this iteration of and interaction between theory and data that we increase scientific understanding.

2. *Cognition is generally adaptive but not in all specific instances.*

When we consider all the ways in which we can make mistakes, it is astonishing how well our cognitive systems operate. Evolution has served us well in shaping the development of a cognitive apparatus that is able accurately to decode environmental stimuli. It also can understand internal stimuli that make the most of the information available to us. We can perceive, learn, remember, reason, and solve problems with great accuracy. And we do so even though we constantly are barraged by a plethora of stimuli. Any of the stimuli easily could distract us from processing information properly. The same processes, however, that lead us to perceive, remember, and reason accurately in most situations also can lead us astray. Our memories and reasoning processes, for example, are susceptible to certain well-identified, systematic errors. For example, we tend to overvalue information that is easily available to us. We do this even when this information is not optimally relevant to the problem at hand. In general, all systems—natural or artificial—are based on tradeoffs. The same characteristics that make them highly efficient in a large variety of circumstances can render them inefficient in specialized circumstances. A system that would be extremely efficient in each specialized circumstance would be inefficient across a wide variety of circumstances simply because it would become too cumbersome and complex. Humans thus represent a highly efficient, but imperfect, adaptation to the environments they face.

3. *Cognitive processes interact with each other and with noncognitive processes.*

Although cognitive psychologists try to study and often to isolate the functioning of specific cognitive processes, they know that these processes work together. For example, memory processes depend on perceptual processes. What you remember depends in part on what you perceive. Similarly, thinking processes depend in part on memory processes: You cannot reflect on what you do not remember. But noncognitive processes also interact with cognitive ones. For example, you learn better when you are motivated to learn. However, your learning likely will be reduced if you are upset about something and cannot concentrate on the learning task at hand. Cognitive psychologists therefore seek to study cognitive processes not only in isolation but also in their interactions with each other and with noncognitive processes.

One of the most exciting areas of cognitive psychology today is at the interface between cognitive and biological levels of analysis. In recent years, for example, it has become possible to localize activity in the brain associated with various kinds of cognitive processes. One has to be careful about assuming that the biological activity is causal of the cognitive activity, however. Research shows that learning that causes changes in the brain—in other words, cognitive processes—can affect biological structures just as biological structures can affect cognitive processes. So the interactions between cognition and other processes occur at many levels. The cognitive system does not operate in isolation. It works in interaction with other systems.

4. *Cognition needs to be studied through a variety of scientific methods.*

There is no one right way to study cognition. Naïve researchers sometimes seek the "best" method by which to study cognition. Their search inevitably will be in vain. All cognitive processes need to be studied through a variety of converging operations. That is, varied methods of study seek a common understanding. The more different kinds of techniques that lead to the same conclusion, the higher the confidence one can have in that conclusion. For example, suppose studies of reaction times, error rates, and patterns of individual differences all lead to the same conclusion. Then one can have much more confidence in the conclusion than if only one method led to that conclusion.

Cognitive psychologists need to learn a variety of different kinds of techniques to do their job well. All these methods, however, must be *scientific.* Scientific methods differ from other methods in that they provide the basis for the self-correcting nature of science. Eventually we correct our errors. The reason is that scientific methods enable us to disconfirm our expectations when those expectations are wrong. Nonscientific methods do not have this feature. For example, methods of inquiry that simply rely on faith or authority to determine truth may have value in our lives. But they are not scientific and hence are not self-correcting. Indeed, the words of one authority may be replaced by the words of another authority tomorrow without anything new being learned about the phenomenon to which the words apply. As the world learned long ago, important dignitaries stating that the Earth is at the center of the universe do not make it so.

5. *All basic research in cognitive psychology may lead to applications, and all applied research may lead to basic understandings.*

Politicians and sometimes even scientists like to draw tidy distinctions between basic and applied research. But the truth is, the distinction often is not clear at all. Research that seems like it will be basic often leads to immediate applications. Similarly, research that seems like it will be applied sometimes leads quickly to basic understandings, whether or not there are immediate applications. For example, a basic finding from research on learning and memory is that learning is superior when it is spaced out over time rather than crammed into a short time interval. This basic finding has an immediate application to study strategies. At the same time, research on eyewitness testimony, which seems on its face to be very applied, has enhanced our basic understanding of memory systems and of the extent to which humans construct their own memories. It does not merely reproduce what happens in the environment.

Before closing this chapter, think about some of the fields of cognitive psychology, described in the remaining chapters, to which these key themes and issues may apply.

Chapter Previews

Cognitive psychologists have been involved in studying a wide range of psychological phenomena. This range includes not only perception, learning, memory, and thinking but also seemingly less cognitively oriented phenomena, such as emotion and motivation. In fact, almost any topic of psychological interest may be studied from a cognitive perspective. Nonetheless, there are some main areas of interest to cognitive psychologists. In this textbook we attempt to describe some of the preliminary answers to questions asked by researchers in the main areas of interest.

Chapter 2 *Cognitive Neuroscience*—What are the structures and processes of the human brain that underlie the structures and processes of human cognition?

Chapter 3 *Attention and Consciousness*—What are the basic processes of the mind that govern how information enters our minds, our awareness, and our high-level processes of information handling?

Chapter 4 *Perception*—How does the human mind perceive what the senses receive? How does the human mind distinctively achieve the perception of forms and patterns?

Chapter 5 *Memory: Models and Research Methods*—How are different kinds of information (e.g., our experiences related to a traumatic event, the names of U.S. presidents, or the procedure for riding a bicycle) represented in memory?

Chapter 6 *Memory Processes*—How do we move information into memory, keep it there, and retrieve it from memory when needed?

Chapter 7 *Representation and Manipulation of Knowledge in Memory: Images and Propositions*—How do we mentally represent information in our minds? Do we do so in words, in pictures, or in some other form for representing meaning? Alternatively, do we have multiple forms of representation?

Chapter 8 *Representation and Organization of Knowledge in Memory:* Concepts, Categories, Networks, and Schemas—How do we mentally organize what we know? How do we manipulate and operate on knowledge—do we do so serially, through parallel processing, or through some combination of processes?

Chapter 9 *Language: Nature and Acquisition*—How do we derive and produce meaning through language? How do we acquire language—both our primary language and any additional languages?

Chapter 10 *Language in Context*—How does our use of language interact with our ways of thinking? How does our social world interact with our use of language?

Chapter 11 *Problem Solving and Creativity*—How do we solve problems? What processes aid and impede us in reaching solutions to problems? Why are some of us more creative than others? How do we become and remain creative?

Chapter 12 *Decision Making and Reasoning*—How do we reach important decisions? How do we draw reasonable conclusions from the information we have available? Why and how do we so often make inappropriate decisions and reach inaccurate conclusions?

Chapter 13 *Human and Artificial Intelligence*—Why do we consider some people more intelligent than others? Why do some people seem better able to accomplish whatever they want to accomplish in their chosen fields of endeavor?

In this book I have tried to emphasize the underlying, common ideas and organizing themes across various aspects of cognitive psychology, rather than simply to state the facts. I have followed this path to help you perceive large, meaningful patterns within the domain of cognitive psychology. I also have tried to give you some idea of how cognitive psychologists think and how they structure their field in their day-to-day work. I hope that this approach will help you to contemplate problems in cognitive psychology at a deeper level than might otherwise be possible. Ultimately, the goal of cognitive psychologists is to understand not only how people may think in their laboratories, but also, to understand how they think in their everyday lives.

Summary

1. **What is cognitive psychology?** Cognitive psychology is the study of how people perceive, learn, remember, and think about information.

2. **How did psychology develop as a science?** Beginning with Plato and Aristotle, people have contemplated how to gain understanding of the truth. Plato held that rationalism offers the clear path to truth, whereas Aristotle espoused empiricism as the route to knowledge. Centuries later, Descartes extended Plato's rationalism, whereas Locke elaborated on Aristotle's empiricism. Kant offered a synthesis of these apparent opposites. Decades after Kant proposed his synthesis, Hegel observed how the history of ideas seems to progress through a *dialectical* process.

3. **How did cognitive psychology develop from psychology?** By the twentieth century, psychology had emerged as a distinct field of study. Wundt focused on the structures of the mind (leading to *structuralism*), whereas James and Dewey focused on the processes of the mind (*functionalism*). Emerging from this dialectic was *associationism*, espoused by Ebbinghaus and Thorndike. It paved the way for behaviorism by underscoring the importance of mental associations. Another step toward behaviorism was Pavlov's discovery of the principles of classical conditioning. Watson and later Skinner were the chief proponents of *behaviorism*. It focused entirely on observable links between an organism's behavior and particular environmental contingencies that strengthen or weaken the likelihood that particular behaviors will be repeated. Most behaviorists dismissed entirely the notion that there is merit in psychologists' trying to understand what is going on in the mind of the individual engaging in the behavior. However, Tolman and subsequent behaviorist researchers noted the role of cognitive processes in influencing behavior. A convergence of developments across many fields led to the emergence of *cognitive psychology* as a discrete discipline, spearheaded by such notables as Neisser.

4. **How have other disciplines contributed to the development of theory and research in cognitive psychology?** Cognitive psychology has roots in philosophy and physiology. They merged to form

the mainstream of psychology. As a discrete field of psychological study, cognitive psychology also profited from cross-disciplinary investigations. Relevant fields include linguistics (e.g., How do language and thought interact?), biological psychology (e.g., What are the physiological bases for cognition?), anthropology (e.g., What is the importance of the cultural context for cognition?), and technological advances like artificial intelligence (e.g., How do computers process information?).

5. **What methods do cognitive psychologists use to study how people think?** Cognitive psychologists use a broad range of methods, including experiments, psychobiological techniques, self-reports, case studies, naturalistic observation, and computer simulations and artificial intelligence.

6. **What are the current issues and various fields of study within cognitive psychology?** Some of the major issues in the field have centered on how to pursue knowledge. Psychological work can be done

- by using both *rationalism* (which is the basis for theory development) and *empiricism* (which is the basis for gathering data); by underscoring

the importance of cognitive structures and of cognitive processes;

- by emphasizing the study of domain-general and of domain-specific processing;

- by striving for a high degree of experimental control (which better permits causal inferences) and for a high degree of *ecological validity* (which better allows generalization of findings to settings outside of the laboratory);

- by conducting basic research seeking fundamental insights about cognition and applied research seeking effective uses of cognition in real-world settings.

Although positions on these issues may appear to be diametrical opposites, often apparently antithetical views may be synthesized into a form that offers the best of each of the opposing viewpoints.

Cognitive psychologists study biological bases of cognition as well as attention, consciousness, perception, memory, mental imagery, language, problem solving, creativity, decision making, reasoning, developmental changes in cognition across the life span, human intelligence, artificial intelligence, and various other aspects of human thinking.

Thinking about Thinking: Factual, Analytical, Creative, and Practical Questions

1. Describe the major historical schools of psychological thought leading up to the development of cognitive psychology.

2. Describe some of the ways in which philosophy, linguistics, and artificial intelligence have contributed to the development of cognitive psychology.

3. Compare and contrast the influences of Plato and Aristotle on psychology.

4. Analyze how various research methods in cognitive psychology reflect empiricist and rationalist approaches to gaining knowledge.

5. Design a rough sketch of a cognitive-psychological investigation involving one of the research

methods described in this chapter. Highlight both the advantages and the disadvantages of using this particular method for your investigation.

6. This chapter describes cognitive psychology as the field is now. How might you speculate that the field will change in the next 50 years?

7. How might an insight gained from basic research lead to practical uses in an everyday setting?

8. How might an insight gained from applied research lead to deepened understanding of fundamental features of cognition?

Key Terms

artificial intelligence (AI)
associationism
behaviorism
cognitive psychology
cognitive science
cognitivism

ecological validity
empiricist
functionalism
Gestalt psychology
hypotheses
introspection

pragmatists
rationalist
statistical significance
structuralism
theory

Annotated Suggested Readings

Nadel, L. (Ed.) (2003). *Encyclopedia of cognitive science* (4 vols.). London, England: Nature Publishing Group. A detailed analysis of topics in the full range of cognitive sciences. Entries are graded for difficulty.

Wilson, R. A., & Keil, F. C. (Eds.) (1999). *The MIT encyclopedia of cognitive sciences*. Cambridge, MA: MIT Press. Entries on the full range of topics that constitute the study of cognitive science.

Cognitive Neuroscience

EXPLORING COGNITIVE PSYCHOLOGY

1. What are the fundamental structures and processes of the cells within the brain?

2. How do researchers study the major structures and processes of the brain?

3. What have researchers found as a result of studying the brain?

An ancient legend from India (Rosenzweig & Leiman, 1989) tells of Sita. She marries one man but is attracted to another. These two frustrated men behead themselves. Sita, bereft of them both, desperately prays to the goddess Kali to bring the men back to life. Sita is granted her wish. She is allowed to reattach the heads to the bodies. In her rush to bring the two men back to life, Sita mistakenly switches their heads. She attaches them to the wrong bodies. Now, to whom is she married? Who is who?

The mind-body issue has long interested philosophers and scientists. Where is the mind located in the body, if at all? How do the mind and body interact? How are we able to think, speak, plan, reason, learn, and remember? What are the physical bases for our cognitive abilities? These questions all probe the relationship between cognitive psychology and neurobiology. Some cognitive psychologists seek to answer such questions by studying the biological bases of cognition. Cognitive psychologists are especially concerned with how the anatomy (physical structures of the body) and the physiology (functions and processes of the body) of the nervous system affect and are affected by human cognition.

Cognitive neuroscience is the field of study linking the brain and other aspects of the nervous system, and especially the brain, to cognitive processing and, ultimately, to behavior. The **brain** is the organ in our bodies that most directly controls our thoughts, emotions, and motivations (Gloor, 1997; Rockland, 2000; Shepherd, 1998). We usually think of the brain as being at the top of the body's hierarchy—as the boss, with various other organs responding to it. Like any good boss, however, it listens to and is influenced by its subordinates, the other organs of the body. Thus, the brain is reactive as well as directive.

A major goal of present work on the brain is to study localization of function. **Localization of function** refers to the specific areas of the brain that control specific skills or behaviors. Before we focus on the brain, however, we will consider how it fits into the overall organization of the nervous system.

The Brain

The **nervous system** is the basis for our ability to perceive, adapt to, and interact with the world around us (Gazzaniga, 1995, 2000; Gazzaniga, Ivry, & Mangun, 1998). Through this system we receive, process, and then respond to information from the environment (Pinker, 1997; Rugg, 1997).

Viewing the Structures and Functions of the Brain

Scientists can use many methods for studying the human brain. These methods include both postmortem (from Latin, "after death") studies and *in vivo* (from Latin, "living") techniques on both humans and animals. Each technique provides important information about the structure and function of the human brain. Even some of the earliest postmortem studies still influence our thinking about how the brain performs certain functions. However, the recent trend is to focus on techniques that provide information about human mental functioning as it is occurring. This trend is in contrast to the earlier trend of waiting to find people with disorders and then studying their brains after they died. Because postmortem studies are the foundation for later work, we discuss them first before moving on to the more modern *in vivo* techniques.

Postmortem Studies

For centuries investigators have been able to dissect a brain after a person has died. Even today dissection often is used for studying the relation between the brain and behavior. Researchers look carefully at the behavior of people who show signs of brain damage while they are alive (Wilson, 2003). The researchers document behavior in these case studies of patients as thoroughly as possible (Fawcett, Rosser, & Dunnett, 2001). Later, after the patients die, the researchers examine the patients' brains for *lesions*—areas where body tissue has been damaged, such as from injury or disease. Then the researchers infer that the lesioned locations may be related to the behavior that was affected.

In this way, researchers may trace a link between an observed type of behavior and anomalies in a particular location in the brain. An early example is Paul Broca's (1824–1880) famous patient, Tan (so named because that was the only syllable he was capable of uttering). Tan had severe speech problems. These problems were linked to lesions in an area of the frontal lobe now called *Broca's area*. This area is involved in certain functions of speech production. In more recent times, postmortem examinations of victims of Alzheimer's disease (an illness that causes devastating losses of memory; see Chapter 5) have led researchers to identify some of the brain structures involved in memory (e.g., the hippocampus, described in a subsequent subsection of this chapter). These examinations also have identified some of the microscopic aberrations associated with the disease process (e.g., distinctive tangled fibers in the brain tissue). Although lesioning techniques provide the basic foundation for understanding the relation of the brain to behavior, they are limited in that they cannot be performed on the living brain. As a result, they do not offer insights into more specific physiological processes of the brain. For this kind of information, we need *in vivo* techniques such as, but not limited to, those described next.

Animal Studies

Scientists also want to understand the physiological processes and functions of the living brain. To study the changing activity of the living brain, scientists must use *in vivo* research. Many early *in vivo* techniques were performed exclusively on animals.

For example, Nobel Prize–winning research on visual perception arose from *in vivo* studies investigating the electrical activity of individual cells in particular regions of the brains of animals (Hubel & Wiesel, 1963, 1968, 1979; see Chapter 4).

In these kinds of studies, microelectrodes are inserted into the brain of an animal (usually a monkey or cat). They obtain single-cell recordings of the activity of a single neuron in the brain. In this way, scientists can measure the effects of certain kinds of stimuli, such as visually presented lines, on the activity of individual neurons. Other animal studies include selective lesioning—surgically removing or damaging part of the brain—to observe resulting functional deficits. Obviously, these techniques cannot be used on human participants. Moreover, we cannot simultaneously record the activity of every neuron. Generalizations based on these studies are somewhat limited. Therefore an array of less invasive imaging techniques for use with humans has been developed. These techniques are described in the following section.

Electrical Recordings

Researchers and practitioners (e.g., psychologists and physicians) often record electrical activity in the brain. This activity appears as waves of various widths (frequencies) and heights (intensities). **Electroencephalograms (EEGs)** are recordings of the electrical frequencies and intensities of the living brain, typically recorded over relatively long periods (Picton & Mazaheri, 2003). Through EEGs, it is possible to study brain-wave activity indicative of changing mental states such as deep sleep or dreaming. To obtain EEG recordings, electrodes are placed at various places along the surface of the scalp. The electrical activity of underlying brain areas is then recorded. Therefore, the information is not well-localized to specific cells. Rather, it is very sensitive to changes over time. For example, EEG recordings taken during sleep reveal changing patterns of electrical activity involving the whole brain. Different patterns emerge during dreaming versus deep sleep.

To relate electrical activity to a particular event or task (e.g., seeing a flash of light or listening to sentences), EEG waves can be averaged over a large number (e.g., 100) of trials to reveal event-related potentials (ERPs). They provide very good information about the time-course of task-related brain activity by averaging out activity that is not task related. The resulting wave forms show characteristic spikes related to the timing of electrical activity. But they reveal only very general information about the location of that activity (because of low spatial resolution, limited by the placement of scalp electrodes). The ERP technique has been used in a wide variety of studies. For example, some studies of intelligence have attempted to relate particular characteristics of ERPs to scores on intelligence tests (e.g., Caryl, 1994). Furthermore, the high degree of temporal resolution afforded by ERPs can be used to complement other techniques. For example, Posner and Raichle (1994) used both ERPs and positron emission tomography (PET; discussed next) to pinpoint areas involved in word association. Using ERPs, they found that participants showed increased activity in certain parts of the brain (left lateral frontal cortex, left posterior cortex, and right insular cortex) when they made rapid associations to given words. As with any technique, EEGs and ERPs provide only a glimpse of brain activity. They are most helpful when used in conjunction with other techniques to converge on particular brain areas involved in cognition.

Static Imaging Techniques

Psychologists also use various techniques for obtaining still images revealing the structures of the brain (Buckner, 2000; Posner & Raichle, 1994; Rosen, Buckner, & Dale, 1998) (Figure 2.1). These techniques include angiograms, computerized axial tomography (CAT) scans, and magnetic resonance imaging (MRI) scans. The X-ray–based techniques (angiogram and CAT scan) allow for the observation of large abnormalities of the brain, such as damage resulting from strokes or tumors. However, they are limited in their resolution and cannot provide much information about smaller lesions and aberrations.

Probably the still-image technique of greatest interest to cognitive psychologists is the **MRI** scan, a technique for revealing high-resolution images of the structure of the living brain by computing and analyzing magnetic changes in the energy of the orbits of nuclear particles in the molecules of the body. It facilitates the detection of lesions *in vivo*, such as lesions associated with particular disorders of language use. In MRI, a strong magnetic field is passed through the brain of a patient. A rotating scanner detects various patterns of electromagnetic changes in the molecules of the brain (Malonek & Grinvald, 1996; Ugurbil, 1999). These molecular changes are analyzed by a computer to produce a three-dimensional picture of the brain. This picture includes detailed information about brain structures. The MRI technique is relatively expensive, however. Moreover, it does not provide much information about physiological processes (Figure 2.2). The final two techniques, discussed in the following section, do provide such information.

Metabolic Imaging

Metabolic imaging techniques rely on changes that take place within the brain as a result of increased consumption of glucose and oxygen in active areas of the brain. The basic idea is that active areas in the brain consume more glucose and oxygen than do inactive areas during some tasks. An area specifically required by one task ought to be more active during that task than during more generalized processing. Scientists attempt to pinpoint specialized areas for a task by using the subtraction method. This method involves subtracting activity during a more general task from activity during the task of interest. The resulting activity then is analyzed statistically. This analysis determines which areas are responsible for performance of a particular task above and beyond the more general activity. For example, suppose the experimenter wishes to determine which area of the brain is most important for something like retrieval of word meanings. The experimenter would have to subtract activity during a task involving reading of words from activity during a task involving the physical recognition of the letters of words. The difference in activity would be presumed to reflect retrieval of meaning. There is one important caveat to remember about these techniques, however. It is that scientists have no way of determining whether the net effect of this activity is excitatory or inhibitory (because some neurons are inhibited by other neurons' neurotransmitters). Therefore, the subtraction technique reveals net brain activity for particular areas. It cannot show whether the area's effect is positive or negative. Moreover, the method assumes that activation is purely additive—that it can be discovered through a subtraction method. This description greatly oversimplifies the subtraction method. But it shows at a general level

FIGURE 2.1

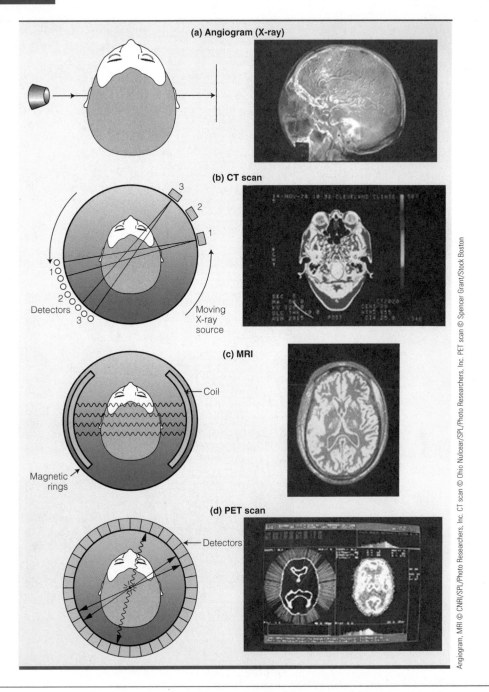

Various techniques have been developed to picture the structures—and sometimes the processes—of the brain. (a) A brain angiogram highlights the blood vessels of the brain. (b) A CAT image of a brain uses a series of rotating scans (one of which is pictured here) to produce a three-dimensional view of brain structures. (c) A rotating series of MRI scans (one of which is pictured here) shows a clearer three-dimensional picture of brain structures than CAT scans show. (d) These still photographs of PET scans of a brain show different metabolic processes during different activities. PET scans permit the study of brain physiology.

FIGURE 2.2

Hoa Qui/Index Stock Imagery

Photodisc/PictureQuest

An MRI machine can provide data that show what areas of the brain are involved in different kinds of cognitive processing.

how scientists determine physiological functioning of particular areas using the imaging techniques described next.

PET scans measure increases in glucose consumption in active brain areas during particular kinds of information processing (Buckner & associates, 1996; Raichle,

1998, 1999). To track their use of glucose, participants are given a mildly radioactive form of glucose that emits positrons as it is metabolized. (Positrons are particles that have roughly the same size and mass as electrons, but that are positively rather than negatively charged.) Next, the brain is scanned to detect positrons. A computer analyzes the data to produce images of the physiological functioning of the brain in action. For example, PET scans have been used to show that blood flow increases to the occipital lobe of the brain during visual processing (Posner & associates, 1988). PET scans also have been used for comparatively studying the brains of people who score high versus low on intelligence tests. When high-scoring people are engaged in cognitively demanding tasks, their brains seem to use glucose more efficiently, in highly task-specific areas of the brain. The brains of people with lower scores appear to use glucose more diffusely, across larger regions of the brain (Haier & associates, 1992; see Chapter 13).

The latest technique, **functional magnetic resonance imaging (fMRI),** is a neuroimaging techinque that uses magnetic fields to construct a detailed representation in three dimensions of levels of activity in various parts of the brain at a given moment in time. This technique builds on MRI (discussed earlier), but it uses increases in oxygen consumption to construct images of brain activity. The basic idea is the same as in PET scans. The fMRI technique does not require the use of radioactive particles. Rather, the participant performs a task while placed inside an MRI machine. This machine creates a magnetic field that induces changes in the particles of oxygen atoms. More active areas draw more oxygenated blood than do less active areas in the brain. The differences in the amounts of oxygen consumed form the basis for fMRI measurements. These measurements then are computer analyzed to provide the most precise information currently available about the physiological functioning of the brain's activity during task performance. This technique is less invasive than PET. It also has higher temporal resolution—measurements can be taken for activity lasting fractions of a second, rather than only for activity lasting minutes to hours. One major drawback, however, is the expense and novelty of fMRI. Relatively few researchers have access to the required machinery. Moreover, testing of participants is very time consuming. See Figure 2.3 for a direct comparison of various brain imaging techniques in terms of spatial and temporal resolution.

The fMRI technique has been used to identify regions of the brain active in many areas, such as vision (Engel & associates, 1994), attention (Cohen & associates, 1994), and memory (Gabrieli & associates, 1996). For example, fMRI has been used to show that the lateral prefrontal cortex is essential for working memory. This is a part of memory that is used to process information that is actively in use at a given time (McCarthy & associates, 1994).

Current techniques still do not provide unambiguous mappings of particular functions to particular brain structures, regions, or even processes. Rather, we have found that some discrete structures, regions, or processes of the brain appear to be involved in particular cognitive functions. Our current understanding of how particular cognitive functions are linked to particular brain structures or processes allows us only to infer suggestive indications of some kind of relationship. Through sophisticated analyses, we can infer increasingly precise relationships. But we are not yet at a point where we can determine the specific cause–effect relationship between a given brain structure or process and a particular cognitive function. Particular functions may be influenced by multiple structures, regions, or processes of the brain. Finally,

FIGURE 2.3

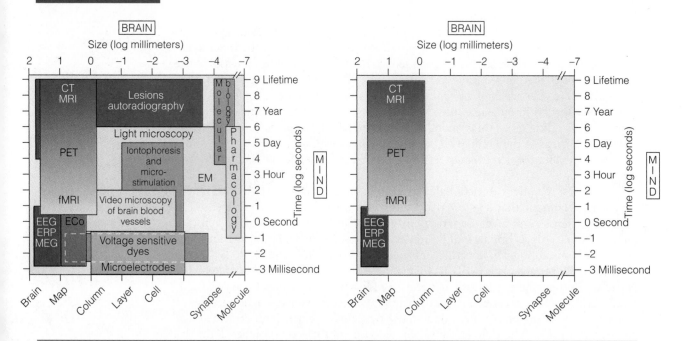

We can view the brain at various levels of spatial resolution ranging from a molecule to the whole brain itself, whereas we can envision the mind as events occurring over times as brief as a few milliseconds—the time it takes one neuron to communicate with another—or as long as a lifetime. Over the past decade or two, scientists have developed a remarkable array of techniques capable of addressing the relationship between brain and mind. Here we graphically summarize the potential contribution of these various techniques to an understanding of this relationship by plotting, logarithmically, the brain on the horizontal axis and the mind on the vertical axis. The techniques then are positioned according to their spatial and temporal precision. Into the left graph we have placed all of the available techniques, including X-ray CAT, MRI, PET, EEG, ERP, electrocorticography (ECo; EEGs recorded from the brain surface at surgery), and electron microscopy (EM). In the right graph we have eliminated all of the techniques that cannot be applied to human subjects. Although the study of the mind-brain relationship in humans clearly will depend on brain-imaging techniques like MRI, PET, and CT in conjunction with electrical techniques, our ultimate understanding of that relationship will require the integration of information from all levels of inquiry. From Images of Mind by Posner and Raichle © 1994, 1997 by Scientific American Library Books. Used with permission of W. H. Freeman and Company.

these techniques provide the best information only in conjunction with other experimental techniques for understanding the complexities of cognitive functioning.

Cognition in the Brain: Cerebral Cortex and Other Structures

So far, we have discussed how scientists determine the structure and function of the brain using various postmortem and *in vivo* techniques. Now we discuss what scientists have discovered about the supreme organ of the nervous system, the human brain. The brain can be viewed as being divided into three major regions: forebrain,

FIGURE 2.4

What does a brain actually look like? Here you can see side and top views of a human brain. Subsequent figures and schematic pictures (i.e., simplified diagrams) point out in more detail some of the main features of the brain.

midbrain, and hindbrain (Figure 2.4 and Table 2.1). These labels do not correspond exactly to locations of regions in an adult's or even a child's head. Rather, the terms come from the front-to-back physical arrangement of these parts in the nervous system of a developing embryo. Initially, the *forebrain* is generally the farthest forward, toward what becomes the face. The *midbrain* is next in line. And the *hindbrain* is generally farthest from the forebrain, near the back of the neck (Figure 2.5[a]). In development, the relative orientations change, so that the forebrain is almost a cap on top of the midbrain and hindbrain. Nonetheless, the terms still are used to designate areas of the fully developed brain. Figure 2.5 (b and c) shows the changing locations and relationships of the forebrain, the midbrain, and the hindbrain over the course of development of the brain. You can see how they develop, from an embryo a few weeks after conception to a fetus of 7 months of age.

Gross Anatomy of the Brain: Forebrain, Midbrain, Hindbrain

Forebrain
The forebrain is the region of the brain located toward the top and front of the brain (Figure 2.6). It comprises the cerebral cortex, the basal ganglia, the limbic system, the thalamus, and the hypothalamus. The cerebral cortex is the outer layer of the cerebral hemispheres. It plays a vital role in our thinking and other mental processes. It therefore merits a special section. This section follows the present discussion of the major structures and functions of the brain. The basal ganglia (singular, ganglion) are collections of neurons crucial to motor function. Dysfunction of the basal ganglia can

TABLE 2.1	Major Structures and Functions of the Brain

The forebrain, midbrain, and hindbrain contain structures that perform essential functions for survival, as well as for high-level thinking and feeling.

REGION OF THE BRAIN	MAJOR STRUCTURES WITHIN THE REGIONS	FUNCTIONS OF THE STRUCTURES
Forebrain	**Cerebral cortex** (outer layer of the cerebral hemispheres)	Involved in receiving and processing sensory information, thinking, other cognitive processing, and planning and sending motor information
	Basal ganglia (collections of nuclei and neural fibers)	Crucial to the function of the motor system
	Limbic systems (hippocampus, amygdala, and septum)	Involved in learning, emotions, and motivation (in particular, the hippocampus influences learning and memory, the amygdala influences anger and aggression, and the septum influences anger and fear)
	Thalamus	Primary relay station for sensory information coming into the brain; transmits information to the correct regions of the cerebral cortex through projection fibers that extend from the thalamus to specific regions of the cortex; comprises several nuclei (groups of neurons) that receive specific kinds of sensory information and project that information to specific regions of the cerebral cortex, including four key nuclei for sensory information: (1) from the visual receptors, via optic nerves, to the visual cortex, permitting us to see; (2) from the auditory receptors, via auditory nerves, to the auditory cortex, permitting us to hear; (3) from sensory receptors in the somatic nervous system, to the primary somatosensory cortex, permitting us to sense pressure and pain; and (4) from the cerebellum (in the hindbrain) to the primary motor cortex, permitting us to sense physical balance and equilibrium

result in motor deficits. These deficits include tremors, involuntary movements, changes in posture and muscle tone, and slowness of movement. Deficits are observed in Parkinson's disease and Huntington's disease. Both of these diseases entail severe motor symptoms (Rockland, 2000; Shepherd, 1998).

The **limbic system** is important to emotion, motivation, memory, and learning. Animals such as fish and reptiles, which have relatively undeveloped limbic systems, respond to the environment almost exclusively by instinct. Mammals and especially humans have

TABLE 2.1	Major Structures and Functions of the Brain (cont.)	
REGION OF THE BRAIN	**MAJOR STRUCTURES WITHIN THE REGIONS**	**FUNCTIONS OF THE STRUCTURES**
	Hypothalamus	Controls the endocrine system; controls the autonomic nervous system, such as internal temperature regulation, appetite and thirst regulation, and other key functions; involved in regulation of behavior related to species survival (in particular, fighting, feeding, fleeing, and mating); plays a role in controlling consciousness (see reticular activating system); involved in emotions, pleasure, pain, and stress reactions
Midbrain	*Superior colliculi* (on top)	Involved in vision (especially visual reflexes)
	Inferior colliculi (below)	Involved in hearing
	Reticular activating system (RAS; also extends into the hindbrain)	Important in controlling consciousness (sleep arousal), attention, cardiorespiratory function, and movement
	Gray matter, red nucelus, substantia nigra, ventral region	Important in controlling movement
Hindbrain	*Cerebellum*	Essential to balance, coordination, and muscle tone
	Pons (also contains part of the RAS)	Involved in consciousness (sleep and arousal); bridges neural transmissions from one part of the brain to another; involved with facial nerves
	Medulla oblongata	Serves as juncture at which nerves cross from one side of the body to opposite side of the brain; involved in cardiorespiratory function, digestion, and swallowing

relatively more developed limbic systems. They seem to allow us to suppress instinctive responses (e.g., the impulse to strike someone who accidentally causes us pain). Our limbic systems make us better able to adapt our behaviors flexibly in response to our changing environment. The limbic system comprises three central interconnected cerebral structures. They are the amygdala, the septum, and the hippocampus.

The **amygdala** plays a role an important role in emotion, especially in anger and aggression (Adolphs, 2003). The **septum** is involved in anger and fear. Stimulation of

FIGURE 2.5

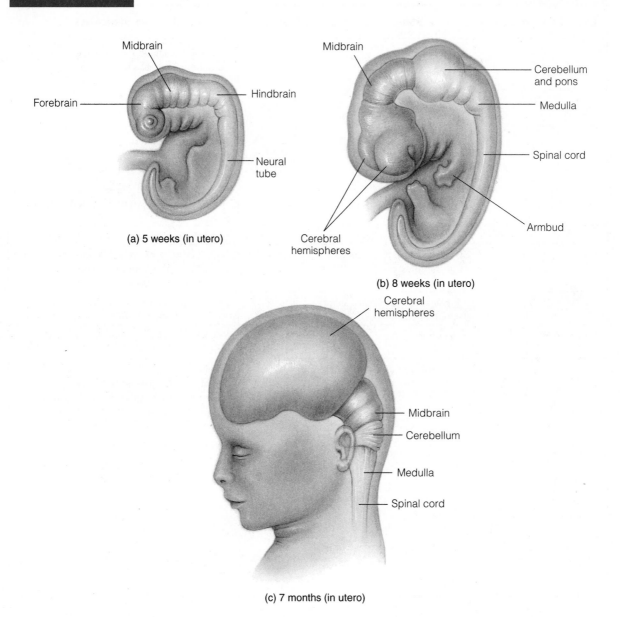

(a) 5 weeks (in utero)

(b) 8 weeks (in utero)

(c) 7 months (in utero)

Over the course of embryonic and fetal development, the brain becomes more highly specialized and the locations and relative positions of the hindbrain, the midbrain, and the forebrain change from conception to term. From In Search of the Human Mind by Robert J. Stern-berg, copyright © 1995 by Harcourt Brace & Company, reproduced by permission of the publisher.

IN THE LAB OF JOHN GABRIELI

Courtesy of Dr. John Gabrieli

Everything we know is either in our genes or learned through experience. Only some experiences, however, are remembered. We quickly forget a great deal of our lives. Selection of what we remember and what we forget is, therefore, important for who we become, what we believe in, and what we are good at. The memories we keep from the past shape our futures.

How does our brain let us selectively remember experiences? I became fascinated with this question when, as a graduate student, I had the opportunity to perform research with perhaps the most famous neuropsychological patient of the twentieth century, H.M. Due to surgery in 1953 intended to treat his epilepsy, H.M. became a globally amnesic patient who could not remember any new events or facts. After a few seconds, he forgot all his new experiences, including materials encountered in laboratory experiments, the most famous public events, and the most important of personal events such as the deaths of his parents.

H.M.'s surgery involved removal of a number of structures located in the medial, or inner, aspects of the temporal lobes. From his case, it was difficult to know what roles these different structures played in normal memory and whether they played a critical role in the initial recording (encoding) of memories (as opposed to retaining or later retrieving those memories). With noninvasive imaging of brain activity via functional magnetic resonance imaging we could examine these issues in the normal human brain.

During the imaging session of normal human brains, people saw pictures of indoor or outdoor scenes while we recorded their brain response to each scene. Next, they received an unexpected memory test with scenes from the brain-scanning session and new scenes. Sometimes they correctly recognized a previously presented scene (a remembered experience), but other times they failed to recognize a scene previously viewed (a forgotten experience). The level of brain activity in the parahippocampal cortex, one particular area in the medial temporal lobe, as a person saw each scene predicted whether they would later remember or forget that scene. Thus, we could visualize brain activity in a specific brain structure that determined whether current experience was fated to be well remembered in the future or doomed to be forgotten in a few moments. In a way, we could see the birth of a memory and the selective recording of experiences destined to be remembered and influence future behavior.

the amygdala commonly results in fear. It can be evidenced in various ways, such as through palpitations, fearful hallucinations, or frightening flashbacks in memory (Frackowiak & associates, 1997; Gloor, 1997; Rockland, 2000). Damage to (lesions) or removal of the amygdala can result in maladaptive lack of fear. The animal approaches potentially dangerous objects without hesitation or fear (Adolphs & associates, 1994; Frackowiak & associates, 1997). Two other effects of lesions to the amygdala can be visual agnosia (inability to recognize objects) and hypersexuality (Stefannaci, 1999).

The **hippocampus** plays an essential role in memory formation (Cohen & Eichenbaum, 1993; Dusek & Eichenbaum, 1997; Eichenbaum, 1999; Gluck, 1996; O'Keefe, 2003). It gets its name from the Greek word for "seahorse," its approximate shape. People who have suffered damage to or removal of the hippocampus still can recall existing memories. For example, they can recognize old friends and places, but they are unable to form new ones (relative to the time of the brain damage). New information—new situations, people, and places—remain forever new. **Korsakoff's syndrome** produces loss of memory function. This loss is believed to be associated with deterioration of the hippocampus. The syndrome can result from excessive alcohol use. The hippocampus also appears to keep track of where things are and how

FIGURE 2.6

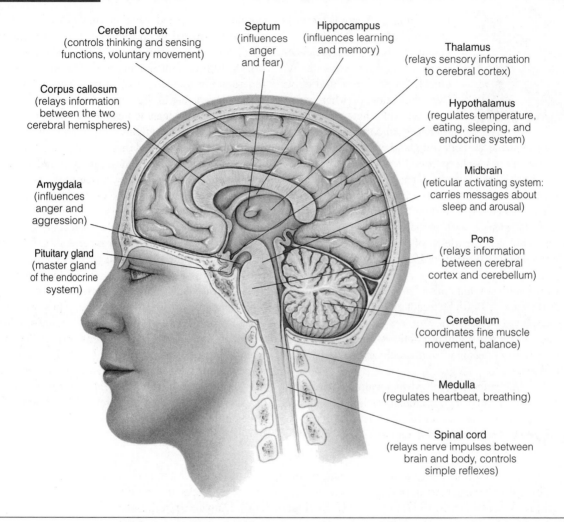

Cerebral cortex
(controls thinking and sensing
functions, voluntary movement)

Septum
(influences
anger
and fear)

Hippocampus
(influences learning
and memory)

Thalamus
(relays sensory information
to cerebral cortex)

Corpus callosum
(relays information
between the two
cerebral hemispheres)

Hypothalamus
(regulates temperature,
eating, sleeping, and
endocrine system)

Amygdala
(influences
anger and
aggression)

Midbrain
(reticular activating system:
carries messages about
sleep and arousal)

Pituitary gland
(master gland
of the endocrine
system)

Pons
(relays information
between cerebral
cortex and cerebellum)

Cerebellum
(coordinates fine muscle
movement, balance)

Medulla
(regulates heartbeat, breathing)

Spinal cord
(relays nerve impulses between
brain and body, controls
simple reflexes)

The forebrain, the midbrain, and the hindbrain contain structures that perform essential functions for survival and for high-level thinking and feeling. From In Search of the Human Mind by Robert J. Sternberg, copyright © 1995 by Harcourt Brace & Company, reproduced by permission of the publisher.

these things are spatially related to each other. In other words, it monitors what is where (McClelland, McNaughton, & O'Reilly, 1995; Tulving & Schacter, 1994). Disruption in the hippocampus appears to result in deficits in declarative memory (i.e., memory for pieces of information). But it does not result in deficits in procedural memory (i.e., memory for courses of action) (Rockland, 2000).

The exact role of the hippocampus in memory and memory formation is yet to be determined. One hypothesis is that the hippocampus provides a cognitive map of sorts. The map represents the space an organism needs to navigate (O'Keefe & Nadel, 1978). Another view is that the hippocampus is essential for flexible learning and for seeing the relations among items learned (Eichenbaum, 1997; Squire, 1992). We return to the role of the hippocampus in Chapter 5.

The **thalamus** relays incoming sensory information through groups of neurons that project to the appropriate region in the cortex. Most of the sensory input into the brain passes through the thalamus. It is located in about the center of the brain, at about the level of the eyes. To accommodate all the different types of information that must be sorted out, the thalamus is divided into a number of nuclei (groups of neurons of similar function). Each nucleus receives information from specific senses. The information is then relayed to corresponding specific areas in the cerebral cortex. (Table 2.2 includes the names and roles of the various nuclei.) The thalamus also helps in the control of sleep and waking. When the thalamus malfunctions, the result can be pain, tremor, amnesia, impairment of language, and disruptions in waking and sleeping (Rockland, 2000; Steriade, Jones, & McCormick, 1997).

The **hypothalamus** regulates behavior related to species survival: fighting, feeding, fleeing, and mating. The hypothalamus also is active in regulating emotions and reactions to stress (Malsbury, 2003). It interacts with the limbic system. The small size of the hypothalamus (from Greek *hypo-*, "under"; located at the base of the forebrain, beneath the thalamus) belies its importance in controlling many bodily functions (see Table 2.1 for more information).

Midbrain

The midbrain helps to control eye movement and coordination. The midbrain is more important in nonmammals than in mammals. In nonmammals it is the main source of control for visual and auditory information. In mammals these functions are dominated by the forebrain. Table 2.1 lists several structures (and corresponding functions) of the midbrain. But by far the most indispensable of these structures is the

TABLE 2.2	Four Major Nuclei of the Thalamus*		
Four key thalamic nuclei relay visual, auditory, somatosensory, and equilibrium-related information			
NAME OF NUCLEUS†	**RECEIVES INFORMATION FROM**	**PROJECTS (TRANSMITS INFORMATION) PRIMARILY TO**	**FUNCTIONAL BENEFIT**
Lateral geniculate nucleus	The visual receptors, via optic nerves	The visual cortex	Permits us to see
Medial geniculate nucleus	The auditory receptors, via auditory nerves	The auditory cortex	Permits us to hear
Ventroposterior nucleus	The somatic nervous system	The primary somatosensory cortex	Permits us to sense pressure and pain
Ventrolateral nucleus	The cerebellum (in the hindbrain)	The primary motor cortex	Permits us to sense physical balance and equilibrium

*Other thalamic nuclei also play important roles.
†The names refer to the relative location of the nuclei within the thalamus: lateral, toward the right or left side of the medial nucleus; ventral, closer to the belly than to the top of the head; posterior, toward the back, behind; ventroposterior, bellyward and in the back; ventrolateral, bellyward and on the side. Also, geniculate means "knee-shaped."

reticular activating system (RAS; also called the "reticular formation"), a network of neurons essential to the regulation of consciousness (sleep, wakefulness, arousal, and even attention to some extent and to such vital functions as heartbeat and breathing) (Sarter, Bruno, & Berntson, 2003).

Actually, the RAS also extends into the hindbrain. Both the RAS and the thalamus are essential to our having any conscious awareness of or control over our existence. The **brain stem** connects the forebrain to the spinal cord. It comprises the hypothalamus, the thalamus, the midbrain, and the hindbrain. A structure called the *periaqueductal gray* (PAG) is in the brain stem. This region seems to be key for certain kinds of adaptive behaviors. Injections of small amounts of excitatory amino acids or, alternatively, electrical stimulation of this area results in any of several responses. One is an aggressive, confrontational response. A second is an avoidance or flight response. A third is a heightened defensive reactivity. And a fourth is reduced reactivity as is experienced after a defeat, when one feels hopeless (Bandler & Shipley, 1994; Rockland, 2000).

Physicians make a determination of brain death based on the function of the brain stem. Specifically, a physician must determine that the brain stem has been damaged so severely that various reflexes of the head (e.g., the pupillary reflex) are absent for more than 12 hours. Or the brain must show no electrical activity or cerebral circulation of blood (Berkow, 1992).

Hindbrain

The hindbrain comprises the medulla oblongata, the pons, and the cerebellum.

The **medulla oblongata** controls heart activity and largely controls breathing, swallowing, and digestion. The medulla is also the place at which nerves from the right side of the body cross over to the left side of the brain. At this point, nerves from the left side of the body cross over to the right side of the brain. The medulla oblongata is an elongated interior structure located at the point where the spinal cord enters the skull and joins with the brain. The medulla oblongata, which contains part of the RAS, helps to keep us alive.

The **pons** serves as a kind of relay station because it contains neural fibers that pass signals from one part of the brain to another. Its name derives from the Latin for "bridge," as it serves a bridging function. The pons also contains a portion of the RAS and nerves serving parts of the head and face. The **cerebellum** (from Latin, "little brain") controls bodily coordination, balance, and muscle tone, as well as some aspects of memory involving procedure-related movements (see Chapters 7 and 8) (Middleton & Helms Tillery, 2003).

The prenatal development of the human brain within each individual roughly corresponds to the evolutionary development of the human brain within the species as a whole. Specifically, the hindbrain is evolutionarily the oldest and most primitive part of the brain. It also is the first part of the brain to develop prenatally. The midbrain is a relatively newer addition to the brain in evolutionary terms. It is the next part of the brain to develop prenatally. Finally, the forebrain is the most recent evolutionary addition to the brain. It is the last of the three portions of the brain to develop prenatally.

Additionally, across the evolutionary development of our species, humans have shown an increasingly greater proportion of brain weight in relation to body weight.

However, across the span of development after birth, the proportion of brain weight to body weight declines. The brain weight of a newborn is proportionately much greater in relation to body weight than is the brain weight of an adult. From infancy through adulthood, the development of the brain centers chiefly on the organizational complexity of the connections within the brain. The individual's developmental increases in neural complexity are paralleled by the evolutionary development of our species. But the changing proportion of brain weight to body weight in evolution is not.

For cognitive psychologists, the most important of these evolutionary trends is the increasing neural complexity of the brain. The evolution of the human brain has offered us the increasing ability to exercise voluntary control over behavior. Is has also increased our ability to plan and to contemplate alternative courses of action. These ideas are discussed in the next section with respect to the cerebral cortex.

Cerebral Cortex and Localization of Function

The **cerebral cortex** forms a 1- to 3-millimeter layer that wraps the surface of the brain somewhat like the bark of a tree wraps around the trunk. In human beings, the many convolutions of the cerebral cortex comprise three different elements. *Sulci* (singular, sulcus) are small grooves. *Fissures* are large grooves. And *gyri* (singular, gyrus) are bulges between adjacent sulci or fissures (see Figure 2.5). These folds greatly increase the surface area of the cortex. If the wrinkly human cortex were smoothed out, it would take up about 2 square feet. The cortex comprises 80% of the human brain (Kolb & Whishaw, 1990). The complexity of brain function increases with the cortical area. The human cerebral cortex enables us to think. Because of it, we can plan, coordinate thoughts and actions, perceive visual and sound patterns, and use language. Without it, we would not be human. The surface of the cerebral cortex is grayish. It is sometimes referred to as *gray matter*. This is because it primarily comprises the grayish neural-cell bodies that process the information that the brain receives and sends. In contrast, the underlying *white matter* of the brain's interior comprises mostly white-colored, myelinated axons.

The cerebral cortex forms the outer layer of the two halves of the brain—the left and right cerebral hemispheres (Davidson & Hugdahl, 1995; Galaburda & Rosen, 2003; Gazzaniga & Hutsler, 1995, 1999; Hellige, 1993, 1995; Levy, 2000; Mangun & associates, 1994). Although the two hemispheres appear to be quite similar, they function differently. The left cerebral hemisphere is specialized for some kinds of activity. The right cerebral hemisphere is specialized for other kinds. For example, receptors in the skin on the right side of the body generally send information through the medulla to areas in the left hemisphere in the brain. The receptors on the left side generally transmit information to the right hemisphere. Similarly, the left hemisphere of the brain directs the motor responses on the right side of the body. The right hemisphere directs responses on the left side of the body. However, not all information transmission is **contralateral**—from one side to another (contra-, "opposite"; lateral, "side"). Some **ipsilateral** transmission—on the same side—occurs as well. For example, odor information from the right nostril goes primarily to the right side of the brain. About half of the information from the right eye goes to the right side of the brain. In addition to this general tendency for contralateral specialization, the hemispheres also communicate directly with one another. The **corpus callosum** is a dense aggregate of neural fibers connecting the two cerebral hemispheres (see Witelson, Kigar, & Walter, 2003). It allows transmission of information back and forth. Once information has reached one hemisphere, the corpus callosum transfers it to the other hemisphere. If the corpus callosum is cut, the two **cerebral hemispheres**—the two halves of the brain—cannot communicate with each other.

Hemispheric Specialization

How did psychologists find out that the two hemispheres have different responsibilities? The study of hemispheric specialization in the human brain can be traced back to Marc Dax, a country doctor in France. By 1836, Dax had treated more than 40 patients suffering from *aphasia*—loss of speech—as a result of brain damage. Dax noticed a relationship between the loss of speech and the side of the brain in which damage had occurred. Dax saw, in studying his patients' brains after death, that in every case there had been damage to the left hemisphere of the brain. He was not able to find even one case of speech loss resulting from damage to the right hemisphere only.

In 1861, French scientist Paul Broca claimed that an autopsy revealed that an aphasic stroke patient had a lesion in the left cerebral hemisphere of the brain. By 1864, Broca was convinced that the left hemisphere of the brain is critical in speech, a view that has held up over time. The specific area Broca identified, *Broca's area*, contributes to speech (Figure 2.7). Another important early researcher, German neurologist Carl Wernicke, studied language-deficient patients who could speak but whose speech made no sense. Like Broca, he traced language ability to the left hemisphere. He studied a different precise location, now known as *Wernicke's area*, which contributes to language comprehension (see Figure 2.7).

Karl Spencer Lashley, often described as the father of neuropsychology, started studying localization in 1915. He found that implantations of crudely built electrodes in apparently identical locations in the brain yielded different results. Different locations sometimes paradoxically yielded the same results (e.g., see Lashley, 1950). Subsequent researchers, using more sophisticated electrodes and measurement procedures, have found that specific locations do correlate with specific motor responses across many test sessions. Apparently, Lashley's research was limited by the technology available to him at the time.

Despite the valuable early contributions by Broca, Lashley, and others, the individual most responsible for modern theory and research on hemispheric specialization was Nobel Prize–winning psychologist Roger Sperry. Sperry (1964) argued that each hemisphere behaves in many respects like a separate brain. In a classic experiment that supports this contention, Sperry and his colleagues severed the corpus callosum connecting the two hemispheres of a cat's brain. They then proved that information presented visually to one cerebral hemisphere of the cat was not recognizable to the other hemisphere. Similar work on monkeys indicated the same discrete performance of each hemisphere (Sperry, 1964). Some of the most interesting information about how the human brain works, and especially about the respective roles of the hemispheres, has emerged from studies of humans with epilepsy in whom the corpus callosum has been severed. Surgically severing this neurological bridge prevents epileptic seizures from spreading from one hemisphere to another. This procedure thereby drastically reduces the severity of the seizures. However, this procedure also results in a loss of

FIGURE 2.7

Motor cortex

Association
cortex

Broca's area
(speech)

Sensory cortex

Association
cortex

Auditory
cortex

Visual
cortex

Wernicke's area
(understanding
language)

Strangely, although people with lesions in Broca's area cannot speak fluently, they can use their voices to sing or shout. From Introduction to Psychology, 11/e, by Richard Atkinson, Rita Atkinson, Daryl Bem, Ed Smith, and Susan Nolen Hoeksema, copyright © 1995 by Harcourt Brace & Company, reproduced by permission of the publisher.

communication between the two hemispheres. It is as if the person has two separate specialized brains processing different information and performing separate functions.

Split-brain patients are people who have undergone operations severing the corpus callosum. Split-brain research reveals fascinating possibilities regarding the ways we think. Many in the field have argued that language is localized in the left hemisphere. Spatial visualization ability appears to be largely localized in the right hemisphere (Farah, 1988a, 1988b; Gazzaniga, 1985; Zaidel, 1983). It appears that roughly 90% of the adult population have language functions predominantly localized within the left hemisphere. More than 95% of right-handers and about 70% of left-handers have left-hemisphere dominance for language. In people who lack left-hemisphere processing, language development in the right hemisphere retains phonemic and semantic abilities. But it is deficient in syntactic competence (Gazzaniga & Hutsler, 1999). Jerre Levy (one of Sperry's students) and her colleagues (Levy, Trevarthen, & Sperry, 1972) have probed the link between the cerebral hemispheres and visuospatial versus language-oriented tasks using participants who have undergone split-brain surgery.

The left hemisphere is important not only in language but also in movement. People with *apraxia*—disorders of skilled movements—often have had damage to the left hemisphere. Such people have lost the ability to carry out familiar purposeful movements (Gazzaniga & Hutsler, 1999).

The right hemisphere is largely "mute" (Levy, 2000). It has little grammatical or phonetic understanding. But it does have very good semantic knowledge. It also is involved in practical language use. People with right-hemisphere damage tend to have deficits in following conversations or stories. They also have difficulties in making inferences from context and in understanding metaphorical or humorous speech (Levy, 2000).

In studies such as the one shown in Figure 2.8, split-brain patients typically are unaware that they saw conflicting information in the two halves of the picture. When asked to give an answer about what they saw in words, they report that they saw the image in the right half of the picture. Recall the contralateral association between hemisphere and side of the body. Given this, it seems that the left hemisphere is controlling their verbal processing (speaking) of visual information. Consider in contrast what happens when they are asked to use the fingers of the left hand (which contralaterally sends and receives information to and from the right hemisphere) to point to what they saw. Participants then choose the image from the left half of the picture. This finding indicates that the right hemisphere appears to control spatial processing (pointing) of visual information. Thus, the task that the participants are asked to perform is crucial in determining what image the participant thinks was shown.

Michael Gazzaniga—another of Sperry's students—has dissociated himself from the position of his former teacher, Sperry, and of his colleagues, such as Levy. Gazzaniga disagrees with their assertion that the two hemispheres function completely independently. Nonetheless, he still holds that each hemisphere serves a complementary role. For instance, according to Gazzaniga, there is no language processing in the right hemisphere (except in rare cases of early brain damage to the left hemisphere). Rather, only visuospatial processing occurs in the right hemisphere. As an example, Gazzaniga has found that before split-brain surgery, people can draw three-dimensional representations of cubes with each hand (Gazzaniga & LeDoux, 1978). After surgery, however, they can draw a reasonable-looking cube only with the left hand. In each patient, the right hand draws pictures unrecognizable either as cubes or as three-dimensional objects. This finding is important because of the contralateral association between each side of the body and the opposite hemisphere of the brain. Recall that the right hemisphere controls the left hand. The left hand is the only one that a split-brain patient can use for drawing recognizable figures. This experiment thus supports the contention that the right hemisphere is dominant in our comprehension and exploration of spatial relations.

Gazzaniga (1985) argues that the brain, and especially the right hemisphere of the brain, is organized into relatively independent functioning units that work in parallel.

FIGURE 2.8

Research on split-brain patients reveals that each hemisphere of the brain processes images and other information distinctively. (a) A composite photograph of two different faces is flashed before a split-brain subject. (b) When shown a group of photographs and asked to pick out a person shown in the composite, the subject will say it is the face from the right half of the composite. (c) However, if asked to point out which one the subject originally saw, she will indicate the picture from the left side of the composite. (After Levy, Trevarthen, & Sperry, 1972)

(a)

"Whom did you see?"
"It was Cher."   (b)

"Point to the person you saw"
(c)

© Kobal Collection

In one study, the participant is asked to focus his or her gaze on the center of screen. Then a chimeric face (a face showing the left side of the face of one person and the right side of another) is flashed on the screen. The participant then is asked to identify what he or she saw, either by speaking or by pointing to one of several normal (not chimeric) faces.

According to Gazzaniga, each of the many discrete units of the mind operates relatively independently of the others. These operations are often outside of conscious awareness. While these various independent and often subconscious operations are taking place, the left hemisphere tries to assign interpretations to these operations. Sometimes the left hemisphere perceives that the individual is behaving in a way that does not intrinsically make any particular sense. It still finds a way to assign some meaning to that behavior.

In addition to studying hemispheric differences in language and spatial relations, researchers have tried to determine whether the two hemispheres think in ways that differ from one another. Levy (1974) has found some evidence that the left hemisphere tends to process information analytically (piece-by-piece, usually in a sequence). She argues that the right hemisphere tends to process it holistically (as a whole).

Lobes of the Cerebral Hemispheres

For practical purposes, four **lobes** divide the cerebral hemispheres and cortex into four parts. These lobes are not distinct units. Rather, they are largely arbitrary anatomical regions. Particular functions have been identified with each lobe. But the lobes also interact. The four lobes, named after the bones of the skull lying directly over them (Figure 2.9), are the frontal, parietal, temporal, and occipital lobes. The lobes are involved in numerous functions. Our discussion of them here describes only part of

FIGURE 2.9

(a) Anatomical areas (left lateral view)   **(a) Anatomical areas (top view)**

The cortex is divided into the frontal, parietal, temporal, and occipital lobes. The lobes have specific functions but also interact to perform complex processes. From In Search of the Human Mind by Robert J. Sternberg, copyright © 1995 by Harcourt Brace & Company, reproduced by permission of the publisher.

what they do. The **frontal lobe** is associated with motor processing and higher thought processes, such as abstract reasoning (Stuss & Floden, 2003). The *prefrontal cortex,* the region toward the front of the frontal lobe, is involved in complex motor control and tasks that require integration of information over time (Gazzaniga, Mangun, & Ivrey, 2002). The **parietal lobe** is associated with somatosensory processing. It receives inputs from the neurons regarding touch, pain, temperature sense, and limb position (Culham, 2003; Gazzaniga & associates, 2002). The **temporal lobe** is associated with auditory processing (Murray, 2003). And the **occipital lobe** is associated with **visual** processing (De Weerd, 2003). There are numerous visual areas in the occipital lobe. Each is specialized to analyze specific aspects of a scene, including color, motion, location, and form (Gazzaniga & associates, 2002).

Projection areas are the areas in the lobes in which sensory processing occurs. This name reflects the fact that the nerves contain sensory information going to the thalamus. It is from here that the sensory information is projected to the appropriate area in the relevant lobe. Similarly, the projection areas project motor information downward through the spinal cord to the appropriate muscles via the peripheral nervous system (PNS). Now let us consider the lobes, and especially the frontal lobe, in somewhat more detail.

The frontal lobe, located toward the front of the head (the face), plays a role in judgment, problem solving, personality, and intentional movement. It contains the **primary motor cortex,** which specializes in the planning, control, and execution of movement, particularly of movement involving any kind of delayed response. If your motor cortex were electrically stimulated, you would react by moving a corresponding body part. The nature of the movement would depend on where in the motor cortex your brain had been stimulated. Control of the various kinds of body movements is located contralaterally on the primary motor cortex. A similar inverse mapping occurs from top to bottom. The lower extremities of the body are represented on the upper (toward the top of the head) side of the motor cortex and the upper part of the body is represented on the lower side of the motor cortex.

Information going to neighboring parts of the body also comes from neighboring parts of the motor cortex. Thus, the motor cortex can be mapped to show where and in what proportions different parts of the body are represented in the brain (Figure 2.10).

The three other lobes are located farther away from the front of the head. These lobes specialize in various kinds of sensory and perceptual activity. For example, in the parietal lobe, the **primary somatosensory cortex** receives information from the senses about pressure, texture, temperature, and pain. It is located right behind the frontal lobe's primary motor cortex. If your somatosensory cortex were electrically stimulated, you probably would report feeling as if you had been touched (Figure 2.11).

From looking at the homunculi (see Figures 2.10 and 2.11), you can see that the relationship of function to form applies in the development of the motor and somatosensory cortex regions. The more need we have for use, sensitivity, and fine control in a particular body part, the larger the area of cortex generally devoted to that part. For example, we humans are tremendously reliant on our hands and faces in our interactions with the world. We show correspondingly large proportions of the cerebral cortex devoted to sensation in, and motor response by, our hands and face.

The region of the cerebral cortex pertaining to hearing is located in the temporal lobe, below the parietal lobe. This lobe performs complex auditory analysis. This

FIGURE 2.10

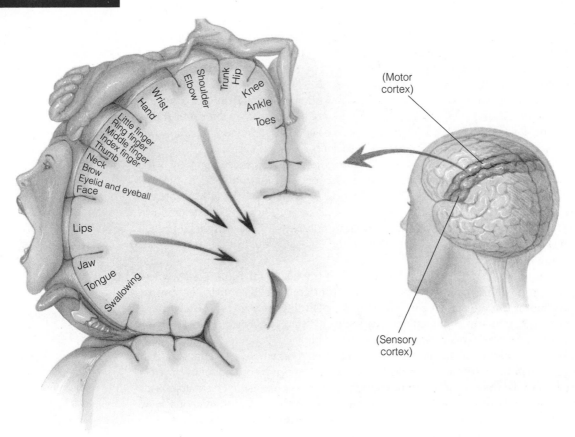

This map of the primary motor cortex is often termed a homunculus *(from Latin, "little person") because it is drawn as a cross section of the cortex surrounded by the figure of a small upside-down person whose body parts map out a proportionate correspondence to the parts of the cortex.*

kind of analysis is needed, for example, in understanding human speech or listening to a symphony. The lobe also is specialized. Some parts are more sensitive to sounds of higher pitch, others to sounds of lower pitch. The auditory region is primarily contralateral, although both sides of the auditory area have at least some representation from each ear. If your auditory cortex were stimulated electrically, you would report having heard some sort of sound.

The visual region of the cerebral cortex is primarily in the occipital lobe. Some neural fibers carrying visual information travel ipsilaterally from the left eye to the left cerebral hemisphere and from the right eye to the right cerebral hemisphere. Other fibers cross over the *optic chiasma* (from Greek, "visual X" or "visual intersection") and go contralaterally to the opposite hemisphere (Figure 2.12). In particular, neural fibers go from the left side of the visual field for each eye to the right side of the vi-

FIGURE 2.11

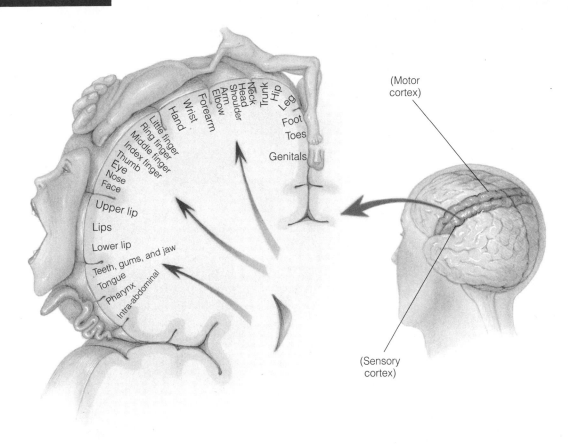

As with the primary motor cortex in the frontal lobe, a homunculus of the somatosensory cortex maps, in inverted form, the parts of the body from which the cortex receives information. From In Search of the Human Mind by Robert J. Sternberg, copyright © 1995 by Harcourt Brace & Company, reproduced by permission of the publisher.

sual cortex. Complementarily, the nerves from the right side of each eye's visual field send information to the left side of the visual cortex.

Association Areas

Association areas of the lobes are regions of the brain that are not part of the somatosensory, motor, auditory, or visual cortices. The term "association area" comes from the belief that an important function of these areas is to link (associate) the activity of the sensory and motor cortices. In humans, association areas make up roughly 75% of the cerebral cortex. In most other animals the association areas are much smaller. When electrical stimulation is applied to association areas, there is no specific observable reaction. However, people with damage to their association areas often do not act, speak, or think normally. The specific abnormal behavior depends

FIGURE 2.12

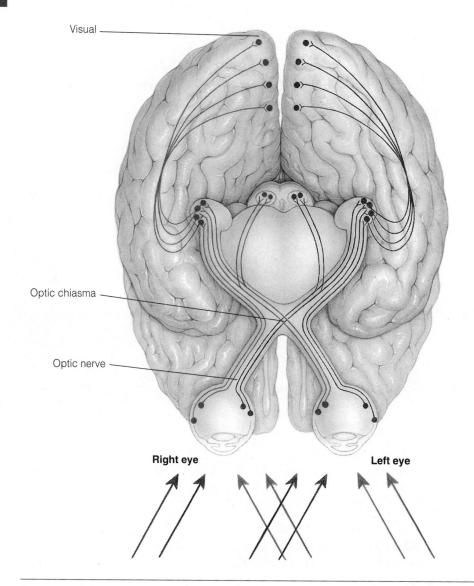

Visual

Optic chiasma

Optic nerve

Right eye   **Left eye**

Some nerve fibers carry visual information ipsilaterally from each eye to each cerebral hemisphere; other fibers cross the optic chiasma and carry visual information contralaterally to the opposite hemisphere. From In Search of the Human Mind by Robert J. Sternberg, copyright © 1995 by Harcourt Brace & Company, reproduced by permission of the publisher.

on the site of damage. The association areas seem somehow to integrate assorted pieces of information from the sensory cortices and to send the integrated information to the motor cortex. They initiate purposeful behavior and expression of logical, reasoned thought.

The frontal association area in the frontal lobes seems to be crucial to problem solving, planning, and judgment. Broca's and Wernicke's speech areas also are located in association areas. Although the roles of association areas in thinking are not completely understood, these areas definitely seem to be places in the brain in which a variety of intellectual abilities are seated.

Consider work that illustrates the function of the association areas in integrating information from various parts of the cortex (Petersen & associates, 1988, 1989; Posner & associates, 1988). Specifically, this work used PET scans to study regional cerebral blood flow during several activities involving the reading of single words. When participants looked at a word on a screen, areas of their visual cortex showed high levels of activity. When they spoke a word, their motor cortex was highly active. When they heard a word spoken, their auditory cortex was activated. When they produced words related to the words they saw (requiring high-level integration of visual, auditory, and motor information), the association areas of the cortex showed the greatest amount of activity.

The brain typically makes up only one fortieth of the weight of an adult human body. Nevertheless, it uses about one fifth of the circulating blood, one fifth of the available glucose, and one fifth of the available oxygen. It is, however, the supreme organ of cognition. Understanding both its structure and function, from the neural to the cerebral levels of organization, is vital to an understanding of cognitive psychology. The recent development of the field of cognitive neuroscience, with its focus on localization of function, reconceptualizes the mind-body question discussed in the beginning of this chapter. The question has changed from "Where is the mind located in the body?" to "Where are particular cognitive operations located in the nervous system?" Throughout the rest of the text, we return to these questions in reference to particular cognitive operations as these operations are discussed in more detail in subsequent chapters.

Michael Posner is a professor of psychology emeritus at the University of Oregon. His groundbreaking research has provided strong evidence of links between cognitive operations and localized brain activity. His work has helped to establish joint cognitive experimental and biological approaches to higher brain function.

Brain Disorders

There are a number of brain disorders that can impair cognitive functioning. The summary here is based in part on the work of Gazzaniga and associates (2002).

Stroke

One type of disorder is a *vascular disorder*, which is caused by a stroke. Strokes occur when the flow of blood to the brain undergoes a sudden disruption. People who experience stroke typically show marked loss of cognitive functioning. The nature of the loss depends on the area of the brain that is affected by the stroke. There may be paralysis, pain, numbness, a loss of speech, a loss of language comprehension, impairments in thought processes, a loss of movement in parts of the body, or other symptoms.

There are two different kinds of stroke (*NINDS stroke information page*). The first kind is an *ischemic stroke*. Usually such a stroke occurs when a buildup of fatty tissue occurs in blood vessels over a period of years, and a piece of this tissue breaks off and gets lodged in arteries of the brain. Ischemic strokes can be treated by clot-busting drugs. The second kind of stroke is a *hemorrhagic stroke*, which occurs when a blood vessel in the brain suddenly breaks. Blood then spills into surrounding tissue. As the blood spills over, brain cells in the affected areas begin to die. This death is either from the lack of oxygen and nutrients or from the rupture of the vessel and the sudden spilling of blood. Symptoms of stroke occur immediately on the occurrence of stroke.

Typical symptoms include

- Numbness or weakness in the face, arms, or legs (especially on one side of the body)
- Confusion, difficulty speaking or understanding speech
- Vision disturbances in one or both eyes
- Dizziness, trouble walking, loss of balance or coordination
- Severe headache with no known cause
  (*NINDS stroke information page*)

The prognosis for stroke victims depends on the type and severity of damage.

Brain Tumors

Brain tumors, also called *neoplasms,* can affect cognitive functioning in very serious ways. Tumors can occur in either the gray or white matter of the brain. Tumors of the white matter are more common (Gazzaniga & associates, 2002). Consider some basic facts about brain tumors (*What you need to know about brain tumors*). There are two types of brain tumors. Primary brain tumors start in the brain. Most childhood brain tumors are of this type. Secondary brain tumors start somewhere else in the body, such as in the lungs. Brain tumors can be either benign or malignant. Benign tumors do not contain cancer cells. They typically can be removed and will not grow back. Cells from benign tumors do not invade surrounding cells or spread to other parts of the body. However, if they press against sensitive areas of the brain, they can result in serious cognitive impairments. They also can be life-threatening, unlike benign tumors in most other parts of the body. Malignant brain tumors, unlike benign ones, contain cancer cells. They are more serious and usually threaten the victim's life. They often grow quickly. They also tend to invade surrounding healthy brain tissue. In rare instances, malignant cells may break away and cause cancer in other parts or the body. Following are the most common symptoms of brain tumors:

- Headaches (usually worse in the morning)
- Nausea or vomiting
- Changes in speech, vision, or hearing
- Problems balancing or walking
- Changes in mood, personality, or ability to concentrate
- Problems with memory
- Muscle jerking or twitching (seizures or convulsions)
- Numbness or tingling in the arms or legs
  (*What you need to know about brain tumors*)

The diagnosis of brain tumors is typically made through neurological examination, CAT scan, and/or MRI. The most common form of treatment is a combination of surgery, radiation, and chemotherapy.

Head Injuries

Head injuries result from many causes, such as car accidents, contact with a hard object, and bullet wounds. Head injuries are of two types (Gazzaniga & associates, 2002). In *closed-head injuries,* the skull remains intact, but there is damage to the brain, typically from the mechanical force of a blow to the head. Slamming one's head against a windshield in a car accident might result in such an injury. In *open-head injuries,* the skull does not remain intact, but rather is penetrated, for example, by a bullet.

Head injuries are surprisingly common. Roughly 700,000 North Americans suffer such injuries each year. Between 70,000 and 90,000 are left permanently disabled (*The anatomy of a head injury*). Loss of consciousness is a sign that there has been some degree of damage to the brain as a result of the injury. Damage resulting from head injury can include spastic movements, difficulty in swallowing, and the slurring of speech, among many other cognitive problems. Immediate symptoms of a head injury include

- Unconsciousness
- Abnormal breathing
- Obvious serious wound or fracture
- Bleeding or clear fluid from the nose, ear, or mouth
- Disturbance of speech or vision
- Pupils of unequal size
- Weakness or paralysis
- Dizziness
- Neck pain or stiffness
- Seizure
- Vomiting more than two to three times
- Loss of bladder or bowel control

  (*Head injuries*)

In summary, brain damage can result from multiple causes, only a few of which are listed here. Others are listed throughout the book. When brain damage occurs, it always should be treated by a medical specialist at the earliest possible time. A neuropsychologist may be called in to assist in diagnosis, and rehabilitation psychologists can be helpful in bringing the patient to the optimal level of psychological functioning possible under the circumstances.

Key Themes

In Chapter 1, we reviewed seven key themes that pervade cognitive psychology. Several of them are relevant here.

One is relative emphases on biological and behavioral mechanisms. The mechanisms described in this chapter are primarily biological. But a major goal of biological researchers is to discover how behavior relates to these biological mechanisms. For example, they study how the hippocampus enables learning. Thus, biology and behavior work together. They are not in any way mutually exclusive.

A second relevant theme is the nature-nurture distinction. One comes into the world with many biological structures and mechanisms in place. But nurture acts to develop them and enable them to reach their potential. The existence of the cerebral cortex is a result of nature, but the memories stored in it derive from nurture. As stated in Chapter 1, nature does not act alone. Rather, its marvels unfold through the interventions of nurture.

A third relevant theme is basic versus applied research. Much of the research in biological approaches to cognition is basic. But this basic research later enables us, as cognitive psychologists, to make applied discoveries. For example, to understand how to treat and, hopefully, help individuals with brain damage, cognitive neuropsychologists first must understand the nature of the damage and its pervasiveness. Many modern antidepressants, for example, affect the reuptake of serontonin in the nervous system. By inhibiting reuptake, they increase serotonin concentrations and ultimately increase feelings of well-being. Interestingly, applied research can help basic research as much as basic research can help applied research. In the case of antidepressants, for example, scientists knew the drugs worked before they knew exactly how they worked. Applied research in creating the drugs helped the scientists understand the biological mechanisms underlying the success of the drugs in relieving symptoms of depression.

People who have strokes on the left sides of their brains have some difficulties in language, whereas those who have strokes on the right side typically have minimal language interferences. If any of you know people who have had strokes, you might have noticed this. This is because our language centers are generally located on the left sides of our brains.

Summary

1. **What are the fundamental structures and processes of the human brain?**   The nervous system, governed by the brain, is divided into two main parts: the central nervous system, consisting of the brain and the spinal cord, and the peripheral nervous system, consisting of the rest of the nervous system (e.g., the nerves in the face, legs, arms, and viscera).

2. **How do researchers study the major structures and processes of the brain?**   For centuries scientists have viewed the brain by dissecting it. Modern dissection techniques include the use of electron microscopes and sophisticated chemical analyses to probe the mysteries of individual cells of the brain. Additionally, surgical techniques on animals (e.g., the use of selective lesioning and single-cell recording) often are used. On humans, studies have included electrical analyses (e.g., electroencephalograms and event-related potentials), studies based on the use of X-ray techniques (e.g., angiograms and computerized axial tomograms), studies based on computer analyses of magnetic fields within the brain (magnetic resonance imaging), and studies based on computer analyses of blood flow and metabolism within the brain (positron emission tomography and functional magnetic resonance imaging).

3. **What have researchers found as a result of studying the brain?**   The major structures of the brain may be categorized as those in the forebrain (e.g., the all-important cerebral cortex and the thalamus, the hypothalamus, and the limbic system, including the hippocampus), the midbrain (including a portion of the brain stem), and the

hindbrain (including the medulla oblongata, the pons, and the cerebellum). The highly convoluted cerebral cortex surrounds the interior of the brain and is the basis for much of human cognition. The cortex covers the left and right hemispheres of the brain. They are connected by the corpus callosum. In general, each hemisphere contralaterally controls the opposite side of the body. Based on extensive split-brain research, many investigators believe that the two hemispheres are specialized: In most people, the left hemisphere seems primarily to control language. The right hemisphere seems primarily to control visuospatial processing. The two hemispheres also may process information differently. Another way to view the cortex is to identify differences among four lobes. Roughly speaking, higher thought and motor processing occur in the frontal lobe. Somatosensory processing occurs in the parietal lobe. Auditory processing occurs in the temporal lobe. And visual processing occurs in the occipital lobe. Within the frontal lobe, the primary motor cortex controls the planning, control, and execution of movement. Within the parietal lobe, the primary somatosensory cortex is responsible for sensations in our muscles and skin. Specific regions of these two cortices can be mapped to particular regions of the body. Association areas within the lobes appear to link the activity of the motor and sensory cortices, allowing for high-level cognitive processes.

Thinking about Thinking: Factual, Analytical, Creative, and Practical Questions

1. How have views of the nature of the relation between the brain and cognition changed over time?

2. Briefly summarize the main structures and functions of the brain.

3. What are some of the reasons that researchers are interested in finding out the localization of function in the human brain?

4. In your opinion, why have the hindbrain, the midbrain, and the forebrain evolved (across the human species) and developed (across human prenatal development) in the sequence mentioned in this chapter? Include the main functions of each in your comments.

5. Researchers already are aware that a deficit of a neurotransmitter, acetylcholine, in the hippocampus is linked to Alzheimer's disease. Given the difficulty of reaching the hippocampus without causing other kinds of brain damage, how might researchers try to treat Alzheimer's disease?

6. In your opinion, why is it that some discoveries, such as that of Marc Dax, go unnoticed? What can be done to maximize the possibility that key discoveries will be noticed?

7. Given the functions of each of the cortical lobes, how might a lesion in one of the lobes be discovered?

8. What is an area of cognition that could be studied effectively by viewing the structure or function of the human brain? Describe how a researcher might use one of the techniques mentioned in this chapter to study that area of cognition.

Key Terms

amygdala
association areas

brain
brain stem

cerebellum
cerebral cortex

cerebral hemispheres

contralateral

corpus callosum

electroencephalogram (EEG)

frontal lobe

functional magnetic resonance imaging (fMRI)

hippocampus

hypothalamus

ipsilateral

Korsakoff's syndrome

limbic system

lobes

localization of function

magnetic resonance imaging (MRI)

medulla oblongata

nervous system

occipital lobe

parietal lobe

pons

positron emission tomography (PET)

primary motor cortex

primary somatosensory cortex

reticular activating ysstem (RAS)

septum

split-brain patients

temporal lobe

thalamus

CogLab Explore CogLab by going to http://coglab.wadsworth.com. Answer the questions required by your instructor from the student manual that accompanies CogLab.

Brain Asymmetry

Annotated Suggested Reading

Gazzaniga, M. (Ed.) (2000). *The new cognitive neuroscience* (2nd ed.). Cambridge, MA: MIT Press. Probably the most comprehensive review of cognitive neuroscience currently available. The level of writing is high.

Attention and Consciousness

EXPLORING COGNITIVE PSYCHOLOGY

1. Can we actively process information even if we are not aware of doing so? If so, what do we do, and how do we do it?

2. What are some of the functions of attention?

3. What are some theories cognitive psychologists have developed to explain what they have observed about attentional processes?

4. What have cognitive psychologists learned about attention by studying the human brain?

The Nature of Attention and Consciousness

[Attention] is the taking possession of the mind, in clear and vivid form, of one out of what seem several simultaneously possible objects or trains of thoughts. . . . It implies withdrawal from some things in order to deal effectively with others.

—William James, Principles of Psychology

You may have found the preceding task awkward, but not impossible. What makes this task difficult, yet possible? **Attention** is the means by which we actively process a limited amount of information from the enormous amount of information available through our senses, our stored memories, and our other cognitive processes (De Weerd, 2003; Duncan, 1999; Motter, 1999; Posner & Fernandez-Duque, 1999; Rao, 2003). It includes both conscious and unconscious processes. Conscious processes are relatively easy to study in many cases. Unconscious processes are harder to study simply because you are not conscious of them (Jacoby, Lindsay, & Toth, 1992; Merikle, 2000). For example, you always have available to you your memory of where you slept when you were 10 years old, but you probably do not often process that information actively. Similarly, you usually have available a wealth of sensory information (e.g., in your body and in your peripheral vision at this very moment). But you attend to only a limited amount of the available sensory information at a given time (Figure 3.1). Moreover, you have very little reliable information about what happens when you sleep. Additionally, the contents of attention can reside either within or outside of awareness (Davies, 1999; Davies & Humphreys, 1993; Metzinger, 1995).

There are many advantages to having attentional processes of some sort. There seem to be at least some limits to our mental resources. There are limits as well to the amount of information on which we can focus those mental resources at any one time. The psychological phenomenon of attention allows us to use our limited mental resources judiciously. By dimming the lights on many stimuli from outside (sensations) and inside (thoughts and memories), we can highlight the stimuli that interest us. This heightened focus increases the likelihood that we can respond speedily and

FIGURE 3.1

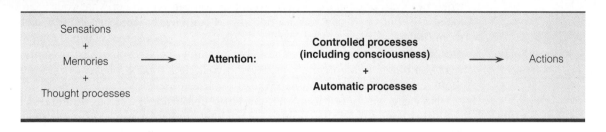

Attention acts as a means of focusing limited mental resources on the information and cognitive processes that are most salient at a given moment.

accurately to interesting stimuli. Heightened attention also paves the way for memory processes. We are more likely to remember information to which we paid attention than information we ignored.

Consciousness includes both the feeling of awareness and the content of awareness, some of which may be under the focus of attention (Block, Flanagan, & Güzeldere, 1997; Bourguignon, 2000; Chalmers, 1995, 1996; Cohen & Schooler, 1997; Farthing, 1992, 2000; Marcel & Bisiach, 1988; Nelkin, 1996; Peacocke, 1998; Velmans, 1996). Therefore, attention and consciousness form two partially overlapping sets (DiGirolamo & Griffin, 2003). At one time, psychologists believed that attention was the same thing as consciousness. Now, however, they acknowledge that some active attentional processing of sensory information, remembered information, and cognitive information proceeds without our conscious awareness (Shear, 1997; Tye, 1995). For example, at this time in your life, writing your own name requires no conscious awareness. You may write it while consciously engaged in other activities—although not if you are completely unconscious.

The benefits of attention are particularly salient when we refer to conscious attentional processes. In addition to the overall value of attention, conscious attention serves three purposes in playing a causal role for cognition. First, it helps in monitoring our interactions with the environment. Through such monitoring, we maintain our awareness of how well we are adapting to the situation in which we find ourselves. Second, it assists us in linking our past (memories) and our present (sensations) to give us a sense of continuity of experience. Such continuity may even serve as the basis for personal identity. Third, it helps us in controlling and planning for our future actions. We can do so based on the information from monitoring and from the links between past memories and present sensations.

Preconscious Processing

Some information that currently is outside of our conscious awareness still may be available to consciousness or at least to cognitive processes. Information that is available for cognitive processing but that currently lies outside of conscious awareness exists at the preconscious level of awareness. Preconscious information includes stored memories that we are not using at a given time but that we could summon when needed. For example, when prompted, you can remember what your bedroom looks like. But obviously you are not always consciously thinking about your bedroom (unless, perhaps, you are extremely tired!). Sensations, too, may be pulled from preconscious to conscious awareness. For example, before you read this sentence, were you highly aware of the sensations in your right foot? Probably not. However, those sensations were available to you.

How can we study things that currently lie outside conscious awareness? Psychologists have solved this problem by studying a phenomenon known as priming. **Priming** occurs when recognition of certain stimuli is affected by prior presentation of the same or similar stimuli (Neely, 2003). Suppose, for example, someone is talking to you about how much he has enjoyed watching television since buying a satellite dish. He speaks at length about the virtues of satellite dishes. Later, you hear the word dish. You are probably more likely to think of a satellite dish, as opposed to a dish served at dinner, than is someone who did not hear the prior conversation about satellite dishes. Most priming is positive. Prior presentation of stimuli facilitates later recognition. But priming on occasion may be negative. It may impede later recognition. Sometimes we are aware of the priming stimuli. For example, you are now primed to read descriptions of studies involving priming. However, priming occurs even when the priming stimulus is presented in a way that does not permit its entry into conscious awareness. In such a case, it is presented at too low an intensity, in too "noisy" a background (i.e., too many other stimuli divert conscious attention from it), or too briefly to be registered in conscious awareness.

For example, in a set of studies Marcel observed processing of stimuli that were presented too briefly to be detected in conscious awareness (Marcel, 1983a, 1983b). In these studies, words were presented to participants very briefly (as measured in milliseconds, or thousandths of a second). After presentation, each word was replaced by a visual mask. The mask blocks the image of the word from remaining on the retina (the rear surface of the eye, comprising the sensory receptors of vision). Marcel timed the presentations to be very brief (20–110 milliseconds). In this way, he was sure that participants could not detect their presence consciously. When participants were asked to guess the word they had seen, their guesses were no better than chance.

In one such study, Marcel presented participants with a series of words to be classified into various categories. Examples would be "leg—body part" and "pine—plant." In this study, the priming stimuli were words having more than one meaning. For example, a palm can be either a tree or a part of the hand. In one condition, participants consciously were aware of seeing a priming word that had two meanings. For these participants, the mental pathway for only one of the two meanings seemed to become activated. In other words, one of the two meanings of the word showed the priming effect. It facilitated (speeded up) the classification of a subsequent related word. However, the other of the two meanings showed a sort of negative priming effect. It actually inhibited (slowing down) the classification of a subsequent unrelated word. For example, if the word "palm" was presented long enough so that the participant was consciously aware of seeing it, the word either facilitated or inhibited the classification of the word "wrist," which it did depending on whether the participant associated "palm" with "hand" or with "tree." Apparently, if the participant was consciously aware of seeing the word "palm," the mental pathway for only one meaning was activated. The mental pathway for the other meaning was inhibited. In contrast, if the word "palm" was presented so briefly that the person was unaware of seeing the word, both meanings of the word appeared to be activated. This procedure facilitated subsequent classification.

Marcel's results were controversial and in need of replication by independent investigators using stringent controls. Such a replication was indeed performed (Cheesman & Merikle, 1984). The investigators used a color-identification task. They found that whether subliminal perception occurred depended on how one defined the threshold of awareness. If one defined the threshold below which perception is subliminal in terms of the level at which participants report a word occuring half the time, then subliminal perception could be said to occur. If, however, one defined subliminal perception in terms of an objective threshold that applies for everyone, then subliminal perception did not occur. This study points out the importance of definition in any cognitive-psychological investigation. Whether a phenomenon occurs sometimes depends on exactly how that phenomenon is defined.

Another example of possible priming effects and preconscious processing can be found in a study described as a test of intuition. This study used a "dyad of triads" task (Bowers & associates, 1990). Participants were presented with pairs (dyads) of three-word groups (triads). One of the triads in each dyad was a potentially coherent grouping. The other triad contained random and unrelated words. For example, the words in Group A, a coherent triad, might have been "playing," "credit," and "report." The words in Group B, an incoherent triad, might have been "still," "pages," and "music." After presentation of the dyad of triads, participants were shown various possible choices for a fourth word related to one of the two triads. The participants then were asked to identify two things. The first was which of the two triads was coherent and related to a fourth word. The second was which fourth word linked the coherent triad. In the preceding example, the words in Group A can be meaningfully paired with a fourth word—"card" (playing card, credit card, report card). The words in Group B bear no such relationship.

Some participants could not figure out the unifying fourth word for a given pair of triads. They were nevertheless asked to indicate which of the two triads was coherent. When participants could not ascertain the unifying word, they still were able to identify the coherent triad at a level well above chance. They seemed to have some preconscious information available to them. This information led them to select one triad over the other. They did so even though they did not consciously know what word unified that triad.

Unfortunately, sometimes pulling preconscious information into conscious awareness is not easy. For example, most of us have experienced the **tip-of-the-tongue phenomenon,** in which we try to remember something that is known to be stored in memory but that cannot readily be retrieved. Psychologists have tried to come up with experiments that measure this phenomenon. For example, they have sought to find out how much people can draw from information that seems to be stuck at the preconscious level. In one study (Brown & McNeill, 1966), participants were read a large number of dictionary definitions. They then were asked to identify the corresponding words having these meanings. This procedure constituted a game similar to the television show *Jeopardy.* For example, they might have been given the clue, "an instrument used by navigators to measure the angle between a heavenly body and a horizon."

In the study, some participants could not come up with the word, but thought they knew it. They then were asked various questions about the word. For example, they might be asked to identify the first letter, indicate the number of syllables, or approximate the word's sounds. The participants often answered these questions accurately. They might have been able to indicate some properties of the appropriate word for the aforementioned instrument. For example, it begins with an *s*, has two syllables, and sounds like sextet. Eventually, some participants realized that the sought-after word is "sextant." These results indicate that particular preconscious information, although not fully accessible to conscious thinking, is still available to attentional processes.

Preconscious perception also has been observed in people who have lesions in some areas of the visual cortex. Typically, the patients are blind in areas of the visual field that correspond to the lesioned areas of the cortex. Some of these patients, however, seem to show **blindsight**—traces of visual perceptual ability in blind areas (Kentridge, 2003). When forced to guess about a stimulus in the "blind" region, they correctly guess locations and orientations of objects at above-chance levels (Weiskrantz, 1994). Similarly, when forced to reach for objects in the blind area, "cortically blind participants . . . will nonetheless preadjust their hands appropriately to size, shape, orientation and 3-D location of that object in the blind field" (Marcel, 1986, p. 41). Yet they fail to show voluntary behavior, such as reaching for a glass of water in the blind region, even when they are thirsty. Some visual processing seems to occur even when participants have no conscious awareness of visual sensations.

An interesting example of blindsight can be found in a case study of a patient called D. B. (Weiskrantz, 1986). The patient was blind on the left side of his visual field as an unfortunate result of an operation. That is, each eye had a blind spot on the left side of its visual field. Consistent with this damage, D. B. reported no awareness of any objects placed on his left side or of any events that took place on this side. But despite his unawareness of vision on this side, there was evidence of vision. The investigator would present objects to the left side of the visual field and then present D. B. with a forced-choice test in which the patient had to indicate which of two objects had been presented to this side. D. B. performed at levels that were significantly better than chance. In other words, he "saw" despite his unawareness of seeing.

The preceding examples show that at least some cognitive functions can occur outside of conscious awareness. We appear able to sense, perceive, and even respond to many stimuli that never enter our conscious awareness (Marcel, 1983a). Just what kinds of processes do or do not require conscious awareness?

INVESTIGATING COGNITIVE PSYCHOLOGY	Repeatedly write your name on a piece of paper while you picture everything you can remember about the room in which you slept when you were 10 years old. While continuing to write your name and picturing your old bedroom, take a mental journey of awareness to notice your bodily sensations, starting from one of your big toes and proceeding up your leg, across your torso, to the opposite shoulder, and down your arm. What sensations do you feel—pressure from the ground, your shoes, or your clothing or even pain anywhere? Are you still managing to write your name while retrieving remembered images from memory and continuing to pay attention to your current sensations?

IN THE LAB OF JOHN F. KIHLSTROM

Courtesy of Dr. John F. Kihlstrom

John Kihlstrom is on the faculty of the Department of Psychology at the University of California, Berkeley, where he is professor in the Department of Psychology and a member of both the Institute for Cognitive and Brain Studies and the Institute for Personality and Social Research. In 1987 he published a lead article in *Science* magazine on "The Cognitive Unconscious," which is widely credited with sparking renewed scientific interest in unconscious mental life after almost a century of Freudianism (Kihlstrom, 1987). A major goal of his research is to use the methods of cognitive psychology to understand the phenomena of hypnosis, a special state of consciousness in which subjects experience various alterations in perception and memory. After coming out of hypnosis, subjects may be unable to remember the things that they did while they were hypnotized. This phenomenon of posthypnotic amnesia has been a major focus of Kihlstrom's research. First, however, the researchers have to find the right subjects. Although there are big individual differences in hypnotizability, there is no personality questionnaire that can predict reliably who can experience hypnosis and who cannot. The only way to find out who is hypnotizable is to try hypnosis and see if it works. For this purpose, the lab relies on a set of standardized scales of hypnotic susceptibility, which are performance-based tests, structured much like tests of intelligence, that measure a subject's ability to experience hypnosis. From this point on, Kihlstrom's experiments look just like anyone else's—except that his subjects are hypnotized.

In one study using a familiar verbal-learning paradigm (Kihlstrom, 1980), the subjects memorized a list of 15 familiar words, such as girl or chair, and then received a suggestion for posthypnotic amnesia. As part of this suggestion, the experiment set up a *reversibility cue* to cancel the amnesia suggestion. After coming out of hypnosis, highly hypnotizable subjects remembered virtually none of the list, whereas insusceptible subjects who had gone through the same procedures remembered the list almost perfectly. This shows that the occurrence of posthypnotic amnesia is highly correlated with hypnotizability.

Then all subjects were given a word-association test, in which they were presented with cues and asked to report the first word that came to mind. Some of these cues were words like boy and table, which were likely to produce the *critical targets* on the study list. Others were control cues, like lamp and dogs, which had an equally high probability of producing neutral targets like light and cats, which had not been studied. Despite their inability to remember the words they had just studied, the hypnotizable, amnesic subjects were no less likely to produce critical targets than were the insusceptible, nonamnesic subjects. This shows that posthypnotic amnesia is a disruption of episodic, but not semantic, memory. In fact, Tulving (1983) cited this experiment as one of the first convincing studies of the difference between these two types of memory.

Even more important, the subjects were more likely to generate critical rather than neutral targets on the free-association test. This is a phenomenon of semantic priming, in which a previous experience, such as studying a list of words, facilitates performance on a subsequent task, such as generating words on a free-association test (Meyer & Schvaneveldt, 1971). The magnitude of the priming effect was the same in the hypnotizable, amnesic subjects as it was in the insusceptible, nonamnesic subjects. In other words, posthypnotic amnesia entails a dissociation between explicit and implicit memory (Schacter, 1987): hypnotizable subjects lacked explicit memory, but retained implicit memory. This experiment is now recognized as one of the first studies to demonstrate the dissociation between these two expressions of memory.

Kihlstrom continues to study posthypnotic amnesia and other aspects of hypnosis, but his original interest in posthypnotic amnesia has expanded to include other aspects of unconscious mental life, and a broader range of topics in memory. In his new work on the *human ecology of memory* (http://socrates.berkeley.edu/~kihlstrm/mnemosyne.htm), he is interested in using memory as a theme to link cognitive psychology to personality and social psychology, and also to link psychology to the other social sciences, the humanities, and the arts.

Controlled versus Automatic Processes

Many cognitive processes also may be differentiated in terms of whether they do or do not require conscious control (Schneider & Shiffrin, 1977; Shiffrin & Schneider, 1977). **Automatic processes** involve no conscious control (see Palmeri, 2003). For the most part, they are performed without conscious awareness. Nevertheless, you may be aware that you are performing them. They demand little or no effort or even intention. They are performed as parallel processes. Many operations occur simultaneously or at least in no particular sequential order. And they are relatively fast. In contrast, **controlled processes** are accessible to conscious control and even require it. Such processes are performed serially. In other words, they occur sequentially, one step at a time. They take a relatively long time to execute, at least as compared with automatic processes.

Three attributes characterize automatic processes (Posner & Snyder, 1975). First, they are concealed from consciousness. Second, they are unintentional. Third, they consume few attentional resources. An alternative view of attention suggests a continuum of processes between fully automatic processes and fully controlled processes. For one thing, the range of controlled processes is so wide and diverse that it would be difficult to characterize all the controlled processes in the same way (Logan, 1988). Similar difficulties arise with characterizing automatic processes. Some automatic processes truly cannot be retrieved into conscious awareness, despite any amount of effort to do so. Examples are preconscious processing and priming. Other automatic processes, such as tying your shoes, can be controlled intentionally. But they rarely are handled in this way. For example, you seldom may think about all of the steps involved in executing many automatic behaviors. Automatic behaviors require no conscious decisions regarding which muscles to move or which actions to take. For example, when you dial a familiar telephone number or drive a car to a familiar place, you do not think about the muscles you move to do so. However, their identities can be pulled into conscious awareness and controlled relatively easily. (Table 3.1 summarizes the characteristics of controlled versus automatic processes.)

In fact, many tasks that start off as controlled processes eventually become automatic ones. For example, driving a car is initially a controlled process. Once we master driving, however, it becomes automatic under normal driving conditions. Such conditions involve familiar roads, fair weather, and little or no traffic. Similarly, when you first learn to speak a foreign language, you need to translate word-for-word from your native tongue. Eventually, however, you begin to think in the second language. This thinking enables you to bypass the intermediate-translation stage. It also allows the process of speaking to become automatic. Your conscious attention can revert to the content, rather than the process, of speaking. A similar shift from conscious control to automatic processing occurs when acquiring the skill of reading.

You may notice that the procedures you learned early in life often are more highly automatic and less accessible to conscious awareness than are procedures acquired later. Examples are tying your shoes, riding a bicycle, or even reading. In general, more recently acquired routine processes and procedures are less fully automatic. At the same time, they are more accessible to conscious control. **Automatization** (also termed *proceduralization*) is the process by which a procedure changes from being highly conscious to being relatively automatic. As you may have guessed based on

TABLE 3.1	Controlled Versus Automatic Processes

There is probably a continuum of cognitive processes from fully controlled processes to fully automatic ones; these features characterize the polar extremes of each.

CHARACTERISTICS	CONTROLLED PROCESSES	AUTOMATIC PROCESSES
Amount of intentional effort	Require intentional effort	Require little or no intention or effort (and intentional effort may even be required to avoid automatic behaviors)
Degree of conscious awareness	Require full conscious awareness	Generally occur outside of conscious awareness, although some automatic processes may be available to consciousness
Use of attentional resources	Consume many attentional resources	Consume negligible attentional resources
Type of processing	Performed serially (one step at a time)	Performed by parallel processing (i.e., with many operations occurring simultaneously or at least in no particular sequential order)
Speed of processing	Relatively time-consuming execution, as compared with automatic processes	Relatively fast
Relative novelty of tasks	Novel and unpracticed tasks or tasks with many variable features	Familiar and highly practiced tasks, with largely stable task characteristics
Level of processing	Relatively high levels of cognitive processing (requiring analysis or synthesis)	Relatively low levels of cognitive processing (minimal analysis or synthesis)
Difficulty of tasks	Usually difficult tasks	Usually relatively easy tasks, but even relatively complex tasks may be automatized, given sufficient practice
Process of acquisition	With sufficient practice, many routine and relatively stable procedures may become automatized, such that highly controlled processes may become partly or even wholly automatic; naturally, the amount of practice required for automatization increases dramatically for highly complex tasks	

your own experience, automatization occurs as a result of practice. Highly practiced activities can be automatized. They thus become highly automatic (LaBerge, 1975, 1976, 1990; LaBerge & Samuels, 1974).

How does automatization occur? A widely accepted view has been that during the course of practice, implementation of the various steps becomes more efficient. The individual gradually combines individual effortful steps into integrated components. These components then are further integrated. Eventually the entire process is a single highly integrated procedure, rather than an assemblage of individual steps (Anderson, 1983; LaBerge & Samuels, 1974). According to this view, people consolidate various discrete steps into a single operation. This operation requires few or no cognitive resources, such as attention. This view of automatization seems to be supported by one of the earliest studies of automatization (Bryan & Harter, 1899). This study investigated how telegraph operators gradually automatized the task of sending and receiving messages. Initially, new operators automatized the transmission of individual letters. However, once the operators had made the transmission of letters automatic, they automatized the transmission of words, phrases, and then other groups of words.

An alternative explanation, called "instance theory," has been proposed. Logan (1988) suggested that automatization occurs because we gradually accumulate knowledge about specific responses to specific stimuli. For example, when a child first learns to add or subtract, he or she applies a general procedure—counting—for handling each pair of numbers. Following repeated practice, the child gradually stores knowledge about particular pairs of particular numbers. Eventually, the child can retrieve from memory the specific answers to specific combinations of numbers. Nevertheless, he or she still can fall back on the general procedure (counting) as needed. Similarly, when learning to drive, the person can draw on an accumulated wealth of specific experiences. These experiences form a knowledge base from which the person quickly can retrieve specific procedures for responding to specific stimuli, such as oncoming cars or stoplights. Preliminary findings suggest that Logan's instance theory may better explain specific responses to specific stimuli, such as calculating arithmetic combinations. The prevailing view may better explain more general responses involving automatization (Logan, 1988).

The effects of practice on automatization show a negatively accelerated curve. In such a curve, early practice effects are great. A graph of improvement in performance would show a steeply rising curve early on. Later practice effects make less and less difference in the degree of automatization. On a graph showing improvement, the curve would eventually level off (Figure 3.2). Clearly, automatic processes generally govern familiar, well-practiced tasks. Controlled processes govern relatively novel tasks. In addition, most automatic processes govern relatively easy tasks. Most difficult tasks require controlled processing. With sufficient practice, however, even many extremely complex tasks, such as reading, can become automatized. Because highly automatized behaviors require little effort or conscious control, we often can engage in multiple automatic behaviors. But we rarely can engage in more than one labor-intensive controlled behavior. Although automatic processes do not require conscious control, they are subject to such control. For example, skilled articulation (speaking) and skilled typing can be stopped almost immediately on signal or in response to detection of an error. However, skilled performance of automatic behaviors often is impaired by conscious control. Try riding a bicycle while consciously monitoring your every movement. It will be extremely difficult to succeed.

It is important to automate various safety practices (Norman, 1976). This is particularly true for people engaging in high-risk occupations, such as pilots, undersea divers, and firefighters. For example, novice divers often complain about the frequent repetition of various safety procedures within the confines of a swimming pool. An example would be releasing a cumbersome weight belt. However, the practice is important, as the novices will learn later. Experienced divers recognize the value of being able to rely on automatic processes in the face of potential panic should they confront a life-threatening deep-sea emergency.

In some situations, automatic processes may be life saving. But in others, they may be life threatening (Langer, 1997). Consider an example of what Langer (1989) calls "mindlessness." In 1982, a pilot and copilot went through a routine checklist

FIGURE 3.2

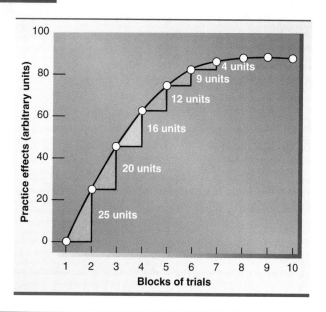

The rate of improvement caused by practice effects shows a pattern of negative acceleration. The negative-acceleration curve attributed to practice effects is similar to the curve shown here, indicating that the rate of learning slows down as the amount of learning increases, until eventually learning peaks at a stable level.

prior to takeoff. They mindlessly noted that the anti-icer was "off," as it should be under most circumstances. But it should not have been off under the icy conditions in which they were preparing to fly. The flight ended in a crash that killed 74 passengers. Typically, our absent-minded implementation of automatic processes has far less lethal consequences. For example, when driving, we may end up routinely driving home instead of stopping by the store, as we had intended to do. Or we may pour a glass of milk and then start to put the carton of milk in the cupboard rather than in the refrigerator.

An extensive analysis of human error notes that errors can be classified either as mistakes or as slips (Reason, 1990). Mistakes are errors in choosing an objective or in specifying a means of achieving it. Slips are errors in carrying out an intended means for reaching an objective. Suppose, for example, you decided that you did not need to study for an examination. Thus you purposely left your textbook behind when leaving for a long weekend. But then you discovered at the time of the exam that you should have studied. In Reason's terms, you made a mistake. However, suppose instead you fully intended to bring your textbook with you. You had planned to study extensively over the long weekend. But in your haste to leave you accidentally left the textbook behind. That would be a slip. In sum, mistakes involve errors in intentional, controlled processes. Slips often involve errors in automatic processes (Reason, 1990).

There are several kinds of slips (Norman, 1988; Reason, 1990—see Table 3.2). In general, slips are most likely to occur when two circumstances occur. First, we must deviate from a routine and automatic processes inappropriately override intentional, controlled processes. Second, our automatic processes are interrupted. Such interruptations are usually a result of external events or data, but sometimes they are a result of internal events, such as highly distracting thoughts. Automatic processes are helpful to us under many circumstances. They save us from needlessly focusing attention on routine tasks, such as tying our shoes or dialing a familiar phone number. We are thus unlikely to forgo them just to avoid occasional slips.

How can we minimize the potential for negative consequences of slips? In everyday situations, we are less likely to slip when we receive appropriate feedback from the environment. For example, the milk carton may be too tall for the cupboard shelf, or a passenger may say, "I thought you were stopping at the store before going home." If we can find ways to obtain useful feedback, we may be able to reduce the likelihood that harmful consequences will result from slips. A particularly helpful kind of feedback involves forcing function. These are physical constraints that make it difficult or impossible to carry out an automatic behavior that may lead to a slip (Norman, 1988). As an example of a forcing function, some modern cars make it difficult or impossible to drive the car without wearing a seatbelt. You can devise your own forcing functions. You may post a small sign on your steering wheel as a reminder to run an errand on the way home. Or you may put items in front of the door. In this way, you block your exit so that you cannot leave without the items you want.

Over a lifetime, we automatize countless everyday tasks. However, one of the most helpful pairs of automatic processes first appears within hours after birth: habituation and its complementary opposite, dishabituation.

Habituation and Adaptation

Habituation involves our becoming accustomed to a stimulus so that we gradually pay less and less attention to it. The counterpart to habituation is dishabituation. In **dishabituation,** a change in a familiar stimulus prompts us to start noticing the stimulus again. Both processes occur automatically. They involve no conscious effort. The relative stability and familiarity of the stimulus govern these processes. Any aspects of the stimulus that seem different or novel (unfamiliar) either prompt dishabituation or make habituation less likely to occur in the first place. For example, suppose that a radio is playing instrumental music while you study your cognitive psychology textbook. At first the sound might distract you. But after a while you become habituated to the sound and scarcely notice it. If the loudness of the noise were suddenly to change drastically, however, you immediately would dishabituate to it. The once-familiar sound to which you had been habituated would become unfamiliar. It thus would enter your awareness. Habituation is not limited to humans. It is found in organisms as simple as the mollusk *Aplysia* (Castellucci & Kandel, 1976).

We usually exert no effort whatsoever to become habituated to our sensations of stimuli in the environment. Nonetheless, although we usually do not consciously control habituation, we can do so. In this way, habituation is an attentional phenomenon that differs from the physiological phenomenon of sensory adaptation. **Sensory adaptation** is a lessening of attention to a stimulus that is not subject to conscious control.

TABLE 3.2	Slips Associated with Automatic Processes

Occasionally, when we are distracted or interrupted during implementation of an automatic process, slips occur. However, in proportion to the number of times we engage in automatic processes each day, slips are relatively rare events (Reason, 1990).

TYPE OF ERROR	DESCRIPTION OF ERROR	EXAMPLE OF ERROR
Capture errors	We intend to deviate from a routine activity we are implementing in familiar surroundings, but at a point where we should depart from the routine we fail to pay attention and to regain control of the process; hence, the automatic process captures our behavior, and we fail to deviate from the routine.	Psychologist William James (1890/1970, cited in Langer, 1989) gave an example in which he automatically followed his usual routine, undressing from his work clothes, then putting on his pajamas and climbing into bed—only to realize that he had intended to remove his work clothes to dress to go out to dinner.
Omissions*	An interruption of a routine activity may cause us to skip a step or two in implementing the remaining portion of the routine.	When going to another room to retrieve something, if a distraction (e.g., a phone call) interrupts you, you may return to the first room without having retrieved the item.
Perseverations*	After an automatic procedure has been completed, one or more steps of the procedure may be repeated.	If, after starting a car, you become distracted, you may turn the ignition switch again.
Description errors	An internal description of the intended behavior leads to performing the correct action on the wrong object.	When putting away groceries, you may end up putting the ice cream in the cupboard and a can of soup in the freezer.
Data-driven errors	Incoming sensory information may end up overriding the intended variables in an automatic action sequence.	While intending to dial a familiar phone number, if you overhear someone call out another series of numbers, you may end up dialing some of those numbers instead of the ones you intended to dial.
Associative-activation errors	Strong associations may trigger the wrong automatic routine.	When expecting someone to arrive at the door, if the phone rings, you may call out, "Come in!"
Loss-of-activation errors	The activation of a routine may be insufficient to carry it through to completion.	All too often, each of us has experienced the feeling of going to another room to do something and getting there only to ask ourselves, "What am I doing here?" Perhaps even worse is the nagging feeling, "I know I should be doing something, but I can't remember what." Until something in the environment triggers our recollection, we may feel extremely frustrated.

*Omissions and perseverations may be considered examples of errors in the sequencing of automatic processes. Related errors include inappropriately sequencing the steps, as in trying to remove socks before taking off shoes.

PRACTICAL
APPLICATIONS
OF COGNITIVE
PSYCHOLOGY

Habituation is not without faults. Becoming bored during a lecture or while reading a textbook is a sign of habituation. Your attention may start to wander to the background noises, or you may find that you have read a paragraph or two with no recollection of the content. Fortunately, you can dishabituate yourself with very little effort. Here are a few tips on how to overcome the negative effects of boredom.

1. Take a break or alternate between different tasks if possible. If you do not remember the last few paragraphs of the text, it is time to stop for a few minutes. Go back and mark the last place in the text you do remember and put the book down. If you feel like a break is a waste of valuable time, do some other work for a while.

2. Take notes while reading or listening. Most people already do so. Note-taking focuses attention on the material more than does simply listening or reading. If necessary, try switching from script to printed handwriting to make the task more interesting.

3. Adjust your attentional focus to increase stimulus variability. Is the instructor's voice droning on endlessly, so that you cannot take a break during lecture? Try noticing other aspects of your instructor, like hand gestures or body movements, while still paying attention to the content. Create a break in the flow by asking a question—even just raising your hand can make a change in a lecturer's speaking pattern. Change your arousal level. If all else fails, you may have to force yourself to be interested in the material. Think about how you can use the material in your everyday life. Also, sometimes just taking a few deep breaths or closing your eyes for a few seconds can change your internal arousal levels.

It occurs directly in the sense organ, not in the brain. We can exert some conscious control over whether we notice something to which we have become habituated, but we have no conscious control over sensory adaptation. For example, we cannot consciously force ourselves to smell an odor to which our senses have become adapted. Nor can we consciously force our pupils to adapt—or not adapt—to differing degrees of brightness or darkness. In contrast, if someone asked us, "Who's the lead guitarist in that song?" we can once again notice background music. Table 3.3 provides some of the other distinctions between sensory adaptation and habituation.

Some of the factors that influence habituation are stimulus internal variation and subjective arousal. Some stimuli involve more internal variation than do others. For example, background music contains more internal variation than does the steady drone of an air conditioner. The relative complexity of the stimulus (e.g., an ornate, intricate Oriental rug versus a gray carpet) does not seem to be important to habituation. Rather, what matters is the amount of change within the stimulus over time. For example, a mobile involves more change than does an ornate but rigid sculpture. Thus, it is relatively difficult to remain continually habituated to the frequently changing noises coming from a television. The reason is that the voices typically speak animatedly and with great inflectional expression. They are constantly changing.

Psychologists can observe habituation occurring at the physiological level by measuring our degree of arousal. **Arousal** is a degree of physiological excitation, responsiv-

TABLE 3.3	Differences Between Sensory Adaptation and Habituation

Responses involving physiological adaptation take place mostly in our sense organs, whereas responses involving cognitive habituation take place mostly in our brains (and relate to learning).

ADAPTATION	**HABITUATION**
Not accessible to conscious control (*Example:* You cannot decide how quickly to adapt to a particular smell or a particular change in light intensity.)	Accessible to conscious control (*Example:* You can decide to become aware of background conversations to which you had become habituated.)
Tied closely to stimulus intensity (*Example:* The more the intensity of a bright light increases, the more strongly your senses will adapt to the light.)	Not tied very closely to stimulus intensity (*Example:* Your level of habituation will not differ much in your response to the sound of a loud fan and to that of a quiet air conditioner.)
Unrelated to the number, length, and recency of prior exposures (*Example:* The sense receptors in your skin will respond to changes in temperature in basically the same way no matter how many times you have been exposed to such changes and no matter how recently you have experienced such changes.)	Tied very closely to the number, length, and recency of prior exposures (*Example:* You will become more quickly habituated to the sound of a chiming clock when you have been exposed to the sound more often, for longer times, and on more recent occasions.)

ity, and readiness for action, relative to a baseline. Arousal often is measured in terms of heart rate, blood pressure, electroencephalograph (EEG) patterns, and other physiological signs. Consider what happens, for example, when an unchanging visual stimulus remains in our visual field for a long time. Our neural activity (as shown on an EEG) in response to that stimulus decreases (see Chapter 2). Both neural activity and other physiological responses (e.g., heart rate) can be measured. These measurements detect heightened arousal in response to perceived novelty or diminished arousal in response to perceived familiarity. In fact, psychologists in many fields use physiological indications of habituation to study a wide array of psychological phenomena in people who cannot provide verbal reports of their responses. Examples of such people are infants and comatose patients. Physiological indicators of habituation tell the researcher whether the person notices changes in the stimulus. Such changes might occur in the color, pattern, size, or form of a stimulus. These indicators signal whether the person notices the changes at all, as well as what changes the person notices in the stimulus.

Among other phenomena, psychologists have used habituation to study visual discrimination (detection of differences among stimuli) in infants. First, they habituate the infant to a particular visual pattern. They do so by presenting it until the infant no longer pays attention to it. Then they introduce a visual pattern that only slightly differs from the one to which the infant has become habituated. If the infant is able to discriminate the difference, the infant will not habituate to (i.e., will notice) the new pattern. If the infant cannot discriminate the difference, however, the infant will appear to be habituated to the new pattern as well.

Habituation definitely gives much more to our attentional system than it receives. That is, habituation itself requires no conscious effort and few attentional resources.

Despite its negligible use of attentional resources, it offers a great deal of support to attentional processes. It allows us easily to turn our attention away from familiar and relatively stable stimuli and toward novel and changing stimuli. We might conjecture about the evolutionary value of habituation. Without habituation, our attentional system would be much more greatly taxed. How easily would we function in our highly stimulating environments if we could not habituate to familiar stimuli? Imagine trying to listen to a lecture if you could not habituate to the sounds of your own breathing, the rustling of papers and books, or the faint buzzing of fluorescent lights.

Attention

Signal Detection

Habituation supports our attentional system. But this system performs many functions other than merely tuning out familiar stimuli and tuning into novel ones. There are three main functions of conscious attention. First, in **signal detection,** we detect the appearance of a particular stimulus. Second, in **selective attention,** we choose to attend to some stimuli and to ignore others (Cohen, 2003; Duncan, 1999). Third, in **divided attention,** we prudently allocate our available attentional resources to coordinate our performance of more than one task at a time. These three functions are summarized in Table 3.4.

First consider signal detection. What factors contribute to your ability to detect important events in the world? How do people search the environment to detect important stimuli? Understanding this function of attention has immediate practical importance. A lifeguard at a busy beach must be ever vigilant. Similarly, an air-traffic controller must be highly vigilant. Many other occupations require vigilance. Examples are those involving communications and warning systems and quality control in almost any setting. Even the work of police detectives, physicians, and research psychologists requires vigilance. We also must search out from among a diverse array of items those that are more important. In each of these settings, people must remain alert to detect the appearance of a stimulus. But each setting also involves the presence of distracters. It also has prolonged periods during which the stimulus is absent.

The Nature of Signal Detection

Signal-detection theory (SDT) is a theory of how we detect stimuli that involves four possible outcomes of the presence or absence of a stimulus and our detection or nondetection of a stimulus. It characterizes our attempts to detect a **signal,** a target stimulus (Table 3.5). First, in *hits* (also called "true positives"), we correctly identify the presence of a target. Second, in *false alarms* (also called "false positives"), we incorrectly identify the presence of a target that is actually absent. Third, in *misses* (also called "false negatives"), we incorrectly fail to observe the presence of a target. Fourth, in *correct rejections* (also called "true negatives"), we correctly identify the absence of a target. Usually, the presence of a target is difficult to detect. Thus we make detection judgments based on inconclusive information with some criteria for target

TABLE 3.4	Four Main Functions of Attention	

Cognitive psychologists have been particularly interested in the study of divided attention, vigilance and signal detection, search, and selective attention.

FUNCTION	DESCRIPTION	EXAMPLE
Divided attention	We often manage to engage in more than one task at a time, and we shift our attentional resources to allocate them prudently, as needed.	Experienced drivers easily can talk while driving under most circumstances, but if another vehicle seems to be swerving toward their car, they quickly switch all of their attention away from talking and toward driving.
Vigilance and signal detection	On many occasions, we vigilantly try to detect whether we did or did not sense a signal, a particular target stimulus of interest. Through vigilant attention to detecting signals, we are primed to take speedy action when we do detect signal stimuli.	In a research submarine, we may watch for unusual sonar blips; in a dark street, we may try to detect unwelcome sights or sounds; or following an earthquake, we may be wary of the smell of leaking gas or of smoke.
Search	We often engage in an active search for particular stimuli.	If we detect smoke (as a result of our vigilance), we may engage in an active search for the source of the smoke. In addition, some of us are constantly in search of missing keys, sunglasses, and other objects; my teenage son often "searches" for missing items in the refrigerator (often without much success—until someone else points them out to him).
Selective attention	We constantly are making choices regarding the stimuli to which we will pay attention and the stimuli that we will ignore. By ignoring or at least deemphasizing some stimuli, we thereby highlight particularly salient stimuli. The concentrated focus of attention on particular informational stimuli enhances our ability to manipulate those stimuli for other cognitive processes, such as verbal comprehension or problem solving.	We may pay attention to reading a textbook or to listening to a lecture while ignoring such stimuli as a nearby radio or television or latecomers to the lecture.

detections. The number of hits is influenced by where you place your criteria for considering something a hit. In other words, how willing are you to make false alarms? For example, sometimes the consequences of making a miss are so grave that we lower the criteria for considering something as a hit. In this way, we increase the number of false alarms we make to boost hit detection. This trade-off often occurs with medical diagnoses. For example, it might occur with highly sensitive screening tests where positive results lead to further tests. Thus, overall sensitivity to targets must reflect the placement of a flexible criterion and is measured in terms of hits minus false alarms. SDT often is used to measure sensitivity to a target's presence. Measurement can

TABLE 3.5	Signal Detection Matrix Used in Signal-Detection Theory	
Signal-detection theory was one of the first theories to suggest an interaction between the physical sensation of a stimulus and cognitive processes such as decision making.		

SIGNAL	DETECT A SIGNAL	DO NOT DETECT A SIGNAL
Present	Hit	Miss
Absent	False alarm	Correct rejection

occcur under conditions of both vigilance and the search for targets. It also is used in memory research to control for effects of guessing.

A practical example of the use of signal-detection theory is the role of screeners in airports. A disturbing finding was that the 9/11 hijackers were screened, and several of them were pulled aside because they set off metal detectors. After further screening, they were let onto their planes anyway, although they were carrying boxcutters. The results of what constituted a "miss" for the screeners were disastrous. As a result of this fiasco, the rules for screening were tightened up considerably. But the tightening of rules created many false alarms. Babies, grandmothers, and other relatively low-risk passengers started to get second and sometimes even third screenings. So the rules were modified to profile passengers by computer. For example, those who bought one-way tickets or changed their flight plans at the last moment became more likely to be subjected to extra screening. This procedure, in turn, has inconvenienced those travelers who need to change their travel plans frequently, such as business travelers. The system for screening passengers is constantly evolving in order to minimize both misses and false alarms (Figure 3.3).

Vigilance

Vigilance refers to a person's ability to attend to a field of stimulation over a prolonged period, during which the person seeks to detect the appearance of a particular target stimulus of interest. When being vigilant, the individual watchfully waits to detect a signal stimulus that may appear at an unknown time. Typically, vigilance is needed in settings where a given stimulus occurs only rarely but requires immediate attention as soon as it does occur. Military officers watching for a sneak attack are engaged in a high-stakes vigilance task.

In one study, participants watched a visual display that looked like the face of a clock (Mackworth, 1948). A clock hand moved in continuous steps. Every once in a while, the clock hand would take a double step. The participants' task was to press a button as soon as possible after observing a double step. Participants' performance began to deteriorate substantially after just half an hour of observation. Indeed, after a half hour, participants were missing close to one fourth of the double steps. It appears that decreases in vigilance are not primarily a result of participants' decreased sensitivity. Rather, they are due to their increased doubtfulness about their perceived

FIGURE 3.3

Reuters/Corbis

Screening hand luggage is an example of signal-detection theory at work in everyday life. Screeners learn techniques to enable them to maximize "hits" and "correct rejections" and to minimize "false alarms" and "misses."

observations (Broadbent & Gregory, 1965). To relate these findings to SDT, over time it appears that participants become less willing to risk reporting false alarms. They err instead by failing to report the presence of the signal stimulus when they are not sure they detect it. They thereby show higher rates of misses. Training can help to increase vigilance (Fisk & Schneider, 1981). But in tasks requiring sustained vigilance, fatigue hinders performance. So there may be no substitute for frequent rest periods to enhance signal detection.

Attentional processes governing signal detection also appear to be highly localized and strongly influenced by expectation (Motter, 1999; Posner, Snyder, & Davidson, 1980). Neurological studies show that signal detection of a visual stimulus is greatest at the point where a signal is expected to appear. Accuracy of signal detection falls off sharply as the appearance of the stimulus occurs farther from the locus of attention

© Peter Menzel/Stock Boston

For some jobs, vigilance is a matter of life and death.

(LaBerge & Brown, 1989; LaBerge, Carter, & Brown, 1992; Mangun & Hillyard, 1990, 1991). Thus, a busy lifeguard or air-traffic controller may respond quickly to a signal within a narrow radius of where a signal is expected to appear. But signals appearing outside the concentrated range of vigilant attention may not be detected as quickly or as accurately.

In vigilance tasks, expectations regarding location strongly affect response efficiency. In this case, efficiency involves the speed and accuracy of detecting a target stimulus. However, expectations regarding the form of the stimulus do not (Posner, Snyder, & Davidson, 1980). Here, form refers to what shape or letter may appear in a visual field. Suppose, now, that a participant is cued to look for a target stimulus in two distant locations. This cueing does not enhance vigilance performance for both locations. Various studies suggest that visual attention may be (very roughly) likened to a spotlight. Stimuli within the region of the attentional spotlight are detected readily. But stimuli outside the spotlight are not (Norman, 1968; Palmer, 1990; Posner & associates, 1980). Furthermore, like a spotlight, the beam of focused attention can be narrowly concentrated on a small area or widened to embrace a larger, more diffuse area (Palmer, 1990). However, the abrupt onset of a stimulus (i.e., the sudden appearance of a stimulus) captures our attention. This effect occurs even when factors such as degree of illuminance (brightness) are controlled (Yantis, 1993). Thus, we seem to be predisposed to notice the sudden appearance of stimuli in our visual field. We might speculate about the adaptive advantage this feature of attention may have offered to our ancestral hunter-gatherer forebears. They presumably needed to avoid various predators. They also had to catch various prey.

Vigilance is extremely important in warding off terrorist attacks of various kinds. For example, repeating announcements at airports often ask travelers to be vigilant in looking for unattended baggage, which may contain explosives. Because luggage is such a common site at airports, it is difficult to spot bags that are lying unattended, not seeming to belong to anyone. Similarly, in many countries, pedestrians are asked to be vigilant for cars or trucks that seem to be unattended and parked in odd places, because they may contain explosives that can be detonated at a distance. The costs of failure of vigilance, in today's world, can be great loss of life as well as property.

Search

Whereas vigilance involves passively waiting for a signal stimulus to appear, search involves actively and often skillfully seeking out a target (Pashler, 1998; Posner & DiGirolamo, 1998; Posner, DiGirolamo, & Fernandez-Duque, 1997; Wolfe, 1994). Specifically, **search** refers to a scan of the environment for particular features—actively looking for something when you are not sure where it will appear. Trying to locate a particular brand of cereal in a crowded aisle at the grocery store—or a particular key term in a crowded textbook—is an example of search. As with vigilance, when we are searching for something, we may respond by making false alarms. Airport screeners look at X-rays of hand luggage, trying to determine whether there are any sharp objects in the baggage that might pose a danger in flight. Search is made more difficult by **distracters,** nontarget stimuli that divert our attention away from the target stimulus. In the case of search, false alarms usually arise when we encounter such distracters while searching for the target stimulus. For instance, consider searching for a product in the grocery store. We often see several distracting items that look something like the item we hope to find. Package designers take advantage of the effectiveness of distracters when creating packaging for products. For example, if a container looks like a box of Cheerios, you may pick it up without realizing that it's really Tastee-Oh's.

As you may have expected, the number of targets and distracters affects the difficulty of the task. For example, try to find the *T* in Figure 3.4 (*a*). Then try to find the *T* in Figure 3.4 (*b*). The display size refers to the number of items in a given visual array. (It does not refer to the size of the items or even the size of the field on which the array is displayed.) The display-size effect is the degree to which the number of items in a display hinders (slows down) the search process. When studying visual-search phenomena, investigators often manipulate the display size. They then observe how various contributing factors increase or decrease the display-size effect.

Distracters cause more trouble under some conditions than under others. Suppose we look for some distinctive features. Examples might be color, size, proximity to like items, distance from unlike items, or orientation, such as vertical, horizontal, or oblique. We are able to conduct a **feature search,** in which we simply scan the environment for that feature or those features (Treisman, 1986, 1992, 1993). Distracters play little role in slowing our search in that case. For example, try to find the O in Figure 3.4 (*c*). The O has some distinctive features, as compared with the *L* distracters in the display. The O thus seems to pop out of the display. Featural singletons, which are items with distinctive features, stand out in the display (Yantis, 1993). When featural singletons are targets, they seem to grab our attention. They

FIGURE 3.4A

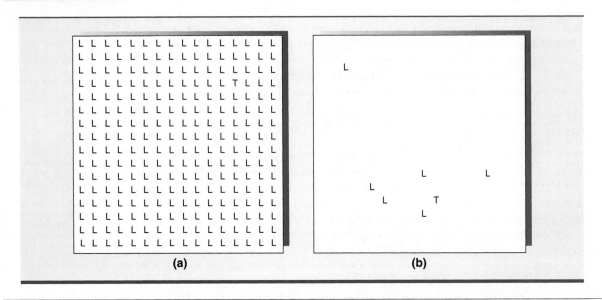

Compare the relative difficulty in finding the T in (a) and (b). The display size affects your ease of performing the task.

FIGURE 3.4B

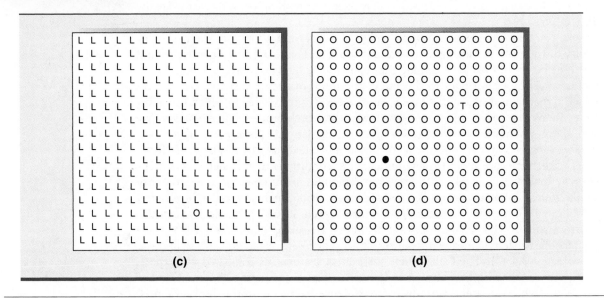

In (c), find the O and in (d), find the T.

make search virtually impossible to avoid. Unfortunately, any featural singletons grab our attention. This includes featural singletons that are distracters. When we are searching for a featural-singleton target stimulus, a featural-singleton distracter stimulus seems to distract us from finding the target (Theeuwes, 1992). For example, find the *T* in Figure 3.4 (*d*). The *T* is a featural singleton. But the presence of the black (filled) circle probably slows you down in your search.

A problem arises, however, when the target stimulus has no unique or even distinctive features. An example might be a particular boxed or canned item in a grocery aisle. In these situations, the only way we can find it is to conduct a conjunction search (Treisman, 1991). In a **conjunction search,** we look for a particular combination (conjunction—joining together) of features. For example, the only difference between a *T* and an *L* is the particular integration (conjunction) of the line segments. The difference is not a property of any single distinctive feature of either letter. Both letters comprise a horizontal line and a vertical line. So a search looking for either of these features would provide no distinguishing information. In Figure 3.4 (*a*), you had to perform a conjunction search to find the *T*. So it probably took you longer to find it than to find the *O* in Figure 3.4 (*c*).

Feature-Integration Theory

According to Anne Treisman, a **feature-integration theory** explains the relative ease of conducting feature searches and the relative difficulty of conducting conjunction searches. Consider Treisman's (1986) model of how our minds conduct visual searches. For each possible feature of a stimulus, each of us has a mental map for representing the given feature across the visual field. For example, there is a map for every color, size, shape, or orientation (e.g., p, q, b, d) of each stimulus in our visual field. For every stimulus, the features are represented in the feature maps immediately. There is no added time required for additional cognitive processing. Thus, during feature searches, we monitor the relevant feature map for the presence of any activation anywhere in the visual field. This process can be done in parallel (all at once). It therefore shows no display-size effects. However, during conjunction searches, an additional stage of processing is needed. During this stage, we must use our attentional resources as a sort of mental "glue." It conjoins two or more features into an object representation at a particular location. This attentional process can only conjoin the features one object at a time. This stage must be carried out sequentially, conjoining each object one by one. Effects of display size (i.e., a larger number of objects with features to be conjoined) therefore appear.

Sometimes people search for information quite effectively, although their attention is divided. How can they do this? One way is through a feature inhibition mechanism (Treisman & Sato, 1990). Here, inhibition or suppression occurs of irrelevant features that might distract an individual from being able to search for a target. There is some neuropsychological support for Treisman's model. For example, Nobel laureates David Hubel and Torsten Wiesel (1979) have identified specific neural feature detectors. These are cortical neurons that respond differentially to visual stimuli of particular orientations. Examples of such orientations would be vertical, horizontal, or diagonal. More recently, investigators have identified additional cortical processes involved in the various distinct steps of feature integration required for a variety of tasks (Bachevalier & Mishkin, 1986; Mishkin & Appenzeller, 1987;

FIGURE 3.4C

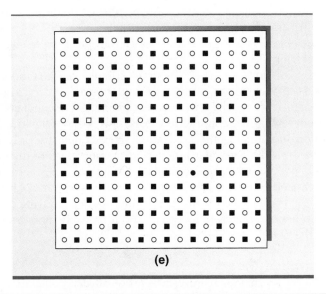

(e)

In (e), find the black circle.

Anne Treisman is a professor of psychology at Princeton University. She is well known for her work in a variety of areas of attention and perception, especially her theory that incoming signals are attenuated rather than filtered when they make their way through the cognitive-processing system.

Mishkin, Ungerleider, & Macko, 1983). These tasks include object recognition and visual discrimination. The researchers observed that during visual search, differing neural activity appears to be involved in the relatively low-level identification of features. This is in contrast to the neural activity during relatively high-level featural integration and synthesis. Today we know that processing is more complex than Hubel and Wiesel originally thought. There is parallel processing of color, orientation, motion, depth, and other features (Maunsell, 1995).

Similarity Theory

Not everyone agrees with Treisman's model, however. According to *similarity theory*, Treisman's data can be reinterpreted. On this view, the data are a result of the fact that as the similarity between target and distracter stimuli increases, so does the difficulty in detecting the target stimuli (Duncan & Humphreys, 1989, 1992). Thus, targets that are highly similar to distracters are hard to detect. Targets that are highly disparate from distracters are easy to detect. For example, try to find the black (filled) circle in Figure 3.4 (e). The target is highly similar to the distracters (black squares or white circles). It is therefore very difficult to find.

According to this theory, another factor that facilitates the search for target stimuli is similarity (uniformity) among the distracters (Duncan & Humphreys, 1989). Searching for target stimuli against a background of relatively uniform (highly similar) distracters is fairly easy. But searching for target stimuli against a background of highly diverse distracters is quite difficult. Furthermore, the difficulty of search tasks depends on the degree of similarity between the targets and the distracters and on the degree of disparity among the distracters. But it does not depend on the number of features to be integrated. For instance, one reason that it is easier to read long strings of text written in lowercase letters than text written in capital letters is that capital letters tend to be more similar to one another in appearance. Lowercase letters, in contrast, have more distinguishing features. However, as in the initial letter of a sentence or of a word in a title, capital letters are quite distinctive from lowercase letters. You can get an idea of how highly dissimilar distracters impede visual search. Try to find the capital letter *R* in Figure 3.4 (*f*) and (*g*).

In addition, some findings do not fit well with Treisman's theory. For example, some features (e.g., size and color) may be conjoined easily even without attentional processes. Search for these integrated features appears to occur about as rapidly as does search for some discrete features (He & Nakayama, 1992; Nakayama, 1990). For example, it would be about as easy to search for objects with conjoined features of size and color as it would be to search for objects of a distinctive color alone. For instance, it would be as easy to search for large red circles (target stimuli) versus. small red circles, large blue circles, and small blue circles (distracters) as it would be to search for red circles (target stimuli) versus. blue circles (distracters). Thus, the difficulty of visual search depends not only on whether discrete features must be integrated. It also depends on which features must be integrated in a given search.

Guided Search Theory

In response to these and other findings, investigators have proposed an alternative to Treisman's model. They call it *guided search* (Cave & Wolfe, 1990). According to

---

FIGURE 3.4D

(f)   (g)

In (f) and (g), find the R.

these researchers, the guided-search model suggests that all searches, whether feature searches or conjunction searches, involve two consecutive stages. The first is a parallel stage. In it, the individual simultaneously activates a mental representation of all the potential targets. The representation is based on the simultaneous activation of each of the features of the target. In a subsequent serial stage, the individual sequentially evaluates each of the activated elements, according to the degree of activation. He or she then chooses the true targets from the activated elements. According to this model, the activation process of the parallel initial stage helps to guide the evaluation and selection process of the serial second stage of the search.

Let's see how guided search might work. Try to find the white circles in Figure 3.4 (h). In this case, the targets are all white circles. The distracters are all black squares. Thus, we have a feature search. So the parallel stage will activate all the circles. But it will activate none of the squares. Therefore, the serial stage quickly will be able to select all the targets. However, look at Figure 3.4 (i). Try to find the black circle. The distracters include white squares, white circles, and black squares. Hence, the parallel stage will activate a mental map for the target black circle. This is the top-priority activation because of the conjunction of features. For the distracter, it will activate black squares and white circles. During the serial stage, you first will evaluate the black circle, which was highly activated. But then you will evaluate the black squares and the white circles, which were less highly activated. You then will dismiss them as distracters.

Cave and Wolfe's guided-search model predicts that some conjunction searches are easier than others. In particular, those involving more items with features similar to those of the target are easier than those involving fewer items with features simi-

FIGURE 3.4E

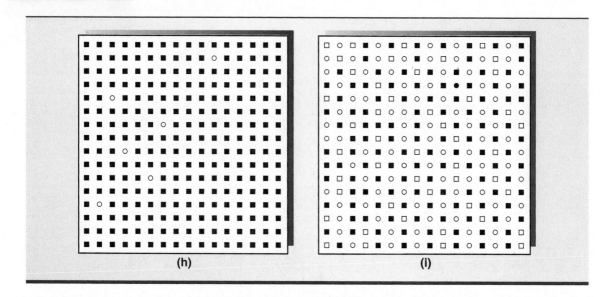

(h)   (i)

In (h), find the white (hollow) circles, and in (i), find the black circle.

lar to those of the target. These researchers found support for their model by creating computer simulations of their model. They then compare the performance of the simulations with the actual performance of participants carrying out searches. Under most circumstances, the simulations of their model produced results that were very similar to those of the actual participants.

Movement-Filter Theory

One feature, movement, shows paradoxical effects when it is combined with other features (McLeod & associates, 1991). Sometimes movement enhances the ease and speed of conducting a visual search. But other times it inhibits visual search. Suppose movement is conjoined with a distinctive feature, such as the shape of a target. Search then occurs more easily and speedily than in the search for the distinctive feature alone. For example, movement particularly facilitates visual search when the conjoining feature is a distinctive shape. An example would be X versus O (McLeod, Driver, & Crisp, 1988; McLeod & associates,1991). For more subtle features, such as a very slight difference in orientation, visual search is slowed when movement is a conjoining feature.

Perhaps we possess a some kind of a movement filter. And suppose it "can direct attention to stimuli with a common movement characteristic" (McLeod & associates, 1991, p. 55), independently of other visual features. Lesion studies even have identified a possible cerebral location for the movement filter: a region of the medial temporal cortex (McLeod & associates, 1989). Other researchers have offered support for the existence of a movement filter. They have identified particular neural pathways for detecting depth and movement. They also have discovered discrete pathways for detecting form and color (Livingstone & Hubel, 1988).

Synchronous movement also enhances the likelihood of illusory conjunctions. In illusory conjunctions, we incorrectly perceive that a particular distracter stimulus possesses conjoined features that are being sought in a target stimulus. Illusory conjunctions occur as a result of mistakenly conjoining in our minds discrete features that we observe in distracter stimuli. Suppose we are looking for a target that is a red triangle. In our peripheral vision we get a quick glance at a red square and a yellow triangle. We incorrectly may form an illusory conjunction. We believe that we saw a red triangle. Illusory conjunctions are predicted by Treisman's (1991, 1992, 1993) model.

Consider when illusory conjunctions occur and movement is a feature. We may identify distracters as targets if they possess some features of the target and are moving in synchrony and in the same direction as the target. For example, suppose the target stimulus is a red square. The observer sees a red circle and a white square moving together in the same direction. The observer may identify incorrectly one or both as red squares. He or she perceives an illusory conjunction of features (Baylis, Driver, & McLeod, 1992). Illusory conjunctions are much more likely under two conditions. The first is when the observer has limited attentional resources. An example would be focusing attention on other stimuli (Treisman & Schmidt, 1982). The second is when the observer has limited information. An example would be incomplete, distorted, or out-of-focus stimuli. Illusory conjunctions also play a role in form and pattern perception (see Chapter 4). Such conjunctions also are influenced by various factors. One factor is other features of the surrounding context. A second is prior knowledge. And a third is preexisting schemas (Treisman, 1990). For example, we are

FIGURE 3.4F

In (j), find the deviant stimuli in each subarray. In (k) and (l), find all instances of the letters p and a.

much more likely to form an illusory conjunction of features that leads us to perceive a yellow banana and a purple plum rather than a purple banana and a yellow plum. The exception might be if the odd fruits were depicted on a canvas along with blue apples and pink limes.

Final Considerations

Suppose we know in advance the general area in which to expect a stimulus to be located. We then can find the stimulus much more readily (Posner & associates, 1980). For example, consider Figure 3.4 (j). Once we detect the spatial pattern regarding where to expect the target stimulus, our search becomes easier. Prior knowledge also influences our ability to use various strategies for conjunctive searches. For example, for most people over age 7 years, it will be relatively easy to find the instances of the letters *a* and *p* in Figure 3.4 (k). Similarly, anyone who is experienced at touch typing can readily find the instances of those letters in Figure 3.4 (l). In both cases, prior knowledge may facilitate visual search.

Selective and Divided Attention

Basic Paradigms for Studying Selective Attention

Suppose you are at a dinner party. It is just your luck that you are sitting next to a salesman. He sells 110 brands of vacuum cleaners. He describes to you in excruciating detail the relative merits of each brand. As you are listening to this blatherer, who happens to be on your right, you become aware of the conversation of the two diners sitting on your left. Their exchange is much more interesting. It contains juicy information you had not known about one of your acquaintances. You find yourself trying to keep up the semblance of a conversation with the blabbermouth on your right. But you are also tuning in to the dialogue on your left.

The preceding vignette describes a naturalistic experiment in selective attention. It was inspired the research of Colin Cherry (1953). Cherry referred to this phenomenon as the **cocktail party problem,** the process of tracking one conversation in the face of the distraction of other conversations. He observed that cocktail parties are often settings in which selective attention is salient. The preceding is a good example.

Cherry did not actually hang out at numerous cocktail parties to study conversations. He studied selective attention in a more carefully controlled experimental setting. He devised a task known as shadowing. In *shadowing,* you listen to two different messages. You are required to repeat back only one of the messages as soon as possible after you hear it. In other words, you are to follow one message (think of a detective "shadowing" a suspect) but ignore the other. For some participants, he used **binaural presentation,** presenting the same two messages or sometimes just one message to both ears simultaneously. For other participants, he used **dichotic presentation,** presenting a different message to each ear. (Figure 3.5 illustrates how these listening tasks might be presented.)

Cherry's participants found it virtually impossible to track only one message during simultaneous binaural presentation of two distinct messages. It is as though in attending to one thing, we divert attention from another (Desimone & Duncan, 1995; Duncan, 1996). His participants much more effectively shadowed distinct messages in dichotic-listening tasks. In such tasks they generally shadowed messages fairly accurately. During dichotic listening, participants also were able to notice

FIGURE 3.5

Colin Cherry discovered that selective attention was much easier during dichotic presentation than during binaural presentation of differing messages.

physical, sensory changes in the unattended message, for example when the message was changed to a tone or the voice changed from a male to a female speaker. However, they did not notice semantic changes in the unattended message. They failed to notice even when the unattended message shifted to English or German or was played backward.

Think of being at a cocktail party or in a noisy restaurant. Three factors help you to selectively attend only to the message of the target speaker to whom you wish to listen. The first is distinctive sensory characteristics of the target's speech. Examples of such characteristics are high versus low pitch, pacing, and rhythmicity. A second is sound intensity (loudness). And a third is location of the sound source. Attending to the physical properties of the target speaker's voice has its advantages. You can avoid being distracted by the semantic content of messages from nontarget speakers in the area. Clearly, the sound intensity of the target also helps. In addition, you probably intuitively can use a strategy for locating sounds. This changes a binaural task into a dichotic one. You turn one ear toward and the other ear away from the target speaker. Note that this method offers no greater total sound intensity. The reason is that with one ear closer to the speaker, the other is farther away. The key advantage is the difference in volume. It allows you to locate the source of the target sound.

Filter and Bottleneck Theories of Selective Attention

Models of selective attention can be of several different kinds (Bundesen, 1996, 2000; Logan, 1996). The models differ in two ways. First, do they have a distinct "filter" for incoming information? Second, if they do, where in the processing of information does the filter occur (Pashler, 1998)?

Broadbent's Model
According to one of the earliest theories of attention, we filter information right after it is registered at the sensory level (Broadbent, 1958; Figure 3.6). In Broadbent's view, multiple channels of sensory input reach an attentional filter. It permits only one channel of sensory information to proceed through the filter to reach the processes of perception. We thereby assign meaning to our sensations. In addition to the target stimuli, stimuli with distinctive sensory characteristics may pass through the attentional system. Examples would be differences in pitch or in loudness. They thereby reach higher levels of processing, such as perception. However, other stimuli will be filtered out at the sensory level. They may never pass through the attentional filter to reach the level of perception. Broadbent's theory was supported by Colin Cherry's findings that sensory information may be noticed by an unattended ear. Examples of such material would be male versus female voices or tones versus words. But information requiring higher perceptual processes is not noticed in an unattended ear. Examples would be German versus English words or even words played backward instead of forward.

Moray's Selective Filter Model
Not long after Broadbent's theory, evidence began to suggest that Broadbent's model must be wrong (e.g., Gray & Wedderburn, 1960). First, an investigator found that even when participants ignore most other high-level (e.g., semantic) aspects of an

FIGURE 3.6

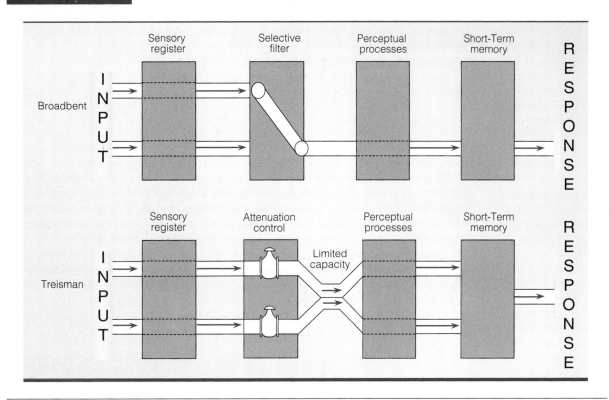

Various mechanisms have been proposed suggesting a means by which incoming sensory information passes through the attentional system to reach high-level perceptual processes.

unattended message, they still recognize their names in an unattended ear (Moray, 1959). He suggested that the reason for this effect is that powerful, highly salient messages may break through the filter of selective attention. But other messages may not. To modify Broadbent's metaphor, one could say that, according to Moray, the selective filter blocks out most information at the sensory level. But some highly salient messages are so powerful that they burst through the filtering mechanism.

Treisman's Attenuation Model

While a participant is shadowing a coherent message in one ear and ignoring a message in the other ear, something interesting occurs. If the message in the attended ear suddenly is switched to the unattended ear, participants will pick up the first few words of the old message in the new ear (Treisman, 1960). This finding suggests that context briefly will lead the participants to shadow a message that should be ignored.

Moreover, if the unattended message was identical to the attended one, all participants noticed it. They noticed even if one of the messages was slightly out of temporal synchronization with the other (Treisman, 1964a, 1964b). Participants typically recognized the two messages to be the same when the shadowed message was as much as 4.5 seconds ahead of the unattended one. They also recognized it if it was as far as 1.5 seconds behind the unattended one. In other words, it is easier to recognize the unattended message when it precedes, rather than follows, the attended one. Treisman also observed fluently bilingual participants. Some of them noticed the identity of messages if the unattended message was a translated version of the attended one.

Moray's modification of Broadbent's filtering mechanism was clearly not sufficient to explain Treisman's (1960) findings that messages switched from the attended ear to the unattended ear were briefly shadowed. They also could not explain her work with bilinguals. Here, as noted, synonymous messages were recognized in the unattended ear (Treisman, 1964a, 1964b). Her findings suggested to Treisman that at least some information about unattended signals is being analyzed. Treisman also interpreted Moray's findings as indicating that some higher-level processing of the information reaching the supposedly unattended ear must be taking place. Otherwise, participants would not recognize the familiar sounds to realize that they were salient. That is, the incoming information cannot be filtered out at the level of sensation. If it were, we would never perceive the message to recognize its salience.

Based on these findings, Treisman proposed a theory of selective attention. It involves a different kind of filtering mechanism. Recall that in Broadbent's theory the filter acts to block stimuli other than the target stimulus. In Treisman's theory, however, the mechanism merely attenuates (weakens the strength of) stimuli other than the target stimulus. For particularly potent stimuli, the effects of the attenuation are not great enough to prevent the stimuli from penetrating the signal-weakening mechanism. Figure 3.5 illustrates Treisman's signal-attenuating mechanism.

According to Treisman, selective attention involves three stages. In the first stage, we preattentively analyze the physical properties of a stimulus. Examples would be loudness (sound intensity) and pitch (related to the "frequency" of the sound waves). This preattentive process is conducted in parallel (simultaneously) on all incoming sensory stimuli. For stimuli that show the target properties, we pass the signal on to the next stage. For stimuli that do not show these properties, we pass on only a weakened version of the stimulus. In the second stage, we analyze whether a given stimulus has a pattern, such as speech or music. For stimuli that show the target pattern, we pass the signal on to the next stage. For stimuli that do not show the target pattern, we pass on only a weakened version of the stimulus. In the third stage we focus attention on the stimuli that make it to this stage. We sequentially evaluate the incoming messages. We assign appropriate meanings to the selected stimulus messages.

Deutsch and Deutsch's Late Filter Model

Consider an alternative to Treisman's attenuation theory. It simply moves the location of the signal-blocking filter to follow, rather than precede, at least some of the perceptual processing needed for recognition of meaning in the stimuli. In this view, the signal-blocking filter occurs later in the process. It has its effects after sensory analysis. Thus, it occurs after some perceptual and conceptual analysis of input have taken place (Deutsch & Deutsch, 1963; Norman, 1968—Figure 3.7). This later filtering would allow people to recognize information entering the unattended ear. For example, they might recognize the sound of their own names or a translation of attended input (for bilinguals). If the information does not perceptually strike some sort of chord, people will throw it out at the filtering mechanism shown in Figure 3.7. If it does, however, as with the sound of an important name, people will pay attention to it. Note that proponents of both the early and the late filtering mechanisms propose that there is an attentional bottleneck through which only a single source of information can pass. The two models differ only in terms of where they hypothesize the bottleneck to be positioned.

The Multimode Theory

Multimode theory (Johnston & Heinz, 1978) proposes that attention is flexible. Selection of one message over another message can be made at any of various different points in the course of information processing. According to this theory, processing occurs in three stages. In Stage 1, the individual constructs sensory representations of stimuli. In Stage 2, the individual constructs semantic representations. Neither of these stages is fully conscious. In Stage 3, the representations of Stages 1 and 2 become conscious. Early selection (Broadbent) would be associated with Stage 1, whereas late selection would be associated with Stage 3. The difficulty of a task requiring selection depends, in part, upon when selection takes place. More effort is required in later than in earlier stages.

Neisser's Synthesis

In 1967, Ulric Neisser synthesized the early-filter and the late-filter models in a way different from Johnston and Heinz (1978). He proposed that there are two processes governing attention: preattentive and attentive processes. Preattentive, automatic processes are rapid and occur in parallel. They can be used to notice only physical sensory characteristics of the unattended message. But they do not discern meaning

FIGURE 3.7

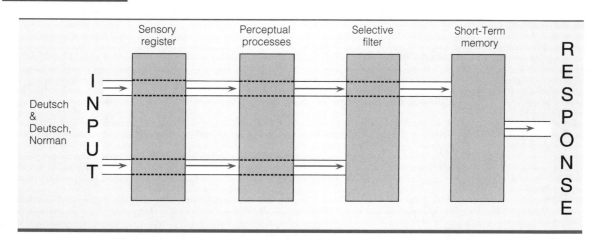

According to some cognitive psychologists, the attentional filtering mechanisms follow, rather than precede, preliminary perceptual processes.

or relationships. Attentive, controlled processes occur later. They are executed serially and consume time and attentional resources, such as working memory. They also can be used to observe relationships among features. They serve to synthesize fragments into a mental representation of an object. More recent work in attention builds on Neisser's distinction between preattentive and attentive processes. It focuses only on the consciously controlled aspects of attention (Cowan, 1995).

Consider a different view of the two processes (McCann & Johnston, 1992). According to these researchers, physical analysis of sensory data occurs continually. But semantic analysis of stimuli occurs only when cognitive capacity (in the form of working memory) is not already overtaxed. and the capacity also must be sufficient to permit such analysis. Supportive evidence is that people show much faster reaction times when responding to physically discriminable stimuli than to semantically discriminable stimuli.

A two-step model of some sort could account for Cherry's, Moray's, and Treisman's data. Evidence of fully automatic versus fully controlled processes also seems to support this model. Automatic processes may be governed only by the first step of attentional processing. Controlled processes additionally may be governed by the second of the two steps. The model also nicely incorporates aspects of Treisman's signal-attenuation theory and of her subsequent feature-integration theory. According to this latter theory, discrete processes for feature detection and for feature integration occur during searches. Again, Treisman's feature-detection process may be linked to the former of the two processes (i.e., speedy, automatic processing). Her feature-integration process may be linked to the latter of the two processes (i.e., slower, controlled processing). Unfortunately, however, the two-step model does not do a good job of explaining the continuum of processes from fully automatic ones to fully controlled ones. Recall, for example, that fully controlled processes appear to be at least partially automatized (Spelke, Hirst, & Neisser, 1976). How does the two-process model explain the automatization of processes in divided-attention phenomena? For example, how can one read for comprehension while writing dictated, categorized words?

Attentional-Resource Theories of Selective Attention

More recent theories have moved away from the notion of signal-blocking or signal-attenuating filters. They have instead moved toward the notion of apportionment of limited attentional resources. Attentional-resource theories help to explain how we can perform more than one attention-demanding task at a time. They posit that people have a fixed amount of attention that they can choose to allocate according to what the task requires. Figure 3.8 shows two examples of such a theory. In panel (a), the system has a single pool of resources that can be divided up, say, among multiple tasks (Kahneman, 1973).

However, it now appears that such a model represents an oversimplification. People are much better at dividing their attention when competing tasks are in different modalities. At least some attentional resources may be specific to the modality in which a task is presented. For example, most people easily can simultaneously listen to music and concentrate on writing. But it is harder to listen to the news station and concentrate on writing at the same time. The reason is that both are verbal tasks. The words from the news interfere with the words you are thinking about. Similarly, two visual tasks are more likely to interfere with each other than are a visual task coupled with an auditory one. Panel (b) of Figure 3.8 shows a model that allows for attentional

FIGURE 3.8

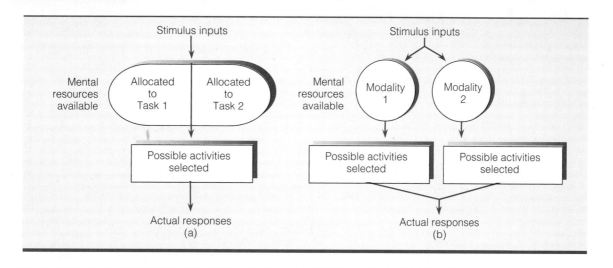

Attentional resources may involve either a single pool or a multiplicity of modality-specific pools. Although the attentional resources theory has been criticized for its imprecision, it seems to complement filter theories in explaining some aspects of attention.

resources to be specific to a given modality (Navon & Gopher, 1979). For someone trying to write while listening to music, the use of two distinctive modality-specific attentional resources probably would not pose serious attentional difficulties. An example would be auditory for music, writing for visual.

Attentional-resources theory has been criticized severely as overly broad and vague (e.g., S. Yantis, personal communication, December 1994). Indeed, it may not stand alone in explaining all aspects of attention. But it complements filter theories quite well. Filter and bottleneck theories of attention seem to be more suitable metaphors for competing tasks that seem to be attentionally incompatible. Examples would be selective-attention tasks or in simple divided-attention tasks involving the PRP (psychological refractory period) effect (Pashler, 1994). For these kinds of tasks, it appears that some preattentive processes may occur simultaneously. But processes requiring attention must be handled sequentially, as if passing one-by-one through an attentional bottleneck. However, resource theory seems to be a better metaphor for explaining phenomena of divided attention on complex tasks. In these tasks, practice effects may be observed. According to this metaphor, as each of the complex tasks becomes increasingly automatized, performance of each task makes fewer demands on the limited-capacity attentional resources. Additionally, for explaining search-related phenomena, theories specific to visual search (e.g., models proposing guided search [Cave & Wolfe, 1990] or similarity [Duncan & Humphreys, 1989]) seem to have stronger explanatory power than do filter or resource theories. However, these two kinds theories are not altogether incompatible. Although the findings from research on visual search do not conflict with filter or resource theories, the task-specific theories more specifically describe the processes at work during visual search.

Additional Considerations in Selective Attention

The Role of Task, Situation, and Person Variables

The existing theoretical models of attention may be too simplistic and mechanistic to explain the complexities of attention. For example, both trait-based anxiety (a personality characteristic) and situation-related anxiety have been found to affect attention (Eysenck & Byrne, 1992; Eysenck & Calvo, 1992; Eysenck & Graydon, 1989). Both types of anxiety tend to place constraints on attention. Other considerations enter in as well. A first is overall arousal. One may be tired, drowsy, or drugged, which may limit attention. Being excited sometimes enhances it. A second consideration is specific interest in a target task and stimuli, as against interest in distracters. A third is the nature of the task. For example, it may be highly difficult, complex, or novel. Such tasks require more attentional resources than do easy, simple, or highly familiar tasks. Task difficulty particularly influences performance during divided attention. A fourth consideration is amount of practice in performing a given task or set of tasks. Related to this is the skill of utilizing attentional resources for a task or tasks. Increased practice and skill enhance attention (Spelke, Hirst, & Nesser, 1976). A fifth consideration is the stage of processing at which attentional demands are needed. This stage may be before, during, or after some degree of perceptual processing.

In sum, some attentional processes occur outside our conscious awareness. Others are subject to conscious control. The psychological study of attention has included diverse phenomena. They include vigilance, search, selective attention, and divided attention during the simultaneous performance of multiple tasks. To explain this diversity of attentional phenomena, current theories emphasize that a filtering mechanism appears to govern some aspects of attention. Limited modality-specific attentional resources appear to influence other aspects of attention. Clearly, findings from cognitive research have yielded many insights into attention. But additional understanding also has been gained through the study of attentional processes in the brain.

The Stroop Effect

Much of the research on selective attention has focused on auditory processing. But selective attention also can be studied through visual processing. One of the tasks most frequently used for this purpose was first formulated by John Ridley Stroop (1935). The Stroop effect is named after him. The way the task works is as follows:

Quickly read aloud the following words: "brown," "blue," "green," "red," "purple." Easy, isn't it? Now quickly name aloud the colors shown in part (a) of the top figure on the back endpaper of this book. In this figure, the colored ink matches the name of the color word. This task, too, is easy. Now, look at part (c) of the same figure. Here, the colors of the inks differ from the color names that are printed with them. Again, name the ink colors you see, out loud, as quickly as possible.

You probably will find the task very difficult: Each of the written words interferes with your naming the color of the ink. The **Stroop effect** demonstrates the psychological difficulty in selectively attending to the color of the ink and trying to ignore the word that is printed with the ink of that color. One explanation of why the Stroop test may be particularly difficult is that, for you and most other adults, reading is now an automatic process. It is not readily subject to your conscious control (MacLeod, 1991, 1996). For that reason, you find it difficult intentionally to refrain from reading and instead to concentrate on identifying the color of the ink, disregarding the word printed in that ink color. An alternative explanation is that the output of a response occurs when the mental pathways for producing the response are activated sufficiently (MacLeod, 1991). In the Stroop test, the color word activates a cortical pathway for saying the word. In contrast, the ink-color name activates a pathway for naming the color. But the former pathway interferes with the latter. In this situation, it takes longer to gather sufficient strength of activation to produce the color-naming response and not the word-reading response.

Divided Attention

In signal detection and selective attention, the attentional system must coordinate a search for the simultaneous presence of many features. This is a relatively simple, if not easy, task. At times, however, the attentional system must perform two or more discrete tasks at the same time. Early work in this area was done by Ulric Neisser and Robert Becklen (1975). They had participants view a videotape in which the display of one activity was superimposed on the display of another activity. The first activity was three-person basketball; the second, two people playing a hand-slapping game. Initially, the task was simply to watch one activity and ignore the other. The participant pressed a button whenever key events occurred in the attended activity. Essentially, this first task required only selective attention.

However, the two researchers then asked participants to attend to both activities simultaneously. They were to signal key events in each of the two activities. Even when the researchers presented the two activities dichoptically (i.e., not in a single visual field, but rather with one activity observed by one eye and the other activity observed by the other eye), participants had great difficulty performing both tasks simultaneously. Neisser and Becklen hypothesized that improvements in performance would have occurred eventually as a result of practice. They also hypothesized that the performance of multiple tasks was based on skill resulting from practice. They believed it not to be based on special cognitive mechanisms.

The following year, investigators used a dual-task paradigm to study divided attention during the simultaneous performance of two activities (Spelke, Hirst, & Neisser, 1976). The dual-task paradigm involves two tasks (Task A and Task B) and three conditions (Task A only, Task B only, and both Tasks A and B). The idea was that the researchers would compare and contrast the latency (response time) and accuracy of performance in each of the three conditions. Of course, higher latencies mean slower responses. Previous research had shown that the speed and accuracy of simultaneous performance of two tasks was quite poor for the simultaneous performance of two controlled processes. There are rare instances in which people demonstrate high levels of speed and accuracy for the simultaneous performance of two tasks. In those instances, at least one of the tasks generally involves automatic processing, and usually both tasks involve such processing.

As expected, initial performance was indeed quite poor for the two controlled tasks they chose. These two tasks were reading for detailed comprehension and writing down dictated words. However, Spelke and her colleagues continued to have the two participants in their study perform these two tasks 5 days a week for many weeks (85 sessions in all). To the surprise of many, given enough practice, the participants' performance improved on both tasks. They showed improvements in their speed of reading and accuracy of reading comprehension, as measured by comprehension tests. They also showed increases in their recognition memory for words they had written during dictation. Eventually, participants' performance on both tasks reached the same levels that the participants previously had shown for each task alone.

The authors then introduced sublists of related words within the full word-dictation lists. Examples would be sublists of words that formed a sentence or rhymed. They asked the participants to report any of the words that had been dictated, or any general properties of the particular list that they remembered. The participants initially recalled very few words and no relationships among any of the words. After repeated practice, however, they noticed words related in various ways. One was by superordinate categories. A second was by rhyming sounds. A third was by strings of words that formed sentences. And a fourth was by parts of speech. They included grammatical classes, such as verbs and plural nouns. Furthermore, simultaneous performance of the more complex dictation task initially led to a dip in performance on the reading-comprehension task. With continued practice, performance on that task soon returned to previous high levels.

Next, the authors modified the word-dictation task. Now, the participants sometimes wrote the dictated words and sometimes wrote the correct one of two categories (e.g., animals vs. furniture) to which the dictated words belonged. At the same time, they still engaged in the reading-comprehension task. As with previous modifications, initial performance on the two tasks dropped. But performance returned to high levels after practice. Spelke and her colleagues suggested that these findings showed that controlled tasks can be automatized so that they consume fewer attentional resources. Further, two discrete controlled tasks may be automatized to function together as a unit. These authors were quick to point out that the tasks do not, however, become fully automatic. For one thing, they continue to be intentional and conscious. For another, they involve relatively high levels of cognitive processing.

An entirely different approach to studying divided attention has focused on extremely simple tasks that require speedy responses. When people try to perform two overlapping speeded tasks, the responses for one or both tasks are almost always slower (Pashler, 1994). When a second task begins soon after the first task has started, speed of performance usually suffers. The slowing resulting from simultaneous engagement in speeded tasks is termed the PRP effect, mentioned earlier in this chapter. Findings from PRP studies indicate that people can accommodate fairly easily perceptual processing of the physical properties of sensory stimuli while engaged in a second speeded task (Pashler, 1994). However, they cannot readily accommodate more than one cognitive task requiring them to choose a response, retrieve information from memory, or engage in various other cognitive operations. When both tasks require performance of any of these cognitive operations, one or both tasks will show the PRP effect.

Consider driving a car, for example. You need constantly to be aware of threats to your safety. Suppose you fail to select one such threat, such as a car that runs a red light and is headed directly at you as you enter an intersection. The result is that you may become an innocent victim of a horrible car accident. Moreover, if you are unsuccessful in dividing your attention, you may cause an accident. For example, most automobile accidents are caused by failures in divided attention. A study of 2700 crashes in the state of Virginia between June and November of 2002 investigated causes of accidents (Warner, 2004). According to the study, rubbernecking (viewing accidents that have already occurred) was the cause of 16% of accidents, followed by driver fatigue (12%); looking at scenery or landmarks (10%); distractions caused by passengers or children (9%); adjusting a radio, tape, or CD player (7%); and cell phone use (5%). On average, distractions occurring inside the vehicle accounted for 62% of the distractions reported. Distractions outside the vehicle accounted for 35%. The other 3% were of undetermined cause. The causes of accidents differed somewhat for rural versus urban areas. Accidents in rural areas were more likely to be due to driver fatigue, insects entering or striking the vehicle, or pet distractions. In urban areas, crashes were more likely to result from rubbernecking, traffic, or cell-phone use. Overall, the study suggested that cell phones are somewhat less responsible for accidents than some people had expected (Figure 3.9).

There are many ways to study divided attention (Egeth, 2000; Luck & associates, 1996; Moore & Egeth, 1997; Pashler, 1998; Pashler & Johnston, 1998; van der Heijden, 1992). One of the simplest starts with our own set of everyday experiences.

One way of studying divided attention makes use of a simulation of the driving situation (Strayer & Johnston, 2001). Researchers had participants perform a tracking task. The participants had control of a joystick, which moved a cursor on a computer screen. The participants needed to keep the cursor in position on a moving target. At various times, the target would flash either green or red. If the color was green, the participants were to ignore the signal. If the color was red, however, the participants were to push a simulated brake. The simulated brake was a button on the joystick.

In one condition, participants did the task singly, that is, by itself. In another condition, participants were involved in a second task. This procedure created a dual-task

FIGURE 3.9

Illustrating a failure of divided attention, drivers who rubberneck at the scene of an accident are a major cause of further accidents.

situation. The participants either listened to a radio broadcast while doing the task or talked on a cell phone to an experimental confederate. Participants talked roughly half the time and also listened roughly half the time. Two different topics were used to ensure that the results were not due to the topic of conversation. The results of the study are shown in Figure 3.10.

As shown in the Figure 3.10, the probability of a miss in the face of the red signal increased substantially in the cell-phone dual-task condition relative to the single-task condition. Reaction times were also substantially slower in this condition than in the single-task condition. In contrast, there was no signifiant difference between probabilities of a miss in the single-task and radio dual-task condition, nor was there a significant difference in reaction time in this condition. Thus, use of cell phones appears to be substantially more risky than listening to the radio while driving.

Consciousness of Complex Mental Processes

No serious investigator of cognition believes that people have conscious access to very simple mental processes. For example, none of us has a good idea of the means by which we recognize whether a printed letter such as "A" is an upper-case or a lower-case one. But now consider more complex processing. How conscious are we of our complex mental processes? Cognitive psychologists have differing views on how this question is best answered.

One view (Ericsson & Simon, 1984) is that people have quite good access to their complex mental processes. Simon and his colleagues, for example, have used *protocol analysis* in analyzing people's solving of problems, such as chess problems and so-called "cryparithmetic" problems, in which one has to figure out what numbers substitute for letters in a mathematical computation problem. These investigations have suggested to Simon and his colleagues that people have quite good conscious access to their complex information processes.

A second view is that people's access to their complex mental processes is not very good (e.g., Nisbett & Wilson, 1977). In this view, people may think they know how they solve complex problems, but their thoughts are frequently erroneous. According to Nisbett and Wilson, we typically are conscious of the products of our thinking, but only vaguely conscious, if at all, of the processes of thinking. For example, suppose you decide to buy one model of bicycle over another. You certainly will know the product of the decision—which model you bought. But you may have only a vague idea of how you arrived at that decision. Indeed, according to this view, you may believe you know why you made the decision, but that belief is likely to be flawed. Advertisers depend on this second view. They try to manipulate your thoughts and feelings toward a product so that, whatever your conscious thoughts may be, your unconscious ones will lead you to buy their product over that of a competitor.

The essence of the second view is that people's conscious access to their thought processes, and even their control over their thought processes, is quite minimal (Wegner, 2002; Wilson, 2002). Consider the problem of getting over someone who has terminated an intimate relationship with you. One technique that is sometimes used to get over someone is thought suppression. As soon as you think of the person, you try to put the individual out of your mind. There is one problem with this technique but it is a major one: It often does not work. Indeed, the more you try not to think about the person, the more you may end up thinking about him or her and

FIGURE 3.10

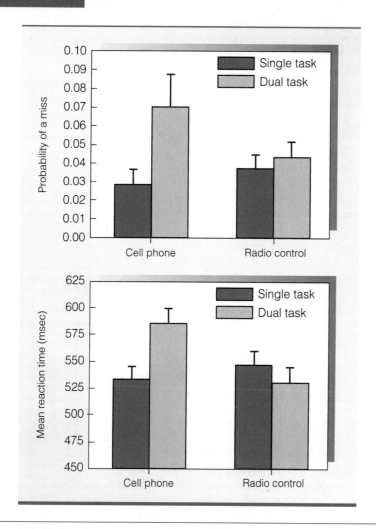

In the top panel, dual-task performance significantly increased the probability of a miss in the cell-phone condition but not in the radio-control condition. In the bottom panel, reaction time increased significantly for a dual task in the cell-phone condition but not in the radio-control condition. From Strayer, D. L., and Johnston, W. A. (2001). Driven to distraction: "Dual-task studies of simulated driving and conversing on a cellular telephone." Psychological Science, 12, 463. Reprinted by permission of Blackwell Publishing.

having trouble getting the person off your mind. Research has actually shown that trying not to think about something usually does not work (Wegner, 1997a, 1997b). Ironically, the more you try not to think about someone or something, the more "obsessed" you may become with the person or object.

Change Blindness

Adaptive behavior requires us to be attentive to changes in our environment because changes cue us to both opportunities and dangers. Evolutionarily, the ability to spot predators suddenly appearing in the visual field would have been a great advantage for the survival of organisms and, ultimately, their genes. It thus may be surprising to discover that people can show remarkable levels of **change blindness,** the inability to detect changes in objects or scenes that are being viewed (O'Regan, 2003; Simons, 2000).

In one study, a stranger asks a bystander for directions. As the interaction proceeds, two workers carrying a wooden door walked between the stranger and the bystander. When the workers have passed by, the original stranger has been replaced by a different stranger (one of the workers). The interaction then continues as before. How likely do you think it is that the bystander would notice that the person to whom he or she is talking is no longer the same person? Oddly enough, only about half of the bystanders notice that a switch has been made. Many do not even notice the change when they are explicitly told that the person to whom they are talking is not the one with whom they originally were conversing (Simons & Levin, 1997, 1998).

In another paradigm, participants see pairs of pictures, separated by brief intervals. Changes are made in the pictures in the interval. For the most part, people have difficulty recognizing the changes. They are more likely to recognize them when they are important to the scene than when they are unimportant. Even when told explicitly to look for changes, people have trouble finding them (Rensink, O'Regan, & Clark, 1997; Levin & Simons, 1997; Shore & Klein, 2000; Simons, 2000).

These results suggest that people are much less astute in recognizing changes in their environments than we might expect. Even fairly blatant changes, such as the identity of a person to whom we speak, may pass us by. When we admire Sherlock Holmes for his astuteness, we probably give him too little credit. In the fictional detective stories in which he plays a role, he notices extremely unobvious things. We tend often not to notice even things that are obvious.

Attention Deficit Hyperactivity Disorder

Most of us take for granted our ability to pay attention and to divide our attention in adaptive ways. But not everyone can do so. People with *attention deficit hyperactivity disorder* (ADHD) have difficulties in focusing their attention in ways that enable them to adapt in optimal ways to their environment (*Attention deficit hyperactivty disorder,* 2004, upon which this section is largely based; see also Swanson & associates, 2003). This condition typically first displays itself during the preschool or early school years. It is estimated that 3% to 5% of children have the disorder, meaning that, in the United States, roughly 2 million children exhibit symptoms. The disorder does not typically leave in adulthood, although it may vary in its severity, becoming either more or less severe.

The condition was first described by Dr. Heinrich Hoffman in 1845. Today, it has been widely investigated. No one know sfor sure the cause of ADHD. It may be a partially heritable condition. There is some evidence of a link to maternal smoking and drinking of alcohol during preganancy. Lead exposure on the part of the child may also be associated with ADHD. Brain injury is another possible cause, as are food additives, and in particular, sugar.

There is some evidence that incidence of ADHD has increased in recent years, although the reasons are not clear. Various hypotheses have been put forward, including increased watching of fast-paced television shows, use of fast-paced video games, additives in foods, increases in unknown toxins in the environment, and so forth.

The three primary characteristics of ADHD are inattention, hyperactivity (i.e., levels of activity that exceed what is normally shown by children of a given age), and impulsiveness. There are three main types. One is predominantly hyperactive-impulsive. The second is predominantly inattentive. The third combines both inattentativeness with hyperactivity and impulsiveness. I describe the inattentive type here because it is most relevant to the topic of this chapter.

Children with the inattentive type of ADHD shows several distinctive symptoms. First, they are easily distracted by irrelevant sights and sounds. Second, they often fail to pay attention to details. Third, they are susceptible to making careless mistakes in their work. Fourth, they often fail to read instructions completely or carefully. Fifth, they are susceptible to forgetting or losing things they need for tasks, such as pencils or books. Finally, they tend to jump from one incompleted task to another.

ADHD is most often treated with a combination of psychotherapy and drugs. Some of the drugs currently used to treat ADHD are Ritalin (methylphenidate), Metadate (methylphenidate), and Strattera (atomoxetine). This last drug differs from other drugs used to treat ADHD in that it is not a stimulant. Rather, it affects the neurotransmitter norepinephrine. The stimulants, in contrast, affect the neurotransmitter dopamine.

Cognitive Neuroscientific Approaches to Attention and Consciousness

The neuroscience of attention has an ever-growing body of literature. Consider an attempt to synthesize diverse studies investigating attentional processes in the brain (Posner, 1992; Posner & Dehaene, 1994; Posner & Raichle, 1994). Is attention a function of the entire brain, or is it a function of discrete attention-governing modules in the brain? According to Posner, the attentional system in the brain "is neither a property of a single brain area nor of the entire brain" (Posner & Dehaene, 1994, p. 75).

Indeed, for other researchers, attention involves mostly the interaction of diverse specific areas of the brain (Cohen & associates, 1994b; Connor & associates, 1996; Farah, 1994; Haxby & associates, 1994; Motter, 1999; Olshausen, Andersen, & Van Essen, 1993; Treue & Maunsell, 1996; Zipser, Lamme, & Schiller, 1996). There are, they believe, no specialized areas responsible only for specific attentional functions. Farah has done work on neglect with patients. *Neglect* is an attentional dysfunction in which participants ignore the half of their visual field that is contralateral to the hemisphere of the brain that has a lesion. It is due mainly to unilateral lesions in the parietal lobes. Research reveals that the problem may be a result of the interaction of systems that mutually inhibit one another. When only one of the pair involved in the system is damaged, as is the case with neglect patients, patients become locked in to one side of the visual field. The reason is that the inhibition normally provided by the other half of the system is no longer working.

One way to test for neglect is to give patients who are suspected of suffering from neglect a sheet of paper with a number of horizontal lines. Patients are then asked to bisect the lines precisely in the middle of each. Patients with lesions in the right hemisphere tend to bisect the lines to the right of the midline. Patients with lesions in the left hemisphere tend to bisect the lines to the left of the midline. The reason is that the former group of patients does not see all of the lines to the left, whereas the latter group does not see all of the lines to the right. Sometimes patients miss the lines altogether (patients who neglect the entire visual field).

Attentional Systems

Posner (1995) has identified an anterior (frontward) attention system (attentional network) within the frontal lobe and a posterior (toward the rear) attention system within the parietal lobe. The anterior attention system becomes increasingly activated during tasks requiring awareness. An example would be tasks in which participants must attend to the meanings of words. This system also is involved in "attention for action." Here, the participant is planning or selecting an action from among alternative courses of action. In contrast, the posterior attention system involves the parietal lobe of the cortex, a portion of the thalamus, and some areas of the midbrain related to eye movements. This system becomes highly activated during tasks involving visuospatial attention. In these tasks, the participant must disengage and shift attention (e.g., visual search or vigilance tasks) (Posner & Raichle, 1994). Attention also involves neural activity in the relevant visual, auditory, motor, and association areas of the cortex involved in particular visual, auditory, motor, or higher order tasks (Posner & associates, 1988). The anterior and posterior attention systems appear to enhance attention across various tasks. This suggests that they may be involved in regulating the activation of relevant cortical areas for specific tasks (Posner & Dehaene, 1994).

Another question has been with regard to the activity of the attentional system. This activity occurs as a result of enhanced activation of attended items, inhibition or suppressed activation of unattended items, or both processes. Apparently, it depends (Posner & Dehaene, 1994) on the particular task and on the area of the brain under investigation. The task at hand is to determine which processes occur in which areas of the brain during the performance of which tasks. For mapping the areas of the brain involved in various tasks, cognitive neuropsychologists often use positron emission tomography (PET). This technique maps regional cerebral blood flow (see Chapter 2 for a more in-depth discussion of this technique). In one such PET study (Corbetta & associates, 1993b), researchers found increased activation in areas responsible for each of the distinct attributes of various search tasks. These include features such as motion, color, and shape and for selected versus divided attentional conditions.

Using Event-Related Potentials to Measure Attention

An alternative way of studying attention in the brain is to focus on studying event-related potentials (ERPs; see Chapter 2). They indicate minute changes in electrical activity in response to various stimuli. Both the PET and the ERP techniques offer information on the geography (localization) of cerebral activity and on the chronology of cerebral events. However, the PET technique provides higher resolution for spatial localization of cerebral function. The ERP provides much more sensitive indications of the chronology of responses (within milliseconds; Näätänen, 1988a, 1988b, 1990, 1992). Thus, through ERP studies, even extremely brief responses to stimuli may be noticed.

The ERP's sensitivity to very brief responses has allowed Näätänen and his colleagues (e.g., Cowan & associates, 1993; Näätänen, 1988a, 1988b; Paavilainen & associates, 1993) to examine the specific conditions in which target versus distracter stimuli do or do not prompt attentional responses. For example, Näätänen has found that at least some response to infrequent, deviant auditory stimuli (e.g., peculiar changes in pitch) seems to be automatic. It occurs even when the participant is focusing attention on a primary task and is not consciously aware of the deviant stimuli. These automatic, preconscious responses to deviant stimuli occur whether the stimuli are targets or distracters. The responses occur whether the deviants are widely different from the standard stimuli or are only slightly different from the standard stimuli (Cowan & associates, 1993; Paavilainen & associates, 1993). There is no performance decrement in the controlled task as a result of the automatic response to deviant stimuli (Näätänen, 1990). So it seems that some automatic superficial analysis and selection of stimuli may occur without taxing attentional resources.

Many of the foregoing studies have involved normal participants. But cognitive neuropsychologists also have learned a great deal about attentional processes in the brain by studying people who do not show normal attentional processes, such as people who show specific attentional deficits and who are found to have either lesions or inadequate blood flow in key areas of the brain. Overall attention deficits have been linked to lesions in the frontal lobe and in the basal ganglia (Lou, Henriksen, & Bruhn, 1984); visual attentional deficits have been linked to the posterior parietal cortex and the thalamus, as well as to areas of the midbrain related to eye movements (Posner & Petersen, 1990; Posner & associates, 1988). Work with split-brain patients (e.g., Ladavas & associates, 1994; Luck & associates, 1989) also has led to some interesting findings regarding attention and brain function, such as the observation that the right hemisphere seems to be dominant for maintaining alertness and that the attentional systems involved in visual search seem to be distinct from other aspects of visual attention. Using the variety of methods described here enables us to study attention in a way that any one method would not permit (Stuss & associates, 1995).

A Psychopharmacological Approach

Another approach to the understanding of attentional processes is psychopharmacological research, which evaluates changes in attention and consciousness associated with various chemicals (e.g., neurotransmitters such as acetylcholine or GABA [see Chapter 2], hormones, and even central nervous system stimulants ["uppers"] or depressants ["downers"]; Wolkowitz, Tinklenberg, & Weingartner, 1985). In addition, researchers study physiological aspects of attentional processes at a global level of analysis. For example, overall arousal can be observed through such responses as pupillary dilation, changes in the autonomic (self-regulating) nervous system (see Chapter 2), and distinctive EEG patterns. An area that has long been recognized as crucial to overall arousal is the reticular activating system (RAS; see Chapter 2). Changes in the RAS and in specific measures of arousal have been linked to habituation and dishabituation, as well as to the orienting reflex, in which an individual reflexively responds to sudden changes by reorienting the position of the body toward the source of the sudden change (e.g., sudden noise or flash of light).

Links among Perception, Attention, and Consciousness

In this chapter, we have focused on attention and consciousness. Before closing this discussion and beginning a discussion of perception, we may appreciate one cognitive psychologist's view of how consciousness and perception interact. Anthony Marcel (1983a) has proposed a model for describing how sensations and cognitive processes that occur outside our conscious awareness may influence our conscious perceptions and cognitions. According to Marcel, our conscious representations of what we perceive often differ qualitatively from our nonconscious representations of sensory stimuli. Outside of conscious awareness, we continually try to make sense of a constant flow of sensory information. Also outside of awareness are perceptual hypotheses regarding how the current sensory information matches with various properties and objects we have encountered previously in our environment. These hypotheses are inferences based on knowledge stored in long-term memory. During the matching process, information from differing sensory modalities is integrated.

According to Marcel's model, once there is a suitable match between the sensory data and the perceptual hypotheses regarding various properties and objects, the match is reported to conscious awareness as "being" particular properties and objects. Consciously, we are aware only of the reported objects or properties; we are not aware of the sensory data, the perceptual hypotheses that do not lead to a match, or even the processes that govern the reported match. Thus, before a given object or property is detected consciously (i.e., is reported to conscious awareness by the nonconscious matching process), we will have chosen a satisfactory perceptual hypothesis and excluded various possibilities that less satisfactorily matched the incoming sensory data to what we already know or can infer.

According to Marcel's model, the sensory data and the perceptual hypotheses are available to and used by various nonconscious cognitive processes in addition to the matching process. Sensory data and cognitive processes that do not reach awareness still exert influence on how we think and how we perform other cognitive tasks. It is widely held that we have limited attentional capacity (e.g., see Norman, 1976). According to Marcel, we accommodate these limitations by making use of nonconscious information and processes as much as possible, while limiting the information and processing that enter our conscious awareness. In this way, our limited attentional capacity is not constantly overtaxed. Hence, our processes of attention are intimately intertwined with our processes of perception. In this chapter, we have described many functions and processes of attention. In the following chapter, we focus on various aspects of perception.

Key Themes

The study of attention and consciousness highlights several key themes in cognitive psychology, as described in Chapter 1.

A first theme is the respective roles of structures and processes. The brain contains various structures and systems of structures, such as the reticular activating system, that generate the processes that contribute to attention. Sometimes, the relationship between structure and process is not entirely clear, and it is the job of cognitive psychologists to better understand it. For example, blindsight is a phenomenon in which a process occurs—sight—in the absence of the structures in the brain that would seem to be necessary for the sight to take place.

A second theme is the relation between biology and behavior. Blindsight is a case of a curious and as yet poorly understood link. The biology does not appear to be there to generate the behavior. Another interesting example is attention deficit hyperactivity disorder. Physicians now have available a number of drugs that treat ADHD. These treatments enable children as well as adults better to focus on tasks that they need to get done. But the mechanisms by which the drugs work are still poorly understood. Indeed, somewhat paradoxically, most of the drugs used to treat ADHD are stimulants, which, when given to children with ADHD, appear to calm them down.

A third theme is validity of causal inference versus ecological validity. Where should one study, say, vigilance? One can study it in a laboratory, of course, to achieve careful experimental control. But if one is studying high-stakes vigilance situations, such as those in which military officers are examining radar screens for possible attacks against the country, one must insist on having a high degree of ecological validity to ensure that the results apply to the actual situation in which the military officers find themselves. The stakes are too high to allow slippage. Yet, when one studies vigilance in the actual-life situation, one cannot and would not want to make attacks against the country happen. So one needs simulations that are as realistic as possible. In this way, one tries to ensure ecological validity of conclusions drawn.

Get two friends to help you with this demonstration. Ask one friend to read something very softly into your other friend's ear (it can be anything—a joke, a greeting card, or a cognitive psychology textbook), and have your other friend try to "shadow" what the other friend is saying. Shadowing is repeating all of the words that another person is saying. In your friend's other ear, say "animal" very softly. Later, ask your friend what you said. Most likely, your friend will not be able to say what you said. Try this again, but this time say your friend's name. Your friend will most likely be able to say that you said his/her name. This demonstrates Triesman's attenuation model.

Summary

1. **Can we actively process information even if we are not aware of doing so? If so, what do we do, and how do we do it?** Whereas attention embraces all of the information that an individual is manipulating (a portion of the information available from memory, sensation, and other cognitive processes), consciousness comprises only the narrower range of information that the individual is aware of manipulating. Attention allows us to use our limited active cognitive resources (e.g., because of the limits of working memory) judiciously, to respond quickly and accurately to interesting stimuli, and to remember salient information. Conscious awareness allows us to monitor our interactions with the environment, to link our past and present experiences and thereby sense a continuous thread of experience, and to control and plan for future actions.

We actively can process information at the preconscious level without being aware of doing so. For example, researchers have studied the phenomenon of priming, in which a given stimulus increases the likelihood that a subsequent related (or identical) stimulus will be readily processed (e.g., retrieval from long-term memory). In contrast, in the tip-of-the-tongue phenomenon, another example of preconscious processing, retrieval of desired information from memory does not occur despite an ability to retrieve related information.

Cognitive psychologists also observe distinctions in conscious versus preconscious attention by distinguishing between controlled and automatic processing in task performance. Controlled processes are relatively slow, sequential in nature, intentional (requiring effort), and under conscious control. Automatic processes are relatively fast, parallel in nature, and for the most part outside of conscious awareness. Actually, a continuum of processing appears to exist, from fully automatic to fully controlled processes. A pair of automatic processes that support our attentional system is habituation and dishabituation, which affect our responses to familiar versus novel stimuli.

2. **What are some of the functions of attention?** One main function involved in attention is identifying important objects and events in the environment. Researchers use measures from signal-detection theory to determine an observer's sensitivity to targets in various tasks. For example, vigilance refers to a person's ability to attend to a field of stimulation over a prolonged period, usually with the stimulus to be detected occurring only infrequently. Whereas vigilance involves passively waiting for an event to occur, search involves actively seeking out a stimulus.

People use selective attention to track one message and simultaneously to ignore others. Auditory selective attention (such as in the cocktail party problem) may be observed by asking participants to shadow information presented dichotically. Visual selective attention may be observed in tasks involving the Stroop effect. Attentional processes also are involved during divided attention, when people attempt to handle more than one task at once; generally, the simultaneous performance of more than one automatized task is easier to handle than the simultaneous performance of more than one controlled task. However, with practice, individuals appear to be capable of handling more than one controlled task at a time, even engaging in tasks requiring comprehension and decision making.

3. **What are some of the theories cognitive psychologists have developed to explain what they have observed about attentional processes?** Some theories of attention involve an attentional filter or bottleneck, according to which information is selectively blocked out or attenuated as it passes from one level of processing to the next. Of the bottleneck theories, some suggest that the signal-blocking or signal-attenuating mechanism occurs just after sensation and prior to any perceptual processing; others propose a later mechanism, after at least some perceptual processing has occurred. Attentional-resource theories offer an alternative way of explaining attention; according to these theories, people have a fixed amount of attentional resources (perhaps modulated by sensory modalities) that they allocate according to the perceived task requirements. Resource theories and bottleneck theories actually may be complementary. In addition to these general theories of attention, some task-specific theories (e.g., feature-integration theory, guided-search theory, and similarity theory) have attempted to explain search phenomena in particular.

4. **What have cognitive psychologists learned about attention by studying the human brain?** Early neuropsychological research led to the discovery of feature detectors, and subsequent work has explored other aspects of feature detection and integration processes that may be involved in visual search. In addition, extensive research on attentional processes in the brain seems to suggest that the attentional system primarily involves two regions of the cortex, as well as the thalamus and some other subcortical structures; the attentional system also governs various specific processes that occur in many areas of the brain, particularly in the cerebral cortex. Attentional processes may be a result of heightened activation in some areas of the brain, of inhibited activity in other areas of the brain, or perhaps of some combination of activation and inhibition. Studies of responsivity to particular stimuli show that even when an individual is focused on a primary task and is not consciously aware of processing other stimuli, the brain of the individual automatically responds to infrequent, deviant stimuli (e.g., an odd tone). By using various approaches to the study of the brain (e.g., PET, ERP, lesion studies, and psychopharmacological studies), researchers are gaining insight into diverse aspects of the brain and also are able to use converging operations to begin to explain some of the phenomena they observe.

Thinking about Thinking: Factual, Analytical, Creative, and Practical Questions

1. Describe some of the evidence regarding the phenomena of priming and preconscious perception.

2. Why are habituation and dishabituation of particular interest to cognitive psychologists?

3. Compare and contrast the theories of visual search described in this chapter.

4. Choose one of the theories of attention and explain how the evidence from signal detection, selective attention, or divided attention supports or challenges the theory you chose.

5. Design one task likely to activate the posterior attentional system and another task likely to activate the anterior attentional system.

6. Design an experiment for studying divided attention.

7. Describe some practical ways in which you can use forcing functions and other strategies for lessening the likelihood that automatic processes will have negative consequences for you in some of the situations you face.

8. How could advertisers use some of the principles of visual search or selective attention to increase the likelihood that people will notice their messages?

Key Terms

arousal
attention
automatic processes
automatization
binaural presentation
blindsight
change blindness
cocktail party problem
conjunction search
consciousness

controlled processes
dichotic presentation
dishabituation
distracters
divided attention
feature-integration theory
feature search
habituation
multimode theory
priming

search
selective attention
sensory adaptation
signal
signal detection
signal-detection theory (SDT)
Stroop effect
tip-of-the-tongue phenomenon
vigilance

 Explore CogLab by going to http://coglab.wadsworth.com. Answer the questions required by your instructor from the student manual that accompanies CogLab.

Attentional Blink
Stroop Effect

Simon Effect
Spatial Cueing

Annotated Suggested Reading

Pashler, H. (1998). *The psychology of attention.* Cambridge, MA: MIT Press. An excellent review of the literature on attention.

Perception

EXPLORING COGNITIVE PSYCHOLOGY

1. How do we perceive stable objects in the environment given variable stimulation?

2. What are two fundamental approaches to explaining perception?

3. What happens when people with normal visual sensations cannot perceive visual stimuli?

Have you ever been told that you "can't see something that's right under your nose"? How about that you "can't see the forest for the trees"? Have you ever listened to your favorite song over and over, trying to decipher the lyrics? In each of these situations, we call on the complex construct of perception. **Perception** is the set of processes by which we recognize, organize, and make sense of the sensations we receive from environmental stimuli (Epstein & Rogers, 1995; Goodale, 2000a, 2000b; Kosslyn & Osherson, 1995; Pomerantz, 2003). Perception encompasses many psychological phenomena. In this chapter, we focus on visual perception. It is the most widely recognized and the most widely studied perceptual modality (system for a particular sense, e.g., touch or smell). To find out about some of the phenomena of perception, psychologists often study situations that pose problems in making sense of our sensations.

Consider, for example, the image displayed in Figure 4.1. To most people, the figure initially looks like a blur of meaningless shadings. There is a recognizable creature staring them in the face. But they may not see it. When people finally realize what is in the figure, they rightfully feel "cowed." In Figure 4.1, the figure of the cow is hidden within the continuous gradations of shading that constitute the picture. Before

FIGURE 4.1

What do you learn about your own perception by trying to identify the object staring at you from this photo? From Dallenbach, K. M. (1951). A puzzle-picture with a new principle of concealment. American Journal of Psychology, 54, 431–433.

FIGURE 4.2

What perceptual changes would make it easier for you to identify the figure depicted here?

you recognized the figure as a cow, you correctly sensed all aspects of the figure. But you had not yet organized those sensations to form a mental *percept*, that is, mental representation of a stimulus that is perceived. Without such a percept of the cow, you could not meaningfully grasp what you previously had sensed. In Figure 4.2, you will see shadings as well. These shadings, however, are discrete. In many instances, they are nothing more than dots. Again, there is a hidden object. If you are dogged in your pursuit of the hidden object, you will no doubt find it.

The preceding examples show that sometimes we cannot perceive what does exist. At other times, however, we perceive things that do not exist. For example, notice the black triangle in the center of the left panel of Figure 4.3. Also note the white triangle in the center of the right panel of Figure 4.3. They jump right out at you. Now look very closely at each of the panels. You will see that the triangles are not really all there. The black that constitutes the center triangle in the left panel looks darker, or blacker, than the surrounding black. But it is not. Nor is the white central triangle in the right panel any brighter, or whiter, than the surrounding white. Both central triangles are optical illusions. They involve the perception of visual information not physically present in the visual sensory stimulus. So, sometimes we do not perceive what is there. Other times, we perceive what is not there. And at still other times, we perceive what cannot be there. Consider, for example, the winding staircase in Figure 4.4. Follow it around until you reach the top. Are you having trouble reaching the top? This illusion is called a "perpetual staircase." It seems always to go up, although this feat is impossible.

FIGURE 4.3

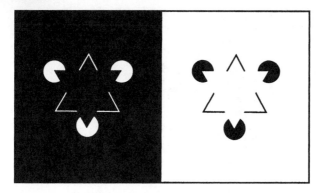

You easily can see the triangles in this figure—or are the triangles just an illusion? From In Search of the Human Mind by Robert J. Sternberg, copyright © 1995 by Harcourt Brace & Company, reproduced by permission of the publisher.

FIGURE 4.4

How can you reach the top of the staircase depicted here?

The existence of perceptual illusions suggests that what we sense (in our sensory organs) is not necessarily what we perceive (in our minds). Our minds must be taking the available sensory information and manipulating that information somehow to create mental representations of objects, properties, and spatial relationships of our environments (Peterson, 1999). Moreover, the way we represent these objects will depend in part on our viewpoint in perceiving the objects (Edelman & Weinshall, 1991; Poggio & Edelman, 1990; Tarr, 1995; Tarr & Bülthoff, 1998). For millennia, people have recognized that what we perceive often differs from the rectilinear sensory stimuli that reach our sense receptors. An example is the use of optical illusions

FIGURE 4.5

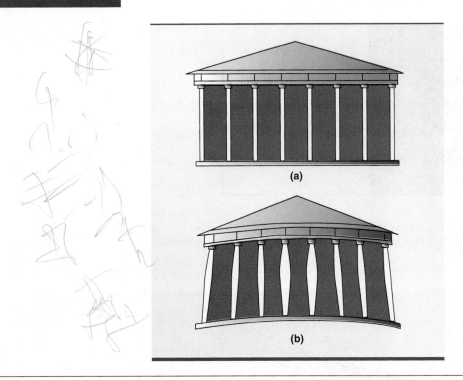

(a)

(b)

Early in the first century A.D., Roman architect Marcus Vitruvius Polio wrote De Architectura, *in which he documented the genius of the Greek architects Ictinus and Callicrates, who designed the Parthenon (dedicated in 438 B.C.). The columns of the Parthenon actually bulge slightly in the middle to compensate for the visual tendency to perceive that straight parallel lines seem to curve inward. Similarly, the horizontal lines of the beams crossing the top of the columns and the top step of the porch bulge slightly upward to counteract the tendency to perceive that they curve slightly downward. In addition, the columns lean ever so slightly inward at the top to compensate for the tendency to perceive them as spreading out as we gaze upward at them. Vitruvius also described many optical illusions in his treatise on architecture, and contemporary architects consider these distortions of visual perception in their designs today.*

in the construction of the Parthenon (Figure 4.5). Were the Parthenon actually constructed the way it appears to us perceptually (with strictly rectilinear form), its appearance would be bizarre.

Architects are not the only ones to have recognized some fundamental principles of perception. For centuries, artists have known how to lead us to perceive three-dimensional (3-D) percepts when viewing two-dimensional (2-D) images. What are some of the principles that guide our perceptions of both real and illusory percepts? First, we consider some of the perceptual information that leads us to perceive 3-D space from 2-D sensory information. Then we discuss some of the ways in which we perceive a stable set of percepts. Such stable perception occurs despite constant changes in the size and shape of what we observe. Then, we move on to theoretical approaches to perception. Finally, we consider some rare failures in normal visual perception among people with brain injuries.

From Sensation to Representation

Some Basic Concepts

If a tree falls in the forest and no one is around to hear it, does it make a sound? An answer to this old riddle can be found by placing the riddle in the context of perception. In his influential and controversial work, James Gibson (1966, 1979) provided a useful framework for studying perception. He introduced the concepts of distal (external) object, informational medium, proximal stimulation, and perceptual object.

The distal (far) object is the object in the external world. In this case, it is the falling tree. This event imposes a pattern on an informational medium. The informational medium is the reflected light, sound waves (here, the sound of the falling tree), chemical molecules, or tactile (relating to touch) information coming from the environment. Thus, the prerequisites for perception of objects in the external world begin early. They start even before sensory information impinges on our sense receptors (neural cells that are specialized to receive particular kinds of sensory information). When the information comes into contact with the appropriate sensory receptors of the eyes, ears, nose, skin, or mouth, proximal (near) stimulation occurs. Finally, perception occurs when an internal perceptual object in some way reflects the properties of the external world.

Table 4.1 summarizes this framework for the occurrence of perception. It lists the various properties of distal objects, informational media, proximal stimuli, and perceptual objects involved in perceiving the environment. To return to the original question, if a tree falls in the forest and no one is around to hear it, it makes no perceived sound. But it does make a sound. So the answer is yes or no, depending on how you look at the question.

The question of where to draw the line between perception and cognition, or even between sensation and perception, arouses much debate. Instead, to be more productive we should view these processes as part of a continuum. Information flows through the system. Different processes address different questions. Questions of sensation focus on qualities of stimulation. Is that shade of red brighter than the red of an apple? Is the sound of that falling tree louder than the sound of thunder? How well do one person's impressions of colors or sounds match someone else's impressions of those same colors or sounds? This same color or sound information answers different questions for perception. These are typically questions of identity and of form, pattern, and movement. Is that red thing an apple? Did I just hear a tree falling? Finally, cognition occurs as this information is used to serve further goals. Is that apple edible? Should I get out of this forest?

We never can experience through vision, hearing, taste, smell, or touch exactly the same set of stimulus properties we have experienced before. Therefore, one fundamental question for perception is "How do we achieve perceptual stability in the face of this utter instability at the level of sensory receptors?" Indeed, given the nature of our sensory receptors, variation seems necessary for perception.

In the phenomenon of sensory adaptation, receptor cells adapt to constant stimulation by ceasing to fire until there is a change in stimulation. Through sensory adaptation, we may stop detecting the presence of a stimulus. This mechanism ensures

TABLE 4.1   Perceptual Continuum

Perception occurs as environmental objects impart structure of the informational medium that ultimately impinges on sensory receptors, leading to internal object identification.

DISTAL OBJECT	INFORMATIONAL MEDIUM	PROXIMAL STIMULATION	PERCEPTUAL OBJECT
Vision—sight (e.g., Grandma's face)	Reflected light from Grandma's face (visible electromagnetic waves)	Photon absorption in the rod and cone cells of the retina, the receptor surface in the back of the eye	Grandma's face
Audition—sound (e.g., a falling tree)	Sound waves generated by the tree's fall	Sound wave conduction to the basilar membrane, the receptor surface within the cochlea of the inner ear	A falling tree
Olfaction—smell (e.g., sizzling bacon)	Molecules released by frying bacon	Molecular absorption in the cells of the olfactory epithelium, the receptor surface in the nasal cavity	Bacon
Gustation—taste (e.g., a bite of ice cream)	Molecules of ice cream both released into the air and dissolved in water	Molecular contact with taste buds, the receptor cells on the tongue and soft palate, combined with olfactory stimulation (see above entry)	Ice cream
Touch (e.g., a computer keyboard)	Mechanical pressure and vibration at the point of contact between the surface of the skin (epidermis) and the keyboard	Stimulation of various receptor cells within the dermis, the innermost layer of skin	Computer keys

that sensory information is changing constantly. Because of sensory adaptation in the retina (the receptor surface of the eye), our eyes constantly are making tiny rapid movements. These movements, termed *saccades*, create constant changes in the location of the projected image inside the eye. To study visual perception without saccades, scientists devised a way to create stabilized images. Such images do not move across the retina because they actually follow the saccades. The use of this technique has confirmed the hypothesis that constant stimulation of the cells of the retina makes the image appear to disappear (Ditchburn, 1980; Riggs & associates, 1953). Thus, stimulus variation is an essential attribute for perception. It paradoxically makes the task of explaining perception more difficult.

Perceptual Constancies

The perceptual system deals with variability by performing a rather remarkable analysis regarding the objects in the perceptual field. For example, picture yourself walking across campus to your cognitive psychology class. Suppose that two students are standing outside the door. They are chatting as you approach. As you get closer to the door, the amount of space on your retina devoted to images of those students becomes increasingly large. On the one hand, this proximal sensory evidence suggests that the students are becoming larger. On the other hand, you perceive that the students have remained the same size. Why?

Your classmates' perceived constancy in size is an example of perceptual constancy. **Perceptual constancy** occurs when our perception of an object remains the same even when our proximal sensation of the distal object changes (Gillam, 2000). The physical characteristics of the external distal object are probably not changing. But because we must be able to deal effectively with the external world, our perceptual system has mechanisms that adjust our perception of the proximal stimulus. Thus, the perception remains constant although the proximal sensation changes. Of the several kinds of perceptual constancies, here we consider two of the main constancies: size and shape constancies.

Size constancy is the perception that an object maintains the same size despite changes in the size of the proximal stimulus. The size of an image on the retina depends directly on the distance of that object from the eye. The same object at two different distances projects different-sized images on the retina. Some striking illusions can be achieved when our sensory and perceptual systems are misled by the very same information that usually helps us to achieve size constancy. For example, look at Figure 4.6. Here we see the Ponzo illusion. In this illusion, two objects that appear to be of different sizes are actually of the same size. The Ponzo illusion stems from the depth cue provided by the converging lines. Equivalent image sizes at different depths usually indicate different-sized objects. Another illusion is the Müller-Lyer illusion, illustrated in Figure 4.7. Here, two line segments that are of the same length appear

FIGURE 4.6

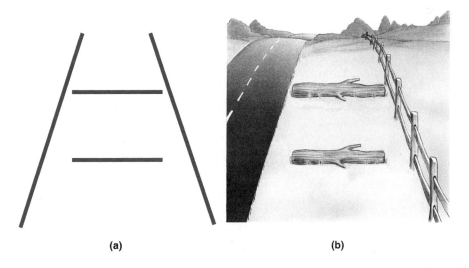

(a)   (b)

We perceive the top line and the top log in a and b as being longer than the bottom line and the bottom log, respectively, although the top and bottom figures are identical in length. We do so because in the real three-dimensional world, the top line and the log would be larger.

FIGURE 4.7

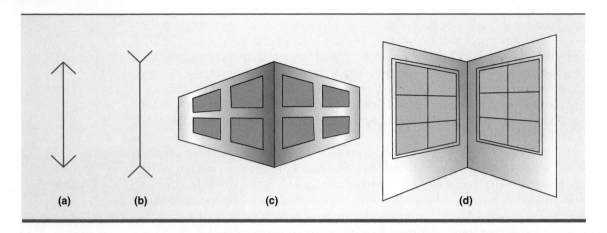

(a)   (b)   (c)   (d)

In this illusion, too, we tend to view two equally long line segments as being of different lengths. In particular, the vertical line segments in panels a and c appear shorter than the line segments in panels b and d, although all the line segments are the same size. Oddly enough, we are not certain why such a simple illusion occurs. Sometimes, the illusion we see in the abstract line segments (panels a and b) is explained in terms of the diagonal lines at the ends of the vertical segments. These diagonal lines may be implicit depth cues similar to the ones we would see in our perceptions of the exterior and interior of a building (Coren & Girgus, 1978; Gregory, 1966). In panel c, a view of the exterior of a building, the sides appear to recede into the distance (with the diagonal lines angling toward the vertical line segment, as in panel a, whereas in panel d, a view of the interior of a building, the sides appear to come toward us (with the diagonal lines angling away from the vertical line segment, as in panel b).

to be of different lengths. Finally, compare the two center circles in the pair of circle patterns in Figure 4.8. Both center circles are actually the same size. But the size of the center circle relative to the surrounding circles affects perception of the center circle's size.

Like size constancy, shape constancy relates to the perception of distances but in a different way. *Shape constancy* is the perception that an object maintains the same shape despite changes in the shape of the proximal stimulus. For example, Figure 4.9 is an illustration of shape constancy. An object's perceived shape remains the same despite changes in its orientation and hence in the shape of its retinal image. As the actual shape of the pictured door changes, some parts of the door seem to be changing differentially in their distance from us. It is possible to use neuropsychological imaging to localize parts of the brain that are used in this shape analysis. They are in the extrastriate cortex (Kanwisher & associates, 1996, 1997). Points near the outer edge of the door seem to move more quickly toward us than do points near the inner edge. Nonetheless, we perceive that the door remains the same shape.

Depth Perception

As you move around in your environment, you constantly look around. You visually orient yourself in 3-D space. As you look forward into the distance, you look into the third dimension of depth. **Depth** is the distance from a surface, usually using your own

FIGURE 4.8

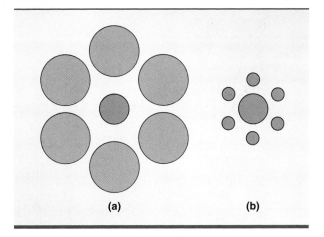

(a)   (b)

Guess which center circle is larger (a or b) and then measure the diameter of each one.

body as a reference surface when speaking in terms of depth perception. Consider what happens when you transport your body, reach for or manipulate objects, or otherwise position yourself in your 3-D world. You must use information regarding depth. This use of depth information even extends beyond the range of your body's reach. When you drive, you use depth to assess the distance of an approaching automobile. When you decide to call out to a friend walking down the street, you determine how loudly to call. Your decision is based on how far away you perceive your friend to be. How do you manage to perceive 3-D space when the proximal stimuli on your retinas comprise only a 2-D projection of what you see?

Refer back to the impossible staircase (see Figure 4.4). Look also at other impossible configurations in Figure 4.10. They are confusing because there is contradictory depth information in different sections of the picture. Small segments of these impossible figures look reasonable to us because there is no inconsistency in their individual depth cues (Hochberg, 1978). However, it is difficult to make sense of the figure as a whole. The reason is that the cues providing depth information in various segments of the picture are in conflict.

Generally, depth cues are either monocular (mon-, "one"; ocular, related to the eyes) or binocular (bin-, "both," "two"). **Monocular depth cues** can be represented in just two dimensions and observed with just one eye. Figure 4.11 illustrates several of the monocular depth cues defined in Table 4.2. They include texture gradients, relative size, interposition, linear perspective, aerial perspective, location in the picture plane, and motion parallax. Before you read about the cues in either the table or the figure caption, look just at the figure. See how many depth cues you can decipher for yourself simply by observing the figure carefully.

Table 4.2 also describes motion parallax, the only monocular depth cue not shown in the figure. Motion parallax requires movement. It thus cannot be used to judge depth within a stationary image, such as a picture. Another means of judging

FIGURE 4.9

Here, you see a rectangular door and door frame, showing the door as closed, slightly opened, more fully opened, or wide open. Of course, the door does not appear to be a different shape in each panel. Indeed, it would be odd if you perceived a door to be changing shapes as you opened it. Yet, the shape of the image of the door sensed by your retinas does change as you open the door. If you look at the figure, you will see that the drawn shape of the door is different in each panel.

depth involves **binocular depth cues,** based on the receipt of sensory information in three dimensions from both eyes (Parker, Cumming, & Dodd, 2000). Table 4.2 also summarizes some of the binocular cues used in perceiving depth.

Binocular depth cues utilize the relative positioning of your eyes. Your two eyes are positioned far enough apart to provide two kinds of information to your brain:

FIGURE 4.10

What cues may lead you to perceive these impossible figures as entirely plausible?

FIGURE 4.11

National Gallery/London/ET Archive/Superstock

M. C. Escher's "Waterfall" © 2005 The M. C. Escher Company-Holland. All Rights Reserved.

In The Annunciation (left), *Carlo Crivelli masterfully illustrated at least five monocular depth cues: (1, 2) Texture gradients and relative size: The floor tiles appear similar both in front of and behind the figures in the forefront of the corridor, but the tiles at the front of the corridor are larger and are spread farther apart than the tiles at the rear. (3) Interposition: The peacock partially blocks our view of the frieze on the wall to the right of the corridor. (4) Linear perspective: The sides of the wall seem to converge inward toward the rear of the corridor. (5) Location in the picture plane: The figures at the rear of the corridor are depicted higher in the picture plane than are the figures at the front of the corridor. M. C. Escher used his mastery of visual perception to create paradoxical depictions such as in his drawing* Waterfall *(right). Can you see how he used various monocular depth cues to lead us to perceive the impossible?*

TABLE 4.2	Monocular and Binocular Cues for Depth Perception

Various perceptual cues aid in our perception of the three-dimensional world. Some of these cues can be observed by one eye alone, whereas others require the use of both eyes.

CUES FOR DEPTH PERCEPTION	APPEARS CLOSER	APPEARS FARTHER AWAY
Monocular depth cues		
Texture gradients	Larger grains, farther apart	Smaller grains, closer together
Relative size	Bigger	Smaller
Interposition	Partially obscures other object	Is partially obscured by other object
Linear perspective	Apparently parallel lines seem to diverge as they move away from the horizon	Apparently parallel lines seem to converge as they approach the horizon
Aerial perspective	Images seem crisper, more clearly delineated	Images seem fuzzier, less clearly delineated
Location in the picture plane	Above the horizon, objects are higher in the picture plane; below the horizon, objects are lower in the picture plane	Above the horizon, objects are lower in the picture plane; below the horizon, objects are higher in the picture plane
Motion parallax	Objects approaching get larger at an ever-increasing speed (i.e., big and moving quickly closer)	Objects departing get smaller at an ever-decreasing speed (i.e., small and moving slowly farther away)
Binocular depth cues		
Binocular convergence	Eyes feel tug inward toward nose	Eyes relax outward toward ears
Binocular disparity	Huge discrepancy between image seen by left eye and image seen by right eye	Minuscule discrepancy between image seen by left eye and image seen by right eye

binocular disparity and binocular convergence. In *binocular disparity*, your two eyes send increasingly disparate (differing) images to your brain as objects approach you. Your brain interprets the degree of disparity as an indication of distance from you. In addition, for objects we view at relatively close locations, we use depth cues based on binocular convergence. In *binocular convergence*, your two eyes increasingly turn inward as objects approach you. Your brain interprets these muscular movements as indications of distance from you. Figure 4.12 illustrates how these two processes work.

Depth perception is a good example of how cues facilitate our perception. There is nothing intrinsic about relative size to indicate that an object that appears smaller is farther away from us. Rather, the brain uses this contextual information to conclude that the smaller object is farther away.

Approaches to Object and Form Perception

Viewer-Centered versus Object-Centered Approaches

Right now I am looking at the computer on which I am typing this text. I depict the results of what I see as a mental representation. What form does this mental representation take? There are two common positions regarding the answer to this question.

FIGURE 4.12

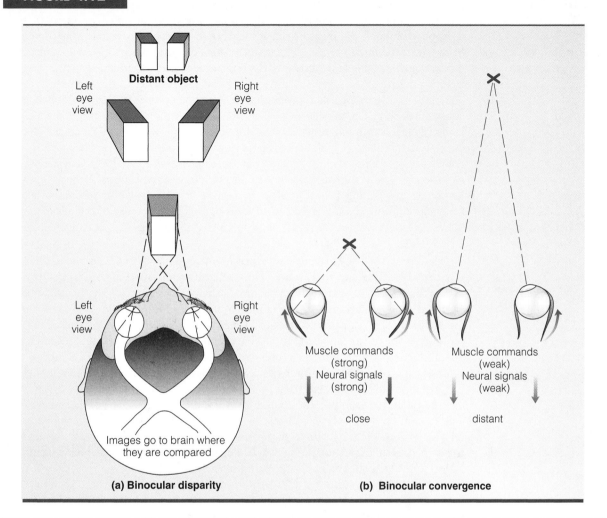

(a) Binocular disparity

(b) Binocular convergence

(a) Binocular disparity: The closer an object is to you, the greater the disparity between the views of it as sensed in each of your eyes. You can test these differing perspectives by holding your finger about an inch from the tip of your nose. Look at it first with one eye covered, then the other: It will appear to jump back and forth. Now do the same for an object 20 feet away, then 100 yards away. The apparent jumping, which indicates the amount of binocular disparity, will decrease with distance. Your brain interprets the information regarding disparity as a cue indicating depth. (b) Binocular convergence: Because your two eyes are in slightly different places on your head, when you rotate your eyes so that an image falls directly on the central part of your eye, in which you have the greatest visual acuity, each eye must turn inward slightly to register the same image. The closer the object you are trying to see, the more your eyes must turn inward. Your muscles send messages to your brain regarding the degree to which your eyes are turning inward, and these messages are interpreted as cues indicating depth.

PRACTICAL
APPLICATIONS
OF COGNITIVE
PSYCHOLOGY

Models and actors often use these depth cues of perception to their advantage while being photographed. For example, some models only allow certain angles or orientations to be photographed. A long nose can appear shorter when photographed from slightly below the facial midline (just look closely at some pictures of Barbara Streisand from different angles) because the bridge of the nose recedes slightly into the distance. Also, leaning forward a little can make the upper body appear slightly larger than the lower body, and vice versa for leaning backward. In group pictures, standing slightly behind another person makes you appear smaller; standing slightly in front makes you appear larger. Women's swimsuit designers create optical-illusion swimsuits to enhance different features of the body, making legs appear longer or waists appear smaller and either enhancing or de-emphasizing bustlines. Some of these processes to alter perceptions are so basic that many animals have special adaptations designed to make them appear larger (e.g., the fanning peacock tail) or to disguise their identity from predators. Take a moment to think about how you could apply perceptual processes to your advantage.

One position, **viewer-centered representation,** is that the individual stores the way the object looks to him or her. Thus, what matters is the appearance of the object to the viewer, not the actual structure of the object. The second position, **object-centered representation,** is that the individual stores a representation of the object, independent of its appearance to the viewer. The key similarity between these two positions is that both can account for how I represent a given object and its parts. The key difference is in whether I represent the object and its parts in relation to me (viewer-centered) or in relation to the entirety of the object itself, independent of my own position (object-centered).

Consider, for example, my computer. It has different parts: a screen, a keyboard, a mouse, and so forth. Suppose I represent the computer in terms of viewer-centered representation. Then its various parts are stored in terms of their relation to me. I see the screen as facing me at perhaps a 20-degree angle. I see the keyboard facing me horizontally. I see the mouse off to the right side and in front of me. Suppose, instead, that I use an object-centered representation. Then I would see the screen at a 70-degree angle relative to the keyboard. And the mouse is directly to the right side of the keyboard, neither in front of it nor in back of it.

One potential reconciliation of these two approaches to mental representation suggests that people may use both kinds of representations. According to this approach, recognition of objects occurs on a continuum (Burgund & Marsolek, 2000; Tarr, 2000; Tarr & Bülthoff, 1995). At one end of this continuum are cognitive mechanisms that are more viewpoint-centered. At the other end of the continuum are cognitive mechanisms that are more object-centered. For example, suppose you see a picture of car that is inverted. How do you know it is a car? Object-centered mechanisms would recognize the object as a car, but viewpoint-centered mechanisms would recognize the car as inverted. In general, decomposition of objects into parts will be useful for recognizing the differences between, say, a Mercedes and a Hyundai, but may not be so useful for recognizing the subtler differences between two different but similar models of Mercedes. In the latter case, viewpoint-centered perception may be more important, as shown in Figure 4.13.

FIGURE 4.13

Image Port/Index Stock Imagery

Getty Images

Ron Avery/Super Stock

Viewpoint-centered mechanisms may be more important in distinguishing two different models of Mercedes-Benz, whereas object-centered mechanisms may be more important in distinguishing the Hyundai from either Mercedes model.

The Gestalt Approach

Perception does much more for us than maintain size and shape constancy in depth. It also organizes objects in a visual array into coherent groups. One way to understand how this organization occurs is from the structuralist approach to psychology. This approach was based on the notion that simple sensations constitute the building blocks of perceived form. The structuralist approach to form perception is focused on breaking wholes into elementary components. This approach does little to address the ways in which these myriad sensations interact. Instead, it emphasizes individual elements. The structuralist approach could not give any inkling as to how—or whether—the dynamic whole of a structure (e.g., a familiar tune) might differ from the sum of its parts (e.g., individual notes). The more functional Gestalt school of psychology emerged largely as a reaction against the extreme approach of structuralism. The Gestaltists' goal was to address directly the more global, holistic processes involved in perceiving structure in the environment.

Iconoclastic psychologists such as Kurt Koffka (1886–1941), Wolfgang Köhler (1887–1968), and Max Wertheimer (1880–1943) founded a new approach. The **Gestalt approach to form perception** was based on the notion that the whole differs from the sum of its individual parts (see Chapter 1). The Gestalt approach has proved to be useful particularly for understanding how we perceive groups of objects or even parts of objects to form integral wholes (Palmer, 1999a, 1999b, 2000; Palmer & Rock, 1994; Prinzmetal, 1995). According to the Gestalt **law of Prägnanz,** we tend to perceive any given visual array in a way that most simply organizes the disparate elements into a stable and coherent form. Thus, we do not merely experience a jumble of unintelligible, disorganized sensations. For example, we tend to perceive a focal figure and other sensations as forming a background for the figure on which we focus.

Consider what happens when you walk into a familiar room. You perceive that some things stand out (e.g., faces in photographs or posters). Others fade into the background (e.g., undecorated walls and floors). A figure is any object perceived as being highlighted. It is almost always perceived against or in contrast to some kind of receding, unhighlighted (back)ground. Figure 4.14 (*a*) illustrates the concept of **figure-ground**—what stands out from versus what recedes into the background. You probably first will notice the light-colored lettering of the word figure, we perceive this light-colored lettering as the figure against the darker-lettered surrounding ground of the word ground. Similarly, in Figure 4.14 (*b*), you can see either a white

IN THE LAB OF STEPHEN PALMER

Courtesy of Dr. Stephen Palmer

One current project in my laboratory is aimed at determining where Gestalt grouping principles operate in the stream of visual processing. Most theorists have assumed that grouping factors (such as proximity, closure, and similarity in shape and color) operate at the level of the two-dimensional (2-D) retinal image, before depth perception and perceptual constancy have been achieved. We wanted to know whether grouping actually might occur after depth and constancy processing. The logic of our experiments is that if we can show that depth information and perceptual constancy influence grouping, then grouping must operate at least partly *after* depth and constancy. Figure *a* shows a stimulus display for which we asked subjects whether the central column of figures (in the gray region) grouped with the columns on the left or on the right. At the level of the 2-D image, these figures are ovals that ought to group with the ovals on the right by 2-D shape similarity. At the later level of three-dimensional (3-D) perception, however, the central

figures are circles slanted in depth and ought to group with the circles on the left by 3-D shape similarity. Our subjects perceived the central column as grouping more strongly with the circles on the left, thus supporting our hypothesis that grouping factors can work after depth and constancy have been perceived. (The control condition shown in Figure *b* demonstrates that when the main cues to depth and constancy have been removed, the central column groups strongly to the right by virtue of 2-D shape similarity.)

Other recent experiments in our lab have shown that grouping takes place *before* depth and constancy processing as well as after them.

(a)   (b)

vase against a black background or two silhouetted faces peering at each other against a white ground. It is virtually impossible to see both sets of objects simultaneously. Although you may switch rapidly back and forth between the vase and the faces, you cannot see them both at the same time.

One of the reasons suggested as to why each figure makes sense is that both figures conform to the Gestalt principle of symmetry. Symmetry requires that features appear to have balanced proportions around a central axis or a central point. Table 4.3 and Figure 4.15 summarize a few of the Gestalt principles of form perception. They include figure-ground perception, proximity, similarity, continuity, closure, and symmetry. Each of these principles supports the overarching law of Prägnanz. Each thereby illustrates how we tend to perceive visual arrays in ways that most simply organize the disparate

FIGURE 4.14

(a)

Courtesy of Kaiser Porcelain, Ltd.

(b)

In these two Gestalt images (a and b), find which is the figure and which is the ground.

TABLE 4.3	Gestalt Principles of Visual Perception	
The Gestalt principles of proximity, similarity, continuity, closure, and symmetry aid in our perception of forms.		

GESTALT PRINCIPLES	PRINCIPLE	FIGURE ILLUSTRATING THE PRINCIPLE
Figure-ground	When perceiving a visual field, some objects (figures) seem prominent, and other aspects of the field recede into the background (ground).	Figure 4.14 shows a figure-ground vase, in which one way of perceiving the figures brings one perspective or object to the fore, and another way of perceiving the figures brings a different object or perspective to the fore and relegates the former foreground to the background.
Proximity	When we perceive an assortment of objects, we tend to see objects that are close to each other as forming a group.	In Figure 4.15 (a), we tend to see the middle four circles as two pairs of circles.
Similarity	We tend to group objects on the basis of their similarity.	In Figure 4.15 (b), we tend to see four columns of xs and os, not four rows of alternating letters.
Continuity	We tend to perceive smoothly flowing or continuous forms rather than disrupted or discontinuous ones.	Figure 4.15 (c) shows two fragmented curves bisecting, which we perceive as two smooth curves, rather than as disjointed curves.
Closure	We tend to perceptually close up, or complete, objects that are not, in fact, complete.	Figure 4.15 (d) shows only disjointed, jumbled line segments, which you close up to see a triangle and a circle.
Symmetry	We tend to perceive objects as forming mirror images about their center.	For example, when viewing Figure 4.15 (e), a configuration of assorted brackets, we see the assortment as forming four sets of brackets, rather than eight individual items, because we integrate the symmetrical elements into coherent objects.

elements into a stable and coherent form. Stop for a moment and look at your environment. You will perceive a coherent, complete, and continuous array of figures and background. You do not perceive holes in objects where your textbook occludes (i.e., covers up) your view of them. If your book obscures part of the edge of a table, you still perceive the table as a continuous entity. You do not see it as having gaping holes. In viewing the environment, we tend to perceive groupings. We see groupings of nearby objects (proximity) or of like objects (similarity). We also see groupings of complete objects rather than partial ones (closure), continuous lines rather than broken ones (continuity), and symmetrical patterns rather than asymmetrical ones.

People tend to use Gestalt principles even when they are confronted with novel stimuli. Palmer (1977) showed participants novel geometric shapes that served as targets. He then showed them fragments of the shapes. For each fragment, the participants had to say whether it was part of the original novel geometric shape. Participants were quicker to recognize the fragments as part of the original target if they conformed to Gestalt principles. Consider, for example, a triangle. It exhibits closure. It was recognized more quickly as part of the original novel figure than were three line segments that were comparable to the triangle except that they were not closed. They

FIGURE 4.15

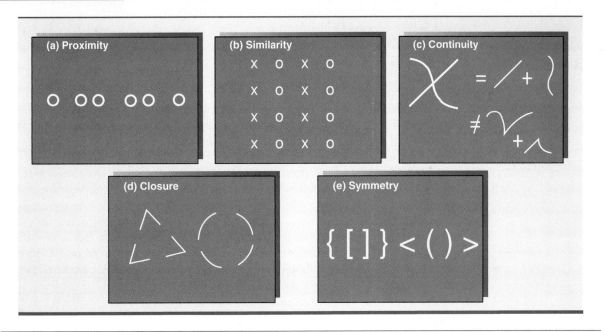

The Gestalt principles of form perception include perception of figure-ground, (a) proximity, (b) similarity, (c) continuity, (d) closure, and (e) symmetry. Each principle demonstrates the fundamental law of law of Prägnanz, which suggests that through perception, we unify disparate visual stimuli into a coherent and stable whole.

thus did not conform to the Gestalt principle. In sum, we seem to use Gestalt principles in our everyday perception. We use them whether the figures to which we apply the principles are familiar or not.

The Gestalt principles of form perception are remarkably simple. Yet they characterize much of our perceptual organization (Palmer, 1992). The Gestalt principles provide valuable descriptive insights into form and pattern perception. But they offer few or no explanations of these phenomena. To understand how or why we perceive forms and patterns, we need to consider explanatory theories of perception.

Pattern-Recognition Systems

How do we recognize patterns? For example, how do we recognize faces? One proposal is that humans have two systems for recognizing patterns (Farah, 1992, 1995; Farah & associates, 1998). The first system specializes in recognition of parts of objects and in assembling those parts into distinctive wholes. For example, when you are in a biology class and notice the elements of a tulip—the stamen, the pistil, and so forth—you look at the flower through this first system. The second system specializes in recognizing larger configurations. It is not well equipped to analyze parts of objects or the construction of the objects. But it is especially well equipped to recognize configurations. For example, if you look at a tulip in a garden and admire its distinctive beauty and form, you look at the flower through the second system.

The second system would typically be most relevant to the recognition of faces. So when you see a friend whom you see on a daily basis, you would recognize him or her using the configurational system. So dependent are you on this system in every-day life that you might not even notice some major change in your friend's appearance, such as his or her having longer hair, or having put on new glasses. But the first system can also be used in face recognition. Suppose you see someone whose face looks vaguely familiar. But you are not sure who it is. You start analyzing features and then realize it is a friend you have not seen for 10 years. In this case, you were able to make the facial recognition only after you analyzed the face by its features.

There is good evidence that there is something special about recognition of faces. In one study, experimental participants were shown sketches of two kinds of objects, faces and houses (Tanaka & Farah, 1993). In each case, the face was paired with the name of the person whom the face represented and the house was paired with the name of the house's owner. There were six pairings per trial. After learning the six pairings, participants were asked to recognize parts of either the faces or the houses or to recognize the faces or houses as a whole. For example, they might see just a nose or ear, or just a window or a doorway. Or they might see a whole face or house. If face recognition is somehow special and especially dependent on the second, configurational system, then people should have more difficulty recognizing parts of faces than parts of houses. The data are shown in Figure 4.16.

FIGURE 4.16

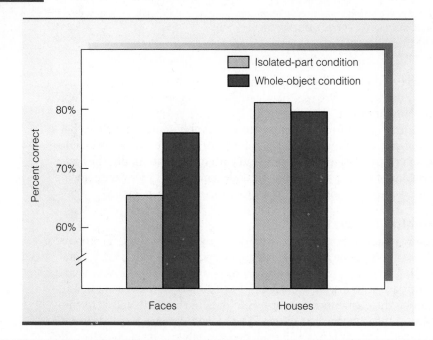

People have more trouble recognizing parts of faces than whole faces. They recognize parts of houses about as well as they recognize whole houses, however. From J. W. Tanaka and M. J. Farah, "Parts and Wholes in Face Recognition," Quarterly Journal of Experimental Psychology, 46A, p. 225–245, Fig. 6. Reprinted by permission of the Experimental Psychology Society.

People generally were better at recognizing houses, whether they were presented in parts or in wholes. But more important, people had relatively more difficulty in recognizing parts of faces than they had in recognizing whole faces. In contrast, they did about the same, whether they had to recognize parts of houses or whole houses. Face recognition, therefore, appears to be special. Presumably, it is especially dependent on the configurational system.

Prosopagnosia—the inability to recognize faces that was discussed earlier—would imply damage of some kind to the configurational system. But other disabilities, such as an early reading disability in which a beginning reader has difficulty in recognizing the features that comprise unique words, might stem from damage to the first, element-based system. Moreover, processing can move from one system to another. A typical reader may learn the appearances of words through the first system—element by element—and then come to recognize the words as wholes. Indeed, some forms of reading disability might stem from the inability of the second system to take over from the first.

Theoretical Approaches to Perception

Gestalt principles of perception focus on aspects of the stimuli that influence perception. Many other theoretical explanations of perception also start from the "bottom." They first consider the physical stimulus—the observable form or pattern—being perceived. They then work their way up to higher order cognitive processes, such as organizing principles and concepts. Theories taking this approach are termed **bottom-up theories,** which are data-driven (i.e., stimulus-driven) theories. Not all theorists focus on the sensory data of the perceptual stimulus, however. Many theorists prefer **top-down theories,** which are driven by high-level cognitive processes, existing knowledge, and prior expectations that influence perception (Clark, 2003). These theories then work their way down to considering the sensory data, such as the perceptual stimulus. Expectations are important. When people expect to see something, they may see it even if it is not there or is no longer there. For example, suppose people expect to see a certain person in a certain location. They may think they see that person, even if they are actually seeing someone else who looks only vaguely similar (Simons, 1996). Top-down and bottom-up approaches have been applied to virtually every aspect of cognition. As applied to perception, there are two major theories of perception. They manifest the bottom-up and top-down approaches. These theories usually are presented in opposition to each other. But to some extent they deal with different aspects of the same phenomenon. Ultimately, a complete theory of perception will need to encompass both bottom-up and top-down processes. First, we start at the bottom.

Bottom-Up Approaches: Direct Perception

How do you know the letter A when you see it? Easy to ask, hard to answer. Of course, it's an A because it looks like an A. What makes it look like an A, though, instead of like an H? Just how difficult it is to answer this question becomes apparent when you look at Figure 4.17. You probably will see the image in Figure 4.17 as the words "THE CAT." Yet the H of "THE" is identical to the A of "CAT." What subjectively feels like

FIGURE 4.17

THE CAT

When you read these words, you probably have no difficulty differentiating the A from the H. Look more closely at each of these two letters. What features differentiate them?

a simple process of pattern recognition is almost certainly quite complex. How do we connect what we perceive to what we have stored in our minds? Gestalt psychologists referred to this problem as the *Hoffding function* (Köhler, 1940). It was named after nineteenth-century Danish psychologist Harald Hoffding. He questioned whether perception can be reduced to a simple view of associating what is seen with what is remembered. An influential and controversial theorist who also questioned associationism is James J. Gibson (1904–1980). His theory of direct perception truly defines the bottom-up approach. In addition to the direct approach, there are four main bottom-up theories of form and pattern perception. They are template theories, prototype theories, feature theories, and structural-description theories.

According to Gibson's theory of **direct perception,** the array of information in our sensory receptors, including the sensory context, is all we need to perceive anything. In other words, we do not need higher cognitive processes or anything else to mediate between our sensory experiences and our perceptions. Existing beliefs or higher-level inferential thought processes are not necessary for perception.

Gibson believed that, in the real world, sufficient contextual information over time usually exists to make perceptual judgments. He claimed that we need not appeal to higher-level intelligent processes to explain perception. For example, Figure 4.18 shows that we do not need to have prior experience with particular shapes to perceive apparent shapes. Gibson (1979) believed that we use this contextual information directly. In essence, we are biologically tuned to respond to it. According to Gibson, we often observe depth cues such as texture gradients. Those cues aid us to perceive directly the relative proximity or distance of objects and of parts of objects. Based on our analysis of the stable relationships among features of objects and settings in the real world, we directly perceive our environment (Gibson, 1950, 1954/1994; Mace, 1986). We do not need the aid of complex thought processes.

Such contextual information might not be readily controlled in a laboratory experiment. But such information is likely to be available in a real-world setting. Gibson's model sometimes is referred to as an ecological model (Turvey, 2003). This is because of Gibson's concern with perception as it occurs in the everyday world (the ecological environment) rather than in laboratory situations, where less contextual information is available. Ecological constraints apply not only to initial perceptions but also to the ultimate internal representations (such as concepts) that are formed

FIGURE 4.18

The perception of these apparent amorphous shapes is consistent with James Gibson's direct-perception view that contextual information alone is sufficient for perception to occur, without additional knowledge or high-level thinking. Prior knowledge about the contexts does not lead to our perception of the triangle or the pear. From The Legacy of Solomon Asch: Essays in Cognition and Social Psychology by Irving Rock. Copyright © 1990 by Lawrence Erlbaum Associates. Reprinted by permission.

from those perceptions (Hubbard, 1995; Shepard, 1984). Continuing to wave the Gibsonian banner was Eleanor Gibson (1991, 1992). She conducted landmark research in infant perception. She observed that infants (who certainly lack much prior knowledge and experience) quickly develop many aspects of perceptual awareness, including depth perception.

The direct-perception viewpoint does not integrate the processes of intelligence, as usually conceived, with the processes of perception. In this viewpoint, the information that we need to understand what we see resides in the stimulus information. Nevertheless, intelligence still plays a role in cognitive processing. Its role occurs after the perceptual processing has been completed. Thus, this model views the roles of perception and intelligence as separate and possibly sequential.

Template Theories

One theory says that we have stored in our minds myriad sets of templates. **Templates** are highly detailed models for patterns we potentially might recognize. We recognize a pattern by comparing it with our set of templates. We then choose the exact template that perfectly matches what we observe (Selfridge & Neisser, 1960). We see examples of template matching in our everyday lives. Fingerprints are matched in this way. Machines rapidly process imprinted numerals on checks by comparing them to templates. Increasingly, products of all kinds are identified with universal product codes (UPCs or "bar codes"). They can be scanned and identified by computers at the time of purchase.

In each of the aforementioned instances, the goal of finding one perfect match and disregarding imperfect matches suits the task. You would be alarmed to find that your bank's numeral-recognition system failed to register a deposit to your account. Such failure might occur because it was programmed to accept an ambiguous character according to what seemed to be a best guess. For template matching, only an exact match will do. This is exactly what you want from a bank computer. However, consider your perceptual system at work in everyday situations. It rarely would work if you required exact matches for every stimulus you were to recognize. Imagine, for example, needing mental templates for every possible percept of the face of someone you love. Imagine one for each facial expression, each angle of viewing, each addition or removal of makeup, each hairdo, and so on.

Letters of the alphabet are simpler than faces and other complex stimuli. Yet template-matching theories also fail to explain some aspects of the perception of letters. For one thing, such theories cannot easily account for our perception of the letters and words in Figure 4.17. We identify two different letters (A and H) from only one physical form. Hoffding (1891) noted other problems. We can recognize an A as an A despite variations in the size, orientation, and form in which the letter is written. Are we to believe that we have mental templates for each possible size, orientation, and form of a letter? Storing organizing, and retrieving so many templates in memory would be unwieldy. Moreover, how could we possibly anticipate and create so many templates for every conceivable object of perception (Figure 4.19)?

Prototype Theories

The unwieldiness and rigidity of template theories soon led to an alternative explanation of pattern perception: prototype-matching theory. A **prototype** is a sort of average of a class of related objects or patterns, which integrates all of the most typical (most frequently observed) features of the class. That is, a prototype is highly representative of a pattern. But it is not intended as a precise, identical match to any pattern or all other patterns for which it is a model. A great deal of research has been found to support the prototype-matching approach (e.g., Franks & Bransford, 1971). The prototype model seems to explain perception of configurations. Examples would include arrays of dots, a triangle, a diamond, an F, an M, or a random array (Posner, Goldsmith, & Welton, 1967; Posner & Keele, 1968), and highly simplified line drawings of faces (Reed, 1972). Prototypes even include rather well-defined faces created with the police called Identikits, which are often used for witness identification (Solso & McCarthy, 1981; Figure 4.20).

Surprisingly, we seem to be able to form prototypes even when we have never seen an exemplar that exactly matches the prototype. That is, the prototypes we form seem to integrate all of the most typical features of a pattern. This occurs even when we have never seen a single instance in which all of the typical features are integrated at one time (Neumann, 1977). Consider an illustration of this point. Some researchers generated various series of patterns, such as the patterns in Figure 4.20 (a and c), based on a prototype. They then showed participants the series of generated patterns. They did not show the prototype on which the patterns were based. Later, they again showed participants the series of generated patterns. They also showed some additional patterns, including both distracters and the prototype pattern. Under these conditions, participants not only identified the prototype pattern as being one they had seen previously (e.g., Posner & Keele, 1968). They also gave particularly high ratings of their confidence in having seen the prototype previously (Solso & McCarthy, 1981).

FIGURE 4.19

Template-matching will distinguish between different bar codes, but not between different versions of the letter A written in different scripts.

Feature Theories

Yet another alternative explanation of pattern and form perception may be found in *feature-matching theories*. According to these theories, we attempt to match features of a pattern to features stored in memory, rather than to match a whole pattern to a template or a prototype (Stankiewicz, 2003). One such feature-matching model has been called *pandemonium*. In it, metaphorical "demons" with specific duties receive and analyze the features of a stimulus (Selfridge, 1959). Figure 4.21 shows this model.

Oliver Selfridge's pandemonium model describes "image demons." They pass on a retinal image to "feature demons." Each feature demon calls out when there are

FIGURE 4.20

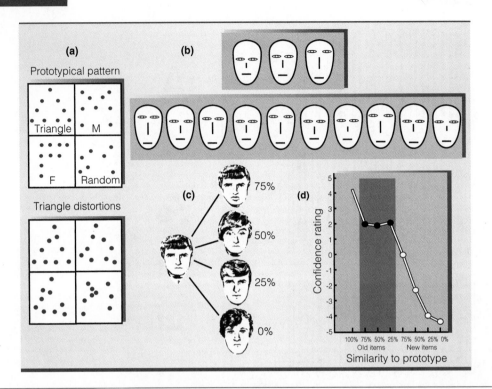

(a) These dot configurations are similar to those used in the experiment by Michael Posner and his colleagues. Michael I. Posner, Ralph Goldsmith, and Kenneth E. Welton, Jr. (1967), "Perceived Distance and the Classification of Distorted Patterns," from Journal of Experimental Psychology, 73(1):28–38. Copyright © 1967 by the American Psychological Association. Reprinted with permission. (b) These highly simplified drawings of faces are similar to those used by Stephen Reed. Stephen K. Reed (1972), "Pattern Recognition and Categorization," Cognitive Psychology, July 1972, 3(3): 382–407. Reprinted by permission of Elsevier. (c) These faces are similar to those created in the experiment by Robert Solso and John McCarthy (1981). Robert Solso and Judith McCarthy (1981), "Prototype Formation of Faces: A Case of Pseudomemory," British Journal of Psychology, November 1981, Vol. 72, No. 4, p. 499–503. Reprinted by permission of The British Psychological Society. (d) This graph illustrates Solso and McCarthy's findings, indicating the frequency of perceived recognition of each face, including the recognition of a prototypical face never observed by the subjects.

matches between the stimulus and the given feature. These matches are yelled out at demons at the next level of the hierarchy, the "cognitive (thinking) demons." They shout out possible patterns stored in memory that conform to one or more of the features noticed by the feature demons. A "decision demon" listens to the pandemonium of the cognitive demons. It decides on what has been seen, based on which cognitive demon is shouting the most frequently (i.e., which has the most matching features).

Although Selfridge's model is one of the most widely known models, other feature models have been proposed. Most feature models also distinguish not only different features. They also distinguish different kinds of features, such as global versus local features. Local features constitute the small-scale or detailed aspects of a given pattern. There is no consensus as to what exactly constitutes a local feature. Never-

FIGURE 4.21

According to Oliver Selfridge's feature-matching model, we recognize patterns by matching observed features to features already stored in memory. We recognize the patterns for which we have found the greatest number of matches.

theless, we generally can distinguish such features from global features, the features that give a form its overall shape. Consider, for example, the stimuli depicted in Figure 4.22 *a* and *b*. These stimuli are of the type used in some research on pattern perception (Navon, 1977). Globally, the stimuli in panels *a* and *b* form the letter *H*. In panel *a*, the local features (small *H*'s) correspond to the global ones. In panel *b*, comprising many local letter *S*'s, they do not.

In one study, participants identified the stimuli at either the global or the local level (Navon, 1977). Consider what happened when the local letters were small and positioned close together. Participants could identify stimuli at the global level more quickly than at the local level. Moreover, when participants were required to identify stimuli at the global level, whether the local features matched the global ones did not matter. They responded equally rapidly whether the global *H* was made up of local *H*'s or of local *S*'s. However, now consider what happened when participants were asked to respond at the local level. They responded more quickly if the global features agreed with the local ones. In other words, they were slowed down if they had to identify local *S*'s combining to form a global *H* instead of identifying local *H*'s combining to form a global *H*. This pattern of results is called the *global precedence effect*.

In contrast, when letters are more widely spaced, as in panels *a* and *b* of Figure 4.23, the effect is reversed. Then a *local-precedence effect* appears. That is, the participants more quickly identify the local features of the individual letters than the global ones, and the local features interfere with the global recognition in cases of contradictory stimuli (Martin, 1979). Other limitations (e.g., the size of the stimuli) hold as well, and other kinds of features also influence perception.

Some support for feature theories comes from neurological and physiological research. Researchers used single-cell recording techniques with animals (Hubel & Wiesel, 1963, 1968, 1979). They carefully measured the responses of individual neurons in the visual cortex. Then they mapped those neurons to corresponding visual stimuli for particular locations in the visual field (see Chapter 2). Their research

FIGURE 4.22

Compare panel *a* (global H's made of local H's) with panel *b* (global H's made of local S's). All the local letters are tightly spaced. D. Navon, "Forest Before Trees: The Precedence to Global Features in Visual Perception," *Cognitive Psychology*, July 1977, Vol. 9, No. 3, p. 353–382. Reprinted by permission of Elsevier.

FIGURE 4.23

H		H	S		S
H		H	S		S
H	H	H	S	S	S
H		H	S		S
H		H	S		S
	(a)			(b)	

Compare panels (a) and (b), in which the local letters are widely spaced. In which figure (Figure 4.22 or Figure 4.23) do you note the global-precedence effect, and in which figure do you note the local-precedence effect? D. Navon, "Forest Before Trees: The Precedence to Global Features in Visual Perception," Cognitive Psychology, July 1977, Vol. 9, No. 3, p. 353–382. Reprinted by permission of Elsevier.

showed that specific neurons of the visual cortex in the brain respond to varying stimuli presented to specific regions of the retina corresponding to these neurons. Each individual cortical neuron, therefore, can be mapped to a specific receptive field on the retina. A disproportionately large amount of the visual cortex is devoted to neurons mapped to receptive fields in the foveal region of the retina.

Most of the cells in the cortex do not respond simply to spots of light. Rather, they respond to "specifically oriented line segments" (Hubel & Wiesel, 1979, p. 9). What's more, these cells seem to show a hierarchical structure in the degree of complexity of the stimuli to which they respond. Consider what happens as the stimulus proceeds through the visual system to higher levels in the cortex. In general, the size of the receptive field increases, as does the complexity of the stimulus required to prompt a response. As evidence of this hierarchy, there are two kinds of visual cortex neurons (Figure 4.24): *simple cells* and *complex cells* (Hubel & Wiesel, 1979).

Simple cells receive input from the neurons projecting from the thalamus (see Chapter 2). They then fire in response to lines of particular orientations and positions in the receptive field. The specifically stimulating orientation or position differs from one cell to another. A particular cell also might respond preferentially to particular light-dark boundaries, bright lines on dark backgrounds, or the reverse. Even the line's thickness may affect whether the cell responds to the stimulus. The various lines are called "features." Thus, the neurons that detect and respond to them are called "feature detectors."

Hubel and Wiesel (1979) guessed that groups of these simple cells feed into complex cells (Figure 4.25). Each complex cell fires in response to lines of particular orientations. These lines can be located anywhere in the receptive field of the group of simple cells that feed into the given complex cell. Complex cells may receive input from one eye only or from both eyes. They appear insensitive to the particular type of

FIGURE 4.24

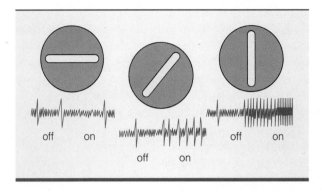

David Hubel and Torsten Wiesel discovered that cells in our visual cortex become activated only when they detect the sensation of line segments of particular orientations. From In Search of the Human Mind by Robert J. Sternberg, copyright © 1995 by Harcourt Brace & Company, reproduced by permission of the publisher.

Irving Biederman is the William M. Keck professor of cognitive neuroscience at the University of Southern California. He is best known for his work in high-level vision and in shape recognition in particular. His theory of geons shows a possible way in which various images of objects can be decomposed into a set of fundamental units.

light-dark contrasts of a line segment, as long as the segment is oriented appropriately (Carlson, 1992). Some complex cells fire only in response to line segments of particular orientations and precise lengths in the receptive field.

Based on Hubel and Wiesel's work, other investigators have found feature detectors that respond to corners and angles (DeValois & DeValois, 1980; Shapley & Lennie, 1985). In some areas of the cortex, there are highly sophisticated complex cells, called *hypercomplex cells*. They fire maximally only in response to very specific shapes, regardless of the size of the given stimulus. Examples would be a hand or a face. As the stimulus decreasingly resembles the optimal shape, these cells are decreasingly likely to fire.

Other work on visual perception has identified separate neural pathways in the cerebral cortex for processing different aspects of the same stimuli (De Yoe & Van Essen, 1988; Köhler & associates, 1995). They are termed the "what" and "where" pathways. The "what" pathway descends from the primary visual cortex in the occipital lobe (see Chapter 2) toward the temporal lobes. It is mainly responsible for processing the color, shape, and identity of visual stimuli. The "where" pathway ascends from the occipital lobe toward the parietal lobe. It is responsible for processing location and motion information. Thus, feature information feeds into at least two different systems for identifying objects and events in the environment.

Once discrete features have been analyzed according to their orientations, how are they integrated into a form we can recognize as particular objects?

Structural-Description Theory

Consider a means by which we may form stable 3-D mental representations of objects, based on the manipulation of a few simple geometric shapes (Biederman, 1987). This means is a set of 3-D geons (for geometrical ions). They include objects such as bricks, cylinders, wedges, cones, and their curved axis counterparts (Biederman, 1990/1993b, p. 314). According to Biederman's **recognition-by-components (RBC) theory,** we

FIGURE 4.25

Fires only in response to detecting specific shapes in the region governed by the complex cells that feed into the given hypercomplex cell		Hypercomplex cell	
Fires only in response to lines of particular orientations in the area governed by the group of simple cells feeding into the given complex cell	Complex cell	Complex cell	Other complex cells
Fires only in response to lines of particular orientations and positions in the receptive field, with particular orientation or position differing from one simple cell to another	Simple cell Simple cell Other simple cells	Simple cell Simple cell Other simple cells	Simple cell Simple cell Other simple cells
Transmit neural information via the thalamus, to an area of the visual cortex corresponding to particular sensory receptors	Neurons projected from the thalamus	Neurons projected from the thalamus	Neurons projected from the thalamus
Transmit neural information to the thalamus from sensory receptors in particular regions of the retina	Sensory receptors in particular locations in the retina of the eye	Sensory receptors in particular locations in the retina of the eye	Sensory receptors in particular locations in the retina of the eye

The process of visual perception appears to involve at least three levels of hierarchically organized neurons: simple cells, complex cells, and hypercomplex cells.

quickly recognize objects by observing the edges of objects and then decomposing the objects into geons. The geons also can be recomposed into alternative arrangements. You know that a small set of letters can be manipulated to compose countless words and sentences. Similarly, a small number of geons can be used to build up many basic shapes and then myriad basic objects (Figure 4.26).

The geons are simple and are viewpoint-invariant (i.e., discernible from various viewpoints). The objects constructed from geons thus are recognized easily from many perspectives, despite visual noise. According to Biederman (1993a), his RBC theory parsimoniously explains how we are able to recognize the general classification for multitudinous objects quickly, automatically, and accurately. This recognition occurs despite changes in viewpoint. It occurs even under many situations in which the stimulus object is degraded in some way. Biederman's RBC theory explains how we may recognize general instances of chairs, lamps, and faces. But it does not adequately explain how we recognize particular chairs or particular faces. An example would be your own face or your best friend's face.

FIGURE 4.26

(a)

(b)

Irving Biederman amplified feature-matching theory by proposing a set of elementary components of patterns, which he based on variations in three-dimensional shapes derived from a cone.

Biederman himself has recognized that aspects of his theory require further work, such as how the relations among the parts of an object can be described (Biederman, 1990/1993b, p. 16). Another problem with Biederman's approach, and the bottom-up approach in general, is how to account for the effects of prior expectations and environmental context on some phenomena of pattern perception.

Top-Down Approaches: Constructive Perception

In contrast to the bottom-up approach to perception is the top-down, constructive approach (Bruner, 1957; Gregory, 1980; Rock, 1983; von Helmholtz, 1909/1962). In **constructive perception,** the perceiver builds (constructs) a cognitive understanding (perception) of a stimulus. He or she uses sensory information as the foundation for the structure but also using other sources of information to build the perception. This viewpoint also is known as *intelligent perception* because it states that higher-order thinking plays an important role in perception. It also emphasizes the role of learning in perception (Fahle, 2003). Some investigators have pointed out that not only does the world affect our perception but also the world we experience is actually formed by our perception (Goldstone, 2003). These ideas go back to the philosophy of Immanuel Kant. In other words, perception is reciprocal with the world we experience. Perception both affects and is affected by the world as we experience it.

Irvin Rock was an adjunct professor of psychology at the University of California at Berkeley. He is well known for his championing of the role of problem solving in perception and the claim that perception is indirect. He also originated the study of one-trial learning and has made major contributions to the study of the moon and other perceptual illusions.

For example, picture yourself driving down a road you have never traveled before. As you approach a blind intersection, you see an octagonal red sign with white lettering. It bears the letters "ST_P." An overgrown vine cuts between the *T* and the *P*. Chances are, you will construct from your sensations a perception of a stop sign. You thus will respond appropriately. Similarly, constructivists would suggest that our perceptions of size and shape constancy indicate that high-level constructive processes are at work during perception. Another type of perceptual constancy can be viewed as illustrating top-down construction of perception. In color constancy, we perceive that the color of an object remains the same despite changes in lighting that alter the hue. Consider lighting that becomes so dim that color sensations are virtually absent. We still perceive bananas as yellow, plums as purple, and so on.

According to constructivists, during perception we quickly form and test various hypotheses regarding percepts. The percepts are based on three things. The first is what we sense (the sensory data). The second is what we know (knowledge stored in memory). The third is what we can infer (using high-level cognitive processes). In perception, we consider prior expectations. An example would be expecting to see an approaching friend whom we had arranged to meet. We also use what we know about the context. Here, an example would be that trains often ride on railroad tracks, but airplanes and automobiles usually do not. And we also may use what we reasonably can infer, based both on what the data are and on what we know about the data. According to constructivists, we usually make the correct attributions regarding our visual sensations. The reason is that we perform unconscious inference, the process by which we unconsciously assimilate information from a number of sources to create a perception (Snow & Mattingley, 2003). In other words, using more than one source of information, we make judgments that we are not even aware of making.

In the stop-sign example, sensory information implies that the sign is a meaningless assortment of oddly spaced consonants. However, your prior learning tells you something important—that a sign of this shape and color posted at an intersection of roadways and containing these three letters in this sequence probably means that you should stop thinking about the odd letters. Instead, you should start slamming on the brakes. Successful constructive perception requires intelligence and thought in combining sensory information with knowledge gained from previous experience.

One reason for favoring the constructive approach is that bottom-up (data-driven) theories of perception do not fully explain context effects. **Context effects** are the influences of the surrounding environment on perception (e.g., our perception of "THE CAT" in Figure 4.16). Fairly dramatic context effects can be demonstrated experimentally (Biederman, 1972; Biederman, Glass, & Stacy, 1973; Biederman & associates, 1974). In one study, people were asked to identify objects after they had viewed the objects in either an appropriate or an inappropriate context for the items (Palmer, 1975). For example, participants might see a scene of a kitchen followed by stimuli such as a loaf of bread, a mailbox, and a drum. Objects that were appropriate to the established context, such as the loaf of bread in this example, were recognized more rapidly than were objects that were inappropriate to the established context.

Perhaps even more striking is a context effect known as the *configural-superiority effect* (Pomerantz, 1981), by which objects presented in certain configurations are easier to recognize than the objects presented in isolation, even if the objects in the configurations are more complex than those in isolation. Suppose you show a participant four stimuli, all of them diagonal lines. Three of the lines are slanting one way, and one line is slanting the other way. The participant's task is to identify which stimulus is unlike the others (Figure 4.27 *a*). Now suppose that you show participants four stimuli. All of them comprise three lines (Figure 4.27 *c*). Three of the stimuli are shaped like triangles. One is not. In each case, the stimulus is a diagonal line (Figure 4.27 *a*) plus other lines (Figure 4.27 *b*). Thus, the stimuli in this second condition are more complex variations of the stimuli in the first condition. Participants can more quickly spot which of the three-sided figures is different from the others than they can spot which of the lines is different from the others.

In a similar vein, there is an object-superiority effect, in which a target line that forms a part of a drawing of a 3-D object is identified more accurately than a target that forms a part of a disconnected 2-D pattern (Lanze, Weisstein, & Harris, 1982; Weisstein & Harris, 1974). These findings parallel findings in the study of letter and word recognition.

The viewpoint of constructive or intelligent perception shows the central relation between perception and intelligence. According to this viewpoint, intelligence is an integral part of our perceptual processing. We do not perceive simply in terms of what is "out there in the world." Rather, we perceive in terms of the expectations and other cognitions we bring to our interaction with the world. On this view, intelligence and perceptual processes interact in the formation of our beliefs about what it is that we are encountering in our everyday contacts with the world at large.

An extreme top-down position would drastically underestimate the importance of sensory data. If it were correct, we would be susceptible to gross inaccuracies of perception. We frequently would form hypotheses and expectancies that inadequately evaluated the sensory data available. For example, if we expected to see a friend and someone else came into view, we might inadequately consider the perceptible differ-

FIGURE 4.27

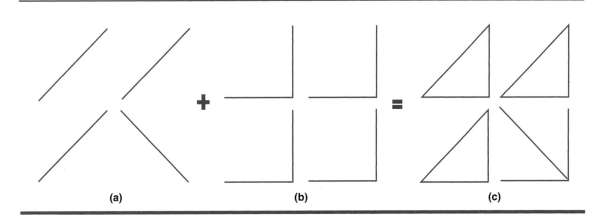

Subjects more readily perceive differences among integrated configurations comprising multiple lines (c) than they do solitary lines (a). In this figure, the lines in (b) are added to the lines in (a) to form shapes in (c), thereby making (c) more complex than (a).

ences between the friend and a stranger. Thus, an extreme constructivist view of perception would be highly error-prone and inefficient. However, an extreme bottom-up position would not allow for any influence of past experience or knowledge on perception. Why store knowledge that has no use for the perceiver? Neither extreme is ideal for explaining perception. It is more fruitful to consider ways in which bottom-up and top-down processes interact to form meaningful percepts.

Synthesizing the Two Approaches

Both theoretical approaches have been able to garner empirical support (cf. Cutting & Kozlowski, 1977, vs. Palmer, 1975). So how do we decide between the two? On one level, the constructive-perception theory, which is more top-down, seems to contradict direct-perception theory, which is more bottom-up. Constructivists emphasize the importance of prior knowledge in combination with relatively simple and ambiguous information from the sensory receptors. In contrast, direct-perception theorists emphasize the completeness of the information in the receptors themselves. They suggest that perception occurs simply and directly. Thus, there is little need for complex information processing.

Instead of viewing these theoretical approaches as incompatible, we may gain deeper insight into perception by considering the approaches to be complementary. Sensory information may be more richly informative and less ambiguous in interpreting experiences than the constructivists would suggest. But it may be less informative than the direct-perception theorists would assert. Similarly, perceptual processes may be more complex than hypothesized by Gibsonian theorists. This would be particularly true under conditions in which the sensory stimuli appear only briefly or are degraded. Degraded stimuli are less informative for various reasons. For example, the stimuli may be partially obscured or weakened by poor lighting. Or they may be incomplete, or distorted by illusory cues or other visual "noise" (distracting visual stimulation analogous to audible noise). We likely use a combination of information from the sensory receptors and our past knowledge to make sense of what we perceive.

Recent work suggests that, whereas early stages of the visual pathway represent only what is in the retinal image of an object, later-stage representations emphasize the viewer's current interest or attention. In other words, the later-stage representations are not independent of our attentional focus. On the contrary, they are directly affected by it (Maunsell, 1995). Moreover, vision for different things can take different forms. Visual control of action is mediated by cortical pathways that are different from those involved in visual control of perception (Ganel & Goodale, 2003). In other words, when we merely see an object, such as a cell phone, we process it differently than if we intend also to pick the object up. In general, according to Ganel and Goodale (2003), we perceive objects holistically. But if we plan to act on them, we perceive them more analytically so that we can act in an effective way.

A Computational Theory of Perception

David Marr (1982) proposed a theory of visual perception that considers the full richness of sensory information. Although a predecessor to Biederman's theory, it nevertheless takes a somewhat different approach to the relation between bottom-up and top-down information. It considers bottom-up processing without dismissing altogether the value of prior knowledge and experience in perception. Although Marr could not be considered a constructivist, he recognized the complexity of the cognitive processes required for perceiving a mental representation of the environment, based on raw sensory data. In addition, Marr's theory incorporates some of the descriptive principles of perception, such as depth cues, perceptual constancies, and Gestalt principles of form perception.

Marr proposed that raw sensory data from the retinas of the eyes can be organized through the use of three kinds of features: edges, contours, and regions of similarity. Edges form the boundaries between and around objects and parts of objects. Contour features differentiate one kind of surface from another. In a map, for example, contour lines indicate the differing elevations of land areas. Similarly, on the retina, various kinds of contours provide different kinds of information. For example, one kind of contour represents a convex surface. Such a surface would be found on a rounded ball of clay. Another kind of contour represents a concave (curving inward) surface. It would be found if someone bashed in the ball of clay and left a sizable indentation (Figure 4.28). Regions of similarity are areas that are largely undifferentiated by distinctive features.

Marr showed how a model of perception could be specified in sufficient detail to be simulated by a computer. Hence, his approach is considered a computational model. According to Marr (1982), the human brain uses a three-step process for computing a 3-D percept of what we see. First, the brain creates a 2-D primal sketch of the sensory information that reaches the eyes. This sketch represents an object, like a chair, in just two dimensions. Then the brain creates a 2½-D sketch of the data.

FIGURE 4.28

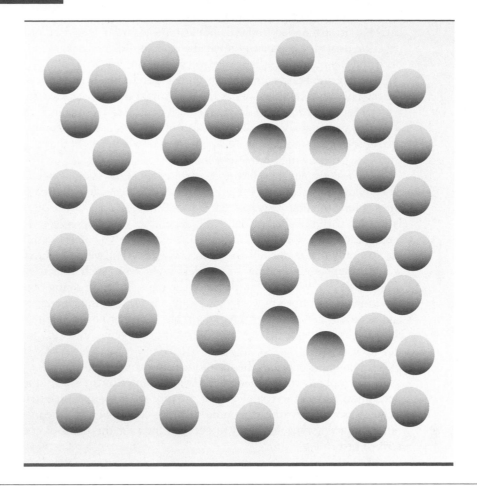

Are these contours concave or convex? Now turn the page upside-down and decide whether the contours are concave or convex. Our sensitivity to contour features is emphasized in David Marr's computational model of perception.

This sketch considers depth cues and surface orientations. For example, now the perception of the chair includes some aspects of depth but not others. So the sketch is incomplete with regard to depth information. This sketch also shows the orientation of the chair in the picture plane. For example, it might be with the right side up or maybe even backward. Finally the brain creates a 3-D model. It represents 3-D objects and the spatial interrelationships among the objects. Now consider these aspects in more detail.

First, the sensory receptors in the retina send information to the visual areas of the brain. These areas map out a 2-D primal sketch of what is observed. This sketch takes sensory data regarding changes in light intensity. It then maps out edges, contours, and regions of similarity. The mapping is based entirely on the observer's sensations from a given viewpoint. For example, a bowl of fruit on a table might be sketched as a pattern of edges between and around fruits, between the bowl and the table, and between the table and the background. Contours might be observed in the convexities of rounded fruits. Examples of such fruits would be oranges, grapes, or peaches. Regions of similarity might be detected in the background, in the expanse of the table surrounding the fruit bowl, and so on.

Second, the brain converts the primal sketch into what Marr termed the *2½-D sketch*. This new sketch enhances the 2-D primal sketch by considering the observer's view of the orientations of surfaces. It also considers depth cues. These cues include shading, texture gradients, motion, and binocular cues. For example, shadings and other depth cues would indicate which fruits or which legs of the table were nearer to the observer and which were farther.

Third, the brain then further elaborates the 2½-D sketch to build a 3-D model. This model fully represents the 3-D shapes of objects and the spatial interrelationships among the objects perceived. The 3-D model includes the observer's spatial relationship with the objects. But it is independent of the observer's viewpoint. For example, each fruit would be represented as a discrete 3-D object despite the observer's view of only one surface of the object. Objects that were obscured from view still would be represented in the 3-D model. Examples of such objects would be fruits at the back of the bowl or a fourth leg of the table. It is in forming the 3-D model that the individual's prior knowledge and experiences may influence perception. For example, knowing that a fourth leg of a table is likely to exist despite its absence from view might influence perception. Marr did not specify, however, how this influence might be exerted.

To summarize, current theories concerning the ways we perceive patterns explain some, but not all, of the phenomena we encounter in the study of form and pattern perception. Given the complexity of the process, it is impressive that we understand as much as we do. At the same time, clearly a comprehensive theory is still some way off. Such a theory would need to account fully for the kinds of context effects described here.

Deficits in Perception

Agnosias

Clearly, cognitive psychologists learn a great deal about normal perceptual processes by studying perception in normal participants. In addition, however, we also often gain understanding of perception by studying people whose perceptual processes differ from the norm (Farah, 1990; Weiskrantz, 1994). An example would be people who suffer from an **agnosia,** a severe deficit in the ability to perceive sensory information (Moscovitch, Winocur, & Behrmann, 1997). There are many kinds of agnosias. Not all of them are visual. Here we focus on a few specific inabilities to see forms and patterns in space. People with visual agnosia have normal sensations of what is in front of them. But they cannot recognize what they see. Agnosias often are caused by brain lesions (Farah, 1990, 1999).

Sigmund Freud (1953), who specialized in neurology in his medical practice before he developed his psychodynamic theory of personality, observed that some of his patients were unable to identify familiar objects. Nevertheless, they seemed to have no particular psychological disturbance or discernible damage to their visual abilities. In fact, people who suffer from visual-object agnosia can sense all parts of the visual field. But the objects they see do not mean anything to them (Kolb & Whishaw, 1985). For example, one agnosic patient, on seeing a pair of eyeglasses, noted first that there was a circle, then that there was another circle, then that there was a crossbar, and finally guessed that he was looking at a bicycle. A bicycle does, indeed, comprise two circles and a crossbar (Luria, 1973). Lesions in particular visual areas of the cortex may be responsible for visual-object agnosia.

Disturbance in the temporal region of the cortex can lead to simultagnosia. In *simultagnosia*, an individual is unable to pay attention to more than one object at a time. For instance, if you were simultagnosic and you were to look at Figure 4.29 (*a*), you would not be able to see each of the objects depicted. Rather, you might report seeing the hammer but not the other objects (Williams, 1970). In *spatial agnosia*, a person has severe difficulty in negotiating the everyday environment. For example, a spatial agnosic can get lost at home, make wrong turns en route to familiar locations, and fail to recognize even the most familiar landmarks. Such individuals also seem to have great difficulty drawing the symmetrical features of symmetrical objects (Heaton, 1968). This disorder seems to stem from lesions in the parietal lobe of the brain. *Prosopagnosia*, mentioned earlier, results in a severely impaired ability to recognize human faces (Farah & associates, 1995; Feinberg & associates, 1994; McNeil & Warrington, 1993; Young, 2003). A prosopagnosic, for example, might not even be

FIGURE 4.29

(a)   (b)

When you view this figure, you see various objects overlapping. People with simultagnosia cannot see more than one of these objects at any one time (a). However, even people with normal perception cannot simultaneously perceive both objects in reversible figures (b). From Sensation and Perception by Stanley Coren and Lawrence M. Ward, copyright © 1989 by Harcourt Brace & Company, reproduced by permission of the publisher.

able to recognize her or his own face in the mirror. Furthermore, there are even extremely rare cases of prosopagnosics who cannot recognize human faces but who can recognize the faces of their farm animals. The problem thus appears to be extremely specific to human faces (McNeil & Warrington, 1993). This fascinating disorder has spawned much research on face identification. It has become the latest "hot topic" in visual perception (Damasio, 1985; Farah & associates, 1995; Farah, Levinson, & Klein, 1995; Haxby & associates, 1996). The functioning of the right-hemisphere fusiform gyrus is strongly implicated in prosopagnosia. In particular, the disorder is associated with damage to the right temporal lobe of the brain.

There are other types of agnosias as well. One type is *auditory agnosia,* which is an impairment in the ability to recognize certain sounds. One patient, C.N., was reported to be unable to distinguish different types of music. She could not recognize melodies from her own collection of records and also could not tell whether two melodies were the same or different (Peretz & associates, 1994). Two other kinds of agnosias pertain to object recognition (Gazzaniga, Ivry, & Mangun, 2002). *Apperceptive agnosia* is a failure in object recognition that is linked to a failure in perceptual processing. *Associative agnosia* is the ability to represent objects visually but not to be able to use this information to recognize things. Thus, in associative agnosia, the problem is not in perceptual processing, but rather in associative cognitive processes operating on perceptual representations.

This kind of extreme specificity of deficits leads to questions about specialization. Specifically, are there distinct processing centers or modules for particular perceptual tasks? This question goes beyond the separation of perceptual processes along different sensory modalities (e.g., the differences between visual and auditory perception). Modular processes are those that are specialized for particular tasks. They may involve only visual processes (as in color perception). Or they may involve an integration of visual and auditory processes (as in certain aspects of speech perception that are discussed in Chapter 10). Jerry Fodor, an influential modern philosopher, has written a book entirely devoted to the delineation of the necessary characteristics of modular processes. For some process to be truly modular, the following properties must exist. First, the modules must work fast and their operation must be mandatory. Second, modules have characteristically shallow outputs (i.e., yielding basic categorizations). Central access to the module's computations is limited. It is not subject to conscious attentional influences. Third, modules are domain specific. They are fine-tuned with respect to the kinds of information used. Information does not necessarily flow freely across various modules. It is sometimes referred to as "encapsulated." Finally, modules are supported by fixed neural architectures and therefore suffer characteristic breakdown patterns. Thus, for face perception to be considered a truly modular process, we would need to have further evidence of domain specificity and informational encapsulation. That is, other perceptual processes should not contribute to, interfere with, or share information with face perception. Moreover, the neurological basis of prosopagnosia is not well understood.

Although cognitive psychologists are intrigued by the fact that a few people are prosopagnosic, they are even more fascinated by the fact that most of us are not. Just how do you recognize your mother or your best friend? In addition, how do you recognize the much simpler and less dynamic forms and patterns of the letters and words in this sentence? This chapter has considered just a few of the many aspects of perception that interest cognitive psychologists. Of particular note are the cognitive processes by which we form mental representations of what we sense. These representations use prior knowledge, inferences, and specialized cognitive operations to make sense of our sensations.

Anomalies in Color Perception

Another kind of deficit in perception is a deficit in color perception. This deficit is much more common in men than in women. It is genetically linked.

There are several kinds of color blindness, although only one kind represents true color-blindness. The most common is red-green color-blindness. People with this form of color-blindness have difficulty in distinguishing red from green, although they may be able to distinguish, say, dark red from light green. People with this form of color-blindness experience either of two syndromes (*Visual diabilities: Color-blindness*, 2004).

One kind is *protanopia*, which is the extreme form of red-green color-blindness. People with this syndrome have trouble seeing the very long wavelengths, namely, reds. These reds appear to them more as beiges, but darker than they really are. The greens look similar to the reds. *Protanomaly* is a less extreme form of red-green color-blindness. The second kind of red-green color-blindness is *deuteranopia*. People with this syndrome have trouble seeing medium wavelengths, namely, greens. *Deuteranomaly* is a less serious form of this condition. Although people with deuteranomaly do not see reds and greens the way normal people do, they still usually can distinguish them.

Much less common than red-green color-blindness is blue-yellow color-blindness. People with this form of color blindness have difficulty distinguishing between blues and yellows. *Tritanopia* is insensitivity to short wavelengths—the blues. Blues and greens can be confused, but yellows also can seem to disappear or to appear as light shades of reds.

Least common of all is *rod monochromacy*, also called *achromacy*. People with this condition have no color vision at all. It is thus the only true form of pure color-blindness. People with this condition have cones that are nonfunctional. They see only shades of gray, as a function of their vision through the rods of the eye.

Akinetopsia

Akinetopsia is a selective loss of motion perception (Gazzaniga, Ivry, & Mangun, 2002). In this disorder, an individual is unable to perceive motion. Rather, motion appears instead as a series of snapshots. The deficit appears to be extremely rare, and there is only one reported case study in the literature (Zihl, von Cramon, & Mai, 1983). The deficit appears to occur only in cases of severe bilateral damage to the temporoparietal cortices.

Key Themes

Several key themes, as outlined in Chapter 1, emerge in our study of perception.

The first theme is that of rationalism versus empiricism. How much of the way we perceive can be understood as due to the some kind of order in the environment that is relatively independent of our perceptual mechanisms? In the Gibsonian view, much of what we perceive derives from the structure of the stimulus, independent of our experience with it. In contrast, in the view of constructive perception, we construct what we perceive. We build up mechanisms for perceiving based on our experience with the environment. As a result, our perception is influenced at least as much by our intelligence as it is by the structure of the stimuli we perceive.

The second important theme is that of basic versus applied research. Research on perception has many applications, for example, in understanding how we can construct machines that perceive. The United States Postal Service, for example, relies heavily on machines that read zip codes on mailed items. To the extent that the machines are inaccurate, mail risks going astray. These machines cannot rely on strict template matching, because people write numbers in different ways. So the machines must do at least some feature analysis. A second example of an application of perception research is in human-factors. Human-factors researchers design machines and user interfaces to be user-friendly. An automobile driver or airplane pilot sometimes needs to make split-second decisions. The cockpits thus must have instrument panels that are well lighted, easy to read, and accessible for quick action.

The third theme is that of domain generality versus domain specificity. Perhaps nowhere is this theme better illustrated than in research on face recognition. Is there something special about face recognition? It appears so. Yet many of the mechanisms that are used for face recognition are used for other kinds of perception as well. Thus, it appears that perceptual mechanisms may be mixed—some general across domains, others specific to domains such as face recognition.

Have you ever noticed that the moon looks very large when it is on the horizon just above the trees and houses but looks relatively small when it is straight up in the air? This is called the "moon illusion." Many people think that the moon looks very close to us when it is on the horizon, but believe it or not, we see the moon as very large on the horizon because we perceive it to be *farther* away from us. Don't believe this? Stand at one end of a room and hold your thumb up to your eye so that it is the same size as the door on the opposite side of the room. Do you *really* think that your thumb is as large as a door? No. You know that your thumb is close to you, so it just *looks* as large as the door. There are numerous cues in the room to tell you that the door is farther away from you than your thumb is. In your mind, you make the door much larger to compensate for the distance away from you. When we look at the moon above us, there are no cues to tell us that the moon is far away. However, when the moon is on the horizon, there are numerous cues that tell us that the moon is far (houses, trees, cars, bushes, etc.). Thus, in your mind, you make the moon much larger than it is to compensate for how *far* the moon appears to be. Want to get rid of the moon illusion? Take a piece of paper and roll it up into a cylinder. Hold this cylinder up to your eye so that you only see the moon and nothing else. The moon will appear to be just as large when it is on the horizon as when it is straight up in the air.

The reason is that the cylinder eliminates all cues telling us that the moon is really far away. Because the moon is in fact just as far away when it is on the horizon as it is when it is straight up in the air, it will appear to be the same size in both locations.

Summary

1. **How do we perceive stable objects in the environment, given variable stimulation?** Perceptual experience involves four elements: distal object, informational medium, proximal stimulation, and perceptual object. Proximal stimulation is constantly changing because of the variable nature of the environment and physiological processes designed to overcome sensory adaptation. Perception therefore must address the fundamental question of constancy.

   Perceptual constancies (e.g., size and shape constancy) result when our perceptions of objects tend to remain constant. That is, we see constancies even as the stimuli registered by our senses change. Some perceptual constancies may be governed by what we know about the world. For example, we have expectations regarding how rectilinear structures usually appear. But constancies also are influenced by invariant relationships among objects in their environmental context.

   One reason we can perceive 3-D space is the use of binocular depth cues. Two such cues are binocular disparity and binocular convergence. Binocular disparity is based on the fact that each of two eyes receives a slightly different image of the same object as it is being viewed. Binocular convergence is based on the degree to which our two eyes must turn inward toward each other as objects get closer to us. We also are aided in perceiving depth by monocular depth cues. These cues include texture gradients, relative size, interposition, linear perspective, aerial perspective, height in the picture plane, and motion parallax. One of the earliest approaches to form and pattern perception is the Gestalt approach to form perception. The Gestalt law of Prägnanz has led to the explication of several principles of form perception. These principles include figure-ground, proximity, similarity, closure, continuity, and symmetry. They characterize how we perceptually group together various objects and parts of objects.

2. **What are two fundamental approaches to explaining perception?** Perception is the set of processes by which we recognize, organize, and make sense of stimuli in our environment. It may be viewed from either of two basic theoretical approaches: top-down, constructive perception, or bottom-up, direct perception. The viewpoint of constructive (or intelligent) perception asserts that the perceiver essentially constructs or builds up the stimulus that is perceived. He or she does so by using prior knowledge, contextual information, and sensory information. In contrast, the viewpoint of direct perception asserts that all the information we need to perceive is in the sensory input (such as from the retina) that we receive.

   Three of the main bottom-up theoretical approaches to pattern perception include template-matching theories, prototype-matching theories, and feature-matching theories. Some support for feature-matching theories comes from neurophysiological studies identifying what are called "feature detectors" in the brain. It appears that various cortical neurons can be mapped to specific receptive fields on the retina. Differing cortical neurons respond to different features. Examples of such features are line segments or edges in various spatial orientations. Visual perception seems to depend on three levels of complexity in the cortical neurons. Each level of complexity seems to be further removed from the incoming information from the sensory receptors. Another bottom-up approach, the recognition-by-components (RBC) theory, more specifically delineates a set of features involved in form and pattern perception. Bottom-up approaches explain some aspects of form and pattern perception.

Other aspects require approaches that suggest at least some degree of top-down processing of perceptual information. For example, top-down approaches better but incompletely explain such phenomena as context effects, including the object-superiority effect and the word-superiority effect.

An alternative to both of these approaches integrates features of each. It suggests that perception may be more complex than direct-perception theorists have suggested, yet perception also may involve more efficient use of sensory data than constructive-perception theorists have suggested. Specifically, a computational approach to perception suggests that our brains compute 3-D perceptual models of the environment, based on information from the 2-D sensory receptors in our retinas.

3. **What happens when people with normal visual sensations cannot perceive visual stimuli?** Agnosias, which are usually associated with brain lesions, are deficits of form and pattern perception.

They cause afflicted people to be insufficiently able to recognize objects that are in their visual fields, despite normal sensory abilities. People who suffer from visual-object agnosia can sense all parts of the visual field. But the objects they see do not mean anything to them. Individuals with simultagnosia are unable to pay attention to more than one object at a time. People with spatial agnosia have severe difficulty in comprehending and handling the relationship between their bodies and the spatial configurations of the world around them. People with prosopagnosia have severe impairment in their ability to recognize human faces including their own. These deficits lead to the question of whether specific perceptual processes are modular—specialized for particular tasks. Other perception deficits include various types of color-blindness and the inability to perceive motion (akinetopsia).

Thinking about Thinking: Factual, Analytical, Creative, and Practical Questions

1. Briefly describe each of the monocular and binocular depth cues listed in this chapter.

2. Describe bottom-up and top-down approaches to perception.

3. How might deficits of perception, such as agnosia, offer insight into normal perceptual processes?

4. Compare and contrast the Gestalt approach to form perception and Marr's computational theory.

5. Design a demonstration that would illustrate the phenomenon of perceptual constancy.

6. Design an experiment to test either the prototype-matching theory of pattern perception or the feature-matching theory.

7. To what extent does perception involve learning? Why?

Key Terms

agnosia
binocular depth cues
bottom-up theories
constructive perception
context effects
depth
direct perception

figure-ground
Gestalt approach to form perception
law of Prägnanz
monocular depth cues
object-centered representation
perception

perceptual constancy
prototype
recognition-by-components (RBC) theory
templates
top-down theories
viewer-centered representation

Explore CogLab by going to http://coglab.wadsworth.com. Answer the questions required by your instructor from the student manual that accompanies CogLab.

Mapping the Blind Spot   Muller-Lyer Illusion
Receptive Fields   Signal Detection
Apparent Motion   Visual Search
Metacontrast Masking   Lexical Decision

Annotated Suggested Reading

Palmer, S. E. (1999). *Vision science*. Cambridge, MA: Bradford Books. A very complete and penetrating analysis of all aspects of the cognitive-scientific study of vision.

Memory: Models and Research Methods

EXPLORING COGNITIVE PSYCHOLOGY

1. What are some of the tasks used for studying memory, and what do various tasks indicate about the structure of memory?

2. What has been the prevailing traditional model for the structure of memory?

3. What are some of the main alternative models of the structure of memory?

4. What have psychologists learned about the structure of memory by studying both exceptional memory and the physiology of the brain?

Who is the president of the United States? What is today's date? What does your best friend look like, and what does your friend's voice sound like? What were some of your experiences when you first started college? How do you tie your shoelaces?

INVESTIGATING COGNITIVE PSYCHOLOGY

How do you know the answers to the preceding questions, or to any questions for that matter? How do you remember any of the information you use every waking hour of every day? **Memory** is the means by which we retain and draw on our past experiences to use that information in the present (Tulving, 2000b; Tulving & Craik, 2000). As a *process*, memory refers to the dynamic mechanisms associated with storing, retaining, and retrieving information about past experience (Bjorklund, Schneider, & Hernández Blasi, 2003; Crowder, 1976). Specifically, cognitive psychologists have identified three common operations of memory: encoding, storage, and retrieval (Baddeley, 1998, 1999, 2000b; Brown & Craik, 2000). Each operation represents a stage in memory processing. In encoding, you transform sensory data into a form of mental representation. In storage, you keep encoded information in memory. In retrieval, you pull out or use information stored in memory. These memory processes are discussed at length in Chapter 6.

This chapter introduces some of the tasks used for studying memory. It then discusses the traditional model of memory. This model includes the sensory, short-term, and long-term storage systems. Although this model still influences current thinking about memory, we consider some interesting alternative perspectives before moving on to discuss exceptional memory and insights provided by neuropsychology.

Tasks Used for Measuring Memory

In studying memory, researchers have devised various tasks that require participants to remember arbitrary information (e.g., numerals) in different ways. Because this chapter includes many references to these tasks, we begin this section with an advance organizer—a basis for organizing the information to be given. In this way, you will know how memory is studied. The tasks involve recall versus recognition memory and implicit versus explicit memory.

Recall versus Recognition Tasks

In **recall,** you produce a fact, a word, or other item from memory. Fill-in-the-blank tests require that you recall items from memory. In **recognition,** you select or otherwise identify an item as being one that you learned previously. (See Table 5.1 for examples and explanations of each type of task.) Multiple-choice and true-false tests involve some degree of recognition. There are three main types of recall tasks used in experiments (Lockhart, 2000). The first is *serial recall,* in which you recall items in the exact order in which they were presented (Crowder & Green, 2000). The second is *free recall,* in which you recall items in any order you choose. The third is *cued recall,* in which you are first shown items in pairs, but during recall you are cued with only one member of each pair and are asked to recall each mate. Cued recall is also called "paired-associates recall" (Lockhart, 2000). Psychologists also can measure *relearning,* which is the number of trials it takes to learn once again items that were learned at some time in the past.

Recognition memory is usually much better than recall (although there are some exceptions, which are discussed in Chapter 6). For example, in one study, participants

---

TABLE 5.1   Types of Tasks Used for Measuring Memory

Some memory tasks involve recall or recognition of explicit memory for declarative knowledge. Other tasks involve implicit memory and memory for procedural knowledge.

TASKS REQUIRING EXPLICIT MEMORY FOR DECLARATIVE KNOWLEDGE	DESCRIPTION OF WHAT THE TASKS REQUIRE	EXAMPLE
Explicit-memory tasks	You must consciously recall particular information.	Who wrote *Hamlet*?
Declarative-knowledge tasks	You must recall facts.	What is your first name?
Recall tasks	You must produce a fact, a word, or other item from memory.	Fill-in-the-blank tests require that you recall items from memory. For example, "The term for persons who suffer severe memory impairment is _____."
Serial-recall task	You must repeat the items in a list in the exact order in which you heard or read them.	If you were shown the digits 2-8-7-1-6-4, you would be expected to repeat "2-8-7-1-6-4," in exactly that order.
Free-recall task	You must repeat the items in a list in any order in which you can recall them.	If you were presented with the word list, "dog, pencil, time, hair, monkey, restaurant," you would receive full credit if you repeated "monkey, restaurant, dog, pencil, time, hair."
Cued-recall task	You must memorize a list of paired items; then when you are given one item in the pair, you must recall the mate for that item.	Suppose that you were given the following list of pairs: "time-city, mist-home, switch-paper, credit-day, fist-cloud, number-branch." Later, when you were given the stimulus "switch" you would be expected to say, "paper," and so on.

could recognize close to 2,000 pictures in a recognition-memory task (Standing, Conezio, & Haber, 1970). It is difficult to imagine anyone recalling 2,000 items of any kind they were just asked to memorize. As you will see later in the section on exceptional memory, even with extensive training the best measured recall performance is around 80 items.

Different memory tasks indicate different levels of learning. Recall tasks generally elicit deeper levels than recognition ones. Some psychologists refer to recognition-memory tasks as tapping *receptive* knowledge. Recall memory tasks, in which you have to produce an answer, instead require *expressive* knowledge. Differences between receptive and expressive knowledge also are observed in areas other than that of simple memory tasks (e.g., language, intelligence, and cognitive development).

Implicit versus Explicit Memory Tasks

Memory theorists distinguish between explicit memory and implicit memory (Mulligan, 2003). Each of the preceding tasks involves **explicit memory,** in which participants engage in conscious recollection. For example, they might recall or recognize

TABLE 5.1	Types of Tasks Used for Measuring Memory *(Continued)*	
TASKS REQUIRING EXPLICIT MEMORY FOR DECLARATIVE KNOWLEDGE	**DESCRIPTION OF WHAT THE TASKS REQUIRE**	**EXAMPLE**
Recognition tasks	You must select or otherwise identify an item as being one that you learned previously.	Multiple-choice and true-false tests involve recognition. For example, "The term for people with outstanding memory ability is (1) amnesics, (2) semanticists, (3) mnemonists, or (4) retrograders."
Implicit-memory tasks	You must draw on information in memory without consciously realizing that you are doing so.	Word-completion tasks tap implicit memory. You would be presented with a word fragment, such as the first three letters of a word; then you would be asked to complete the word fragment with the first word that comes to mind. For example, suppose that you were asked to supply the missing three letters to fill in these blanks and form a word: _e_or_. Because you had recently seen the word *memory*, you would be more likely to provide the three letters m-m-y for the blanks than would someone who had not recently been exposed to the word.
Tasks involving procedural knowledge	You must remember learned skills and automatic behaviors, rather than facts.	If you were asked to demonstrate a "knowing-how" skill, you might be given experience in solving puzzles or in reading mirror writing, and then you would be asked to show what you remember of how to use those skills. Or, you might be asked to master or to show what you already remember about particular motor skills (e.g., riding a bicycle or ice skating).

words, facts, or pictures from a particular prior set of items. A related phenomenon is **implicit memory,** in which we recollect something but are not consciously aware that we are trying to do so (Schacter, 1995a, 2000; Schacter, Chiu, & Ochsner, 1993; Schacter & Graf, 1986a, 1986b). Every day you engage in many tasks that involve your unconscious recollection of information. Even as you read this book, you unconsciously are remembering various things. They include the meanings of particular words, some of the cognitive-psychological concepts you read about in earlier chapters, and even how to read. These recollections are aided by implicit memory.

In the laboratory, people sometimes perform word-completion tasks, which involve implicit memory. In a word-completion task, participants receive a word fragment, such as the first three letters of a word. They then complete it with the first word that comes to mind. For example, suppose that you are asked to supply the missing five letters to fill in these blanks to form a word: imp_ _ _ _ _. Because you recently have seen the word *implicit*, you would be more likely to provide the five letters "l-i-c-i-t" for the blanks than would someone who had not recently been exposed to the word. You have been primed. **Priming** is the facilitation in your ability to utilize missing information. In general, participants perform better when they have seen the word on a recently presented list, although they have not been explicitly instructed to remember words from that list (Tulving, 2000a).

Traditional Model of Memory

There are several different major models of memory (Murdock, 2003; Roediger, 1980b). In the mid-1960s, based on the data available at the time, researchers proposed a model of memory distinguishing two structures of memory first proposed by William James (1890/1970): primary memory, which holds temporary information currently in use, and secondary memory, which holds information permanently or at least for a very long time (Waugh & Norman, 1965). Three years later, Richard Atkinson and Richard Shiffrin (1968) proposed an alternative model that conceptualized memory in terms of three memory stores: (1) a **sensory store,** capable of storing relatively limited amounts of information for very brief periods; (2) a **short-term store,** capable of storing information for somewhat longer periods but also of relatively limited capacity; and (3) a **long-term store,** of very large capacity, capable of storing information for very long periods, perhaps even indefinitely (Richardson-Klavehn & Bjork, 2003).

The model differentiates among structures for holding information, termed *stores*, and the information stored in the structures, termed *memory*. Today, however, cognitive psychologists commonly describe the three stores as sensory memory, short-term memory, and long-term memory. Also, Atkinson and Shiffrin were not suggesting that the three stores are distinct physiological structures. Rather, the stores are **hypothetical constructs**—concepts that are not themselves directly measurable or observable but that serve as mental models for understanding how a psychological phenomenon works. Figure 5.1 shows a simple information-processing model of these stores (Atkinson & Shiffrin, 1971). As this figure shows, the Atkinson-Shiffrin model emphasizes

FIGURE 5.1

the passive receptacles in which memories are stored. But it also alludes to some control processes that govern the transfer of information from one store to another.

The three-stores model is not the only way to conceptualize memory, however. First, the chapter presents what we know about memory in terms of the three-stores model. Then it describes some alternative ways in which to conceptualize memory. For now, however, let's begin with the sensory store in the three-stores model.

Sensory Store

The *sensory store* is the initial repository of much information that eventually enters the short- and long-term stores. Strong (although not undisputed; see Haber, 1983) evidence argues in favor of the existence of an iconic store. The **iconic store** is a discrete visual sensory register that holds information for very short periods of time. Its name derives from the fact that information is stored in the form of icons. These in turn are visual images that represent something. Icons usually resemble whatever is being represented.

If you have ever "written" your name with a lighted sparkler (or stick of incense) against a dark background, you have experienced the persistence of a visual memory. You briefly "see" your name, although the sparkler leaves no physical trace. This visual persistence is an example of the type of information held in the iconic store.

Sperling's Discovery

The initial discovery regarding the existence of the iconic store came from a doctoral dissertation by a graduate student at Harvard named George Sperling (1960).

He addressed the question of how much information we can encode in a single, brief glance at a set of stimuli. Sperling flashed an array of letters and numbers on a screen for a mere 50 milliseconds (thousandths of a second). Participants were asked to report the identity and location of as many of the symbols as they could recall. Sperling could be sure that participants got only one glance because previous research had shown that 0.050 seconds is long enough for only a single glance at the presented stimulus.

Sperling found that when participants were asked to report on what they saw, they remembered only about four symbols. The finding confirmed an earlier one made by Brigden in 1933. The number of symbols recalled was pretty much the same, without regard to how many symbols had been in the visual display. Some of Sperling's participants mentioned that they had seen all the stimuli clearly. But while reporting what they saw they forgot the other stimuli. Sperling then conceived an ingenious idea for how to measure what the participants saw. The procedure used by R. Brigden and initially by Sperling is a *whole-report procedure*. In this procedure, participants report *every* symbol they have seen. Sperling then introduced a *partial-report procedure*. Here, participants need to report only part of what they see.

Sperling found a way to obtain a sample of his participants' knowledge. He then extrapolated from this sample to estimate their total knowledge. His logic was similar to that of school examinations, which also are used as samples of an individual's total knowledge of course material. Sperling presented symbols in three rows of four symbols each. Figure 5.2 shows a display similar to one that Sperling's participants might have seen. Sperling informed participants that they would have to recall only a single row of the display. The row to be recalled was signaled by a tone of high, medium, or low pitch. The pitches corresponded to the need to recall the top, middle, or bottom row, respectively.

To estimate the duration of iconic memory, Sperling manipulated the interval between the display and the tone. The range of the interval was from 0.10 seconds

FIGURE 5.2

H B S T
A H M G
E L W C

This symbolic display is similar to the one used for George Sperling's visual-recall task. From Psychology, Second Edition by Margaret W. Matlin, copyright © 1995 by Holt, Rinehart and Winston, reproduced by permission of the publisher.

before the onset of the display to 1.0 seconds *after* the offset of the display. The partial-report procedure dramatically changed how much participants could recall. Sperling then multiplied the number of symbols recalled with this procedure by three. The reason was that participants had to recall only one third of the information presented but did not know beforehand which of the three lines they would be asked to report.

Using this partial-report procedure, Sperling found that participants had available roughly nine of the twelve symbols if they were cued immediately before or immediately after the appearance of the display. However, when they were cued 1 second later, their recall was down to four or five of the twelve items. This level of recall was about the same as that obtained through the whole-report procedure. These data suggest that the iconic store can hold about nine items. They also suggest that information in this store decays very rapidly (Figure 5.3). Indeed, the advantage of the partial-report procedure is reduced drastically by 0.3 seconds of delay. It essentially is obliterated by 1 second of delay for onset of the tone.

Sperling's results suggest that information fades rapidly from iconic storage. Why are we subjectively unaware of such a fading phenomenon? First, we rarely are

FIGURE 5.3

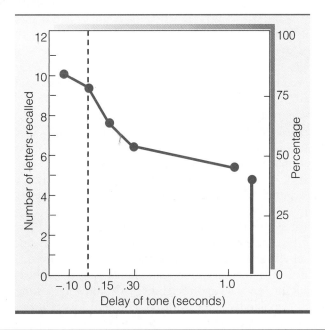

The figure shows the average number of letters recalled (left axis; percentage equivalents indicated on right axis) by a subject, based on using the partial-report procedure, as a function of the delay between the presentation of the letters and the tone signaling when to demonstrate recall. The bar at the lower-right corner indicates the average number of letters recalled when subjects used the whole-report procedure. (After Sperling, 1960.)

subjected to stimuli such as the ones in his experiment. They appeared for only 50 milliseconds and then disappeared before participants needed to recall them. Second and more important, however, we are unable to distinguish what we see in iconic memory from what we actually see in the environment. What we see in iconic memory is what we take to be in the environment. Participants in Sperling's experiment generally reported that they could still see the display up to 150 milliseconds after it actually had been terminated.

Elegant as it was, Sperling's use of the partial-report procedure was imperfect. It still suffered, at least to some small extent, from the problem inherent in the full-report procedure: Participants had to report multiple symbols. They may have experienced fading of memory during the report. Indeed, a distinct possibility of output interference exists. In this case, the production of output interferes with the phenomenon being studied. That is, verbally reporting multiple symbols may interfere with reports of iconic memory.

Subsequent Refinement

In subsequent work, participants were shown displays of two rows of eight randomly chosen letters for a duration of 50 milliseconds (Averbach & Coriell, 1961). In this investigation, a small mark appeared just above one of the positions where a letter had appeared (or was about to appear). Its appearance was at varying time intervals before or after presentation of the letters. In this research, then, participants needed to report only a single letter at a time. The procedure thus minimized output interference. These investigators found that when the bar appeared immediately before or after the stimulus display, participants could report accurately on about 75% of the trials. Thus, they seemed to be holding about twelve items (75% of 16) in sensory memory. Sperling's estimate of the capacity of iconic memory, therefore, may have been conservative. The evidence in this study suggests that when output interference is greatly reduced, the estimates of the capacity of iconic memory may greatly increase. Iconic memory may comprise as many as twelve items.

A second experiment (Averbach & Coriell, 1961) revealed an additional important characteristic of iconic memory: it can be erased. The erasable nature of iconic memory definitely makes our visual sensations more sensible. We would be in serious trouble if everything we saw in our visual environment persisted for too long. For example, if we are scanning the environment at a rapid pace, we need the visual information to disappear quickly.

The investigators found that when a stimulus was presented after a target letter in the same position that the target letter had occupied, it could erase the visual icon (Averbach & Coriell, 1961). This interference is called backward visual masking. *Backward visual masking* is mental erasure of a stimulus caused by the placement of one stimulus where another one had appeared previously. If the mask stimulus is presented in the same location as a letter and within 100 milliseconds of the presentation of the letter, the mask is superimposed on the letter. For example, F followed by L would be E. At longer intervals between the target and the mask, the mask erases the original stimulus. For example, only the L would remain if F and then L had been presented. At still longer intervals between the target and the mask, the mask no longer interferes. This noninterference is presumably because the target information already has been transferred to more durable memory storage.

To summarize, visual information appears to enter our memory system through an iconic store. This store holds visual information for very short periods. In the normal course of events, this information may be transferred to another store. Or it may be erased. Erasure occurs if other information is superimposed on it before there is sufficient time for the transfer of the information to another memory store.

Short-Term Store

Most of us have little or no introspective access to our sensory memory stores. Nevertheless, we all have access to our short-term memory store. It holds memories for matters of seconds and, occasionally, up to a couple of minutes. For example, can you remember the name of the researcher who discovered the iconic store? What about the names of the researchers who subsequently refined this work? If you can recall those names, you used some memory-control processes for doing so. According to the Atkinson-Shiffrin model, the short-term store holds not only a few items. It also has available some control processes that regulate the flow of information to and from the long-term store. Here, we may hold information for longer periods. Typically, material remains in the short-term store for about 30 seconds, unless it is rehearsed to retain it. Information is stored acoustically—by the way it sounds—rather than visually—by the way it looks.

How many items of information can we hold in short-term memory at any one time? In general, our immediate (short-term) memory capacity for a wide range of items appears to be about seven items, plus or minus two (Miller, 1956). An item can be something simple, such as a digit, or something more complex, such as a word. If we chunk together a string of, say, twenty letters or numbers into seven meaningful items, we can remember them. We could not, however, remember twenty items and repeat them immediately. For example, most of us cannot hold in short-term memory this string of twenty-one numbers: 101001000100001000100. Suppose, however, we chunk it into larger units, such as 10, 100, 1000, 10000, 1000, and 100. We probably will be able to reproduce easily the twenty-one numerals as six items (Miller, 1956).

Other factors also influence memory capacity for temporary storage. For example, the number of syllables we pronounce with each item affects the number of items we can recall. When each item has a larger number of syllables, we can recall fewer items (Baddeley, Thomson, & Buchanan, 1975; Naveh-Benjamin & Ayres, 1986; Schweickert & Boruff, 1986). In addition, any delay or interference can cause our seven-item capacity to drop to about three items. Indeed, in general the capacity limit may be closer to three to five than it is to seven (Cowan, 2001), and some estimates are even lower (e.g., Waugh & Norman, 1965).

Most studies have used verbal stimuli to test the capacity of the short-term store. But people can also hold visual information in short-term memory. For example, they can hold information about shapes as well as their colors and orientations. What is the capacity of the short-term store of visual information? Is it less, the same, or perhaps greater?

A team of investigators set out to discover the capacity of the short-term store for visual information (Luck & Vogel, 1997; Vogel, Woodman, & Luck, 2001). They presented experimental participants with two visual displays. The displays were presented in sequence, on following the other. The stimuli were of three types: colored squares, black lines at varying orientations, and colored lines at different orientations. Thus, the third kind of stimulus combined the features of the first two. The kind of stimulus was the same in each of the two displays. For example, if the first display contained colored squares, so did the second. The two displays could be either the same or different from each other. If they were different, then it was by only one feature. The participants needed to indicate whether the two displays were the same or different from each other. The investigators found that participants could hold roughly four items in memory, within the estimates suggested by Cowan (2001). The results were the same whether just individual features were varied (i.e., colored squares; black lines at varying orientation) or pairs of features (i.e., colored lines at different orientations). Thus, storage seems to depend on numbers of objects rather than numbers of features.

This work contained a possible confound (i.e., other responsible factor that cannot be easily disentangled from the supposed causal factor). In the stimuli with colored lines at different orientations, the added feature was at the same spatial location as the original one. That is, color and orientation were with respect to the same object in the same place in the display. A further study thus was done to separate the effects of spatial location from number of objects (Lee & Chun, 2001). In this research, stimuli comprising boxes and lines could be either at separate locations or at overlapping locations. The overlapping locations thus separated the objects from the fixed locations. The research would thus enable one to determine whether people can remember four objects, as suggested in the previous work, or four spatial locations. The results were the same as in the earlier research. Participants still could remember four objects, regardless of spatial locations. Thus, memory was for objects, not spatial locations.

Long-Term Store

We constantly use short-term memory throughout our daily activities. When most of us talk about memory, however, we usually are talking about long-term memory. Here we keep memories that stay with us over long periods, perhaps indefinitely. All of us rely heavily on our long-term memory. We hold in it information we need to get us by in our day-to-day lives. Examples are what people's names are, where we keep things, how we schedule ourselves on different days, and so on. We also worry when we fear that our long-term memory is not up to snuff.

How much information can we hold in long-term memory? How long does the information last? The question of storage capacity can be disposed of quickly because the answer is simple. We do not know. Nor do we know how we would find out. We can design experiments to tax the limits of short-term memory. But we do not know how to test the limits of long-term memory and thereby find out its capacity. Some theorists have suggested that the capacity of long-term memory is infinite, at least in practical terms (Bahrick, 1984a, 1984b, 2000; Bahrick & Hall, 1991; Hintzman, 1978). It turns out that the question of how long information lasts in long-term memory is not easily answerable, At present, we have no proof even that there is an absolute outer limit to how long information can be stored.

What is stored in the brain? Wilder Penfield addressed this question while performing operations on the brains of conscious patients afflicted with epilepsy. He used electrical stimulation of various parts of the cerebral cortex to locate the origins of each patient's problem. In fact, his work was instrumental in plotting the motor and sensory areas of the cortex described in Chapter 2 of this text.

Harry Bahrick is a research professor of psychology at Ohio Wesleyan University. He is best known for his studies of the lifetime retention of information in semantic memory. He has shown that unrehearsed knowledge can remain in memory for a quarter of a century or even longer, as, for example, in the case of recognizing fellow students known during the high school years but not seen or thought of since.

During the course of such stimulation, Penfield (1955, 1969) found that patients sometimes would appear to recall memories from way back in their childhoods. These memories may not have been called to mind for many, many years. (Note that the patients could be stimulated to recall episodes such as events from their childhood, not facts such as the names of U.S. presidents.) These data suggested to Penfield that long-term memories may be permanent.

Some researchers have disputed Penfield's interpretations (e.g., Loftus & Loftus, 1980). For example, they have noted the small number of such reports in relation to the hundreds of patients on whom Penfield operated. In addition, we cannot be certain that the patients actually were recalling these events. They may have been inventing them. Other researchers, using empirical techniques on older participants, found contradictory evidence.

Some researchers tested participants' memory for names and photographs of their high-school classmates (Bahrick, Bahrick, & Wittlinger, 1975). Even after 25 years, there was little forgetting of some aspects of memory. Participants tended to recognize names as belonging to classmates rather than to outsiders. Recognition memory for matching names to graduation photos was quite high. As you might expect, recall of names showed a higher rate of forgetting. The term *permastore* refers to the very long-term storage of information, such as knowledge of a foreign language (Bahrick, 1984a, 1984b; Bahrick & associates, 1993) and of mathematics (Bahrick & Hall, 1991).

The Levels-of-Processing Model

A radical departure from the three-stores model of memory is the **levels-of-processing framework,** which postulates that memory does not comprise three or even any specific number of separate stores but rather varies along a continuous dimension in terms of depth of encoding (Craik & Lockhart, 1972). In other words, there are theoretically an infinite number of levels of processing (LOP) at which items can be encoded. There are no distinct boundaries between one level and the next. The emphasis in this model is on processing as the key to storage. The level at which information is stored will depend, in large part, on how it is encoded. Moreover, the deeper the level of processing, the higher, in general, is the probability that an item may be retrieved (Craik & Brown, 2000).

A set of experiments seemed to support the LOP view (Craik & Tulving, 1975). Participants received a list of words. A question preceded each word. Questions were varied to encourage three different levels of processing. In progressive order of depth, they were *physical, acoustic,* and *semantic.* Samples of the words and the questions are shown in Table 5.2. The results of the research were clear. The deeper the level of processing encouraged by the question, the higher the level of recall achieved. Similar results emerged independently in Russia (Zinchenko, 1962, 1981). Words that were logically (e.g., taxonomically) connected (e.g., *dog* and *animal*) were recalled more easily than were words that were concretely connected (e.g., *dog* and *leg*). At the same time, concretely connected words were more easily recalled than were words that were unconnected.

An even more powerful inducement to recall has been termed the self-reference effect (Rogers, Kuiper, & Kirker, 1977). In the *self-reference effect,* participants show

TABLE 5.2	Levels-of-Processing Framework	

Among the levels of processing proposed by Fergus Craik and Endel Tulving are the physical, acoustic, and semantic levels, as shown in this table.

LEVEL OF PROCESSING	BASIS FOR PROCESSING	EXAMPLE	
Physical	Visually apparent features of the letters	**Word:** TABLE **Question:** Is the word written in capital letters?	
Acoustic	Sound combinations associated with the letters (e.g., rhyming)	**Word:** CAT **Question:** Does the word rhyme with "MAT"?	
Semantic	Meaning of the word	**Word:** DAFFODIL **Question:** Is the word a type of plant?	

very high levels of recall when asked to relate words meaningfully to themselves by determining whether the words describe them. Even the words that participants assess as not describing themselves are recalled at high levels. This high recall is a result of considering whether the words do or do not describe the participants. However, the highest levels of recall occur with words that people consider self-descriptive. Similar self-reference effects have been found by many other researchers (e.g., Bower & Gilligan, 1979; Brown, Keenan, & Potts, 1986; Ganellen & Carver, 1985; Halpin & associates, 1984; Katz, 1987; Reeder, McCormick, & Esselman, 1987).

Some researchers suggest that the self-reference effect is distinctive, but others suggest that it is explained easily in terms of the LOP framework or other ordinary memory processes (e.g., Mills, 1983). Specifically, each of us has a very elaborate self-schema. This self-schema is an organized system of internal cues regarding ourselves, our attributes, and our personal experiences. Thus, we can richly and elaborately encode information related to ourselves much more so than information about other topics (Bellezza, 1984, 1992). Also, we easily can organize new information pertaining to ourselves. When other information is also readily organized, we may recall non-self-referent information easily as well (Klein & Kihlstrom, 1986). Finally, when we generate our own cues, we demonstrate much higher levels of recall than when someone else generates cues for us to use (Greenwald & Banaji, 1989).

Despite much supporting evidence, the LOP framework as a whole has its critics. For one thing, some researchers suggest that the particular levels may involve a circular definition. On this view, the levels are defined as deeper because the information is retained better. But the information is viewed as being retained better because the levels are deeper. In addition, some researchers noted some paradoxes in retention. For example, under some circumstances, strategies that use rhymes have produced better retention than those using just semantic rehearsal. For example, focusing on superficial sounds and not underlying meanings can result in better retention than focusing on repetition of underlying meanings. Specifically, consider what happens when the context for retrieval involves attention to phonological (acoustic) properties of words (e.g., rhymes). Here, performance is enhanced when the context for encoding involves rehearsal based on phonological properties, rather than on semantic properties of words (Fisher & Craik, 1977, 1980). Nonetheless, consider what happened when semantic retrieval, based on semantic encoding, was compared with acoustic (rhyme) retrieval, based on rhyme encoding. Performance was greater for semantic retrieval than for acoustic retrieval (Fisher & Craik, 1977).

In light of these criticisms and some contrary findings, the LOP model has been revised. The sequence of the levels of encoding may not be as important as the match between the type of elaboration of the encoding and the type of task required for retrieval (Morris, Bransford, & Franks, 1977). Furthermore, there appear to be two kinds of strategies for elaborating the encoding. The first is within-item elaboration. It elaborates encoding of the particular item (e.g., a word or other fact) in terms of its characteristics, including the various levels of processing. The second kind of strategy is between-item elaboration. It elaborates encoding by relating each item's features (again, at various levels) to the features of items already in memory. Thus, suppose you wanted to be sure to remember something in particular. You could elaborate it at various levels for each of the two strategies.

Elaboration strategies have practical applications: In studying, you may wish to match the way in which you encode the material to the way in which you will be expected to retrieve it in the future. Furthermore, the more elaborately and diversely you encode material, the more readily you are likely to recall it later in a variety of task settings. Just looking over material again and again in the same way is less likely to be productive for learning the material than is finding more than one way in which to learn it. If the context for retrieval will require you to have a deep understanding of the information, you should find ways to encode the material at deep levels of processing, such as by asking yourself meaningful questions about the material.	**PRACTICAL APPLICATIONS OF COGNITIVE PSYCHOLOGY**

An Integrative Model: Working Memory

The working-memory model is probably the most widely used and accepted today. Psychologists who use it view short-term and long-term memory from a different perspective (e.g., Baddeley, 1990a, 1995; Cantor & Engle, 1993; Daneman & Carpenter, 1980; Daneman & Tardif, 1987; Engle, 1994; Engle, Cantor, & Carullo, 1992). Table 5.3 shows the contrasts between the Atkinson-Shiffrin model and an alternative perspective. Note the semantic distinctions, the differences in metaphorical representation, and the differences in emphasis for each view. The key feature of the alternative view is the role of working memory. **Working memory** holds only the most recently activated portion of long-term memory, and it moves these activated elements into and out of brief, temporary memory storage (Dosher, 2003).

	TABLE 5.3	Traditional Versus Nontraditional Views of Memory

Since Richard Atkinson and Richard Shiffrin first proposed their three-stores model of memory (which may be considered a traditional view of memory), various other models have been suggested.

	TRADITIONAL THREE-STORES VIEW	**ALTERNATIVE VIEW OF MEMORY***
Terminology: definition of memory stores	Working memory is another name for short-term memory, which is distinct from long-term memory.	Working memory (active memory) is that part of long-term memory that comprises all the knowledge of facts and procedures that recently has been activated in memory, including the brief, fleeting short-term memory and its contents.
Metaphor for envisioning the relationships	Short-term memory may be envisioned as being distinct from long-term memory, perhaps either alongside it or hierarchically linked to it.	Short-term memory, working memory, and long-term memory may be envisioned as nested concentric spheres, in which working memory contains only the most recently activated portion of long-term memory and short-term memory contains only a very small, fleeting portion of working memory.
Metaphor for the movement of information	Information moves directly from long-term memory to short-term memory and then back—never in both locations at once.	Information remains within long-term memory; when activated, information moves into long-term memory's specialized working memory, which actively will move information into and out of the short-term memory store contained within it.
Emphasis	Distinction between long- and short-term memory.	Role of activation in moving information into working memory and the role of working memory in memory processes.

*Examples of researchers holding this view: Cantor & Engle, 1993; Engle, 1994; Engle, Cantor, & Carullo, 1992.

Alan Baddeley has suggested an integrative model of memory (Baddeley, 1990b; 1992; 1993; 1997; Baddeley & Hitch, 1974). It synthesizes the working-memory model with the LOP framework. Essentially, he views the LOP framework as an extension of, rather than as a replacement for, the working-memory model.

Baddeley originally suggested that working memory comprises four elements. The first is a **visuospatial sketchpad,** which briefly holds some visual images. The second is a **phonological loop,** which briefly holds inner speech for verbal comprehension and for acoustic rehearsal. Two components of this loop are critical. One is phonological storage, which holds information in memory. The other is subvocal rehearsal, which is used to put the information into memory in the first place. Without this loop, acoustic information decays after about 2 seconds. The third element is a **central executive,** which both coordinates attentional activities and governs responses. The central executive is critical to working memory because it is the gating mechanism that decides what information to process further and how to process it. It decides what resources to allocate to memory and related tasks, and how to allocate them. It is also involved in higher order reasoning and comprehension, and is central to human intelligence. The fourth element is a number of other *"subsidiary slave sys-*

tems" that perform other cognitive or perceptual tasks (Baddeley, 1989, p. 36). Recently, another component has been added to working memory (Baddeley, 2000a). This is the episodic buffer. The **episodic buffer** is a limited-capacity system that is capable of binding information from the subsidiary systems and from long-term memory into a unitary episodic representation. This component integrates information from different parts of working memory so that they make sense to us.

Baddeley's model can be related to that of Craik and Lockhart. Baddeley's visuospatial sketchpad might be used for Craik's physical processing. Baddeley's articulatory loop might be used for Craik's acoustic processing. To integrate the various levels of processing, Baddeley's central executive moves items in and out of short-term memory. It integrates the information arriving from the senses and from long-term memory.

Neuropsychological methods, and especially brain imaging, can be very helpful in understanding the nature of memory (Buckner, 2000; Cabeza & Nyberg, 1997; Markowitsch, 2000; Nyberg & Cabeza, 2000; Rosenzweig, 2003; Rugg & Allan, 2000; Ungerleider, 1995). Support for a distinction between working memory and long-term memory comes from neuropsychological research. Neuropsychological studies have shown abundant evidence of a brief memory buffer. The buffer is used for remembering information temporarily. It is distinct from long-term memory, which is used for remembering information for long periods (Schacter, 1989a; Smith & Jonides, 1995; Squire, 1986; Squire & Knowlton, 2000). Furthermore, through some promising new research using positron emission tomography (PET) techniques, investigators have found evidence for distinct brain areas involved in the different aspects of working memory. The phonological loop, maintaining speech-related information, appears to involve bilateral activation of the frontal and parietal lobes (Cabeza & Nyberg, 1997). It is interesting that the visuospatial sketchpad appears to activate slightly different areas. Which ones it activates depends on the length of the retention interval. Shorter intervals activate areas of the occipital and right frontal lobes. Longer intervals activate areas of the parietal and left frontal lobes (Haxby & associates, 1995). Finally, the central executive functions appear to involve activation mostly in the frontal lobes (Roberts, Robbins, & Weiskrantz, 1996).

Whereas the three-stores view emphasizes the structural receptacles for stored information, the working-memory model underscores the functions of working memory in governing the processes of memory. These processes include encoding and integrating information. Examples are integrating acoustic and visual information through cross-modality, organizing information into meaningful chunks, and linking new information to existing forms of knowledge representation in long-term memory. We can conceptualize the differing emphases with contrasting metaphors. For example, we can compare the three-stores view to a warehouse, in which information is passively stored. The sensory store serves as the loading dock. The short-term store comprises the area surrounding the loading dock. Here, information is stored temporarily until it is moved to or from the correct location in the warehouse. A metaphor for the working-memory model might be a multimedia production house. It continuously generates and manipulates images and sounds. It also coordinates the integration of sights and sounds into meaningful arrangements. Once images, sounds, and other information are stored, they still are available for reformatting and reintegration in novel ways, as new demands and new information become available.

Different aspects of working memory are represented in the brain differently. Figure 5.4 shows some of these differences.

Alan Baddeley is past director of the MRC Applied Psychology Unit, Cambridge, England, and is a professor of cognitive psychology at Bristol University. Baddeley is best known for his work on the concept of working memory, which has shown that working memory can be viewed as an interface among many of the varied aspects of cognition.

| FIGURE 5.4 | Sternberg's Triarchic Theory of Intelligence |

Different areas of the cerebral cortex are involved in different aspects of working memory. The figure shows those aspects involved primarily in the articulatory loop, including phonological storage and subvocal rehearsal. From E. Awh, et al. (1996). Dissociation of storage and rehearsal in verbal working memory: Evidence from positron emission tomography. Psychological Science, 7, 25–31. Copyright 1996 by Blackwell, Inc. Reprinted by permission.

Working memory can be measured through a number of different tasks. The most commonly used are shown in Figure 5.5.

Task (a) is a retention-delay task. It is the simplest task shown in the figure. An item is shown, in this case, a geometric shape. (The + at the beginning is merely a focus point to indicate that the series of items is beginning.) There is then a retention interval, which may be filled with other tasks, or unfilled, in which case time passes without any specifically designed intervening activity. The participant is then presented with a stimulus and must say whether it is old or new. In the figure, the stimulus being tested is new. So "new" would be the correct answer.

Task (b) is a temporally ordered working-memory load task. A series of items is presented. After a while, the series of asterisks indicates that a test item will be presented. The test item is presented, and the participant must say whether the item is old or new. Because "4," the number in the figure, has not been presented before, the correct answer is "new."

Task (c) is a temporal order task. A series of items is presented. Then the asterisks indicate a test item will be given. The test item shows two previously presented items, 3 and 7. The participant must indicate which of the two numbers, 3 or 7, appeared more recently. The correct answer is 7, as 7 occurred after 3 in the list.

Task (d) is an n-back task. Stimuli are presented. At specified points, one is asked to repeat the stimulus that occurred n presentations back. For example, one might be asked to repeat the digit that occurred 1 back—or just before (as with the 6). Or one might be asked to repeat the digit that occurred 2 back (as with the 7).

Task (e) is a temporally ordered working-memory load task. It can also be referred to simply as a digit-span task (when digits are used). One is presented with a series of stimuli. After they are presented, one repeats them back in the order they were presented. A variant of this task has the participant repeat them back in the order opposite to that in which they were presented—from the end to the beginning.

Finally, Task (f) is a temporally ordered working-memory load task. One is given a series of simple arithmetic problems. For each problem, one indicates whether the sum or difference is correct. At the end, one repeats the results of the arithmetic problems in their correct order.

Multiple-Memory-Systems

The working-memory model is consistent with the notion that multiple systems may be involved in the storage and retrieval of information. Recall that when Wilder Penfield electrically stimulated the brains of his patients, the patients often asserted that they vividly recalled particular episodes and events. They did not, however, recall semantic facts that were unrelated to any particular event. These findings suggest that there may be at least two separate memory systems. One would be for organizing and storing information with a distinctive time referent. It would address questions such as, "What did you eat for lunch yesterday?" or "Who was the first person you saw this morning?" The second system would be for information that has no particular time referent. It would address questions such as, "Who were the two psychologists who first proposed the three-stores model of memory?" and "What is a mnemonist?"

FIGURE 5.5

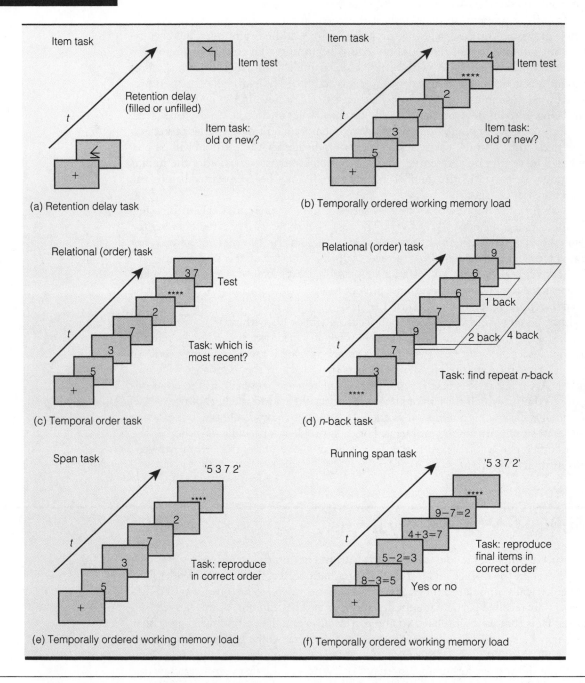

Tasks and Working Memory. From Encyclopedia of Cognitive Science, Vol. 4, p. 571. Copyright © 2003. Reproduced with perimission of B. Dosher.

IN THE LAB OF M. K. JOHNSON

Courtesy of Dr. M. K. Johnson

A memory is a mental experience that is taken to be a veridical (truthful) representation of an event from one's past. Memories can be false in relatively minor ways (e.g., believing one last saw the keys in the kitchen when they were in the living room) and in major ways that have profound implications for oneself and others (e.g., mistakenly believing one is the originator of an idea or believing that one was sexually abused as a child when one was not). Such memory distortions reflect errors arising from imperfect *source monitoring* processes—the processes by which we make attributions about the origin of activated information in mental experience. Source monitoring errors include both confusions between internal and external sources of information and between various external sources (e.g., attributing something that was imagined to perception, an intention to an action, something one heard about to something one witnessed, something read in a tabloid to a television program, an incident that occurred in place A or time A to place B or time B). The integration of information across individual experiences from different sources is necessary for all higher-order, complex thought. But this very creativity makes us vulnerable to having false memories because we sometimes misattribute the sources of the information that comes to mind. Several types of evidence indicate that the prefrontal cortex (PFC) plays a key role in identifying the sources of mental experiences: Damage to the PFC produces deficits in source memory. Source memory deficits are more likely in children (whose frontal lobes are slow to develop) and in older adults (who are likely to show increased neural disease in the PFC with age). PFC dysfunction may play a role in schizophrenia, which sometimes includes severe source monitoring deficits in the form of delusions. My lab is currently using fMRI to help clarify the brain regions involved in source monitoring. In one type of study, participants saw a series of items of two types (pictures and words). Later they were given a memory test in which they were shown some words that corresponded to the items seen earlier (old items) intermixed with some that did not correspond to any of the items seen earlier (new items). We compared the brain activity when participants were asked to make source judgments (e.g., say "yes" to items previously seen as pictures) with brain activity when they were simply asked to decide whether a test item was familiar (say "yes" to any previously presented item). We found greater activity in the left PFC in the source identification compared with the old/new condition (and sometimes greater activity in the right PFC as well). Furthermore, several other labs have reported related findings providing converging evidence that the left PFC is recruited in monitoring the origin of memories. It is interesting that when we reviewed published studies of patients who confabulate, we found that patients with right and left frontal damage were equally represented. This is consistent with the idea that processes subserved by both the right and left PFC contribute to evaluating the origin of mental experiences, possibly in different ways, and that interactions between right and left hemispheres are likely important. Thus, one goal for future research is to more specifically relate component processes of memory to patterns of activity across various regions of PFC.

Suggested Reading

Johnson, M. K., Hayes, S. M., D'Esposito, M., & Raye, C. L. (2000). Confabulation. In J. Grafman & F. Boller, *Handbook of neuropsychology (2nd Ed.) Vol. 2 Memory and Its Disorders*, L. S. Cermak (Ed.), pp. 359–383. Amsterdam, Netherlands: Elsevier Science.

Johnson, M. K., & Raye, C. L. (1998). False memories and confabulation. *Trends in Cognitive Sciences, 2*, 137–145.

Mitchell, K. J., Johnson, M. K., Raye, C. L., & Greene, E. J. (2004). Prefrontal cortex activity associated with source monitoring in a working memory task. *Journal of Cognitive Neuroscience, 16*, 921–934.

Ranganath, C., Johnson, M. K., & D'Esposito, M. (2000). Left anterior prefrontal activation increases with demands to recall specific perceptual information. *Journal of Neuroscience, 20*, RC108.

Raye C. L., Johnson, M. K., Mitchell, K. J., Nolde, S. F., & D'Esposito, M. (2000). Left and right PFC contributions to episodic remembering: An fMRI study. *Psychobiology, 28*, 197–206.

Based on such findings, Endel Tulving (1972) proposed a distinction between two kinds of memory. **Semantic memory** stores general world knowledge. It is our memory for facts that are not unique to us and that are not recalled in any particular temporal context. **Episodic memory** stores personally experienced events or episodes. According to Tulving, we use episodic memory when we learn lists of words or when we need to recall something that occurred to us at a particular time or in a particular context. For example, suppose I needed to remember that I saw Harrison Hardimanowitz in the dentist's office yesterday. I would be drawing on an episodic memory. But if I needed to remember the name of the person I now see in the waiting room ("Harrison Hardimanowitz"), I would be drawing on a semantic memory. There is no particular time tag associated with the name of that individual as being Harrison. But there is a time tag associated with my having seen him at the dentist's office yesterday.

Tulving (1983, 1989) and others (e.g., Shoben, 1984) provide support for the distinction between semantic and episodic memory. It is based on both cognitive research and neurological investigation. The neurological investigations have involved electrical-stimulation studies, studies of patients with memory disorders, and cerebral blood flow studies. For example, lesions in the frontal lobe appear to affect recollection regarding *when* a stimulus was presented. But they do not affect recall or recognition memory *that* a particular stimulus was presented (Schacter, 1989a). It is not clear that semantic and episodic memories are two distinct systems. Nevertheless, they sometimes appear to function in different ways. Many cognitive psychologists question this distinction (e.g., Baddeley, 1984; Eysenck & Keane, 1990; Humphreys, Bain, & Pike, 1989; Johnson & Hasher, 1987; Ratcliff & McKoon, 1986; Richardson-Klavehn & Bjork, 1988). They point to blurry areas on the boundary between these two types of memory. They also note methodological problems with some of the supportive evidence. Perhaps episodic memory is merely a specialized form of semantic memory (Tulving, 1984, 1986). The question is open.

A neuroscientific model attempts to account for differences in hemispheric activation for semantic versus episodic memories. According to this model, *HERA* (hemispheric encoding/retrieval asymmetry), there is greater activation in the left than in the right prefrontal hemisphere for tasks requiring retrieval from semantic memory (Nyberg, Cabeza, & Tulving, 1996; Tulving & associates, 1994). In contrast, there is more activation in the right than in the left prefrontal hemisphere for episodic-retrieval tasks. This model, then, proposes that semantic and episodic memories must be distinct because they draw on separate areas of the brain. For example, if one is asked to generate verbs that are associated with nouns (e.g., "drive" with "car"), this task requires semantic memory. It results in greater left-hemispheric activation (Nyberg, Cabeza, & Tulving, 1996). In contrast, if people are asked to freely recall a list of words, an episodic-memory task, they show more right-hemispheric activation.

A third discrete memory system is *procedural memory,* or memory for procedural knowledge (Tulving, 1985). The cerebellum of the brain seems to be centrally involved in this type of memory. The neuropsychological and cognitive evidence supporting a discrete procedural memory has been quite well documented (Cohen & associates, 1985; Cohen & Squire, 1980; Rempel-Clower & associates, 1996; Squire, 1987; Squire, Knowlton, & Musen, 1993). An alternative taxonomy of memory is shown in Figure 5.6 (Squire, 1986, 1993). It distinguishes declarative (explicit) mem-

FIGURE 5.6

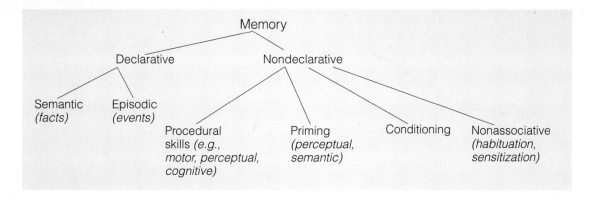

Based on extensive neuropsychological research, Larry Squire has posited that memory comprises two fundamental types: declarative (explicit) memory and various forms of nondeclarative (implicit) memory, each of which may be associated with discrete cerebral structures and processes.

ory from various kinds of nondeclarative (implicit) memory. Nondeclarative memory comprises procedural memory, priming effects, simple classical conditioning, habituation, sensitization, and perceptual aftereffects. In yet another view, there are five memory systems in all: episodic, semantic, perceptual (i.e., recognizing things on the basis of their form and structure), procedural, and working (Schacter, 2000).

A Connectionist Perspective

The network model provides the structural basis for a *connectionist model*, also known as a parallel distributed processing (PDP) model. (Frean, 2003; Sun, 2003). According to the PDP model, the key to knowledge representation lies in the connections among various nodes, not in each individual node (Feldman & Shastri, 2003). Activation of one node may prompt activation of a connected node. This process of spreading activation may prompt the activation of additional nodes. The PDP model fits nicely with the notion of working memory as comprising the activated portion of long-term memory. In this model, activation spreads through nodes within the network. This spreading continues as long as the activation does not exceed the limits of working memory. A **prime** is a node that activates a connected node. A **priming effect** is the resulting activation of the node. The priming effect has been supported by considerable evidence. Examples are the aforementioned studies of priming as an aspect of implicit memory. In addition, some evidence supports the notion that priming is due to spreading activation (McClelland & Rumelhart, 1985, 1988). But not everyone agrees about the mechanism for the priming effect (see McKoon & Ratcliff, 1992b).

Connectionist models also have some intuitive appeal in their ability to integrate several contemporary notions about memory: *Working memory* comprises the *activated* portion of long-term memory and operates through at least some amount of *parallel processing*. *Spreading activation* involves the simultaneous (parallel) activation (*priming*) of multiple links among *nodes* within the *network*. Many cognitive psychologists who hold this integrated view suggest that part of the reason we humans are as efficient as we are in processing information is that we can handle many operations at once. Thus, the contemporary cognitive-psychological conceptions of working memory, network models of memory, spreading activation, priming, and parallel processes mutually enhance and support one another.

Some of the research supporting the connectionist model of memory has come directly from experimental studies of people performing cognitive tasks in laboratory settings. Connectionist models effectively explain priming effects, skill learning (procedural memory), and several other phenomena of memory. Thus far, however, connectionist models have failed to provide clear predictions and explanations of recall and recognition memory that occurs following a single episode or a single exposure to semantic information.

In addition to using laboratory experiments on human participants, cognitive psychologists have used computer models to simulate various aspects of information processing. The three-stores model is based on serial (sequential) processing of information. Serial processing can be simulated on individual computers that handle only one operation at a time. In contrast, the parallel-processing model of working memory, which involves simultaneous processing of multiple operations, cannot be simulated on a single computer. Parallel processing requires neural networks. In these networks, multiple computers are linked and operate in tandem. Alternatively, a single special computer may operate with parallel networks. Many cognitive psychologists now prefer a parallel-processing model to describe many phenomena of memory. The parallel-processing model was actually inspired by observing how the human brain seems to process information. Here, multiple processes go on at the same time. In addition to inspiring theoretical models of memory function, neuropsychological research has offered specific insights into memory processes. It also has provided evidence regarding various hypotheses of how human memory works.

Not all cognitive researchers accept the connectionist model. Some believe that human thought is more systematic than connectionist models will allow (Fodor & Pylyshyn, 1988; Matthews, 2003). They believe that complex behavior displays a degree of orderliness and purposefulness that connectionist models cannot incorporate. Connectionist modelers dispute this claim. The issue will be resolved as cognitive psychologists explore the extent to which connectionist models can reproduce and even explain complex behavior.

Memory in the Real World

How is memory used in everyday situations and what is memory for? Some researchers believe we should study memory in more real-world settings, in addition to laboratory settings (Cohen, 1989; Neisser, 1978, 1982). The basic idea is that memory research should have ecological validity and apply to natural memory phenomena in natural settings. The techniques used therefore examine naturalistic settings using self-reports and questionnaires. Although this approach has been criticized for its lack of control and generalizability (Banaji & Crowder, 1989), it has generated some interesting new conceptualizations into the nature of memory research in general.

For example, one set of researchers has called for a change in the metaphor used in conceptualizing memory, rather than a change in the research setting. The traditional *storehouse* metaphor of memory, in which memory is conceived of as a repository of information and events, inevitably leads to questions of quantity. The question thus becomes: How many items can be remembered from or used in a particular occasion (Koriat & Goldsmith, 1996a, 1996b)? The laboratory setting is most congenial to this approach, allowing for control over the variables of quantity. In contrast, the everyday or real-world approach calls for more of a *correspondence* metaphor. Here, memory is conceived of as a vehicle for interaction with the real world. Thus, the questions shift toward accuracy in representing past events. How closely does memory correspond to particular events? Here, memory would be viewed as a structure fulfilling a particular purpose in our interactions with the world.

We may see this new trend broadening as more researchers become increasingly interested in the functional properties of memory. Already some promising new insights into the question of what memory is for offer some concrete proposals into the structure of memory. For example, one view calls for a memory system centered around bodily interactions with the environment (Glenberg, 1997). Thus, correspondence with the real world is achieved via representations that reflect the structural relationship between the body and the external world, rather than the encoding of abstract symbolic representations.

Whether this approach will take the lead in memory research or be overcome by the impetus of the laboratory-storehouse metaphor remains to be seen. Whatever the case may be, new metaphors and controversies are essential for the survival of the field. Without a constant flow of new ideas or rethinking of old ideas, science would stagnate and die. Another approach that already is beginning to dominate much of memory research is the neuropsychological study of memory. It developed in part from the study of people with exceptional memory.

Exceptional Memory and Neuropsychology

Up to this point, the discussion of memory has focused on tasks and structures involving normally functioning memory. However, there are rare cases of people with exceptional memory (either enhanced or deficient) that provide some interesting insights into the nature of memory in general. The study of exceptional memory leads directly to neuropsychological investigations of the physiological mechanisms underlying memory.

Outstanding Memory: Mnemonists

Imagine what your life would be like if you had outstanding memory abilities. Suppose, for example, you were able to remember every word printed in this book. In this case, you would be considered a **mnemonist,** someone who demonstrates extraordinarily keen memory ability, usually based on using special techniques for memory enhancement. Perhaps the most famous of mnemonists was a man called "S."

Russian psychologist Alexander Luria (1968) reported that one day S. appeared in his laboratory and asked to have his memory tested. Luria tested him. He discovered that the man's memory appeared to have virtually no limits. S. could reproduce extremely long strings of words, regardless of how much time had passed since the words had been presented to him. Luria studied S. over 30 years. He found that even when S.'s retention was measured 15 or 16 years after a session in which S. had learned words, S. still could reproduce the words. S. eventually became a professional entertainer. He dazzled audiences with his ability to recall whatever was asked of him.

What was S.'s trick? How did he remember so much? Apparently, he relied heavily on the mnemonic of visual imagery. He converted material that he needed to remember into visual images. For example, he reported that when asked to remember the word *green*, he would visualize a green flowerpot. For the word *red*, he visualized a man in a red shirt coming toward him. Even numbers called up images. For example, *1* was a proud, well-built man. The number *3* was a gloomy person. The number *6* was a man with a swollen foot and so on.

For S., much of his use of visual imagery in memory recall was not intentional. Rather, it was the result of a rare psychological phenomenon. This phenomenon, termed *synesthesia*, is the experience of sensations in a sensory modality different from the sense that has been physically stimulated. For example, S. automatically would convert a sound into a visual impression. He even reported experiencing a word's taste and weight. Each word to be remembered evoked a whole range of sensations. They automatically would come to S. when he needed to recall that word.

Other mnemonists have used different strategies. V. P., a Russian immigrant, could memorize long strings of material such as rows and columns of numbers (Hunt & Love, 1972). Whereas S. relied primarily on visual imagery, V. P. apparently relied more on verbal translations. He reported memorizing numbers by transforming them into dates. Then he would think about what he had done on that day.

Another mnemonist, S. F., remembered long strings of numbers by segmenting them into groups of three or four digits each. He then encoded them into running times for different races (Ericsson, Chase, & Faloon, 1980). An experienced long-distance runner, S. F. was familiar with the times that would be plausible for different races. S. F. did not enter the laboratory as a mnemonist. Rather, he had been selected to represent the average college student in terms of intelligence and memory ability.

S. F.'s original memory for a string of numbers was about seven digits, average for a college student. After 200 practice sessions distributed over a period of 2 years, however, S. F. had increased his memory for digits more than 10-fold. He could recall up to about 80 digits. His memory was impaired severely, however, when the experimenters purposely gave him sequences of digits that could not be translated into running times. The work with S. F. suggests that a person with a fairly typical level of memory ability can, at least in principle, be converted into one with quite an extraordinary memory. At least, this is possible in some domains, following a great deal of concerted practice.

Many of us yearn to have memory abilities like those of S. or V. P. In this way, we may believe we could ace our exams virtually effortlessly. However, we should consider that S. was not particularly happy with his life. And part of the reason was his exceptional memory. He reported that his synesthesia, which was largely involuntary, interfered with his ability to listen to people. Voices gave rise to blurs of sensations. They in turn interfered with his ability to follow a conversation. Moreover, S.'s heavy reliance on imagery created difficulty for him when he tried to understand abstract concepts. For example, he found it hard to understand concepts such as *infinity* or *nothing*. These concepts do not lend themselves well to visual images. He also sometimes was overwhelmed when he read. Earlier memories also sometimes intruded on later ones. Of course, we cannot say how many of S.'s problems in life were caused by his exceptional memory. But clearly S. himself believed that his exceptional memory had a down side as well as an up side. It was often as likely to be a hindrance as a help.

These exceptional mnemonists offer some insight into processes of memory. Each of the three described here did more or less the same thing—consciously or almost automatically. Each translated arbitrary, abstract, meaningless information into more meaningful or more sensorially concrete information. Whether the translated information was racing times, dates and events, or visual images, the key was their meaning for the mnemonist.

If you are unable to retrieve a memory that you need, does it mean that you have forgotten it? Not necessarily. Cognitive psychologists have studied a phenomenon called **hypermnesia,** which is a process of producing retrieval of memories that would have seem to have been forgotten (Erdelyi & Goldberg, 1979; Holmes, 1991; Turtle & Yuille, 1994). Hypermnesia is sometimes loosely referred to as "unforgetting," although the terminology cannot be correct, because strictly speaking, the memories that are retrieved were never unavailable (i.e., forgotten), but rather, inaccessible (i.e., hard to retrieve). Hypermnesia is usually achieved by trying many and diverse retrieval cues to unearth a memory. Psychodynamic therapy, for example, is some-

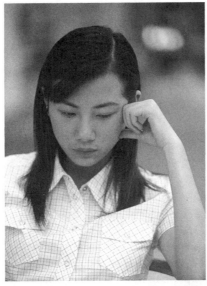

If the patient uses hypermnesia to dredge up what has seemed to be a forgotten memory, we often cannot be certain that the memory is a genuine old one rather than one newly created by suggestion.

times used to try to achieve hypermnesia. This therapy also points out the risk of trying to achieve hypermnesia. The individual may create a new memory, believing it is an old one, rather than retrieving a genuine old memory.

We usually take for granted the ability to remember, much like the air we breathe. However, just as we become more aware of the importance of air when we do not have enough to breathe, we are less likely to take memory for granted when we observe people with serious memory deficiencies.

Deficient Memory

Several different syndromes are associated with memory loss. The most well known is amnesia.

Amnesia

Amnesia is severe loss of explicit memory (Mayes & Hunkin, 2003). One type is **retrograde amnesia,** in which individuals lose their purposeful memory for events prior to whatever trauma induces memory loss (Squire, 1999). Mild forms of retrograde amnesia can occur fairly commonly when someone sustains a concussion. Usually, events immediately prior to the concussive episode are not well remembered.

W. Ritchie Russell and P. W. Nathan (1946) reported a more severe case of retrograde amnesia. A 22-year-old greenkeeper was thrown from his motorcycle in August 1933. A week after the accident, the young man was able to converse sensibly. He seemed to have recovered. However, it quickly became apparent that he had suffered a severe loss of memory for events that had occurred prior to the trauma. On questioning, he gave the date as February 1922. He believed himself to be a schoolboy. He had no recollection of the intervening years. Over the next several weeks, his memory for past events gradually returned. The return started with the least recent and proceeded toward more recent events. By 10 weeks after the accident, he had recovered his memory for most of the events of the previous years. He finally was able to recall everything that had happened up to a few minutes prior to the accident. In retrograde amnesia, the memories that return typically do so starting from the more distant past. They then progressively return up to the time of the trauma. Often events right before the trauma are never recalled.

Another kind of amnesia is one that almost all of us experience. It is **infantile amnesia,** the inability to recall events that happened when we were very young (Spear, 1979). Generally, we can remember little or nothing that has happened to us before the age of about 5 years. It is extremely rare for someone to recall many memories before age 3 years. Reports of childhood memories usually involve memories of significant events. Examples are the birth of a sibling or the death of a parent (Fivush & Hamond, 1991). For example, some adults have recalled their own hospitalization or the birth of a sibling as far back as age 2 years. The death of a parent or a family move may be recalled from as far back as age 3 years (Usher & Neisser, 1993).

The accuracy of reported childhood memories has come into question recently, however. In fact, many psychologists suggest that the accuracy of children's recollections of events may be questionable even shortly after these events occurred (e.g., Ceci & Bruck, 1993). The memories are particularly suspect if the children are exposed to covert or overt suggestions regarding the remembered material. (The unreliability of our memories for events is discussed more fully in the next chapter.)

One of the most famous cases of amnesia is the case of H. M. (Scoville & Milner, 1957). H. M. underwent brain surgery to save him from continual disruptions due to uncontrollable epilepsy. The operation took place on September 1, 1953. It was largely experimental. The results were highly unpredictable. At the time of the operation, H. M. was 29 years old. He was above average in intelligence. After the operation, his recovery was uneventful with one exception. He suffered severe **anterograde amnesia,** the inability to remember events that occur after a traumatic event. However, he had good (although not perfect) recollection of events that had occurred before his operation. H. M.'s memory loss severely affected his life. On one occasion, he remarked, "Every day is alone in itself, whatever enjoyment I've had, and whatever sorrow I've had" (Milner, Corkin, & Teuber, 1968, p. 217). Apparently, H. M. lost his ability purposefully to recollect any new memories of the time following his operation. As a result, he lived suspended in an eternal present.

Amnesia and the Explicit-Implicit Memory Distinction

Research psychologists study amnesia patients in part to gain insight into memory functioning in general. One of the general insights gained by studying amnesia victims highlights the distinction between explicit and implicit memories. Explicit memory is typically impaired in amnesia. Implicit memory, such as priming effects on word-completion tasks and procedural memory for skill-based tasks, is typically not impaired. Apparently two kinds of abilities need to be distinguished. The first is the ability to reflect consciously on prior experience, which is required for tasks involving explicit memory of declarative knowledge. The second is the ability to demonstrate remembered learning in an apparently automatic way, without conscious recollection of the learning (Baddeley, 1989). Amnesia victims perform extremely poorly on most explicit memory tasks. But they may show normal or almost-normal performance on tasks involving implicit memory such as cued-recall tasks (Warrington & Weiskrantz, 1970) and word-completion tasks (Baddeley, 1989). Consider what happens following word-completion tasks. When amnesics were asked whether they previously had seen the word they just completed, they were unlikely to remember the specific experience of having seen the word (Graf, Mandler, & Haden, 1982; Tulving, Schacter, & Stark 1982). Furthermore, these amnesics do not explicitly recognize words they have seen at better than chance levels. Although the distinction between implicit memory and explicit memory has been readily observed in amnesics, both amnesics and normal participants show the presence of implicit memory.

Likewise, amnesia victims also show paradoxical performance in another regard. Consider two kinds of tasks. *Procedural knowledge* tasks involve "knowing how." They involve skills such as how to ride a bicycle. *Declarative knowledge* tasks involve "knowing that." They tap factual information, such as the terms in a psychology textbook. On the one hand, amnesia victims may perform extremely poorly on the traditional memory tasks requiring recall or recognition memory of declarative knowledge. On the other hand, they may demonstrate improvement in performance resulting from learning—remembered practice—when engaged in tasks that require procedural knowledge. Such tasks would include solving puzzles, learning to read mirror writing, or mastering motor skills (Baddeley, 1989).

Amnesia and Neuropsychology

Studies of amnesia victims have revealed much about the way in which memory depends on the effective functioning of particular structures of the brain. By looking for matches between particular lesions in the brain and particular deficits of function, researchers come to understand how normal memory functions. Thus, when studying different kinds of cognitive processes in the brain, neuropsychologists frequently look for dissociations of function. In *dissociations*, normal individuals show the presence of a particular function (e.g., explicit memory). But people with specific lesions in the brain show the absence of that particular function. This absence occurs despite the presence of normal functions in other areas (e.g., implicit memory).

By observing people with disturbed memory function, we know that memory is volatile. It may be affected by a blow to the head, a disturbance in consciousness, or any number of other injuries to or diseases of the brain. We cannot determine, however, the specific cause-effect relationship between a given structural lesion and a particular memory deficit. The fact that a particular structure or region is associated with an interruption of function does not mean that the region is solely responsible for controlling that function. Indeed, functions can be shared by multiple structures or regions. A broad physiological analogy may help to explain the difficulty of determining localization based on an observed deficit. The normal functioning of a portion of the brain—the reticular activating system (RAS)—is essential to life. But life depends on more than a functioning brain. If you doubt the importance of other structures, ask a patient with heart or lung disease. Thus, although the RAS is essential to life, a person's death may be the result of malfunction in other structures of the body. Tracing a dysfunction within the brain to a particular structure or region poses a similar problem.

For the observation of simple dissociations, many alternative hypotheses may explain a link between a particular lesion and a particular deficit of function. Much more compelling support for hypotheses about cognitive functions comes from observing double dissociations. In *double dissociations*, people with different kinds of neuropathological conditions show opposite patterns of deficits. For some functions and some areas of the brain, neuropsychologists have managed to observe the presence of a double dissociation. For example, some evidence for distinguishing brief memory from long-term memory comes from just such a double dissociation (Schacter, 1989b). People with lesions in the left parietal lobe of the brain show profound inability to retain information in short-term memory. But they show no impairment of long-term memory. They continue to encode, store, and retrieve information in long-term memory, apparently with little difficulty (Shallice & Warrington, 1970; Warrington & Shallice, 1972). In contrast, persons with lesions in the medial (middle) temporal regions of the brain show relatively normal short-term memory of verbal materials, such as letters and words. But they show serious inability to retain new verbal materials in long-term memory (Milner, Corkin, & Teuber, 1968; Shallice, 1979; Warrington, 1982).

Double dissociations offer strong support for the notion that particular structures of the brain play particular vital roles in memory (Squire, 1987). Disturbances or lesions in these areas cause severe deficits in memory formation. But we cannot say that memory—or even part of memory—resides in these structures. Nonetheless, studies of brain-injured patients are informative and at least suggestive of how memory works. At present, cognitive neuropsychologists have found that double dissociations support several distinctions. These distinctions are those between brief memory and long-term memory and between declarative (explicit) and nondeclarative (implicit) memory. There also are some preliminary indications of other distinctions.

Alzheimer's Disease

Although amnesia is the syndrome most associated with memory loss, it is often less devastating than a disease that includes memory loss as one of many symptoms. **Alzheimer's disease** is a disease of older adults that causes dementia as well as progressive memory loss (Kensinger & Corkin, 2003). Dementia is a loss of intellectual function that is severe enough to impair one's everyday life. The memory loss in Alzheimer's disease can be seen in comparative brain scans of individuals with and without Alzheimer's disease. Note in Figure 5.7 that as the disease advances, there is diminishing cognitive activity in the areas of the brain associated with memory function.

FIGURE 5.7

Brain scans of a normal individual, an individual with early-stage Alzheimer's, and an individual with late-stage Alzheimer's. As the disease progresses, cognitive activity decreases in the brain associated with memory function.

The disease was first identified by Alois Alzheimer in 1907. It is typically recognized on the basis of loss of intellectual function in daily life. Formally, a definitive diagnosis is possible only after death. The brains of people with the disease show plaques and tangles that are not found in normal brains. Plaques are dense deposits found outside the nerve cells of the brain. They are spherical structures with a dense core of amyloid-β protein (Kensinger & Corkin, 2003). Tangles are pairs of filaments that become twisted around each other. They are found in the cell body and dendrites of neurons and often are shaped like a flame (Kensinger & Corkin, 2003). Alzheimer's disease is diagnosed when memory is impaired and there is at least one other area of dysfunction in the domains of language, motor, attention, executive function, personality, or object recognition. The symptoms are of gradual onset, and the progression is continuous and irreversible.

Although the progression of disease is irreversible, it can be slowed somewhat. The main drug currently being used for this purpose is Aricept. Research evidence is mixed (Fischman, 2004). It suggests that, at best, Aricept may slightly slow progression of the disease, but that it cannot reverse it. A more recent drug, memantine (sold as Namenda), can supplement Aricept and slow progression of the disease somewhat more. The two drugs have different mechanisms. Aricept slows destruction of the neurotransmitter acetylcholine in the brain. Memantine inhibits a chemical that overexcites brain cells and leads to cell damage and death (Fischman, 2004).

The incidence of Alzheimer's increases exponentially with age (Kensinger & Corkin, 2003). The incidence at ages 70 to 75 is about 1% per year. But between ages 80 and 85, the incidence is over 6% a year. By age 70, 30% to 50% of adults have Alzheimer's symptoms, and after 80 years, the percentage is in excess of 50%.

A special kind of Alzheimer's disease is familial, or early-onset Alzheimer's disease. It has been linked to a genetic mutation. People with the genetic mutation always develop the disease. It results in the disease exhibiting itself early, often before even 50 years of age and sometimes as early as the 20s (Kensinger & Corkin, 2003). Late-onset Alzheimer's, in contrast, appears to be complexly determined and related to a variety of possible genetic and environmental influences, none of which have been conclusively identified.

The earliest signs of Alzheimer's disease typically include impairment of episodic memory. People have trouble remembering things that were learned in a temporal or spatial context. As the disease progresses, semantic memory also begins to go. Whereas people without the disease tend to remember emotionally charged information better than they remember nonemotionally charged information, people with the disease show no difference in the two kinds of memory (Kensinger & associates, 2002). Most forms of nondeclarative memory are spared in Alzheimer's disease until near the very end of its course. The end is inevitably death unless the individual dies first of other causes.

Role of the Hippocampus and Other Structures

Where in the brain are memories stored, and what structures and areas of the brain are involved in memory processes, such as encoding and retrieval? Many early attempts at localization of memory were unfruitful. For example, after literally hundreds of experiments, renowned neuropsychologist Karl Lashley reluctantly stated that he could find no specific locations in the brain for specific memories. In the decades since Lashley's admission, psychologists have been able to locate many cerebral structures involved in memory. For example, they know of the importance of the hippocampus and other nearby structures. However, the physiological structure may not be such that we will find Lashley's elusive localizations of specific ideas, thoughts, or events. Even Penfield's findings regarding links between electrical stimulation and episodic memory of events have been subject to question.

Some studies show encouraging, although preliminary, findings regarding the structures that seem to be involved in various aspects of memory. First, specific sensory properties of a given experience appear to be organized across various areas of the cerebral cortex (Squire, 1986). For example, the visual, spatial, and olfactory (odor) features of an experience may be stored discretely in each of the areas of the cortex responsible for processing of each type of sensation. Thus, the cerebral cortex appears to play an important role in memory in terms of the long-term storage of information (Zola & Squire, 2000; Zola-Morgan & Squire, 1990).

In addition, the hippocampus and some related nearby cerebral structures appear to be important for explicit memory of experiences and other declarative information. The hippocampus also seems to play a key role in the encoding of declarative information (Squire & Zola-Morgan, 1991; Thompson, 2000; Thompson & Krupa, 1994; Zola-Morgan & Squire, 1990). Its main function appears to be in the integration and consolidation of separate sensory information (Moscovitch, 2003). Most important, it is involved in the transfer of newly synthesized information into long-term structures supporting declarative knowledge. Perhaps such transfer provides a means of cross-referencing information stored in different parts of the brain (Reber, Knowlton, & Squire, 1996; Squire, 1986; Squire, Cohen, & Nadel, 1984). Additionally, the hippocampus seems to play a crucial role in complex learning (McCormick & Thompson, 1984). The amygdala also appears to play an important role in memory consolidation, especially where emotional experience is involved (Cahill & associates, 1995; Cahill & McGaugh, 1996; Ledoux, 1996; McGaugh, 1999; Packard, Cahill, & McGaugh, 1994; McGaugh, Cahill, & Roozendaal, 1996).

In evolutionary terms, the aforementioned cerebral structures (chiefly, the cortex and the hippocampus) are relatively recent acquisitions. Declarative memory also may be considered a relatively recent phenomenon. At the same time, other memory structures may be responsible for nondeclarative forms of memory. For example, the basal ganglia seem to be the primary structures controlling procedural knowledge (Mishkin & Petri, 1984). But they are not involved in controlling the priming effect (Heindel, Butters, & Salmon, 1988), which may be influenced by various other kinds of memory (Schacter, 1989b). Furthermore, the cerebellum also seems to play a key role in memory for classically conditioned responses and contributes to many cognitive tasks in general (Cabeza & Nyberg, 1997; Thompson, 1987). Thus, various forms of nondeclarative memory seem to rely on differing cerebral structures.

In addition to these preliminary insights regarding the macrolevel structures of memory, we are beginning to understand the microlevel structure of memory. For example, we know that repeated stimulation of particular neural pathways tends to strengthen the likelihood of firing. In particular, at a particular synapse, there appear to be physiological changes in the dendrites of the receiving neuron. These changes make the neuron more likely to reach the threshold for firing again.

We also know that some neurotransmitters disrupt memory storage. Others enhance memory storage. Both serotonin and acetylcholine seem to enhance neural transmission associated with memory. Norepinephrine also may do so. High concentrations of acetylcholine have been found in the hippocampus of normal people (Squire, 1987).

But low concentrations are found in victims of Alzheimer's disease. In fact, Alzheimer's patients show severe loss of the brain tissue that secretes acetylcholine.

Memory tests may be given to assess whether an individual has Alzheimer's disease. But definitive diagnosis is possible only through analysis of brain tissue, which, as mentioned earlier, shows plaques and tangles in case of disease. In one test, individuals see a sheet of paper containing four words (Buschke & associates, 1999). Each word belongs to a different category. The examiner says the category name for one of the words. The individual must point to the appropriate word. For example, if the category is animal, the individual might point to a picture of a cow. A few minutes after the words have been presented, individuals make an attempt to recall all the words they saw. If they cannot recall a word, they are given the category to which the word belongs. Some individuals cannot remember the words, even when prompted with the categories. Alzheimer's patients score much worse on this test than do other individuals.

Researchers have been better able to track down the cause of another form of memory dysfunction. But they have not devised a way to eliminate this preventable deficit. Alcohol consumption has been shown to disrupt the activity of serotonin. It thereby impairs the formation of memories (Weingartner & associates, 1983). In fact, severe or prolonged abuse of alcohol can lead to Korsakoff's syndrome, a devastating form of anterograde amnesia. This syndrome is often accompanied by at least some retrograde amnesia (Parkin, 1991; Shimamura & Squire, 1986). Korsakoff's syndrome has been linked to damage in the diencephalon (the region comprising the thalamus and the hypothalamus) of the brain (Jernigan & associates, 1991; Langlais, Mandel, & Mair, 1992). It also has been linked to dysfunction or damage in other areas (Jacobson & Lishman, 1990), such as in the frontal (Parsons & Nixon, 1993; Squire, 1982) and the temporal (Blansjaar & associates, 1992) lobes of the cortex.

Other physiological factors also affect memory function. Some of the naturally occurring hormones also stimulate increased availability of glucose in the brain, which enhances memory function. These hormones are often associated with highly arousing events. Examples of such events are traumas, achievements, first-time experiences (e.g., first passionate kiss), crises, or other peak moments (e.g., reaching a major decision). They may play a role in remembering these events.

The amygdala is often associated with emotional events, so a natural question to ask is whether, in memory tasks, there is involvement of the amygdala in memory for emotionally charged events. In one study, participants saw two video presentations presented on separate days (Cahill & associates, 1996). Each presentation involved twelve clippings, half of which had been judged as involving relatively emotional content and the other half as involving relatively unemotional content. As participants watched the video clippings, brain activity was assessed by means of PET (see Chapter 2). After a gap of 3 weeks, the participants returned to the lab and were asked to recall the clips. For the relatively emotional clips, amount of activation in the amygdala was associated with recall; for the relatively unemotional clips, there was no association. This pattern of results suggests that when memories are emotionally charged, level of amygdala activation is associated with recall. In other words, the more emotionally charged the emotional memory, the greater the probability the memory will later be retrieved. There also may be a sex difference with regard to recall of emotional memories. There is some evidence that women recall emotionally charged pictures better than do men (Canli & associates, 2002).

Some of the most fascinating work has focused more on the strategies used in regard to memory. Memory strategies and memory processes are the subject of the following chapter.

Key Themes

This chapter illustrates some of the key themes noted in Chapter 1.

First, it shows how basic and applied research can interact. An example is research on Alzheimer's disease. At the present time, the disease is not curable. But it is treatable. It can be treated with drugs and with guidance provided in a structured living environment. Basic research into the biological structures (e.g., tangles and plaques) and cognitive functions (e.g., impaired memory) associated with Alzheimer's may one day help us better understand and treat the disease.

Second, the chapter shows the interaction of biology with behavior. The hippocampus has become one of the most carefully studied parts of the brain. Current functional magnetic resonance imaging (fMRI) research is showing how the hippocampus and other parts of the brain, such as the amygdala (in the case of emotionally based memories) and the cerebellum (in the case of procedural memories) function to enable us to remember what we need to know.

Third, the chapter shows how structure and function are both important to understanding human memory. The Atkinson-Shiffrin model proposed control processes that operated on three structures: a very short-term store, a short-term store, and a long-term store. The more recent working-memory model proposes how executive function controls and activates portions of long-term memory to provide the information needed to solve tasks at hand.

After you use an ATM with a friend, ask him or her to fill in the blank: A_M. Your friend will most likely say "ATM." If you were to do this without visiting an ATM, most people will most likely say "ARM." The first response is an example of implicit memory.

Ask some friends and/or family members to help you with a memory experiment. Give half of them the instruction to count the number of letters in the words you are about to recite. Give the other half of your friends and/or family members the instruction to think of three words related to the words you are about to recite. Recite the following words about 5 seconds apart: beauty, ocean, competitor, bad, decent, happy, brave, beverage, artistic, dejected. About 5 or 10 minutes later, ask your friends to write down as many of the ten words they can remember. In general, those who were asked to think of three related words to the words you read will remember more than those who were asked to count the number of letters in the words. This is a demonstration of levels of processing. Those friends who thought of three related words processed the words more deeply than those who merely counted up the number of letters in the words. Words that are processed more deeply are remembered better.

Summary

1. **What are some of the tasks used for studying memory, and what do various tasks indicate about the structure of memory?** Among the many tasks used by cognitive psychologists, some of the main ones have been tasks assessing explicit recall of information (e.g., free recall, serial recall, and cued recall) and tasks assessing explicit recognition of information. By comparing memory performance on these explicit tasks with performance on implicit tasks (e.g., word-completion tasks), cognitive psychologists have found evidence of differing memory systems or processes governing each type of task (e.g., as shown in studies of amnesics).

2. **What has been the prevailing traditional model of the structure of memory?** Memory is the means by which we draw on our knowledge of the past to use this knowledge in the present. According to one model, memory is conceived as involving three stores. A sensory store is capable of holding relatively limited amounts of information for very brief periods. A short-term store is capable of holding small amounts of information for somewhat longer periods. And a long-term store is capable of storing large amounts of information virtually indefinitely. Within the sensory store, the iconic store refers to visual sensory memory.

3. **What are some of the main alternative models of the structure of memory?** An alternative model uses the concept of working memory, usually defined as being part of long-term memory and also comprising short-term memory. From this perspective, working memory holds only the most recently activated portion of long-term memory. It moves these activated elements into and out of short-term memory. A second model is the levels-of-processing framework, which hypothesizes distinctions in memory ability based on the degree to which items are elaborated during encoding. A third model is the multiple-memory-systems model, which posits not only a distinction between procedural memory and declarative (semantic) memory but also a distinction between semantic and episodic memory. In addition, psychologists have proposed other models for the structure of memory. They include a parallel-distributed-processing (PDP; connectionist) model. The PDP model incorporates the notions of working memory, semantic memory networks, spreading activation, priming, and parallel processing of information. Finally, many psychologists call for a complete change in the conceptualization of memory, focusing on memory functioning in the real world. This call leads to a shift in memory metaphors from the traditional storehouse to the more modern correspondence metaphor.

4. **What have psychologists learned about the structure of memory by studying exceptional memory and the physiology of the brain?** Among other findings, studies of mnemonists have shown the value of imagery in memory for concrete information. They also have demonstrated the importance of finding or forming meaningful connections among items to be remembered. The main forms of amnesia are anterograde amnesia, retrograde amnesia, and infantile amnesia. The last form of amnesia is qualitatively different from the other forms and occurs in everyone. Through the study of the memory function of people with each form of amnesia, it has been possible to differentiate various aspects of memory. These include long-term versus temporary forms of memory, procedural versus declarative memory processes, and explicit versus implicit memory.

Although specific memory traces have not yet been identified, many of the specific structures involved in memory function have been located. To date, the subcortical structures involved in memory appear to include the hippocampus, the thalamus, the hypothalamus, and even the basal ganglia and the cerebellum. The cortex also governs much of the long-term storage of declarative knowledge. The neurotransmitters serotonin and acetylcholine appear to be vital to memory function. Other physiological chemicals, structures, and processes also play important roles, although further investigation is required to identify these roles.

Thinking about Thinking: Factual, Analytical, Creative, and Practical Questions

1. Describe two characteristics each of sensory memory, short-term memory, and long-term memory.

2. What are double dissociations, and why are they valuable to understanding the relationship between cognitive function and the brain?

3. Compare and contrast the three-stores model of memory with one of the alternative models of memory.

4. Critique one of the experiments described in this chapter. What is a problem you see regarding the interpretation given? How could subsequent research be designed to enhance the interpretation of the findings?

5. How would you design an experiment to study some aspect of implicit memory?

6. Imagine what it would be like to recover from one of the forms of amnesia. Describe your impressions of and reactions to your newly recovered memory abilities.

7. How would your life be different if you could greatly enhance your own mnemonic skills in some way?

Key Terms

Alzheimer's disease
amnesia
anterograde amnesia
central executive
episodic buffer
episodic memory
explicit memory
hypermnesia
hypothetical constructs
iconic store

implicit memory
infantile amnesia
levels-of-processing framework
long-term store
memory
mnemonist
prime
priming
phonological loop
priming effect

recall
recognition
retrograde amnesia
semantic memory
sensory store
short-term store
visuospatial sketchpad
working memory

 Explore CogLab by going to http://coglab.wadsworth.com. Answer the questions required by your instructor from the student manual that accompanies CogLab.

Memory Span	Modality Effect
Partial Report	Position Error
Absolute Identification	Irrelevant Speech
Operation Span	Phonological Similarity
Implicit Learning	Levels of Processing

Annotated Suggested Reading

Tulving, E., & Craik, F. I. M. (Eds.) (2000). *The Oxford handbook of memory*. New York: Oxford University Press. This handbook provides perhaps the most comprehensive account of memory phenomena that is currently available.

Memory Processes

EXPLORING COGNITIVE PSYCHOLOGY

1. What have cognitive psychologists discovered regarding how we encode information for storing it in memory?

2. What affects our ability to retrieve information from memory?

3. How does what we know or what we learn affect what we remember?

4. How does memory develop with age?

> *The procedure is actually quite simple. First you arrange items into different groups. Of course one pile may be sufficient depending on how much there is to do. If you have to go somewhere else due to lack of facilities that is the next step; otherwise, you are pretty well set. It is important not to overdo things. That is, it is better to do too few things at once than too many. In the short run this may not seem important but complications can easily arise. A mistake can be expensive as well. At first, the whole procedure will seem complicated. Soon, however, it will become just another facet of life. It is difficult to foresee any end to the necessity for this task in the immediate future, but then, one can never tell. After the procedure is completed one arranges the materials into different groups again. Then they can be put into their appropriate places. Eventually they will be used once more and the whole cycle will then have to be repeated. However, that is part of life.*

John Bransford and Marcia Johnson (1972, p. 722) asked their participants to read the preceding passage and to recall the steps involved. To get an idea of how easy it was for their participants to do so, try to recall those steps now yourself. Bransford and Johnson's participants (and probably you, too) had a great deal of difficulty understanding this passage and recalling the steps involved. What makes this task so difficult? What are the mental processes involved in this task?

As mentioned in the previous chapter, cognitive psychologists generally refer to the main processes of memory as comprising three common operations: encoding, storage, and retrieval. Each one represents a stage in memory processing. **Encoding** refers to how you transform a physical, sensory input into a kind of representation that can be placed into memory. **Storage** refers to how you retain encoded information in memory. **Retrieval** refers to how you gain access to information stored in memory. Our emphasis in discussing these processes will be on recall of verbal and pictorial material. Remember, however, that we have memories of other kinds of stimuli as well, such as odors (Herz & Engen, 1996).

Encoding, storage, and retrieval often are viewed as sequential stages. You first take in information. Then you hold it for a while. Later you pull it out. However, the processes interact with each other and are interdependent. For example, you may have found the text in the chapter-opening paragraph difficult to encode, thereby also making it hard to store and to retrieve the information. However, a verbal label can facilitate encoding and hence storage and retrieval. Most people do much better with the passage if given its title, "Washing Clothes." Try now to recall the steps described in the passage. The verbal label helps us to encode, and therefore to remember, a passage that otherwise seems incomprehensible.

Encoding and Transfer of Information

Forms of Encoding

Short-Term Storage

When you encode information for temporary storage and use, what kind of code do you use? Participants were visually presented with several series of six letters at the rate of 0.75 seconds per letter (Conrad, 1964). The letters used in the various lists were B, C, F, M, N, P, S, T, V, and X. Immediately after the letters were presented, participants had to write down each list of six letters in the order given. What kinds of errors did participants make? Despite the fact that letters were presented visually, errors tended to be based on acoustic confusability. In other words, instead of recalling the letters they were supposed to recall, participants substituted letters that sounded like the correct letters. Thus, they were likely to confuse F for S, B for V, P for B, and so on. Another group of participants simply listened to single letters in a setting that had noise in the background. They then immediately reported each letter as they heard it. Participants showed the same pattern of confusability in the listening task as in the visual memory task (Conrad, 1964). Thus, we seem to encode visually presented letters by how they sound, not by how they look.

The Conrad experiment shows the importance in short-term memory of an acoustic code rather than a visual code. But the results do not rule out the possibility that there are other codes. One such code would be a *semantic code*—one based on word meaning. One researcher argued that short-term memory relies primarily on an acoustic rather than a semantic code (Baddeley, 1966). He compared recall performance for lists of acoustically confusable words—such as *map, cab, mad, man,* and *cap*—with that for lists of acoustically distinct words—such as *cow, pit, day, rig,* and *bun.* He found that performance was much worse for the visual presentation of acoustically similar words.

He also compared performance for lists of semantically similar words—such as *big, long, large, wide,* and *broad*—with performance for lists of semantically dissimilar words—such as *old, foul, late, hot,* and *strong.* There was little difference in recall between the two lists. Suppose performance for the semantically similar words had been much worse. It would have indicated that participants were confused by the semantic similarities and hence were processing the words semantically. However, performance for the semantically similar words was only *slightly* worse than that for the semantically dissimilar words.

Subsequent work investigating how information is encoded in short-term memory has shown clear evidence of at least some semantic encoding in short-term memory (Shulman, 1970; Wickens, Dalezman, & Eggemeier, 1976). Thus, encoding in short-term memory appears to be primarily acoustic. But there may be some secondary semantic encoding as well. In addition, we sometimes temporarily encode information visually as well (Posner, 1969; Posner & associates, 1969; Posner & Keele,

1967). But visual encoding appears to be even more fleeting (about 1.5 seconds). It also is more vulnerable to decay than acoustic encoding. Thus, initial encoding is primarily acoustic in nature. But other forms of encoding may be used under some circumstances.

Long-Term Storage

As mentioned, information stored temporarily in working memory is encoded primarily in acoustic form. Hence, when we make errors in retrieving words from short-term memory, the errors tend to reflect confusions in sound. How is information encoded into a form that can be transferred into storage and available for subsequent retrieval?

Most information stored in long-term memory seems to be primarily semantically encoded. In other words, it is encoded by the meanings of words. Consider some relevant evidence.

Participants learned a list of 41 different words (Grossman & Eagle, 1970). Five minutes after learning took place, participants were given a recognition test. Included in the recognition test were distracters. These are items that appear to be legitimate choices but that are not correct alternatives. That is, they were not presented previously. Nine of the distracters were semantically related to words on the list. Nine were not. The data of interest were false alarms to the distracters. These are responses in which the participants indicated that they had seen the distracters, although they had not. Participants falsely recognized an average of 1.83 of the synonyms but only an average of 1.05 of the unrelated words. This result indicated a greater likelihood of semantic confusion.

Another way to show semantic encoding is to use sets of semantically related test words, rather than distracters. Participants learn a list of 60 words that included 15 animals, 15 professions, 15 vegetables, and 15 names of people (Bousfield, 1953). The words were presented in random order. Thus, members of the various categories were intermixed thoroughly. After participants heard the words, they were asked to free-recall the list in any order they wished. The investigator then analyzed the order of output of the recalled words. Did participants recal successive words from the same category more frequently than would be expected by chance? Indeed, successive recalls from the same category did occur much more often than would be expected by chance occurrence. Participants were remembering words by clustering them into categories.

Encoding of information in long-term memory is not exclusively semantic. There also is evidence for visual encoding. Participants received 16 drawings of objects, including four items of clothing, four animals, four vehicles, and four items of furniture (Frost, 1972). The investigator manipulated not only the semantic category but also the visual category. The drawings differed in visual orientation. Four were angled to the left, four angled to the right, four horizontal, and four vertical. Items were presented in random order. Participants were asked to recall them freely. The order of participants' responses showed effects of both semantic and visual categories. These results suggested that participants were encoding visual as well as semantic information.

In addition to semantic and visual information, acoustic information can be encoded in long-term memory (Nelson & Rothbart, 1972). Thus, there is considerable flexibility in the way we store information that we retain for long periods. Those who seek to know the single correct way we encode information are seeking an answer to the wrong question. There is no one correct way. A more useful question involves asking, "In what *ways* do we encode information in long-term memory?" From a more psychological perspective, however, the most useful question to ask is, "*When* do we encode in *which* ways?" In other words, under what circumstances do we use one form of encoding, and under what circumstances do we use another? These questions are the focus of present and future research.

Transfer of Information from Short-Term Memory to Long-Term Memory

Given the problems of decay and interference, how do we move information from short-term memory to long-term memory? The means of moving information depend on whether the information involves declarative or nondeclarative memory. Some forms of nondeclarative memory are highly volatile and decay quickly. Examples are priming and habituation. Other nondeclarative forms are maintained more readily, particularly as a result of repeated practice (of procedures) or repeated conditioning (of responses). Examples are procedural memory and simple classical conditioning.

For entrance into long-term declarative memory, various processes are involved. One method of accomplishing this goal is by deliberately attending to information to comprehend it. Another is by making connections or associations between the new information and what we already know and understand. We make connections by integrating the new data into our existing schemas of stored information. **Consolidation** is this process of integrating new information into stored information. In humans, the process of consolidating declarative information into memory can continue for many years after the initial experience (Squire, 1986).

The disruption of consolidation has been studied effectively in amnesics. Studies have particularly examined people who have suffered brief forms of amnesia as a consequence of electroconvulsive therapy (ECT; Squire, 1986). For these amnesics, the source of the trauma is clear. Confounding variables can be minimized. A patient history before the trauma can be obtained, and follow-up testing and supervision after the trauma are more likely to be available. A range of studies suggests that during the process of consolidation, our memory is susceptible to disruption and distortion.

To preserve or enhance the integrity of memories during consolidation, we may use various metamemory strategies (Koriat & Goldsmith, 1996; Metcalfe, 2000; Nelson & Narens, 1994; Schwartz & Metcalfe, 1994). **Metamemory** strategies involve reflecting on our own memory processes with a view to improving our memory. Such strategies are especially important when we are transferring new information to long-term memory by rehearsing it. Metamemory strategies are just one component of **metacognition,** our ability to think about and control our own processes of thought and ways of enhancing our thinking.

Rehearsal

One technique people use for keeping information active is **rehearsal,** the repeated recitation of an item. The effects of such rehearsal are termed practice effects. Rehearsal may be *overt*, in which case it is usually aloud and obvious to anyone watching. Or it may be *covert*, in which case it is silent and hidden. Just repeating words over and over again to oneself is not enough to achieve effective rehearsal (Tulving, 1962). One needs also to think about the words and, possibly, their inter-relationships. Whether rehearsal is overt or covert, what is the best way to organize your time for rehearsing new information?

More than a century ago, Hermann Ebbinghaus (1885, cited in Schacter, 1989a) noticed that the distribution of study (memory rehearsal) sessions over time affects the consolidation of information in long-term memory. Much more recently, researchers have offered support for Ebbinghaus's observation as a result of their studies of people's long-term recall of Spanish vocabulary words the people had learned 8 years earlier (Bahrick & Phelps, 1987). They observed that people's memory for information depends on how they acquire it. Their memories tend to be good when they use **distributed practice**, learning in which various sessions are spaced over time. Their memories for information are not as good when the information is acquired through **massed practice**, learning in which sessions are crammed together in a very short space of time. The greater the distribution of learning trials over time, the more the participants remembered over long periods.

Research has linked the spacing effect to the process by which memories are consolidated in long-term memory (Glenberg, 1977, 1979; Leicht & Overton, 1987). That is, the spacing effect may occur because at each learning session, the context for encoding may vary. The individuals may use alternative strategies and cues for encoding. They thereby enrich and elaborate their schemas for the information. The principle of the spacing effect is important to remember in studying. You will recall information longer, on average, if you distribute your learning of subject matter and you vary the context for encoding. Do not try to mass or cram it all into a short period.

Why would distributing learning trials over days make a difference? One possibility is that information is learned in variable contexts. These diverse contexts help strengthen and begin to consolidate it. Another possible answer comes from studies of the influences of sleep on memory. Of particular importance is the amount of REM sleep, a particular stage of sleep characterized by rapid-eye-movement, dreaming, and rapid brain waves (Karni & associates, 1994). Specifically, disruptions in REM sleep patterns the night after learning reduced the amount of improvement on a visual-discrimination task that occurred relative to normal sleep. Furthermore, this lack of improvement was not observed for disrupted stage-three or stage-four sleep patterns (Karni & associates, 1994). Other research also shows better learning with increases in the proportion of REM stage sleep after exposure to learning situations (Smith, 1996). Thus, apparently a good night's sleep, which includes plenty of REM-stage sleep, aids in memory consolidation.

Is there something special occurring in the brain that could explain why REM sleep is so important for memory consolidation? Neuropsychological research on animal learning may offer a tentative answer to this question. Recall that the hippocampus has been found to be an important structure for memory. In recording studies of rat hippocampal cells, researchers have found that cells of the hippocampus that were activated during initial learning are reactivated during subsequent periods of sleep. It is as if they are replaying the initial learning episode to achieve consolidation into long-term storage (Scaggs & McNaughton, 1996; Wilson & McNaughton, 1994).

In a recent review, investigators have proposed that the hippocampus acts as a rapid learning system (McClelland, McNaughton, & O' Reilly, 1995). It temporarily maintains new experiences until they can be appropriately assimilated into the more gradual neocortical representation system of the brain. Such a complementary system is necessary to allow memory to represent more accurately the structure of the environment. McClelland and his colleagues have used connectionist models of learning to show that integrating new experiences too rapidly leads to disruptions in long-term memory systems. Thus, the benefits of distributed practice seem to occur because we have a relatively rapid learning system in the hippocampus. It becomes activated during sleep. Repeated exposure on subsequent days and repeated reactivation during subsequent periods of sleep help learning. These rapidly learned memories become integrated into our more permanent long-term memory system.

The spacing of practice sessions affects memory consolidation. However, the distribution of learning trials within any given session does not seem to affect memory. According to the *total-time hypothesis*, the amount of learning depends on the amount of time spent mindfully rehearsing the material. This relation occurs more or less without regard to how that time is divided into trials in any one session. The total-time hypothesis does not always hold, however. Moreover, the total-time hypothesis of rehearsal has at least two apparent constraints (Cooper & Pantle, 1967). First, the full amount of time allotted for rehearsal actually must be used for that purpose. Second, to achieve beneficial effects, the rehearsal should include various kinds of elaboration or mnemonic devices that can enhance recall.

To move information into long-term memory, an individual must engage in elaborative rehearsal. In *elaborative rehearsal*, the individual somehow elaborates the items to be remembered. Such rehearsal makes the items either more meaningfully integrated into what the person already knows or more meaningfully connected to one another and therefore more memorable. Consider, in contrast, maintenance rehearsal. In *maintenance rehearsal*, the individual simply repetitiously rehearses the items to be repeated. Such rehearsal temporarily maintains information in short-term memory without transferring the information to long-term memory. Without any kind of elaboration, the information cannot be organized and transferred.

Organization of Information

Stored memories are organized. One way to show this organization is through the measurement of subjective organization in free recall. This refers to our individually determined ways of organizing our memories. To measure subjective organization, researchers may give participants a multitrial free-recall task. Participants have multiple trials during which to learn to recall in any order they choose a list of unrelated words. Recall that if sets of test words can be divided into categories (e.g., names of fruits or of furniture), participants spontaneously will cluster their recall output by these categories. They do so even if the order of presentation is random (Bousfield, 1953). Similarly, participants will tend to show consistent patterns of word order in their recall protocols, even if there are no apparent relations among words in the list (Tulving, 1962). In other words, participants create their own consistent organization. They then group their recall by the subjective units they create. Although most adults spontaneously tend to cluster items into categories, categorical clustering also may be used intentionally as an aid to memorization.

PRACTICAL APPLICATIONS OF COGNITIVE PSYCHOLOGY	You can use these memory strategies to help you study for exams: 1. Study throughout the course rather than cram the night before an exam. This distributes the learning sessions, allowing for consolidation into more permanent memory systems. 2. Link new information to what you already know by rehearsing new information in meaningful ways. Organize new information to relate it to other coursework or areas of your life. 3. Use the various mnemonic devices shown in Table 6.1.

Mnemonic devices are specific techniques to help you memorize lists of words (Best, 2003). Essentially, such devices add meaning to otherwise meaningless or arbitrary lists of items. As Table 6.1 shows, a variety of methods—categorical clustering, acronyms, acrostics, interactive imagery among items, pegwords, and the method of loci—can help you to memorize lists of words and vocabulary items. Although the techniques described in Table 6.1 are not the only available ones, they are among the most frequently used.

- In *categorical clustering*, one organizes a list of items into a set of categories. For example, one might organize one's shopping list by the types of foods to be bought (e.g., fruits, vegetables, meats).

- In *interactive images*, one imagines (as vividly as possible) the objects represented by words one has to remember interacting with each other in some active way. For example, suppose you have to remember to buy socks, apples, and a pair of scissors. You might imagine cutting a sock that has an apple stuffed in it with a pair of scissors.

- In the *pegword system*, one associates each word with a word on a previously memorized list and forms an interactive image between the two words. For example, you might memorize a list such as "One is a bun," "Two is a shoe," "Three is a tree," and so on. To remember that you need to buy socks, apples, and a pair of scissors, you might imagine an apple between two buns, a sock stuffed inside a shoe, and a pair of scissors cutting a tree.

- In the *method of loci*, one visualizes walking around an area with distinctive landmarks that one knows well. One then links the various landmarks to specific items to be remembered. For example, suppose you have three landmarks on your route to school—a strange-looking house, a tree, and a baseball diamond. You might imagine a big sock on top of the house in place of the chimney, the pair of scissors cutting the tree, and apples replacing bases on the baseball diamond.

- In using *acronyms*, one devises a word or expression in which each of its letters stands for a certain other word or concept. An example is UK for the United Kingdom.

- In using *acrostics*, one forms a sentence rather than a single word to help one remember new words. For example, one might remember that "every good boy does fine" to recall the names of notes found on the lines of the treble clef in music.

- In using the *keyword system*, one forms an interactive image that links the sound and meaning of a foreign word with the sound and meaning of a familiar word. To remember the word *libro*, for example, which means "book" in Spanish, one might associate *libro* with *liberty*. Then think of the Statue of Liberty holding up a large book instead of a torch.

What is the comparative effectiveness of various mnemonic strategies, including verbal elaborative rehearsal, mental imagery for isolated items, interactive images (linking a sequence of items), the method of loci, and the pegword system (Table 6.2)? The relative effectiveness of the methods for encoding is influenced by the kind

TABLE 6.1	Mnemonic Devices: Assorted Techniques

Of the many mnemonic devices available, the ones described here rely either on organization of information into meaningful chunks—such as categorical clustering, acronyms, and acrostics; or on visual images—such as interactive images, a pegword system, and the method of loci.

TECHNIQUE	**EXPLANATION/DESCRIPTION**	**EXAMPLE**
Categorical clustering	Organize a list of items into a set of categories	If you needed to remember to buy apples, milk, bagels, grapes, yogurt, rolls, Swiss cheese, grapefruit, and lettuce, you would be better able to do so if you tried to memorize the items by categories: *fruits*—apples, grapes, grapefruit; *dairy products*—milk, yogurt, Swiss cheese; *breads*—bagels, rolls; *vegetables*—lettuce.
Interactive images	Create interactive images that link the isolated words in a list	Suppose, for example, that you need to remember a list of unrelated words: *aardvark, table, pencil, book, radio, Kansas, rain, electricity, stone, mirror*. You might better remember these words by generating interactive images. For example, you might imagine an *aardvark* sitting on a *table* holding a *pencil* in its claws and writing in a *book*, with *rain* pouring over *Kansas* (as pictured on a map) that lands on a *radio* that is sitting on a *stone*, which generates *electricity* reflected in a *mirror*.
Pegword system	Associate each new word with a word on a previously memorized list, and form an interactive image between the two words	One such list is from a nursery rhyme: One is a bun. Two is a shoe. Three is a tree. Four is a door. Five is a hive. Six is a stick. Seven is heaven. Eight is a gate. Nine is a dime. Ten is a hen. To recall the list of words you used for the interactive images system, you might visualize an *aardvark* eating a delicious *bun*. You might imagine a *shoe* atop a tall *table*. You might visualize one large branch of a *tree* that ends with a sharp *pencil* point. Then you would go on forming interactive images for each of the words in the list. When you need to remember the words, you first recall the numbered images and then recall the words as you visualize them in the interactive images.

Continued

TABLE 6.1	Mnemonic Devices: Assorted Techniques *(Continued)*	
TECHNIQUE	**EXPLANATION/DESCRIPTION**	**EXAMPLE**
Method of loci	Visualize walking around an area with distinctive landmarks that you know well, and then link the various landmarks to specific items to be remembered	When you need to memorize a list of words, mentally walk past each of the distinctive landmarks, depositing each word to be memorized at one of the landmarks. Visualize an interactive image between the new word and the landmark. For example, if you wished to remember the list of items mentioned previously, you might envision an *aardvark* nibbling at the roots of a familiar tree, a *table* sitting on the sidewalk in front of an empty lot, a *pencil*-shaped statue in the center of a fountain, and so on. When you wished to remember the list, you would take your mental walk and pick up the words you had linked to each of the landmarks along the walk.
Acronym	Devise a word or expression in which each of its letters stands for a certain other word or concept (e.g., USA, IQ, and laser)	Suppose that you want to remember the names of the mnemonic devices described in this chapter. The acronym "IAM PACK" might prompt you to remember Interactive images, Acronyms, Method of loci, Pegwords, Acrostics, Categories, and Keywords. Of course, this technique is more useful if the first letters of the words to be memorized actually can be formed into a word phrase, or something close to one, even if the word or phrase is nonsensical, as in this example.
Acrostic	Form a sentence rather than a single word to help you remember the new words	For example, music students trying to memorize the names of the notes found on lines of the treble clef (the higher notes; specifically E, G, B, D, and F above middle C) learn that "*Every Good Boy Does Fine.*"
Keyword system	Form an interactive image that links the sound and meaning of a foreign word with the sound and meaning of a familiar word	For example, suppose that you needed to learn that the French word for *butter* is *beurre*. First, you would note that *beurre* sounds something like "bear." Next, you would associate the keyword *bear* with *butter* in an image or sentence. For instance, you might visualize a bear eating a stick of butter. Later, *bear* would provide a retrieval cue for *beurre*.

of task (free recall vs. serial recall) required at the time of retrieval (Roediger, 1980a). Thus, when choosing a method for encoding information for subsequent recall, one should consider the purpose for recalling the information. The individual should choose not only strategies that allow for effectively encoding the information (moving it into long-term memory). He or she also should choose strategies that offer appropriate cues for facilitating subsequent retrieval when needed. For example, prior to taking an exam in cognitive psychology, using a strategy for retrieving an alphabetical list of prominent cognitive psychologists would probably be relatively ineffective. Using a strategy for linking particular theorists with the key ideas of their theories is likely to be more effective.

The use of mnemonic devices and other techniques for aiding memory involves metamemory. Most adults spontaneously use categorical clustering. So its inclusion in this list of mnemonic devices is actually just a reminder to use this common memory strategy. In fact, each of us often uses various kinds of *reminders*—external memory aids—to enhance the likelihood we will remember important information. For example, by now you have surely learned the benefits of various external memory aids. These include taking notes during lectures, writing shopping lists for items to purchase, setting timers and alarms, and even asking other people to help you remember

TABLE 6.2	Mnemonic Devices: Comparative Effectiveness

Henry Roediger conducted a study of recall memory, in which initial recall of a series of items was compared with recall following brief training in each of several memory strategies. For both free recall and serial recall, training in interactive imagery, the method of loci, and the pegword system was more effective than either elaborative (verbal) rehearsal or imagery for isolated items. However, the beneficial effects of training were most pronounced for the serial-recall condition. In the free-recall condition, imagery of isolated items was modestly more effective than elaborative (verbal) rehearsal, but for serial recall, elaborative (verbal) rehearsal was modestly more effective than imagery for isolated items.

Condition (type of mnemonic training)	Number of participants	FREE-RECALL CRITERION *Average number of items recalled correctly following training*			SERIAL-RECALL CRITERION *Average number of items recalled correctly following training*		
		Number of correct items recalled on practice list, prior to training	*Immediate recall*	*Recall following a 24-hour delay*	*Number of correct items recalled on practice list, prior to training*	*Immediate recall*	*Recall following a 24-hour delay*
Elaborative rehearsal (verbal)	32	13.2	11.4	6.3	7.0	5.8	1.3
Isolated images of individual items	25	12.4	13.1	6.8	6.8	4.8	1.0
Interactive imagery (with links from one item to the next)	31	13.0	15.6	11.2	7.6	9.6	5.0
Method of loci	29	12.6	15.3	10.6	6.8	13.6	5.8
Pegword system	33	13.1	14.2	8.2	7.7	12.5	4.9
Mean *performance across conditions*	—	12.9	13.9	8.6	7.2	9.4	3.6

H. L. Roediger (1980), "The Effectiveness of Four Mnemonics in Ordering Recall," Journal of Experimental Psychology: HLM, 6(5): 558–567. Copyright © 1980 by the American Psychological Association. Adapted with permission.

things. In addition, we can design our environment to help us remember important information through the use of *forcing functions* (Norman, 1988). These are physical constraints that prevent us from acting without at least considering the key information to be remembered. For example, to ensure that you remember to take your notebook to class, you might lean the notebook against the door through which you must pass to go to class.

Most of the time, we try to improve our *retrospective memory*—our memory for the past. At times we also try to improve our *prospective memory*—memory for things we need do or remember in the future. For example, we may need to remember to call someone, to buy cereal at the supermarket, or to finish a homework assignment due the next day. We use a number of strategies to improve prospective memory. Examples are keeping a to-do list, asking someone to remind us to do something, or tying a string around our finger to remind us that we need to do something. Research suggests that having to do something regularly on a certain day does not necessarily improve prospective memory for doing that thing. But being monetarily reinforced for doing the thing does tend to improve prospective memory (Meacham, 1982; Meacham & Singer, 1977).

Retrieval

Once we have stored information, how do we retrieve it when we want to do so? If we have problems retrieving information, how do we know whether we even stored the information in the first place?

Retrieval from Short-Term Memory

Once information is encoded and stored in short-term memory, how do people retrieve that information?

INVESTIGATING COGNITIVE PSYCHOLOGY	Memorize the following list of numbers: 6, 3, 8, 2, 7. Now, was 8 on the list? How do people make decisions such as this one?

Participants received a short list including from one to six digits (Sternberg, 1966). Participants were expected to be able to hold it in short-term memory. After a brief pause, a test digit was flashed on a screen. Participants had to say whether this digit appeared in the set that they had been asked to memorize. Thus, if the list comprised the digits 4, 1, 9, 3, and the digit 9 flashed on the screen, the correct response would be "yes." If, instead, the test digit was 7, the correct response would be "no." The digits that were presented are termed the *positive set*. Those that were not presented are termed the *negative set*.

Are items retrieved all at once (parallel processing) or sequentially (serial processing)? If retrieved serially, the question then arises, "Are all items retrieved, regardless of the task (exhaustive retrieval), or does retrieval stop as soon as an item seems to accomplish the task (self-terminating retrieval)?"

Parallel versus Serial Processing

As mentioned previously, parallel processing refers to the simultaneous handling of multiple operations. As applied to short-term memory, the items stored in short-term memory would be retrieved all at once, not one at a time. The prediction in Figure

6.1 (*a*) shows what would happen if parallel processing were the case in the memory-scanning task. Response times should be the same, regardless of the size of the positive set. This is because all comparisons would be done at once.

Serial processing refers to operations being done one after another. In other words, on the digit-recall task, the digits would be retrieved in succession, rather than all at once (as in the parallel model). According to the serial model, it should take longer to retrieve four digits than to retrieve two digits (as shown in Figure 6.1 [*b*]).

Exhaustive versus Self-Terminating Processing

Suppose information processing were serial. Then there would be two ways in which to gain access to the stimuli: exhaustive or self-terminating processing. *Exhaustive serial processing* implies that the participant always would check the test digit against *all* digits in the positive set, even if a match were found partway through the list.

FIGURE 6.1

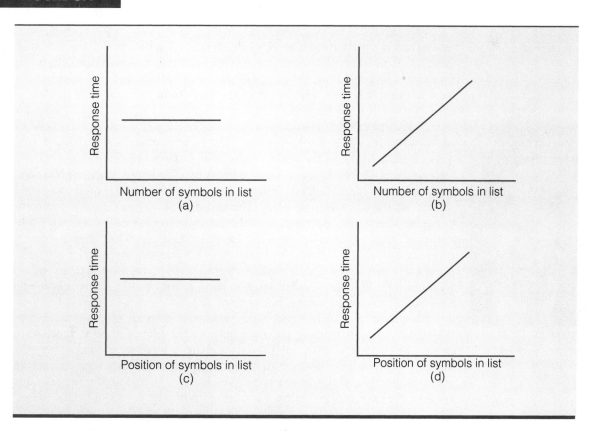

Panel a illustrates findings suggestive of parallel processing; b illustrates serial processing; c shows exhaustive serial processing; and d shows self-terminating serial processing. Based on S. Sternberg (1966), "High Speed in S. Sternberg's Short-Term Memory-Scanning Task," Science, Vol. 153, p. 652–654. Copyright © 1966 American Association for the Advancement of Science.

Exhaustive processing would predict the pattern of data shown in Figure 6.1 (c). Note that positive responses all would take the same amount of time, regardless of the serial position of a positive test probe. In other words, in an exhaustive search, you would take the same amount of time to find any digit. Where in the list it was located would not matter.

Self-terminating serial processing implies that the participant would check the test digit against only those digits needed to make a response. Consider Figure 6.1 (d). It shows that response time now would increase linearly as a function of where a test digit was located in the positive set. The later the serial position, the longer is the response time.

The Winner—a Serial, Exhaustive Model—with Some Qualifications

The actual pattern of data was crystal clear. The data looked like those in Figures 6.1 (b) and (c). Response times increased linearly with set size. But they were the same, regardless of serial position. Later, this pattern of data was replicated (Sternberg, 1969). Moreover, the mean response times for positive and negative responses were essentially the same. This fact further supported the serial exhaustive model. Comparisons took roughly 38 milliseconds (0.038 seconds) apiece (Sternberg, 1966, 1969).

Although many investigators considered the question of parallel versus serial processing to have been answered decisively, in fact, a parallel model could account for the data (Corcoran, 1971). Imagine a horse race that involves parallel processing. The race is not over until the last horse passes the finish line. Now suppose we add more horses to the race. The length of the race (from the start until the last of the horses crosses the finishing line) is likely to increase. For example, if horses are selected randomly, the slowest horse in an eight-horse race is likely to be slower than the slowest horse in a four-horse race. That is, with more horses, a wider range of speeds is more likely. So the entire race will take longer because the race is not complete until the slowest horse crosses the finish line. Similarly, when applying a parallel model to a retrieval task involving more items, a wider range of retrieval speeds for the various items is also more likely. The entire retrieval process is not complete until the last item has been retrieved. Mathematically, it is impossible to distinguish parallel from serial models unequivocally (Townsend, 1971). There always exists some parallel model that will mimic any serial model in its predictions and vice versa. The two models may not be equally plausible, but they still exist. Moreover, it appears that what processes individuals use depends in part on the stimuli that are processed (e.g., Naus, 1974; Naus, Glucksberg, & Ornstein, 1972).

Some cognitive psychologists have suggested that we should seek not only to understand the *how* of memory processes but also the *why* of memory processes (e.g., Bruce, 1991). That is, what functions does memory serve for individual persons and for humans as a species? To understand the functions of memory, we must study memory for relatively complex information. We also need to understand the relationships between the information presented and other information available to the individual, both within the informational context and as a result of prior experience.

Retrieval from Long-Term Memory

It is difficult to separate storage from retrieval phenomena. Participants in one study were tested on their memory for lists of categorized words (Tulving & Pearlstone,

Gordon H. Bower is a professor of psychology at Stanford University. His earlier contributions were in mathematical learning theories. Later, with John Anderson, he developed a theoretical framework for linking laboratory studies of verbal memory with psycholinguistic theories of memory. He also has investigated how people's emotional states influence memory storage and retrieval.

1966). Participants would hear words within a category together in the list. They even would be given the name of the category before the items within it were presented. For example, the participants might hear the category "article of clothing" followed by the words, "shirt, socks, pants, belt." Participants then were tested for their recall.

The recall test was done in one of two ways. In the free-recall condition, participants merely recalled as many words as they could in any order they chose. In a cued-recall condition, however, participants were tested category by category. They were given each category label as a cue. They then were asked to recall as many words as they could from that category. The critical result was that cued recall was far better, on average, than free recall. Had the researchers tested only free recall, they might have concluded that participants had not stored quite so many words. However, the comparison to the cued-recall condition demonstrated that apparent memory failures were largely a result of retrieval rather than storage failures.

Categorization dramatically can affect retrieval. Investigators had participants learn lists of categorized words (Bower & associates, 1969). Either the words were presented in random order or they were presented in the form of a hierarchical tree that showed the organization of the words. For example, the category "minerals" might be at the top, followed by the categories of "metals and stones," and so on. Participants given hierarchical presentation recalled 65% of the words. In contrast, recall was just 19% by participants given the words in random order.

Another problem that arises when studying memory is figuring out why we sometimes have trouble retrieving information. Cognitive psychologists often have difficulty finding a way to distinguish between availability and accessibility of items. **Availability** is the presence of information stored in long-term memory. **Accessibility** is the degree to which we can gain access to the available information. Memory performance depends on the accessibility of the information to be remembered. Ideally, memory researchers would like to assess the availability of information in memory. Unfortunately, they must settle for assessing the accessibility of such information.

Processes of Forgetting and Memory Distortion

Why do we so easily and so quickly forget phone numbers we have just looked up or the names of people whom we have just met? Several theories have been proposed as to why we forget information stored in working memory. The two most well-known theories are interference theory and decay theory. **Interference** occurs when competing information causes us to forget something; **decay** occurs when simply the passage of time causes us to forget.

Interference versus Decay Theory

Interference theory refers to the view that forgetting occurs because recall of certain words interferes with recall of other words. Evidence for interference goes back many years (Brown, 1958; Peterson & Peterson, 1959). In one study, participants to recall *trigrams* (strings of three letters) at intervals of 3, 6, 9, 12, 15, or 18 seconds after the presentation of the last letter (Peterson & Peterson, 1959). The investigator used only consonants, so that the trigrams would not be easily pronounceable—for example, "K B F." Each participant was tested eight times at each of the six delay intervals for a total of 48 trials. Figure 6.2 shows percentages of correct recalls after the various intervals of time. Why does recall decline so rapidly? Because after the oral presentation of each trigram, participants counted backward by threes from a three-digit number spoken immediately after the trigram. The purpose of having the participants count backward was to prevent them from rehearsing during the *retention interval*. This is the time between the presentation of the last letter and the start of the recall phase of the experimental trial.

Clearly, the trigram is almost completely forgotten after just 18 seconds if participants are not allowed to rehearse it. Moreover, such forgetting also occurs when words rather than letters are used as the stimuli to be recalled (Murdock, 1961). Thus, counting backward interfered with recall from short-term memory, supporting the interference account of forgetting in short-term memory. At that time, it seemed surprising that counting backward with numbers would interfere with the recall of letters. The previous view had been that verbal information would interfere only with verbal (words) memory. Similarly, it was thought that quantitative (numerical) information would interfere only with quantitative memory.

Although the foregoing discussion has construed interference as though it were a single construct, at least two kinds of interference figure prominently in psychological theory and research: retroactive interference and proactive interference. **Retroactive interference** (or retroactive inhibition) is caused by activity occurring *after* we learn something but *before* we are asked to recall that thing. The interference in the Brown-Peterson task appears to be retroactive, because counting backward by threes occurs after learning of the trigram. It interferes with our ability to remember information we learned previously.

FIGURE 6.2

The percentage of recall of three consonants (a trigram) drops off quickly if participants are not allowed to rehearse the trigrams. G. Keppel and B. J. Underwood (1962), "Proactive Inhibition in Short-Term Retention of Single Items," Journal of Verbal Learning and Verbal Behavior, Vol. 1, p. 153–161. Reprinted by permission of Elsevier.

A second kind of interference is proactive interference (or proactive inhibition). **Proactive interference** occurs when the interfering material occurs *before,* rather than *after,* learning of the to-be-remembered material. Proactive as well as retroactive interference may play a role in short-term memory (Keppel & Underwood, 1962). Thus, retroactive interference appears to be important (Reitman, 1971; Shiffrin, 1973; Waugh & Norman, 1965), but not the only factor.

Some early psychologists recognized the need to study memory retrieval for connected texts and not just for unconnected strings of digits, words, or nonsense syllables. In one study, participants learned a text and then recalled it (Bartlett, 1932). Participants in Britain learned what was to them a strange and difficult-to-understand North American Indian legend called "The War of the Ghosts." (The text is depicted in its entirety in Table 6.3.)

Participants distorted their recall to render the story more comprehensible to themselves. In other words, their prior knowledge and expectations had a substantial effect on their recall. Apparently, people bring into a memory task their already existing schemas, or organized relevant knowledge structures, which affect the way in which they recall what they learn. The later work using the Brown-Peterson paradigm confirms the notion that prior knowledge has an enormous effect on memory, sometimes leading to interference or distortion.

Yet another method often used for determining the causes of forgetting draws inferences from a serial-position curve: The serial-position curve represents the probability of recall of a given word, given its serial position (order of presentation) in a list. Suppose that you are presented with a list of words and are asked to recall them. You even might try it on yourself with the "Investigating Cognitive Psychology" box.

Say the following list of words once to yourself, and then, immediately thereafter, try to recall all the words, in any order, without looking back at them: *Table, Cloud, Book, Tree, Shirt, Cat, Light, Bench, Chalk, Flower, Watch, Bat, Rug, Soap, Pillow.*

INVESTIGATING COGNITIVE PSYCHOLOGY

If you are like most people, you will find that your recall of words is best for items at and near the end of the list. Your recall will be second best for items near the beginning of the list, and poorest for items in the middle of the list. A typical serial-position curve is shown in Figure 6.3.

The **recency effect** refers to superior recall of words at and near the end of a list. The **primacy effect** refers to superior recall of words at and near the beginning of a list. As Figure 6.3 shows, both the recency effect and the primacy effect seem to influence recall. The serial-position curve makes sense in terms of interference theory. Words at the end of the list are subject to proactive but not to retroactive interference. Words at the beginning of the list are subject to retroactive but not to proactive interference. And words in the middle of the list are subject to both types of interference. Hence, recall would be expected to be poorest in the middle of the list. Indeed, it is poorest.

The amount of proactive interference generally climbs with increases in the length of time between when the information is presented (and encoded) and when the information is retrieved (Underwood, 1957). Also as you might expect, proactive

TABLE 6.3	Bartlett's Legend

Read the legend described in this table, and then turn the page and try to recall the legend in its entirety.

(A) ORIGINAL INDIAN MYTH	(B) TYPICAL RECALL BY A STUDENT IN ENGLAND
The War of the Ghosts	*The War of the Ghosts*
One night two young men from Egulac went down to the river to hunt seals, and while they were there it became foggy and calm. Then they heard war-cries, and they thought: "Maybe this is a war-party." They escaped to the shore, and hid behind a log. Now canoes came up, and they heard the noise of paddles, and saw one canoe coming up to them. There were five men in the canoe, and they said: "What do you think? We wish to take you along. We are going up the river to make war on the people." One of the young men said, "I have no arrows." "Arrows are in the canoe," they said. "I will not go along. I might be killed. My relatives do not know where I have gone. But you," he said, turning to the other, "may go with them." So one of the young men went, but the other returned home. And the warriors went on up the river to a town on the other side of Kalama. The people came down to the water, and they began to fight, and many were killed. But presently the young man heard one of the warriors say: "Quick, let us go home; that Indian has been hit." Now he thought: "Oh, they are ghosts." He did not feel sick, but they said he had been shot. So the canoes went back to Egulac, and the young man went ashore to his house, and made a fire. And he told everybody and said: "Behold I accompanied the ghosts, and we went to fight. Many of our fellows were killed, and many of those who attacked us were killed. They said I was hit, and I did not feel sick." He told it all, and then he became quiet. When the sun rose he fell down. Something black came out of his mouth. His face became contorted. The people jumped up and cried. He was dead.	Two men from Edulac went fishing. While thus occupied by the river they heard a noise in the distance. "It sounds like a cry," said one, and presently there appeared some in canoes who invited them to join the party of their adventure. One of the young men refused to go, on the ground of family ties, but the other offered to go. "But there are no arrows," he said. "The arrows are in the boat," was the reply. He thereupon took his place, while his friend returned home. The party paddled up the river to Kaloma, and began to land on the banks of the river. The enemy came rushing upon them, and some sharp fighting ensued. Presently someone was injured, and the cry was raised that the enemy were ghosts. The party returned down the stream, and the young man arrived home feeling none the worse for his experience. The next morning at dawn he endeavoured to recount his adventures. While he was talking something black issued from his mouth. Suddenly he uttered a cry and fell down. His friends gathered round him. But he was dead.

"The War of the Ghosts," from Remembering: A Study in Experimental and Social Psychology by F. C. Bartlett. Copyright © 1932 by Cambridge University Press. Reprinted with permission of Cambridge University Press.

interference increases as the amount of prior—and potentially interfering—learning increases (Greenberg & Underwood, 1950). The effects of proactive interference appear to dominate under conditions in which recall is delayed. But proactive and retroactive interference now are viewed as complementary phenomena. Yet another theory for explaining how we forget information is decay theory.

FIGURE 6.3

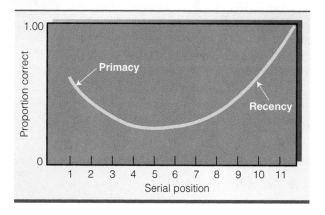

When asked to recall a list of words, we show superior recall of words close to the end of a list (the recency effect), pretty good recall of words close to the beginning of the list (primacy effect), and relatively poor recall of words in the middle of the list.

Decay theory asserts that information is forgotten because of the gradual disappearance, rather than displacement, of the memory trace. Thus, decay theory views the original piece of information as gradually disappearing unless something is done to keep it intact. This view contrasts with interference theory, just discussed, in which one or more pieces of information block recall of another.

Decay theory turns out to be exceedingly difficult to test. Why? First, under normal circumstances, preventing participants from rehearsing is difficult. Through rehearsal, participants maintain the to-be-remembered information in memory. Usually participants know that you are testing their memory. They may try to rehearse the information or they may even inadvertently rehearse it to perform well during testing. However, if you do prevent them from rehearsing, the possibility of interference arises. The task you use to prevent rehearsal may interfere retroactively with the original memory.

For example, try not to think of white elephants as you read the next two pages. When instructed not to think about them, you actually find it quite difficult not to. The difficulty persists even if you try to follow the instructions. Unfortunately, as a test of decay theory, this experiment is itself a white elephant, because preventing people from rehearsing is so difficult.

Despite these difficulties, it is possible to test decay theory. Such a test involves using a task intervening between learning and testing that (1) prevents rehearsal and (2) presents no interfering learning. In one such study, the intervening task, involving tone detection, required a great deal of effort and attention but no new learning (Reitman, 1971, 1974). Participants heard a very faint tone presented through earphones. They were to press a button each time they heard the tone. Of course, there was no guarantee that participants would not rehearse at all. Nor was there any guarantee that all information would be blocked from entering short-term memory. However, the test was about as close to ideal as one could realistically produce.

Participants saw five words (Reitman, 1974). The display lasted for 2 seconds. As soon as the display went off, participants engaged in the tone-detection task for 15 seconds, after which they tried to recall as many of the five words as they could. Recall declined by about 24% over the 15 seconds. Reitman interpreted this decline as evidence of decay.

To conclude, evidence exists for both interference and decay, at least in short-term memory. The evidence for decay is not airtight. But it is certainly suggestive. The evidence for interference is rather strong. But the extent to which the interference is retroactive, proactive, or both is unclear. In addition, interference also affects material in long-term memory, leading to memory distortion.

The Constructive Nature of Memory

An important lesson about memory is that memory retrieval is not just **reconstructive,** involving the use of various strategies (e.g., searching for cues, drawing inferences) for retrieving the original memory traces of our experiences and then rebuilding the original experiences as a basis for retrieval (see Kolodner, 1983, for an artificial-intelligence model of reconstructive memory). Rather, in real-life situations, memory is also **constructive,** in that prior experience affects how we recall things and what we actually recall from memory (Grant & Ceci, 2000; Sutton, 2003). Recall the Bransford and Johnson (1972) study, cited at the opening of this chapter. In this study participants could remember a passage about washing clothes quite well but only if they realized that it was about washing clothes.

In a further demonstration of the constructive nature of memory, participants read an ambiguous passage that could be interpreted meaningfully in two ways (Bransford & Johnson, 1973). Either it could be viewed as being either about watching a peace march from the fortieth floor of a building or about a space trip to an inhabited planet. Participants omitted different details, depending on what they thought the passage was about. Consider, for example, a sentence mentioning that the atmosphere did not require the wearing of special clothing. Participants were more likely to remember it when they thought the passage was about a trip into outer space than when they thought it was about a peace march.

Consider a comparable demonstration in a different domain (Bower, Karlin, & Dueck, 1975). Investigators showed participants 28 different *droodles*—nonsense pictures that can be given various interpretations (see also Chapter 10, Figure 10.2). Half of the participants in their experiment were given an interpretation by which they could label what they saw. The other half did not receive an interpretation prompting a label. Participants in the label group correctly reproduced almost 20% more droodles than did participants in the control group.

Autobiographical Memory

Autobiographical memory refers to memory of an individual's history. Autobiographical memory is constructive. One does not remember exactly what has happened. Rather, one remembers one's construction or reconstruction of what happened. Peo-

Photo Credits

This page constitutes an extension of the copyright page. We have made every effort to trace the ownership of all copyrighted material and to secure permission from copyright holders. In the event of any question arising as to the use of any material, we will be pleased to make the necessary corrections in future printings. Thanks are due to the following authors, publishers, and agents for permission to use the material indicated.

Chapter 1. 5, 6: Archives of the History of American Psychology, University of Akron **10:** Courtesy of Dr. Ulric Neisser **11:** Courtesy of Dr. Herbert A. Simon **12:** Courtesy of Dr. Ludy T. Benjamin, Jr. **Chapter 2. 33, top:** CNRI/SPL/Photo Researchers, Inc. **33, center:** Ohio Nuclear/SPL/Photo Researchers, Inc. **33, center:** CNRI/SPL/Photo Researchers, Inc. **33, bottom:** Spencer Grant/Stock Boston **34, top:** Hoa Qui/Index Stock Imagery **34, bottom:** Photodisc/PictureQuest **37, left:** Biophoto Associates/Science Source/Photo Researchers, Inc. **37, right:** A. Glauberman/Photo Researchers, Inc. **41:** Courtesy of Dr. John Gabrieli **49, all:** The Kobal Collection **55:** Courtesy of Dr. Michael Posner **Chapter 3. 67:** Courtesy of Dr. John F. Kilstrom **79:** Reuters/Corbis **80:** © Peter Menzel/Stock Boston **84:** Courtesy of

Dr. Anne Treisman **99:** Tony Freeman/PhotoEdit **Chapter 4. 121, left:** National Gallery/London/ET Archive/Superstock **121, right:** M. C. Escher's "Waterfall" © 2005 The M. C. Escher Company–Holland. All Rights Reserved. **125, top:** Image Port/Index Stock Imagery **125, bottom:** Ron Avery/SuperStock **125, center:** Getty Images **126:** Courtesy of Dr. Stephen Palmer **127:** Courtesy of Kaiser Porcelain, Ltd. **140:** Courtesy of Dr. Irving Biederman **143:** Courtesy of Dr. Irvin Rock **Chapter 5. 166:** Courtesy of Dr. Harry Bahrick **171:** Courtesy of Dr. Alan Baddeley **175:** Courtesy of Dr. M. K. Johnson **181:** Yang Liu/Corbis **185, left:** CNRI/Phototake **185, right:** Zephyr/Photo Researchers, Inc. **185, bottom:** CNRI/Phototake **Chapter 6. 206:** Courtesy of Dr. Gordon H. Bower **214:** Courtesy of Dr. Elizabeth Loftus **216:** Courtesy of Dr. Elizabeth Loftus **Chapter 7. 230, top left:** AP/Wide World Photos **230, top right:** AP/Wide World Photos **230, bottom left:** AP/Wide World Photos **230, bottom right:** AP/Wide World Photos **233:** Courtesy of Dr. Stephen M. Kosslyn **235:** Courtesy of Dr. Stephen M. Kosslyn **247:** Courtesy of Dr. Roger N. Shepard **258:** Courtesy of Dr. Martha Farah **Chapter 8. 293:** Courtesy of Dr. John R. Anderson **299:** Courtesy of Dr. James L.

McClelland **304:** Courtesy of Dr. James L. McClelland **Chapter 9. 313:** Bill Gillette/Stock Boston **332:** Courtesy of Dr. Paul Bloom **Chapter 10. 359:** Courtesy of Dr. Michael Cole **377:** Courtesy of Dr. Walter Kintsch **382, left:** SuperStock **382, right:** CNRI/Phototake **382, bottom:** WDCN/University of London/Photo Researchers, Inc. **Chapter 11. 408:** © SuperStock **414:** Courtesy of Dr. Dedre Genter **423:** Courtesy of Dr. Michelene Chi **428, top:** George Tiedemann/New Sport/Corbis **428, bottom left:** AGE Fotostock/SuperStock **428, bottom right:** Ed Lallo/PictureQuest **430, left:** Biblioteca Reale, Turin, Italy/Pixtal/SuperStock **430, center:** SuperStock **430, right:** Omikron/Photo Researchers, Inc. **Chapter 12. 443:** Bob Daemmrich/PhotoEdit **444:** Courtesy of Dr. Amos Tversky **447, left:** Digital Vision/PictureQuest **447, right:** Comstock/SuperStock **450, top:** Tom Carter/Index Stock Imagery **450, bottom:** Tom Carter/PhotoEdit **453:** Courtesy of Dr. Baruch Fischhoff **455:** Courtesy of Dr. Gerd Gigerenzer **467:** Courtesy of Dr. Philip Johnson-Laird **Chapter 13. 495:** Courtesy of Dr. Earl Hunt **499:** Courtesy of Dr. Randall Engle **506:** © George Holton/Photo Researchers, Inc. **507:** Courtesy of Dr. Howard Gardner

ple's autobiographical memories are generally quite good. Nevertheless, they are subject to distortions (as will be discussed later). They are differentially good for different periods of life. Middle-aged adults often remember events from their youthful and early-adult periods better than they remember events from their more recent past (Rubin, 1982, 1996).

One way of studying autobiographical memory is through diary studies. In such studies, individuals, often researchers, keep detailed autobiographies (e.g., Linton, 1982; Wagenaar, 1986). One investigator, for example, kept a diary for a 6-year period (Linton, 1982). She recorded at least two experiences per day on index cards. Then, each month she chose two cards at random and tried to recall the events she had written on the cards as well as the dates of the events. She further rated each memory for its salience and its emotional content. Surprisingly, her rate of forgetting of events was linear. It was not curvilinear, as is usually the case. In other words, a typical memory curve shows substantial forgetting over short time intervals and then a slowing in the rate of forgetting over longer time intervals. Linton's forgetting curve, however, did not show any such pattern. Her rate of forgetting was about the same over the entire 6-year interval. She also found little relationship between her ratings of the salience and emotionality of memories, on the one hand, and their memorability, on the other. Thus, she surprised herself in what she did and did not remember.

In another study of autobiographical memory, a researcher attempted to recall information regarding performances attended at the Metropolitan Opera house over a period of 25 years (Sehulster, 1989). A total of 284 performances comprised the data for the study. The results were more in line with traditional expectations. Operas seen near the beginning and end of the 25-year period were remembered better (serial-position effect). Important performances also were better recalled than less important ones.

Memory Distortions

People have tendencies to distort their memories (Ayers & Reder, 1998; Balota & associates, 1999; Garry & associates, 1996; Goff & Roediger, 1998; Heaps & Nash, 1999; Johnson & Raye, 1998; Norman & Schacter, 1997; Roediger & McDermott, 2000; Schacter, 1995b; Schacter & Curran, 2000). For example, just saying something has happened to you makes you more likely to think it really happened. This is true, whether it happened or not (Ackil & Zaragoza, 1998). There are seven specific ways in which these distortions tend to occur (which Schacter, 2001, refers to as the "seven sins of memory"). Here are Schacter's "seven sins":

1. *Transience*. Memory fades quickly. For example, although most people know that O. J. Simpson was acquitted of criminal charges in the murder of his wife, they do not remember how they found out about his acquittal. At one time they could have said, but they no longer can.

2. *Absent-mindedness*. People sometimes brush their teeth after already having brushed them or enter a room looking for something only to discover that they have forgotten what they were seeking.

3. *Blocking*. People sometimes have something that they know they should remember, but they can't. It's as though the information is on the tip of

their tongue, but they cannot retrieve it. For example, people may see someone they know but the person's name escapes them. Or they may try to think of a synonym for a word, knowing that there is an obvious synonym but are unable to recall it.

4. *Misattribution*. People often cannot remember where they heard what they heard or read what they read. Sometimes people think they saw things they did not see or heard things they did not hear. For example, eyewitness testimony is sometimes clouded by what we think we should have seen, rather than what we actually saw.

5. *Suggestibility*. People are susceptible to suggestion, so that if it is suggested to them that they saw something, they may think they remember seeing it. For example, in Holland, when asked whether they had seen a television film of a plane crashing into an apartment building, many people said they had seen it. There was no such film.

6. *Bias*. People often are biased in their recall. For example, people who currently are experiencing chronic pain in their lives are more likely to remember pain in their past, whether or not they actually experienced it. People who are not experiencing such pain are less likely to recall pain in the past, again with little regard to their actual past experience.

7. *Persistence*. People sometimes remember things as consequential that, in a broad context, are inconsequential. For example, someone with many successes but one notable failure may remember the single failure better than the many successes.

What are some of the specific ways in which memory distortions are studied?

The Eyewitness Testimony Paradigm

A survey of U.S. prosecutors estimated that about 77,000 suspects are arrested each year after being identified by eyewitnesses (Dolan, 1995). Studies of more than 1,000 known wrongful convictions have pointed to errors in eyewitness identification as being "the single largest factor leading to those false convictions" (Wells, 1993, p. 554). What proportion of eyewitness identifications are mistaken? The answer to that question varies widely ("from as low as a few percent to greater than 90%"; Wells, 1993, p. 554), but even the most conservative estimates of this proportion suggest frightening possibilities.

Consider the story of a man named Timothy. In 1986, Timothy was convicted of brutally murdering a mother and her two young daughters (Dolan, 1995). He was then sentenced to die, and for 2 years and 4 months, Timothy lived on death row. Although the physical evidence did not point to Timothy, eyewitness testimony placed him near the scene of the crime at the time of the murder. Subsequently, it was discovered that a man who looked like Timothy was a frequent visitor to the neighborhood of the murder victims, and Timothy was given a second trial and was acquitted.

Some of the strongest evidence for the constructive nature of memory has been obtained by those who have studied the validity of eyewitness testimony. In a now-classic study, participants saw a series of 30 slides in which a red Datsun drove down a street, stopped at a stop sign, turned right, and then appeared to knock down a

Elizabeth Loftus is a professor of psychology at the University of California, Irvine. She has made major contributions to the study of human memory, particularly in the areas of eyewitness testimony and so-called repressed memories, which she has argued can be planted in the minds of unwitting individuals so that the individuals believe they are remembering events that they never actually experienced.

pedestrian crossing at a crosswalk (Loftus, Miller, & Burns, 1978). As soon as the participants finished seeing the slides, they had to answer a series of 20 questions about the accident. One of the questions contained information that was either consistent or inconsistent with what they had been shown. For example, half of the participants were asked: "Did another car pass the red Datsun while it was stopped at the stop sign?" The other half of the participants received the same question, except with the word *yield* replacing the word *stop*. In other words, the information in the question given this second group was inconsistent with what the participants had seen.

Later, after engaging in an unrelated activity, all participants were shown two slides and asked which they had seen. One had a stop sign, the other had a yield sign. Accuracy on this task was 34% better for participants who had received the consistent question (stop sign question) than for participants who had received the inconsistent question (yield sign question). This experiment and others (e.g., Loftus, 1975, 1977) have shown people's great susceptibility to distortion in eyewitness accounts. This distortion may be due, in part, to phenomena other than just constructive memory. But it does show that we easily can be led to construct a memory that is different from what really happened. As an example, you might have had a disagreement with a roommate or a friend regarding an experience in which both of you were in the same place at the same time. But what each of you remembers about the experience may differ sharply. And *both* of you may feel that you are truthfully and accurately recalling what happened.

There are serious potential problems of wrongful conviction when using eyewitness testimony as the sole or even the primary basis for convicting accused people of crimes (Loftus & Ketcham, 1991; Loftus, Miller, & Burns, 1987; Wells & Loftus, 1984). Moreover, eyewitness testimony is often a powerful determinant of whether a jury will convict an accused person. The effect particularly is pronounced if eyewitnesses appear highly confident of their testimony. This is true even if the eyewitnesses can provide few perceptual details or offer apparently conflicting responses. People sometimes even think they remember things simply because they have imagined or thought about them (Garry & Loftus, 1994). It has been estimated that as many as 10,000 people per year may be convicted wrongfully on the basis of mistaken eyewitness testimony (Cutler & Penrod, 1995; Loftus & Ketcham, 1991). In general, then, people are remarkably susceptible to mistakes in eyewitness testimony. In general, they are prone to imagine that they have seen things they have not seen (Loftus, 1998).

Lineups can lead to faulty conclusions (Wells, 1993). Eyewitnesses assume that the perpetrator is in the lineup. This is not always the case, however. When the perpetrator of a staged crime was not in a lineup, participants were susceptible to naming someone other than the perpetrator as the perpetrator. In this way, they can recognize *someone* in the lineup as having committed the crime. The identities of the nonperpetrators in the lineup also can affect judgments (Wells, Luus, & Windschitl, 1994). In other words, whether a given person is identified as a perpetrator can be influenced simply by who the others in the lineup are. So the choice of the "distracter" individuals is important. Police may inadvertently affect the likelihood of whether an identification occurs or not and also whether a false identification is likely to occur.

Eyewitness identification is particularly weak when identifying people of a race other than the race of the witness (e.g., Bothwell, Brigham, & Malpass, 1989;

Brigham & Malpass, 1985; Shapiro & Penrod, 1986). Even infants seem to be influenced by postevent information when recalling an experience, as shown through their behavior in operant-conditioning experiments (Rovee-Collier & associates, 1993).

IN THE LAB OF ELIZABETH LOFTUS

Courtesy of Dr. Elizabeth Loftus

Remember the time when you were a kid and your family went to Disneyland? The highlight of your trip was meeting Mickey Mouse who shook your hand. Remember that? Marketers use autobiographical advertising like this to create nostalgia for their products. With two collaborators, Kathy Braun and Rhiannon Ellis, we have been exploring whether such referencing can cause people to believe that they had experiences as children that are mentioned in the ads (Braun, Ellis, & Loftus, 2002). In our first study, participants viewed an ad for Disney that suggested that as a child they shook hands with Mickey Mouse. Later on they answered questions about their childhood experiences at Disney. Relative to controls, the ad increased their confidence that as a child they personally had shaken hands with Mickey at Disneyland. Of course we realized that the increased confidence could be due to either (1) a revival of a true memory or (2) the creation of a new, false one. Because some people could have actually met Mickey at Disney, both are possibilities. So, we conducted a second study in which our participants viewed a fake ad for Disney that suggested that they shook hands with an impossible character—Bugs Bunny. Again, relative to controls, the ad increased confidence that they personally had shaken hands with the impossible character as a child at Disneyland. Although this could not possibly have happened because Bugs Bunny is a Warner Brothers character and would not be caught dead at a Disney property, about 16% of the subjects later said that they remembered or knew that the event actually had happened to them.

In later research, we wondered whether the mode of presenting the false information would affect the likelihood that subjects would accept it. In our original study Bugs Bunny was introduced both visually, and also in the text of the ad. In more recent research, we prepared three different false ads that included Bugs Bunny (Braun-LaTour, LaTour, Pickrell & Loftus, 2004/2005). In the "picture" condition, the ad featured a picture of Bugs at the bottom of the ad. In the "text" condition, Bugs was introduced with a headline on the ad saying, "Bugs says it's time to remember the magic," and then within the text by mentioning him as a character that they might have shaken hands with. In the "both" condition, the ad contained both picture and text. Once again, the ad copy led many people to claim later that they had personally met and shaken hands with Bugs. And it mattered whether the ad contained a picture. We found that including the picture of Bugs substantially enhanced the false memory effect. For example, the picture alone led to a significantly higher false memory rate than the text only (48% versus 17%). The "both" condition produced an intermediate rate, contrary to our expectation that it would be the most effective; however, this intermediate rate was not significantly different from the other two conditions.

These findings suggest that advertisements that contain autobiographical referencing can tamper with our personal childhood memories. Advertisers are probably not mentioning false details; they mention details that could be true. However, they are not true for everyone. You may have seen a picture of Mickey Mouse when you were at Disney, but you never actually met him or shaken hands with him. An ad may make you think you did. Because we view thousands of advertisements in the course of a typical month, could we all be unwitting subjects in a mass experiment on memory distortion?

Not everyone views eyewitness testimony with such skepticism, however (e.g., see Zaragoza, McCloskey, & Jamis, 1987). It is still not clear whether the information about the original event actually is displaced by, or is simply competing with, the subsequent misleading information. Some investigators have argued that psychologists need to know a great deal more about the circumstances that impair eyewitness testimony before impugning such testimony before a jury (McKenna, Treadway, & McCloskey, 1992). At present, the verdict on eyewitness testimony is still not in. The same can be said for repressed memories, considered in the next section.

Whatever may be the validity of eyewitness testimony for adults, it clearly is suspect for children (Ceci & Bruck, 1993, 1995). Children's recollections are particularly susceptible to distortion. Such distortion is especially likely when the children are asked leading questions, as in a courtroom setting. Consider some relevant facts (Ceci & Bruck, 1995). First, the younger the child is, the less reliable the testimony of that child can be expected to be. In particular, children of preschool age are much more susceptible to suggestive questioning that tries to steer them to a certain response than are school-age children or adults. Second, when a questioner is coercive or even just seems to want a particular answer, children can be quite susceptible to providing the adult with what he or she wants to hear. Given the pressures involved in court cases, such forms of questioning may be unfortunately prevalent. Third, children may believe that they recall observing things that others have said they observed. In other words, they hear a story about something that took place and then believe that they have observed what allegedly took place. Perhaps even more than eyewitness testimony from adults, the testimony of children must be interpreted with great caution.

Steps can be taken to enhance eyewitness identification (e.g., using methods to reduce potential biases, to reduce the pressure to choose a suspect from a limited set of options, and to ensure that each member of an array of suspects fits the description given by the eyewitness, yet offers diversity in other ways; described in Wells, 1993). In addition, some psychologists (e.g., Loftus, 1993a, 1993b) and many defense attorneys believe that jurors should be advised that the degree to which the eyewitness feels confident of her or his identification does not necessarily correspond to the degree to which the eyewitness is actually accurate in her or his identification of the defendant as being the culprit. At the same time, some psychologists (e.g., Egeth, 1993; Yuille, 1993) and many prosecutors believe that the existing evidence, based largely on simulated eyewitness studies rather than on actual eyewitness accounts, is not strong enough to risk attacking the credibility of eyewitness testimony when such testimony might send a true criminal to prison, preventing the person from committing further crimes.

Repressed Memories

Might you have been exposed to a traumatic event as a child but have been so traumatized by this event that you now cannot remember it? Some psychotherapists have begun using hypnosis and related techniques to elicit from people what are alleged to be repressed memories. Repressed memories are memories that are alleged to have been pushed down into unconsciousness because of the distress they cause. Such memories, according to the view of psychologists who believe in their existence, are very inaccessible. But they can·be dredged out (Briere & Conte, 1993).

Do repressed memories actually exist? Many psychologists strongly doubt their existence (Ceci & Loftus, 1994; Lindsay & Read, 1994; Loftus & Ketcham, 1994; Pennebaker & Memon, 1996; Roediger & McDermott, 1995, 2000). Others are at least highly skeptical (Bowers & Farvolden, 1996). First, some therapists inadvertently may be planting ideas in their clients' heads. In this way, they may be creating false memories of events that never took place. Indeed, creating false memories is relatively easy, even in people with no particular psychological problems. Such memories can be implanted by using ordinary, nonemotional stimuli (Roediger & McDermott, 1995). Second, showing that implanted memories are false is often extremely hard to do. Reported incidents often end up, as in the case of childhood sexual abuse, merely pitting one person's word against another (Schooler, 1994). At the present time, no compelling evidence points to the existence of such memories. But psychologists also have not reached the point where their existence can be ruled out definitively. Therefore, no clear conclusion can be reached at this time.

The Roediger-McDermott (1995) paradigm, which is adapted from work of Deese (1959), shows the effects of memory distortion. Participants receive a list of 15 words strongly associated with a critical but nonpresented word. For example, the participants might receive 15 words strongly related to the word "sleep" but never receive the word "sleep." The recognition rate for the nonpresented word (in this case, "sleep") was comparable to that for presented words.

This result has been replicated multiple times (McDermott, 1996; Schacter, Verfaellie, & Pradere, 1996).

Why are people so weak in distinguishing what they have heard from what they have not heard? One possibility is a *source-monitoring error*, which occurs when a person attributes a memory derived from one source to another source. Research by Marcia Johnson and her colleagues (Johnson, 1996; Johnson, Hashtroudi, & Lindsay, 1993; Lindsay & Johnson, 1991) suggests that people frequently have difficulties in *source monitoring*, or figuring out the origins of a memory. They may believe they read an article in a prestigious newspaper, such as the *New York Times*, when in fact they saw it in a tabloid on a supermarket shelf while waiting to check out. When people hear a list of words not containing a word that is highly associated with the other words, they may believe that their recall of that central word is from the list rather than from their minds.

Context Effects on Encoding and Retrieval

As studies of constructive memory show, our cognitive contexts for memory clearly influence our memory processes of encoding, storing, and retrieving information. Studies of expertise also show how existing schemas may provide a cognitive context for encoding, storing, and retrieving new information. Specifically, experts generally have more elaborated schemas than do novices in regard to their areas of expertise (e.g., Chase & Simon, 1973; Frensch & Sternberg, 1989). These schemas provide a cognitive context in which the experts can operate. They relatively easily can integrate and organize new information. They fill in gaps when provided with partial or even distorted information and visualize concrete aspects of verbal information. They also can implement appropriate metacognitive strategies for organizing and rehearsing new information. Clearly, expertise enhances our confidence in our recollected memories.

Another factor that enhances our confidence in recall is the perceived clarity—the vividness and richness of detail—of the experience and its context. When we are recalling a given experience, we often associate the degree of perceptual detail and intensity with the degree to which we are accurately remembering the experience (Johnson & associates, 1988; Johnson, Hatroudi, & Lindsay, 1993; Johnson, Nolde, & De Leonardis, 1996; Johnson & Raye, 1981). We feel greater confidence that our recollections are accurate when we perceive them with greater richness of detail. Although this heuristic for reality monitoring is generally effective, there are some situations in which factors other than accuracy of recall may lead to enhanced vividness and detail of our recollections (Neisser, 1982).

In particular, an oft-studied form of vivid memory is the **flashbulb memory**—a memory of an event so powerful that the person remembers the event as vividly as if it were indelibly preserved on film (Brown & Kulik, 1977). People old enough to recall the assassination of President John Kennedy may have flashbulb memories of this event. Some people also have flashbulb memories for the explosion of the space shuttle *Challenger*, the destruction of the World Trade Center on 9/11, or momentous events in their personal lives. The emotional intensity of an experience may enhance the likelihood that we will recall the particular experience (over other experiences) ardently and perhaps accurately (Bohannon, 1988). A related view is that a memory is most likely to become a flashbulb memory under three circumstances. These are that the memory trace is important to the individual, is surprising, and has an emotional effect on the individual (Conway, 1995).

Some investigators suggest that flashbulb memories may be more vividly recalled because of their emotional intensity. Other investigators, however, suggest that the vividness of recall may be the result of the effects of rehearsal. The idea here is that we frequently retell, or at least silently contemplate, our experiences of these momentous events. Perhaps our retelling also enhances the perceptual intensity of our recall (Bohannon, 1988). Other findings suggest that flashbulb memories may be perceptually rich (Neisser & Harsch, 1993). On this view, they may be recalled with relatively greater confidence in the accuracy of the memories (Weaver, 1993) but not actually be any more reliable or accurate than any other recollected memory, (Neisser & Harsch, 1993; Weaver, 1993). Suppose flashbulb memories are indeed more likely to be the subject of conversation or even silent reflection. Then perhaps, at each retelling of the experience, we reorganize and construct our memories such that the accuracy of our recall actually diminishes while the perceived vividness of recall increases over time. At present, researchers heatedly debate whether studies of such memories as a special process are a flash in the pan (e.g., Cohen, McCloskey, & Wible, 1990) or a flash of insight into memory processes (e.g., Schmidt & Bohannon, 1988).

The emotional intensity of a memorable event is not the only way in which emotions, moods, and states of consciousness affect memory. Our moods and states of consciousness also may provide a context for encoding that affects later retrieval of semantic memories. Thus, when we encode semantic information during a particular mood or state of consciousness, we may more readily retrieve that information when in the same state again (Baddeley, 1989; Bower, 1983). Regarding state of consciousness, something that is encoded when we are influenced by alcohol or other drugs may be re-trieved more readily while under those same influences again (Eich, 1995; J. E. Eich, 1980). On the whole, however, the "main effect" of alcohol and many drugs is stronger than the interaction. In other words, the depressing effect of alcohol and many drugs on memory is greater than the facilitating effect of recalling something in the same drugged state as when one encoded it.

In regard to mood, some investigators have suggested a factor that may maintain depression. In particular, the depressed person can more readily retrieve memories of previous sad experiences, which may further the continuation of the depression (Bad-deley, 1989). If psychologists or others can intervene to prevent the continuation of this vicious cycle, the person may begin to feel happier. As a result, other happy mem-ories may be more easily retrieved, thus further relieving the depression, and so on. Perhaps the folk-wisdom advice to "think happy thoughts" is not entirely unfounded. In fact, under laboratory conditions, participants seem more accurately to recall items that have pleasant associations than they recall items that have unpleasant associa-tions (Matlin & Underhill, 1979).

Emotions, moods, states of consciousness, schemas, and other features of our in-ternal context clearly affect memory retrieval. In addition, even our external contexts may affect our ability to recall information. We appear to be better able to recall in-formation when we are in the same physical context as the one in which we learned the material (Godden & Baddeley, 1975). In one experiment, 16 underwater divers were asked to learn a list of 40 unrelated words. Learning occurred either while the divers were on shore or while they were 20 feet beneath the sea. Later, they were asked to recall the words when either in the same environment as where they had learned them or in the other environment. Recall was better when it occurred in the same place as did the learning.

Even infants demonstrate context effects on memory. Consider an operant-conditioning experiment in which the infants could make a crib mobile move in interesting ways by kicking it. Three-month-olds (Butler & Rovee-Collier, 1989) or 6-month-olds (Borovsky & Rovee-Collier, 1990) were given an opportunity to kick a distinctive crib mobile in the same context (i.e., surrounded by a distinctive bumper lining the periphery of the crib) in which they first learned to kick it or in a different context. They kicked more strongly in the same context. The infants showed much less kicking when in a different context or when presented with a different mobile.

From these results, such learning seems highly context-dependent. However, in one set of studies, 3-month-olds (Rovee-Collier & DuFault, 1991) or 6-month-olds (Amabile & Rovee-Collier, 1991) were offered operant-conditioning experiences in multiple contexts for kicking a distinctive mobile. They were soon thereafter placed in a novel context. It was unlike any of the contexts for conditioning. The infants re-tained the memory. They kicked the mobile at high rates in the novel context. Thus, when information is encoded in various contexts, the information also seems to be re-trieved more readily in various contexts. This effect occurs at least when there is min-imal delay between the conditioning contexts and the novel context. However, con-sider what happened when the novel context occurred after a long delay. The infants did not show increased kicking. Nevertheless, they still showed context-dependent memory for kicking in the familiar contexts (Amabile & Rovee-Collier, 1991).

All of the preceding context effects may be viewed as an interaction between the context for encoding and the context for retrieval of encoded information. The results of various experiments on retrieval suggest that how items are encoded has a strong effect both on how and on how well items are retrieved. This relationship is called **encoding specificity**—what is recalled depends on what is encoded (Tulving & Thomson, 1973). Consider a rather dramatic example of encoding specificity. We know that recognition memory is virtually always better than recall. For example, generally recognizing a word that you have learned is easier than recalling it. After all, in recognition you have only to say whether you have seen the word. In recall, you only have to generate the word and then mentally confirm whether it appeared on the list.

In one experiment, Watkins and Tulving (1975) had participants learn a list of 24 paired associates, such as *ground-cold* and *crust-cake*. Participants were instructed to learn to associate each response (such as *cold*) with its stimulus word (such as *ground*). After participants had studied the word pairs, they were given an irrelevant task. Then they were given a recognition test with distracters. Participants were asked simply to circle the words they had seen previously. Participants recognized an average of 60% of the words from the list. Then, participants were provided with the 24 stimulus words. They were asked to recall the responses. Their cued recall was 73%. Thus, recall was better than recognition. Why? According to the encoding-specificity hypothesis, the stimulus was a better cue for the word than the word itself. The reason was that the words had been learned as paired associates.

As mentioned previously (see Chapter 5), the link between encoding and retrieval also may explain the self-reference effect (Greenwald & Banaji, 1989). Specifically, the main cause of the self-reference effect is not due to unique properties of self-referent cues. Rather, it is due to a more general principle of encoding and retrieval: When individuals generate their own cues for retrieval, they are much more potent than when other individuals do so. Other researchers have confirmed the importance of making cues meaningful to the individual to enhance memory. For example, consider what happened when participants made up their own retrieval cues. They were able to remember, almost without errors, lists of 500 and 600 words (Mantyla, 1986). For each word on a list, participants were asked to generate another word (the cue) that to them was an appropriate description or property of the target word. Later, they were given a list of their cue words. They were asked to recall the target word. Cues were most helpful when they were both *compatible* with the target word, and *distinctive*, in that they would not tend to generate a large number of related words. For example, if you are given the word "coat," then "jacket" might be both compatible and distinctive as a cue. However, suppose you came up with the word "wool" as a cue. That cue might make you think of a number of words, such as "fabric" and "sheep," that are not the target word.

To summarize, retrieval interacts strongly with encoding. Suppose you are studying for a test and want to recall well at the time of testing. Organize the information you are studying in a way that appropriately matches the way in which you will be expected to recall it. Similarly, you will recall information better if the level of processing for encoding matches the level of processing for retrieval (Moscovitch & Craik, 1976).

Memory Development

Many changes occur in memory with development (Bauer & Van Abbema, 2003). What are some of these changes?

Metacognitive Skills and Memory Development

Some researchers also have suggested that older children may have greater processing resources (Kail & Bisanz, 1992), such as attentional resources and working memory. These resources may underlie the overall greater speed of cognitive processing of older children. According to this view, the reason that older children seem able to process information more quickly than younger children may be because the older children can hold more information for active processing. Hence, in addition to being able to organize information into increasingly large and complex chunks, older children may be able to hold more chunks of information in working memory.

Children appear to develop and use increasing metamemory skills and various other kinds of metacognitive skills. These skills involve the understanding and control of cognitive processes. Examples are monitoring and modifying one's own cognitive processes while one is engaged in tackling cognitive tasks (Brown, 1978; Flavell & Wellman, 1977). Many information-processing researchers have been interested in the specific metacognitive skills of older children. An example is work on the understanding of appearance and reality. For example, 4- and 5-year-old children were shown imitation objects such as a sponge that looked exactly like a rock (Flavell, Flavell, & Green, 1983). The researchers encouraged the children to play with the imitations so they could become thoroughly familiar with the objects. In this way, the children would see clearly that the fakes were not what they appeared to be. Children then had to answer questions about the identity of the objects. Afterward, the children were asked to view the objects through a blue plastic sheet and to make color judgments about the objects. The sheet distorted the perceived hues of the objects. The children also were asked to make size judgments while viewing the objects through a magnifying glass. The children were fully aware that they were viewing the objects through these intermediaries.

The children's errors formed an interesting pattern. There were two fundamental kinds of errors. When asked to report reality (the way the object actually was), the children would sometimes report appearance (the way the object looked through the blue plastic or the magnifying glass). When asked to report appearance, they would sometimes report the reality. In other words, 4- and 5-year-old children did not yet clearly perceive the distinction between appearance and reality.

Actually, many scholars would agree with the observation that young children often fail to distinguish appearance from reality. Their failure to conserve quantity also may be attributed to their attention to the change in appearance, rather than to the stability of the quantity. Children also increasingly profit from and eventually even seek out feedback regarding the outcomes of their cognitive efforts. These changes in encoding, memory organization and storage, metacognition, and use of feedback seem to affect children's cognitive development across many specific domains. In addition, however, some cognitive-developmental changes seem to be domain specific.

The use of external memory aids, rehearsal, and many other memory strategies seems to come naturally to almost all of us as adults—so much so that we may take for granted that we have always done it; we have not. Lynne Appel and her colleagues (1972) designed an experiment to discover the extent to which young children spontaneously rehearse. They showed colored pictures of common objects to children at three grade levels: preschoolers, first-graders, and fifth-graders. Children were instructed either to "look at" the names of 15 pictures or to "remember" the names for a later test.

When children were instructed just to look at the pictures, almost no children exhibited rehearsal. In the memory condition, some of the young children showed some—but not much—rehearsal. Very few of the preschoolers seemed to know that rehearsing would be a good idea when they would later be asked to recall information. Moreover, the performance of the preschoolers was no better in the memory condition than in the looking condition.

Older children performed better. A major difference between the memory of younger and older children (as well as adults) is not in basic mechanisms, but in learned strategies, such as rehearsal (Flavell & Wellman, 1977). Young children seriously overestimate their ability to recall information. They rarely spontaneously use rehearsal strategies when asked to recall items. That is, young children seem not to know about many memory-enhancing strategies.

In addition, even when young children do know about such strategies, they do not always use them. For example, even when trained to use rehearsal strategies in one task, most do not transfer the use of that strategy. They do not carry over their learning from one task to other tasks (Flavell & Wellman, 1977). Thus, young children appear to lack not only the knowledge of strategies, but also the inclination to use them when they do know about them. Older children understand that to retain words in short-term memory, they need to rehearse. Younger children do not have this understanding. In a nutshell, younger children lack metamemory skills.

Whether children rehearse is not just a function of age. Mentally retarded children are much less likely to rehearse spontaneously than are children of normal intelligence (Brown & associates, 1973). Indeed, if such children are trained to rehearse, their performance can be improved greatly (Belmont & Butterfield, 1971; Butterfield, Wambold, & Belmont, 1973). However, the mentally retarded performers will not always spontaneously transfer their learning to other tasks. For example, if the children are taught to rehearse with lists of numbers but then are presented with a list of animals, they may have to be taught all over again to rehearse for the new kinds of items, as well as for the old.

Culture, experience, and environmental demands also affect the use of memory-enhancing strategies. For example, Western children generally have more formal schooling than non-Western children do. As a result, they are given much more practice using rehearsal strategies for remembering isolated bits of information. In contrast, Guatemalan children and Australian aboriginal children generally have many more opportunities to become adept at using memory-enhancing strategies that rely on spatial location and arrangements of objects (Kearins, 1981; Rogoff, 1986).

Another aspect of metamemory skill involves cognitive monitoring. In monitoring, the individual tracks and, as needed, readjusts an ongoing train of thought. Cognitive monitoring may consist of several related skills (Brown, 1978; see also Brown

& DeLoache, 1978). For instance, you are realizing "what you know and what you do not know" (Brown, 1978, p. 82). You learn to be aware of your own mind and the degree of your own understanding (Holt, 1964). Other work on the development of cognitive monitoring proposes a distinction between self-monitoring and self-regulation strategies (Nelson & Naren, 1994). Self-monitoring is a bottom-up process of keeping track of current understanding, involving the improving ability to predict memory performance accurately. Self-regulation is a top-down process of central executive control over planning and evaluation. Children benefit from training in using such cognitive monitoring processes to enhance their use of appropriate strategies (see Schneider & Bjorklund, 1998).

Recall also that physiological maturation of the brain and increasing content knowledge may partially explain why adults and older children generally perform better on memory tests than do younger children. These physiological and experience-based changes augment the changes in memory processes. Examples are increased knowledge about and inclination to use metamemory strategies. The goal of such strategies is to be able eventually to retrieve stored information at will.

An important metacognitive development is the acquisition of a theory of mind—that is, an understanding of how the mind operates (Keil, 1999; Perner, 1998; 1999). As children grow older, their theory of mind becomes more sophisticated. Consider an example (Perner, 1999, p. 207): "Maxi puts his chocolate into the cupboard. He goes out to play. While he is outside he can't see that his mother comes and transfers the chocolate from the cupboard into the table drawer. She then leaves to visit a friend. When Maxi comes home to get his chocolate, where will he look for it?" Children below the age of 3 typically give the wrong answer, believing that Maxi will search for the chocolate in the drawer where it actually is. By age 3, some children start to get the problem right. By 4 years of age, most children solve the problem correctly, although even some 5- and 6-year-olds still make errors (Ruffman & associates, 1998). Autistic children seem to lack or have a seriously defective theory of mind (Baron-Cohen, Leslie, & Frith, 1985; Perner, 1999).

This chapter and the previous chapter have indicated many situations in which knowledge and memory interact, such as when prior knowledge influences encoding and retrieval. The following two chapters describe how we represent knowledge. They emphasize the roles of mental imagery and semantic knowledge.

Key Themes

This chapter illustrates several of the key themes first presented in Chapter 1.

First, it highlights the issue of validity of causal inference versus ecological validity. Some researchers, such as Mahzarin Banaji and Robert Crowder, have argued that laboratory research yields findings that maximize not only experimental control, but also ecological validity. Ulric Neisser has disagreed, suggesting that if one wishes to study everyday memory, one must study it in everyday settings. Ultimately, the two kinds of research together are likely to maximize our understanding of memory phenomena. Typically, there is no one right way to do research. Rather, we learn the most when we use a variety of methods that converge on a set of common findings.

Secondly, the chapter raises the issue of domain specificity versus domain generality. Mnemonics discussed in this chapter work better in certain domains than they do in others. For example, you may be able to devise mnemonics better if you are highly familiar with a domain, such as was the case for the runner studied by Chase, Ericsson, and Faloon (discusssed in Chapter 5). In general, the more knowledge you have about a domain, the easier it will be to chunk information in that domain.

Thirdly, the chapter raises an interesting issue of rationalism versus empiricism. This issue is the extent to which courts should rely on empirical evidence from psychological research to guide what they do. To what extent should the credibility of witnesses be determined by rational considerations (e.g., were they at the scene of a crime, or are they known to be trustworthy?) and to what extent by empirical considerations revealed by psychological research (e.g., being at the scene of a crime does not guarantee credible testimony, and people's judgments of trustworthiness are often incorrect)? Court systems often work on the basis of rational considerations—of what should be. Psychological research reveals what is.

Get some friends and/or family members to help you again. Tell them that you are going to read a list of words, and as soon as you finish, they are to write down as many words as they can remember in any order they wish. Read the following words to them about one second apart: book, peace, window, run, box, harmony, hat, voice, tree, begin, anchor, hollow, floor, area, tomato, concept, arm, rule, lion, hope. After giving them enough time to try to remember the words, total up their number of recollections in the following groups of four: (1) book, peace, window, run; (2) box, harmony, hat, voice; (3) tree, begin, anchor, hollow; (4) floor, area, tomato, concept; (5) arm, rule, lion, hope. Most likely, your friends and family members will remember more from groups 1 and 5 than from groups 2, 3, and 4, with group 3 the least recalled group. This exercise demonstrates the serial-position curve. Save the recollections for a demonstration for Chapter 7.

Summary

1. **What have cognitive psychologists discovered regarding how we encode information for storing it in memory?** Encoding of information in short-term memory appears to be largely, although not exclusively, acoustic in form. Information in short-term memory is susceptible to acoustic confusability—that is, errors based on sounds of words. But there is some visual and semantic encoding of information in short-term memory. Information in long-term memory appears to be encoded primarily in a semantic form. Thus, confusions tend to be in terms of meanings rather than in terms of the sounds of words. In addition, some evidence points to the existence of visual encoding, as well as of acoustic encoding, in long-term storage.

Transfer of information into long-term storage may be facilitated by several factors. One is rehearsal of the information, particularly if the information is elaborated meaningfully. A second is organization, such as categorization of the information. A third is the use of mnemonic devices. And a fourth is the use of external memory aids, such as writing lists or taking notes. In addition, people tend to remember better when knowledge is acquired through distributed practice across various study sessions, rather than through massed practice. But the distribution of time during any given study session does not seem to affect transfer into long-term memory. The effects of distributed practice may be due to a hippocampal-based mechanism that results in rapid encoding of new information to be integrated with existing memory systems over time, perhaps during sleep.

2. **What affects our ability to retrieve information from memory?** Studying retrieval from long-term memory is difficult due to problems of differentiating retrieval from other memory processes. It also is difficult to differentiate accessibility from availability. Retrieval of information from short-term memory appears to be in the form of serial, exhaustive processing. This implies that a person always sequentially checks all information on a list. Nevertheless, some data may be interpreted as allowing for the possibility of self-terminating serial processing and even of parallel processing.

3. **How does what we know or what we learn affect what we remember?** Two of the main theories of forgetting in short-term memory are decay theory and interference theory. Interference theory distinguishes between retroactive interference and proactive interference. Assessing the effects of decay, while ruling out both interference and rehearsal effects, is much harder. But some evidence of distinctive decay effects has been found. Interference also seems to influence long-term memory, at least during the period of consolidation. This period may continue for several years after the initial memorable experience.

Memory appears to be not only reconstructive—a reproduction of what was learned, based on recalled data and on inferences from only those data. It also is constructive—influenced by attitudes, subsequently acquired information, and schemas based on past knowledge. As shown by the effects of existing schemas on the construction of memory, schemas affect memory processes. So do other internal contextual factors, such as emotional intensity of a memorable experience, mood, and even state of consciousness. In addition, environmental context cues during encoding seem to affect later retrieval. Encoding specificity refers to the fact that what is recalled depends largely on what is encoded. How information is encoded at the time of learning will greatly affect how it is later recalled. One of the most effective means of enhancing recall is for the individual to generate meaningful cues for subsequent retrieval.

4. **How does memory develop with age?** Memory generally improves with age. The causes are many, but increased metacognitive skills seem to be essential for memory development to occur. Older children develop more advanced theories of mind. Children with autism may lack such theories.

Thinking about Thinking: Factual, Analytical, Creative, and Practical Questions

1. In what forms do we encode information for brief memory storage versus long-term memory storage?

2. What is the evidence for encoding specificity? Cite at least three sources of supporting evidence.

3. What is the main difference between two of the proposed mechanisms by which we forget information?

4. Compare and contrast some of the views regarding flashbulb memory.

5. Suppose that you are an attorney defending a client who is being prosecuted solely on the basis of eyewitness testimony. How could you demonstrate to members of the jury the frailty of eyewitness testimony?

6. Use the chapter-opening example from Bransford and Johnson as an illustration to make up a description of a common procedure without labeling the procedure. Try having someone read your description and then recall the procedure.

7. Make a list of 10 or more unrelated items you need to memorize. Choose one of the mnemonic devices mentioned in this chapter, and describe how you would apply the device to memorizing the list of items. Be specific.

8. What are three things you have learned about memory that can help you to learn new information so that you can effectively recall the information over the long term?

Key Terms

accessibility
autobiographical memory
availability
consolidation
constructive
decay
decay theory
distributed practice
encoding

encoding specificity
flashbulb memory
interference
interference theory
massed practice
metacognition
metamemory
mnemonic devices
primacy effect

proactive interference
recency effect
reconstructive
rehearsal
retrieval (memory)
retroactive interference
storage (memory)

 Explore CogLab by going to http://coglab.wadsworth.com. Answer the questions required by your instructor from the student manual that accompanies CogLab.

Brown-Peterson
False Memory
Serial Position
Sternberg Search

Von Restorff Effect
Encoding Specificity
Forgot It All Along
Remember/Know

Annotated Suggested Reading

Schacter, D. L. (2002). *The seven sins of memory*. New York: Mariner. An interesting account of why people forget things they might otherwise remember. The book can be read by people with only a minimal background in cognitive psychology.

Representation and Manipulation of Knowledge in Memory: Images and Propositions

EXPLORING COGNITIVE PSYCHOLOGY

1. What are some of the major hypotheses regarding how knowledge is represented in the mind?

2. What are some of the characteristics of mental imagery?

3. How does knowledge representation benefit from both analogical images and symbolic propositions?

4. How may conceptual knowledge and expectancies influence the way we use images?

5. How do spatial skills develop?

Look carefully at the photos depicted in Figure 7.1. Describe to yourself what two of these people look like and sound like. Clearly, none of these people can truly exist in a physical form inside your mind. How are you able to imagine and describe them? You must have in your mind some form of *mental representation*, something that stands for something else, of what you know about them (Thagard, 1995; Von Eckardt, 1993, 1999). More generally, you use **knowledge representation,** the form for what you know in your mind about things, ideas, events, and so on that exist outside of your mind.

Mental Representation of Knowledge

Ideally, cognitive psychologists would love to be able to observe directly how each of us represents knowledge. It would be as if we could take a videotape or a series of snapshots of ongoing representations of knowledge in the human mind. Unfortunately, direct empirical methods for observing knowledge representation are not available now. Moreover, such methods are unlikely to be available in the immediate future. When direct empirical methods are unavailable, several alternative methods remain. For one thing, we can ask people to describe their own knowledge representations and knowledge-representation processes. Unfortunately, none of us has conscious access to our own knowledge-representation processes. And self-report information about these processes is highly unreliable (Pinker, 1985).

Another possibility is the rationalist approach. In this approach, we try to deduce logically the most reasonable account of how people represent knowledge. For centuries, philosophers have done exactly that. In classic epistemology—the study of the nature, origins, and limits of human knowledge—philosophers distinguished between two kinds of knowledge structures. The first is **declarative knowledge**, knowledge of facts that can be stated. Examples are the date of your birth, the name of your best friend, or the way a rabbit looks. The second kind of knowledge is **procedural knowledge**, knowledge of procedures that can be implemented. Examples are the steps involved in tying your shoelaces, adding a column of numbers, or driving a car. The distinction is between *knowing that* and *knowing how* (Ryle, 1949).

FIGURE 7.1

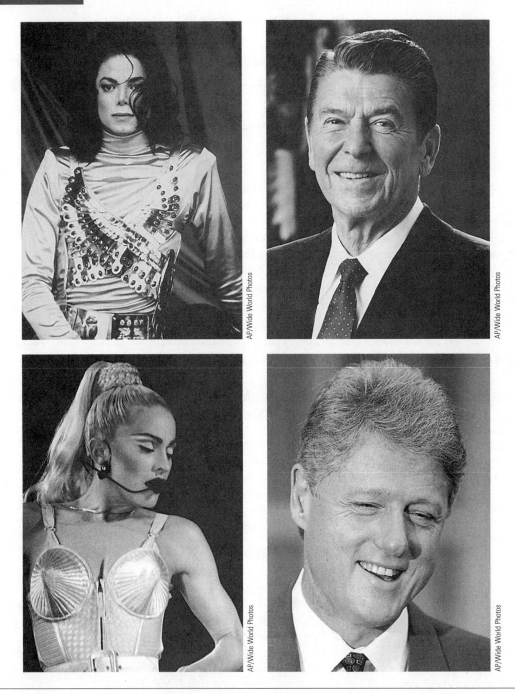

Look at each of these photos carefully. Next, close your eyes, and picture two of the people represented—people whom you have heard speak or sing. Without looking again at the photos, mentally compare the voices and the appearances of the two people you have chosen.

Cognitive psychologists have made extensive use of rationalist insights as a starting-point for understanding cognition. But they rarely are content with rationalist descriptions alone. Instead, they seek some kind of empirical support for the insights proposed in rationalist accounts of cognition. There are two main sources of empirical data on knowledge representation. These are standard laboratory experiments and neuropsychological studies.

In experimental work, researchers indirectly study knowledge representation. They do so by observing how people handle various cognitive tasks that require the manipulation of mentally represented knowledge. In neuropsychological studies, researchers typically use one of two methods. One is to observe how the normal brain responds to various cognitive tasks involving knowledge representation. The other is to observe the links between various deficits in knowledge representation and associated pathologies in the brain.

External Representations: Pictures versus Words

In this chapter, we focus on the distinction between knowledge represented in mental pictures and knowledge represented in more symbolic forms, such as words or abstract propositions. Of course, cognitive psychologists chiefly are interested in our internal, mental representations of what we know. But to help our understanding, we consider first how external representations in words differ from such representations in pictures.

Some ideas are better and more easily represented in pictures and others in words. For example, suppose someone asks you, "What is the shape of a chicken egg?" You may find drawing easier than describing an egg. For many geometric shapes and concrete objects, pictures do seem to express myriad words about the object in an economical form. However, what if someone asks you, "What is justice?" Describing such an abstract concept in words would be very difficult. Doing so pictorially would be even harder.

As Figure 7.2 (a) and (b) show, both pictures and words may be used to represent things and ideas. But neither form of representation actually retains all of the characteristics of what is being represented. For example, neither the word "cat" nor the picture of the cat actually eats fish, meows, or purrs when petted. Both the word "cat" and the picture of this cat are distinctive representations of "catness." Each type of representation has distinctive characteristics.

As you just observed, the picture is relatively *analogous* to the real-world object it represents. The picture shows concrete attributes, such as shape and relative size. These attributes are similar to the features and properties of the real-world object the picture represents. Even if you cover up a portion of the figure of the cat, what remains is still analogous to a part of a cat. Under typical circumstances, most aspects of the picture may be grasped simultaneously. But you may scan the picture, zoom in for a closer look, or zoom out to see the big picture. Even when scanning or zooming, however, you do not have to follow any arbitrary rules for looking at features of the picture from top to bottom, left to right, and so on.

Unlike a picture of a cat, the word "cat" is a **symbolic representation**, meaning that the relationship between the word and what it represents is simply arbitrary. There is nothing inherently catlike about the word. Suppose you cover up part of the

FIGURE 7.2

(a)

(b) The cat is under the table.

(c) UNDER (CAT, TABLE)

We may represent things and ideas in pictures or in words. Neither pictures nor words capture all the characteristics of what they represent, and each more readily captures some kinds of information than other kinds. Some cognitive psychologists have suggested that we have (a) some mental representations that resemble pictorial, analogous images; (b) other mental representations that are highly symbolic, like words; and perhaps even (c) more fundamental propositional representations that are in a pure abstract "mentalese" that is neither verbal nor pictorial, which cognitive psychologists often represent in this highly simplified shorthand.

INVESTIGATING COGNITIVE PSYCHOLOGY

Observe Figure 7.2. What is the shape of the word "cat"? What is the shape of the picture of the cat? Cover part of the word. Now explain how what is left relates to the characteristics of a cat. Cover part of the picture. Now explain how what is left relates to the characteristics of a cat.

word. The remaining visible part no longer bears even a symbolic relationship to any part of the object it represents. Furthermore, because symbols are arbitrary, their use requires the application of rules. For example, in forming words, the sounds or letters also must be sequenced according to rules (e.g., "c-a-t," not "a-c-t" or "t-c-a"). In forming sentences, the words also must be sequenced according to rules. For example, one can say "the cat is under the table," not "table under cat the is").

Symbolic representations such as the word "cat" capture some kinds of information but not other kinds of information. The dictionary defines "cat" as "a carnivorous mammal (*Felis catus*) long domesticated as a pet and for catching rats and mice" (*Merriam-Webster's Collegiate Dictionary*, 1993). Suppose our own mental representations for the meanings of words resemble those of the dictionary. Then the word "cat" connotes an animal that eats meat ("carnivorous"), nurses its young ("mammal"), and so on. This information is abstract and general. It may be applied to any number of specific cats having any fur color or pattern. To represent additional characteristics, we must use additional words. Examples would be black, Persian, or calico.

The picture of the cat does not convey any of the abstract information conveyed by the word regarding what the cat eats, whether it nurses its young, and so on. However, the picture conveys a great deal of concrete information about this specific cat. For example, it communicates the exact position of the cat's legs, the angle at which we are viewing the cat, the length of the cat's tail, whether both of its eyes are open, and so on.

Pictures and words also represent relationships in different ways. The picture in Figure 7.2 (a) shows the spatial relationship between the cat and the table. For any given picture showing a cat and a table, the spatial (positional) relationship (e.g., beside, above, below, behind) will be represented concretely in the picture. In contrast, when using words, spatial relationships between things must be stated explicitly by a discrete symbol, such as a preposition. An example would be, "The cat is *under* the table." More abstract relationships, however, such as class membership, often are implied by the meanings of the words. Examples would be that cats are mammals or that tables are items of furniture. But abstract relationships rarely are implied through pictures.

To summarize, pictures aptly capture concrete and spatial information in a manner analogous to whatever they represent. Words handily capture abstract and categorical information in a manner that is symbolic of whatever they represent. Pictorial representations convey all features simultaneously. In general, any rules for creating or understanding pictures pertain to the analogous relationship between the picture and what it represents. They help ensure as much similarity as possible between the two. Representations in words usually convey information sequentially. They do so according to arbitrary rules that have little to do with what the words represent. But the words have a lot to do with the structure of the symbol system for using words. Each kind of representation is well suited to some purposes but not to others. For example, blueprints and identification photos serve different purposes than essays and memos do.

Now we have some preliminary ideas about external representations of knowledge. Let's turn to considering internal representations of knowledge. Specifically, how do we represent what we know in our minds? Do we have mental scenarios (pictures) and mental narratives (words)? In subsequent chapters on information processing and language, we discuss various kinds of symbolic mental representations. In this chapter, we focus on mental pictures.

Courtesy of Dr. Stephen M. Kosslyn

Stephen M. Kosslyn is a professor of psychology at Harvard University. He is best known for his research showing that imagery is not a single, undifferentiated faculty but rather involves a number of distinct processes. He also has made major contributions to neuropsychology by identifying discrete areas of the brain associated with specific imagery processes.

Mental Imagery

Imagery is the mental representation of things that are not currently being sensed by the sense organs (Behrmann, Kosslyn, & Jeannerod, 1996; Thomas, 2003). We often have images for objects, events, settings. For example, recall one of your first experiences on a college campus. What were some of the sights, sounds, and even smells you sensed at that time? Might they have included cut grass, tall buildings, or tree-lined paths? These sensations are not immediately available to you at this moment. But you still can imagine them. In fact, mental imagery may represent things that have never been observed by your senses at any time. For example, imagine what it would be like to travel down the Amazon River. Mental images even may represent things that do not exist at all outside the mind of the person creating the image. For example, imagine how you would look if you had a third eye in the center of your forehead.

Imagery may involve mental representations in any of the sensory modalities, such as hearing, smell, or taste. Imagine the sound of a fire alarm, your favorite song, or your nation's anthem. Now imagine the smell of a rose, of fried bacon, or of an onion. Finally, imagine the taste of a lemon, of a pickle, or of your favorite candy. At least hypothetically, each form of mental representation is subject to investigation. Researchers have studied each of the sensory representations (e.g., Intons-Peterson, 1992; Intons-Peterson, Russell, & Dressel, 1992; Reisberg & associates, 1989; Reisberg, Wilson, & Smith, 1991; Smith, Reisberg, & Wilson, 1992).

Nonetheless, most research on imagery in cognitive psychology has focused on visual imagery. Such imagery includes the mental representation of visual knowledge such as objects or settings that are not presently visible to the eyes. Apparently, researchers are just like other people. Most of us are more aware of visual imagery than of other forms of imagery. When students kept a diary of their mental images, the students reported many more visual images than auditory, smell, touch, or taste images (Kosslyn & associates, 1990).

We use visual images to solve problems and to answer questions involving objects (Kosslyn, 1990; Kosslyn & Rabin, 1999). Which is darker red—a cherry or an apple? How many windows are there in your house or apartment? How do you get from your home to your first class of the day? How do you fit together the pieces of a puzzle or the component parts of an engine, a building, or a model? According to Kosslyn, to solve problems and answer questions such as these, we visualize the objects in question. In doing so, we mentally represent the images.

Many psychologists outside of cognitive psychology are interested in applications of mental imagery to other fields in psychology. Such applications include using guided-imagery techniques for controlling pain and for strengthening immune responses and otherwise promoting health. Such techniques are also helpful in overcoming psychological problems, such as phobias and other anxiety disorders. Design engineers, biochemists, physicists, and many other scientists and technologists use imagery to think about various structures and processes and to solve problems in their chosen fields. Not everyone is equally facile in creating and manipulating mental images, however. Research in applied settings and in the laboratory indicates that some of us are better able to create mental images than are others (Reisberg & associates, 1986).

In just what form do we represent images in our minds? According to an extreme view of imagery, all images of everything we ever sense may be stored as exact copies of physical images. Realistically, to store every observed physical image in the brain seems impossible. The capacity of the brain and the structures and processes used by the brain would be inadequate to such a task (Kosslyn, 1981; Kosslyn & Pomerantz, 1977). Note the simple example in the "Investigating Cognitive Psychology" box.

Dual-Code Theory: Analogical Images versus Symbols

According to dual-code theory, we use both imagined and verbal codes for representing information (Paivio, 1969, 1971). These two codes organize information into

IN THE LAB OF S. M. KOSSLYN

Courtesy of Dr. Stephen M. Kosslyn

Most cognitive abilities—such as memory, perception, reasoning, or imagery—intuitively seem to be accomplished by individual faculties. However, research in cognitive neuroscience has shown that these abilities are not unitary and undifferentiated but instead correspond to a collection of distinct functions. Recent work in our laboratory is aimed at discovering how people differ in their abilities to use different aspects of imagery. For example, try to answer the following questions. Are some of them easier than others?

- Does a Star of David contain two overlapping triangles?
- Do tigers tend to have narrower stripes than do zebras?
- If you imagine a block letter F superimposed on a block letter L, would the combination produce a new letter?
- If the upper case version of the letter "n" were rotated 90 degrees clockwise, would it be another letter?

Although imagery tends to be used in every case, distinct processes are used to answer the different types of questions. The first one concerns "seeing" an embedded property of a shape; the second one requires visualizing with high resolution; the third one requires mentally amalgamating separate shapes to form a whole; and the fourth question requires "mentally rotating" a pattern in an image. We asked whether people differ in their abilities to carry out these sorts of im-

agery, and whether those differences reflect the way their brains work. In one study, Kosslyn & associates (2004) used positron emission tomography (PET) to examine variations in the amount of blood flow in different people's brains while they performed different imagery tasks. We sought to discover whether differences in blood flow in different parts of the brain (which reflect differences in how strongly activated the parts are) predict how well people perform different imagery tasks. In this study, the tasks were specifically designed to assess how well people can: a) divide up imaged forms while "looking" for specific parts; b) create images with high resolution; c) build up images from separate segments; and, d) transform (rotate) images. In addition to monitoring the participants' brains, we recorded the amount of time they required to evaluate each stimulus and their accuracy level. After the study was complete, we computed a mean response time and accuracy level for each person for each task, and correlated these measures with the amount of blood flow in different brain areas while they performed the task. The most interesting finding was that performance in different tasks was predicted by variations in blood flow in different brain areas. This finding shows that the four facets of imagery rely on largely distinct processes. In more recent work, using functional magnetic resonance imaging (fMRI), we (Ganis & associates, in preparation) have found that changes in activation in different brain areas predict changes in performance of different tasks. The emerging bottom line is that different tasks draw on different combinations of processes, and that these processes rely (at least in part) on different brain areas.

knowledge that can be acted on, stored somehow, and even later retrieved for subsequent use. According to Paivio, mental images are analogue codes. **Analogue codes** are a form of knowledge representation that preserves the main perceptual features of whatever is being represented for the physical stimuli we observe in our environment. For example, trees and rivers might be represented by analogue codes. Just as the movements of the hands on an analogue clock are analogous to the passage of time, the mental images we form in our minds are analogous to the physical stimuli we observe.

INVESTIGATING COGNITIVE PSYCHOLOGY	Look at your face in a mirror. Gradually turn your head from far right (to see yourself out of your left peripheral vision) to far left. Now tilt your head as far forward as you can then tilt it as far back as you can. All the while, make sure you still are seeing your reflection. Now make a few different expressions, perhaps even talking to yourself to exaggerate your facial movements. How could you possibly store a moving picture or even a series of separate images of your face or of other rotating objects?

In contrast, according to Paivio, our mental representations for words chiefly are represented in a symbolic code. A *symbolic code* is a form of knowledge representation that has been chosen arbitrarily to stand for something and that does not perceptually resemble whatever is being represented. Just as a digital watch uses arbitrary symbols (typically, numerals) to represent the passage of time, our minds use arbitrary symbols (words and combinations of words) to represent many ideas. A symbol may be anything that is arbitrarily designated to stand for something other than itself. For example, we recognize that the numeral "9" is a symbol for the concept of "nineness." It represents a quantity of nine of something. But nothing about the symbol in any way would suggest its meaning. Concepts like *justice* and *peace* would be represented symbolically. We arbitrarily have designated this symbol to represent the concept. But "9" has meaning only because we use it to represent a deeper concept.

INVESTIGATING COGNITIVE PSYCHOLOGY	To get an intuitive sense of how you may use each of the two kinds of representations, think about how you mentally represent all the facts you know about cats. Use your mental definition of the word "cat" and all the inferences you may draw from your mental image of a cat. Which kind of representation is more helpful for answering the following questions: Is a cat's tail long enough to reach the tip of the cat's nose if the cat is stretching to full length? Do cats like to eat fish? Are the back legs and the front legs of a cat exactly the same size and shape? Are cats mammals? Which is wider—a cat's nose or a cat's eye? Which kinds of mental representations were the most valuable for answering each of these questions?

Paivio also found some empirical support for his dual-code theory. He noted that verbal information seems to be processed differently than is imaginal information. For example, in one study, participants were shown both a rapid sequence of pictures and a sequence of words (Paivio, 1969). They then were asked to recall the words or the pictures in one of two ways. One way was at random, so that they recalled as many as possible, regardless of the order in which the items were presented. The other way was in the correct sequence. Participants more easily recalled the pictures when they were allowed to do so in any order. But they more readily recalled the sequence in which the words were presented than the sequence for the pictures.

Other researchers also supported the notion that our minds use one system for representing verbal information and a different system for representing imaginal information. For example, it has been hypothesized that actual visual perception could interfere with simultaneous visual imagery. Similarly, the need to produce a verbal response could interfere with the simultaneous mental manipulation of words. A classic investigation tested this notion (Brooks, 1968). Participants performed either a visual task or a verbal task. The visual task involved answering questions requiring judgments about a picture that was presented briefly. The verbal task involved answering questions requiring judgments about a sentence that was stated briefly. Participants expressed their responses verbally (saying "yes" or "no" aloud), visually (pointing to an answer), or manually (tapping with one hand to agree and the other to disagree). The two interference conditions were a visual task requiring a visual (pointing) response and a verbal task requiring a verbal response. Interference was measured by slow-downs in response times. Brooks confirmed his hypothesis. Participants did show slower response times in performing the imaginal task when asked to respond using a competing visual display, as compared with when they were using a noninterfering response medium (i.e., either verbal or manual). Similarly, his participants showed more interference in performing the verbal task when asked to respond using a competing verbal form of expression, as compared with how they performed when responding manually or by using a visual display. Thus, a response involving visual perception can interfere with a task involving manipulations of a visual image. Similarly, a response involving verbal expression can interfere with a task involving mental manipulations of a verbal statement. These findings suggest the use of two distinct codes for mental representation of knowledge. The two codes are an imaginal (analogical) code and a verbal (symbolic) code.

Propositional Theory

Not everyone subscribes to the dual-code theory. An alternative theory of knowledge representation is sometimes termed a conceptual-propositional theory, or just a propositional theory (Anderson & Bower, 1973; Pylyshyn, 1973, 1978, 1981, 1984). According to this view, we do not store mental representations in the form of images. Rather, our mental representations (sometimes called "mentalese") more closely resemble the abstract form of a proposition. A proposition is the meaning underlying a particular relationship among concepts. According to this view, images are *epiphenomena*, secondary phenomena that occur as a result of other cognitive processes. Anderson and Bower have moved beyond their original conceptualization. Neither believes today in the idea that propositions are at the base of all mental representations. Others, such as Pylyshyn, however, still hold to this position.

How would a propositional representation work? Consider an example. To describe Figure 7.2 (*a*), you could say, "The table is above the cat." You also could say, "The cat is beneath the table." Both of these statements indicate the same relationship as "Above the cat is the table." With a little extra work, you probably could come up with a dozen or more ways of verbally representing this relationship. See this notion in Figure 7.2 (*a*). Of course, imagery theorists would discount these explanations. They would explain the visual phenomena largely in terms of visual imagery and the neuropsychological mechanisms underlying it (Farah, 2000; Farah & Ratcliff, 1994; Hampson, Marks, & Richardson, 1990; Kosslyn, 1994a, 1994b; Kosslyn & Thompson, 2000; Logie & Denis, 1991).

Logicians have devised a shorthand means, called "predicate calculus," of expressing the underlying meaning of a relationship. It attempts to strip away the various superficial differences in the ways we describe the deeper meaning of a proposition:

[Relationship between elements]([Subject element],[Object element])

The logical expression for the proposition underlying the relationship between the cat and the table is shown in Figure 7.2 (*c*). This logical expression, of course, would need to be translated by the brain into a format suitable for its internal mental representation.

Using Propositions

It is easy to see why the hypothetical construct of propositions is so widely accepted among cognitive psychologists. Propositions may be used to describe any kind of relationship. Examples of relationships include actions of one thing on another, attributes of a thing, positions of a thing, class membership of a thing, and so on, as shown in Table 7.1. In addition, any number of propositions may be combined to represent more complex relationships, images, or series of words. An example would be "The furry mouse bit the cat, who is now hiding under the table." The key idea is that the propositional form of mental representation is neither in words nor in images. Rather, it is in an abstract form representing the underlying meanings of knowledge. Thus, a proposition for a sentence would not retain the acoustic or visual properties of the words. Similarly, a proposition for a picture would not retain the exact perceptual form of the picture (Clark & Chase, 1972).

According to the propositional view (Clark & Chase, 1972), both images (e.g., of the cat and the table in Figure 7.2 [*a*]) and verbal statements (e.g., in Figure 7.2 [*b*]) are mentally represented in terms of their deep meanings. That is, they are represented as propositions, not as specific images or statements. According to propositional theory, imaginal and verbal information are encoded and stored as propositions. Then, when we wish to retrieve the information from storage, the propositional representation is retrieved. From it, our minds re-create the verbal or the imaginal code relatively accurately.

Analogical Limitations

Some evidence does suggest limits to analogical representation of images. For example, look quickly at Figure 7.3. Then look away. Does Figure 7.3 contain a *parallelogram* (a four-sided figure that has two pairs of parallel lines of equal length)? Participants in one study looked at figures such as this one. They had to determine whether particular shapes (e.g., a parallelogram) were or were not part of a given whole figure (as shown in Figure 7.3) (Reed, 1974). Overall performance was little better than chance. The participants appeared unable to call up a precise analogical mental image. They could not use a mental image to trace the lines to determine which component shapes were or were not part of a whole figure. To Reed, these findings suggested the use of a propositional code rather than an analogical one. Examples of a propositional code would be "a Star of David" or "two overlapping triangles, one of which is inverted." Another possible explanation is that people have analogical mental images that are imprecise in some ways.

TABLE 7.1	Propositional Representations of Underlying Meanings

We may use propositions to represent any kind of relationship, including actions, attributes, spatial positions, class membership, or almost any other conceivable relationship. The possibility for combining propositions into complex propositional representational relationships makes the use of such representations highly flexible and widely applicable.

TYPE OF RELATIONSHIP	REPRESENTATION IN WORDS	PROPOSITIONAL REPRESENTATION*	IMAGINAL REPRESENTATION
Actions	A mouse bit a cat.	Bite [action] (mouse [agent of action], cat [object])	
Attributes	Mice are furry.	[external surface characteristic] (furry [attribute], mouse [object])	
Spatial positions	A cat is under the table.	[vertically higher position] (table, cat)	
Class membership	A cat is an animal.	[categorical membership] (animal [category], cat [member])	

*In this table, propositions are expressed in a shorthand form (known as "predicate calculus") commonly used to express underlying meaning. This shorthand is intended only to give some idea of how the underlying meaning of knowledge might be represented. It is not believed that this form is literally the form in which meaning is represented in the mind. In general, the shorthand form for representing propositions is this: [Relationship between elements] ([subject element], [object element]).

There are additional limits to analogical representation (Chambers & Reisberg, 1985, 1992). Look now at Figure 7.4 (*a*). Imagine the rabbit shown in the figure. Actually, the figure shown here is an *ambiguous figure*, meaning that it can be interpreted in more than one way. Ambiguous figures often are used in studies of perception. But these researchers decided to use such figures to determine whether mental representations of images are truly analogical to perceptions of physical objects. Without looking back at the figure, can you determine the alternative interpretation of Figure 7.4 (*a*)? When the participants in Chambers and Reisberg's study had difficulty, the researchers offered cues. But even participants with high visualization skills often were unable to conjure the alternative interpretation.

Finally, the investigators suggested to participants that they should call on their memory to draw their mental representations of the figures. Without looking again at the figure, briefly sketch Figure 7.4 (*a*), based on your own mental representation of

FIGURE 7.3

Quickly glance at this figure and then cover it with your hand. Imagine the figure you just saw. Does it contain a parallelogram? From Cognition, Third Edition by Margaret W. Matlin, copyright © 1994 by Holt, Rinehart and Winston, reproduced by permission of the publisher.

it. Once you have completed your sketch, try once more to see whether you can find an alternative interpretation of the figure. If you are like most of Chambers and Reisberg's participants, not until you have in front of you an actual *percept* (object of perception) of the figure can you guess at an alternative interpretation of the figure. These studies indicate that mental representations of figures are not the same as percepts of these figures. In case you have not yet guessed it, the alternative interpretation of the rabbit is a duck. In this interpretation, the rabbit's ears are the duck's bill.

One interpretation of Chambers and Reisberg's findings—an implausible one—is that there is no discrete imaginal code. An alternative and more plausible explanation is that a propositional code may override the imaginal code in some circumstances. That is, the initial interpretation of the figure in propositional code may override the imaginal code for the figure. Much earlier work suggested that semantic (verbal) information (e.g., labels for figures) tends to distort recall of visual images in the direction of the meaning of the images (Carmichael, Hogan, & Walter, 1932). For example, for each of the figures in the center column of Figure 7.5, observe the alternative interpretations for the figures recalled. Base your recall on the differing labels given for the figures.

Propositional Limits

In contrast to the above work, there is some evidence that mental imagery may be manipulated directly, rather than via a propositional code (Finke, Pinker, & Farah, 1989). Participants in this study manipulated mental images by combining two distinct images to form a different mental image altogether. This manipulation of mental images may be viewed as an imaginal Gestalt experience. In the combined image,

FIGURE 7.4

(a)

(b)

(c)

(a) Look closely at the rabbit, then cover it with your hand and re-create it in your mind. Can you see a different animal in this image, just by mentally shifting your perspective? (b) What animal do you observe in this figure? Create a mental image of this figure, and try to imagine the front end of this animal as the back end of another animal and the tail end of this animal as the front end of another animal. (c) Observe the animal in this figure, and create a mental image of the animal; cover the figure, and try to reinterpret your mental image as a different kind of animal (both animals probably are facing in the same direction). (a) D. Chambers and D. Reisberg (1985), "Can Mental Images be Ambiguous?," Journal of Experimental Psychology: Human Perception and Performance, 11: 317–328. Copyright © 1985 by the American Psychological Association. Reprinted with permission. (b, c) Peterson, M. A., Kihlstrom, J. F., Rose, P. M., and Glisky, M. L. (1992). Mental images can be ambiguous: Reconstruals and reference-frame reversals. Memory & Cognition, 20, 107–123.

the whole of the two combined images differed from the sum of its two distinct parts. The study showed that in some situations, mental images can be combined effectively (e.g., the letter H and the letter X) to create mental images. They may be of geometric shapes (e.g., right triangles), of letters (e.g., M), or of objects (e.g., a bow tie). It appears that propositional codes are less likely to influence imaginal ones when participants create their own mental images, rather than when participants are presented with a picture to be represented. However, propositional codes may influence imaginal ones. This is especially likely when the picture used for creating an image is ambiguous (as in Figure 7.4 [a–c]) or rather abstract (as in Figure 7.3).

Other investigators have built on Finke's work regarding the construction of mental images (Finke, Pinker, & Farah, 1989). They presented an alternative view of Chambers and Reisberg's findings regarding the manipulation of ambiguous figures (see Figure 7.4 [a]) (Peterson & associates, 1992). They believe that the mental reinterpretation of ambiguous figures involves two manipulations. The first is a mental *realignment*

FIGURE 7.5

Reproduced figure	Verbal labels	Stimulus figures	Verbal labels	Reproduced figure
	Curtains in a window		Diamond in a rectangle	
	Seven		Four	
	Ship's wheel		Sun	
	Hourglass		Table	
	Kidney bean		Canoe	
	Pine tree		Trowel	
	Gun		Broom	
	Two		Eight	

Semantic labels clearly influence mental images, as shown here in the differing drawings based on mental images of objects given differing semantic (verbal) labels. (After Carmichael, Hogan, & Walter, 1932)

of the reference frame. This would be a shift in the positional orientations of the figures on the mental "page" or "screen" on which the image is displayed. In Figure 7.4 (*a*), the shift would be of the duck's back to the rabbit's front, and the duck's front to the rabbit's back. The second manipulation is a mental *reconstrual* (reinterpretation) of parts of the figure. This would be the duck's bill as the rabbit's ears. Participants may be unlikely to manipulate mental images spontaneously to reinterpret ambiguous figures. But such manipulations occur when participants are given the right context.

Under what conditions do participants mentally reinterpret their image of the duck-rabbit figure (Figure 7.4 [*a*]) and some other ambiguous figures (Peterson & associates, 1992)? Some experiments differed in terms of the types of supporting hints.

Across experiments, from 20% to 83% of participants were able to reinterpret ambiguous figures, using one or more of the following hints:

1. *Implicit reference-frame hint*—in which participants first were shown another ambiguous figure involving realignment of the reference frame (e.g., see Figure 7.4 [*b*]; a hawk's head/a goose's tail, and a hawk's tail/a goose's head).

2. *Explicit reference-frame hint*—in which participants were asked to modify the reference frame by considering either "the back of the head of the animal they had already seen as the front of the head of some other animal" (Peterson & associates, 1992, p. 111; considered a conceptual hint) or "the front of the thing you were seeing as the back of something else" (p. 115; considered an abstract hint).

3. *Attentional hint*—in which participants were directed to attend to regions of the figure where realignments or reconstruals were to occur.

4. *Construals from "good" parts*—in which participants were asked to construe an image from parts determined to be "good" (according to both objective [geometrical] and empirical [inter-rater agreement] criteria), rather than from parts determined to be "bad" (according to similar criteria).

Additionally, some spontaneous reinterpretation of mental images for ambiguous figures may occur. This is particularly likely for images of figures that may be reinterpreted without realigning the reference frame. See, for example, Figure 7.4 (*c*), which may be either a whole snail or an elephant's head, or possibly even a bird, a helmet, a leaf, or a seashell.

The investigators went on to suggest that the processes involved in constructing and manipulating mental images are similar to the processes involved in perceptual processes (Peterson & associates, 1992). An example would be the recognition of forms (discussed in Chapter 4). Not everyone agrees with this view. But some support for their views has been found by cognitive psychologists who hold that mental imagery and visual perception are functionally equivalent. Here, *functional equivalence* refers to individuals using about the same operations to serve about the same purposes for their respective domains. Overall, the weight of the evidence seems to indicate there are multiple codes rather than just a single code. But the controversy continues (Barsalou, 1994).

Mental Manipulations of Images

According to the **functional-equivalence hypothesis,** although visual imagery is not identical to visual perception, it is functionally equivalent to it. That is, as Paivio suggested decades ago, although we do not construct images that are exactly identical to percepts, we do construct images that are functionally equivalent to percepts. These functionally equivalent images are analogous to the physical percepts they represent. This view has many advocates (e.g., Farah, 1988b; Finke, 1989; Jolicoeur & Kosslyn, 1985a, 1985b; Rumelhart & Norman, 1988; Shepard & Metzler, 1971).

TABLE 7.2	Principles of Visual Imagery: Questions

According to the functional-equivalence hypothesis, we represent and use visual imagery in a way that is functionally equivalent to that for physical percepts. Ronald Finke has suggested several principles of visual imagery that may be used to guide research and theory development.

PRINCIPLE	POSSIBLE QUESTIONS GENERATED FROM PRINCIPLES
1. Our mental transformations of images and our mental movements across images correspond to similar transformations of and movements across physical objects and percepts.	Do our mental images follow the same laws of motion and space that are observed in physical percepts? For example, does it take longer to manipulate a mental image at a greater angle of rotation than at a smaller one? Does it take longer to scan across a large distance in a mental image than across a smaller distance?
2. The spatial relations among elements of a visual image are analogous to those relations in actual physical space.	Are the characteristics of mental images analogous to the characteristics of percepts? For example, is it easier to see the details of larger mental images than of smaller ones? Are objects that are closer together in physical space also closer together in mental images of space?
3. Mental images can be used to generate information that was not explicitly stored during encoding.	After participants have been asked to form a mental image, can they answer questions that require them to infer information, based on the image, that was not specifically encoded at the time they created the image? For example, suppose that participants are asked to picture a tennis shoe. Can they later answer questions such as "How many lace-holes are there in the tennis shoe?"
4. The construction of mental images is analogous to the construction of visually perceptible figures.	Does it take more time mentally to construct a more complex mental image than a simpler one? Does it take longer to construct a mental image of a larger image than of a smaller one?
5. Visual imagery is functionally equivalent to visual perception in terms of the processes of the visual system used for each.	Are the same regions of the brain involved in manipulating mental imagery as are involved in manipulating visual percepts? For example, are similar areas of the brain activated when mentally manipulating an image, as compared with those involved when physically manipulating an object?

One investigator has suggested some principles of how visual imagery may be functionally equivalent to visual perception (Finke, 1989). These principles may be used as a guide for designing and evaluating research on imagery. Table 7.2 offers an idea of some of the research questions that may be generated, based on Finke's principles.

Mental Rotations

Basic Phenomena

Mental rotation involves rotationally transforming an object's visual mental image (Takano & Okubo, 2003). In a classic experiment, participants were asked to observe pairs of two-dimensional (2-D) pictures showing three-dimensional (3-D) geometric forms (Figure 7.6) (Shepard & Metzler, 1971). As the figure shows, the forms were rotated from 0 to 180 degrees. The rotation was either in the picture plane (i.e., in 2-D

FIGURE 7.6

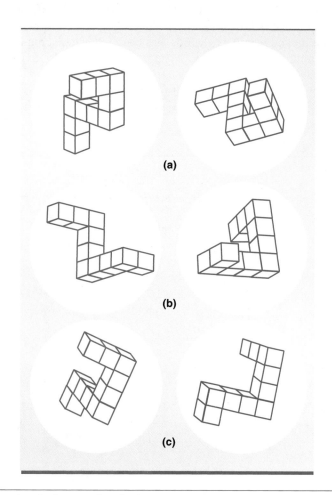

(a)

(b)

(c)

For which of these pairs of figures does the figure on the right show an accurate rotation of the figure on the left? Reprinted with permission from "Mental Rotation," by R. Shepard and J. Metzler. Science, Vol. 171(3972), p. 701–703. Copyright © 1971 American Association for the Advancement of Science.

space, as in Figure 7.6 [*a*]) or in depth (i.e., in 3-D space, as in Figure 7.6 [*b*]). In addition, participants were shown distracter forms. These were not rotations of the original stimuli (as in Figure 7.6 [*c*]). Participants then were asked to tell whether a given image was or was not a rotation of the original stimulus.

As shown in Figure 7.7, the response times for answering the questions about the figures formed a *linear function* of the degree to which the figures were rotated. For each increase in the degree of rotation of the figures, there was a corresponding increase in the response times. Furthermore, there was no significant difference between rotations in the picture plane and rotations in depth. These findings are functionally equivalent to what we might expect if the participants had been rotating physical objects in space. To rotate objects at larger angles of rotation takes longer. Whether the objects are rotated clockwise, counterclockwise, or in the third dimension of depth makes little difference. The finding of a relation between degree of angular rotation and reaction time now has been replicated a number of times with a variety of stimuli (e.g., Jordan & Huntsman, 1990; Van Selst & Jolicoeur, 1994; see also Tarr, 1999).

To try your own hand at mental rotations, do the demonstration in the "Investigating Cognitive Psychology" box for yourself (based on Hinton, 1979).

FIGURE 7.7

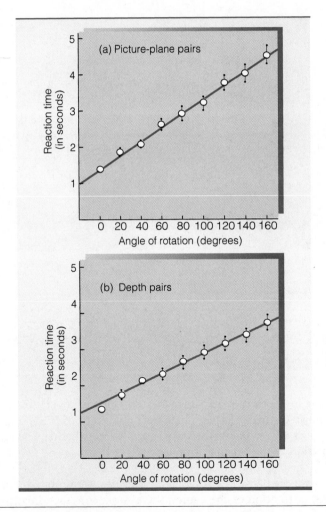

Response times to questions about mental rotations of figures show a linear relationship to the angle of rotation, and this relationship is preserved, whether the rotations are in the picture plane or are in depth. Reprinted with permission from "Mental Rotation," by R. Shepard and J. Metzler. Science, Vol. 171(3972), p. 701–703. Copyright © 1971 American Association for the Advancement of Science.

Imagine a cube floating in the space in front of you. Now, mentally grasp the left front bottom corner of the cube with your left hand. Also grasp the right back top corner of the cube with your right hand. While mentally holding those corners, rotate the cube so that the corner in your left hand is directly below the corner in your right hand (as if to form a vertical axis around which the cube would spin). How many corners of the imaginary cube are in the middle (i.e., not being grasped by your hands)? Describe the positions of the corners.

Other researchers have supported these original findings in other studies of mental rotations. For example, they have found similar results in rotations of 2-D figures, such as letters of the alphabet (Jordan & Huntsman, 1990) and cubes (Just & Carpenter, 1985). In addition, response times are longer for *degraded stimuli*—stimuli that are blurry, incomplete, or otherwise less informative (Duncan & Bourg, 1983)—than for intact stimuli. They also are longer for unfamiliar figures than for familiar ones (Jolicoeur, Snow, & Murray, 1987).

The benefits of increased familiarity also may lead to *practice effects*—improvements in performance associated with increased practice. When participants have practice in mentally rotating particular figures (increasing their familiarity), their performance improves. But this improvement appears not to carry over to rotation tasks for novel figures (Jolicoeur, 1985). For example, few people have extensive experience with rotating actual geometrical cubes. Hence, in the demonstration with the mental cube, most people imagine that there are four remaining corners of the cube being held by the two corners in their hands. They further imagine that all four corners are aligned on a horizontal plane, parallel to the ground. In fact, six corners remain. Only two corners are aligned in a given horizontal plane (parallel to the ground) at any one time. Try it yourself, using whatever nonimaginary cube you can put your hands on.

The work of Shepard and others on mental rotation provides a direct link between research in cognitive psychology and research on intelligence. The kinds of problems studied by Shepard and his colleagues are very similar to problems that can be found on conventional psychometric tests of spatial ability. For example, the Primary Mental Abilities test of Louis Thurstone and Thelma Thurstone (1962) requires mental rotation of two-dimensionally pictured objects in the picture plane. Similar problems appear on other tests. Shepard's work points out a major contribution of cognitive research toward our understanding of intelligence. This contribution is the identification of the mental representations and cognitive processes that underlie adaptations to the environment and thus, ultimately, human intelligence.

Roger N. Shepard is the Ray Lyman Wilbur professor emeritus of social science at Stanford University. Shepard is known best for his seminal work on the study of mental imagery, as well as his work on multidimensional scaling, on establishing general laws of cognition, and on visual thinking in general.

Neuropsychological Evidence

Is there any physiological evidence for mental rotation? Researchers often are unable to study directly the cerebral activity associated with many cognitive processes in the living brain of a human. Sometimes we may gain insight into these processes by studying the brains of primates, animals whose cerebral processes seem most closely analogous to our own. Using single-cell recordings in the motor cortex of monkeys, investigators found some physiological evidence of mental rotations by the monkeys (Georgopoulos & associates, 1989). Each monkey had been trained to physically move a handle in a direction that was perpendicular and counterclockwise to a target light. This light was used as a reference point. Wherever the target light appeared, the monkeys were to use that point as a reference for the perpendicular and counterclockwise physical rotation of the handle. During these physical rotations, the monkey's cortical activity was recorded. Later, in the absence of the handle, the target light again was presented at various locations. The cortical activity again was recorded. During these presentations, activity in the motor cortex showed an interesting pattern. The same individual cortical cells tended to respond as if the monkeys were anticipating the movements of the particular rotations associated with particular locations of the target light.

Preliminary findings based on primate research suggest that areas of the cerebral cortex have mappings that resemble the 2-D spatial arrangements of visual receptors in the retina of the eye (see Kosslyn, 1994b). These mappings may be construed as relatively depictive (Cohen & associates, 1996; Kosslyn & associates, 1995). Perhaps if these same regions of the cortex are active in humans during tasks involving mental imagery, mental imagery may be similarly depictive in representation. The rise of current brain-imaging techniques have allowed researchers to image human brain activity noninvasively to address such speculations. For example, in a study using functional magnetic resonance imaging, investigators found that the same brain areas involved in perception also are involved in mental-rotation tasks (Cohen & associates, 1996; see also Kosslyn & Sussman, 1995).

Thus, not only are imagery and perception functionally equivalent in psychological studies but neuropsychological techniques verify the equivalence by demonstrating overlapping brain activity. However, does mental imagery involve the same mechanisms as memory processes? If so, the functional-equivalence hypothesis for perception would lose some ground. If imagery is "functionally equivalent" to everything, then it is really equivalent to nothing. A careful review cites many psychological studies that find differences between human-imagery and memory tasks (Georgopoulos & Pellizzer, 1995). Furthermore, this review addresses single-cell recording studies of primates performing analogous tasks to verify the distinction between imagery and memory. In sum, there is converging evidence, both from traditional and neuropsychological studies, to lend support to the hypothesis of functional equivalence between perception and mental imagery. Further neuropsychological work will be discussed later in the chapter.

Image Scaling

The key idea underlying research on image size and scaling is that we represent and use mental images in ways that are functionally equivalent to our representations and uses of percepts. For example, in visual perception, there are limitations on *resolution*, our ability to distinguish individual elements, such as parts of an object or physically adjacent objects. There may also be limits on the clarity with which we perceive details in what we observe. In general, seeing featural details of large objects is easier than seeing such details of small ones. We respond more quickly to questions about large objects we observe than to questions about small ones we observe. Thus, if imaginal representation is functionally equivalent to perception, participants also should respond more quickly to questions about features of imaginally large objects than to questions about features of imaginally small ones.

However, what happens when we zoom in closer to objects to perceive featural details? Sooner or later we reach a point at which we can no longer see the entire object. To see the whole object once more, we must zoom out. See the "Investigating Cognitive Psychology" box to observe perceptual zooming for yourself.

Find a large bookcase (floor to ceiling, if possible; if not, observe the contents of a large refrigerator with an open door). Stand as close to the bookcase as you can while still keeping all of it in view. Now, read the smallest writing on the smallest book in the bookcase. Without changing your gaze, can you still see all of the bookcase? Can you read the title of the book farthest from the book on which you are focusing your perception?

INVESTIGATING COGNITIVE PSYCHOLOGY

Researchers fairly easily can control the sizes of percepts in perceptual research. However, for research on image size, controlling the sizes of people's mental images is more difficult. How do I know that the image of the elephant in my head is the same size as the image of the elephant in your head? There are some ways to get around this problem (Kosslyn, 1975).

One of the ways is to use relative size as a means of manipulating image size (Kosslyn, 1975). Specifically, participants imagine four different pairs of animals. They are an elephant and a rabbit, a rabbit and a fly, a rabbit and an elephant-sized fly, and a rabbit and a fly-sized elephant. Participants answer specific questions about the features of the rabbit and are timed in their responses. In such a situation, it takes longer to describe the details of smaller objects than to describe the details of the larger objects. That is, it takes longer to respond to rabbits paired with elephants or with elephant-sized flies than to respond to rabbits paired with flies or with fly-sized elephants. Consider a metaphor to explain this phenomenon (Kosslyn, 1983). Imagine we each have mental screen for visual images. Our screen resolution is finer and more detailed for objects that take up a larger area of the mental screen than it is for objects taking up a smaller area (Kosslyn & Koenig, 1992).

In another study, children in the first and fourth grades and adult college undergraduates were asked whether particular animals can be characterized as having various physical attributes (Kosslyn, 1976). Examples would be "Does a cat have claws?" and "Does a cat have a head?". In one condition, participants were asked to visualize each animal. They were to use this mental image in answering the questions. In the other condition, they were not asked to use mental images. It was presumed that they used verbal-propositional knowledge to respond to the verbal questions.

In the imagery condition, all participants responded more quickly to questions about physical attributes that are larger than to questions about attributes that are smaller. For example, they might be asked about a cat's head (larger) and a cat's claws (smaller). Different results were found in the nonimagery condition. In the nonimagery condition, fourth graders and adults responded more quickly to questions about physical attributes based on the distinctiveness of the characteristic for the animal. For example, they responded more quickly to questions about whether cats have claws (which are distinctive) than to questions about whether cats have heads (which are not particularly distinctive to cats alone). The physical size of the features did not have any effect on performance in the nonimagery condition for either fourth graders or adults.

In contrast, first graders constantly responded more quickly regarding larger attributes. They did so in both the imagery and the nonimagery conditions. Many of these younger children indicated that they used imagery even when not instructed to do so. Furthermore, in both conditions, adults responded more quickly than did children. But the difference was much greater for the nonimagery condition than for the imagery condition. These findings support the functional-equivalence hypothesis. The reason is that physical size influences perceptual-resolution ability. The findings also support the dual-code view in two ways. First, for adults and older children, responses based on the use of imagery (an imaginal code) differed from responses based on propositions (a symbolic code). Second, the development of propositional knowledge and ability does not occur at the same rate as the development of imaginal knowledge and ability. The distinction in the rate of development of each form of representation also seems to support Paivio's notion of two distinct codes.

INVESTIGATING COGNITIVE PSYCHOLOGY	Look at the rabbit and the fly in Figure 7.8. Close your eyes and picture them both in your mind. Now imaginally look only at the fly, and determine the exact shape of the fly's head. Do you notice yourself having to take time to zoom in to "see" the detailed features of the fly? If you are like most people, you are able to zoom the focus on your mental images to give the features or objects a larger portion of your mental screen, much as you might physically move toward an object you wanted to observe more closely. Now, look at the rabbit and the elephant, and picture them both in your mind. Next, close your eyes and look at the elephant. Imagine walking toward the elephant, watching it as it gets closer to you. Do you find that there comes a point when you can no longer see the rabbit or even all of the elephant? If you are like most people, you will find that the image of the elephant will appear to overflow the size of your image space. To "see" the whole elephant, you probably have to mentally zoom out again.

Image Scanning

Kosslyn has found additional support for the use of imaginal representation in his studies of image scanning. The key idea underlying image-scanning research is that images can be scanned, in much the same way as physical percepts can be scanned. Furthermore, our strategies and responses for imaginal scanning are expected to be functionally equivalent to those we use for perceptual scanning. A means of testing the functional equivalence of imaginal scanning is to observe some aspects of per-

FIGURE 7.8

Stephen Kosslyn (1983) asked participants to imagine either a rabbit and a fly (to observe zooming in to "see" details) or a rabbit and an elephant (to observe whether zooming in may lead to apparent overflow of the image space).

formance during perceptual scanning. One then compares that performance with performance during imaginal scanning.

For example, in perception, to scan across longer distances takes longer than to scan across shorter ones. In one of Kosslyn's experiments, participants were shown a map of an imaginary island, which you can see in Figure 7.9 (Kosslyn, Ball, & Reiser, 1978). The map shows various objects on the island, such as a hut, a tree, and a lake. Participants studied the map until they could reproduce it accurately from memory. At this point, they placed the locations of each of the six objects in the map no more than a quarter of an inch from their correct locations. Once the memorization phase of the experiment was completed, the critical phase began.

Participants were instructed that, on hearing the name of an object read to them, they should picture the map. They then should mentally scan directly to the mentioned object. Finally, they should press a key as soon as they arrived at the location of the named object. An experimenter then read to the participants the name of a first object. Five seconds later, the experimenter read to the participants the name of a second object. Participants again had to scan mentally to the proper location. They then pressed a button when they found the object. This procedure was repeated a number of times. In each case, the participants mentally moved between various pairs of objects on successive trials. The experimenter kept track of response times for participants on each trial. These response times indicated the amounts of time it took

FIGURE 7.9

Stephen Kosslyn and his colleagues used a map of an imaginary island with various landmarks to determine whether mental scanning across the image of a map was functionally equivalent to perceptual scanning of a perceived map.

participants to scan from one object to another. The critical finding was an almost perfect linear relation between the distances separating successive pairs of objects in the mental map and the amount of time it took participants to press the button. In other words, participants seem to have encoded the map in the form of an image. They actually scanned that image as needed for a response.

Findings supporting an imaginal code have been shown in several other domains. For example, the same pattern of results obtained for scanning objects in three dimensions (Pinker, 1980). Specifically, participants observed and then mentally represented a 3-D array of objects—toys suspended in an open box. Then they mentally scanned from one object to another.

Synthesizing Images and Propositions

In this chapter, we have discussed two opposing views of knowledge representation. One is a **dual-code theory**, suggesting that knowledge is represented both in images and in symbols. The second is a **propositional theory**, suggesting that knowledge is represented only in underlying propositions, not in the form of images or of words and other symbols. Before we consider some proposed syntheses of the two hypotheses, let's review the findings described thus far. We do so in light of Finke's principles of visual imagery (Table 7.3). In the discussion thus far, we have addressed the first three of Finke's criteria for imaginal representations. Mental imagery appears functionally equivalent to perception in many ways. This conclusion is based on studies of mental rotations, image scaling (sizing), and image scanning. However, the studies involving ambiguous figures and unfamiliar mental manipulations suggest that there are limits to the analogy between perception and imagery.

Epiphenomena and Demand Characteristics

Although there seems to be good evidence for the existence of both propositions and mental images (Kosslyn, 1994), the debate is not over. Perhpas some of the results found in image research could be the result of demand characteristics (Intons-Peterson, 1983). On this view, experimenters' expectancies regarding the performance of participants on a particular task create an implicit demand for the participants to perform as expected.

Intons-Peterson (1983) manipulated experimenter expectancies by suggesting to one group of experimenters that task performance would be expected to be better for perceptual tasks than for imaginal ones. She suggested the opposite outcome to a second group of experimenters. She found that experimenter expectancies did influence participants' responses in three tasks. The tasks were image scanning, mental rotations, and another task comparing perceptual performance with imaginal performance. When experimenters expected imaginal performance to be better than perceptual performance, participants responded accordingly and vice versa. This result occurred even when the experimenters were not present while participants were responding and when the cues were presented via computer. Thus, experimental participants performing visualization tasks may be responding in part to the demand characteristics of the task. These demand characteristics result from the experimenters' expectations regarding the outcomes.

Other investigators responded (Jolicoeur & Stephen Kosslyn, 1985a, 1985b). In one set of experiments, the researchers modified the procedure for the task. They completely omitted all instructions to scan the mental image. Furthermore, questions that involved responses requiring image scanning were intermixed with questions that did not require any image scanning. Even when image scanning was not an implicit task demand, participants' responses still showed that mental images were scanned in a manner analogous to perceptual scanning.

In another set of experiments, Jolicoeur and Kosslyn led experimenters to expect a pattern of responses that differed from the one analogous to perceptual scanning. Specifically, experimenters were led to expect that the pattern of responses would show a U-shaped curve, rather than a linear function. In this study, too, responses still showed a linear relation between distance and time. They did not show the U-shaped response pattern expected by the experimenters. The hypothesis regarding the functional equivalence of imagery and perception thus appears to have strong empirical support.

The debate between the propositional hypothesis and the functional-equivalence (analogical) hypothesis has been suggested to be intractable, based on existing knowledge (Keane, 1994). For each empirical finding that supports the view that imagery is

TABLE 7.3	Principles of Visual Imagery: Findings

How well did the studies reported in this chapter satisfy the criteria suggested by Ronald Finke's principles of visual imagery?

PRINCIPLE	POSSIBLE HYPOTHESES GENERATED FROM PRINCIPLES
1. Our mental transformations of images and our mental movements across images correspond to similar transformations of and movements across physical objects and percepts.	Mental rotations generally conform to the same laws of motion and space that are observed in physical percepts (e.g., Shepard & Metzler, 1971), even showing performance decrements associated with degraded stimuli (E. Duncan & Bourg, 1983; cf. also Chapter 4, for comparisons with perceptual stimuli). However, it appears that for some mental images, mental rotations of imaginal objects do not fully and accurately represent the physical rotation of perceived objects (e.g., Hinton, 1979); hence, some nonimaginal knowledge representations or cognitive strategies appear influential in some situations. In image scanning, it takes longer to scan across a large distance in a mental image than across a smaller distance (Kosslyn, Ball, & Reiser, 1978).
2. The spatial relations among elements of a visual image are analogous to those relations in actual physical space.	It appears that cognitive manipulations of mental images are analogous to manipulations of percepts in studies involving image size. As in visual perception, there are limits to the resolution of the featural details of an image, as well as limits to the size of the image space (analogous to the visual field) that can be "observed" at any one time. To observe greater detail of individual objects or parts of objects, a smaller size or number of objects or parts of objects may be observed and vice versa (Kosslyn, 1975). In related work (Kosslyn, 1976), it appears easier to see the details of larger mental images (e.g., a cat's head) than of smaller ones (e.g., a cat's claws). It appears also that just as we perceive the physical proximity (closeness) of objects that are closer together in physical space, we also imagine the closeness of mental images in our mental image space (Kosslyn, Ball, & Reiser, 1978).
3. Mental images can be used to generate information that was not explicitly stored during encoding.	After participants have been asked to form a mental image, they can answer some kinds of questions that require them to infer information, based on the image, which was not specifically encoded at the time they created the image. The studies by S. Reed (1974) and by Chambers and Reisberg (1985) suggest that propositional representations may play a role; studies by Finke (1989) and by M. Peterson et al. (1992) suggest that imaginal representations are sometimes sufficient for drawing inferences.
4. The construction of mental images is analogous to the construction of visually perceptible figures.	Studies of lifelong blind people suggest that mental imagery in the form of spatial arrangements may be constructed from haptic, rather than visual, information. Based on the findings regarding cognitive maps (e.g., Hirtle & Mascolo, 1986; Saarinen, 1987b; Stevens & Coupe, 1978; B. Tversky, 1981), it appears that both propositional and imaginal knowledge representations influence the construction of spatial arrangements.
5. Visual imagery is functionally equivalent to visual perception in terms of the processes of the visual system used for each.	It appears that some of the same regions of the brain that are involved in manipulating visual percepts may be involved in manipulating mental imagery (e.g., see Farah, et al., 1988a, 1988b), but it also appears that spatial and visual imagery may be represented differently in the brain.

analogous to perception, a rationalist reinterpretation of the finding may be offered. The reinterpretation offers an alternative explanation of the finding. Although the rationalist alternative may be a less parsimonious explanation than the empiricist explanation, the alternative cannot be refuted outright. Hence, the debate between the functional-equivalence view and the propositional view may boil down to a debate between empiricism and rationalism.

Johnson-Laird's Mental Models

An alternative synthesis of the literature suggests that mental representations may take any of three forms (Johnson-Laird, 1983, 1989, 1995, 1999; Johnson-Laird & Goldvarg, 1997). These forms are of propositions, mental models, or images. Here, propositions are fully abstracted representations of meaning that are verbally expressible. The criterion of verbal expressibility distinguishes Johnson-Laird's view from that of other cognitive psychologists. **Mental models** are knowledge structures that individuals construct to understand and explain their experiences (Brewer, 2003; Halford, 1993; Schaeken, Johnson-Laird, & D'Ydewalle, 1996; Tversky, 2000). The models are constrained by the individuals' implicit theories about these experiences. These conceptions can be more or less accurate. For example, you may have a mental model to account for how planes fly into the air. But the model depends not on physical or other laws but rather on your beliefs about them. The same would apply to the creation of mental models from text or symbolic reasoning problems as from accounts of planes flying in the air (Byrne, 1996; Ehrlich, 1996; Garnham, 1987; Garnham & Oakhill, 1996; Rogers, Rutherford, & Bibby, 1992; Schwartz, 1996; Stevenson, 1993; Zwaan, Magliano, & Graesser, 1995).

Images are much more specific representations. They retain many of the perceptual features of particular objects, viewed from a particular angle, with the particular details of a given instantiation (Katz, 2000; Kunzendorf, 1991; Schwartz & Black, 1996). For example, "The cat is under the table" may be represented in several ways. It may be represented as a proposition (because it is verbally expressible), as a mental model (of any cat and table, perhaps resembling prototypical ones—see Chapter 4), or as an image (of a particular cat in a particular position under a particular table).

Consider an experiment (Mani & Johnson-Laird, 1982). Some participants received determinate descriptions for a spatial layout. It indicated a precise location for each object in the spatial array. Other participants received indeterminate descriptions for a spatial layout. They were given ambiguous locations for objects in the array. As an analogy, consider a relatively determinate description of the location of Washington, D.C. It lies between Alexandria, Virginia, and Baltimore, Maryland. An indeterminate description of the location is that it lies between the Pacific Ocean and the Atlantic Ocean. When participants were given determinate descriptions for the spatial layout of objects, they inferred additional spatial information not included in the descriptions. But they did not recall the verbatim details well. Their having inferred additional spatial information suggests that the participants formed a mental model of the information. That they then did not recall the verbatim descriptions very well suggests that they relied on the mental models. They did not rely on the verbal descriptions for their mental representations.

In contrast, consider what happened when participants were given indeterminate descriptions for the spatial layout of objects. They seldom inferred spatial information not given in the descriptions. But they remembered the verbatim descriptions better than the other participants did. The authors suggested that participants did not infer a mental model for the indeterminate descriptions because of the multitude of possibilities for mental models of the given information. Instead, the participants appear to have mentally represented the descriptions as verbally expressible propositions. The notion of mental models as a form of knowledge representation has been applied to a broad range of cognitive phenomena. These phenomena include visual perception, memory, comprehension of text passages, and reasoning (Johnson-Laird, 1983, 1989).

Perhaps the use of mental models may offer a possible explanation of some findings that cannot be fully explained in terms of visual imagery. A series of experiments studied people who were born blind (Kerr, 1983). Because these participants have never experienced visual perception, we may assume that they have never formed visual images. At least, they have not done so in the ordinary sense of the term. Some of Kosslyn's tasks were adapted to work comparably for sighted and for blind participants (Kerr, 1983). For example, for a map-scanning task, the experimenter used a board with topographical features and landmarks that could be detected by using touch. She then asked participants to form a mental image of the board. For a task similar to Kosslyn's image-size tasks, Kerr asked participants to imagine various common objects of various sizes.

The blind participants responded more slowly to all tasks than did the sighted participants. But Kerr's blind participants still showed similar response patterns to those of sighted participants. They showed faster response times when scanning shorter distances than when scanning longer distances. They also were faster when answering questions about images of larger objects than about images of smaller objects. At least in some respects, spatial imagery appears not to involve representations that are actual analogues to visual percepts. The use of haptic (touch-based) "imagery" suggests alternative modalities for mental imagery.

Imaginal representation also may occur in an auditory modality (based on hearing). As an example, investigators found that participants seem to have auditory mental images, just as they have visual mental images (Intons-Peterson, Russell, & Dressel, 1992). Specifically, participants took longer mentally to shift a sound upward in pitch than downward. In particular, they were slower in going from the low-pitched purring of a cat to the high-pitched ringing of a telephone than in going from the cat's purring to a clock's ticking. The relative response times were analogous to the time needed physically to change sounds up or down in pitch. Consider what happened, in contrast, when individuals were asked to make psychophysical judgments involving discriminations between stimuli. Participants took longer to determine whether purring was lower-pitched than was ticking (two relatively close stimuli) than to determine whether purring was lower-pitched than was ringing (two relatively distant stimuli). Psychophysical tests of auditory sensation and perception reveal findings analogous to these.

Faulty mental models are responsible for many errors in thinking. Consider several examples (Brewer, 2003). One is that school children tend to think of heat and cold as moving through objects much as fluids do. These children also believe that plants obtain their food from the ground and that boats made of iron should sink. Even adults have trouble understanding the trajectory of an object dropped from a moving airplane.

Neuropsychological Evidence for Multiple Codes

An argument can be made that experimenter expectancies and demand characteristics may influence performance on cognitive tasks. But it seems implausible that such factors would influence the results of psychobiological research. For example, suppose you remembered every word in Chapter 2 regarding which particular parts of your brain govern which kinds of perceptual and cognitive functions. (This is, of course, an unlikely assumption for you or for most participants in psychobiological research.) How would you go about conforming to experimenters' expectancies? You would have to control directly your brain's activities and functions so that you would simulate what experimenters expected in association with particular perceptual or cognitive functions. Likewise, brain-damaged patients do not know that particular lesions are supposed to lead to particular deficits. Indeed, the patients rarely know where a lesion is until after deficits are discovered. Thus, neuropsychological findings may circumvent issues of demand characteristics in resolving the dual-code controversy. But this research does not eliminate experimenter biases as far as where to look for lesions or their corresponding deficits.

Lateralization of Function

Some investigators followed the longstanding tradition of studying patterns of brain lesions and relating them to cognitive deficits. They noted that lesions in particular areas of the brain seem to affect symbol-manipulation functions such as language (Luria, 1976; Milner, 1968). In contrast, lesions in other areas of the brain seem to affect imagery-manipulation functions such as the ability to recognize faces. Specifically, lesions in the right hemisphere are associated more strongly with impaired visual memory and visual perception. Lesions in the left hemisphere are associated more strongly with impaired verbal memory and verbal comprehension.

Initial psychobiological research on imagery came from studies of patients with identified lesions and from split-brain patients (see Chapter 2). Recall from Chapter 2 the studies of patients who underwent surgery that severed their right hemisphere from their left hemisphere. Researchers found that the right hemisphere appears to be more proficient in representing and manipulating knowledge of a visuospatial nature in a manner that may be analogous to perception (Gazzaniga & Sperry, 1967). In contrast, the left hemisphere appears to be more proficient in representing and manipulating verbal and other symbol-based knowledge.

One investigator has gone so far as to suggest that cerebral asymmetry has evolutionary origins (Corballis, 1989). As in the brains of other animals, the right hemisphere of the human brain represents knowledge in a manner that is analogous to our physical environment. Unlike the brains of other animals, however, the left hemisphere of only the human brain has the ability to manipulate imaginal components and symbols and to generate entirely new information. Examples of such imaginal components would be consonant and vowel sounds and geometric shapes. According to Corballis, humans alone can conceive what they have never perceived. However,

Martha Farah is a professor of psychology at the University of Pennsylvania. She is most well known for her seminal work on mental imagery and its relation to the brain. She has shown, for example, that imagery uses many of the same parts of the brain as does visual perception.

a recent review of the findings on lateralization has led to a modified view (Corballis, 1997). Specifically, recent neuropsychological studies of mental rotation in both animals and humans show that both hemispheres may be partially responsible for task performance. The apparent right hemisphere dominance observed in humans may be the result of the overshadowing of left hemisphere functions by linguistic abilities. Thus, it would be nice to have clear evidence of a cerebral hemispheric dissociation between analogue imagery functions and symbolic propositional functions. But scientists will have to look deeper into brain functioning before this issue is resolved completely.

Visual versus Spatial Images

In attempting to understand the nature of visual imagery, some investigators found evidence that visual and spatial imagery may be represented differently (Farah, 1988a, 1988b; Farah & associates, 1988a). Here, visual imagery refers to the use of images that represent visual characteristics such as colors and shapes. Spatial imagery refers to images that represent spatial features such as depth dimensions, distances, and orientations. Consider the case of L. H., a 36-year-old who had a head injury at age 18 years. The injury resulted in lesions in the right and the left temporo-occipital regions, the right temporal lobe, and the right inferior frontal lobe. L. H.'s injuries implicated possible impairment of his ability to represent and manipulate both visual and spatial images. Figure 7.10 shows those areas of L. H.'s brain where there was damage.

Despite L. H.'s injuries, L. H.'s ability to see was intact. He was able satisfactorily to copy various pictures (Figure 7.11 [*a*] and [*b*]). Nonetheless, he could not recognize any of the pictures he copied. In other words, he could not link verbal labels to the objects pictured. He performed very poorly when asked to respond verbally to questions requiring visual imagery, such as those regarding color or shape. Surprisingly, however, L. H. showed relatively normal abilities in several kinds of tasks. These involved (1) rotations (2-D letters, 3-D objects); (2) mental scanning, size scaling, matrix memory, and letter corners; and (3) state locations (Figure 7.11 [*c*] and [*d*]).

The investigators also used ERP (event-related potential, see Chapter 2, Table 2.1) studies. They thereby compared brain processes associated with visual perception to brain processes associated with visual imagery (Farah & associates, 1988b). As you may recall, the primary visual cortex is located in the occipital region of the brain. During visual perception, ERPs generally are elevated in the occipital region. Suppose visual imagery were analogous to visual perception. We could expect that during tasks involving visual imagery, there would be analogous elevations of ERPs in the occipital region.

In this study, ERPs were measured during a reading task. In one condition, participants were asked to read a list of concrete words (e.g., *cat*). In the other condition, participants were asked to read a comparable list of concrete words. They also had to imagine the objects as they read the words. Each word was presented for 200 milliseconds. ERPs were recorded from the different sites in the occipital-lobe and temporal-lobe regions. The researchers found that the ERPs were similar during the first 450 milliseconds. After this time period, however, participants in the imaginal condition showed greater neural activity in the occipital lobe than did participants in the nonimaginal (reading only) condition.

According to the researchers, "Neurophysiological evidence suggests that our cognitive architecture includes both representations of the visual appearance of ob-

FIGURE 7.10

Regions in which the brain of L. H. was damaged. The right temporal lobe and right inferior frontal lobe, as shown in the figure at the top; and the temporo-occipital region, as shown in the figure at the bottom. From Cognitive Psychology, 6/e by R. Solso, p. 306. © 2000 Elsevier.

jects in terms of their form, color, and perspective and of the spatial structure of objects in terms of their three-dimensional layout in space" (Farah & associates, 1988a, p. 459). The knowledge of object labels (recognizing the objects by name) and attributes (answering questions about the characteristics of the objects) taps propositional, symbolic knowledge about the pictured objects. In contrast, the ability to manipulate the orientation (rotation) or the size of images taps imaginal, analogous knowledge of the objects. Thus, both forms of representation seem to answer particular kinds of questions for knowledge use.

Spatial Cognition and Cognitive Maps

Rats, Bees, and Humans

Most of the studies described thus far have involved the way in which we represent imaginal knowledge. The studies are based on what we have perceived by looking at and then imagining visual stimuli. Other research suggests that we may form imaginal maps based solely on our physical interactions with and navigations through our

FIGURE 7.11

L. H. was able to draw accurately various objects. Panel a shows what he was shown, and Panel b shows what he drew. However, he could not recognize the objects he copied. Despite L. H.'s severe deficits on visual-imagery tasks (Panel c, regarding colors, sizes, shapes, etc.), L. H. showed normal ability on spatial-imagery tasks (Panel d, regarding rotations, scanning, scaling, etc.). Reprinted from Cognitive Psychology, Vol. 20, p. 439–462, © 1988, with permission from Elsevier.

How do you benefit from having a dual code for knowledge representation? Although a dual code may seem redundant and inefficient, having a code for analogue physical and spatial features that is distinct from a code for symbolic propositional knowledge actually can be very efficient. Consider how you learn material in your cognitive psychology course. Most people go to the lecture. Here they obtain information from an instructor. They also read material from a textbook, as you are doing now. If you had only an analogue code for knowledge representation, you would have a much harder time integrating the verbal information you received from your instructor in class with the printed information in your textbook. All of your information would be in the form of auditory–visual images gleaned from listening to and watching your instructor in class and visual images of the words in your textbook. Thus, a symbolic code that is distinct from the analogue features of encoding is helpful for integrating across different modes of knowledge acquisition. Furthermore, analogue codes preserve important aspects of experience without interfering with underlying propositional information. For the purposes of performing well on a test, it is irrelevant whether the information was obtained in class or in the text. But later you may need to verify the source of information to prove that your answer is correct. In this case, analogical information might help.

PRACTICAL APPLICATIONS OF COGNITIVE PSYCHOLOGY

physical environment. This is true even when we never have a chance to "see the whole picture," as from an aerial photograph or a map. **Cognitive maps** are internal representations of our physical environment, particularly centering on spatial relationships. Cognitive maps seem to offer internal representations that simulate particular spatial features of our external environment (Rumelhart & Norman, 1988).

Some of the earliest work on cognitive maps was done by Edward Tolman during the 1930s. At this time, it was considered almost unseemly for psychologists to try to understand cognitive processes that could not be observed or measured directly. In one study, the researchers were interested in the ability of rats to learn a maze, such as that shown in Figure 7.12 (Tolman & Honzik, 1930). Rats were divided into three groups:

1. In the first group, the rats had to learn the maze. Their reward for getting from the start box to the end box was food. Eventually, these rats learned to run the maze without making any errors. In other words, they did not make wrong turns or follow blind alleys.

2. A second group of rats also was placed in the maze. But these rats received no reinforcement for successfully getting to the end box. Although their performance improved over time, they continued to make more errors than the reinforced group. These results are hardly surprising. We would expect the rewarded group to have more incentive to learn.

3. Finally, consider the third group. These rats received no reward for 10 days of learning trials. On the eleventh day, however, food was placed in the end box for the first time. With just one reinforcement, the learning of these rats improved dramatically. These rats ran the maze about as well as the rats in the first group in fewer trials.

FIGURE 7.12

Edward Tolman found that rats seemed to have formed a mental map of a maze during behavioral experiments.

What, exactly, were the rats in Tolman and Honzik's experiment learning? It seems unlikely that they were learning simply "turn right here, turn left there," and so on. Rather, according to Tolman, the rats were learning a cognitive map, an internal representation of the maze. Through this argument, Tolman became one of the earliest cognitive theorists. He argued for the importance of the mental representations that give rise to behavior.

Decades later, even very simple creatures were shown to appear able to form some cognitive maps. They even may be able to translate imaginal representations into a primitive, prewired, analogical, and perhaps even symbolic form. For example, a Nobel Prize-winning German scientist studied the behavior of bees when they return to their hive after having located a source of nectar (von Frisch, 1962, 1967). Apparently, bees not only can form imaginal maps for getting to food sources. They also can use a somewhat symbolic form of communicating that information to other bees. Specifically, different patterns of dances can be used to represent different meanings. For example, a round dance indicates a source less than 100 yards from the hive. A figure-eight dance indicates a source at a greater distance. The details of the dance (e.g., in regard to wiggle patterns) differ from one species to another. But the basic dances appear to be the same across all species of bees. If the lowly bee appears able to imagine the route to nectar, what kinds of cognitive maps may be conceived in the minds of humans?

Humans seem to use three types of knowledge when forming and using cognitive maps. The first is *landmark* knowledge, which is information about particular features at a location and which may be based on both imaginal and propositional representations (Thorndyke, 1981). The second is *route-road* knowledge, which involves specific pathways for moving from one location to another (Thorndyke & Hayes-Roth, 1982).It may be based on both procedural knowledge and declarative knowledge. The third is *survey* knowledge, which involves estimated distances between landmarks, much as they might appear on survey maps (Thorndyke & Hayes-Roth, 1982). It may be represented imaginally or propositionally (e.g., in numerically specified distances). Thus, people use both an analogical code and a propositional code for imaginal representations such as images of maps (McNamara, Hardy, & Hirtle, 1989; Russell & Ward, 1982).

Mental Shortcuts

When we use these three kinds of knowledge (landmark, route-road, and survey knowledge), we sometimes seem to take mental shortcuts that influence our estimations of distance. These mental shortcuts are cognitive strategies termed heuristics, often described as rules of thumb. For example, in regard to landmark knowledge, the density of the landmarks sometimes appears to affect our mental image of an area. Specifically, as the density of intervening landmarks increases, estimates of distances increase correspondingly. In other words, people tend to distort their mental images such that their mental estimates of distances increase in relation to the number of intervening landmarks (Thorndyke, 1981).

In estimations of distances between particular physical locations (e.g., cities), route-road knowledge appears often to be weighted more heavily than survey knowledge. This is true even when participants form a mental image based on looking at a map (McNamara, Ratcliff, & McKoon, 1984). Consider what happened when participants were asked to indicate whether particular cities had appeared on a map. They showed more rapid response times between names of cities when the two cities were closer together in route-road distance than when the two cities were physically closer together "as the crow flies" (Figure 7.13).

The use of heuristics in manipulating cognitive maps suggests that propositional knowledge affects imaginal knowledge (Tversky, 1981). This is so at least when people are solving problems and answering questions about images. In some situations, conceptual information seems to lead to distortions in mental images. In these situations, propositional strategies, rather than imaginal strategies, may better explain people's responses. In general, these distortions seem to reflect a tendency to regularize features of mental maps. Thus, angles, lines, and shapes are represented as more like pure abstract geometric forms than they really are.

1. *Right-angle bias:* People tend to represent intersections (e.g., street crossings) as forming 90-degree angles more often than the intersections really do (Moar & Bower, 1983).

FIGURE 7.13

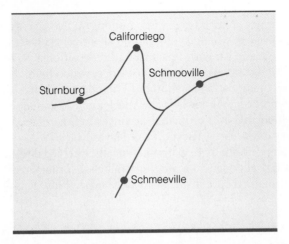

Which city is closer to Sturnburg: Schmeeville or Schmooville? It appears that our use of cognitive maps often emphasizes the use of route-road knowledge, even when it contradicts survey knowledge. Based on Timothy R. McNamara, Roger Ratcliff, and Gail McKoon (1984), "The Mental Representation of Knowledge Acquired from Maps," Journal of Experimental Psychology: LMC, 10(4): 723–732. Copyright © 1984 by the American Psychological Association.

2. *Symmetry heuristic:* People tend to represent shapes (e.g., states or countries) as being more symmetrical than they really are (Tversky & Schiano, 1989).

3. *Rotation heuristic:* When representing figures and boundaries that are slightly slanted (i.e., oblique), people tend to distort the images as being either more vertical or more horizontal than they really are (Tversky, 1981).

4. *Alignment heuristic:* People tend to represent landmarks and boundaries that are slightly out of alignment by distorting their mental images to be better aligned than they really are (i.e., we distort the way we line up a series of figures or objects; Tversky, 1981).

5. *Relative-position heuristic:* People tend to represent the relative positions of particular landmarks and boundaries by distorting their mental images in ways that more accurately reflect their conceptual knowledge about the contexts in which the landmarks and boundaries are located, rather than reflecting the actual spatial configurations.

To see how the relative-position heuristic might work, close your eyes and picture a map of the United States. Is Reno, Nevada, west of San Diego, California, or east of it? In a series of experiments, investigators asked participants questions such as this one (Stevens & Coupe, 1978). They found that the large majority of people believe San Diego to be west of Reno. That is, for most of us, our mental map looks something like that in panel *a* of Figure 7.14. Actually, however, Reno is west of San Diego. See the correct map in panel *b* of Figure 7.14.

FIGURE 7.14

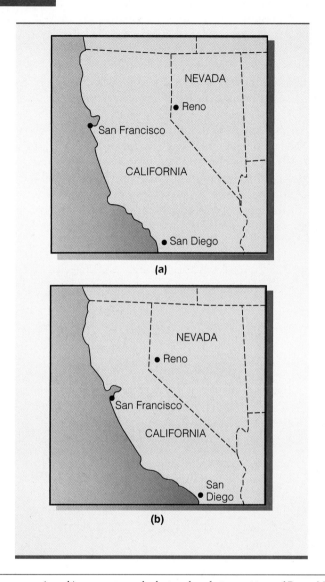

Which of these two maps (a or b) more accurately depicts the relative positions of Reno, Nevada, and San Diego, California?

Some of these heuristics also affect our perception of space and of forms (see Chapter 4). For example, the symmetry heuristic seems to be equally strong in memory and in perception (Tversky, 1991). Nonetheless, there are differences between perceptual processes and representational (imaginal or propositional) processes. For example, the relative-position heuristic appears to influence mental representation much more strongly than it does perception (Tversky, 1991).

There is evidence of powerful influences of semantic or propositional knowledge (or beliefs) on imaginal representations of world maps (Saarinen, 1987b). Specifically, students from 71 sites in 49 countries were asked to draw a sketch map of the world. Most (even Asians) drew maps showing a Eurocentric view of the world. Many Americans drew Americentric views. A few others showed views centered on and highlighting their own countries. (Figure 7.15 shows an Australia-centered view of the world.) In addition, most students showed modest distortions that enlarged the more prominent, well-known countries. They also diminished the sizes of less well-known countries (e.g., in Africa).

Finally, further work suggests that propositional knowledge about semantic categories may affect imaginal representations of maps. In one study, the researchers studied the influence of semantic clustering on estimations of distances (Hirtle & Mascolo, 1986). Hirtle's participants were shown a map of many buildings and then were asked to estimate distances between various pairs of buildings. They tended to distort the distances in the direction of guessing shorter distances for more similar landmarks and longer distances for less similar landmarks. Investigators found similar distortions

FIGURE 7.15

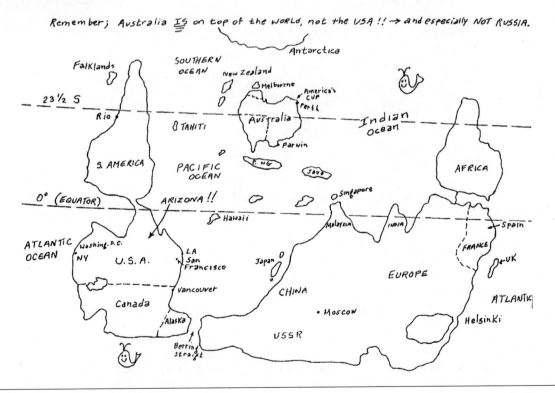

Based on this Australian student's map, can you infer that this student mentally represents the world in the same way you do? From Robert Solso, Cognitive Psychology, 3/e. Published by Allyn and Bacon, Boston, MA. Copyright © 1991 by Pearson Education. Reprinted by permission of the publisher.

in students' mental maps for the city in which they lived (Ann Arbor, Michigan) (Hirtle & Jonides, 1985).

The work on cognitive maps shows once again how the study of mental imagery can help elucidate our understanding of human adaptation to the environment—that is, of human intelligence. To survive, we need to find our way around the environment in which we live. We need to get from one place to another. Sometimes, to imagine the route we will need to traverse to navigate within our environment. Mental imagery provides a key basis for this adaptation. In some societies (Gladwin, 1970), the ability to navigate with the help of very few cues is a life-or-death issue. If sailors cannot do so, they eventually get lost and potentially die of dehydration or starvation. Thus, our imagery abilities are potential keys to our survival and to what makes us intelligent in our everyday lives.

There are also sex differences in spatial and related skills. Women find it easier to remember where they saw things (spatial-location memory). Men find it easier to do mental rotation of spatial images (Silverman & Eals, 1992). Most tests of spatial abilities involve mental rotation, however. So men tend to perform better on common tests of spatial skills than do women.

Text Maps

Thus far we have discussed the construction of cognitive maps based on procedural knowledge (e.g., following a particular route, as a rat in a maze), on propositional information (e.g., using mental heuristics), and on observation of a graphic map. In addition, we may be able to create cognitive maps from a verbal description (Franklin & Tversky, 1990; Taylor & Tversky, 1992a, 1992b). These cognitive maps may be as accurate as those created from looking at a graphic map. Others have found similar results in studies of text comprehension (Glenberg, Meyer, & Lindem, 1987).

Tversky noted that her research involved having the readers envision themselves in an imaginal setting as participants, not as observers, in the scene. She wondered whether people might create and manipulate images differently when envisioning themselves in different settings. Specifically, Tversky wondered whether propositional information might play a stronger role in mental operations when we think about settings in which we are participants, as compared with settings in which we are observers. As Item 4 in Table 7.3 indicates, the findings regarding cognitive maps suggest that the construction of mental imagery may involve both processes analogous to perception and processes relying on propositional representations.

Whether the debate regarding propositions versus imagery can be resolved in the terms in which it traditionally has been presented remains unclear. The various forms of mental representation sometimes are considered to be mutually exclusive. In other words, we think in terms of the question, "Which representation of information is correct?" Often, however, we create false dichotomies. We suggest that alternatives are mutually exclusive, when, in fact, they might be complementary. For example, models postulating mental imagery and those positing propositions can be seen as opposed to each other. However, this opposition does not inhere in the nature of things. Rather, it is in our construction of a relation. People possibly could use both representations. Propositional theorists might like to believe that all representations are fundamentally propositional. Quite possibly, though, both images and propositions are way stations toward some more basic and primitive form of representation in the mind of which we do not yet have any knowledge. A good case can be made in favor of both propositional and imaginal representations of knowledge. Neither is necessarily more basic than the other. The question we presently need to address is when we use which.

Development of Visuospatial Skills

Young children develop basic spatial understandings that form the basis for geometry. One such basic understanding is *spatial visualization*. This is our ability to orient ourselves in our surroundings and to manipulate images of objects mentally. Although many studies have examined spatial visualization in children (e.g., Huttenlocher, Hedges, & Duncan, 1991; Huttenlocher & Presson, 1973, 1979; Kail, 1991, 1997; Marmor, 1975, 1977), consider just one typical example of this research (Kail, Pellegrino, & Carter, 1980).

Participants in grades 3, 4, and 6 and in college judged whether pairs of stimuli were identical or were mirror-image reversals of each other. One stimulus in each pair was presented in an upright position. The other was rotated 0, 30, 60, 90, 120, or 150 degrees from the standard upright position. The pairs comprising each stimulus item were either alphanumeric (alphabetic and/or numeric) symbols—such as 4, 5, F, and G—or unfamiliar abstract geometric forms. See Figure 7.15. The speed of mental rotation increases with age and with the degree of familiarity of the objects (Kail, Pellegrino, & Carter, 1980). Thus, older participants can mentally rotate more quickly. All participants can rotate familiar objects more quickly than they can rotate unfamiliar ones.

The findings raised several questions, two of which particularly intrigued researchers. First, why might the speed of mental rotation improve with age? The researchers suggested that younger children must rotate the entire stimulus. Older children may rotate stimuli more analytically. So that they rotate each component separately and may need only to rotate a part of the stimulus. Thus, the change in cognitive development may involve more than a simple change in processing speed. A second question is why participants encoded and rotated the unusual geometric forms more slowly than the familiar, alphanumeric ones. The difference might be because of the activation of an already existing, easily accessible pattern in memory for the familiar characters. This is in contrast to the requirement that the participants form a new representation for the unfamiliar stimuli.

Investigators also found that children and young adults showed speedier response times in mental-rotation tasks when given opportunities for practice (Kail & Park, 1990). The performance of both school-aged children and young adults on mental-rotation tasks is not impaired as a function of their engaging in simultaneous tasks involving memory recall (Kail, 1991). These findings suggest that mental rotation may be an automatic process for school-aged children and adults. Given that familiarity with the items and practice with mental rotation appear to enhance response times, his study suggests that mental rotation may be an automatic process. It may permit us to infer that enhanced response times may be the result of increasing automatization of the task across childhood and adolescence. Furthermore, such automatic processes may be a sign of more effective visuospatial skills because increased speed is associated with increased accuracy in spatial memory (Kail, 1997).

At the other end of the life span, two investigators studied whether processing speed or other factors may influence age-related changes in mental rotation by adults (Dror & Kosslyn, 1994). They found that older participants (55–71 years; mean 65 years) responded more slowly and less accurately than younger participants (18–23 years; mean 20 years) on mental-rotation tasks. However, they also found that older and younger participants showed comparable response times and error rates on tasks involving image scanning. Based on these and other findings, these authors concluded that aging affects some aspects of visual imagery more than others.

The authors also analyzed their data for mental rotation, image-scanning, and other imagery tasks. For example, participants were asked to generate or maintain a mental image within a visual region and then indicate whether the image would obscure a probe stimulus within that region. General effects of aging may lead to a reduction in response times across tasks. However, age differences in error rates may arise because of specific effects of aging. They may influence selectively particular aspects of mental imagery. The authors also speculated that if the participants had been urged to minimize their error rates, perhaps older people would have shown even slower response times to ensure lower error rates. However, other work directly testing that speculation failed to confirm the authors' hypothesis (Hertzog, Vernon, & Rypma, 1993). Other researchers have suggested that a factor contributing to task-specific differences in age-related decline in mental imagery is whether the task requires multiple simultaneous transformations or multiple sequential ones (Mayr & Kliegl, 1993).

Key Themes

This chapter illustrates some of the key themes mentioned in Chapter 1.

A first theme is that of structures and processes. The debate as to whether images are phenomenal or epiphenomenal hinges upon what kinds of mental structures are used to process stimuli. For example, when people mentally rotate objects, is the structural representation imaginal or propositional? Either kind of mental representation could generate processes that would enable people to see objects at different angular viewpoints. But the kinds of processes would be different—either mental manipulation of images or mental manipulation of propositions. In order to understand cognition, we need to understand how structures and processes interact.

A second theme is that of validity of causal inferences versus ecological validity. Suppose you wish to hire air-traffic controllers. Can you assess their mental-imagery and spatial-visualization skills using paper-and-pencil tests of manipulation of geometric forms? Or do you need to test them in a setting that is more similar to that of air-traffic control, as through a simulation of the actual job? The paper-and-pencil test probably will yield more precise measurements, but will these measurements be valid? There is no final answer to the question. Rather, researchers are studying this kind of question in order to understand how best to assess people's real-life skills.

A third theme is biological and behavioral studies. As an example, early work by Stephen Kosslyn and his collaborators was all behavioral. The researchers investigated how people mentally manipulate various kinds of images. As time went by, the team started using biological techniques, such as functional magnetic resonance imaging (fMRI), to supplement their behavioral studies. But they never saw the two kinds of research as in opposition to each other. Rather, they viewed them as wholly complementary, and do even today.

Look at the list of words that your friends and/or family members recalled in the demonstration in Chapter 6. Add up the total number of recollections for every other word (i.e., book, window, box, hat, etc.—the words in odd-numbered positions in the list). Now add up the total number of recollections for the other words (i.e., peace, run, harmony, voice, etc.—the words in even-numbered positions in the list). Most people will recall more words from the first set than from the second set. This is because the first set is made up of words that are concrete, or those words that are easily visualizable. The second set of words is made up of words that are abstract, or not easily visualizable. This is a demonstration of the dual coding hypothesis (or its more contemporary version, the functional-equivalence hypothesis).

Which is larger in land area, India or Germany? If you are used to seeing the world in terms of the popular Mercator map, in which the map is flat and the equator is in the bottom half of the map, you might think that India and Germany are about the same size. In fact, you might think that Germany may be a bit larger than India. Now look at a globe of the world. You will see that India is actually about five times as large as Germany. This is an example of how our cognitive maps may not be based in reality but rather in our exposure to the topic and to our constructions and heuristics.

Summary

1. **What are some of the major hypotheses regarding how knowledge is represented in the mind?** Knowledge representation comprises the various ways in which our minds create and modify mental structures that stand for what we know about the world outside of our minds. Knowledge representation involves both declarative (knowing that) and nondeclarative (knowing how) forms of knowledge. Through mental imagery, we create analogue mental structures that stand for things that are not presently being sensed in the sense organs. Imagery may involve any of the senses. But the form of imagery most commonly reported by laypeople and most commonly studied by cognitive psychologists is visual imagery. Some studies (e.g., studies of blind participants and some studies of the brain) suggest that visual imagery itself may comprise two discrete systems of mental representation. One system involves nonspatial visual attributes, such as color and shape. Another involves spatial attributes, such as location, orientation, and size or distance scaling.

According to Paivio's dual-code hypothesis, two discrete mental codes for representing knowledge exist. One code is for images and another for words and other symbols. Images are represented in a form analogous to the form we perceive through our senses. In contrast, words and concepts are encoded in a symbolic form, which is not analogical.

An alternative view of image representation is the propositional hypothesis. It suggests that both images and words are represented in a propositional form. The proposition retains the underlying meaning of either images or words, without any of the perceptual features of either. For example, the acoustic features of the sounds of the words are not stored. Nor are the visual features of the colors or shapes of the images. Furthermore, propositional codes, more than imaginal codes, seem to influence mental representation when participants are shown ambiguous or abstract figures. Apparently, unless the context facilitates performance, the use of visual images does not always readily lead to successful performance on some tasks requiring mental manipulations of either abstract figures or ambiguous figures.

2. **What are some of the characteristics of mental imagery?** Based on a modification of the dual-code view, Shepard and others have espoused a functional-equivalence hypothesis. It asserts that images are represented in a form functionally equivalent to percepts, even if images are not truly identical to percepts. Studies of mental rotations, image scaling, and image scanning suggest that imaginal task performance is functionally equivalent to perceptual task performance. Even performance on some tasks involving comparisons of auditory images seems to be functionally equivalent to performance on tasks involving comparisons of auditory percepts. Propositional codes seem less likely to influence mental representation than imaginal ones when participants are given an opportunity to create their own mental images. For example, they might do so in tasks involving image sizing or mental combinations of imaginal letters. Some researchers have suggested that experimenter expectancies may have influenced cognitive studies of imagery. But others have refuted these suggestions. In any case, psychobiological studies are not subject to such influences. They seem to support the functional-equivalence hypothesis by finding overlapping brain areas involved in visual perception and mental rotation.

3. **How does knowledge representation benefit from both analogical images and symbolic propositions?** Kosslyn has synthesized these various hypotheses to suggest that images may involve both analogous and propositional forms of knowledge representation. In this case, both forms influence our mental representation and manipulation of images. Thus, some of what we know about images is represented in a form that is analogous to perception. Other things we know about images are represented in a propositional form. Johnson-Laird has proposed an alternative synthesis. He has suggested that knowledge may be represented as verbally expressible propositions, as somewhat abstracted analogical mental models, or as highly concrete and analogical mental images.

Studies of split-brain patients and patients with lesions indicate some tendency toward hemispheric specialization. Visuospatial information may be processed primarily in the right hemisphere. Linguistic (symbolic) information may be processed primarily in the left hemisphere of right-handed individuals. A case study suggests that spatial imagery also may be processed in a different region of the brain than the regions in which other aspects of visual imagery are processed. Studies of normal participants show that visual-perception tasks seem to involve regions of the brain similar to the regions involved in visual-imagery tasks.

4. **How may conceptual knowledge and expectancies influence the way we use images?** People tend to distort their own mental maps in ways that regularize many features of the maps. For example, they may tend to imagine right angles, symmetrical forms, either vertical or horizontal boundaries (not oblique ones), and well-aligned figures and objects. People also tend to employ distortions of their mental maps in ways that support their propositional knowledge about various landmarks. They tend to cluster similar landmarks, to segregate dissimilar ones, and to modify relative positions to agree with conceptual knowledge about the landmarks. In addition, people tend to distort their mental maps. They increase their estimates regarding the distances between endpoints as the density of intervening landmarks increases.

Some of the heuristics that affect cognitive maps support the notion that propositional information influences imaginal representations. The influence of propositional information may be particularly potent when participants are not shown a graphic map, Instead, they are asked to read a narrative passage and to envision themselves as participants in a setting described in the narrative.

5. **How do spatial skills develop?** As children grow older, their spatial skills improve. For example, they are more rapid in performing mental rotations. Age differences can also appear during adulthood.

Thinking about Thinking: Factual, Analytical, Creative, and Practical Questions

1. Describe some of the characteristics of pictures versus of words as external forms of knowledge representation.

2. What factors might lead a person's mental model to be inaccurate with respect to how radio transmissions lead people to be able to hear music on a radio?

3. In what ways is mental imagery analogous (or functionally equivalent) to perception?

4. In what ways do propositional forms of knowledge representation influence performance on tasks involving mental imagery?

5. What are some strengths and weaknesses of ERP studies?

6. Some people report never experiencing mental imagery, yet they are able to solve mental-rotation problems. How might they solve such problems?

7. What are some practical applications of having two codes for knowledge representation? Give an example applied to your own experiences, such as applications to studying for examinations.

8. Based on the heuristics described in this chapter, what are some of the distortions that may be influencing your cognitive maps for places with which you are familiar (e.g., a college campus or your home town)?

Key Terms

analogue code	functional-equivalence hypothesis	mental rotation
cognitive maps	imagery	procedural knowledge
declarative knowledge	knowledge representation	propositional theory
dual-code theory	mental models	symbolic representation

Explore CogLab by going to http://coglab.wadsworth.com. Answer the questions required by your instructor from the student manual that accompanies CogLab.

Mental Rotation   Mental Scanning
Link Word

Annotated Suggested Reading

Denis, M., Mellet. E., & Kosslyn, S. M. (2004). *Neu-roimaging of mental imagery*. Philadelphia: Taylor & Francis. An up-to-date review of studies that seek to understand mental-imagery skills through the use of neuroimaging techniques.

Representation and Organization of Knowledge in Memory: Concepts, Categories, Networks, and Schemas

EXPLORING COGNITIVE PSYCHOLOGY

1. **How are representations of words and symbols organized in the mind?**

2. **How do we represent other forms of knowledge in the mind?**

3. **How does declarative knowledge interact with procedural knowledge?**

Once we have represented knowledge, how do we organize it so that we can retrieve and then use it? The preceding chapter described how knowledge may be represented in the form of propositions and images. In this chapter, we continue the discussion of knowledge representation. We expand this discussion to include various means of organizing declarative knowledge that can be expressed in words and other symbols (i.e., "knowing that"). Consider, for example, your knowledge of facts about cognitive psychology, about world history, about your personal history, and about mathematics. It relies on your mental organization of declarative knowledge. In addition, this chapter describes a few of the various models for representing procedural knowledge. This is knowledge about how to follow various procedural steps for performing actions (i.e., "knowing how"). For example, your knowledge of how to ride a bicycle, how to write your signature, how to drive a car to a familiar location, and how to catch a ball depends on your mental representation of procedural knowledge. Some theorists even have suggested integrative models for representing both declarative and procedural knowledge.

To get an idea of how declarative and procedural knowledge may interact, get out a piece of scrap paper and a pen or pencil. Try the demonstration in the "Investigating Cognitive Psychology" box.

As quickly and as legibly as possible, write your normal signature, from the first letter of your first name to the last letter of your last name. Don't stop to think about which letters come next. Just write as quickly as possible.

Turn the paper over. As quickly and as legibly as possible, write your signature backward. Start with the last letter of your last name and work toward the first letter of your first name.

Now, compare the two signatures. Which signature was more easily and accurately created?

For both signatures, you had available extensive declarative knowledge of which letters preceded or followed one another. But for the first task, you also could call on procedural knowledge, based on years of knowing how to sign your name.

INVESTIGATING COGNITIVE PSYCHOLOGY

In addition to seeking to understand the *what* (the form or structure) of knowledge representation, cognitive psychologists also try to grasp the *how* (the processes) of knowledge representation and manipulation. That is, what are some of the general processes by which we select and control the disorganized array of raw data available to us through our sense organs? How do we relate that sensory information to the information we have available from internal sources of information (i.e., our memories and our thought processes)? How do we organize and reorganize our mental representations during various cognitive processes? Through what mental processes do we operate on the knowledge we have in our minds? To what extent are these processes domain-general—common to multiple kinds of information, such as verbal and quantitative information? Conversely, to what extent are they domain-specific—used only for particular kinds of information, such as verbal or quantitative information?

Knowledge representation and processing have been investigated by researchers from several different disciplines. Among these researchers are cognitive psychologists, computer scientists studying artificial intelligence (AI; attempts to program machines to perform intelligently), and neuropsychologists. Their diverse approaches to investigating knowledge representation promote exploration of a wide range of phenomena. They also encourage multiple perspectives of similar phenomena. Finally, they offer the strength of **converging operations**—the use of multiple approaches and techniques to address a problem.

Other than to satisfy their own idle curiosity, why do so many different researchers want to understand how knowledge is represented? The way in which knowledge is represented profoundly influences how effectively knowledge can be manipulated for performing any number of cognitive tasks. To illustrate the influence of knowledge representation through a very crude analogy, try the following multiplication task, using a representation in either Roman or Arabic numerals:

$$\begin{array}{r} \text{CMLIX} \\ \underline{\times\ \text{LVIII}} \end{array} \qquad \begin{array}{r} 959 \\ \underline{\times\ 58} \end{array}$$

Organization of Declarative Knowledge

The fundamental unit of symbolic knowledge is the **concept**—an idea about something that provides a means of understanding the world (Bruner, Goodnow, & Austin, 1956; Fodor, 1994; Hampton, 1997b, 1999; Kruschke, 2003; Love, 2003). Often, a single concept may be captured in a single word, such as *apple*. Each concept relates to other concepts, such as *redness, roundness,* or *fruit*. One way to organize concepts can be captured by the notion of a category. A **category** is a concept that functions to organize or point out aspects of equivalence among other concepts based on common features or similarity to a prototype (Coley, Atran, & Medin, 1997; Hampton, 1995; Mayer, 2000b; Medin, 1998; Medin & Aguilar, 1999; Wattenmaker, 1995; Wisniewski & Medin, 1994). For example, the word *apple* can act as a category, as in a collection of different kinds of apples. But it also can act as a concept within the category *fruit*. We later discuss a number of different ways to organize concepts into categories. These ways include the use of defining features, prototypes and exemplars, and hierarchically organized semantic **networks**. Later in the chapter, we discuss how concepts also may be organized into **schemas**, which are mental frameworks for representing knowledge that encompass an array of interrelated concepts in a meaningful organization (Bartlett, 1932; Brewer, 1999). For example, we might have a schema for a kitchen. It tells us the kinds of things one might find in a kitchen and where we might find them.

A problem with schemas is that they can give rise to stereotypes. We might, for example, have a schema for the kind of person we believe was responsible for the destruction of the World Trade Center on September 11, 2001. This schema can easily generate a stereotype of certain groups of people as likely terrorists.

Concepts and Categories

In general, concepts and categories can be divided in various ways. One commonly used distinction is that between natural categories and artifact categories (Medin & Heit, 1999; Medin, Lynch, & Solomon, 2000). **Natural categories** are groupings that occur naturally in the world. For example, birds or trees form natural categories. **Artifact categories** are groupings that are designed or invented by humans to serve particular purposes or functions. Examples of artifact categories are automobiles and kitchen appliances.

Natural and artifact categories are relatively stable categories. Moreover, people tend to agree on criteria for membership. A tiger is always a mammal, for example. A knife is always an implement used for cutting. But concepts are not always stable. They can change (Dunbar, 2003; Thagard, 2003). Some categories are referred to as *ad hoc categories*, which are categories that are formed with a particular purpose in mind (Barsalou, 1983). Whereas natural and artifact categories are likely to appear in a dictionary, ad hoc categories are not. An example would be "things you need to write a paper." If you are writing a paper for a course, you need certain things. But what are they? Well, they vary across persons, across subject matters, and across time. Similarly, "things you need to attract a romantic partner" may vary widely from one person to the next.

An additional kind of entity is a **nominal kind,** which is the arbitrary assignment of a label to an entity that meets a certain set of prespecified conditions. In some cases, the features for nominal kinds are clear. For example, a widow is a woman whose husband is deceased. A quadrilateral is any four-sided figure. In other cases, the features are not so clear, as for "lover" or "annoyance." In these cases, it is particularly difficult to ascertain how meaning is constructed. Several theories have been proposed that attempt to do so.

Feature-Based Categories: A Defining View

The classic view of conceptual categories involves disassembling a concept into a set of featural components. These components are singly necessary and jointly sufficient to define the category (Katz, 1972; Katz & Fodor, 1963). In other words, each feature is an essential element of the category. Together, the properties uniquely define the category. These components may be viewed as defining features because they constitute the definition of a category, according to the feature-based, componential point of view. A **defining feature** is a necessary attribute: For a thing to be an "X," it must have that feature. Otherwise, it is not an "X."

Consider, for example, the term *bachelor*. In addition to being human, a bachelor can be viewed as comprising three features: male, unmarried, and adult. The features are each singly necessary. Thus, even the absence of one feature makes the category inapplicable. Thus, an unmarried male who is not an adult would not be a bachelor. We would not refer to a 12-year-old unmarried boy as a bachelor because he is not an adult. Nor would we refer to just any male adult as a bachelor. If he is married, he is out of the running. An unmarried female adult is not a bachelor, either. Moreover, the three features are jointly sufficient. If a person has all three features, then he is automatically a bachelor. According to this view, you cannot be male, unmarried, and adult, and at the same time not be a bachelor. The feature-based view applies to more than bachelorhood, of course. For example, the term *wife* is made up of the features *married*, *female*, and *adult*. *Husband* comprises the features *married*, *male*, and *adult*.

The feature-based view is especially common among linguists, those who study language (Clark & Clark, 1977). This view is attractive because it makes categories of meaning appear so orderly. Unfortunately, it does not work as well as it appears to at first glance. Some categories do not readily lend themselves to featural analysis. *Game* is one such category. Finding anything at all that is a common feature of all games is actually difficult to do (Wittgenstein, 1953). Some are fun; some are not. Some involve multiple players; others, such as solitaire, do not. Some are competitive; others, such as children's circle games (e.g., ring-around-the-rosy), are not. The more you consider the concept of a game, the more you begin to wonder whether there is anything at all that holds the category together. It is not clear that there are any defining features of a game at all. Nonetheless, we all know what we mean, or think we do, by the word *game*.

Some things may seem to have clear defining features. Yet a violation of those defining features does not seem to change the category we use to define them. Consider a zebra (see Keil, 1989). We all know that a zebra is a black-and-white striped horselike animal. However, suppose that someone were to paint a zebra all black. A zebra painted black is missing the critical attribute of stripes. But we still would call it a "zebra." We run into the same problem with birds. We might think of the ability to fly as critical to being a bird. But certainly we would agree that a robin whose wings have been clipped is still a robin and still a bird. So is an ostrich, which does not fly.

The examples of the robin and the ostrich point out another problem with the feature-based theory. Both a robin and an ostrich share the same defining features of birds. They are, therefore, birds. However, loosely speaking, a robin seems somehow to be a better example of a bird than is an ostrich. Indeed, suppose people are asked to rate the typicality of a robin versus an ostrich as a bird. The former virtually always will get a higher rating than the latter (Malt & Smith, 1984; Mervis, Catlin, & Rosch, 1976; Rosch, 1975). Moreover, children learn typical instances of a category earlier than they learn atypical ones (Rosch, 1978). Table 8.1 shows some ratings of typicality for various instances of birds (Malt & Smith, 1984). Clearly, there are enormous differences. On the 7-point scale used by Malt and Smith for ratings of the typicality of birds, *bat* received a rating of 1.53. This rating is despite the fact that a bat, strictly speaking, is not even a bird at all.

In sum, the feature-based theory has some attractive features. But it does not seem to give a complete account of categories. Some specific examples of a category such as *bird* seem to be better examples than others. Yet they all have the same defining features. However, the various examples may be differentially typical of the category of birds. Thus, we need a theory of knowledge representation that better characterizes how people truly represent knowledge.

TABLE 8.1	Typicality Ratings for Birds		

Barbara Malt and Edward Smith (1984) found enormous differences in the typicality ratings for various instances of birds (or birdlike animals). (After Malt & Smith, 1984)

BIRD	RATING*	BIRD	RATING*
Robin	6.89	Vulture	4.84
Bluebird	6.42	Sandpiper	4.47
Seagull	6.26	Chicken	3.95
Swallow	6.16	Flamingo	3.37
Falcon	5.74	Albatross	3.32
Mockingbird	5.47	Penguin	2.63
Starling	5.16	Bat	1.53
Owl	5.00		

*Ratings were made on a 7-point scale, with 7 corresponding to the highest typicality.

Prototype Theory: A Characteristic View

The **prototype theory** suggests that categories are formed on the basis of a (prototypical, or averaged) model of the category. Crucial to this theory are **characteristic features,** which describe (characterize or typify) the prototype but are not necessary for it. Characteristic features commonly are present in exemplars of concepts. But they are not always present. For example, consider the prototype of a game. It might include that it usually is enjoyable, has two or more players, and presents some degree of challenge. But a game does not have to be enjoyable. It does not have to have two or more players. And it does not have to be challenging. Similarly, a bird usually has wings and flies. This theory introduces a new wrinkle into our attempt to understand knowledge organization by basing categorization on a prototype. A *prototype* is usually the original item on which subsequent models are based. But in this theory, the prototype may be whichever model best represents the class on which the category is based. This theory can handle the facts that (1) games seem to have no defining features at all and (2) a robin seems to be a better example of a bird than is an ostrich.

To understand how these problems are handled, you need to understand the concept of a characteristic feature. Whereas a defining feature is possessed by every instance of a category, a characteristic feature need not be. Instead, many or most instances possess each characteristic feature. Thus, the ability to fly is typical of birds. But it is not a defining feature of a bird. An ostrich cannot fly. It also lacks some other characteristic features of birds. According to prototype theory, it thus seems less birdlike than a robin, which can fly. Similarly, a typical game may be enjoyable; but it need not be so. Indeed, consider what happens when people are asked to list the features of a category, such as *fruit* or *furniture*. Most features that the people list are characteristic rather than defining (Rosch & Mervis, 1975). Suppose one lists the properties typical of a category such as *fruit* and then assesses how many of those properties a given instance has. One actually can compute a score of family resemblance that indicates how typical an instance is, overall, of the more general category (Rosch & Mervis, 1975).

Psychologists, in reflecting on how people seem to think about concepts and categories, came to differentiate two kinds of categories. These are called *classical concepts* and *fuzzy concepts*. Classical concepts are categories that can be readily defined through defining features, such as bachelor. Fuzzy concepts are categories that cannot be so easily defined. Their borders are, as their name implies, fuzzy. Classical concepts tend to be inventions that experts have devised for arbitrarily labeling a class that has associated defining features. Fuzzy concepts tend to evolve naturally (Smith, 1988, 1995). Thus, the concept of a bachelor is an arbitrary concept we invented. Some experts may suggest that we use the word *fruit* to describe any part of a plant that has seeds, pulp, and skin. Nevertheless, our natural, fuzzy concept of fruit usually does not easily extend to tomatoes, pumpkins, and cucumbers. Check the dictionary definitions for tomatoes, pumpkins, and cucumbers if you doubt their fruitiness. All of them really are subordinates (lower levels) of their superordinate (higher level) category, fruit.

Classical concepts and categories—and the words that label them—may be built on defining features. Fuzzy concepts and categories are built around prototypes. According to the prototype view, an object will be classified as an instance of a category if it is sufficiently similar to the prototype. Exactly what is meant by similarity to a prototype can be a complex issue. There are actually different theories of how this similarity should be measured (Smith & Medin, 1981). For our purposes, we view similarity in terms of the number of features shared between an object and the prototype. Perhaps some features even should be weighted more heavily as being more central to the prototype than are other features (e.g., Komatsu, 1992).

Actually, some psychologists suggest that instead of using a single prototype for categorizing a concept, we use multiple exemplars. **Exemplars** are typical representatives of a category (Murphy, 1993; Ross, 2000; Ross & Spalding, 1994). For example, in considering birds, we might think of not only the prototypical songbird, which is small, flies, builds nests, sings, and so on. We might also think of exemplars for birds of prey, for large flightless birds, for medium-sized water fowl, and so on. Some investigators use this approach in explaining how categories are both formed and used in speeded classification situations (Nosofsky & Palmeri, 1997; Nosofsky, Palmeri, & McKinley, 1994; see also Estes, 1994). In particular, categories are set up by creating a rule and then storing exceptions as exemplars. Later during recognition, exemplars race in memory. The speed of each item is determined by similarity to the target item. Likely candidates then enter a selection process. Thus, the category is coherent and stable. Storing exceptions allows categories to remain flexible. Indeed, suppose we have multiple exemplars. Then when we see an instance of a bird we can more flexibly match this instance to an appropriate exemplar than to a single prototype (Ross & Spalding, 1994).

A Synthesis: Combining Feature-Based and Prototype Theories

It is interesting that even classical categories seem to have prototypes. Consider two classical concepts (Armstrong, Gleitman, & Gleitman, 1983): *odd number* and *plane geometry figure*. Both of these concepts are defined easily. For example, an *odd number* is any integer not evenly divisible by 2. People found different instances of these categories to be more or less prototypical of their respective categories. For example, 7 and 13 are typical examples of odd numbers that are viewed as quite close to the prototype for an odd number. In contrast, 15 and 21 are not seen as so prototypically odd. In other words, people view 7 and 13 as better exemplars of odd numbers than 15 and 21. Nevertheless, all four numbers are actually odd. Similarly, a triangle is viewed as typical of plane geometry figures. In contrast, an ellipse is not.

A full theory of categorization might need to combine both defining and characteristic features (see also Hampton, 1997a; Smith & associates, 1988; Smith, Shoben, & Rips, 1974; Wisniewski, 1997, 2000). On this view, each category has both a prototype and a core. A **core** refers to the defining features something must have to be considered an example of a category. In contrast, the prototype encompasses the characteristic features that tend to be typical of an example but that are not necessary for being considered an example.

Consider the concept of a robber, for example. The core requires that someone labeled as a robber be a person who takes from others without permission. The prototype, however, tends to identify particular people as more likely to be robbers. White-collar criminals are hard to catch. In part, the reason is that they do not look like our prototypes of robbers, no matter how much they may steal from other people. In contrast, unkempt denizens of our inner cities sometimes are arrested for crimes they did not commit. In part, the reason is that they more closely match the police prototype of a robber, regardless of whether they steal.

Two researchers tested the notion that we come to understand the importance of defining features only as we grow older (Keil & Batterman, 1984). Younger children, they hypothesized, view categories largely in terms of characteristic features. The investigators presented children in the age range from 5 to 10 years with descriptions. Among them were two unusual individuals. The first was "a smelly, mean old man with a gun in his pocket who came to your house and took your TV set because your parents didn't want it anymore and told him he could have it." The second was "a very friendly and cheerful woman who gave you a hug, but then disconnected your toilet bowl and took it away without permission and with no intention to return it." Younger children often characterized the first description as a better depiction of a robber than the second description. It was not until close to age 10 years that children began to shift toward characterizing the second individual as more robberlike. In other words, the younger children viewed someone as a robber, even if the person did not steal anything. What mattered was that the person had the characteristic features of a robber. However, the transition is never fully complete. We might suspect that the first individual would be at least as likely to be arrested as the second. Thus, the issue of categorization itself remains somewhat fuzzy. But it appears to include some aspects of defining features and some aspects of prototypicality.

Theory-Based View

A departure from feature-based, prototype-based, and exemplar-based views of meaning is a theory-based view of meaning, also sometimes called an explanation-based view. A **theory-based view of meaning** holds that people understand and categorize concepts in terms of implicit theories, or general ideas they have regarding those concepts (Markman, 2003). For example, what makes someone a "good sport"? In the componential view, you would try to isolate features of a good sport. In the prototype view, you would try to find characteristic features of a good sport. In the exemplar view, you might try to find some good examples you have known in your life. In the theory-based view, you would use your experience to construct an explanation for what makes someone a good sport. Such a theory might go something like this: A good sport is someone who, when he or she wins, is gracious in victory and does not mock losers or otherwise make them feel bad about losing. It is also someone who, when he or she loses, loses graciously and does not blame the winner or the referee or find excuses. Rather, he or she takes the defeat in stride, congratulates the winner, and then moves on. Note that in the theory-based view, it is difficult to capture the essence of the theory in a word or two. Rather, the view of a concept is more complex.

The theory-based view suggests that people can distinguish between essential and incidental, or accidental features of concepts because they have complex mental representations of these concepts. One study showed how such theories might manifest themselves in judgments about newly learned concepts (Rips, 1989). Participants received stories about hypothetical creature. The stimuli were presented under two experimental conditions.

In this study (Rips, 1989), one condition involved a birdlike creature called a sorp that, through an accident, came to look like an insect. It was never stated that the sorp was birdlike or insectlike. Rather, the circumstances of the transformation were described in some detail. The sorp was described as having a diet consisting of seeds and berries, as having two wings and two legs, and as nesting high in the branches of a tree. The nest, like that of a bird, was composed of twigs and similar materials. Moreover, the sorp was covered with bluish-gray feathers, like many birds. But a particular sorp had a misfortune. Its nest was near the burial place of hazardous chemicals. As the chemicals contaminated the vegetation that the sorp ate, its appearance gradually started to change. The sorp lost its feathers and instead grew a new pair of wings that had a transparent membrane. The sorp left its nest and developed an outer shell that was brittle and iridescent. It grew two more pairs of legs, so that it now had six legs in all. It came to be able to hold on to smooth surfaces and it started sustaining itself solely on the nectar of flowers. In due course, the sorp mated with another sorp, a normal female. The female laid the fertilized eggs that resulted from the mating in her nest and incubated them. Then, after 3 weeks, normal young sorps emerged from their shells. Note that, in this description, the fact of the sorp's being able to mate with a normal sorp to produce normal sorps shows that the unfortunate sorp never really changed its basic biological makeup. It remained, in essence, a sorp.

The second condition involved an essential change in the nature of a creature. In other words, the change was one of essence rather than of accident. The change involved a creature known as a doon. During an early stage of the doon's life, it is known as a sorp. It has all the characteristics of a sorp (as previously described). But after a few months, the doon sheds its feathers and then develops the same characteristics that resulted from the unfortunate sorp's accident. Note that in this second condition, there is a transformation identical to that of the sorp described in the first condition, but the transformation is represented as a natural biological one rather than an accidental one caused by proximity to hazardous chemicals.

A control group read only the decription of sorps, but experimental participants in the study were asked to provide two ratings after reading about the sorp and the doon. The first rating was of the degree to which the sorp (in the sorp condition) or the doon (in the doon) condition fit into the category of "bird." The second rating was the similarity of the sorp or doon to birds. Thus, one rating was for category membership, and the other for similarity. Control-group participants were asked merely to rate the similarity of sorps to birds.

According to prototype and exemplar theories, there is no particular reason to expect the two sets of ratings from experimental participants to show different patterns. According to these theories, people categorize objects on the basis of their similarity to a prototype or an exemplar, so the results should be the same for both sets of ratings. Figure 8.1 shows the actual data.

The results for the categorization and similarity ratings are dramatically different. Note that in the accidental-change condition, category membership ratings are higher than in the essential-change condition. In other words, people were less likely to see the accidental change than the essential change as affecting fundamental category membership. In contrast, similarity ratings were higher in the accidental-change condition than in the essential-change condition. Control-group participants had no trouble recognizing the similarity of the sorp to a bird. The difference in patterns between the category-membership and similarity ratings is consistent with the theory-based view of meaning.

Further support for the theory-based view comes from work with children. A number of investigators have studied a view of meaning called *essentialism*. This view holds that certain categories, such as those of "lion" or "female," have an underlying reality that cannot be observed directly (Gelman, 2003, 2004). For example, someone could be, say, a female even if another individual were unable in his or her observations on

FIGURE 8.1

Effects of Changes on Categorizing and Similarity Ratings

the street to be able to detect that femaleness. One instance is having short hair. Having short hair might be more typical of males than females, yet females can have short hair. Gelman (2004) showed that even young children look beyond obvious features to understand the essential nature of things. This view contradicts Piaget's theory. According to that theory, children in the age range from roughly 8 to 11 years are "concrete" thinkers. They cannot abstract features that are formal in nature. Yet, the work of psychologists studying essentialism suggests that young children can and do look for hidden features that are in no way obvious.

For example, in one study, 165 children ages 4 to 5 years were asked to make inferences about things like a tiger or gold (Gelman & Markman, 1986). They could use either category membership, which is abstract, or perceptual similarity, which is concrete, to make their inferences. The inferences they would make by the two different means were different. The researchers found that even by the age of 4 years, children could make inferences using the abstract categories, even when these categories conflicted with appearances.

How people learn about concepts and categories depends, in part, on the task they will do with those concepts and categories. For example, people learn about categories one way if they need to make classifications (e.g., "Is this particular animal a cat or a dog?") and another way if they need to make inferences (e.g., "If this animal is a dog, how many toes will it have?") (Yamauchi & Markman, 1998). Learning, therefore, is strategically flexible, depending on the task that the individual will have to do; it does not occur with a "one-size-fits-all" rigidity (Markman & Ross, 2003; Ross, 1997).

What all this means is that meaning is not just a matter of a set of features or exemplars. From the time children are very young, they start to form theories about the nature of objects. These theories develop with age. For example, you probably have a theory about what makes a car a car. You could see cars looking all kinds of strange ways. As long as they conformed to your theory, you would nevertheless label them as cars. Theories enable us to view meaning deeply rather than just to assign meaning on the basis of superficial features of objects.

Semantic Network Models

An older model still in use today is that knowledge is represented in terms of a hierarchical semantic (related to meaning as expressed in language—i.e., in linguistic symbols) network. A semantic network is a web of interconnected elements of meaning (Collins & Quillian, 1969). **Nodes** are the elements of a network. In a semantic network, they typically represent concepts. The connections between nodes are *labeled relationships*. They might involve category membership (e.g., an "is a" relationship connecting "pig" to "mammal"), attributes (e.g., connecting "furry" to "mammal"), or some other semantic relationship. Thus, a **network** provides a means for organizing concepts. The exact form of a semantic network differs from one theory to another. But most networks look something like the highly simplified network shown in Figure 8.2. The labeled relationships form links that enable the individual to connect the various nodes in a meaningful way.

In a seminal study, the participants were given statements relating concepts, such as "A robin is a bird" and "A robin is an animal" (Collins & Quillian, 1969). They

FIGURE 8.2

In a simple semantic network, nodes serve as junctures representing concepts linked by labeled relationships: (a) a basic network structure showing that relationship R links the nodes a and b; (b) a simple network diagram of the sentence "Mary hit the ball."

were asked to verify the truth of the statements. The participants received only *class-inclusion statements*, in which the subject was a single word. The *predicate*, describing the subject, took the form "is a [category noun]." Some of the statements were true. Others were not. As the conceptual category of the predicate became more hierarchically remote from the category of the subject of the statement, people generally took longer to verify a true statement. Thus, we could expect people to take longer to verify "A robin is an animal" than "A robin is a bird." The reason is that *bird* is an immediate superordinate category for *robin*. *Animal*, however, is a more remote superordinate category. Collins and Quillian concluded that a hierarchical network representation, such as the one shown in Figure 8.3, adequately accounted for the response times in their study. According to this model, organized knowledge representation takes the form of a hierarchical tree diagram.

A hierarchical model seemed ideal to the investigators. Within a hierarchy we can store information efficiently that applies to all members of a category at the highest possible level in the hierarchy. We do not have to repeat the information at all of the lower levels in the hierarchy. Therefore, a hierarchical model contains a high degree of cognitive economy. The system allows for a maximum of efficient capacity use with a minimum of redundancy. Thus, if you know that dogs and cats are mammals, you store everything you know about mammals at the mammals level. For example, you might store that mammals have fur and give birth to live young whom they nurse. You do not have to repeat that information again at the hierarchically lower level for dogs and cats. Whatever was known about items at higher levels in a hierarchy was applied to all items at lower levels in the hierarchy. This concept of *inheritance* implies that lower-level items inherit the properties of higher-level items. This concept, in turn, is the key to the economy of hierarchical models. Computer models of the network clearly demonstrated the value of cognitive economy.

The Collins and Quillian study instigated a whole line of research into the structure of semantic networks. However, many of the psychologists who studied the Collins and Quillian data disagreed with Collins and Quillian's interpretations. For one thing, numerous anomalies in the data could not be explained by the model. For example, participants take longer to verify, "A lion is a mammal," than to verify "A

FIGURE 8.3

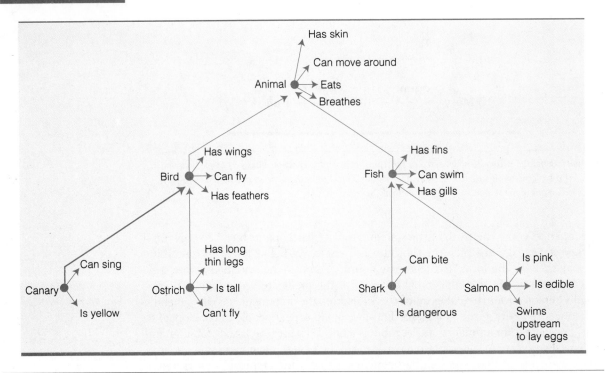

From *In Search of the Human Mind* by Robert J. Sternberg, copyright © 1995 by Harcourt Brace & Company, reproduced by permission of the publisher.

lion is an animal." Yet, in a strictly hierarchical view, verification should be faster for the mammal statement than for the animal one. After all, the category *mammal* is hierarchically closer to the category *lion* than is the category *animal*.

An alternative theory is that knowledge is organized based on a comparison of semantic features, rather than on a strict hierarchy of concepts (Smith, Shoben, & Rips, 1974). This theory differs from the feature-based theory of categorization in a key way. Features of different concepts are compared directly, rather than serving as the basis for forming a category.

Consider, for example, members of the set of mammal names. Mammal names can be represented in terms of a psychological space organized by three features: size, ferocity, and humanness (Henley, 1969). A lion, for example, would be high in all three. An elephant would be particularly high in size but not so high in ferocity. A rat would be small in size but relatively high in ferocity. Figure 8.4 shows how information might be organized within a nonhierarchical feature-based theory. Note that this representation, too, leaves a number of questions unanswered. For example, how does the word *mammal* itself fit in? It does not seem to fit into the space of mammal names. Where would other kinds of objects fit?

FIGURE 8.4

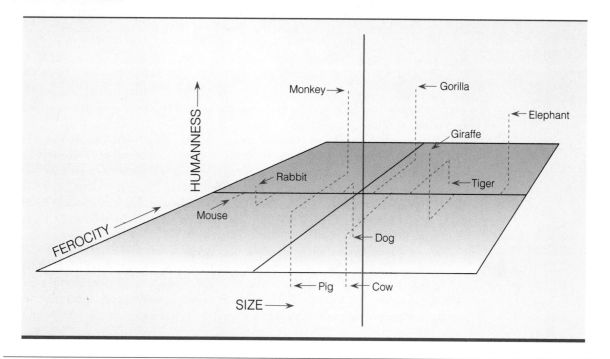

One alternative to hierarchical network models of semantic memory involves representations highlighting the comparison of semantic features. The features model, too, fails to explain all the data regarding semantic memory.

Neither of the preceding two theories of representation completely specifies how all information might be organized in a semantic network. Perhaps some kind of combination of representations is used (e.g., Collins & Loftus, 1975). Other network models tend to emphasize mental relationships that we think about more frequently rather than just any hierarchical relationships. For example, they might emphasize the link between birds and robins or sparrows, or the link between birds and flying. They would not emphasize the link between birds and turkeys or penguins, or the link between birds and standing on two legs.

Concepts appear to have a **basic level** (sometimes termed a natural level) of specificity, a level within a hierarchy that is preferred to other levels (Medin, Proffitt, & Schwartz, 2000; Rosch, 1978). Suppose I show you a red, roundish edible object that has a stem and that came from a tree. You might characterize it as a fruit, an apple, a Delicious apple, a Red Delicious apple, and so on. Most people, however, would characterize the object as an apple. The basic, preferred level is *apple*. In general, the basic level is neither the most abstract nor the most specific. Of course, this basic level can be manipulated by context or expertise (Tanaka & Taylor, 1991). Suppose the object were held up at a fruit stand that sold only apples. You might describe it as a Red Delicious apple to distinguish it from the other apples around it. Similarly, an apple farmer talking to a horticulture student might be more specific than would be a hurried shopper.

How can we tell what the basic level is? Why is the basic level the *apple*, rather than *Red Delicious apple* or *fruit*? Or why is it *cow*, rather than *mammal* or *Guernsey*? Perhaps the basic level is the one that has the largest number of distinctive features that set it off from other concepts at the same level (Rosch & associates, 1976). Thus, most of us would find more distinguishing features between an apple and a cow, say, than between a Red Delicious apple and a Pippin apple. Similarly, we would find few distinguishing features between a Guernsey cow and a Holstein cow. Again, not everyone necessarily would have the same basic level, as in the case of farmers. However, most people would. For our purposes, the basic level is the one that most people find to be maximally distinctive.

When people are shown pictures of objects, they identify the objects at a basic level more quickly than they identify objects at higher or lower levels (Rosch & associates, 1976). Objects appear to be recognized first in terms of their basic level. Only afterward are they classified in terms of higher- or lower-level categories. Thus, the picture of the roundish red edible object from a tree probably first would be identified as an apple. Only then, if necessary, would it be identified as a fruit or a Red Delicious apple.

We may broaden our understanding of concepts further if we consider not only the hierarchical and basic levels of a concept (Komatsu, 1992). We also should take into account other relational information the concept contains. Specifically, we may better understand the ways in which we derive meanings from concepts by considering their relations with other concepts, as well as the relations among attributes contained within a concept.

Schematic Representations

Schemas

One main approach to understanding how concepts are related in the mind is through schemas. They are very similar to semantic networks except that schemas are often more task oriented. Recall that a schema is a mental framework for organizing knowledge. It creates a meaningful structure of related concepts. Of course, both concepts and schemas may be viewed at many levels of analysis. It all depends on the mind of the individual and the context (Barsalou, 2000). For example, most of us probably view *cow* as a fundamental concept within, perhaps, a more elaborate schema for farm animals. However, for a cattle breeder or a dairy farmer, *cow* may not be at all fundamental. Both the breeder and the farmer may recognize many different kinds of cows. Each one may have various distinctive characteristics. Similarly, most people do not have an elaborate schema for *cognitive psychology*. However, for most cognitive psychologists, the schema for *cognitive psychology* is richly elaborated. It encompasses many subschemas, such as subschemas for attention, memory, and perception.

Schemas have several characteristics that ensure wide flexibility in their use (Rumelhart & Ortony, 1977; Thorndyke, 1984):

1. Schemas can include other schemas. For example, a schema for animals includes a schema for cows, a schema for apes, and so on.

2. Schemas encompass typical, general facts that can vary slightly from one specific instance to another. For example, although the schema for mam-

mals includes a general fact that mammals typically have fur, it allows for humans, who are less hairy than most other mammals. It also allows for porcupines, which seem more prickly than furry.

3. Schemas can vary in their degree of abstraction. For example, a schema for *justice* is much more abstract than a schema for *apple* or even a schema for *fruit*.

Schemas also can include information about relationships (Komatsu, 1992). Some of this information includes relationships among the following:

- Concepts (e.g., the link between trucks and cars)
- Attributes within concepts (e.g., the height and the weight of an elephant)
- Attributes in related concepts (e.g., the redness of a cherry and the redness of an apple)
- Concepts and particular contexts (e.g., fish and the ocean)
- Specific concepts and general background knowledge (e.g., concepts about particular U.S. presidents and general knowledge about the U.S. government and about U.S. history)

Relationships within schemas that particularly interest cognitive psychologists are causal ("if-then") relationships. For example, consider our schema for glass. It probably specifies that if an object made of glass falls onto a hard surface, then the object may break. Schemas also include information that we can use as a basis for drawing inferences in novel situations. For instance, suppose that a 75-year-old woman, a 45-year-old man, a 30-year-old nun, and a 25-year-old woman are sitting on park benches surrounding a playground. A young child falls from some playground equipment. He calls out "Mama!" To whom is the child calling? Chances are, to determine your answer you would be able to draw an inference by calling on various schemas. They would include ones for mothers, for men and women, for people of various ages, and even for people who join religious orders.

Early conceptions of schemas centered on how we represent information in memory (e.g., Bartlett, 1932). They also focused on how children develop cognitive understandings of how the world works (Piaget, 1928, 1952, 1955). Researchers interested in AI have adapted the notion of schemas to fit various computer models of human intelligence. As a part of their overall interest in developing computer models of intelligence, these researchers devised computer models of how knowledge is represented and used.

Scripts

One notion about schematic representations is termed a script (Schank & Abelson, 1977). A **script** is ". . . a structure that describes appropriate sequences of events in a particular context. A script is made up of slots and requirements about what can fill those slots. The structure is an interconnected whole, and what is in one slot affects what can be in another. Scripts handle stylized everyday situations. They are not subject to much change, nor do they provide the apparatus for handling totally novel situations" (Schank & Abelson, 1977, p. 41).

Thus, scripts are much less flexible than are schemas in general. However, scripts include default values for the actors, the props, the setting, and the sequence of events expected to occur.

Consider the restaurant script. The script may be applied to one particular kind of restaurant, the coffee shop. A script has several features. One is props. These include tables, a menu, food, a check, and money. A second is roles to be played. They include a customer, a waiter, a cook, a cashier, and an owner. A third feature is opening conditions for the script. For example, the customer is hungry and he or she has money. A fourth feature is scenes. These include entering, ordering, eating, and exiting. And a fifth feature is a set of results. The customer has less money. The owner has more money. The customer is no longer hungry. And, sometimes, the customer and the owner are pleased.

Various empirical studies have been conducted to test the validity of the script notion. In one, researchers presented their participants with eighteen brief stories (Bower, Black, & Turner, 1979). Consider one of these, representing the doctor's office script, in the "Investigating Cognitive Psychology" box.

INVESTIGATING COGNITIVE PSYCHOLOGY

THE DOCTOR

John was feeling bad today so he decided to go see the family doctor. He checked in with the doctor's receptionist and then looked through several medical magazines that were on the table by his chair. Finally the nurse came and asked him to take off his clothes. The doctor was very nice to him. He eventually prescribed some pills for John. Then John left the doctor's office and headed home.

Did John take off his clothes?

This "scripted" description of a visit to a doctor's office is fairly typical. Notice that in this description, as would probably happen in any verbal description of a script, some details are missing. The speaker (or scriptwriter, in this case) may have omitted mentioning these details. Thus, we do not know for sure that John actually took off his clothes. Moreover, the nurse probably beckoned John at some point. She or he then escorted him to an examination room. The nurse then probably took John's temperature and his blood pressure and weighed him. The doctor probably asked John to describe his symptoms, and so on. But we do not know any of these things for sure.

In the research, participants were asked to read eighteen stories. Later, they were asked to perform one of two tasks. In a recall task, participants were asked to recall as much as they could about each of the stories. Here, participants showed a significant tendency to recall, as parts of the stories, elements that were not actually in the stories but that were parts of the scripts that the stories represented. In the recognition task, participants were presented with sentences. They were asked to rate on a 7-point scale their confidence that they had seen each of the sentences. Some of the sentences were from the stories. Others were not. Of the sentences that were *not* from the stories, some were from the relevant scripts. Others were not from these scripts. Participants were more likely to characterize particular nonstory sentences as having come from the stories if the nonstory sentences were script-relevant than if the nonstory sentences were not script-relevant. The Bower, Black, and Turner research suggested that scripts seem to guide what people recall and recognize—ultimately, what people know.

In a related context, scripts also may come into play in regard to the ways in which experts converse with and write for one another. Certainly, experts share a **jargon**—specialized vocabulary commonly used within a group, such as a profession or a trade. In addition, however, experts share a common understanding of scripts that are known by insiders to the field of expertise. This understanding is not shared by outsiders. When trying to understand technical manuals and technical conversations outside your own area of expertise, you may run into vocabulary difficulties and information gaps. You lack the proper script for interpreting the language being spoken.

Take a closer look at the scripts you use in your everyday life. Is your going-to-class script different from your going-to-meals script or other scripted activities? In what ways do your scripts differ—in structure or in details? Try making changes to your script, either in details or in structure. See how things work. For example, you may find that you rush in the morning to get to school or work and forget things or arrive late. Aside from the obvious adjustment of getting up earlier, analyze the structure of your script. See if you can combine or remove steps. You could try laying out your clothes and packing your backpack or briefcase the night before to simplify your morning routine. The bottom line? The best way to make your scripts work better for you is first to analyze what they are and then to correct them.

PRACTICAL APPLICATIONS OF COGNITIVE PSYCHOLOGY

Despite the flaws in the script model, it has helped cognitive psychologists gain insight into knowledge organization. Scripts may enable us to use a mental framework for acting in certain situations when we must fill in apparent gaps within a given context. Without access to mental scripts, we probably would be at a loss the first time we entered a new restaurant or a new doctor's office. Imagine what it would be like if the nurse at the doctor's office had to explain each step to you. When everyone in a given situation follows a similar script, the day flows much more smoothly.

Whether we subscribe to the notion of categories, semantic networks, or schemas, the important issue is that knowledge is organized. These forms of organization can serve different purposes. The most adaptive and flexible use of knowledge would allow us to use any form of organization, depending on the situation. We need some means to define aspects of the situation, to relate these concepts to other concepts and categories, and to select the appropriate course of action given the situation. Next, we move on to discuss theories about how the mind represents procedural knowledge.

Representations of Procedural Knowledge

Some of the earliest models for representing procedural knowledge come from AI and computer-simulation research (see Chapter 1). With these models, researchers try to get computers to perform tasks intelligently, particularly in ways that simulate intelligent performance of humans. In fact, cognitive psychologists have learned a great deal about representing and using procedural knowledge. They have had to because of the distinctive problems posed in getting computers to implement procedures based on a series of instructions compiled in programs. Through trial-and-error attempts at getting computers to simulate intelligent cognitive processes, cognitive psychologists have come to understand some of the complexities of human information processing. As a result of their efforts, they have developed a variety of models for how information is represented and processed. Each of these models involves the **serial processing** of information, in which information is handled through a linear sequence of operations, one operation at a time. One way in which computers can represent and organize procedural knowledge is in the form of sets of rules governing a **production,** a generation and output of a procedure (Jones & Ritter, 2003). Specifically, computer simulations of productions follow production rules ("if-then" rules), comprising an "if" clause and a "then" clause (Newell & Simon, 1972). People may use this same form of organizing knowledge or something very close to it. For example, suppose your car is veering toward the left side of the road. Then you should steer toward the right side of the road if you wish to avoid hitting the curb. The "if" clause includes a set of conditions that must be met to implement the "then" clause. The "then" clause is an action or a series of actions.

For a given clause, each condition may contain one or more variables. For each of these conditions, there may be one or more possibilities. For example, *if* you want to go somewhere by car, and *if* you know how to drive a car, and *if* you are licensed and insured to drive, and *if* you have a car available to you, and *if* you do not have other constraints (e.g., no keys, no gas, broken engine, dead battery), *then* you may execute the actions for driving a car somewhere.

When the rules are described precisely and all of the relevant conditions and actions are noted, a huge number of rules are required to perform even a very simple task. These rules are organized into a structure of *routines* (instructions regarding procedures for implementing a task) and *subroutines* (instructions for implementing a subtask within a larger task governed by a routine). Many of these routines and subroutines are *iterative*, meaning that they are repeated many times during the performance of a task. The various routines and subroutines execute component tasks and subtasks required for implementing the main production. For the performance of a particular task or the use of a particular skill, knowledge representation involves a production system (Anderson, 1983; Newell & Simon, 1972). It comprises the entire set of rules (productions) for executing the task or using the skill (Anderson, 1993; Simon, 1999).

Consider an example of a simple production system for a pedestrian to cross the street at an intersection with a traffic light (Newell & Simon, 1972). It is shown here (with the "if" clauses indicated to the left of the arrows and the "then" clauses indicated to the right of the arrows):

traffic-light red → stop

traffic-light green → move

move and left foot on pavement → step with right foot

move and right foot on pavement → step with left foot

In this production system, the individual first tests to see whether the light is red. If it is red, the person stops and again tests to see whether the light is red. This sequence is repeated until the light turns green. At that point, the person starts moving. If the person is moving and the left foot is on the pavement, the person will step with the right foot. If the person is moving and the right foot is on the pavement, the person will step with the left foot.

Sometimes, production systems, like computer programs, contain bugs. *Bugs* are flaws in the instructions for the conditions or for executing the actions. For example, in the cross-the-street program, if the last line read "move and right foot on pavement → step with right foot," the individual executing the production system would get nowhere. According to the production-system model, human representations of procedural knowledge may contain some occasional bugs (VanLehn, 1990).

Until about the mid-1970s, researchers interested in knowledge representation followed either of two basic strands of research. AI and information-processing researchers were refining various models for representing procedural knowledge. Cognitive psychologists and other researchers were considering various alternative models for representing declarative knowledge. By the end of the 1970s, some integrative models of knowledge representation began to emerge.

Integrative Models for Representing Declarative and Nondeclarative Knowledge

Combining Representations: ACT-R

An excellent example of a theory that combines forms of mental representation is the **ACT** (adaptive control of thought) model of knowledge representation and information processing (Anderson, 1976, 1993; Anderson, Budiu, & Reder, 2001). In his ACT model, John Anderson synthesized some of the features of serial information-processing models and some of the features of semantic-network models. In ACT, procedural knowledge is represented in the form of production systems. Declarative knowledge is represented in the form of propositional networks. Anderson (1985) defined a proposition as being the smallest unit of knowledge that can constitute a separate assertion. Recall from Chapter 7 that propositions are abstracted underlying meanings of relationships among elements. ACT is an evolved form of earlier models (Anderson, 1972; Anderson & Bower, 1973).

Anderson intended his model to be so broad in scope that it would offer an overarching theory regarding the entire architecture of cognition. In Anderson's view, individual cognitive processes such as memory, language comprehension, problem solving, and reasoning are merely variations on a central theme. They all reflect an underlying system of cognition. The most recent version of ACT, **ACT-R,** is a model of information processing that integrates a network representation for declarative knowledge and a production-system representation for procedural knowledge (Anderson, 1983; Figure 8.5).

In ACT-R, networks include images of objects and corresponding spatial configurations and relationships. They also include temporal information, such as relationships involving the sequencing of actions, events, or even the order in which items appear. Anderson referred to the temporal information as "temporal strings." He noted

John R. Anderson is a professor of psychology at Carnegie-Mellon University. He is best known for his ACT-R model of human cognition. Anderson also has made major contributions in his work on the application of psychology to real-world learning, such as in learning the computer language LISP.

Courtesy of Dr. John R. Anderson

FIGURE 8.5

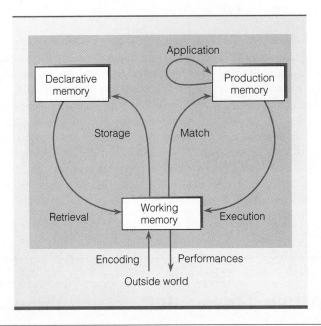

Relationship between declarative memory, production memory, and working memory. From The Legacy of Solomon Asch: Essays in Cognition and Social Psychology by Irwin Rock. Copyright © 1990 by Lawrence Erlbaum Associates. Reprinted by permission.

that they contain information about the relative time sequence. Examples would be before/after, first/second/third, and yesterday/tomorrow. These relative time sequences can be compared with absolute time referents, such as 2 P.M., September 4, 2004. The model is under constant revision and currently includes information about statistical regularities in the environment (Anderson, 1991, 1996; Anderson & Fincham, 1996).

Anderson's declarative network model, like many other network models (e.g., Collins & Loftus, 1975), contains a mechanism by which information can be retrieved and a structure for storing information. Recall that within a semantic network, concepts are stored at various nodes within the network. According to Anderson's model (and various other network models), the nodes can be either inactive or active at a given time. An active node is one that is, in a sense, "turned on." A node can be turned on—activated—directly by external stimuli such as sensations. Or it can be activated by internal stimuli, such as memories or thought processes. Or it can be activated indirectly, by the activity of one or more neighboring nodes.

Given each node's receptivity to stimulation from neighboring nodes, activation easily can spread from one node to another. But there are limits on the amount of information (number of nodes) that can be activated at any one time. Within the limited capacity of the overall cognitive system, this **spreading activation** is excitation that fans out along a set of nodes within a given network (Shastri, 2003). Of course, as more nodes are activated and the spread of activation reaches greater distances from the initial source of the activation, the activation weakens.

ACT-R also suggests means by which the network changes as a result of activation. For one thing, the more often particular links between nodes are used, the stronger the links become. In a complementary fashion, activation is likely to spread along the routes of frequently traveled connections. It is less likely to spread along infrequently used connections between nodes.

Consider an analogy. Imagine a complex set of water pipes interlinking various locations. When the water is turned on at one location, the water starts moving through various pipes. It is showing a sort of spreading activation. At various interconnections, a valve is either open or closed. It thus either permits the flow to continue through or diverts the flow (the activation) to other connections.

To carry the analogy a bit further, processes such as attention can influence the degree of activation throughout the system. Consider the water system again. The higher the water pressure in the system, the farther along the water will spread through the system of pipes. To relate this metaphor back to spreading activation, think about what happens when we are thinking about an issue and various associations seem to come to mind regarding that issue. We are experiencing the spread of activation along the nodes that represent our knowledge of various aspects of the problem and, possibly, its solution.

To help explain some aspects of spreading activation, picture the pipes as being more flexible than normal pipes. These pipes gradually can expand or contract. It all depends on how frequently they are used. The pipes along routes that are traveled frequently may expand to enhance the ease and speed of travel along those routes. The pipes along routes that are seldom traveled gradually may contract. Similarly, in spreading activation, connections that frequently are used are strengthened. Connections that are seldom used are weakened. Thus, within semantic networks, declarative knowledge may be learned and maintained through the strengthening of connections as a result of frequent use.

How does Anderson explain the acquisition of procedural knowledge? Such knowledge is represented in production systems rather than in semantic networks. Knowledge representation of procedural skills occurs in three stages: cognitive, associative, and autonomous (Anderson, 1980). During the cognitive stage, we think about explicit rules for implementing the procedure. During the associative stage, we practice using the explicit rules extensively, usually in a highly consistent manner. Finally, during the autonomous stage, we use these rules automatically and implicitly. We show a high degree of integration and coordination, as well as speed and accuracy.

For example, while we are in the cognitive stage for learning how to drive a standard-shift car, we must explicitly think about each rule for stepping on the clutch pedal, the gas pedal, or the brake pedal. Simultaneously, we also try to think about when and how to shift gears. During the associative stage, we carefully and repeatedly practice following the rules in a consistent manner. We gradually become more familiar with the rules. We learn when to follow which rules and when to implement which procedures. Eventually, we reach the autonomous stage. At this time we have integrated all of the various rules into a single, coordinated series of actions. We no longer need to think about what steps to take to shift gears. We can concentrate instead on listening to our favorite radio station. We simultaneously can think about going to our destination, avoiding accidents, stopping for pedestrians, and so on.

Our progress through these stages is proceduralization. *Proceduralization* is the overall process by which we transform slow, explicit information about procedures ("knowing that") into speedy, implicit, implementations of procedures ("knowing how"). (Recall the discussion of *automatization* in Chapter 3. This is a term used by other cognitive psychologists to describe essentially the same process as proceduralization.) One means by which we make this transformation is through composition. During this stage, we construct a single production rule that effectively embraces two or more production rules. It thus streamlines the number of rules required for executing the procedure. For example, consider what happens when we learn to drive a standard-shift car. We may compose a single procedure for what were two separate procedures. One was for pressing down on the clutch. The other was for applying the brakes when we reach a stop sign.

Another aspect of proceduralization is "production tuning." It involves the two complementary processes of generalization and discrimination. We learn to generalize existing rules to apply them to new conditions. For example, we can generalize our use of the clutch, the brakes, and the accelerator to a variety of standard-shift cars. Finally, we learn to discriminate new criteria for meeting the conditions we face. For example, what happens after we have mastered driving a particular standard-shift car? If we drive a car with a different number of gears or with different positions for the reverse gear, we must discriminate the relevant information about the new gear positions from the irrelevant information about the old gear positions.

Thus far, the models of knowledge representation presented in this chapter have been based largely on computer models of human intelligence. As the foregoing discussion shows, information-processing theories based on computer simulations of human cognitive processes have greatly advanced our understanding of human knowledge representation and information processing. An alternative approach to understanding knowledge representation in humans has been to study the human brain itself. Much of the research in psychobiology has offered evidence that many operations of the human brain do not seem to process information step-by-step, bit-by-bit. Rather, the human brain seems to engage in multiple processes simultaneously. It acts on myriad bits of knowledge all at once. Such models do not necessarily contradict step-by-step models. First, people seem likely to use both serial and parallel processing. Second, different kinds of processes may be occurring at different levels. Thus, our brains may be processing multiple pieces of information simultaneously. They combine into each of the steps of which we are aware when we process information step-by-step.

Models Based on the Human Brain

As mentioned previously, knowledge traditionally has been described as either declarative or procedural. Procedural knowledge usually involves some degree of skill. Examples would be skill in problem solving or numerical, linguistic, or musical operations. These skills increase as a result of practice. Eventually, performance requires little conscious attention, at least under most circumstances (see Chapter 3). For example, knowledge of a telephone number is declarative knowledge. Knowing how to memorize a phone number involves procedural knowledge. By now, you have become very skilled at knowing how to memorize information. As a result, you are no longer aware of many of the procedures you use for doing so. When you were a child, however, you were still learning how mentally to represent the procedural knowledge for memorizing simple facts. You were probably keenly conscious of learning to do so.

One can expand the traditional distinction between declarative and procedural knowledge to suggest that nondeclarative knowledge may encompass a broader range of mental representations than just procedural knowledge (Squire, 1986; Squire & associates, 1990). Specifically, in addition to declarative knowledge, we mentally represent the following forms of nondeclarative knowledge:

- Perceptual, motor, and cognitive skills (procedural knowledge)
- Simple associative knowledge (classical and operant conditioning)
- Simple nonassociative knowledge (habituation and sensitization)
- Priming (fundamental links within a knowledge network, in which the activation of information along a particular mental pathway facilitates the subsequent retrieval of information along a related pathway or even the same mental pathway; see Chapter 3)

According to Squire, all of these nondeclarative forms of knowledge are usually implicit (unstated). They are not easily made explicit.

Squire's primary inspiration for his model came from three sources. The first was his own work. The second was a wide range of neuropsychological research done by others (e.g., Baddeley & Warrington, 1970; Milner, 1972). This range included studies of amnesic patients, animal studies, and studies of the *microanatomy* of the brain (using microscopes to study brain cells). The third source was human cognitive experiments. Consider an example: Work with amnesic patients reveals clear distinctions between the neural systems for representing declarative knowledge versus neural systems for some of the nondeclarative forms of knowledge. For instance, amnesic patients often continue to show procedural knowledge even when they cannot remember that they possess such knowledge. Often they show improvements in performance on tasks requiring skills. These improvements indicate some form of new knowledge representation despite an inability to remember ever having previous experience with the tasks. For example, an amnesic patient who is given repeated practice in reading mirror writing will improve as a result of practice. But he or she will not recall ever having engaged in the practice (Baddeley, 1989).

Nondeclarative knowledge representation occurs as a result of experience in implementing a procedure. It is not merely a result of reading, hearing, or otherwise acquiring information from explicit instructions. Once a mental representation of nondeclarative knowledge is constructed, that knowledge is implicit. It is not easily made explicit. In fact, the process of enhancing the mental representation of nondeclarative knowledge tends actually to decrease explicit access to that knowledge. For example, suppose you recently have learned how to drive a standard-shift car. You may find it easier to describe how to do so than may someone who learned that skill long ago. As your explicit access to nondeclarative knowledge decreases, however, your speed and ease of gaining implicit access to that knowledge increases. Eventually, most nondeclarative knowledge can be retrieved for use much more quickly than declarative knowledge can be retrieved.

Another paradox of human knowledge representation also is demonstrated by amnesics. Although amnesics do not show normal memory abilities under most circumstances, they do show the priming effect. Recall from Chapter 3 that, in priming, particular cues and stimuli seem to activate mental pathways. These pathways in turn enhance the retrieval or cognitive processing of related information. For example, if someone asks you to spell the word *sight*, you will probably spell it differently, depending on several factors. These factors include whether you have been primed to think about sensory modalities ("s-i-g-h-t"), about locations for an archaeological dig ("s-i-t-e"), or about lists of references ("c-i-t-e"). Consider what happens when the amnesic participants have no recall of the priming and cannot explicitly recall the experience during which priming occurred. Nevertheless, priming still affects their performance.

If you can recruit at least two (and preferably more) volunteers, try the experiment on priming in the "Investigating Cognitive Psychology" box. It requires you to draw on your store of declarative knowledge.

INVESTIGATING COGNITIVE PSYCHOLOGY

Separate your volunteers into two groups. For one group, ask them to unscramble the following anagrams (puzzles in which you must figure out the correct order of letters to make a sensible word): ZAZIP, GASPETHIT, POCH YUSE, OWCH MINE, ILCHI, ACOT.

Ask the members of the other group to unscramble the following anagrams: TECKAJ, STEV, ASTEREW, OLACK, ZELBAR, ACOT.

For the first group, the correct answers are *pizza*, *spaghetti*, *chop suey*, *chow mein*, *chili*, and a sixth item. The correct answers for the second group are *jacket*, *vest*, *sweater*, *cloak*, *blazer*, and a sixth item. The sixth item in each group may be either *taco* or *coat*. Did your volunteers show a tendency to choose one or the other answer, depending on the preceding list with which they were primed?

The preceding examples illustrate situations in which an item may prime another item that is somehow related in meaning. We actually may differentiate two types of priming: semantic priming and repetition priming (Posner & associates, 1988). In semantic priming, we are primed by a meaningful context or by meaningful information. Examples are fruits or green things, which may prime "lime." In repetition priming, a prior exposure to a word or other stimulus primes a subsequent retrieval of that information. For example, hearing the word "lime" primes subsequent stimulation for the word "lime." Both types of priming have generated a great deal of research. But semantic priming often particularly interests cognitive psychologists.

For example, there is evidence of priming from research on normal participants. In one study, participants received two short paragraphs (McKoon & Ratcliff, 1980). After reading the paragraphs, the participants took a recognition-memory test. Participants then stated whether they had seen a given word in one of the stories and were timed in their responses. Some of the words they saw were from one of the stories they had just read. Others were from neither story. The critical aspect of the experiment was whether a given test word was preceded by a word from the *same* story or by a word from the *other* story. The first kind of trial is a primed trial. The second kind is an unprimed control trial. Suppose priming does indeed occur. Then participants should respond more quickly to a test item if it has just been preceded by a test item from the same story than if it has just been preceded by a test item from the other story. The researchers verified this prediction in a series of experiments.

According to spreading-activation theories, the amount of activation between a prime and a given target node is a function of two things. The first is the number of links connecting the prime and the target. The second is the relative strengths of each connection. This view holds that increasing the number of intervening links tends to decrease the likelihood of the priming effect. But increasing the strength of each link between the prime and its target tends to increase the likelihood of the priming effect. This model has been well supported (e.g., McNamara, 1992). Furthermore, the occurrence of priming through spreading activation is taken by most psychologists as support for a network model of knowledge representation in memory processes. In particular, the notions of priming effects through spreading activation within a network model have led to the emergence of a newer model. It is called a connectionist model of knowledge representation.

Parallel Processing: The Connectionist Model

The computer-inspired information-processing theories assume that humans, like computers, process information serially. That is, information is processed one step after another. Some aspects of human cognition may indeed be explained in terms of serial processing. But psychobiological findings and other cognitive research seem to indicate other aspects of human cognition. These aspects involve **parallel processing,** in which multiple operations go on all at once. We have seen how the information processing of a computer has served as a metaphor for many models of cognition. Similarly, our increasing understanding of how the human brain processes information also serves as a metaphor for many of the recent models of knowledge representation in humans. The human brain seems to handle many operations and to process information from many sources simultaneously—in parallel. Thus, many contemporary models of knowledge representation emphasize the importance of parallel processing in human cognition. As a further result of interest in parallel processing, some computers have been made to simulate parallel processing, such as through so-called neural networks of interlinked computer processors.

At present, many cognitive psychologists are exploring the limits of parallel processing models. According to **parallel distributed processing (PDP) models** or **connectionist models,** we handle very large numbers of cognitive operations at once through a network distributed across incalculable numbers of locations in the brain (McClelland, Rumelhart, & the PDP Research Group, 1986; McLeod, Plunkett, & Rolls, 1998; Plaut, 2000; Rumelhart, McClelland, & the PDP Research Group, 1986; Seidenberg & McClelland, 1989). A computer can begin responding to an input within nanoseconds (millionths of a second). But an individual neuron may take up to 3 milliseconds to fire in response to a stimulus. Consequently, serial processing in the human brain would be far too slow to manage the amount of information it handles. For example, most of us can recognize a complex visual stimulus within about

James L. McClelland is a professor of psychology and computer science at Carnegie-Mellon University and is a codirector of the Center for the Neural Basis of Cognition. McClelland is best known for his seminal work with David Rumelhart on introducing PDP (connectionist) models into the mainstream of psychology and for the revelation that such models can be formulated, implemented, and tested in a number of different domains of cognitive functioning.

300 milliseconds. If we processed the stimulus serially, only a few hundred neurons would have had time to respond. Rather, according to PDP models, the distribution of parallel processes better explains the speed and accuracy of human information processing.

The mental structure within which parallel processing is believed to occur is the network. In connectionist networks, all forms of knowledge are represented within the network structure. Recall that the fundamental element of the network is the node. Each node is connected to many other nodes. These interconnected patterns of nodes enable the individual to organize meaningfully the knowledge contained in the connections among the various nodes. In many network models, each node represents a concept.

The network of the PDP model is different in key respects from the semantic network described earlier. In the PDP model, the network comprises neuronlike units (McClelland & Rumelhart, 1981, 1985; Rumelhart & McClelland, 1982). They do not, in and of themselves, actually represent concepts, propositions, or any other type of information. Thus, the pattern of connections represents the knowledge, not the specific units. The same idea governs our use of language. Individual letters (or sounds) of a word are relatively uninformative. But the pattern of letters (or sounds) is highly informative. Similarly, no single unit is very informative. But the pattern of interconnections among units is highly informative. Figure 8.6 illustrates how just six units (dots) may be used to generate many more than six patterns of connections between the dots.

The PDP model demonstrates another way in which a brain-inspired model differs from a computer-inspired one. Differing cognitive processes are handled by differing patterns of activation, rather than as a result of a different set of instructions from a computer's central processing unit. In the brain, at any one time a given neuron may be inactive, excitatory, or inhibitory.

- *Inactive* neurons are not stimulated beyond their threshold of excitation. They do not release any neurotransmitters into the synapse (the interneuronal gap).
- *Excitatory* neurons release neurotransmitters that stimulate receptive neurons at the synapse. They increase the likelihood that the receiving neurons will reach their threshold of excitation.
- *Inhibitory* neurons release neurotransmitters that inhibit receptive neurons. They reduce the likelihood that the receiving neurons will reach their threshold of excitation.

Furthermore, although the action potential of a neuron is all or none, the amounts of neurotransmitters and neuromodulators released may vary. The frequency of firing also may vary. This variation affects the degree of excitation or inhibition of other neurons at the synapse.

Similarly, in the PDP model, individual units may be inactive. Or they may send excitatory or inhibitory signals to other units. That is not to say that the PDP model actually indicates specific neural pathways for knowledge representation. We are still a long way from having more than a faint glimmer of knowing how to map specific neural information. Rather, the PDP model uses the physiological processes of the

FIGURE 8.6

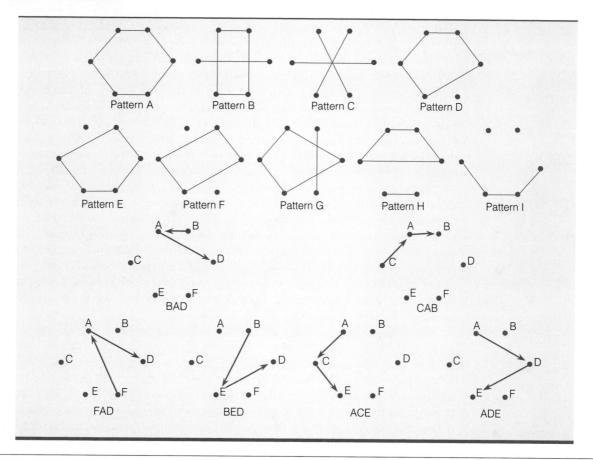

Each individual unit (dot) is relatively uninformative, but when the units are connected into various patterns, each pattern may be highly informative, as illustrated in the patterns at the top of this figure. Similarly, individual letters are relatively uninformative, but patterns of letters may be highly informative. Using just three-letter combinations, we can generate many different patterns, such as DAB, FED, and other patterns shown in the bottom of this figure.

brain as a metaphor for understanding cognition. According to the PDP model, connections between units can possess varying degrees of potential excitation or inhibition. These differences can occur even when the connections are currently inactive. The more often a particular connection is activated, the greater is the strength of the connection, whether the connection is excitatory or inhibitory.

According to the PDP model, whenever we use knowledge, we change our representation of it. Thus, knowledge representation is not really a final product. Rather, it is a process or even a potential process. What is stored is not a particular pattern of connections. It is a pattern of potential excitatory or inhibitory connection strengths. The brain uses this pattern to re-create other patterns when stimulated to do so.

When we receive new information, the activation from that information either strengthens or weakens the connections between units. The new information may come from environmental stimuli, from memory, or from cognitive processes. The ability to create new information by drawing inferences and making generalizations allows for almost infinite versatility in knowledge representation and manipulation.

This versatility is what makes humans—unlike computers—able to accommodate incomplete and distorted information. Information that is distorted or incomplete is considered to be *degraded*. According to the PDP model, human minds are flexible. They do not require that all aspects of a pattern precisely match to activate a pattern. Thus, consider what happens when enough distinctive (but not all) aspects of a particular pattern have been activated by other attributes in the description. The degraded information does not prevent us from re-creating the correct pattern. This cognitive flexibility also greatly enhances our ability to learn new information.

By using the PDP model, cognitive psychologists attempt to explain various general characteristics of human cognition. These characteristics include our ability to respond flexibly, dynamically, rapidly, and relatively accurately, even when we are given only partial or degraded information. In addition, cognitive psychologists attempt to use the model to explain specific cognitive processes. Examples of such processes are perception, reasoning, reading, language comprehension, and priming, as well as other memory processes (Elman & associates, 1996; Hinton, 1991; Hinton & Shallice, 1991; O'Reilly, 1996; Plaut & associates, 1996; Plaut & Shallice, 1994; Smolensky, 1999).

Although connectionist models of knowledge representation explain many phenomena of knowledge representation and processing, these models are not flawless. They explain many cognitive processes. These processes include, for example, those involving perception and memory. They may be learned gradually by our storing knowledge through gradual strengthening of patterns of connections within the network. However, many aspects of the model are not yet well defined. For example, the model is less effective in explaining how people can remember a single event (Schacter, 1989a). For example, how do we suddenly construct a whole new interconnected pattern for representing what we know about a memorable event, such as graduation day?

Similarly, connectionist models do not satisfactorily explain how we often quickly can unlearn established patterns of connections when we are presented with contradictory information (Ratcliff, 1990; Treadway & associates, 1992). For example, suppose that you are told that the criteria for classifying parts of plants as fruits are that they must have seeds, pulp, and skin. You also are told that whether they are sweeter than other plant parts is not important. Suppose now you are given the task of sorting various photos of plant parts into groups that are or are not fruits. You will sort tomatoes and pumpkins with apples and other fruits, even if you did not previously consider them to be fruits.

These shortcomings of connectionist systems can be bypassed. It may be that there are two learning systems in the brain (McClelland, McNaughton, & O'Reilly, 1995). One system corresponds to the connectionist model in resisting change and in being relatively permanent. The complementary system handles rapid acquisition of new information. It holds the information for a short time. It then integrates the newer information with information in the connectionist system. Evidence from neuropsychology and connectionist network modeling seem to corroborate this account

(McClelland, McNaughton, & O'Reilly, 1997). Thus, the connectionist system is spared. But we still need a satisfactory account of the other learning system.

The preceding models of knowledge representation and information processing clearly have profited from technological advances in computer science, in brain imaging, and in the psychobiological study of the human brain in action. These are techniques that few would have predicted to have been so promising 40 years ago. Thus, it would be foolish to predict that specific avenues of research will lead us in particular directions. Nonetheless, particular avenues of research do hold promise. For example, using powerful computers, researchers are attempting to create parallel-processing models via neural networks. Increasingly sophisticated techniques for studying the brain offer intriguing possibilities for research. Case studies, naturalistic studies, and traditional laboratory experiments in the field of cognitive psychology also offer rich opportunities for further exploration. Some researchers are trying to explore highly specific cognitive processes, such as auditory processing of speech sounds. Others are trying to investigate fundamental processes that underlie all aspects of cognition. Which type of research is more valuable?

Comparing Connectionist with Network Representations

How do connectionist models compare with network models? Figure 8.7 shows the concept of a robin as represented by both a network model and a connectionist model.

In the network representation, an individual builds up a knowledge base about a robin over time as more and more information is acquired about robins. Note that information about robins is embedded in a general network representation that goes beyond just robins. One's understanding of robins partly depends on the relationship of the robin to other birds and even other kinds of living things. Indeed, perhaps the

FIGURE 8.7

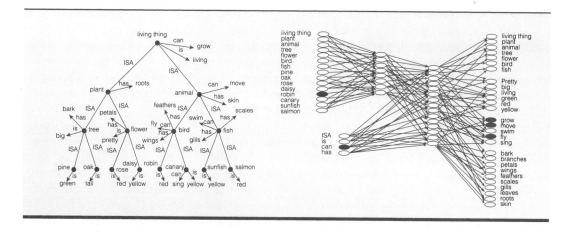

Network and connectionist representations of concepts relating to birds. From J. L. McClelland, "Connectionist Model of Memory," in E. Tulving & F. I. M. Craik (Eds.), The Oxford Handbook of Memory, p. 583–596. © 2000 Oxford University Press.

IN THE LAB OF JAMES L. McCLELLAND

Courtesy of Dr. James L. McClelland

In my laboratory we attempt to understand the implications of the idea that human cognitive processes arise from the interactions of neurons in the brain. We develop computational models that directly carry out some human cognitive tasks with simple, neuronlike processing units. Some psychologists and cognitive neuroscientists have supposed that worrying about the nature of the underlying hardware is a mistake. According to their approach, human cognitive processes should be understood at a more abstract level of analysis. My collaborators and I believe, however, that the properties of the underlying hardware have important implications for the nature and organization of cognitive processes in the brain. An important case in point is the process of assigning the past tense to a word in English. Consider the formation of the past tense of *like*, *take*, and *gleat* (*gleat* is not a word in English, but it could be. For example, we might coin the word *gleat* to refer to the act of saluting in a particular way). In any case, most people agree that the past tense of *like* is liked, the past tense of *take* is *took*, and the past tense of *gleat* is *gleated*. Before the advent of neural network models, everyone in the field assumed that to form the past tense of a novel verb like *gleat*, one would need to use a rule (e.g., to form the past tense of a word, add -[e]d). Also, developmental psychologists observed that young children occasionally made interesting errors such as saying *taked* instead of *took*, and they interpreted this as indicating that the children were overapplying the past tense rule. They also assumed that to produce the past tense of an exception word like *take* correctly (e.g., to produce *took*), a child would need to memorize this particular item. For familiar but regular words such as *like*, either the rule or the lookup mechanism might be used. Dave Rumelhart and I (1986) thought about this issue and observed that neural network models have a tendency to be sensitive to both general regularities and specific exceptions. On the basis of this, we thought that a single mechanism might be used in the brain to produce the past tenses of both regular and exceptional words. To explore this possibility, we created a simple neural network model, as illustrated in the figure. The model takes as its input a pattern of activity representing the present tense of a word and produces on its output another pattern of activity representing the past tense of the word. The network operates by propagating activation from the input units to the output units via connections from the input units to the output units. The connections are like synapses between neurons, and each has a strength or "weight" that can be positive or negative that modulates the effect of an input on an output. Units sum up the weighted inputs they receive. If the summed input is positive, the unit comes on; if the input is negative, the unit goes off. Rumelhart and I trained this network with pairs of items representing the present and past tenses of familiar words. After we trained it with the 10 most frequent words (most of which are exceptions), the network knew how to produce the past tenses of these words, but it did not know how to deal with other words. We then trained it with the 10 frequent words plus 400 more words, most of which were regular, and we found that early in training, it tended to overregularize most of the exceptions (e.g., it said *taked* instead of *took*), even for those words that it had previously produced correctly. We trained it for a long time, and at the end of training it recovered its ability to produce exceptions correctly, while still producing past tenses for regular words such as *like* and for many novel words such as *gleat*. Thus, as a first approximation the model accounted for the developmental pattern in which children first deal correctly with exceptions; then learn how to deal with regular words and novel words and overregularize exceptions; and then deal correctly with regular words, novel words, and exceptions when they are older. Our model, then, illustrates that in a neural network, it is not necessary to have separate mechanisms to deal with rules and exceptions. Furthermore, this illustrates the general point that the nature of the underlying processing machinery may have implications for higher-level characterizations of the cognitive processes. However, I should make clear that our initial work did not by any means settle the issue. Several critics rushed to the defense of the two-process approach, criticizing several features of our models (Pinker &

Continues

IN THE LAB OF JAMES L. McCLELLAND—cont'd

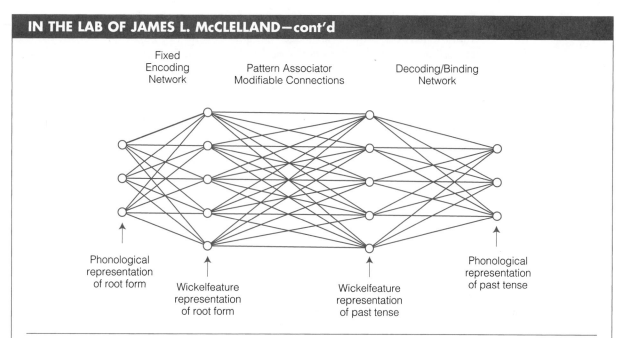

The neural network model used by Rumelhart and McClelland to model the formation of past tenses of English verbs. The fixed encoding network and fixed decoding network were used to encode and decode the patterns of activation corresponding to the present and past tenses of words. The connections in the pattern association were trained by presenting the encoded present tense of a word together with the encoded form of its past tense, then adjusting the connections so that the network would tend to produce the correct past tense on its own given the present tense as input (From D. E. Rumelhart, & J. L. McClelland, [1986]. On learning the past tenses of English verbs. In J. L. McClelland, D. E. Rumelhart, et al. [Eds.], Parallel distribution processing. Explorations in the microstructure of cognition. Vol. 2. Psychological and biological models, p. 222. Reprinted with permission from MIT Press.)

Prince, 1988; Lachter & Bever, 1988). Others responded to these criticisms with improved neural network models (MacWhinney & Leinbach, 1991; Plunkett & Marchman, 1991). Debate about these issues is still ongoing (McClelland and Patterson, 2002; Pinker and Ullman, 2002). Thus our modeling work has not finally settled this issue. It simply has raised an alternative to earlier conceptualizations and suggested that we cannot ignore the nature of the underlying processing mechanisms whose activity gives rise to cognition.

McClelland, J. L., and Patterson, K. (2002). Rules or connections in past-tense inflections: What does the evidence rule out? *Trends in Cognitive Sciences, 6,* 465–472.

Pinker, S., and Ullman, M. T. (2002). The past and future of the past tense. *Trends in Cognitive Sciences, 6,* 456–463.

most fundamental feature of the robin is that it is a living thing. So this information is represented at the top to show it is an extremely general characteristic of a robin. Living things are living and can grow, so this information is also represented at a very general level. As one moves down the network, information gets more and more specific. For example, we learn that a robin is a bird and that it is partly red.

In contrast, the connectionist network represents patterns of activation. Here, too, the network shows knowledge that goes beyond just birds. The knowledge is in the connections rather than in the nodes. Through activation of certain connections, knowledge about a robin is built up. A strong connection is one that is activated many times, whereas a weak one is activated only on rare occasions.

How Domain General or Domain Specific Is Cognition?

Should cognitive psychologists try to find a set of mental processes that is common across all domains of knowledge representation and processing? Or should they study mental processes specific to a particular domain? In early AI research, investigators believed that the ideal was to write programs that were as domain general as possible. Although none of the programs truly worked in all domains, they were a good start. Similarly, in the broader field of cognitive psychology, the trend in the 1960s through the mid-1970s was to strive for domain-general understandings of cognitive processes (Miller, Galanter, & Pribram, 1960; Simon, 1976).

During the late 1970s and the 1980s, the balance shifted toward domain specificity. In part this was because of striking demonstrations regarding the role of specific knowledge in chess playing (Chase & Simon, 1973; De Groot, 1965; see Chapter 11). A key book, *The Modularity of Mind*, presented an argument for extreme domain specificity (Fodor, 1983). On this view, the mind is **modular,** divided into discrete modules that operate more or less independently of each other. According to Fodor, each independently functioning module can process only one kind of input (language [e.g., words]; visual percepts [e.g., faces], etc.).

Fodor (1983) asserted the modularity of lower level processes, such as the basic perceptual processes involved in lexical access (see Chapter 4). However, the application of modularity has been extended to higher intellectual processes as well (Gardner, 1983). Also, the book emphasized the modularity of specific cognitive functions, such as lexical access to word meanings, as distinct from word meanings derived from context. These functions primarily have been observed in cognitive experiments. However, issues of modularity also have been important in psychobiological research. For example, there are discrete pathological conditions associated with discrete cognitive deficits.

Recently, there has been more of an attempt to integrate domain-specific and domain-general perspectives in our thinking about knowledge representation and processing. In the chapters that follow, you may wish to reflect on whether the processes and forms of knowledge representation being described may be seen as primarily domain general or primarily domain specific.

Key Themes

This chapter brings out several of the key themes described in Chapter 1.

One theme is that of rationalism versus empiricism. How do we assign meaning to concepts? The featural view is largely a rationalistic one. Concepts have sets of features that are largely a priori and that are the same from one person to another. The underlying notion is that one could understand a concept by a detailed dictionary definition, pretty much without reference to people's experience. The prototype, exemplar, and theory-based views are much more empirically based. They assign a major role to experience. For example, theories may change with experience. The theory of a concept such as a "dog" that a 3-year-old child has may be very different from that of a 10-year-old child.

A second theme is that of the validity of causal inference versus ecological validity. Early research on concepts, such as that of Bruner, Goodnow, and Austin, used abstract concepts, such as geometric forms that could be of different colors, shapes, and sizes. But in her work, Eleanor Rosch called this approach into question. Rosch argued that natural concepts show few of the characteristics of artificial ones. Studying artificial concepts, therefore, might yield information that applied to those concepts, but not necessarily to real-world ones. Modern researchers tend to study real-world concepts more than artificial ones.

A third theme is that of basic versus applied research. Basic research on concepts has generated a great deal of applied research. For example, market researchers are very interested in people's conceptualizations of commercial products. They use empirical and statistical techniques to understand how products are conceived. Often, then, advertising serves to reposition the products in customers' minds. For example, a car that is viewed as in the category of "economy cars" may be, through advertising, moved to a more "upscale car" category.

Ask a friend if he or she would like to win $20. The $20 can be won if your friend can recite the months of the year within 30 seconds—in alphabetical order. Go! In the years that we have offered this cash to the students in our courses, not a single student has ever won, so your $20 is probably safe. This demonstration shows how something as common and frequently used as the months of the year is bundled together in a certain order. It is very difficult to rearrange their names in an order that is different from their commonly used or more familiar order.

Summary

1. **How are representations of words and symbols organized in the mind?** The fundamental unit of symbolic knowledge is the concept. Concepts may be organized into categories, which may include other categories. They may be organized into schemas, which may include other schemas. They also may vary in application and in abstractness. Finally, they may include information about relationships between concepts, attributes, contexts, and general knowledge and information about causal relationships. There are different general theories of categorization. They include feature-based definitional categories, prototype-based categories, and exemplar-based approaches. One of the forms for schemas is the script. An alternative model for knowledge organization is a semantic network, involving a web of labeled relations between conceptual nodes. An early network model was strictly hierarchical. It was based on the notion of cognitive economy. But subsequent ones have tended to emphasize the frequency with which particular associations are used.

2. **How do we represent other forms of knowledge in the mind?** Many cognitive psychologists have developed models for procedural knowledge. These are based on computer simulations of such representations. An example of such a model is the production system.

3. **How does declarative knowledge interact with procedural knowledge?** An important model in cognitive psychology is ACT, as well as its various updated revisions, ACT* and ACT-R It represents both procedural knowledge in the form of production systems and declarative knowledge in the form of a semantic network. In each of these models, the metaphor for understanding both knowledge representation and information processing is based on the way in which a computer processes information. For example, these models underscore the serial processing of information.

Research on how the human brain processes information has shown that brains, unlike computers, use parallel processing of information. In addition, it appears that much of information processing is not localized only to particular areas of the brain. Instead it is distributed across various regions of the brain all at once. At a microscopic level of analysis, the neurons within the brain may be inactive. Or they may be excited or inhibited by the actions of other neurons with which they share a synapse. Finally, studies of how the brain processes information have shown that some stimuli seem to prime a response to subsequent stimuli so that it becomes easier to process the subsequent stimuli.

A model for human knowledge representation and information processing based on what we know about the brain is the parallel distributed processing (PDP) model. It is also called a connectionist model. In such models, it is held that neuronlike units may be excited or inhibited by the actions of other units. Or they may be inactive. Further, knowledge is represented in terms of patterns of excitation or inhibition strengths, rather than in particular units. Most PDP models also explain the priming effect by suggesting the mechanism of spreading activation.

Many cognitive psychologists believe that the mind is at least partly modular. It has different activity centers in the mind operate fairly independently of each other. However, other cognitive psychologists believe that human cognition is governed by many fundamental operations. On this view, specific cognitive functions are merely variations on a theme. In all likelihood, cognition involves some modular, domain-specific processes and some fundamental, domain-general processes.

Thinking about Thinking: Factual, Analytical, Creative, and Practical Questions

1. Define declarative knowledge and procedural knowledge, and give examples of each.

2. What is a script that you use in your daily life? How might you make it work better for you?

3. Describe some of the attributes of schemas, and compare and contrast two of the schema models mentioned in this chapter.

4. In your opinion, why have many of the models for knowledge representation come from people with a strong interest in artificial intelligence?

5. What are some advantages and disadvantages of hierarchical models of knowledge representation?

6. How would you design an experiment to test whether a particular cognitive task was better explained in terms of modular components or in terms of some fundamental underlying domain-general processes?

7. What are some practical examples of the forms of nondeclarative knowledge in Squire's model? (For ideas on conditioning, see Chapter 1; for ideas on habituation or on priming, see Chapter 3.)

8. How might you use semantic priming to enhance the likelihood that a person will think of something you would like the person to think of (e.g., your birthday, a restaurant to visit, or a movie to view)?

Key Terms

ACT

ACT-R

artifact category

basic level

category

characteristic features

concept

connectionist models

converging operations

core

defining features

exemplars

jargon

modular

natural category

networks

nodes

nominal kind

parallel distributed processing
(PDP) models

parallel processing

production

production system

prototype theory

schemas

script

serial processing

spreading activation

theory-based view of meaning

Explore CogLab by going to http://coglab.wadsworth.com. Answer the questions required by your instructor from the student manual that accompanies CogLab.

Prototypes   Implicit Learning

Absolute Identification

Annotated Suggested Reading

McLeod, P., Plunkett K., & Rolls, E. T. (1998). *Introduction to connectionist modeling of cognitive processes*.
New York: Oxford University Press. There is no
simple introduction to connectionism. But this exposition is about as clear as one can find on the use
of connectionist modeling to characterize a wide
variety of cognitive processes.

Language: Nature and Acquisition

EXPLORING COGNITIVE PSYCHOLOGY

1. **What properties characterize language?**

2. **What are some of the processes involved in language?**

3. **How do we acquire the ability to use language?**

> *I stood still, my whole attention fixed upon the motions of her fingers. Suddenly, I felt a misty consciousness as of something forgotten—a thrill of returning thought; and somehow the mystery of language was revealed to me. I knew then that "w-a-t-e-r" meant the wonderful cool something that was flowing over my hand. That living word awakened my soul, gave it light, joy, set it free! . . . Everything had a name, and each name gave birth to a new thought. As we returned to the house every object which I touched seemed to quiver with life. . . . I learned a great many new words that day . . . words that were to make the world blossom for me.*

—Helen Keller, *Story of My Life*

Helen Keller was both blind and deaf by 19 months after her birth. She was first awakened to a sentient, thought-filled, comprehensible world through her teacher, Anne Sullivan. The miracle worker held one of Helen's hands under a spigot from which a stream of water gushed over Helen's hand. All the while she spelled with a manual alphabet into Helen's other hand the mind-awakening word "w-a-t-e-r."

Language is the use of an organized means of combining words in order to communicate. It makes it possible for us to communicate with those around us. It also makes it possible to think about things and processes we currently cannot see, hear, feel, touch, or smell. These things include ideas that may not have any tangible form. As Helen Keller demonstrated, the words we use may be written, spoken, or otherwise signed (e.g., via American Sign Language [ASL]). Even so, not all **communication**—exchange of thoughts and feelings—is through language. Communication encompasses other aspects. One is such nonverbal means as gestures, which can be used, for example, to embellish or to indicate. A second aspect includes glances. Glances may serve many purposes. For example, sometimes they are deadly, other times, seductive. A third aspect includes touches, such as handshakes, hits, and hugs. These are only a few of the means by which we can communicate.

Psycholinguistics is the psychology of our language as it interacts with the human mind. It considers both production and comprehension of language (Gernsbacher & Kaschak, 2003a, 2003b; Indefrey & Levelt, 2000; Wheeldon, Meyer, & Smith, 2003). Four areas of study have contributed greatly to an understanding of psycholinguistics. One is linguistics, the study of language structure and change. A second is neurolinguistics, the study of the relationships among the brain, cognition, and language. A third is sociolinguistics, the study of the relationship between social behavior and language (Carroll, 1986). A fourth is computational linguistics and psycholinguistics, which is the study of language via computational methods (Coleman,

2003; Gasser, 2003; Lewis, 2003). This chapter first briefly describes some general properties of language. The next sections discuss the processes of language. These processes include how we understand the meanings of particular words and how we structure words into meaningful sentences. Then, the final section more fully elaborates the linguistic approach to language. It describes how each of us has acquired at least one language. As you might expect, this discussion brings up the nature-nurture debate that so often arises in regard to psychological issues. But it focuses on how acquired abilities interact with experience. Chapter 10 describes the broader context within which we use language. This context includes the psychological and social contexts of language.

Properties of Language

General Description

What properties characterize language? The answer to this question depends on whom you ask. Linguists may offer somewhat different answers than may cognitive psychologists. Nonetheless, there seems to be some consensus regarding six properties that are distinctive of language (Brown, 1965; Clark & Clark, 1977; Glucksberg & Danks, 1975). Specifically, language is:

1. *Communicative:* Language permits us to communicate with one or more people who share our language.
2. *Arbitrarily symbolic:* Language creates an arbitrary relationship between a symbol and its referent: an idea, a thing, a process, a relationship, or a description.
3. *Regularly structured:* Language has a structure; only particularly patterned arrangements of symbols have meaning, and different arrangements yield different meanings.
4. *Structured at multiple levels:* The structure of language can be analyzed at more than one level (e.g., in sounds, in meaning units, in words, in phrases).
5. *Generative, productive:* Within the limits of a linguistic structure, language users can produce novel utterances. The possibilities for creating new utterances are virtually limitless.
6. *Dynamic:* Languages constantly evolve.

The communicative property of language is listed first. Despite its being the most obvious feature of language, it is also the most remarkable one. As an example, I can write what I am thinking and feeling so that you may read and understand my thoughts and feelings. This is not to say that there are not occasional flaws in the communicative property of language. Countless cognitive psychologists and others dedicate their lives to the study of how we fail to communicate through language. Despite the frustrations of miscommunications, however, for one person to be able to use language to communicate to another is impressive.

Signs that resemble their referents in some way are termed icons. These pictographs are icons that were used in ancient Egyptian hieroglyphics. In contrast, most language involves the manipulation of symbols, which bear only an arbitrary relation to their referents.

What may be more surprising is the second property of language. We communicate through our shared system of arbitrary symbolic reference to things, ideas, processes, relationships, and descriptions (Steedman, 2003). The arbitrary nature of the system alludes to the lack of any reason for choosing a particular symbol. Indeed, all words are symbols. In this context, a *symbol* is something that represents, indicates, or suggests something else. It refers, points, or alludes to a particular thing, process, or description, such as *professor, amuse,* or *brilliant*. By consensual agreement, a particular combination of letters or sounds may be meaningful to us. But the particular symbols do not themselves lead to the meaning of the word. The sound combination is arbitrary. This arbitrariness can be seen from the fact that different languages use very different sounds to refer to the same thing (e.g., *baum, árbol, tree*).

A convenient feature of symbols is that we can use them to refer to things, ideas, processes, relationships, and descriptions that are not currently present, such as the Amazon River. We even can use symbols to refer to things that never have existed, such as dragons or elves. And we can use symbols to refer to things that exist in a form that is not physically tangible, such as calculus, truth, or justice. Without arbitrary symbolic reference, we would be limited to symbols that somehow resembled the things they are supposed to symbolize. For example, we would need a treelike symbol to represent a tree. Two principles underlying word meanings are the *principle of conventionality* and the *principle of contrast* (Clark, 1993, 1995). The first principle simply states that meanings of words are determined by conventions. In other words, words mean what conventions make them mean. According to the second principle, different words have different meanings. The point of having different words is precisely to have them symbolize things that are at least slightly different.

The third property is the regular structure of language. It makes possible this shared system of communication. Later in this chapter we describe more specifically the structure of language. For now, however, it suffices that you already know two things. The first is that particular patterns of sounds and of letters form meaningful words. Random sounds and letters, however, usually do not. The second is that particular patterns of words form meaningful sentences, paragraphs, and discourse. Most others make no sense.

The fourth property is the multiplicity of structure. Any meaningful utterance can be analyzed at more than one level. Subsequent sections describe several levels at which we can analyze the structure of language. These various levels convey varying degrees of meaningful content. For example, psycholinguists study language at the level of sounds, such as *p* and *t*. They also examine the level of words, such as "pat," "tap," "pot," "top," "pit," and "tip." They also analyze the level of sentences, such as "Pat said to tap the top of the pot, then tip it into the pit." Finally, they analyze things at the level of larger units of language, such as this paragraph or even this book.

A fifth property of language is productivity (sometimes termed *generativity*). Productivity refers here to our limitless ability to produce language creatively. On the one hand, our use of language does have limitations. We have to conform to a particular structure and to use a particular shared system of arbitrary symbols. We can use language to produce an infinite number of unique sentences and other meaningful combinations of words. Although the number of sounds (e.g., *s* as in "hiss") used in a language may be finite, the various sounds can be combined endlessly to form new words and new sentences. Among them are many novel utterances. These are linguistic expressions that are brand new and never have been spoken before by anyone. Thus, language is inherently creative. None of us possibly could have heard previously all the sentences we are capable of producing and that we actually produce in the course of our everyday lives. Any language appears to have the potential to express any idea in it that can be expressed in any other language. However, the ease, clarity, and succinctness of expression of a particular idea may vary greatly from one language to the next. Thus, the creative potential of different languages appears to be roughly the same.

Finally, the productive aspect of language quite naturally leads to the dynamic, evolutionary nature of language. Individual language users coin words and phrases and modify language usage. The wider group of language users either accepts or rejects the modifications. To imagine that language would never change is almost as incomprehensible as to imagine that people and environments would never change. For example, the modern English we speak now evolved from Middle English. This language in turn evolved from Old English.

Although we can delineate various properties of language, it is important always to keep in mind what the main purpose of language is. Language facilitates our being able to construct a mental representation of a situation that enables us to understand the situation and communicate about it (Budwig, 1995; Zwaan & Radvansky, 1998).

In other words, ultimately, language is primarily about use, not just about one set of properties or another. For example, it provides the basis for linguistic encoding in memory. You are able to remember things better because you can use language to help you recall or recognize them.

To conclude, many differences exist among languages. Nevertheless, there are some common properties. Among them are communication, arbitrary symbolic reference, regularity of structure, multiplicity of structure, productivity, and change. Next, we consider how language is used in more detail. Then we observe some universal aspects of how we humans acquire our primary language.

Fundamental Aspects of Language

Essentially, there are two fundamental aspects of language. The first is receptive comprehension and decoding of language input. The second is expressive encoding and production of language output. Decoding refers to deriving the meaning from whatever symbolic reference system is being used (e.g., while listening or reading). In Chapters 5 and 6, we used the term *encoding* to refer to both semantic and nonsemantic encoding of information into a form that can be stored in both working memory and long-term memory (Waters & Caplan, 2003). As applied to language, encoding involves transforming our thoughts into a form that can be expressed as linguistic output (e.g., speech, signing, or writing). In this chapter, we use the terms *encoding* and *decoding* to describe only semantic encoding and decoding.

Related terms are verbal comprehension and verbal fluency. **Verbal comprehension** is the receptive ability to comprehend written and spoken linguistic input, such as words, sentences, and paragraphs (Starr & Rayner, 2003). **Verbal fluency** is the expressive ability to produce linguistic output. When we deal specifically with spoken communication, we can refer to vocal comprehension or fluency. Verbal comprehension and verbal fluency appear to be relatively distinct abilities (Thurstone, 1938). People may be able to understand language well but not produce it well or vice versa. The dissociation becomes particularly apparent in the case of second language. For example, many people around the world can understand substantial amounts of English without being able to read or write it adequately.

Language can be broken down into many smaller units. It is much like the analysis of molecules into basic elements by chemists. The smallest unit of speech sound is the *phone,* which is simply a single vocal sound. A given phone may or may not be part of the speech system of a particular language (Archangeli, 2003; Jusczyk, 2003; Meyer & Wheeldon, 2003; Munhall, 2003; Roca, 2003b). A click of your tongue, a pop of your cheek, or a gurgling sound may be a phone. A **phoneme** is the smallest unit of speech sound that can be used to distinguish one utterance in a given language from another. In English, phonemes are made up of vowel and consonant sounds. For example, we distinguish among "sit," "sat," "fat," and "fit," so the /s/ sound, the /f/ sound, the /I/ sound, and the /ae/ sound are all phonemes in English (as is the /t/ sound). These sounds are produced by alternating sequences of opening and closing of the vocal tract. Different languages use different numbers and combinations of phonemes. Hawaiian has about thirteen phonemes. Some African dialects have up to sixty. North American English has about forty phonemes, as shown in Table 9.1. The following set of examples highlights the difference between phones and phonemes.

TABLE 9.1	North American English Phonetic Symbols

The phonemes of a language constitute the repertoire of the smallest units of sound that can be used to distinguish one meaningful utterance from another in the given language. (After H. H. Clark & Clark, 1977)

CONSONANTS				VOWELS		DIPHTHONGS	
p	*pill*	θ	*thigh*	i	b*ee*t	Ay	b*i*te
B	*bill*		*thy*		b*i*t	Æw	*abou*t
M	*mill*	Š	*shallow*	e	b*ai*t	Oy	b*oy*
T	*till*	Ž	mea*s*ure		b*e*t		
D	*dill*	Č	*ch*ip	Æ	b*a*t		
N	*nil*		*gyp*	U	b*oo*t		
K	*kill*	L	*l*ip	U	p*u*t		
G	*gill*	R	*r*ip		b*u*t		
ŋ	si*ng*	Y	*y*et	o	b*oa*t		
F	*fill*	W	*w*et		b*ou*ght		
v	*v*at		*wh*et	A	p*o*t		
S	*s*ip	h	*h*at	ə	s*o*fa		
Z	*z*ip				m*a*rry		

In English, the difference between the /p/ and the /b/ sound is an important distinction. These sounds function as phonemes in English because they comprise the difference between different words. For example, English speakers distinguish between "they bit the buns from the bin" and "they pit the puns from the pin" (a well-structured but meaningless sentence). At the same time, there are some phones that English speakers may produce but that do not function to distinguish words. They therefore do not serve as phonemes in English. These often are called *allophones,* which are sound variants of the same phoneme.

To illustrate the difference between the allophones of the phoneme /p/, try putting your open hand about 1 inch from your lips. Then say aloud, "Put the paper cup to your lip." If you are like most English speakers, you felt a tiny puff of air when you pronounced the /ph/ in "Put" and "paper." But you felt no puffs of air when you pronounced the /p/ in "cup" or "lip." If you somehow managed to stifle the puff of air when saying, "Put" or "paper" or to add a puff of air when saying "cup" or "lip," you would be producing different (allo)phones. But you would not be making a meaningful distinction in the phonemes of English. There is no meaningful difference between /ph/ut and /p/ut in English. In contrast, the difference between /k/ut and /g/ut is potentially meaningful. However, in some languages, such as Thai, a distinction considered irrelevant in English is meaningful. In these languages, the difference between /p/ and /ph/ is phonemic rather than merely allophonic (Fromkin & Rodman, 1988).

Phonemics is the study of the particular phonemes of a language. *Phonetics* is the study of how to produce or combine speech sounds or to represent them with written symbols (Roca, 2003a). Linguists may travel to remote villages to observe, record, and analyze different languages. Some of these languages are dying as members leave tribal areas in favor of more urban areas. The study of phonetic inventories of diverse languages is one way linguists gain insight into the nature of language (Ladefoged & Maddieson, 1996).

At the next level of the hierarchy is the **morpheme**—the smallest unit that denotes meaning within a particular language. English courses may have introduced you to two forms of morphemes. One is root words. We add the second form, affixes, to these root words. Affixes include suffixes, which follow the root word, and prefixes, which precede the root word. The word *affixes* itself comprises the root "fix," a prefix, and a suffix. The prefix is "af-." This prefix is a variant of the prefix "ad-," meaning "toward," "to," or "near." The suffix is "-es," which indicates the plural form of a noun. The word *recharge* contains two morphemes, "re-" and "charge."

Linguists analyze the structure of morphemes and words in a way that goes beyond the analysis of roots and affixes. **Content morphemes** are the words that convey the bulk of the meaning of a language. **Function morphemes** add detail and nuance to the meaning of the content morphemes or help the content morphemes fit the grammatical context. Examples are the suffix "-ist," the prefix "de-," the conjunction "and," or the article "the." A subset of function morphemes are inflections, the common suffixes we add to words to fit the grammatical context. For example, most American kindergartners know to add special suffixes to indicate the following:

- *Verb tense:* You study often. You studied yesterday. You are studying now.
- *Verb and noun number:* The professor assigns homework. The teaching assistants assign homework.
- *Noun possession:* The student's textbook is fascinating.
- *Adjective comparison:* The wiser of the two professors taught the wisest of the three students.

The **lexicon** is the entire set of morphemes in a given language or in a given person's linguistic repertoire. The average adult speaker of English has a lexicon of about 80,000 morphemes (Miller & Gildea, 1987). Children in grade 1 in the United States have somewhat more than 10,000 words in their vocabularies. By grade 3, they are at about 20,000. By grade 5, they have reached about 40,000, or half of their eventual adult level of attainment (Anglin, 1993). By combining morphemes, most adult English speakers have a vocabulary, a repertoire of words, of hundreds of thousands of words. For example, by attaching just a few morphemes to the root content morpheme *study*, we have *student, studious, studied, studying,* and *studies*. Vocabulary is built up slowly. It develops through many diverse exposures to words and clues as to their meanings (Akhtar & Montague, 1999; Hoff & Naigles, 1999; Woodward & Markman, 1998). One of the ways in which English has expanded to embrace an increasing vocabulary is by combining existing morphemes in novel ways. Some suggest that a part of William Shakespeare's genius lay in his enjoying the creation of new words by combining existing morphemes. He is alleged to have coined more than 1,700 words—8.5% of his written vocabulary—and countless expressions—including the word *countless* itself (Lederer, 1991).

The next level of analysis is termed syntax. **Syntax** refers to the way in which users of a particular language put words together to form sentences. Syntax plays a major role in our understanding of language. A sentence comprises at least two parts. The first is a **noun phrase,** which contains at least one noun (often the subject of the sentence) and includes all the relevant descriptors of the noun. The second is a **verb phrase,** which contains at least one verb and whatever the verb acts on, if anything. The verb phrase also may be termed the *predicate* because it affirms or states something about the subject. Typically, it is an action or a property of the subject. Linguists consider the study of syntax to be fundamental to understanding the structure of language. The syntactical structure of language specifically is addressed later in this chapter.

INVESTIGATING COGNITIVE PSYCHOLOGY	Identify which of the following are noun phrases: (1) the round, red ball on the corner; (2) and the; (3) round and red; (4) the ball; (5) water; (6) runs quickly. (*Hint:* Noun phrases can be the subject or object of a sentence, e.g., "____[NP]____ bounces ____[NP]____.")
	Identify which of the following are verb phrases: (1) the boy bounced the ball; (2) and the bouncing ball; (3) rolled; (4) ran across the room; (5) gave her the ball; (6) runs quickly. (*Hint:* Verb phrases contain verbs, as well as anything on which the verb acts [but not the subject of the action]. For example, "The psychology student ____[VP]____.")

Complementary to syntax is **semantics,** the study of meaning in a language. A semanticist would be concerned with how words express meaning The final level of analysis is that of **discourse,** which encompasses language use at the level beyond the sentence, such as in conversation, paragraphs, stories, chapters, and entire works of literature. Table 9.2 summarizes the various aspects of language. The next section discusses how we understand language through speech perception and further analysis. We will reserve discussion of discourse for Chapter 10 and the social context for language.

Processes of Language Comprehension

How do we understand language, given its multifaceted encoding? One approach to this question centers on the psychological processes involved in speech perception (Hickok & Poeppel, 2000). It also considers how listeners deal with the peculiarities resulting from the acoustic (relating to sound) transmission of language. A second, more linguistically oriented approach focuses on descriptions of the grammatical structure of languages. Finally, a third approach examines the psycholinguistic processes involved in language comprehension at the discourse macrolevel of analysis. All three approaches overlap to some degree and offer interesting insights into the nature of language and its use.

Speech Perception

Have you ever been in a situation where you needed to communicate with someone over the phone, but the speech you heard was garbled by a faulty telephone trans-

TABLE 9.2	Summary Description of Language

All human languages can be analyzed at many levels.

LANGUAGE INPUT			**LANGUAGE OUTPUT**
↓ D e c o d i n g ↓	Phonemes (distinctive subset of all possible phones)	…/t/ + /ā/ + /k/ + /s/…	↑ E n c o d i n g ↑
	Morphemes (from the distinctive lexicon of morphemes)	…take (content morpheme) + s (plural function morpheme)…	
	Words (from the distinctive vocabulary of words)	It + takes + a + heap + of + sense + to + write + good + nonsense.	

	Phrases:
	  Noun phrases (NP: a noun and its descriptors)
	  Verb phrases (VP: a verb and whatever it
	    acts on)
		NP = It
		+
		VP = takes a heap of sense to write good nonsense.	

	Sentences (based on the language's syntax— syntactical structure)	It takes a heap of sense to write good nonsense.	
	Discourse	"It takes a heap of sense to write good nonsense," was first written by Mark Twain (Lederer, 1991, p. 131)…	

COMPREHEND LANGUAGE			**PRODUCE LANGUAGE**

mission? If so, you will agree that speech perception is fundamental to language use in our everyday lives. To understand speech is crucial to human communication. To understand speech perception, we consider some interesting phenomena of speech. We also reflect on the question of whether speech is somehow special among all of the various kinds of sounds we can perceive.

We are able to perceive speech with amazing rapidity. On the one hand, we can perceive as many as fifty phonemes *per second* in a language in which we are fluent (Foulke & Sticht, 1969). On the other hand, we can perceive only about two thirds of a phone per second of nonspeech sounds (Warren & associates, 1969). Consider why foreign languages are difficult to understand when we hear them. Even if we can read them, the sounds of their letters and letter combinations may be different from the sounds corresponding to the same letters and letter combinations in our native language. For example, my Spanish sounds "American" because I tend to reinterpret Spanish sounds in terms of the American English phonetic system rather than the Spanish one.

How are we able to perceive fifty phonemes per second if, paradoxically, we only can perceive less than one phone per second of nonspeech sounds? One answer to this question lies in the fact that speech sounds show coarticulation. **Coarticulation** occurs when phonemes or other units are produced in a way that overlaps them in time. One or more phonemes begin while other phonemes still are being produced. The articulations coincide. Not only do phonemes within a word overlap. The boundaries between words in continuous speech also tend to overlap. This overlapping of speech sounds may seem to create additional problems for perceiving speech. But coarticulation is viewed as necessary for the effective transmission of speech information, given the previously mentioned deficiencies in perceiving other sounds (Liberman & associates, 1967). Thus, speech perception is viewed as different from other perceptual abilities because of both the linguistic nature of the information and the particular way in which information must be encoded for effective transmission.

So how do we perceive speech with such ease? There are many alternative theories of speech perception to explain our facility. These theories differ mainly as to whether speech perception is viewed as special or ordinary with respect to other types of auditory perception.

The View of Speech Perception as Ordinary

One main approach equates processes of speech perception with processes of auditory perception of other sounds. These kinds of theories emphasize either template-matching or feature-detection processes. Such theories postulate that there are distinct stages of neural processing. In one stage speech sounds are analyzed into their components. In another stage these components are analyzed for patterns and matched to a prototype or template (Kuhl, 1991; Massaro, 1987; Stevens & Blumstein, 1981). One theory of this kind is the *phonetic refinement theory* (Pisoni & associates, 1985). It says that we start with an analysis of auditory sensations and shift to higher level processing. We identify words on the basis of successively paring down the possibilities for matches between each of the phonemes and the words we already know from memory. In this theory, the initial sound that establishes the set of possible words we have heard need not be the first phoneme alone. You may have observed this phenomenon yourself on a conscious level. Have you ever been watching a movie or listening to a lecture when you heard only garbled sound. It takes you a few moments to figure out what the speaker must have said. To decide what you heard, you may have gone through a conscious process of phonetic refinement. A similar theoretical idea is embodied by the TRACE model (McClelland & Elman, 1986). According to this model, speech perception begins with three levels of feature detection: the level of acoustic features, the level of phonemes, and the level of words. According to this theory, speech perception is highly interactive. Lower levels affect higher levels and vice versa.

One attribute these theories have in common is that they all require decision-making processes above and beyond feature detection or template matching. Thus, the speech we perceive may differ from the speech sounds that actually reach our ears. The reason is that cognitive and contextual factors influence our perception of the sensed signal. For example, the phonemic-restoration effect involves integrating what we know with what we hear when we perceive speech (Samuel, 1981; Warren, 1970; Warren & Warren, 1970).

Suppose that you were in an experiment. You are listening to a sentence having the following pattern: "It was found that the *eel was on the _____." For the final word, one of the following words is inserted: *axle, shoe, table,* or *orange.* In addition, the speaker inserts a cough instead of the initial sound where the asterisk appeared in "*eel." Virtually all participants are unaware that a consonant has been deleted. The sound they recall having heard differs according to the context. The participants recall hearing "the *wheel* was on the axle," "the *heel* was on the shoe," "the *meal* was on the table," or "the *peel* was on the orange." In essence, they restore the missing phoneme that best suits the context of the sentence.

Phonemic restoration is similar to the visual phenomenon of closure, which is based on incomplete visual information. Indeed, one main approach to auditory perception attempts to extend, to various acoustic events, including speech, the Gestalt principles of visual perception (Bregman, 1990). These principles include, for example, symmetry, proximity, and similarity. Thus, theories that consider speech perception as ordinary use general perceptual principles of feature-detection and Gestalt psychology. They thereby attempt to explain how listeners understand speech. Other theorists, however, view speech perception as special.

The View of Speech Perception as Special

One phenomenon in speech perception that led to the notion of specialization was the finding of **categorical perception**—discontinuous categories of speech sounds. That is, although the speech sounds we actually hear comprise a continuum of variation in sound waves, we experience speech sounds categorically. This phenomenon can be seen in the perception of the consonant–vowel combinations, *ba*, *da*, and *ga*. The acoustic difference between these syllables centers on distinct patterns of variation in the speech signal. Some patterns lead to perception of *ba*. Others lead to perception of *da*. And still others lead to perception of *ga*. Moreover, within each syllable category there are differences in the sound patterns for different instances that do not influence speech perception. The *ba* that you said yesterday differs from the *ba* you say today. But it is not perceived as different. This categorical form of perception does not apply to a nonspeech sound, such as a tone. Here continuous differences in pitch (how high or low the tone is) are heard as continuous and distinct.

In a classic study, researchers used a speech synthesizer to mimic this natural variation in syllable acoustic patterns. By this means, they also were able to control the acoustic difference between the syllables (Liberman & associates, 1957). They created a series of consonant–vowel sounds that changed in equal increments from *ba* to *da* to *ga*. People who listened to the synthesized syllables, however, heard a sudden switch. It was from the sound category of *ba* to the sound category of *da* (and likewise from the category of *da* to that of *ga*). Furthermore, this difference in labeling the syllables led to poorer discrimination within a phoneme category. It also enhanced discrimination across phoneme boundaries. Thus, although the tokens were physically equal in acoustic distance from one another, people only heard the tokens that also differed in phonetic label as different. Discrimination of two neighboring *ba*s was poor, whereas discrimination of *ba* from its neighboring *da* was preserved. Normal perceptual processing should discriminate equally between all equally spaced pairs of the different tokens along the continuum, however. The researchers thus concluded that speech is perceived via specialized processes.

These and other findings led the researchers to investigate the notion that speech perception relies on special processes. They also proposed the early but still influential motor theory of speech perception (Liberman & associates, 1967; Liberman & Mattingly, 1985). The theory was developed to explain how listeners overcome the context-sensitivity of phonetic segments that arise from coarticulation, resulting in categorical perception phenomena. To return to an earlier example, the /p/ spoken in the word *lip* differs acoustically from the /ph/ spoken in the word *put*. This largely results from the differences in the coarticulatory context of the two instances of the phoneme. The overlapping of /p/ with *li-* versus *-ut* causes the /p/ to sound different. Why do English-speakers treat the /p/ and /ph/ as the same phoneme? According to the motor theory, speech perception depends on what we hear a speaker articulate (in this case, /p/ and /ph/). It also depends on what we infer as the intended articulations of the speaker (in this case, only /p/). Thus, the listener uses specialized processes involved in producing speech to perceive speech. He or she thereby overcomes the effects of coarticulation, which leads to categorical perception. Since the early work of Liberman and colleagues, the phenomenon of categorical perception has been extended to the perception of other kinds of stimuli, such as color and facial emotion. This extension weakens the claim that speech perception is special (Jusczyk, 1997). However, supporters of the speech-is-special position still maintain that other forms of evidence indicate that speech is perceived via specialized processes.

One such distinctive aspect of human speech perception can be seen in the so-called McGurk effect (McGurk & MacDonald, 1976). This effect involves the synchrony of visual and auditory perceptions. Imagine yourself watching a movie. As long as the soundtrack corresponds to the speakers' lip movements, you encounter no problems. However, suppose that the soundtrack indicates one thing, such as *da*. At the same time, the actor's lips clearly make the movements for another sound, such as *ba*. You are likely to hear a compromise sound, such as *tha*. It is neither what was said nor what was seen. You somehow synthesize the auditory and visual information. You thereby come up with a result that is unlike either. For this reason, poorly dubbed movies of foreign origin can be confusing.

In normal conversation, we use lip reading to augment our perception of speech. It is particularly important in situations in which background noise may make speech perception more difficult. The motor theory accounts for this integration quite easily because articulatory information includes visual and auditory information. However, believers in other theories interpret these findings as support for more general perceptual processes. They believe these processes naturally integrate information across sensory modalities (Massaro, 1987; Massaro & Cohen, 1990).

Is a synthesis of these opposing views possible? Perhaps one reason for the complexity of this issue lies in the nature of speech perception itself. It involves both linguistic and perceptual attributes. From a purely perceptual perspective, speech is just a relatively complex signal that is not treated qualitatively differently from other signals. From a psycholinguistic perspective, speech is special because it lies within the domain of language, a special human ability. Indeed, cognitive psychology textbooks differ in terms of where speech perception is discussed. Sometimes it is discussed in the context of language, other times in the context of perception. Thus, the diversity of views on the nature of speech perception can be seen as reflecting the differences in how researchers treat speech. They view it either as regular acoustic signals or as more special phonetic messages (Remez, 1994).

Semantics and Syntax

Language is very difficult to put into words.

Voltaire

Semantics

The opening of this chapter quoted from Helen Keller's description of her first awareness that words had meanings. You probably do not remember the moment that words first came alive to you. But your parents surely do. In fact, one of the greatest joys of being a parent is watching your children's amazing discovery that words have meanings. In semantics, **denotation** is the strict dictionary definition of a word. **Connotation** is a word's emotional overtones, presuppositions, and other nonexplicit meanings.

How do we understand word meanings in the first place? Recall from previous chapters that we encode meanings into memory through concepts. These include ideas, to which we may attach various characteristics and with which we may connect various other ideas, such as through propositions (Rey, 2003). They also include images and perhaps motor patterns for implementing particular procedures. Here, we are concerned only with concepts, particularly in terms of words as arbitrary symbols for concepts.

Actually, when we think of words as representing concepts, words are economical ways in which to manipulate related information. For example, when you think about the single word *desk,* you also may conjure all these things:

- All the instances of desks in existence anywhere
- Instances of desks that exist only in your imagination
- All of the characteristics of desks
- All of the things you might do with desks
- All of the other concepts you might link to desks (e.g., things you put on or in desks or places where you might find desks)

Having a word for something helps us to add new information to our existing information about that concept. For example, you have access to the word *desk.* When you have new experiences related to desks or otherwise learn new things about desks, you have a word around which to organize all this related information.

Recall, too, the constructive nature of memory. Having word labels (e.g., "washing clothes," "peace march") has several effects. First, it facilitates the ease of understanding and remembering a text passage. Second, it enhances subjects' recall of the shape of a droodle. Third, it affects the accuracy of eyewitness testimony. Having words as concepts for things helps us in our everyday nonverbal interactions. For example, our concepts of *skunk* and of *dog* allow us more easily to recognize the difference between the two, even if we see an animal only for a moment (Ross & Spalding, 1994). This rapid recognition enables us to respond appropriately, depending on which we saw. Clearly, being able to comprehend the conceptual meanings of words is important. Just how do words combine to convey meaning, however?

Syntax

An equally important part of the psychology of language is the analysis of linguistic structure. *Syntax* is the systematic way in which words can be combined and sequenced to make meaningful phrases and sentences (Carroll, 1986). Whereas speech perception chiefly studies phonetic structure of language, syntax focuses on the study of the grammar of phrases and sentences. In other words, it considers the regularity of structure.

Although you have doubtless heard the word *grammar* before in regard to how people *ought* to structure their sentences, psycholinguists use the word *grammar* in a slightly different way. Specifically, **grammar** is the study of language in terms of noticing regular patterns. These patterns relate to the functions and relationships of words in a sentence. They extend as broadly as the level of discourse and as narrowly as the pronunciation and meaning of individual words. In your English courses, you may have been introduced to prescriptive grammar. This kind of grammar prescribes the "correct" ways in which to structure the use of written and spoken language. Of greater interest to psycholinguists is descriptive grammar, in which an attempt is made to describe the structures, functions, and relationships of words in language.

Consider an example of a sentence that illustrates the contrast between prescriptive and descriptive approaches to grammar: When Junior observes his father carrying upstairs an unappealing bedtime book, Junior responds, "Daddy, what did you bring that book that I don't want to be read to out of up for?" (Pinker, 1994, p. 97). Junior's utterance might shiver the spine of any prescriptive grammarian. But Junior's ability to produce such a complex sentence, with such intricate internal interdependencies, would please descriptive grammarians.

Why can syntax prompt such pleasure? First, the study of syntax allows analysis of language in manageable—and therefore relatively easily studied—units. Second, it offers limitless possibilities for exploration. There are virtually no bounds to the possible combinations of words that may be used to form sentences. Earlier, we referred to this property as the productivity of language. In English, as in any language, we can take a particular set of words (or morphemes, to be more accurate) and a particular set of rules for combining the items and produce a breathtakingly vast array of meaningful utterances. Suppose you were to go to the U.S. Library of Congress and randomly select any sentence from any book. You then searched for an identical sentence in the vast array of sentences in the books therein. Barring intentional quotations, you would be unlikely to find the identical sentence (Pinker, 1994).

INVESTIGATING COGNITIVE PSYCHOLOGY	Mark an asterisk next to the sentences that are not grammatical, regardless of whether the sentences are meaningful or accurate: 1. The student the book. 2. Bought the book. 3. Bought the student the book. 4. The book was bought by the student. 5. By whom was the book bought? 6. By student the bought book. 7. The student was bought by the book. 8. Who bought the book? 9. The book bought the student. 10. The book bought.

The Syntax Tendency

People demonstrate a remarkable knack for understanding syntactical structure. As the preceding demonstration showed, you, I, and other fluent speakers of a language can recognize syntactical structure immediately. We can do so whether particular sentences and particular word orders are or are not grammatical (Bock, 1990; Pinker, 1994). We can do so even when the sentences are meaningless. For example, we can evaluate Chomsky's sentence, "Colorless green ideas sleep furiously." Or we can evaluate a sentence composed of nonsense words, as in Lewis Carroll's poem "Jabberwocky," "'Twas brillig and the slithy toves did gyre and gimble in the wabe."

Also, just as we show semantic priming of word meanings in memory, we show syntactical priming of sentence structures. We spontaneously tend to use syntactical structures that parallel the structures of sentences we have just heard (Bock, 1990; Bock, Loebell, & Morey, 1992). For example, a speaker will be more likely to use a passive construction (e.g., "The student was praised by the professor") after hearing a passive construction. He or she will do so even when the topics of the sentences differ.

Other evidence of our uncanny aptitude for syntax is shown in the speech errors we produce (Bock, 1990). Even when we accidentally switch the placement of two words in a sentence, we still form grammatical, if meaningless or nonsensical, sentences. We almost invariably switch nouns for nouns, verbs for verbs, prepositions for prepositions, and so on. For example, we may say, "I put the oven in the cake." But we will probably not say, "I put the cake oven in the." We usually even attach (and detach) appropriate function morphemes to make the switched words fit their new positions. For example, when meaning to say, "The butter knives are in the drawer," we may say, "The butter drawers are in the knife." Here, we change "drawer" to plural and "knives" to singular to preserve the grammaticality of the sentence. Consider even so-called agrammatic aphasics, who have extreme difficulties in both comprehending and producing language. Their substitution errors in speech seem to preserve syntactical categories (Butterworth & Howard, 1987; Garrett, 1992).

The preceding examples seem to indicate that we humans have some mental mechanism for classifying words according to syntactical categories. This classification mechanism is separate from the meanings for the words (Bock, 1990). When we compose sentences, we seem to parse the sentences. We assign appropriate syntactical categories (often called "parts of speech," e.g., noun, verb, article) to each component of the sentence. We then use the syntax rules for the language to construct grammatical sequences of the parsed components.

Using the following ten words, create five strings of words that make grammatical sentences. Also create five sequences of words that violate the syntax rules of English grammar: *ball, basket, bounced, into, put, red, rolled, tall, the, woman.*

To complete the preceding task, you mentally classified the words into syntactical categories, even if you did not know the correct labels for the categories. You then arranged the words into grammatical sequences according to the syntactical categories for the words and your implicit knowledge of English syntax rules. You will see later in the chapter that most 4 year olds can demonstrate the same ability to parse words into categories and to arrange them into grammatical sentences. Of course, most 4 year olds probably cannot label the syntactical categories for any of the words.

INVESTIGATING COGNITIVE PSYCHOLOGY

Early in the twentieth century, linguists who studied syntax largely focused on how sentences could be analyzed in terms of sequences of phrases, such as noun phrases and verb phrases, which were mentioned previously. They also focused on how phrases could be parsed into various syntactical categories, such as nouns, verbs, and adjectives. Such analyses are of **phrase-structure grammars,** which analyze the structure of phrases as they are used. The rules governing the sequences of words are termed *phrase-structure rules.* To observe the interrelationships of phrases within a sentence, linguists often use tree diagrams, such as the ones shown in Figure 9.1. Various other models also have been proposed (e.g., relational grammar, Perlmutter, 1983; lexical-functional grammar, Bresnan, 1982).

Tree diagrams help to reveal the interrelationships of syntactical classes within the phrase structures of sentences (Bock, 1990; Wasow, 1989). In particular, such diagrams show that sentences are not merely organized chains of words, strung together sequentially. Rather, they are organized into hierarchical structures of embedded phrases. The use of tree diagrams helps to highlight many aspects of how we use language, including both our linguistic sophistication and our difficulties in using language. Look again at Figure 9.1. Focus on the two possible tree diagrams for one sentence, showing its two possible meanings. By observing tree diagrams of ambiguous sentences, psycholinguists can better pinpoint the source of confusion.

In 1957, Noam Chomsky revolutionized the study of syntax. He suggested that to understand syntax, we must observe not only the interrelationships among phrases within sentences but also the syntactical relationships between sentences. Specifically, Chomsky observed that particular sentences and their tree diagrams show peculiar relationships.

Consider, for example, the following sentences:

S_1: Susie greedily ate the crocodile.

S_2: The crocodile was eaten greedily by Susie.

Oddly enough, a phrase-structure grammar would not show any particular relation at all between sentences S_1 and S_2 (Figure 9.2). Indeed, phrase-structure analyses of S_1 and S_2 would look almost completely different. Yet, the two sentences differ only in voice. The first sentence is expressed in the active voice and the second in the passive voice. Recall from Chapter 7 an important fact about propositions. They may be used for illustrating that the same underlying meanings can be derived through alternative means of representation. The preceding two sentences represent the same proposition: "ate (greedily) (Susie, crocodile)."

Consider another pair of paraphrased sentences:

S_3: The crocodile greedily ate Susie.

S_4: Susie was eaten greedily by the crocodile.

Phrase-structure grammar similarly would show no relationship between S_3 and S_4. What's more, phrase-structure grammar would show some similarities of surface structure between corresponding sentences in the first and second pairs (S_1 and S_3; S_2 and S_4). They clearly have quite different meanings, particularly to Susie and the crocodile. Apparently, an adequate grammar would address the fact that sentences with similar surface structures can have very different meanings.

FIGURE 9.1

Phrase-structure grammars illustrate the hierarchies of phrases within sentences. (a) The sentence, "The girl looked at the boy with the red shirt" may be diagrammed as shown here. (b) Linguists usually abbreviate tree diagrams as shown here, in the abbreviated linguistic tree diagram of the sentence shown in (a). Tree diagrams (c) and (d) show the possible ways for analyzing the sentence, "The girl looked at the boy with the telescope."

FIGURE 9.2

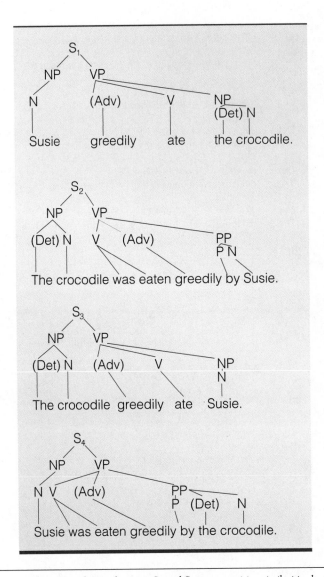

Phrase-structure grammars show surprising dissimilarities between S_1 and S_2, yet surprising similarities between S_1 and S_3 or between S_2 and S_4. Noam Chomsky suggested that to understand syntax, we also must consider a way of viewing the interrelationships among various phrase structures.

This observation and other observations of the interrelationships among various phrase structures led linguists to go beyond merely describing various individual phrase structures. They began to focus their attention on the relationships among different phrase structures. Linguists may gain deeper understanding of syntax by studying the relationships among phrase structures that involve transformations of elements within sentences (Chomsky, 1957). Specifically, Chomsky suggested a way to augment the study of phrase structures. He proposed the study of **transformational grammar,** which involves the study of transformational rules that guide the ways in which underlying propositions can be rearranged to form various phrase structures.

A simple way of looking at Chomsky's transformational grammar is to say that "Transformations . . . are rules that map tree structures onto other tree structures" (Wasow, 1989, p. 170). For example, transformational grammar considers how the tree-structure diagrams in Figure 9.2 are interrelated. With application of the transformational rules, the tree structure of S_1 can be mapped onto the tree structure of S_2. Similarly, the structure of S_3 can be mapped onto the tree structure of S_4.

In transformational grammar, **deep structure** refers to an underlying syntactical structure that links various phrase structures through the application of various transformation rules. In contrast, **surface structure** refers to any of the various phrase structures that may result from such transformations. Many casual readers of Chomsky have misconstrued Chomsky's terms. They incorrectly inferred that deep structures signify profound underlying meanings for sentences, whereas surface structures refer only to superficial interpretations of sentences. Chomsky meant only to show that differing phrase structures may have a relationship that is not immediately apparent by using phrase-structure grammar alone. This notion would apply in the example of "Susie greedily ate the crocodile" and "The crocodile was eaten greedily by Susie." For detection of the underlying relationship between two phrase structures, transformation rules must be applied.

Relationships between Syntactical and Lexical Structures

Chomsky (1965, cited in Wasow, 1989) also addressed how syntactical structures may interact with lexical structures. In particular, Chomsky suggested that our mental lexicon contains more than the semantic meanings attached to each word (or morpheme). According to Chomsky, each lexical item also contains syntactical information. This syntactical information for each lexical item indicates three things. The first is the syntactical category of the item, such as noun versus verb. The second is the appropriate syntactical contexts in which the particular morpheme may be used, such as pronouns as subjects versus as direct objects. The third is any idiosyncratic information about the syntactical uses of the morpheme, such as the treatment of irregular verbs.

For example, there would be separate lexical entries for the word *spread* categorized as a noun and for *spread* as a verb. Each lexical entry also would indicate which syntactical rules to use for positioning the word. The rules that were applicable depend on which category was applicable in the given context. For example, as a verb, *spread* would not follow the article *the*. As a noun, however, spread would be allowed to do so. Even the peculiarities of syntax for a given lexical entry would be stored in the lexicon. For example, the lexical entry for the verb *spread* would indicate that this verb deviates from the normal syntactical rule for forming past tenses. This normal rule is to add *-ed* to the stem used for the present tense.

You may wonder why we would clutter up our mental lexicon with so much syntactical information. There is an advantage to attaching syntactical, context-sensitive, and idiosyncratic information to the items in our mental lexicon. If we add to the complexity of our mental lexicon, we can simplify drastically the number and complexity of the rules we need in our mental syntax. For example, by attaching the idiosyncratic treatment of irregular verbs (e.g., *spread* or *fall*) to our mental lexicon, we do not have to endure different syntactical rules for each verb. By making our lexicon more complex, we allow our syntax to be simpler. In this way, appropriate transformations may be simple and relatively context free. Once we know the basic syntax of a language, we easily can apply the rules to all items in our lexicon. We then can gradually expand our lexicon to provide increasing complexity and sophistication.

Not all cognitive psychologists agree with all aspects of Chomsky's theories (e.g., Bock, Loebell, & Morey, 1992; Garrett, 1992; Jackendoff, 1991). Many particularly disagree with his emphasis on syntax (form) over semantics (meaning). Nonetheless, several cognitive psychologists have proposed models of language comprehension and production that include key ideas of syntax. How do we link the elements in our mental lexicon to the elements in our syntactical structures? Various models for such bridging have been proposed (Bock, Loebell, & Morey, 1992; Jackendoff, 1991). According to some of these models, when we parse sentences by syntactical categories, we create slots for each item in the sentence. Consider, for example, the sentence, "Juan gave María the book from the shelf." There is a slot for a noun used as (1) a subject (Juan), (2) as a direct object (the book), (3) as an indirect object (María), and (4) as objects of prepositions (the shelf). There are also slots for the verb, the preposition, and the articles.

In turn, lexical items contain information regarding the kinds of slots into which the items can be placed. The information is based on the kinds of thematic roles the items can fill. **Thematic roles** are ways in which items can be used in the context of communication. Several roles have been identified. A first is that of agent, the "doer" of any action. A second is that of patient, the direct recipient of the action. A third role is that of the beneficiary, the indirect recipient of the action. A fourth role is the instrument, the means by which the action is implemented. A fifth role is location, the place where the action occurs. A sixth is source, where the action originated. And a seventh is the goal, where the action is going (Bock, 1990; Fromkin & Rodman, 1988). According to this view of how syntax and semantics are linked, the various syntactical slots can be filled by lexical entries with corresponding thematic roles. For example, the slot of subject noun might be filled by the thematic role of agent. As a further example, nouns that can fill agent roles can be inserted into slots for subjects of phrases. Patient roles correspond to slots for direct objects. Beneficiary roles fit with indirect objects, and so on. Nouns that are objects of prepositions may be filled with various thematic roles. These include location, such as at the beach; source, such as from the kitchen; and goal, such as to the classroom. So far, we have concentrated on describing the structure and processes of language in its most developed state. How do we acquire this remarkable ability?

PRACTICAL APPLICATIONS OF COGNITIVE PSYCHOLOGY	Given what you now know about processes of speech perception, semantics, and syntax, think about ways to make your speech production easier for others to perceive. If you are speaking to someone whose primary language differs from yours, try slowing down your speech, exaggerating the length of time between words. Be sure to enunciate consonant sounds carefully, without making your vowels sounds too long. Use simpler sentence constructions. Break down lengthy and involved sentences into smaller units. Insert longer pauses between sentences to give the person time to translate the sentence into propositional form. Communication may feel more effortful but will probably be more effective.

Language Acquisition

In the past, debates about the acquisition of language centered on the same theme as debates about the acquisition of any ability—the nature versus nurture theme. However, current thinking about language acquisition has incorporated the understanding that acquiring language really involves a natural endowment modified by the environment (Bates & Goodman, 1999; Lightfoot, 2003; MacWhinney, 1999; Maratsos, 2003; Wexler, 1996). For example, the social environment, in which infants use their social capacities to interact with others, provides one source of information for language acquisition (Carpenter, Nagell, & Tomasello, 1998; Snow, 1999; Tomasello, 1999). Thus, the approach to studying language acquisition now revolves around discovering what abilities are innately given and how these abilities are tempered by the environment of the child. This process is aptly termed "innately guided learning" (see Elman & associates, 1996; Jusczyk, 1997). Before examining the nature-nurture debate, let's take a look at a series of stages that seems to be universal in language acquisition.

Stages of Language Acquisition

Around the world, people seem to acquire their primary language in pretty much the same sequence and in just about the same way. In recent years, research on the development of speech perception finds the same overall pattern of progression. This pattern is from more general to more specific abilities. That is, as infants we are initially able to distinguish among all possible phonetic contrasts. But over time we lose the ability to distinguish nonnative contrasts in favor of those used in our native language environment (see Jusczyk, 1997). Thus, some aspects of infants' speech perception and production abilities mirror each other. They develop from more general to more specific abilities. From day one, infants appear to be programmed to tune into their linguistic environment with the specific goal of acquiring language. A current debate is whether this ability is especially used in learning concepts and their meanings, connections between concepts and their meanings, or both (Fodor, 1997; Marcus, 1998; Pinker, 1999; Plunkett, 1998). Whatever may be the case, infants clearly have remarkably acute language-learning abilities. They show these abilities even from an early age (Marcus & associates, 1999; Pinker, 1997, 1999).

For example, newborns seem to respond preferentially to their mothers' voices (DeCasper & Fifer, 1980). They also seem to respond motorically in synchrony with the speech of the caregivers who interact with them directly (Field, 1978; Martin, 1981; Schaffer, 1977; Snow, 1977; Stern, 1977). Infants also prefer to listen to someone speaking in what will be their native language over a future nonnative language. Perhaps they are focusing on the rhythmic structure of the language (Bertoncini, 1993; Mehler & associates, 1996). Suppose you were to videotape infants' motor responses while the infants were attending to someone speaking to them. Their movements would seem to be dancing in time with the rhythm of the speech. The emotional expression of infants also seems to be matched to that of their caregivers (Fogel, 1991).

IN THE LAB OF PAUL BLOOM

Courtesy of Dr. Paul Bloom

The research done in my lab is fairly eclectic, but one major focus is the development of social cognition, also known as "theory of mind." Some of this work involves the origins of social knowledge. In collaboration with Valerie Kuhlmeier at Queens University and Karen Wynn at Yale, I am looking at what young babies know about mental states. There is an important body of recent research showing that babies have a rich understanding of objects—they know that they are solid, for instance, and that they move on continuous paths through space. The methods used typically involve measurements of how long babies look at different scenes, exploiting the fact that babies show different looking patterns when shown normal events (such as an object bumping into a wall) than when shown surprising or magical events (such as an object going through a wall).

We have been using a similar method to explore their understanding of social beings. In one set of studies, we showed movies in which a circle tries to get up a hill to 12-month-old babies. On some occasions, a triangle would gently push the circle from the bottom, apparently helping it up; on other occasions, a square would push it down from the top, seeming to thwart its desire. These are adult interpretations of these movies; we were interested in whether babies would interpret the movies in the same way.

To test this, we then showed the babies movies where the three characters are together, and then the circle either approaches the triangle or approaches the square. We found that babies look differently at these events; they seem to expect the circle to approach the character that helped it and to avoid the character that hindered it. One interpretation of these findings is that babies know enough about mental states to expect the ball to *like* the triangle and *dislike* the square, and we are exploring this in further studies.

Other research involves the implications that our social cognition has for how we think about domains like religion, morality, and fiction. For instance, in collaboration with a graduate student at Yale, Deena Skolnick, I am looking at how people reason about the mental states of fictional characters. It is clear from previous research that young children understand the difference between fiction and reality; they know that Batman and Harry Potter are not real. But philosophers have pointed out that our natural conception of fiction is that there are many distinct fictional worlds that are intricately related to one another. One implication of this is that the characters themselves should have intuitions about who is real and who is fictional. When we ask adults, "Does Batman think Robin is real or make-believe?" they answer "real," but when we ask, "Does Batman think Harry Potter is real or make-believe?" the answer is not so clear. Batman and Robin live in the same world, after all, and this is a different world from that of Harry Potter and Hermione Granger.

This research is ongoing, but we are finding that young children share the same sorts of intuitions. Our capacity to reason about knowledge and emotions exists so that we can make sense of other people, but it extends in interesting ways to other realms, including our understanding of fictional worlds.

Suggested Readings

Bloom, P. (2004). *Descartes' baby: How the science of child development explains what makes us human.* New York: Basic Books.

Kuhlmeier, V., Wynn, K., & Bloom, P. (2003). Attribution of dispositional states by 12-month-olds. *Psychological Science, 14,* 402–408.

Within the first years of life, we humans seem to progress through the following stages in producing language:

1. Cooing, which comprises mostly vowel sounds
2. Babbling, which comprises consonant as well as vowel sounds; to most people's ears, the babbling of infants growing up among speakers from different language groups sounds very similar (Oller & Eilers, 1998)
3. One-word utterances; these utterances are limited in both the vowels and the consonants they utilize (Ingram, 1999)
4. Two-word utterances and telegraphic speech
5. Basic adult sentence structure (present by about age 4 years), with continuing vocabulary acquisition (see Bloom, 2000, for a discussion of the mechanisms of this acquisition)

Consider these stages in more detail. Infants also have been known to produce sounds of their own. Most obviously, the communicative aspect of crying—whether intentional or not—works quite well. In terms of language acquisition, however, it is the cooing of infants that most intrigues linguists. **Cooing** is the infant's oral expression that explores the production of vowel sounds. The cooing of infants around the world, including deaf infants, is indistinguishable across babies and across languages. Infants are actually better than adults at being able to discriminate sounds that carry no meaning for them (Werker, 1989). They can make phonetic distinctions that adults have lost. Thus, there are things that extremely young children do better than adults.

During the cooing stage, hearing infants also can discriminate among all phones, not just the phonemes characteristic of their own language. For example, during this stage, both Japanese and American infants can discriminate the /l/ from the /r/ phoneme. However, as Japanese infants move into the next stage, they gradually lose this ability. By 1 year of age, Japanese infants—for whom the distinction does not make a phonemic difference—no longer make this discrimination (Eimas, 1985; Tsushima & associates, 1994).

Loss of discrimination ability is not limited to Japanese infants. Consider a skill of infants who grow up in homes where English is spoken. They are able to distinguish early in life between phonemes that are different in the Hindi language of India but that are not different in English (Werker, 1994; Werker & Tees, 1984). In English, the phonemes are allophones of the /t/ sound. In particular, the English-speaking infants are able to make the discrimination with roughly 95% accuracy at between 6 and 8 months of age. By 8 to 10 months, the infants' accuracy is down to 70%. By 10 to 12 months, it is down to a mere 20%. As they grow older, infants clearly lose the capacity to make discriminations that are not relevant to their language.

At the babbling stage, deaf infants no longer vocalize. The sounds produced by hearing infants change. **Babbling** is the infant's preferential production largely of those distinct phonemes—both vowels and consonants—that are characteristic of the infant's own language (Locke, 1994; Petitto & Marentette, 1991). Thus, the cooing of infants around the world is essentially the same. But infant babbling is more differentiated. As suggested previously, the ability of the infant to perceive, as well as to produce, nonphonemic phones recedes during this stage.

Eventually, the infant utters his or her first word. It is followed shortly by one or two more. Soon after, yet a few more follow. The infant uses these one-word utterances—termed *holophrases*—to convey intentions, desires, and demands. Usually, the words are nouns describing familiar objects that the child observes (e.g., *car, book, ball, baby, nose*) or wants (e.g., *Mama, Dada, juice, cookie*).

By 18 months of age, children typically have vocabularies of 3 to 100 words (Siegler, 1986). The young child's vocabulary cannot yet encompass all the child wishes to describe. As a result, the child commits overextension errors. An **overextension error** is erroneously extending the meaning of words in the existing lexicon to cover things and ideas for which a new word is lacking. For example, the general term for a man may be "Dada"—which can be quite distressing to a new father in a public setting. The general term for any kind of four-legged animal may be "doggie." Young children have to overextend the meanings of the words they know. They have too few words in their vocabulary to do otherwise. How do they decide which words to use when overextending the meanings of the words they know?

A *feature hypothesis* suggests that children form definitions that include too few features (Clark, 1973). Thus, a child might refer to a cat as a dog because of a mental rule that if an animal has the feature of four legs, it is a "doggie." An alternative *functional hypothesis* (Nelson, 1973) suggests that children first learn to use words that describe important functions or purposes. For example, lamps give light. Blankets make us warm. According to this view, overextension errors result from functional confusions. A dog and a cat both do similar things and serve the same purposes as pets. So a child is likely to confuse them. The functional hypothesis usually has been viewed as an alternative to the feature hypothesis. But both mechanisms possibly could be at work in children's overextensions.

Gradually, between 1.5 and 2.5 years of age, children start combining single words to produce two-word utterances. Thus begins an understanding of syntax. These early syntactical communications seem more like telegrams than conversations. The articles, prepositions, and other function morphemes are usually left out. Hence, linguists refer to these early utterances with rudimentary syntax as telegraphic speech. **Telegraphic speech** can be used to describe two- or three-word utterances and even slightly longer ones, if they have omissions of some function morphemes.

Vocabulary expands rapidly. It more than triples from about 300 words at about 2 years of age to about 1,000 words at about 3 years of age. Almost incredibly, by age 4 years children acquire the foundations of adult syntax and language structure (Table 9.3). By age 5 years, most children also can understand and produce quite complex and uncommon sentence constructions. By age 10 years, children's language is fundamentally the same as that of adults.

Nature and Nurture

Neither nature alone nor nurture alone adequately explains all aspects of language acquisition. Just how might nature then facilitate nurture in the process? Perhaps humans have a **language-acquisition device (LAD)**, a biologically innate mechanism that facilitates language acquisition (Chomsky, 1965, 1972). That is, we humans seem to be biologically preconfigured to be ready to acquire language.

TABLE 9.3	Developmental Changes Associated with Language Acquisition

Regardless of the language children acquire, children around the world seem to follow the same developmental pattern, at about the same ages.

Approximate Age	Characteristics of Age	Interaction With Information Processing
Prenatal First several months About the second 6 months after birth	Responsivity to human voices Cooing, which comprises largely vowel sounds Babbling, which comprises the distinct phonemes—vowels and consonants—that characterize the primary language of the infant	As sounds become more meaningful, the infant's perception of the sounds becomes more selective and the infant's ability to remember sounds increases.
About 1 to 3 years of age	One-word utterances Two-word utterances Telegraphic speech	As fluency and comprehension increase, the ability mentally to manipulate linguistic symbols increases, as does conceptual development; overextension errors occur when children try to apply their limited vocabulary to a variety of situations, but as children's vocabulary becomes more specialized, these errors occur less often.
About 3 to 4 years	Simple sentences that reflect tremendous expansion of vocabulary, as well as remarkably adept understanding of syntax, despite errors of overregularization	Vocabulary and concepts continue to expand in terms of both comprehension and fluency, and the child internalizes rules of syntax; overregularization errors offer insights into how children form rules about language structures.
By about 4 years of age	Basic adult sentence structure; some increases in complexity of structure continue through adolescence; vocabulary continues to increase, although at a declining rate	Children's language patterns and strategies for language acquisition are studied in much the same ways as those for adults; however, their metacognitive strategies for acquiring vocabulary become increasingly sophisticated throughout childhood.

Several observations of humans support the notion that we are predisposed to acquire language. For one thing, human speech perception is quite remarkable, given the nature of auditory processing capacities for other sounds. Moreover, all children within a broad normal range of abilities and of environments seem to acquire language at an incredibly rapid rate. In fact, deaf children acquire sign language in about the same way and at about the same rate as hearing children acquire spoken language. If you have ever struggled to acquire a second language, you can appreciate the relative ease and speed with which young children seem to acquire their first language. This accomplishment is quite remarkable. Consider that children are offered a relatively modest quantity and variety of linguistic input (whether speech or signs) in relation to the highly sophisticated internalized language structures children create. Children seem to have a knack for acquiring an implicit understanding of the many rules of language structure. They also have a knack for applying those rules to new vocabulary and new contexts. However, many adults still can learn new languages quite well if placed in the right context, such as an immersion program. Their learning may be good, although they are likely to retain an accent that reflects the phonemes of their first language when they speak the new language. For example, a Spaniard learning English may speak English with a Spanish accent. In the same way, the American would be likely to speak Spanish with some degree of an American accent.

Metacognition is our understanding and control of our cognition (Scheck & Nelson, 2003). It provides one of our best aids in learning language. As adults, we have a great advantage in learning language. We have greater familiarity with the structure of language than we do when we are young. The extent to which metacognition helps, however, depends on how similar a new language is to the language or languages we already know. For example, most English-speaking adults find Spanish much easier to acquire than Russian. The reason is that the structure of Spanish is much more like that of English than is the structure of Russian. Chinese is still harder to acquire, on average, because it is even more different from English than is Russian.

Perhaps even more surprising, almost all children seem to acquire these aspects of language in the same progression and at more or less the same time. However, the linguistic environment clearly plays a role in the language-acquisition process. There seem to be *critical periods*—times of rapid development, during which a particular ability must be developed if it is ever to develop adequately—for acquiring these understandings of language (Newport, 2003; Stromswold, 2000). No one knows exactly why critical periods occur. Perhaps young children are at an advantage in language learning because limitations in their perceptual and memory abilities render them more likely to process smaller chunks of speech information (Newport, 1991). These smaller chunks may make it easier for them to see the structure of language. This view has by no means been unanimously accepted, however (Rohde & Plaut, 1999). Nor has any other explanation been universally accepted for the existence of critical periods. During such periods, the environment plays a crucial role. For example, the cooing and babbling stages seem to be a critical period for acquiring a native speaker's discrimination and production of the distinctive phonemes of a particular language. During this critical period, the child's linguistic context must provide those distinctive phonemes.

There seems to be a critical period for acquiring a native understanding of a language's syntax, too. Perhaps the greatest support for this view comes from studies of adult users of ASL. Consider adults who have signed ASL for 30 years or more. Researchers could discernibly differentiate among those who acquired ASL before age 4 years, between ages 4 and 6 years, and after age 12 years. Despite 30 years of signing, those who acquired ASL later in childhood showed less profound understanding of the distinctive syntax of ASL (Meier, 1991; Newport, 1990).

Studies of linguistically isolated children seem to provide additional support for the notion of the interaction of both physiological maturation and environmental support. Consider the rare children who have been linguistically isolated. Those who are rescued at younger ages seem to acquire more sophisticated language structures than do those who are rescued when they are older. The research on critical periods for language acquisition is much more equivocal for the acquisition of additional languages, after acquiring a first one (Bahrick & associates, 1994; see also Chapter 10).

Two additional observations, which apply to all humans at all ages, also support the notion that nature contributes to language acquisition. First, humans possess several physiological structures that serve no purpose other than to produce speech (G. S.

Dell, personal communication, November 1994). Second, myriad universal characteristics have been documented across the vast array of human languages. By 1963, a lone linguist documented forty-five universal characteristics across thirty languages (e.g., Finnish, Hindi, Swahili, Quechua, and Serbian). Since then, hundreds of universal patterns have been documented across languages around the globe (see Pinker, 1994).

Neither nature nor nurture alone appears to determine language acquisition. According to the **hypothesis testing** view, children acquire language by mentally forming tentative hypotheses regarding language, based on their inherited facility for language acquisition and then testing these hypotheses in the environment. Thus, nature and nurture work together. The implementation of this process is said to follow several operating principles (Slobin, 1971, 1985). In forming hypotheses, young children look for and attend to these things:

1. Patterns of changes in the forms of words
2. Morphemic inflections that signal changes in meaning, especially suffixes
3. Sequences of morphemes, including both the sequences of affixes and roots and the sequences of words in sentence

In addition, children learn to avoid exceptions. They also figure out various other patterns characteristic of their native tongue. Although not all linguists support the hypothesis-testing view, two phenomena support it. The first is overregularization, or using and sometimes overapplying rules. The second is language productivity, creating novel utterances based on some kind of understanding of how to do so.

A variant of the hypothesis-testing view is that while children are acquiring language, they do not pay attention to all aspects of language. Instead, children focus on the perceptually most salient aspects of language. These aspects happen to be the most meaningful aspects in most cases (Newport, 1990). Although Newport's studies have focused on deaf children's acquisition of ASL, this phenomenon may apply to spoken language as well. Indeed, one study finds that hearing infants do attend to the salient acoustic cues in sentences that mark grammatically critical attributes of sentences (Hirsh-Pasek & associates, 1987).

Although few psychologists (if any) have asserted that language is entirely a result of nature, many researchers have emphasized the genetic component (e.g., Gilger, 1996; Pinker, 1994; Stromswold, 1998, 2000). Some focus on the environmental mechanisms that children use to acquire language. Three such mechanisms are imitation, modeling, and conditioning.

Imitation

In imitation, children do exactly what they see others do. Sometimes children do imitate the language patterns of others, especially their parents. Imitation, however, would not in itself be sufficient for acquisition of language. Children must be doing something more. More often, children loosely follow what they hear. This phenomenon is referred to as *modeling*.

Modeling

Even amateur observers of children notice that children's speech patterns and vocabulary model the patterns and vocabulary of the people in their environment. From infancy, children listen to and try to imitate speech sounds they hear (Kuhl & Meltzoff,

1997). In fact, parents of very young children seem to go to great lengths to make it easy for children to attend to and to understand what they are saying. Almost without thinking, parents and other adults tend to use a higher pitch than usual. In this way, they exaggerate the vocal inflection of their speech. For example, they raise and lower pitch and volume more extremely than normal. They also use **child-directed speech**—simpler sentence constructions when speaking with infants and young children (Rice, 1989). This distinctive form of adult speech also has been termed *motherese*. For example, a mother might say to her baby, "Baby come to mama." In this way, she attempts to speak to the child in a way that the child will understand.

Through child-directed speech, adults seem to go out of their way to make language interesting and comprehensible to infants and other young children. Their goal is to communicate successfully with their infants (Acredolo & Goodwyn, 1998). In this way, they also make it possible for the infants to model aspects of the adults' behavior. Indeed, infants do seem to prefer listening to child-directed speech more than to other forms of adult speech (Fernald, 1985). These exaggerations serve at least two purposes. First, they seem to gain and hold infants' attention. Second, they signal the infants when to take turns in vocalizing and communicate affect (emotion-related information). Across cultures, parents seem to use this specialized form of speech. They further tailor it to particular circumstances. They use rising intonations to gain children's attention. They use falling intonations to comfort the children. And they use brief, discontinuous, rapid-fire explosions of speech to warn against prohibited behavior (Fernald & associates, 1989).

Parents even seem to model the correct format for verbal interactions. Early caregiver–child verbal interactions are characterized by verbal turn taking. The caregiver says something. She or he then uses vocal inflection to cue the infant to respond. The infant babbles, sneezes, burps, or otherwise makes some audible response. The caregiver then accepts whatever noises the infant makes as valid communicative utterances and replies. Next the infant further responds to the cue. And the process continues on for as long as they both show interest in continuing.

Parents also seem to work hard to understand children's early utterances. In these utterances, one or two words may be used for conveying an entire array of concepts. As the child grows older and more sophisticated and acquires more language, parents gradually provide less linguistic support. They demand increasingly sophisticated utterances from the child. They initially seem to provide a scaffold from which the child can construct an edifice of language. As the child's language develops, the parents gradually remove the scaffolding.

Do parental models of language use provide the chief means by which children acquire language? The mechanism of imitation is quite appealing in its simplicity. Unfortunately, it does not explain many aspects of language acquisition. For example, suppose imitation is the primary mechanism. Why, in this case, do children universally begin by producing one-word utterances, then two-word and other telegraphic utterances, and later complete sentences? Why not start out with complete sentences? In addition, perhaps the most compelling argument against imitation alone relates to our linguistic productivity. Shakespeare may have been more productive than most of us. But each of us is quite innovative in the speech we produce. Most of the utterances we produce are ones that we have never heard or read before.

Yet another argument against imitation alone is a phenomenon that occurs when young children have acquired an understanding of how language usually works. **Over-regularization** occurs when individuals apply the general rules of language to the exceptional cases that vary from the norm. For example, instead of imitating her parents' sentence pattern, "The mice fell down the hole, and they ran home," the young child might overregularize the irregular forms. She or he would then say, "The mouses falled down the hole, and they runned home." The fact that children say things like "mouses" shows that the next mechanism to be considered—conditioning—could not tell the entire story of language acquisition.

Conditioning

The mechanism of conditioning is also exquisitely simple. Children hear utterances and associate those utterances with particular objects and events in their environment. They then produce those utterances and are rewarded by their parents and others for having spoken. Initially their utterances are not perfect. But through successive approximations children come to speak just as well as native adult speakers of their language. The progression from babbling to one-word utterances to more complex utterances would seem to support the notion that children begin with simple associations. Their utterances gradually increase in complexity and in the degree to which they approximate adult speech.

As with imitation, the simplicity of the proposed conditioning mechanism does not suffice to explain actual language acquisition fully. For one thing, parents are much more likely to respond to whether the statement of the child is true or false than to the relative correctness of the child's grammar and pronunciation (Brown, Cazden, & Bellugi, 1969). Of course, parents sometimes do respond to the grammatical correctness of children's speech. But their responses only explain why children eventually stop overregularizing their speech. They do not explain why the children ever begin doing so. Also, just as linguistic productivity argues against imitation alone, it contradicts conditioning: Children constantly use novel utterances for which they have never previously been rewarded. They consistently apply the words and language structures they already know to novel situations and contexts for which they have never before received reinforcement. Thus, through the combined effects of innately given linguistic abilities and exposure to a linguistic environment, infants acquire a language automatically and seemingly effortlessly.

Beyond the First Years

The foregoing theories offer explanations of how children acquire the foundations of adult language structure by age 4 years or so. Indeed, 4-year-old language achievements are remarkable. But few of us would have difficulty recognizing that the vocabulary and the linguistic sophistication of 4 year olds differ from those of most older children and adults. What changes occur in children's use of language after age 4? And what do such changes imply regarding developmental changes in cognition?

To understand these changes, we explore both verbal comprehension and verbal fluency. In general, children's ability to comprehend language and to process information efficiently increases with age (Hunt, Lunneborg, & Lewis, 1975; Keating &

Bobbitt, 1978). Older children also demonstrate greater verbal fluency than do younger children (Sincoff & Sternberg, 1988). We do not want to look only at increases in verbal comprehension and fluency abilities that develop with age. We also want to understand development by looking at the specific strategies a child of a given age uses to comprehend or generate verbal material. Much of what develops is not just verbal ability. It also is the ability to generate useful strategies for verbal comprehension and fluency. These strategies are at the intersection of language acquisition and metacognition. They are important aspects of human intelligence (Sternberg, 1985a).

An interesting aspect of research on strategies of verbal comprehension has been research on comprehension monitoring (Markman, 1977, 1979). This research hypothesizes that one of the ways in which we enhance our understanding of verbal information is to monitor what we hear and read. We thereby check it for accuracy, logic, and cohesiveness. To study the influence of comprehension monitoring, researchers observed children and adults and attempted to correlate comprehension-monitoring skills with assessments of overall comprehension.

Consider a typical experiment. Children between the ages of 8 and 11 years heard passages containing contradictory information. This description of how to make the dessert Baked Alaska is an example (Markman, 1979, p. 656):

> To make it they put the ice cream in a very hot oven. The ice cream in
> Baked Alaska melts when it gets that hot. Then they take the ice cream out
> of the oven and serve it right away. When they make Baked Alaska, the ice
> cream stays firm and does not melt.

Note that the passage contains a blatant internal contradiction. It says both that the ice cream melts and that it does not. Almost half of the young children who saw this passage did not notice the contradiction at all. Even when they were warned in advance about problems with the story, many of the youngest children still did not detect the inconsistency. Thus, young children are not very successful at comprehension monitoring. They are less than successful even when cued to be aware of inconsistencies in the text they read. An important aspect of development of all cognitive skills, including comprehension monitoring, is the improvement that people show in their use of these skills.

Animal Language

Some cognitive psychologists specialize in the study of nonhuman animals. Why would they study such animals, when humans are so readily available? There are several reasons.

First, nonhuman animals often are presumed to have somewhat simpler cognitive systems. It is therefore easier to model their behavior. These models can then be bootstrapped to the study of humans, as has happened most notably in the study of learning. For example, a model of conditioning that originally was proposed for nonhuman animals such as white rats has proven to be extremely useful in understanding human learning (Rescorla & Wagner, 1972). The model, when first proposed, was unique in suggesting that nonhuman animal cognition is more complex than had previously been thought. Robert Rescorla and Allan Wagner showed that classical conditioning depends not just on simple contiguity of an unconditioned and conditioned stimulus, but rather on the contingency involved in the situation. In other words, classical conditioning occurs when animals reduce uncertainty in a learning situation—when they learn the relation between occurrences of two kinds of stimuli. In sum, research on simpler animals often leads to important insights about human learning.

Second, nonhuman animals can be subject to procedures that would not be possible for human ones. For example, a rat may be sacrificed at the end of a learning experiment to study changes that have occurred in the brain as a result of learning. All such studies must, of course, must be subject to institutional approval for the ethics of experimentation before they are conducted.

Third, nonhuman animals that are not in the wild can serve as full-time subjects, or at least, regularly available subjects. They are typically there when the experimenter needs them. In contrast, college students and other humans have many other obligations, such as classes, homework, and personal commitments. Moreover, sometimes, even when they sign up for research, they fail to show up.

Fourth, an understanding of the comparative and evolutionary as well as developmental bases of human behavior requires studies of nonhuman animals of various kinds (Rumbaugh & Beran, 2003). If cognitive psychologists want to understand the origins of human cognition in the distant past, they need to study other kinds of animals besides humans.

Fifth and finally, the study of humans enables cognitive psychologists to explore which cognitive skills are uniquely human and which ones are shared with other animals. The philosopher René Descartes suggested that language is what qualitatively distinguishes human beings from other species. Was he right? Before we get into the particulars of language in nonhuman species, we should emphasize the distinction between communication and language. Few would doubt that nonhuman animals communicate in one way or another. What is at issue is whether they do so through what reasonably can be called a language. Whereas *language* is an organized means of combining words to communicate, *communication* more broadly encompasses not only the exchange of thoughts and feelings through language, but also nonverbal expression. Examples include gestures, glances, distancing, and other contextual cues.

Primates—especially chimpanzees—offer our most promising insights into nonhuman language. Jane Goodall, the well-known investigator of chimpanzees in the wild, has studied diverse aspects of chimp behavior. One is vocalizations. Goodall considers many of them to be clearly communicative, although not necessarily indicative of language. For example, chimps have a specific cry indicating that they are about to be attacked. They have another for calling their fellow chimps together. Nonetheless, their repertoire of communicative vocalizations seems to be small, nonproductive (new utterances are not produced), limited in structure, lacking in structural complexity, and relatively nonarbitrary. It also is not spontaneously acquired. The chimps' communications thus do not satisfy our criteria for a language.

By using sign language, R. Allen and Beatrice Gardner were able to teach their tame chimp, Washoe, rudimentary language skills (Brown, 1973) beyond the stages a human toddler could reach. Subsequently, David Premack (1971) had even greater success with his chimpanzee, Sarah. She acquired a vocabulary of more than 100 words of various parts of speech and showed at least rudimentary linguistic skills. She modeled her trainer and was able to use the instruction she received to construct what appeared to be a rudimentary language of her own.

A less positive view of the linguistic capabilities of chimpanzees was taken by Herbert Terrace (1981), who raised a chimp named Nim Chimpsky, a takeoff on Noam Chomsky, the eminent linguist. Over the course of several years, Nim made more than 19,000 multiple-sign utterances in a slightly modified version of ASL. Most of his utterances consisted of two-word combinations.

Terrace's careful analysis of these utterances, however, revealed that most of them were repetitions of what Nim had seen. Terrace concluded that, despite what appeared to be impressive accomplishments, Nim did not show even the rudiments of syntactical expression. The chimp could produce single- or even multiple-word utterances, but not in a syntactically organized way. For example, Nim would alternate signing "Give Nim banana," "Banana give Nim," and "Banana Nim give," showing no preference for the grammatically correct form. Moreover, Terrace also studied films showing other chimpanzees supposedly producing language. He came to the same conclusion for them that he had reached for Nim. His position, then, is that although chimpanzees can understand and produce utterances, they do not have linguistic competence in the same sense that even very young humans do. Their communications lack structure and particularly multiplicity of structure.

Susan Savage-Rumbaugh and her colleagues (Savage-Rumbaugh & associates, 1986, 1993) have found the best evidence yet in favor of language use among chimpanzees. Their pygmy chimpanzees spontaneously combined the visual symbols (such as red triangles and blue squares) of an artificial language the researchers taught them. They even appear to have understood some of the language spoken to them. One pygmy chimp in particular (Greenfield & Savage-Rumbaugh, 1990) seemed to possess remarkable skill, even possibly demonstrating a primitive grasp of language structure. It may be that the difference in results across groups of investigators is due to the particular kind of chimp tested or to the procedures used. The chimp's language may not meet all the constraints posed by the properties of language described at this beginning of the chapter. For example, the language used by the chimps is not spontaneously acquired. Rather, they learn it only through very deliberate and systematic programs of instruction. At this point, we just cannot be sure if the chimps truly show the full range of language abilities.

Whether nonhuman species can use language, it seems almost certain that the language facility of humans far exceeds that of other species we have studied. Noam Chomsky (1991) has stated the key question regarding nonhuman language quite eloquently: "If an animal had a capacity as biologically advantageous as language but somehow hadn't used it until now, it would be an evolutionary miracle, like finding an island of humans who could be taught to fly."

Common Themes

This chapter deals with a number of the major themes reviewed in Chapter 1.

First and foremost is the theme of nature versus nurture. To what extent is language the result of some innate language acquisition device and to what extent is it the result of experience? Earlier research during the times of behaviorism very heavily emphasized the role of nurture. Much modern research, since the work in the 1960s of Noam Chomsky, has emphasized the role of innate factors (nature). But clearly nature interacts with nurture. Children who receive minimal verbal experiences in their early years will be at a disadvantage in the development of language skills.

A second theme is that of rationalism versus empiricism. Most psychologists emphasize empirical techniques in their research. But linguists such as Chomsky have emphasized more rationalistic techniques. They analyze language, typically without formally collecting empirical data at all, at least in the cognitive psychologists' sense of what constitute such data. The stunning insights of Chomsky show that the two methods complement each other. Many insights can evolve from rationalism. They then can be tested by empirical methods.

A third theme is that of domain generality versus domain specificity. In particular, to what extent is language special? Is it a domain apart from other domains, or simply one more cognitive domain like any other? Many psychologists today believe that there is indeed something special about language. At the same time, cognitive processes operate on it so that people use their language in practically all of the other domains in which they work. For example, many mathematical and physical problems are presented with words.

Say to any number of people, "In mud eels are, in clay none are." Ask them what you just said. Our experience is that almost no one can understand this sentence. The reason is that they are not applying the appropriate schema to understand your utterance. If you were to ask them to think of themselves as fish who don't want to be eaten by eels and then if you were to repeat this sentence, many will be able to understand what you say. (Our experience is that there are still some who will not be able to understand this utterance, so you will have to give them stronger hints.)

Summary

1. **What properties characterize language?** There are at least six properties of language, the use of an organized means of combining words in order to communicate. (1) Language permits us to communicate with one or more people who share our language. (2) Language creates an arbitrary relationship between a symbol and its referent—an idea, a thing, a process, a relationship, or a description. (3) Language has a regular structure; only particular sequences of symbols (sounds and words) have meaning. Different sequences yield different meanings. (4) The structure of language can be analyzed at multiple levels (e.g., phonemic and morphemic). (5) Despite having the limits of a structure, language users can produce novel utterances; the possibilities for generating new utterances are virtually limitless. (6) Languages constantly evolve.

Language involves verbal comprehension—the ability to comprehend written and spoken linguistic input, such as words, sentences, and paragraphs. It also involves verbal fluency—the ability to produce linguistic output. The smallest units of sound produced by the human vocal tract are phones. Phonemes are the smallest units of sound that can be used to differentiate meaning in a given language. The smallest semantically meaningful unit in a language is a morpheme. Morphemes may be either roots or affixes—prefixes or suffixes. Affixes in turn may be either content morphemes, conveying the bulk of the word's meaning, or function morphemes, augmenting the meaning of the word. A lexicon is the repertoire of morphemes in a given language (or for a given language user). The study of the meaningful sequencing of words within phrases and sentences in a given language is syntax. Larger units of language are embraced by the study of discourse.

2. **What are some of the processes involved in language?** In speech perception, listeners must overcome the influence of coarticulation (overlapping) of phonemes on the acoustic structure of the speech signal. Categorical perception is the phenomenon in which listeners perceive continuously varying speech sounds as distinct categories. It lends support to the notion that speech is perceived via specialized processes. The motor theory of speech perception attempts to explain these processes in relation to the processes involved in speech production. Those who believe speech perception is ordinary explain speech perception in terms of feature-detection, prototype, and Gestalt theories of perception.

Syntax is the study of the linguistic structure of sentences. Phrase-structure grammars analyze sentences in terms of the hierarchical relationships among words in phrases and sentences. Transformational grammars analyze sentences in terms of transformational rules that describe interrelationships among the structures of various sentences. Some linguists have suggested a mechanism for linking syntax to semantics. By this mechanism, grammatical sentences contain particular slots for syntactical categories. These slots may be filled by words that have particular thematic roles within the sentences. According to this view, each item in a lexicon contains information regarding appropriate thematic roles, as well as appropriate syntactical categories.

3. **How do we acquire the ability to use language?** Humans seem to progress through stages in acquiring language. The first is cooing, which comprises all possible phones. The second is babbling, which comprises only the distinct phonemes that characterize the primary language of the infant. The third is one-word utterances. The fourth is two-word utterances and telegraphic speech. And the fifth is basic adult sentence structure (present by about age 4 years). This progression includes changes in perception that reduce the number of phonemes that can be distinguished. After the cooing stage, the infant tunes in only to those phonemes of the native language environment.

During language acquisition, children engage in overextension errors, in which they extend the meaning of a word to encompass more concepts than the word is intended to encompass. Neither nature alone nor nurture alone can account for human language acquisition. The mechanism of hypothesis testing suggests an integration of nature and nurture. Children acquire language by mentally forming tentative hypotheses regarding language (based on nature) and then testing these hypotheses in the environment (based on nurture). Children are guided in the formation of these hypotheses by an innate language-acquisition device (LAD), which facilitates language acquisition. Over the course of development, language complexity, vocabulary, and even strategies for vocabulary acquisition become increasingly sophisticated.

Thinking about Thinking: Factual, Analytical, Creative, and Practical Questions

1. Describe the six key properties of language.

2. What evidence is there that both nature and nurture influence language acquisition?

3. In your opinion, why do some view speech perception as special, whereas others consider speech perception ordinary?

4. Compare and contrast the speech-is-ordinary and speech-is-special views, particularly in reference to categorical perception and phoneme restoration.

5. How do phrase-structure diagrams reveal the alternative meanings of ambiguous sentences?

6. Make up a sentence that illustrates several of the thematic roles mentioned in this chapter (i.e., agent, patient, beneficiary, instrument, location, source, and goal).

7. In this chapter, we saw that passive-voice sentences can be transformed into active-voice sentences using transformation rules. What are some other kinds of sentence structures that are related to one another? In your own words, state the transformation rules that would govern the changes from one form to another.

8. Give a sample of an utterance you might reasonably expect to hear from an 18-month-old child.

Key Terms

babbling

categorical perception

child-directed speech

coarticulation

communication

connotations

content morphemes

cooing

deep structure

denotation

discourse

function morphemes

grammar

hypothesis testing

language

language-acquisition device (LAD)

lexicon

metacognition

morpheme

noun phrase

overextension error

overregularization

phoneme

phrase-structure grammars

psycholinguistics

semantics

surface structure

syntax

telegraphic speech

thematic roles

transformational grammar

verb phrase

verbal comprehension

verbal fluency

Explore CogLab by going to http://coglab.wadsworth.com. Answer the questions required by your instructor from the student manual that accompanies CogLab.

Categorical Perception
    Identification
Discrimination

Suffix Effect
Lexical Decision

Annotated Suggested Reading

Bloom, P. (2000). *How children learn the meanings of words*. Cambridge, MA: MIT Press. A comprehensive and empirically supported account of vocabulary acquisition in young children.

Language in Context

EXPLORING COGNITIVE PSYCHOLOGY

1. How does language affect the way we think?

2. How does our social context influence our use of language?

3. How can we find out about language by studying the human brain, and what do such studies reveal?

"My surgeon was a butcher."

"His house is a rat's nest."

"Her sermons are sleeping pills."

"He's a real toad, and he always dates real dogs."

"Abused children are walking time bombs."

"My boss is a tiger in board meetings but a real pussycat with me."

"Billboards are warts on the landscape."

"My cousin is a vegetable."

"John's last girlfriend chewed him up and spit him out."

Not one of the preceding statements is literally true. Yet fluent readers of English have little difficulty comprehending these metaphors and other nonliteral forms of language. How do we comprehend them? One of the reasons that we can understand nonliteral uses of language is that we can interpret the words we hear within a broader linguistic, cultural, social, and cognitive context. In this chapter, we first focus on the cognitive context of language. We look at how people use language in context to learn how to read and be proficient readers. Then, we look at how language and thought interact. Next, we discuss some uses of language in its social context. Finally, we examine some neuropsychological insights into language. Although the topics in this chapter are diverse, they all have one element in common. They address the issue of how language is used in the everyday contexts in which we need it to communicate with others and to make our communications as meaningful as we possibly can.

Reading: Bottom-Up and Top-Down Processes

Because reading is such a complex process, a discussion of how we engage in this process could be placed in any of a number of chapters in this book. At a minimum, reading involves language, memory, thinking, intelligence, and perception (Adams, 1990, 1999; Adams, Treiman, & Pressley, 1997; Garrod & Daneman, 2003; Just & Carpenter, 1987). The ability to read is fundamental to our everyday lives.

People who have **dyslexia**—difficulty in deciphering, reading, and comprehending text—can suffer greatly in a society that puts a high premium on fluent reading (Benasich & Thomas, 2003; Coltheart, 2003; Galaburda, 1999; National Reading Council, 1998; Shankweiler & associates, 1995; Spear-Swerling & Sternberg, 1996;

Sternberg & Grigorenko, 1999; Sternberg & Spear-Swerling, 1999; Torgesen, 1997; Vellutino & associates, 1996). Problems in phonological processing, and thus in word identification, pose "the major stumbling block in learning to read" (Grodzinsky, 2003; Pollatsek & Rayner, 1989, p. 403; see also Rayner & Pollatsek, 2000). Several different processes may be impaired in dyslexia.

The first is phonological awareness. It refers to awareness of the sound structure of spoken language. A typical way of assessing phonological awareness is through a phoneme-deletion task. Children are asked to say, for example, "goat" without the "-t." Another task that is used is phoneme counting. Children might be asked how many different sounds there are in the word "fish." The correct answer is three.

A second process is phonological reading. It entails reading words in isolation. Teachers sometimes call this skill "word decoding" or "word attack." For measurement of the skill, children might be asked to read words in isolation. Some of the words might be quite easy; others, difficult. Individuals with dyslexia often have more trouble recognizing the words in isolation than in context. When given context, they use the context to figure out what the word means.

A third process is phonological coding in working memory. This process is involved in remembering strings of phonemes that are sometimes confusing. It might be measured by comparing working memory for confusable versus nonconfusable phonemes. For example, a child might be assessed for how well he or she remembers the string "t, b, z, v, g" versus "o, x, r, y, q." Most people will have more difficulty with the first string. But individuals with dyslexia who have problems in phonological coding in working memory will have particular trouble.

A fourth process is lexical access. This process refers to one's ability to retrieve phonemes from long-term memory. The question here is whether one can quickly retrieve a word from long-term memory when it is seen. For example, if you see the word "pond," do you immediately recognize the word as "pond," or does it take you a while to retrieve it?

There are several different kinds of dyslexia. The most well-known kind is *developmental dyslexia,* which is difficulty in reading that starts in childhood and typically continues throughout adulthood. Most commonly, children with developmental dyslexia have difficult in learning the rules that relate letters to sounds. A second kind of dyslexia is *acquired dyslexia,* which is typically caused by traumatic brain damage. A perfectly good reader who experiences a brain injury may acquire dyslexia.

Developmental dyslexia is believed to have both biological and environmental causes. A major dispute in the field is the role of each (Sternberg & Spear-Swerling, 1999). People with developmental dyslexia often have been found to have abnormalities in certain chromosomes, most notably, 6 and 15. But educational interventions can help reduce the impairments in reading cause by dyslexia.

Perceptual Issues in Reading

If you view your own text processing, you can see that the ability to read is truly remarkable. You somehow manage to perceive the correct letter when it is presented in a wide array of typestyles and typefaces. For example, you can perceive it correctly in capital and lowercase forms, and even in cursive forms. Such processes involve the perception of aspects of printed words relating to visual form. Such aspects are referred to as *orthographic*. You then must translate the letter into a sound, creating a phonological code (relating to sound). This translation is particularly difficult in English because English does not always ensure a direct correspondence between a letter and a sound. George Bernard Shaw, playwright and lover of the English language, observed the illogicality of English spellings. He suggested that, in English, it would be perfectly reasonable to pronounce "ghoti" as "fish." You would pronounce the "gh" as in rough, the "o" as in women, and the "ti" as in nation. That brings up another perplexing "Englishism": How do you pronounce "ough"? Try the words *dough, bough, bought, through,* and *cough*—had *enough?*

After you somehow manage to translate all those visual symbols into sounds, you must sequence those sounds to form a word (Pollatsek & Miller, 2003). Then you need to identify the word and figure out what the word means. Ultimately you move on to the next word and repeat the process all over again. You continue this process with subsequent words to formulate a single sentence. You continue this process for as long as you read. Clearly, the normal ability to read is not at all simple. About 36 million American adults have not yet learned to read at an eighth-grade level (Conn & Silverman, 1991). On the one hand, the statistics on low literacy and illiteracy should alarm us and provoke us to action. On the other hand, we may need to reconsider our possibly less-than-favorable appraisal of those who have not yet mastered the task of reading. To undertake such a challenge—at any age—is difficult indeed.

When learning to read, novice readers must come to master two basic kinds of perceptual processes: lexical processes and comprehension processes. **Lexical processes** are used to identify letters and words. They also activate relevant information in memory about these words. **Comprehension processes** are used to make sense of the text as a whole (and are discussed later in this chapter). The separation and integration of both bottom-up and top-down approaches to perception can be seen as we consider the lexical processes of reading.

Lexical Processes in Reading

Fixations and Reading Speed

When we read, our eyes do not move smoothly along a page or even along a line of text. Rather, our eyes move in *saccades*—rapid sequential movements as they fixate on successive clumps of text. the fixations are like a series of "snapshots" (Pollatsek & Rayner, 1989). Fixations are of variable length (Carpenter & Just, 1981). Readers fixate for a longer time on longer words than on shorter words. They also fixate longer on less familiar words (i.e., words that appear less frequently in the English language) than on more familiar words (i.e., words of higher frequency). The last word of a sentence also seems to receive an extra long fixation time. This can be called "sentence wrap-up time" (Carpenter & Just, 1981).

Although most words are fixated, not all of them are. Readers fixate up to about 80% of the content words in a text. These words include nouns, verbs, and other words that carry the bulk of the meaning. (Function words, such as "the" and "of," serve a supporting role to the content words.) Just what is the visual span of one of these fixations? It appears that we can extract useful information from a perceptual window of characters about four characters to the left of a fixation point and about fourteen or fifteen characters to the right of it. These characters include letters, numerals, punctuation marks, and spaces. Saccadic movements leap an average of about seven to nine characters between successive fixations. So some of the information we extract may be preparatory for subsequent fixation (Pollatsek & Rayner, 1989; Rayner & associates, 1995). When students speed-read, they show fewer and shorter fixations (Just, Carpenter, & Masson, 1982). But apparently their greater speed is at the expense of comprehension of anything more than just the gist of the passage (Homa, 1983).

Lexical Access

An important aspect of reading is **lexical access**—the identification of a word that allows us to gain access to the meaning of the word from memory. Most psychologists who study reading believe that lexical access is an interactive process. It combines information from multiple levels of processing, such as the features of letters, the letters themselves, and the words comprising the letters (Morton, 1969). Consider some of the basics of an interactive-activation model (Rumelhart & McClelland, 1981, 1982). The hypothesis of this model is that activation of particular lexical elements occurs at multiple levels. Moreover, activity at each of the levels is interactive.

The model distinguishes among three levels of processing following visual input. These are the feature level, the letter level, and the word level. The model assumes that information at each level is represented separately in memory. Information passes from one level to another bidirectionally. In other words, processing occurs in each of two directions. First, it is bottom-up, starting with sensory data and working up to higher levels of cognitive processing. Second, it is top-down, starting with high-level cognition operating on prior knowledge and experiences related to a given context (Figure 10.1). The interactive view implies that not only do we use the sensorially perceptible features of letters, say, to help us identify words. We also use the features we already know about words to help us identify letters. For this reason, the model is referred to as "interactive." Moreover, the top-down aspect of the model allows for generalized context effects (see also Plaut & associates, 1996).

Other theorists have suggested alternatives to Rumelhart and McClelland's model (e.g., Meyer & Schvaneveldt, 1976; Paap & associates, 1982). But the distinctions among interactive models go beyond the scope of this introductory text. Support for word-recognition models involving discrete levels of processing comes from studies of cerebral processing (Petersen & associates, 1988; Posner & associates, 1988, 1989). Studies that map brain metabolism indicate that different regions of the brain become activated during passive visual processing of word forms, as opposed to semantic analysis of words or even spoken pronunciation of the words. These studies involve the use of techniques such as positron emission tomography and functional magnetic resonance imaging (fMRI), discussed in Chapter 2.

In addition to neuropsychological support, at least two of the word-recognition models have been simulated on computer (the McClelland and Rumelhart model and the model proposed by Paap & associates, 1982). Both models aptly predicted a word-superiority effect as well as a pseudoword-superiority effect. The word-superiority effect is similar to the configural-superiority effect and the object-superiority effect (mentioned in regard to top-down influences on perception). In the **word-superiority effect,** letters are read more easily when they are embedded in words than when they

FIGURE 10.1

David Rumelhart and James McClelland used this figure to illustrate how activation at the feature level, the letter level, and the word level may interact during word recognition. In this figure, lines terminating in arrows prompt activation, and lines terminating in dots (black circles) prompt inhibition. For example, the feature for a solid horizontal bar at the top of a letter leads to activation of the T character but to inhibition of the N character. Similarly, at the letter level, activation of T as the first letter leads to activation of TRAP and TRIP but to inhibition of ABLE. Going from the top down, activation of the word TRAP leads to inhibition of A, N, G, and S as the first letter but to activation of T as the first letter. From Richard E. Meyer, "The Search for Insight: Grappling with Gestalt Psychology's Unanswered Questions," in The Nautre of Insight, edited by R. J. Sternberg and J. E. Davidson. © 1995 MIT Press. Reprinted with permission from MIT Press.

are presented either in isolation or with letters that do not form words. People take substantially longer to read unrelated letters than to read letters that form a word (Cattell, 1886). People take about twice as long to read unrelated words as to read words in a sentence (Cattell, 1886).

Further demonstrations of the effect were offered by Gerald Reicher (1969) and Daniel Wheeler (1970), so it sometimes is called the "Reicher-Wheeler effect." Typically, the word-superiority effect is observed in an experimental paradigm known as the *lexical-decision task*. In this paradigm, a string of letters is presented very briefly. It then is either removed or covered by a *visual mask*, a pattern that wipes out the previously presented stimulus from iconic memory. The participant then is asked to make a decision about the string of letters.

In studying the word-superiority effect, experimenters present participants very briefly with either a word or a single letter, followed by a visual mask. The participant then is given a choice of two letters. The participants then must decide which he or she just saw. For example, suppose the test stimulus is the word "WORK." The alternatives might be "_ _ _ D" and "_ _ _ K." If the test stimulus is "K," the alternatives might be "D" and "K." Participants are more accurate in choosing the correct letter when it is presented in the context of a word than they are in choosing the correct letter when it is presented in isolation (Johnston & McClelland, 1973). Even letters in pronounceable pseudowords (e.g., "MARD") are identified more accurately than letters in isolation. However, strings of letters that cannot be pronounced as words (e.g., "ORWK") do not aid in identification (Pollatsek & Rayner, 1989).

There is also a "sentence-superiority effect" (Cattell, 1886; Perfetti, 1985; Perfetti & Roth, 1981). For example, suppose that a reader very briefly sees a degraded stimulus. The word *window*, for example, might be shown but in degraded form (Figure 10.2). When the word is standing by itself in this form, it is more difficult to recognize than when it is preceded by a sentence context. An example of such a context would be "There were several repair jobs to be done. The first was to fix the _____" (Perfetti, 1985). Having a meaningful context for a stimulus helps the reader to perceive it.

Also, apparently context effects work at both conscious and preconscious levels. At the conscious level, we have active control over the use of context to determine

---

FIGURE 10.2

This figure shows instances of the word window and of the word pepper, in which each word is clearly legible, somewhat legible, or almost completely illegible. Percentages are percentages of degradation.

word meanings. At the preconscious level, the use of context is probably automatic and outside our active control (Stanovich, 1981; see also Posner & Snyder, 1975). A series of experiments involving the lexical-decision task offers evidence of context effects in making lexical decisions (Meyer & Schvaneveldt, 1971; Schvaneveldt, Meyer, & Becker, 1976). Participants seem to make lexical decisions more quickly when presented with strings of letters that commonly are associated pairs of words (e.g., "doctor" and "nurse" or "bread" and "butter"). They respond more slowly when presented with unassociated pairs of words, with pairs of nonwords, or with pairs involving a word and a nonword.

How well we read is determined largely by how well we reflect on and think about what we are reading. What is the relation between the language in which material is presented—either visually or verbally—and the thinking we do?

Language and Thought

One of the most interesting areas in the study of language is the relationship between language and the thinking human mind (Harris, 2003). Many different questions have been asked about this relationship. We consider only some of them here. Studies comparing and contrasting users of differing languages and dialects form the basis of this section.

Differences among Languages

Why are there so many different languages around the world? And how does using any language in general and using a particular language influence human thought? As you know, different languages comprise different lexicons. They also use different syntactical structures. These differences often reflect variations in the physical and cultural environments in which the languages arose and developed. For example, in terms of lexicon, the Garo of Burma distinguish among many different kinds of rice, which is understandable because they are a rice-growing culture. Nomadic Arabs have more than 20 different words for camels. These peoples clearly conceptualize rice and camels more specifically and in more complex ways than do people outside their cultural groups. As a result of these linguistic differences, do the Garo think about rice differently than we do? And do the Arabs think about camels differently than we do?

The syntactical structures of languages differ, too. Almost all languages permit some way in which to communicate actions, agents of actions, and objects of actions (Gerrig & Banaji, 1994). What differs across languages is the order of subject, verb, and object in a typical declarative sentence. Also differing is the range of grammatical inflections and other markings that speakers are obliged to include as key elements of a sentence. For example, in describing past actions in English, we indicate whether an action took place in the past by changing (inflecting) the verb form. For example, walk changes to walked in the past tense. In Spanish and German, the verb also must indicate whether the agent of action was singular or plural and whether it is being referred to in the first, second, or third person. In Turkish, the verb form must indicate past action, singular or plural, and the person. It also must indicate whether the action was witnessed or experienced directly by the speaker or was noted only indirectly. Do these differences and other differences in obligatory syntactical structures influence—or perhaps even constrain—the users of these languages to think about things differently because of the language they use while thinking?

Linguistic Relativity: The Sapir-Whorf Hypothesis

The concept relevant to this question is **linguistic relativity,** the assertion that the speakers of different languages have differing cognitive systems and that these different cognitive systems influence the ways in which people speaking the various languages think about the world. Thus, according to the relativity view, the Garo would think about rice differently than we do. For example, the Garo would develop more cognitive categories for rice than would an English-speaking counterpart. What would happen when the Garo contemplated rice? They purportedly would view it differently—and perhaps with greater complexity of thought—than would English speakers, who have only a few words for rice. Thus, language would shape thought. There is some evidence that word learning may occur, in part, as a result of infants' mental differentiation among various kinds of concepts (Carey, 1994; Xu & Carey, 1995, 1996). So it might make sense that infants who encounter different kinds of objects might make different kinds of mental differentiations. These differentiations would be a function of the culture in which the infants grew up.

The linguistic relativity hypothesis is sometimes referred to as the Sapir-Whorf hypothesis, after the two men who were most forceful in propagating it. Edward Sapir (1941/1964) said that "we see and hear and otherwise experience very largely as we do because the language habits of our community predispose certain choices of interpretation" (p. 69). Benjamin Lee Whorf (1956) stated this view even more strongly:

> We dissect nature along lines laid down by our native languages. The categories and types that we isolate from the world of phenomena we do not find there because they stare every observer in the face; on the contrary, the world is presented in a kaleidoscopic flux of impressions which has to be organized by our minds—and this means largely by the linguistic systems in our minds. (p. 213)

The Sapir-Whorf hypothesis has been one of the most widely mentioned ideas in all of the social and behavioral sciences (Lonner, 1989). However, some of its implications appear to have reached mythical proportions. For example, "many social scientists have warmly accepted and gladly propagated the notion that Eskimos have multitudinous words for the single English word *snow.* Contrary to popular beliefs, Eskimos do *not* have numerous words for snow (Martin, 1986). No one who knows anything about Eskimo (or more accurately, about the Inuit and Yupik families of related languages spoken from Siberia to Greenland) has ever said they do" (Pullum, 1991, p. 160). Laura Martin, who has done more than anyone else to debunk the myth, understands why her colleagues might consider the myth charming. But she has been quite "disappointed in the reaction of her colleagues when she pointed out the fallacy; most, she says, took the position that true or not 'it's still a great example'" (Adler, 1991, p. 63). Apparently, we must exercise caution in our interpretation of findings regarding linguistic relativity.

FIGURE 10.3

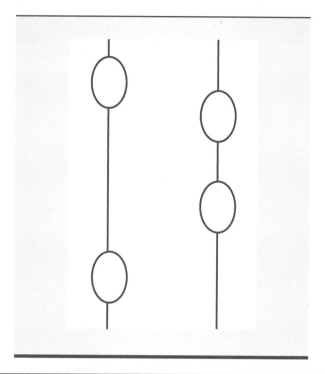

How does your label for this image affect your perception, your mental representation, and your memory of the image? From Psychology, Fifth Edition by John Daley, et al., © 1998 Pearson Education. Reprinted by permission of John Daley.

Consider a milder form of linguistic relativism. It is that language may not determine thought, but that language certainly may influence thought. Our thoughts and our language interact in myriad ways, only some of which we now understand. Clearly, language facilitates thought. It even affects perception and memory. For some reason, we have limited means by which to manipulate nonlinguistic images (Hunt & Banaji, 1988). Such limitations make desirable the use of language to facilitate mental representation and manipulation. Even nonsense pictures ("droodles") are recalled and redrawn differently, depending on the verbal label given to the picture (Bower, Karlin, & Dueck, 1975).

To see how this phenomenon might work, look at Figure 10.3 right now. Suppose, instead of being labeled as it is, it had been entitled "beaded curtain." You might have perceived it differently. However, once a particular label has been given, viewing the same figure from the alternative perspective is much harder (Glucksberg, 1988). Psychologists have used other ambiguous figures (see Chapter 3) and have found similar results. Figure 10.4 illustrates three other figures that can be given alternative labels. When participants are given a particular label, they tend to draw their recollection of the figure in a way more similar to the given label. For example, they will draw a figure differently as a function of whether it is labeled "eyeglasses" or "dumbbells."

FIGURE 10.4

When the original figures (in the center) are redrawn from memory, the new drawings tend to be distorted to be more like the labeled figures. From Psychology, Fifth Edition by John Daley, et al., © 1998 Pearson Education. Reprinted by permission of John Daley.

Language also affects in other ways how we encode, store, and retrieve information in memory. Remember the examples in Chapter 6 regarding the label "Washing Clothes?" It enhanced people's responses to recall and comprehension questions about text passages (Bransford & Johnson, 1972, 1973). In a similar vein, eyewitness testimony is powerfully influenced by the distinctive phrasing of questions posed to eyewitnesses (Loftus & Palmer, 1974). Even when participants generated their own descriptions, the subsequent accuracy of their eyewitness testimony declined (Schooler & Engstler-Schooler, 1990). In other words, accurate recall actually declined following an opportunity to write a description of an observed event, a particular color, or a particular face. When given an opportunity to identify statements about an event, the actual color, or a face, participants were less able to do so accurately if they had previously described it. Paradoxically, when participants were allowed to take their time in responding, their performance was even less accurate than when they were forced to respond quickly. In other words, given time to reflect on their answers, participants were more likely to respond in accord with what they had said or written than with what they had seen.

Is the Sapir-Whorf hypothesis relevant to everyday life? Almost certainly it is. If language constrains our thought, then we may fail to see solutions to problems because we do not have the right words to express these solutions. Consider the misunderstandings we have with people who speak other languages, such as what happens all the time at the United Nations. On this view, the misunderstandings may result from the fact that the languages of the others parse the word differently than we do.

One must be grateful that extreme versions of the Sapir-Whorf hypothesis do not appear to be justified. Such versions would suggest that we are, figuratively, slaves to the words available to us.

Linguistic Universals

There has been some research that addresses **linguistic universals**—characteristic patterns across all languages of various cultures—and relativity. Recall from Chapter 9 that linguists have identified hundreds of linguistic universals related to phonology (the study of phonemes), morphology (the study of morphemes), semantics, and syntax. An area that illustrates much of this research well focuses on color names. These words provide an especially convenient way of testing for universals. Why? Because people in every culture can be expected to be exposed, at least potentially, to pretty much the same range of colors.

In actuality, different languages name colors quite differently. But the languages do not divide the color spectrum arbitrarily. A systematic pattern seems universally to govern color naming across languages. Consider the results of investigations of color terms across a large number of languages (Berlin & Kay, 1969; Kay, 1975). Two apparent linguistic universals about color naming have emerged across languages. First, all of the languages surveyed took their basic color terms from a set of just eleven color names. These are black, white, red, yellow, green, blue, brown, purple, pink, orange, and gray. Languages ranged from using all eleven color names, as in English, to using just two of the names. Second, when only some of the color names are used, the naming of colors falls into a hierarchy of five levels. The levels are (1) black, white; (2) red; (3) yellow, green, blue; (4) brown; and (5) purple, pink, orange, gray. Thus, if a language names only two colors, they will be black and white. If it names three colors, they will be black, white, and red. A fourth color will be taken from the set of yellow, green, and blue. The fifth and sixth will be taken from this set as well. Selection will continue until all eleven colors have been labeled.

Syntactical as well as semantic structural differences across languages may affect thought. For example, Spanish has two forms of the verb *to be*—*ser* and *estar*. However, they are used in different contexts. One investigator studied the uses of *ser* and *estar* in adults and in children (Sera, 1992).

When *to be* indicated the identity of something (e.g., in English, "This is José") or the class membership of something (e.g., "José is a carpenter"), both adults and children used the verb form *ser*. Moreover, both adults and children used different verb forms when *to be* indicated attributes of things. Ser was used to indicate permanent attributes (e.g., "Maria is tall"). *Estar* was used to indicate temporary attributes (e.g., "Maria is busy"). When using forms of *to be* to describe the locations of objects, including of people, animals, and other things, both adults and children used *estar*. However, when using forms of *to be* to describe the locations of events (e.g., meetings or parties), adults used *ser*, whereas children continued to use *estar*.

Sera (1992) interprets these findings as indicating two things. First, *ser* seems to be used primarily for indicating permanent conditions, such as identity; class inclusion; and relatively permanent, stable attributes of things. *Estar* seems to be used primarily for indicating temporary conditions, such as short-term attributes of things and the location of objects. These things often are subject to change from one place to another. Moreover, children treat the location of events in the same way as the location of objects. They view it as temporary and hence use *estar*. Adults, in contrast, differentiate between events and objects. In particular, adults consider the locations of events to be unchanging. Because they are permanent, they require the use of *ser*.

Other researchers have also suggested that young children have difficulty distinguishing between objects and events (e.g., Keil, 1979). Young children also find it difficult to recognize the permanent status of many attributes (Marcus & Overton, 1978). Thus, the developmental differences regarding the use of *ser* to describe the location of events may indicate developmental differences in cognition. Sera's work suggests that differences in language use may indeed indicate differences in thinking. However, her work leaves open an important psychological question. Do native Spanish speakers have a more differentiated sense of the temporary and the permanent than do native English speakers, who use the same verb form to express both senses of *to be*? Thus far, the answer is unclear.

Other languages also have been used in investigations of linguistic relativity. For example, in the Navaho language, the choice of verb depends on the shape of the object engaging in the action of the verb. In English, it does not (Carroll & Casagrande, 1958). Might the use of different verb forms for different shapes suggest that Navaho children would learn to perceive and organize information by shapes earlier than do children who speak English?

Early research indicated that young English-speaking children group objects by color before they group them by shape (Brian & Goodenough, 1929). In contrast, Navaho-speaking children are more likely than English-speaking Navaho children to classify objects on the basis of shape. However, these findings are problematic. The reason is that English-speaking children from Boston perform more like the Navaho-speaking Navaho children than like the English-speaking Navaho children (Carroll & Casagrande, 1958). Furthermore, other research comparing adults' and children's generalizations of novel nouns among novel objects finds that young English-speaking children actually will overuse shape in classifying objects (Smith, Jones, & Landau, 1996). What would happen for people who speak both of the languages being studied? Also consider another fact. Children who learn Mandarin Chinese tend to use more verbs than nouns. In contrast, children acquiring English or Italian tend to use more nouns than verbs (Tardif, 1996; Tardif, Shatz, & Naigles, 1997). Moreover, Korean-speaking children use verbs earlier than English-speaking children do. In contrast, English-speaking children have larger naming vocabularies earlier than do Korean-speaking children (Gopnik & Choi, 1995; Gopnik, Choi, & Baumberger, 1996).

What differences in thinking might such differences in acquisition imply? No one knows for sure.

An intriguing experiment assessed the possible effects of linguistic relativity by studying people who speak more than one language (Hoffman, Lau, & Johnson, 1986). In Chinese, a single term, *shì gÈ*, specifically describes a person who is "worldly, experienced, socially skillful, devoted to his or her family, and somewhat reserved" (p. 1098). English clearly has no comparable single term to embrace these diverse characteristics. Hoffman and his colleagues composed text passages in English and in Chinese describing various characters. They included the *shì gÈ* stereotype, without, of course, specifically using the term *shì gÈ* in the descriptions. The researchers then asked participants who were fluent in both Chinese and English to read the passages either in Chinese or in English. Then they rated various statements about the characters, in terms of the likelihood that the statements would be true of the characters. Some of these statements involved a stereotype of a *shì gÈ* person.

Their results seemed to support the notion of linguistic relativity. The participants were more likely to rate the various statements in accord with the *shì gÈ* stereotype when they had read the passages in Chinese than when they had read the passages in English. Similarly, when participants were asked to write their own impressions of the characters, their descriptions conformed more closely to the *shì gÈ* stereotype if they previously read the passages in Chinese. These authors do not suggest that it would be impossible for English speakers to comprehend the *shì gÈ* stereotype. Rather, they suggest that having that stereotype readily accessible facilitates its mental manipulation.

Research on linguistic relativity is a good example of the dialectic in action. Before Sapir and Whorf, the issue of how language constrains thought was not salient in the minds of psychologists. Sapir and Whorf then presented a thesis that language largely controls thought. After they presented their thesis, a number of psychologists tried to show the antithesis. This is that they were wrong and that language did not control thought. Today, many psychologists believe in a synthesis. This is that language has some influence on thought but not nearly so extreme an influence as Sapir and Whorf believed.

The question of whether linguistic relativity exists and, if so, to what extent, remains open. There may be a mild form of relativity. In other words, language can influence thought. However, a stronger deterministic form of relativity is less likely. Based on the available evidence, language does not seem to determine differences in thought among members of various cultures Finally, it is probably the case that language and thought interact with each other throughout the life span (Vygotsky, 1986).

Bilingualism and Dialects

Suppose a person can speak and think in two languages. Does the person think differently in each language? In fact, do **bilinguals**—people who can speak two languages—think differently from **monolinguals**—people who can speak only one language? (Multilinguals speak at least two and possibly more languages.) What differences, if any, emanate from the availability of two languages versus just one? Might bilingualism affect intelligence, positively or negatively?

Does bilingualism make thinking in any one language more difficult, or does it enhance thought processes? The data are somewhat self-contradictory (Hakuta, 1986). Different participant populations, different methodologies, different language groups, and different experimenter biases may have contributed to the inconsistency in the literature. Consider what happens when bilinguals are balanced bilinguals, who are roughly equally fluent in both languages, and when they come from middle-class backgrounds. In these instances, positive effects of bilingualism tend to be found. But negative effects may result under other circumstances. What might be the causes of this difference?

Let us distinguish between what might be called additive versus subtractive bilingualism (Cummins, 1976). In *additive bilingualism*, a second language is acquired in addition to a relatively well-developed first language. In *subtractive bilingualism*, elements of a second language replace elements of the first language. It appears that the

Michael Cole is a professor of psychology and communication at the University of California, San Diego. He is well known for his contributions to cultural and cross-cultural cognitive psychology, having shown that tests that are valid in one culture cannot simply be translated and directly carried over to another culture and remain valid. During the past 20 years, Cole also has been seminal in reviving psychological interest in the work of Lev Vygotsky.

additive form results in increased thinking ability. In contrast, the subtractive form results in decreased thinking ability (Cummins, 1976). In particular, there may be something of a threshold effect. Individuals may need to be at a certain relatively high level of competence in both languages for a positive effect of bilingualism to be found. Children from backgrounds with lower socioeconomic status (SES) may be more likely to be subtractive bilinguals than are children from the middle SES. Their SES may be a factor in their being hurt rather than helped by their bilingualism.

Researchers also distinguish between *simultaneous bilingualism*, which occurs when a child learns two languages from birth, and *sequential bilingualism*, which occurs when an individual first learns one language and then another (Bhatia & Ritchie, 1999). Either form of language learning can contribute to fluency. It depends on the particular circumstances in which the languages are learned (Pearson & associates, 1997). It is known, however, that infants begin babbling at roughly the same age. This happens regardless of whether they consistently are exposed to one or two languages (Oller & associates, 1997). In the United States, many people make a big deal of bilingualism, perhaps because relatively few Americans born in the United States of nonimmigrant parents learn a second language to a high degree of fluency. In other cultures, however, the learning of multiple languages is taken for granted. For example, in parts of India, people routinely may learn as many as four languages (Khubchandani, 1997). In Flemish-speaking Belgium, many people learn at least some French, English, and/or German. Often, they learn one or more of these other languages to a high degree of fluency.

A significant factor believed to contribute to acquisition of a language is age. Some researchers have suggested that nativelike mastery of some aspects of a second language rarely are acquired after adolescence. Other researchers disagree with this view (Bahrick & associates, 1994). They found that some aspects of a second language, such as vocabulary comprehension and fluency, seem to be acquired just as well after adolescence as before. Furthermore, these researchers found that even some aspects of syntax seem to be acquired readily after adolescence. These results are contrary to prior findings (Johnson & Newport, 1989, 1991; Newport, 1990). The mastery of nativelike pronunciation, however, seems to depend on early acquisition (Asher & Garcia, 1969; Oyama, 1976). It may seem surprising that learning completely novel phonemes in a second language may be easier than learning phonemes that are highly similar to the phonemes of the first language (Flege, 1991). In any case, there do not appear to be critical periods for second-language acquisition (Birdsong, 1999). The possible exception is the acquisition of native accent. Adults may appear to have a harder time learning second languages because they can retain their native language as their dominant language. Young children, in contrast, who typically need to attend school in the new language, may have to switch dominant language. They thus learn the new language to a higher level of mastery (Jia & Aaronson, 1999).

What kinds of learning experiences facilitate second-language acquisition? There is no single correct answer to that question (Bialystock & Hakuta, 1994). One reason is that each individual language learner brings distinctive cognitive abilities and knowledge to the language-learning experience. In addition, the kinds of learning experiences that facilitate second-language acquisition should match the context and uses for the second language once it is acquired.

For example, consider four different individuals. Caitlin, a young child, may not need to master a wealth of vocabulary and complex syntax to get along well with other children. If she can master the phonology, some simple syntactical rules, and some basic vocabulary, she may be considered fluent. Similarly, José needs only to get by in a few everyday situations, such as shopping, handling routine family business transactions, and getting around town. He may be considered proficient after mastering some simple vocabulary and syntax, as well as some pragmatic knowledge regarding context-appropriate manners of communicating. Kim Yee must be able to communicate regarding her specialized technical field. She may be considered proficient if she masters the technical vocabulary, a primitive basic vocabulary, and the rudiments of syntax. Sumesh is a student who studies a second language in an academic setting. Sumesh may be expected to have a firm grasp of syntax and a rather broad, if shallow, vocabulary. Each of these language learners may require different kinds of language experiences to gain the proficiency being sought. Different kinds of experiences may be needed to enhance their competence in the phonology, vocabulary, syntax, and pragmatics of the second language.

When speakers of one language learn other languages, they find the languages differentially difficult. For example, it is much easier, on average, for a native speaker of English to acquire Spanish as a second language than it is to acquire Russian. One reason is that English and Spanish share more roots than do English and Russian. Moreover, Russian is much more highly inflected than are English and Spanish. English and Spanish are more highly dependent on word order. The difficulty of learning a language as a second language, however, does not appear to have much to do with its difficulty as a first language. Russian infants probably learn Russian about as easily as U.S. infants learn English (Maratsos, 1998).

Single-System versus Dual-System Hypotheses

One way of approaching bilingualism is to apply what we have learned from cognitive-psychological research to practical concerns regarding how to facilitate acquisition of a second language. Another approach is to study bilingual individuals to see how bilingualism may offer insight into the human mind. For example, some cognitive psychologists have been interested in finding out how the two languages are represented in the bilingual's mind. The **single-system hypothesis** suggests that two languages are represented in just one system. Alternatively, the **dual-system hypothesis** suggests that two languages are represented somehow in separate systems of the mind (De Houwer, 1995; Paradis, 1981). For instance, might German language information be stored in a physically different part of the brain than English language information? Figure 10.5 shows schematically the difference in the two points of view.

One way to address this question is through the study of bilinguals who have experienced brain damage. Suppose a bilingual person has brain damage in a particular part of the brain. An inference consistent with the dual-system hypothesis would be that the individual would show different degrees of impairment in the two languages. The single-system view would suggest roughly equal impairment in the two languages. The logic of this kind of investigation is compelling. But the results are not. When recovery of language after trauma is studied, sometimes the first language recovers first, sometimes the second language recovers first. And sometimes recovery is about equal for the two languages (Albert & Obler, 1978; Paradis, 1977).

FIGURE 10.5

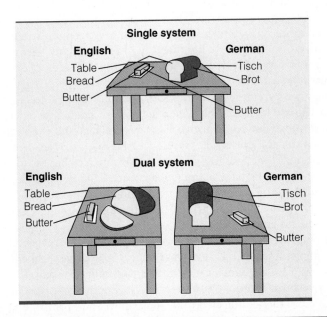

The single-system conceptualization hypothesizes that both languages are represented in a unified cognitive system. The dual-system conceptualization of bilingualism hypothesizes that each language is represented in a separate cognitive system.

Based on this methodology, the conclusions that can be drawn are equivocal. Nevertheless the results seem to suggest at least some duality of structure.

A different method of study has led to an alternative perspective on bilingualism. Two investigators mapped the region of the cerebral cortex relevant to language use in two of their bilingual patients being treated for epilepsy (Ojemann & Whitaker, 1978). Mild electrical stimulation was applied to the cortex of each patient. Electrical stimulation tends to inhibit activity where it is applied. It leads to reduced ability to name objects for which the memories are stored at the location being stimulated. The results for both patients were the same. They may help explain the contradictions in the literature. Some areas of the brain showed equal impairments for object-naming in both languages. But other areas of the brain showed differential impairment in one or the other language. The results also suggested that the weaker language was more diffusely represented across the cortex than was the stronger language. In other words, asking the question of whether two languages are represented singly or separately may be asking the wrong question. The results of this study suggest that some aspects of the two languages may be represented singly. Other aspects may be represented separately.

To summarize, two languages seem to share some, but not all, aspects of mental representation. Learning a second language is often a plus. But it is probably most useful if the individual learning the second language is in an environment in which the learning of the second language adds to rather than subtracts from the learning of the first language. Moreover, for beneficial effects to appear, the second language must be learned well. In the approach usually taken in schools, students may receive as little as 2 or 3 years of second-language instruction spread out over a few class periods a week. This approach probably will not be sufficient for the beneficial effects of bilingualism to appear. However, schooling does seem to yield beneficial effects on acquisition of syntax. This is particularly so when a second language is acquired after adolescence. Furthermore, individual learners should choose specific kinds of language-acquisition techniques to suit their personal attributes. These attributes include abilities, preferences, and personal goals for using the second language.

Language Mixtures and Change

Bilingualism is not a certain outcome of linguistic contact between different language groups. Sometimes when people of two different language groups are in prolonged contact with one another, the language users of the two groups begin to share some vocabulary that is superimposed onto each group's syntax. This superimposition results in what is known as a pidgin. Over time, this admixture can develop into a distinct linguistic form. It has its own grammar and hence becomes a creole. One linguist has studied the similarities across different creoles (Bickerton, 1990). He has postulated that modern creoles may resemble an evolutionarily early form of language, termed *protolanguage*. The existence of pidgins and creoles, and possibly a protolanguage, supports the universality notion discussed earlier. That is, linguistic ability is so natural and universal that given the opportunity, humans actually invent new languages quite rapidly.

Creoles and pidgins arise when two linguistically distinctive groups meet. The counterpart—a dialect—occurs when a single linguistic group gradually diverges toward somewhat distinctive variations. A **dialect** is a regional variety of a language distinguished by features such as vocabulary, syntax, and pronunciation. The study of dialects provides insights into such diverse phenomena as auditory discrimination, test development, and social discrimination.

Dialectical differences often represent harmless regional variations. They create few serious communication difficulties. But these can lead to some confusion. In the United States, for example, when national advertisers give toll-free numbers to call, they sometimes route the calls to the Midwest. They do so because they have learned that the Midwestern form of speech seems to be the most universally understood form within the country. Other forms, such as southern and northeastern ones, may be harder for people from diverse parts of the country to understand. And when calls are routed to other countries, such as India, there may be serious difficulties in achieving effective communication because of differences in dialect as well as accent. Many radio announcers try to learn something close to a standard form of English, often called "network English." In this way, they can maximize their comprehensibility to as many listeners as possible.

Sometimes, differing dialects are assigned different social statuses. In these cases, *standard* forms having higher status than *nonstandard* ones. The distinction between standard and nonstandard forms of a language can become unfortunate when speakers of one dialect start to view themselves as speakers of a superior dialect. Usually, the standard dialect is that of the class in society that has the most political or economic power. Virtually any thought can be expressed in any dialect.

Slips of the Tongue

Thus far, much of the discussion has assumed that people use—or at least attempt to use—language correctly. An area of particular interest to cognitive psychologists, however, is how people use language incorrectly. One way of using language incorrectly is through **slips of the tongue,** inadvertent linguistic errors in what we say. They may occur at any level of linguistic analysis: phonemes, morphemes, or larger units of language (Crystal, 1987; McArthur, 1992). In such cases, what we think and mean to say do not correspond to what we actually do say. Freudian psychoanalysts have suggested that in Freudian slips, the verbal slip reflects some unconscious processing that has psychological significance. The slips are alleged often to indicate repressed emotions. For example, a business competitor may say, "I'm glad to beat you," when what was overtly intended was, "I'm glad to meet you."

Most cognitive psychologists see things differently from the psychoanalytic view. They are intrigued by slips of the tongue because of what the lack of correspondence between what is thought and what is said may tell us about how language is produced. In speaking, we have a mental plan for what we are going to say. Sometimes, however, this plan is disrupted when our mechanism for speech production does not cooperate with our cognitive one. Often, such errors result from intrusions by other thoughts or by stimuli in the environment. Examples would be a radio talk show or a neighboring conversation (Garrett, 1980). Slips of the tongue may be taken to indicate that the language of thought differs somewhat from the language through which we express our thoughts (Fodor, 1975). Often we have the idea right. But its expression comes out wrong. Sometimes we are not even aware of the slip until it is pointed out to us. In the language of the mind, whatever it may be, the idea is right although the expression represented by the slip is inadvertently wrong.

There are various kinds of slips that people tend to make in their conversations (Fromkin, 1973; Fromkin & Rodman, 1988):

- In anticipation, the speaker uses a language element before it is appropriate in the sentence because it corresponds to an element that will be needed later in the utterance. For example, instead of saying, "an inspiring expression," a speaker might say, "an expiring expression."
- In perseveration, the speaker uses a language element that was appropriate earlier in the sentence but that is not appropriate later on. For example, a speaker might say, "We sat down to a bounteous beast" instead of a "bounteous feast."
- In substitution, the speaker substitutes one language element for another. For example, you may have warned someone to do something "after it is too late," when you meant "before it is too late."
- In reversal (also called "transposition"), the speaker switches the positions of two language elements. An example is the reversal that reportedly led *flutterby* to become *butterfly*. This reversal captivated language users so much that it is now the preferred form. Sometimes, reversals can be fortuitously opportune.

They create spoonerisms, in which the initial sounds of two words are reversed and make two entirely different words. The term is named after the Reverend William Spooner, who was famous for them. Some of his choicest slips include, "You have hissed all my mystery lectures," and "Easier for a camel to go through the knee of an idol" (Clark & Clark, 1977).

- In malapropism, one word is replaced by another that is similar in sound but different in meaning (e.g., furniture dealers selling "naughty pine" instead of "knotty pine").

- Additionally, slips may occur because of insertions of sounds (e.g., "mischievi-ous" instead of "mischievous" or "drownded" instead of "drowned") or other linguistic elements. The opposite kind of slip involves deletions (e.g., sound deletions such as "prossing" instead of "processing"). Such deletions often in-volve blends (e.g., "blounds" for "blended sounds").

Each kind of slip of the tongue may occur at different hierarchical levels of lin-guistic processing (Dell, 1986). That is, it may occur at the acoustical level of phonemes, as in "bounteous beast" instead of "bounteous feast." It may occur at the semantic level of morphemes, as in "after it's too late" instead of "before it's too late." Or it may occur at even higher levels, as in "bought the bucket" instead of "kicked the bucket" or "bought the farm." The patterns of errors (e.g., reversals, substitutions) at each hierarchical level tend to be parallel (Dell, 1986). For example, in phonemic errors, initial consonants tend to interact with initial consonants, as in "tasting wime" instead of "wasting time." Final consonants tend to interact with final consonants, as in "bing his tut" instead of "bit his tongue." Prefixes often interact with prefixes, as in "expiring expression," and so on.

Also, errors at each level of linguistic analysis suggest particular kinds of insights into how we produce speech. Consider, for example, phonemic errors. A stressed word, which is emphasized through speech rhythm and tone, is more likely to influ-ence other words than is an unstressed word (Crystal, 1987). Furthermore, even when sounds are switched, the basic rhythmic and tonal patterns usually are preserved. An example is the emphasis on "hissed" and the first syllable of "mystery" in the first spoonerism quoted here.

Even at the level of words, the same parts of speech tend to be involved in the errors we produce (e.g., nouns interfere with other nouns, and verbs with verbs; Bock, 1990; Bock, Loebell, & Morey, 1992). In the second spoonerism quoted here, Spooner managed to preserve the syntactical categories, the nouns *knee* and *idol*. He also preserved the grammaticality of the sentence by changing the articles from "*a* needle" to "*an* idol." Even in the case of word substitutions, syntactic categories are preserved. In speech errors, semantic categories, too, may be preserved. An example would be naming a category when intending to name a member of the category, such as "fruit" for "apple." Another example would be naming the wrong member of the category, such as "peach" for "apple." A last example would be naming a member of a category when intending to name the category as a whole, as in "peach" for "fruit" (Garrett, 1992). Data from studies of speech errors may help us better understand nor-mal language processing. Another aspect of language that offers us a distinctive view is the study of metaphorical language.

Metaphorical Language

Until now, we have discussed primarily the literal uses of language. At least as interesting to poets and to many others are its omnipresent figurative uses. A notable example is the use of metaphors as a way of expressing thoughts. **Metaphors** juxtapose two nouns in a way that positively asserts their similarities, while not disconfirming their dissimilarities. Related to metaphors are similes. **Similes** introduce the words *like* or *as* into a comparison between items.

Metaphors contain four key elements. Two are the items being compared, a tenor and a vehicle. And two are ways in which the items are related. The *tenor* is the topic of the metaphor. The *vehicle* is what the tenor is described in terms of. For example, consider the metaphor, "Billboards are warts on the landscape." The tenor is "billboards." The vehicle is "warts." The *ground* of the metaphor is the set of similarities between the tenor and the vehicle. And the *tension* of the metaphor is the set of dissimilarities between the two. We may conjecture that a key similarity (ground) between billboards and warts is that they are both considered unattractive. The dissimilarities (tension) between the two are many, including that billboards appear on buildings, highways, and other impersonal public locations. But warts appear on diverse personal locations on an individual.

Of the various theories that have been proposed to explain how metaphors work, the main traditional views have highlighted either the ways in which the tenor and the vehicle are similar or the ways in which they differ. For example, the traditional comparison view highlights the importance of the comparison. It underscores the comparative similarities and analogical relationship between the tenor and the vehicle (Malgady & Johnson, 1976; Miller, 1979; Ortony, 1979; cf. also Sternberg & Nigro, 1983). As applied to the metaphor, "Abused children are walking time bombs," the comparison view would underscore the similarity between the elements: their potential for explosion. In contrast, the anomaly view of metaphor emphasizes the dissimilarity between the tenor and the vehicle (Beardsley, 1962; Bickerton, 1969; Clark & Lucy, 1975; Gerrig & Healy, 1983; Lyons, 1977; Searle, 1979; van Dijk, 1975). The anomaly view would highlight the many dissimilarities between abused children and time bombs.

The domain-interaction view integrates aspects of each of the preceding views. It suggests that a metaphor is more than a comparison and more than an anomaly. According to this view, a metaphor involves an interaction of some kind between the domain (area of knowledge, such as animals, machines, plants) of the tenor and the domain of the vehicle (Black, 1962; Hesse, 1966). The exact form of this interaction differs somewhat from one theory to another. The metaphor often is more effective when two circumstances occur. First, the tenor and the vehicle share many similar characteristics (e.g., the potential explosiveness of abused children and time bombs). Second, the domains of the tenor and the vehicle are highly dissimilar (e.g., the domain of humans and the domain of weapons) (Tourangeau & Sternberg, 1981, 1982).

Consider another view: that metaphors are essentially a nonliteral form of class-inclusion statements (Glucksberg & Keysar, 1990). According to this view, the tenor of each metaphor is a member of the class characterized by the vehicle of the given metaphor. That is, we understand metaphors not as statements of comparison but as statements of category membership, in which the vehicle is a prototypical member of the category.

For example, suppose I say, "My colleague's partner is an iceberg." I am thereby saying that the partner belongs to the category of things that are characterized by an utter lack of personal warmth, extreme rigidity, and the ability to produce a massively chilling effect on anyone in the surrounding environment For a metaphor to work well, the reader should find the salient features of the vehicle ("iceberg") to be unexpectedly relevant as features of the tenor ("my colleague's partner"). That is, the reader should be at least mildly surprised that prominent features of the vehicle may characterize the tenor. But after consideration, the reader should agree that those features do describe the tenor.

Metaphors enrich our language in ways that literal statements cannot match. Our understanding of metaphors seems to require not only some kind of comparison. It also requires that the domains of the vehicle and of the tenor interact in some way. Reading a metaphor can change our perception of both domains. It therefore can educate us in a way that is perhaps more difficult to transmit through literal speech.

Metaphors can enrich our speech in social contexts. For example, suppose we say to someone that "you are a prince." Chances are that we do not mean that the person is literally a prince. Rather, we mean that the person has characteristics of a prince. How, in general, do we use language to negotiate social contexts?

Language in a Social Context

The study of the social context of language is a relatively new area of linguistic research. One aspect of context is the investigation of **pragmatics,** the study of how people use language. It includes sociolinguistics and other aspects of the social context of language.

Under most circumstances, you change your use of language in response to contextual cues without giving these changes much thought. Similarly, you usually unself-consciously change your language patterns to fit different contexts.

INVESTIGATING COGNITIVE PSYCHOLOGY

To get an idea of how you change your use of language in different contexts, suppose that you and your friend are going to meet right after work. Suppose also that something comes up. You must call your friend to change the time or place for your meeting. When you call your friend at work, your friend's supervisor answers and offers to take a message. Exactly what will you say to your friend's supervisor to ensure that your friend will know about the change in time or location? Suppose, instead, that the 4-year-old son of your friend's supervisor answers. Exactly what will you say in this situation? Finally, suppose that your friend answers directly. How will you have modified your language for each context, even when your purpose (underlying message) in all three contexts was the same?

For example, in speaking with a conversational partner, you seek to establish common ground, or a shared basis for engaging in a conversation (Clark & Brennan, 1991). When we are with people who share background, knowledge, motives, or goals, establishing common ground is likely to be easy and scarcely noticeable. When little is shared, however, such common ground may be hard to find.

Gestures and vocal inflections, which are forms of nonverbal communication, can help establish common ground. One aspect of nonverbal communication is *personal space*—the distance between people in a conversation or other interaction that is considered comfortable for members of a given culture. *Proxemics* is the study of interpersonal distance or its opposite, proximity. It concerns itself with relative distancing and the positioning of you and your fellow conversants. In the United States, 18 to 24 inches is considered about right (Hall, 1966). Scandinavians expect more distance. Middle Easterners, southern Europeans, and South Americans expect less (Sommer, 1969; Watson, 1970).

When on our own familiar turf, we take our cultural views of personal space for granted. Only when we come into contact with people from other cultures do we notice these differences. For example, when I was visiting Venezuela, I noticed my cultural expectations coming into conflict with the expectations of those around me. I often found myself in a comical dance. I would back off from the person with whom I was speaking. Meanwhile, that person was trying to move closer. Within a given culture, greater proximity generally indicates one or more of three things. First, the people see themselves in a close relationship. Second, the people are participating in a social situation that permits violation of the bubble of personal space, such as close dancing. Third, the "violator" of the bubble is dominating the interaction.

Speech Acts

Direct Speech Acts

Another key aspect of the way in which you use language depends on what purpose you plan to achieve with language. In the earlier example, you were using language to try to ensure that your friend would meet you at the new location and time. When you speak, what kinds of things can you accomplish?

Speech acts address the question of what you can accomplish with speech. All speech acts seem to fall into five basic categories, based on the purpose of the acts (Searle, 1975a; see also Harnish, 2003). In other words, there are essentially five things you can accomplish with speech—no more, no less. Table 10.1 identifies these categories and gives examples of each.

1. The first category of speech acts is representatives. A *representative* is a speech act by which a person conveys a belief that a given proposition is true. The speaker can use various sources of information to support the given belief. But the statement is nothing more, nor less, than a statement of belief. We can put in various qualifiers to show our degree of certainty. But we still are stating a belief, which may or may not be verifiable.

2. A second category of speech act is a directive. A *directive* represents an attempt by a speaker to get a listener to do something. Sometimes a directive is quite indirect. For example, almost any sentence structured as a question probably is serving a directive function. Any attempt to elicit assistance of any kind, however indirect, falls into this category.

3. A third category is a commissive. In uttering a *commissive*, the speaker is committing himself or herself to some future course of action.

TABLE 10.1	Speech Acts

The five basic categories of speech acts encompass the various tasks that can be accomplished through speech (or other modes of using language).

SPEECH ACT	DESCRIPTION	EXAMPLE
Representative	A speech act by which a person conveys a belief that a given proposition is true	If I say that "The Marquis de Sade is a sadist," I am conveying my belief that the marquis enjoyed seeing others feel pain. I can use various sources of information to support my belief, including the fact that the word "sadist" derives from this marquis. Nonetheless, the statement is nothing more nor less than a statement of belief. Similarly, I can make a statement that is more directly verifiable, such as "As you can see here on this thermometer, the temperature outside is 31 degrees Fahrenheit."
Directive	An attempt by a speaker to get a listener to do something, such as supplying the answer to a question	I can ask my son to help me shovel snow in various ways, some of which are more direct than others, such as, "Please help me shovel the snow," or "It sure would be nice if you were to help me shovel the snow," or "Would you help me shovel the snow?" The different surface forms are all attempts to get him to help me. Some directives are quite indirect. If I ask, "Has it stopped raining yet?" I am still uttering a directive, in this case seeking information rather than physical assistance. In fact, almost any sentence structured as a question probably serves a directive function.
Commissive	A commitment by the speaker to engage in some future course of action	If my son responds, "I'm busy now, but I'll help you shovel the snow later," he is uttering a commissive, in that he is pledging his future help. If my daughter then says, "I'll help you," she too is uttering a commissive because she is pledging her assistance now. Promises, pledges, contracts, guarantees, assurances, and the like all constitute commissives.
Expressive	A statement regarding the speaker's psychological state	If I tell my son later, "I'm really upset that you didn't come through in helping me shovel the snow," that, too, would be an expressive. If my son says, "I'm sorry I didn't get around to helping you out," he would be uttering an expressive. If my daughter says, "Daddy, I'm glad I was able to help out," she is uttering an expressive.
Declaration (also termed *performative*)	A speech act by which the very act of making a statement brings about an intended new state of affairs	Suppose that you are called into your boss's office and told that you are responsible for the company losing $50,000 and then your boss says, "You're fired." The speech act results in your being in a new state—that is, unemployed. You might then tell your boss, "That's fine because I wrote you a letter yesterday saying that the money was lost because of your glaring incompetence, not mine, and I resign." You are again making a declaration.

Promises, pledges, contracts, guarantees, assurances, and the like all constitute commissives.

4. A fourth category of speech act is an expressive. An *expressive* is a statement regarding the speaker's psychological state.

5. The fifth kind of speech act is a declaration. A *declaration* is a speech act by which the very act of making a statement brings about an intended new state of affairs. When a cleric says, "I now pronounce you husband and wife," the speech act is a declaration. Once the speech act is accomplished,

the marriage rite is completed. Declarations also are termed *performatives* (Clark & Clark, 1977).

The appealing thing about Searle's taxonomy is that it classifies almost any statement that might be made. It shows exhaustively, at least at one level, the different kinds of things speech can accomplish. It also shows the close relationship between language structure and language function.

Indirect Speech Acts

Sometimes speech acts are indirect, meaning that we accomplish our goals in speaking in an oblique fashion. One way of communicating obliquely is through **indirect requests,** through which we make a request without doing so straightforwardly (Gordon & Lakoff, 1971; Searle, 1975b). An example would be "Won't you please take out the garbage?"

There are four basic ways of making indirect requests: (1) asking or making statements about abilities, (2) stating a desire, (3) stating a future action, and (4) citing reasons. Examples of these forms of indirect requests are illustrated in Table 10.2. In each case, the indirect request is aimed at having a waitress tell the speaker where to find the restroom in a restaurant.

When are indirect speech acts interpreted literally, and when is the indirect meaning understood by the listener? When an indirect speech act such as "Must you open the window?" is presented in isolation, it usually first is interpreted literally, for example, as "Do you need to open the window?" (Gibbs, 1979). When the same speech act is presented in a story context that makes the indirect meaning clear, the sentence first is interpreted in terms of the indirect meaning. For instance, suppose a character in a story had a cold and asked, "Must you open the window?" It would be interpreted as an indirect request, "Do not open the window."

TABLE 10.2	Indirect Speech Acts

One way of using speech is to communicate obliquely, rather than directly.

TYPE OF INDIRECT SPEECH ACT	EXAMPLE OF AN INDIRECT REQUEST FOR INFORMATION
Abilities	If you say, "Can you tell me where the rest room is?" to a waitress at a restaurant, and she says, "Yes, of course I can," the chances are she missed the point. The question about her ability to tell you the location of the rest room was an indirect request for her to tell you exactly where it is.
Desire	"I would be grateful if you told me where the rest room is." Your statements of thanks in advance are really ways of getting someone to do what you want.
Future action	"Would you tell me where the rest room is?" Your inquiry into another person's future actions is another way to state an indirect request.
Reasons	You need not spell out the reasons to imply that there are good reasons to comply with the request. For example, you might imply that you have such reasons for the waitress to tell you where the rest room is by saying, "I need to know where the rest room is."

Subsequent work showed that indirect speech acts often anticipate what potential obstacles the respondent might pose. These obstacles are specifically addressed through the indirect speech act (Gibbs, 1986). For example, the question, "May I have..." addresses potential obstacles of permission. "Would you mind..." addresses potential obstacles regarding a possible imposition on the respondent. "Do you have..." addresses potential obstacles regarding availability.

Conversational Postulates

In speaking to each other, we implicitly set up a cooperative enterprise. Indeed, if we do not cooperate with each other when we speak, we often end up talking past rather than to each other. We thereby fail to communicate what we intended. Conversations thrive on the basis of a **cooperative principle,** by which we seek to communicate in ways that make it easy for our listener to understand what we mean (Grice, 1967). According to Grice, successful conversations follow four maxims: the maxim of quantity, the maxim of quality, the maxim of relation, and the maxim of manner. (Examples of these maxims are provided in Table 10.3.)

According to the *maxim of quantity*, you should make your contribution to a conversation as informative as required but no more informative than is appropriate. For example, suppose that someone says to you, "Hi, how are you?" You subsequently enter into a 3-hour soliloquy on how your life is not quite what you were hoping it to be. Here, you are violating the maxim of quantity. The social convention is to answer with a short response, even if you might like to go into greater detail. Sometimes we violate the maxim of quantity for a specific end. Suppose I have been seeking a chance to tell the chairperson of our department about problems I see with our educational program. The chairperson is taking a big risk by asking me, "How are things going?" while hoping for only a short reply.

According to the *maxim of quality*, your contribution to a conversation should be truthful. You are expected to say what you believe to be the case. If you have ever sought directions when in a strange city, you know the extreme frustration that can result if people are not truthful in telling you that they do not know where to find a particular location. Irony, sarcasm, and jokes might seem to be exceptions to the maxim of quality, but they are not. The listener is expected to recognize the irony or sarcasm and to infer the speaker's true state of mind from what is said. Similarly, a joke often is expected to accomplish a particular purpose. It usefully contributes to a conversation when that purpose is clear to everyone.

According to the *maxim of relation*, you should make your contributions to a conversation relevant to the aims of the conversation. Sometimes, of course, people purposely violate this maxim. Suppose a romantic partner says to you, "I think we need to talk about our relationship." You reply, "The weather sure is beautiful today." You are violating the maxim to make the point that you do not want to talk about the relationship. When you do so, however, you are being uncooperative. Unless the two of you can agree on how to define the conversation, you will talk past each other and have a very frustrating conversation.

According to the *maxim of manner*, you should be clear and try to avoid obscure expressions, vague utterances, and purposeful obfuscation of your point. To these four maxims noted by Grice, we might add an additional maxim: Only one person speaks

TABLE 10.3	Conversational Postulates	
To maximize the communication that occurs during conversation, speakers generally follow four maxims.		
POSTULATE	**MAXIM**	**EXAMPLE**
Maxim of quantity	Make your contribution to a conversation as informative as required but no more informative than is appropriate.	If someone asks you the temperature outside and you reply, "It's 31.297868086298 degrees out there," you are violating the maxim of quantity because you are giving more information than was probably wanted. In the old TV series *Star Trek,* Mr. Spock, a "Vulcan" with a computer-like mind, elicits shrugs when he gives much more information in answer to a question than anyone would expect or want, as in the preceding answer to the temperature question.
Maxim of quality	Your contribution to a conversation should be truthful; you are expected to say what you believe to be the case.	Clearly, there are awkward circumstances in which each of us is unsure of just how much honesty is being requested, such as for the response to, "Honey, how do I look?" Under most circumstances, however, communication depends on an assumption that both parties to the communication are being truthful.
Maxim of relation	You should make your contributions to a conversation relevant to the aims of the conversation.	Almost any large meeting I attend seems to have someone who violates this maxim. This someone inevitably goes into long digressions that have nothing to do with the purpose of the meeting and that hold up the meeting. That reminds me of a story a friend once told me about a meeting he once attended, where…
Maxim of manner	You should try to avoid obscure expressions, vague utterances, and purposeful obfuscation of your point.	Nobel Prize–winning physicist Richard Feynman (1985) described how he once read a paper by a well-known sociologist, and he found that he could not make heads or tails of it. One sentence went something like this: "The individual member of the social community often receives information via visual, symbolic channels" (p. 281). Feynman concluded, in essence, that the sociologist was violating the maxim of manner when Feynman realized that the sentence meant, "People read."

at a time (Sacks, Schegloff, & Jefferson, 1974). Given that maxim, the situational context and the relative social positions of the speakers affect turn taking (Keller, 1976; Sacks, Schegloff, & Jefferson, 1974). Sociolinguists have noted many ways in which speakers signal to one another when and how to take turns. Sometimes people flaunt the conversational postulates to make a point. For example, suppose one says, "My parents are wardens." One is not providing full information (what, exactly, does it mean for one's parents to be wardens?). But the ambiguity is intentional. Or sometimes when a conversation on a topic is becoming heated, one purposely may switch topics and bring up an irrelevant issue. One's purpose in doing so is to get the conversation to another, safer topic. When we flaunt the postulates, we are sending an explicit message by doing so: The postulates retain their importance because their absence is so notable.

Gender and Language

Within our own culture, do men and women speak a different language? Gender differences have been found in the content of what we say. Young girls are more likely to ask for help than are young boys (Thompson, 1999). Older adolescent and young adult males prefer to talk about political views, sources of personal pride, and what they like about the other person. In contrast, females in this age group prefer to talk about feelings toward parents, close friends, classes, and their fears (Rubin & associates, 1980). Also, in general, women seem to disclose more about themselves than do men (Morton, 1978).

Conversations between men and women are sometimes regarded as cross-cultural communication (Tannen, 1986, 1990, 1994). According to Tannen, young girls and boys learn conversational communication in essentially separate cultural environments through their same-sex friendships. As men and women, we then carry over the conversational styles we have learned in childhood into our adult conversations.

Tannen has suggested that male–female differences in conversational style largely center on differing understandings of the goals of conversation. These cultural differences result in contrasting styles of communication. These in turn can lead to misunderstandings and even breakups as each partner somewhat unsuccessfully tries to understand the other. Men see the world as a hierarchical social order in which the purpose of communication is to negotiate for the upper hand, to preserve independence, and to avoid failure (Tannen, 1990, 1994). Each man strives to one-up the other and to "win" the contest. Women, in contrast, seek to establish a connection between the two participants, to give support and confirmation to others, and to reach consensus through communication.

To reach their conversational goals, women use conversational strategies that minimize differences, establish equity, and avoid any appearances of superiority on the part of one or another conversant. Women also affirm the importance of and the commitment to the relationship. They handle differences of opinion by negotiating to reach a consensus that promotes the connection and ensures that both parties at least feel that their wishes have been considered. They do so even if they are not entirely satisfied with the consensual decision.

Men enjoy connections and rapport. But because men have been raised in a gender culture in which status plays an important role, other goals take precedence in conversations. Tannen has suggested that men seek to assert their independence from their conversational partners. In this way, they indicate clearly their lack of acquiescence to the demands of others, which would indicate lack of power. Men also prefer to inform (thereby indicating the higher status conferred by authority) rather than to consult (indicating subordinate status) with their conversational partners. The male partner in a close relationship thus may end up informing his partner of their plans. In contrast, the female partner expects to be consulted on their plans. When men and women are engaged in cross-gender communications, their crossed purposes often result in miscommunication because each partner misinterprets the other's intentions.

Tannen has suggested that men and women need to become more aware of their cross-cultural styles and traditions. In this way, they may at least be less likely to misinterpret one another's conversational interactions. They are also both more likely to achieve their individual aims, the aims of the relationship, and the aims of the other people and institutions affected by their relationship. Such awareness is important not only in conversations between men and women. It is also important in conversations among family members in general (Tannen, 2001). Tannen may be right. But at present, converging operations are needed in addition to Tannen's sociolinguistic case-based approach to pin down the validity and generality of her interesting findings.

PRACTICAL APPLICATIONS OF COGNITIVE PSYCHOLOGY	Think about how your gender influences your conversational style. Construct some ways to communicate more effectively with people of the opposite sex. How might your speech acts and conversational postulates differ? If you are a man, do you tend to use and prefer directives and declarations over expressives and commissives? If you are a woman, do you use and prefer expressives and commissives over directives and declarations? If so, speaking to people of the opposite sex can lead to misinterpretations of meaning based on differences in style. For example, when you want to get another person to do something, it may be best to use the style that more directly reflects the other person's style. In this case, you might use a directive with men ("Would you go to the store?") and an expressive with women ("I really enjoy going shopping."). Also, remember that your responses should match the other person's expectations regarding how much information to provide, honesty, relevance, and directness. The art of effective communication really involves listening carefully to another person, observing body language, and interpreting the person's goals accurately. This can be accomplished only with time, effort, and sensitivity.

Discourse and Reading Comprehension

The preceding sections discussed some of the more general aspects of social uses of language. This section discusses more specifically the processes involved in understanding and using language in the social context of discourse. Discourse involves communicative units of language larger than individual sentences—in conversations, lectures, stories, essays, and even textbooks (Di Eugenio, 2003). Just as grammatical sentences are structured according to systematic syntactical rules, passages of discourse are structured systematically.

INVESTIGATING COGNITIVE PSYCHOLOGY	The following series of sentences is taken from a short story by O. Henry (William Sydney Porter, 1899–1953) entitled, "The Ransom of Red Chief." Actually, the following sequence of sentences is incorrect. Without knowing anything else about the story, try to figure out the correct sequence of sentences. 1. The father was respectable and tight, a mortgage financier and a stern, upright collection-plate passer and forecloser. 2. We selected for our victim the only child of a prominent citizen named Ebenezer Dorset. 3. We were down South in Alabama—Bill Driscoll and myself—when this kidnapping idea struck us. 4. Bill and me figured that Ebenezer would melt down for a ransom of two thousand dollars to a cent. *Hint:* O. Henry was a master of irony, and by the end of the story the would-be kidnappers paid the father a hefty ransom to take back his son so that they could quickly escape from the boy. The sequence used by O. Henry, ex-convict and expert storyteller, was 3, 2, 1, 4. Is that the order you chose? How did you know the correct sequence for these sentences?

By adulthood, most of us have a firm grasp of how sentences are sequenced into a discourse structure. From our knowledge of discourse structure, we can derive meanings of sentence elements that are not apparent by looking at isolated sentences. To see how some of these discourse-dependent elements work, read the sentences about Rita and Thomas in the "Investigating Cognitive Psychology" box. Then answer the questions that follow them.

INVESTIGATING COGNITIVE PSYCHOLOGY

Rita gave Thomas a book about problem solving. He thanked her for the book. She asked, "Is it what you wanted?" He answered enthusiastically, "Yes, definitely." Rita asked, "Should I get you the companion volume on decision making?" He responded, "Please do."

In the second and third sentences, who were the people and things being referred to with the pronouns "He," "her," "She," and "it"? Why was the noun "book" preceded by the article "a" in the first sentence and by the article "the" in the second one? How do you know what Thomas's answer, "Yes, definitely," means? What is the action being requested in the response, "Please do"?

Cognitive psycholinguists who analyze discourse particularly are intrigued by how we are able to answer the questions posed in the preceding example. When grasping the meanings of pronouns (e.g., *he, she, him, her, it, they, them, we, us*), how do we know to whom (or to what) the pronouns are pointing? How do we know the meanings of ellipsed utterances (e.g., "Yes, definitely")? What does the use of the definite article *the* (as opposed to the indefinite article *a*) preceding a noun signify to listeners regarding whether a noun was mentioned previously? How do you know what event is being referenced by the verb *do*? The meanings of pronouns, ellipses, definite articles, event references, and other local elements within sentences usually depend on the discourse structure within which these elements appear (Grosz, Pollack, & Sidner, 1989).

Often, for understanding discourse we rely not only on our knowledge of discourse structure. We also rely on our knowledge of a broad physical, social, or cultural context within which the discourse is presented. For example, observe how your understanding of the meaning of a paragraph is influenced by your existing knowledge and expectations. For example, this cognitive psychology textbook will be easier to read, on average, if you have taken an introductory psychology course than if you have not taken such a course. When reading the following sentences in the "Investigating Cognitive Psychology" box, pause between sentences and think about what you know and what you expect, based on your knowledge.

Semantic Encoding: Retrieving Word Meaning from Memory

Semantic encoding is the process by which we translate sensory information into a meaningful representation that we perceive. This representation is based on our understanding of the meanings of words. In lexical access we identify words, based on letter combinations. We thereby activate our memory in regard to the words. In semantic encoding we take the next step and gain access to the meaning of the word stored in memory. Sometimes we cannot semantically encode the word because its meaning

INVESTIGATING COGNITIVE PSYCHOLOGY

1. Susan became increasingly anxious as she prepared for the upcoming science exam. (What do you know about Susan?)
2. She had never written an exam before, and she wasn't sure how to construct an appropriate test of the students' knowledge. (How have your beliefs about Susan changed?)
3. She was particularly annoyed that the principal had even asked her to write the exam.
4. Even during a teachers' strike, a school nurse should not be expected to take on the task of writing an examination. (How did your expectations change over the course of the four sentences?)

In the preceding example, your understanding at each point in the discourse was influenced by your existing knowledge and expectations based on your own experiences within a particular context. Thus, just as prior experience and knowledge may aid us in lexical processing of text, they also may aid us in comprehending the text itself. What are the main reading comprehension processes? The process of reading comprehension is so complex that many entire courses and myriad volumes are devoted exclusively to the topic, but we focus here on just a few processes. These include semantic encoding, acquiring vocabulary, comprehending ideas in text, creating mental models of text, and comprehending text based on context and point of view.

does not already exist in memory. We then must find another way in which to derive the meanings of words, such as from noting the context in which we read them.

To engage in semantic encoding, the reader needs to know what a given word means. Knowledge of word meanings (vocabulary) very closely relates to the ability to comprehend text. People who are knowledgeable about word meanings tend to be good readers and vice versa. A reason for this relationship appears to be that readers simply cannot understand text well unless they know the meanings of the component words. For example, in one study, recall of the semantic content of a passage differed by 8% between two groups of participants when the two groups differed in their passage-relevant vocabulary knowledge by 9% (Beck, Perfetti, & McKeown, 1982).

People with larger vocabularies are able to access lexical information more rapidly than are those with smaller vocabularies (Hunt, 1978). Verbal information often is presented rapidly—whether in listening or in reading. The individual who can gain access to lexical information rapidly is able to process more information per unit of time than can one who can only gain access to such information slowly.

Acquiring Vocabulary: Deriving Word Meanings from Context

Another way in which having a larger vocabulary contributes to text comprehension is through learning from context. Whenever we cannot semantically encode a word because its meaning is not already stored in memory, we must engage in some kind of strategy to derive meaning from the text. In general, we must either search for a meaning, using external resources (such as dictionaries or teachers), or formulate a meaning. We formulate the meaning based on the existing information stored in memory, using context cues with which to do so.

IN THE LAB OF WALTER KINTSCH

Courtesy of Dr. Walter Kintsch

High-level cognition, such as language comprehension and problem solving, is heavily knowledge dependent. It is often not possible to understand (and model) comprehension and thinking without explicitly considering the exact nature of the knowledge that people rely on—language knowledge, world knowledge, and personal experience. Thus, a precondition for modeling much of higher-level cognition is that we are able to represent accurately, objectively, and comprehensively the knowledge people have. That is a tall order, and in consequence investigators often work on problems where the role of prior knowledge is minimized, shying away from the knowledge-intensive problems that characterize everyday discourse comprehension and problem solving.

We have taken a different course and have chosen to base our research on a statistical model of human knowledge called Latent Semantic Analysis or LSA, which was invented by my colleague Tom Landauer in 1997. LSA is a computer program that observes how words are used in a large amount of text—say 11 million words in 36,000 documents containing about 90,000 word types —and then constructs a map of the semantic relations among these words and documents. Such a map shows how the meanings of words, sentences, and whole texts are related. In constructing this map, LSA considers only which words were grouped together, not their order and syntax. Once we have such a map we can easily look up the semantic distance between any words, whether or not they have ever been observed together in the original corpus. Even better, we can place sentences and whole texts on that map, and compute their semantic distance or similarity. The map is not like the two-dimensional maps we are familiar with, however. A much larger number of dimensions—about 300—are required to faithfully represent the exceedingly complex semantic relationships on which our language is based. Words and texts are represented as vectors in that space, and their similarity can be measured by the cosine of the angle between these vectors. Words that are close in meaning have a high cosine; unrelated words have a low cosine or even a negative one. For example, the cosine between *tree* and *oak* is 0.80, whereas the cosine between *tree* and *liberty* is 0.04; the cosine between *liberty* and *freedom*, on the other hand, is 0.70. Similarly the cosine between the paraphrases *Men love their liberty* and *People cherish their freedom* is 0.79, whereas the cosine between the unrelated sentence pair *People cherish their freedom* and *Birds flap their wings* is 0.06. The website lsa.colorado.edu allows anyone to perform such calculations.

A problem we have focused on is how to model a person's knowledge of what words mean. The word vector that represents meaning in LSA is decontextualized: LSA infers that vector by observing how the word is used in many different contexts, but it lumps together different meanings and senses of a word. Psychologists and linguists typically describe word meanings in terms of a mental lexicon—a list in the mind of all meanings and senses of a word together with brief definitions, much like in a real lexicon. There are many problems with this idea of a fixed mental lexicon, such as how to retrieve the right meaning at the right time, how to account for novel uses of the language, and even how to decide when a word is used in the same sense and when we are dealing with a different sense. LSA suggests a different model in which word meanings and word senses are generated anew every time a word is used in context. This can be done by allowing the context to modify the word vector so that a new, contextualized word meaning emerges. Sometimes these contextual modifications are small, as when a word is used in a familiar context, but sometimes they are very large. So most of the time when we are talking about a *house*, we use the word in its most familiar sense and the context has only a slight effect; if we are talking about the House of Representatives, quite a different sense of house is generated. The effects of context are particularly strong when a word is used metaphorically. Thus, the shark in *My lawyer is a shark* is quite different from the fish with fins that swims in the ocean.

LSA is important in research on language comprehension, but it is also a powerful educational tool because it allows computers to understand what students write about. Thus, the computer can provide

Continues

IN THE LAB OF WALTER KINTSCH—cont'd

feedback to a writer about the content of what has been written. We have put this ability to good use in a program called *Summary Street*, which is currently used in several dozen classrooms all over Colorado. Suppose a sixth-grade student has to write a summary of a chapter she has read in her social studies textbook. Her first draft is surely in need of improvement, but it is nearly impossible for a teacher to check and correct all the individual essays in a classroom. Here the computer can help: it compares what has been written with the original text, notes portions of the text not represented or underrepresented in the student's essay, and provides immediate feedback. It also flags redundant sentences or irrelevant sentences. It never tells the student what to do; it just identifies potential problems with a summary. The student can reread the chapter, fix what she has written, or accept the computer's advice. Students write better summaries when they receive this kind of feedback that is delivered instantly as needed. They like it when somebody is paying attention to them, even if it is only a computer. A number of other related applications of LSA are currently in use or being developed, such as software that grades essays automatically and a system that matches readers to instructional texts appropriate to their skill level. Thus, basic research on how people comprehend language goes hand in hand with the development of useful practical applications of the knowledge we have gained.

People learn most of their vocabulary indirectly. They do so not by using external resources but by figuring out the meanings of the flidges from the surrounding information (Werner & Kaplan, 1952).

For example, if you tried to look up the word *flidges* in the dictionary, you did not find it there. From the structure of the sentence you probably figured out that *flidges* is a noun. From the surrounding context you probably figured out that it is a noun having something to do with words or vocabulary. In fact, *flidges* is a nonsense word I used as a placeholder for the word *words* to show how you would gain a fairly good idea of a word's meaning from its context.

Investigators had adult participants learn meanings of words from sentence contexts (van Daalen-Kapteijns & Elshout-Mohr, 1981; see also Sternberg & Powell, 1983). They found that high- and low-verbal participants (i.e., people with large or small vocabularies, respectively) learn word meanings differently. High-verbal participants perform a deeper analysis of the possibilities for a new word's meaning than do low-verbal participants. In particular, the high-verbal participants used a well-formulated strategy for figuring out word meanings. The low-verbal participants seemed to have no clear strategy at all.

Comprehension of Ideas in Text: Propositional Representations

What factors influence our comprehension of what we read? Walter Kintsch has developed a model of text comprehension based on his observations (Kintsch, 1990; Kintsch & van Dijk, 1978). According to the model, as we read we try to hold as much information as possible in working (active) memory to understand what we read. However, we do not try to store the exact words we read in working (active) memory. Rather, we try to extract the fundamental ideas from groups of words. We then store those fundamental ideas in a simplified representational form in working memory.

The representational form for these fundamental ideas is the proposition. Propositions were defined in more detail in Chapter 7. For now it suffices to say that a proposition is the briefest unit of language that can be independently found to be true or false. For example, the sentence, "Penguins are birds, and penguins can fly" contains two propositions. You can verify independently whether penguins are birds and whether penguins can fly. In general, propositions assert either an action (e.g., flying) or a relationship (e.g., membership of penguins in the category of birds).

According to Kintsch, working memory holds propositions rather than words. Its limits are thus taxed by large numbers of propositions, rather than by any particular number of words (Kintsch & Keenan, 1973). When a string of words in text requires us to hold a large number of propositions in working memory, we have difficulty comprehending the text. When information stays in working memory a longer time, it is better comprehended and better recalled subsequently. Because of the limits of working memory, however, some information must be moved out of working memory to make room for new information.

According to Kintsch, propositions that are thematically central to the understanding of the text will remain in working memory longer than propositions that are irrelevant to the theme of the text passage. Kintsch calls the thematically crucial propositions *macropropositions*. He further calls the overarching thematic structure of a passage of text the *macrostructure*. In an experiment testing his model, Kintsch and an associate asked participants to read a 1,300-word text passage (Kintsch & van Dijk, 1978). The participants then had to summarize the key propositions in the passage immediately, at 1 month, or at 3 months after reading the passage. What happened after 3 months? Participants recalled the macropropositions and the overall macrostructure of the passage about as well as could participants who summarized it immediately after reading it. However, the propositions providing nonthematic details about the passage were not recalled as well after 1 month and not at all well after 3 months.

Representing the Text in Mental Models

Once words are semantically encoded or their meaning is derived from the use of context, the reader still must create a mental model of the text that is being read. This model simulates the world being described rather than the particular words being used to describe it (Craik, 1943; see Johnson-Laird, 1989). A mental model may be viewed as a sort of internal working model of the situation described in the text as the reader understands it. In other words, the reader creates some sort of mental representation that contains within it the main elements of the text. They are represented in a way that is relatively easy to grasp or at least that is simpler and more concrete than the text itself. For example, suppose that you read the sentence, "The loud bang scared Alice." You may form a picture of Alice becoming scared on hearing a loud noise. Or you may access propositions stored in memory regarding the effects of loud bangs.

A given passage of text or even a given set of propositions (to refer back to Kintsch's model) may lead to more than one mental model (Johnson-Laird, 1983). For example, you may need to modify your mental model. Whether you do depends on whether the next sentence is, "She tried to steer off the highway without losing control of the car," or "She ducked to avoid being shot." In representing the loud bang that scared Alice, more than one mental model is possible. If you start out with a different model than the one required in a given passage, your ability to comprehend the text depends on your ability to form a new mental model.

Note that to form mental models, you must make at least tentative inferences (preliminary conclusions or judgments) about what is meant but not said. In the first case, you are likely to assume that a tire blew out. In the second case, you may infer that someone is shooting a gun. Note that neither of these things is stated explicitly. The construction of mental models illustrates that, in addition to comprehending the words themselves, we also need to understand how words combine into meaningfully integrated representations of narratives or expositions. Passages of text that lead unambiguously to a single mental model are easier to comprehend than are passages that may lead to multiple mental models (Johnson-Laird, 1989).

Inferences can be of different kinds. One of the most important kinds is a bridging inference (Haviland & Clark, 1974). This is an inference a reader (or listener) makes when a sentence seems not to follow directly from the sentence preceding it. In essence, what is new in the second sentence goes one step too far beyond what is given in the previous sentences. Consider, for example, two pairs of two sentences:

1. John took the picnic out of the trunk. The beer was warm.
2. John took the beer out of the trunk. The beer was warm.

Readers took about 180 milliseconds longer to read the first pair of sentences than the second. Haviland and Clark suggested a reason for this greater processing time. It was that, in the first pair, information needed to be inferred (the picnic included beer) that was directly stated in the second pair.

Although most researchers emphasize the importance of inference making in reading and forms of language comprehension (e.g., Graesser & Kreuz, 1993), not all researchers do. According to the minimalist hypothesis, readers make inferences based only on information that is easily available to them. They do so only when they need to make such inferences to make sense of adjoining sentences (McKoon & Ratcliff, 1992a). I believe that the bulk of the evidence regarding the minimalist position indicates that it is itself too minimalist. Readers appear to make more inferences than this position suggests (Suh & Trabasso, 1993, Trabasso & Suh, 1993).

Comprehending Text Based on Context and Point of View

What we remember from a given passage of text often depends on our point of view. For example, suppose that you were reading a text passage about the home of a wealthy family. It described many of the features of the house, such as a leaky roof, a fireplace, and a musty basement. It also described the contents of the house, such as valuable coins, silverware, and television set. How might your encoding and comprehension of the text be different if you were reading it from the point of view of a prospective purchaser of the home as opposed to the viewpoint of a prospective cat burglar? In a study using just such a passage, people who read the passage from the viewpoint of a cat burglar remembered far more about the contents of the home. In contrast, those who read from the viewpoint of a home buyer remembered more about the condition of the house (Anderson & Pichert, 1978).

To summarize, our comprehension of what we read depends on several abilities. First is gaining access to the meanings of words, either from memory or on the basis of context. Second is deriving meaning from the key ideas in what we read. Third is forming mental models that simulate the situations about which we read. And fourth is extracting the key information from the text, based on the contexts in which we read and on the ways in which we intend to use what we read.

Thus far we have discussed the social and cognitive contexts for language. Language use interacts with, but does not completely determine, the nature of thought. Social interactions influence the ways in which language is used and comprehended in discourse and reading. Next, we highlight some of the insights we have gained by studying the physiological context for language. Specifically, how do our brains process language?

Neuropsychology of Language

Recall from Chapter 2 that some of our earliest insights into brain localization related to an association between specific language deficits and specific organic damage to the brain, as first discovered by Marc Dax, Paul Broca, and Carl Wernicke (see also Brown & Hagoort, 1999; Garrett, 2003). Broca's aphasia and Wernicke's aphasia are particularly well-documented instances in which brain lesions affect linguistic functions (see Chapter 2). Let's consider these and related syndromes in more detail.

Aphasia

Aphasia is an impairment of language functioning caused by damage to the brain (Caramazza & Shapiro, 2001; Garrett, 2003; Hillis & Caramazza, 2003). There are several types of aphasias (Figure 10.6).

Wernicke's aphasia is caused by damage to Wernicke's area of the brain (see Chapter 2). It is characterized by notable impairment in the understanding of spoken words and sentences. It also typically involves the production of sentences that have the basic structure of the language spoken but that make no sense. They are sentences that are empty of meaning. Two examples are "Yeah, that was the pumpkin furthest from my thoughts" and "the scroolish prastimer ate my spanstakes" (Hillis & Caramazza, 2003, p. 176). In the first case, the words makes sense, but not in the context they are presented. In the second case, the words themselves are neologisms, or newly created words.

Broca's aphasia is caused by damage to Broca's area of the brain (see Chapter 2). It is characterized by the production of agrammatical speech at the same time that verbal comprehension ability is largely preserved. It thus differs from Wernicke's aphasia in two key respects. First is that speech is agrammatical rather than grammatical, as in Wernicke's. Second is that verbal comprehension is largely preserved. An example of a production by a patient with Broca's aphasia is "Stroke . . . Sunday . . . arm, talking – bad" (Hillis & Caramazza, 2003, p. 176). The gist of the intended sentence is maintained, but the expression of it is badly distorted.

FIGURE 10.6

Brain scans comparing brain of (a) normal patient with brains of patients with (b) Wernicke's aphasia and (c) Broca's aphasia.

Global aphasia is the combination of highly impaired comprehension and production of speech. It is caused by lesions to both Broca's and Wernicke's areas.

Anomic aphasia involves difficulties in naming objects or in retrieving words. The patient may look at an object and simply be unable to retrieve the word that corresponds to the object. Sometimes, specific categories of things cannot be recalled, such as names of living things (Warrington & Shallice, 1984).

Autism

Autism is a developmental disorder characterized by abnormalities in social behavior, language, and cognition (Jarrold & Happé, 2003; Pierce & Courchesne, 2003). It is biological in its origins, although the genes responsible for it have not been conclusively identified (Lamb & associates, 2000). Children with autism show abnormalities in many areas of the brain, including the frontal and parietal lobes, as well as the cerebellum, brain stem, corpus callosum, basal ganglia, amygdala, and hippocampus. The disease was first identified in the middle of the twentieth century (Kanner, 1943). It is five times more common in males than in females, and occurs in roughly 1 out of every 600 live births. Children with autism usually are identified by around 14 months of age, when they fail to show the normal patterns of interactions with others that would be expected. Children with autism display repetitive movements and stereotyped patterns of interests and activities (Pierce & Courchesne, 2003). Often they repeat the same motion, over and over again, with no obvious purpose to the movement. When they interact with someone, they are more likely to view their lips than their eyes. About half of children with autism fail to develop functional speech. What speech they do develop tends to be characterized by *echolalia*, meaning they repeat, over and over again, speech they have heard. Sometimes the repetition occurs several hours after the original use of the words by someone else (Pierce & Courchesne, 2003).

There are a variety of theories of autism. One recent theory suggests that autism can be understood in terms of sex differences in the wiring of the human brain. According to this theory (Baron-Cohen, 2003), male brains are, on average, stronger than female ones at understanding and building systems. These systems can be concrete ones, such as those involved in building machinery, or they can be abstract ones, such as those in politics or writing or music. Females' brains, in contrast, are stronger at empathizing and communicating. According to Baron-Cohen, autism results from an extreme male brain. This brain is almost totally inept in empathy and communication, but very strong in systematizing. As a result, autistic individuals sometimes can perform tasks that require a great deal of systematization, such as figuring out the day corresponding to a date well in the future. As it happens, autism is also much more common among males than among females. Although this theory has not been conclusively proven, it is intriguing, and currently under further investigation.

Lesion Studies and Event-Related Potentials Research

Through studies of patients with brain lesions, researchers have learned a great deal about the relations between particular areas of the brain (the areas of lesions observed in patients) and particular linguistic functions (the observed deficits in the brain-injured patients). For example, we can broadly generalize that many linguistic functions are located primarily in the areas identified by Broca and Wernicke. Damage to Wernicke's area, in the posterior of the cortex, is now believed to entail more grim consequences for linguistic function than does damage to Broca's area, closer to the front of the brain (Kolb & Whishaw, 1990). Also, lesion studies have shown that linguistic function is governed by a much larger area of the posterior cortex than just the area identified by Wernicke. In addition, other areas of the cortex also play a role. Examples are association-cortex areas in the left hemisphere and a portion of the left temporal cortex. Moreover, recent imaging studies of the post-traumatic recovery of linguistic functioning find that neurological language functioning appears to redistribute to other areas of the brain. These areas include analogous areas in the right hemisphere and some frontal areas. Thus, damage to the major left hemisphere areas responsible for language functioning sometimes can lead to enhanced involvement of other areas as language functioning recovers. It is as if previously dormant or overshadowed areas take over the duties left vacant (Cappa, & associates, 1997). Finally, some subcortical structures (e.g., the basal ganglia and the posterior thalamus) also are involved in linguistic function (Kolb & Whishaw, 1990).

Geschwind (1970) proposed a model, sometimes known as the Geschwind-Wernicke model, for how language is processed by the brain. According to this model, speech sounds signaling language travel to the inner ear. The auditory nerve then carries these signals to the primary auditory cortex of the temporal lobe. From there, the signal travels to an association area of the brain at a region in which the temporal, occipital, and parietal lobes join. Here sense is made from what was said. In other words, meaning is assigned at this point. From there, the processed information travels to Wernicke's area. It then moves on to Broca's area. Although the model as originally formulated localized language comprehension in Wernicke's area and language production in Broca's area, this view is now known to be an oversimplification. Wernicke's area seems to have some involvement in language production and Broca's area in language comprehension (Zurif, 1990).

Event-related potentials, or ERPs (see Chapter 2), also can be used to study the processing of language in the brain. For one thing, a certain ERP called N400 (a negative potential 400 milliseconds after stimulus onset) typically occurs when individuals hear an anomalous sentence (Kutas & Hillyard, 1980). Thus, if people are presented a sequence of normal sentences but also anomalous sentences (such as "The leopard is a very good napkin"), the anomalous sentences will elicit the N400 potential. Moreover, the more anomalous a sentence is, the greater the response shown in another ERP, P600 (a positive potential 600 milliseconds after the stimulus onset; Kutas & Van Patten, 1994).

Men and women appear to process language differently, at least at the phonological level (Shaywitz & associates, 1995). An fMRI study of men and women asked participants to perform one of four tasks:

1. Indicate whether a pair of letters was identical.
2. Indicate whether two words have the same meaning.
3. Indicate whether a pair of words rhymes.
4. Compare the lengths of two lines (a control task).

The researchers found that when both male and female participants were performing the letter-recognition and word-meaning tasks, they showed activation in the left temporal lobe of the brain. When they were performing the rhyming task, however, different areas were activated for men versus women. Only the inferior (lower) frontal region of the left hemisphere was activated for men. The inferior frontal region of both the left and right hemispheres was activated in women. These results suggested that men localized their phonological processing more than did women.

Some intriguing sex differences emerge in the ways that linguistic function appears to be localized in the brain (Kimura, 1987). Men seem to show more left-hemisphere dominance for linguistic function than the women show. Women show more bilateral, symmetrical patterns of linguistic function. Furthermore, the brain locations associated with aphasia seemed to differ for men and women. Most aphasic women showed lesions in the anterior region, although some aphasic women showed lesions in the temporal region. In contrast, aphasic men showed a more varied pattern of lesions. Aphasic men were more likely to show lesions in posterior regions rather than in anterior regions. One interpretation of Kimura's findings is that the role of the posterior region in linguistic function may be different for women than it is for men. Another interpretation relates to the fact that women show less lateralization of linguistic function. Women may be better able to compensate for any possible loss of function due to lesions in the left posterior hemisphere through functional offsets in the right posterior hemisphere. The possibility that there also may be subcortical sex differences in linguistic function further complicates the ease of interpreting Kimura's findings. (Recall also the earlier discussion of communication differences between men and women.)

Kimura (1981) also has studied hemispheric processing of language in people who use sign language rather than speech to communicate. She found that the locations of lesions that would be expected to disrupt speech also disrupt signing. Further, the hemispheric pattern of lesions associated with signing deficits is the same pattern shown with speech deficits. That is, all right-handers with signing deficits show left-hemisphere lesions, as do most left-handers. But some left-handers with signing deficits show right-hemisphere lesions. This finding supports the view that the brain processes both signing and speech similarly in terms of their linguistic function. It refutes the view that signing involves spatial processing or some other nonlinguistic form of cognitive processing.

There is some evidence that the brain mechanisms responsible for language learning are different from those responsible for the use of language by adults (Stiles & associates, 1998). In general, the left hemisphere seems to be better at processing well-practiced routines. The right hemisphere is better at dealing with novel stimuli (Mills, Coffey-Corina, & Neville, 1997). A possibly related finding is that individuals who have learned language later in life show more right-hemisphere involvement (Neville, 1995). Perhaps the reason is that language remains somewhat more novel for them than for others. This finding points out that one cannot precisely map linguistic or other kinds of functioning to hemispheres in a way that works for all people. Rather, the mappings differ somewhat from one person to another (Zurif, 1995).

Despite the many findings that have resulted from studies of brain-injured patients, there are three key difficulties in drawing conclusions based only on studies of patients with lesions:

1. Naturally occurring lesions are often not easily localized to a discrete region of the brain, with no untoward effects on other regions. For example, when hemorrhaging or insufficient blood flow (such as impairment due to clotting) causes lesions, the lesions also may affect other areas of the brain. Thus, many patients who show cortical damage also have suf-

fered some damage in subcortical structures. This may confound the findings of cortical damage.

2. Researchers are able to study the linguistic function of patients only after the lesions have caused damage. Typically they are unable to document the linguistic function of patients prior to the damage.

3. Because it would be unethical to create lesions merely to observe their effects on patients, researchers are able to study the effects of lesions only in those areas where lesions happen to have occurred naturally. Other areas therefore are not studied.

Other Methods

Although lesion studies are valuable, researchers also investigate brain localization of linguistic function via other methods. One example is evaluating the effects on linguistic function that follow electrical stimulation of the brain (Ojemann, 1982; Ojemann & Mateer, 1979). Through stimulation studies, researchers have found that stimulation of particular points in the brain seems to yield discrete effects on particular linguistic functions (such as the naming of objects) across repeated, successive trials. For example, in a given person, repeated stimulation of one particular point might lead to difficulties in recalling the names of objects on every trial. In contrast, stimulation of another point might lead to incorrect naming of objects. In addition, information regarding brain locations in a specific individual may not apply across individuals. Thus, for a given individual, a discrete point of stimulation may seem to affect only one particular linguistic function. But across individuals, these particular localizations of function vary widely. The effects of electrical stimulation are transitory. Linguistic function returns to normal soon after the stimulation has ceased. These brain-stimulation studies also show that many more areas of the cortex are involved in linguistic function than was thought previously.

Using electrical-stimulation techniques, sex differences in linguistic function can be identified. There is a somewhat paradoxical interaction of language and the brain (Ojemann, 1982). Although females generally have superior verbal skills to males, males have a proportionately larger (more diffusely dispersed) language area in their brains than do females. Counterintuitively, therefore, the size of the language area in the brain may be inversely related to the ability to use language. This interpretation seems further bolstered by Ojemann's findings with bilinguals, mentioned earlier. These findings regard the diffuse distribution of the nondominant language versus the more concentrated localization of the dominant language.

Yet another avenue of research involves the study of the metabolic activity of the brain and the flow of blood in the brain during the performance of various verbal tasks. For example, preliminary metabolic and blood-flow studies of the brain have indicated that many areas of the brain appear to be involved simultaneously during linguistic processing (Petersen & associates, 1988). However, most studies confirm the left hemisphere bias indicated by lesion studies (see Cabeza & Nyberg, 1997). Through these kinds of studies, researchers can examine multiple simultaneous cerebral processes involved in various linguistic tasks.

For all right-handed individuals and for most left-handed people, the left hemisphere of the brain seems clearly implicated in syntactical aspects of linguistic processing. It is essential to speech and to signing. The left hemisphere also seems to be essential to the ability to write. However, the right hemisphere seems capable of quite a bit of auditory comprehension. This is so, particularly in terms of semantic processing, as well as some reading comprehension and post-traumatic linguistic recovery. The right hemisphere also seems to be important in several of the subtle nuances of linguistic comprehension and expression. Examples are understanding and expressing vocal inflection and gesture and comprehending metaphors and other nonliteral aspects of language (e.g., jokes and sarcasm; Kolb & Whishaw, 1990).

Finally, some subcortical structures, especially the basal ganglia and the posterior thalamus, seem to be involved in linguistic function. The thalamus seems to be involved in linguistic function, particularly in coordinating the activities of the cortical areas involved in speech (Hughlings-Jackson, 1866/1932; Penfield & Roberts, 1959). Investigators have linked lesions in the thalamus to specific difficulties in speaking (e.g., perseveration or impairment of speed, fluency, or naming—Ojemann, 1975). Also, the thalamus may play a role in activating the cortex for understanding and remembering language. Because of the difficulty of studying subcortical structures, the specific role of the thalamus and other subcortical structures is not yet well defined (Kolb & Whishaw, 1990).

Much of this chapter has revealed the many ways in which language and thought interact. The following chapter focuses on problem solving and creativity. But it also further reveals the interconnectedness of the ways in which we use language and the ways in which we think.

Common Themes

This chapter deals with several of the themes highlighted in Chapter 1.

A first theme is that of validity of causal inference versus ecological validity. Some researchers study language comprehension and production in controlled laboratory settings. For example, studies of phonology are likely to occur in a laboratory where it is possible to gain precise experimental control of stimuli. But work on language and thought often is done in remote parts of the world where tight experimental controls are only a dream. Studies of language usage in remote African villages, for example, cannot be done with tight controls, although some control is possible. As always, a combination of methodologies best enables cognitive psychologists to understand psychological phenomena to their fullest.

A second theme is that of biological versus behavioral methods. Lesion studies are a particularly good example of a combination of the two methodologies. On the one hand, they require a deep understanding of the nature of the brain and the parts of the brain affected by particular lesions. On the other hand, researchers examine behavior to understand how the particular lesions, and by inference, parts of the brain, are related to behavioral functioning.

A third theme is structure versus process. To understand any linguistic phenomena, one must analyze thoroughly the structure of the language under investigation.

One can then investigate the processes that are used to comprehend and produce this language. Without an understanding of both structure and process, it would be impossible to fully understand language and thought.

Suppose you are on a camping trip and are sitting around the campfire at night, admiring the numerous stars in the sky. Suppose you were to say to someone the following metaphorical question, "Would you like to see the sun paint a picture across the morning sky?" What does this question mean? Some people might say that it means that you are asking if they would like to wake up early to see how beautiful the sunrise will be the next morning. Some people might say that it means that it is getting late and that you should go to sleep to wake up early to see the beautiful sunrise. Now, suppose you ask this same question not on a camping trip but in a sleazy bar. What do you think the utterance will mean in that context?

Read the following passage:

> Aoccdrnig to a rseearch at an Elingsh uinervtisy, it dseon't mttaer in waht oredr the ltteers in a wrod are, the olny iprmoatnt tihng is that the frist and lsat ltteres are at the rghit pclae. The rset can be a toatl mses and you can sitll raed it wouthit porbelm. Tihs is bcuseae we do not raed ervey lteter by itslef but the wrod as a wlohe.

Although most people cannot read the above passage as quickly as they can if all the letters are in the right order, they still can understand what the passage says.

Summary

1. **How do perceptual processes interact with the cognitive processes of reading?** The reading difficulties of people with dyslexia often relate to problems with the perceptual aspects of reading. Reading comprises two basic kinds of processes: (1) lexical processes, which include sequences of eye fixations and lexical access; and (2) comprehension processes.

2. **How does language affect the way we think?** According to the linguistic relativity view, cognitive differences that result from using different languages cause people speaking the various languages to perceive the world differently. However, the linguistic universals view stresses cognitive commonalities across different language users. No single interpretation explains all of the available evidence regarding the interaction of language and thought.

Research on bilinguals seems to show that environmental considerations also affect the interaction of language and thought. For example, additive bilinguals have established a well-developed primary language. The second language adds to their linguistic and perhaps even their cognitive skills. In contrast, subtractive bilinguals have not yet firmly established their primary language when portions of a second language partially displace the primary language. This displacement may lead to difficulties in verbal skills. Theorists differ in their views as to whether bilinguals store two or more languages separately (dual-system hypothesis) or together (single-system hypothesis). Some aspects of multiple languages possibly could be stored separately and others unitarily. Creoles and pidgins arise when two or more distinct linguistic groups come into contact. A dialect appears when a regional variety of a language becomes distinguished by features such as distinctive vocabulary, grammar, and pronunciation.

Slips of the tongue may involve inadvertent verbal errors in phonemes, morphemes, or larger units of language. Slips of the tongue include anticipations, perseverations, reversals (including spoonerisms), substitutions, insertions, and deletions. Alternative views of metaphor include the comparison view, the anomaly view, the domain-interaction view, and the class-inclusion view.

3. **How does our social context influence our use of language?** Psychologists, sociolinguists, and others who study pragmatics are interested in how language is used within a social context. Their research looks into various aspects of nonverbal as well as verbal communication. Speech acts comprise representatives, directives, commissives, expressives, and declarations. Indirect requests, ways of asking for something without doing so straightforwardly, may refer to abilities, desires, future actions, and reasons. Conversational postulates provide a means for establishing language as a cooperative enterprise. They comprise several maxims, including the maxims of quantity, quality, relation, and manner. Sociolinguists have observed that people engage in various strategies to signal turn taking in conversations.

Sociolinguistic research suggests that male–female differences in conversational style center largely on men's and women's differing understandings of the goals of conversation. It has been suggested that men tend to see the world as a hierarchical social order in which their communication aims involve the need to maintain a high rank in the social order. In contrast, women tend to see communication as a means for establishing and maintaining their connection to their communica-

tion partners. To do so, they seek ways to demonstrate equity and support and to reach consensual agreement.

In discourse and reading comprehension, we use the surrounding context to infer the reference of pronouns and ambiguous phrases. The discourse context also can influence the semantic interpretation of unknown words in passages and aid in acquiring new vocabulary. Propositional representations of information in passages can be organized into mental models for text comprehension. Finally, a person's point of view likewise influences what will be remembered.

4. **How can we find out about language by studying the human brain, and what do such studies reveal?** Neuropsychologists, cognitive psychologists, and other researchers have managed to link quite a few language functions with specific areas or structures in the brain. They observe what happens when a particular area of the brain is injured, is electrically stimulated, or is studied in terms of its metabolic activity. For most people, the left hemisphere of the brain is vital to speech. It affects many syntactical aspects and some semantic aspects of linguistic processing. For most people, the right hemisphere handles a more limited number of linguistic functions. They include auditory comprehension of semantic information, as well as comprehension and expression of some nonliteral aspects of language use. These aspects involves vocal inflection, gesture, metaphors, sarcasm, irony, and jokes.

Thinking about Thinking: Factual, Analytical, Creative, and Practical Questions

1. Based on the discussion of reading in this chapter, what is a practical suggestion you could recommend that might make reading easier for someone who is having difficulty reading?

2. Why are researchers interested in the number of color words used by different cultures?

3. Describe the five basic kinds of speech acts proposed by Searle.

4. How should cognitive psychologists interpret evidence of linguistic universals when considering the linguistic-relativity hypothesis?

5. Compare and contrast the kinds of understandings that can be gained by studying speech errors made by normal people with those that can be gained by studying the language produced by people who have particular brain lesions.

6. Write an example of a pidgin conversation between two people and a creole conversation, focusing on the differences between pidgins and creoles.

7. Draft an example of a brief dialogue between a male and a female in which each may misunderstand the other, based on their differing beliefs regarding the goals of communication.

8. Suppose that you are an instructor of English as a second language. What kinds of things will you want to know about your students to determine how much to emphasize phonology, vocabulary, syntax, or pragmatics in your instruction?

9. Give an example of a humorous violation of one of Grice's four maxims of successful conversation.

Key Terms

aphasia
bilinguals
comprehension processes
cooperative principle
dialect
dual-system hypothesis
dyslexia

indirect requests
lexical access
lexical processes
linguistic relativity
linguistic universals
metaphors
monolinguals

pragmatics
similes
single-system hypothesis
slips of the tongue
speech acts
word-superiority effect

Explore CogLab by going to http://coglab.wadsworth.com. Answer the questions required by your instructor from the student manual that accompanies CogLab.

Word Superiority

Annotated Suggested Reading

Tomasello, M. (1999). *The cultural origins of human cognition*. Cambridge, MA: Harvard University Press. This book discusses the role of culture in the evolution of human cognition, with special emphasis on language.

Problem Solving and Creativity

EXPLORING COGNITIVE PSYCHOLOGY

1. What are some key steps involved in solving problems?

2. What are the differences between problems that have a clear path to a solution versus problems that do not?

3. What are some of the obstacles and aids to problem solving?

4. How does expertise affect problem solving?

5. What is creativity, and how can it be fostered?

How do you solve problems that arise in your relationships with other people? How do you solve the "two-string" problem illustrated in Figure 11.1? How does anyone solve any problem for that matter? This chapter considers the process of solving problems, as well as some of the hindrances and aids to **problem solving,** an effort to overcome obstacles obstructing the path to a solution (Reed, 2000). At the conclusion of this chapter, we discuss creativity and its role in problem solving. Throughout the whole chapter, we discuss how people make the "mental leaps" that lead them from having a set of givens to having a solution to a problem (Holyoak & Thagard, 1995).

FIGURE 11.1

Imagine that you are the person standing in the middle of this room, in which two strings are hanging down from the ceiling. Your goal is to tie together the two strings, but neither string is long enough so that you can reach out and grab the other string while holding either of the two strings. You have available a few clean paintbrushes, a can of paint, and a heavy canvas tarpaulin. How will you tie together the two strings? From Richard E. Meyer, "The Search for Insight: Grappling with Gestalt Psychology's Unanswered Questions," in The Nature of Insight, edited by R. J. Sternberg and J. E. Davidson. © 1995 MIT Press. Reprinted with permission from MIT Press.

The focus of this chapter is on individual problem solving. It is worth remembering, however, that working in groups often facilitates problem solving. The solutions reached by groups often are better than those reached by individuals (Williams & Sternberg, 1988). Therefore, we can ease our burden in problem solving not just by improving our problem-solving skills. We also can facilitate our problem-solving efforts by working with others who will bring their skills to bear on the problems we face.

The Problem-Solving Cycle

We engage in problem solving when we need to overcome obstacles to answer a question or to achieve a goal. If we quickly can retrieve an answer from memory, we do not have a problem. If we cannot retrieve an immediate answer, then we have a problem to be solved. This section describes the steps of the **problem-solving cycle,** which include problem identification, problem definition, strategy formulation, organization of information, allocation of resources, monitoring, and evaluation (shown in Figure 11.2; see Bransford & Stein, 1993; Hayes, 1989; Pretz, Naples, & Sternberg, 2003; Sternberg, 1986).

FIGURE 11.2

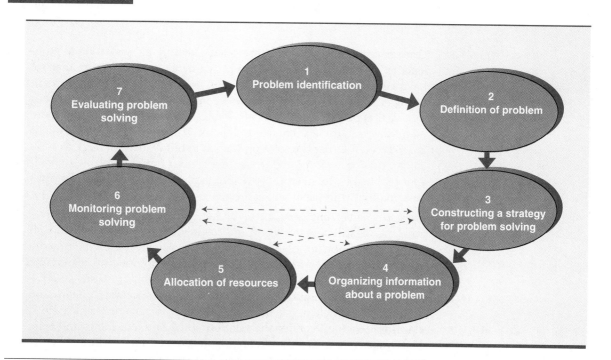

The steps of the problem-solving cycle include problem identification, problem definition, strategy formulation, organization of information, allocation of resources, monitoring, and evaluation.

In considering the steps, remember also the importance of flexibility in following the various steps of the cycle. Successful problem solving may involve occasionally tolerating some ambiguity regarding how best to proceed. Rarely can we solve problems by following any one optimal sequence of problem-solving steps. Moreover, we may go back and forth through the steps. We can change their order as need be, or even skip or add steps when it seems appropriate. How people solve problems depends partly on how they understand them (Whitten & Graesser, 2003). Consider an example of how understanding matters.

People are told the following about a drug (Stanovich, 2003; Stanovich & West, 1998):

150 people received the drug and were not cured.

150 people received the drug and were cured.

75 people did not receive the drug and were not cured.

300 people did not receive the drug and were cured.

Will they understand exactly what they were told? Many people believe that the drug in this instance was helpful. In fact, the drug described is not helpful at all. On the contrary, it is harmful. Only 50% of the people who received the drug were cured (i.e., 150 of 300). In contrast, 80% of the people who did not receive the drug were cured (300 of 375).

We also need to remember that our emotions can influence the ways in which we implement the problem-solving cycle (Schwarz & Skurnik, 2003). Motivation also greatly affects how we solve problems and whether we ever complete them (Zimmerman & Campillo, 2003).

1. *Problem identification:* As odd as it sounds, identifying a situation as problematic is sometimes a difficult step. We may fail to recognize that we have a goal. For example, we might need to stay out of the path of an oncoming car we fail to observe. Or we might fail to recognize that our path to a goal is obstructed. An example would be needing to obtain more money because we lack enough to buy something we want. Or we might fail to recognize that the solution we had in mind does not work. For example, the job we expected to get might not now be available to us. If your problem is the need to write a term paper, you must first identify a question that your paper will address.

2. *Problem definition and representation:* Once we identify the existence of a problem, we still have to define and represent the problem well enough to understand how to solve it. Consider, for example, preparing to write your term paper. You must define your topic well enough to determine the research you will gather and your overall strategy for writing your paper. The problem-definition step is crucial. If you inaccurately define and represent the problem, you are much less able to solve it (Funke, 1991; Hegarty, 1991). In fact, for the solution of the problem shown in Figure 11.1, this step is crucial to your finding the answer. That is, in solving the two-string problem, are you constraining your answer in ways that are limiting your ability to solve the problem?

"Relax, honey. Change is good."

Sometimes we don't recognize an important problem that confronts us. © *The New Yorker Collection 1993 Robert Mankoff from cartoonbank.com. All right reserved.*

3. *Strategy formulation:* Once the problem has been defined effectively, the next step is to plan a strategy for solving it. The strategy may involve **analysis**—breaking down the whole of a complex problem into manageable elements. Instead, or perhaps in addition, it may involve the complementary process of **synthesis**—putting together various elements to arrange them into something useful. In writing your term paper, you must analyze the components of your topic, research the various components, and then synthesize the topics into a rough draft of your paper. As in most dichotomies, one must be careful of drawing too much of a distinction (Kotovsky, 2003). People use analysis to help in synthesizing information. They also may use synthesis to help in analysis.

Another pair of complementary strategies involves divergent and convergent thinking. In **divergent thinking,** you try to generate a diverse assortment of possible alternative solutions to a problem. Once you have considered a variety of possibilities, however, you must engage in **convergent thinking** to narrow down the multiple possibilities to converge on a single best answer. Sometimes, you merely find what you believe to be the most likely solution, which you will try first. When you came up with the topic for your paper, you first used divergent thinking to generate many possible topics. You then used convergent thinking to select the most suitable topic that interested you. In solving real-life problems, you may need both analysis and synthesis and both divergent and convergent thinking. There is no single ideal strategy for addressing every problem. Instead, the optimal strategy depends on both the problem and the problem solvers' personal preferences in problem-solving methods.

4. *Organization of information:* In this stage, you try to integrate all of the information that you believe you will need to effectively do the task at hand. It might involve collecting references or even collecting your own ideas. This stage is critical to good problem solving. Sometimes, people fail to solve a problem not because they cannot solve it, but because they do not realize what information they have or how it fits together. Once a strategy (at least a tentative strategy) has been formulated, you are ready to organize the available information in a way that enables you to implement the strategy. Of course, throughout the problem-solving cycle you constantly are organizing and reorganizing the available information. At this step, however, you organize the information strategically, finding a representation that best enables you to implement your strategy. For example, if your problem is to organize the information for your term paper, you may use an outline to organize your ideas. If your problem is to find a location, you may need to organize and represent the available information in the form of a map. If your problem is to earn a particular amount of money by a particular date, you may represent the available information in the form of a timetable for intervening dates by which you must have earned a particular portion of the total amount.

5. *Resource allocation:* In addition to our other problems, most of us face the problem of having limited resources. These resources include time, money, equipment, and space. Some problems are worth a lot of time and other resources. Others are worth very few resources. Moreover, we need to know when to allocate which resources. Studies show that expert problem solvers (and better students) tend to devote more of their mental resources to global (big-picture) planning than do novice problem solvers. Novices (and poorer students) tend to allocate more time to local (detail-oriented) planning than do experts (Larkin & associates, 1980; Sternberg, 1981). For example, better students are more likely than poorer students to spend more time in the initial phase, deciding how to solve a problem, and less time actually solving it (Bloom & Broder, 1950). By spending more time in advance deciding what to do, effective students are less likely to fall prey to false starts, winding paths, and all kinds of errors. When a person allocates more mental resources to planning on a large scale, he or she is able to save time and energy and to avoid frustration later on. Thus, when writing your term paper, you probably will spend much of your time conducting your research, organizing your notes, and planning your paper.

6. *Monitoring:* A prudent expenditure of time includes monitoring the process of solving the problem. Effective problem solvers do not set out

on a path to a solution and then wait until they have reached the end of the path to check where they are (Schoenfeld, 1981). Rather, they check up on themselves all along the way to make sure that they are getting closer to their goal. If they are not, they reassess what they are doing. They may conclude that they made a false start, that they got off track somewhere along the way, or even that they see a more promising path if they take a new direction. If you are writing a term paper, you will want to be monitoring whether you are making good progress. If you are not making good progress, you will want to figure out why.

7. *Evaluation:* Just as you need to monitor a problem while you are in the process of solving it, you need to evaluate your solution after you have finished. Some of the evaluation may occur right away. The rest may occur a bit later or even much later. For example, after drafting your term paper, you probably will evaluate your draft. You will want to revise and edit it quite a few times before turning in your paper. Often key advances occur through the evaluation process. Through evaluation, new problems may be recognized. Moreover, the problem may be redefined, and new strategies may come to light. New resources may also become available, or existing ones may be used more efficiently. Hence, the cycle is completed when it leads to new insights and begins anew.

Types of Problems

Problems can be categorized according to whether they have clear paths to a solution (Davidson & Sternberg, 2003). **Well-structured problems** have clear solution paths to solutions. These problems also are termed *well-defined problems*. An example would be "How do you find the area of a parallelogram?" **Ill-structured problems** lack clear paths to solutions. These problems are also termed *ill-defined problems*. An example would be "How do you tie together two suspended strings, when neither string is long enough to allow you to reach the other string while holding either of the strings?" Of course, in the real world of problems, these two categories may represent a continuum of clarity in problem solving rather than two discrete classes with a clear boundary between the two. Nonetheless, the categories are useful in understanding how people solve problems. We next consider each of these kinds of problems in turn.

Well-Structured Problems

On tests in school, your teachers have asked you to tackle countless well-structured problems in specific content areas (e.g., math, history, geography). These problems had clear paths—if not necessarily easy paths—to their solutions. In psychological research, cognitive psychologists might ask you to solve less content-specific kinds of well-structured problems. For example, cognitive psychologists often have studied a particular type of well-structured problem: the class of *move problems*, so termed because such problems require a series of moves to reach a final goal state. Perhaps the most well known of the move problems is one involving two antagonistic parties, whom we call "hobbits" and "orcs" in the "Investigating Cognitive Psychology" box.

<table>
<tr>
<td>

INVESTIGATING COGNITIVE PSYCHOLOGY

</td>
<td>

Three hobbits and three orcs are on a river bank. The hobbits and orcs need to cross over to the other side of the river. They have for this purpose a small rowboat that will hold just two people. There is one problem, however. If the number of orcs on either river bank exceeds the number of hobbits on that bank, the orcs will eat the hobbits on that bank. How can all six creatures get across to the other side of the river in a way that guarantees that they all arrive there with the forest intact? Try to solve the problem before reading on.

The solution to the problem is shown in Figure 11.3. The solution contains several features worth noting. First, the problem can be solved in a minimum of eleven steps, including the first and last steps. Second, the solution is essentially *linear* in nature. There is just one valid move (connecting two points with a line segment) at most steps of problem solution. At all but two steps along the solution path, only one error can be made without violating the rules of the move problem: to go directly backward in the solution. At two steps, there are two possible forward-moving responses. But both of these lead toward the correct answer. Thus, again, the most likely error is to return to a previous state in the solution of the problem.

</td>
</tr>
</table>

A second kind of error is to make an illegal move. That is, a move that is not permitted according to the terms of the problem. For example, a move that resulted in having more than two individuals in the boat would be illegal. According to those who have studied the problem, there are three main kinds of errors that people seem to make (Greeno, 1974; Simon & Reed, 1976; Thomas, 1974). They are (1) inadvertently moving backward, (2) making illegal moves, and (3) not realizing the nature of the next legal move.

One method for studying how to solve well-defined problems is to develop computer simulations. Here, the researcher's task is to create a computer program that can solve these problems. By developing the instructions a computer must execute to solve problems, the researcher may better understand how humans solve similar kinds of problems. According to one model of problem solving (Newell & Simon, 1972), the problem solver (which may be using human or artificial intelligence) must view the initial problem state and the goal state within a problem space (Wenke & Frensch, 2003). A **problem space** is the universe of all possible actions that can be applied to solving a problem, given any constraints that apply to the solution of the problem. According to this model, the fundamental strategy for solving problems is to decompose the problem task into a series of steps. These steps eventually will lead to the solution of the problem at hand. Each step involves a set of rules for procedures ("operations") that can be implemented. The set of rules is organized hierarchically into programs containing various internal levels of subprograms (called "routines" and "subroutines").

FIGURE 11.3

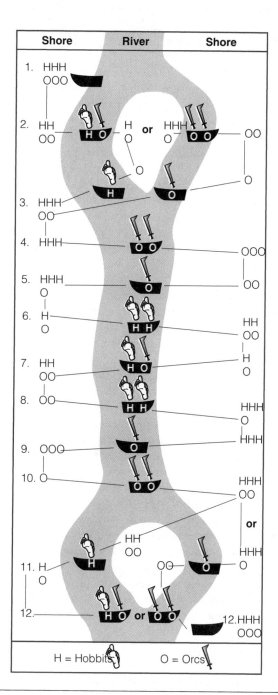

(Refer to the box for an explanation of the solution.) What can you learn about your own methods of solving problems by seeing how you approached this particular problem? From In Search of the Human Mind by Robert J. Sternberg, copyright © 1995 by Harcourt Brace & Company, reproduced by permission of the publisher.

Many of the sublevel programs are **algorithms,** sequences of operations that may be repeated over and over again and that, in theory, guarantee the solution to a problem (Hunt, 1975; Sternberg, 2000). Generally, an algorithm continues until it satisfies a condition determined by a program. Suppose a computer is provided with a well-defined problem and an appropriate hierarchy (program) of operations organized into procedural algorithms. The computer can readily calculate all possible operations and combinations of operations within the problem space. It also can determine the best possible sequence of steps to take to solve the problem.

Unlike computers, however, the human mind does not specialize in high-speed computations of numerous possible combinations. The limits of our working memory prohibit us from considering more than just a few possible operations at one time (Hambrick & Engle, 2003; Kintsch & associates, 1999). Newell and Simon recognized these limits and observed that humans must use mental shortcuts for solving problems. These mental shortcuts are termed **heuristics**—informal, intuitive, speculative strategies that sometimes lead to an effective solution and sometimes do not (Fischhoff, 1999; Holyoak, 1990; Korf, 1999; Stanovich, 2003; Sternberg, 2000). Suppose we store in long-term memory several simple heuristics that we can apply to a variety of problems. We thereby can lessen the burden on our limited-capacity working memory.

Newell and Simon observed that when problem solvers were confronted with a problem for which they could not immediately see an answer, effective problem solvers used the heuristic of means–ends analysis. In this strategy, the problem solver continually compares the current state and the goal state and takes steps to minimize the differences between the two states. Various other problem-solving heuristics include *working forward, working backward,* and *generate and test.* Table 11.1 illustrates how a problem solver might apply these heuristics to the aforementioned move problem (Greeno & Simon, 1988) and to a more common everyday problem (Hunt, 1994). Figure 11.4 shows a rudimentary problem space for the move problem. It illustrates that there may be any number of possible strategies for solving it.

You enter a bookstore seeking out a certain book, Hortense Hortigan's *Make a Million in a Month.* You are not sure where in the bookstore, if anywhere, you can find the book. What would be an algorithm for solving this problem? How about a heuristic?

The only algorithm that guarantees your discovering whether the book is in the bookstore is to check each book in the store. Eventually, you will either have found Hortigan's book or searched unsuccessfully through all titles. There are many possible heuristics you could apply, however. One is to ask a clerk for help. A second is to look through an index of books in the store, if one is available. A third is to start your search in more plausible sections (financial or self-help), only then moving to less plausible sections; and so on. Notice, however, that if you use the heuristics and do not find the book, you cannot be certain the book is not there. For example, it may be misplaced or not yet in the index.

Isomorphic Problems

Sometimes, two problems are **isomorphic;** that is, their formal structure is the same, and only their content differs. Sometimes, as in the case of the hobbits and orcs problem and a similar missionaries and cannibals problem, in which cannibals eat missionaries when they outnumber them, the isomorphism is obvious. Similarly, you can

		EXAMPLE OF HEURISTIC APPLIED TO THE MOVE PROBLEM (GREENO & SIMON, 1988)	**EXAMPLE OF HEURISTIC APPLIED TO AN EVERYDAY PROBLEM: HOW TO TRAVEL BY AIR FROM YOUR HOME TO ANOTHER LOCATION USING THE MOST DIRECT ROUTE POSSIBLE (HUNT, 1994)**
HEURISTIC	**DEFINITION OF HEURISTIC**		
Means–ends analysis	The problem-solver analyzes the problem by viewing the end—the goal being sought—and then tries to decrease the distance between the current position in the problem space and the end goal in that space.	Try to get as many people on the far bank and as few people on the near bank as possible.	Try to minimize the distance between home and the destination.
Working forward	The problem-solver starts at the beginning and tries to solve the problem from the start to the finish.	Evaluate the situation carefully with the six people on one bank and then try to move them step by step to the opposite bank.	Find the possible air routes leading from home toward the destination, and take the routes that seem most directly to lead to the destination.
Working backward	The problem-solver starts at the end and tries to work backward from there.	Start with the final state—having all hobbits and all orcs on the far bank—and try to work back to the beginning state.	Find the possible air routes that reach the destination, and work backward to trace which of these routes can be most directly traced to originate at home.
Generate and test	The problem-solver simply generates alternative courses of action, not necessarily in a systematic way, and then notices in turn whether each course of action will work.	This method works fairly well for the move problem because at most steps in the process, there is only one allowable forward move, and there are never more than two possibilities, both of which eventually will lead to the solution.	Find the various possible alternative routes leading from home, then see which of these routes might be used to end up at the destination. Choose the most direct route. Unfortunately, given the number of possible combinations of routes for air travel, this heuristic may not be very helpful.

TABLE 11.1   Four Heuristics

These four heuristics may be used in solving the move problem illustrated in Figures 11.3 and 11.4.

readily detect the isomorphism of many games that involve constructing words from jumbled or scrambled letters. Figure 11.5 also shows a different set of isomorphic problems. The problems illustrate some of the puzzles associated with isomorphic problems.

It often is extremely difficult to observe the underlying structural isomorphism of problems (Reed, 1987; Reed, Dempster, & Ettinger, 1985). It is also difficult to be

FIGURE 11.4

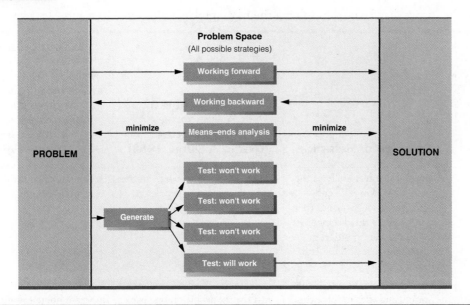

A problem space contains all of the possible strategies leading from the initial problem state to the solution (the goal state). This problem space, for example, shows four of the heuristics that might be used in solving the move problem illustrated in Figure 11.3. From In Search of the Human Mind by Robert J. Sternberg, copyright © 1995 by Harcourt Brace & Company, reproduced by permission of the publisher.

able to apply problem-solving strategies from one problem to another. For example, it may not be clear how an example from a textbook applies to another problem (e.g., one on a test). Problem solvers are particularly unlikely to detect isomorphisms when two problems are similar but not identical in structure. Further, when the content or the surface characteristics of the problems differ sharply, detecting the isomorphism of the structure of problems is harder. For example, school-aged children may find it difficult to see the structural similarity between various word problems that are framed within different story situations. Similarly, physics students may have difficulty seeing the structural similarities among various physics problems when different kinds of materials are used. The problem of recognizing isomorphisms across varying contexts returns us to the recurring difficulties in problem representation.

Problems of Problem Representation

What is the key reason that some problems are easier to solve than their isomorphisms? Consider the various versions of a problem known as the Tower of Hanoi. In this problem, the problem solver must use a series of moves to transfer a set of rings (usually three) from the first of three pegs to the third of the three pegs, using as few moves as possible (Figure 11.6). Researchers presented this same basic problem in many different isomorphic forms (Kotovsky, Hayes, & Simon, 1985). They found that

FIGURE 11.5

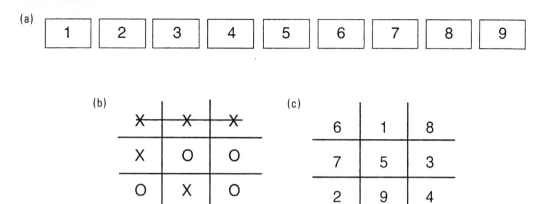

Compare the problems illustrated in the games of (a) number scrabble, (b) tic-tac-toe, and (c) magic square. Number scrabble is based on equations. Which triples of numbers satisfy the equation X + Y + Z = 15? Tic-tac-toe requires one to produce three X's or three O's in a row, column, or diagonal. The magic square requires one to place numbers in the tic-tac-toe board so that every row, column, and major diagonal adds to 15. In what ways are these problems isomorphic? How do their differences in presentation affect the ease of representing and solving these problems?

some forms of the problem took up to 16 times as long to solve as other forms. Although many factors influenced these findings, a major determinant of the relative ease of solving the problem was how the problem was represented. For example, in the form shown in Figure 11.6, the physically different sizes of the discs facilitated the mental representation of the restriction against moving larger discs onto smaller discs. Other forms of the problem did not.

Problems such as the Tower of Hanoi challenge problem-solving skills, in part through their demands on working memory. Researchers had experimental participants do what they called the "Tower of London" task, which was very similar to the Tower of Hanoi (Welsh, Satterlee-Cartmell, & Stine, 1999). In this task, the goal was to move a set of colored balls across different-sized pegs in order to match a target configuration. As in the Tower of Hanoi, there were constraints on which balls could be moved at a given time. They also gave participants two tests of working-memory capacity. They found that the measures of working-memory capacity accounted for between 25% and 36% of the variance in how successful participants were in solving the problem. Interestingly, mental-processing speed, sometimes touted as a key to intelligence (see Chapter 13) showed no correlation with success in solution.

Recall the two-string problem, posed at the outset of this chapter. The solution to the "two-string problem" is shown in Figure 11.7. As this figure shows, the two-string problem can be solved. However, many people find it extremely difficult to arrive at the solution. Many never do, no matter how hard they try. People who find the problem insoluble often err at Step 2 of the problem-solving cycle, after which

FIGURE 11.6

There are three discs of unequal sizes, positioned on the leftmost of three pegs so that the largest disc is at the bottom, the middle-sized disc is in the middle, and the smallest disc is on the top. Your task is to transfer all three discs to the rightmost peg, using the middle peg as a stationing area, as needed. You may move only one disc at a time, and you may never move a larger disc on top of a smaller disc. From Intelligence Applied: Understanding and Increasing Your Intellectual Skills by Robert J. Sternberg, copyright © 1986 by Harcourt Brace & Company, reproduced by permission of the publisher.

they never recover. That is, by defining the problem as being one in which they must be able to move toward one string while holding another, they impose on themselves a constraint that makes the problem virtually insoluble. Unfortunately, all of us are subject to misdefining problems from time to time, as the case of the two-string problem shows.

Ill-Structured Problems and the Role of Insight

The two-string problem is an example of an ill-structured problem. In fact, although we occasionally may misrepresent well-structured problems, we are much more likely to have difficulty representing ill-structured problems. Before we explain the nature of ill-structured problems, try to solve a couple more such problems. The following problems illustrate some of the difficulties created by the representation of ill-structured problems (after Sternberg, 1986a). Be sure to try all three problems before you read about their solutions.

1. Haughty Harry and several other job seekers were looking for work as carpenters. The site supervisor handed each applicant two sticks (a 1" × 2" × 60" stick and a 1" × 2" × 43" stick) and a 2" C-clamp. This situation is represented in Figure 11.8. The opening of the clamp is wide enough so that both sticks can be inserted and held together securely when the clamp is tightened. The supervisor ushered the job applicants into a room 12'3" × 13'5", with an 8' ceiling. Mounted on the ceiling were two 1' × 1' beams, dividing the ceiling into thirds lengthwise. She told

FIGURE 11.7

Many people assume that they must find a way to move themselves toward each string and then bring the two strings together. They fail to consider the possibility of finding a way to get one of the strings to move toward them, such as by tying something to one of the strings, then swinging the object as a pendulum, and grabbing the object when it swings close to the other string. There is nothing in the problem that suggests that the person must move, rather than that the string may move. Nevertheless, most people presuppose that the constraint exists. By placing an unnecessary and unwarranted constraint on themselves, people make the problem insoluble. From Richard E. Mayer, "The Search for Insight: Grappling with Gestalt Psychology's Unanswered Questions," in The Nature of Insight, edited by R. J. Sternberg and J. E. Davidson. Copyright © 1995 by MIT Press. Reprinted by permission.

the applicants that she would hire the first applicant who could build a hat rack capable of supporting her hard hat, using just the two sticks and the C-clamp. She could hire only one person. So she recommended that the applicants not try to help one another. What should Harry do?

2. A woman who lived in a small town married twenty different men in that same town. All of them are still living, and she never divorced any of them. Yet she broke no laws. How could she do this?

3. You have loose black and brown socks in a drawer, mixed in a ratio of five black socks for every brown one. How many socks do you have to take out of that drawer to be assured of having a pair of the same color?

Both the two-string problem and each of the three preceding problems are ill-structured problems. There are no clear, readily available paths to solution. By definition, ill-structured problems do not have well-defined problem spaces. Problem solvers

FIGURE 11.8

Using just the materials shown here, how can you construct a hat rack in the room shown in this figure? From Richard E. Meyer, "The Search for Insight: Grappling with Gestalt Psychology's Unanswered Questions," in The Nature of Insight, edited by R. J. Sternberg and J. E. Davidson. © 1995 MIT Press. Reprinted with permission from MIT Press.

have difficulty constructing appropriate mental representations for modeling these problems and their solutions. For such problems, much of the difficulty is in constructing a plan for sequentially following a series of steps that inch ever closer to their solution. These three particular ill-structured problems are termed *insight problems*. To solve each problem you need to see the problem in a novel way. In particular, you need to see it differently from how you would probably see the problem at first, and differently from how you would probably solve problems in general. That is, you must restructure your representation of the problem to solve it.

Insight is a distinctive and sometimes seemingly sudden understanding of a problem or of a strategy that aids in solving the problem. Often, an insight involves reconceptualizing a problem or a strategy for its solution in a totally new way. Insight often involves detecting and combining relevant old and new information to gain a novel view of the problem or of its solution. Although insights may feel as though they are sudden, they are often the result of much prior thought and hard work. Without this work, the insight would never have occurred. Insight can be involved in solving well-structured problems. But it more often is associated with the rocky and twisting path to solution that characterizes ill-structured problems. For many years, psychologists interested in problem solving have been trying to figure out the true nature of insight.

To understand some of the alternative views on insightful problem solving, you may find it useful knowing the solutions to the preceding insight problems. Consider first the hat-rack problem. Harry was unable to solve the problem before Sally quickly whipped together a hat rack like the one shown in Figure 11.9. To solve the problem,

FIGURE 11.9

Were you able to modify your definition of the materials available in a way that helped you solve the problem? From Intelligence Applied: Understanding and Increasing Your Intellectual Skills by Robert J. Sternberg, copyright © 1986 by Harcourt Brace & Company, reproduced by permission of the publisher.

Sally had to redefine her view of the materials in a way that allowed her to conceive of a C-clamp as a hat holder.

The woman who was involved in multiple marriages is a minister. The critical element for solving this problem is to recognize that the word "married" may be used to describe the performance of the marriage ceremony. So the minister married the twenty men but did not herself become wedded to any of them. To solve this problem, you had to redefine your interpretation of the term *married*. Others have suggested yet additional possibilities. For example, perhaps the woman was an actress and only married the men in her role as an actress. Or perhaps the woman's multiple marriages were annulled so she never technically divorced any of the men.

As for the socks, you need only to take out three socks to be assured of having a pair of the same color. The ratio information is irrelevant. Whether the first two socks you withdraw match in color, the third certainly will match at least one of the first two.

Early Gestaltist Views

Gestalt psychologists emphasized the importance of the whole as more than a collection of parts. In regard to problem solving, Gestalt psychologists held that insight problems require problem solvers to perceive the problem as a whole. Gestalt psychologist Max Wertheimer (1945/1959) wrote about **productive thinking,** which involves insights that go beyond the bounds of existing associations. He distinguished it from *reproductive thinking*, which is based on existing associations involving what is already known. According to Wertheimer, insightful (productive) thinking differs fundamentally from reproductive thinking. In solving the insight problems given in this chapter, you had to break away from your existing associations and see each problem in an entirely new light. Productive thinking also can be applied to well-structured problems.

Wertheimer's colleague Wolfgang Köhler (1927) studied insight in nonhuman primates, particularly a caged chimpanzee named Sultan (Figure 11.10). In Köhler's view, the ape's behavior illustrated insight. To Köhler and other Gestaltists, insight is a special process. It involves thinking that differs from normal, linear information processing.

Gestalt psychologists described examples of insight. They speculated on a few ways in which the special process of insight might occur: It might result from (1) extended unconscious leaps in thinking, (2) greatly accelerated mental processing, or (3) some kind of short-circuiting of normal reasoning processes (Perkins, 1981). Unfortunately, the early Gestaltists did not provide convincing evidence for any of these mechanisms. Nor did they specify exactly what insight is. Therefore, we need to consider alternative views as well.

The Nothing-Special View

According to the nothing-special view, insight is merely an extension of ordinary perceiving, recognizing, learning, and conceiving (Langley & associates, 1987; Perkins, 1981; Weisberg, 1986, 1995). They suggested that Gestalt psychologists failed to pin down insight because there is no special thinking process called "insight." Additionally, sometimes people seem to have solved so-called insight problems without expe-

FIGURE 11.10

In the study depicted here, Gestalt psychologist Wolfgang Köhler placed an ape in an enclosure with a few boxes. At the top of the cage, just out of reach, was a bunch of bananas. After the ape unsuccessfully tried to jump and to stretch to reach the bananas, the ape showed sudden insight: The ape realized that the boxes could be stacked on top of one another to make a structure tall enough to reach the bunch of bananas.

riencing any sudden mental restructuring of the problem. At other times, people seem to show sudden mental restructuring of so-called routine problems (Weisberg, 1995). Insights are merely significant products of ordinary thinking processes.

The Neo-Gestaltist View

Some researchers have found that insightful problem solving can be distinguished from noninsightful problem solving in two ways (Metcalfe, 1986; Metcalfe & Wiebe, 1987). For one thing, when given routine problems to solve, problem solvers show remarkable accuracy in their ability to predict their own success in solving a problem prior to any attempt to solve it. In contrast, when given insight problems, problem solvers show poor ability to predict their own success prior to trying to solve the problems. Not only were successful problem solvers pessimistic about their ability to solve insight problems but unsuccessful problem solvers were often optimistic about their ability to solve them.

In addition, the investigators used a clever methodology to observe the problem-solving process while participants were solving routine versus insight problems. At 15-second intervals, participants paused briefly to rate how close ("warm") versus far ("cold") they felt they were to reaching a solution. Consider first what happened for routine problems, such as algebra, Tower of Hanoi, and deductive reasoning problems. Participants showed incremental increases in their feelings of warmth as they drew closer to reaching a correct solution. For insight problems, however, participants showed no such incremental increases. Figure 11.11 shows a comparison of participants' reported feelings of warmth for solving algebra problems versus insight problems. In solving insight problems, participants showed no increasing feelings of warmth until moments before abruptly realizing the solution and correctly solving the problem. Metcalfe's findings certainly seem to support the Gestaltist view that there is something special about insightful problem solving, as distinct from noninsightful, routine problem solving. The specific nature and underlying mechanisms of insightful problem solving have yet to be addressed by this research, however.

The Three-Process View

Yet another view of insight has focused specifically on the possible mechanisms for insightful problem solving (Davidson, 1995, 2003; Davidson & Sternberg, 1984). According to this view, insights are of three kinds. The three kinds correspond to three different processes: selective encoding, selective comparison, and selective combination. These processes may be used either with insight or with little insight.

Selective-encoding insights involve distinguishing relevant from irrelevant information. Recall from earlier chapters that encoding involves representing information in memory. All of us have available much more information than we possibly can handle. Thus, each of us must select the information that is important for our purposes. At the same time, we must filter out the unimportant or irrelevant information. Selective encoding is the process by which this filtering is done. For example, when you are taking notes during a lecture, you must selectively encode which points are crucial. You need to identify which points are supportive and explanatory, and which are not necessary.

Selective-comparison insights involve novel perceptions of how new information relates to old information. The creative use of analogies is a form of selective comparison. When solving important problems, we almost always need to call on our

FIGURE 11.11

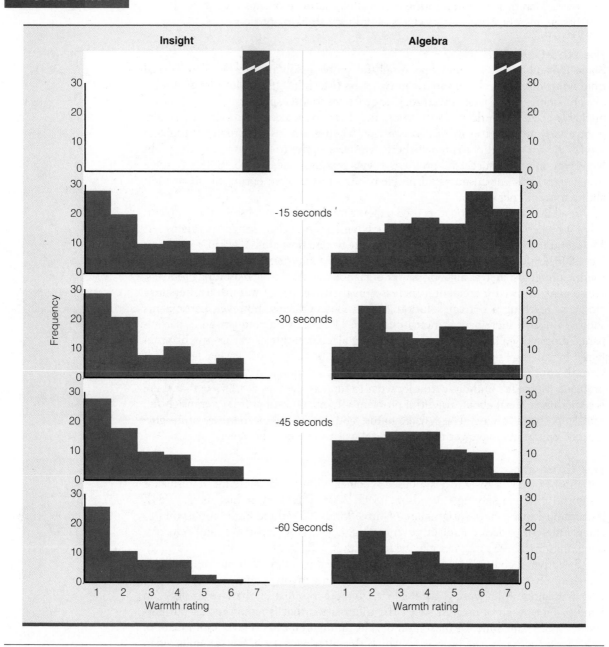

When Janet Metcalfe presented participants with routine problems and insight problems, they showed clear differences in their feelings of warmth as they approached a solution to the problems. These frequency histograms (bar graphs in which the area of each bar indicates the frequency for the given interval of time) show comparative feelings of warmth during the four 15-second intervals prior to solving the problems. When solving insight problems, participants showed no incremental increases in feelings of warmth, whereas when solving routine problems, participants showed distinct incremental increases in feelings of warmth. Routine problems included algebra problems such as "$(3 \times^2 + 2 \times + 10)(3 \times) = $." Insight problems included problems such as "A prisoner was attempting escape from a tower. He found in his cell a rope which was half long enough to permit him to reach the ground safely. He divided the rope in half and tied the two parts together and escaped. How could he have done this?" (From Metcalfe & Wiebe, 1987, pp. 242, 245.)

existing knowledge. We then need to compare that information with our new knowledge of the current problem. Insights of selective comparison are the basis for this relating. For example, suppose that you must master a whole list of new terms for your cognitive psychology class. For some of the terms, you may be able to compare the new terms with synonymous words that you already know. For others, you may be able to expand on and elaborate words you already know to define the new terms.

Selective-combination insights involve taking selectively encoded and compared snippets of relevant information and combining that information in a novel, productive way. Often, for us just to identify analytically the important information for solving a problem is not enough. We also must figure out how to synthesize the information. For example, to solve either the hat-rack problem or the two-string problem, you had to find a way to put together the available materials in a novel way. To write a term paper, you must synthesize your research notes in a way that addresses the central question in your paper.

Additional Insights into Insight

There is yet another view of routine versus insightful problem solving (Smith, 1995). One can distinguish between the insight experience and insight. An insight experience is a special process involving an abrupt mental restructuring. Insight is an understanding that may involve either the special insight experience or normal cognitive processes that occur incrementally, rather than suddenly. Thus, routine problems may demand insight. But they may not require the insight experience. Insight problems, however, require the insight experience. According to Smith, therefore, insights need not be sudden "ah-ha" experiences. They may and often do occur gradually and incrementally over time.

Unfortunately, insights—like many other aspects of human thinking—can be both startlingly brilliant and dead wrong. How do we fall into mental traps that lead us down false paths as we try to reach solutions?

Obstacles and Aids to Problem Solving

Several factors can hinder problem solving.

Mental Sets, Entrenchment, and Fixation

One factor that can hinder problem solving is **mental set**—a frame of mind involving an existing model for representing a problem, a problem context, or a procedure for problem solving. Another term for mental set is *entrenchment*. When problem solvers have an entrenched mental set, they fixate on a strategy that normally works well in solving many problems but that does not work well in solving this particular problem. For example, in the two-string problem, you may fixate on strategies that involve moving yourself toward the string, rather than moving the string toward you. In the oft-marrying minister problem, you may fixate on the notion that to marry someone is to become wedded to the person.

Mental sets also can influence the solution of rather routine problems. For example, consider "water-jar" problems (Luchins, 1942). In water-jar problems, participants are asked how to measure out a certain amount of water using three different jars. Each jar holds a different amount of water. Table 11.2 shows the problems used by Luchins.

If you are like many people solving these problems, you will have found a formula that works for all of the remaining problems. You fill up Jar B. Then you pour out of it the amount of water you can put into Jar A. Then you twice pour out of it the amount of water you can put into Jar C. The formula, therefore, is $B - A - 2C$. However, Problems 7 through 11 can be solved in a much simpler way. One need use just two of the jars. For example, Problem 7 can be solved by $A - C$. Problem 8 can be solved by $A + C$, and so on. People who are given Problems 1 through 6 to solve generally continue to use the $B - A - 2C$ formula in solving Problems 7 through 11. Consider, in Luchins's original experiment, those participants who solved the first set of problems. Between 64% and 83% of them went on to solve the last set of problems by using the less simple strategy. What happened to the control participants, who were not given the first set of problems? Only 1% to 5% failed to apply the simpler solutions to the last set of problems. They had no established mental set that interfered with their seeing things in a new and simpler way.

Another type of mental set involves fixation on a particular use (function) for an object. Specifically, **functional fixedness** is the inability to realize that something known to have a particular use may also be used for performing other functions. Functional fixedness prevents us from solving new problems by using old tools in novel ways. Becoming free of functional fixedness is what first allowed people to use a reshaped coat

---

TABLE 11.2	Luchins's Water-Jar Problems

How do you measure out the right amount of water using Jars A, B, and C? You need to use up to three jars to obtain the required amounts of water (measured in numbers of cups) in the last column. Columns A, B, and C show the capacity of each jar. The first problem, for example, requires you to get 20 cups of water from just two of the jars, a 29-cup one (Jar A) and a 3-cup one (Jar B). Easy: Just fill Jar A, and then empty out 9 cups from this jar by taking out 3 cups three times, using Jar B. Problem 2 isn't too hard, either. Fill Jar B with 127 cups, then empty out 21 cups using Jar A, and then empty out 6 cups, using Jar C twice. Now try the rest of the problems yourself. (After Luchins, 1942)

	JARS AVAILABLE FOR USE			REQUIRED AMOUNT
PROBLEM NUMBER	A	B	C	(CUPS)
1	29	3	0	20
2	21	127	3	100
3	14	163	25	99
4	18	43	10	5
5	9	42	6	21
6	20	59	4	31
7	23	49	3	20
8	15	39	3	18
9	28	76	3	25
10	18	48	4	22
11	14	36	8	6

hanger to get into a locked car. It is also what first allowed thieves to pick simple spring door locks with a credit card. Another type of mental set is considered an aspect of social cognition. **Stereotypes** are beliefs that members of a social group tend more or less uniformly to have particular types of characteristics. We seem to learn many stereotypes during childhood. For example, cross-cultural studies of children show their increasing knowledge about—and use of—gender stereotypes across the childhood years (Neto, Williams, & Widner, 1991). Stereotypes often arise in the same way that other kinds of mental sets develop. We observe a particular instance or set of instances of some pattern. We then may overgeneralize from those limited observations. We may assume that all future instances similarly will demonstrate that pattern. Of course, when the stereotypes are used to target particular scapegoats for societal mistreatment, grave social consequences result for the targets of stereotypes. The targets are not the only ones to suffer from stereotypes, however. Like other kinds of mental sets, stereotypes hinder the problem-solving abilities of the individuals who used them. These people limit their thinking by using set stereotypes.

Negative and Positive Transfer

Often, people have particular mental sets that prompt them to fixate on one aspect of a problem or one strategy for problem solving to the exclusion of other possible relevant ones. They are carrying knowledge and strategies for solving one kind of problem to a different kind of problem. **Transfer** is any carryover of knowledge or skills from one problem situation to another (Detterman & Sternberg, 1993; Gentile, 2000). Transfer can be either negative or positive. **Negative transfer** occurs when solving an earlier problem makes it harder to solve a later one. Sometimes an early problem gets an individual on a wrong track. For example, police may have difficulty solving a political crime because such a crime differs so much from the kinds of crime that they typically deal with. **Positive transfer** occurs when the solution of an earlier problem makes it easier to solve a new problem. That is, sometimes the transfer of a mental set can be an aid to problem solving.

From a broad perspective, positive transfer may be considered to involve the transfer of factual knowledge or skills from one setting to another. For example, you may apply your general knowledge about psychology and your study skills acquired during a lifetime of studying for tests to the problem of studying for an examination in cognitive psychology. More narrowly, however, during positive transfer, you effectively apply a strategy or a type of solution that worked well for one particular problem or set

Imagine that you are a doctor treating a patient with a malignant stomach tumor. You cannot operate on the patient because of the severity of the cancer. But unless you destroy the tumor somehow, the patient will die. You could use high-intensity X-rays to destroy the tumor. Unfortunately, the intensity of X-rays needed to destroy the tumor also will destroy healthy tissue through which the rays must pass. X-rays of lesser intensity will spare the healthy tissue. But they will be insufficiently powerful to destroy the tumor. Your problem is to figure out a procedure that will destroy the tumor without also destroying the healthy tissue surrounding the tumor.

INVESTIGATING COGNITIVE PSYCHOLOGY

IN THE LAB OF DEDRE GENTNER

Courtesy of Dr. Dedre Gentner

Dedre Gentner is a professor of psychology at Northwestern University. She is best known for her work on analogy and similarity. According to her *structure-mapping* theory, comparison involves a process of finding a maximal alignment of common conceptual relations and mapping inferences based on this alignment (Gentner, 1983; Gentner & Markman, 1997). She has shown that such processes operate across a wide range of cognitive domains (Gentner, 2003).

Much of Gentner's work focuses on learning. As predicted by structure-mapping theory, she has found that comparison processing fosters learning by highlighting common relational systems and promoting inferences. Her studies show that carrying out a comparison during learning can greatly improve people's ability to transfer knowledge to new contexts. For example, business schools invest considerable effort in teaching students how to negotiate; yet even highly motivated students are typically unable to apply the techniques outside the classroom. Gentner and her colleagues investigated the effects of adding comparison to the training (Gentner, Loewenstein, & Thompson, 2003; Loewenstein, Thompson & Gentner, 1999). Business school students studied two cases that both demonstrated a particular negotiating technique before entering into a simulated negotiation. Half the students were told to compare the two cases, and the other half studied each case in turn and wrote out significant commonalities. The comparison group was over twice as likely to use the technique in the subsequent negotiation as the group that studied the cases separately. This *comparison-based learning* technique may have wide application in overcoming the "inert knowledge" problem in education.

Gentner has applied the structure-mapping theory to ordinary similarity, yielding some surprising results. For example, people are faster to point out differences for highly similar pairs, such as *hotel/motel*, than for very dissimilar pairs, such as *traffic light/shopping mall* (Gentner & Markman, 1994). Another surprising

finding concerns the way similarity operates in memory. When thinking about a topic, people are often reminded of past similar situations. But the kind of similarity that leads to similarity-based remindings follows a very different pattern from the kind of similarity used in reasoning. Gentner, Rattermann and Forbus (1993) devised pairs of stories that could either match in their deep causal structure or in their surface characteristics (such as similar characters and context). As expected, people rated the structural matches (analogical pairs) higher in similarity and in inferential soundness—defined as whether one could reason about one story based on the other—than the surface pairs. Yet when a new group of participants was given a memory test, the pattern was quite different. This group first read half of the stories, then later saw the other half and wrote down any remindings to the first set. They were highly likely to be reminded of stories that were surface-similar to the new stories and only rarely reminded of structurally similar stories. Interestingly, despite this reminding pattern, this group did not consider the surface pairs to be good matches. When asked to rate the pairs (after the reminding task), they showed the same pattern as the first group: They rated the surface-matching pairs very low in similarity and soundness, even though they had failed to retrieve them, and gave high ratings to structurally matching pairs that they had rarely retrieved on their own. These findings were simulated in a model of similarity-based reminding and reasoning called MAC/FAC (many are called but few are chosen) (Forbus, Gentner & Law, 1995). The implications of this research for everyday life are that our memorial reminding processes are more superficial than our judgment and reasoning processes. To increase our learning power, we should seek ways to make our memories more effective, such as using analogies during learning, as discussed in the text.

In her work on cognitive development, Gentner has shown that there is a relational shift from a focus on object similarity to a focus on relational similarity as children learn more domain knowledge (Gentner, 1988). For example, asked to explain the metaphor "A cloud is like a sponge," a 5-year-old replies that both are round and fluffy, while a 9-year-old replies

IN THE LAB OF DEDRE GENTNER—cont'd

that both hold water and give it back at a later time. Gentner has also extended her comparison-based learn
ing technique to work with children. For example, she finds that if young children are led to compare two highly similar rooms, they show increased ability to carry out a challenging analogical mapping to a different room, relative to children who see the same two initial rooms separately, without comparing them (Loewenstein & Gentner, 2000).

Gentner has also studied how word meanings are represented and learned. She proposes that there is a deep distinction between object terms (e.g., concrete nouns) and relational terms (e.g., verbs and prepositions). Her prediction that concrete object nouns will be dominant across languages in children's early word learning (Gentner, 1982) has inspired a large number of cross-linguistic studies. She is currently investigating the interaction of language with analogical processing in cognitive development and learning.

Gentner is Director of the Cognitive Science Program at Northwestern University. She is a fellow of the American Psychological Association, the American Psychological Society, the Cognitive Science Society, and the Society for Experimental Psychology. She is a member of the American Academy of Arts and Sciences and a past fellow of the Center for Advanced Study in the Behavioral Sciences at Stanford. She is a past president of the Cognitive Science Society. She serves as an Associate Editor of the journal *Cognitive Science* and is on the editorial boards of several other journals, including *Metaphor and Symbol* and the *Journal of the Learning Sciences*. She has co-edited three books: *Mental Models*, *The Analogical Mind*, and *Language in Mind*.

Forbus, K. D., Gentner, D., & Law, K. (1995). MAC/FAC: A model of similarity-based retrieval. *Cognitive Science, 19*(2), 141-205.

Gentner, D. (1982). Why nouns are learned before verbs: Linguistic relativity versus natural partitioning. In S. A. Kuczaj (Ed.), *Language development: Vol. 2. Language, thought and culture* (pp. 301-334). Hillsdale, NJ: Erlbaum.

Gentner, D. (1983). Structure-mapping: A theoretical framework for analogy. *Cognitive Science, 7,* 155-170.

Gentner, D. (1988). Metaphor as structure mapping: The relational shift. *Child Development, 59,* 47-59.

Gentner, D. (2003). Why we're so smart. In D. Gentner and S. Goldin-Meadow (Eds.), *Language in mind: Advances in the study of language and cognition* (pp. 195-236). Cambridge, MA: MIT Press.

Gentner, D., Loewenstein, J., & Thompson, L. (2003). Learning and transfer: A general role for analogical encoding. *Journal of Educational Psychology 95* (2), 393-408.

Gentner, D., & Markman, A. B. (1994). Structural alignment in comparison: No difference without similarity. *Psychological Science, 5*(3), 152-158.

Gentner, D., & Markman, A. B. (1997). Structure mapping in analogy and similarity. *American Psychologist, 52,* 45-56.

Gentner, D., Rattermann, M. J., & Forbus, K. D. (1993). The roles of similarity in transfer: Separating retrieval from inferential soundness. *Cognitive Psychology, 25,* 524-575.

Holyoak, K. J., & Koh, K. (1987). Surface and structural similarity in analogical transfer. *Memory & Cognition, 15,* 332-340.

Loewenstein, J., & Gentner, D. (2001). Spatial mapping in preschoolers: Close comparisons facilitate far mappings. *Journal of Cognition and Development, 2*(2), 189-219.

Loewenstein, J., & Gentner, D. (in press). Relational language and the development of relational mapping. *Cognitive Psychology.*

Loewenstein, J., Thompson, L., & Gentner, D. (1999). Analogical encoding facilitates knowledge transfer in negotiation. *Psychonomic Bulletin & Review, 6*(4), 586-597.

of problems when you are trying to solve an analogous problem. How do people realize that particular problems are analogous and can be solved through positive transfer of strategies or even of solutions?

Transfer of Analogies

Researchers designed some elegant studies of positive transfer involving analogies (Gick & Holyoak, 1980, 1983). To appreciate their results, you need to become familiar with a problem first used by Karl Duncker (1945), often called the "radiation problem." It is described in the "Investigating Cognitive Psychology" box.

INVESTIGATING COGNITIVE PSYCHOLOGY	A general wishes to capture a fortress located in the center of a country. There are many roads radiating outward from the fortress. All have been mined. Although small groups of men can pass over the roads safely, any large force will detonate the mines. A full-scale direct attack is therefore impossible. What should the general do?

Duncker had in mind a particular insightful solution as the optimal one for this problem. Figure 11.12 shows the solution pictorially.

Prior to presenting Duncker's radiation problem, participants received another, easier problem. This particular problem was called the "military problem" (Holyoak, 1984, p. 205). It is described in the "Investigating Cognitive Psychology" box.

Table 11.3 shows the correspondence between the radiation and the military problems. It turns out to be quite close, although not perfect. The question is whether producing a group-convergence solution to the military problem helped participants in solving the radiation problem. Consider participants who received the military problem with the convergence solution and then were given a hint to apply it in some way to the radiation problem. About 75% of the participants reached the correct solution to the radiation problem. This figure compared with less than 10% of the participants who did not receive the military story first but instead received no prior story or only an irrelevant one.

In another experiment, participants were not given the convergence solution to the military problem. They had to figure it out for themselves. About 50% of the participants generated the convergence solution to the military problem. Of these, 41% went on to generate a parallel solution to the radiation problem. That is, positive transfer was *weaker* when participants produced the original solution themselves than when the solution to the first problem was given to them (41%, as compared with 75%).

The investigators found that the usefulness of the military problem as an analogue to the radiation problem depended on the induced mental set with which the problem solver approached the problems. Consider what happened when participants were asked to memorize the military story under the guise that it was a story–recall experiment and then were given the radiation problem to solve. Only 30% of participants produced the convergence solution to the radiation problem. The investigators also found that positive transfer improved if two, rather than just one, analogous problems were given in advance of the radiation problem. Researchers have expanded

FIGURE 11.12

The solution to the X-ray problem involves dispersion. The idea is to direct weak X-radiation toward the tumor from a number of different points outside the body. No single set of rays would be strong enough to destroy either the healthy tissue or the tumor. However, the rays would be aimed so that they all converged at one spot within the body—the spot that houses the tumor. This solution actually is used today in some X-ray treatments, except that a rotating source of X-rays is used for dispersing rays. From In Search of the Human Mind by Robert J. Sternberg, copyright © 1995 by Harcourt Brace & Company, reproduced by permission of the publisher.

these findings to encompass problems other than the radiation problem. They found that when the domains or the contexts for the two problems were more similar, participants were more likely to see and apply the analogy (see Holyoak, 1990).

Similar patterns of data were found with various types of problems involving electricity (Gentner & Gentner, 1983). Related results also have emerged in studies of mathematical insight (Davidson & Sternberg, 1984). Perhaps the most crucial aspect of these studies is that people have trouble noticing the analogy unless they explicitly are told to look for it. Consider studies involving physics problems. Positive transfer from solved examples to unsolved problems was more likely among students who specifically tried to understand *why* particular examples were solved as they were, as compared with students who sought only to understand *how* particular problems were solved as they were (Chi & associates, 1989). Based on these findings, we generally need to be looking for analogies to find them. We often will not find them unless we explicitly seek them.

People sometimes do not recognize the surface similarities of problems (Bassock, 2003). Other times they are fooled by surface similarities into believing two different

TABLE 11.3	Correspondence Between the Radiation and the Military Problems

What are the commonalities between the two problems, and what is an elemental strategy that can be derived by comparing the two problems? (After Gick & Holyoak, 1983)

Military Problem
    Initial State
        Goal: Use army to capture fortress
        Resources: Sufficiently large army
        Constraint: Unable to send entire army along one road
    Solution Plan: Send small groups along multiple roads simultaneously
    Outcome: Fortress captured by army

Radiation Problem
    Initial State
        Goal: Use rays to destroy tumor
        Resources: Sufficiently powerful rays
        Constraint: Unable to administer high-intensity rays from one direction only
    Solution Plan: Administer low-intensity rays from multiple directions simultaneously
    Outcome: Tumor destroyed by rays

Convergence Schema
    Initial State
        Goal: Use force to overcome a central target
        Resources: Sufficiently great force
        Constraint: Unable to apply full force along one path alone
    Solution Plan: Apply weak forces along multiple paths simultaneously
    Outcome: Central target overcome by force

M. L. Gick and K. J. Holyoak (1983), "Schema Induction and Analogical Transfer," Cognitive Psychology, Vol. 15, p. 1-38. Reprinted by permission of Elsevier.

kinds of problems are the same (Bassock, Wu, & Olseth, 1995; Gentner, 2000; Gentner & Markman, 1997). Sometimes even experienced problem solvers are led astray. They believe that similar surface structures indicate comparable deep structures. For example, problem solvers may use the verbal content rather than the mathematical operations required in a mathematical problem to classify the problem as being of a certain kind (Blessing & Ross, 1996). So, in a way, it can make sense to err on the side of caution. Often, it is best not to immediately assume that two problems that look like they are essentially the same necessarily are (Ben-Zeev, 1996).

Intentional Transfer: Searching for Analogies

In looking for analogies, we need to be careful not to be misled by associations between two things that are analogically irrelevant. For example, one study investigated children's solutions to verbal analogies of the form "A is to B as C is to X" (Sternberg & Nigro, 1980). The children are given multiple-choice options for X. Children often will choose an answer that is associatively close but analogically incorrect. (In representing analogies, a single colon [:] indicates the "is to" expression and a double colon [::] is used to indicate the "as" expression.) For example, in the analogy LAWYER : CLIENT :: DOCTOR : (a. NURSE, b. PATIENT, c. MEDICINE,

d. MD), children might choose option a. because NURSE is more strongly associated with DOCTOR than is the correct answer, PATIENT.

Analogies between problems involve mappings of relationships between problems (Gentner, 1983, 2000). The actual content attributes of the problems are irrelevant. In other words, what matters in analogies is not the similarity of the content, but how closely their structural systems of relationships match. Because we are accustomed to considering the importance of the content, we find it difficult to push the content to the background. It also is difficult to bring form (structural relationships) to the foreground. For example, the differing content makes the analogy between the military problem and the radiation problem hard to recognize and impedes positive transfer from one problem to the other.

The opposite phenomenon is **transparency,** in which people see analogies where they do not exist because of similarity of content. In making analogies, we need to be sure we are focusing on the relationships between the two terms being compared, not just their surface content attributes. For example, in studying for final exams in two psychology courses, you may need different strategies when studying for a closed-book essay exam than for an open-book, multiple-choice exam. Transparency of content may lead to negative transfer between nonisomorphic problems if care is not taken to avoid such transfer.

Incubation

For solving many problems, the chief obstacle is not the need to find a suitable strategy for positive transfer. Rather, it is to avoid obstacles resulting from negative transfer. **Incubation**—putting the problem aside for a while without consciously thinking about it—offers one way in which to minimize negative transfer. It involves taking a pause from the stages of problem solving. For example, suppose you find that you are unable to solve a problem. None of the strategies you can think of seem to work. Try setting the problem aside for a while to let it incubate. During incubation, you must not consciously think about the problem. You do, however, allow for the possibility that the problem will be processed subconsciously. Some investigators of problem solving have even asserted that incubation is an essential stage of the problem-solving process (e.g., Cattell, 1971; Helmholtz, 1896). Others have failed to find experimental support for the phenomenon of incubation (e.g., Baron, 1988). Nevertheless, extensive anecdotal support for it has been offered (e.g., Poincaré, 1913). Still other investigators suggest that incubation may be particularly helpful in solving insight problems (e.g., Smith, 1995).

Several possible mechanisms for the beneficial effects of incubation have been proposed, such as the following:

1. When we no longer keep something in active memory, we let go of some of the unimportant details. We keep only the more meaningful aspects in memory. From these meaningful aspects, we then are free to reconstruct them anew. Fewer of the limitations of the earlier mental set remain (Anderson, 1975).

2. As time passes, more recent memories become more integrated with existing memories (Anderson, 1985). During this reintegration, some associations of the mental set may weaken.

3. As time passes, new stimuli—both internal and external—may activate new perspectives on the problem. These stimuli may weaken the effects of the mental set (Bastik, 1982).

4. An internal or external stimulus may lead the problem solver to see an analogy between the current problem and another problem. As a result, the problem solver can either readily find a comparable solution or perhaps even simply apply a known solution (Langley & Jones, 1988; Seifert & associates, 1995).

5. Consider what happens when problem solvers are in a low state of cortical arousal, such as in the shower, in bed, or taking a walk. Increases in attention span—and perhaps working-memory capacity—may allow increasingly remote cues to be perceived and held in active memory simultaneously. The person, while relaxed, may toy with cues that otherwise might be perceived as irrelevant or distracting when in a high state of cortical arousal. For example, the cues might be ignored while trying actively to solve the problem (Luria, 1973/1984). Some of the preceding mechanisms also may interact. Such interaction may be through the process of spreading activation or through some sort of priming effect.

The benefits of incubation can be enhanced in two ways (Kaplan & Davidson, 1989). First, invest enough time in the problem initially. Explore all aspects of the problem. Investigate several possible avenues of solving it. Second, allow sufficient time for incubation to permit your old associations resulting from negative transfer to weaken somewhat. A drawback of incubation is that it takes time. If you have a deadline for problem solution, you must begin solving the problem early enough to meet the deadline. This includes the time you need for incubation.

PRACTICAL APPLICATIONS OF COGNITIVE PSYCHOLOGY	These suggestions can be used directly to help you solve everyday problems. If you have an assignment due at some later date, take the time immediately on being given the assignment to plan a course of action. For example, in writing a term paper, scan the outlines of future readings in the course. Find the general topic that interests you. Then get some idea on how much information is available on your topic. Do not get too involved in the details. This procedure can help you narrow down the focus. Choosing a topic you are relatively unfamiliar with for shorter paper assignments is generally a good option. In this way, you will learn something new. Moreover, you will be more likely to have entrenched ideas or fixations concerning topics of higher familiarity. However, try positively to transfer major themes across different topics. For example, the nature-nurture issue often plays out in diverse topics in psychology. Finally, put the topic to the side for a while. Allow the course material to integrate itself with your existing knowledge and with your developing topic ideas. Then, about 2 to 3 weeks before the paper is due, start working on a draft that you can set aside again for a few days before final polishing. Overall, the total amount of distributed time involved in completing an assignment this way will be only slightly more than if you cram the work into a few days before the paper is due. But the quality of the paper is almost sure to be better.

Expertise: Knowledge and Problem Solving

Even people who do not have expertise in cognitive psychology recognize that knowledge, particularly expert knowledge, greatly enhances problem solving. Expertise is superior skills or achievement reflecting a well-developed and well-organized knowledge base. What interests cognitive psychologists is the reason that expertise enhances problem solving. Why can experts solve problems in their field more successfully than novices can? Do experts know more problem-solving algorithms, heuristics, and other strategies? Do experts know better strategies? Or do they just use these strategies more often? What do experts know that makes the problem-solving process more effective for them than for novices in a field? Is it all talent or just acquired skill?

Organization of Knowledge

A team of researchers set out to discover what experts know and do (Chase & Simon, 1973). They sought to determine what distinguishes expert from novice chess players. In one of their studies, they had expert and novice players briefly view a display of a chessboard with the chess pieces on it, and the players then had to recall the positions of the chess pieces on the board. In general, the experts performed quite a bit better than the novices. But they performed better only if the positions of the chess pieces on the board made sense in terms of an actual game of chess (see also De Groot, 1965; Vicente & De Groot, 1990). If the pieces were distributed around the board randomly, experts recalled the positions of the pieces no better than did the novices (Figure 11.13).

Knowledge can interact with understanding in problem solving (Whitten & Graesser, 2003). Consider a study investigating how knowledge interacts with coherence of a text. Investigators presented children with biology texts (McNamara & associates, 1996). Half of the children in the study had high levels of domain knowledge about biology and half had low levels. In addition, half the texts were highly coherent, meaning that they made clear how the various concepts in the text related to each other. The other half of the texts were of low coherence, meaning that they were more difficult to read because the ideas did not flow smoothly. Readers then had to do a variety of problem-solving tasks based on what they had read. As the authors predicted, participants with low domain knowledge performed better when the texts were highly coherent. This finding suggests that, in general, learners do better when they are presented new material in a coherent way. Surprisingly, however, the high-knowledge group performed better when the texts were of low rather than high coherence. The authors of the study suggested that high-knowledge readers may have been, essentially, on automatic pilot when reading the high-coherence texts, not paying much attention because they thought they knew what was in the texts. The low-coherence texts forced them to pay attention. These results point out the importance of attentional processes when people solve problems. This is particularly relevant in domains in which they are expert and in which they therefore may not feel they have to pay attention.

FIGURE 11.13

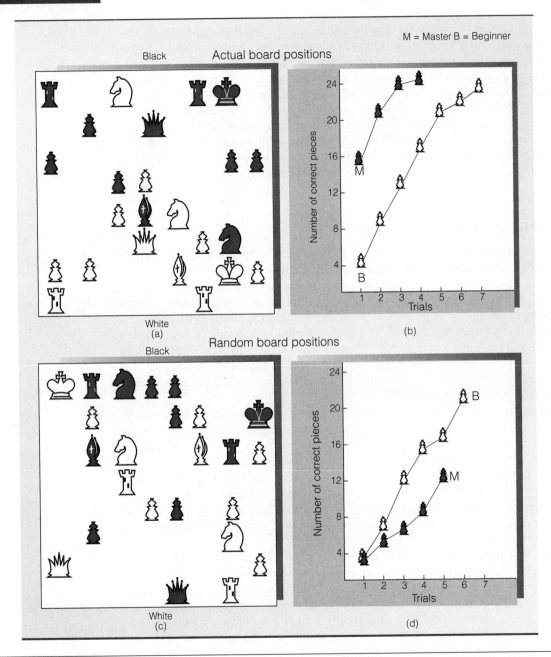

When experts and novices were asked to recall realistic patterns of chess pieces, as in (a), experts demonstrated much better performance, as shown in (b). However, when experts and novices were asked to recall random arrangements of chess pieces, as shown in (c), experts performed no better than novices, as shown in (d). From William G. Chase and Herbert A. Simon (1973), "The Mind's Eye in Chess," in Visual Information Processing, edited by William G. Chase. Reprinted by permission of Elsevier.

Elaboration of Knowledge

This work suggested that what differentiated the experts from the novices was in the amount, organization, and use of knowledge. There were two tasks. One involved a random array of pieces and the other a meaningful arrangement of pieces. Both chess tasks required the experts to use heuristics for storing and retrieving information about the positions of the pieces on the chess board. The key difference was that chess experts had stored and organized in memory tens of thousands of particular board positions. When they saw sensible board positions, they could use the knowledge they had in memory to help them. They were able to remember the various board positions as integrated, organized chunks of information. For random scatterings of pieces on the board, however, the knowledge of the experts was of no use. The experts had no advantage over the novices. Like the novices, they had to try to memorize the distinctive interrelations among many discrete pieces and positions.

Other work demonstrates that retrieval processes involving recognition of board arrangements are instrumental in grand master–level chess players' success when compared with novices' play (Gobet & Simon, 1996a, 1996b, 1996c). Even when grand masters are time-constrained so that look-ahead processes are curtailed, their constrained performance does not differ substantially from their unconstrained playing. Thus, an organized knowledge system is relatively more important to experts' performance in chess than even the processes involved in predicting future moves.

Other studies have examined experts in different domains. Examples of such domains are the game of Go (Reitman, 1976), radiology (Lesgold & associates, 1988), and physics (Larkin & associates, 1980). These studies revealed the same thing again and again. What differentiated experts from novices were their schemas for solving problems within their own domains of expertise (Glaser & Chi, 1988). The schemas of experts involve large, highly interconnected units of knowledge. They are organized according to underlying structural similarities among knowledge units. In contrast, the schemas of novices involve relatively small and disconnected units of knowledge. They are organized according to superficial similarities (Bryson & associates, 1991). This same observation applies to various activities of experts versus novices. One is in how they classify various problems (Chi, Glaser, & Rees, 1982). Another is in how they describe the essential nature of various problems (Larkin & associates, 1980). And a third is in how they determine and describe a solution method for various problems (Chi, Glaser, & Rees, 1982).

An interesting study looked at the role of knowledge on understanding and interpreting a news broadcast regarding a baseball game (Hambrick & Engle, 2002). A total of 181 adults having a wide range of knowledge about baseball listened to radio broadcasts recorded by a professional baseball announcer. The announcements sounded like a real game. After each broadcast, memory for changes in the status of the game were measured. For example, participants would be asked questions about which bases were occupied after each player's turn at bat and about the numbers of outs and of runs scored during the inning. Baseball knowledge accounted for more than half of the reliable variation in participants' performance. Working memory capacity also mattered, but not nearly so much as knowledge. Thus, people can remember things better and solve problems with what they remember better if they have a solid knowledge base with which to work.

Michelene Chi is a professor of psychology at the University of Pittsburgh. She is most well known for showing that the organization of experts' knowledge in their domain of expertise allows them to represent this knowledge more profoundly than can novices. She also has shown that the initial organization of a learner's knowledge can be fundamentally flawed so that it prevents the learner from understanding the true meaning of a concept.

Setting Up the Problem

Another difference between experts and novices can be observed by asking problem solvers to report aloud what they are thinking as they are attempting to solve various problems (Bryson & associates, 1991; De Groot, 1965; Lesgold, 1988). Observers can compare various aspects of problem solving. One includes the statements made by problem solvers, so-called *verbal protocols*. Another is the time spent on various aspects of problems, and the relationship between problem-solving strategies and the solutions reached. Experts appear to spend proportionately more time determining how to represent a problem than do novices (Lesgold, 1988; Lesgold & associates, 1988). But they spend much less time than do novices actually implementing the strategy for solution.

The differences between experts and novices in their expenditure of time can be viewed in terms of the focus and direction of their problem solving. Experts seem to spend relatively more time than do novices figuring out how to match the given information in the problem with their existing schemas. In other words, they try to compare what they know about the problem with how the information they have matches what they already know, based on their expertise. Once experts find a correct match, they quickly can retrieve and implement a problem strategy. Thus, experts seem to be able to work forward from the given information ("What do I know?") to find the unknown information ("What do I need to find out?"). They implement the correct sequence of steps, based on the strategies they have retrieved from their schemas in long-term memory (Chi & associates, 1982).

Consider, for example, the ways an expert doctor and a novice medical student might handle a patient with a set of symptoms. The novice is not sure what to make of the symptoms. He somewhat haphazardly orders a long and expensive series of medical tests. He is hoping that with a more nearly complete set of symptomatic information, he may be able to make a correct diagnosis. The more experienced doctor, however, is more likely to immediately recognize the symptoms as fitting into a diagnostic pattern or one of a small number of patterns. This doctor orders only a small number of highly targeted tests. She is able to choose the correct diagnosis from among the limited number of possibilities. She then moves on to treat the diagnosed illness.

In contrast, novices seem to spend relatively little time trying to represent the problem. Instead, they choose to work backward from the unknown information to the given information. That is, they go from asking what they need to find out to asking what information is offered and what strategies do they know that can help them find the missing information. Often, novices use means–ends analysis (see Hunt, 1994). Thus, novices often consider more possible strategies than experts consider (see Holyoak, 1990). For experts, means–ends analysis of problems serves only as a backup strategy. They turn to it only if they are unable to retrieve an appropriate strategy, based on their existing schemas.

Thus, experts have not only more knowledge but also better-organized knowledge. They use their knowledge more effectively. Furthermore, the schemas of experts involve not only greater declarative knowledge about a problem domain. They also involve more procedural knowledge about strategies relevant to that domain. Perhaps because of their better grasp of the strategies required, experts more accurately predict the difficulty of solving problems than do novices (Lesgold & Lajoie, 1991). Experts also monitor their problem-solving strategies more carefully than novices do (Schoenfeld, 1981).

Automatic Expert Processes

Through practice in applying strategies, experts may automatize various operations. They can retrieve and execute these operations easily while working forward (see VanLehn, 1989). They use two important processes. One is *schematization*, which involves developing rich, highly organized schemas. The other is *automatization*, which involves consolidating sequences of steps into unified routines that require little or no conscious control. Through these two processes, experts may shift the burden of solving problems from limited-capacity working memory to infinite-capacity long-term memory. They thereby become increasingly efficient and accurate in solving problems. The freeing of their working-memory capacity may better enable them to monitor their progress and their accuracy during problem solving. Novices, in contrast, must use their working memory for trying to hold multiple features of a problem and various possible alternative strategies. This effort may leave novices with less working memory available for monitoring their accuracy and their progress toward solving the problem.

A good example of how automatization enhances performance can be seen in studies of reading ability. Consider the issue of expertise in reading. Why would some people, particularly children learning to read, be better than others at reading? Reading is believed by some to involve two distinct processes (Wagner & Stanovich, 1996). The first is a process of conversion from the *orthographic* (relating to visual appearance of letters) code to the *phonological* (relating to the sounds of the language) code. The second is a phonology-based word recognition process. Extensive exposure to text can enhance the orthographic-to-phonological conversion process by increasing automaticity at this level of processing. Thus, a portion of the differences in reading ability appears to be the result of increased automaticity in the conversion of orthographic to phonological encoding of words through increased reading practice (see Samuels, 1999, pp. 176–179; Sternberg & Wagner, 1982).

However, the automaticity of experts actually may hinder problem solving. This can occur when experts are tackling problems that differ structurally from the problems they normally encounter (Frensch & Sternberg, 1989). Initially, novices may perform better than experts when the problems appear structurally different from the norm. Eventually, however, the performance of experts generally catches up to and surpasses that of novices (Frensch & Sternberg, 1989; Lesgold, 1988). Perhaps this difference results from the experts' richly developed schemas and their enhanced self-monitoring skills. Table 11.4 summarizes the various characteristics of expert problem solving.

Innate Talent and Acquired Skill

Although a richly elaborated knowledge base is crucial to expertise in a domain, there remain differences in performance that are not explainable in terms of knowledge level alone. There is considerable debate as to whether differences between novices and experts and among different experts themselves are due either to innate talent or to the quantity and quality of practice in a domain. Many espouse the "practice makes perfect" point of view (see Ericsson, 1996, 1999, 2003; Ericsson, Krampe, & Tesch-Römer, 1993; Ericsson & Lehmann, 1996; Sloboda, 1996; Sloboda & associates, 1996; Sternberg, 1998). The practice should be deliberate, or focused.

| **TABLE 11.4** | What Characterizes Expertise? |

Although many aspects of expertise remain to be explored, several characteristics of expert problem solving have been discovered.

EXPERTS	NOVICES
Have large, rich schemas containing a great deal of declarative knowledge about domain	Have relatively impoverished schemas containing relatively less declarative knowledge about domain
Have well-organized, highly interconnected units of knowledge in schemas	Have poorly organized, loosely interconnected, scattered units of knowledge
Spend proportionately more time determining how to represent a problem than in searching for and executing a problem strategy	Spend proportionately more time searching for and executing a problem strategy than in determining how to represent a problem
Develop sophisticated representation of problems, based on structural similarities among problems	Develop relatively poor and naive representation of problems, based on superficial similarities among problems
Work forward from given information to implement strategies for finding unknown	Work backward from focusing on unknown to finding problem strategies that make use of given information
Generally choose a strategy based on elaborate schema of problem strategies; use means-ends analysis only as a backup strategy for handling unusual, atypical problems	Frequently use means-ends analysis as a strategy for handling most problems; sometimes choose a strategy based on knowledge of problem strategies
Schemas contain a great deal of procedural knowledge about problem strategies relevant to domain	Schemas contain relatively little procedural knowledge about problem strategies relevant to domain
Have automatized many sequences of steps within problem strategies	Show little or no automatization of any sequences of steps within problem strategies
Show highly efficient problem solving; when time constraints are imposed, solve problems more quickly than novices	Show relatively inefficient problem solving; solve problems less quickly than experts
Accurately predict the difficulty of solving particular problems	Do not accurately predict the difficulty of solving particular problems
Carefully monitor own problem-solving strategies and processes	Show poor monitoring of own problem-solving strategies and processes
Show high accuracy in reaching appropriate solutions	Show much less accuracy than experts in reaching appropriate solutions
When confronting highly unusual problems with atypical structural features, take relatively more time than novices both to represent the problem and to retrieve appropriate problem strategies	When confronting highly unusual problems with atypical structural features, novices take relatively less time than experts both to represent the problem and to retrieve problem strategies
When provided with new information that contradicts initial problem representation, show flexibility in adapting to a more appropriate strategy	Show less ability to adapt to new information that contradicts initial problem representation and strategy

It should emphasize acquisition of new skills rather than mindless repetition of what the developing expert already knows how to do. However, some take an alternative approach. It acknowledges the importance of practice in building a knowledge and skill base. It also underscores the importance of something like talent. Indeed, the interaction between innate abilities modified by experience is widely accepted in the domain of language acquisition (as discussed in Chapter 9) as well as other domains. Certainly, some skill domains are heavily dependent on nurture. For example, wisdom is partly knowledge-based. The knowledge one uses to make wise judgments is necessarily a result of experience (Baltes & Smith, 1990).

Experts in some domains perform at superior levels by virtue of prediction skills. For example, expert typists move their fingers toward keys corresponding to the letters they will need to type more quickly than do novice typers (Norman & Rumelhart, 1983). Indeed, the single best predictor of typing speed is how far ahead in the text a typist looks when typing (Ericsson, 2003). The farther ahead he or she looks, the better the typist is able to have fingers in position as needed. When typists are not allowed to look ahead in their typing, the advantage of expert typists is largely eliminated (Salthouse, 1984). Expert musicians, too, are better able to sight-read than novices by virtue of their looking farther ahead in the music so they can anticipate what notes will be coming up (Sloboda, 1984). Even in sports, such as tennis, experts are superior to novices in part by virtue of their being able to predict the trajectory of an approaching ball more rapidly and accurately than novices (Abernethy, 1991).

Another characteristic of experts is that they tend to use a more systematic approach to difficult problems within their domain of expertise in a more systematic way than do novices. For example, one study compared strategies used by problem solvers in a simulated biology laboratory (Vollmeyer, Burns, & Holyoak, 1996). The investigators found that better problem solvers were more systematic in their approach to the lab than were poorer problem solvers. For example, in seeking an explanation of a biological phenomenon, they were more likely to hold one variable constant while varying other variables.

Many scientists in the field of expertise prefer to minimize the contributions of talent to expertise by locking talent in the trunk of "folk" psychology (Sternberg, 1996). This tendency is not surprising, given two factors. The first is the widespread use of the term *talent* outside the scientific community. The second is the lack of an adequate, testable definition of talent.

Genetic heritage seems to make some difference in the acquisition of at least some kinds of expertise. Studies of the heritability of reading disabilities, for example, seem to point to a strong role for genetic factors in people with a reading disability (see DeFries & Gillis, 1993; Olson, 1999). Furthermore, differences in the phonological awareness required for reading ability could be a factor in reading for which individual differences are at least partially genetic (Wagner & Stanovich, 1996). In general, even if the role of practice is found to account for much of the expertise shown in a given domain, the contributions of genetic factors to the remaining portion of expertise could make some difference in a world of intense competition (Shiffrin, 1996).

The application of expertise to problem solving generally involves converging on a single correct solution from a broad range of possibilities. A complementary asset to expertise in problem solving involves creativity. Here, an individual extends the range of possibilities to consider never-before-explored options. In fact, many problems can be solved only by inventing or discovering strategies to answer a complex question.

George Tiedemann/New Sport/Corbis

AGE Fotostock/SuperStock

Ed Lallo/PictureQuest

A common trait among experts in various skills is that they put in tremendous numbers of hours of deliberate practice to perfect their skills.

Creativity

How can we possibly define creativity as a single construct that unifies the work of Leonardo da Vinci and Marie Curie, of Vincent Van Gogh and Isaac Newton, and of Toni Morrison and Albert Einstein? There may be about as many narrow definitions of creativity as there are people who think about creativity (Figure 11.14). However, most investigators in the field of creativity would broadly define **creativity** as the process of producing something that is both original and worthwhile (Csikszentmihalyi, 1999, 2000; Lubart & Mouchiroud, 2003; Runco, 1997, 2000; Sternberg & Lubart, 1996). The *something* could take many forms. It might be a theory, a dance, a chemical, a process or procedure, a story, a symphony, or almost anything else.

What does it take to create something original and worthwhile? What are creative people like? Almost everyone would agree that creative individuals show creative productivity. They produce inventions, insightful discoveries, artistic works,

FIGURE 11.14

CREATIVITY IS...

DIGGING DEEPER

CREATIVITY IS...

LOOKING TWICE

CREATIVITY IS...

LISTENING FOR SMELLS

CREATIVITY IS...

~~TALKING~~ LISTENING TO A CAT

CROSSING OUT MISTAKES

Here are some original and worthwhile ways of defining creativity. How do you define creativity? (Torrance, 1988, pp. 50–53). From "The Nature of Creativity as Manifest in its Testing," by E.P. Torrance in The Nature of Creativity, *edited by Robert J. Sternberg. Copyright © 1988 by Cambridge University Press. Reprinted by permission of Cambridge University Press and E.P. Torrance.*

revolutionary paradigms, or other products that are both original and worthwhile. Conventional wisdom suggests that highly creative individuals also have creative lifestyles. These lifestyles are characterized by flexibility, nonstereotyped behaviors, and nonconforming attitudes. What characteristics do cognitive psychologists notice in creative individuals? The answer to this question depends on the perspective of the psychologist you ask. This section of this chapter describes a number of different approaches to creativity. They include psychometric and cognitive approaches; personality and motivational approaches; and social, societal, and historical approaches to understanding creativity. The chapter concludes with a couple of integrative perspectives. These perspectives attempt to incorporate key features of the other approaches to creativity.

It's How Much You Produce

Do creative individuals simply produce more? We have yet to develop a method for detecting highly creative individuals at a glance. But highly creative individuals seem to share several characteristics. Psychologists who take a psychometric (*-metric*, measurement) approach emphasize performance on tasks involving specific aspects of creativity (Guilford, 1950). These tasks involve *divergent production*—the generation of a diverse assortment of appropriate responses. Therefore, creativity reflects simply the ability to create more.

For example, creative individuals often have high scores on tests of creativity. An example of such a test is includes the *Torrance Tests of Creative Thinking* (Torrance, 1974, 1984). They measure the diversity, numerosity, and appropriateness of responses to open-ended questions. Examples of such questions are to think of all the possible ways in which to use a paper clip or a ballpoint pen. Torrance's test also as-

What do creative people such as these have in common?

sesses creative figural responses. For example, a person might be given a sheet of paper displaying some circles, squiggles, or lines. The test would assess how many different ways the person had used the given shapes to complete a drawing. Assessment of the Torrance test would consider particularly how much the person had used unusual or richly elaborated details in completing a figure.

It's What You Know

Other psychological researchers have focused on creativity as a cognitive process by studying problem solving and insight (Finke, 1995; Langley & Jones, 1988; Smith, 1995; Weisberg, 1988, 1995, 1999). Are creative people smarter than the rest of us? Some researchers believe that what distinguishes remarkably creative individuals from less remarkable people is their expertise and commitment to their creative endeavor (Weisberg, 1988, 1995, 1999). Highly creative individuals work long and hard. They study the work of their predecessors and their contemporaries. They thereby become thoroughly expert in their fields. They then build on and diverge from what they know to create innovative approaches and products (Weisberg, 1988, 1995, 1999). To these researchers, creativity in itself is nothing special. The processes involved in creativity are used by all of us every day in solving problems. What differentiates the remarkable from the mundane is the extraordinary content on which these ordinary processes operate. This notion feeds back to those discussed previously in expertise. Indeed, creativity often is treated as related to expertise.

Not every cognitive psychologist agrees with the nothing-special view of creative insight. For example, to one investigator, "insight is what distinguishes . . . the inspiring from the denigrating, the magical from the mediocre" (Finke, 1995, p. 255). On this view, there are two types of creative thinking. First, in convergent insight, the individual converges on a unifying pattern or structure within a scattered assortment of data. Second, in divergent insight, the individual diverges from a particular form or structure to explore what kinds of uses may be found for it. Divergent insight may be used to understand various creative endeavors (Finke, 1995). They include architectural design, physical or biological models, product development, or scientific invention.

Other investigators focus on creativity as it is manifested in scientific insight (Langley & Jones, 1988). These researchers suggest that memory processes such as spreading activation (see Chapter 8) and thinking processes such as analogical reasoning (see Chapter 12) account for much of scientific insight. Another investigator distinguishes between scientific insight and the insight experience (Smith, 1995). He has suggested that the abruptness of the insight experience may result from a sudden release from a mental rut (a mental set such as functional fixedness). This sudden release may be more likely to arise after a period of incubation in a context other than the context in which the individual became fixated on the problem.

Some computer programs that can do work such as composing music (Johnson-Laird, 1988) or rediscovering scientific principles (Langley & associates, 1986) can be viewed as creative. The question one always need ask, with these programs, is whether their accomplishments truly are comparable to those of creative humans and whether the processes they use to be creative are the same as those used by humans (Boden, 1999). For example, Langley and colleagues' (1986) programs *rediscover* scientific ideas rather than discover them for the first time. Even Deep Blue, the computer program that beat world-champion chess player Gary Kasparov, did so not by playing chess more creatively than Kasparov did. Rather, it won through its enormous powers of rapid computation.

It's Who You Are

Other psychologists have turned their focus away from cognition to consider the role of personality and motivation in creativity. Is there a creative personality—either you have it or you don't? Consider the importance of personal style:

> ". . . openness to new ways of seeing, intuition, alertness to opportunity, a liking for complexity as a challenge to find simplicity, independence of judgment that questions assumptions, willingness to take risks, unconventionality of thought that allows odd connections to be made, keen attention, and a drive to find pattern and meaning—these, coupled with the motive and the courage to create." (Barron, 1988, p. 95)

Also important is the role of personal philosophy in creativity (Barron, 1988). This includes flexible beliefs and broadly accepting attitudes toward other cultures, other races, and other religious creeds. Some investigators have focused on the importance of motivation in creative productivity (e.g., Amabile, 1996; Collins & Amabile, 1999; Hennessey & Amabile, 1988). One may differentiate intrinsic motivation, which is internal to the individual, from extrinsic motivation, which is external to the individual. For example, intrinsic motivators might include sheer enjoyment of the creative process or personal desire to solve a problem. Extrinsic motivators might include a desire for fame or fortune. Intrinsic motivation is essential to creativity. Extrinsic motivators actually may impede creativity under many but not all circumstances (Amabile, 1996; Ruscio, Whitney, & Amabile, 1998).

In a review of the literature, certain traits seem consistently to be associated with creative individuals (Feist, 1998, 1999). In particular, creative individuals tend to be more open to new experiences, self-confident, self-accepting, impulsive, ambitious, driven, dominant, and hostile than less creative individuals. They also are less conventional.

It's Where You Are

Some researchers focus on the importance of external factors that contribute to creativity. Do you have to be in the right place at the right time? "We cannot study creativity by isolating individuals and their works from the social and historical milieu in which their actions are carried out . . . what we call creative is never the result of individual action alone" (Csikszentmihalyi, 1988, p. 325). In regard to the context for creativity, we should note two contexts (Csikszentmihalyi, 1996): the domain and the field. The domain comprises existing knowledge in a particular area of creative endeavor, such as particle physics or painting. The field comprises the social context surrounding creativity. It includes both the collegial network in the domain and the broader social and public institutions of the society.

One can seek to understand creativity by going beyond the immediate social, intellectual, and cultural context to embrace the entire sweep of history (Simonton,

1988, 1994, 1997, 1999). Creative contributions, almost by definition, are unpredictable because they violate the norms established by the forerunners and the contemporaries of the creator. Among the many attributes of creative individuals are the abilities to make serendipitous discoveries and to pursue such discoveries actively (Simonton, 1994).

Evolutionary thinking also can be used to study creativity (Cziko, 1998; Simonton, 1998). Underlying such models is the notion that creative ideas evolve much as organisms do. The idea is that creativity occurs as an outcome of a process of blind variation and selective retention (Campbell, 1960). In blind variation, creators first generate an idea. They have no real sense of whether the idea will be successful (selected for) in the world of ideas. As a result, their best bet for producing lasting ideas is to go for a large quantity of ideas. Some of these ideas then will be valued by their field. That is, they will be selectively retained by virtue of their being labeled as creative.

All of the Above

Consider an integrated view of what characterizes creative individuals (Gardner, 1993a; Policastro & Gardner, 1999). Like some case-study researchers (e.g., Gruber, 1974/1981; Gruber & Davis, 1988), Gardner (1993a) used in-depth study of seven creative individuals. Like Simonton, he attempted to relate these creative individuals to the historical context in which they developed and worked. He noted that great creators seemed to be in the right place at the right time for revolutionary change in their chosen domain. Like Csikszentmihalyi, Gardner studied how both the domain (e.g., physics, politics, music) and the field (e.g., collaborators, mentors, rivals) influence the way in which the creative individual demonstrates creativity. In addition, he studied both the kinds of early experiences leading to creative achievement and the development of creativity across the life span.

Creative individuals tended to have moderately supportive but rather strict and relatively chilly (i.e., not warmly affectionate and nurturing) early family lives. Most showed an early interest in their chosen field. But most were not particularly noteworthy. They generally tended to show an early interest in exploring uncharted territory. But only after gaining mastery of their chosen field, after about a decade of practicing their craft, did they have their initial revolutionary breakthrough. Most creators seemed to have obtained at least some emotional and intellectual support at the time of their breakthrough. However, following this initial breakthrough (and sometimes before), highly creative individuals generally dedicated all their energies to their work. They sometimes abandoned, neglected, or exploited close relationships during adulthood. About a decade after their initial creative achievement, most of the creators Gardner studied made a second breakthrough. It was more comprehensive and more integrative but less revolutionary. Whether a creator continued to make significant contributions depended on the particular field of endeavor. Poets and scientists were less likely to do so than musicians and painters.

An alternative integrative theory of creativity suggests that multiple individual and environmental factors must converge for creativity to occur (Sternberg & Lubart, 1991, 1993, 1995, 1996). What distinguishes the highly creative individual from the only modestly creative one is the confluence of multiple factors, rather than extremely high levels of any particular factor or even the possession of a distinctive trait. This theory is termed the *investment theory of creativity*. The theme unifying these various factors is that the creative individual takes a buy-low, sell-high approach to ideas (Sternberg & Lubart, 1995, 1996). In buying low, the creator initially sees the hidden potential of ideas that are presumed by others to have little value. The creative person then focuses attention on this idea. It is, at the time of the creator's interest, unrecognized or under-valued by contemporaries. But it has great potential for creative development. The creator then develops the idea into a meaningful, significant creative contribution until at last others also can recognize the merits of the idea. Once the idea has been developed and its value is recognized, the creator then sells high. He or she moves on to other pursuits and looks for the hidden potential in other undervalued ideas. Thus, the creative person influences the field most by always staying a step ahead of the rest.

Despite the diversity of views, most researchers would agree that most of the preceding individual characteristics and environmental conditions are necessary. None alone would be sufficient. In fact, extraordinary creative productivity may be as rare as it is precisely because so many variables must come together, in the right amounts, in a single person. A further complication is that many of these variables do not show a linear relationship to creativity. If the relation were linear, an increase in a particular characteristic or condition always would be associated with an increase in creativity. The contrary appears to be true. Many seem to show paradoxical effects and other nonlinear relationships.

Types of Creative Contributions

According to one set of investigators, creative contributions may be of eight kinds (Sternberg, 1999; Sternberg, Kaufman, & Pretz, 2001, 2002). The eight types of creative contributions include the following:

1. *Replication*. The creative contribution represents an effort to show that a given field is where it should be.

2. *Redefinition*. The creative contribution represents an effort to redefine where the field currently is. The current status of the field is thus seen from a new point of view.

3. *Forward movement*. The creative contribution represents an attempt to move the field forward in the direction in which it already is moving, and the contribution takes the field to a point where others are ready for the field to go.

4. *Advance forward movement*. The creative contribution represents an attempt to move the field forward in the direction it is already going. But the contribution moves beyond where others are ready for the field to go.

5. *Redirection*. The creative contribution represents an attempt to move the field from where it is toward a new and different direction.

6. *Redirection from a point in the past*. The creative contribution represents an attempt to move the field back to where it once was (a reconstruction of the past) so that the field may move onward from that point.

7. *Starting over.* The creative contribution represents an attempt to move the field to a different and as yet not reached starting point. It then moves the field in a different direction from that point.

8. *Integration.* The creative contribution represents an attempt to move the field by putting together aspects of two or more past kinds of creative contributions that formerly were viewed as distinct or even opposed. Now they are seen as synthesized (Sternberg, 1999).

The eight types of creative contributions described are viewed as qualitatively distinct. However, within each type, there can be quantitative differences. For example, a forward incrementation may represent a fairly small step forward or a substantial leap for a given field. A starting over may restart an entire field or just a small area of it. Moreover, a given contribution may overlap categories.

The eight kinds of creative contributions may differ in the extent of the creative contribution they make. But there is no *a priori* way of evaluating the *amount* of creativity on the basis of the *type* of creative contribution. Certain types of creative contributions probably tend, on average, to be greater in amounts of novelty than are others. For example, replications tend, on average, not to be highly novel. But creativity also involves the quality of work, and the type of creative contribution a work makes does not necessarily predict the quality of the work.

When people have new ideas, they have to use their reasoning skills to analyze these ideas and ultimately to decide if the ideas are truly creative. How do they do such reasoning and decision making? These issues are discussed in the next chapter.

Common Themes

This chapter highlights several of the themes first presented in Chapter 1.

The first theme is domain generality versus domain specificity. Early work on problem solving, such as that by Allen Newell and Herbert Simon and their colleagues, emphasized the domain generality of problem solving. These investigators sought to write computer routines, such as the General Problem Solver, that would solve a broad array of problems. Later theorists have more emphasized domain specificity in problem solving. They have especially called attention to the need for a broad knowledge base to solve problems successfully.

A second theme is validity of causal inference versus ecological validity. Most studies of creativity have occurred in laboratory settings. For example, Paul Torrance gave students paper-and-pencil tests of creative thinking administered in classrooms. In contrast Howard Gruber has been interested only in creativity as it occurred in natural settings, such as when Darwin generated his many ideas behind the theory of evolution.

A third theme is basic versus applied research. The field of creativity has generated many insights regarding fundamental processes used in creative thought. But the field has also spawned a large industry of "creativity enhancement"—programs designed to make people more creative. Some of these programs utilize insights of basic research. Others represent little more than the intuitions of their inventors. It is important that training be based, where possible, on psychological theory and research rather than guesswork.

Line up six toothpicks. Ask a friend to make four equilateral triangles with these six toothpicks without breaking the toothpicks into pieces. Most people will not be able to do this task because they will try to make the four triangles on a single plane. When they give up, make a single triangle flat on the table with three of the toothpicks, then with the other three toothpicks make a pyramid by joining the three toothpicks at the top and having the sides connect with the intersections of the three toothpicks on the table. Your friend was fixated on the plane of the alignment of the toothpicks. See if any of your friends can figure out this problem if you give them the toothpicks standing up in a toothpick holder.

Summary

1. **What are some key steps involved in solving problems?** Problem solving involves mentally working to overcome obstacles that stand in the way of reaching a goal. The key steps of problem solving are problem identification, problem definition and representation, strategy construction, organization of information, allocation of resources, monitoring, and evaluation. In everyday experiences, these steps may be implemented very flexibly. Various steps may be repeated, may occur out of sequence, or may be implemented interactively.

2. **What are the differences between problems that have a clear path to a solution versus problems that do not?** Although well-structured problems may have clear paths to solution, the route to solution still may be difficult to follow. Some well-structured problems can be solved using algorithms. They may be tedious to implement but are likely to lead to an accurate solution if applicable to a given problem. Computers are likely to use algorithmic problem-solving strategies. Humans are more likely to use rather informal heuristics (e.g., means–ends analysis, working forward, working backward, and generate and test) for solving problems. When ill-structured problems are solved, the choice of an appropriate problem representation powerfully influences the ease of reaching an accurate solution. Additionally, in solving ill-structured problems, people may need to use more than a heuristic or an algorithmic strategy; insight may be required.

Many ill-structured problems cannot be solved without the benefit of insight. There are several alternative views of how insightful problem solving takes place. According to the Gestaltist and the neo-Gestaltist views, insightful problem solving is a special process. It comprises more than the sum of its parts and may be evidenced by the suddenness of realizing a solution. According to the nothing-special view, insightful problem solving is no different from any other kind of problem solving. And according to the three-process view, insight involves a special use of three processes: selective encoding, selective combination, and selective comparison.

3. **What are some of the obstacles and aids to problem solving?** A mental set (also termed entrenchment) is a strategy that has worked in the past but that does not work for a particular problem that needs to be solved in the present. A particular type of mental set is functional fixedness. It involves the inability to see that something that is known to have a particular use also may be used for serving other purposes. Transfer may be either positive or negative. It refers to the carry-over of problem-solving skills from one problem

or kind of problem to another. Positive transfer across isomorphic problems rarely occurs spontaneously, particularly if the problems appear to be different in content or in context. Incubation follows a period of intensive work on a problem. It involves laying a problem to rest for a while and then returning to it. In this way, subconscious work can continue on the problem while the problem is consciously ignored.

4. **How does expertise affect problem solving?** Experts differ from novices in both the *amount* and the *organization of knowledge* that they bring to bear on problem solving in the domain of their expertise. For experts, many aspects of problem solving may be governed by automatic processes. Such automaticity usually facilitates the expert's ability to solve problems in the given area of expertise. When problems involve novel elements requiring novel strategies, however, the automaticity of some procedures actually may impede problem solving, at least temporarily. Expertise in a given domain is viewed mostly from the practice-makes-perfect perspective. However, many point out that the notion of talent should not be ignored and probably contributes much to the differences between different experts.

5. **What is creativity, and how can it be fostered?** Creativity involves producing something that is both original and worthwhile. Several factors characterize highly creative individuals. One is extremely high motivation to be creative in a particular field of endeavor (e.g., for the sheer enjoyment of the creative process). A second is both nonconformity in violating any conventions that might inhibit the creative work and dedication in maintaining standards of excellence and self-discipline related to the creative work. A third factor is deep belief in the value of the creative work, as well as willingness to criticize and improve the work. A fourth is careful choice of the problems or subjects on which to focus creative attention. A fifth is thought processes characterized by both insight and divergent thinking. A sixth factor is risk taking. A seventh factor is extensive knowledge of the relevant domain. And an eighth factor is profound commitment to the creative endeavor. In addition, the historical context and the domain and field of endeavor influence the expression of creativity.

Thinking about Thinking: Factual, Analytical, Creative, and Practical Questions

1. Describe the steps of the problem-solving cycle and give an example of each step.

2. What are some of the key characteristics of expert problem solvers?

3. What are some of the insights into problem solving gained through studying computer simulations of problem solving? How might a computer-based approach limit the potential for understanding problem solving in humans?

4. Compare and contrast the various approaches to creativity.

5. Design a problem that would require insight for its solution.

6. Design a context for problem solving that would enhance the ease of reaching a solution.

7. Given what we know about some of the hindrances to problem solving, how could you minimize those hindrances in your handling of the problems you face?

8. Given some of the ideas regarding creativity presented in this chapter, what can you do to enhance your own creativity?

Key Terms

algorithms	insight	selective-combination insights
analysis	isomorphic	selective-comparison insights
convergent thinking	mental set	selective-encoding insights
creativity	negative transfer	stereotypes
divergent thinking	positive transfer	synthesis
functional fixedness	problem solving	transfer
heuristics	problem-solving cycle	transparency
ill-structured problems	problem space	well-structured problem
incubation	productive thinking	

 Explore CogLab by going to http://coglab.wadsworth.com. Answer the questions required by your instructor from the student manual that accompanies CogLab.

Monty Hall

Annotated Suggested Reading

Davidson, J. E., & Sternberg, R. J. (Eds.) (2003). *The psychology of problem solving.* New York: Cambridge University Press. A complete review of contemporary literature on problem solving.

Decision Making and Reasoning

EXPLORING COGNITIVE PSYCHOLOGY

1. What are some of the strategies that guide human decision making?

2. What are some of the forms of deductive reasoning that people may use and what factors facilitate or impede deductive reasoning?

3. How do people use inductive reasoning to make causal inferences and to reach other types of conclusions?

4. Are there any alternative views of reasoning?

INVESTIGATING COGNITIVE PSYCHOLOGY

Linda is 31 years old, single, outspoken, and very bright. She majored in philosophy. As a student, she was deeply concerned with issues of discrimination and social justice and also participated in antinuclear demonstrations.

Based on the preceding description, list the likelihood that the following statements about Linda are true:

(a) Linda is a teacher in elementary school.
(b) Linda works in a bookstore and takes yoga classes.
(c) Linda is active in the feminist movement.
(d) Linda is a psychiatric social worker.
(e) Linda is a member of the League of Women Voters.
(f) Linda is a bank teller.
(g) Linda is an insurance salesperson.
(h) Linda is a bank teller and is active in the feminist movement.

(Tversky & Kahneman, 1983, p. 297).

If you are like 85% of the people Tversky and Kahneman studied, you rated the likelihood of item (h) above as greater than the likelihood of item (f). Stop for a minute, however. Imagine a huge convention hall filled with the entire population of bank tellers. Now think about how many of them would be at a hypothetical booth for feminist bank tellers—a subset of the entire population of bank tellers. If Linda is at the booth for feminist bank tellers, she must, by definition, be in the convention hall of bank tellers. Hence, the likelihood that she is at the booth (i.e., she is a feminist bank teller) cannot logically be greater than the likelihood that she is in the convention hall (i.e., she is a bank teller). Nonetheless, given the description of Linda, we intuitively feel more likely to find her at the booth than in the convention hall. This intuitive feeling is an example of a **fallacy**—erroneous reasoning—in judgment and reasoning.

In this chapter we consider many ways in which we make judgments and decisions and use reasoning to draw conclusions. The first section deals with how we make choices and judgments. **Judgment and decision making** are used to select from among choices or to evaluate opportunities. An example would be choosing the car that would please you the most for the amount of money you have. The second section addresses various forms of reasoning. The goal of reasoning is to draw conclusions deductively from principles or inductively from evidence. An example of deductive reasoning would be applying the general laws of physics to reach conclusions regarding the mechanics of a particular car engine. An example of inductive reasoning would be reading consumer-oriented statistics to find out the reliability, economy, and safety of various cars.

Judgment and Decision Making

In the course of our everyday lives, we constantly are making judgments and decisions. One of the most important decisions you may have made is that of whether and where to go to college. Once in college, you still need to decide on which courses to take. Later on, you may need to choose a major field of study. You make decisions about friends and dates, about how to relate to your parents, and about how to spend money. How do you go about making these decisions?

Classical Decision Theory

The earliest models of how people make decisions are referred to as "classical decision theory." Most of these models were devised by economists, statisticians, and philosophers, not by psychologists. Hence, they reflect the strengths of an economic perspective. One such strength is the ease of developing and using mathematical models for human behavior. Among the early models of decision making crafted in the twentieth century was *economic man and woman*. This model assumed three things. First, decision makers are fully informed regarding all possible options for their decisions and of all possible outcomes of their decision options. Second, they are infinitely sensitive to the subtle distinctions among decision options. Third, they are fully rational in regard to their choice of options (Edwards, 1954; see also Slovic, 1990). The assumption of infinite sensitivity means that people can evaluate the difference between two outcomes, no matter how subtle the distinctions among options may be. The assumption of rationality means that people make their choices to maximize something of value, whatever that something may be.

Consider an example of how this model works. Suppose that a decision maker is considering which of two job offers to accept. Assume that both provide the same starting salaries. Suppose also that people at Company A have a 50% chance of getting a 20% salary increase the first year. People at Company B have a 90% chance of getting a 10% salary increase the first year. The decision maker will calculate the expected value for each option, which is the probability times the corresponding value (utility), which here is the increase in salary ($0.50 \times 0.20 = 0.10$; $0.90 \times 0.10 = 0.09$). For all of the potential benefits (additive calculations) and costs (subtractive calculations) of each job, the person would perform similar calculations. He or she would then choose the job with the highest expected value. In other words, he or she would pick the one offering the highest calculated benefit at the lowest calculated cost. Assuming all other things are equal, we should choose Company A. A great deal of economic research has been based on this model.

An alternative model makes greater allowance for the psychological makeup of each individual decision maker. According to *subjective expected utility theory,* the goal of human action is to seek pleasure and avoid pain. According to this theory, in making decisions people will seek to maximize pleasure (referred to as positive utility) and to minimize pain (referred to as negative utility). In doing so, however, each of us uses calculations of two things. One is **subjective utility,** which is a calculation based on the individual's judged weightings of utility (value), rather than on objective criteria. and the second is **subjective probability,** which is a calculation based on the individual's estimates of likelihood, rather than on objective statistical computations.

Ponder an example of how this model works. In deciding which of two job offers to accept, different people would give different subjective positive or negative utilities to each feature of each job offer. Consider someone with a husband and four children. She might give a higher positive utility to benefits such as health insurance, dental care, vacation time, paid holidays, and so on, than would a single person who is strongly career oriented. Similarly, the woman with a family might assign a higher negative utility to the warning that a job involves a lot of travel requiring the person to be out of state for many days each month.

Two job seekers also might assign differing subjective probabilities to various potential positive or negative utilities. A pessimist probably would expect a higher likelihood of negative utilities and a lower likelihood of positive utilities than would an optimist. Hence, according to subjective expected utility theory, each person will go through a series of steps. First the person will multiply each subjective probability by each subjective positive utility for each job offer. Then he or she will subtract the calculation of the subjective probability of each subjective negative utility. Finally, he or she will reach a decision based on the relative expected values obtained from these calculations. The alternative that has the highest expected value is chosen. Subjective utility theory takes into account the many subjective variables that arise when people are involved. But theorists soon noticed that human decision making is more complex than even this modified theory implies.

For most decisions, there is no one perfect option that will be selected by all people. How, then, can we predict the optimal decision for a particular person? According to subjective expected utility theory, we need know only the person's subjective expected utilities. These are based on both subjective estimates of probability and subjective weightings of costs and benefits. We then can predict the optimal decision for that person. This prediction is based on the belief that people seek to reach well-reasoned decisions based on five factors. The first factor is consideration of all possible known alternatives, given that unpredictable alternatives may be available. The second is use of a maximum amount of available information, given that some relevant information may not be available. The third is careful, if subjective, weighing of the potential costs (risks) and benefits of each alternative. The fourth is careful (although subjective) calculation of the probability of various outcomes, given that certainty of outcomes cannot be known. And the fifth is a maximum degree of sound reasoning, based on considering all of the aforementioned factors. Now, answer the following question. When was the last time you implemented the five preceding aspects of optimal decision making, even allowing for limits on your knowledge and for unpredictable elements? Probably not recently.

Satisficing

As early as the 1950s some researchers were beginning to challenge the notion of unlimited rationality. Not only did these researchers recognize that we humans do not always make ideal decisions and that we usually include subjective considerations in our decisions. They also suggested that we humans are not entirely and boundlessly rational in making decisions. In particular, we humans are not necessarily irrational. Rather, we show **bounded rationality**—we are rational, but within limits. (Simon, 1957).

Perhaps we typically use a decision-making strategy he termed satisficing (Simon, 1957). In **satisficing,** we consider options one by one, and then we select an option as soon as we find one that is satisfactory or just good enough to meet our minimum level of acceptability. We do not consider all possible options and then carefully compute which of the entire universe of options will maximize our gains and minimize our losses. Thus, we will consider the minimum possible number of options needed to arrive at a decision that we believe will satisfy our minimum requirements. Of course, satisficing is only one of several suboptimal strategies people can use.

Suppose, for example, that you are looking for a used car. There are probably a staggering number of used-car lots near where you live. You probably have neither the time nor the inclination to visit them all. Such extensive visits would allow you to

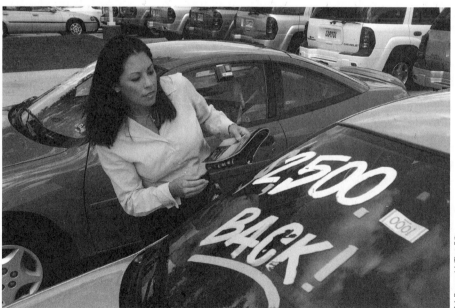

According to Herbert Simon, people often satisfice when they make important decisions, such as which car to buy. They decide for the first acceptable alternative that comes along.

Amos Tversky, now deceased, was the Davis-Brack professor of behavioral science at Stanford University. Tversky was best known for his work on human judgment and decision making, including work with Daniel Kahneman on heuristics and biases in judgment under conditions of uncertainty. Tversky also made major contributions to the study of similarity and psychological measurement.

pick the car that seems best on all of the many dimensions on which you might judge a car. So you go to one lot to see what is available. If you see a car there that you find satisfactory in terms of your major criteria for making the purchase, you buy it. If you do not find a car there that is good enough, you move on to the next lot. You keep looking only until you find a car that meets your needs. Then you buy it. On the one hand, you have probably not picked the optimal car of all those available. On the other hand, you have not spent 4 months looking through all of the lots in town.

You also may use satisficing when considering research topics for a term project or paper. There are countless possible topics. You probably can consider quite a few. But then you need to settle on a satisfactory or even pretty good topic without continuing your exploration indefinitely. A decision maker may find that an uncomfortably high number of options have failed to reach the initial minimum level of acceptability. He or she may then decide to adjust the minimum level deemed adequate for satisficing. For example, suppose I decide that I want to buy a new luxury car with an excellent consumer track record and high fuel efficiency for less than $3,000. I may end up having to adjust my minimum level of acceptability way downward.

Elimination by Aspects

We sometimes use a different strategy when faced with far more alternatives than we feel that we reasonably can consider in the time we have available (Tversky, 1972a, 1972b). In such situations, we do not try to manipulate mentally all the weighted attributes of all the available options. Rather, we use a process of elimination by aspects. In **elimination by aspects,** we eliminate alternatives by focusing on aspects of each alternative, one at a time. In particular, we focus on one aspect (attribute) of the various options. We form a minimum criterion for that aspect. We then eliminate all options that do not meet that criterion. For the remaining options, we then select a second aspect for which we set a minimum criterion by which to eliminate additional options. We continue using a sequential process of elimination of options by considering a series of aspects until a single option remains (Dawes, 2000).

For example, in choosing a car to buy we may focus on total price as an aspect. We may choose to dismiss factors such as maintenance costs, insurance costs, or other factors that realistically might affect the money we will have to spend on the car in addition to the sale price. Once we have weeded out the alternatives that do not meet our criterion, we choose another aspect. We set a criterion value and weed out additional alternatives. We continue in this way. We weed out more alternatives, one aspect at a time, until we are left with a single option. In practice, it appears that we may use some elements of elimination by aspects or satisficing to narrow the range of options to just a few. Then we use more thorough and careful strategies. Examples would be those suggested by subjective expected utility theory. They can be useful for selecting among the few remaining options (Payne, 1976).

We often use mental shortcuts and even biases that limit and sometimes distort our ability to make rational decisions. One of the key ways in which we use mental shortcuts centers on our estimations of probability. Consider, for example, some of the strategies used by statisticians when calculating probability. They are shown in Table 12.1.

You easily may be able to calculate the simple probability that a given cost or benefit will occur (shown on the first row of the table). You also can calculate the

TABLE 12.1	Rules of Probability
HYPOTHETICAL EXAMPLE	**CALCULATION OF PROBABILITY**
Lee is one of ten highly qualified candidates applying for one scholarship. What are Lee's chances of getting the scholarship?	Lee a 0.1 chance of getting the scholarship.
If Lee is one of ten highly qualified scholarship students applying for one scholarship, what are Lee's chances of *not* getting the scholarship?	$1 - 0.1 = 0.9$ Lee has a 0.9 chance of not getting the scholarship.
Lee's roommate and Lee are among ten highly qualified scholarship students applying for one scholarship. What are the chances that one of the two will get he scholarship?	$0.1 + 0.1 = 0.2$ There is a 0.2 chance that one of the two roommates will get the scholarship.
Lee owns four pairs of shoes—blue, white, black, and brown. Lee rotates randomly among the pairs of shoes he wears. What are the chances that one of the two roommates will be awarded the scholarship and that Lee will be wearing black shoes at the time?	$0.25 \times 0.2 = 0.05$ There is a 0.05 chance that one of the two roommates will be awarded the scholarship and that Lee will be wearing black shoes at the time of the announcement.

simple probability that a given cost or benefit will not occur (shown on the second line of the table). However, the calculations of combined probabilities for the occurrence or nonoccurrence of various costs and benefits can be quite cumbersome (see the third and fourth rows of the table).

Another probability is *conditional probability*. It is the likelihood of one event, given another. For example, you might want to calculate the likelihood of receiving an "A" for a cognitive psychology course, given that you receive an "A" on the final exam. The formula for calculating conditional probabilities in light of evidence is known as Bayes's theorem. It is quite complex. So most people do not use it in everyday reasoning situations. Nonetheless, such calculations are essential to evaluating scientific hypotheses, forming realistic medical diagnoses, analyzing demographic data, and performing many other real-world tasks. (For a highly readable explanation of Bayes's theorem, see Eysenck & Keane, 1990, pp. 456–458. For a detailed description of Bayes's theorem from a cognitive psychological perspective, see Osherson, 1990.)

Heuristics and Biases

People make many decisions based on biases and heuristics (short-cuts) in their thinking (Kahneman & Tversky, 1972, 1990; Stanovich, Sái, & West, 2004; Tversky & Kahneman, 1971, 1993). These mental shortcuts lighten the cognitive load of making decisions. But they also allow for a much greater chance of error.

Representativeness

Before you read about representativeness, try the following problem from Kahneman and Tversky (1972a, 1972b).

INVESTIGATING COGNITIVE PSYCHOLOGY	All the families having exactly six children in a particular city were surveyed. In seventy-two of the families, the exact order of births of boys and girls was G B G B B G (G girl; B boy). What is your estimate of the number of families surveyed in which the exact order of births was B G B B B B?

Most people judging the number of families with the B G B B B B birth pattern estimate the number to be less than seventy-two. Actually, the best estimate of the number of families with this birth order is seventy-two, the same as for the G B G B B G birth order. The expected number for the second pattern would be the same because the gender for each birth is independent (at least, theoretically) of the gender for every other birth. For any one birth, the chance of a boy (or a girl) is one of two. Thus, any particular pattern of births is equally likely $(1/2)^6$, even B B B B B B or G G G G G G.

Why do many of us believe some birth orders to be more likely than others? In part, the reason is that we use the heuristic of representativeness. In **representativeness,** we judge the probability of an uncertain event according to (1) how obviously it is similar to or representative of the population from which it is derived and (2) the degree to which it reflects the salient features of the process by which it is generated (such as randomness) (see also Fischhoff, 1999; Johnson-Laird, 2000, 2004). For example, people believe that the first birth order is more likely because (1) it is more representative of the number of females and males in the population and (2) it looks more random than the second birth order. In fact, of course, either birth order is equally likely to occur by chance.

Similarly, suppose people are asked to judge the probability of flips of a coin yielding the sequence—H T H H T H (H, heads; T, tails). Most people will judge it as higher than they will if asked to judge the sequence—H H H H T H. If you expect a sequence to be random, you tend to view as more likely a sequence that "looks random." Indeed, people often comment that the numbers in a table of random numbers "don't look random." The reason is that people underestimate the number of runs of the same number that will appear wholly by chance. We frequently reason in terms of whether something appears to represent a set of accidental occurrences, rather than actually considering the true likelihood of a given chance occurrence. This tendency makes us more vulnerable to the machinations of magicians, charlatans, and con artists. Any of them may make much of their having predicted the realistic probability of a nonrandom-looking event. For example, the odds are 9 to 1 that two people in a group of forty people (e.g., in a classroom or a small nightclub audience) will share a birthday (the same month and day, not necessarily the same year). In a group of fourteen people, there are better than even odds that two people will have birthdays within a day of each other (Krantz, 1992).

Another example of the representativeness heuristic is the gambler's fallacy. *Gambler's fallacy,* is a mistaken belief that the probability of a given random event, such as winning or losing at a game of chance, is influenced by previous random events. For example, a gambler who loses five successive bets may believe that a win

People often mistakenly believe in the gambler's fallacy. They think that if they have been unlucky in their gambles, it is time for their luck to change. In fact, success or failure in past gambles has no effect on the likelihood of success in future ones.

Research shows that the "hot hand" effect is in our minds, not in the players' games. Making a past shot does not increase the player's chance of making future shots.

is therefore more likely the sixth time. In truth, of course, each bet (or coin toss) is an independent event. It has an equal probability of winning or losing. The gambler is no more likely to win on the sixth bet than on the first—or on the 1,001st.

A related fallacy is the misguided belief in the "hot hand" or the "streak shooter" in basketball. Apparently, both professional and amateur basketball players, as well as their fans, believe that a player's chances of making a basket are greater after making a previous shot than after missing one. However, the statistical likelihoods (and the actual records of players) show no such tendency (Gilovich, Vallone, & Tversky, 1985). Shrewd players will take advantage of this belief and will closely guard opponents immediately after they have made baskets. The reason is that the opposing players will be more likely to try to get the ball to these perceived "streak shooters."

That we frequently rely on the representativeness heuristic may not be terribly surprising. It is easy to use and often works. For example, suppose we have not heard a weather report prior to stepping outside. We informally judge the probability that it will rain. We base our judgment on how well the characteristics of this day (e.g., the month of the year and the presence or absence of clouds in the sky) represent the characteristics of days on which it rains. Another reason that we often use the representativeness heuristic is that we mistakenly believe that small samples (e.g., of events, of people, of characteristics) resemble in all respects the whole population from which the sample is drawn (Tversky & Kahneman, 1971). We particularly tend to underestimate the likelihood that the characteristics of a small sample (e.g., the people whom we know well) of a population inadequately represent the characteristics of the whole population.

We also tend to use the representativeness heuristic more frequently when we are highly aware of anecdotal evidence based on a very small sample of the population. This reliance on anecdotal evidence has been referred to as a "man-who" argument (Nisbett & Ross, 1980). When presented with statistics, we may refute those data with our own observations of, "I know a man who . . . ." For example, faced with statistics on coronary disease and high-cholesterol diets, someone may counter with, "I know a man who ate whipped cream for breakfast, lunch, and dinner and lived to be 110 years old. He would have kept going but he was shot through his perfectly healthy heart by a jealous lover."

One reason that people misguidedly use the representativeness heuristic is because they fail to understand the concept of base rates. **Base rate** refers to the prevalence of an event or characteristic within its population of events or characteristics. In everyday decision making, people often ignore base-rate information. But it is important to effective judgment and decision making. In many occupations, the use of base-rate information is essential for adequate job performance. For example, suppose a doctor were told that a 10-year-old boy was suffering chest pains. The doctor would be much less likely to worry about an incipient heart attack than if told that a 50-year-old man had the identical symptom. Why? Because the base rate of heart attacks is much higher in 50-year-old men than in 10-year-old boys. Of course, people use other heuristics as well. People can be taught how to use base rates to improve their decision making (Gigerenzer, 1996; Koehler, 1996).

Availability

Most of us at least occasionally use the **availability heuristic,** in which we make judgments on the basis of how easily we can call to mind what we perceive as relevant instances of a phenomenon (Tversky & Kahneman, 1973; see also Fischhoff, 1999; Sternberg, 2000). For example, consider the letter R. Are there more words in the English language that begin with the letter R or that have R as their third letter? Most respondents say that there are more words beginning with the letter R (Tversky & Kahneman, 1973). Why? Because generating words beginning with the letter R is easier than generating words having R as the third letter. In fact, there are more English-language words with R as their third letter. The same happens to be true of some other letters as well, such as K, L, N, and V.

The availability heuristic also has been observed in regard to everyday situations. In one study, married partners individually stated which of the two partners performed a larger proportion of each of twenty different household chores (Ross & Sicoly, 1979). These tasks included mundane chores such as grocery shopping or preparing breakfast. Each partner stated that he or she more often performed about sixteen of the twenty chores. Suppose each partner was correct. Then, to accomplish 100% of the work in a household, each partner would have to perform 80% of the work. Similar outcomes emerged from questioning of members of college basketball teams and joint participants in laboratory tasks. For all participants, the greater availability of their own actions made it seem that each had performed a greater proportion of the work in joint enterprises.

Although clearly 80% + 80% does not equal 100%, we can understand why people may engage in using the availability heuristic when it confirms their beliefs about themselves. However, people also use the availability heuristic when its use leads to a logical fallacy that has nothing to do with their beliefs about themselves. Two groups of participants were asked to estimate the number of words of a particular form that would be expected to appear in a 2,000-word passage. For one group the form was _ _ _ ing (i.e., seven letters ending in -ing). For the other group the form was _ _ _ _ _n_ (i.e., seven letters with n as the second-to-the-last letter). Clearly, there cannot be more seven-letter words ending in -ing than seven-letter words with n as the second-to-the-last letter. But the greater availability of the former led to estimates of probability that were more than twice as high for the former, as compared with the latter (Tversky & Kahneman, 1983). This example illustrates how the availability heuristic might lead to the conjunction fallacy. In the *conjunction fallacy*, an individual gives a higher estimate for a subset of events (e.g., the instances of -ing) than for the larger set of events containing the given subset (e.g., the instances of n as the second-to-the-last letter). This fallacy also is illustrated in the chapter-opening vignette regarding Linda.

Another heuristic—the representativeness heuristic—also may induce individuals to engage in the conjunction fallacy during probabilistic reasoning (Tversky & Kahneman, 1983; see also Dawes, 2000). Tversky and Kahneman asked college students:

> Please give your estimate of the following values: What percentage of the men surveyed [in a health survey] have had one or more heart attacks? What percentage of the men surveyed both are over 55 years old and have had one or more heart attacks? (p. 308)

The mean estimates were 18% for the former and 30% for the latter. In fact, 65% of the respondents gave higher estimates for the latter (which is clearly a subset of the former).

However, people do not always engage in the conjunction fallacy. Only 25% of respondents gave higher estimates for the latter question than for the former when the questions were rephrased as frequencies rather than as percentages. In other words, the questions were in terms of numbers of individuals within a given sample of the population. Also, the researchers found that the conjunction fallacy was less likely when the conjunctions are defined by the intersection of concrete classes than by a combination of properties. For example, they were less likely for types of objects or individuals such as dogs or beagles than they were for features of objects or individuals such as conservatism or feminism (Tversky & Kahneman, 1983). Although classes and properties are equivalent from a logical standpoint, they generate different mental representations (Stenning & Monaghan, 2004). Different rules and relations are used in each of the two cases. Thus, the formal equivalence of properties to classes is not intuitively obvious to most people (Tversky & Kahneman, 1983).

A variant of the conjunction fallacy is the *inclusion fallacy*. In the inclusion fallacy, the individual judges a greater likelihood that every member of an inclusive category has a particular characteristic than that every member of a subset of the inclusive category has that characteristic (Shafir, Osherson, & Smith, 1990). For example,

Although riding in a car is statistically much more risky than riding in a plane, people often feel less safe in a plane, in part because of the availability heuristic. People hear about every major U.S. plane crash that takes place. But they hear about relatively few car accidents.

participants judged a much greater likelihood that "every single lawyer" (i.e., every lawyer) is conservative than that every single labor-union lawyer is conservative. According to the researchers, we tend to judge the likelihood that the members of a particular class (e.g., lawyers) or subclass (e.g., labor-union lawyers) of individuals will demonstrate a particular characteristic (e.g., conservatism) based on the perceived typicality (i.e., representativeness) of the given characteristic for the given category. We should, however, judge likelihood based on statistical probability.

Heuristics such as representativeness and availability do not always lead to wrong judgments or poor decisions. Indeed, we use these mental shortcuts because they are so often right. For example, one of the factors that leads to the greater availability of an event is in fact the greater frequency of the event. However, availability also may be influenced by recency of presentation (as in implicit-memory cueing, mentioned in Chapter 7), unusualness, or distinctive salience of a particular event or event category for the individual. Nonetheless, when the available information is not biased for some reason the instances that are most available are generally the most common ones. Examples of biased coverage might be sensationalized press coverage, extensive advertising, recency of an uncommon occurrence, or personal prejudices. We generally make decisions in which the most common instances are the most relevant and valuable ones. In such cases, the availability heuristic is often a convenient shortcut with few costs. However, when particular instances are better recalled because of biases (e.g., your views of your own behavior, in comparison with that of other people), the availability heuristic may lead to less than optimal decisions.

Other Judgment Phenomena

A heuristic related to availability is the *anchoring-and-adjustment heuristic*, by which people adjust their evaluations of things by means of certain reference points called *end-anchors*. Before you read on, quickly (in less than 5 seconds) calculate in your head the answer to the following problem:

$$8 \times 7 \times 6 \times 5 \times 4 \times 3 \times 2 \times 1$$

Now, quickly calculate your answer to the following problem:

$$1 \times 2 \times 3 \times 4 \times 5 \times 6 \times 7 \times 8$$

Two groups of participants estimated the product of one or the other of the preceding two sets of eight numbers (Tversky & Kahneman, 1974). The median (middle) estimate for the participants given the first sequence was 2,250. For the participants given the second sequence, the median estimate was 512. (The actual product is 40,320 for both.) The two products are the same, as they must be because the numbers are exactly the same (applying the commutative law of multiplication). Nonetheless, people provide a higher estimate for the first sequence than for the second. The reason is that their computation of the anchor—the first few digits multiplied by each other—renders a higher estimate from which they make an adjustment to reach a final estimate.

Another consideration in decision theory is the influence of *framing effects*, in which the way that the options are presented influences the selection of an option (Tversky & Kahneman, 1981). For instance, we tend to choose options that demonstrate risk aversion when we are faced with an option involving potential gains. That is, we tend to choose options offering a small but certain gain rather than a larger but uncertain gain, unless the uncertain gain is either tremendously greater or only modestly less than certain. The example in the "Investigating Cognitive Psychology" box is only slightly modified from one used by Tversky and Kahneman (1981).

INVESTIGATING COGNITIVE PSYCHOLOGY	Suppose that you were told that 600 people were at risk of dying of a particular disease. Vaccine A could save the lives of 200 of the people at risk. For Vaccine B, there is a 0.33 likelihood that all 600 people would be saved, but there is a 0.66 likelihood that all 600 people will die. Which option would you choose?

We tend to choose options that demonstrate risk seeking when we are faced with options involving potential losses. That is, we tend to choose options offering a large but uncertain loss rather than a smaller but certain loss, unless the uncertain loss is either tremendously greater or only modestly less than certain. The next "Investigating Cognitive Psychology" box provides an interesting example.

INVESTIGATING COGNITIVE PSYCHOLOGY	Suppose that for the 600 people at risk of dying of a particular disease, if Vaccine C is used, 400 people will die. However, if Vaccine D is used, there is a 0.33 likelihood that no one will die and a 0.66 likelihood that all 600 people will die. Which option would you choose?

In the preceding situations, most people will choose Vaccine A and Vaccine D. Now, compare the number of people whose lives will be lost or saved by using Vaccines A or C. Similarly, compare the number of people whose lives will be lost or saved by using Vaccines B or D. In both cases, the expected value is identical. Our predilection for risk aversion versus risk seeking leads us to quite different choices based on the way in which a decision is framed, even when the actual outcomes of the choices are the same.

Another judgment phenomenon is **illusory correlation,** in which we tend to see particular events or particular attributes and categories as going together because we are predisposed to do so (Hamilton & Lickel, 2000). In the case of events, we may see spurious cause-effect relationships. In the case of attributes, we may use personal prejudices to form and use stereotypes (perhaps as a result of using the representativeness heuristic). For example, suppose we expect people of a given political party to show particular intellectual or moral characteristics. The instances in which people show those characteristics are more likely to be available in memory and recalled more easily than are instances that contradict our biased expectations. In other words, we perceive a correlation between the political party and the particular characteristics.

Illusory correlation even may influence psychiatric diagnoses based on projective tests such as the Rorschach and the Draw-a-Person tests (Chapman & Chapman,

1967, 1969, 1975). Researchers suggested a false correlation in which particular responses would be associated with particular diagnoses. For example, they suggested that people diagnosed with paranoia tend to draw people with large eyes more than do people with other diagnoses. In fact, diagnoses of paranoia were no more likely to be linked to depictions of large eyes than were any other diagnoses. However, what happened when individuals expected to observe a correlation between the particular responses and the associated diagnoses? They tended to see the illusory correlation, although no actual correlation existed.

Another common error is **overconfidence**—an individual's overvaluation of her or his own skills, knowledge, or judgment. For example, people answered 200 two-alternative statements, such as "Absinthe is (a) a liqueur, (b) a precious stone." (Absinthe is a licorice-flavored liqueur.) People were asked to choose the correct answer and to state the probability that their answer was correct (Fischhoff, Slovic, & Lichtenstein, 1977). People were overconfident. For example, when people were 100% confident in their answers, they were right only 80% of the time. In general, people tend to overestimate the accuracy of their judgments (Kahneman & Tversky, 1996). Why are people overconfident? One reason is that people may not realize how little they know. A second reason is that they may realize what they are assuming when they call on the knowledge they have. A third reason may be their ignorance of the fact that their information comes from unreliable sources (Carlson, 1995; Griffin & Tversky, 1992).

Baruch Fischhoff is a professor of social and decision sciences and a professor of engineering and public policy at Carnegie-Mellon University. He has studied psychological processes such as hindsight bias, risk perception, and value elicitation. He also has done policy-making work in areas such as risk and environmental management.

Because of overconfidence, people often make poor decisions. These decisions are based on inadequate information and ineffective decision-making strategies. Why we tend to be overconfident in our judgments is not clear. One simple explanation is that we prefer not to think about being wrong (Fischhoff, 1988).

An error in judgment that is quite common in people's thinking is the *sunk-cost fallacy* (Dupuy, 1998, 1999; Nozick, 1990). This is the decision to continue to invest in something simply because one has invested in it before and one hopes to recover one's investment. For example, suppose you have bought a car. It is a lemon. You already have invested thousands of dollars in getting it fixed. Now you have another major repair on it confronting you. You have no reason to believe that this additional repair really will be the last in the string of repairs. You think how much money you have spent on repairs. You reason that you need to do the additional repair to justify the amount you already have spent on repairs. So you do the repair rather than buy a new car. You have just committed the sunk-cost fallacy. The problem is that you already have lost the money on those repairs. Throwing more money into the repairs will not get that money back. Your best bet may well be to view the money already spent on repairs as a "sunk cost." You then buy a new car. Similarly, suppose you go on a vacation. You intend to stay on vacation for two weeks. You are having a miserable time. You are trying to decide whether to go home a week early. Should you go home a week early? You decide not to. In this way, you attempt to justify the investment you already have made in the vacation. Again, you have committed the sunk-cost fallacy. Instead of viewing the money simply as lost on an unfortunate decision, you have decided to throw more money away. But you do so without any hope that the vacation will get any better.

Taking *opportunity costs* into account is important when judgments are made. These are the prices paid for availing oneself of certain opportunities. For example, suppose you see a great job offer in San Francisco. You always wanted to live there. You are ready to take it. Before you do, you need to ask yourself a question. What other things you will have to forego to take advantage of this opportunity? An example might be the chance, on your budget, of having more than 500 square feet of living space. Another might be the chance to live in a place where you probably do not have to worry about earthquakes. Any time you take advantage of an opportunity, there are opportunity costs. They may, in some cases, make what looked like a good opportunity look like not such a great opportunity at all. Ideally, you should try to look at these opportunity costs in an unbiased way.

Finally, a bias that often affects all of us is **hindsight bias**—when we look at a situation retrospectively, we believe we easily can see all the signs and events leading up to a particular outcome (Fischhoff, 1982; Wasserman, Lempert, & Hastie, 1991). For example, suppose people are asked to predict the outcomes of psychological experiments in advance of the experiments. People rarely are able to predict the outcomes at better than chance levels. However, when people are told of the outcomes of psychological experiments, they frequently comment that these outcomes were obvious. They say the outcomes easily would have been predicted in advance. Similarly, when intimate personal relationships are in trouble, people often fail to observe signs of the difficulties until the problems reach crisis proportions. By then, it may be too late to save the relationship. In retrospect, however, people may slap their foreheads. They ask themselves, "Why didn't I see it coming? It was so obvious! I should have seen the signs."

Much of the work on judgment and decision making has focused on the errors we make. Human rationality is limited. Still, human irrationality also is limited (Cohen, 1981). We do act rationally in many instances. Also, each of us can improve our decision making through practice. We are most likely to do so if we obtain specific feedback regarding how to improve our decision-making strategies. Another key way to improve decision making is to gain accurate information for the calculation of probabilities. Then we must use probabilities appropriately in decision making. In addition, although subjective expected utility theory may offer a limited description of actual human decision making, it is far from useless. It offers a good prescription for enhancing the effectiveness of decision making when confronting a decision important enough to warrant the time and mental effort required (Slovic, 1990). Furthermore, we can try to avoid overconfidence in our intuitive guesses regarding optimal choices. Yet another way to enhance our decision making is to use careful reasoning in drawing inferences about the various options available to us.

The work on heuristics and biases shows the importance of distinguishing between intellectual competence and intellectual performance as it manifests itself in daily life. Even experts in the use of probability and statistics can find themselves falling into faulty patterns of judgment and decision making in their everyday lives. People may be intelligent in a conventional, test-based sense. Yet they may show exactly the same biases and faulty reasoning that someone with a lower test score would show. People often fail to fully utilize their intellectual competence in their daily life. There even can be a wide gap between the two. Thus, if we wish to be intelligent in our daily lives and not just on tests, we have to be street-smart. In particular, we must be mindful of applying our intelligence to the problems that continually confront us.

Heuristics do not always lead us astray. Sometimes, they are amazingly simple ways of drawing sound conclusions. For example, a simple heuristic, *take the best*, can

IN THE LAB OF GERD GIGERENZER

Courtesy of Dr. Gerd Gigerenzer

Which city has a larger population, San Diego or San Antonio? Two-thirds of University of Chicago undergraduates got the answer right: San Diego. Then we asked German students who knew very little about San Diego, and many of whom had never even heard of San Antonio (Goldstein & Gigerenzer, 2002). What proportion of the German students do you think got the answer right? 100%. How can it be that people who know less about a subject get more correct answers? The answer is that the German students used the recognition heuristic. For the present case, this heuristic says:

If one of two objects is recognized and the other is not, then infer that the recognized object has the higher value with respect to the criterion.

Note that the American students could not use the recognition heuristic, they had heard of both cities. They had to rely on recall knowledge (i.e., facts) rather than recognition. The recognition heuristic can only be used by people who have a sufficient degree of ignorance, that is, who recognize only some objects—but not all. In such cases, the less-is-more effect can result, that is, less knowledge can lead to more accurate judgments. Similar surprising results have been obtained in predicting the outcome of British soccer games (e.g., Manchester United versus Shrewsbury Town) by people in England as opposed to Turkey. The recognition heuristic is also used in the supermarket when customers must choose among several similar products, preferring one whose name they have heard of. This heuristic is exploited by advertisements, like those of Bennetton, which give no information about the product but simply try to increase name recognition. Finally, the recognition heuristic has also been successful on the stock market, where it managed to outperform major mutual funds and the Dow in picking stock investments (Borges & associates, 1999).

The recognition heuristic does not always apply, however, nor can it always make correct inferences. The effectiveness of the apparently simplistic heuristic depends on its ecological rationality: its ability to exploit the structure of the information in natural environments. The heuristic is successful when ignorance—specifically, a lack of recognition—is systematically rather than randomly distributed, that is, when it is strongly correlated with the criterion. Experimental studies indicate that 90% or more of the participants rely on the recognition heuristic in situations in which it is ecologically rational.

In the Center for Adaptive Behavior and Cognition (ABC) at the Max Planck Institute for Human Development, we study not only this heuristic but a whole adaptive toolbox of heuristics. Part of the fun in the lab springs from the interdisciplinary nature of the ABC group. Psychologists collaborate with economists, mathematicians, computer scientists, and evolutionary biologists, among others. Using multiple methods, we attempt to open the adaptive toolbox.

The adaptive toolbox is, in two respects, a Darwinian metaphor for decision making. First, evolution does not follow a grand plan, but results in a patchwork of solutions for specific problems. The same goes for the toolbox: Its heuristics are domain specific, not general. Second, the heuristics in the adaptive toolbox are not good or bad, rational or irrational, *per se,* only relative to an environment, just as adaptations are context-bound. In these two restrictions lie their potential: heuristics can perform astonishingly well when used in a suitable environment. The rationality of the adaptive toolbox is not logical, but rather ecological.

The ABC program aims at providing the building blocks, or, if you like, the ABC's of cognitive heuristics for choice, categorization, inference, estimation, preference, and other tasks. These heuristics are fast because they involve little computation, frugal because they search only for little information, and robust because their simplicity makes it likely they can be generalized effectively to new environments. Herbert Simon once introduced the metaphor of a pair of scissors to exemplify what we call ecological rationality. One blade is the mind, the other the environment. To understand cognition, we study the match between the structure of cognitive heuristics and the environment. Studying one blade alone, as much of cognitive science today does, will not reveal why and how cognition works.

be amazingly effective in decision situations (Gigerenzer & Goldstein, 1996; Gigerenzer, Todd, & the ABC Research Group, 1999; Marsh, Todd, & Gigerenzer, 2004). The rule is simple. In making a decision, identify the single most important criterion to you for making that decision. For example, when you choose a new automobile, the most important factor might be good gas mileage, safety, or appearance. This heuristic would seem on its face to be inadequate. In fact, it often leads to very good decisions. It produces even better decisions, in many cases, than far more complicated heuristics. Thus, heuristics can be used for good as well as for bad decision making. Indeed, when we take people's goals into account, heuristics often are amazingly effective (Evans & Over, 1996).

Judgment and decision making involve evaluating opportunities and selecting one choice over another. A related kind of thinking is reasoning. **Reasoning** is the process of drawing conclusions from principles and from evidence (Leighton, 2004a, 2004b; Leighton & Sternberg, 2004; Sternberg, 2004b; Wason & Johnson-Laird, 1972). In reasoning, we move from what is already known to infer a new conclusion or to evaluate a proposed conclusion.

Reasoning is often divided into two types: deductive and inductive reasoning. **Deductive reasoning** is the process of reasoning from one or more general statements regarding what is known to reach a logically certain conclusion (Johnson-Laird, 2000; Rips, 1999; Williams, 2000). It often involves reasoning from one or more general statements regarding what is known to a specific application of the general statement. In contrast, **inductive reasoning** is the process of reasoning from specific facts or observations to reach a likely conclusion that may explain the facts. The inductive reasoner then may use that probable conclusion to attempt to predict future specific instances (Johnson-Laird, 2000). The key feature distinguishing inductive from deductive reasoning is that in inductive reasoning, we never can reach a logically certain conclusion. We only can reach a particularly well-founded or probable conclusion.

Deductive Reasoning

Deductive reasoning is based on logical propositions. A **proposition** is basically an assertion, which may be either true or false. Examples are "Cognitive psychology students are brilliant," "cognitive psychology students wear shoes," or "cognitive psychology students like peanut butter." In a logical argument, **premises** are propositions about which arguments are made. Cognitive psychologists are interested particularly in propositions that may be connected in ways that require people to draw reasoned conclusions. That is, deductive reasoning is useful because it helps people connect various propositions to draw conclusions. Cognitive psychologists want to know how people connect propositions to draw conclusions. Some of these conclusions are well reasoned. Others are not. Much of the difficulty of reasoning is in even understanding the language of problems (Girotto, 2004). Some of the mental processes used in language understanding, and the cerebral functioning underlying them, are used in reasoning too (Lawson, 2004).

Conditional Reasoning

One of the primary types of deductive reasoning is **conditional reasoning,** in which the reasoner must draw a conclusion based on an if-then proposition. The conditional if-then proposition states that if antecedent condition p is met, then consequent event q follows. For example, "If students study hard, then they score high on their exams." Under some circumstances, if you have established a conditional proposition, then you may draw a well-reasoned conclusion. The usual set of conditional propositions from which you can draw a well-reasoned conclusion is "If p, then q. p. Therefore, q." This inference illustrates deductive validity. That is, it follows logically from the propositions on which it is based. The following is also logical: "If students eat pizza, then they score high on their exams. They eat pizza. Therefore, they score high on their exams." As you may have guessed, deductive validity does not equate with truth. You can reach deductively valid conclusions that are completely untrue with respect to the world. Whether the conclusion is true depends on the truthfulness of the premises. In fact, people are more likely mistakenly to accept an illogical argument as logical if the conclusion is factually true. For now, however, we put aside the issue of truth and focus only on the **deductive validity,** or logical soundness, of the reasoning.

One set of propositions and its conclusion is the argument "If p, then q. p. Therefore, q," which is termed a *modus ponens* argument. In the modus ponens argument, the reasoner affirms the antecedent. For example, take the argument, "If you are a husband, then you are married. Harrison is a husband. Therefore, he is married." The set of propositions for the *modus ponens* argument is shown in Table 12.2. In addition to the *modus ponens* argument, you may draw another well-reasoned conclusion from a conditional proposition, given a different second proposition: "If p, then q. Not q. Therefore, not p." This inference is also deductively valid. This particular set of propositions and its conclusion is termed a *modus tollens* argument, in which the reasoner denies the consequent. For example, we modify the second proposition of the argument to deny the consequent: "If you are a husband, then you are married. Harrison is not married. Therefore, he is not a husband." Table 12.2 shows two conditions in which a well-reasoned conclusion can be reached. It also shows two conditions in which such a conclusion cannot be reached. As the examples illustrate, some inferences based on conditional reasoning are fallacies. They lead to conclusions that are not deductively valid. When using conditional propositions, we cannot reach a deductively valid conclusion based either on denying the antecedent condition or on affirming the consequent. Let's return to the proposition, "If you are a husband, then you are married." We would not be able to confirm or to refute the proposition based on denying the antecedent: "Joan is not a husband. Therefore, she is not married." Even if we ascertain that Joan is not a husband, we cannot conclude that she is not married. Similarly, we cannot deduce a valid conclusion by affirming the consequent: "Joan is married. Therefore, she is a husband." Even if Joan is married, her spouse may not consider her a husband.

Conditional reasoning can be studied in the laboratory using a "selection task" (Wason, 1968, 1969, 1983; Wason & Johnson-Laird, 1970, 1972). Participants are presented with a set of four two-sided cards. Each card has a numeral on one side and

TABLE 12.2	Conditional Reasoning: Deductively Valid Inferences and Deductive Fallacies

Two kinds of conditional propositions lead to valid deductions, and two others lead to deductive fallacies.

TYPE OF ARGUMENT		CONDITIONAL PROPOSITION	EXISTING CONDITION	INFERENCE
Deductively valid inferences	Modus ponens	$p \rightarrow q$ If you are a mother, then you have a child.	p You are a mother.	$\therefore q$ Therefore, you have a child.
	Modus tollens	$p \rightarrow q$ If you are a mother, then you have a child.	$\neg q$ You do not have a child.	$\therefore \neg p$ Therefore, you are not a mother.
Deductive fallacies	Denying the antecedent	$p \rightarrow q$ If you are a mother, then you have a child.	$\neg p$ You are not a mother.	$\therefore \neg q$ Therefore, you do not have a child.
	Affirming the consequent	$p \rightarrow q$ If you are a mother, then you have a child.	q You have a child.	$\therefore p$ Therefore, you are a mother.

a letter on the other side. Face up are two letters and two numerals. The letters are a consonant and a vowel. The numbers are an even number and an odd number. For example, participants may be faced with the following series of cards:

S 3 A 2

Each participant then is told a conditional statement. An example would be "If a card has a consonant on one side, then it has an even number on the other side." The task is to determine whether the conditional statement is true or false. One does so by turning over the exact number of cards necessary to test the conditional statement. That is, the participant must not turn over any cards that are not valid tests of the statement. But the participant must turn over all cards that are valid tests of the conditional proposition.

Table 12.3 illustrates the four possible tests participants might perform on the cards. Two of the tests (affirming the antecedent and denying the consequent) are both necessary and sufficient for testing the conditional statement. That is, to evaluate the deduction, the participant must turn over the card showing a consonant to see whether it has an even number on the other side. He or she thereby affirms the antecedent (the *modus ponens* argument). In addition, the participant must turn over the card showing an odd number (i.e., not an even number) to see whether it has a vowel (i.e., not a consonant) on the other side. He or she thereby denies the consequent (the *modus tollens* argument). The other two possible tests (denying the an-

TABLE 12.3	Conditional Reasoning: Wason's Selection Task

In the Wason selection task, Peter Wason presented participants with a set of four cards, from which the participants were to test the validity of a given proposition. This table illustrates how a reasoner might test the conditional proposition ($p \rightarrow q$), "If a card has a consonant on one side (p), then it has an even number on the other side (q)."

PROPOSITION BASED ON WHAT SHOWS ON THE FACE OF THE CARD	TEST	TYPE OF REASONING	
p A given card has a consonant on one side (e.g., "S," "F," "V," or "P")	∴ q Does the card have an even number on the other side?	Based on *modus ponens*	Deductively valid inferences
¬ q A given card does not have an even number on one side. That is, a given card has an odd number on one side (e.g., "3," "5," "7," or "9").	∴¬ p Does the card *not* have a consonant on the other side? That is, does the card have a vowel on the other side?	Based on *modus tollens*	
¬ p A given card does not have a consonant on one side. That is, a given card has a vowel on one side (e.g., "A," "E," "I," or "O").	∴¬ q Does the card *not* have an even number on the other side? That is, does the card have an odd number on the other side?	Based on denying the antecedent.	Deductive fallacies
q A given card has an even number on one side (e.g., "2," "4," "6," or "8").	∴ p Does the card have a consonant on the other side?	Based on affirming the consequent	

tecedent and affirming the consequent) are irrelevant. That is, the participant need not turn over the card showing a vowel. (i.e., not a consonant). To do so would be to deny the antecedent. He or she also need not turn over the card showing an even number (i.e., not a odd number). To do so would be to affirm the consequent. Most participants knew to test for the *modus ponens* argument. However, many participants failed to test for the *modus tollens* argument. Some of these participants instead tried to deny the antecedent as a means of testing the conditional proposition.

Most people of all ages (at least starting in elementary school) appear to have little difficulty in recognizing and applying the *modus ponens* argument. However, few people spontaneously recognize the need for reasoning by means of the *modus tollens* argument. Many people do not recognize the logical fallacies of denying the antecedent or affirming the consequent, at least as these fallacies are applied to abstract reasoning problems (Braine & O'Brien, 1991; O'Brien, 2004; Rips, 1988, 1994; Rumain, Connell, & Braine, 1983). In fact, some evidence suggests that even people who have taken a course in logic fail to demonstrate deductive reasoning across various situations (Cheng & associates, 1986). However, most people do demonstrate conditional reasoning under two kinds of circumstances. The first is conditions that minimize possible linguistic ambiguities. The second is conditions that activate schemas that provide a meaningful context for the reasoning.

Why might both children and adults fallaciously affirm the consequent or deny the antecedent? Perhaps they do because of invited inferences that follow from normal discourse comprehension of conditional phrasing (Rumain, Connell, & Braine, 1983). For instance, suppose that my publisher advertises, "If you buy this textbook, then we will give you a $5 rebate." Consider everyday situations. You probably correctly infer that if you do not buy this textbook, the publisher will not give you a $5 rebate. However, formal deductive reasoning would consider this denial of the antecedent to be fallacious. The statement says nothing about what happens if you do *not* buy the textbook. Similarly, you may infer that you must have bought this textbook (affirm the consequent) if you received a $5 rebate from the publisher. But the statement says nothing about the range of circumstances that lead you to receive the $5 rebate. There may be other ways to receive it. Both inferences are fallacious according to formal deductive reasoning. But both are quite reasonable invited inferences in everyday situations. It helps when the wording of conditional-reasoning problems either explicitly or implicitly disinvites these inferences. Both adults and children are then much less likely to engage in these logical fallacies.

The demonstration of conditional reasoning also is influenced by the presence of contextual information that converts the problem from one of abstract deductive reasoning to one that applies to an everyday situation. For example, participants received both the Wason selection task and a modified version of the Wason selection task (Griggs & Cox, 1982). In the modified version, the participants were asked to suppose that they were police officers. As officers, they were attempting to enforce the laws applying to the legal age for drinking alcoholic beverages. The particular rule to be enforced was "If a person is drinking beer, then the person must be over 19 years of age." Each participant was presented with a set of four cards: (1) "drinking a beer," (2) "drinking a Coke," (3) "16 years of age," and (4) "22 years of age." The participant then was instructed to "Select the card or cards that you definitely need to turn over to determine whether or not the people are violating the rule" (p. 414). On the one hand, none of Griggs and Cox's participants had responded correctly on the abstract version of the Wason selection task. On the other hand, a remarkable 72% of the participants correctly responded to the modified version of the task.

A more recent modification of this task has shown that beliefs regarding plausibility influence whether people choose the *modus tollens* argument. This is one's denying the consequent by checking to see whether a person who is not older than 19 years of age is not drinking beer. Specifically, people are far more likely to try to deny the consequent when the test involves checking to see whether an 18-year-old is drinking beer than checking to see whether a 4-year-old is drinking beer. Nevertheless, the logical argument is the same in both cases (Kirby, 1994). How do people use deductive reasoning in realistic situations? Two investigators have suggested that, rather than using formal inference rules, people often use pragmatic reasoning schemas (Cheng & Holyoak, 1985). **Pragmatic reasoning schemas** are general organizing principles or rules related to particular kinds of goals, such as permissions, obligations, or causations. These schemas sometimes are referred to as *pragmatic rules*. These pragmatic rules are not as abstract as formal logical rules. Yet they are sufficiently general and broad so that they can apply to a wide variety of specific situations. Prior beliefs, in other words, matter in reasoning (Evans & Feeney, 2004).

Alternatively, one's performance may be affected by *perspective effects*—that is, whether one takes the point of view of the police officers or of the people drinking the alcoholic beverages (Almor & Sloman, 1996; Staller, Sloman, & Ben-Zeev, 2000). So it may not be permissions *per se* that matter. Rather, what may matter are the perspectives one takes when solving such problems.

Thus, consider situations in which our previous experiences or our existing knowledge cannot tell us all we want to know. Pragmatic reasoning schemas help us deduce what might reasonably be true. Particular situations or contexts activate particular schemas. For example, suppose that you are walking across campus. You see someone who looks extremely young. Then you see the person walk to a car. He unlocks it, gets in, and drives away. This observation would activate your permission schema for driving. "If you are to be permitted to drive alone, then you must be at least 16 years old." You might now deduce that the person you saw is at least 16 years old. In one experiment, 62% of participants correctly chose *modus ponens* and *modus tollens* arguments but not the two logical fallacies when the conditional-reasoning task was presented in the context of permission statements. Only 11% did so when the task was presented in the context of arbitrary statements unrelated to pragmatic reasoning schemas (Cheng & Holyoak, 1985).

Researchers conducted an extensive analysis comparing the standard abstract Wason selection task with an abstract form of a permission problem (Griggs & Cox, 1993). The standard abstract form might be "If a card has an 'A' on one side, then it must have a '4' on the other side. The abstract permission form might be "If one is to take action 'A,' then one must first satisfy precondition 'P.'" Performance on the abstract permission task was still superior (49% correct overall) to performance on the standard abstract task (only 9% correct overall). This was so even when the authors added to the standard abstract task a statement that framed the task in a checking context. An example would be "Suppose you are an authority checking whether or not certain rules are being followed." The permission form was still better if a rule-clarification statement was added. An example of this would be "In other words, in order to have an 'A' on one side, a card must first have a '4' on the other side." And the permission form was better even for explicit negations. For example, "NOT A" and "NOT 4" would be used instead of implicit negations for "A" and "4"—namely, "B" and "7." Thus, although both the standard selection task and the permission-related task involve deductive reasoning, the two tasks actually appear to pose different problems (Griggs & Cox, 1993; Manktelow & Over, 1990, 1992). Pragmatic reasoning schemas do not, therefore, fully explain all aspects of conditional reasoning (Braine & O'Brien, 1991; Braine, Reiser, & Rumain, 1984; Rips, 1983, 1988, 1994) Indeed, people do not always use rules of reasoning at all (Garcia-Madruga & associates, 2000; Johnson-Laird & Savary, 1999; Smith, Langston, & Nisbett, 1992).

An altogether different approach to conditional reasoning takes an evolutionary view of cognition (Cummins, 2004). On this view, we should consider what kinds of thinking skills would provide a naturally selective advantage for humans in adapting to our environment across evolutionary time (Cosmides, 1989; Cosmides & Tooby, 1996). To gain insight into human cognition, we should look to see what kinds of adaptations would have been most useful in the distant past. So, we hypothesize on how human hunters and gatherers would have thought during the millions of years of evolutionary time that predated the relatively recent development of agriculture and the very recent development of industrialized societies.

How has evolution influenced human cognition? Humans may possess something like a schema-acquisition device (Cosmides, 1989). According to Cosmides, it facilitates our ability to quickly glean important information from our experiences. It also helps us to organize that information into meaningful frameworks. In her view, these schemas are highly flexible. But they also are specialized for selecting and organizing the information that will most effectively aid us in adapting to the situations we face. According to Cosmides, one of the distinctive adaptations shown by human hunters and gatherers has been in the area of social exchange. Hence, evolutionary development of human cognition should facilitate the acquisition of schemas related to social exchange.

According to Cosmides, there are two kinds of inferences in particular that social-exchange schemas facilitate. One kind is inferences related to cost-benefit relationships. The other kind is inferences that help people detect when someone is cheating in a particular social exchange. Across nine experiments, participants demonstrated deductive reasoning that confirmed the predictions of social-exchange theory, rather than predictions based on permissions-related schemas or on abstract deductive-reasoning principles (Cosmides, 1989).

Syllogistic Reasoning

In addition to conditional reasoning, the other key type of deductive reasoning is syllogistic reasoning, which is based on the use of syllogisms. **Syllogisms** are deductive arguments that involve drawing conclusions from two premises (Rips, 1994, 1999). All syllogisms comprise a major premise, a minor premise, and a conclusion. Unfortunately, sometimes the conclusion may be that no logical conclusion may be reached based on the two given premises.

Linear Syllogisms

In a syllogism, each of the two premises describes a particular relationship between two items and at least one of the items is common to both premises. The items may be objects, categories, attributes, or almost anything else that can be related to something. Logicians designate the first term of the major premise as the subject. The common term is the middle term (which is used once in each premise). And the second term of the minor premise is the predicate.

In alinear syllogism, the relationship among the terms is linear. It involves a quantitative or qualitative comparison. Each term shows either more or less of a particular attribute or quantity. Suppose, for example, that you are presented with the problem in the "Investigating Cognitive Psychology" box.

Each of the two premises describes a linear relationship between two items; Table 12.4 shows the terms of each premise and the relationship of the terms in each premise. The deductive-reasoning task for the linear syllogism is to determine a relationship between two items that do not appear in the same premise. In the preceding linear syllogism, the problem solver needs to infer that you are smarter than your roommate to realize that you are the smartest of the three.

You are smarter than your best friend.
Your best friend is smarter than your roommate.
Which of you is the smartest?

INVESTIGATING COGNITIVE PSYCHOLOGY

When the linear syllogism is deductively valid, its conclusion follows logically from the premises. We correctly can deduce with complete certainty that you are the smartest of the three. Your roommate or your best friend may, however, point out an area of weakness in your conclusion. Even a conclusion that is deductively valid may not be objectively true. Of course, it is true in this example.

How do people solve linear syllogisms? Several different theories have been proposed. Some investigators have suggested that linear syllogisms are solved spatially, through mental representations of linear continua (DeSoto, London, & Handel, 1965; Huttenlocher, 1968). The idea here is that people imagine a visual representation laying out the terms on a linear continuum. For example, the premise "You are smarter than your roommate" might be represented mentally as an image of a vertical continuum. Your name is above your roommate's. The linear continuum usually is visualized vertically, although it can be visualized horizontally. When answering the question, people consult this continuum and choose the item in the correct place along the continuum.

Other investigators have proposed that people solve linear syllogisms using a semantic model involving propositional representations (Clark, 1969). For example, the premise "You are smarter than your roommate" might be represented as [smarter (you, your roommate)]. According to this view, people do not use images at all but rather combine semantic propositions.

A third view is that people use a combination of spatial and propositional representations in solving the syllogisms (Sternberg, 1980). According to this view, people use propositions initially to represent each of the premises. They then form mental images based on the contents of these propositions. Model testing has tended to support the combination (or mixture) model over exclusively propositional or exclusively spatial representations (Sternberg, 1980).

None of the three models appear to be quite right, however. They all represent performance averaged over many individuals. Rather, there seem to be individual

TABLE 12.4 Linear Syllogisms

What logical deduction can you reach, based on the premises of this linear syllogism? Is deductive validity the same as truth?

	FIRST TERM (ITEM)	LINEAR RELATIONSHIP	SECOND TERM (ITEM)
Premise A Premise B Conclusion: Who is smartest?	You Your best friend _____	are smarter than is smarter than is/are the smartest of the three.	your best friend. your roommate.

differences in strategies, in which some people tend to use a more imaginal strategy and others tend to use a more propositional strategy (Sternberg & Weil, 1980). This result points out an important limitation on many psychological findings: Unless we consider each individual separately, we risk jumping to conclusions based on a group average that does not necessarily apply to each person individually (see Siegler, 1988). Whereas most people may use a combination strategy, not everyone does. The only way to find out which each person uses is to examine each individual.

Categorical Syllogisms

Probably the most well-known kind of syllogism is the categorical syllogism. Like other kinds of syllogisms, categorical syllogisms comprise two premises and a conclusion. In the case of the **categorical syllogism,** the premises state something about the category memberships of the terms. In fact, each term represents all, none, or some of the members of a particular class or category. As with other syllogisms, each premise contains two terms. One of them must be the middle term, common to both premises. The first and the second terms in each premise are linked through the categorical membership of the terms. That is, one term is a member of the class indicated by the other term. However the premises are worded, they state that some (or all or none) of the members of the category of the first term are (or are not) members of the category of the second term. To determine whether the conclusion follows logically from the premises, the reasoner must determine the category memberships of the terms. An example of a categorical syllogism would be as follows:

All cognitive psychologists are pianists.

All pianists are athletes.

Therefore, all cognitive psychologists are athletes.

Logicians often use circle diagrams to illustrate class membership. They make it easier to figure out whether a particular conclusion is logically sound. The conclusion for this syllogism does in fact follow logically from the premises. This is shown in the circle diagram in Figure 12.1. However, the conclusion is false because the premises are false. For the preceding categorical syllogism, the subject is cognitive psychologists, the middle term is pianists, and the predicate is athletes. In both premises, we asserted that all members of the category of the first term were members of the category of the second term.

Statements of the form "All A are B" sometimes are referred to as *universal affirmatives* because they make a positive (affirmative) statement about all members of a class (universal). In addition, there are three other kinds of possible statements in a categorical syllogism. One kind comprises *universal negative statements* (e.g., "No cognitive psychologists are flutists"). A second kind is *particular affirmative statements* (e.g., "Some cognitive psychologists are left-handed"). The last kind is *particular negative statements* (e.g., "Some cognitive psychologists are not physicists"). These are summarized in Table 12.5.

In all kinds of syllogisms, some combinations of premises lead to no logically valid conclusion. In categorical syllogisms, in particular, we cannot draw logically valid conclusions from categorical syllogisms with two particular premises or with two negative premises. For example, "Some cognitive psychologists are left-handed. Some

FIGURE 12.1

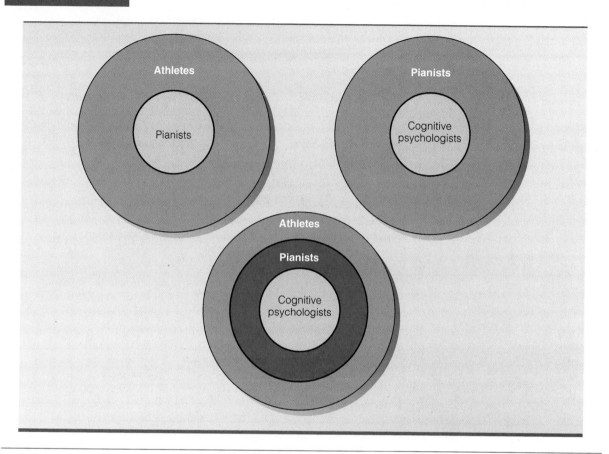

Circle diagrams may be used to represent categorical syllogisms such as the one shown here: "All pianists are athletes. All cognitive psychologists are pianists. Therefore, all cognitive psychologists are athletes." From In Search of the Human Mind by Robert J. Sternberg, copyright © 1995 by Harcourt Brace & Company, reproduced by permission of the publisher.

left-handed people are smart." Based on these premises, you cannot conclude even that some cognitive psychologists are smart. The left-handed people who are smart might not be the same left-handed people who are cognitive psychologists. We just don't know. Consider a negative example; "No students are stupid. No stupid people eat pizza." We cannot conclude anything one way or the other about whether students eat pizza, based on these two negative premises. As you may have guessed, people appear to have more difficulty (work more slowly and make more errors) when trying to deduce conclusions based on one or more particular premises or negative premises.

Various theories have been proposed as to how people solve categorical syllogisms. One of the earliest theories was the atmosphere bias (Begg & Denny, 1969; Woodworth & Sells, 1935). There are two basic ideas of this theory. The first is that if there is at least one negative in the premises, people will prefer a negative solution.

TABLE 12.5	Categorical Syllogisms: Types of Premises

The premises of categorical syllogisms may be universal affirmatives, universal negatives, particular affirmatives, or particular negatives.

TYPE OF PREMISE	FORM OF PREMISE STATEMENTS	DESCRIPTION	EXAMPLES	REVERSIBILITY*
Universal affirmative	All A are B.	The premise positively (affirmatively) states that all members of the first class (universal) are members of the second class.	All men are males.	All males are men. ≠ **Nonreversible** All A are B. All B are A.
Universal negative	No A are B. (Alternative: All A are *not* B.)	The premise states that none of the members of the first class are members of the second class.	No men are females. *or* All men are not females.	No men are females = No females are men. ↔Reversible↔ No A are B = No B are A.
Particular affirmative	Some A are B.	The premise states that only some of the members of the first class are members of the second class.	Some females are women.	Some females are women. ≠ Some women are females. **Nonreversible** Some A are B. ≠ Some B are A.
Particular negative	Some A are not B.	The premise states that some members of the first class are not members of the second class.	Some women are not females.	Some females are not women. ≠ **Nonreversible** Some A are not B. ≠ Some B are not A.

*In formal logic, the word some means "some and possibly all." In common parlance, and as used in cognitive psychology, *some* means "some and not all." Thus, in formal logic, the particular affirmative also would be reversible. For our purposes, it is not.

The second is that if there is at least one particular in the premises, people will prefer a particular solution. For example, if one of the premises is "No pilots are children," people will prefer a solution that has the word "no" in it. Nonetheless, it does not account very well for large numbers of responses.

Other researchers focused attention on the conversion of premises (Chapman & Chapman, 1959). Here, the terms of a given premise are reversed. People sometimes believe that the reversed form of the premise is just as valid as the original form. The idea here is that people tend to convert statements like "If A, then B," into "If B, then A." They do not realize that the statements are not equivalent. These errors are made by children and adults alike (Markovits, 2004).

A more widely accepted theory is based on the notion that people solve syllogisms by using a semantic (meaning-based) process based on mental models (Johnson-Laird, 1997; Johnson-Laird & associates, 1999; Johnson-Laird, Byrne, & Schaeken, 1992; Johnson-Laird & Savary, 1999; Johnson-Laird & Steedman, 1978). This view is of reasoning as involving semantic processes based on mental models may be contrasted with rule-based ("syntactic") processes, such as those characterized by formal logic. A **mental model** is an internal representation of information that corresponds analogously with whatever is being represented (see Johnson-Laird, 1983). Some mental models are more likely to lead to a deductively valid conclusion than are others. In particular, some mental models may not be effective in disconfirming an invalid conclusion.

For example, in the Johnson-Laird study, participants were asked to describe their conclusions and their mental models for the syllogism, "All of the artists are bee-keepers. Some of the beekeepers are clever." One participant said, "I thought of all the little...artists in the room and imagined they all had beekeeper's hats on" (Johnson-Laird & Steedman, 1978, p. 77). Figure 12.2 shows two different mental models for this syllogism. As the figure shows, the choice of a mental model may affect the reasoner's ability to reach a valid deductive conclusion. Because some models are better than others for solving some syllogisms, a person is more likely to reach a deductively valid conclusion by using more than one mental model.

In the figure, the mental model shown in part (*a*) may lead to the deductively invalid conclusion that some artists are clever. By observing the alternative model in part (*b*), we can see an alternative view of the syllogism. It shows that the conclusion that some artists are clever may not be deduced on the basis of this information alone. Specifically, perhaps the beekeepers who are clever are not the same as the beekeepers who are artists.

Two types of representations of syllogisms are often used by logicians. As mentioned previously, circle diagrams are often used to represent categorical syllogisms. In circle diagrams, you can use overlapping, concentric, or nonoverlapping circles to represent the members of different categories (Figures 12.1 and 12.2). An alternative representation often used by logicians is a truth table. It can be used to represent the truth value of various combinations of propositions, based on the truth value of each of the component propositions. People can learn how to improve their reasoning by being taught how to circle diagrams or truth tables (Nickerson, 2004).

On this view, the difficulty of many problems of deductive reasoning relates to the number of mental models needed for adequately representing the premises of the deductive argument (Johnson-Laird, Byrne, & Schaeken, 1992). Arguments that entail only one mental model may be solved quickly and accurately. However, to infer accurate conclusions based on arguments that may be represented by multiple alternative models is much harder. Such inferences place great demands on working memory (Gilhooly, 2004). In these cases, the individual must simultaneously hold in working memory each of the various models. Only in this way can he or she reach or evaluate a conclusion. Thus, limitations of working-memory capacity may underlie at least some of the errors observed in human deductive reasoning (Johnson-Laird, Byrne, & Schaeken, 1992).

In two experiments, the role of working memory was studied in syllogistic reasoning (Gilhooly & associates, 1993). In the first, syllogisms were simply presented either orally or visually. Oral presentation placed a considerably higher load on working memory because participants had to remember the premises. In the visual-presentation condition, participants could look at the premises. As predicted, performance was lower in the oral-presentation condition. In a second experiment, participants needed to solve syllogisms while at the same time they performed another task. Either the task

Philip Johnson-Laird is a professor of psychology at Princeton University. He is best known for his work on mental models, deductive reasoning, and creativity. In particular, Johnson-Laird has shown how the concept of mental models can be applied toward understanding a wide variety of psychological processes.

FIGURE 12.2

Philip Johnson-Laird and Mark Steedman hypothesized that people use various mental models analogously to represent the items within a syllogism. Some mental models are more effective than others, and for a valid deductive conclusion to be reached, more than one model may be necessary, as shown here. (See text for explanation.)

drew on working-memory resources, or it did not. The researchers found that the task that drew on working-memory resources interfered with syllogistic reasoning. The task that did not draw on these resources did not.

As children get older, their effective use of working memory increases. So their ability to use mental models that draw on working-memory resources increases. Researchers asked children of different ages to look at cards with objects displayed on them, such as shirts and trousers of different colors (Barrouillet & Lecas, 1998). Then they were given premises, such as "If you wear a white shirt, you wear green trousers." They were asked to indicate which combinations of cards were consistent with the premises. For example, cards with white shirts and green trousers would be consistent with this premise, but so would shirts and trousers of other colors because the statement also implies that if you do not wear green trousers, you do not wear a white shirt.

Older children, who were able to hold more combinations in working memory, chose more different card combinations to represent the premises.

Other factors also may contribute to the ease of forming appropriate mental models. People seem to solve logical problems more accurately and more easily when the terms have high imagery value (Clement & Falmagne, 1986). This situation probably facilitates their mental representation. Similarly, when propositions showed high relatedness in terms of mental images, participants could more easily and accurately solve the problems and judge the accuracy of the conclusions. An example would be one premise about dogs and the other about cats, rather than one about dogs and the other about tables. For example, it would be relatively easy to solve a high-imagery, high-relatedness syllogism, such as "Some artists are painters. Some painters use black paint." It would be relatively hard to solve a low-imagery, low-relatedness syllogism, such as "Some texts are prose. Some prose is well-written." High imagery value and high relatedness may make it easier for reasoners to come up with counterexamples that reveal an argument to be deductively invalid (Clement & Falmagne, 1986).

Some deductive-reasoning problems comprise more than two premises. For example, transitive-inference problems, in which problem solvers must order multiple terms, can have any number of premises linking large numbers of terms. Mathematical and logical proofs are deductive in character and can have many steps as well.

Further Aids and Obstacles to Deductive Reasoning

In deductive reasoning, as in many other cognitive processes, we engage in many heuristic shortcuts. They sometimes lead to inaccurate conclusions. In addition to these shortcuts, we often are influenced by biases that distort the outcomes of our reasoning.

Heuristics in syllogistic reasoning include *overextension errors*. In these errors, we overextend the use of strategies that work in some syllogisms to syllogisms in which the strategies fail us. For example, although reversals work well with universal negatives, they do not work with other kinds of premises. We also experience *foreclosure effects* when we fail to consider all of the possibilities before reaching a conclusion. For example, we may fail to think of contrary examples when inferring conclusions from particular or negative premises. In addition, premise-phrasing effects may influence our deductive reasoning. Examples would be the sequence of terms or the use of particular qualifiers or negative phrasing. Premise-phrasing effects may lead us to leap to a conclusion without adequately reflecting on the deductive validity of the syllogism.

Biases that affect deductive reasoning generally relate to the content of the premises and the believability of the conclusion. They also reflect the tendency toward *confirmation bias*. In confirmation bias, we seek confirmation rather than disconfirmation of what we already believe. Suppose the content of the premises and a conclusion seem to be true. In such cases, reasoners tend to believe in the validity of the conclusion, even when the logic is flawed (Evans, Barston, & Pollard, 1983). To a lesser extent, people also show the opposite tendency to disconfirm the validity of the conclusion when the conclusion or the content of the premises contradicts the reasoner's existing beliefs (Evans, Barston, & Pollard, 1983; Janis & Frick, 1943). This is not to say that people fail to consider logical principles when reasoning deductively. In general, explicit attention to the premises seems more likely to lead to valid inferences. Explicit attention to irrelevant information more often leads to inferences based on prior beliefs regarding the believability of the conclusion (Evans, Barston, & Pollard, 1983).

To enhance our deductive reasoning, we may try to avoid heuristics and biases that distort our reasoning. We also may engage in practices that facilitate reasoning. For example, we may take longer to reach or to evaluate conclusions. Effective reasoners also consider more alternative conclusions than do poor reasoners (Galotti, Baron, & Sabini, 1986). In addition, training and practice seem to increase performance on reasoning tasks. The benefits of training tend be strong when the training relates to pragmatic reasoning schemas (Cheng & associates, 1986) or to such fields as law and medicine (Lehman, Lempert, & Nisbett, 1987). The benefits are weaker for abstract logical problems divorced from our everyday life (see Holland & associates, 1986; Holyoak & Nisbett, 1988).

One factor that affects syllogistic reasoning is mood. When people are in a sad mood, they tend to pay more attention to details (Schwarz & Skurnik, 2003). Hence, perhaps surprisingly, they tend to do better in syllogistic reasoning tasks when they are in a sad mood than when they are in a happy mood (Fiedler, 1988; Melton, 1995). People in a neutral mood tend to show performance in between the two extremes.

PRACTICAL APPLICATIONS OF COGNITIVE PSYCHOLOGY	Even without training you can improve your own deductive reasoning through developing strategies to avoid making errors. Make sure you are using the proper strategies in solving syllogisms. Remember that reversals only work with universal negatives. Sometimes translating abstract terms to concrete ones (e.g., the letter C to cows) can help. Also, take the time to consider contrary examples and create more mental models. The more mental models you use for a given set of premises, the more confident you can be that if your conclusion is not valid, it will be disconfirmed. Thus, the use of multiple mental models increases the likelihood of avoiding errors. The use of multiple mental models also helps you to avoid the tendency to engage in confirmation bias. Circle diagrams also can be helpful in solving deductive-reasoning problems.

Inductive Reasoning

With deductive reasoning, reaching logically certain—deductively valid—conclusions is at least theoretically possible. In inductive reasoning, which is based on our observations, reaching any logically certain conclusion is not possible. The most that we can strive to reach is only a strong, or highly probable, conclusion (Johnson-Laird, 2000; Thagard, 1999).

For example, suppose that you notice that all of the people enrolled in your cognitive psychology course are on the dean's list (or honor roll). From these observations, you could reason inductively that all students who enroll in cognitive psychology are excellent students (or at least earn the grades to give that impression). However, unless you can observe the grade-point averages of all people who ever have taken or ever will take cognitive psychology, you will be unable to prove your conclusion. Further, a single poor student who happened to enroll in a cognitive psychology course would disprove your conclusion. Still, after large numbers of observations, you might conclude that you had made enough observations to reason inductively.

The fundamental riddle of induction is how we can make any inductions at all. As the future has not happened, how can we predict what it will bring? There is also an important so-called new riddle of induction (Goodman, 1983). Given possible alternative futures, how do we know *which one* to predict? For example, in the number series problem, 2, 4, 6, ?, most people would replace the question mark with an 8. But we cannot know for sure that the correct number is 8. A mathematical formula could be proposed that would yield any number at all as the next number. So why choose the pattern of ascending even numbers (2x, where x is increasing integers)? Partly we choose it because it seems simple to us. It is a less complex formula than others we might choose. And partly we choose it because we are familiar with it. We are used to ascending series of even numbers. But we are not used to other complex series in which 2, 4, 6, may be embedded, such as 2, 4, 6, 10, 12, 14, 18, 20, 22, and so forth.

In this situation and in many others requiring reasoning, you were not given clearly stated premises or obvious, certain relationships between the elements. Such information could lead you to deduce a surefire conclusion. In its absence, you cannot deduce a logically valid conclusion at all. At these times, an alternative kind of reasoning is needed. Inductive reasoning involves reasoning where there is no logically certain conclusion. Often it involves reasoning from specific facts or observations to a general conclusion that may explain the facts.

Inductive reasoning forms the basis of the empirical method. In it, we cannot logically leap from saying, "All observed instances to date of X are Y" to saying, "Therefore, all X are Y." It is always possible that the next observed X will not be a Y. Furthermore, regardless of the number of observations or the soundness of the reasoning, no inductively based conclusions can be proved. Such conclusions only can be supported, to a greater or lesser degree, by available evidence. Thus, we return to the need to consider probability. The inductive reasoner must state any conclusions about a hypothesis in terms of likelihoods. Examples are "There is a 99% chance of rain tomorrow," or "The probability is only 0.05 that the null hypothesis is correct in asserting that these findings are a result of random variation."

Cognitive psychologists probably agree on at least two of the reasons why people use inductive reasoning. First, it helps them to become increasingly able to make sense out of the great variability in their environment. Second, it also helps them to predict events in their environment, thereby reducing their uncertainty. Thus, cognitive psychologists seek to understand the *how* rather than the *why* of inductive reasoning. We may (or may not) have some innate schema-acquisition device. But we certainly are not born with all the inferences we manage to induce. We already have implied that inductive reasoning often involves the processes of generating and testing hypotheses. We may further figure out that we reach inferences by generalizing some broad understandings from a set of specific instances. As we observe additional instances, we may further broaden our understanding. Or we may infer specialized exceptions to the general understandings. For example, after observing quite a few birds, we may infer that birds can fly. But after observing penguins and ostriches, we may add to our generalized knowledge specialized exceptions for flightless birds.

During generalization, we observe that particular properties vary together across diverse instances of a concept. Or we may observe that particular procedures covary across different events. We then can induce some general principles for those covariations. The great puzzle of inductive reasoning is how we manage to infer useful general principles based on the huge number of observations of covariation to which we are constantly exposed. Humans do not approach induction with mind-staggering computational abilities to calculate every possible covariation. Nor can we derive inferences from just the most frequent or the most plausible of these covariations. Rather, we seem to approach this task as we approach so many other cognitive tasks. We look for shortcuts. Inductive reasoners, like other probabilistic reasoners, use heuristics. Examples are representativeness, availability, the law of large numbers, and the unusualness heuristic. When using the unusualness heuristic, we pay particular attention to unusual events. When two unusual events co-occur or occur in proximity to one another, we tend to assume that the two events are connected in some way. For example, we might infer that the former unusual event caused the latter one (Holyoak & Nisbett, 1988).

Reaching Causal Inferences

One approach to studying inductive reasoning is to examine **causal inferences**—how people make judgments about whether something causes something else (Cheng, 1997, 1999; Cheng & Holyoak, 1995; Koslowski, 1996; Spellman, 1997). One of the first investigators to propose a theory of how people make causal judgments was John Stuart Mill (1887). He proposed a set of canons—widely accepted heuristic principles on which people may base their judgments. For example, one of Mill's canons is the *method of agreement*. It involves making separate lists of the possible causes that are present and those that are absent when a given outcome occurs. If, of all the possible causes, only one is present in all instances of the given outcome, the observer can conclude inductively that the one cause present in all instances is the true cause. That is, despite all the differences among possible causes, there is agreement in terms of one cause and one effect.

For example, suppose a number of people in a given community contracted hepatitis. The local health authorities would try to track down all the various possible means by which each of the hepatitis sufferers had contracted the disease. Now suppose it turned out that they all lived in different neighborhoods, shopped at different grocery stores, had different physicians and dentists, and otherwise led very different lives but that they all ate in the same restaurant on a given night. The health authorities probably inductively would conclude that they contracted hepatitis while eating at that restaurant.

Another of Mill's canons is the *method of difference*. In this method, you observe that all the circumstances in which a given phenomenon occurs are just like those in which it does not occur except for one way in which they differ. For example, suppose that a particular group of students all live in the same dormitory, eat the same food in the same dining halls, sleep on the same schedule, and take all the same classes. But some of the students attend one discussion group, and other students attend another. The students in discussion group A get straight As. But the students in discussion group B get straight Cs. We could conclude inductively that something is happening in the discussion groups to lead to this difference. Does this method sound familiar? If the observer manipulated the various aspects of this method, the method might be called an empirical experiment: You would hold constant all the variables but one. You would manipulate this variable to observe whether it is distinctively associated with the predicted outcome. In fact, inductive reasoning may be viewed as hypothesis testing (Bruner, Goodnow, & Austin, 1956).

One study investigated causal inference by giving people scenarios such as the one shown in Table 12.6 (Schustack & Sternberg, 1981). Participants were to use the information describing the consequences for each company. They needed to figure out whether a company's stock values would drop if the company's major product were under suspicion as a carcinogen. People used four pieces of information to make causal judgments, as shown in Table 12.7. Specifically, they tended to confirm that an event was causal in one of two ways. The first was based on the joint presence of the possibly causal event and the outcome. The second was based on the joint absence of the possibly causal event and the outcome. They tended to disconfirm the causality of a particular antecedent event in two ways as well. One was based either on the presence of the possibly causal event but the absence of the outcome. The other was based on the absence of the possibly causal event but the presence of the outcome. In these ways, people can be quite rational in making causal judgments. However, we do fall prey to various common errors of inductive reasoning. One common error of induction relates to the law of large numbers. Under some circumstances, we recognize that a greater number of observations strengthens the likelihood of our conclusions. At other times, however, we fail to consider the size of the sample we have observed when assessing the strength or the likelihood of a particular inference. In addition, most of us tend to ignore base-rate information. Instead, we focus on unusual variations or salient anecdotal ones. Awareness of these errors can help us improve our decision making.

Perhaps our greatest failing is one that extends to psychologists, other scientists, and nonscientists: We demonstrate confirmation bias, which may lead us to errors such as illusory correlations (Chapman & Chapman, 1967, 1969, 1975). Furthermore, we frequently make mistakes when attempting to determine causality based on correlational evidence alone. As has been stated many times, correlational evidence cannot indicate the direction of causation. Suppose we observe a correlation between Factor A and Factor B. We may find one of three things. First, it may be that Factor A causes Factor B. Second, it may be that Factor B causes Factor A. Third, some higher order Factor C may be causing both Factors A and B to occur together.

TABLE 12.6	Market Analyst Observations Regarding Cosmetics Manufacturers
Based on the information given here, how would you determine causality?	

Company 1	The office staff of the company organized and joined a union. The company's major product was under suspicion as a carcinogen.	There was a drastic drop in the value of the company's stock.
Company 2	The office staff of the company did not organize and join a union. The company's major product was under suspicion as a carcinogen.	There was a drastic drop in the value of the company's stock.
Company 3	Illegal campaign contributions were traced to the company's managers. The company's major product was not under suspicion as a carcinogen.	There was no drastic drop in the value of the company's stock.

TABLE 12.7	Four Bases for Inferring Causality		
Even nonlogicians often use available information effectively when assessing causality.			
CAUSAL INFERENCE	**BASIS FOR INFERENCE**	**EXPLANATION**	**EXAMPLE**
Confirmation	The joint presence of the possibly causal event and the outcome	If an event and an outcome tend to co-occur, people are more likely to believe that the event causes the outcome.	If some other company had a major product suspected to be a carcinogen and its stock went down, that pairing of facts would increase people's belief that having a major product labeled as a carcinogen depresses stock values.
Confirmation	The joint absence of the possibly causal event and the outcome	If the outcome does not occur in the absence of the possibly causal event, then people are more likely to believe that the event causes the outcome.	If other companies' stocks have not gone down when they had no products labeled as carcinogens, then the absence of both the carcinogens among the major products and the stock drops is at least consistent with the notion that having a product labeled as a carcinogen might cause stocks to drop.
Disconfirmation	The presence of the possibly causal event but the absence of the outcome	If the possibly causal event is present but not the outcome, then the event is seen as less likely to lead to the outcome.	If other companies have had major products labeled as carcinogens but their stocks have not gone down, people would be more likely to conclude that having a major product labeled as a carcinogen does not lead to drops in stock prices.
Disconfirmation	The absence of the possibly causal event but the presence of the outcome	If the outcome occurs in the absence of the possibly causal event, then the event is seen as less likely to lead to the outcome. (This rule is one of Mill's canons.)	If other companies have had stock prices drop without having products labeled as carcinogens, people would be less likely to infer that having a product labeled as a carcinogen leads to decreases in stock prices.

A related error occurs when we fail to recognize that many phenomena have multiple causes. For example, a car accident often involves several causes. For example, it may have originated with the negligence of several drivers, rather than just one. Once we have identified one of the suspected causes of a phenomenon, we may commit what is known as a *discounting error*. We stop searching for additional alternative or contributing causes.

Confirmation bias can have a major effect on our everyday lives. For example, we may meet someone, expecting not to like him. As a result, we may treat him in ways that are different from how we would treat him if we expected to like him. He then may respond to us in less favorable ways. He thereby "confirms" our original belief that he is not likable. Confirmation bias thereby can play a major role in schooling. Teachers often expect little of students when they think them low in ability. The students then give the teachers little. The teachers' original beliefs are thereby "confirmed" (Sternberg, 1997).

Research has investigated the relationship between covariation (correlation) information and causal inferences (Ahn & associates, 1995; Ahn & Bailenson, 1996). For some information to contribute to causal inferences, the information necessarily must be correlated with the event. But this covariation information is not sufficient to imply causality. The researchers proposed that the covariation information also must provide information about a possible causal mechanism for the information to contribute to causal inferences. Consider their example. In attempting to determine the cause of Jane's car accident last night, one could use purely covariation information. An example would be "Jane is more likely than most to have a car accident" and "car accidents were more likely to have occurred last night." However, people prefer information specifically about causal mechanisms (Ahn & associates, 1995). An example would be "Jane was not wearing her glasses last night" and "the road was icy," in making causal attributions over information that only covaries with the car accident event. Both of these latter pieces of information about Jane's car accident can be considered covariation information. But the descriptions provide additional causal mechanism information.

In Chapter 8, we discussed the theory-based model of concepts. People's theories affect not only the concepts they have but also the causal inferences they make with these concepts. Consider a set of studies investigating how clinical psychologists make inferences about patients who come to them with various kinds of disorders. Typically, they use the *Diagnostic and Statistical Manual of Mental Disorders* (fourth edition; *DSM-IV*, American Psychiatric Association, 1994) to make such diagnoses. The *DSM-IV* is *atheoretical*. In other words, it is based on no theory. In five experiments, clinicians were asked to diagnose patients with disorders that were either causally central or causally peripheral to the clinicians' own theories of disorders. Participants were more likely to diagnose a hypothetical patient as having a disorder if that disorder was more causally central to the clinicians' own belief system. In other words, the clinicians' own implicit theories trumped the *DSM-IV* in their diagnosing.

The theory-based model of categorization posits that concepts are represented as theories, not feature lists. Thus, it is interesting that the *DSM-IV* established atheoretical guidelines for mental disorder diagnosis. Five experiments investigated how clinicians handled an atheoretical nosology (Kim & Ahn, 2002). The investigators used a variety of methods to ascertain clinicians' implicit personal theories of disorders. In this way, it was possible to discover the clinicians' causal theories of disorders. Then, the clinicians' responses on diagnostic and memory tasks were measured. Of particular interest here is how the clinicians decided on whether a patient had a particular disorder. Did they primarily use the *DSM-IV*, the standard reference manual in the field? Or did they use their own causal theories of disorders? Participants were more likely to diagnose a hypothetical patient with a disorder if that patient had causally central rather than causally peripheral symptoms according to their theory of the disorder. In other words, the more causally central to their own implicit theory a diagnosis was, the more likely they were to give that diagnosis in response to a set of symptoms. Their memory for causally central symptoms was also better than their memory for symptoms they saw as causally peripheral. Clinicians are thus driven to use their own implicit causal theories, even if they have had decades of practice with the atheoretical *DSM*. This set of studies provides strong support for the theory-based notion of concepts discussed in Chapter 8. But it also shows that these theories do not just "sit" in the head. They are actively used when we do causal reasoning. Even experts prefer their causal theories over a standard reference work in their field (*DSM-IV*).

An alternative view is that people act as naive scientists in positing unobservable theoretical causal power entities to explain observable covariations (Cheng, 1997). Thus, people are somewhat rational in making causal attributions based on the right kinds of covariation information.

Categorical Inferences

On what basis do people draw inferences? People generally use both bottom-up strategies and top-down strategies for doing so (Holyoak & Nisbett, 1988). That is, they use both information from their sensory experiences and information based on what they already know or have inferred previously. Bottom-up strategies are based on observing various instances and considering the degree of variability across instances. From these observations, we abstract a prototype (see Chapters 6 and 9). Once a prototype or a category has been induced, the individual may use focused sampling to add new instances to the category. He or she focuses chiefly on properties that have provided useful distinctions in the past. Top-down strategies include selectively searching for constancies within many variations and selectively combining existing concepts and categories.

Reasoning by Analogy

Inductive reasoning may be applied to a broader range of situations than those requiring causal or categorical inferences. For example, inductive reasoning may be applied to reasoning by analogy. Consider an example analogy problem: "Fire is to asbestos as water is to (a) vinyl, (b) air, (c) cotton, (d) faucet." In reasoning by analogy, the reasoner must observe the first pair of items ("fire" and "asbestos" in this example) and must induce from those two items one or more relations (in this case, surface resistance because surfaces coated with asbestos can resist fire). The reasoner then must apply the given relation in the second part of the analogy. In the example analogy, the reasoner chooses the solution to be "vinyl" because surfaces coated with vinyl can resist water.

Some investigators have used reaction-time methodology to figure out how people solve induction problems. For example, using mathematical modeling I was able to break down the amounts of time participants spent on various processes of analogical reasoning. I found that most of the time spent in solving simple verbal analogies is spent in encoding the terms and in responding (Sternberg, 1977). Only a small part actually is spent in doing reasoning operations on these encodings.

The difficulty of encoding can become even greater in various puzzling analogies. For example, in the analogy RAT : TAR :: BAT : (a. CONCRETE, b. MAMMAL, c. TAB, d. TAIL), the difficulty is in encoding the analogy as one involving letter reversal rather than semantic content for its solution. In a problematic analogy such as AUDACIOUS : TIMOROUS :: MITIGATE : (a. ADUMBRATE, b. EXACERBATE, c. EXPOSTULATE, d. EVISCERATE), the difficulty is in recognizing the meanings of the words. If reasoners know the meanings of the words, they probably will find it relatively easy to figure out that the relation is one of antonyms. (Did this example audaciously exacerbate your difficulties in solving problems involving analogies?)

Development of Inductive Reasoning

Young children do not have the same inductive-reasoning skills as do older children. For example, 4-year-olds appear not to induce generalized biological principles about animals when given specific information about individual animals (Carey, 1985). By age 10 years, however, children are much more likely to do so. For example, if 4-year-olds are told that both dogs and bees have a particular body organ, they still assume that only animals that are highly similar either to dogs or to bees have this organ and that other animals do not. In contrast, 10-year-olds would induce that if animals as dissimilar as dogs and bees have this organ, many other animals are likely to have this organ as well. Also, 10-year-olds would be much more likely than 4-year-olds to induce biological principles that link humans to other animals.

Along the same lines, when 5-year-olds learn new information about a specific kind of animal, they seem to add the information to their existing schemas for the particular kind of animal but not to modify their overall schemas for animals or for biology as a whole (see Keil, 1989, 1999). However, first- and second-graders have shown an ability to choose and even to spontaneously generate appropriate tests for gathering indirect evidence to confirm or disconfirm alternative hypotheses (Sodian, Zaitchik, & Carey, 1991).

Even children as young as 3 years seem to induce some general principles from specific observations, particularly those principles that pertain to taxonomic categories for animals (Gelman, 1984/1985; Gelman & Markman, 1987). For example, preschoolers were able to induce principles that correctly attribute the cause of phenomena (such as growth) to natural processes rather than to human intervention (Gelman & Kremer, 1991; Hickling & Gelman, 1995). In related work, preschoolers were able to reason correctly that a blackbird was more likely to behave like a flamingo than like a bat because blackbirds and flamingos are both birds (Gelman & Markman, 1987). Note that in this example, preschoolers are going against their perception that blackbirds look more like bats than like flamingos, basing their judgment instead on the fact that they are both birds (although the effect is admittedly strongest when the term "bird" also is used in regard to both the flamingo and the blackbird).

Although the purpose of words is largely to express meaning—for example, to indicate a dog by the use of the word "dog" or a flamingo by the use of the word "flamingo"—there is some evidence that the process is not wholly one directional. Sometimes, children use words whose meanings they do not understand and only gradually acquire the correct meaning after they have started to use the words (Kessler Shaw, 1999). Nelson (1999) refers to this phenomenon as "use without meaning."

Other work supports the view that preschoolers may make decisions based on induced general principles rather than on perceptual appearances. For example, they may induce taxonomic categories based on functions (such as means of breathing) rather than on perceptual appearances (such as apparent weight) (Gelman & Markman, 1986). When given information about the internal parts of objects in one category, preschoolers also induced that other objects in the same category were likely to have the same internal parts (Gelman & O'Reilly, 1988; see also Gelman & Wellman, 1991).

However, when inducing principles from discrete information, young preschoolers were more likely than older children to emphasize external, superficial features of animals than to give weight to internal structural or functional features. Also, given the same specific information, older children seem to induce richer inferences regarding biological properties than do younger children (Gelman, 1989).

It is important to maintain both forms of knowledge, appearance based and principled, for flexible use across different situations and domains (Wellman & Gelman, 1998). Knowledge about deep internal functional relationships is important for inducing properties of objects. But similarity in appearance is also important under other circumstances. Knowledge acquisition develops via the use of framework theories, or models, for drawing inferences about the environment in various domains (such as physics, psychology, and biology) (Wellman & Gelman, 1998). Numerous studies demonstrate children's early and rapid acquisition of expertise in understanding physical objects and causal relations among events, psychological entities and casual-explanatory reasoning, and biological entities and forces. The changes in reasoning about factors in these domains appear to show enhanced understanding of the relation between appearances and deeper functional principles. Thus, children use foundational knowledge within different domains to build framework understandings of the world.

An Alternative View of Reasoning

By now you have reasonably inferred that cognitive psychologists often disagree—sometimes rather heatedly—about how and why people reason as they do. An alternative perspective on reasoning has been proposed. It is that two complementary systems of reasoning can be distinguished. The first is an associative system, which involves mental operations based on observed similarities and temporal contiguities (i.e., tendencies for things to occur close together in time). The second is a rule-based system, which involves manipulations based on the relations among symbols (Sloman, 1996).

The associative system can lead to speedy responses that are highly sensitive to patterns and to general tendencies. Through this system we detect similarities between observed patterns and patterns stored in memory. We may pay more attention to salient features (e.g., highly typical or highly atypical ones) than to defining features of a pattern. This system imposes rather loose constraints that may inhibit the selection of patterns that are poor matches to the observed pattern. It favors remembered patterns that are better matches to the observed pattern. An example of associative reasoning is use of the representativeness heuristic. Another example is the belief-bias effects in syllogistic reasoning. This effect occurs when we agree more with syllogisms that affirm our beliefs, whether or not these syllogisms are logically valid. An example of the workings of the associative system may be in the *false-consensus effect*. Here, people believe that their own behavior and judgments are more common and more appropriate than those of other people (Ross, Greene, & House, 1977). Suppose people have an opinion on an issue. They are likely to believe that, because it is their opinion, it is likely to be shared and believed to be correct by others. Of course, there is some diagnostic value in one's own opinions. It is quite possible that others do indeed believe what one believes (Dawes & Mulford, 1996; Krueger, 1998). On the whole, however, associating others' views with our own simply because they are our own is a questionable practice.

The rule-based system usually requires more deliberate, sometimes painstaking procedures for reaching conclusions. Through this system, we carefully analyze relevant features (e.g., defining features) of the available data, based on rules stored in memory. This system imposes rigid constraints that rule out possibilities that violate the rules. Evidence of rule-based reasoning are several. First, we can recognize logical arguments when they are explained to us. Second, we can recognize the need to make categorizations based on defining features despite similarities in typical features. For example, we can recognize that a coin with a 3-inch diameter, which looks exactly like a quarter, must be a counterfeit. Third, we can rule out impossibilities, such as cats conceiving and giving birth to puppies. Fourth, we can recognize many improbabilities. For example, it is unlikely that the U.S. Congress will pass a law that provides annual salaries to all full-time college students. According to Sloman, we need both complementary systems. We need to respond quickly and easily to everyday situations, based on observed similarities and temporal contiguities. Yet we also need a means for evaluating our responses more deliberately.

The two systems may be conceptualized within a connectionist framework (Sloman, 1996). The associative system is represented easily in terms of pattern activation and inhibition, which readily fits the connectionist model. The rule-based system may be represented as a system of production rules (see Chapter 11).

An alternative connectionist view suggests that deductive reasoning may occur when a given pattern of activation in one set of nodes (e.g., those associated with a particular premise or set of premises) entails or produces a particular pattern of activation in a second set of nodes (Rips, 1994). Similarly, a connectionist model of inductive reasoning may involve the repeated activation of a series of similar patterns across various instances. This repeated activation then may strengthen the links among the activated nodes. It thereby leads to generalization or abstraction of the pattern for a variety of instances.

Connectionist models of reasoning and the various other approaches described in this chapter offer diverse views of the available data regarding how we reason and make judgments. At present, no one theoretical model explains all the data well. But each model explains at least some of the data satisfactorily. Together, the theories help us understand human intelligence, the topic of the next and final chapter.

Common Themes

Several of the themes discussed in Chapter 1 are relevant to this chapter.

A first theme is rationalism versus empiricism. Consider, for example, errors in syllogistic reasoning. One way of understanding such errors is in terms of the particular logical error made, independently of the mental processes the reasoner has used. For example, affirming the consequent is a logical error. One need do no empirical research to understand at the level of symbolic logic the errors that have been made.

Moreover, deductive reasoning is itself based on rationalism. A syllogism such as "All toys are chairs. All chairs are hot dogs. Therefore, all toys are hot dogs" is logically valid, but factually incorrect. Thus, deductive logic can be understood at a rational level, independently of its empirical content. But if we wish to know psychologically why people make errors or what is factually true, than we need to combine empirical observations with rational logic.

A second theme is domain generality versus domain specificity. The rules of deductive logic apply equally in all domains. One can apply them, for example, to abstract or to concrete content. But research has shown that psychologically, deductive reasoning with concrete content is easier than reasoning with abstract content. So, although the rules apply in exactly the same way generally across domains, ease of application is not psychologically equivalent across those domains.

A third theme is nature versus nurture. Are people preprogrammed to be logical thinkers? Piaget, the famous Swiss cognitive-developmental psychologist, believed so. He believed that the development of logical thinking follows an inborn sequence of stages that unfold over time. According to Piaget, there is not much one can do to alter either the sequence of timing of these stages. But research has suggested that the sequence Piaget proposed does not unfold as he thought. For example, many people never reach his highest stage. And some children are able to reason in ways he would not have predicted they would be able to reason until they were older. So once again, nature and nurture interact.

Consider this passage from Shakespeare's *Macbeth*:

> First Apparition: *Macbeth! Macbeth! Beware Macduff; Beware the thane of Fife. Dismiss me: enough. . . .*

> Second Apparition: *Be bloody, bold, and resolute; laugh to scorn the power of man, for none of woman born shall harm Macbeth.*

> Macbeth: *Then live, Macduff: what need I fear of thee? But yet I'll make assurance double sure, and take a bond of fate: thou shalt not live; that I may tell pale-hearted fear it lies, and sleep in spite of thunder.*

In this passage, Macbeth mistakenly took the Second Apparition's vision to mean that no man could kill him, so he boldly decided to confront Macduff. However, as we all know, Macduff was born by abdominal delivery (Cesarean delivery), so he did not fall into the category of men who could not harm Macbeth. Macduff eventually killed Macbeth because Macbeth came to a wrong conclusion based on the Second Apparition's premonition. The First Apparition's warning about Macduff should have been heeded.

Suppose you are trying to decide between buying an SUV or a subcompact car. You would like the room of the SUV, but you would like the fuel efficiency of the subcompact car. Whichever one you choose, did you make the right choice? This is a difficult question to answer because most of our decisions are made under conditions of uncertainty. Thus, let us say that you bought the SUV. You can carry a number of people, you have the power to pull a trailer easily up a hill, and you sit higher so your road vision is much better. However, every time you fill up the gas tank, you are reminded of how much fuel this vehicle takes. On the other hand, let us say that you bought the subcompact car. When picking friends up at the airport, you have difficulty fitting all of them in with their luggage; you cannot pull trailers up hills (or at least, not very easily); and you sit so low that when there is an SUV in front of you, you can hardly see what is on the road. However, every time you fill up your gas tank or hear someone with an SUV complaining about how much it costs to fill up his or her tank, you see how little you have to pay for gas. Again, did you make the right choice? There are no right nor wrong answers to most of the decisions we make. We use our best judgment at the time of our decisions and think that they are more right than wrong as opposed to definitively right or wrong.

Summary

1. **What are some of the strategies that guide human decision making?** Early theories were designed to achieve practical mathematical models of decision making and assumed that decision makers are fully informed, infinitely sensitive to information, and completely rational. Subsequent theories began to acknowledge that humans often use subjective criteria for decision making, that chance elements often influence the outcomes of decisions, that humans often use subjective estimates for considering the outcomes, and that humans are not boundlessly rational in making decisions. People apparently often use satisficing strategies, settling for the first minimally acceptable option, and strategies involving a process of elimination by aspects to weed out an overabundance of options.

   One of the most common heuristics most of us use is the representativeness heuristic. We fall prey to the fallacious belief that small samples of a population resemble the whole population in all respects. Our misunderstanding of base rates and other aspects of probability often leads us to other mental shortcuts as well, such as in the conjunction fallacy and the inclusion fallacy. Another common heuristic is the availability heuristic, in which we make judgments based on information that is readily available in memory, without bothering to seek less available information. The use of heuristics such as anchoring and adjustment, illusory correlation, and framing effects also often impair our ability to make effective decisions. Once we have made a decision (or better yet, another person has made a decision) and the out-

come of the decision is known, we may engage in hindsight bias, skewing our perception of the earlier evidence in light of the eventual outcome. Perhaps the most serious of our mental biases, however, is overconfidence, which seems to be amazingly resistant to evidence of our own errors.

2. **What are some of the forms of deductive reasoning that people may use, and what factors facilitate or impede deductive reasoning?** Deductive reasoning involves reaching conclusions from a set of conditional propositions or from a syllogistic pair of premises. Among the various types of syllogisms are linear syllogisms and categorical syllogisms. In addition, deductive reasoning may involve complex transitive-inference problems or mathematical or logical proofs involving large numbers of terms. Also, deductive reasoning may involve the use of pragmatic reasoning schemas in practical, everyday situations.

   In drawing conclusions from conditional propositions, people readily apply the *modus ponens* argument, particularly regarding universal affirmative propositions. Most of us have more difficulty, however, in using the *modus tollens* argument and in avoiding deductive fallacies such as affirming the consequent or denying the antecedent, particularly when faced with propositions involving particular propositions or negative propositions. In solving syllogisms, we have similar difficulties with particular premises and negative premises and with terms that are not presented in the customary sequence. Frequently, when trying to draw conclusions, we overextend a strategy from a situation in which it leads to a deductively valid conclusion to one in which it leads to a deductive fallacy. We also may foreclose on a given conclusion before considering the full range of possibilities that may affect the conclusion. These mental shortcuts may be exacerbated by situations in which we engage in confirmation bias (tending to confirm our own beliefs).

We can enhance our ability to draw well-reasoned conclusions in many ways, such as by taking time to evaluate the premises or propositions carefully and by forming multiple mental models of the propositions and their relationships. We also may benefit from training and practice in effective deductive reasoning. We are particularly likely to reach well-reasoned conclusions when such conclusions seem plausible and useful in pragmatic contexts, such as during social exchanges.

3. **How do people use inductive reasoning to reach causal inferences and to reach other types of conclusions?** Although we cannot reach logically certain conclusions through inductive reasoning, we can at least reach highly probable conclusions through careful reasoning. More than a century ago, John Stuart Mill recommended that people use various canonical strategies for reaching inductive conclusions. When making categorical inferences, people tend to use both top-down and bottom-up strategies. Processes of inductive reasoning generally form the basis of scientific study and hypothesis testing as a means to derive causal inferences. In addition, in reasoning by analogy people often spend more time encoding the terms of the problem than in performing the inductive reasoning. It appears that people sometimes may use reasoning based on formal rule systems, such as by applying rules of formal logic, and sometimes use reasoning based on associations, such as by noticing similarities and temporal contiguities.

4. **Are there any alternative views of reasoning?** Steven Sloman has suggested that people have two distinct systems of reasoning: an associative system that is sensitive to observed similarities and temporal contiguities and a rule-based system that involves manipulations based on relations among symbols.

Thinking about Thinking: Factual, Analytical, Creative, and Practical Questions

1. Describe some of the heuristics and biases people use while making judgments or reaching decisions.

2. What are the two logical arguments and the two logical fallacies associated with conditional reasoning, as in the Wason selection task?

3. Which of the various approaches to conditional reasoning seems best to explain the available data? Give reasons for your answer.

4. Some cognitive psychologists question the merits of studying logical formalisms such as linear or categorical syllogisms. What do you think can be gained by studying how people reason in regard to syllogisms?

5. Based on the information in this chapter, design a way to help college students more effectively apply deductive reasoning to the problems they face.

6. Design a question, such as the ones used by Kahneman and Tversky, which requires people to estimate subjective probabilities of two different events. Indicate the fallacies that you may expect to influence people's estimates or tell why you think people would give realistic estimates of probability.

7. Suppose that you need to rent an apartment. How would you go about finding one that most effectively meets your requirements and your preferences? How closely does your method resemble the methods described by subjective expected utility theory, by satisficing, or by elimination by aspects?

8. Give two examples showing how you use rule-based reasoning and associative reasoning in your everyday experiences.

Key Terms

availability heuristic
base rate
bounded rationality
categorical syllogism
causal inferences
conditional reasoning
deductive reasoning
deductive validity
elimination by aspects

fallacy
hindsight bias
illusory correlation
inductive reasoning
judgment and decision making
mental model
overconfidence
pragmatic reasoning schema
premises

proposition
reasoning
representativeness
satisficing
subjective probability
subjective utility
syllogism

Explore CogLab by going to http://coglab.wadsworth.com. Answer the questions required by your instructor from the student manual that accompanies CogLab.

Risky Decisions   Wason Selection Task
Typical Reasoning

Annotated Suggested Reading

Leighton, J. P., & Sternberg, R. J. (Eds.) (2004). *The nature of reasoning*. New York: Cambridge University Press. A complete review of contemporary theories and research on reasoning.

Human and Artificial Intelligence

EXPLORING COGNITIVE PSYCHOLOGY

1. What are the key issues in measuring intelligence? How do different researchers and theorists approach the issues?

2. What are some information-processing approaches to intelligence?

3. What are some alternative views of intelligence?

4. How have researchers attempted to simulate intelligence using machines such as computers?

5. Can intelligence be improved, and if so, how?

6. How does intelligence develop in adults?

INVESTIGATING COGNITIVE PSYCHOLOGY

Before you read about how cognitive psychologists view intelligence, try responding to a few tasks that require you to use your own intelligence:

1. Candle is to tallow as tire is to (a) automobile, (b) round, (c) rubber, (d) hollow.
2. Complete this series: 100%, 0.75, ½; (a) whole, (b) one eighth, (c) one fourth.
3. The first three items form one series. Complete the analogous second series that starts with the fourth item:

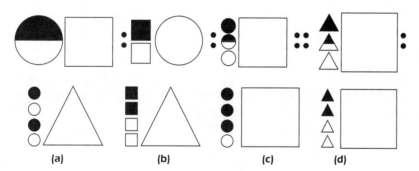

(a)   (b)   (c)   (d)

4. You are at a party of truth-tellers and liars. The truth-tellers always tell the truth, and the liars always lie. You meet someone new. He tells you that he just heard a conversation in which a girl said she was a liar. Is the person you met a liar or a truth-teller?

Each of the preceding tasks is believed, at least by some cognitive psychologists, to require some degree of intelligence. (The answers are at the end of this section.) Intelligence is a concept that can be viewed as tying together all of cognitive psychology. Just what is intelligence? In 1921, when the editors of the *Journal of Educational Psychology* asked fourteen famous psychologists that question, the responses varied but generally embraced these two themes. First, intelligence involves the capacity to learn from experience. Second, it involves the ability to adapt to the surrounding environment. Sixty-five years later, twenty-four cognitive psychologists with expertise in intelligence research were asked the same question (Sternberg & Detterman, 1986). They, too, underscored the importance of learning from experience and adapting to the environment. They also broadened the definition to emphasize the importance of *metacognition*—people's understanding and control of their own thinking processes. Contemporary experts also more heavily emphasized the role of culture. They pointed out that what is considered intelligent in one culture may be considered stupid in another culture (Serpell, 2000). To summarize, **intelligence** is the capacity to learn from experience, using metacognitive processes to enhance learning, and the ability to adapt to the surrounding environment. It may require different adaptations within different social and cultural contexts.

According to the *Oxford English Dictionary*, the word *intelligence* entered our language in about the twelfth century. Today, we can look up intelligence in numerous dictionaries. But most of us still have our own implicit (unstated) ideas about what it means to be smart. That is, we have our own *implicit theories* (usually unstated conceptions) of intelligence. We use our implicit theories in many social situations. For example, we use them when we meet people and evaluate their intelligence. We also use them when we describe people we know as being very smart or not so smart.

Within our implicit theories of intelligence, we also recognize that intelligence has somewhat different meanings in different contexts. A smart salesperson may show a different kind of intelligence than a smart neurosurgeon or a smart accountant. Each of them may show a different kind of intelligence than a smart choreographer, composer, athlete, or sculptor. Often, we use our implicit and context-relevant definitions of intelligence to make assessments of intelligence. Is your mechanic smart enough to find and fix the problem in your car? Is your physician smart enough to find and treat your health problem? Is this attractive person smart enough to hold your interest in a conversation?

Implicit theories of intelligence may differ from one culture to another. For example, there is evidence that Chinese people in Taiwan include interpersonal and intrapersonal (self-understanding) skills as part of their conception of intelligence (Yang & Sternberg, 1997). Rural Kenyan conceptions of intelligence encompass moral as well as cognitive skills (Grigorenko & associates, 2001). Thus, what might count as a comprehensive assessment of intelligence could differ from one culture to another (Sternberg & Kaufman, 1998).

Even within the United States, many people today have started viewing as important not only the cognitive aspects of intelligence but also the emotional aspects of intelligence. **Emotional intelligence** is "the ability to perceive and express emotion, assimilate emotion in thought, understand and reason with emotion, and regulate emotion in the self and others" (Mayer, Salovey, & Caruso, 2000, p. 396). There is good evidence for the existence of some kind of emotional intelligence (Ciarrochi, Forgas, & Mayer, 2001; Mayer & Salovey, 1997; Salovey & Sluyter, 1997), although the evidence is mixed (Davies, Stankov, & Roberts, 1998). The concept of emotional intelligence has also become very popular in recent years (Goleman, 1995, 1998). A related concept is that of social intelligence. *Social intelligence* is the ability to understand and interact with other people (Kihlstrom & Cantor, 2000). Research also shows that personality variables are related to intelligence (Ackerman, 1996).

Explicit definitions of intelligence also frequently take on an assessment-oriented focus. In fact, some psychologists have been content to define intelligence as whatever it is that the tests measure (Boring, 1923). This definition, unfortunately, is circular. According to it, the nature of intelligence is what is tested. But what is tested must necessarily be determined by the nature of intelligence. Moreover, what different tests of intelligence test is not always the same thing. Different tests measure somewhat different constructs (Daniel, 1997, 2000; Kaufman, 2000; Kaufman & Lichtenberger, 1998). So it is not feasible to define intelligence by what tests test as though they all measured the same thing. By the way, the answers to the questions in the chapter opener are as follows:

1. Rubber. Candles are frequently made of tallow, just as tires are frequently made of (c) rubber.

2. 100%, 0.75, and ½ are quantities that successively decrease by ¼; to complete the series, the answer is (c) one fourth, which is a further decrease by ¼.

3. The first series was a circle and a square, followed by two squares and a circle, followed by three circles and a square; the second series was three triangles and a square, which would be followed by (b), four squares and a triangle.

4. The person you met is clearly a liar. If the girl about whom this person was talking were a truth-teller, she would have said that she was a truth-teller. If she were a liar, she would have lied and said that she was a truth-teller also. Thus, regardless of whether the girl was a truth-teller or a liar, she would have said that she was a truth-teller. Because the man you met has said that she said she was a liar, he must be lying and hence must be a liar.

Measures and Structures of Intelligence

Contemporary measurements of intelligence usually can be traced to one of two very different historical traditions. One tradition concentrated on lower-level, psychophysical abilities. These include sensory acuity, physical strength, and motor coordination. The other focused on higher-level, judgmental abilities. We traditionally describe these abilities as related to thinking (Nęčka & Orzechowski, 2005). Stop for a moment to think about yourself and your close associates. How would you assess yourself and your associates in terms of intelligence? When you make these assessments, do psychophysical abilities seem more important? Or do judgment abilities seem more important to you?

Francis Galton (1822–1911) believed that intelligence is a function of psychophysical abilities. For several years, Galton maintained a well-equipped laboratory where visitors could have themselves measured on a variety of psychophysical tests. These tests measured a broad range of psychophysical skills and sensitivities. One example was weight discrimination, the ability to notice small differences in the weights of objects. Another example was pitch sensitivity, the ability to hear small differences between musical notes. A third example was physical strength (Galton, 1883). One of the many enthusiastic followers of Galton attempted to detect links among the assorted tests (Wissler, 1901). He hoped such links would unify the various dimensions of psychophysically based intelligence. But he detected no unifying associations. Moreover, the psychophysical tests did not predict college grades. Thus, the psychophysical approach to assessing intelligence soon faded almost into oblivion. Nevertheless, it would reappear many years later in a somewhat different guise.

An alternative to the psychophysical approach was developed by Alfred Binet (1857–1911). He and his collaborator, Theodore Simon, also attempted to assess intelligence, but their goal was much more practical than purely scientific. Binet had been asked to devise a procedure for distinguishing normal from mentally retarded learners (Binet & Simon, 1916). Thus, Binet and his collaborator set out to measure intelligence as a function of the ability to learn within an academic setting. In Binet's view, judgment is the key to intelligence; the key is not psychophysical acuity, strength, or skill.

For Binet (Binet & Simon, 1916), intelligent thought (mental judgment) comprises three distinct elements: direction, adaptation, and criticism. Think about how you are intelligently using these elements yourself at this moment: Direction involves knowing what has to be done and how to do it; adaptation refers to customizing a strategy for performing a task and then monitoring that strategy while implementing it; and criticism is your ability to critique your own thoughts and actions. The importance of direction and adaptation certainly fits with contemporary views of intelligence, and Binet's notion of criticism actually seems prescient, considering the current appreciation of metacognitive processes as a key aspect of intelligence.

Initially, when Binet and Simon developed their intelligence test, they were interested in some means of comparing the intelligence of a given child with that of other children of the same chronological (physical) age. For their purposes, they sought to determine each child's *mental age*—the average level of intelligence for a person of a given age. Thus, a mental age of 7 refers to the level of thinking reached by an average 7-year-old child. Mental ages worked just fine for comparing a given 7-year-old child with other 7-year-old children, but the use of mental ages made it difficult to compare relative intelligence in children of differing chronological ages.

William Stern (1912) suggested instead that we evaluate people's intelligence by using an *intelligence quotient* (IQ): a ratio of mental age (MA) divided by chronological age (CA), multiplied by 100 (Figure 13.1). This ratio can be expressed mathematically as follows: IQ = (MA/CA)(100). Thus, if Joan's mental age of 5 equals her chronological age of 5, then her intelligence is average and her IQ is 100 because $(5/5)(100) = 100$. When mental age exceeds chronological age, the ratio will lead to an IQ score above 100, and when chronological age exceeds mental age, the ratio will lead to an IQ score below 100. Intelligence scores that are expressed in terms of a ratio of mental age to chronological age are termed *ratio IQs*.

For various reasons, ratio IQs, too, proved inadequate. For example, increases in mental age slow down at about age 16 years. An 8-year-old child with a mental age of 12 years is pretty smart. However, do you feel sure that a 40-year-old adult with a mental age of 60 is similarly intelligent, although the ratio IQ is the same for the 8-year-old child and the 40-year-old adult? What does a mental age of 60 mean? Today, psychologists rarely use IQs based on mental ages. Instead, researchers have turned to measurement comparisons based on assumed normal distributions of test scores within large populations. Scores based on deviations from the middle score in

FIGURE 13.1

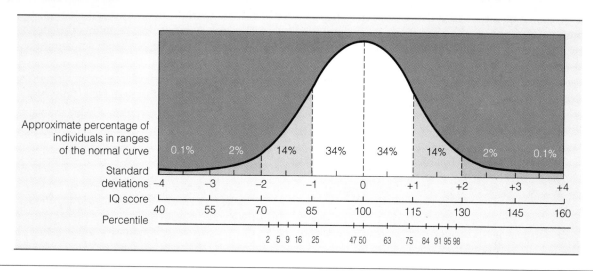

This figure shows a normal distribution as it applies to IQ, including identifying labels that are sometimes used to characterize different levels of IQ. It is important not to take these labels too seriously because they only are loose characterizations, not scientific descriptions of performance. From Intelligence Applied: Understanding and Increasing Your Intellectual Skills by Robert J. Sternberg, copyright © 1986 by Harcourt Brace & Company, reproduced by permission of the publisher.

a normal distribution of scores on a test of intelligence are termed *deviation IQs*. Many cognitive theorists believe that IQs provide only incomplete measurement of intelligence, as is discussed later.

Lewis Terman of Stanford University built on Binet and Simon's work in Europe and constructed the earliest version of what has come to be called the Stanford-Binet Intelligence Scale (Terman & Merrill, 1937, 1973; Thorndike, Hagen, & Sattler, 1986; Table 13.1). For years, the Stanford-Binet test was the standard for intelligence tests, and it still is used widely. The competitive Wechsler scales, named for their creator, David Wechsler, are probably even more widely used, however.

There are three levels of the Wechsler intelligence scales, including the third edition of the Wechsler Adult Intelligence Scale (WAIS-III), the fourth edition of the Wechsler Intelligence Scale for Children (WISC-IV), and the Wechsler Preschool and Primary Scale of Intelligence (WPPSI). The Wechsler tests yield three scores. They are a verbal score, a performance score, and an overall score. The verbal score is based on tests such as vocabulary and verbal similarities. In verbal similarities, the test-taker has to say how two things are similar. The performance score is based on several tests. One is picture completion, which requires identification of a missing part in a picture of an object. Another is picture arrangement, which requires rearrangement of a scrambled set of cartoonlike pictures into an order that tells a coherent story. The overall score is a combination of the verbal and the performance scores. Table 13.2 shows the types of items from each of the Wechsler adult-scale subtests, which you may wish to compare with those of the Stanford-Binet.

TABLE 13.1	The Stanford-Binet Intelligence Scale

The sample questions used throughout this chapter are not actual questions from any of the scales; they are intended only to illustrate the types of questions that might appear in each of the main content areas of the tests. How would you respond to these questions? What do your responses indicate about your intelligence?

CONTENT AREA	EXPLANATION OF TASKS/QUESTIONS	EXAMPLE OF A POSSIBLE TASK/QUESTION
Verbal Reasoning		
Vocabulary Comprehension	Define the meaning of a word. Show an understanding of why the world works as it does.	What does the word diligent mean? Why do people sometimes borrow money?
Absurdities	Identify the odd or absurd feature of a picture.	(Recognize that ice hockey players do not ice skate on lakes into which swimmers in bathing suits are diving.)
Verbal relations	Tell how three of four items are similar to one another yet different from the fourth item.	(Note that an apple, a banana, and an orange can be eaten, but a mug cannot be.)
Quantitative Reasoning		
Number series	Complete a series of numbers.	Given the numbers 1, 3, 5, 7, 9, what number would you expect to come next?
Quantitative	Solve simple arithmetic-word problems.	If Maria has six apples, and she wants to divide them evenly among herself and her two best friends, how many apples will she give to each friend?
Figural/Abstract Reasoning		
Pattern analysis	Figure out a puzzle in which the test-taker must combine pieces representing parts of geometric shapes, fitting them together to form a particular geometric shape.	Fit together these pieces to form a (geometric shape).
Short-Term Memory		
Memory for sentences Memory for digits Memory for objects	Listen to a sentence, then repeat it back exactly as the examiner said it. Listen to a series of digits (numbers), then repeat the numbers either forward or backward or both. Watch the examiner point to a series of objects in a picture, then point to the same objects in exactly the same sequence in which the examiner did so.	Repeat this sentence back to me: "Harrison went to sleep late and awoke early the next morning." Repeat these numbers backward: "9, 1, 3, 6." (Point to the carrot, then the hoe, then the flower, then the scarecrow, then the baseball.)

Wechsler, like Binet, had a conception of intelligence that went beyond what his own test measured. Wechsler clearly believed in the worth of attempting to measure intelligence. But he did not limit his conception of intelligence to test scores. Wechsler believed that intelligence is central in our everyday lives. Intelligence is not represented

TABLE 13.2	The Wechsler Adult Intelligence Scale

Based on the content areas and the kinds of questions shown here, how does the Wechsler differ from the Stanford-Binet?

CONTENT AREA	EXPLANATION OF TASKS/QUESTIONS	EXAMPLE OF A POSSIBLE TASK/QUESTION
Verbal Scale		
Comprehension	Answer questions of social knowledge.	What does it mean when people say, "A stitch in time saves nine"? Why are convicted criminals put into prison?
Vocabulary	Define the meaning of a word.	What does persistent mean? What does archaeology mean?
Information	Supply generally known information.	Who is Laura Bush? What are six New England states?
Similarities	Explain how two things or concepts are similar.	In what ways are an ostrich and a penguin alike? In what ways are a lamp and a heater alike?
Arithmetic	Solve simple arithmetic-word problems.	If Paul has $14.43, and he buys two sandwiches, which cost $5.23 each, how much change will he receive? How many hours will it take to travel 1200 miles if you are traveling 60 miles per hour?
Digit span	Listen to a series of digits (numbers), then repeat the numbers either forward, backward, or both.	Repeat these numbers backward: "9, 1, 8, 3, 6." Repeat these numbers, just as I am telling you: "6, 9, 3, 2, 8."
Performance Scale		
Object assembly	Put together a puzzle by combining pieces to form a particular common object.	Put together these pieces to make something.
Block design	Use patterned blocks to form a design that looks identical to a design shown by the examiner.	Assemble the blocks at the left to match the design at the right.
Picture completion	Tell what is missing from each picture.	What is missing from this picture?
Picture arrangement	Put a set of cartoonlike pictures into chronological order, so that they tell a coherent story.	Arrange these pictures in an order that tells a story, and then tell what is happening in the story.
Digit symbol	When given a key matching particular symbols to particular numerals, use the sequence of symbols to transcribe from symbols to numerals using the key.	Look carefully at the key, showing which symbols correspond to which numerals. In the blanks, write the correct numeral for the symbol above each blank.

just by a test score or even by what we do in school. We use our intelligence not just in taking tests and in doing homework. We also use it in relating to people, in performing our jobs effectively, and in managing our lives in general.

A focus on the measurement of intelligence is only one of several approaches to theory and research on intelligence. At least two of the key issues in the approach to studying intelligence have arisen in earlier chapters of this book in regard to other topics in cognitive psychology. One is whether cognitive psychologists should focus on the measurement of intelligence or on the processes of intelligence. A second is that of what underlies intelligence: a person's genetic inheritance, a person's acquired attributes, or some kind of interaction between the two.

Psychologists interested in the structure of intelligence have relied on factor analysis as the indispensable tool for their research. **Factor analysis** is a statistical method for separating a construct—intelligence in this case—into a number of hypothetical factors or abilities that the researchers believe to form the basis of individual differences in test performance. The specific factors derived, of course, still depend on the specific questions being asked and the tasks being evaluated.

Factor analysis is based on studies of correlation. The idea is that the more highly two tests are correlated, the more likely they are to measure the same thing. In research on intelligence, a factor analysis might involve these steps. First, give a large number of people several different tests of ability. Second, determine the correlations among all those tests. Third, statistically analyze those correlations to simplify them into a relatively small number of factors that summarize people's performance on the tests. The investigators in this area generally have agreed on and followed this procedure. Yet the resulting factorial structures of intelligence have differed among different theorists. Among the many competing factorial theories, the main ones probably have been those of Spearman, Thurstone, Guilford, Cattell, Vernon, and Carroll. Figure 13.2 contrasts four of these theories.

Spearman: The "g" Factor

Charles Spearman (1863–1945) usually is credited with inventing factor analysis (Spearman, 1927). Using factor-analytic studies, Spearman concluded that intelligence can be understood in terms of two kinds of factors. A single general factor pervades performance on all tests of mental ability. A set of specific factors is involved in performance on only a single type of mental-ability test (e.g., arithmetic computations). In Spearman's view, the specific factors are of only casual interest because of the narrow applicability of these factors. To Spearman, the general factor, which he labeled "**g**," provides the key to understanding intelligence. Spearman believed "g" to be the result of "mental energy." Many psychologists still believe Spearman's theory to be essentially correct (e.g., Jensen, 1998, 2005; see essays in Sternberg & Grigorenko, 2002).

Thurstone: Primary Mental Abilities

In contrast to Spearman, Louis Thurstone (1887–1955) concluded that the core of intelligence resides not in one single factor but in seven such factors (Thurstone,

FIGURE 13.2

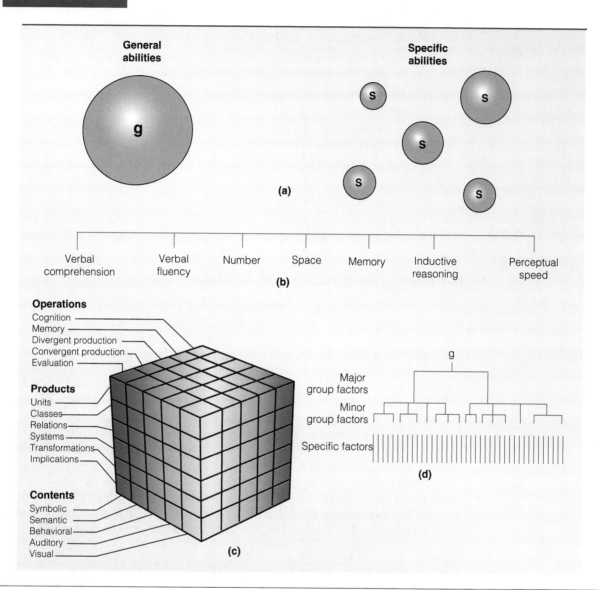

Although Spearman, Thurstone, Guilford, and Vernon all used factor analysis to determine the factors underlying intelligence, they all reached different conclusions regarding the structure of intelligence. Which model most simply yet comprehensively describes the structure of intelligence as you understand it? How do particular models of intelligence shape our understanding of intelligence? From In Search of the Human Mind by Robert J. Sternberg, copyright © 1995 by Harcourt Brace & Company, reproduced by permission of the publisher.

1938). He referred to them as primary mental abilities. According to Thurstone, the primary mental abilities are as follows:

1. *Verbal comprehension:* measured by vocabulary tests
2. *Verbal fluency:* measured by time-limited tests requiring the test-taker to think of as many words as possible that begin with a given letter
3. *Inductive reasoning:* measured by tests such as analogies and number-series completion tasks
4. *Spatial visualization:* measured by tests requiring mental rotation of pictures of objects
5. *Number:* measured by computation and simple mathematical problem-solving tests
6. *Memory:* measured by picture and word-recall tests
7. *Perceptual speed:* measured by tests that require the test-taker to recognize small differences in pictures or to cross out the *a*'s in strings of varied letters

Guilford: The Structure of Intellect

At the opposite extreme from Spearman's single g-factor model is the **structure-of-intellect (SOI)** model (Guilford, 1967, 1982, 1988). It includes up to 150 factors of the mind in one version of the theory. According to Guilford, intelligence can be understood in terms of a cube that represents the intersection of three dimensions (Figure 13.2). The dimensions are operations, contents, and products. According to Guilford, operations are simply mental processes, such as memory and evaluation. Evaluation involves making judgments, such as determining whether a particular statement is of fact or opinion. Contents are the kinds of terms that appear in a problem. Examples are semantic (words) and visual (pictures). Products are the kinds of responses required. They include units (single words, numbers, or pictures), classes (hierarchies), and implications (Figure 13.2).

Several psychologists have believed that Guilford posited more factors than he could prove (e.g., Eysenck, 1967; Horn & Knapp, 1973). Perhaps Guilford's most valuable contribution was to suggest that we consider various kinds of mental operations, contents, and products in our views and our assessments of intelligence.

Cattell, Vernon, and Carroll: Hierarchical Models

A more parsimonious way of handling a number of factors of the mind is through a hierarchical model of intelligence. One such model proposed that general intelligence comprises two major subfactors. They are fluid ability and crystallized ability. Fluid ability is speed and accuracy of abstract reasoning, especially for novel problems. Crystallized ability is accumulated knowledge and vocabulary (Cattell, 1971). Subsumed within these two major subfactors are other, more specific factors. A similar view is a general division between practical-mechanical and verbal-educational abilities (Vernon, 1971).

A more recent model is a hierarchy comprising three strata (Carroll, 1993). Stratum I includes many narrow, specific abilities (e.g., spelling ability, speed of reasoning). Stratum II includes various broad abilities (e.g., fluid intelligence, crystallized intelligence). And Stratum III is just a single general intelligence, much like Spearman's g. Of these strata, the most interesting is the middle stratum, which is neither too narrow nor too all encompassing.

In addition to fluid intelligence and crystallized intelligence, Carroll includes in the middle stratum several other abilities. They are learning and memory processes, visual perception, auditory perception, facile production of ideas (similar to verbal fluency), and speed (which includes both sheer speed of response and speed of accurate responding). Carroll's model is probably the most widely accepted of the psychometric models. Whereas the factor-analytic approach it exemplifies has tended to emphasize the structures of intelligence, the information-processing approach has tended to emphasize the operations of intelligence.

Information Processing and Intelligence

Information-processing theorists are interested in studying how people mentally manipulate what they learn and know about the world (Hunt, 2005). The ways in which various information-processing investigators study intelligence differ primarily in terms of the complexity of the processes being studied (Stankov, 2005). Researchers has considered both the speed and the accuracy of information processing to be important factors in intelligence.

Process-Timing Theories

Inspection time is the amount of time it takes you to inspect items and make a decision about them. It is measured through an inspection-time experimental paradigm (Nettelbeck, 1987; Nettelbeck & Lally, 1976; Nettelbeck & Rabbitt, 1992; see also Deary, 2000b; Deary & Stough, 1996; Neubauer & Fink, 2005). Here is a typical use of the paradigm. For each of a number of trials, a computer monitor displays a fixation cue (a dot in the area where a target figure will appear) for 500 milliseconds. There is then a pause of 360 milliseconds. Following this period, the computer presents the target stimulus for a particular interval of time. Finally, it presents a visual mask (a stimulus that erases the trace in iconic memory).

The target stimulus typically comprises two vertical lines of unequal length. For example, one might be 25 millimeters and the other 35 millimeters. The two lines are aligned at the top by a horizontal crossbar. The shorter of the two lines may appear on either the right or the left side of the stimulus. The visual mask is a pair of lines that are thicker and longer than the two lines of the target stimulus. The task is to inspect the target stimulus and then indicate the side on which the shorter line appeared. One indicates the left-hand stimulus by pressing a left-hand button on a keypad connected to a computer that records the responses. One indicates the right-hand stimulus by pressing the right-hand button.

The key variable is the length of time for the presentation of the target stimulus, not the speed of responding by pressing the button. Nettelbeck defined inspection time operationally. It is the length of time for presentation of the target stimulus after which the participant still responds with at least 90% accuracy in indicating the

Courtesy of Dr. Earl Hunt

Earl Hunt is a professor of psychology and adjunct professor of computer science at the University of Washington. He has done major work on computer-simulation models of inductive reasoning, on the nature of intelligence, and on drug-induced alterations of memory and reasoning.

side on which the shorter line appeared. He found that shorter inspection times correlate with higher scores on intelligence tests (e.g., various subscales of the WAIS) among differing populations of participants (Nettelbeck, 1987). Other investigators have confirmed this finding (e.g., Deary & Stough, 1996).

Choice Reaction Time

Some investigators have proposed that intelligence can be understood in terms of speed of neuronal conduction (e.g., Jensen, 1979, 1998). In other words, the smart person is someone whose neural circuits conduct information rapidly. When Arthur Jensen proposed this notion, direct measures of neural-conduction velocity were not readily available. So Jensen primarily studied a proposed proxy for measuring neural-processing speed. The proxy was *choice reaction time*—the time it takes to select one answer from among several possibilities.

Consider a typical choice-reaction-time paradigm. The participant is seated in front of a set of lights on a board (Figure 13.3). When one of the lights flashes, he or she extinguishes it by pressing as rapidly as possible a button beneath the correct light. The experimenter would then measure the participant's speed in performing this task.

Participants with higher IQs are faster than participants with lower IQs in their reaction time (RT) (Jensen, 1982). In this particular version of the task, RT is defined as the time between when a light comes on and the finger leaves the home (central) button. In some studies, participants with higher IQs also showed a faster movement time (MT). MT is defined as the time between letting the finger leave the home button and hitting the button under the light. These findings may be due to increased central nerve-conduction velocity, although at present this proposal remains speculative (Reed & Jensen, 1991, 1993).

FIGURE 13.3

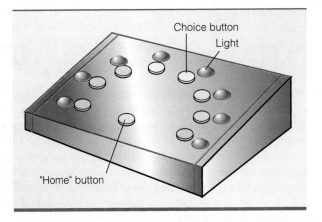

To measure choice reaction time, Jensen used an apparatus like the one shown here. *Reprinted with permission of The Free Press, a division of Simon & Schuster Adult Publishing Group, from* Bias in Mental Testing *by Arthur R. Jensen. Copyright © 1980 by Arthur R. Jensen. All rights reserved.*

Various findings regarding choice reaction time may be influenced by extraneous factors. They include the number of response alternatives and the visual-scanning requirements of Jensen's apparatus. In this case, RT as measured would not be a result of speed of reaction time alone (Bors, MacLeod, & Forrin, 1993). In particular, manipulating the number of buttons and the size of the visual angle of the display (how much of the visual field it consumes) can reduce the correlation between IQ and reaction time (Bors, MacLeod, & Forrin, 1993). Thus, the relation between reaction time and intelligence is unclear.

Lexical-Access Speed and Speed of Simultaneous Processing

Some investigations have focused on *lexical-access speed*—the speed with which we can retrieve information about words (e.g., letter names) stored in our long-term memories (Hunt, 1978). This speed can be measured with a letter-matching, reaction-time task first proposed by Posner and Mitchell, 1967 (Hunt, 1978).

Participants are shown pairs of letters, such as "A A," "A a," or "A b." For each pair, they indicate whether the letters constitute a match in name (e.g., "A a" match in name of letter of the alphabet but "A b" do not). They also are given a simpler task. In it, they are asked to indicate whether the letters match physically (e.g., "A A" are physically identical, whereas "A a" are not). The variable of interest is the difference between their speed for the first set of tasks, involving name matching, and their speed for the second set, involving matching of physical characteristics. The difference in reaction time between the two kinds of tasks is said to provide a measure of speed of lexical access. This score is based on a *subtraction* of name-match minus physical-match reaction time. The subtraction controls for mere perceptual-processing time. Students with lower verbal ability take longer to gain access to lexical information than do students with higher verbal ability (Hunt, 1978).

Intelligence is also related to people's ability to divide their attention (Hunt & Lansman, 1982). For example, suppose that participants are asked to solve mathematical problems and simultaneously to listen for a tone and press a button as soon as they hear it. We can expect that they both would solve the math problems effectively and respond quickly to hearing the tone. According to Hunt and Lansman, more intelligent people are better able to timeshare between two tasks and to perform both effectively.

In sum, process-timing theories attempt to account for differences in intelligence by appealing to differences in the speed of various forms of information processing. Inspection time, choice reaction time, and lexical access timing all have been found to correlate with measures of intelligence. These findings suggest that, on average, higher intelligence may be related to the speed of various information-processing abilities. More intelligent people encode information more rapidly into working memory. They access information in long-term memory more rapidly. And they respond more rapidly. Why would more rapid encoding, retrieval, and responding be associated with higher intelligence test scores? Do rapid information processors learn more?

Is there a link between age-related slowing of information processing and (1) initial encoding and recall of information and (2) long-term retention (Nettelbeck & associates, 1996; see also Bors & Forrin, 1995). It appears that the relation between inspection time and intelligence may not be related to learning. In particular, there is a difference between initial recall and actual long-term learning (Nettelbeck & associates, 1996). Initial recall performance is mediated by processing speed. Older, slower participants showed deficits. Longer-term retention of new information, preserved in older participants, is mediated by cognitive processes other than speed of processing. These processes include rehearsal strategies. Thus, speed of information processing may influence initial performance on recall and inspection time tasks. But speed is not related to long-term learning. Perhaps faster information-processing aids participants in performance aspects of intelligence test tasks, rather than contributing to actual learning and intelligence. Clearly, this area requires more research to determine how information-processing speed relates to intelligence.

Working Memory

Recent work suggests that a critical component of intelligence may be working memory. Indeed, some investigators have argued that intelligence may be little more than working memory (Kyllonen & Christal, 1990). In one study, participants read sets of passages and, after they had read the passages, tried to remember the last word of each passage (Daneman & Carpenter, 1983). Recall was highly correlated with verbal ability. In another study, participants performed a variety of working-memory tasks. In one task, for example, the participants saw a set of simple arithmetic problems, each of which was followed by a word or a digit. An example would be "Is $(3 \cdot 5) - 6 = 7$? TABLE" (Turner & Engle, 1989; see also Hambrick, Kane, & Engle, 2005). The participants saw sets of from two to six such problems and solved each one. After solving the problems in the set, they tried to recall the words that followed the problems. The number of words recalled was highly correlated with measured intelligence. Thus, it appears that the ability to store and manipulate information in working memory may be an important aspect of intelligence. It is probably not all there is to intelligence, however.

Componential Theory and Complex Problem Solving

Cognitive approaches for studying information processing can be applied to more complex tasks, such as analogies, series problems (e.g., completing a numerical or figural series), and syllogisms (Sternberg, 1977, 1983, 1984a; see Chapter 12). The idea is to take the kinds of tasks used on conventional intelligence tests and to isolate components of intelligence. *Components* are the mental processes used in performing these tasks, such as translating a sensory input into a mental representation, transforming one conceptual representation into another, or translating a conceptual representation into a motor output (Sternberg, 1982b). Many investigators have elaborated on and expanded this basic approach (Lohman, 2000, 2005; Wenke, Frensch, & Funke, 2005).

Componential analysis breaks down people's reaction times and error rates on these tasks in terms of the processes that make up the tasks. This kind of analysis revealed that people may solve analogies and similar tasks by using several component processes. Among them are several processes. A first is encoding the terms of the problem A second is inferring relations among at least some of the terms. A third is mapping the inferred relations to other terms, which would be presumed to show similar relations. And a fourth is applying the previously inferred relations to the new situations.

IN THE LAB OF RANDALL ENGLE

Courtesy of Dr. Randall Engle

The amount of information we can think about at one time is quite limited, and the role this limitation plays in real-world cognition has been an important focus of cognitive psychology for nearly 50 years. If temporary memory or capacity limits are important to cognition, then we should see a relationship between measures of short-term memory such as simple digit or word span and performance on such important cognitive tasks as reading comprehension, complex learning, and reasoning. Although such relationships between simple span tasks and other cognitive tasks are not reliably found, span tasks that interleave items-to-be-remembered with other attention-demanding tasks do reliably predict a wide range of real-world cognition (Engle, 2001). In the operation span task, for example, participants read aloud a series of two to five operation-word strings such as "Is 6/3 + 3 = 6? (yes or no) CAT" and then see a question mark which indicates they are to recall the two to five words from the series. Recall on this and other working memory capacity (WMC) tasks reliably predict performance on a wide range of higher-level cognitive tasks, including those that reflect the concept known as general fluid intelligence. This is important because fluid intelligence tasks show the greatest decline with aging and also decrease with damage to the frontal cortex of the brain. Therefore, WMC tasks clearly reflect some critical aspect of the information processing system. But, what mechanisms are responsible for that relationship? I have argued that individual differences in WMC reflect an abiding difference in the ability to control attention so as to keep thought directed to the service of task goals. Individuals with low working memory are less able to prevent the capture of thought by retrieved memories or by external events that lead thought away from performance of current tasks. In other words, WMC reflects an ability to prevent distraction from internally generated thoughts or from events in the external environment. Take, for example, findings using the antisaccade task. In this task, participants face a computer screen with a central fixation point and two white boxes 11.5° to the right and left of fixation. At some point, one of the boxes would flicker, and the participant was to resist the natural tendency to look at the flickering box and to quickly move his or her fixation to the box on the other side of screen. If individual differences in WMC reflect differences in the ability to control attention, then we should see a relationship between measures of WMC and performance on this antisaccade task, and, in fact, we do. Individuals with low WMC make many more errors on this task than high WMC individuals do, even though there are no group differences in a control task that requires the participant to look toward the flickering box (Unsworth, Schrock, and Engle, 2004). Participants with high WMC are better able to resist the strong pull to look toward something that suggests movement. We have also shown that individuals with low WMC are much more vulnerable to the internally generated distractions that occur as a result of proactive interference. Individuals with high WMC are more able to prevent interfering events from coming to mind and from intruding into the thought process, again as a result of their greater ability to prevent attention from being captured. Although individual differences in WMC appear to be a relatively abiding characteristic of the individual, we now know that many other variables lead to reduced WMC temporarily (Engle and Kane, 2004), and this reduction in turn will lead to deterioration of performance on a wide range of cognitive tasks.

Consider the analogy, LAWYER : CLIENT :: DOCTOR : (a. PATIENT b. MEDICINE). To solve this analogy, you need to *encode* each term of the problem. This includes perceiving a term and retrieving information about it from memory. You then *infer* the relationship between lawyer and client. In particular, the former provides professional services to the latter. You then *map* the relationship in the first half of the analogy to the second half of the analogy. Here, you note that it will involve that same relationship. Finally, you *apply* that inferred relationship to generate the final term of the analogy. This leads to the appropriate response of PATIENT. Figure 13.4 shows how componential analysis would be applied to an analogy problem, A is to B as C is to D, where D is the solution. Studying these components of information processing reveals more than measuring mental speed alone.

There are significant correlations between speed in executing these processes and performance on other, traditional intelligence tests. However, a more intriguing discovery is that participants who score higher on traditional intelligence tests take longer to encode the terms of the problem than do less intelligent participants. But they make up for the extra time by taking less time to perform the remaining components of the task. In general, more intelligent participants take longer during *global planning*—encoding the problem and formulating a general strategy for attacking the problem (or set of problems). But they take less time for *local planning*—forming and implementing strategies for the details of the task (Sternberg, 1981).

The advantage of spending more time on global planning is the increased likelihood that the overall strategy will be correct. Thus, when taking more time is advantageous, brighter people may take longer to do something than will less bright people. For example, the brighter person might spend more time researching and planning for writing a term paper but less time in the actual writing of it. This same differential in time allocation has been shown in other tasks as well. An example

FIGURE 13.4

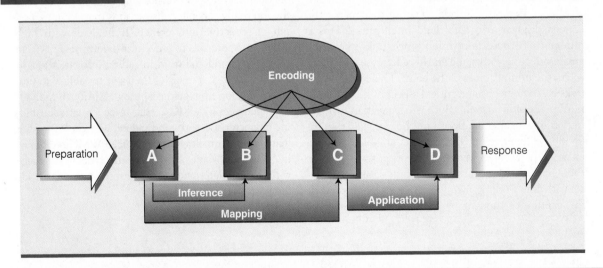

In the solution of an analogy problem, the problem solver must first encode the problem A is to B as C is to D. The problem solver then must infer the relationship between A and B. Next, the problem solver must map the relationship between A and B to the relationship between C and each of the possible solutions to the analogy. Finally, the problem solver must apply the relationship to choose which of the possible solutions is the correct solution to the problem.

would be in solving physics problems (Larkin & associates, 1980; see Sternberg, 1979, 1985a). That is, more intelligent people seem to spend more time planning for and encoding the problems they face. But they spend less time engaging in the other components of task performance. This may relate to the previously mentioned metacognitive attribute many include in their notions of intelligence.

Researchers have also studied information processing of people engaged in complex problem-solving situations. Examples are playing chess and performing logical derivations (Newell & Simon, 1972; Simon, 1976). For example, a simple, brief task might require the participants first to view an arithmetic or geometric series. Then they must figure out the rule underlying the progression. And finally they must guess what numeral or geometric figure might come next. More complex tasks might include some of the tasks mentioned in Chapter 11 (e.g., the water jugs problems; see Estes, 1982). Can performance on these or other tasks be analyzed at a biological level?

An Integrative Approach

An integrative approach would combine models of various kinds of cognitive functioning as bases for intelligence. In such an approach, four sources of individual differences in intelligence might be detected (Ackerman, 1988, 2005). These are (1) breadth of declarative knowledge, (2) breadth of procedural skills, (3) capacity of working memory, and (4) speed of processing. The advantage of this approach is that it does not try to localize individual differences in intelligence as coming from one source. Rather, multiple sources are involved.

Biological Bases of Intelligence

The human brain is clearly the organ that serves as a biological basis for human intelligence. Early studies, such as those of Karl Lashley, studied the brain to find biological indices of intelligence and other aspects of mental processes. They were a resounding failure, despite great efforts. As tools for studying the brain have become more sophisticated, however, we are beginning to see the possibility of finding physiological indicators of intelligence. Some investigators believe that we will soon have clinically useful psychophysiological indices of intelligence (e.g., Matarazzo, 1992). But widely applicable indices will be much longer in coming. In the meantime, the biological studies we now have are largely correlational. They show statistical associations between biological and psychometric or other measures of intelligence. They do not establish causal relations.

One line of research looks at the relationship of brain size to intelligence (see Jerison, 2000; Vernon & associates, 2000). The evidence suggests that, for humans, there is a modest but significant statistical relationship between brain size and intelligence. However, it is difficult to know what to make of this relationship. Greater brain size may cause greater intelligence, greater intelligence may cause greater brain size, or both may be dependent on some third factor. Moreover, it is probably at least as important how efficiently the brain is used than what its size is. For example, on average, men have larger brains than women have. But women, on average, have better connections through the corpus callosum of the two hemispheres of the brain. So it is not clear which sex would be, on average, at an advantage. Probably neither would be. It is important to note that the relationship between brain size and intelligence does not hold across species (Jerison, 2000). Rather, what holds seems to be a relationship between intelligence and brain size, relative to the rough general size of the organism.

For now, some of the current studies offer some appealing possibilities. For example, complex patterns of electrical activity in the brain, which are prompted by specific stimuli, appear to correlate with scores on IQ tests (Barrett & Eysenck, 1992). Several studies initially suggested that speed of conduction of neural impulses may correlate with intelligence, as measured by IQ tests (McGarry-Roberts, Stelmack, & Campbell, 1992; Vernon & Mori, 1992). A follow-up study, however, failed to find a strong relation between neural-conduction velocity and intelligence (Wickett & Vernon, 1994). In this study, conduction velocity was measured by neural-conduction speeds in a main nerve of the arm. Intelligence was measured by a Multidimensional Aptitude Battery. Surprisingly, neural-conduction velocity appears to be a more powerful predictor of IQ scores for men than for women. So sex differences may account for some of the differences in the data (Wickett & Vernon, 1994). Additional studies on both males and females are needed.

More recent work suggests it may be the flexibility of neural circuitry, rather than speed of conduction, that is key (Newman & Just, 2005). Hence, we would want to study not just speed, but neural circuitry. An alternative approach to studying the brain suggests that neural efficiency may be related to intelligence. Such an approach is based on studies of how the brain metabolizes glucose (a simple sugar required for brain activity) during mental activities. (See Chapter 2 for more on positron emission tomography and other brain-imaging techniques.) Higher intelligence correlates with reduced levels of glucose metabolism during problem-solving tasks (Haier & associates, 1992). That is, smarter brains consume less sugar and hence expend less effort than do less smart brains doing the same task. Furthermore, cerebral efficiency increases as a result of learning on a relatively complex task involving visuospatial manipulations, the computer game Tetris (Haier & associates, 1992). As a result of practice, more intelligent participants not only show lower cerebral glucose metabolism overall, but also show more specifically localized metabolism of glucose. In most areas of their brains, smarter participants show less glucose metabolism. But in selected areas of their brains, believed to be important to the task at hand, they show higher levels of glucose metabolism. Thus, more intelligent participants may have learned how to use their brains more efficiently. They carefully focus their thought processes on a given task.

Other research, however, suggests that the relationship between glucose metabolism and intelligence may be more complex (Haier & associates, 1995; Larson & associates, 1995). On the one hand, one study confirmed the earlier findings of increased glucose metabolism in less smart participants, in this case, mildly retarded participants (Haier & associates, 1995). On the other hand, another study found, contrary to the earlier findings, that smarter participants had increased glucose metabolism relative to their average comparison group (Larson & associates, 1995).

There was a problem with earlier studies. It was that the tasks participants received were not matched for difficulty level across groups of smart and average individuals. The study by Larson and colleagues used tasks that were matched to the ability levels of the smarter and average participants. They found that the smarter participants used more glucose. Moreover, the glucose metabolism was highest in the right hemisphere of the more intelligent participants performing the hard task. These results again suggest selectivity of brain areas. What could be driving the increases in glucose metabolism? Currently, the key factor appears to be subjective task difficulty. In earlier studies smarter participants simply found the tasks to be too easy. Matching task difficulty to participants' abilities seems to indicate that smarter participants increase glucose metabolism when the task demands it. The preliminary findings in this area will need to be investigated further before any conclusive answers arise.

Some neuropsychological research suggests that performance on intelligence tests may not indicate a crucial aspect of intelligence. This is the ability to set goals, to plan how to meet them, and to execute those plans (Dempster, 1991). Specifically, people with lesions on the frontal lobe of the brain frequently perform quite well on standardized IQ tests. These tests require responses to questions within a highly structured situation. But they do not require much in the way of goal setting or planning. Intelligence involves the ability to learn from experience and to adapt to the surrounding environment. Thus the ability to set goals and to design and implement plans cannot be ignored. An essential aspect of goal setting and planning is the ability to attend appropriately to relevant stimuli. Another related ability is that of ignoring or discounting irrelevant stimuli.

We cannot realistically study a brain or its contents and processes in isolation without also considering the entire human being. We must consider the interactions of that human being with the entire environmental context within which the person acts intelligently. Hence, many researchers and theorists urge us to take a more contextual view of intelligence. Furthermore, some alternative views of intelligence attempt to broaden the definition of intelligence to be more inclusive of people's varied abilities.

Alternative Approaches to Intelligence

Cultural Context and Intelligence

According to **contextualism,** intelligence must be understood in its real-world context. The context of intelligence may be viewed at any level of analysis. It may be focused narrowly, as on the home and family environment, or it may be extended broadly, to entire cultures. For example, even cross-community differences have been correlated with differences in performance on intelligence tests. Such context-related differences include those of rural versus urban communities, low versus high proportions of teenagers to adults within communities, and low versus high socioeconomic status of communities (see Coon, Carey, & Fulker, 1992). Contextualists have been intrigued particularly by the effects of cultural context on intelligence.

Contextualists consider intelligence to be inextricably linked to culture. They view intelligence as something that a culture creates to define the nature of adaptive performance in that culture. It further accounts for why some people perform better than others on the tasks that the culture happens to value (Sternberg, 1985a). Theorists who endorse this model study just how intelligence relates to the external world in which the model is being applied and evaluated. In general, definitions and theories of intelligence will more effectively encompass cultural diversity by broadening in scope. Before exploring some of the contextual theories of intelligence, we will look at what prompted psychologists to believe that culture might play a role in how we define and assess intelligence.

There have been many definitions of culture (e.g., Brislin, Lonner, & Thorndike, 1973; Kroeber & Kluckhohn, 1952). Culture is defined here as "the set of attitudes, values, beliefs and behaviors shared by a group of people, communicated form one generation to the next via language or some other means of communication (Barnouw, 1985)" (Matsumoto, 1994, p. 4). The term *culture* can be used in many ways and has a long history (Benedict, 1946; Boas, 1911; Mead, 1928; see Matsumoto, 1996; Sternberg, 2004a). Berry and colleagues (1992) described six uses of the term: descriptively to characterize a culture, historically to describe the traditions of a group, normatively to express rules and norms of a group, psychologically to emphasize how a group learns and solves problems, structurally to emphasize the organizational elements of a culture, and genetically to describe cultural origins.

One reason to study culture and intelligence is that they are so inextricably interlinked. Indeed, Tomasello (2001) has argued that culture is what, in large part, separates human from animal intelligence. Humans have evolved as they have, he believes, in part because of their cultural adaptations, which in turn develop from their ability, even in infancy from about 9 months onward, to understand others as intentional agents.

Many research programs demonstrate the potential hazards of single-culture research. For example, Greenfield (1997) found that it means a different thing to take a test among Mayan children than it does among most children in the United States. The Mayan expectation is that collaboration is permissible and that it is rather unnatural *not* to collaborate. Such a finding is consistent with the work of Markus and Kitayama (1991), which suggests different cultural constructions of the self in individualistic versus collectivistic cultures. Indeed, Nisbett (2003) has found that some cultures, especially Asian ones, tend to be more dialectical in their thinking, whereas other cultures, such as European and North American ones, tend to be more linear. And individuals in different cultures may construct concepts in quite different ways, rendering results of concept-formation or identification studies in a single culture suspect (Atran, 1999; Coley & associates, 1999; Medin & Atran, 1999). Thus, groups may think about what appears superficially to be the same phenomenon—whether a concept or the taking of a test—differently. What appear to be differences in general intelligence may in fact be differences in cultural properties (Helms-Lorenz, Van de Vijver, & Poortinga, 2003). Helms-Lorenz and colleagues (2003) have argued that measured differences in intellectual performance may result from differences in cultural complexity; but complexity of a culture is extremely hard to define, and what appears to be simple or complex from the point of view of one culture may appear differently from the point of view of another.

People in different cultures may have quite different ideas of what it means to be smart. For example, one of the more interesting cross-cultural studies of intelligence was performed by Michael Cole and his colleagues (Cole & associates, 1971). These investigators asked adult members of the Kpelle tribe in Africa to sort terms representing concepts. Consider what happens in Western culture when adults are given a sorting task on an intelligence test. More intelligent people typically will sort hierarchically. For example, they may sort names of different kinds of fish together. Then they place the word "fish" over that. They place the name "animal" over "fish" and over "birds," and so on. Less intelligent people will typically sort functionally. They may sort "fish" with "eat," for example. Why? Because we eat fish. Or they may sort "clothes" with "wear" because we wear clothes. The Kpelle sorted functionally. They did so even after investigators unsuccessfully tried to get the Kpelle spontaneously to sort hierarchically.

Finally, in desperation, one of the experimenters (Glick) asked a Kpelle to sort as a foolish person would sort. In response, the Kpelle quickly and easily sorted hierarchically. The Kpelle had been able to sort this way all along. They just had not done it because they viewed it as foolish. And they probably considered the questioners rather unintelligent for asking such stupid questions.

The Kpelle people are not the only ones who might question Western understandings of intelligence. In the Puluwat culture of the Pacific Ocean, for example, sailors navigate incredibly long distances. They use none of the navigational aids that sailors from technologically advanced countries would need to get from one place to another (Gladwin, 1970). Suppose Puluwat sailors were to devise intelligence tests for us and our fellow Americans. We and our compatriots might not seem very intelligent. Similarly, the highly skilled Puluwat sailors might not do well on American-crafted tests of intelligence. These and other observations have prompted quite a few theoreticians to recognize the importance of considering cultural context when intelligence is assessed.

A study provides an example a little closer to home regarding the effects of cultural differences on intelligence tests (Sarason & Doris, 1979). It tracked the IQs of an immigrant population: Italian Americans. Less than a century ago, first-generation Italian-American children showed a median IQ of 87 (low average; range 76–100). Their IQs were relatively low even when nonverbal measures were used and when so-called mainstream American attitudes were considered. Some social commentators and intelligence researchers of the day pointed to heredity and other nonenvironmental factors as the basis for the low IQs. Today, some commentators do the same for other minority groups (Herrnstein & Murray, 1994).

For example, a leading researcher of the day, Henry Goddard, pronounced that 79% of immigrant Italians were "feebleminded." He also asserted that about 80% of immigrant Jews, Hungarians, and Russians were similarly unendowed (Eysenck & Kamin, 1981). Goddard (1917) also asserted that moral decadence was associated with this deficit in intelligence. He recommended that the intelligence tests he used be administered to all immigrants and that all those he deemed substandard selectively be excluded from entering the United States. But subsequent generations of Italian-American students who take IQ tests today show slightly above-average IQs (Ceci, 1991). Other immigrant groups that Goddard had denigrated have shown similar "amazing" increases. Even the most fervent hereditarians would be unlikely to attribute such remarkable gains in so few generations to heredity. Cultural assimilation, including integrated education, seems a much more plausible explanation.

The preceding arguments may make it clear why it is so difficult to come up with a test that everyone would consider **culture-fair**—equally appropriate and fair for members of all cultures. If members of different cultures have different ideas of what it means to be intelligent, then the very behaviors that may be considered intelligent in one culture may be considered unintelligent in another. Take, for example, the concept of mental quickness. In mainstream U.S. culture, quickness usually is associated with intelligence. To say someone is "quick" is to say that the person is intelligent. Indeed, most group tests of intelligence are strictly timed. Even on individual tests of intelligence, the test-giver times some responses of the test-taker. Many information-processing theorists and even psychophysiological theorists focus on the study of intelligence as a function of mental speed.

In many cultures of the world, however, quickness is not at a premium. In these cultures, people may believe that more intelligent people do not rush into things. Even in our own culture, no one will view you as brilliant if you rush things that should not be rushed. For example, it generally is not smart to decide on a marital partner, a job, or a place to live in the 20 to 30 seconds you normally might have to solve an intelligence-test problem. Thus, there exist no perfectly culture-fair tests of intelligence, at least at present. How then should we consider context when assessing and understanding intelligence?

Several researchers have suggested that providing culture-relevant tests is possible (e.g., Baltes, Dittmann-Kohli, & Dixon, 1984; Jenkins, 1979; Keating, 1984). **Culture-relevant tests** measure skills and knowledge that relate to the cultural experiences of the test-takers can be offered. Baltes and his colleagues, for example, have designed tests measuring skill in dealing with the pragmatic aspects of everyday life. Designing culture-relevant tests requires creativity and effort. But it is probably not impossible. For example, one study investigated memory abilities—one aspect of intelligence as our culture

Intricate patterns on Moroccan rugs were more easily remembered by Moroccan rug merchants than by Westerners. In contrast, Westerners more easily remembered information unfamiliar to Moroccan rug merchants.

defines it—in our culture versus the Moroccan culture (Wagner, 1978). It found that the level of recall depended on the content that was being remembered. Culture-relevant content was remembered more effectively than nonrelevant content. For example, when compared with Westerners, Moroccan rug merchants were better able to recall complex visual patterns on black-and-white photos of Oriental rugs. Sometimes tests just are not designed to minimize the effects of cultural differences. In such cases, the key to culture-specific differences in memory may be the knowledge and use of metamemory strategies, rather than actual structural differences in memory (e.g., memory span and rates of forgetting) (Wagner, 1978).

Research has shown that rural Kenyan school children have substantial knowledge about natural herbal medicines they believe fight illnesses. Western children, of course, would not be able to identify any of these medicines (Sternberg & associates, 2001; Sternberg & Grigorenko, 1997). In short, making a test culturally relevant appears to involve much more than just removing specific linguistic barriers to understanding.

Similar context effects appear in children's and adults' performance on a variety of tasks. Three kinds of context affect performance (Ceci & Roazzi, 1994). The first is the social context. An example would be whether a task is considered masculine or feminine. The second is the mental context. An example would be whether a visuospatial task involves buying a home or burgling it. The third is the physical context. Here, an example would be whether a task is presented at the beach or in a laboratory. For example, 14-year-old boys performed poorly on a task when it was couched as a cupcake-baking task. But they performed well when it was framed as a battery-charging task (Ceci & Bronfenbrenner, 1985). Brazilian maids had no difficulty with proportional reasoning when hypothetically purchasing food. But they had great difficulty with it when hypothetically purchasing medicinal herbs (Schliemann & Magalhües, 1990). Brazilian children whose poverty had forced them to become street vendors showed no difficulty in performing complex arithmetic computations when selling things. But they had great difficulty performing similar calculations in a classroom (Carraher, Carraher, & Schliemann, 1985). Thus, test performance may be affected by the context in which the test terms are presented. The extent to which the context of performance resembles the context of learning of an intelligent action may partially determine the extent to which the behavior shows transfer from the first situation to the second (Barnett & Ceci, 2005).

In these studies, the investigators looked at the interaction of cognition and context. Several investigators have proposed theories that seek explicitly to examine this interaction within an integrated model of many aspects of intelligence. Such theories view intelligence as a complex system and are discussed in the next two sections.

Gardner: Multiple Intelligences

Howard Gardner (1983, 1993b, 1999) has proposed a **theory of multiple intelligences,** in which intelligence comprises multiple independent constructs, not just a single, unitary construct. However, instead of speaking of multiple abilities that together constitute intelligence (e.g., Thurstone, 1938), this theory distinguishes eight distinct intelligences that are relatively independent of each other (Table 13.3). Each is a separate system of functioning, although these systems can interact to produce what we see

Howard Gardner is a professor of education and adjunct professor of psychology at Harvard University. He is best known for his theory of multiple intelligences and for showing how the theory can be applied in educational settings. He has also done important work in neuropsychology and in the psychology of creativity.

TABLE 13.3	Gardner's Eight Intelligences

On which of Howard Gardner's eight intelligences do you show the greatest ability? In what contexts can you use your intelligences most effectively? (After Gardner, 1999)

TYPE OF INTELLIGENCE	TASKS REFLECTING THIS TYPE OF INTELLIGENCE
Linguistic intelligence	Used in reading a book; writing a paper, a novel, or a poem; and understanding spoken words
Logical-mathematical intelligence	Used in solving math problems, in balancing a checkbook, in solving a mathematical proof, and in logical reasoning
Spatial intelligence	Used in getting from one place to another, in reading a map, and in packing suitcases in the trunk of a car so that they all fit into a compact space
Musical intelligence	Used in singing a song, composing a sonata, playing a trumpet, or even appreciating the structure of a piece of music
Bodily-kinesthetic intelligence	Used in dancing, playing basketball, running a mile, or throwing a javelin
Interpersonal intelligence	Used in relating to other people, such as when we try to understand another person's behavior, motives, or emotions
Intrapersonal intelligence	Used in understanding ourselves—the basis for understanding who we are, what makes us tick, and how we can change ourselves, given our existing constraints on our abilities and our interests
Naturalist intelligence	Used in understanding patterns in nature

From Multiple Intelligences by Howard Gardner. Copyright © 1993 by Howard Gardner. Reprinted by perimssion of Basic Books, a member of Perseus Books, L.L.C.

as intelligent performance. Looking at Gardner's list of intelligences, you might want to evaluate your own intelligences, perhaps rank ordering your strengths in each.

In some respects, Gardner's theory sounds like a factorial one. It specifies several abilities that are construed to reflect intelligence of some sort. However, Gardner views each ability as a separate intelligence, not just as a part of a single whole. Moreover, a crucial difference between Gardner's theory and factorial ones is in the sources of evidence Gardner used for identifying the eight intelligences. Gardner used converging operations, gathering evidence from multiple sources and types of data.

In particular, the theory uses eight "signs" as criteria for detecting the existence of a discrete kind of intelligence (Gardner, 1983, pp. 63–67):

1. Potential isolation by brain damage. The destruction or sparing of a discrete area of the brain (e.g., areas linked to verbal aphasia) may destroy or spare a particular kind of intelligent behavior
2. The existence of exceptional individuals (e.g., musical or mathematical prodigies). They demonstrate extraordinary ability (or deficit) in a particular kind of intelligent behavior
3. An identifiable core operation or set of operations (e.g., detection of relationships among musical tones). It is essential to performance of a particular kind of intelligent behavior

4. A distinctive developmental history leading from novice to master. It is accompanied by disparate levels of expert performance (i.e., varying degrees of expressing this type of intelligence)

5. A distinctive evolutionary history. Increases in intelligence plausibly may be associated with enhanced adaptation to the environment

6. Supportive evidence from cognitive-experimental research. An example would be task-specific performance differences across discrete kinds of intelligence (e.g., visuospatial tasks versus verbal tasks). They would need to be accompanied by cross-task performance similarities within discrete kinds of intelligence (e.g., mental rotation of visuospatial imagery and recall memory of visuospatial images)

7. Supportive evidence from psychometric tests indicating discrete intelligences (e.g., differing performance on tests of visuospatial abilities versus on tests of linguistic abilities)

8. Susceptibility to encoding in a symbol system (e.g., language, math, musical notation) or in a culturally devised arena (e.g., dance, athletics, theater, engineering, or surgery as culturally devised expressions of bodily-kinesthetic intelligence)

Gardner does not dismiss entirely the use of psychometric tests. But the base of evidence used by Gardner does not rely on the factor analysis of various psychometric tests alone. In thinking about your own intelligences, how fully integrated do you believe them to be? How much do you perceive each type of intelligence as depending on any of the others?

Gardner's view of the mind is modular. Modularity theorists believe that different abilities—such as Gardner's intelligences—can be isolated as emanating from distinct portions or modules of the brain. Thus, a major task of existing and future research on intelligence is to isolate the portions of the brain responsible for each of the intelligences. Gardner has speculated as to at least some of these locales. But hard evidence for the existence of these separate intelligences has yet to be produced. Furthermore, some scientists question the strict modularity of Gardner's theory (Nettelbeck & Young, 1996). Consider the phenomenon of preserved specific cognitive functioning in autistic savants. Savants are people with severe social and cognitive deficits but with corresponding high ability in a narrow domain. They suggest that such preservation fails as evidence for modular intelligences. The narrow long-term memory and specific aptitudes of savants may not really be intelligent (Nettelbeck & Young, 1996). Thus, there may be reason to question the intelligence of inflexible modules.

Sternberg: The Triarchic Theory

Whereas Gardner emphasizes the separateness of the various aspects of intelligence, I tend to emphasize the extent to which they work together in my triarchic theory of human intelligence (Sternberg, 1985a, 1988c, 1996b, 1999). According to the **triarchic theory of human intelligence,** intelligence comprises three aspects, dealing with the

FIGURE 13.5

According to Robert Sternberg, intelligence comprises analytical, creative, and practical abilities. In analytical thinking, we try to solve familiar problems by using strategies that manipulate the elements of a problem or the relationships among the elements (e.g., comparing, analyzing); in creative thinking, we try to solve new kinds of problems that require us to think about the problem and its elements in a new way (e.g., inventing, designing); and in practical thinking, we try to solve problems that apply what we know to everyday contexts (e.g., applying, using).

relation of intelligence (1) to the internal world of the person, (2) to experience, and (3) to the external world. Figure 13.5 illustrates the parts of the theory and their interrelations.

How Intelligence Relates to the Internal World

This part of the theory emphasizes the processing of information. Information processing can be viewed in terms of three different kinds of components. First are meta-components—higher order executive processes (i.e., metacognition) used to plan, monitor, and evaluate problem solving. Second are performance components—lower order processes used for implementing the commands of the metacomponents. And third are knowledge-acquisition components—the processes used for learning how to solve the problems in the first place. The components are highly interdependent.

Suppose that you were asked to write a term paper. You would use metacomponents for higher order decisions. Thus, you would use them to decide on a topic, plan the paper, monitor the writing, and evaluate how well your finished product succeeds in accomplishing your goals for it. You would use knowledge-acquisition components for research to learn about the topic. You would use performance components for the actual writing. In practice, the three kinds of components do not function in isolation. Before actually writing the paper, you first would have to decide on a topic. Then you would have to do some research. Similarly, your plans for writing the paper might change as you gather new information. It may turn out that there is not enough information on particular aspects of the chosen topic. This scarcity of information may force you to shift your emphasis. Your plans also may change if particular aspects of the writing go more smoothly than others.

How Intelligence Relates to Experience

The theory also considers how prior experience may interact with all three kinds of information-processing components. That is, each of us faces tasks and situations with which we have varying levels of experience. They range from a completely novel task, with which we have no previous experience, to a completely familiar task, with which we have vast, extensive experience. As a task becomes increasingly familiar, many aspects of the task may become *automatic*. They require little conscious effort for determining what step to take next and how to implement that next step. A novel task makes demands on intelligence different from those of a task for which automatic procedures have been developed.

According to the triarchic theory, relatively novel tasks—such as visiting a foreign country, mastering a new subject, or acquiring a foreign language—demand more of a person's intelligence. A completely unfamiliar task may demand so much of the person as to be overwhelming. Suppose, for example, you were visiting a foreign country. You probably would not profit from enrolling in a course with unfamiliar abstract subject matter taught in a language you do not understand. The most intellectually stimulating tasks are those that are challenging and demanding but not overwhelming.

How Intelligence Relates to the External World

The triarchic theory also proposes that the various components of intelligence are applied to experience to serve three functions in real-world contexts. The first is adapting ourselves to our existing environments. The second is shaping our existing environments to create new environments. And the third is selecting new environments. You use adaptation when you learn the ropes in a new environment and try to figure out how to succeed in it. For example, when you first start college, you probably try to figure out the explicit and implicit rules of college life. You then try to use these rules to succeed in the new environment. You also shape your environment. For example, you may decide what courses to take and what activities to pursue. You even may try to shape the behavior of those around you. Finally, if you are unable either to adapt yourself or to shape your environment to suit you, you might consider selecting another environment. For example, you might transfer to a different college.

According to the triarchic theory, people may apply their intelligence to many different kinds of problems. For example, some people may be more intelligent in the face of abstract, academic problems. Others may be more intelligent in the face of concrete, practical problems. An intelligent person does not necessarily excel in all aspects of intelligence. Rather, intelligent people know their strengths and weaknesses. They find ways in which to capitalize on their strengths and either to compensate for or to correct their weaknesses. For example, a person who is strong in psychology but not in physics might choose as a physics project the creation of a physics aptitude test (which I did when I took physics). The point is to make the most of your strengths and to find ways to improve on or at least to live comfortably with your weaknesses.

We performed a comprehensive study testing the validity of the triarchic theory and its usefulness in improving performance. We predicted that matching students' instruction and assessment to their abilities would lead to improved performance (Sternberg & associates, 1996; Sternberg & associates, 1999). Students were selected for one of five ability patterns: high only in analytical ability, high only in creative ability, high only in practical ability, high in all three abilities, or not high in any of the three abilities. Then students were assigned at random to one of four instructional groups. They emphasized either memory-based, analytical, creative, or practical learning. Then the memory-based, analytical, creative, and practical achievement of all students was assessed. We found that students who were placed in an instructional condition that matched their strength in terms of pattern of ability outperformed students who were mismatched. Thus, the prediction of the experiment was confirmed. For example, a high-analytical student being placed in an instructional condition that emphasized analytical thinking outperformed a high-analytical student being placed in an instructional condition that emphasized practical thinking.

Teaching all students to use all of their analytic, creative, and practical abilities has resulted in improved school achievement for all students, whatever their ability pattern (Grigorenko, Jarvin, & Sternberg, 2002; Sternberg, Torff, & Grigorenko, 1998). One important consideration in light of such findings is the need for changes in the assessment of intelligence (Sternberg & Kaufman, 1996). Current measures of intelligence are somewhat one-sided. They measure mostly analytic abilities. They involve little or no assessment of creative and practical aspects of intelligence (Sternberg & associates, 2000; Wagner, 2000). A more well-rounded assessment and instruction system could lead to greater benefits of education for a wider variety of students—a nominal goal of education.

Thus far, we have described various models of human intelligence. These models do not, in themselves, state whether intelligence can be taught or improved through instruction. A number of investigators have addressed this issue, however. Can intelligence actually be modified with instruction, and if so, how? What strategies are effective, and which ones, less so? Consider the answers.

PRACTICAL APPLICATIONS OF COGNITIVE PSYCHOLOGY	What is your dominant cognitive style? Defining your preferred way of interacting with the environment could help you perform better in school or on the job. The "Thinking about Thinking" section at the end of each of the chapters in this text was designed to appeal to different cognitive styles to more meaningfully integrate the information in each chapter. Which questions were more appealing to you or helped you most? Analytical questions asked you to compare, analyze, or evaluate ideas; creative questions asked you to design or create; and practical questions asked you to apply information to other situations. Try to apply your knowledge in all three ways for the most effective and flexible use.

Improving Intelligence: Effective, Ineffective, and Questionable Strategies

Human intelligence is highly malleable. It can be shaped and even increased through various kinds of interventions (Detterman & Sternberg, 1982; Grotzer & Perkins, 2000; Perkins & Grotzer, 1997; Sternberg & colleagues, 1996; Sternberg & colleagues, 1997). Moreover, the malleability of intelligence has nothing to do with the extent to which intelligence has a genetic basis (Sternberg, 1997). An attribute (such as height) can be partly or even largely genetically based and yet can be environmentally malleable.

The Head Start program was initiated in the 1960s. It was to be a way of providing preschoolers with an edge on intellectual abilities and accomplishments when they started school. Long-term follow-ups have indicated that by mid-adolescence, children who participated in the program were more than a grade ahead of matched controls who did not receive the program (Lazar & Darlington, 1982; Zigler & Berman, 1983). The children in the program also scored higher on a variety of tests of scholastic achievement. They were also less likely to need remedial attention. And they were less likely to show behavioral problems. Although such measures are not truly measures of intelligence, they show strong positive correlations with intelligence tests.

An alternative to intellectual enrichment outside the home may be to provide an enriched home environment. A particularly successful project has been the

---

INVESTIGATING COGNITIVE PSYCHOLOGY

A number of training programs have also shown some success. One such program is Reuven Feuerstein's (1980) Instrumental Enrichment program. It involves training in a variety of abstract-reasoning skills. It appears to be particularly effective for improving the skills of retarded performers. Another program, the Odyssey program (see Adams, 1986), was shown to be effective in raising the intellectual performance of Venezuelan children of junior high school age. The Philosophy for Children program (Lipman, Sharp, & Oscanyan, 1980) was also shown to teach logical thinking skills to children throughout the primary and secondary levels of schooling. Aspects of the Intelligence Applied program (Sternberg, 1986a; Sternberg & Grigorenko, 2002a) for teaching intellectual skills have been shown to be effective. It can improve both insight skills (Davidson & Sternberg, 1984) and the ability to learn meanings of words from context, a primary means for acquiring new vocabulary (Sternberg, 1987a). Practical intelligence also can be taught (Gardner & associates, 1994; Sternberg, Okagaki, & Jackson, 1990).

Abecedarian Project. It showed that the cognitive skills and achievements of lower socioeconomic status children could be increased through carefully planned and executed interventions (Ramey & Ramey, 2000).

Several factors in the early (preschool) home environment appear to be correlated with high IQ scores (Bradley & Caldwell, 1984). They are emotional and verbal responsivity of the primary caregiver and the caregiver's involvement with the child, avoidance of restriction and punishment, organization of the physical environment and activity schedule, provision of appropriate play materials, and opportunities for variety in daily stimulation. Further, Bradley and Caldwell found that these factors more effectively predicted IQ scores than did socioeconomic status or family-structure variables. It should be noted, however, that the Bradley-Caldwell study is correlational. It therefore cannot be interpreted as indicating causality. Furthermore, their study pertained to preschool children. Children's IQ scores do not begin to predict adult IQ scores well until age 4 years. Moreover, before age 7 years, the scores are not very stable (Bloom, 1964). Other work has suggested that factors such as maternal social support and interactive behavior may play a key role in the instability of scores on tests of intellectual ability between ages 2 and 8 years (Pianta & Egeland, 1994).

The Bradley and Caldwell data should not be taken to indicate that demographic variables have little effect on IQ scores. On the contrary, throughout history and across cultures, many groups of people have been assigned pariah status as inferior members of the social order. Across cultures, these disadvantaged groups (e.g., native Maoris versus. European New Zealanders) have shown differences in tests of intelligence and aptitude (Steele, 1990; Zeidner, 1990). Such was the case of the Burakumin tanners in Japan. In 1871, they were granted emancipation but not full acceptance into Japanese society. On the one hand, they show poor performance and underprivileged status in Japan. On the other hand, those who immigrate to America—and are treated like other Japanese immigrants—perform on IQ tests and in school achievement at a level comparable to that of their fellow Japanese Americans (Ogbu, 1986).

Similar positive effects of integration were shown on the other side of the world. In Israel, the children of European Jews score much higher on IQ tests than do children of Arabic Jews. The exception is when the children are reared on kibbutzim. Here, the children of all national ancestries are raised by specially trained caregivers, in a dwelling separate from their parents. When these children shared the same child-rearing environments, there were no national-ancestry–related differences in IQ (Smilansky, 1974).

Altogether, there is now abundant evidence that a variety of factors can affect intellectual skills. One factor is people's environments (Ceci, Nightingale, & Baker, 1992; Reed, 1993; Sternberg & Wagner, 1994). Another is their motivation (Collier, 1994; Sternberg & Ruzgis, 1994). A third is their training (Feuerstein, 1980; Sternberg, 1987c). Thus, the controversial claims made by Herrnstein and Murray (1994) in their book, *The Bell Curve*, regarding the futility of intervention programs, are unfounded. One needs to consider all the evidence in favor of the possibility of improving cognitive skills. Likewise, Herrnstein and Murray's appeal to "a genetic factor in cognitive ethnic differences" (Herrnstein & Murray, 1994, p. 270) seems dicey in light of the direct evidence against such genetic differences (see Sternberg, 1996b). It appears to result in part from a misunderstanding of the heritability of traits in general.

Heredity certainly plays a role in individual differences in intelligence (Loehlin, Horn, & Willerman, 1997; Plomin, 1997), as does the environment (Sternberg & Grigorenko, 1999; Wahlsten & Gottlieb, 1997). Genetic inheritance may set some kind of upper limit on how intelligent a person may become. However, we now know that for any attribute that is partly genetic, there is a *reaction range*. This is the range of broad limits of possibilities in which an attribute can be expressed in various ways. Thus, each person's intelligence can be developed further within this broad range of potential intelligence (Grigorenko, 2000). We have no reason to believe that people now reach their upper limits in the development of their intellectual skills. To the contrary, the evidence suggests that we can do quite a bit to help people become more intelligent (for further discussion of these issues, see Mayer, 2000a; Sternberg, 1995; see also Neisser & associates, 1996).

Ultimately, we can help people to become more intelligent. To do so, we help them to better perceive, learn, remember, represent information, reason, decide, and solve problems. In other words, what we do is help them improve the cognitive functions that have been the focus of this book. The connection between improving intelligence and improving cognition is not a casual one. On the contrary, human cognition forms the core of human intelligence. Thus intelligence is a construct that helps us unify all the diverse aspects of cognition. Cultural and other contextual factors may influence the expression of our intelligence. For example, behavior that is considered intelligent in one culture may be considered unintelligent in another culture. But the cognitive processes underlying behavior are largely the same. In every culture people need to learn, to reason, to solve problems, and so on. Thus, when we study cognitive psychology, we are learning about the fundamental core of human intelligence that helps people the world over adapt to their environmental circumstances. And these processes apply, no matter how different those circumstances may be. No wonder, then, that the study of cognition is so fundamental to psychology in particular and to the understanding of human behavior in general.

Development of Intelligence in Adults

Intelligence, of course, develops with age (Anderson, 2005). Do scores on cognitive-ability tests continue to increase indefinitely? The available data suggest that they may not (Berg, 2000). Although crystallized intelligence is higher, on average, for older adults than for younger adults, fluid intelligence is higher, on average, for younger adults than for older ones (Horn & Cattell, 1966). At the college level, then, both fluid and crystallized abilities are increasing. Later in life, however, the picture often changes.

For example, the performance of older adults on many information-processing tasks appears to be slower, particularly on complex tasks (Bashore, Osman, & Hefley, 1989; Cerella, 1990, 1991; Poon, 1987; Schaie, 1989). In general, crystallized cognitive abilities seem to increase throughout the life span, whereas fluid cognitive abilities seem to increase up until the 20s or 30s or possibly 40s and slowly decrease thereafter. The preservation of crystallized abilities suggests that long-term memory and the structure and organization of knowledge representation are preserved across the life span (Salthouse, 1992, 1996, 2005). Moreover, many adults find ways of compensating for later deficits in skills so that their actual performance is unaffected. For example, older typists may type less quickly but look further ahead in their typing to compensate for the loss of processing speed (Salthouse, 1996). Or if they are forgetful, they may write notes to themselves more often than they did when they were younger.

Although psychometric researchers disagree about the age when fluid intelligence starts to decline, many researchers agree that eventually some decline does indeed occur, on average. The rate and extent of decline varies widely across people. Some cognitive abilities also seem to decline under some circumstances but not others, on average. For example, effectiveness of performance on some problem-solving tasks appears to show age-related decline (Denny, 1980), although even brief training appears to improve scores on problem-solving tasks for older adults (Rosenzweig & Bennett, 1996; Willis, 1985).

Not all cognitive abilities decline, however. For example, one book (Cerella & associates, 1993) devotes twenty chapters to describing studies showing little or no intellectual decline in various areas of cognition, including object and word perception, language comprehension, and problem solving. Some researchers (e.g., Schaie & Willis, 1986) have found that some kinds of learning abilities seem to increase, and others (Graf, 1990; Labouvie-Vief & Schell, 1982; Perlmutter, 1983b) have found that the ability to learn and remember meaningful skills and information shows little decline. Also, even in a single domain, such as memory, decreases in one kind of performance may not imply decreases in another. For example, although short-term memory performance seems to decline (Hultsch & Dixon, 1990; West, 1986), long-term memory (Bahrick, Bahrick, & Wittlinger, 1975) and recognition memory (Schonfield & Robertson, 1966) remain quite good.

Some researchers (e.g., Schaie, 1974, 1996) even question much of the evidence for intellectual decline. For one thing, our views of memory and aging may be confounded by reports of pathological changes that occur in some older adults. Such changes do not result from general intellectual decline but from specific neurophysiological disorders. These neurophysiological disorders, such as Alzheimer's disease, are fairly uncommon even among the most elderly. Preventive screening tools for Alzheimer's disease, which capitalize on differences in typical aging adult abilities, currently are being investigated with mixed success (Mirmiran, von Someren, & Swaab, 1996). Cognitive abilities seem to decline most in the last 10 years before death.

Another qualification on findings of decline in older age is the use of cross-sectional research designs, which involve testing different cohorts (generations) of individuals at the same time. Such designs tend to overestimate the extent of decline of cognitive abilities. For unknown reasons more recent generations of individuals show higher cognitive abilities—at least as measured by IQ (Flynn, 1984, 1987)—than do earlier generations. Consequently, the lower IQs of the older individuals may be a generational effect rather than an aging effect. Indeed, longitudinal research designs, which test the same individuals repeatedly over an extended period, suggest less decline in mental abilities with age. These studies, however, may underestimate the extent of decline resulting from selective dropout. The less able participants drop out of the study over the years, perhaps because they find the taking of the cognitive tests to be discouraging or even humiliating.

Although the debate about intellectual decline with age continues, positions have converged somewhat. For instance, there is a consensus (Cerella, 1990, 1991; Kliegl, Mayr, & Krampe, 1994; Salthouse, 1994, 1996) that some slowing of the rate of cognitive processing occurs across the span of adulthood, and the evidence of slowing remains even when the experimental methodology and analyses rule out the disproportionate representation of demented adults among the elderly (Salthouse, Kausler, & Saults, 1990). Among the general factors that have been suggested as contributing to age-related slowing of cognitive processing have been a generalized decline in central nervous system functioning (Cerella, 1991), a decline in working-memory capacity (Salthouse, 1993), and a decline in attentional resources (see Horn & Hofer, 1992).

Slowed processing might lead to cognitive deficits through two speed-related issues in cognitive functioning—limited time and simultaneity (Salthouse, 1996). Slowed processing may prevent certain operations from being computed. Such operations may need to occur within a limited amount of time. The operations may need to overlap because of storage limitations. For example, auditory memory exhibits rapid decay, leading to the necessity for rapid classification of auditory signals. Slowing of upper-level processing can result in incomplete or inaccurate processing of auditory signals. Given the semi-parallel nature of much of cognitive processing along with the nature of synaptic transmission, that speed would be an issue is not surprising—such processing is very time dependent.

In addition to these general factors, many cognitive-developmental psychologists have suggested that specific factors also affect age-related changes in cognitive processing. The specific factors differentially may affect various cognitive tasks. For example, specific factors include greater slowing of higher-order cognitive processes than of sensory-motor processes (Cerella, 1985). They also include differential slowing of high- versus low-complexity tasks (Kliegl, Mayr, & Krampe, 1994). A further cognitive factor is greater slowing for tasks requiring coordinative complexity (requiring simultaneous processing of multiple stimuli) than for sequential complexity (requiring sequential processing of multiple stimuli; Mayr & Kliegl, 1993). A final factor is greater age-related decline in processes of information retrieval than in processes of encoding (see Salthouse, 1992). In addition, priming effects and tasks requiring implicit memory seem to show little or no evidence of decline. But tasks involving explicit memory do show age-related decline (see Salthouse, 1992).

Based on existing research, three basic principles of cognitive development in adulthood have been suggested (Dixon & Baltes, 1986). First, fluid abilities and other aspects of information processing may decline in late adulthood. But this decline is balanced by stabilization and even advancement of well-practiced and pragmatic aspects of mental functioning (crystallized abilities). Second, despite the age-related decline in information processing, sufficient reserve capacity allows at least temporary increases in performance, especially if the older adult is motivated to perform well. Third, when adults lose some of the speed and physiology-related efficiency of information processing, they often compensate, in a given task, with other knowledge and expertise-based information-processing skills (Salthouse, 1991, 1996; see also Salthouse & Somberg, 1982). In other words, older adults develop practical strategies to retain relatively high levels of functioning (Berg & associates, 1998; Berg, Meegan, & Deviney, 1998; Sternberg, Grigorenko, & Oh, 2001). They also can draw on practical knowledge that younger people may not have (Berg, 2000; Colonia-Willner, 1998; Torff & Sternberg, 2001).

Although the evidence regarding age-related differences in the selection of cognitive strategies is mixed, there appear to be no age-related differences in self-monitoring of cognitive processes (see Salthouse, 1992). So it would appear that older adults may be able effectively to utilize information regarding how to enhance their cognitive performance. Also, when task performance is based more on accuracy than on speed, older adults may at least partly compensate for speed deficits with increased carefulness and persistence (see Horn & Hofer, 1992). Further, at all times throughout the life span, there is considerable *plasticity*—modifiability—of abilities (Baltes, 1997; Baltes & Willis, 1979; Mirmiran & associates, 1996; Rosenzweig & Bennett, 1996). None of us is stuck at a particular level of performance. Each of us can improve.

In recent years, some psychologists have become particularly interested in the development of wisdom in adulthood (see Sternberg, 1990). Most theorists have argued that wisdom increases with age, although there are exceptions (Meacham, 1990).

Psychologists' definitions of wisdom have been diverse. Some (Baltes & associates, 1995; Baltes & Smith, 1990) define *wisdom* as exceptional insight into human development and life matters, including exceptionally good judgment and advice and commentary about difficult life problems. Furthermore, wisdom can be seen as reflecting a positive gain in culture-based cognitive pragmatics (meaningful uses of cognitive skills) in the face of the more physiologically controlled losses in cognitive mechanics (Baltes, 1993). Other research has found six factors in people's conceptions of wisdom. They are reasoning ability, sagacity (shrewdness), learning from ideas and from the environment, judgment, expeditious use of information, and perspicacity (intensely keen awareness, perception, and insight) (Sternberg, 1985b). In wisdom, to know what you do not know is also important (Meacham, 1983, 1990). Whatever the definition (Moshman, 1998), the study of wisdom represents an exciting new direction for discovering what abilities may be developed during later adulthood at the same time that fluid abilities or the mechanical aspects of information processing may be flagging.

Adults are sometimes called on to do tasks that challenge their intelligence in ways that are quite specific. For example, pilots use their intelligence to make decisions that, for their passengers as well as themselves, can be matters of life and death. Psychology can be used to help design cockpits that optimize the conditions for their making these decisions. Research shows that cockpits in which there is a high degree of similarity of colors of various elements, or in which background elements are moving, interfere with pilots' ability to read instrumentation (Nikolic, Orr, & Sarter, 2004). The branch of psychology that helps in the intelligent design of instruments, such as cockpit instruments, is called "human-factors" psychology. The errors pilots make can be of various kinds. For example, they may make a slip, which they intend to do one thing but do another; or they may show a lapse, in which case they fail to attend to a signal that needs attention (Sarter & Alexander, 2000). Human-factors psychologists study not just the instrumentation but also the ways workers react to it. Their goal is to optimize the human-machine interaction as a whole.

Artificial Intelligence: Computer Simulations

Can a Computer Program Be "Intelligent"?

Much of the early information-processing research centered on work based on computer simulations of human intelligence as well as computer systems that use optimal methods to solve tasks. Programs of both kinds can be classified as examples of **artificial intelligence (AI),** or intelligence in symbol-processing systems such as computers (see Schank & Towle, 2000). Computers cannot actually think. They must be programmed to behave as though they are thinking. That is, they must be programmed to simulate cognitive processes. In this way, they give us insight into the details of how people process information cognitively. Essentially, computers are just pieces of hardware—physical components of equipment—that respond to instructions. Other kinds of hardware (other pieces of equipment) also respond to instructions. For example, if you can figure out how to give the instructions, a VCR (videocassette recorder) will respond to your instructions and will do what you tell it to do.

What makes computers so interesting to researchers is that they can be given highly complex instructions, known as computer programs or even more commonly as software. Programs tell the computer how to respond to new information.

Before we consider any intelligent programs, we need to consider seriously the issue of what, if anything, would lead us to describe a computer program as being "intelligent."

The Turing Test

Probably the first serious attempt to deal with the issue of whether a computer program can be intelligent was made by Alan Turing (1963), based on ideas Turing first presented in 1950. Specifically, Turing devised a test by which a human could assess the intelligence of a respondent (see Chapter 1). The basic idea behind the Turing Test is whether an observer can distinguish the performance of a computer from that of a human. For the test to work, everyone must agree that the human is intelligent in at least some degree. In the specific form proposed by Turing, the test is conducted with a computer, a human respondent, and an interrogator. The interrogator has two different "conversations" with an interactive computer program. The goal of the interrogator is to figure out which of two parties is a person communicating through the computer and which is the computer itself. The interrogator can ask the two parties any questions at all. However, the computer will try to fool the interrogator into believing that it is human. The human, in contrast, will be trying to show the interrogator that he or she truly is human. The computer passes the Turing Test if an interrogator is unable to distinguish the computer from the human.

The test of indistinguishability of computer from human commonly is used in assessing the intelligence of a computer program. The test is not usually performed in quite the way described by Turing. For example, outputs of some kind generated by a computer might be scanned and assessed for their comparability to human performance. In some cases, human data from a problem-solving task are compared with computer-generated data. The degree of relation between them is then evaluated. For example, suppose a computer solves number-series problems such as 1, 4, 9, 16, . . . (where each number is the next larger perfect square). The response times and error patterns of the computer can be compared to those of human participants who have solved the same problems (Kotovsky & Simon, 1973; Simon & Kotovsky, 1963). Of course, the response times of the computer are typically much faster than those of humans. But the researchers are less interested in overall reaction times than in patterns of reaction times. In other words, what matters is not whether computers take more or less time on each problem than do humans. Rather, it is whether the problems that take the computer relatively longer to solve also take human participants relatively longer.

Sometimes, the goal of a computer model is not to match human performance but to exceed it. In this case, maximum AI, rather than simulation of human intelligence, is the goal of the program. The criterion of whether computer performance matches that of humans is no longer relevant. Instead, the criterion of interest is that of how well the computer can perform the task assigned to it. Computer programs that play chess, for example, typically play in a way that emphasizes "brute force." The programs evaluate extremely large numbers of possible moves. Many of them are moves humans would never even consider evaluating (Berliner, 1969; Bernstein,

1958). Using brute force, the IBM program "Deep Blue" beat world champion Gary Kasparov in a 1997 chess match. The same brute-force method is used in programs that play checkers (Samuel, 1963). These programs generally are evaluated in terms of how well they can beat each other or even more important, human contenders playing against them.

Having considered some issues of what constitutes an intelligent computer program, we now turn to some of the actual programs. The discussion of these programs will give you an idea of how AI research has evolved. It will also show you how AI models have influenced the work of cognitive psychologists. As the preceding examples have shown, many early AI programs focused on problem solving.

Early Programs

One of the very earliest intelligent programs was the Logic Theorist (LT) (Newell, Shaw, & Simon, 1957b). It was designed to discover proofs for theorems in elementary symbolic logic.

A successor to the LT was called the General Problem Solver (GPS) (Newell, Shaw, & Simon, 1957a). This program used a method of solving problems called *means–ends analysis*. It involves solving problems by successively reducing the difference between the present status (where you are now) and the goal status (where you want to be; see Chapter 11). Figure 13.6 shows a schematic **flow chart**—a model path for reaching a goal or solving a problem. The flow chart shows how GPS can transform one object (or one problem state) into another using means–ends analysis.

Means–ends analysis can be applied to a wide range of problems. An example would be the "MOVE" problems described in Chapter 11, in which hobbits and orcs needed to cross a river using just one two-person boat. GPS, as it was formulated back in the 1950s and 1960s, could apply the heuristic to problems such as proving logic theorems or to some of the other problems described in Chapter 11. The GPS program and the LT program were typical of the early work carried out at Carnegie-Mellon University. But the Newell-Simon group at Carnegie was not the only group

---

FIGURE 13.6

In developing GPS, Allen Newell, Clifford Shaw, and Herbert Simon suggested a flow chart for implementing a means-ends analysis to reach a goal.

busy trying to create intelligent programs. At MIT, a group led primarily by Marvin Minsky also was interested in creating AI programs. The MIT programs differed from the Carnegie programs in their greater emphasis on the retrieval of semantic information—that is, the use of meaningful verbal information (Minsky, 1968). For example, by the early 1970s, MIT Researcher Terry Winograd (1972) had developed SHRDLU. This program commanded a robot arm manually to manipulate various blocks in a "block world." Figure 13.7 shows examples of the kinds of elements that inhabit the block world of SHRDLU.

Whereas SHRDLU processes information in terms of a block world, other programs operate in very different worlds. One of the more interesting is that of the psychotherapist, on the one hand, and the patient, on the other.

Two programs that operate in the world of psychotherapy are ELIZA and PARRY. The former takes on the role of a nondirective psychotherapist. The latter takes on the role of a paranoid patient of a psychotherapist. The goal of the nondirective therapist is to elicit a patient's feelings. The therapist then reflects these feelings back to the patient and helps the patient understand and figure out what to do about these feelings. Consider, for example, a segment of an interaction between ELIZA and a patient working with ELIZA, as shown in Table 13.4. In this segment, ELIZA seems to show clinical

FIGURE 13.7

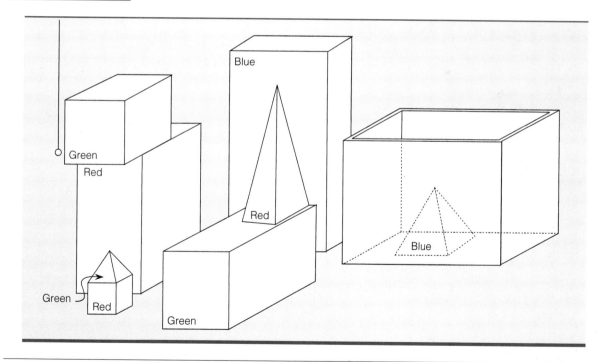

Terry Winograd's robot was programmed to operate within a three-dimensional block world containing elements such as the blocks shown here. From Understanding Natural Languages by Terry Winograd. Copyright © 1972 by Terry Winograd. Reprinted by permission of Elsevier.

TABLE 13.4   Programs That Simulate Belief Systems: ELIZA and PARRY

Joseph Weizenbaum's ELIZA was developed to simulate a nondirective psychotherapist, and Kenneth Colby's PARRY was developed to simulate a paranoid patient. What might happen if PARRY were to seek psychotherapeutic guidance from ELIZA? (Adapted from Weizenbaum, 1966, and from Colby, 1963)

ELIZA*	PARRY†
Men are all alike.	Why are you in the hospital?
IN WHAT WAY?	I SHOULDN'T BE HERE.
They're always bugging us about something or other.	Who brought you here?
CAN YOU THINK OF A SPECIFIC EXAMPLE?	THE POLICE.
Well, my boyfriend made me come here.	What trouble did you have with the police?
YOUR BOYFRIEND MADE YOU COME HERE.	COPS DON'T DO THEIR JOB.
He says I'm depressed much of the time.	What do they do instead?
I AM SORRY TO HEAR THAT YOU ARE DEPRESSED.	COPS ARREST THE WRONG PEOPLE.
It's true. I am unhappy.	They arrest the right ones sometimes.
DO YOU THINK COMING HERE WILL HELP YOU NOT TO BE UNHAPPY?	THE LAW SHOULD GET THOSE ITALIAN CROOKS.
I need some help, that much seems certain.	Are you Italian?
WHAT WOULD IT MEAN TO YOU IF YOU GOT SOME HELP?	MY BACKGROUND IS BRITISH BUT I WAS BORN IN THIS COUNTRY.
Perhaps I could learn to get along with my mother.	Do you know any Italian crooks?
TELL ME MORE ABOUT YOUR FAMILY.	I TRY TO AVOID THE UNDERWORLD.
My mother takes care of me.	Are you afraid of the underworld?
WHO ELSE IN YOUR FAMILY TAKES CARE OF YOU?	THE MAFIA ARE THE WORST GANGSTERS.
My father.	Are you connected with the Mafia?
YOUR FATHER?	YOU KNOW, THEY KNOW ME.
You are like my father in some ways.	How do they know you?
WHAT RESEMBLANCE DO YOU SEE?	THEY SPY ON ME.
You are not very aggressive, but I think you don't want me to notice that.	Why do they?
WHAT MAKES YOU THINK I AM NOT VERY AGGRESSIVE?	THEY WANT TO GET FALSE EVIDENCE TO FRAME ME.
You don't argue with me.	What do they have against you?
WHY DO YOU THINK I DON'T ARGUE WITH YOU?	THEY ARE OUT TO GET ME.
You are afraid of me.	What for?
DOES IT PLEASE YOU TO THINK THAT I AM AFRAID OF YOU?	I HAVE INCRIMINATING EVIDENCE AGAINST THE MAFIA.
My father is afraid of everybody.	Are you sure of all this?
WHAT ELSE COMES TO MIND WHEN YOU THINK OF YOUR FATHER?	YOU DON'T BELIEVE ME?
Bullies.	I am doing my best.
DOES THAT HAVE ANYTHING TO DO WITH THE FACT THAT YOUR BOYFRIEND MADE YOU COME HERE?	(SILENCE ON THE "PATIENT'S" PART)
	(Silence on the psychiatrist's part)
	CAN'T YOU THINK OF A DECENT QUESTION TO ASK?
	You seem hostile to me.
	SOME OF YOUR REMARKS ANNOY ME.
	I am sorry.
	FORGET THE EXCUSES, YOU GUYS ARE ALL ALIKE.

*J. Weizenbaum (1966) "Eliza—A Computer Program for the Study of Natural Language Communication Between Man & Machine," Communications of the Association for Computing Machinery, Vol. 9, p. 36–45. © 1966 Association of Computing Machinery. Reprinted by permission.
†"Computer Simulation of a Neurotic Process," by Perry Colby. In Tomkins/Messick, Computer Simulation and Personality. Copyright © 1963 by John Wiley & Sons, Inc.

insight about her patient. However, ELIZA is not as bright as she appears here. She uses key words and phrases in the interlocutor's (patient's) remarks to choose her own remarks. She does not understand in any larger sense what the patient is saying. Indeed, the creator of ELIZA chose the domain of nondirective psychotherapy because he believed simulating the responses of a nondirective psychotherapist would be relatively easy (Weizenbaum, 1966). He avoided simulating people in other occupations who more directively show their knowledge and expertise in their interactions with others.

If therapists can be simulated, why not patients? Kenneth Colby (1963), a trained psychiatrist, created a simulation of a paranoid patient who is especially concerned that the Mafia is after him. The workings of the program are shown in the segment of dialogue reproduced in Table 13.4. Colby's simulation of a paranoid is not just a set of responses that "sounds paranoid." Rather, the simulation is generated from a theory of the neurotic process of a paranoid. The primary intention of the paranoid is to determine another person's intentions. Messages from the other are scanned to assist in this determination. Messages are classified as malevolent, benevolent, or neutral. The paranoid person is particularly susceptible to an interpretation of malevolence. This interpretation can emanate from a belief that the other intends either physical or psychological harm to the person who is paranoid.

Colby performed a somewhat more formal evaluation of his program than is typical. He asked a group of thirty-three psychiatrists to read transcripts of "interviews" with PARRY and with actual paranoid patients. None of the psychiatrists were told that a computer model was involved. Roughly half of them rated the model as more paranoid than actual patients.

Colby's program differs fundamentally from many others. It simulates not just abstract cognitive processes but also a belief system. Another program by Colby uses cognitive therapy for the treatment of mild depression. It involves both a text and dialogue mode of interaction with a person (Colby, 1995).

Programs That Simulate Expertise

Unlike the East Coast research at Yale, MIT, and Carnegie-Mellon, AI research on the West Coast, especially at Stanford, tended to emphasize **expert systems:** computer programs that can perform the way an expert does in a fairly specific domain. No attempt was made to more globally model human intelligence or even to extend the particular expert systems, even in theory. Rather, the researchers attempted to simulate performance in just one domain, often a narrow one. They sought a level of expertise that surpasses what would be possible for a program that was fairly domain general.

For example, several programs were developed to diagnose various kinds of medical disorders. Such programs are obviously of enormous potential significance, given the very high costs (financial and personal) of incorrect diagnoses. Probably the most well-known and certainly the oldest of these programs is MYCIN (Buchanan & Shortliffe, 1984; Shortliffe, 1976). MYCIN can be used for detecting and potentially even treating certain bacterial infections. Table 13.5 shows a fragment of a system of statements used by MYCIN, translated to be readable by humans. Note that the program gives an indication of its certainty (0.6) regarding the identification of the offending microorganism as being bacteroides. The 0.6 is not, strictly speaking, a probability. But it is on a scale where 0 indicates total lack of certainty regarding truth and 1 indicates total certainty. MYCIN contains roughly 500 rules (if-then statements). It can deal with about 100 different kinds of bacterial infections.

TABLE 13.5	A Program That Simulates Expertise: MYCIN
At Stanford, the development of expert systems, such as the one excerpted here, has been a focus of AI research.	

If:	(1) The gram stain of the organism is gramneg [i.e., not a particular type of microorganism],
	(2) The morphology of the organism is rod, and
	(3) The aerobicity of the organism is anaerobic
Then:	There is suggestive evidence (.6) that the identity of the organism is bacteroides.

From Computer Based Medical Consultations by E. H. Shortliffe. Copyright © 1974 by Elsevier Science Publishing.

MYCIN has been tested for its validity in making diagnoses and treatment suggestions. MYCIN's performance compared favorably with that of faculty members in the Stanford School of Medicine. MYCIN outperformed medical students and residents in the same school (Yu & associates, 1984). Earlier, it had been shown to be quite effective in prescribing medication for meningitis. Thus, within its relatively narrow domain of expertise, MYCIN is clearly an impressive expert system.

Other expert systems also have been created for medical diagnosis. For example, INTERNIST (Miller, Pople, & Myers, 1982) diagnoses a broader spectrum of diseases than does MYCIN. Within its broader domain, its diagnostic powers do not measure up to those of an experienced internist. This program illustrates what sometimes is termed the *bandwidth-fidelity problem*. The broader the bandwidth of a radio or other receiver, the poorer its fidelity (faithfulness, reliability) tends to be. Similarly, the wider the spectrum of problems to which an AI program addresses itself, the less reliable it is likely to be in solving any one of those kinds of problems.

Other expert systems solve other types of problems, including some of the problems found by scientists. For example, DENDRAL, another early expert system developed at Stanford, helps scientists identify the molecular structure of newly discovered organic compounds (Buchanan & associates, 1976).

Questions about the Intelligence of Intelligent Programs

Artificially intelligent programs such as the ones described here are not without their critics, of course. Consider some of the main objections that have been raised in regard to some of the aforementioned programs. Experts differ as to how much credence they give to these various objections. Ultimately, each of us needs to evaluate the objections for ourselves.

Serial Processing

Some of the objections to AI pertain to the limitations of the existing hardware and software designs. For one thing, human brains can process many sources of information simultaneously. However, because of the architectural structure of computer hardware, most computers (virtually all early computers, and even most contemporary ones) can handle only one instruction at a time. Hence, models based on computer simulations have tended to depend on serial processing (step-by-step, one-at-a-time) of information. However, with various computers linked into neural networks of computers, computers now may simulate parallel processing (multiple steps being performed simultaneously). Hence, the serial-processing limitation no longer applies to all computer-based models of AI.

Absence of Intuition

Another of the limitations of AI relates to a different characteristic of human intelligence: intuition. Some have argued that whereas computers can be good and competent manipulators of symbols according to prepackaged algorithms, they lack intuition (Dreyfus & Dreyfus, 1990). To these investigators, intuition is found in the kinds of hunches that distinguish genuine experts from those with book knowledge. Intuition does not necessarily involve the expertise that will enable people to exploit their knowledge maximally when confronted with a difficult situation. Basically, the Dreyfuses are arguing that computers excel in the mathematical and deductive aspect of thinking but not in the intuitive one.

For example, some years ago, a United Airlines DC-10 airliner crash-landed. All three of its hydraulic systems were severed by debris from an engine that was torn off in midair. They hit the tail of the plane, where the three hydraulic systems were interlinked. The pilot of the DC-10 radioed to technical headquarters for guidance as to what to do when all three hydraulic systems go down. The technical experts were unable to help the crew. They had never encountered the situation before and had no guidelines to follow. The crew, nevertheless, working on intuition, managed to steer the plane roughly by varying engine thrust. The news media and others applauded the pilot and his crew for their intuitions as to what to do in the face of a very thorny problem. In this instance, there were no guidelines, and no computer program had been written to solve the problem. As a result of these intuitions, roughly two thirds of the passengers in the plane survived a crash landing in Sioux City, Iowa.

The argument that computers cannot show intuitive intelligence does not go unchallenged. Several researchers interested in human problem solving (see Chapter 11) have studied computer simulations of problem solving. Their research has led them to infer that at least some characteristics of intuition can be modeled on computers. For example, one set of programs (the "Bacon" programs) simulates the processes involved in various important scientific discoveries in the past (Langley & associates, 1987). The investigators behind the programs argued that their programs do display intuition. Moreover, they argued that there is nothing mystical about intuition. Rather, according to these researchers, intuition can be understood in terms of the same information-processing mechanisms that are applied to conventional forms of problem solving.

Along a similar line, other investigators simulated large parts of a theory of how we reason inductively (Holland & associates, 1986). Their programs were inductive ones, going beyond the information given in a problem to come up with a solution that is not deductively determined by the problem elements. One can easily argue that such programs are intuitive, at least in some sense. They go beyond the information given. Other programs also make inferences that go well beyond the simple facts stored in their databases.

Intelligence versus the Appearance of Intelligence

A philosopher has raised an objection to the basic idea that computers can be considered truly intelligent (Searle, 1980). To make his objection, he uses what is known as the "Chinese Room" problem. Imagine that Searle, the philosopher, is locked in a room. He is given a large batch of Chinese writing to translate. He knows no Chinese at all. However, suppose that, in addition to the Chinese writing, Searle is given a second batch of Chinese script. He also receives a set of rules for translating the Chinese into English. Next, Searle is given a third batch. It gives him a set of rules for formulating responses to questions that were raised in the first batch of Chinese writing. Searle then responds to the original batch of writing with a response that makes sense and is in perfect Chinese. Presumably, over time, Searle could become extremely good at manipulating the rules. His responses would be every bit as good as those of a native Chinese speaker who understood exactly what was being asked. However, in fact, Searle still knows no Chinese at all. He is simply following a set of rules.

According to Searle, programs that seem to understand various kinds of inputs and to respond in a seemingly intelligent way (such as Winograd's SHRDLU) are like Searle in the Chinese room. The computers understand the input being given to them no better than Searle understands Chinese. They are simply operating according to a set of preprogrammed rules. Searle's notion is that the computer does not really see and understand the connections between input and output. Rather, it uses pre-established connections that make it seem intelligent on the surface. To Searle, these programs do not demonstrate AI. They only appear to show intelligence.

Predictably, AI researchers have not competed with each other to be the first to accept Searle's argument. They generally have not been eager to acknowledge any folly in their attempts to model AI. A number of researchers have offered responses to Searle's charge that the computer is not anything like what it is cracked up to be. One scientist, for example, argued that Searle's use of the rule systems in the second and third batches of input is, in fact, intelligent (Abelson, 1980). He further argued that children learning a language also at first apply rules rather blindly. Only later do they come to understand the rules and how they are being used. Others argue that the system as a whole (comprising Searle as well as the set of instructions) does indeed exhibit understanding. In addition, some computer programs even have shown an ability to simulate at least a modest degree of skill development and knowledge acquisition. Nevertheless, existing computer programs do not begin to approach our human ability to enhance our own intelligence.

Common Themes

This chapter addresses several of the themes described in Chapter 1.

First and most prominent, perhaps, is the nature-nurture theme. This theme has played a major part in intelligence research since the nineteenth century. Investigators are in general agreement that nature plays a role. Intelligence is partially heritable. The estimates of heritability actually increase with age. The older you are, the more nature plays a role and the less nurture plays a role. This may be because of differential effects of early rearing environments that start to wear off. But the kind of environment an individual has affects the extent to which people can utilize and make the most of their genetic potential. Moreover, research shows that environment can affect biology. The brain changes as a result of learning experiences.

A second theme is validity of causal inference versus ecological validity. Some studies of intelligence have been done in the laboratory. Others, especially studies of practical intelligence and cultural studies of intelligence, have more often been done in the field. For example, studies of practical intelligence in rural Kenya simply cannot be done in a highly controlled setting. Both kinds of studies enhance our knowledge of intelligence. They complement each other.

A third theme is basic versus applied research. In the twentieth century, much of the early research done on intelligence was applied. It was designed to create, standardize, and validate intelligence tests. But later in the twentieth century, researchers started to realize that they had very little idea of the cognitive processes that contribute to performance on the tests. So more basic research ensued in which investigators tried to understand these cognitive processes. The research suggested that the tests gave useful information. But other kinds of tests also emerged as useful for understanding human intelligence and individual differences in it.

Robert L. Williams developed a test he called the BITCH Test (Black Intelligence Test of Cultural Homogeneity). Many "standard" intelligence tests rely heavily on vocabulary (e.g., The Shipley Test, a major section on the Wechsler intelligence tests). Williams scored very poorly on an intelligence test when he was in high school, so he was advised not to go to college but to develop trade skills. Because Williams knew he had "street smarts," he ignored this advice, went to college, and eventually earned his Ph.D. To demonstrate that knowledge of vocabulary does not capture all of what goes into intelligence, Williams' BITCH test asked people to define various "Black" terms of the time, such as "alley apple," "deuce-and-a-quarter," and "Mother's Day." Not surprisingly, most Blacks did better on this test than their White counterparts. The items on the test were culturally relevant to most Blacks at the time (many of the terms are outdated now), and they were culturally irrelevant to most Whites.

PRACTICAL APPLICATIONS OF COGNITIVE PSYCHOLOGY

Summary

1. **What are the key issues in intelligence research? How do different researchers and theorists respond to those issues?** An early issue in the study of intelligence centered on how to measure intelligence. Francis Galton and his followers emphasized psychophysical acuity. Binet and his followers emphasized judgment. Two common themes that run through the definitions of intelligence proposed by many experts are the capacity to learn from experience and the ability to adapt to the environment. In addition, the importance of metacognition and of cultural context increasingly are recognized by researchers and theorists of intelligence. Nonetheless, psychologists often disagree regarding the relative importance of context (nurture) versus inheritance (nature) in determining intelligence. Also, different researchers disagree regarding whether to focus on studying the structures of intelligence (e.g., Spearman, Thurstone, Cattell) or the processes of intelligence (e.g., Hunt,

Jensen, Simon). Some researchers (e.g., Gardner, Sternberg) also have focused on trying to integrate the various approaches to intelligence into comprehensive systems models of intelligence. One approach to intelligence is to understand it in terms of factor analysis. This is a statistical technique that seeks to identify latent sources of individual differences in performance on tests. There are several principal factor-analytic models of the mind. One is the g-factor model of Spearman. Another is the primary-mental-abilities model of Thurstone. A third is the structure-of-intellect (SOI) model of Guilford. And a fourth comprises the hierarchical models of Cattell, of Vernon, and of Carroll, among others.

2. **What are some information-processing approaches to intelligence?** An alternative approach to intelligence is to understand it in terms of information processing. Information-processing theorists have sought to understand intelligence in terms of a number of constructs and tasks. They include inspection time, choice reaction time, speed of lexical access, the ability to divide attention successfully, the components of reasoning and problem solving, and complex problem solving that can be simulated via computers. A related approach is the biological model. It uses increasingly sophisticated means of viewing the brain while the brain is engaged in intelligent behaviors. Preliminary findings suggest that speed of neural conduction may play a role in intelligence. Particularly intriguing are findings suggesting that neural efficiency and specialization of cerebral function may be influential in intelligent cognitive processing.

3. **What are some alternative views of intelligence?** Another main approach to understanding intelligence (based on an anthropological model) is a contextual approach. According to this approach, intelligence is viewed as wholly or partly determined by cultural values. Contextual theorists differ in the extent to which they believe that the meaning of intelligence differs from one culture to another. What is considered to be intelligent behavior is, to some extent, culturally rela-

tive. The same behavior that is considered to be intelligent in one culture may be considered unintelligent in another culture. To create a test of intelligence that is culture-fair—that is, equally fair for members of different cultures—is difficult, and perhaps impossible. Members of different cultures have different conceptions of what constitutes intelligent behavior.

Systems models of intelligence seek to go beyond cultural content. Gardner's theory of multiple intelligences specifies that intelligence is not a unitary construct. Rather, there are multiple intelligences, each relatively independent of the others. Sternberg's triarchic theory of human intelligence conceives of intelligence in terms of information-processing components. They are applied to experience to serve the functions of adaptation to the environment, shaping of the environment, and selection of new environments

4. **Can intelligence be improved, and if so, how?** Intellectual skills can be taught. Thus, intelligence is malleable rather than fixed. Researchers largely agree that some improvements are possible. They disagree regarding both the degree to which they believe that such improvements can be achieved and the means by which to do so.

5. **How does intelligence continue to develop in adults?** Intelligence continues to change in adulthood. Crystallized abilities appear to increase fairly steadily. Fluid abilities sometimes decline, especially within the last ten years before death. A number of researchers have investigated wisdom, which can be seen as an extension of intelligence. Wisdom involves knowledge of the pragmatics of life. Wise people, according to some theorists, seek a common good.

6. **How have researchers attempted to simulate intelligence using machines such as computers?** AI research is conducted on the premise that having machines simulate intelligence is both possible and valuable. The Turing Test is designed to evaluate the extent to which particular AI programs have succeeded in simulating humanlike intelligence.

Critics of AI, however, question both the possibility and the worth of trying to get machines to simulate human intelligence. They sometimes use the "Chinese Room" problem to illustrate a distinction between simulated intelligence and true understanding. Arguments can be made to support either perspective. Many now classic AI programs have been developed. Among the earliest ones are the Logic Theorist, which proves theorems in symbolic logic, and the General Problem Solver, which solves various kinds of problems using means–ends analysis. A later program was SHRDLU. It simulated a robot performing various operations in a block world, such as placing one block on top of another or placing a block in a box. Programs that modeled belief systems include ELIZA. It was designed to simulate a nondirective psychotherapist. Another is PARRY, designed to simulate the thinking of a paranoid psychiatric patient. Expert systems, programs designed to demonstrate expertise, include MYCIN, which diagnoses certain bacterial diseases by analyzing the results of blood tests. They also include DENDRAL, which analyzes the structure of organic compounds.

Thinking about Thinking: Factual, Analytical, Creative, and Practical Questions

1. Briefly summarize the key strands of AI research and name an example of a program in each strand.

2. What are some of the main reasons that intelligence tests have been devised and used?

3. In what ways is the theory of multiple intelligences different from factor-analytic theories of intelligence?

4. What are some of the strengths and limitations of the information-processing approach to intelligence?

5. How would you design a program to improve intelligence (as you define the concept)?

6. Design an experiment that would link a physiological approach to a cognitive approach to intelligence.

7. How might any of the structural approaches to intelligence lead to practical applications?

8. Contextualists underscore the importance of viewing intelligence within a given context. What are some aspects of your social, mental, or physical context that you consider important to the expression of your intelligence?

Key Terms

artificial intelligence (AI)
contextualism
culture-fair
culture-relevant tests
emotional intelligence

expert systems
factor analysis
flow chart
intelligence
structure-of-intellect (SOI)

theory of multiple intelligences
triarchic theory of human intelligence

Annotated Suggested Reading

Sternberg, R. J., & Pretz, J. E. (Eds.) (2005). *Cognition and intelligence*. New York: Cambridge University Press. A comprehensive review of the relation between cognition and intelligence, covering virtually all of aspects of cognition addressed in this book.

Glossary

accessibility—the degree to which we can gain access to the available information

agnosia—a severe deficit in the ability to perceive sensory information

algorithms—sequences of operations that may be repeated over and over again and that, in theory, guarantee the solution to a problem

Alzheimer's disease—a disease primarily of older adults that causes dementia as well as progressive memory loss

amnesia—severe loss of explicit memory

amygdala—plays a role an important role in emotion, especially in anger and aggression

analogue codes—a form of knowledge representation that preserves the main perceptual features of whatever is being represented for the physical stimuli we observe in our environment

analysis—breaking down the whole of a complex problem into manageable elements

anterograde amnesia—the inability to remember events that occur after a traumatic event

aphasia—an impairment of speech functioning caused by damage to the brain

arousal—a degree of physiological excitation, responsivity, and readiness for action, relative to a baseline

artifact categories—groupings that are designed or invented by humans to serve particular purposes or functions

artificial intelligence (AI)—the attempt by humans to construct systems that show intelligence and, particularly, the intelligent processing of information; intelligence in symbol-processing systems such as computers

association areas—regions of the lobes of the brain that are not part of the somatosensory, motor, auditory, or visual cortices

associationism—examines how events or ideas can become associated with one another in the mind to result in a form of learning

attention—the means by which we actively process a limited amount of information from the enormous amount of information available through our senses, our stored memories, and our other cognitive processes

autobiographical memory—refers to memory of an individual's history

automatic process—involves no conscious control

automatization—the process by which a procedure changes from being highly conscious to being relatively automatic; also termed *proceduralization*

availability—the presence of information stored in long-term memory

availability heuristic—cognitive shortcut that occurs when we make judgments on the basis of how easily we can call to mind what we perceive as relevant instances of a phenomenon

babbling—the infant's preferential production largely of those distinct phonemes—both vowels and consonants—that are characteristic of the infant's own language

base rate—refers to the prevalence of an event or characteristic within its population of events or characteristics

basic level—degree of specificity of a concept that seems to be a level within a hierarchy that is preferred to other levels; sometimes termed *natural level*

behaviorism—a theoretical outlook that psychology should focus only on the relation between observable behavior, on the one hand, and environmental events or stimuli, on the other

bilinguals—people who can speak two languages

binaural presentation—presenting the same two messages or sometimes just one message to both ears simultaneously

binocular depth cues—based on the receipt of sensory information in three dimensions from both eyes

blindsight—traces of visual perceptual ability in blind areas

bottom-up theories—data-driven (i.e., stimulus-driven) theories

bounded rationality—belief that we are rational, but within limits

brain—the organ in our bodies that most directly controls our thoughts, emotions, and motivations

brain stem—connects the forebrain to the spinal cord

categorical perception—discontinuous categories of speech sounds

category—a concept that functions to organize or point out aspects of equivalence among other concepts based on common features or similarity to a prototype

causal inferences—how people make judgments about whether something causes something else

central executive—both coordinates attentional activities and governs responses

cerebellum—controls bodily coordination, balance, and muscle tone, as well as some aspects of memory involving procedure-related movements; from Latin, "little brain"

cerebral cortex—forms a 1- to 3-millimeter layer that wraps the surface of the brain somewhat like the bark of a tree wraps around the trunk

cerebral hemispheres—the two halves of the brain

change blindness—the inability to detect changes in objects or scenes that are being viewed

characteristic features—qualities that describe (characterize or typify) the prototype but are not necessary for it

child-directed speech—the use of simpler sentence constructions when speaking with infants and young children

coarticulation—occurs when phonemes or other units are produced in a way that overlaps them in time

cocktail party problem—the process of tracking one conversation in the face of the distraction of other conversations

cognitive maps—internal representations of our physical environment, particularly centering on spatial relationships

cognitive psychology—the study of how people perceive, learn, remember, and think about information

cognitive science—a cross-disciplinary field that uses ideas and methods from cognitive psychology, psychobiology, artificial intelligence, philosophy, linguistics, and anthropology

cognitivism—the belief that much of human behavior can be understood in terms of how people think

communication—exchange of thoughts and feelings

comprehension processes—used to make sense of the text as a whole

concept—an idea about something that provides a means of understanding the world

conditional reasoning—occurs when the reasoner must draw a conclusion based on an if-then proposition

conjunction search—looking for a particular combination (conjunction—joining together) of features

connotation—a word's emotional overtones, presuppositions, and other nonexplicit meanings

consciousness—includes both the feeling of awareness and the content of awareness

consolidation—the process of integrating new information into stored information

constructive—prior experience affects how we recall things and what we actually recall from memory

constructive perception—the perceiver builds (constructs) a cognitive understanding (perception) of a stimulus; he or she uses sensory information as the foundation for the structure but also uses other sources of information to build the perception

content morphemes—the words that convey the bulk of the meaning of a language

context effects—the influences of the surrounding environment on perception

contextualism—belief that intelligence must be understood in its real-world context

contralateral—from one side to another

controlled processes—accessible to conscious control and even require it

convergent thinking—attempt to narrow down the multiple possibilities to converge on a single best answer

converging operations—the use of multiple approaches and techniques to address a problem

cooing—the infant's oral expression that explores the production of vowel sounds

cooperative principle—principle in conversation that holds that we seek to communicate in ways that make it easy for our listener to understand what we mean

core—refers to the defining features something must have to be considered an example of a category

corpus callosum—a dense aggregate of neural fibers connecting the two cerebral hemispheres

creativity—the process of producing something that is both original and worthwhile

culture-fair—equally appropriate and fair for members of all cultures

culture-relevant tests—measure skills and knowledge that relate to the cultural experiences of the test-takers

decay—occurs when simply the passage of time causes an individual to forget

decay theory—asserts that information is forgotten because of the gradual disappearance, rather than displacement, of the memory trace

declarative knowledge—knowledge of facts that can be stated

deductive reasoning—the process of reasoning from one or more general statements regarding what is known to reach a logically certain conclusion

deductive validity—logical soundness

deep structure—refers to an underlying syntactic structure that links various phrase structures through the application of various transformation rules

defining feature—a necessary attribute

denotation—the strict dictionary definition of a word

depth—the distance from a surface, usually using your own body as a reference surface when speaking in terms of depth perception

dialect—a regional variety of a language distinguished by features such as vocabulary, syntax, and pronunciation

dichotic presentation—presenting a different message to each ear

direct perception theory—belief that the array of information in our sensory receptors, including the sensory context, is all we need to perceive anything

discourse—encompasses language use at the level beyond the sentence, such as in conversation, paragraphs, stories, chapters, and entire works of literature

dishabituation—change in a familiar stimulus that prompts us to start noticing the stimulus again

distracters—nontarget stimuli that divert our attention away from the target stimulus

distributed practice—learning in which various sessions are spaced over time

divergent thinking—when one tries to generate a diverse assortment of possible alternative solutions to a problem

divided attention—the prudent allocation of available attentional resources to coordinate the performance of more than one task at a time

dual-code theory—belief suggesting that knowledge is represented both in images and in symbols

dual-system hypothesis—suggests that two languages are represented somehow in separate systems of the mind

dyslexia—difficulty in deciphering, reading, and comprehending text

ecological validity—the degree to which particular findings in one environmental context may be considered relevant outside of that context

electroencephalograms (EEGs)—recordings of the electrical frequencies and intensities of the living brain, typically recorded over relatively long periods

elimination by aspects—occurs when we eliminate alternatives by focusing on aspects of each alternative, one at a time

emotional intelligence—the ability to perceive and express emotion, assimilate emotion in thought, understand and reason with emotion, and regulate emotion in the self and others

empiricist—one who believes that we acquire knowledge via empirical evidence

encoding—refers to how you transform a physical, sensory input into a kind of representation that can be placed into memory

encoding specificity—what is recalled depends on what is encoded

episodic buffer—a limited-capacity system that is capable of binding information from the subsidiary systems and from long-term memory into a unitary episodic representation

episodic memory—stores personally experienced events or episodes

exemplars—typical representatives of a category

expert systems—computer programs that can perform the way an expert does in a fairly specific domain

explicit memory—when participants engage in conscious recollection

factor analysis—a statistical method for separating a construct—intelligence in this case—into a number of hypothetical factors or abilities that the researchers believe form the basis of individual differences in test performance

fallacy—erroneous reasoning

feature search—simply scanning the environment for a particular feature or features

feature-integration theory—explains the relative ease of conducting feature searches and the relative difficulty of conducting conjunction searches

figure-ground—what stands out from versus what recedes into the background

flashbulb memory—a memory of an event so powerful that the person remembers the event as vividly as if it were indelibly preserved on film

flow chart—a model path for reaching a goal or solving a problem

frontal lobe— associated with motor processing and higher thought processes, such as abstract reasoning

function morphemes—a morpheme that adds detail and nuance to the meaning of the content morphemes or helps the content morphemes fit the grammatical context

functional fixedness—the inability to realize that something known to have a particular use may also be used for performing other functions

functional magnetic resonance imaging (fMRI)—a neuroimaging techinque that uses magnetic fields to construct a detailed representation in three dimensions of levels of activity in various parts of the brain at a given moment in time

functional-equivalence hypothesis—belief that although visual imagery is not identical to visual perception, it is functionally equivalent to it

functionalism—seeks to understand what people *do*, and *why* they do it

general factor—provides the key to understanding intelligence; labeled "g" by Spearman

gestalt approach to form perception—based on the notion that the whole differs from the sum of its individual parts

gestalt psychology—states that we best understand psychological phenomena when we view them as organized, structured wholes

grammar—the study of language in terms of noticing regular patterns

habituation—involves our becoming accustomed to a stimulus so that we gradually pay less and less attention to it

heuristics—informal, intuitive, speculative strategies that sometimes lead to an effective solution and sometimes do not

hindsight bias—when we look at a situation retrospectively, we believe we easily can see all the signs and events leading up to a particular outcome

hippocampus—plays an essential role in memory formation

hypermnesia—a process of producing retrieval of memories that seem to have been forgotten

hypothalamus—regulates behavior related to species survival: fighting, feeding, fleeing, and mating; also active in regulating emotions and reactions to stress

hypotheses—tentative proposals regarding expected empirical consequences of the theory

hypothesis testing—a view of language acquisition that asserts that children acquire language by mentally forming tentative hypotheses regarding language, based on their inherited facility for language acquisition and then testing these hypotheses in the environment

hypothetical constructs—concepts that are not themselves directly measurable or observable but that serve as mental models for understanding how a psychological phenomenon works

iconic store—a discrete visual sensory register that holds information for very short periods of time

ill-structured problems—problems that lack well-defined paths to solution

illusory correlation—occurs when we tend to see particular events or particular attributes and categories as going together because we are predisposed to do so

imagery—the mental representation of things that are not currently being sensed by the sense organs

implicit memory—when we recollect something but are not consciously aware that we are trying to do so

incubation—putting the problem aside for a while without consciously thinking about it

indirect requests—the making of a request without doing so straightforwardly

inductive reasoning—the process of reasoning from specific facts or observations to reach a likely conclusion that may explain the facts

infantile amnesia—the inability to recall events that happened when we were very young

insight—a distinctive and sometimes seemingly sudden understanding of a problem or of a strategy that aids in solving the problem

intelligence—the capacity to learn from experience, using metacognitive processes to enhance learning, and the ability to adapt to the surrounding environment

interference—occurs when competing information causes an individual to forget something

interference theory—refers to the view that forgetting occurs because recall of certain words interferes with recall of other words

introspection—a looking inward at pieces of information passing through consciousness

ipsilateral transmission—on the same side

isomorphic—the formal structure is the same, and only the content differs

jargon—specialized vocabulary commonly used within a group, such as a profession or a trade

judgment and decision making—used to select from among choices or to evaluate opportunities

knowledge representation—the form for what you know in your mind about things, ideas, events, and so on that exist outside of your mind

Korsakoff's syndrome—produces loss of memory function

language—the use of an organized means of combining words in order to communicate

language-acquisition device (LAD)—a biologically innate mechanism that facilitates language acquisition

law of Prägnanz—tendency to perceive any given visual array in a way that most simply organizes the disparate elements into a stable and coherent form

levels-of-processing framework—postulates that memory does not comprise three or even any specific number of separate stores but rather varies along a continuous dimension in terms of depth of encoding

lexical access—the identification of a word that allows us to gain access to the meaning of the word from memory

lexical processes—used to identify letters and words

lexicon—the entire set of morphemes in a given language or in a given person's linguistic repertoire

limbic system—important to emotion, motivation, memory, and learning

linguistic relativity—the assertion that speakers of different languages have differing cognitive systems and that these different cognitive systems influence the ways in which people speaking the various languages think about the world

linguistic universals—characteristic patterns across all languages of various cultures

lobes—divide the cerebral hemispheres and cortex into four parts

localization of function—refers to the specific areas of the brain that control specific skills or behaviors

long-term store—very large capacity, capable of storing information for very long periods, perhaps even indefinitely

magnetic resonance imaging (MRI) scan—a technique for revealing high-resolution images of the structure of the living brain by computing and analyzing magnetic changes in the energy of the orbits of nuclear particles in the molecules of the body

massed practice—learning in which sessions are crammed together in a very short space of time

medulla oblongata—controls heart activity and largely controls breathing, swallowing, and digestion

memory—the means by which we retain and draw on our past experiences to use this information in the present

mental models—knowledge structures that individuals construct to understand and explain their experiences; an internal representation of information that corresponds analogously with whatever is being represented

mental rotation—involves rotationally transforming an object's visual mental image

mental set—a frame of mind involving an existing model for representing a problem, a problem context, or a procedure for problem solving

metacognition—our understanding and control of our cognition; our ability to think about and control our own processes of thought and ways of enhancing our thinking

metamemory—strategies involve reflecting on our own memory processes with a view to improving our memory

metaphor—two nouns juxtaposed in a way that positively asserts their similarities, while not disconfirming their dissimilarities

mnemonic devices—specific techniques to help you memorize lists of words

mnemonist—someone who demonstrates extraordinarily keen memory ability, usually based on the use of special techniques for memory enhancement

modular—divided into discrete modules that operate more or less independently of each other

monocular depth cues—can be represented in just two dimensions and observed with just one eye

monolinguals—people who can speak only one language

morpheme—the smallest unit that denotes meaning within a particular language

natural categories—groupings that occur naturally in the world

negative transfer—occurs when solving an earlier problem makes it harder to solve a later one

nodes—the elements of a network

nominal kind—the arbitrary assignment of a label to an entity that meets a certain set of prespecified conditions

noun phrase—syntactic structure that contains at least one noun (often, the subject of the sentence) and includes all the relevant descriptors of the noun

object-centered representation—the individual stores a representation of the object, independent of its appearance to the viewer

occipital lobe—associated with visual processing, the primary motor cortex, which specializes in the planning, control, and execution of movement, particularly of movement involving any kind of delayed response

overconfidence—an individual's overvaluation of her or his own skills, knowledge, or judgment

overextension error—erroneously extending the meaning of words in the existing lexicon to cover things and ideas for which a new word is lacking

overregularization—occurs when individuals apply the general rules of language to the exceptional cases that vary from the norm

parallel distributed processing (PDP) models or connectionist models—the handling of very large numbers of cognitive operations at once through a network distributed across incalculable numbers of locations in the brain

parallel processing—occurs when multiple operations are executed all at once

parietal lobe—associated with somatosensory processing

perception—the set of processes by which we recognize, organize, and make sense of the sensations we receive from environmental stimuli

perceptual constancy—occurs when our perception of an object remains the same even when our proximal sensation of the distal object changes

phoneme—is the smallest unit of speech sound that can be used to distinguish one utterance in a given language from another

phonological loop—briefly holds inner speech for verbal comprehension and for acoustic rehearsal

phrase-structure grammar—syntactical analysis of the structure of phrases as they are used

pons—serves as a kind of relay station because it contains neural fibers that pass signals from one part of the brain to another

positive transfer—occurs when the solution of an earlier problem makes it easier to solve a new problem

positron emission tomography (PET) scans—measure increases in glucose consumption in active brain areas during particular kinds of information processing

pragmatic reasoning schemas—general organizing principles or rules related to particular kinds of goals, such as permissions, obligations, or causations

pragmatics—the study of how people use language

pragmatists—ones who believe that knowledge is validated by its usefulness

premises—are propositions about which arguments are made

primacy effect—refers to superior recall of words at and near the beginning of a list

primary somatosensory cortex—receives information from the senses about pressure, texture, temperature, and pain

prime—a node that activates a connected node; this activation is known as the priming effect

priming—the facilitation in one's ability to utilize missing information; occurs when recognition of certain stimuli is affected by prior presentation of the same or similar stimuli

priming effect—the resulting activation of the node

proactive interference—occurs when the interfering material occurs *before*, rather than *after*, learning of the to-be-remembered material

problem solving—an effort to overcome obstacles obstructing the path to a solution

problem-solving cycle—includes problem identification, problem definition, strategy formulation, organization of information, allocation of resources, monitoring, and evaluation

problem space—the universe of all possible actions that can be applied to solving a problem, given any constraints that apply to the solution of the problem

procedural knowledge—knowledge of procedures that can be implemented

production—the generation and output of a procedure

productive thinking—involves insights that go beyond the bounds of existing associations

proposition—basically an assertion, which may be either true or false

propositional theory—belief suggesting that knowledge is represented only in underlying propositions, not in the form of images or of words and other symbols

prototype—a sort of average of a class of related objects or patterns, which integrates all of the most typical (most frequently observed) features of the class

prototype theory—suggests that categories are formed on the basis of a (prototypical, or averaged) model of the category

psycholinguistics—the psychology of our language as it interacts with the human mind

rationalist—one who believes that the route to knowledge is through logical analysis

reasoning—the process of drawing conclusions from principles and from evidence

recall—to produce a fact, a word, or other item from memory

recency effect—refers to superior recall of words at and near the end of a list

recognition—to select or otherwise identify an item as being one that you learned previously

recognition-by-components (RBC) theory—belief that we quickly recognize objects by observing the edges of objects and then decomposing the objects into geons

reconstructive—involving the use of various strategies (e.g., searching for cues, drawing inferences) for retrieving the original memory traces of our experiences and then rebuilding the original experiences as a basis for retrieval

rehearsal—the repeated recitation of an item

representativeness—occurs when we judge the probability of an uncertain event according to (1) its obvious similarity to or representation of the population from which it is derived and (2) the degree to which it reflects the salient features of the process by which it is generated (such as randomness)

reticular activating system (RAS)—a network of neurons essential to the regulation of consciousness (sleep, wakefulness, arousal, and even attention to some extent and to such vital functions as heartbeat and breathing); also called *reticular formation*

retrieval—refers to how you gain access to information stored in memory

retroactive interference—caused by activity occurring *after* we learn something but *before* we are asked to recall that thing; also called *retroactive inhibition*

retrograde amnesia—occurs when individuals lose their purposeful memory for events prior to whatever trauma induces memory loss

satisficing—occurs when we consider options one by one, and then we select an option as soon as we find one that is satisfactory or just good enough to meet our minimum level of acceptability

schemas—mental frameworks for representing knowledge that encompass an array of interrelated concepts in a meaningful organization

script—a structure that describes appropriate sequences of events in a particular context

search—refers to a scan of the environment for particular features—actively looking for something when you are not sure where it will appear

selective attention—choosing to attend to some stimuli and to ignore others

selective-combination insight—involves taking selectively encoded and compared snippets of relevant information and combining that information in a novel, productive way

selective-comparison insight—involves novel perceptions of how new information relates to old information

selective-encoding insight—involves distinguishing relevant from irrelevant information

semantic memory—stores general world knowledge

semantic network—a web of interconnected elements of meaning

semantics—the study of meaning in a language

sensory adaptation—a lessening of attention to a stimulus that is not subject to conscious control

sensory store—capable of storing relatively limited amounts of information for very brief periods

septum—is involved in anger and fear

sequential bilingualism—occurs when an individual first learns one language and then another

serial processing—means by which information is handled through a linear sequence of operations, one operation at a time

short-term store—capable of storing information for somewhat longer periods but also of relatively limited capacity

signal—a target stimulus

signal detection—the detection of the appearance of a particular stimulus

signal-detection theory (SDT)—a theory of how we detect stimuli that involves four possible outcomes of the presence or absence of a stimulus and our detection or nondetection of a stimulus

simile—introduces the words *like* or *as* into a comparison between items

simultaneous bilingualism—occurs when a child learns two languages from birth

single-system hypothesis—suggests that two languages are represented in just one system

slips of the tongue—inadvertent linguistic errors in what we say

speech acts—addresses the question of what you can accomplish with speech

split-brain patients—people who have undergone operations severing the corpus callosum

spreading activation—excitation that fans out along a set of nodes within a given network

statistical significance—indicates the likelihood that a given set of results would be obtained if only chance factors were in operation

stereotypes—beliefs that members of a social group tend more or less uniformly to have particular types of characteristics

storage—refers to how you retain encoded information in memory

Stroop effect—demonstrates the psychological difficulty in selectively attending to the color of the ink and trying to ignore the word that is printed with the ink of that color

structuralism—seeks to understand the structure (configuration of elements) of the mind and its perceptions by analyzing those perceptions into their constituent components

structure-of-intellect (SOI)—Guilford's model for a three-dimensional structure of intelligence, embracing various contents, operations, and products of intelligence

subjective probability—a calculation based on the individual's estimates of likelihood, rather than on objective statistical computations

subjective utility—a calculation based on the individual's judged weightings of utility (value), rather than on objective criteria

surface structure—a level of syntactic analysis that involves the specific syntactical sequence of words in a sentence and any of the various phrase structures that may result

syllogisms—deductive arguments that involve drawing conclusions from two premises

symbolic representation—meaning that the relationship between the word and what it represents is simply arbitrary

syntax—refers to the way in which users of a particular language put words together to form sentences

synthesis—putting together various elements to arrange them into something useful

telegraphic speech—can be used to describe two- or three-word utterances and even slightly longer ones, if they have omissions of some function morphemes

templates—highly detailed models for patterns we potentially might recognize

temporal lobe—associated with auditory processing

thalamus—relays incoming sensory information through groups of neurons that project to the appropriate region in the cortex

thematic roles—are ways in which items can be used in the context of communication

theory—an organized body of general explanatory principles regarding a phenomenon

theory of multiple intelligences—belief that intelligence comprises multiple independent constructs, not just a single, unitary construct

theory-based view of meaning—holds that people understand and categorize concepts in terms of implicit theories, or general ideas they have regarding those concepts

tip-of-the-tongue phenomenon—experience of trying to remember something that is known to be stored in memory but that cannot readily be retrieved

top-down theories—driven by high-level cognitive processes, existing knowledge, and prior expectations

transfer—any carryover of knowledge or skills from one problem situation to another

transformational grammar—involves the study of transformational rules that guide the ways in which underlying propositions can be rearranged to form various phrase structures

transparency—occurs when people see analogies where they do not exist because of similarity of content

triarchic theory of human intelligence—belief that intelligence comprises three aspects, dealing with the relation of intelligence (1) to the internal world of the person, (2) to experience, and (3) to the external world

verb phrase—syntactic structure that contains at least one verb and whatever the verb acts on, if anything

verbal comprehension—the receptive ability to comprehend written and spoken linguistic input, such as words, sentences, and paragraphs

verbal fluency—the expressive ability to produce linguistic output

viewer-centered representation—an individual stores the way the object looks to him or her

vigilance—refers to a person's ability to attend to a field of stimulation over a prolonged period, during which the person seeks to detect the appearance of a particular target stimulus of interest

visuospatial sketchpad—briefly holds some visual images

vocabulary—a repertoire of words

well-structured problems—problems that have well-defined paths to solution

word-superiority effect—letters are read more easily when they are embedded in words than when they are presented either in isolation or with letters that do not form words

working memory—holds only the most recently activated portion of long-term memory, and it moves these activated elements into and out of brief, temporary memory storage

References

Abelson, R. P. (1980). Searle's argument is just a set of Chinese symbols. *Behavioral and Brain Sciences, 3,* 424–425.

Abernethy, B. (1991). Visual search strategies and decision-making in sport. *International Journal of Sport Psychology, 22,* 189–210.

Ackerman, P. (1988). Determinants of individual differences during skill acquisition: Cognitive abilities and information processing. *Journal of Experimental Psychology: General, 117,* 288–318.

Ackerman, P. (2005). Ability determinants of individual differences in skilled performance. In R. J. Sternberg & J. E. Pretz (Eds.), *Cognition and intelligence* (pp. 142–159). New York: Cambridge University Press.

Ackerman, P. L. (1996). A theory of adult intellectual development: Process, personality, interests, and knowledge. *Intelligence, 22,* 227–257.

Ackil, J. K., & Zaragoza, M. S. (1998). Memorial consequences of forced confabulation: Age differences in susceptibility to false memories. *Developmental Psychology, 34,* 1358–1372.

Acredolo, L. P., & Goodwyn, S. W. (1998). *Baby signs: How to talk with your baby before your baby can talk.* Chicago: NTB/Contemporary Publishers.

Adams, M. (1990). *Beginning to read: Thinking and learning about print.* Cambridge, MA: MIT Press.

Adams, M. (1999). Reading. In R. A. Wilson & F. C. Keil (Eds.), *The MIT encyclopedia of the cognitive sciences* (pp. 705–707). Cambridge, MA: MIT Press.

Adams, M. J. (Ed.). (1986). *Odyssey: A curriculum for thinking* (Vols. 1–6). Watertown, MA: Charlesbridge Publishing.

Adams, M. J., Treiman, R., & Pressley, M. (1997). Reading, writing and literacy. In I. Sigel & A. Renninger (Eds.), *Handbook of child psychology* (5th ed., vol. 4). *Child psychology in practice* (pp. 275–357). New York: Wiley.

Adler, J. (1991, July 22). The melting of a mighty myth. *Newsweek,* 63.

Adolphs, R. (2003). Amygdala. In L. Nadel (Ed.), *Encyclopedia of cognitive science, Vol. 1,* pp. 98–105. London, England: Nature Publishing Group.

Adolphs, R., Tranel, D., Damasio, H., & Damasio, A. (1994). Impaired recognition of emotion in facial expressions following bilateral damage to the human amygdala. *Nature, 372,* 669–672.

Ahn, W., & Bailenson, J. (1996). Causal attribution as a search for underlying mechanisms. An explanation of the conjunction fallacy and the discounting principle. *Cognitive Psychology, 31,* 82–123.

Ahn, W., Kalish, C. W., Medin, D. L., & Gelman, S. A. (1995). The role of covariation versus mechanism information in causal attribution. *Cognition, 54,* 299–352.

Akhtar, N. & Montague, L. (1999). Early lexical acquisition: The role of cross-situational learning. *First Language, 19,* 347–358.

Albert, M. L., & Obler, L. (1978). *The bilingual brain: Neuro-psychological and neurolinguistic aspects of bilingualism.* New York: Academic Press.

Almor, A., & Sloman, S. A. (1996). Is deontic reasoning special? *Psychological Review, 103,* 503–546.

Amabile, T. A., & Rovee-Collier, C. (1991). Contextual variation and memory retrieval at six months. *Child Development, 62*(5), 1155–1166.

Amabile, T. M. (1996). *Creativity in context.* Boulder, CO: Westview.

American Psychiatric Association. (1994). *Diagnostic and statistical manual of mental disorders* (4th ed.). Washington, DC: Author.

Anderson, B. F. (1975). *Cognitive psychology.* New York: Academic Press.

Anderson, J. R. (1972). FRAN: A simulation model of free recall. In G. H. Bower (Ed.), *The psychology of learning and motivation* (Vol. 5, pp. 315–378). New York: Academic Press.

Anderson, J. R. (1976). *Language, memory, and thought.* Hillsdale, NJ: Erlbaum.

Anderson, J. R. (1980). Concepts, propositions, and schemata: What are the cognitive units? *Nebraska Symposium on Motivation, 28,* 121–162.

Anderson, J. R. (1983). *The architecture of cognition.* Cambridge, MA: Harvard University Press.

Anderson, J. R. (1985). *Cognitive psychology and its implications.* New York: Freeman.

Anderson, J. R. (1991). The adaptive nature of human categorization. *Psychological Review, 98,* 409–429.

Anderson, J. R. (1993). *Rules of the mind.* Hillsdale, NJ: Erlbaum.

Anderson, J. R. (1996). ACT: A simple theory of complex cognition. *American Psychologist, 51,* 355–365.

Anderson, J. R., & Bower, G. H. (1973). *Human associative memory.* New York: Wiley.

Anderson, J. R., & Fincham, J. M. (1996). Categorization and sensitivity to correlation. *Journal of Experimental Psychology: Learning, Memory, and Cognition, 22,* 259–277.

Anderson, J. R., Budiu, R., & Reder, L. M. (2001). A theory of sentence memory as part of a general theory of memory. *Journal of Memory & Language, 45,* 277–367.

Anderson, M. (2005). Marrying intelligence and cognition. In R. J. Sternberg & J. E. Pretz (Eds.), *Cognition and intelligence* (pp. 268–287). New York: Cambridge University Press.

Anderson, R. C., & Pichert, J. W. (1978). Recall of previously unrecallable information following a shift in perspective. *Journal of Verbal Learning and Verbal Behavior, 17,* 1–12.

Anglin, J. M. (1993). Vocabulary development: A morphological analysis. *Monographs of the Society for Research in Child Development, 58,* (No. 10).

Appel, L. F., Cooper, R. G., McCarrell, N., Sims-Knight, J., Yussen, S. R., & Flavell, J. H. (1972). The development of the distinction between perceiving and memorizing. *Child Development, 43,* 1365–1381.

Armstrong, S. L., Gleitman, L. R., & Gleitman, H. (1983). What some concepts might not be. *Cognition, 13,* 263–308.

Asher, J. J., & Garcia, R. (1969). The optimal age to learn a foreign language. *Modern Language Journal, 53*(5), 334–341.

Atkinson, R. C., & Shiffrin, R. M. (1968). Human memory: A proposed system and its control processes. In K. W. Spence & J. T. Spence (Eds.), *The psychology of learning and motivation: Vol. 2. Advances in research and theory.* New York: Academic Press.

Atkinson, R. C., & Shiffrin, R. M. (1971). The control of short-term memory. *Scientific American, 225,* 82–90.

Atran, S. (1999). Itzaj Maya folkbiological taxonomy: Cognitive universals and cultural particulars. In D. L. Medin & S. Atran (Eds.), *Folkbiology* (pp. 119–213). Cambridge, MA: MIT Press.

Attention deficit hyperactivity disorder. (http://www.nimh.nih.gov/Publicat/ADHD.cfm, retrieved 8/11/04).

Averbach, E., & Coriell, A. S. (1961). Short-term memory in vision. *Bell System Technical Journal, 40,* 309–328.

Ayers, M. S., & Reder, L. M. (1998). A theoretical review of the misinformation effect: Predictions from an activation-based memory model. *Psychonomic Bulletin & Review, 5,* 1–21.

Bachevalier, J., & Mishkin, M. (1986). Visual recognition impairment follows ventromedial but not dorsolateral frontal lesions in monkeys. *Behavioral Brain Research, 20*(3), 249–261.

Baddeley, A. D. (1966). Short-term memory for word sequences as function of acoustic, semantic, and formal similarity. *Quarterly Journal of Experimental Psychology, 18,* 362–365.

Baddeley, A. D. (1984). The fractionation of human memory. *Psychological Medicine, 14*(2), 259–264.

Baddeley, A. D. (1989). The psychology of remembering and forgetting. In T. Butler (Ed.), *Memory: History, culture and the mind.* London: Basil Blackwell.

Baddeley, A. D. (1990a). *Human memory.* Hove, England: Erlbaum.

Baddeley, A. D. (1990b). *Human memory: Theory and practice.* Needham Heights, MA: Allyn & Bacon.

Baddeley, A. D. (1992). Working memory. *Science, 255,* 556–559.

Baddeley, A. D. (1993). Verbal and visual subsystems of working memory. *Current Biology, 3,* 563–565.

Baddeley, A. D. (1995). Working memory. In M. S. Gazzaniga (Ed.), *The cognitive neurosciences* (pp. 755–764). Cambridge, MA: MIT Press.

Baddeley, A. D. (1998). *Human memory: Theory and practice* (rev. ed.). Needham Heights, MA: Allyn & Bacon.

Baddeley, A. D. (1999). Memory. In R. A. Wilson & F. C. Keil (Eds.), *The MIT encyclopedia of the cognitive sciences* (pp. 514–517). Cambridge, MA: MIT Press.

Baddeley, A. D. (2000a). The episodic buffer: A new component of working memory. *Trends in Cognitive Sciences, 4,* 417–423.

Baddeley, A. D. (2000b). Short-term and working memory. In E. Tulving & F. I. M. Craik (Eds.), *The Oxford handbook of memory* (pp. 77–92). New York: Oxford University Press.

Baddeley, A. D., & Hitch, G. J. (1974). Working memory. In G. Bower (Ed.), *Advances in learning and motivation* (Vol. 8, pp. 47–90). New York: Academic Press.

Baddeley, A., & Warrington, E. (1970). Amnesia and the distinction between long- and short-term memory. *Journal of Verbal Learning & Verbal Behavior, 9*(2), 176–189.

Baddeley, A., Thomson, N., & Buchanan, M. (1975). Word length and the structure of short-term memory. *Journal of Verbal Learning & Verbal Behavior, 14*(6), 575–589.

Bahrick, H. P. (1984a). Fifty years of second language attrition: Implications for programmatic research. *Modern Language Journal, 68*(2), 105–118.

Bahrick, H. P. (1984b). Semantic memory content in permastore: Fifty years of memory for Spanish learned in school. *Journal of Experimental Psychology: General, 113*(1), 1–29.

Bahrick, H. P. (2000). Long-term maintenance of knowledge. In E. Tulving & F. I. M. Craik (Eds.), *The Oxford handbook of memory* (pp. 347–362). New York: Oxford University Press.

Bahrick, H. P., & Hall, L. K. (1991). Lifetime maintenance of high school mathematics content. *Journal of Experimental Psychology: General, 120*(1), 20–33.

Bahrick, H. P., & Phelps, E. (1987). Retention of Spanish vocabulary over eight years. *Journal of Experimental Psychology: Learning, Memory, & Cognition, 13,* 344–349.

Bahrick, H. P., Bahrick, L. E., Bahrick, A. S., & Bahrick, P. E. (1993). Maintenance of foreign language vocabulary and the spacing effect. *Psychological Science, 4*(5), 316–321.

Bahrick, H. P., Bahrick, P. O., & Wittlinger, R. P. (1975). Fifty years of memory for names and faces: A cross-sectional approach. *Journal of Experimental Psychology: General, 104,* 54–75.

Bahrick, H. P., Hall, L. K., Goggin, J. P., Bahrick, L. E., & Berger, S. A. (1994). Fifty years of language maintenance and language dominance in bilingual Hispanic immigrants. *Journal of Experimental Psychology: General, 123*(3), 264–283.

Balota, D. A., Cortese, M. J., Duchek, J. M., Adams, D., Roediger, H. L., McDermott, K. B., et al. (1999). Veridical and false memories in healthy older adults and in dementia and Alzheimer's types. *Cognitive Neuropsychology, 16,* 361–384.

Baltes, P. B. (1993). The aging mind: Potential and limits. *Gerontologist, 33,* 580–594.

Baltes, P. B. (1997). On the incomplete architecture of human ontogeny: Selection, optimization, and compensation as foundations of developmental theory. *American Psychologist, 52,* 366–380.

Baltes, P. B., & Smith, J. (1990). Toward a psychology of wisdom and its ontogenesis. In R. J. Sternberg (Ed.), *Wisdom: Its nature, origins, and development* (pp. 87–120). New York: Cambridge University Press.

Baltes, P. B., & Willis, S. L. (1979). Toward psychological theories of aging and development. In J. E. Birren & K. W. Schaie (Eds.), *Handbook of the psychology of aging.* New York: Van Nostrand Reinhold.

Baltes, P. B., Dittmann-Kohli, F., & Dixon, R. A. (1984). New perspectives on the development of intelligence in adulthood: Toward a dual-process conception and a model of selective optimization with compensation. In P. B. Baltes & O. G. Brim, Jr. (Eds.), *Life-span development and behavior* (Vol. 6, pp. 33–76). New York: Academic Press.

Baltes, P. B., Staudinger, U. M., Maercker, A., & Smith, J. (1995). People nominated as wise: A comparative study of wisdom-related knowledge. *Psychology & Aging, 10,* 155–166.

Banaji, M. R., & Crowder, R. G. (1989). The bankruptcy of everyday memory. *American Psychologist, 44,* 1185–1193.

Bandler, R., & Shipley, M. T. (1994). Columnar organization in the midbrain periaqueductal gray: modules for emotional expression? *Trends in Neuroscience, 17,* 379–389.

Bandura, A. (1977). *Social learning theory.* Englewood Cliffs, NJ: Prentice-Hall.

Barnett, S. M., & Ceci, S. J. (2005). The role of transferable knowledge in intelligence. In R. J. Sternberg & J. E. Pretz (Eds.), *Cognition and intelligence* (pp. 208–224). New York: Cambridge University Press.

Barnouw, V. (1985). *Culture and personality.* Chicago: Dorsey Press.

Baron, J. (1988). *Thinking and deciding.* New York: Cambridge University Press.

Baron-Cohen, S. (2003). *The essential difference: The truth about the male and female brain.* New York; Basic Books.

Baron-Cohen, S., Leslie, A. M., & Frith, U. (1985). Does the autistic child have a "theory of mind"? *Cognition, 21,* 37–46.

Barrett, P. T., & Eysenck, H. J. (1992). Brain evoked potentials and intelligence: The Hendrickson paradigm. *Intelligence, 16*(3,4), 361–381.

Barron, F. (1988). Putting creativity to work. In R. J. Sternberg (Ed.), *The nature of creativity* (pp. 76–98). New York: Cambridge University Press.

Barrouillet, P., & Lecas, J. F. (1998). How can mental models account for content effects in conditional reasoning: A developmental perspective. *Cognition, 67*, 209–253.

Barsalou, L. (1983). Ad hoc categories. *Memory and Cognition, 11*, 211–227.

Barsalou, L. W. (1994). Flexibility, structure, and linguistic vagary in concepts: Manifestations of a compositional system of perceptual symbols. In A. F. Collins, S. E. Gathercole, M. A. Conway, & P. E. Morris (Eds.), *Theories of memory* (pp. 29–101). Hillsdale, NJ: Erlbaum.

Barsalou, L. W. (2000). Concepts: Structure. In A. E. Kazdin (Ed.), *Encyclopedia of psychology* (Vol. 2, pp. 245-248). Washington, DC: American Psychological Association.

Bartlett, F. C. (1932). *Remembering: A study in experimental and social psychology*. Cambridge, England: Cambridge University Press.

Bashore, T. R., Osman, A., & Hefley, E. F. (1989). Mental slowing in elderly persons: A cognitive psychophysiological analysis. *Psychology & Aging, 4*, 235–244.

Bassock, M. (2003). Analogical transfer in problem solving. In J. E. Davidson & R. J. Sternberg (Eds.), *The psychology of problem solving* (pp. 343–369). New York: Cambridge University Press.

Bassock, M., Wu, L., & Olseth, K. L. (1995). Judging a book by its cover: Interpretative effects of content on problem solving transfer. *Memory and Cognition, 23*, 354–367.

Bastik, T. (1982). *Intuition: How we think and act*. Chichester, England: Wiley.

Bates, E., & Goodman, J. (1999). On the emergence of grammar from the lexicon. In B. MacWhinney (Ed.), *The emergence of language* (pp. 29–80). Mahwah, NJ: Erlbaum.

Bauer, P. J., & Van Abbema, D. L. (2003). Memory, development of. In L. Nadel (Ed.), *Encyclopedia of cognitive science, Vol. 2*, pp. 1090-1095. London, England: Nature Publishing Group.

Baylis, G., Driver, J., & McLeod, P. (1992). Movement and proximity constrain miscombinations of colour and form. *Perception, 21*(2), 201–218.

Beardsley, M. (1962). The metaphorical twist. *Philosophical Phenomenological Research, 22*, 293–307.

Beck, I. L., Perfetti, C. A., & McKeown, M. G. (1982). Effects of long-term vocabulary instruction on lexical access and reading comprehension. *Journal of Educational Psychology, 74*, 506–521.

Begg, I., & Denny, J. (1969). Empirical reconciliation of atmosphere and conversion interpretations of syllogistic reasoning. *Journal of Experimental Psychology, 81*, 351–354.

Behrmann, M., Kosslyn, S. M., & Jeannerod, M. (Eds.) (1996). *The neuropsychology of mental imagery*. New York: Pergamon.

Bellezza, F. S. (1984). The self as a mnemonic device: The role of internal cues. *Journal of Personality and Social Psychology, 47*, 506–516.

Bellezza, F. S. (1992). Recall of congruent information in the self-reference task. *Bulletin of the Psychonomic Society, 30*(4), 275–278.

Belmont, J. M., & Butterfield, E. C. (1971). Learning strategies as determinants of memory deficiencies. *Cognitive Psychology, 2*, 411–420.

Benasich, A. A., & Thomas, J. J. (2003). Developmental disorders of language. In L. Nadel (Ed.), *Encyclopedia of cognitive science, Vol. 1*, pp. 959–967. London, England: Nature Publishing Group.

Benedict, R. (1946). *The crysanthemum and the sword*. Boston: Houghton Mifflin.

Ben-Zeev, T. (1996). When erroneous mathematical thinking is just as "correct": The oxymoron of rational errors. In R. J. Sternberg & T. Ben-Zeev (Eds.), *The nature of mathematical thinking* (pp. 55–79). Mahwah, NJ: Erlbaum.

Berg, C. A. (2000). Adult intellectual development. In R. J. Sternberg (Ed.), Handbook of human intelligence. Cambridge.

Berg, C. A., Meegan, S. P., & Deviney, F. P. (1998). A social contextual model of coping with everyday problems across the lifespan. *International Journal of Behavioral Development, 22*, 239–261.

Berg, C. A., Strough, J., Calderone, K. S., Sansone, C., & Weir, C. (1998). The role of problem definitions in understanding age and context effects on strategies for solving everyday problems. *Psychology and Aging, 13*, 29–44.

Berkow, R. (1992). *The Merck manual of diagnosis and therapy* (16th ed.). Rahway, NJ: Merck Research Laboratories.

Berlin, B., & Kay, P. (1969). *Basic color terms: Their universality and evolution*. Los Angeles: University of California Press.

Berliner, H. J. (1969, August). Chess playing program. *SICART Newsletter, 19*, 19–20.

Bernstein, A. (1958, July). A chess-playing program for the IBM704. *Chess Review*, 208–209.

Berry, J. W., Poortinga, Y. H., Segall, M. H., & Dasen, P. R. (1992). *Cross-cultural psychology: Research and applications*. New York: Cambridge University Press.

Bertoncini, J. (1993), Infants' perception of speech units: Primary representation capacities. In B. B. De Boysson-Bardies, S. De Schonen, P. Jusczyk, P. MacNeilage, & J. Morton (Eds.), *Developmental neurocognition: Speech and face processing in the first year of life*. Dordrecht: Kluwer.

Best, J. (2003). Memory mnemonics. In L. Nadel (Ed.), *Encyclopedia of cognitive science, Vol. 2*, pp. 1081-1084. London, England: Nature Publishing Group.

Bhatia, T. T., & Ritchie, W. C. (1999). The bilingual child: Some issues and perspectives. In W. C. Ritchie & T. K. Bhatia (Eds.), *Handbook of child language acquisition* (pp. 569–646). San Diego: Academic Press.

Bialystok, E., & Hakuta, K. (1994). *In other words: The science and psychology of second-language acquisition*. New York: Basic Books.

Bickerton, D. (1969). Prolegomena to a linguistic theory of metaphor. *Foundations of Language, 5*, 36–51.

Bickerton, D. (1990). *Language and species*. Chicago: University of Chicago Press.

Biederman, I. (1972). Perceiving real-world scenes. *Science, 177*(4043), 77–80.

Biederman, I. (1987). Recognition-by-components: A theory of human image understanding. *Psychological Review, 94*, 115–147.

Biederman, I. (1993a). Geon theory as an account of shape recognition in mind and brain. *Irish Journal of Psychology, 14*(3), 314–327.

Biederman, I. (1993b). Visual object recognition. In A. I. Goldman (Ed.), *Readings in philosophy and cognitive science* (pp. 9–21). Cambridge, MA: MIT Press. (Original work published 1990)

Biederman, I., Glass, A. L., & Stacy, E. W. (1973). Searching for objects in real-world scenes. *Journal of Experimental Psychology, 97*(1), 22–27.

Biederman, I., Rabinowitz, J. C., Glass, A. L., & Stacy, E. W. (1974). On the information extracted from a glance at a scene. *Journal of Experimental Psychology, 103*(3), 597–600.

Binet, A., & Simon, T. (1916). *The development of intelligence in children* (E. S. Kite, Trans.). Baltimore: Williams & Wilkins.

Birdsong, D. (1999). Introduction: Whys and why nots of the critical period hypothesis for second language acquisition. In D. Birdsong (Ed.), *Second language acquisition and the critical period hypothesis* (pp. 1–22). Mahwah, NJ: Erlbaum.

Bjorklund, D. F., Schneider, W., & Hernández Blasi, C. (2003). Memory. In L. Nadel (Ed.), *Encyclopedia of cognitive science, Vol. 2*, pp. 1059–1065. London, England: Nature Publishing Group.

Black, M. (1962). *Models and metaphors*. Ithaca, NY: Cornell University Press.

Blansjaar, B. A., Vielvoye, G. J., Van Dijk, J. Gert, & Rinders, R. J. (1992). Similar brain lesions in alcoholics and Korsakoff patients: MRI, psychometric and clinical findings. *Clinical Neurology & Neurosurgery, 94*(3), 197–203.

Blessing, S. B., & Ross, B. H. (1996). Content effects in problem categorization and problem solving. *Journal of Experimental Psychology: Learning, Memory, and Cognition, 22*, 792–810.

Block, N., Flanagan, O., & Güzeldere, G. (Eds.) (1997). *The nature of consciousness: Philosophical debates*. Cambridge, MA: MIT Press.

Bloom, B. S. (1964). *Stability and change in human characteristics*. New York: Wiley.

Bloom, B. S., & Broder, L. J. (1950). *Problem-solving processes of college students*. Chicago: University of Chicago Press.

Bloom, P. (2000). *How children learn the meanings of words*. Cambridge, MA: MIT Press.

Boas, F. (1911). *The mind of primitive man*. New York: Macmillan.

Bock, K. (1990). Structure in language: Creating form in talk. *American Psychologist, 45*(11), 1221–1236.

Bock, K., Loebell, H., & Morey, R. (1992). From conceptual roles to structural relations: Bridging the syntactic cleft. *Psychological Review, 99*(1), 150–171.

Boden, M. A. (1999). Computer models of creativity. In R. J. Sternberg (Ed.), *Handbook of creativity* (pp. 351–372). New York: Cambridge University Press.

Bohannon, J. (1988). Flashbulb memories for the space shuttle disaster: A tale of two theories. *Cognition, 29*(2), 179–196.

Borges, B., Goldstein, D. G., Ortmann, A. & Gigerenzer, G. (1999). Can ignorance beat the stock market? In Gigerenzer, G., Todd, P. M. & the ABC Research Group, *Simple heuristics that make us smart*. New York: Oxford University Press (59-72).

Boring, E. G. (1923, June 6). Intelligence as the tests test it. *New Republic*, 35–37.

Boring, E. G. (1942). *Sensation and perception in the history of experimental psychology*. New York: Appleton-Century-Crofts.

Borovsky, D., & Rovee-Collier, C. (1990). Contextual constraints on memory retrieval at six months. *Child Development, 61*(5), 1569–1583.

Bors, D. A., & Forrin, B. (1995). Age, speed of information processing, recall, and fluid intelligence. *Intelligence, 20*, 229–248.

Bors, D. A., MacLeod, C. M., & Forrin, B. (1993). Eliminating the IQ–RT correlation by eliminating an experimental confound. *Intelligence, 17*(4), 475–500.

Bothwell, R. K., Brigham, J. C., & Malpass, R. S. (1989). Cross-racial identification. *Personality & Social Psychology Bulletin, 15*(1), 19–25.

Bourguignon, E. (2000). Consciousness and unconsciousness: Cross-cultural experience. In A. E. Kazdin (Ed.), *Encyclopedia of psychology* (pp. 275–277). Washington, DC: American Psychological Association.

Bousfield, W. A. (1953). The occurrence of clustering in the recall of randomly arranged associates. *Journal of General Psychology, 49*, 229–240.

Bower, G. H. (1983). Affect and cognition. *Philosophical Transaction: Royal Society of London* (Series B), *302*, 387–402.

Bower, G. H., & Gilligan, S. G. (1979). Remembering information related to one's self. *Journal of Research in Personality, 13*, 420–432.

Bower, G. H., Black, J. B., & Turner, T. J. (1979). Scripts in memory for texts. *Cognitive Psychology, 11*, 177–220.

Bower, G. H., Clark, M. C., Lesgold, A. M., & Winzenz, D. (1969). Hierarchical retrieval schemes in recall of categorized word lists. *Journal of Verbal Learning and Verbal Behavior, 8*, 323–343.

Bower, G. H., Karlin, M. B., & Dueck, A. (1975). Comprehension and memory for pictures. *Memory & Cognition, 3*, 216–220.

Bowers, K. S., & Farvolden, P. (1996). Revisiting a century-old Freudian slip: From suggestion disavowed to the truth repressed. *Psychological Bulletin, 119*, 355–380.

Bowers, K. S., Regehr, G., Balthazard, C., & Parker, K. (1990). Intuition in the context of discovery. *Cognitive Psychology, 22*, 72–110.

Bradley, R. H., & Caldwell, B. M. (1984). 174 Children: A study of the relationship between home environment and cognitive development during the first 5 years. In A. W. Gottfried (Ed.), *Home environment and early cognitive development: Longitudinal research*. San Diego, CA: Academic Press.

Braine, M. D. S., & O'Brien, D. P. (1991). A theory of if: A lexical entry, reasoning program, and pragmatic principles. *Psychological Review, 98*(2), 182–203.

Braine, M. D. S., Reiser, B. J., & Rumain, B. (1984). Some empirical justification for a theory of natural propositional logic. In G. H. Bower (Ed.), *The psychology of learning and motivation* (Vol. 18). New York: Academic Press.

Bransford, J. D., & Johnson, M. K. (1972). Contextual prerequisites for understanding: Some investigations of comprehension and recall. *Journal of Verbal Learning and Verbal Behavior, 11*, 717–726.

Bransford, J. D., & Johnson, M. K. (1973). Considerations of some problems of comprehension. In W. G. Chase (Ed.), *Visual information processing* (pp. 383–438). New York: Academic Press.

Bransford, J. D., & Stein, B. S. (1993). *The ideal problem solver: A guide for improving thinking, learning, and creativity* (2nd ed.). New York: W. H. Freeman.

Braun, K.A., Ellis, R. & Loftus, E.F. (2002). Make My Memory: How Advertising Can Change Our Memories of the Past. *Psychology and Marketing, 19*, 1-23.

Braun-LaTour, LaTour, M.S., Pickrell, J., & Loftus, E.F. (2004-05). How and when advertising can influence memory for consumer experience. Journal of Advertising, 33, 7-25.

Bregman, A. S. (1990). *Auditory scene analysis: The perceptual organization of sound*. Cambridge, MA: MIT Press.

Bresnan, J. W. (Ed.). (1982). *The mental representation of grammatical relations*. Cambridge, MA: MIT Press.

Brewer, W. F. (1999). Schemata. In R. A. Wilson & F. C. Keil (Eds.), *The MIT encyclopedia of the cognitive sciences* (pp. 729–730). Cambridge, MA: MIT Press.

Brewer, W. F. (2003). Mental models. In L. Nadel (Ed.), *Encyclopedia of cognitive science* (Vol. 3, pp. 1–6). London, England: Nature Publishing Group.

Brian, C. R., & Goodenough, F. L. (1929). The relative potency of color and form perception at various ages. *Journal of Experimental Psychology, 12*, 197–213.

Briere, J., & Conte, J. R. (1993). Self-reported amnesia for abuse in adults molested as children. *Journal of Traumatic Stress, 6*, 21–31.

Brigden, R. (1933). A tachistoscopic study of the differentiation of perception. *Psychological Monographs, 44*, 153–166.

Brigham, J. C., & Malpass, R. S. (1985). The role of experience and contact in the recognition of faces of own and other-race persons. *Journal of Social Issues, 41*(3), 139–155.

Brislin, R. W., Lonner, W. J., & Thorndike, R. M. (Eds.) (1973). *Cross-cultural research methods*. New York: Wiley.

Broadbent, D. E. (1958). *Perception and communication*. Oxford, England: Pergamon.

Broadbent, D. E., & Gregory, M. (1965). Effects of noise and of signal rate upon vigilance analyzed by means of decision theory. *Human Factors, 7*, 155–162.

Brooks, L. R. (1968). Spatial and verbal components of the act of recall. *Canadian Journal of Psychology, 22*(5), 349–368.

Brown, A. L. (1978). Knowing when, where, and how to remember: A problem of metacognition. In R. Glaser (Ed.), *Advances in instructional psychology* (Vol. 1, pp. 77–165). Hillsdale, NJ: Erlbaum.

Brown, A. L., & DeLoache, J. S. (1978). Skills, plans, and self-regulation. In R. Siegler (Ed.), *Children's thinking: What develops?* (pp. 3–35). Hillsdale, NJ: Erlbaum.

Brown, A. L., Campione, J. C., Bray, N. W., & Wilcox, B. L. (1973). Keeping track of changing variables: Effects of rehearsal training and rehearsal prevention in normal and retarded adolescents. *Journal of Experimental Psychology, 101*, 123–131.

Brown, C. M., & Hagoort, P. (Eds.) (1999). *Neurocognition of language*. Oxford, England: Oxford University Press.

Brown, J. A. (1958). Some tests of the decay theory of immediate memory. *Quarterly Journal of Experimental Psychology, 10*, 12–21.

Brown, P., Keenan, J. M., & Potts, G. R. (1986). The self-reference effect with imagery encoding. *Journal of Personality & Social Psychology, 51*(5), 897–906.

Brown, R. (1965). *Social psychology*. New York: Free Press.

Brown, R. (1973). *A first language: The early stages*. Cambridge, MA: Harvard University Press.

Brown, R., & Kulik, J. (1977). Flashbulb memories. *Cognition, 5*, 73–99.

Brown, R., & McNeill, D. (1966). The "tip of the tongue" phenomenon. *Journal of Verbal Learning and Verbal Behavior, 5*, 325–337.

Brown, R., Cazden, C. B., & Bellugi, U. (1969). The child's grammar from 1 to 3. In J. P. Hill (Ed.), *Minnesota Symposium on Child Psychology* (Vol. 2). Minneapolis: University of Minnesota Press.

Brown, S. C., & Craik, F. I. M. (2000). Encoding and retrieval of information. In E. Tulving & F. I. M. Craik (Eds.), *The Oxford handbook of memory* (pp. 93–108). New York: Oxford University Press.

Bruce, D. (1991). Mechanistic and functional explanations of memory. *American Psychologist, 46*(1), 46–48.

Bruner, J. S. (1957). On perceptual readiness. *Psychological Review, 64*, 123–152.

Bruner, J. S., Goodnow, J. J., & Austin, G. A. (1956). *A study of thinking*. New York: Wiley.

Bryan, W. L., & Harter, N. (1899). Studies on the telegraphic language: The acquisition of a hierarchy of habits. *Psychological Review, 6*, 345–375.

Bryson, M., Bereiter, C., Scarmadalia, M., & Joram, E. (1991). Going beyond the problem as given: Problem solving in expert and novice writers. In R. J. Sternberg & P. A. Frensch (Eds.), *Complex problem solving: Principles and mechanisms* (pp. 61–84). Hillsdale, NJ: Erlbaum.

Buchanan, B. G., & Shortliffe, E. H. (1984). *Rule-based expert systems: The MYCIN experiments of the Stanford Heuristic Programming Project*. Reading, MA: Addison-Wesley.

Buchanan, B. G., Smith, D. H., White, W. C., Gritter, R., Feigenbaum, E. A., Lederberg, J., & Djerassi, C. (1976). Applications of artificial intelligence for chemical inference: XXII. Automatic rule formation in mass spectrometry by means of the meta-Dendral program. *Journal of the American Chemistry Society, 98*, 6168–6178.

Buckner, R. (2000a). Brain imaging techniques. In A. E. Kazdin (Ed.), *Encyclopedia of psychology* (Vol. 1, pp. 457–459). Washington, DC: American Psychological Association.

Buckner, R. L. (2000b). Neuroimaging of memory. In M. S. Gazzaniga (Ed.), *The new cognitive neurosciences* (2nd ed., pp. 817–828). Cambridge, MA: MIT Press.

Buckner, R. L., Bandettini, P. A., O'Craven, K. M., Savoy, R. L., Petersen, E., Raichle, M. E., et al. (1996). Detection of cortical activation during averaged single trials of a cognitive task using functional magnetic resonance imaging. *Proceedings of the National Academy of Sciences, 93*, 14878–14883.

Budwig, N. (1995). *A developmental-functionalist approach to child language*. Mahwah, NJ: Erlbaum.

Bundesen, C. (1996). Formal models of visual attention: A tutorial review. In A. F. Kramer, M. G. H. Coles, & G. D. Logan (Eds.), *Converging operations in the study of visual selective attention* (pp. 1–43). Washington, DC: American Psychological Association.

Bundesen, C. (2000). Attention: Models of attention. In A. E. Kazdin (Ed.), *Encyclopedia of psychology* (Vol. 1, pp. 295–299). Washington, DC: American Psychological Association.

Burgund, E. D., & Marsolek, C. J. (2000). Viewpoint-invariant and viewpoint-dependent object recognition in dissociable neural subsystems. *Psychonomic Bulletin & Review, 7*, 480–489.

Buschke, H., Kulansky, G., Katz, M., Stewart, W. F., Sliwinski, M. J., Eckholdt, H. M., et al. (1999). Screening for dementia with the Memory Impairment Screen. *Neurology, 52*, 231–238.

Butler, J., & Rovee-Collier, C. (1989). Contextual gating of memory retrieval. *Developmental Psychobiology, 22*, 533–552.

Butterfield, E. C., Wambold, C., & Belmont, J. M. (1973). On the theory and practice of improving short-term memory. *American Journal of Mental Deficiency, 77*, 654–669.

Butterworth, B., & Howard, D. (1987). Paragrammatisms. *Cognition, 26*(1), 1–37.

Byrne, R. M. J. (1996). A model theory of imaginary thinking. In J. Oakhill & A. Garnham (Eds.), *Mental models in cognitive science* (pp. 155–174). Hove, England: Taylor & Francis.

Cabeza, R., & Nyberg, L. (1997). Imaging cognition: An empirical review of PET studies with normal subjects. *Journal of Cognitive Neuroscience, 9*(1), 1–26.

Cahill, L., Babinsky, R., Markowitsch, H. J., & McGaugh, J. L. (1995). The amygdala and emotional memory. *Nature, 377*, 295–296.

Cahill, L., Haier, R. J., Fallon, J., Alkire, M. T., Tang, C., Keator, D., Wu, J., & McGaugh, J. L. (1996). Amygdala activity at encoding correlated with long-term, free recall of emotional information. *Proceedings of the National Academy of Sciences, 93*, 8016–8021.

Campbell, D. A. (1960). Blind variation and selective retention in creative thought as in other knowledge processes. *Psychological Review, 67*, 380–400.

Canli, T., Desmond, J. E., Zhao, Z., & Gabrieli, J. D. (2002). Sex differences in the neural basis of emotional memories. *Proceedings of the National Academies of Sciences, 99*, 10789–10794.

Cantor, J., & Engle, R. W. (1993). Working memory capacity as long-term memory activation: An individual differences approach. *Journal of Experimental Psychology: Learning, Memory, & Cognition, 19*(5), 1101–1114.

Cappa, S. F., Perani, D., Grassli, F., Bressi, S., Alberoni M., Franceschi M., et al. (1997). A PET follow-up study of recovery after stroke in acute aphasics. *Brain and Language, 56*, 55–67.

Carey, S. (1985). *Conceptual change in childhood*. Cambridge, MA: MIT Press.

Caramazza, A., & Shapiro, K. (2001). Language categories in the brain: evidence from aphasia. In L. Rizzi & A.Belletti (Eds.), *Structures and beyond*. Oxford, England: Oxford University Press.

Carey, S. (1994). Does learning a language require the child to reconceptualize the world? In L. Gleitman & B. Landau (Eds.), *The acquisition of the lexicon* (pp. 143–168). Cambridge, MA: Elsevier/MIT Press.

Carlson, E. R. (1995). Evaluating the credibility of sources: A missing link in the teaching of critical thinking. *Teaching of Psychology, 22*, 39–41.

Carlson, N. R. (1992). *Foundations of physiological psychology* (2nd ed.). Boston: Allyn & Bacon.

Carmichael, L., Hogan, H. P., & Walter, A. A. (1932). An experimental study of the effect of language on the reproduction of visually perceived form. *Journal of Experimental Psychology, 15*, 73–86.

Carpenter, M., Nagell, K., & Tomasello, M. (1998). Social cognition, joint attention, and communicative competence from 9 to 15 months of age. *Monographs of the Society for Research in Child Development, 63* (4, Serial No. 255).

Carpenter, P. A., & Just, M. A. (1981). Cognitive processes in reading: Models based on readers' eye fixations. In A. M. Lesgold & C. A. Perfetti (Eds.), *Interactive processes in reading* (pp. 177–213). Hillsdale, NJ: Erlbaum.

Carraher, T. N., Carraher, D., & Schliemann, A. D. (1985). Mathematics in the streets and in the schools. *British Journal of Developmental Psychology, 3*, 21–29.

Carroll, D. W. (1986). *Psychology of language*. Monterey, CA: Brooks/Cole.

Carroll, J. B. (1993). *Human cognitive abilities: A survey of factor-analytic studies*. New York: Cambridge University Press.

Carroll, J. B., & Casagrande, J. B. (1958). The function of language classification in behavior. In E. E. Maccoby, T. Newcomb, & E. L. Hartley (Eds.), *Readings in social psychology* (3rd ed., pp. 18–31). New York: Holt, Rinehart and Winston.

Caryl, P. G. (1994). Early event-related potentials correlate with inspection time and intelligence. *Intelligence, 18*(1), 15–46.

Castellucci, V. F., & Kandel, E. R. (1976). Presynaptic facilitation as a mechanism for behavioral sensitization in *Aplysia. Science, 194*, 1176–1178.

Cattell, J. M. (1886). The influence of the intensity of the stimulus on the length of the reaction time. *Brain, 9*, 512–514.

Cattell, R. B. (1971). *Abilities: Their structure, growth, and action*. Boston: Houghton Mifflin.

Cave, K. R., & Wolfe, J. M. (1990). Modeling the role of parallel processing in visual search. *Cognitive Psychology, 22*(2), 225–271.

Ceci, S. J. (1991). How much does schooling influence general intelligence and its cognitive components? A reassessment of the evidence. *Developmental Psychology, 27*(5), 703–722.

Ceci, S. J., & Bronfenbrenner, U. (1985). Don't forget to take the cupcakes out of the oven: Strategic time-monitoring, prospective memory and context. *Child Development, 56*, 175–190.

Ceci, S. J., & Bruck, M. (1993). Suggestibility of the child witness: A historical review and synthesis. *Psychological Bulletin, 113*(3), 403–439.

Ceci, S. J., & Bruck, M. (1995). *Jeopardy in the courtroom*. Washington, DC: American Psychological Association.

Ceci, S. J., & Loftus, E. F. (1994). "Memory work": A royal road to false memories? *Applied Cognitive Psychology, 8*, 351–364.

Ceci, S. J., & Roazzi, A. (1994). The effects of context on cognition: Postcards from Brazil. In R. J. Sternberg & R. K. Wagner (Eds.), *Mind in context: Interactionist perspectives on human intelligence* (pp. 74–101). New York: Cambridge University Press.

Ceci, S. J., Nightingale, N. N., & Baker, J. G. (1992). The ecologies of intelligence: Challenges to traditional views. In D. K. Detterman (Ed.), *Current topics in human intelligence: Vol. 2. Is mind modular or unitary?* (pp. 61–82). Norwood, NJ: Ablex.

Cerella, J. (1985). Information processing rates in the elderly. *Psychological Bulletin, 98*(1), 67–83.

Cerella, J. (1990). Aging and information-processing rate. In J. E. Birren & K. W. Schaie (Eds.), *Handbook of the psychology of aging* (3rd ed., pp. 201–221). San Diego, CA: Academic Press.

Cerella, J. (1991). Age effects may be global, not local: Comment on Fisk and Rogers (1991). *Journal of Experimental Psychology: General, 120*(2), 215–223.

Cerella, J., Rybash, J. M., Hoyer, W., & Commons, M. L. (1993). *Adult information processing: Limits on loss*. San Diego, CA: Academic Press.

Chalmers, D. J. (1995). The puzzle of conscious experience. *Scientific American, 273*, 80–86.

Chalmers, D. J. (1996). *The conscious mind: In search of a fundamental theory*. New York: Oxford University Press.

Chambers, D., & Reisberg, D. (1985). Can mental images be ambiguous? *Journal of Experimental Psychology: Human Perception & Performance, 11*(3), 317–328.

Chambers, D., & Reisberg, D. (1992). What an image depicts depends on what an image means. *Cognitive Psychology, 24*(2), 145–174.

Chapman, L. J., & Chapman, J. P. (1959). Atmosphere effect reexamined. *Journal of Experimental Psychology, 58*, 220–226.

Chapman, L. J., & Chapman, J. P. (1967). Genesis of popular but erroneous psychodiagnostic observations. *Journal of Abnormal Psychology, 72*(3), 193–204.

Chapman, L. J., & Chapman, J. P. (1969). Illusory correlation as an obstacle to the use of valid psychodiagnostic signs. *Journal of Abnormal Psychology, 74*, 271–280.

Chapman, L. J., & Chapman, J. P. (1975). The basis of illusory correlation. *Journal of Abnormal Psychology, 84*(5), 574–575.

Chase, W. G., & Simon, H. A. (1973). The mind's eye in chess. In W. G. Chase (Ed.), *Visual information processing* (pp. 215–281). New York: Academic Press.

Cheesman, J., & Merikle, P. M. (1984). Priming with and without awareness. *Perception & Psychophysics, 36*, 387–395.

Cheng, P. (1999). Causal reasoning. In R. A. Wilson & F. C. Keil (Eds.), *The MIT encyclopedia of the cognitive sciences* (pp. 106–108). Cambridge, MA: MIT Press.

Cheng, P., & Holyoak, K. (1995). Complex adaptive systems as intuitive statisticians: causality, contingency, and prediction. In H. L. Roitblat & J. A. Meyer (Eds.), *Comparative approaches to cognitive science* (pp. 271–302). Cambridge, MA: MIT Press.

Cheng, P. W. (1997). From covariation to causation: A causal power theory. *Psychological Review, 104*, 367–405.

Cheng, P. W., & Holyoak, K. J. (1985). Pragmatic reasoning schemas. *Cognitive Psychology, 17*, 391–416.

Cheng, P. W., Holyoak, K. J., Nisbett, R. E., & Oliver, L. M. (1986). Pragmatic versus syntactic approaches to training deductive reasoning. *Cognitive Psychology, 17*(3), 391–416.

Cherry, E. C. (1953). Some experiments on the recognition of speech with one and two ears. *Journal of the Acoustical Society of America, 25*, 975–979.

Chi, M. T. H., Bassok, M., Lewis, M., Reimann, P., & Glaser, R. (1989). Self-explanations: How students study and use examples in learning to solve problems. *Cognitive Science, 13,* 145–182.

Chi, M. T. H., Glaser, R., & Rees, E. (1982). Expertise in problem solving. In R. J. Sternberg (Ed.), *Advances in the psychology of expertise* (Vol. 1, pp. 7–76). Hillsdale, NJ: Erlbaum.

Chomsky, N. (1957). *Syntactic structures.* The Hague, Netherlands: Mouton.

Chomsky, N. (1959). [Review of the book *Verbal behavior*] *Language, 35,* 26–58.

Chomsky, N. (1965). *Aspects of the theory of syntax.* Cambridge, MA: MIT Press.

Chomsky, N. (1972). *Language and mind* (2nd ed.). New York: Harcourt Brace Jovanovich.

Chomsky, N. (1991, March). [Quoted in] *Discover, 12*(3), 20.

Ciarrochi, J., Forgas, J. P., & Mayer, J. D. (Eds.) (2001). *Emotional intelligence in everyday life: A scientific inquiry.* Philadelphia: Psychology Press.

Clark, A. (2003). Perception, philosophical issues about. In L. Nadel (Ed.), *Encyclopedia of cognitive science, Vol. 3,* pp. 512–517. London, England: Nature Publishing Group.

Clark, E. V. (1973). What's in a word? On the child's acquisition of semantics in his first language. In T. E. Moore (Ed.), *Cognitive development and the acquisition of language.* New York: Academic Press.

Clark, E. V. (1993). *The lexicon in acquisition.* Cambridge, England: Cambridge University Press.

Clark, E. V. (1995). Later lexical development and word formation. In P. Fletcher & B. MacWhinney (Eds.), *The handbook of child language* (pp. 393–412). Oxford, Blackwell.

Clark, H. H. (1969). Linguistic processes in deductive reasoning. *Psychological Review, 76,* 387–404.

Clark, H. H., & Brennan, S. E. (1991). Grounding in communication. In L. B. Resnick, J. M. Levine, & S. P. Tansley (Eds.), *Perspectives on socially shared cognition* (pp. 127–149). Washington, DC: American Psychological Association.

Clark, H. H., & Chase, W. G. (1972). On the process of comparing sentences against pictures. *Cognitive Psychology, 3,* 472–517.

Clark, H. H., & Clark, E. V. (1977). *Psychology and language: An introduction to psycholinguistics.* New York: Harcourt Brace Jovanovich.

Clark, H. H., & Lucy, P. (1975). Understanding what is meant from what is said: A study in conversationally conveyed requests. *Journal of Verbal Learning and Verbal Behavior, 14,* 56–72.

Clement, C. A., & Falmagne, R. J. (1986). Logical reasoning, world knowledge, and mental imagery: Interconnections in cognitive processes. *Memory & Cognition, 14*(4), 299–307.

Cohen, A. (2003). Selective attention. In L. Nadel (Ed.), *Encyclopedia of cognitive science, Vol. 3,* pp. 1033–1037. London, England: Nature Publishing Group.

Cohen, G. (1989). *Memory in the real world.* Hillsdale, NJ: Erlbaum.

Cohen, J. (1981). Can human irrationality be experimentally demonstrated? *Behavioral and Brain Sciences, 4,* 317–331.

Cohen, J. D., & Schooler, J. W. (Eds.) (1997). *Scientific approaches to consciousness.* Mahwah, NJ: Erlbaum.

Cohen, J. D., Forman, S. D., Braver, T. S., Casey, B. J., Servan-Schreiber, D., & Noll, D. C. (1994a). Activation of prefrontal cortex in a non-spatial working memory task with functional MRI. *Human Brain Mapping, 1,* 293–304.

Cohen, J. D., Romero, R. D., Servan-Schreiber, D., & Farah, M. J. (1994b). Mechanisms of spatial attention: The relation of macrostructure to microstructure in parietal neglect. *Journal of Cognitive Neuroscience, 6,* 377–387.

Cohen, M. S., Kosslyn, S. M., Breiter, et al. (1996). Changes in cortical activity during mental rotation: A mapping study using functional MRI. *Brain, 119,* 89–100.{AU: Please list first 6 authors}

Cohen, N. J., & Eichenbaum, H. (1993). *Memory, amnesia, and the hippocampal system.* Cambridge, MA: MIT Press.

Cohen, N. J., & Squire, L. (1980). Preserved learning and retention of pattern-analyzing skill in amnesia: Dissociation of knowing how and knowing that. *Science, 210*(4466), 207–210.

Cohen, N. J., Eichenbaum, H., Deacedo, B. S., & Corkin, S. (1985). Different memory systems underlying acquisition of procedural and declarative knowledge. *Annals of the New York Academy of Sciences, 444,* 54–71.

Cohen, N. J., McCloskey, M., & Wible, C. G. (1990). Flashbulb memories and underlying cognitive mechanisms: Reply to Pillemer. *Journal of Experimental Psychology: General, 119*(1), 97–100.

Colby, K. M. (1963). Computer simulation of a neurotic process. In S. S. Tomkins & S. Messick (Eds.), *Computer simulation of personality: Frontier of psychological research* (pp. 165–180). New York: Wiley.

Colby, K. M. (1995). A computer program using cognitive therapy to treat depressed patients. *Psychiatric Services, 46,* 1223–1225.

Cole, M., Gay, J., Glick, J., & Sharp, D. W. (1971). *The cultural context of learning and thinking.* New York: Basic Books.

Coleman, J. (2003). Phonology, computational. In L. Nadel (Ed.), *Encyclopedia of cognitive science* (Vol. 3, pp. 650-654). London, England: Nature Group Press.

Coley, J. D., Atran, S., & Medin, D. L. (1997). Does rank have its privilege? Inductive inferences within folk biological taxonomies. *Cognition, 64,* 73–112.

Coley, J. D., Medin, D. L., Proffitt, J. B., Lynch, E., & Atran, S. (1999). Inductive reasoning in folkbiological thought. In D. L. Medin & S. Atran (Eds.), *Folkbiology* (pp. 205–232). Cambridge, MA: MIT Press.

Collier, G. (1994). *Social origins of mental ability.* New York: Wiley.

Collins, A. M., & Loftus, E. F. (1975). A spreading-activation theory of semantic processing. *Psychological Review, 82,* 407–429.

Collins, A. M., & Quillian, M. R. (1969). Retrieval time from semantic memory. *Journal of Verbal Learning and Verbal Behavior, 8,* 240–248.

Collins, M. A., & Amabile, T. M. (1999). Motivation and creativity. In R. J. Sternberg (Ed.), *Handbook of creativity* (pp. 297–312). New York: Cambridge University Press.

Colonia-Willner, R. (1998). Practical intelligence at work: Relationship between aging and cognitive efficiency among managers in a bank environment. *Psychology and Aging, 13,* 45–57.

Coltheart, M. (2003). Dyslexia. In L. Nadel (Ed.), *Encyclopedia of cognitive science, Vol. 1,* pp. 1049–1052. London, England: Nature Publishing Group.

Conn, C., & Silverman, I., (Eds.). (1991). *What counts: The complete Harper's index.* New York: Henry Holt.

Connor, C. E., Gallant, J. L., Preddie, D. C., & Van Essen, D. C. (1996). Responses in area V4 depend on the spatial relationship between stimulus and attention. *Journal of Neurophysiology, 75,* 1306–1308.

Conrad, R. (1964). Acoustic confusions in immediate memory. *British Journal of Psychology, 55,* 75–84.

Conway, M. A. (1995). *Flashbulb memories.* Hove, England: Erlbaum.

Coon, H., Carey, G., & Fulker, D. W. (1992). Community influences on cognitive ability. *Intelligence, 16*(2), 169–188.

Cooper, E. H., & Pantle, A. J. (1967). The total-time hypothesis in verbal learning. *Psychological Bulletin, 68*, 221–234.

Corballis, M. C. (1989). Laterality and human evolution. *Psychological Review, 96*(3), 49–50.

Corballis, M. C. (1997). Mental rotation and the right hemisphere. *Brain and Language, 57*, 100–121.

Corbetta, M., Miezin, F. M., Shulman, G. L., & Petersen, S. E. (1993). A PET study of visuospatial attention. *Journal of Neuroscience, 13*(3), 1202–1226.

Corcoran, D. W. J. (1971). *Pattern recognition*. Harmondsworth: Penguin.

Coren, S., & Girgus, J. S. (1978). *Seeing is deceiving: The psychology of visual illusions*. Hillsdale, NJ: Erlbaum.

Cosmides, L. (1989). The logic of social exchange: Has natural selection shaped how humans reason? Studies with the Wason selection task. *Cognition, 31*, 187–276.

Cosmides, L., & Tooby, J. (1996). Are humans good intuitive statisticians after all? Rethinking some conclusions from the literature on judgment under uncertainty. *Cognition, 58*, 1–73.

Cowan, N. (1995). *Attention and memory: An integrated framework*. New York: Oxford University Press.

Cowan, N. (2001). The magical number 4 in short-term memory: A reconsideration of mental storage capacity. *Behavioral and Brain Sciences, 24*.

Cowan, N., Winkler, I., Teder, W., & Näätänen, R. (1993). Memory prerequisites of mismatch negativity in the auditory event-related potential (ERP). *Journal of Experimental Psychology: Learning, Memory, & Cognition, 19*(4), 909–921.

Craik, F. I. M., & Brown, S. C. (2000). Memory: Coding processes. In A. E. Kazdin (Ed.), *Encyclopedia of psychology* (Vol. 5, pp. 162–166). Washington, DC: American Psychological Association.

Craik, F. I. M., & Lockhart, R. S. (1972). Levels of processing: A framework for memory research. *Journal of Verbal Learning and Verbal Behavior, 11*, 671–684.

Craik, F. I. M., & Tulving, E. (1975). Depth of processing and the retention of words in episodic memory. *Journal of Experimental Psychology: General, 104*, 268–294.

Craik, K. (1943). *The nature of exploration*. Cambridge, England: Cambridge University Press.

Crowder, R. G. (1976). *Principles of learning and memory*. Hillsdale, NJ: Erlbaum.

Crowder, R. G., & Green, R. L. (2000). Serial learning: Cognition and behavior. In E. Tulving & F. I. M. Craik (Eds.), *The Oxford handbook of memory* (pp. 125–136). New York: Oxford University Press.

Crystal, D. (Ed.). (1987). *The Cambridge encyclopedia of language*. New York: Cambridge University Press.

Csikszentmihalyi, M. (1988). Society, culture, and person: A systems view of creativity. In R. J. Sternberg (Ed.), *The nature of creativity* (pp. 325–339). New York: Cambridge University Press.

Csikszentmihalyi, M. (1999). Creativity. In R. A. Wilson & F. C. Keil (Eds.), *The MIT encyclopedia of the cognitive sciences* (pp. 205–206). Cambridge, MA: MIT Press.

Csikszentmihalyi, M. (2000). Creativity: An overview. In A. E. Kazdin (Ed.), *Encyclopedia of psychology* (Vol. 2, p. 342). Washington, DC: American Psychological Association.

Culham, J. C. (2003). Parietal cortex. In L. Nadel (Ed.), *Encyclopedia of cognitive science, Vol. 3*, pp. 451–457. London, England: Nature Publishing Group.

Cummins, D. D. (2004). The evolution of reasoning. In J. P. Leighton & R. J. Sternberg (Eds.), *The nature of reasoning* (pp. 339–374). New York: Cambridge University Press.

Cummins, J. (1976). The influence of bilingualism on cognitive growth: A synthesis of research findings and explanatory hypothesis. *Working Papers on Bilingualism, 9*, 1–43.

Cutler, B. L., & Penrod, S. D. (1995). *Mistaken identification: The eyewitness, psychology, and the law*. New York: Cambridge University Press.

Cutting, J., & Kozlowski, L. (1977). Recognizing friends by their walk: Gait perception without familiarity cues. *Bulletin of the Psychonomic Society, 9*(5), 353–356.

Cziko, G. A. (1998). From blind to creative: In defense of Donald Campbell's selectionist theory of human creativity. *Journal of Creative Behavior, 32*, 192–208.

Damasio, A. R. (1985). Prosopagnosia. *Trends in Neurosciences, 8*, 132–135.

Daneman, M., & Carpenter, P. A. (1980). Individual differences in working memory and reading. *Journal of Verbal Learning and Verbal Behavior, 19*, 450–466.

Daneman, M., & Carpenter, P. A. (1983). Individual differences in integrating information between and within sentences. *Journal of Experimental Psychology: Learning, Memory, and Cognition, 9*, 561–583.

Daneman, M., & Tardif, T. (1987). Working memory and reading skill reexamined. In M. Coltheart (Ed.), *Attention and performance: Vol. 12. The psychology of reading* (pp. 491–508). Hove, England: Erlbaum.

Daniel, M. H. (1997). Intelligence testing: Status and trends. *American Psychologist, 52*, 1038–1045.

Daniel, M. H. (2000). Interpretation of intelligence test scores. In R. J. Sternberg (Ed.), *Handbook of intelligence* (pp. 477–491). New York: Cambridge University Press.

Davidson, J. E. (1995). The suddenness of insight. In R. J. Sternberg & J. E. Davidson (Eds.), *The nature of insight* (pp. 125–155). Cambridge, MA: MIT Press.

Davidson, J. E. (2003). Insights about insightful problem solving. In J. E. Davidson & R. J. Sternberg (Eds.), *The psychology of problem solving* (pp. 149–175). New York: Cambridge University Press.

Davidson, J. E., & Sternberg, R. J. (1984). The role of insight in intellectual giftedness. *Gifted Child Quarterly, 28*, 58–64.

Davidson, J. E., & Sternberg, R. J. (1985). Competence and performance in intellectual development. In E. Neimark, R. deLisi, & J. H. Newman (Eds.), *Moderators of competence* (pp. 43–76). Hillsdale, NJ: Erlbaum.

Davidson, J. E., & Sternberg, R. J. (Eds.). (2003). *The psychology of problem solving*. New York: Cambridge University Press.

Davidson, R. J., & Hugdahl, K. (Eds.) (1995). *Cerebral asymmetry*. Cambridge, MA: MIT Press.

Davies, M. (1999). Consciousness. In R. A. Wilson & F. C. Keil (Eds.), *The MIT encyclopedia of the cognitive sciences* (pp. 190–193). Cambridge, MA: MIT Press.

Davies, M., & Humphreys, G. W. (1993). *Consciousness: Psychological and philosophical essays*. Oxford: Blackwell.

Davies, M., Stankov, L., & Roberts, R. D. (1998). Emotional intelligence: In search of an elusive construct. *Journal of Personality & Social Psychology, 75*, 989–1015.

Dawes, R. (2000). Tversky, Amos. In A. Kazdin (Ed.), *Encyclopedia of psychology* (Vol. 8, pp. 127–128). Washington, DC: American Psychological Association.

Dawes, R. M., Mulford, M. (1996). The false consensus effect and overconfidence: Flaws in judgment or flaws in how we study judgment? *Organizational Behavior & Human Decision Processes, 65*(3), 201–211.

De Groot, A. D. (1965). *Thought and choice in chess.* The Hague, Netherlands: Mouton.

De Weerd, P. (2003a). Attention, neural basis of. In L. Nadel (Ed.), *Encyclopedia of cognitive science, Vol. 1,* pp. 238–246. London, England: Nature Publishing Group.

De Weerd, P. (2003b). Occipital cortex. In L. Nadel (Ed.), *Encyclopedia of cognitive science, Vol. 3,* pp. 408–414. London, England: Nature Publishing Group.

De Yoe, E. A., & Van Essen, D. C, (1988). Concurrent processing streams in monkey visual cortex. *Trends in Neurosciences, 11,* 219–226.

Deary, I. J. (2000a). *Looking down on human intelligence: from psychometrics to the brain.* Oxford: Oxford University Press.

Deary, I J. (2000b). Simple information processing and intelligence. In R. J. Sternberg (Ed.), *Handbook of intelligence* (pp. 267–284). New York: Cambridge University Press.

Deary, I. J., & Stough, C. (1996). Intelligence and inspection time: Achievements, prospects, and problems. *American Psychologist, 51,* 599–608.

DeCasper, A. J., & Fifer, W. P. (1980). Of human bonding: Newborns prefer their mothers' voices. *Science, 208,* 1174–1176.

Deese, J. (1959). On the prediction of occurrence of particular verbal intrusions in immediate recall. *Journal of Experimental Psychology, 58,* 17–22.

DeFries, J. C., Gillis, J. J. (1993). Genetics of reading disability. In R. Plomin and G. McClearn (Eds.), *Nature, nurture & psychology* (pp. 121–145). Washington, DC, US: American Psychological Association.

DeHouwer, A. (1995). Bilingual language acquisition. In P. Fletcher & B. MacWhinney (Eds.), *The handbook of child language* (pp. 219–250). Oxford: Blackwell.

Dell, G. S. (1986). A spreading-activation theory of retrieval in sentence production. *Psychological Review, 93*(3), 283–321.

Dempster, F. N. (1991). Inhibitory processes: A neglected dimension of intelligence. *Intelligence, 15*(2), 157–173.

Denny, N. W. (1980). Task demands and problem-solving strategies in middle-aged and older adults. *Journal of Gerontology, 35,* 559–564.

Desimone, R., & Duncan, J. (1995). Neural mechanisms of selective visual attention. *Annual Review of Neuroscience, 18,* 193–222.

DeSoto, C. B., London, M., & Handel, S. (1965). Social reasoning and spatial paralogic. *Journal of Personality and Social Psychology, 2,* 513–521.

Detterman, D. K., & Sternberg, R. J. (Eds.). (1982). *How and how much can intelligence be increased.* Norwood, NJ: Ablex.

Detterman, D. K., & Sternberg, R. J. (Eds.) (1993). *Transfer on trial: Intelligence, cognition, and instruction.* Norwood, NJ: Ablex.

Deutsch, J. A., & Deutsch, D. (1963). Attention: Some theoretical considerations. *Psychological Review, 70,* 80–90.

DeValois, R. L., & DeValois, K. K. (1980). Spatial vision. *Annual Review of Psychology, 31,* 309–341.

Di Eugenio, B. (2003). Discourse processing. In L. Nadel (Ed.), *Encyclopedia of cognitive science, Vol. 1,* pp. 976–983. London, England: Nature Publishing Group.

DiGirolamo, G. J., & Griffin, H. J. (2003). Consciousness and attention. In L. Nadel (Ed.), *Encyclopedia of cognitive science, Vol. 1,* pp. 711–717. London, England: Nature Publishing Group.

Ditchburn, R. W. (1980). The function of small saccades. *Vision Research, 20,* 271–272.

Dixon, R. A., & Baltes, P. B. (1986). Toward life-span research on the functions and pragmatics of intelligence. In R. J. Sternberg & R. K. Wagner (Eds.), *Practical intelligence: Nature and origins of competence in the everyday world* (pp. 203–235). New York: Cambridge University Press.

Dolan, M. (1995, February 11). When the mind's eye blinks. *Los Angeles Times,* pp. A1, A24, A25.

Dosher, B. A. (2003). Working memory. In L. Nadel (Ed.), *Encyclopedia of cognitive science, Vol. 4,* pp. 569–577. London, England: Nature Publishing Group.

Doyle, C. L. (2000). Psychology: Definition. In A. E. Kazdin (Ed.), *Encyclopedia of psychology* (Vol. 6, pp. 375–376). Washington, DC: American Psychological Association.

Dreyfus, H. L., & Dreyfus, S. E. (1990). Making a mind versus modelling the brain: Artificial intelligence back at a branch-point. In M. A. Boden (Ed.), *The philosophy of artificial intelligence: Oxford readings in philosophy* (pp. 309–333). Oxford, England: Oxford University Press.

Dror, I. E., & Kosslyn, S. M. (1994). Mental imagery and aging. *Psychology and Aging, 9*(1), 90–102.

Dunbar, K. (2003). Scientific thought. In L. Nadel (Ed.), *Encyclopedia of cognitive science, Vol. 3,* pp. 1006–1009. London, England: Nature Publishing Group.

Duncan, E., & Bourg, T. (1983). An examination of the effects of encoding and decision processes on the rate of mental rotation. *Journal of Mental Imagery, 7*(2), 3–55.

Duncan, J. (1996). Cooperating brain systems in selective perception and action. In T. Inui & J. L. McClelland (Eds.), *Attention and performance XVI* (pp. 549–578). Cambridge, MA: MIT Press.

Duncan, J. (1999). Attention. In R. A. Wilson & F. C. Keil (Eds.), *The MIT encyclopedia of the cognitive sciences* (pp. 39–41). Cambridge, MA: MIT Press.

Duncan, J., & Humphreys, G. (1989). Visual search and stimulus similarity. *Psychological Review, 96*(3), 433–458.

Duncan, J., & Humphreys, G. (1992). Beyond the search surface: Visual search and attentional engagement. *Journal of Experimental Psychology: Human Perception & Performance, 18*(2), 578–588.

Duncker, K. (1945). On problem-solving. *Psychological Monographs, 58*(5, Whole No. 270).

Dupuy, J. P. (1998). Rationality and self-deception. In J. P. Dupuy (Ed.), *Self-deception and paradoxes of rationality* (pp. 113–150). Stanford, CA: CSLI Publications.

Dupuy, J. P. (1999). Rational choice theory. In R. A. Wilson & F. C. Keil (Eds.), *The MIT encyclopedia of the cognitive sciences* (pp. 699–701). Cambridge, MA: MIT Press.

Dusek, J. A., & Eichenbaum, H. (1997). The hippocampus and memory for orderly stimulus relations. *Proceedings of the National Academy of Sciences, USA, 94,* 7109–7114.

Ebbinghaus, H. (1885). *Uber das Gedächtnis.* Leipzig, Germany: Duncker and Humblot.

Edelman, S., & Weinshall, D. (1991). A self-organizing multiple-view representation of 3D objects. *Biological Cybernetics, 64,* 209–219.

Edwards, W. (1954). The theory of decision making. *Psychological Bulletin, 51,* 380–417.

Egeth, H. (2000). Attention: An overview. In A. E. Kazdin (Ed.), *Encyclopedia of psychology* (Vol. 1, pp. 293–295). Washington, DC: American Psychological Association.

Egeth, H. E. (1993). What do we not know about eyewitness identification? *American Psychologist, 48*(5), 577–580.

Ehrlich, K. (1996). Applied mental models in human-computer interaction. In J. Oakhill & A. Garnham (Eds.), *Mental models in cognitive science* (pp. 313–339). Hillsdale, NJ: Erlbaum.

Eich, E. (1995). Searching for mood dependent memory. *Psychological Science, 6,* 67–75.

Eich, J. E. (1980). The cue-dependent nature of state-dependent retrieval. *Memory & Cognition, 8,* 157–158.

Eichenbaum, H. (1997). Declarative memory: Insights from cognitive neurobiology. *Annual Review of Psychology, 48,* 547–572.

Eichenbaum, H. (1999). Hippocampus. In R. A. Wilson & F. C. Keil (Eds.), *The MIT encyclopedia of the cognitive sciences* (pp. 377–378). Cambridge, MA: MIT Press.

Eimas, P. D. (1985). The perception of speech in early infancy. *Scientific American, 252,* 46–52.

Elman, J. L., Bates, E. A., Johnson, M. H., Karmiloff-Smith, A., Parisi, D., & Plunkett, K. (1996). *Rethinking innateness: A connectionist perspective on development.* Cambridge, MA: MIT Press.

Engel, A. S., Rumelhart, D. E., Wandell, B. A., Lee, A. T., Gover, G. H., Chichilisky, E. J., et al. (1994). MRI measurement of language lateralization in Wada-tested patients. *Brain, 118,* 1411–1419.

Engle, R. W. (1994). Individual differences in memory and their implications for learning. In R. J. Sternberg (Ed.), *Encyclopedia of intelligence* (pp. 700–704). New York: Macmillan.

Engle, R. W. (2001). What is working-memory capacity? In H. L. Roediger III & J. S. Nairne (Eds.), *The nature of remembering: Essays in honor of Robert G. Crowder* (pp. 297–314). Washington, DC: American Psychological Association.

Engle, R. W., & Kane, M. J. (2004). Executive attention, working memory capacity, and a two-factor theory of cognitive control. In B. Ross (Ed.). *The psychology of learning and motivation ,Vol. 44,* pp. 145–199. New York: Elsevier

Engle, R. W., Cantor, J., & Carullo, J. J. (1992). Individual differences in working memory and comprehension: A test of four hypotheses. *Journal of Experimental Psychology: Learning, Memory, & Cognition, 18*(5), 972–992.

Epstein, W., & Rogers, S. (Eds.), (1995). Handbook of perception and cognition (Vol. 5): Perception of space and motion. San Diego, CA: Academic Press.

Erdelyi, M., & Goldberg, B. (1979). Let's now sweep repression under the rug: Toward a cognitive psychology of repression. In J. F. Kihlstrom & F. J. Evans (Eds.), *Functional disorders of memory.* Hillsdale, NJ: Erlbaum.

Ericsson, K. A. (1999). Expertise. In R. A. Wilson & F. C. Keil (Eds.), *The MIT encyclopedia of the cognitive sciences* (pp. 298–300). Cambridge, MA: MIT Press.

Ericsson, K. A. (2003). The acquisition of expert performance as problem solving: Construction and modification of mediating mechanisms through deliberate practice. In J. E. Davidson & R. J. Sternberg (Eds.), *The psychology of problem solving* (pp. 31–83). New York: Cambridge University Press.

Ericsson, K. A. (Ed.). (1996). *The road to excellence.* Mahwah, NJ: Erlbaum.

Ericsson, K. A. & Lehmann, A. C. (1996). Expert and exceptional performance: evidence on maximal adaptations on task constraints. *Annual Review of Psychology, 47,* 273–305.

Ericsson, K. A., Chase, W. G., & Faloon, S. (1980). Acquisition of a memory skill. *Science, 208,* 1181–1182.

Ericsson, K. A., Krampe, R. T., & Tesch-Römer, C. (1993). The role of deliberate practice in the acquisition of expert performance. *Psychological Review, 100,* 363–406.

Estes, W. K. (1982). Learning, memory, and intelligence. In R. J. Sternberg (Ed.), *Handbook of intelligence* (pp. 170–224). New York: Cambridge University Press.

Estes, W. K. (1994). *Classification and cognition.* New York: Oxford University Press.

Evans, J. St. B. T., & Feeney, A. (2004). The role of prior belief in reasoning. In J. P. Leighton & R. J. Sternberg (Eds.), *The nature of reasoning* (pp.78–102). New York: Cambridge University Press.

Evans, J. St. B. T., & Over, D. E. (1996). Rationality in the selection task: Epistemic utility versus uncertainty reduction. *Psychological Review, 103,* 356–363.

Evans, J. St. B. T., Barston, J. I., & Pollard, P. (1983). On the conflict between logic and belief in syllogistic reasoning. *Memory and cognition, 11*(3), 295–306.

Evans, T. G. (1968). A program for the solution of geometric-analogy intelligence question. In M. L. Minsky (Ed.), *Semantic information processing* (pp. 271–353). Cambridge, MA: MIT Press.

Eysenck, H. J. (1967). Intelligence assessment: A theoretical and experimental approach. *British Journal of Educational Psychology, 37,* 81–98.

Eysenck, H. J., & Kamin, L. (1981). *The intelligence controversy: H. J. Eysenck vs. Leon Kamin.* New York: Wiley.

Eysenck, M., & Byrne, A. (1992). Anxiety and susceptibility to distraction. *Personality & Individual Differences, 13*(7), 793–798.

Eysenck, M., & Calvo, M. G. (1992). Anxiety and performance: The processing efficiency theory. *Cognition & Emotion, 6*(6), 409–434.

Eysenck, M., & Graydon, J. (1989). Susceptibility to distraction as a function of personality. *Personality & Individual Differences, 10*(6), 681–687.

Eysenck, M., & Keane, M. T. (1990). *Cognitive psychology: A student's handbook.* Hove, England: Erlbaum.

Fahle, M. (2003). Perceptual learning. In L. Nadel (Ed.), *Encyclopedia of cognitive science, Vol. 3,* pp. 548–552. London, England: Nature Publishing Group.

Farah, M. J. (1988a). Is visual imagery really visual? Overlooked evidence from neuropsychology. *Psychological Review, 95*(3), 307–317.

Farah, M. J. (1988b). The neuropsychology of mental imagery: Converging evidence from brain-damaged and normal subjects. In J. Stiles-Davis, M. Kritchevsky, & U. Bellugi (Eds.), *Spatial cognition: Brain bases and development* (pp. 33–56). Hillsdale, NJ: Erlbaum.

Farah, M. J. (1990). *Visual agnosia: Disorders of object recognition and what they tell us about normal vision.* Cambridge, MA: MIT Press.

Farah, M. J. (1992). Is an object an object an object? Cognitive and neuropsychological investigations of domain specificity in visual object recognition. *Current Directions in Psychological Science, 1,* 164–169.

Farah, M. J. (1994). Neuropsychological inference with an interactive brain: A critique of the "locality" assumption. *Behavioral and Brain Sciences, 17,* 43–104.

Farah, M. J. (1995). Dissociable systems for visual recogniiton: A cognitive neuropsycohlogy approach. In S. M. Kosslyn & D. N. Osherson (Eds.), *Visual cognition: An invitation to cognitive science, Vol. 2.* Cambridge, MA: MIT Press.

Farah, M. J. (1999). Object recognition, human neuropsychology. In R. A. Wilson & F. C. Keil (Eds.), *The MIT encyclopedia of the cognitive sciences* (pp. 615–618). Cambridge, MA: MIT Press.

Farah, M. J. (2000). The neural bases of mental imagery. In M. S. Gazzaniga (Ed.), *The new cognitive neurosciences* (2nd ed., pp. 965–974). Cambridge, MA: MIT Press.

Farah, M. J., & Ratcliff, G. (Eds.) (1994). *The neural bases of mental imagery*. Hillsdale, NJ: Erlbaum.

Farah, M. J., Hammond, K. M., Levine, D. N., & Calvanio, R. (1988a). Visual and spatial mental imagery: Dissociable systems of representation. *Cognitive Psychology, 20*(4), 439–462.

Farah, M. J., Levinson, K. L., & Klein, K. L. (1995). Face perception and within category discrimination in prosopagnosia. *Neuropsychologia, 33*, 661–674.

Farah, M. J., Peronnet, F., Gonon, M. A., & Giard, M. H. (1988b). Electrophysiological evidence for a shared representational medium for visual images and visual percepts. *Journal of Experimental Psychology: General, 117*(3), 248–257.

Farah, M. J., Wilson, K. D., Drain, H. M., & Tanaka, J. R. (1995). The inverted face inversion effect in prosopagnosia: Evidence for mandatory, face-specific, perceptual mechanisms. *Vision Research, 35*, 2089–2093.

Farah, M. J., Wilson, K. D., Drain, M., & Tanaka, J. (1998). What is "special" about face perception? *Psychological Review, 105*, 482–498.

Farthing, G. W. (1992). *The psychology of consciousness*. Englewood Cliffs, NJ: Prentice-Hall.

Farthing, G. W. (2000). Consciousness and unconsciousness: An overview. In A. E. Kazdin (Ed.), *Encyclopedia of psychology* (Vol. 2, pp. 268–272). Washington, DC: American Psychological Association.

Fawcett, J. W., Rosser, A. E., & Dunnett, S. B. (2001). *Brain damage, brain repair*. New York: Oxford University Press.

Feinberg, T. E., Schindler, R. J., Ochoa, E.; Kwan, P. C., et al. (1994). Associative visual agnosia and alexia without prosopagnosia. *Cortex, 30*(3), 395–412.

Feist, G. J. (1998). A meta-analysis of personality in scientific and artistic creativity. *Personality and Social Psychology Review, 2*, 290–309.

Feist, G. J. (1999). The influence of personality on artistic and scientific creativity. In R. J. Sternberg (Ed.), *Handbook of creativity* (pp. 273–296). New York: Cambridge University Press.

Feldman, J. A., & Shastri, L. (2003). Connectionism. In L. Nadel (Ed.), *Encyclopedia of cognitive science, Vol. 1*, pp. 680–687. London, England: Nature Publishing Group.

Fernald, A. (1985). Four-month-old infants prefer to listen to motherese. *Infant Behavior and Development, 8*, 118–195.

Fernald, A., Taeschner, T., Dunn, J., Papousek, M., De Boysson-Bardies, B., & Fukui, I. (1989). A cross-cultural study of prosodic modification in mothers' and fathers' speech to preverbal infants. *Journal of Child Language, 16*, 477–501.

Feuerstein, R. (1980). *Instrumental enrichment: An intervention program for cognitive modifiability*. Baltimore: University Park Press.

Fiedler, K. (1988). Emotional mood, cognitive style, and behavior regulation. In K. Fiedler & J. Forgas (Eds.), *Affect, cognition, and social behavior* (pp. 100–119). Toronto: Hogrefe International.

Field, T. (1978). Interaction behaviors of primary versus secondary caregiver fathers. *Developmental Psychology, 14*, 183–184.

Finke, R. A. (1989). *Principles of mental imagery*. Cambridge, MA: MIT Press.

Finke, R. A. (1995). Creative insight and preinventive forms. In R. J. Sternberg & J. E. Davidson (Eds.), *The nature of insight* (pp. 255–280). Cambridge, MA: MIT Press.

Finke, R. A., Pinker, S., & Farah, M. J. (1989). Reinterpreting visual patterns in mental imagery. *Cognitive Science, 13*(3), 252–257.

Fischhoff, B. (1982). For those condemned to study the past: Heuristics and biases in hindsight. In D. Kahneman, P. Slovic, & A. Tversky (Eds.), *Judgment under uncertainty: Heuristics and biases* (pp. 335–351). Cambridge, England: Cambridge University Press.

Fischhoff, B. (1988). Judgment and decision making. In R. J. Sternberg & E. E. Smith (Eds.), *The psychology of human thought* (pp. 153–187). New York: Cambridge University Press.

Fischhoff, B. (1999). Judgment heuristics. In R. A. Wilson & F. C. Keil (Eds.), *The MIT encyclopedia of the cognitive sciences* (pp. 423–425). Cambridge, MA: MIT Press.

Fischhoff, B., Slovic, P., & Lichtenstein, S. (1977). Knowing with certainty: The appropriateness of extreme confidence. *Journal of Experimental Psychology: Human Perception and Performance, 3*, 552–564.

Fischman, J. (2004, August 2). Vanishing minds: New research is helping Alzheimer's patients cope-and hope. *U.S. News & World Report, 137, 3*, 74–78.

Fisher, R. P., & Craik, F. I. (1977). Interaction between encoding and retrieval operations in cued recall. *Journal of Experimental Psychology: Human Learning & Memory, 3*(6), 701–711.

Fisher, R. P., & Craik, F. I. (1980). The effects of elaboration on recognition memory. *Memory & Cognition, 8*(5), 400–404.

Fisk, A. D., & Schneider, W. (1981). Control and automatic processing during tasks requiring sustained attention: A new approach to vigilance. *Human Factors, 23*, 737–750.

Fivush, R., & Hamond, N. R. (1991). Autobiographical memory across the preschool years: Toward reconceptualizing childhood memory. In R. Fivush & N. R. Hamond (Eds.), *Knowing and remembering in young children* (pp. 223–248). New York: Cambridge University Press.

Flavell, J. H., & Wellman, H. M. (1977). Metamemory. In R. V. Kail, Jr., & J. W. Hagen (Eds.), *Perspectives on the development of memory and cognition* (pp. 3–33). Hillsdale, NJ: Erlbaum.

Flavell, J. H., Flavell, E. R., & Green, F. L. (1983). Development of the appearance–reality distinction. *Cognitive Psychology, 15*, 95–120.

Flege, J. (1991). The interlingual identification of Spanish and English vowels: Orthographic evidence. *Quarterly Journal of Experimental Psychology: Human Experimental Psychology, 43*, 701–731.

Flynn, J. R. (1984). The mean IQ of Americans: massive gains 1932 to 1978. *Psychological Bulletin, 95*, 29–51.

Flynn, J. R. (1987). Massive IQ gains in fourteen nations: What IQ tests really measure. *Psychological Bulletin, 95*, 29–51.

Fodor, J. A. (1975). *The language of thought*. New York: Crowell.

Fodor, J. A. (1983). *The modularity of mind*. Cambridge, MA: MIT Press.

Fodor, J. A. (1994). Concepts-a pot-boiler. *Cognition, 50*, 95–113.

Fodor, J. A. (1997). Do we have it in us? (Review of Elman et al., *Rethinking innateness*). *Times Literary Supplement*, May 16, pp. 3–4.

Fodor, J., & Pylyshyn, Z. (1988). Connectionism and cognitive architecture: A critical analysis. *Cognition, 28*, 3–71.

Fogel, A. (1991). *Infancy: Infant, family, and society* (2nd ed.). St. Paul, MN: West.

Foulke, E., & Sticht, T. (1969). Review of research on the intelligibility and comprehension of accelerated speech. *Psychological Bulletin, 72*, 50–62.

Frackowiak, R. S. J., Friston, K. J., Frith, C. D., Dolan, R. J., & Mazziotta, J. C. (Eds.). (1997). *Human brain function*. San Diego, CA: Academic Press USA.

Franklin, N., & Tversky, B. (1990). Searching imagined environments. *Journal of Experimental Psychology: General, 119*(1), 63–76.

Franks, J. J., & Bransford, J. D. (1971). Abstraction of visual patterns. *Journal of Experimental Psychology, 90*(1), 65–74.

Frean, M. (2003). Connectionist architectures: Optimization. In L. Nadel (Ed.), *Encyclopedia of cognitive science, Vol. 1*, pp. 691–697. London, England: Nature Publishing Group.

Frensch, P. A., & Sternberg, R. J. (1989). Expertise and intelligent thinking: When is it worse to know better? In R. J. Sternberg (Ed.), *Advances in the psychology of human intelligence* (Vol. 5, pp. 157–188). Hillsdale, NJ: Erlbaum.

Freud, S. (1953). *An aphasia*. London: Imago.

Frisch, K. von. (1962). Dialects in the language of the bees. *Scientific American, 207*, 79–87.

Frisch, K. von. (1967). Honeybees: Do they use direction and distance information provided by their dances? *Science, 158*, 1072–1076.

Fromkin, V. A. (1973). *Speech errors as linguistic evidence*. The Hague, Netherlands: Mouton.

Fromkin, V. A., & Rodman, R. (1988). *An introduction to language* (4th ed.). Fort Worth, TX: Holt, Rinehart and Winston.

Frost, N. (1972). Encoding and retrieval in visual memory tasks. *Journal of Experimental Psychology, 95*, 317–326.

Funke, J. (1991). Solving complex problems: Exploration and control of complex social systems. In R. J. Sternberg & P. A. Frensch (Eds.), *Complex problem solving: Principles and mechanisms* (pp. 159–183). Hillsdale, NJ: Erlbaum.

Gabrieli, J. D. E., Desmond, J. E., Demb, J. B., Wagner, A. D., Stone, M. V., Vaidya, C. J., et al. (1996). Functional magnetic resonance imaging of semantic memory processes in the frontal lobes. *Psychological Science, 7*, 278–283.

Galaburda, A. M. (1999). Dyslexia. In R. A. Wilson & F. C. Keil (Eds.), *The MIT encyclopedia of the cognitive sciences* (pp. 249–251). Cambridge, MA: MIT Press.

Galaburda, A. M., & Rosen, G. D. (2003). Brain asymmetry. In L. Nadel (Ed.), *Encyclopedia of cognitive science, Vol. 1*, pp. 406–410. London, England: Nature Publishing Group.

Galotti, K. M., Baron, J., & Sabini, J. P. (1986). Individual differences in syllogistic reasoning: Deduction rules or mental models? *Journal of Experimental Psychology: General, 115*(1), 16–25.

Galton, F. (1883). *Inquiry into human faculty and its development*. London: Macmillan.

Ganel, T., & Goodale, M. A. (2003). Visual control of action but not perception requires analytical processing of object shape. *Nature, 426*, 664–667.

Ganellen, R. J., & Carver, C. S., (1985). Why does self-reference promote incidental encoding? *Journal of Experimental Social Psychology, 21*(3), 284–300.

Garcia-Madruga, J. A., Moreno, S., Carriedo, N., & Gutierrez, F. (2000). Task, premise order, and strategies in Rips's conjunction-disjunction and conditionals problems. In W. Schaeken & G. De Vooght (Eds.), *Deductive reasoning and strategies* (pp. 49–71). Mahwah, NJ: Erlbaum.

Gardner, H. (1983). *Frames of mind: The theory of multiple intelligences*. New York: Basic Books.

Gardner, H. (1985). *The mind's new science: A history of the cognitive revolution*. New York: Basic Books.

Gardner, H. (1993a). *Creating minds: An anatomy of creativity seen through the lives of Freud, Einstein, Picasso, Stravinsky, Eliot, Graham, and Gandhi*. New York: HarperCollins.

Gardner, H. (1993b). *Multiple intelligences: The theory in practice*. New York: Basic Books.

Gardner, H. (1999). *Intelligence reframed*. New York: Basic Books.

Gardner, H., Krechevsky, M. Sternberg, R. J. & Okagaki, L. (1994). Intelligence in context: Enhancing students' practical intelligence for school. In K. McGilly (Ed.), *Classroom lessons: Integrating cognitive theory and classroom practice* (pp. 105–127). Cambridge, MA: Bradford Books.

Garnham, A. (1987). *Mental models as representations of discourse and text*. Chichester, England: Ellis Horwood.

Garnham, A., & Oakhill, J. V. (1996). The mental models theory of language comprehension. In B. K. Britton & A. C. Graesser (Eds.), *Models of understanding text* (pp. 313–339). Hillsdale, NJ: Erlbaum.

Garrett, M. F. (1980). Levels of processing in sentence production. In B. Butterworth (Ed.), *Language production: Vol. 1. Speech and talk* (pp. 177–210). London: Academic Press.

Garrett, M. F. (1992). Disorders of lexical selection. *Cognition, 42*(1–3), 143–180.

Garrett, M. F. (2003). Language and brain. In L. Nadel (Ed.), *Encyclopedia of cognitive science, Vol. 2*, pp. 707–717. London, England: Nature Group Press.

Garrod, S., & Daneman, M. (2003). Reading, psychology of. In L. Nadel (Ed.), *Encyclopedia of cognitive science, Vol. 3*, pp. 848–854. London, England: Nature Publishing Group.

Garry, M., & Loftus, E. F. (1994). Pseudomemories without hypnosis. *International Journal of Clinical and Experimental Hypnosis, 42*, 363–378.

Garry, M., Manning, C. G., Loftus, E. F., & Sherman, S. J. (1996). Imagination inflation: Imaging a childhood event inflates confidence that it occurred. *Psychonomic Bulletin & Review, 3*, 208–214.

Gasser, M. (2003). Language learning, computational models of. In L. Nadel (Ed.), *Encyclopedia of cognitive science* (Vol. 2, pp. 747-753). London, England: Nature Group Press.

Gazzaniga, M. (1995a). Principles of human brain organization derived from split-brain studies. *Neuron, 14*, 217–228.

Gazzaniga, M. (Ed.) (2000). *The new cognitive neurosciences* (2nd ed.). Cambridge, MA: MIT Press.

Gazzaniga, M., Ivry, R. B., & Mangun, G. (1998). *Cognitive neuroscience: The biology of the mind*. New York: Norton.

Gazzaniga, M. S. (1985). *The social brain: Discovering the networks of the mind*. New York: Basic Books.

Gazzaniga, M. S. (Ed.). (1995b). *The cognitive neurosciences*. Cambridge, MA: MIT Press.

Gazzaniga, M. S., & Hutsler, J. J. (1999). Hemispheric specialization. In R. A. Wilson & F. C. Keil (Eds.), *The MIT encyclopedia of the cognitive sciences* (pp. 369–372). Cambridge, MA: MIT Press.

Gazzaniga, M. S., & LeDoux, J. E. (1978). *The integrated mind*. New York: Plenum.

Gazzaniga, M. S., & Sperry, R. W. (1967). Language after section of the cerebral commissures. *Brain, 90*(1), 131–148.

Gazzaniga, M. S., Ivry, R. B., & Mangun, G. R. (2002). *Cognitive neuroscience: The biology of the mind* (2nd ed.). New York: Norton.

Gelman, S. A. (1985). Children's inductive inferences from natural kind and artifact categories. (Doctoral dissertation, Stanford University, 1984). *Dissertation Abstracts International, 45*(10B), 3351–3352.

Gelman, S. A. (1989). Children's use of categories to guide biological inferences. *Human Development, 32*(2), 65–71.

Gelman, S. A. (2003). *The essential child: Origins of essentialism in everyday thought*. New York: Oxford University Press.

Gelman, S. A. (2004). Psychological essentialism in children. *Trends in Cognitive Sciences, 8*, 404–409.

Gelman, S. A., & Kremer, K. E. (1991). Understanding natural causes: Children's explanations of how objects and their properties originate. *Child Development, 62*(2), 396–414.

Gelman, S. A., & Markman, E. M. (1986). Categories and induction in young children. *Cognition, 23,* 183–209.

Gelman, S. A., & Markman, E. M. (1987). Young children's inductions from natural kinds: The role of categories and appearances. *Child Development, 58*(6), 1532–1541.

Gelman, S. A., & O'Reilly, A. W. (1988). Children's inductive inferences within superordinate categories: The role of language and category structure. *Child Development, 59*(4), 876–887.

Gelman, S. A., & Wellman, H. M. (1991). Insides and essence: Early understandings of the non-obvious. *Cognition, 38*(3), 213–244.

Gentile, J. R. (2000). Learning, transfer of. In A. E. Kazdin (Ed.), *Encyclopedia of psychology* (Vol. 5, pp. 13–16). Washington, DC: American Psychological Association.

Gentner, D. (1983). Structure-mapping: A theoretical framework for analogy. *Cognitive Science, 7,* 155–170.

Gentner, D. (2000). Analogy. In R. A. Wilson & F. C. Keil (Eds.), *The MIT encyclopedia of the cognitive sciences* (pp. 17–20). Cambridge, MA: MIT Press.

Gentner, D., & Gentner, D. R. (1983). Flowing waters or teeming crowds: Mental models of electricity. In D. Gentner & A. Stevens (Eds.), *Mental models*. Hillsdale, NJ: Erlbaum.

Gentner, D., & Markman, A. B. (1997). Structure-mapping in analogy and similarity. *American Psychologist, 52,* 45–56.

Georgopoulos, A. P., & Pellizzer, G. (1995). The mental and the neural: Psychological and neural studies of mental rotation and memory scanning. *Neuropsychologia, 33,* 1531–1547.

Georgopoulos, A. P., Lurito, J. T., Petrides, M., & Schwartz, A. B., Massey, J. T. (1989). Mental rotation of the neuronal population vector. *Science, 243*(4888), 234–236.

Gernsbacher, M. A., & Kaschak, M. P. (2003a). Language comprehension. In L. Nadel (Ed.), *Encyclopedia of cognitive science* (Vol. 2, pp. 723-726). London, England: Nature Group Press.

Gernsbacher, M. A., & Kaschak, M. P. (2003b). Psycholinguistics. In L. Nadel (Ed.), *Encyclopedia of cognitive science* (Vol. 3, pp. 783-786). London, England: Nature Group Press.

Gerrig, R. J., & Banaji, M. R. (1994). Language and thought. In R. J. Sternberg (Ed.), *Thinking and problem solving* (pp. 235–261). New York: Academic Press.

Gerrig, R. J., & Healy, A. F. (1983). Dual processes in metaphor understanding: Comprehension and appreciation. *Journal of Experimental Psychology: Learning, Memory, & Cognition, 9,* 667–675.

Geschwind, N. (1970). The organization of language and the brain. *Science, 170,* 940–944.

Gibbs, R. W. (1979). Contextual effects in understanding indirect requests. *Discourse Processes, 2,* 1–10.

Gibbs, R. W. (1986). What makes some indirect speech acts conventional? *Journal of Memory and Language, 25,* 181–196.

Gibson, E. J. (1991). The ecological approach: A foundation for environmental psychology. In R. M. Downs, L. S. Liben, & D. S. Palermo (Eds.), *Visions of aesthetics, the environment & development: The legacy of Joachim F. Wohlwill* (pp. 87–111). Hillsdale, NJ: Erlbaum.

Gibson, E. J. (1992). How to think about perceptual learning: Twenty-five years later. In H. L. Pick, Jr., P. W. van den Broek, & D. C. Knill (Eds.), *Cognition: Conceptual and methodological issues* (pp. 215–237). Washington, DC: American Psychological Association.

Gibson, J. J. (1950). *The perception of the visual world*. Boston: Houghton Mifflin.

Gibson, J. J. (1966). *The senses considered as perceptual systems*. New York: Houghton Mifflin.

Gibson, J. J. (1979). *The ecological approach to visual perception*. Boston: Houghton Mifflin.

Gibson, J. J. (1994). The visual perception of objective motion and subjective movement. *Psychological Review, 101*(2), 318–323. (Original work published 1954)

Gick, M. L., & Holyoak, K. J. (1980). Analogical problem solving. *Cognitive Psychology, 12,* 306–355.

Gick, M. L., & Holyoak, K. J. (1983). Schema induction and analogical transfer. *Cognitive Psychology, 15,* 1–38.

Gigerenzer, G. (1996). On narrow norms and vague heuristics: A reply to Kahneman and Tversky. *Psychological Review, 103,* 592–596.

Gigerenzer, G., & Goldstein, D. G. (1996). Reasoning the fast and frugal way: Models of bounded rationality. *Psychological Review, 103,* 650–669.

Gigerenzer, G., Todd, P. M., & the ABC Research Group (1999). *Simple heuristics that make us smart*. New York: Oxford University Press.

Gilger, J. W. (1996). How can behavioral genetic research help us understand language development and disorders? In M. L. Rice (Ed.), *Toward a genetics of language* (pp. 77–110). Mahwah, NJ: Erlbaum.

Gilhooly, K. J. (2004). Working memory and reasoning. In J. P. Leighton & R. J. Sternberg (Eds.), *The nature of reasoning* (pp.49–77). New York: Cambridge University Press.

Gilhooly, K. J., Logie, R. H., Wetherick, N. E., & Wynn, V. (1993). Working memory and strategies in syllogistic reasoning tasks. *Memory and Cognition, 21,* 115–124.

Gillam, B. (2000). Perceptual constancies. In A. E. Kazdin (Ed.), *Encyclopedia of psychology* (Vol. 6, pp. 89–93). Washington, DC: American Psychological Association.

Gilovich, T., Vallone, R., & Tversky, A. (1985). The hot hand in basketball: On the misperception of random sequences. *Cognitive Psychology, 17*(3), 295–314.

Girotto, V. (2004). Task understanding. In J. P. Leighton & R. J. Sternberg (Eds.), *The nature of reasoning* (pp.103–125). New York: Cambridge University Press.

Gladwin, T. (1970). *East is a big bird*. Cambridge, MA: Harvard University Press.

Glaser, R., & Chi, M. T. H. (1988). Overview. In M. T. H. Chi, R. Glaser, & M. Farr (Eds.), *The nature of expertise* (pp. xv–xxxvi). Hillsdale, NJ: Erlbaum.

Glenberg, A. M. (1977). Influences of retrieval processes on the spacing effect in free recall. *Journal of Experimental Psychology: Human Learning & Memory, 3*(3), 282–294.

Glenberg, A. M. (1979). Component-levels theory of the effects of spacing of repetitions on recall and recognition. *Memory & Cognition, 7*(2), 95–112.

Glenberg, A. M. (1997). What memory is for. *Behavioral and Brain Sciences, 20,* 1–55.

Glenberg, A. M., Meyer, M., & Lindem, K. (1987). Mental models contribute to foregrounding during text comprehension. *Journal of Memory & Language, 26*(1), 69–83.

Gloor, P. (1997). *The temporal lobe and limbic system*. New York: Oxford University Press.

Gluck, M. A. (Ed.) (1996). Computational models of hippocampal function in memory. Special issue of *Hippocampus, 6,* #6.

Glucksberg, S. (1988). Language and thought. In R. J. Sternberg & E. E. Smith (Eds.), *The psychology of human thought* (pp. 214–241). New York: Cambridge University Press.

Glucksberg, S., & Danks, J. H. (1975). *Experimental psycholinguistics.* Hillsdale, NJ: Erlbaum.

Glucksberg, S., & Keysar, B. (1990). Understanding metaphorical comparisons: Beyond similarity. *Psychological Review, 97*(1), 3–18.

Gobet, F., & Simon, H. A. (1996a). Recall of random and distorted chess positions: Implications for the theory of expertise. *Memory and Cognition, 24,* 493–503.

Gobet, F., & Simon, H. A. (1996b). Roles of recognition processes and look-ahead search in time-constrained expert problem solving: Evidence from grand-master-level chess. *Psychological Science, 7,* 52–55.

Gobet, F., & Simon, H. A. (1996c). Templates in chess memory: A mechanism for recalling several boards. *Cognitive Psychology, 31,* 1–40.

Goddard, H. H. (1917). Mental tests and immigrants. *Journal of Delinquency, 2,* 243–277.

Godden, D. R., & Baddeley, A. D. (1975). Context-dependent memory in two natural environments: On land and underwater. *British Journal of Psychology, 66,* 325–331.

Goff, L. M., & Roediger, H. L. (1998). Imagination inflation for action events: Repeated imaginings lead to illusory recollections. *Memory and Cognition, 26,* 20–33.

Goldstein, D. G. & Gigerenzer, G. (2002). Models of ecological rationality: The recognition heuristic. *Psychological Review, 109*(1), 75–90.

Goldstone, R. L. (2003). Perceptual organizatoin in vision: Behavioral and neural perspectives. In R. Kimchi & M. Behrmann (Eds.), *Perceptual organization in vision: Behavioral and neural perspectives* (pp. 233-280). Mahwah, NJ: Erlbaum.

Goleman, D. (1995). *Emotional intelligence.* New York: Bantam.

Goleman, D. (1998). *Working with emotional intelligence.* New York: Bantam.

Goodale, M. A. (2000a). Perception and action. In A. E. Kazdin (Ed.), *Encyclopedia of psychology* (Vol. 6, pp. 86–89). Washington, DC: American Psychological Association.

Goodale, M. A. (2000b). Perception and action in the human visual system. In M. Gazzaniga (Ed.), *The new cognitive neurosciences* (pp. 365–378). Cambridge, MA: MIT Press.

Goodman, N. (1983). *Fact, fiction, and forecast* (4th ed). Cambridge, MA: Harvard University Press.

Gopnik, A., & Choi, S. (1995). Names, relational words, and cognitive development in English and Korean speakers: Nouns are not always learned before verbs. In M. Tomasello & W. E. Merriman (Eds.), *Beyond names for things: Young children's acquisition of verbs* (pp. 83–90). Hillsdale, NJ: Erlbaum.

Gopnik, A., Choi, S., & Baumberger, T. (1996). Cross-linguistic differences in early semantic and cognitive development. *Cognitive Development, 11,* 197–227.

Gordon, D., & Lakoff, G. (1971). Conversational postulates. In *Papers from the Seventh Regional Meeting, Chicago Linguistic Society* (pp. 63–84). Chicago: Chicago Linguistic Society.

Graesser, A. C., & Kreuz, R. J. (1993). A theory of inference generation during text comprehension. *Discourse Processes, 16,* 145–160.

Graf, P. (1990). Life-span changes in implicit and explicit memory. *Bulletin of the Psychonomic Society, 28,* 353–358.

Graf, P., Mandler, G., & Haden, P. E. (1982). Simulating amnesic symptoms in normal subjects. *Science, 218*(4578), 1243–1255.

Grant, E. R., & Ceci, S. J. (2000). Memory: Constructive processes. In A. E. Kazdin (Ed.), *Encyclopedia of psychology* (Vol. 5, pp. 166–169). Washington, DC: American Psychological Association.

Gray, J. A., & Wedderburn, A. A. I. (1960). Grouping strategies with simultaneous stimuli. *Quarterly Journal of Experimental Psychology, 12,* 180–184.

Greenberg, R., & Underwood, B. J. (1950). Retention as a function of stage of practice. *Journal of Experimental Psychology, 40,* 452–457.

Greenfield, P. M. (1997). You can't take it with you: Why abilities assessments don't cross cultures. *American Psychologist, 52,* 1115–1124.

Greenfield, P. M., & Savage-Rumbaugh, S. (1990). Grammatical combination in Pan paniscus: Processes of learning and invention in the evolution and development of language. In S. Parker & K. Gibson (Eds.), *"Language" and intelligence in monkeys and apes: Comparative developmental perspectives.* New York: Cambridge University Press.

Greeno, J. G. (1974). Hobbits and orcs: Acquisition of a sequential concept. *Cognitive Psychology, 6,* 270–292.

Greeno, J. G., & Simon, H. A. (1988). Problem solving and reasoning. In R. C. Atkinson, R. Herrnstein, G. Lindzey, & R. D. Luce (Eds.), *Stevens' handbook of experimental psychology* (Rev. ed., pp. 589–672). New York: Wiley.

Greenwald, A. G., & Banaji, M. (1989). The self as a memory system: Powerful, but ordinary. *Journal of Personality & Social Psychology, 57*(1), 41–54.

Gregory, R. L. (1980). Perceptions as hypotheses. *Philosophical Transactions of the Royal Society of London, Series B, 290,* 181–197.

Grice, H. P. (1967). William James Lectures, Harvard University, published in part as "Logic and conversation." In P. Cole & J. L. Morgan (Eds.), *Syntax and semantics: Vol. 3. Speech acts* (pp. 41–58). New York: Seminar Press.

Griffin, D., & Tversky, A. (1992). The weighing of evidence and the determinants of confidence. *Cognitive Psychology, 24,* 411–435.

Griggs, R. A., & Cox, J. R. (1982). The elusive thematic-materials effect in Wason's selection task. *British Journal of Psychology, 73,* 407–420.

Griggs, R. A., & Cox, J. R. (1993). Permission schemas and the selection task. *The Quarterly Journal of Experimental Psychology, 46A*(4), 637–651.

Grigorenko, E. L. (2000). Heritability and intelligence. In R. J. Sternberg (Ed.), *Handbook of intelligence* (pp. 53–91). New York: Cambridge University Press.

Grigorenko, E. L., Geissler, P. W., Prince, R., Okatcha, F., Nokes, C., Kenny, D. A., et al. (2001). The organization of Luo conceptions of intelligence: A study of implicit theories in a Kenyan village. *International Journal of Behavioral Development, 25,* 367–378.

Grigorenko, E. L., Jarvin, L., & Sternberg, R. J. (2002). School-based tests of the triarchic theory of intelligence: Three settings, three samples, three syllabi. *Contemporary Educational Psychology, 27,* 167–208.

Grodzinsky, Y. (2003). Language disorders. In L. Nadel (Ed.), *Encyclopedia of cognitive science, Vol. 2,* pp. 740–746. London, England: Nature Group Press.

Grossman, L., & Eagle, M. (1970). Synonymity, antonymity, and association in false recognition responses. *Journal of Experimental Psychology, 83,* 244–248.

Grosz, B. J., Pollack, M. E., & Sidner, C. L. (1989). Discourse. In M. I. Posner (Ed.), *Foundations of cognitive science* (pp. 437–468). Cambridge, MA: MIT Press.

Grotzer, T. A., & Perkins, D. N. (2000). Teaching intelligence: A performance conception. In R. J. Sternberg (Ed.), *Handbook of intelligence* (pp. 492–515). New York: Cambridge University Press.

Gruber, H. E. (1981). *Darwin on man: A psychological study of scientific creativity* (2nd ed.). Chicago: University of Chicago Press. (Original work published 1974)

Gruber, H. E., & Davis, S. N. (1988). Inching our way up Mount Olympus: The evolving-systems approach to creative thinking. In R. J. Sternberg (Ed.), *The nature of creativity* (pp. 243–270). New York: Cambridge University Press.

Guilford, J. P. (1950). Creativity. *American Psychologist, 5*(9), 444–454.

Guilford, J. P. (1967). *The nature of human intelligence.* New York: McGraw Hill.

Guilford, J. P. (1982). Cognitive psychology's ambiguities: Some suggested remedies. *Psychological Review, 89,* 48–59.

Guilford, J. P. (1988). Some dangers in the structure-of-intellect model. *Educational & Psychological Measurement, 48,* 1–4.

Haber, R. N. (1983). The impending demise of the icon: A critique of the concept of iconic storage in visual information processing. *Behavioral and Brain Sciences, 6*(1), 1–54.

Haier, R. J., Chueh, D., Touchette, P., Lott, I., Buchbaum, M. S., MacMillan, D., et al. (1995). Brain size and cerebral glucose metabolic rate in nonspecific mental retardation and Down syndrome. *Intelligence, 20,* 191–210.

Haier, R. J., Siegel, B., Tang, C., Abel, L., & Buchsbaum, M. S. (1992). Intelligence and changes in regional cerebral glucose metabolic rate following learning. *Intelligence, 16*(3–4), 415–426.

Hakuta, K. (1986). *Mirror of language.* New York: Basic Books.

Halford, G. S. (1993). *Children's understanding: The development of mental models.* Hillsdale, NJ: Erlbaum.

Hall, E. T. (1966). *The hidden dimension.* New York: Doubleday.

Halpin, J. A., Puff, C. R., Mason, H. F., & Marston, S. P. (1984). Self-reference and incidental recall by children. *Bulletin of the Psychonomic Society, 22,* 87–89.

Hambrick, D. Z., & Engle, R. W. (2002). Effects of domain knowledge, working memory capacity, and age on cognitive performance: An investigation of the knowledge-is-power hypothesis. *Cognitive Psychology, 44,* 339–387.

Hambrick, D. Z., & Engle, R. W. (2003). The role of working memory in problem solving. In J. E. Davidson & R. J. Sternberg (Eds.), *The psychology of problem solving* (pp. 176–206). New York: Cambridge University Press.

Hambrick D. Z., Kane, M. J., & Engle, R. W. (2005). The role of working memory in higher-level cognition. In R. J. Sternberg & J. E. Pretz (Eds.), *Cognition and intelligence* (pp. 104–121). New York: Cambridge University Press.

Hamilton, D. L., & Lickel, B. (2000). Illusory correlation. In A. E. Kazdin (Ed.), *Encyclopedia of psychology* (Vol. 4, pp. 226–227). Washington, DC: American Psychological Association.

Hampson, P. J., Marks, D. F., & Richardson, J. T. E. (1990). *Imagery: Current developments.* London: Routledge.

Hampton, J. A. (1995). Testing the prototype theory of concepts. *Journal of Memory and Language, 32,* 68–708.

Hampton, J. A. (1997a). Emergent attributes of combined concepts. In T. B. Ward, S. M. Smith, & J. Vaid (Eds.), *Conceptual structures and processes: Emergence, discovery, and change* (pp. 83–110). Washington, DC: American Psychological Association.

Hampton, J. A. (1997b). Psychological representations of concepts. In M. A. Conway & S. E. Gathercole (Eds.), *Cognitive models of memory* (pp. 81–110). Hove, England: Psychology Press.

Hampton, J. A. (1999). Concepts. In R. A. Wilson & F. C. Keil (Eds.), *The MIT encyclopedia of the cognitive sciences* (pp. 177–179). Cambridge, MA: MIT Press.

Harnish, R. M. (2003). Speech acts. In L. Nadel (Ed.), *Encyclopedia of cognitive science, Vol. 4,* pp. 150–156. London, England: Nature Publishing Group.

Harris, C. L. (2003). Language and cognition. In L. Nadel (Ed.), *Encyclopedia of cognitive science, Vol. 2,* pp. 717–722. London, England: Nature Group Press.

Haviland, S. E., & Clark, H. H. (1974). What's new? Acquiring new information as a process in comprehension. *Journal of Verbal Learning and Verbal Behavior, 13,* 512–521.

Haxby, J., Horwitz, B., Ungerleider, L. G., Maisog, J., Pietrini, P., & Grady, C. (1994). The functional organization of human extrastriate cortex: a PET-rCBF study of selective attention to faces and locations. *Journal of Neuroscience, 14,* 6336–6353.

Haxby, J. V., Ungerleider, L. G., Horwitz, B., Maisog, J. M., Rappaport, S. L., & Grady, C. L. (1996). Face encoding and recognition in the human brain. *Proceedings of he National Academy of Sciences USA, 98,* 922–927.

Haxby, J. V., Ungerleider, L. G., Horwitz, B., Rapoport, S., & Grady, C. L. (1995). Hemispheric differences in neural systems for face working memory: A PET-rCBF study. *Human Brain Mapping, 3,* 68–82.

Hayes, J. R. (1989). *The complete problem solver* (2nd ed.). Hillsdale, NJ: Erlbaum.

He, Z., & Nakayama, K. (1992). Apparent motion determined by surface layout not by disparity or three-dimensional distance. *Nature, 367*(6459), 173–175.

Head injuries. (http://kidshealth.org/parent/firstaid_safe/emergencies/head_injury.html, retrieved 12/29/04).

Heaps, C., & Nash, M. (1999). Individual differences in imagination inflation. *Psychonomic Bulletin & Review, 6,* 313–318.

Heaton, J. M. (1968). *The eye: Phenomenology and psychology of function and disorder.* London: Tavistock.

Hebb, D. O. (1949). *The organization of behavior: A neuropsychological theory.* New York: Wiley.

Hegarty, M. (1991). Knowledge and processes in mechanical problem solving. In R. J. Sternberg & P. A. Frensch (Eds.), *Complex problem solving: Principles and mechanisms* (pp. 159–183). Hillsdale, NJ: Erlbaum.

Heindel, W. C., Butters, N., & Salmon, D. P. (1988). Impaired learning of a motor skill in patients with Huntington's disease. *Behavioral Neuroscience, 102*(1), 141–147.

Hellige, J. B. (1993). *Hemispheric asymmetry.* Cambridge, MA: Harvard University Press.

Hellige, J. B. (1995). Hemispheric asymmetry for components of visual information processing. In R. J. Davidson & K. Hugdahl (Eds.), *Brain asymmetry.* Cambridge, MA: MIT Press.

Helmholtz, H. L. F. von. (1962). *Treatise on physiological optics* (3rd ed., J. P. C. Southall, Ed. and Trans.). New York: Dover. (Original work published 1909)

Helmholtz, H. von. (1896). *Vorträge und Reden.* Braunschweig, Germany: Vieweg und Sohn.

Helms-Lorenz, M., Van de Vijver, F. J. R., & Poortinga, Y. H. (2003). Cross-cultural differences in cognitive performance and Spearman's hypothesis: g or c? *Intelligence, 31,* 9–29.

Henley, N. M. (1969). A psychological study of the semantics of animal terms. *Journal of Verbal Learning and Verbal Behavior, 8,* 176–184.

Hennessey, B. A., & Amabile, T. M. (1988). The conditions of creativity. In R. J. Sternberg (Ed.), *The nature of creativity* (pp. 11–38). New York: Cambridge University Press.

Herrnstein, R., & Murray, C. (1994). *The bell curve: Intelligence and class structure in American life.* New York: Free Press.

Hertzog, C., Vernon, M. C., & Rypma, B. (1993). Age differences in mental rotation task performance: The influence of speed/accuracy tradeoffs. *Journal of Gerontology, 48*(3), 150–156.

Herz, R. S., & Engen, T. (1996). Odor memory: Review and analysis. *Psychonomic Bulletin and Review, 3*, 300–313.

Hesse, M. (1966). *Models and analogies in science*. South Bend, IN: University of Notre Dame Press.

Hickling, A. K., & Gelman, S. A. (1995). How does your garden grow? Early conceptualization of seeds and their place in the plant growth cycle. *Child Development, 66*, 856–867.

Hickok, G., & Poeppel, D. (2000). Towards a functional neuroanatomy of speech perception. *Trends in Cognitive Sciences, 4*, 131–138.

Hillis, A. E., & Caramazza, A. (2003). Aphasia. In L. Nadel (Ed.), *Encyclopedia of cognitive science, Vol. 1*, pp. 175–184. London, England: Nature Publishing Group.

Hinton, G. E. (1979). Some demonstrations of the effects of structural descriptions in mental imagery. *Cognitive Science, 3*, 231–251.

Hinton, G. E. (Ed.) (1991). *Connectionist symbol processing*. Cambridge, MA: MIT Press.

Hinton, G. E., & Shallice, T. (1991). Lesioning an attractor network: Investigations of acquired dyslexia. *Psychological Review, 98*, 74–95.

Hintzman, D. L. (1978). *The psychology of learning and memory*. San Francisco: Freeman.

Hirsh-Pasek, K., Kemler Nelson, D. G., Jusczyk, P. W., Cassidy, K. W., Druss, B., & Kennedy, L. (1987). Clauses are perceptual units for young infants. *Cognition, 26*, 269–286.

Hirst, W., Spelke, E., Reaves, C. C., Caharack, G., & Neisser, U. (1980). Dividing attention without alternation or automaticity. *Journal of Experimental Psychology: General, 109*, 98–117.

Hirtle, S. C., & Jonides, J. (1985). Evidence of hierarchies in cognitive maps. *Memory & Cognition, 13*(3), 208–217.

Hirtle, S. C., & Mascolo, M. F. (1986). Effect of semantic clustering on the memory of spatial locations. *Journal of Experimental Psychology: Learning, Memory, & Cognition, 12*(2), 182–189.

Hochberg, J. (1978). *Perception* (2nd ed.). Englewood Cliffs, NJ: Prentice-Hall.

Hoff, E., & Naigles, L. (1999). *Fast mapping is only the beginning: Complete word learning requires multiple exposures*. Paper presented at the VIIIth International Congress for the Study of Child Language. July 12–16. San Sebastian, Spain.

Hoffding, H. (1891). *Outlines of psychology*. New York: Macmillan.

Hoffman, C., Lau, I., & Johnson, D. R. (1986). The linguistic relativity of person cognition: An English–Chinese comparison. *Journal of Personality and Social Psychology, 51*, 1097–1105.

Holland, J. H., Holyoak, K. J., Nisbett, R. E., & Thagard, P. R. (1986). *Induction processes of inference, learning, and discovery*. Cambridge, MA: MIT Press.

Holmes, D. (1991). The evidence for repression: an examination of sixty years of research. In J. L. Singer (Ed.), *Repression and dissociation: Implications for personality theory, psychopathology and health* (pp. 85–102). Chicago: University of Chicago Press.

Holt, J. (1964). *How children fail*. New York: Pitman.

Holyoak, K. J. (1984). Analogical thinking and human intelligence. In R. J. Sternberg (Ed.), *Advances in the psychology of human intelligence* (Vol. 2, pp. 199–230). Hillsdale, NJ: Erlbaum.

Holyoak, K. J. (1990). Problem solving. In D. N. Osherson & E. E. Smith (Eds.), *An invitation to cognitive science: Vol. 3. Thinking* (pp. 116–146). Cambridge, MA: MIT Press.

Holyoak, K. J., & Nisbett, R. E. (1988). Induction. In R. J. Sternberg & E. E. Smith (Eds.), *The psychology of human thought* (pp. 50–91). New York: Cambridge University Press.

Holyoak, K. J., & Thagard, P. (1995). *Mental leaps*. Cambridge, MA: MIT Press.

Homa, D. (1983). An assessment of two extraordinary speed-readers. *Bulletin of the Psychonomic Society, 21*, 115–118.

Horn, J. L., & Cattell, R. B. (1966). Refinement and test of the theory of fluid and crystallized ability intelligences. *Journal of Educational Psychology, 57*, 253–270.

Horn, J. L., & Hofer, S. M. (1992). Major abilities and development in the adult period. In R. J. Sternberg & C. A. Berg (Eds.), *Intellectual development* (pp. 44–99). New York: Cambridge University Press.

Horn, J. L., & Knapp, J. R. (1973). On the subjective character of the empirical base of Guilford's structure-of-intellect model. *Psychological Bulletin, 80*, 33–43.

Hubbard, T. L. (1995). Environmental invariants in the representation of motion: Implied and representational momentum, gravity, friction, and centripetal force. *Psychonomic Bulletin and Review, 2*, 322–338.

Hubel, D., & Wiesel, T. (1963). Receptive fields of cells in the striate cortex of very young, visually inexperienced kittens. *Journal of Neurophysiology, 26*, 994–1002.

Hubel, D., & Wiesel, T. (1968). Receptive fields and functional architecture of the monkey striate cortex. *Journal of Physiology, 195*, 215–243.

Hubel, D. H., & Wiesel, T. N. (1979). Brain mechanisms of vision. *Scientific American, 241*, 150–162.

Hughlings-Jackson, J. (1932). In J. Taylor (Ed.), *Selected writings of John Hughlings-Jackson*. London: Hodder and Stoughton. (Original work published 1866)

Hultsch, D. F., & Dixon, R. A. (1990). Learning and memory in aging. In J. E. Birren & K. W. Schaie (Eds.), *Handbook of the psychology of aging* (3rd ed. pp. 258–274). San Diego, CA: Academic Press.

Humphreys, M., Bain, J. D., & Pike, R. (1989). Different ways to cue a coherent memory system: A theory for episodic, semantic, and procedural tasks. *Psychological Review, 96*(2), 208–233.

Hunt, E. (2005). Information processing and intelligence. In R. J. Sternberg & J. E. Pretz (Eds.), *Cognition and intelligence* (pp. 1–25). New York: Cambridge University Press.

Hunt, E. B. (1975). *Artificial intelligence*. New York: Academic Press.

Hunt, E. B. (1978). Mechanics of verbal ability. *Psychological Review, 85*, 109–130.

Hunt, E. B. (1994). Problem solving. In R. J. Sternberg (Ed.), *Handbook of perception and cognition: Vol. 12. Thinking and problem solving* (pp. 215–232). New York: Academic Press.

Hunt, E. B., & Banaji, M. (1988). The Whorfian hypothesis revisited: A cognitive science view of linguistic and cultural effects on thought. In J. W. Berry, S. H. Irvine, & E. Hunt (Eds.), *Indigenous cognition: Functioning in cultural context*. Dordrecht, The Netherlands: Martinus Nijhoff Publishers.

Hunt, E. B., & Lansman, M. (1982). Individual differences in attention. In R. J. Sternberg (Ed.), *Advances in the psychology of human intelligence* (Vol. 1, pp. 207–254). Hillsdale, NJ: Erlbaum.

Hunt, E. B., & Love, T. (1972). How good can memory be? In A. W. Melton & E. Martin (Eds.), *Coding processes in human memory*. Washington, DC: V. H. Winston & Sons.

Hunt, E. B., Lunneborg, C., & Lewis, J. (1975). What does it mean to be high verbal? *Cognitive Psychology, 7,* 194–227.

Huttenlocher, J. (1968). Constructing spatial images: A strategy in reasoning. *Psychological Review, 75,* 550–560.

Huttenlocher, J., & Presson, C. C. (1973). Mental rotation and the perspective problem. *Cognitive Psychology, 4,* 277–299.

Huttenlocher, J., & Presson, C. C. (1979). The coding and transformation of spatial information. *Cognitive Psychology, 11*(3), 375–394.

Huttenlocher, J., Hedges, L. V., & Duncan, S. (1991). Categories and particulars: Prototype effects in spatial location. *Psychological Review, 98*(3), 352–376.

Indefrey, P., & Levelt, W. J. M. (2000). The neural correlates of language production. In M. Gazzaniga (Ed.), *The new cognitive neurosciences* (2nd ed., pp. 845–865). Cambridge, MA: MIT Press.

Ingram, D. (1999). Phonological acquisition. In M. Barrett (Ed.), *The development of language* (pp. 73–98). East Sussex, UK: Psychology Press.

Intons-Peterson, M. J. (1983). Imagery paradigms: How vulnerable are they to experimenters' expectations? *Journal of Experimental Psychology: Human Perception & Performance, 9*(3), 394–412.

Intons-Peterson, M. J. (1992). Components of auditory imagery. In D. Reisberg (Ed.), *Auditory imagery* (pp. 45–71). Hillsdale, NJ: Erlbaum.

Intons-Peterson, M. J., Russell, W., & Dressel, S. (1992). The role of pitch in auditory imagery. *Journal of Experimental Psychology: Human Perception & Performance, 18*(1), 233–240.

Jackendoff, R. (1991). Parts and boundaries. *Cognition, 41*(1–3), 9–45.

Jacobson, R. R., & Lishman, W. A. (1990). Cortical and diencephalic lesions in Korsakoff's syndrome: A clinical and CT scan study. *Psychological Medicine, 20*(1), 63–75.

Jacoby, L. L., Lindsay, D. S., & Toth, J. P. (1992). Unconscious influences revealed: Attention, awareness, and control. *American Psychologist, 47,* 802–209.

James, W. (1970). *The principles of psychology* (Vol. 1). New York: Holt. (Original work published 1890)

Janis, I. L., & Frick, F. (1943). The relationship between attitudes toward conclusions and errors in judging logical validity of syllogisms. *Journal of Experimental Psychology, 33,* 73–77.

Jarrold, C., & Happé, F. (2003). Austism, psychology of. In L. Nadel (Ed.), *Encyclopedia of cognitive science, Vol. 1,* pp. 283–286. London, England: Nature Publishing Group.

Jenkins, J. J. (1979). Four points to remember: A tetrahedral model of memory experiments. In L. S. Cermak & F. I. M. Craik (Eds.), *Levels of processing in human memory* (pp. 429–446). Hillsdale, NJ: Erlbaum.

Jensen, A. R. (1979). g: Outmoded theory or unconquered frontier? *Creative Science and Technology, 2,* 16–29.

Jensen, A. R. (1982). The chronometry of intelligence. In R. J. Sternberg (Ed.), *Advances in the psychology of human intelligence.* (Vol. 1, pp. 255–310). Hillsdale, NJ: Erlbaum.

Jensen, A. R. (1998). *The g factor.* Westport, CT: Praeger/Greenwood.

Jensen, A. R. (2005). Mental chronometry and the unification of differential psychology. In R. J. Sternberg & J. E. Pretz (Eds.), *Cognition and intelligence* (pp. 26–50). New York: Cambridge University Press.

Jerison, H. J. (2000). The evolution of intelligence. In R. J. Sternberg (Ed.), *Handbook of intelligence* (pp. 216–244). New York: Cambridge University Press.

Jernigan, T. L., Schafer, K., Butters, N., & Cermak, L. S. (1991). Magnetic resonance imaging of alcoholic Korsakoff patients. *Neuropsychopharmacology, 4*(3), 175–186.

Jia, G., & Aaronson, D. (1999). Age differences in second language acquisition: The dominant language switch and maintenance hypothesis. In A. Greenhill, H. Littlefield, & C. Tano, *Proceedings of the 23rd Annual Boston University Conference on Language Development* (pp. 301–312). Somerville, MA: Cascadilla Press.

Johnson, J. S., & Newport, E. L. (1989). Critical period effects in second language learning: The influence of maturational state on the acquisition of English as a second language. *Cognitive Psychology, 21,* 60–99.

Johnson, J. S., & Newport, E. L. (1991). Critical period effects on universal properties of language: The status of subjacency in the acquisition of a second language. *Cognition, 39*(3), 215–258.

Johnson, M. K. (1996). Fact, fantasy, and public policy. In D. J. Herrmann, C. McEvoy, C. Hertzog, P. Hertel, & M. K. Johnson (Eds.), *Basic and applied memory research: Theory in context* (Vol. 1). Mahwah, NJ: Erlbaum.

Johnson, M. K., & Hasher, L. (1987). Human learning and memory. *Annual Review of Psychology, 38,* 631–668.

Johnson, M. K., & Raye, C. L. (1981). Reality monitoring. *Psychological Review, 88,* 67–85.

Johnson, M. K., & Raye, C. L. (1998). False memories and confabulation. *Trends in Cognitive Sciences, 2,* 137–145.

Johnson, M. K., Foley, M. A., Suengas, A. G., & Raye, C. L. (1988). Phenomenal characteristics of memories for perceived and imagined autobiographical events. *Journal of Experimental Psychology: General, 117*(4), 371–376.

Johnson, M. K., Hashtroudi, S., & Lindsay, D. S. (1993). Source monitoring. *Psychological Bulletin, 114,* 3–28.

Johnson, M. K., Nolde, S. F., & De Leonardis, D. M. (1996). Emotional focus and source monitoring. *Journal of Memory and Language, 35,* 135–156.

Johnson-Laird, P. N. (1983). *Mental models.* Cambridge, MA: Harvard University Press.

Johnson-Laird, P. N. (1988). Freedom and constraint in creativity. In R. J. Sternberg (Ed.), *The nature of creativity* (pp. 202–219). New York: Cambridge University Press.

Johnson-Laird, P. N. (1989). Mental models. In M. I. Posner (Ed.), *Foundations of cognitive science* (pp. 469–499). Cambridge, MA: MIT Press.

Johnson-Laird, P. N. (1995). Mental models, deductive reasoning, and the brain. In M. S. Gazzaniga (Ed.), *The cognitive neurosciences* (pp. 999–1008). Cambridge, MA: MIT Press.

Johnson-Laird, P. N. (1997). Rules and illusions: A critical study of Rips's *The psychology of proof: Minds and machines, 7,* 387–407.

Johnson-Laird, P. N. (1999). Mental models. In R. A. Wilson & F. C. Keil (Eds.), *The MIT encyclopedia of the cognitive sciences* (pp. 525–527). Cambridge, MA: MIT Press.

Johnson-Laird, P. N. (2000). Thinking: Reasoning. In A. Kazdin (Ed.), *Encyclopedia of psychology* (Vol. 8, pp. 75–79). Washington, DC: American Psychological Association.

Johnson-Laird, P. N. (2004). Mental models and reasoning. In J. P. Leighton & R. J. Sternberg (Eds.), *The nature of reasoning* (pp. 169–204). New York: Cambridge University Press.

Johnson-Laird, P. N., & Goldvarg, Y. (1997). How to make the impossible seem possible. In *Proceedings of the Nineteenth Annual Conference of the Cognitive Science Society* (pp. 354–357), Stanford, CA. Hillsdale, NJ: Erlbaum.

Johnson-Laird, P. N., & Savary, F. (1999). Illusory inference: A novel class of erroneous deductions. *Cognition, 71*, 191–229.

Johnson-Laird, P. N., & Steedman, M. (1978). The psychology of syllogisms. *Cognitive Psychology, 10*, 64–99.

Johnson-Laird, P. N., Byrne, R. M. J., & Schaeken, W. (1992). Propositional reasoning by model. *Psychological Review, 99*(3), 418–439.

Johnson-Laird, P. N., Legrenzi, P., Girotto, V., Legrenzi, M. S., & Caverni, J. P. (1999). Naïve probability: A model theory of extensional reasoning. *Psychological Review, 106*, 62–88.

Johnston, J. C., & McClelland, J. L. (1973). Visual factors in word perception. *Perception & Psychophysics, 14*, 365–370.

Jolicoeur, P. (1985). The time to name disoriented natural objects. *Memory & Cognition, 13*(4), 289–303.

Jolicoeur, P., & Kosslyn, S. (1985a). Demand characteristics in image scanning experiments. *Journal of Mental Imagery, 9*(2), 41–49.

Jolicoeur, P., & Kosslyn, S. (1985b). Is time to scan visual images due to demand characteristics? *Memory & Cognition, 13*(4), 320–332.

Jolicoeur, P., Snow, D., & Murray, J. (1987). The time to identify disoriented letters: Effects of practice and font. *Canadian Journal of Psychology, 41*(3), 303–316.

Jones, G., & Ritter, F. E. (2003). Production systems and rule-based inference. In L. Nadel (Ed.), *Encyclopedia of cognitive science, Vol. 3*, pp. 741–747. London, England: Nature Publishing Group.

Jordan, K., & Huntsman, L. A. (1990). Image rotation of misoriented letter strings: Effects of orientation cuing and repetition. *Perception & Psychophysics, 48*(4), 363–374.

Jusczyk, P. W. (1997). *The discovery of spoken language.* Cambridge, MA: MIT Press.

Jusczyk, P. W. (2003). Phonology and phonetics, acquisition of. In L. Nadel (Ed.), *Encyclopedia of cognitive science, Vol. 3*, pp. 645–650. London, England: Nature Group Press.

Just, M., & Carpenter, P. A. (1985). Cognitive coordinate systems: Accounts of mental rotation and individual differences in spatial ability. *Psychological Review, 92*(2), 137–172.

Just, M. A., & Carpenter, P. A. (1987). *The psychology of reading and language comprehension.* Boston: Allyn and Bacon.

Just, M. A., Carpenter, P. A., & Masson, M. E. J. (1982). *What eye fixations tell us about speed reading and skimming* (EyeLab Tech. Rep.). Pittsburgh, PA: Carnegie-Mellon University.

Kahneman, D. (1973). *Attention and effort.* Englewood Cliffs, NJ: Prentice-Hall.

Kahneman, D., & Tversky, A. (1972). Subjective probability: A judgment of representativeness. *Cognitive Psychology, 3*, 430–454.

Kahneman, D., & Tversky, A. (1990). Prospect theory: An analysis of decision under risk. In P. K. Moser (Ed.), *Rationality in action: Contemporary approaches* (pp. 140–170). New York: Cambridge University Press.

Kahneman, D., & Tversky, A. (1996). On the reality of cognitive illusions. *Psychological Review, 103*, 582–591.

Kail, R. V. (1991). Controlled and automatic processing during mental rotation. *Journal of Experimental Child Psychology, 51*(3), 337–347.

Kail, R. V. (1997). Processing time, imagery, and spatial memory. *Journal of Experimental Child Psychology, 64*, 67–78.

Kail, R. V., & Bisanz, J. (1992). The information-processing perspective on cognitive development in childhood and adolescence. In R. J. Sternberg & C. A. Berg (Eds.), *Intellectual development* (pp. 229–260). New York: Cambridge University Press.

Kail, R. V., & Park, Y. S. (1990). Impact of practice on speed of mental rotation. *Journal of Experimental Child Psychology, 49*(2), 227–244.

Kail, R. V., Pellegrino, J. W., & Carter, P. (1980). Developmental changes in mental rotation. *Journal of Experimental Child Psychology, 29*, 102–116.

Kanner, L. (1943). Autistic disturbances of affective contact. *Nervous Child, 2*, 217–250.

Kanwisher, N., Chun, M. M., McDermott, J., & Ledden, P. J. (1996). Functional imaging of human visual recognition. *Cognitive Brain Research, 5*, 55–67.

Kanwisher, N., Woods, R., Ioacoboni, M., & Mazziotta, J. (1997). A locus in human extrastriate cortex for visual shape analysis. *Journal of Cognitive Neuroscience, 9*, 133–142.

Kaplan, C. A., & Davidson, J. E. (1989). *Incubation effects in problem solving.* Manuscript submitted for publication.

Karni, A., Tanne, D., Rubenstein, B. S., Askenasy, J. J. M., & Sagi, D. (1994). Dependence on REM sleep of overnight improvement of a perceptual skill. *Science, 265*, 679.

Katz, A. N. (1987). Self-reference in the encoding of creative-relevant traits. *Journal of Personality, 55*, 97–120.

Katz, A. N. (2000). Mental imagery. In A. E. Kazdin (Ed.), *Encyclopedia of psychology* (Vol. 5, pp. 187–191). Washington, DC: American Psychological Association.

Katz, J. J. (1972). *Semantic theory.* New York: Harper & Row.

Katz, J. J., & Fodor, J. A. (1963). The structure of a semantic theory. *Language, 39*, 170–210.

Kaufman, A. S. (2000). Tests of intelligence. In R. J. Sternberg (Ed.), *Handbook of intelligence* (pp. 445–476). New York: Cambridge University Press.

Kaufman, A. S., & Lichtenberger, E. O. (1998). Intellectual assessment. In C. R. Reynolds (Ed.), *Comprehensive clinical psychology: Volume 4: Assessment* (pp. 203–238). Tarrytown, NY : Elsevier Science.

Kay, P. (1975). Synchronic variability and diachronic changes in basic color terms. *Language in Society, 4*, 257–270.

Keane, M. T. (1994). Propositional representations. In M. W. Eysenck (Ed.), *The Blackwell dictionary of cognitive psychology.* Cambridge, MA: Blackwell.

Kearins, J. M. (1981). Visual spatial memory in Australian aboriginal children of desert regions. *Cognitive Psychology, 13*(3), 434–460.

Keating, D. P. (1984). The emperor's new clothes: The "new look" in intelligence research. In R. J. Sternberg (Ed.), *Advances in the psychology of human intelligence* (Vol. 2, pp. 1–45). Hillsdale, NJ: Erlbaum.

Keating, D. P., & Bobbitt, B. L. (1978). Individual and developmental differences in cognitive-processing components of mental ability. *Child Development, 49*, 155–167.

Keil, F. C. (1979). *Semantic and conceptual development.* Cambridge, MA: Harvard University Press.

Keil, F. C. (1989). *Concepts, kinds, and cognitive development.* Cambridge, MA: MIT Press.

Keil, F. C. (1999). Cognition, content, and development. In M. Bennett (Ed.), *Developmental psychology: Achievements and prospects* (pp. 165–184). Philadelphia: Psychology Press.

Keil, F. C., & Batterman, N. (1984). A characteristic-to-defining shift in the development of word meaning. *Journal of Verbal Learning and Verbal Behavior, 23*, 221–236.

Keller, E. (1976). Gambits. *TESL Talk, 7*(2), 18–21.

Keller, H. (1988). *The story of my life.* New York: Signet. (Original work published 1902).

Kensinger, E. A., & Corkin, S. (2003). Alzheimer's disease. In L. Nadel (Ed.), *Encyclopedia of cognitive science, Vol. 1*, pp. 83–89. London, England: Nature Publishing Group.

Kensinger, E. A., Brierley, B., Medford, N., Growdon, J. H., & Corkin, S. (2002). Effects of normal aging and Alzheimer's disease on emotional memory. *Emotion, 2,* 118–134.

Kentridge, R. W. (2003). Blindsight. In L. Nadel (Ed.), *Encyclopedia of cognitive science, Vol. 1,* pp. 390–397. London, England: Nature Publishing Group.

Keppel, G., & Underwood, B. J. (1962). Proactive inhibition in short-term retention of single items. *Journal of Verbal Learning and Verbal Behavior, 1,* 153–161.

Kerr, N. (1983). The role of vision in "visual imagery" experiments: Evidence from the congenitally blind. *Journal of Experimental Psychology: General, 112*(2), 265–277.

Kessler Shaw, L. (1999). *Acquiring the meaning of know and think.* Unpublished doctoral dissertation. City University of New York Graduate Center.

Khubchandani, L. M. (1997). Bilingual education for indigenous groups in India. In J. Cummins & D. Corson (Eds.), *Encyclopedia of language and education: Vol. 5. Bilingual education* (pp. 67–76). Dordrecht, Netherlands: Kluwer.

Kihlstrom, J. F., & Cantor, N. (2000). Social intelligence. In R. J. Sternberg (Ed.), *Handbook of intelligence* (pp. 359–379). New York: Cambridge University Press.

Kim, N. S., & Ahn, W. K. (2002). Clinical psychologists' theory-based representations of mental disorders predict their diagnostic reasoning and memory. *Journal of Experimental Psychology: General, 131,* 451–476.

Kimura, D. (1981). Neural mechanisms in manual signing. *Sign Language Studies, 33,* 291–312.

Kimura, D. (1987). Are men's and women's brains really different? *Canadian Psychology, 28*(2), 133–147.

Kintsch, W. (1990). The representation of knowledge and the use of knowledge in discourse comprehension. In C. Graumann & R. Dietrich (Eds.), *Language in the social context.* Amsterdam: Elsevier.

Kintsch, W., & Keenan, J. (1973). Reading rate and retention as a function of the number of propositions in the base structure of sentences. *Cognitive Psychology, 5,* 257–274.

Kintsch, W., & van Dijk, T. A. (1978). Toward a model of text comprehension and production. *Psychological Review, 85*(5), 363–394.

Kintsch, W., Healy, A. F., Hegarty, M., Pennington, B. F., & Salthouse, T. A. (1999). Models of working memory: Eight questions and some general issues. In A. Miyake & P. Shah (Eds.), *Models of working memory: Mechanisms of active maintenance and executive control* (pp. 412–441). New York: Cambridge University Press.

Kirby, K. N. (1994). Probabilities and utilities of fictional outcomes in Wason's selection task. *Cognition, 51*(1), 1–28.

Klein, S. B., & Kihlstrom, J. F. (1986). Elaboration, organization, and the self-reference effect in memory. *Journal of Experimental Psychology: General, 115*(1), 26–38.

Kliegl, R., Mayr, U., & Krampe, R. T. (1994). Time–accuracy functions for determining process and person differences: An application to cognitive aging. *Cognitive Psychology, 26*(2), 134–164.

Koehler, J. J. (1996). The base rate fallacy reconsidered: Descriptive, normative, and methodological challenges. *Behavioral and Brain Sciences, 19,* 1–53.

Köhler, S., Kapur, S., Moscovitch, M., Winocur, G., & Houle, S. (1995). Dissociation of pathways for object and spatial vision in the intact human brain. *Neuroreport, 6,* 1865–1868.

Köhler, W. (1927). *The mentality of apes.* New York: Harcourt Brace.

Köhler, W. (1940). *Dynamics in psychology.* New York: Liveright.

Kolb, B., & Whishaw, I. Q. (1985). *Fundamentals of human neuropsychology* (2nd ed.). New York: Freeman.

Kolb, B., & Whishaw, I. Q. (1990). *Fundamentals of human neuropsychology* (3rd ed.). New York: Freeman.

Kolodner, J. L. (1983). Reconstructive memory: A computer model. *Cognitive Science, 7*(4), 281–328.

Komatsu, L. K. (1992). Recent views on conceptual structure. *Psychological Bulletin, 112*(3), 500–526.

Korf, R. (1999). Heuristic search. In R. A. Wilson & F. C. Keil (Eds.), *The MIT encyclopedia of the cognitive sciences* (pp. 372–373). Cambridge, MA: MIT Press.

Koriat, A., & Goldsmith, M. (1996a). Memory metaphors and the everyday–laboratory controversy: The correspondence versus the storehouse conceptions of memory. *Behavioral and Brain Sciences, 19,* 167–228.

Koriat, A., & Goldsmith, M. (1996b). Monitoring and control processes in the strategic regulation of memory accuracy. *Psychological Review, 103,* 490–517.

Koslowski, B. (1996). *Theory and evidence: The development of scientific reasoning.* Cambridge, MA: MIT Press.

Kosslyn, S. M. (1975). Information representation in visual images. *Cognitive Psychology, 7*(3), 341–370.

Kosslyn, S. M. (1976). Using imagery to retrieve semantic information: A developmental study. *Child Development, 47*(2), 434–444.

Kosslyn, S. M. (1981). The medium and the message in mental imagery: A theory. *Psychological Review, 88*(1), 46–66.

Kosslyn, S. M. (1983). *Ghosts in the mind's machine: Creating and using images in the brain.* New York: Norton.

Kosslyn, S. M. (1990). Mental imagery. In D. N. Osherson, S. M. Kosslyn, & J. M. Hollerbach (Eds.), *Visual cognition and action: Vol. 2. An invitation to cognitive science* (pp. 73–97). Cambridge, MA: MIT Press.

Kosslyn, S. M. (1994a). Computational theory of imagery. In M. W. Eysenck (Ed.), *The Blackwell dictionary of cognitive psychology* (pp. 177–181). Cambridge, MA: Blackwell.

Kosslyn, S. M. (1994b). Image and brain: The resolution of the imagery debate. Cambridge, MA: MIT Press.

Kosslyn, S. M., & Koenig, O. (1992). *Wet mind: The new cognitive neuroscience.* New York: Free Press.

Kosslyn, S. M., & Osherson, D. N. (Eds.), (1995). *An Invitation to Cognitive Science, 2nd edition, Volume 2., Visual cognition.* Cambridge, MA: MIT Press.

Kosslyn, S. M., & Pomerantz, J. R. (1977). Imagery, propositions, and the form of internal representations. *Cognitive Psychology, 9*(1), 52–76.

Kosslyn, S. M., & Rabin, C. S. (1999). Imagery. In R. A. Wilson & F. C. Keil (Eds.), *The MIT encyclopedia of the cognitive sciences* (pp. 387–389). Cambridge, MA: MIT Press.

Kosslyn, S. M., & Sussman, A. L. (1995). Roles of memory in perception. In M. S. Gazzaniga (Ed.), *The cognitive neurosciences* (pp. 1035–1042). Cambridge, MA: MIT Press.

Kosslyn, S. M., & Thompson, W. L. (2000). Shared mechanisms in visual imagery and visual perception: Insights from cognitive neuroscience. In M. S. Gazzaniga (Ed.), *The new cognitive neurosciences* (2nd ed., pp. 975–986). Cambridge, MA: MIT Press.

Kosslyn, S. M., Ball, T. M., & Reiser, B. J. (1978). Visual images preserve metric spatial information: Evidence from studies of image scanning. *Journal of Experimental Psychology: Human Perception and Performance, 4,* 47–60.

Kosslyn, S. M., Seger, C., Pani, J. R., & Hillger, L. A. (1990). When is imagery used in everyday life? A diary study. *Journal of Mental Imagery, 14*(3–4), 131–152.

Kosslyn, S. M., Thompson, W. L., Kim, J. J., & Alpert, N. M. (1995). Topographical representations of mental images in primary visual cortex. *Nature*, 378, 496–498.

Kotovsky, K. (2003). Problem solving-large/small, hard/easy, conscious/nonconscious, problem-space/problem-solver: The issue of dichotomization. In J. E. Davidson & R. J. Sternberg (Eds.), *The psychology of problem solving* (pp. 385–383). {AU: Is page range ok: "385-383"?} New York: Cambridge University Press.

Kotovsky, K., & Simon, H. A. (1973). Empirical tests of a theory of human acquisition of concepts for sequential events. *Cognitive Psychology*, 4, 399–424.

Kotovsky, K., Hayes, J. R., & Simon, H. A. (1985). Why are some problems hard? Evidence from the tower of Hanoi. *Cognitive Psychology*, 17, 248–294.

Krantz, L. (1992). *What the odds are: A-to-Z odds on everything you hoped or feared could happen*. New York: Harper Perennial.

Kreuger, J. (1998, October). The bet on bias: A foregone conclusion? *Psychology*, 9.

Kroeber, A. L., & Kluckhohn, C. (1952). *Culture: A critical review of concepts and definitions*. Cambridge, MA: Peabody Museum.

Kruschke, J. K. (2003). Concept learning and categorization: Models. In L. Nadel (Ed.), Encyclopedia of cognitive science, *Vol. 1*, pp. 646–652. London, England: Nature Publishing Group.

Kuhl, P. K. (1991). Human adults and infants show a "perceptual magnet effect" for the prototypes of speech categories, monkeys do not. *Perception & Psycholinguistics*, 50, 93–107.

Kuhl, P. K., & Meltzoff, A. N. (1997). Evolution, nativism, and learning in the development of language and speech. In M. Gopnik (Ed.), *The inheritance and innateness of grammars* (pp. 7–44). New York: Oxford University Press.

Kunzendorf, R. (Ed.) (1991). *Mental imagery*. New York: Plenum.

Kutas, M., & Hillyard, S. A. (1980). Reading senseless sentences: Brain potentials reflect semantic incongruity. *Science*, 207, 203–205.

Kutas, M., & Van Patten, C. (1994). Psycholinguistics electrified: Event-related brain potential investigations. In M. A. Gernsbacher (Ed.), *Handbook of psycholinguistics* (pp. 83–143). San Diego, CA: Academic Press.

Kyllonen, P. C., & Christal, R. E. (1990). Reasoning ability is (little more than) working-memory capacity?! *Intelligence*, 14, 389–433.

LaBerge D., & Samuels, S. J. (1974). Toward a theory of automatic information processing in reading. *Cognitive Psychology*, 6(2), 293–323.

LaBerge, D. (1975). Acquisition of automatic processing in perceptual and associative learning. In P. M. A. Rabbit & S. Dornic (Eds.), *Attention and performance*. London: Academic Press.

LaBerge, D. (1976). Perceptual learning and attention. In W. Estes (Ed.), *Handbook of learning and cognitive processes: Vol. 4. Attention and memory*. Hillsdale, NJ: Erlbaum.

LaBerge, D. (1990). Attention. *Psychological Science*, 1(3), 156–162.

LaBerge, D., & Brown, V. (1989). Theory of attentional operations in shape identification. *Psychological Review*, 96(1), 101–124.

LaBerge, D., Carter, M., & Brown, V. (1992). A network simulation of thalamic circuit operations in selective attention. *Neural Computation*, 4(3), 318–331.

Labouvie-Vief, G., & Schell, D. A. (1982). Learning and memory in later life. In B. B. Wolman (Ed.), *Handbook of developmental psychology*. Englewood Cliffs, NJ: Prentice-Hall.

Ladavas, E., del Pesce, M., Mangun, G. R., & Gazzaniga, M. S. (1994). Variations in attentional bias of the disconnected cerebral hemispheres. *Cognitive Neuropsychology*, 11(1), 57–74.

Ladefoged, P., & Maddieson, I. (1996). *The sounds of the world's languages*. Cambridge: Blackwell.

Lamb, J. A., Moore, J., Bailey, A., & Monaco, A. P. (2000). Autism: Recent molecular genetic advances. *Human Molecular Genetics*, 9, 861–868.

Langer, E. J. (1989). *Mindfulness*. New York: Addison-Wesley.

Langer, E. J. (1997). *The power of mindful learning*. Needham Heights, MA: Addison-Wesley.

Langlais, P. J., Mandel, R. J., & Mair, R. G. (1992). Diencephalic lesions, learning impairments, and intact retrograde memory following acute thiamine deficiency in the rat. *Behavioural Brain Research*, 48(2), 177–185.

Langley, P., & Jones, R. (1988). A computational model of scientific insight. In R. J. Sternberg (Ed.), *The nature of creativity* (pp. 117–201). New York: Cambridge University Press.

Langley, P., Simon, H. A., Bradshaw, G. L., & Zytkow, J. M. (1987). *Scientific discovery: Computational explorations of the creative process*. Cambridge, MA: MIT Press.

Lanze, M., Weisstein, N., & Harris, J. R. (1982). Perceived depth versus structural relevance in the object-superiority effect. *Perception & Psychophysics*, 31(4), 376–382.

Larkin, J. H., McDermott, J., Simon, D. P., & Simon, H. A. (1980). Expert and novice performance in solving physics problems. *Science*, 208, 1335–1342.

Larson, G. E., Haier, R. J., LaCasse, L. & Hazen, K. (1995). Evaluation of a "mental effort" hypothesis for correlation between cortical metabolism and intelligence. *Intelligence*, 21, 267–278.

Lashley, K. S. (1950). In search of the engram. *Symposia of the Society for Experimental Biology*, 4, 454–482.

Lawson, A. E. (2004). Reasoning and brain function. In J. P. Leighton & R. J. Sternberg (Eds.), *The nature of reasoning* (pp.12–48). New York: Cambridge University Press.

Lazar, I., & Darlington, R. (1982). Lasting effects of early education: A report from the consortium for longitudinal studies. *Monographs of the Society for Research in Child Development*, 47(2–3, Serial No. 195).

Lederer, R. (1991). *The miracle of language*. New York: Pocket Books.

Ledoux, J. (1996). *The emotional brain*. New York: Simon & Schuster.

Lee, D., & Chun, M. M. (2001). What are the units of visual short-term memory, objects or spatial locations? *Perception & Psychophysics*, 63, 253–257.

Lehman, D., Lempert, R., & Nisbett, R. E. (1987). *The effects of graduate education on reasoning: Formal discipline and thinking about everyday-life events*. Unpublished manuscript, University of British Columbia.

Leicht, K. L., & Overton, R. (1987). Encoding variability and spacing repetitions. *American Journal of Psychology*, 100(1), 61–68.

Leighton, J. P. (2004a). The assessment of logical reasoning. In J. P. Leighton & R. J. Sternberg (Eds.), *The nature of reasoning*. New York: Cambridge University Press.

Leighton, J. P. (2004b). Defining and describing reason. In J. P. Leighton & R. J. Sternberg (Eds.), *The nature of reasoning* (pp.3–11). New York: Cambridge University Press.

Leighton, J. P., & Sternberg, R. J. (Eds). (2004). *The nature of reasoning*. New York: Cambridge University Press.

Lesgold, A. M. (1988). Problem solving. In R. J. Sternberg & E. E. Smith (Eds.), *The psychology of human thought* (pp. 188–213). New York: Cambridge University Press.

Lesgold, A. M., & Lajoie, S. (1991). Complex problem solving in electronics. In R. J. Sternberg & P. A. Frensch (Eds.), *Complex problem solving: Principles and mechanisms* (pp. 287–316). Hillsdale, NJ: Erlbaum.

Lesgold, A. M., Rubinson, H., Feltovich, P., Glaser, R., Klopfer, D., & Wang, Y. (1988). Expertise in a complex skill: Diagnosing x-ray pictures. In M. T. H. Chi, R. Glaser, & M. Farr (Eds.), *The nature of expertise*. Hillsdale, NJ: Erlbaum.

Levin, D. T., & Simons, D. J. (1997). Failure to detect changes in attended objects in motion pictures. *Psychonomic Bulletin & Review, 4*, 501–506.

Levy, J. (1974). Cerebral asymmetries as manifested in split-brain man. In M. Kinsbourne & W. L. Smith (Eds.), *Hemispheric disconnection and cerebral function*. Springfield, IL: Charles C. Thomas.

Levy, J. (2000). Hemispheric functions. In A. E. Kazdin (Ed.), *Encyclopedia of psychology* (Vol. 4, pp. 113–115). Washington, DC: American Psychological Association.

Levy, J., Trevarthen, C., & Sperry, R. W. (1972). Perception of bilateral chimeric figures following hemispheric deconnexion. *Brain, 95*(1), 61–78.

Lewis, R. L. (2003). Psycholinguistics, computational. In L. Nadel (Ed.), *Encyclopedia of cognitive science, Vol. 3*, pp. 787–794. London, England: Nature Group Press.

Liberman, A. M., & Mattingly, I. G. (1985). The motor theory of speech perception revised. *Cognition, 21*, 1–36.

Liberman, A. M., Cooper, F. S., Shankweiler, D. P., & Studdert-Kennedy, M. (1967). Perception of the speech code. *Psychological Review, 74*, 431–461.

Liberman, A. M., Harris, K. S., Hoffman, H. S., & Griffith, B. C. (1957). The discrimination of speech sounds within and across phoneme boundaries. *Journal of Experimental Psychology, 54*, 358–368.

Lightfoot, D. W. (2003). Language acquisition and language change. In L. Nadel (Ed.), *Encyclopedia of cognitive science, Vol. 2*, pp. 697–700. London, England: Nature Group Press.

Lindsay, D. S., & Johnson, M. K. (1991). Recognition memory and source monitoring. *Bulletin of the Psychonomic Society, 29*, 203–205.

Lindsay, D. S., & Read, J. D. (1994). Psychotherapy and memories of childhood sexual abuse: A cognitive perspective. *Applied Cognitive Psychology, 8*, 281–338.

Linton, M. (1982). Transformations of memory in everyday life. In U. Neisser (Ed.), *Memory observed: Remembering in natural contexts*. San Francisco: Freeman.

Lipman, M., Sharp, A. M., & Oscanyan, F. S. (1980). *Philosophy in the classroom*. Philadelphia,: Temple University Press.

Livingstone, M., & Hubel, D. (1988). Segregation of form, color, movement, and depth: Anatomy, physiology, and perception. *Science, 240*(4853), 740–749.

Locke, J. L. (1994). Phases in the child's development of language. *American Scientist, 82*, 436–445.

Lockhart, R. S. (2000). Methods of memory research. In E. Tulving & F. I. M. Craik (Eds.), *The Oxford handbook of memory* (pp. 45–58). New York: Oxford University Press.

Loehlin, J. C., Horn, J. M., & Willerman, L. (1997). Heredity, environment, and IQ in the Texas Adoption Project. In R. J. Sternberg & E. L. Grigorenko (Eds.), *Intelligence, heredity, and environment* (pp. 105–125). New York: Cambridge University Press.

Loftus, E. F. (1975). Leading questions and the eyewitness report. *Cognitive Psychology, 7*, 560–572.

Loftus, E. F. (1977). Shifting human color memory. *Memory & Cognition, 5*, 696–699.

Loftus, E. F. (1993a). Psychologists in the eyewitness world. *American Psychologist, 48*(5), 550–552.

Loftus, E. F. (1993b). The reality of repressed memories. *American Psychologist, 48*(5), 518–537.

Loftus, E. F. (1998). Imaginary memories. In M. A. Conway, S. E. Gathercole, & C. Cornoldi (Eds.), *Theory of memory II* (pp. 135–145). Hove, England: Psychology Press.

Loftus, E. F., & Ketcham, K. (1991). *Witness for the defense: The accused, the eyewitness, and the expert who puts memory on trial*. New York: St. Martin's Press.

Loftus, E. F., & Ketcham, K. (1994). *The myth of repressed memory*. New York: St. Martin's Press.

Loftus, E. F., & Loftus, G. R. (1980). On the permanence of stored information in the human brain. *American Psychologist, 35*, 409–420.

Loftus, E. F., & Palmer, J. C. (1974). Reconstruction of automobile destruction: An example of the interaction between language and memory. *Journal of Verbal Learning and Verbal Behavior, 13*, 585–589.

Loftus, E. F., Miller, D. G., & Burns, H. J. (1978). Semantic integration of verbal information into a visual memory. *Journal of Experimental Psychology: Human Learning and Memory, 4*, 19–31.

Loftus, E. F., Miller, D. G., & Burns, H. J. (1987). Semantic integration of verbal information into a visual memory. In L. S. Wrightsman, C. E. Willis, S. M. Kassin (Eds.), *On the witness stand: Vol. 2. Controversies in the courtroom* (pp. 157–177). Newbury Park, CA: Sage.

Logan, G. (1988). Toward an instance theory of automatization. *Psychological Review, 95*(4), 492–527.

Logan, G. D. (1996). The CODE theory of visual attention: An integration of space-based and object-based attention. *Psychological Review, 103*, 603–649.

Logie, R. H., & Denis, M. (1991). *Mental images in human cognition*. Amsterdam: North Holland.

Lohman, D. F. (2000). Complex information processing and intelligence. In R. J. Sternberg (Ed.), *Handbook of intelligence* (pp. 285–340). New York: Cambridge University Press.

Lohman, D. F. (2005). Reasoning abilities. In R. J. Sternberg & J. E. Pretz (Eds.), *Cognition and intelligence* (pp. 225–250). New York: Cambridge University Press.

Lonner, W. J. (1989). The introductory psychology text: Beyond Ekman, Whorf, and biased IQ tests. In D. M. Keats, D. Munro, & L. Mann (Eds.), *Heterogeneity in cross-cultural psychology* (pp. 4–22). Amsterdam: Swets & Zeitlinger.

Lou, H. C., Henriksen, L., & Bruhn, P. (1984). Focal cerebral hypoperfusion in children with dyphasia and/or attention deficit disorder. *Archives of Neurology, 41*(8), 825–829.

Love, B. C. (2003). Concept learning. In L. Nadel (Ed.), *Encyclopedia of cognitive science* (Vol. 1, pp. 646-652). London, England: Nature Publishing Group.

Lubart, T. I., & Mouchiroud, C. (2003). Creativity: A source of difficulty in problem solving. In J. E. Davidson & R. J. Sternberg (Eds.), *The psychology of problem solving* (pp. 127–148). New York: Cambridge University Press.

Luchins, A. S. (1942). Mechanization in problem solving. *Psychological Monographs, 54*(6, Whole No. 248).

Luck, S. J., & Vogel, E. K. (1997). The capacity of visual working memory for features and conjunctions. *Nature, 390*, 279–281.

Luck, S. J., Hillyard, S. A., Mangun, G. R., & Gazzaniga, M. S. (1989). Independent hemispheric attentional systems mediate visual search in split-brain patients. *Nature, 342*(6249), 543–545.

Luck, S. J., Hillyard, S. A., Mouloua, M., & Hawkins, H. L. (1996). Mechanisms of visual-spatial attention-Resource allocation or uncertainty reduction? *Journal of Experimental Psychology: Human Perception and Performance, 22*, 725–737.

Luria, A. R. (1968). *The mind of a mnemonist.* New York: Basic Books.

Luria, A. R. (1973). *The working brain.* London: Penguin.

Luria, A. R. (1976). *Basic problems of neurolinguistics.* The Hague, Netherlands: Mouton.

Luria, A. R. (1984). *The working brain: An introduction to neuropsychology* (B. Haigh, Trans.). Harmondsworth, England: Penguin. (Original work published 1973)

Lycan, W. (2003). Perspectival representation and the knowledge argument. In Q. Smith & A. Jokic (Eds.), *Consciousness. New philosophical perspectives.* Oxford: Oxford University Press.

Lyons, J. (1977). *Semantics.* New York: Cambridge University Press.

Mace, W. M. (1986). J. J. Gibson's ecological theory of information pickup: Cognition from the ground up. In T. J. Knapp & L. C. Robertson (Eds.), *Approaches to cognition: Contrasts and controversies* (pp. 137–157). Hillsdale, NJ: Erlbaum.

Mackworth, N. H. (1948). The breakdown of vigilance during prolonged visual search. *Quarterly Journal of Experimental Psychology, 1*, 6–21.

MacLeod, C. (1991). Half a century of research on the Stroop effect: An integrative review. *Psychological Bulletin, 109*(2), 163–203.

MacLeod, C. M. (1996). How priming affects two speeded implicit tests of remembering: Naming colors versus reading words. *Consciousness and Cognition: An International Journal, 5*, 73–90.

MacWhinney, B. (1999). *The emergence of language.* Mahwah, NJ: Erlbaum.

Malgady, R., & Johnson, M. (1976). Modifiers in metaphors: Effects of constituent phrase similarity on the interpretation of figurative sentences. *Journal of Psycholinguistic Research, 5*, 43–52.

Malonek, D., & Grinvald, A. (1996). Interactions between electrical activity and cortical microcirculation revealed by imaging spectroscopy: Implication for functional brain mapping. *Science, 272*, 551–554.

Malsbury, C. W. (2003). Hypothalamus. In L. Nadel (Ed.), *Encyclopedia of cognitive science, Vol. 2*, pp. 445–451. London, England: Nature Publishing Group.

Malt, B. C., & Smith, E. E. (1984). Correlated properties in natural categories. *Journal of Verbal Learning and Verbal Behavior, 23*, 250–269.

Mangun, G. R., & Hillyard, S. A. (1990). Electrophysiological studies of visual selective attention in humans. In A. B. Scheibel & A. F. Wechsler (Eds.), *Neurobiology of higher cognitive function* (pp. 271–295). New York: Guilford.

Mangun, G. R., & Hillyard, S. A. (1991). Modulations of sensory-evoked brain potentials indicate changes in perceptual processing during visual-spatial priming. *Journal of Experimental Psychology: Human Perception & Performance, 17*(4), 1057–1074.

Mangun, G. R., Plager, R., Loftus, W., Hillyard, S. A., Luck, S. J., Clark, V., et al. (1994). Monitoring the visual world: Hemispheric asymmetries and subcortical processes in attention. *Journal of Cognitive Neuroscience, 6*, 265–273.

Mani, K., & Johnson-Laird, P. N. (1982). The mental representation of spatial descriptions. *Memory & Cognition, 10*(2), 181–187.

Manktelow, K. I., & Over, D. E. (1990). Deontic thought and the selection task. In K. J. Gilhooly, M. T. G. Keane, & G. Erdos (Eds.), *Lines of thinking* (Vol. 1, pp. 153–164). London: Wiley.

Manktelow, K. I., & Over, D. E. (1992). Obligation, permission, and mental models. In V. Rogers, A. Rutherford, & P. Bibby (Eds.), *Models in the mind* (pp. 249–266). London: Academic Press.

Mantyla, T. (1986). Optimizing cue effectiveness: Recall of 500 and 600 incidentally learned words. *Journal of Experimental Psychology: Learning, Memory, & Cognition, 12*, 66–71.

Maratsos, M. (1998). The acquisition of grammar. In D. Kuhn & R. S. Siegler (Eds.), *Handbook of child psychology: Vol. 2: Cognition, perception, and language* (5th ed., pp. 421–466). New York: Wiley.

Maratsos, M. P. (2003). Language acquisition. In L. Nadel (Ed.), *Encyclopedia of cognitive science, Vol. 2*, pp. 691–696. London, England: Nature Group Press.

Marcel, A. J. (1983a). Conscious and unconscious perception: An approach to the relations between phenomenal experience and perceptual processes. *Cognitive Psychology, 15*(2), 238–300.

Marcel, A. J. (1983b). Conscious and unconscious perception: Experiments on visual masking and word recognition. *Cognitive Psychology, 15*(2), 197–237.

Marcel, A. J. (1986). Consciousness and processing: Choosing and testing a null hypothesis. *Brain and Behavioral Sciences, 9*, 40–41.

Marcel, A. J., & Bisiach, E. (Eds.) (1988). *Consciousness in contemporary science.* New York: Oxford University Press.

Marcus, D., & Overton, W. (1978). The development of gender constancy and sex role preferences. *Child Development, 49*, 434–444.

Marcus, G. F. (1998). Rethinking eliminative connectionism. *Cognitive Psychology, 37*, 243–282.

Marcus, G. F., Vijayan, S., Bandi Rao, S., & Vishton, P. M. (1999). Rule learning by seven-month-old infants. *Science, 283*, 77–80.

Markman, A. B. (2003). Conceptual representations in psychology. In L. Nadel (Ed.), *Encyclopedia of cognitive science, Vol. 1*, pp. 670–673. London, England: Nature Publishing Group.

Markman, A. B., & Ross, B. (2003). Category use and category learning. *Psychological Bulletin, 129*, 592–613.

Markman, E. M. (1977). Realizing that you don't understand: A preliminary investigation. *Child Development, 48*, 986–992.

Markman, E. M. (1979). Realizing that you don't understand: Elementary school children's awareness of inconsistencies. *Child Development, 50*, 643–655.

Markovits, H. (2004). The development of deductive reasoning. In J. P. Leighton & R. J. Sternberg (Eds.), *The nature of reasoning* (pp. 313–338). New York: Cambridge University Press.

Markowitsch, H. J. (2000). Neuroanatomy of memory. In E. Tulving & F. I. M. Craik (Eds.), *The Oxford handbook of memory* (pp. 465–484). New York: Oxford University Press.

Markus, H. R., & Kitayama, S. (1991). Culture and the self: Implications for cognition, emotion, and motivation. *Psychological Review, 98*, 224–253.

Marmor, G. S. (1975). Development of kinetic images: When does the child first represent movement in mental images? *Cognitive Psychology, 7*, 548–559.

Marmor, G. S. (1977). Mental rotation and number conservation: Are they related? *Developmental Psychology, 13*, 320–325.

Marr, D. (1982). *Vision.* San Francisco: Freeman.

Marsh, B., Todd, P. M., & Gigerenzer, G. (2004). Cognitive heuristics: Reasoning the fast and frugal way. In J. P. Leighton & R. J. Sternberg (Eds.), *The nature of reasoning* (pp. 273–287). New York: Cambridge University Press.

Martin, J. A. (1981). A longitudinal study of the consequences of early mother–infant interaction: A microanalytic approach. *Monographs of the Society for Research in Child Development, 46*(203, Serial No. 190).

Martin, L. (1986). Eskimo words for snow: A case study in the genesis and decay of an anthropological example. *American Psychologist*, 88, 418–423.

Martin, M. (1979). Local and global processing: The role of sparsity. *Memory & Cognition*, 7, 476–484.

Massaro, D. W. (1987). *Speech perception by ear and eye: A paradigm for psychological inquiry*. Hillsdale, NJ: Erlbaum.

Massaro, D. W., & Cohen, M. M. (1990). Perception of synthesized audible and visible speech. *Psychological Science*, 1, 55–63.

Matarazzo, J. D. (1992). Biological and physiological correlates of intelligence. *Intelligence*, 16(3,4), 257–258.

Matlin, M. W., & Underhill, W. A. (1979). Selective rehearsal and selective recall. *Bulletin of the Psychonomic Society*, 14(5), 389–392.

Matsumoto, D. (1994). *People: Psychology from a cultural perspective*. Pacific Grove, CA: Brooks Cole Publishing Co.

Matsumoto, D. (1996). *Culture and psychology*. Pacific Grove, CA: Brooks Cole Publishing Co.

Matthews, R. J. (2003). Connectionism and systematicity. In L. Nadel (Ed.), *Encyclopedia of cognitive science, Vol. 1*, pp. 687–690. London, England: Nature Publishing Group.

Maunsell, J. H. (1995). The brain's visual world: Representation of visual targets in cerebral cortex. *Science*, 270, 764–769.

Mayer, J. D., & Salovey, P. (1997). What is emotional intelligence? In P. Salovey & D. Sluyter (Eds.), *Emotional development and emotional intelligence: Implications for educators* (pp. 3–31). New York: Basic.

Mayer, J. D., Salovey, P., & Caruso, D. (2000a). Emotional intelligence. In R. J. Sternberg (Ed.), *Handbook of intelligence* (pp. 396–420). New York: Cambridge University Press.

Mayer, R. E. (2000a). Concepts: Conceptual change. In A. E. Kazdin (Ed.), *Encyclopedia of psychology* (Vol. 2, pp. 253–255). Washington, DC: American Psychological Association.

Mayer, R. E. (2000b). Intelligence and education. In R. J. Sternberg (Ed.), *Handbook of intelligence* (pp. 519–533). New York: Cambridge University Press.

Mayes, A. R., & Hunkin, N. M. (2003). Amnesia. In L. Nadel (Ed.), *Encyclopedia of cognitive science, Vol. 1*, pp. 90–97. London, England: Nature Publishing Group.

Mayr, U., & Kliegl, R. (1993). Sequential and coordinative complexity: Age-based processing in figural transformations. *Journal of Experimental Psychology: Learning, Memory, & Cognition*, 19(6), 1297–1320.

McArthur, T. (Ed.). (1992). *The Oxford companion to the English language*. New York: Oxford University Press.

McCann, R. S., & Johnston, J. C. (1992). Locus of single-channel bottleneck in dual-task interference. *Journal of Experimental Psychology: Human Perception & Performance*, 18(2), 471–484.

McCarthy, G., Blamire, A. M., Puce, A., Nobe, A. C., Bloch, G., Hyder, F., et al. (1994). Functional magnetic resonance imaging of human prefrontal cortex activation during a spatial working memory task. *Proceedings of the National Academy of Sciences, USA, 90*, 4952–4956.

McClelland, J. L., & Elman, J. L. (1986). The TRACE model of speech perception. *Cognitive Psychology*, 18, 1–86.

McClelland, J. L., & Rumelhart, D. E. (1981). An interactive activation model of context effects in letter perception: Part 1. An account of basic findings. *Psychological Review*, 88, 483–524.

McClelland, J. L., & Rumelhart, D. E., (1985). Distributed memory and the representation of general and specific information. *Journal of Experimental Psychology: General*, 114(2), 159–188.

McClelland, J. L., & Rumelhart, D. E. (1988). *Explorations in parallel distributed processing: A handbook of models, programs, and exercises*. Cambridge, MA: MIT Press.

McClelland, J. L., McNaughton, B. C., & O'Reilly, R. C. (1995). Why there are complementary learning systems in the hippocampus and neocortex: Insights from the successes and failures of connectionist models of learning and memory. *Psychological Review, 102*, 419–457.

McClelland, J. L., Rumelhart, D. E., & the PDP Research Group (1986). *Parallel distributed processing: Explorations in the microstructure of cognition: Vol. 2. Psychological and biological models*. Cambridge, MA: MIT Books.

McCormick, D. A., & Thompson, R. F. (1984). Cerebellum: Essential involvement in the classically conditioned eyelid response. *Science*, 223, 296–299.

McDermott, K. B. (1996). The persistence of false memories in list recall. *Journal of Memory and Language*, 35, 212–230.

McGarry-Roberts, P. A., Stelmack, R. M., & Campbell, K. B. (1992). Intelligence, reaction time, and event-related potentials. *Intelligence*, 16(3,4), 289–313.

McGaugh, J. L. (1999). Memory storage, modulation of. In R. A. Wilson & F. C. Keil (Eds.), *The MIT encyclopedia of the cognitive sciences* (pp. 522–524). Cambridge, MA: MIT Press.

McGaugh, J. L., Cahill, L., & Roozendall, B. (1996). Modulation of memory storage. *Current Opinion in Neurobiology*, 6, 237–242.

McGurk, H., & MacDonald, J. (1976). Hearing lips and seeing voices. *Nature*, 264, 746–748.

McKenna, J., Treadway, M., & McCloskey, M. E. (1992). Expert psychological testimony on eyewitness reliability: Selling psychology before its time. In P. Suedfeld & P. E. Tetlock (Eds.), *Psychology and social policy* (pp. 283–293). New York: Hemisphere.

McKoon, G., & Ratcliff, R. (1980). Priming in item recognition: The organization of propositions in memory for text. *Journal of Verbal Learning and Verbal Behavior*, 19, 369–386.

McKoon, G., & Ratcliff, R. (1992a). Inference during reading. *Psychological Review*, 99, 440–466.

McKoon, G., & Ratcliff, R. (1992b). Spreading activation versus compound cue accounts of priming: Mediated priming revisited. *Journal of Experimental Psychology: Learning, Memory, & Cognition*, 18(6), 1155–1172.

McLeod, P., Driver, J., & Crisp, J. (1988). Visual search for a conjunction of movement and form is parallel. *Nature, 332*(6160), 154–155.

McLeod, P., Driver, J., Dienes, Z., & Crisp, J. (1991). Filtering by movement in visual search. *Journal of Experimental Psychology: Human Perception & Performance*, 17(1), 55–64.

McLeod, P., Heywood, C., Driver, J., & Zihl, J. (1989). Selective deficit of visual search in moving displays after extrastriate damage. *Nature, 339*(6224), 466–467.

McLeod, P., Plunkett, K., & Rolls, E. T. (1998). *Introduction to connectionist modelling of cognitive processes*. Oxford: Oxford University Press.

McNamara, D. S., Kintsch, E., Songer, N. B., & Kintsch, W. (1996). Learning from text: Effect of prior knowledge and text coherence. *Discourse Processes*, 30, 201–236.

McNamara, T. P. (1992). Theories of priming: I. Associative distance and lag. *Journal of Experimental Psychology: Learning, Memory, & Cognition*, 18(6), 1173–1190.

McNamara, T. P., Hardy, J. K., & Hirtle, S. C. (1989). Subjective hierarchies in spatial memory. *Memory & Cognition*, 17(4), 444–453.

McNamara, T. P., Ratcliff, R., & McKoon, G. (1984). The mental representation of knowledge acquired from maps. *Journal of Experimental Psychology: Learning, Memory, & Cognition, 10*(4), 723–732.

McNeil, J. E., & Warrington, E. K. (1993). Prosopagnosia: A face specific disorder. *Quarterly Journal of Experimental Psychology: Human Experimental Psychology, 46*, 1–10.

Meacham, J. (1982). A note on remembering to execute planned actions. *Journal of Applied Developmental Psychology, 3*, 121–133.

Meacham, J. A. (1983). Wisdom and the context of knowledge: Knowing that one doesn't know. In D. Kuhn & J. A. Meacham (Eds.), *On the development of developmental psychology* (pp. 111–134). Basel, Switzerland: Karger.

Meacham, J. A. (1990). The loss of wisdom. In R. J. Sternberg (Ed.), *Wisdom: Its nature, origins, and development* (pp. 181–211). New York: Cambridge University Press.

Meacham, J. A., & Singer, J. (1977). Incentive in prospective remembering. *Journal of Psychology, 97*, 191–197.

Medin, D. L. (1998). Concepts and conceptual structure. In P. Thagard (Ed.), *Mind readings* (pp. 93–126). Cambridge, MA: MIT Press.

Medin, D. L., & Aguilar, C. (1999). Categorization. In R. A. Wilson & F. C. Keil (Eds.), *The MIT encyclopedia of the cognitive sciences* (pp. 104–106). Cambridge, MA: MIT Press.

Medin, D. L., & Atran, S. (Eds.) (1999). *Folkbiology.* Cambridge, MA: MIT Press.

Medin, D. L., & Heit, E. (1999). Categorization. In D. Rumelhart & B. Martin (Eds.), *Handbook of cognition and perception* (pp. 99–143). New York: Academic Press.

Medin, D. L., Lynch, J., & Solomon, H. (2000). Are there kinds of concepts? *Annual Review of Psychology, 51*, 121–147.

Medin, D. L., Proffitt, J. B., & Schwartz, H. C. (2000). Concepts: An overview. In A. E. Kazdin (Ed.), *Encyclopedia of psychology* (Vol. 2, pp. 242–245). Washington, DC: American Psychological Association.

Mehler, J., Dupoux, E., Nazzi, T., & Dahaene-Lambertz, G. (1996). Coping with linguistic diversity: The infant's viewpoint. In J. L. Morgan & K. Demuth (Eds.), *Signal to Syntax: Bootstrapping from speech to grammar in early acquisition* (pp. 101–116). Mahwah, NJ: Erlbaum.

Meier, R. P. (1991). Language acquisition by deaf children. *American Scientist, 79*, 60–76.

Melton, R. J. (1995). The role of positive affect in syllogism performance. *Personality and Social Psychology Bulletin, 21*, 788–794.

Merikle, P. (2000). Consciousness and unconsciousness: Processes. In A. E. Kazdin (Ed.), *Encyclopedia of psychology* (Vol. 2, pp. 272–275). Washington, DC: American Psychological Association.

Merriam-Webster's collegiate dictionary (10th ed.). (1993). Springfield, MA: Merriam-Webster.

Mervis, C. B., Catlin, J., & Rosch, E. (1976). Relationships among goodness-of-example, category norms, and word frequency. *Bulletin of the Psychonomic Society, 7*, 268–284.

Metcalfe, J. (1986). Feeling of knowing in memory and problem solving. *Journal of Experimental Psychology: Learning, Memory, & Cognition, 12*(2), 288–294.

Metcalfe, J. (2000). Metamemory: Theory and data. In E. Tulving & F. I. M. Craik (Eds.), *The Oxford handbook of memory* (pp. 197–211). New York: Oxford University Press.

Metcalfe, J., & Wiebe, D. (1987). Intuition in insight and noninsight problem solving. *Memory & Cognition, 15*(3), 238–246.

Metzinger, T. (Ed.) (1995). *Conscious experience.* Paderborn: Schoningh.

Meyer, A. S., & Wheeldon, L. R. (2003). Phonological encoding of words. In L. Nadel (Ed.), *Encyclopedia of cognitive science, Vol. 3,* pp. 627–629. London, England: Nature Group Press.

Meyer, D. E., & Schvaneveldt, R. W. (1971). Facilitation in recognizing pairs of words: Evidence of a dependence between retrieval operations. *Journal of Experimental Psychology, 90*(2), 227–234.

Meyer, D. E., & Schvaneveldt, R. W. (1976). Meaning, memory structure, and mental processes. *Science, 192*(4234), 27–33.

Middleton, F. A., & Helms Tillery, S. I. (2003). Cerebellum. In L. Nadel (Ed.), *Encyclopedia of cognitive science, Vol. 1,* pp. 467–475. London, England: Nature Publishing Group.

Mill, J. S. (1887). *A system of logic.* New York: Harper & Brothers.

Miller, G. A. (1956). The magical number seven, plus or minus two: Some limits on our capacity for processing information. *Psychological Review, 63*, 81–97.

Miller, G. A. (1979). Images and models, similes and metaphors. In A. Ortony (Ed.), *Metaphor and thought* (pp. 202–250). New York: Cambridge University Press.

Miller, G. A., & Gildea, P. M. (1987). How children learn words. *Scientific American, 257*(3), 94–99.

Miller, G. A., Galanter, E. H., & Pribram, K. H. (1960). *Plans and the structure of behavior.* New York: Holt, Rinehart and Winston.

Miller, R. A., Pople, H., & Myers, J. (1982). INTERNIST, an experimental computer-based diagnostic consultant for general internal medicine. *New England Journal of Medicine, 307*(8), 494.

Mills, C. J. (1983). Sex-typing and self-schemata effects on memory and response latency. *Journal of Personality & Social Psychology, 45*(1), 163–172.

Mills, D., Coffey, S., & Neville, H. (1994). Changes in cerebral organization in infancy during primary language acquisition. In G. Dawson & K. Fischer (Eds.), *Human behavior and the developing brain.* New York: Guilford.

Milner, B. (1968). Disorders of memory loss after brain lesions in man: Preface-Material-specific and generalized memory loss. *Neuropsychologia, 6*(3), 175–179.

Milner, B. (1972). Disorders of learning and memory after temporal lobe lesions in man. *Clinical Neurosurgery, 19*, 421–446.

Milner, B., Corkin, S., & Teuber, H. L. (1968). Further analysis of the hippocampal amnesic syndrome: 14-year follow-up study of H. M. *Neuropsychologia, 6*, 215–234.

Minsky, M. (Ed.). (1968). *Semantic information processing.* Cambridge, MA: MIT Press.

Mirmiran, N., von Someren, E. J. W., & Swaab, D. F. (1996). Is brain plasticity preserved during aging and in Alzheimer's disease? *Behavioral Brain Research, 78*, 43–48.

Mishkin, M., & Appenzeller, T. (1987). The anatomy of memory. *Scientific American, 256*(6), 80–89.

Mishkin, M., & Petri, H. L. (1984). Memories and habits: Some implications for the analysis of learning and retention. In L. R. Squire & N. Butters (Eds.), *Neurophysiology of memory* (pp. 287–296). New York: Guilford.

Mishkin, M., Ungerleider, L. G., & Macko, K. A. (1983). Object vision and spatial vision: Two cortical pathways. *Trends in Neurosciences, 6*(10), 414–417.

Moar, I., & Bower, G. H. (1983). Inconsistency in spatial knowledge. *Memory & Cognition, 11*(2), 107–113.

Moore, C. M., & Egeth, H. (1997). Perception without attention: Evidence of grouping under conditions of inattention. *Journal of Experimental Psychology: Human Perception and Performance, 23*, 339–352.

Morawski, J. (2000). Psychology: Early twentieth century. In A. E. Kazdin (Ed.), *Encyclopedia of psychology* (Vol. 6, pp. 403–410). Washington, DC: American Psychological Association.

Moray, N. (1959). Attention in dichotic listening: Affective cues and the influence of instructions. *Quarterly Journal of Experimental Psychology, 11*, 56–60.

Morris, C. D., Bransford, J. D., & Franks, J. (1977). Levels of processing versus transfer appropriate processing. *Journal of Verbal Learning & Verbal Behavior, 16*(5), 519–533.

Morton, J. (1969). Interaction of information in word recognition. *Psychological Review, 76*, 165–178.

Morton, T. U. (1978). Intimacy and reciprocity of exchange: A comparison of spouses and strangers. *Journal of Personality and Social Psychology, 36*, 72–81.

Moscovitch, M. (2003). Memory consolidation. In L. Nadel (Ed.), *Encyclopedia of cognitive science, Vol. 2*, pp. 1066-1081. London, England: Nature Publishing Group.

Moscovitch, M., & Craik, F. I. M. (1976). Depth of processing, retrieval cues, and uniqueness of encoding as factors in recall. *Journal of Verbal Learning and Verbal Behavior, 15*, 447–458.

Moscovitch, M., Winocur, G., & Behrmann, M. (1997). What is special about face recognition? Nineteen experiments on a person with visual object agnosia and dyslexia but normal face recognition. *Journal of Cognitive Neuroscience, 9*, 555–604.

Moshman, E. (1998). Cognitive development beyond childhood. In W. Damon (Ed.-in-Chief), D. Kuhn, & R. S. Siegler (Vol. Eds.), *Handbook of child psychology: Vol. 2. Cognitive Development* (pp. 947–978). New York: Wiley.

Motter, B. (1999). Attention in the animal brain. In R. A. Wilson & F. C. Keil (Eds.), *The MIT encyclopedia of the cognitive sciences* (pp. 41–43). Cambridge, MA: MIT Press.

Mulligan, N. W. (2003). Memory: Implicit versus explicit. In L. Nadel (Ed.), *Encyclopedia of cognitive science, Vol. 2*, pp. 1114–1120. London, England: Nature Publishing Group.

Munhall, K. G. (2003). Phonology, neural basis of. In L. Nadel (Ed.), *Encyclopedia of cognitive science, Vol. 3*, pp. 655–658. London, England: Nature Group Press.

Murdock, B. B. (2003). Memory models. In L. Nadel (Ed.), *Encyclopedia of cognitive science, Vol. 2*, pp. 1084–1089. London, England: Nature Publishing Group.

Murdock, B. B., Jr. (1961). Short-term retention of single paired-associates. *Psychological Reports, 8*, 280.

Murphy, G. L. (1993). Theories and concept formation. In I. Van Mechelen, J. A. Hampton, R. S. Michalski, & P. Theuns (Eds.), *Categories and concepts: Theoretical views and inductive data analysis* (pp. 173–200). London: Academic Press.

Murray, E. A. (2003). Temporal cortex. In L. Nadel (Ed.), *Encyclopedia of cognitive science, Vol. 4*, pp. 353–360. London, England: Nature Publishing Group.

Näätänen, R. (1988a). Implications of ERP data for psychological theories of attention. *Biological Psychology, 26*(1–3), 117–163.

Näätänen, R. (1988b). Regional cerebral blood-flow: Supplement to event-related potential studies of selective attention. In G. C. Galbraith, M. L. Kietzman, & E. Donchin (Eds.), *Neurophysiology and psychophysiology: Experimental and clinical applications* (pp. 144–156). Hillsdale, NJ: Erlbaum.

Näätänen, R. (1990). The role of attention in auditory information processing as revealed by event-related potentials and other brain measures of cognitive function. *Behavioral & Brain Sciences, 13*(2), 201–288.

Näätänen, R. (1992). *Attention and brain function*. Hillsdale, NJ: Erlbaum.

Nairne, J. S., & Crowder, R. G. (1982). On the locus of the stimulus suffix effect. *Memory & Cognition, 10*, 350–357.

Nakayama, K. (1990). Visual inference in the perception of occluded surfaces (Summary). *Proceedings of the 125th Annual Conference of the Cognitive Science Society* (p. 1019). Hillsdale, NJ: Erlbaum.

National Research Council (1998). *Preventing reading difficulties in young children*. Washington, DC: National Academy Press.

Naus, M. J. (1974). Memory search of categorized lists: A consideration of alternative self-terminating search strategies. *Journal of Experimental Psychology, 102*, 992–1000.

Naus, M. J., Glucksberg, S., & Ornstein, P. A. (1972). Taxonomic word categories and memory search. *Cognitive Psychology, 3*, 643–654.

Naveh-Benjamin, M., & Ayres, T. J. (1986). Digit span, reading rate, and linguistic relativity. *Quarterly Journal of Experimental Psychology: Human Experimental Psychology, 38*(4), 739–751.

Navon, D. (1977). Forest before trees: The precedence of global features in visual perception. *Cognitive Psychology, 9*, 353–383.

Navon, D., & Gopher, D. (1979). On the economy of the human-processing system. *Psychological Review, 86*, 214–255.

Nečka, E., & Orzechowski, J. (2005). Higher-order cognition and intelligence. In R. J. Sternberg & J. E. Pretz (Eds.), *Cognition and intelligence* (pp. 122–141). New York: Cambridge University Press.

Neely, J. H. (2003). Priming. In L. Nadel (Ed.), *Encyclopedia of cognitive science, Vol. 3*, pp. 721–724. London, England: Nature Publishing Group.

Neisser, U. (1967). *Cognitive psychology*. New York: Appleton-Century-Crofts.

Neisser, U. (1978). Memory: What are the important questions? In M. M. Gruneberg, P. Morris, & R. Sykes (Eds.), *Practical aspects of memory* (pp. 3–24). London: Academic Press.

Neisser, U. (1982). Snapshots or benchmarks? In U. Neisser (Ed.), *Memory observed: Remembering in natural contexts*. San Francisco: Freeman.

Neisser, U., & Becklen, R. (1975). Selective looking: Attending to visually specified events. *Cognitive Psychology, 7*(4), 480–494.

Neisser, U., & Harsch, N. (1993). Phantom flashbulbs: False recollections of hearing the news about Challenger. In E. Winograd & U. Neisser (Eds.), *Affect and accuracy in recall: Studies of "flashbulb" memories* (pp. 9–31). New York: Cambridge University Press.

Neisser, U., Boodoo, G., Bouchard, T. J., Boykin, W. A., Brody, N., Ceci, S. J., et al. (1996). Intelligence: Knowns and Unknowns. *American Psychologist, 51*, 77–101.

Nelkin, N. (1996). *Consciousness and the origins of thought*. Cambridge, UK: Cambridge University Press.

Nelson, K. (1973). Structure and strategy in learning to talk. *Monograph of the Society for Research in Child Development, 38*(Serial No. 149).

Nelson, K. (1999). Language and thought. In M. Bennett (Ed.), *Developmental psychology* (pp. 185–204). Philadelphia: Psychology Press.

Nelson, T. O., & Narens, L. (1994). Why investigate metacognition? In J. Metcalfe & A. P. Shimamura (Eds.), *Metacognition-Knowing about knowing* (pp. 1–26). Cambridge, MA: MIT Press.

Nelson, T. O., & Rothbart, R. (1972). Acoustic savings for items forgotten from long-term memory. *Journal of Experimental Psychology, 93*, 357–360.

Neto, F., Williams, J. E., & Widner, S. C. (1991). Portuguese children's knowledge of sex stereotypes: Effects of age, gender, and socioeconomic status. *Journal of Cross-Cultural Psychology, 22*(3), 376–388.

Nettelbeck, T. (1987). Inspection time and intelligence. In P. A. Vernon (Ed.), *Speed of information-processing and intelligence* (pp. 295–346). Norwood, NJ: Ablex.

Nettelbeck, T., & Lally, M. (1976). Inspection time and measured intelligence. *British Journal of Psychology, 67,* 17–22.

Nettelbeck, T., & Rabbitt, P. M. A. (1992). Aging, cognitive performance, and mental speed. *Intelligence, 16*(2), 189–205.

Nettelbeck, T., & Young, R. (1996). Intelligence and savant syndrome: Is the whole greater than the sum of the fragments? *Intelligence, 22,* 49–67.

Nettelbeck, T., Rabbitt, P. M. A., Wilson, C., & Batt, R. (1996). Uncoupling learning from initial recall: The relationship between speed and memory deficits in old age. *British Journal of Psychology, 87,* 593–607.

Neubauer, A. C., & Fink, A. (2005). Basic information processing and the psychophysiology of intelligence. In R. J. Sternberg & J. E. Pretz (Eds.), *Cognition and intelligence* (pp. 68–87). New York: Cambridge University Press.

Neumann, P. G. (1977). Visual prototype formation with discontinuous representation of dimensions of variability. *Memory & Cognition, 5*(2), 187–197.

Neville, H. J. (1995). Developmental specificity in neurocognitive development in humans. In M. S. Gazzaniga (Ed.), *The cognitive neurosciences* (pp. 219–231). Cambridge, MA: MIT Press.

Newell, A., & Simon, H. A. (1972). *Human problem solving.* Englewood Cliffs, NJ: Prentice-Hall.

Newell, A., Shaw, J. C., & Simon, H. A. (1957a). Empirical explorations of the logic theory machine: A case study in heuristics. *Proceedings of the Western Joint Computer Conference,* 230–240.

Newell, A., Shaw, J. C., & Simon, H. A. (1957b). Problem solving in humans and computers. *Carnegie Technical, 21*(4), 34–38.

Newman, S. D., & Just, M. A. (2005). The neural bases of intelligence. In R. J. Sternberg & J. E. Pretz (Eds.), *Cognition and intelligence* (pp. 88–103). New York: Cambridge University Press.

Newport, E. L. (1990). Maturational constraints on language learning. *Cognitive Science, 14,* 11–28.

Newport, E. L. (1991). Constraining concepts of the critical period of language. In S. Carey & R. Gelman (Eds.), *The epigenesis of mind: Essays on biology and cognition* (pp. 111–130). Hillsdale, NJ: Erlbaum.

Newport, E. L. (2003). Language development, critical periods in. In L. Nadel (Ed.), *Encyclopedia of cognitive science, Vol. 2,* pp. 737–740. London, England: Nature Group Press.

Nickerson, R. S. (2004). Teaching reasoning. In J. P. Leighton & R. J. Sternberg (Eds.), *The nature of reasoning* (pp. 410–442). New York: Cambridge University Press.

Nikolic, M. I., Orr, J. M., & Sarter, N. B. (2004). Why pilots miss the green box: How display context undermines attention capture. *International Journal of Aviation Psychology, 14,* 39–52.

NINDS stroke information page (http://www.ninds.nih.gov/disorders/stroke/stroke.htm, retrieved 12/27/04).

Nisbett, R., & Ross, L. (1980). *Human inference: Strategies and shortcomings of social judgment.* Englewood Cliffs, NJ: Prentice-Hall.

Nisbett, R. E. (2003). *The geography of thought: Why we think the way we do.* New York, NY: The Free Press.

Nisbett, R. E., & Wilson, T. D. (1977). Telling more than we can know: Verbal reports on mental processes. *Psychological Review, 84,* 231–259.

Norman, D. A. (1968). Toward a theory of memory and attention. *Psychological Review, 75,* 522–536.

Norman, D. A. (1976). *Memory and attention: An introduction to human information processing* (2nd ed.). New York: Wiley.

Norman, D. A. (1988). *The design of everyday things.* New York: Doubleday.

Norman, D. A., & Rumelhart, D. E. (1975). *Explorations in cognition.* San Francisco: Freeman.

Norman, D. A., & Rumelhart, D. E. (1983). Studies of typing from the LNR research group. In W. E. Cooper (Ed., *Cognitive aspects of skilled typing* (pp. 45–65). New York: Springer-Verlag.

Norman, K. A., & Schacter, D. L. (1997). False recognition in younger and older adults: Exploring the characteristics of illusory memories. *Memory and Cognition, 25,* 838–848.

Nosofsky, R. M., & Palmeri, T. J. (1997). An exemplar-based random walk model of speeded classification. *Psychological Review, 104,* 266–300.

Nosofsky, R. M., Palmeri, T. J., & McKinley, S. C. (1994). Rule-plus-exception model of classification learning. *Psychological Review, 101,* 53–79.

Nozick, R. (1990). Newcomb's problem and two principles of choice. In P. K. Moser (Ed.), *Rationality in action: Contemporary approaches.* (pp. 207–234). New York: Cambridge University Press.

Nyberg, L., & Cabeza, R. (2000). Brain imaging of memory. In E. Tulving & F. I. M. Craik (Eds.), *The Oxford handbook of memory* (pp. 501–520). New York: Oxford University Press.

Nyberg, L., Cabeza, R. & Tulving, E. (1996). PET studies of encoding and retrieval: The HERA model. *Psychonomic Bulletin and Review, 3,* 135–148.

O'Brien, D. P. (2004). Mental-logic theory: What it proposes, and reasons to take this proposal seriously. In J. P. Leighton & R. J. Sternberg (Eds.), *The nature of reasoning* (pp. 205–233). New York: Cambridge University Press.

O'Keefe, J. (2003). Hippocampus. In L. Nadel (Ed.), *Encyclopedia of cognitive science, Vol. 1,* pp. 336–347. London, England: Nature Publishing Group.

O'Keefe, J. A., & Nadel, L. (1978). *The hippocampus as a cognitive map.* New York: Oxford University Press.

O'Reilly, R. C. (1996). Biologically plausible error-driven learning using local activation differences: The generalized recirculation algorithm. *Neural Computation, 8,* 895–938.

Ogbu, J. U. (1986). The consequences of the American caste system. In U. Neisser (Ed.), *The school achievement of minority children.* Hillsdale, NJ: Erlbaum.

Ojemann, G. A. (1975). The thalamus and language. *Brain and Language, 2,* 1–120.

Ojemann, G. A. (1982). Models of the brain organization for higher integrative functions derived with electrical stimulation techniques. *Human Neurobiology, 1,* 243–250.

Ojemann, G. A., & Mateer, C. (1979). Human language cortex: Localization of memory, syntax, and sequential motor–phoneme identification systems. *Science, 205,* 1401–1403.

Ojemann, G. A., & Whitaker, H. A. (1978). The bilingual brain. *Archives of Neurology, 35,* 409–412.

Oller, D. K., & Eilers, R. E. (1998). Interpretive and methodological difficulties in evaluating babbling drift. *Parole, 7/8,* 147–164.

Oller, D. K., Eilers, R. E., Urbano, R., & Cobo-Lewis, A. B. (1997). Development of precursors to speech in infants exposed to two languages. *Journal of Child Language, 24,* 407–425.

Olshausen, B., Andersen, C., & Van Essen, D. C. (1993). A neural model of visual attention and invariant pattern recognition. *Journal of Neuroscience, 13,* 4700–4719.

Olson, R. K. (1999). Genes, environment, and reading disabilities. In R. J. Sternberg & L. Spear-Swerling (Eds.), *Perspectives on learning disabilities: Biological, cognitive, contextual.* Boulder, CO: Westview Press.

O'Regan, J. K. (2003). Change blindness. In L. Nadel (Ed.), *Encyclopedia of cognitive science, Vol. 1,* pp. 486–490. London, England: Nature Publishing Group.

Ortony, A. (1979). The role of similarity in similes and metaphors. In A. Ortony (Ed.), *Metaphor and thought* (pp. 186–201). New York: Cambridge University Press.

Osherson, D. N. (1990). Judgment. In D. N. Osherson & E. E. Smith (Eds.), *An invitation to cognitive science: Vol. 3. Thinking* (pp. 55–87). Cambridge, MA: MIT Press.

Oxford English Dictionary (2nd ed.). (1989). Oxford, England: Clarendon Press.

Oyama, S. (1976). A sensitive period for the acquisition of a nonnative phonological system. *Journal of Psycholinguistic Research, 5*(3), 261–283.

Paap, K. R., Newsome, S. L., McDonald, J. E., & Schvaneveldt, R. W. (1982). An activation-verification model for letter and word recognition: The word-superiority effect. *Psychological Review, 89*(5), 573–594.

Paavilainen, P., Tiitinen, H., Alho, K., & Näätänen R. (1993). Mismatch negativity to slight pitch changes outside strong attentional focus. *Biological Psychology, 37*(1), 23–41.

Packard, M. G., Cahill, L., & McGaugh, J. L. (1994). Amygdala modulation of hippocampal-dependent and caudate nucleus-dependent memory processes. *Proceedings of the National Academy of Sciences, U.S.A., 91,* 8477–8481.

Paivio, A. (1969). Mental imagery in associative learning and memory. *Psychological Review, 76*(3), 241–263.

Paivio, A. (1971). *Imagery and verbal processes.* New York: Holt, Rinehart and Winston.

Palmer, J. (1990). Attentional limits on the perception and memory of visual information. *Journal of Experimental Psychology: Human Perception & Performance, 16*(2), 332–350.

Palmer, S. E. (1975). The effects of contextual scenes on the identification of objects. *Memory & Cognition, 3,* 519–526.

Palmer, S. E. (1977). Hierarchical structure in perceptual representation. *Cognitive Psychology, 9,* 441–474.

Palmer, S. E. (1992). Modern theories of Gestalt perception. In G. W. Humphreys (Ed.), *Understanding vision: An interdisciplinary perspective-Readings in mind and language* (pp. 39–70). Oxford, England: Blackwell.

Palmer, S. E. (1999a). Gestalt perception. In R. A. Wilson & F. C. Keil (Eds.), *The MIT encyclopedia of the cognitive sciences* (pp. 344–346). Cambridge, MA: MIT Press.

Palmer, S. E. (1999b). *Vision science: Photons to phenomenology.* Cambridge, MA: MIT Press.

Palmer, S. E. (2000). Perceptual organization. In A. E. Kazdin (Ed.), *Encyclopedia of psychology* (Vol. 6, pp. 93–97). Washington, DC: American Psychological Association.

Palmer, S. E., & Rock, I. (1994). Rethinking perceptual organization: The role of uniform connectedness. *Psychonomic Bulletin & Review, 1,* 29–55.

Palmeri, T. J. (2003). Automaticity. In L. Nadel (Ed.), *Encyclopedia of cognitive science, Vol. 1,* pp. 290–301. London, England: Nature Publishing Group.

Paradis, M. (1977). Bilingualism and aphasia. In H. A. Whitaker & H. Whitaker (Eds.), *Studies in neurolinguistics* (Vol. 3). New York: Academic Press.

Paradis, M. (1981). Neurolinguistic organization of a bilingual's two languages. In J. E. Copeland & P. W. Davis (Eds.), *The seventh LACUS forum.* Columbia, SC: Hornbeam Press.

Parker, A. J., Cumming, B. G., & Dodd, J. V. (2000). Binocular neurons and the perception of depth. In M. Gazzaniga (Ed.), *The new cognitive neurosciences* (pp. 263–278). Cambridge, MA: MIT Press.

Parkin, A. J. (1991). Recent advances in the neuropsychology of memory. In J. Weinman & J. Hunter (Eds.), *Memory: Neurochemical and abnormal perspectives* (pp. 141–162). London: Harwood Academic Publishers.

Parsons, O. A., & Nixon, S. J. (1993). Neurobehavioral sequelae of alcoholism. *Neurologic Clinics, 11*(1), 205–218.

Pashler, H. (1994). Dual-task interference in simple tasks: Data and theory. *Psychological Bulletin, 116*(2), 220–244.

Pashler, H. (1998). *The psychology of attention.* Cambridge, MA: MIT Press.

Pashler, H. E., & Johnston, J. (1998). Attentional limitations in dual task performance. In H. Pashler (Ed.), *Attention* (pp. 155–189). East Sussex, UK: Psychology Press.

Pavlov, I. P. (1955). *Selected works.* Moscow: Foreign Languages Publishing House.

Payne, J. (1976). Task complexity and contingent processing in decision making: An information search and protocol analysis. *Organizational Behavior and Human Performance, 16,* 366–387.

Peacocke, C. (1998). Conscious attitudes, attention and self-knowledge. In C. Wright, B. C. Smith, & C. Macdonald (Eds.), *Knowing our own minds* (pp. 63–98). Oxford, UK: Oxford University Press.

Pearson, B. Z., Fernandez, S. C., Lewedeg, V., & Oller, D. K. (1997). The relation of input factors to lexical learning by bilingual infants. *Applied Psycholinguistics, 18,* 41–58.

Penfield, W. (1955). The permanent record of the stream of consciousness. *Acta Psychologica, 11,* 47–69.

Penfield, W. (1969). Consciousness, memory, and man's conditioned reflexes. In K. H. Pribram (Ed.), *On the biology of learning* (pp. 129–168). New York: Harcourt, Brace & World.

Penfield, W., & Roberts, L. (1959). *Speech and brain mechanisms.* Princeton, NJ: Princeton University Press.

Pennebaker, J. W., & Memon, A. (1996). Recovered memories in context: Thoughts and elaborations on Bowers and Farvolden. *Psychological Bulletin, 119,* 381–385.

Peretz, I., Kolinsky, R., Tramo, M., Labrecque, R., Hublet, C., Demeurisse, G., & Belleville, S. (1994). Functional dissociations following bilateral lesions of auditory cortex. *Brain, 117,* 1283–1301.

Perfetti, C. A. (1985). *Reading ability.* New York: Oxford University Press.

Perfetti, C. A., & Roth, S. F. (1981). Some of the interactive processes in reading and their role in reading skill. In A. M. Lesgold & C. A. Perfetti (Eds.), *Interactive processes in reading* (pp. 269–297). Hillsdale, NJ: Erlbaum.

Perkins, D. N. (1981). *The mind's best work.* Cambridge, MA: Harvard University Press.

Perkins, D. N., & Grotzer, T. A. (1997). Teaching intelligence. *American Psychologist, 52,* 1125–1133.

Perlmutter, D. (Ed.). (1983a). *Studies in relational grammar* (Vol. 1). Chicago: University of Chicago Press.

Perlmutter, M. (1983b). Learning and memory through adulthood. In M. W. Riley, B. B. Hess, & K. Bond (Eds.), *Aging in society: Selected reviews of recent research*. Hillsdale, NJ: Erlbaum.

Perner, J. (1998). The meta-intentional nature of executive functions and theory of mind. In P. Carruthers & J. Boucher (Eds.), *Language and thought* (pp. 270–283). Cambridge, UK: Cambridge University Press.

Perner, J. (1999). Theory of mind. In M. Bennett (Ed.), *Developmental psychology: Achievements and prospects* (pp. 205–230). Philadelphia: Psychology Press.

Petersen, S. E., Fox, P. T., Posner, M. I., Mintun, M., & Raichle, M. E. (1988). Positron emission tomographic studies of the cortical anatomy of single-word processing. *Nature, 331*(6157), 585–589.

Petersen, S. E., Fox, P. T., Posner, M. I., Mintun, M., & Raichle, M. E. (1989). Positron emission tomographic studies of the processing of single words. *Journal of Cognitive Neuroscience, 1*(2), 153–170.

Peterson, L. R., & Peterson, M. J. (1959). Short-term retention of individual verbal items. *Journal of Experimental Psychology, 58*, 193–198.

Peterson, M. A. (1999). What's in a stage name? *Journal of Experimental Psychology: Human Perception and Performance, 25*, 276–286.

Peterson, M. A., Kihlstrom, J. F., Rose, P. M., & Glisky, M. L. (1992). Mental images can be ambiguous: Reconstruals and reference-frame reversals. *Memory & Cognition, 20*(2), 107–123.

Petitto, L., & Marentette, P. F. (1991). Babbling in the manual mode: Evidence for the ontogeny of language. *Science, 251*(5000), 1493–1499.

Piaget, J. (1928). *Judgment and reasoning in the child*. London: Routledge & Kegan Paul.

Piaget, J. (1952). *The origins of intelligence in children*. New York: International Universities Press.

Piaget, J. (1955). *The language and thought of the child*. New York: Meridian Books.

Pianta, R. C., & Egeland, B. (1994). Predictors of instability in children's mental test performance at 24, 48, and 96 months. *Intelligence, 18*(2), 145–163.

Picton, T. W., & Mazaheri, A. (2003). Electroencephalography. In L. Nadel (Ed.), *Encyclopedia of cognitive science, Vol. 1*, pp. 1083–1087. London, England: Nature Publishing Group.

Pierce, K., & Courchesne, E. (2003). Austism. In L. Nadel (Ed.), *Encyclopedia of cognitive science, Vol. 1*, pp. 278–283. London, England: Nature Publishing Group.

Pinker, S. (1980). Mental imagery and the third dimension. *Journal of Experimental Psychology: General, 109*(3), 354–371.

Pinker, S. (1985). Visual cognition: An introduction. In S. Pinker (Ed.), *Visual cognition* (pp. 1–63). Cambridge, MA: MIT Press.

Pinker, S. (1994). *The language instinct*. New York: William Morrow.

Pinker, S. (1997a). *How the mind works*. New York: Norton.

Pinker, S. (1997b). Letter to the editor. *Science, 276*, 1177–1178.

Pinker, S. (1999). *Words and rules*. New York: Basic Books.

Pisoni, D. B., Nusbaum, H. C., Luce, P. A., & Slowiaczek, L. M. (1985). Speech perception, word recognition and the structure of the lexicon. *Speech Communication, 4*, 75–95.

Plaut, D. C. (2000). Connectionism. In A. E. Kazdin (Ed.), *Encyclopedia of psychology* (pp. 265–268). Washington, DC: American Psychological Association.

Plaut, D. C., & Shallice, T. (1994). *Connectionist modelling in cognitive neuropsychology: A case study*. Hillsdale, NJ: Erlbaum.

Plaut, D. C., McClelland, J. L., Seidenberg, M. S., & Patterson, K. (1996). Understanding normal and impaired word reading: Computational principles in quasi-regular domains. *Psychological Review, 103*, 56–115.

Plomin, R. (1997). Identifying genes for cognitive abilities and disabilities. In R. J. Sternberg & E. L. Grigorenko (Eds.), *Intelligence, heredity, and environment* (pp. 89–104). New York: Cambridge University Press.

Plunkett, K. (1998). Language acquisition and connectionism. *Language and Cognitive Processes, 13*, 97–104.

Poggio, T., & Edelman, S. (1990). A network that learns to recognize three-dimensional objects. *Nature, 343*, 263–266.

Poincaré, H. (1913). *The foundations of science*. New York: Science Press.

Policastro, E., & Gardner, H. (1999). From case studies to robust generalizations: An approach to the study of creativity. In R. J. Sternberg (Ed.), *Handbook of creativity* (pp. 213–225). New York: Cambridge University Press.

Pollatsek, A., & Miller, B. (2003). Reading and writing. In L. Nadel (Ed.), *Encyclopedia of cognitive science, Vol. 3*, pp. 841–847. London, England: Nature Publishing Group.

Pollatsek, A., & Rayner, K. (1989). Reading. In M. I. Posner (Ed.), *Foundations of cognitive science* (pp. 401–436). Cambridge, MA: MIT Press.

Pomerantz, J. R. (1981). Perceptual organization in information processing. In M. Kubovy & J. R. Pomerantz (Eds.), *Perceptual organization* (pp. 141–180). Hillsdale, NJ: Erlbaum.

Pomerantz, J. R. (2003). Perception: Overview. In L. Nadel (Ed.), *Encyclopedia of cognitive science, Vol. 3*, pp. 527–537. London, England: Nature Publishing Group.

Poon, L. W. (1987). *Myths and truisms: Beyond extant analyses of speed of behavior and age*. Address to the Eastern Psychological Association Convention.

Posner, M., & Keele, S. W. (1968). On the genesis of abstract ideas. *Journal of Experimental Psychology, 77*(3, Pt. 1), 353–363.

Posner, M. I. (1969). Abstraction and the process of recognition. In G. H. Bower & J. T. Spence (Eds.), *The psychology of learning and motivation: Vol. 3. Advances in learning and motivation*. New York: Academic Press.

Posner, M. I. (1992). Attention as a cognitive and neural system. *Current Directions in Psychological Science, 1*(1), 11–14.

Posner, M. I. (1995). Attention in cognitive neuroscience: An overview. In M. Gazzaniga (Ed.), *The cognitive neurosciences* (pp. 615–624). Cambridge, MA: MIT Press.

Posner, M. I., & Dehaene, S. (1994). Attentional networks. *Trends in Neurosciences, 17*(2), 75–79.

Posner, M. I., & DiGirolamo, G. J. (1998). Conflict, target detection and cognitive control. In R. Parasuraman (Ed.), *The attentive brain*. Cambridge, MA: MIT Press.

Posner, M. I., & Fernandez-Duque, D. (1999). Attention in the human brain. In R. A. Wilson & F. C. Keil (Eds.), *The MIT encyclopedia of the cognitive sciences* (pp. 43–46). Cambridge, MA: MIT Press.

Posner, M. I., & Keele, S. W. (1967). Decay of visual information from a single letter. *Science, 158*(3797), 137–139.

Posner, M. I., & Petersen, S. E. (1990). The attention system of the human brain. *Annual Review of Neuroscience, 13*, 25–42.

Posner, M. I., & Raichle, M. E. (1994). *Images of mind*. New York: Freeman.

Posner, M. I., & Snyder, C. R. R. (1975). Attention and cognitive control. In R. Solso (Ed.), *Information processing and cognition: The Loyola Symposium* (pp. 55–85). Hillsdale, NJ: Erlbaum.

Posner, M. I., Boies, S., Eichelman, W., & Taylor, R. (1969). Retention of visual and name codes of single letters. *Journal of Experimental Psychology, 81,* 10–15.

Posner, M. I., DiGirolamo, G. J., & Fernandez-Duque, D. (1997). Brain mechanisms of cognitive skills. *Consciousness and Cognition, 6,* 267–290.

Posner, M. I., Goldsmith, R., & Welton, K. E., Jr. (1967). Perceived distance and the classification of distorted patterns. *Journal of Experimental Psychology, 73*(1), 28–38.

Posner, M. I., Petersen, S. E., Fox, P. T., & Raichle, M. E. (1988). Localization of cognitive operations in the human brain. *Science, 240*(4859), 1627–1631.

Posner, M. I., Sandson, J., Dhawan, M., & Shulman, G. L. (1989). Is word recognition automatic? A cognitive-anatomical approach. *Journal of Cognitive Neuroscience, 1,* 50–60.

Posner, M. I., Snyder, C. R. R., & Davidson, B. J. (1980). Attention and the detection of signals. *Journal of Experimental Psychology: General, 109*(2), 160–174.

Premack, D. (1971). Language in chimpanzees? *Science, 172,* 808–822.

Pretz, J. E., Naples, A. J., & Sternberg, R J. (2003). Recognizing, defining, and representing problems. In J. E. Davidson & R. J. Sternberg (Eds.), The *psychology of problem solving* (pp. 3–30). New York: Cambridge University Press.

Prinzmetal, W. P. (1995). Visual feature integration in a world of objects. *Current Directions in Psychological Science, 4,* 90–94.

Pullum, G. K. (1991). *The Great Eskimo vocabulary hoax and other irreverent essays on the study of language.* Chicago: University of Chicago Press.

Pylyshyn, Z. (1978). Imagery and artificial intelligence. In C. W. Savage (Ed.), *Minnesota studies in the philosophy of science: Vol. 9. Perception and cognition issues in the foundations of psychology* (pp. 19–56). Minneapolis: University of Minnesota Press.

Pylyshyn, Z. (1981). The imagery debate: Analogue media versus tacit knowledge. *Psychological Review, 88*(1), 16–45.

Pylyshyn, Z. (1984). *Computation and cognition.* Cambridge, MA: MIT Press.

Pylyshyn, Z. W. (1973). What the mind's eye tells the mind's brain: A critique of mental imagery. *Psychological Bulletin, 80,* 1–24.

Raichle, M. E. (1998). Behind the scenes of function brain imaging: A historical and physiological perspective. *Proceedings of the National Academy of Sciences, 95,* 765–772.

Raichle, M. E. (1999). Positron emission tomography. In R. A. Wilson & F. C. Keil (Eds.), *The MIT encyclopedia of the cognitive sciences* (pp. 656–659). Cambridge, MA: MIT Press.

Ramey, C. T., & Ramey, S. L. (2000). Intelligence and public policy. In R. J. Sternberg (Ed.), *Handbook of intelligence* (pp. 534–548). New York: Cambridge University Press.

Rao, R. P. N. (2003). Attention, models of. In L. Nadel (Ed.), *Encyclopedia of cognitive science, Vol. 1,* pp. 231–237. London, England: Nature Publishing Group.

Ratcliff, R. (1990). Connectionist models of recognition memory: Constraints imposed by learning and forgetting functions. *Psychological Review, 97*(2), 285–308.

Ratcliff, R., & McKoon, G. (1986). More on the distinction between episodic and semantic memories. *Journal of Experimental Psychology: Learning, Memory, & Cognition, 12*(2), 312–313.

Rayner, K., & Pollatsek, A. (2000). Reading. In A. E. Kazdin (Ed.), *Encyclopedia of psychology* (Vol. 7, pp. 14–18). Washington, DC: American Psychological Association.

Rayner, K., Sereno, S. C., Lesch, M. F., & Pollatsek, A. (1995). Phonological codes are automatically activated during reading: Evidence from an eye movement priming paradigm. *Psychological Science, 6,* 26–31.

Reason, J. (1990). *Human error.* New York: Cambridge University Press.

Reber, P. J., Knowlton, B. J, & Squire, L. R. (1996). Dissociable properties of memory systems: Differences in the flexibility of declarative and nondeclarative knowledge. *Behavioral Neurosciences, 110,* 861–871.

Reed, S. (1972). Pattern recognition and categorization. *Cognitive Psychology, 3*(3), 382–407.

Reed, S. (1974). Structural descriptions and the limitations of visual images. *Memory & Cognition, 2*(2), 329–336.

Reed, S. K. (1987). A structure-mapping model for word problems. *Journal of Experimental Psychology: Learning, Memory, & Cognition, 13*(1), 125–139.

Reed, S. K. (2000). Thinking: Problem solving. In A. E. Kazdin (Ed.), *Encyclopedia of psychology* (Vol. 8, pp. 71–75). Washington, DC: American Psychological Association.

Reed, S. K., Dempster, A., & Ettinger, M. (1985). Usefulness of analogous solutions for solving algebra word problems. *Journal of Experimental Psychology: Learning, Memory, & Cognition, 11*(1), 106–125.

Reed, T. E. (1993). Effect of enriched (complex) environment on nerve conduction velocity: New data and review of implications for the speed of information processing. *Intelligence, 17*(4), 533–540.

Reed, T. E,. & Jensen, A. R. (1991). Arm nerve conduction velocity (NCV), brain NCV, reaction time, and intelligence. *Intelligence, 15,* 33–47.

Reed, T. E., & Jensen, A. R. (1993). Choice reaction time and visual pathway nerve conduction velocity both correlate with intelligence, but appear not to correlate with each other: Implications for information processing. *Intelligence, 17,* 191–203.

Reeder, G. D., McCormick, C. B., & Esselman, E. D. (1987). Self-referent processing and recall of prose. *Journal of Educational Psychology, 79,* 243–248.

Reicher, G. M. (1969). Perceptual recognition as a function of meaningfulness of stimulus material. *Journal of Experimental Psychology, 81,* 275–280.

Reisberg, D. (Ed.). (1992). *Auditory imagery.* Hillsdale, NJ: Erlbaum.

Reisberg, D., Culver, L. C., Heuer, F., & Fischman, D. (1986). Visual memory: When imagery vividness makes a difference. *Journal of Mental Imagery, 10*(4), 51–74.

Reisberg, D., Smith, J. D., Baxter, D. A., & Sonenshine, M. (1989). "Enacted" auditory images are ambiguous: "Pure" auditory images are not. *Quarterly Journal of Experimental Psychology: Human Experimental Psychology, 41*(3–A), 619–641.

Reisberg, D., Wilson, M., & Smith, J. D. (1991). Auditory imagery and inner speech. In R. H. Logie & M. Denis (Eds.), *Advances in psychology: Vol. 80. Mental images in human cognition* (pp. 59–81). Amsterdam: North-Holland.

Reitman, J. S. (1971). Mechanisms of forgetting in short-term memory. *Cognitive Psychology, 2,* 185–195.

Reitman, J. S. (1974). Without surreptitious rehearsal, information in short-term memory decays. *Journal of Verbal Learning and Verbal Behavior, 13,* 365–377.

Reitman, J. S. (1976). Skilled perception in Go: Deducing memory structures from inter-response times. *Cognitive Psychology, 8,* 336–356.

Remez, R. E. (1994). A Guide to research on the perception of speech. In M. A. Gernsbacher (Ed.), *Handbook of psycholinguistics* (pp. 145–172). San Diego: Academic Press.

Rempel-Clower, N., Zola, S. M., Squire, L. R., & Amaral, D. G. (1996). Three cases of enduring memory impairment following bilateral damage limited to the hippocampal formation. *Journal of Neuroscience, 16,* 5233–5255.

Rensink, R. A., O'Regan, J. K., & Clark, J. J. (1997). To see or not to see: The need for attention to perceive changes in scenes. *Psychological Science, 8,* 368–373.

Rescorla, R. A. (1967). Pavlovian conditioning and its proper control procedures. *Psychological Review, 74,* 71–80.

Rescorla, R. A., & Wagner, A. R. (1972). A theory of Pavlovian conditioning: Variations in the effectiveness of reinforcement and non-reinforcement. In A. H. Black & W. F. Prokasy (Eds.), *Classical conditioning: Vol. 2. Current research and theory.* New York: Appleton-Century-Crofts.

Rey, G. (2003). Language of thought. In L. Nadel (Ed.), *Encyclopedia of cognitive science, Vol. 2,* pp. 753–760. London, England: Nature Group Press.

Rice, M. L. (1989). Children's language acquisition. *American Psychologist, 44,* 149–156.

Richardson-Klavehn, A., & Bjork, R. A. (1988). Measures of memory. *Annual Review of Psychology, 39,* 475–543.

Richardson-Klavehn, A. R., & Bjork, R. A. (2003). Memory, long-term. In L. Nadel (Ed.), *Encyclopedia of cognitive science, Vol. 2,* pp. 1096–1105. London, England: Nature Publishing Group.

Riggs, L. A., Ratliff, F., Cornsweet, J. C., & Cornsweet, T. N. (1953). The disappearance of steadily fixated visual test objects. *Journal of the Optical Society of America, 43,* 495–501.

Rips, L. J. (1983). Cognitive processes in propositional reasoning. *Psychological Review, 90*(1), 38–71.

Rips, L. J. (1988). Deduction. In R. J. Sternberg & E. E. Smith (Eds.), *The psychology of human thought* (pp. 116–152). New York: Cambridge University Press.

Rips, L. J. (1989). Similarity, typicality, and categorization. In S. Vosniadou & A. Ortony (Eds.), *Similarity and analogical reasoning* (pp. 21–59). New York: Cambridge University Press.

Rips, L. J. (1994). Deductive reasoning. In R. J. Sternberg (Ed.), *Handbook of perception and cognition: Thinking and problem solving* (pp. 149–178). New York: Academic Press.

Rips, L. J. (1999). Deductive reasoning. In R. A. Wilson & F. C. Keil (Eds.), *The MIT Encyclopedia of the cognitive sciences* (pp. 225–226). Cambridge, MA: MIT Press.

Roberts, A. C., Robbins, T. W., & Weiskrantz, L. (1996). Executive and cognitive functions of the pre-frontal cortex. *Philosophical Transactions of the Royal Society (London), B, 351,* (1346).

Roca, I. M. (2003a). Phonetics. In L. Nadel (Ed.), *Encyclopedia of cognitive science, Vol. 3,* pp. 619–625. London, England: Nature Group Press.

Roca, I. M. (2003b). Phonology. In L. Nadel (Ed.), *Encyclopedia of cognitive science, Vol. 3,* pp. 637–645. London, England: Nature Group Press.

Rock, I. (1983). *The logic of perception.* Cambridge, MA: MIT Press.

Rockland, K. S. (2000). Brain. In A. E. Kazdin (Ed.), *Encyclopedia of psychology* (Vol. 1, pp. 447–455). Washington, DC: American Psychological Association.

Roediger, H. L. (1980a). The effectiveness of four mnemonics in ordering recall. *Journal of Experimental Psychology: Human Learning & Memory, 6*(5), 558–567.

Roediger, H. L., & McDermott, K. B. (2000). Distortions of memory. In E. Tulving & F. I. M. Craik (Eds.), *The Oxford handbook of memory* (pp. 149–162). New York: Oxford University Press.

Roediger, H. L., III. (1980b). Memory metaphors in cognitive psychology. *Memory & Cognition, 8*(3), 231–246.

Roediger, H. L., III., & McDermott, K. B. (1995). Creating false memories: Remembering words not presented in lists. *Journal of Experimental Psychology: Learning, Memory, and Cognition, 21,* 803–814.

Rogers, T. B., Kuiper, N. A., & Kirker, W. S. (1977). Self-reference and the encoding of personal information. *Journal of Personality & Social Psychology, 35*(9), 677–688.

Rogers, Y., Rutherford, A, & Bibby, P. A. (Eds.) (1992). *Models in the mind: Theory, perspective and application.* London: Academic Press.

Rogoff, B. (1986). The development of strategic use of context in spatial memory. In M. Perlmutter (Ed.), *Perspectives on intellectual development.* Hillsdale, NJ: Erlbaum.

Rohde, D. L. T., & Plaut, D. (1999). Language acquisition in the absence of explicit negative evidence: How important is starting small? *Cognition, 72,* 67–109.

Rosch, E. (1975). Cognitive representations of semantic categories. *Journal of Experimental Psychology: General, 104,* 192–233.

Rosch, E. (1978). Principles of categorization. In E. Rosch & B. B. Lloyd (Eds.), *Cognition and categorization.* Hillsdale, NJ: Erlbaum.

Rosch, E. H., & Mervis, C. B. (1975). Family resemblances: Studies in the internal structure of categories. *Cognitive Psychology, 7,* 573–605.

Rosch, E. H., Mervis, C. B., Gray, W. D., Johnson, D. M., & Boyes-Braem, P. (1976). Basic objects in natural categories. *Cognitive Psychology, 8,* 382–439.

Rosen, B. R., Buckner, R. L., & Dale, A. M. (1998). Event-related fMRI: Past, present, and future. *Proceedings of the National Academy of Sciences USA, 95,* 773–780.

Rosenzweig, M. R. (2003). Memory, neural basis of: Cellular and molecular mechanisms. In L. Nadel (Ed.), *Encyclopedia of cognitive science, Vol. 2,* pp. 1105–1109. London, England: Nature Publishing Group.

Rosenzweig, M. R. & Bennett, E. L. (1996). Psychobiology of plasticity: Effects of training and experience on brain and behavior. *Behavior and Brain Research, 78,* 57–65.

Rosenzweig, M. R., & Leiman, A. L. (1989). *Physiological psychology* (2nd ed.). New York: Random House.

Ross, B. H. (1997). The use of categories affects classification. *Journal of Memory and Language, 37,* 165–192.

Ross, B. H. (2000). Concepts: Learning. In A. E. Kazdin (Ed.), *Encyclopedia of psychology* (Vol. 2, pp. 248–251). Washington, DC: American Psychological Association.

Ross, B. H., & Spalding, T. L. (1994). Concepts and categories. In R. J. Sternberg (Ed.), *Handbook of perception and cognition: Vol. 12. Thinking and problem solving* (pp. 119–148). New York: Academic Press.

Ross, L., Greene, D., & House, P. (1977). The false consensus effect: An egocentric bias in social perception and attribution processes. *Journal of Experimental Social Psychology, 13*(3), 279–301.

Ross, M., & Sicoly, F. (1979). Egocentric biases in availability and attribution. *Journal of Personality and Social Psychology, 37,* 322–336.

Rovee-Collier, C., & DuFault, D. (1991). Multiple contexts and memory retrieval at three months. *Developmental Psychobiology, 24*(1), 39–49.

Rovee-Collier, C., Borza, M. A., Adler, S. A., & Boller, K. (1993). Infants' eyewitness testimony: Effects of postevent information on a prior memory representation. *Memory & Cognition, 21*(2), 267–279.

Rubin, D. C. (1982). On the retention function for autobiographical memory. *Journal of Verbal Learning and Verbal Behavior, 19*, 21–38.

Rubin, D. C. (Ed.). (1996). *Remembering our past: Studies in autobiographical memory.* New York: Cambridge University Press.

Rubin, Z., Hill, C. T., Peplau, L. A., & Dunkel-Schetter, C. (1980). Self-disclosure in dating couples: Sex roles and the ethic of openness. *Journal of Marriage and the Family, 42*, 305–317.

Ruffman, T., Perner, J., Naito, M., Parkin, L., & Clements, W. A. (1998). Older (but not younger) siblings facilitate false belief understanding. *Developmental Psychology, 34*, 161–174.

Rugg, M. D. (Ed.) (1997). *Cognitive neuroscience.* Hove East Sussex, UK: Psychology Press.

Rugg, M. D., & Allan, K. (2000). Event-related potential studies of memory. In E. Tulving & F. I. M. Craik (Eds.), *The Oxford handbook of memory* (pp. 521–538). New York: Oxford University Press.

Rumain, B., Connell, J., & Braine, M. D. S. (1983). Conversational comprehension processes are responsible for reasoning fallacies in children as well as adults: If is not the biconditional. *Developmental Psychology, 19*(4), 471–481.

Rumbaugh, D. M., & Beran, M. J. (2003). Language acquisition by animals. In L. Nadel (Ed.), *Encyclopedia of cognitive science, Vol. 2,* pp. 700–707. London, England: Nature Group Press.

Rumelhart, D. E., & McClelland, J. L. (1981). Interactive processing through spreading activation. In A. M. Lesgold & C. A. Perfetti (Eds.), *Interactive processes in reading* (pp. 37–60). Hillsdale, NJ: Erlbaum.

Rumelhart, D. E., & McClelland, J. L. (1982). An interactive activation model of context effects in letter perception: Part 2. The contextual enhancement effect and some tests and extensions of the model. *Psychological Review, 89*, 60–94.

Rumelhart, D. E., & Norman, D. (1988). Representation in memory. In R. C. Atkinson, R. J. Herrnstein, G. Lindzey, R. D. Luce (Eds.), *Stevens' handbook of experimental psychology: Vol. 2. Learning and cognition* (2nd ed., 511–587). New York: Wiley.

Rumelhart, D. E., & Ortony, A. (1977). The representation of knowledge in memory. In R. C. Anderson, R. J. Spiro, & W. E. Montague (Eds.), *Schooling and the acquisition of knowledge* (pp. 99–135). Hillsdale, NJ: Erlbaum.

Rumelhart, D. E., McClelland, J. L., & the PDP Research Group. (1986). *Parallel distributed processing. Explorations in the microstructure of cognition: Vol. 1. Foundations.* Cambridge, MA: MIT Press.

Runco, M. A. (2000). Creativity: Research on the process of creativity. In A. E. Kazdin (Ed.), *Encyclopedia of psychology* (Vol. 2, pp. 342–346). Washington, DC: American Psychological Association.

Runco, M. A. (Ed.) (1997). *Creativity research handbook* (Vols. 1–3). Cresskill, NJ: Hampton Press.

Ruscio, J., Whitney, D. M., & Amabile, T. M. (1998). Looking inside the fishbowl of creativity: Verbal and behavioral predictors of creative performance. *Creativity Research Journal, 11*, 243–263.

Russell, J. A., & Ward, L. M. (1982). Environmental psychology. *Annual Review of Psychology, 33*, 651–688.

Russell, W. R., & Nathan, P. W. (1946). Traumatic amnesia. *Brain, 69*, 280–300.

Rychlak, J. E., & Struckman, A. (2000). Psychology: Post-World War II. In A. E. Kazdin (Ed.), *Encyclopedia of psychology* (Vol. 6, pp. 410–416). Washington, DC: American Psychological Association.

Ryle, G. (1949). *The concept of mind.* London: Hutchinson.

Saarinen, J. (1987a). Perception of positional relationships between line segments in eccentric vision. *Perception, 16*(5), 583–591.

Saarinen, T. F. (1987b). *Centering of mental maps of the world* (discussion paper). University of Arizona, Tucson: Department of Geography and Regional Development.

Sacks, H., Schegloff, E. A., & Jefferson, G. (1974). A simplest systematics for the organization of turn-taking for conversation. *Language, 50*, 696–735.

Salovey, P., & Sluyter, D. J. (1997). *Emotional development and emotional intelligence: Implications for educators.* New York: Basic Books.

Salthouse, T. A. (1984). Effects of age and skill in typing. *Journal of Experimental Psychology: General, 113*, 345–371.

Salthouse, T. A. (1991). Expertise as the circumvention of human processing limitations. In K. A. Ericsson & J. Smith (Eds.), *Toward a general theory of expertise: Prospects and limits* (pp. 286–300). New York: Cambridge University Press.

Salthouse, T. A. (1992). The information-processing perspective on cognitive aging. In R. J. Sternberg & C. A. Berg (Eds.), *Intellectual development* (pp. 261–277). New York: Cambridge University Press.

Salthouse, T. A. (1993). Influence of working memory on adult age differences in matrix reasoning. *British Journal of Psychology, 84*(2), 171–199.

Salthouse, T. A. (1994). The nature of the influence of speed on adult age differences in cognition. *Developmental Psychology, 30*(2), 240–259.

Salthouse, T. A. (1996). The processing-speed theory of adult age differences in cognition. *Psychological Review, 103*, 403–428.

Salthouse, T. A. (2005). From description to explanation in cognitive aging. In R. J. Sternberg & J. E. Pretz (Eds.), *Cognition and intelligence* (pp. 288–305). New York: Cambridge University Press.

Salthouse, T. A., & Somberg, B. L. (1982). Skilled performance: Effects of adult age and experience on elementary processes. *Journal of Experimental Psychology: General, 111*(2), 176–207.

Salthouse, T. A., Kausler, D. H., & Saults, J. S. (1990). Age, self-assessed health status, and cognition. *Journal of Gerontology, 45*(4), P156–P160.

Samuel, A. G. (1981). Phonemic restoration: Insights from a new methodology. *Journal of Experimental Psychology: General, 110*, 474–494.

Samuel, A. L. (1963). Some studies in machine learning using the game of checkers. In E. A. Feigenbaum & J. Feldman (Eds.), *Computers and thought* (pp. 71–105). New York: McGraw-Hill.

Samuels, J. J. (1999). Developing reading fluency in learning disabled students. In R. J. Sternberg & L. Spear-Swerling (Eds.), *Perspectives on learning disabilities: Biological, cognitive, contextual* (pp. 176–189). Boulder, CO: Westview Press.

Sapir, E. (1964). *Culture, language and personality.* Berkeley, CA: University of California Press. (Original work published 1941)

Sarason, S. B., & Doris, J. (1979). *Educational handicap, public policy, and social history.* New York: Free Press.

Sarter, M., Bruno, J. P., & Berntson, G. G. (2003). Reticular activating system. In L. Nadel (Ed.), *Encyclopedia of cognitive science, Vol. 3,* pp. 963–967. London, England: Nature Publishing Group.

Sarter, N. B., & Alexander, H. M. (2000). Error types and related error detection mechanisms in the vaiation domain: An analysis of aviation safety reporting system incident reports. *International Journal of Aviation Psychology, 10,* 189–206.

Savage-Rumbaugh, S., McDonald, K., Sevcik, R. A., Hopkins, W. D., & Rubert, E. (1986). Spontaneous symbol acquisition and communicative use by pygmy chimpanzees (*Pan paniscus*). *Journal of Experimental Psychology: General, 115,* 211–235.

Savage-Rumbaugh, S., Murphy, J., Sevcik, R., Brakke, K., Williams, S., & Rumbaugh, D. M. (1993). Language comprehension in ape and child. *Monographs of the Society for Research in Child Development, 58*(3–4, Serial No. 233).

Scaggs, W. E., & McNaughton, B. L. (1996). Replay of neuronal firing sequences in rat hippocampus during sleep following spatial experience. *Science, 271,* 1870–1873.

Schacter, D. L. (1989a). Memory. In M. I. Posner (Ed.), *Foundations of cognitive science* (pp. 683–725). Cambridge, MA: MIT Press.

Schacter, D. L. (1989b). On the relation between memory and consciousness: Dissociable interactions and conscious experience. In H. L. Roediger & F. I. M. Craik (Eds.), *Varieties of memory and consciousness: Essays in honor of Endel Tulving.* Hillsdale, NJ: Erlbaum.

Schacter, D. L. (1995a). Implicit memory. In M. S. Gazzaniga (Ed.), *The cognitive neurosciences* (pp. 815–824). Cambridge, MA: MIT Press.

Schacter, D. L. (1995b). Memory distortion: History and current status. In D. L. Schacter, J. T. Coyle, G. D. Fischbach, M. M. Mesulam, & L. E. Sullivan (Eds.), *Memory distortions* (pp. 1–43). Cambridge, MA: Harvard University Press.

Schacter, D. L. (2000). Memory: Memory systems. In A. E. Kazdin (Ed.) *Encyclopedia of psychology* (Vol. 5, pp. 169–172). Washington, DC: American Psychological Association.

Schacter, D. L. (2001). *The seven sins of memory: How the mind forgets and remembers.* Boston: Houghton Mifflin.

Schacter, D. L., & Curran, T. (2000). Memory without remembering and remembering without memory: Implicit and false memories. In M. S. Gazzaniga (Ed.), *The new cognitive neurosciences* (2nd ed., pp. 829–840). Cambridge, MA: MIT Press.

Schacter, D. L., & Graf, P. (1986a). Effects of elaborative processing on implicit and explicit memory for new associations. *Journal of Experimental Psychology: Learning, Memory, & Cognition, 12*(3), 432–444.

Schacter, D. L., & Graf, P. (1986b). Preserved learning in amnesic patients: Perspectives from research on direct priming. *Journal of Clinical & Experimental Neuropsychology, 8*(6), 727–743.

Schacter, D. L., Chiu, C. Y. P., & Ochsner, K. N. (1993). Implicit memory: A selective review. *Annual Review of Neuroscience, 16,* 159–182.

Schacter, D. L., Verfaellie, M., & Pradere, D. (1996). The neuropsychology of memory illusions: False recall and recognition in amnesic patients. *Journal of Memory and Language, 35,* 319–334.

Schaeken, W., Johnson-Laird, P. N., & D'Ydewalle, G. (1996). Mental models and temporal reasoning. *Cognition, 60,* 205-234.

Schaffer, H. R. (1977). *Mothering.* Cambridge, MA: Harvard University Press.

Schaie, K. W. (1974). Translations in gerontology-from lab to life. *American Psychologist, 29,* 802–807.

Schaie, K. W. (1989). Perceptual speed in adulthood: Cross-sectional and longitudinal studies. *Psychology and Aging, 4,* 443–453.

Schaie, K. W. (1996). *Intellectual development in adulthood: The Seattle longitudinal study.* New York: Cambridge University Press.

Schaie, K. W., & Willis, S. L. (1986). Can decline in intellectual functioning in the elderly be reversed? *Developmental Psychology, 22,* 223–232.

Schank, R. C., & Abelson, R. P. (1977). *Scripts, plans, goals, and understanding.* Hillsdale. NJ: Erlbaum.

Schank, R. C., & Towle, B. (2000). Artificial intelligence. In R. J. Sternberg (Ed.,) *Handbook of intelligence* (pp. 341–356). New York: Cambridge University Press.

Scheck, P., & Nelson, T. O. (2003). Metacognition. In L. Nadel (Ed.), *Encyclopedia of cognitive science, Vol. 3,* pp. 11–15. London, England: Nature Publishing Group.

Schliemann, A. D., & Magalhües, V. P. (1990). *Proportional reasoning: From shops, to kitchens, laboratories, and, hopefully, schools.* Proceedings of the Fourteenth International Conference for the Psychology of Mathematics Education, Oaxtepec, Mexico.

Schmidt, S. R., & Bohannon, J. N. (1988). In defense of the flash-bulb-memory hypothesis: A comment on McCloskey, Wible, & Cohen (1988). *Journal of Experimental Psychology: General, 117*(3), 332–335.

Schneider, W., & Bjorklund, D. F. (1998). Memory. In W. Damon (Ed.-in-Chief), D. Kuhn, & R. S. Siegler (Vol. Eds.), *Handbook of child psychology: Vol. 2. Cognitive development* (pp. 467–521). New York: Wiley.

Schneider, W., & Shiffrin, R. (1977). Controlled and automatic human information processing. *Psychological Review, 84,* 1–66.

Schoenfeld, A. H. (1981). *Episodes and executive decisions in mathematical problem solving.* Paper presented at the annual meeting of the American Educational Research Association, Los Angeles, CA.

Schonbein, W., & Bechtel, W. (2003). History of computational modeling and cognitive science. *Encyclopedia of Cognitive Science.* London, England: Nature Publishing Group.

Schonfield, D., & Robertson, D. A. (1966). Memory storage and aging. *Canadian Journal of Psychology, 20,* 228–236.

Schooler, J. W. (1994). Seeking the core: The issues and evidence surrounding recovered accounts of sexual trauma. *Consciousness and Cognition, 3,* 452–469.

Schooler, J. W., & Engstler-Schooler, T. Y. (1990). Verbal overshadowing of visual memories: Some things are better left unsaid. *Cognitive Psychology, 22,* 36–71.

Schustack, M. W., & Sternberg, R. J. (1981). Evaluation of evidence in causal inference. *Journal of Experimental Psychology: General, 110,* 101–120.

Schvaneveldt, R. W., Meyer, D. E., & Becker, C. A. (1976). Lexical ambiguity, semantic context, and visual word recognition. *Journal of Experimental Psychology: Human Perception & Performance, 2*(2), 243–256.

Schwartz, B. L., & Metcalfe, J. (1994). Methodological problems and pitfalls in the study of human metacognition. In J. Metcalfe & A. P. Shimamura (Eds.), *Metacognition: Knowing about knowing* (pp. 93–114). Cambridge, MA: MIT Press.

Schwartz, D. (1996). Analog imagery in mental model reasoning: Depictive models. *Cognitive Psychology, 30,* 154–219.

Schwartz, D. L., & Black, J. B. (1996). Analog imagery in mental model reasoning: Depictive models. *Cognitive Psychology, 30,* 154–219.

Schwarz, N., & Skurnik, I.(2003). Feeling and thinking: Implications for problem solving. In J. E. Davidson & R. J. Sternberg (Eds.), *The psychology of problem solving* (pp. 263–290). New York: Cambridge University Press.

Schweickert, R., & Boruff, B. (1986). Short-term memory capacity: Magic number or magic spell? *Journal of Experimental Psychology: Learning, Memory, & Cognition, 12*(3), 419–425.

Scoville, W. B., & Milner, B. (1957). Loss of recent memory after bilateral hippocampal lesions. *Journal of Neurology, Neurosurgery, and Psychiatry, 20,* 11–19.

Searle, J. R. (1975a). Indirect speech acts. In P. Cole & J. L. Morgan (Eds.), *Syntax and semantics: Speech acts* (Vol. 3, pp. 59–82). New York: Seminar Press.

Searle, J. R. (1975b). A taxonomy of elocutionary acts. In K. Gunderson (Ed.), *Minnesota studies in the philosophy of language* (pp. 344–369). Minneapolis: University of Minnesota Press.

Searle, J. R. (1979). *Expression and meaning: Studies in the theory of speech acts.* Cambridge, England: Cambridge University Press.

Searle, J. R. (1980). Minds, brains, and programs. *Behavioral and Brain Sciences, 3,* 417–424.

Sehulster, J. R. (1989). Content and temporal structure of autobiographical knowledge: Remembering twenty five seasons at the Metropolitan Opera. *Memory and Cognition, 17,* 290–606.

Seidenberg, M. S., & McClelland, J. L. (1989). A distributed, developmental model of word recognition and naming. *Psychological Review, 96,* 523–568.

Seifert, C. M., Meyer, D. E., Davidson, N., Palatano, A. L., & Yaniv, I. (1995). Demystification of cognitive insight: Opportunistic assimilation and the prepare-mind perspective. In R. J. Sternberg & J. E. Davidson (Eds.), *The nature of insight* (pp. 65–124). Cambridge, MA: MIT Press.

Selfridge, O. G. (1959). Pandemonium: A paradigm for learning. In D. V. Blake & A. M. Uttley (Eds.), *Proceedings of the Symposium on the Mechanization of Thought Processes* (pp. 511–529). London: Her Majesty's Stationery Office.

Selfridge, O. G., & Neisser, U. (1960). Pattern recognition by machine. *Scientific American, 203,* 60–68.

Sera, M. D. (1992). To be or to be: Use and acquisition of the Spanish copulas. *Journal of Memory and Language, 31,* 408–427.

Serpell, R. (2000). Intelligence and culture. In R. J. Sternberg (Ed.), *Handbook of intelligence* (pp. 549–577). New York: Cambridge University Press.

Shafir, E. B., Osherson, D. N., & Smith, E. E. (1990). Typicality and reasoning fallacies. *Memory & Cognition, 18*(3), 229–239.

Shallice, T. (1979). Neuropsychological research and the fractionation of memory systems. In L. G. Nilsson (Ed.), *Perspectives on memory research.* Hillsdale, NJ: Erlbaum.

Shallice, T., & Warrington, E. (1970). Independent functioning of verbal memory stores: A neuropsychological study. *Quarterly Journal of Experimental Psychology, 22*(2), 261–273.

Shankweiler, D., Crain, D. S., Katz, L., Fowler, A. E., Liberman, A. M., Brady, S. A., et al. (1995). Cognitive profiles of reading-disabled children: Comparison of language skills in phonology, morphology, and syntax. *Psychological Science, 6,* 149–156.

Shapiro, P., & Penrod, S. (1986). Meta-analysis of facial identification studies. *Psychological Bulletin, 100*(2), 139–156.

Shapley, R., & Lennie, P. (1985). Spatial frequency analysis in the visual system. *Annual Review of Neuroscience, 8,* 547–583.

Shastri, L. (2003). Spreading-activation networks. In L. Nadel (Ed.), *Encyclopedia of cognitive science, Vol. 4,* pp. 211–218. London, England: Nature Publishing Group.

Shear, J. (Ed.) (1997). *Explaining consciousness: The hard problem.* Cambridge, MA: MIT Press.

Shepard, R. N. (1984). Ecological constraints on internal representation. Resonant kinematics of perceiving, imaging, thinking, and dreaming. *Psychological Review, 91,* 417–447.

Shepard, R. N., & Metzler, J. (1971). Mental rotation of three-dimensional objects. *Science, 171*(3972), 701–703.

Shepherd, G. (Ed.) (1998). *The synaptic organization of the brain.* New York; Oxford University Press.

Shiffrin, R. M. (1973). Information persistence in short-term memory. *Journal of Experimental Psychology, 100,* 39–49.

Shiffrin, R. M. (1996). Laboratory experimentation on the genesis of expertise. In K. A. Ericsson (Ed.), *The road to excellence* (pp. 337–347). Mahwah, NJ: Erlbaum.

Shiffrin, R. M., & Schneider, W. (1977). Controlled and automatic human information processing: II. Perceptual learning, automatic attending, and a general theory. *Psychological Review, 84,* 127–190.

Shimamura, A. P., & Squire, L. R. (1986). Korsakoff's syndrome: A study of the relation between anterograde amnesia and remote memory impairment. *Behavioral Neuroscience, 100*(2), 165–170.

Shoben, E. J. (1984). Semantic and episodic memory. In R. W. Wyer, Jr., & T. K. Srull (Eds.), *Handbook of social cognition* (Vol. 2, pp. 213–231). Hillsdale, NJ: Erlbaum.

Shore, D. I., & Klein, R. M. (2000). The effects of scene inversion on change blindness. *Journal of General Psychology, 127,* 27–43.

Shortliffe, E. H. (1976). *Computer-based medical consultations: MYCIN.* New York: American Elsevier.

Shulman, H. G. (1970). Encoding and retention of semantic and phonemic information in short-term memory. *Journal of Verbal Learning and Verbal Behavior, 9,* 499–508.

Siegler, R. S. (1986). *Children's thinking.* Englewood Cliffs, NJ: Prentice-Hall.

Siegler, R. S. (1988). Individual differences in strategy choices: Good students, not-so-good students, and perfectionists. *Child Development, 59*(4), 833–851.

Silverman, I., & Eals, M. (1992). Sex differences in spatial abilities: Evolutionary theory and data. In J. Barkow, L. Cosmides, & J. Tooby (Eds.), *The adapted mind* (pp. 533–549). New York: Oxford.

Simon, H. A. (1957). *Administrative behavior* (2nd ed.). Totowa, NJ: Littlefield, Adams.

Simon, H. A. (1976). Identifying basic abilities underlying intelligent performance of complex tasks. In L. B. Resnick (Ed.), *The nature of intelligence* (pp. 65–98). Hillsdale, NJ: Erlbaum.

Simon, H. A. (1999a). Problem solving. In R. A. Wilson & F. C. Keil (Eds.), *The MIT encyclopedia of the cognitive sciences* (pp. 674–676). Cambridge, MA: MIT Press.

Simon, H. A. (1999b). Production systems. In R. A. Wilson & F. C. Keil (Eds.), *The MIT encyclopedia of the cognitive sciences* (pp. 676–678). Cambridge, MA: MIT Press.

Simon, H. A., & Kotovsky, K. (1963). Human acquisition of concepts for sequential patterns. *Psychological Review, 70,* 534–546.

Simon, H. A., & Reed, S. K. (1976). Modeling strategy shifts in a problem-solving task. *Cognitive Psychology, 8,* 86–97.

Simons, D. (1996). In sight, out of mind: when object representations fail. *Psychological Science, 5,* 301–305.

Simons, D. J. (2000). Attentional capture and inattentional blindness. *Trends in Cognitive Science, 4,* 147–155.

Simons, D. J, & Levin, D. T. (1997). Change blindness. *Trends in Cognitive Science, 1,* 261–267.

Simons, D. J., & Levin, D. T. (1998). Failure to detect changes to people during a real-world interaction. *Psychonomic Bulletin & Review, 5,* 644–649.

Simonton, D. K. (1988). Creativity, leadership, and chance. In R. J. Sternberg (Ed.), *The nature of creativity* (pp. 386–426). New York: Cambridge University Press.

Simonton, D. K. (1994). *Greatness: Who makes history and why.* New York: Guilford.

Simonton, D. K. (1997). Creativity in personality, developmental, and social psychology: Any links with cognitive psychology? In T. B. Ward, S. M. Smith, & J. Vaid (Eds.), *Creative thought: Conceptual structures and processes* (pp. 309–324). Washington, DC: American Psychological Association.

Simonton, D. K. (1998). Donald Campbell's model of the creative process: Creativity as blind variation and selective retention. *Journal of Creative Behavior, 32*, 153–158.

Simonton, D. K. (1999). Creativity from a historiometric perspective. In R. J. Sternberg (Ed.), *Handbook of creativity* (pp. 116–133). New York: Cambridge University Press.

Sincoff, J. B., & Sternberg, R. J. (1988). Development of verbal fluency abilities and strategies in elementary-school-age children. *Developmental Psychology, 24*, 646–653.

Skinner, B. F. (1957). *Verbal behavior.* New York: Appleton-Century-Crofts.

Slobin, D. I. (1971). Cognitive prerequisites for the acquisition of grammar. In C. A. Ferguson & D. I. Slobin (Eds.), *Studies of child language development.* New York: Holt, Rinehart and Winston.

Slobin, D. I. (Ed.). (1985). *The cross-linguistic study of language acquisition.* Hillsdale, NJ: Erlbaum.

Sloboda, J. A. (1984). Experimental studies in music reading: A review. *Music Perception, 22*, 222–236.

Sloboda, J. A. (1996). The acquisition of musical performance expertise: Deconstructing the "talent" account of individual differences in musical expressivity. In K. A. Ericsson (Ed.), *The road to excellence* (pp. 107–127). Mahwah, NJ: Erlbaum.

Sloboda, J. A., Davidson, J. W., Howe, M. J. A., & Moore, D. G. (1996). The role of practice in the development of performing musicians. *British Journal of Psychology, 87*, 287–309.

Sloman, S. (1996). The empirical case for two systems of reasoning. *Psychological Bulletin, 119*, 3–22.

Slovic, P. (1990). Choice. In D. N. Osherson & E. E. Smith (Eds.), *An invitation to cognitive science: Vol. 3. Thinking* (pp. 89–116). Cambridge, MA: MIT Press.

Smilansky, B. (1974). Paper presented at the meeting of the American Educational Research Association, Chicago.

Smith, C. (1996). Sleep states, memory phases, and synaptic plasticity. *Behavior and Brain Research, 78*, 49–56.

Smith, E. E. (1988). Concepts and thought. In R. J. Sternberg & E. E. Smith (Eds.), *The psychology of human thought* (pp. 19–49). New York: Cambridge University Press.

Smith, E. E. (1995a). Concepts and categorization. In E. E. Smith & D. N. Osherson (Eds.), *An invitation to cognitive science* (Vol. 3, *Thinking*) (2nd ed., pp. 3–33). Cambridge, MA: MIT Press.

Smith, E. E., & Jonides, J. (1995). Working memory in humans: Neuropsychological evidence. In M. Gazzaniga (Ed.), *The cognitive neurosciences* (pp. 1009–1020). Cambridge, MA: MIT Press.

Smith, E. E., & Medin, D. L. (1981). *Categories and concepts.* Cambridge, MA: Harvard University Press.

Smith, E. E., Langston, C., & Nisbett, R. E. (1992). The case for rules in reasoning. *Cognitive Science, 16*(1), 1–40.

Smith, E. E., Osherson, D. N., Rips, L. J., & Keane, M. (1988). Combining prototypes: A modification model. *Cognitive Science, 12*, 485–527.

Smith, E. E., Shoben, E. J., & Rips, L. J. (1974). Structure and process in semantic memory: A featural model for semantic decisions. *Psychological Review, 81*, 214–241.

Smith, J. D., Reisberg, D., & Wilson, M. (1992). Subvocalization and auditory imagery: Interactions between the inner ear and inner voice. In D. Reisberg (Ed.), *Auditory imagery* (pp. 95–119). Hillsdale, NJ: Erlbaum.

Smith, L. B., Jones, S. S., & Landau, B. (1996). Naming in young children: A dumb attentional mechanism? *Cognition, 60*, 143–171.

Smith, S. M. (1995b). Getting into and out of mental ruts: A theory of fixation, incubation, and insight. In R. J. Sternberg & J. E. Davidson (Eds.), *The nature of insight* (pp. 229–251). Cambridge, MA: MIT Press.

Smolensky, P. (1999). Connectionist approaches to language. In R. A. Wilson & F. C. Keil (Eds.), *The MIT encyclopedia of the cognitive sciences* (pp. 188–190). Cambridge, MA: MIT Press.

Snow, C. (1999). Social perspectives on the emergence of language. In B. MacWhinney (Ed.), *The emergence of language* (pp. 257–276). Mahwah, NJ: Erlbaum.

Snow, C. E. (1977). The development of conversation between mothers and babies. *Journal of Child Language, 4*, 1–22.

Snow, J. C., & Mattingley, J. B. (2003). Perception, unconscious. In L. Nadel (Ed.), *Encyclopedia of cognitive science, Vol. 3*, pp. 517–526. London, England: Nature Publishing Group.

Sodian, B., Zaitchik, D., & Carey, S. (1991). Young children's differentiation of hypothetical beliefs from evidence. *Child Development, 62*(4), 753–766.

Solso, R., & McCarthy, J. E. (1981). Prototype formation of faces: A case of pseudomemory. *British Journal of Psychology, 72*, 499–503.

Sommer, R. (1969). *Personal space.* Englewood Cliffs, NJ: Prentice-Hall.

Spear, N. E. (1979). Experimental analysis of infantile amnesia. In J. E. Kihlstrom & F. J. Evans (Eds.), *Functional disorders of memory.* Hillsdale, NJ: Erlbaum.

Spearman, C. (1927). *The abilities of man.* New York: Macmillan.

Spear-Swerling, L., & Sternberg, R. J. (1996). *Off-track: When poor readers become learning disabled.* Boulder, CO: Westview.

Spelke, E., Hirst, W., & Neisser, U. (1976). Skills of divided attention. *Cognition, 4*, 215–230.

Spellman, B. A. (1997). Crediting causality. *Journal of Experimental Psychology: General, 126*, 1–26.

Sperling, G. (1960). The information available in brief visual presentations. *Psychological Monographs: General and Applied, 74*, 1–28.

Sperry, R. W. (1964). The great cerebral commissure. *Scientific American, 210*(1), 42–52.

Squire, L. (1999). Memory, human neuropsychology. In R. A. Wilson & F. C. Keil (Eds.), *The MIT encyclopedia of the cognitive sciences* (pp. 521–522). Cambridge, MA: MIT Press.

Squire, L. R. (1982). The neuropsychology of human memory. *Annual Review of Neuroscience, 5*, 241–273.

Squire, L. R. (1986). Mechanisms of memory. *Science, 232*(4578), 1612–1619.

Squire, L. R. (1987). *Memory and the brain.* New York: Oxford University Press.

Squire, L. R. (1992). Memory and the hippocampus: A synthesis of findings with rats, monkeys, and humans. *Psychological Review, 99*, 195–231.

Squire, L. R. (1993). The organization of declarative and nondeclarative memory. In T. Ono, L. R. Squire, M. E. Raichle, D. I. Perrett, & M. Fukuda (Eds.), *Brain mechanisms of perception and memory: From neuron to behavior* (pp. 219–227). New York: Oxford University Press.

Squire, L. R., & Knowlton, B. J. (2000). The medial temporal lobe, the hippocampus, and the memory systems of the brain. In M.

Gazzaniga (Ed.), *The new cognitive neurosciences* (2nd ed., pp. 765–780). Cambridge, MA: MIT Press.

Squire, L. R., & Zola-Morgan, S. (1991). The medial temporal lobe memory system. *Science, 253*, 1380–1386.

Squire, L. R., Cohen, N. J., & Nadel, L. (1984). The medial temporal region and memory consolidations: A new hypothesis. In H. Weingardner & E. Parker (Eds.), *Memory consolidation*. Hillsdale, NJ: Erlbaum.

Squire, L. R., Knowlton, B. J., & Musen, G. (1993). The structure and organization of memory. *Annual Review of Psychology, 44*, 453–495.

Squire, L. R., Zola-Morgan, S., Cave, C. B., Haist, F., Musen, G., & Suzuki, W. P. (1990). Memory: Organization of brain systems and cognition. In D. E. Meyer & S. Kornblum (Eds.), *Attention and performance: Vol. 14. Synergies in experimental psychology, artificial intelligence, and cognitive neuroscience* (pp. 393–424). Cambridge, MA: MIT Press.

Staller, A., Sloman, S. A., & Ben-Zeev, T. (2000). Perspective effects in non-deontic version of the Wason selection task. *Memory and Cognition, 28*, 396–405.

Stanciewicz, B. J. (2003). Perceptual systems: The visual model. In L. Nadel (Ed.), *Encyclopedia of cognitive science, Vol. 3*, pp. 552-560. London, England: Nature Publishing Group.

Standing, L., Conezio, J., & Haber, R. N. (1970). Perception and memory for pictures: Single-trial learning of 2500 visual stimuli. *Psychonomic Science, 19*, 73–74.

Stankov, L. (2005). Reductionism versus charting. In R. J. Sternberg & J. E. Pretz (Eds.), *Cognition and intelligence* (pp. 51–67). New York: Cambridge University Press.

Stanovich, K. E. (1981). Attentional and automatic context effects in reading. In A. M. Lesgold & C. A. Perfetti (Eds.), *Interactive processes in reading* (pp. 241–267). Hillsdale, NJ: Erlbaum.

Stanovich, K. E. (2003). The fundamental computational biases of human cognition: Heuristics that (sometimes) impair decision making and problem solving. In J. E. Davidson & R. J. Sternberg (Eds.), *The psychology of problem solving* (pp. 291–342). New York: Cambridge University Press.

Stanovich, K. E., Sái, W. C., & West, R. F. (2004). Individual differences in thinking, reasoning, and decision making. In J. P. Leighton & R. J. Sternberg (Eds.), *The nature of reasoning* (pp. 375–409). New York: Cambridge University Press.

Starr, M S., & Rayner, K. (2003). Language comprehension, methodologies for studying. In L. Nadel (Ed.), *Encyclopedia of cognitive science, Vol. 2*, pp. 730–736. London, England: Nature Group Press.

Steedman, M. (2003). Language, connectionist and symbolic representations of. In L. Nadel (Ed.), *Encyclopedia of cognitive science, Vol. 2*, pp. 765–771. London, England: Nature Group Press.

Steele, C. (1990, May). A conversation with Claude Steele. *APS Observer*, pp. 11–17.

Steffanaci, L. (1999). Amygdala, primate. In R. A. Wilson & F. C. Keil (Eds.), *The MIT encyclopedia of the cognitive sciences* (pp. 15–17). Cambridge, MA: MIT Press.

Stenning, K., & Monaghan, P. (2004). Strategies and knowledge representation. In J. P. Leighton & R. J. Sternberg (Eds.), *The nature of reasoning* (pp.129–168). New York: Cambridge University Press.

Steriade, M., Jones, E. G., & McCormick, D. A. (1997). *Thalamus, organization and function* (Vol. 1). New York: Elsevier.

Stern, D. (1977). *The first relationship: Mother and infant*. Cambridge, MA: Harvard University Press.

Stern, W. (1912). *Psychologische Methoden der Intelligenz-Prüfung*. Leipzig, Germany: Barth.

Sternberg, R. J. (1977). *Intelligence, information processing, and analogical reasoning: The componential analysis of human abilities*. Hillsdale, NJ: Erlbaum.

Sternberg, R. J. (1979, September). Beyond IQ: Stalking the IQ quark. *Psychology Today*, pp. 42–54.

Sternberg, R. J. (1980). Representation and process in linear syllogistic reasoning. *Journal of Experimental Psychology: General, 109*, 119–159.

Sternberg, R. J. (1981). Intelligence and nonentrenchment. *Journal of Educational Psychology, 73*, 1–16.

Sternberg, R. J. (1983). Components of human intelligence. *Cognition, 15*, 1–48.

Sternberg, R. J. (1985a). *Beyond IQ: A triarchic theory of human intelligence*. New York: Cambridge University Press.

Sternberg, R. J. (1985b). Implicit theories of intelligence, creativity, and wisdom. *Journal of Personality and Social Psychology, 49*, 607–627.

Sternberg, R. J. (1986). *Intelligence applied: Understanding and increasing your intellectual skills*. San Diego, CA: Harcourt Brace Jovanovich.

Sternberg, R. J. (1987a). Most vocabulary is learned from context. In M. McKeown (Ed.), *The nature of vocabulary acquisition* (pp. 89–105). Hillsdale, NJ: Erlbaum.

Sternberg, R. J. (1987b). Teaching intelligence: The application of cognitive psychology to the improvement of intellectual skills. In J. B. Baron & R. J. Sternberg (Eds.), *Teaching thinking skills: Theory and practice* (pp. 182–218). New York: W. H. Freeman.

Sternberg, R. J. (1988). *The triarchic mind*. New York: Viking.

Sternberg, R. J. (1995). For whom the bell curve tolls: A review of *The Bell Curve. Psychological Science, 6*, 257-261.

Sternberg, R. J. (1996a). Costs of expertise. In K. A. Ericsson (Ed.), *The road to excellence* (pp. 347–355). Mahwah, NJ: Erlbaum.

Sternberg, R. J. (1996b). Myths, countermyths, and truths about human intelligence. *Educational Researcher, 25*(2), 11–16.

Sternberg, R. J. (1997). *Successful intelligence*. New York: Simon & Schuster.

Sternberg, R. J. (1998). Abilities are forms of developing expertise. *Educational Researcher, 27*(3), 11–20.

Sternberg, R. J. (1999). A dialectical basis for understanding the study of cognition. In R. J. Sternberg (Ed.), *The nature of cognition* (pp. 51–78). Cambridge, MA: MIT Press.

Sternberg, R. J. (2000). Thinking: An overview. In A. Kazdin (Ed.), *Encyclopedia of psychology* (Vol. 8, pp. 68–71). Washington, DC: American Psychological Association.

Sternberg, R. J. (2004a). Culture and intelligence. *American Psychologist, 59*, 325–338.

Sternberg, R. J. (2004b). What do we know about the nature of reasoning? In J. P. Leighton & R. J. Sternberg (Eds.), *The nature of reasoning* (pp. 443–455). New York: Cambridge University Press.

Sternberg, R. J. (Ed.). (1982). *Handbook of human intelligence*. New York: Cambridge University Press.

Sternberg, R. J. (Ed.). (1984). *Human abilities: An information-processing approach*. San Francisco: Freeman.

Sternberg, R. J. (Ed.). (1990). *Wisdom: Its nature, origins, and development*. New York: Cambridge University Press.

Sternberg, R. J., & Detterman, D. K. (Eds.). (1986). *What is intelligence? Contemporary viewpoints on its nature and definition*. Norwood, NJ: Ablex.

Sternberg, R. J., & Grigorenko, E. L. (1997, Fall). The cognitive costs of physical and mental ill health: Applying the psychology of the developed world to the problems of the developing world. *Eye on Psi Chi, 2*(1), 20–27.

Sternberg, R. J., & Grigorenko, E. L. (1999). *Our labeled children: What every parent and teacher needs to know about learning disabilities*. Somerville, MA: Perseus.

Sternberg, R. J., & Grigorenko, E. L. (Eds.) (2002a). *Intelligence applied* (2nd ed.). New York: Oxford University Press.

Sternberg, R. J., & Grigorenko, E. L. (Eds.) (2002b). *The general factor of intelligence: How general is it?* Mahwah, NJ: Erlbaum.

Sternberg, R. J., & Kaufman, J. C. (1998). Human abilities. *Annual Review of Psychology, 49*, 479–502.

Sternberg, R. J., & Kaufman, J. L. (1996). Innovation and intelligence testing: The curious case of the dog that didn't bark. *European Journal of Psychological Assessment, 12*, 175–182.

Sternberg, R. J., & Lubart, T. I. (1991). An investment theory of creativity and its development. *Human Development, 34*, 1–31.

Sternberg, R. J., & Lubart, T. I. (1993). Investing in creativity. *Psychological Inquiry, 4*(3), 229–232.

Sternberg, R. J., & Lubart, T. I. (1995). *Defying the crowd*. New York: Free Press.

Sternberg, R. J., & Lubart, T. I. (1996). Investing in creativity. *American Psychologist, 51*, 677–688.

Sternberg, R. J., & Nigro, G. (1980). Developmental patterns in the solution of verbal analogies. *Child Development, 51*, 27–38.

Sternberg, R. J., & Nigro, G. (1983). Interaction and analogy in the comprehension and appreciation of metaphors. *Quarterly Journal of Experimental Psychology, 35A*, 17–38.

Sternberg, R. J., & Powell, J. S. (1983). Comprehending verbal comprehension. *American Psychologist, 38*, 878–893.

Sternberg, R. J., & Ruzgis, P. (Eds.). (1994). *Personality and intelligence*. New York: Cambridge University Press.

Sternberg, R. J., & Spear-Swerling, L. (Eds.) (1999). *Perspectives on learning disabilities*. Boulder, CO: Westview.

Sternberg, R. J., & Wagner, R. K. (1982, July). Automization failure in learning disabilities. *Topics in Learning and Learning Disabilities, 2*, 1–11.

Sternberg, R. J., & Wagner, R. K. (Eds.). (1994). *Mind in context: Interactionist perspectives on human intelligence*. New York: Cambridge University Press.

Sternberg, R. J., & Weil, E. M. (1980). An aptitude–strategy interaction in linear syllogistic reasoning. *Journal of Educational Psychology, 72*, 226–234.

Sternberg, R. J., Ferrari, M., Clinkenbeard, P. R., & Grigorenko, E. L. (1996). Identification, instruction, and assessment of gifted children: A construct validation of a triarchic model. *Gifted Child Quarterly, 40*, 129–137.

Sternberg, R. J., Forsythe, G. B., Hedlund, J., Horvath, J., Snook, S., Williams, W. M., et al. (2000). *Practical intelligence in everyday life*. New York: Cambridge University Press.

Sternberg, R. J., Grigorenko, E. L., & Oh, S. (2001). The development of intelligence at midlife. In M. E. Lachman (Ed.), *Handbook of midlife development* (pp. 217–247). New York: Wiley.

Sternberg, R. J., Grigorenko, E. L., Ferrari, M., & Clinkenbeard, P. (1999). A triarchic analysis of an aptitude-treatment interaction. *European Journal of Psychological Assessment, 15*, 1–11.

Sternberg, R. J., Kaufman, J. C., & Pretz, J. E. (2001). The propulsion model of creative contributions applied to the arts and letters. *Journal of Creative Behavior, 35*, 75–101.

Sternberg, R. J., Kaufman, J. C., & Pretz, J. E. (2002). *The creativity conundrum: A propulsion model of kinds of creative contributions*. New York: Psychology Press.

Sternberg, R. J., Nokes, K., Geissler, P. W., Price, R. , Okatcha, F., Bundy, D. A., et al. (2001). The relationship between academic and practical intelligence: A case study in Kenya. *Intelligence, 29*, 401–418.

Sternberg, R. J., Okagaki, L., & Jackson, A. (1990). Practical intelligence for success in school. *Educational Leadership, 48*, 35–39.

Sternberg, R. J., Powell, C., McGrane, P. A., & McGregor, S. (1997). Effects of a parasitic infection on cognitive functioning. *Journal of Experimental Psychology: Applied, 3*, 67–76.

Sternberg, R. J., Torff, B., & Grigorenko, E. L. (1998). Teaching for successful intelligence raises school achievement. *Phi Delta Kappan, 79*(9), 667–669.

Sternberg, S. (1966). High-speed memory scanning in human memory. *Science, 153*, 652–654.

Sternberg, S. (1969). Memory-scanning: Mental processes revealed by reaction-time experiments. *American Scientist, 4*, 421–457.

Stevens, A., & Coupe, P. (1978). Distortions in judged spatial relations. *Cognitive Psychology, 10*, 422–437.

Stevens, K. N., & Blumstein, S. E. (1981). The search for invariant acoustic correlates of phonetic features. In P. K. Eimas & J. L. Miller (Eds.), *Perspectives on the study of speech* (pp. 1–38). Hillsdale: Erlbaum.

Stevenson, R. J. (1993). *Language, thought, and representation*. New York: Wiley.

Stiles, J., Bates, E. A., Thal, D., Trauner, D., & Reilly, J. (1998). Linguistic, cognitive, and affective development in children with pre- and perinatal focal brain injury: A ten-year overview from the San Diego longitudinal project. In C. Rovee-Collier, L. Lipsitt, & H. Hayne (Eds.), *Advances in infancy research* (Vol. 12, pp. 131–164). Stamford, CT: Ablex.

Strayer, D. L., & Johnston, W. A. (2001). Driven to distraction: Dual-task studies of simulated driving and conversing on a cellular telephone. *Psychological Science,12*, 462–466.

Stromswold, K. (1998). The genetics of spoken language disorders. *Human Biology, 70*, 297–324.

Stromswold, K. (2000). The cognitive neuroscience of language acquisition. In M. Gazzaniga (Ed.), *The new cognitive neurosciences* (2nd ed., pp. 909–932). Cambridge, MA: MIT Press.

Stroop, J. R. (1935). Studies of interference in serial verbal reactions. *Journal of Experimental Psychology, 18*, 624–643.

Stuss, D. T., & Floden, D. (2003). Frontal cortex. In L. Nadel (Ed.), *Encyclopedia of cognitive science, Vol. 2*, pp. 163–169. London, England: Nature Publishing Group.

Stuss, D. T., Shallice, T., Alexander, M. P., & Picton, T. W. (1995). A multidisciplinary approach to anterior attention functions. In J. Grafman, K. J. Holyoak, & F. Boller (Eds.), *Structure and functions of the human prefrontal cortex*. New York: New York Academy of Sciences.

Suh, S., & Trabasso, T. (1993). Inferences during reading: Converging evidence from discourse analysis, talk-aloud protocols, and recognition priming. *Journal of Memory and Language, 32*, 279–300.

Sun, R. (2003). Connectionist implementation and hybrid systems. In L. Nadel (Ed.), *Encyclopedia of cognitive science, Vol. 1*, pp. 697–703. London, England: Nature Publishing Group.

Sutton, J. (2003). Memory, philosophical issues about. In L. Nadel (Ed.), *Encyclopedia of cognitive science, Vol. 2*, pp. 1109-1113. London, England: Nature Publishing Group.

Swanson, J. M., Volkow, N. D., Newcorn, J., Casey, B. J., Moyzis, R., Grandy, D., & Posner, M. (2003). Attention deficit hyperactivity disorder. In L. Nadel (Ed.), *Encyclopedia of cognitive science, Vol. 1*, pp. 226–231. London, England: Nature Publishing Group.

Takano, Y., & Okubo, M. (2003). Mental rotation. In L. Nadel (Ed.), *Encyclopedia of cognitive science* (Vol. 3, pp. 7–10). London, England: Nature Publishing Group.

Tanaka, J. W., & Taylor, M. (1991). Object categories and expertise: Is the basic level in the eye of the beholder? *Cognitive Psychology, 23*, 457–482.

Tannen, D. (1986). *That's not what I meant! How conversational style makes or breaks relationships*. New York: Ballantine.

Tannen, D. (1990). *You just don't understand: Women and men in conversation*. New York: Ballantine.

Tannen, D. (1994). *Talking from 9 to 5: How women's and men's conversational styles affect who gets heard, who gets credit, and what gets done at work*. New York: Morrow.

Tannen, D. (2001). *I only say this because I love you: How the way we talk can make or break family relationships throughout our lives*. New York: Random House.

Tardif, T. (1996). Nouns are not always learned before verbs: Evidence from Mandarin speakers' early vocabularies. *Developmental Psychology, 32*, 492–504.

Tardif, T., Shatz, M., & Naigles, L. (1997). Caregiver speech and children's use of nouns versus verbs: A comparison of English, Italian, and Mandarin. *Journal of Child Language, 24*, 535–565.

Tarr, M. (1999). Mental rotation. In R. A. Wilson & F. C. Keil (Eds.), *The MIT encyclopedia of the cognitive sciences* (pp. 531–533). Cambridge, MA: MIT Press.

Tarr, M. J. (1995). Rotating objects to recognize them: a case study on the role of viewpoint dependency in the recognition of three-dimensional objects. *Psychonomic Bulletin and Review, 2*, 55–82.

Tarr, M. J. (2000). Pattern recognition. In A. Kazdin (Ed.), *Encyclopedia of psychology, Vol. 6*, pp. 66–71). Washington, DC: American Psychological Association.

Tarr, M. J., & Bülthoff, H. H. (1995). Is human object recognition better described by geon structural descriptions or by multiple views? Comment on Biederman and Gerhardstein (1993). *Journal of Experimental Psychology: Human Perception and Performance, 21*, 1494–1505.

Tarr, M. J., & Bülthoff, H. H. (1998). Image-based object recognition in man, monkey, and machine. *Cognition, 67*, 1–20.

Taylor, H., & Tversky, B. (1992a). Descriptions and depictions of environments. *Memory & Cognition, 20*(5), 483–496.

Taylor, H., & Tversky, B. (1992b). Spatial mental models derived from survey and route descriptions. *Journal of Memory & Language, 31*(2), 261–292.

Terman, L. M., & Merrill, M. A. (1937). *Measuring intelligence*. Boston: Houghton Mifflin.

Terman, L. M., & Merrill, M. A. (1973). *Stanford–Binet Intelligence Scale: Manual for the third revision*. Boston: Houghton Mifflin.

Thagard, P. (1995). *Mind: Introduction to cognitive science*. Cambridge, MA: MIT Press.

Thagard, P. (1999). Induction. In R. A. Wilson & F. C. Keil (Eds.), *The MIT encyclopedia of the cognitive sciences* (pp. 399–400). Cambridge, MA: MIT Press.

Thagard, P. (2003). Conceptual change. In L. Nadel (Ed.), *Encyclopedia of cognitive science, Vol. 1*, pp. 666–670). London, England: Nature Publishing Group.

The anatomy of a head injury. (http://www.ahs.uwaterloo.ca/~cahr/headfall.html, retrieved 12/29/04).

Theeuwes, J. (1992). Perceptual selectivity for color and form. *Perception & Psychophysics, 51*(6), 599–606.

Thomas, J. C., Jr. (1974). An analysis of behavior in the hobbits–orcs problem. *Cognitive Psychology, 6*, 257–269.

Thomas, N. J. T. (2003). Mental imagery, philosphical issues about. In L. Nadel (Ed.), *Encyclopedia of cognitive science* (Vol. 2, pp. 1147–1153). London, England: Nature Publishing Group.

Thompson, R. B. (1999). Gender differences in preschoolers' help–eliciting communication. *The Journal of Genetic Psychology, 160*, 357–368.

Thompson, R. F. (1987). The cerebellum and memory storage: A response to Bloedel. *Science, 238*, 1729–1730.

Thompson, R. F. (2000). Memory: Brain systems. In A. E. Kazdin (Ed.), *Encyclopedia of psychology* (Vol. 5, pp. 175–178). Washington, DC: American Psychological Association.

Thompson, R. F., & Krupa, D. J. (1994). Organization of memory traces in the mammalian brain. *Annual Review of Neuroscience, 17*, 519–549.

Thorndike, E. L. (1905). *The elements of psychology*. New York: Seiler.

Thorndike, R. L., Hagen, E. P., & Sattler, J. M. (1986). *Stanford–Binet Intelligence Scale: Guide for administering and scoring the fourth edition*. Chicago: Riverside.

Thorndyke, P. W. (1981). Distance estimation from cognitive maps. *Cognitive Psychology, 13*, 526–550.

Thorndyke, P. W. (1984). Applications of schema theory in cognitive research. In J. R. Anderson & S. M. Kosslyn (Eds.), *Tutorials in learning and memory* (pp. 167–192). San Francisco: Freeman.

Thorndyke, P. W., & Hayes-Roth, B. (1982). Differences in spatial knowledge acquired from maps and navigation. *Cognitive Psychology, 14*, 580–589.

Thurstone, L. L. (1938). *Primary mental abilities*. Chicago: University of Chicago Press.

Thurstone, L. L., & Thurstone, T. G. (1962). *Tests of primary abilities* (Rev. ed.). Chicago: Science Research Associates.

Tolman, E. C. (1932). *Purposive behavior in animals and men*. New York: Appleton-Century-Crofts.

Tolman, E. C., & Honzik, C. H. (1930). "Insight" in rats. *University of California Publications in Psychology, 4*, 215–232.

Tomasello, M. (1999). *The cultural origins of human cognition*. Cambridge, MA: Harvard University Press.

Tomasello, M. (2001). *The cultural origins of human cognition*. Cambridge, MA: Harvard University Press.

Torff, B., & Sternberg, R. J. (2001). Intuitive conceptions among learners and teachers. In B. Torff & R. J. Sternberg (Eds.), *Understanding and teaching the intuitive mind: Student and teacher learning (pp. 3–26). Mahwah, NJ: Erlbaum.

Torgesen, J. K. (1997). The prevention and remediation of reading disabilities: Evaluating what we know from research. *Journal of Academic Language Therapy, 1*, 11–47.

Torrance, E. P. (1974). *The Torrance tests of creative thinking: Technical-norms manual*. Bensenville, IL: Scholastic Testing Services.

Torrance, E. P. (1984). *Torrance tests of creative thinking: Streamlined (revised) manual, Figural A and B*. Bensenville, IL: Scholastic Testing Services.

Tourangeau, R., & Sternberg, R. J. (1981). Aptness in metaphor. *Cognitive Psychology, 13*, 27–55.

Tourangeau, R., & Sternberg, R. J. (1982). Understanding and appreciating metaphors. *Cognition, 11*, 203–244.

Townsend, J. T. (1971). A note on the identifiability of parallel and serial processes. *Perception and Psychophysics, 10*, 161–163.

Trabasso, T., & Suh, S. (1993). Understanding text: achieving explanatory coherence through on-line inferences and mental operations in working memory. *Discourse Processes, 16,* 3–34.

Treadway, M., McCloskey, M., Gordon, B., & Cohen, N. J. (1992). Landmark life events and the organization of memory: Evidence from functional retrograde amnesia. In S. A. Christianson (Ed.), *The handbook of emotion and memory: Research and theory* (pp. 389–410). Hillsdale, NJ: Erlbaum.

Treisman, A. M. (1960). Contextual cues in selective listening. *Quarterly Journal of Experimental Psychology, 12,* 242–248.

Treisman, A. M. (1964a). Monitoring and storage of irrelevant messages in selective attention. *Journal of Verbal Learning and Verbal Behavior, 3,* 449–459.

Treisman, A. M. (1964b). Selective attention in man. *British Medical Bulletin, 20,* 12–16.

Treisman, A. M. (1986). Features and objects in visual processing. *Scientific American, 255*(5), 114B–125.

Treisman, A. M. (1990). Visual coding of features and objects: Some evidence from behavioral studies. In National Research Council (Ed.), *Advances in the modularity of vision: Selections from a symposium on frontiers of visual science* (pp. 39–61). Washington, DC: National Academy Press.

Treisman, A. M. (1991). Search, similarity, and integration of features between and within dimensions. *Journal of Experimental Psychology: Human Perception & Performance, 17,* 652–676.

Treisman, A. M. (1992). Perceiving and re-perceiving objects. *American Psychologist, 47,* 862–875.

Treisman, A. M. (1993). The perception of features and objects. In A. Baddeley & C. L. Weiskrantz (Eds.), *Attention: Selection, awareness, and control* (pp. 5–35). Oxford: Clarenden.

Treisman, A. M., & Sato, S. (1990). Conjunction search revisited. *Journal of Experimental Psychology: Human Perception and Performance, 16,* 459–478.

Treisman, A. M., & Schmidt, H. (1982). Illusory conjunctions in the perception of objects. *Cognitive Psychology, 14*(1), 107–141.

Treue, S., & Maunsell, J. H. R. (1996). Attentional modulation of visual motion processing in cortical areas MT and MST. *Nature, 382,* 539–541.

Tsushima, T., Takizawa, O., Saski, M., Siraki, S., Nishi, K., Kohno, M., et al. (1994). Discrimination of English /r-l/ and w-y/ by Japanese infants at 6–12 months: Language specific developmental changes in speech perception abilities. Paper presented at International Conference on Spoken Language Processing, 4. Yokohama, Japan.

Tulving, E. (1962). Subjective organization in free recall of "unrelated" words. *Psychological Review, 69,* 344–354.

Tulving, E. (1972). Episodic and semantic memory. In E. Tulving & W. Donaldson (Eds.), *Organization of memory.* New York: Academic Press.

Tulving, E. (1983). *Elements of episodic memory.* New York: Oxford University Press.

Tulving, E. (1984). Precis: Elements of episodic memory. *Behavioral and Brain Sciences, 7,* 223–268.

Tulving, E. (1985). How many memory systems are there? *American Psychologist, 40*(4), 385–398.

Tulving, E. (1986). What kind of a hypothesis is the distinction between episodic and semantic memory? *Journal of Experimental Psychology: Learning, Memory, & Cognition, 12*(2), 307–311.

Tulving, E. (1989, July/August). Remembering and knowing the past. *American Scientist, 77,* 361–367.

Tulving, E. (2000a). Concepts of memory. In E. Tulving & F. I. M. Craik (Eds.), *The Oxford handbook of memory* (pp. 33–44). New York: Oxford University Press.

Tulving, E. (2000b). Memory: An overview. In A. E. Kazdin (Ed.), *Encyclopedia of psychology* (Vol. 5, pp. 161–162). Washington, DC: American Psychological Association.

Tulving, E., & Craik, F. I. M. (Eds.) (2000). *The Oxford handbook of memory.* New York: Oxford University Press.

Tulving, E., & Pearlstone, Z. (1966). Availability versus accessibility of information in memory for words. *Journal of Verbal Learning and Verbal Behavior, 5,* 381–391.

Tulving, E., & Schacter, D. L. (1994). *Memory systems 1994.* Cambridge, MA: MIT Press.

Tulving, E., & Thomson, D. M. (1973). Encoding specificity and retrieval processes in episodic memory. *Psychological Review, 80,* 352–373.

Tulving, E., Kapur, S., Craik, F. I.M., Moscovitch, M., & Houle, S. (1994). Hemispheric encoding/retrieval asymmetry in episodic memory: Positron emission tomography findings. *Proceedings of the National Academy of Sciences, 91,* 2016–2020.

Tulving, E., Schacter, D. L., & Stark, H. A. (1982). Priming effects in word-fragment completion are independent of recognition memory. *Journal of Experimental Psychology: Learning, Memory, & Cognition, 8*(4), 336–342.

Turing, A. (1950). Computing machinery and intelligence. *Mind, 59,* 433–460.

Turing, A. M. (1963). Computing machinery and intelligence. In E. A. Feigenbaum & J. Feldman (Eds.), *Computers and thought.* New York: McGraw-Hill.

Turner, M. L., & Engle, R. W. (1989). Is working-memory capacity task dependent? *Journal of Memory and Language, 28,* 127–154.

Turtle, J., & Yuille, J. (1994). Lost but not forgotten details: Repeated eyewitness recall leads to reminiscence but not hypermnesia. *Journal of Applied Psychology, 79,* 260–271.

Turvey, M. T. (2003). Perception: The ecological approach. In L. Nadel (Ed.), *Encyclopedia of cognitive science, Vol. 3,* pp. 538–541. London, England: Nature Publishing Group.

Tversky, A. (1972a). Choice by elimination. *Journal of Mathematical Psychology, 9*(4), 341–367.

Tversky, A. (1972b). Elimination by aspects: A theory of choice. *Psychological Review, 79,* 281–299.

Tversky, A., & Kahneman, D. (1971). Belief in the law of small numbers. *Psychological Bulletin, 76*(2), 105–110.

Tversky, A., & Kahneman, D. (1973). Availability: A heuristic for judging frequency and probability. *Cognitive Psychology, 5,* 207–232.

Tversky, A., & Kahneman, D. (1974). Judgment under uncertainty: Heuristics and biases. *Science, 185,* 1124–1131.

Tversky, A., & Kahneman, D. (1981). The framing of decisions and the psychology of choice. *Science, 211,* 453–458.

Tversky, A., & Kahneman, D. (1983). Extensional versus intuitive reasoning: The conjunction fallacy in probability judgment. *Psychological Review, 90*(4), 293–315.

Tversky, A., & Kahneman, D. (1993). Belief in the law of small numbers. In G. Keren & C. Lewis (Eds.), *A handbook for data analysis in the behavioral sciences: Methodological issues* (pp. 341–349). Hillsdale, NJ: Erlbaum.

Tversky, B. (1981). Distortions in memory for maps. *Cognitive Psychology, 13*(3), 407–433.

Tversky, B. (1991). Distortions in memory for visual displays. In S. R. Ellis, M. Kaiser, & A. Grunewald (Eds.), *Spatial instruments and spatial displays* (pp. 61–75). Hillsdale, NJ: Erlbaum.

Tversky, B. (2000). Mental models. In A. E. Kazdin (Ed.), *Encyclopedia of psychology* (Vol. 5, pp. 191–193). Washington, DC: American Psychological Association.

Tversky, B., & Schiano, D. J. (1989). Perceptual and conceptual factors in distortions in memory for graphs and maps. *Journal of Experimental Psychology: General, 118*, 387–398.

Tye, M. (1995). *Ten problems of consciousness: A representational theory of the phenomenal mind.* Cambridge, MA: MIT Press.

Ugurbil, K. (1999). Magnetic resonance imaging. In R. A. Wilson & F. C. Keil (Eds.), *The MIT encyclopedia of the cognitive sciences* (pp. 505–507). Cambridge, MA: MIT Press.

Underwood, B. J. (1957). Interference and forgetting. *Psychological Review, 64*, 49–60.

Ungerleider, L. G. (1995). Functional brain imaging studies of cortical mechanisms for memory. *Science, 270*, 760–775.

Unsworth, N., Schrock, J. C., & Engle, R. W. (2004). Working memory capacity and the antisaccade task: Individual differences in voluntary saccade control. *Journal of Experimental Psychology: Learning, Memory, and Cognition, 30*, 1302–1321

Usher, J. A., & Neisser, U. (1993). Childhood amnesia and the beginnings of memory for four early life events. *Journal of Experimental Psychology: General, 122*(2), 155–165.

van Daalen-Kapteijns, M., & Elshout-Mohr, M. (1981). The acquisition of word meanings as a cognitive learning process. *Journal of Verbal Learning & Verbal Behavior, 20*(4), 386–399.

Van der Heijden, A. H. C. (1992). *Selective attention in vision.* London: Routledge.

van Dijk, T. A. (1975). Formal semantics of metaphorical discourse. *Poetics, 4*, 173–198.

Van Selst, M., & Jolicoeur, P. (1994). Can mental rotation occur before the dual-task bottleneck? *Journal of Experimental Psychology: Human Perception and Performance, 20*, 905–921.

VanLehn, K. (1989). Problem solving and cognitive skill acquisition. In M. I. Posner (Ed.), *Foundations of cognitive science* (pp. 526–579). Cambridge, MA: MIT Press.

VanLehn, K. (1990). *Mind bugs: The origins of procedural misconceptions.* Cambridge, MA: MIT Press.

Vellutino, F. R., Scanlon, D. M., Sipay, E., Small, S., Pratt, A., Chen, R., et al. (1996). Cognitive profiles of difficult-to-remediate and readily remediated poor readers: Early intervention as a vehicle for distinguishing between cognitive and experiential deficits as basic causes of specific reading disability. *Journal of Educational Psychology, 88*, 601–638.

Velmans, M. (Ed.) (1996). *Science of consciousness: Psychological, neuropsychological, and clinical reviews.* London: Routledge.

Vernon, P. A., & Mori, M. (1992). Intelligence, reaction times, and peripheral nerve conduction velocity. *Intelligence, 16*(3–4), 273–288.

Vernon, P. A., Wickett, J. C., Bazana, P. G., & Stelmack, R. M. (2000). The neuropsychology and psychophysiology of human intelligence. In R. J. Sternberg (Ed.), *Handbook of intelligence* (pp. 245–264). New York: Cambridge University Press.

Vernon, P. E. (1971). *The structure of human abilities.* London: Methuen.

Vicente, K. J., & DeGroot, A. D. (1990). The memory recall paradigm: straightening out the historical record. *American Psychologist, 45*, 285–287.

Visual disabilities: *Color-blindness.* (http://www.webaim.org/techniques/visual/colorblind, retrieved 12/28/04).

Vogel, E. K., Woodman, G. F., & Luck, S. J. (2001). Storage of features, conjunctions, and objects in visual working memory. *Journal of Experimental Psychology: Human Perception and Performance, 27*, 92–114.

Vollmeyer, R., Burns, B. D., & Holyoak, K. J. (1996). The impact of goal specificity on strategy use and the acquisition of problem structure. *Cognitive Science, 20*, 75–100.

Von Eckardt, B. (1993). *What is cognitive science?* Cambridge, MA: MIT Press.

Von Eckardt, B. (1999). Mental representation. In R. A. Wilson & F. C. Keil (Eds.), *The MIT encyclopedia of the cognitive sciences* (pp. 527–529). Cambridge, MA: MIT Press.

Vygotsky, L. S. (1986). *Thought and language.* Cambridge, MA: MIT Press.

Wagenaar, W. (1986). My memory: A study of autobiographic memory over the past six years. *Cognitive Psychology, 18*, 225–252.

Wagner, A. R., & Rescorla, R. A. (1972). Inhibition in Pavlovian conditioning: Application of a theory. In R. A. Boakes & M. S. Halliday (Eds.), *Inhibition and learning.* New York: Academic Press.

Wagner, D. A. (1978). Memories of Morocco: The influence of age, schooling, and environment on memory. *Cognitive Psychology, 10*, 1–28.

Wagner, R. K. (2000). Practical intelligence. In R. J. Sternberg (Ed.,), *Practical intelligence in everyday life.* New York: Cambridge University Press.

Wagner, R. K., & Stanovich, K. E. (1996). Expertise in reading. In K. A. Ericsson (Ed.), *The road to excellence* (pp. 159–227). Mahwah, NJ: Erlbaum.

Wahlsten, D., & Gottlieb, G. (1997). The invalid separation of effects of nature and nurture: Lessons from animal experimentation. In R. J. Sternberg & E. L. Grigorenko (Eds.), *Intelligence, heredity, and environment* (pp. 163–192). New York: Cambridge University Press.

Warner, J. Rubbernecking distracts more than phone. (http://content.health.msn.com/content/article/62/71477.htm, retrieved 8/11/04).

Warren, R. M. (1970). Perceptual restoration of missing speech sounds. *Science, 167*, 392–393.

Warren, R. M., & Warren, R. P. (1970). Auditory illusions and confusions. *Scientific American, 223*, 30–36.

Warren, R. M., Obusek, C. J., Farmer, R. M., & Warren, R. P. (1969). Auditory sequence: Confusion of patterns other than speech or music. *Science, 164*, 586–587.

Warrington, E. (1982). The double dissociation of short- and long-term memory deficits. In L. S. Cermak (Ed.), *Human memory and amnesia.* Hillsdale, NJ: Erlbaum.

Warrington, E., & Shallice, T. (1972). Neuropsychological evidence of visual storage in short-term memory tasks. *Quarterly Journal of Experimental Psychology, 24*(1), 30–40.

Warrington, E., & Shallice, T. (1984). Category specific semantic impairments. *Brain, 107*, 829–853.

Warrington, E., & Weiskrantz, L. (1970). Amnesic syndrome: Consolidation or retrieval? *Nature, 228*(5272), 628–630.

Wason, P., & Johnson-Laird, P. (1970). A conflict between selecting and evaluating information in an inferential task. *British Journal of Psychology, 61*(4), 509–515.

Wason, P. C. (1968). Reasoning about a rule. *Quarterly Journal of Experimental Psychology, 20*(3), 273–281.

Wason, P. C. (1969). Regression in reasoning? *British Journal of Psychology, 60*(4), 471–480.

Wason, P. C. (1983). Realism and rationality in the selection task. In J. St. B. T. Evans (Ed.), *Thinking and reasoning: Psychological approaches* (pp. 44–75). Boston: Routledge & Kegan Paul.

Wason, P. C., & Johnson-Laird, P. N. (1972). *Psychology of reasoning: Structure and content.* London: B. T. Batsford.

Wasow, T. (1989). Grammatical theory. In M. I. Posner (Ed.), *Foundations of cognitive science* (pp. 208–243). Cambridge, MA: MIT Press.

Wasserman, D., Lempert, R. O., & Hastie, R. (1991). Hindsight and causality. *Personality & Social Psychology Bulletin, 17*(1), 30–35.

Waters, G. S., & Caplan, D. (2003). Language comprehension and verbal working memory. In L. Nadel (Ed.), *Encyclopedia of cognitive science, Vol. 2,* pp. 726–730. London, England: Nature Group Press.

Watkins, M. J., & Tulving, E. (1975). Episodic memory: When recognition fails. *Journal of Experimental Psychology: General, 104,* 5–29.

Watson, O. M. (1970). *Proxemic behavior: A cross-cultural study.* The Hague, Netherlands: Mouton.

Wattenmaker, W. D. (1995). Knowledge structures and linear separability: integrating information in object and social categorization. *Cognitive Psychology, 28,* 274–328.

Waugh, N. C., & Norman, D. A. (1965). Primary memory. *Psychological Review, 72,* 89–104.

Weaver, C. A. (1993). Do you need a "flash" to form a flashbulb memory? *Journal of Experimental Psychology: General, 122*(1), 39–46.

Wegner, D. M. (1997a). When the antidote is the poison: Ironic mental control processses. *Psychological Science, 8,* 148–153.

Wegner, D. M. (1997b). Why the mind wanders. In J. D Cohen & J. W. Schooler (Eds.), *Scientific approaches to consciousness* (pp. 295–315). Mahwah, NJ: Erlbaum.

Wegner, D. M. (2002). *The illusion of conscious will.* Cambridge, MA: Bradford Books.

Weingartner, H., Rudorfer, M. V., Buchsbaum, M. S., & Linnoila, M. (1983). Effects of serotonin on memory impairments produced by ethanol. *Science, 221,* 442–473.

Weisberg, R. W. (1986). *Creativity: Genius and other myths.* New York: Freeman.

Weisberg, R. W. (1988). Problem solving and creativity. In R. J. Sternberg (Ed.), *The nature of creativity* (pp. 148–176). New York: Cambridge University Press.

Weisberg, R. W. (1995). Prolegomena to theories of insight in problem solving: A taxonomy of problems. In R. J. Sternberg & J. E. Davidson (Eds.), *The nature of insight* (pp. 157–196). Cambridge, MA: MIT Press.

Weisberg, R. W. (1999). Creativity and knowledge: A challenge to theories. In R. J. Sternberg (Ed.), *Handbook of creativity* (pp. 226–250). New York: Cambridge University Press.

Weiskrantz, L. (1994). Blindsight. In M. W. Eysenck (Ed.), *The Blackwell dictionary of cognitive psychology.* Cambridge, MA: Blackwell.

Weisstein, N., & Harris, C. S. (1974). Visual detection of line segments: An object-superiority effect. *Science, 186,* 752–755.

Weizenbaum, J. (1966). ELIZA-A computer program for the study of natural language communication between man and machine. *Communications of the Association for Computing Machinery, 9,* 36–45.

Wellman, H. M., & Gelman, S. A. (1998). Knowledge acquisition in foundational domains. In W. Damon (Ed.-in-Chief), D. Kuhn, &

R. S. Siegler (Vol. Eds.), *Handbook of child psychology: Vol. 2. Cognitive development* (pp. 523–573). New York: Wiley.

Wells, G. L. (1993). What do we know about eyewitness identification? *American Psychologist, 48,* 553–571.

Wells, G. L., & Loftus, E. G. (1984). *Eyewitness testimony: Psychological perspectives.* New York: Cambridge University press.

Wells, G. L., Luus, C. A. E., & Windschitl, P. D. (1994). Maximizing the utility of eyewitness identification evidence. *Current Directions in Psychological Science, 6,* 194–197.

Welsh, M. C., Satterlee-Cartmell, T., & Stine, M. (1999). Towers of Hanoi and London: Contribution of working memory and inhibition to performance. *Brain & Cognition, 41,* 231–242.

Wenke, D., & Frensch, P. A. (2003). Is success or failure at solving complex problems related to intellectual ability? In J. E. Davidson & R. J. Sternberg (Eds.), *The psychology of problem solving* (pp. 87–126). New York: Cambridge University Press.

Wenke, D., Frensch, P. A., & Funke, J. (2005). Complex problem solving and intelligence. In R. J. Sternberg & J. E. Pretz (Eds.), *Cognition and intelligence* (pp. 160–187). New York: Cambridge University Press.

Werker, J. F. (1989). Becoming a native listener. *American Scientist, 77,* 54–59.

Werker, J. F. (1994). Cross-language speed perception: developmental change does not involve loss. In J. C. Goodman & H. L. Nusbaum (Eds.), *The development of speech perception: The transition from speech sounds to spoken words* (pp. 93–120). Cambridge, MA: MIT Press.

Werker, J. F., & Tees, R. L. (1984). Cross-language speech perception: evidence for perceptual reorganization during the first year of life. *Infant Behavior and Development, 7,* 49–63.

Werner, H., & Kaplan, B. (1952). The acquisition of word meanings: A developmental study. *Monographs of the Society for Research in Child Development,* No. 51.

Wertheimer, M. (1959). *Productive thinking* (Rev. ed.). New York: Harper & Row. (Original work published 1945)

West, R. L. (1986). Everyday memory and aging. *Developmental Neuropsychology, 2*(4), 323–344.

Wexler, K. (1996). The development of inflection in a biologically based theory of language acquisition. In M. L. Rice (Ed.), *Toward a genetics of language* (pp. 113–144). Mahwah, NJ: Erlbaum.

What you need to know about brain tumors (http://www.cancer.gov/cancertopics/wyntk/brain, retrieved 12/29/04.)

Wheeldon, L. R., Meyer, A. S., & Smith, M. (2003). Language production, incremental. In L. Nadel (Ed.), *Encyclopedia of cognitive science, Vol. 2,* pp. 760-764. London, England: Nature Group Press.

Wheeler, D. D. (1970). Processes in word recognition. *Cognitive Psychology, 1,* 59–85.

Whitten, S., & Graesser, A. C. (2003). Comprehension of text in problem solving. In J. E. Davidson & R. J. Sternberg (Eds.), *The psychology of problem solving* (pp. 207–229). New York: Cambridge University Press.

Whorf, B. L. (1956). In J. B. Carroll (Ed.), *Language, thought and reality: Selected writings of Benjamin Lee Whorf.* Cambridge, MA: MIT Press.

Wickens, D. D., Dalezman, R. E., & Eggemeier, F. T. (1976). Multiple encoding of word attributes in memory. *Memory & Cognition, 4*(3), 307–310.

Wickett, J. C., & Vernon, P. (1994). Peripheral nerve conduction velocity, reaction time, and intelligence: An attempt to replicate Vernon and Mori. *Intelligence, 18,* 127–132.

Williams, M. (1970). *Brain damage and the mind*. London: Penguin.

Williams, R. N. (2000). Epistemology. In A. E. Kazdin (Ed.), *Encyclopedia of psychology* (Vol. 3, pp. 225–232). Washington, DC: American Psychological Association.

Williams, W. M., & Sternberg, R. J. (1988). Group intelligence: Why some groups are better than others. *Intelligence, 12*, 351–377.

Willis, S. L. (1985). Towards an educational psychology of the older adult learner: Intellectual and cognitive bases. In J. E. Birren & K. W. Schaie (Eds.), *Handbook of the psychology of aging* (2nd ed.). New York: Van Nostrand Reinhold.

Wilson, B. A. (2003). Brain damage, treatment and recovery from. In L. Nadel (Ed.), *Encyclopedia of cognitive science, Vol. 1,* pp. 410–416. London, England: Nature Publishing Group.

Wilson, M. A., & McNaughton, B. L. (1994). Reactivation of hippocampal ensemble memories during sleep. *Science, 265*, 676–679.

Wilson, T. D. (2002). *Strangers to ourselves: Discovering the adaptive unconscious*. Cambridge, MA: Belknap.

Winograd, T. (1972). *Understanding natural language*. New York: Academic Press.

Wisniewski, E. J. (1997). When concepts combine. *Psychonomic Bulletin and Review, 4*, 167–183.

Wisniewski, E. J. (2000). Concepts: Combinations. In A. E. Kazdin (Ed.), *Encyclopedia of psychology* (Vol. 2, pp. 251-253). Washington, DC: American Psychological Association

Wisniewski, E. J., & Medin, D. L. (1994). On the interaction of theory and data in concept learning. *Cognitive Science, 18*, 221–281.

Wissler, C. (1901). The correlation of mental and physical tests. *Psychological Review, Monograph Supplement 3(6)*.

Witelson, S. F., Kigar, D. L., & Walter, A. (2003). Cerebral commissures. In L. Nadel (Ed.), *Encyclopedia of cognitive science, Vol. 1,* pp. 476–485. London, England: Nature Publishing Group.

Wittgenstein, L. (1953). *Philosophical investigations*. New York: Macmillan.

Wolfe, J. M. (1994). Guided search 2.0: A revised model of visual search. *Psychonomic Bulletin & Review, 1*, 202–238.

Wolkowitz, O. M., Tinklenberg, J. R., & Weingartner, H. (1985). A psychopharmacological perspective of cognitive functions: II. Specific pharmacologic agents. *Neuropsychobiology, 14(3)*, 133–156.

Woodward, A. L., & Markman. E. M. (1998). Early word learning. In D. Kuhn & R. S. Siegler (Eds.), *Handbook of child psychology: Vol. 2, Cognition, perception, and language* (5th ed., pp. 371–420). New York: Wiley.

Woodworth, R. S., & Sells, S. B. (1935). An atmosphere effect in formal syllogistic reasoning. *Journal of Experimental Psychology, 18*, 451–460.

Xu, F., & Carey, S. (1995). Do children's first object names map onto adult-like conceptual representations? In D. MacLaughlin & S. McEwen (Eds.), *Proceedings of the 19th Annual Boston University Conference on Language Development* (pp. 679–688). Somerville, MA: Cascadilla Press.

Xu, F., & Carey, S. (1996). Infants' metaphysics: The case of numerical identity. *Cognitive Psychology, 30*, 111–153.

Yamauchi, T., & Markman. A. B. (1998). Category learning by inference and classification. *Journal of Memory and Language, 39*, 124–148.

Yang, S. Y., & Sternberg, R. J. (1997). Taiwanese Chinese people's conceptions of intelligence. *Intelligence, 25*, 21–36.

Yantis, S. (1993). Stimulus-driven attentional capture. *Current Directions in Psychological Science, 2(5)*, 156–161.

Young, A. W. (2003). Prosopagnosia. In L. Nadel (Ed.), *Encyclopedia of cognitive science, Vol. 3*, pp. 768–771. London, England: Nature Publishing Group.

Yu, V. L., Fagan, L. M., Bennet, S. W., Clancey, W. J., Scott, A. C., Hannigan, J. F., Blum, R. L., Buchanan, B. G., & Cohen, S. N. (1984). An evaluation of MYCIN's advice. In B. G. Buchanan & E. H. Shortliffe (Eds.), *Rule-based expert systems*. Reading, MA: Addison-Wesley.

Yuille, J. C. (1993). We must study forensic eyewitnesses to know about them. *American Psychologist, 48(5)*, 572–573.

Zaidel, E. (1983). A response to Gazzaniga: Language in the right hemisphere, convergent perspectives. *American Psychologist, 38(5)*, 542–546.

Zaragoza, M. S., McCloskey, M., & Jamis, M. (1987). Misleading postevent information and recall of the original event: Further evidence against the memory impairment hypothesis. *Journal of Experimental Psychology: Learning, Memory, & Cognition, 13(1)*, 36–44.

Zeidner, M. (1990). Perceptions of ethnic group modal intelligence scores: Reflections of cultural stereotypes or intelligence test scores? *Journal of Cross-Cultural Psychology, 21*, 214–231.

Zigler, E., & Berman, W. (1983). Discerning the future of early childhood intervention. *American Psychologist, 38*, 894–906.

Zihl, J., von Cramon, D., & Mai, N. (1983). Selective disturbance of movement vision after bilateral brain damage. *Brain, 106*, 313–340.

Zimmerman, B. J., & Campillo, M. (2003). Motivating self-regulated problem solvers. In J. E. Davidson & R. J. Sternberg (Eds.), *The psychology of problem solving* (pp. 233–262). New York: Cambridge University Press.

Zinchenko, P. I. (1962). *Neproizvol'noe azpominanie* [Involuntary memory] (pp. 172–207). Moscow: USSR APN RSFSR.

Zinchenko, P. I. (1981). Involuntary memory and the goal-directed nature of activity. In J. V. Wertsch, *The concept of activity in Soviet psychology*. Armonk, NY: Sharpe.

Zipser, K. Lamme, V. A. F., & Schiller, P. H. (1996). Contextual modulation in primary visual cortex. *Journal of Neuroscience, 16*, 7376–7389.

Zola, S. M., & Squire, L. R. (2000). The medial temporal lobe and the hippocampus. In E. Tulving & F. I. M. Craik (Eds.), *The Oxford handbook of memory* (pp. 485–500). New York: Oxford University Press.

Zola-Morgan, S. M., & Squire, L. R. (1990). The primate hippocampal formation: Evidence for a time-limited role in memory storage. *Science, 250*, 228–290.

Zurif, E. B. (1990). Language and the brain. In D. N. Osherson & H. Lasnik (Eds.), *Language* (pp. 177–198). Cambridge, MA: MIT Press.

Zurif, E. B. (1995). Brain regions of relevance to syntactic processing. In L. R. Gleitman & M. Liberman (Eds.), *Language: An invitation to cognitive science* (Vol. 1, 2nd ed., pp. 381–398). Cambridge, MA: MIT Press.

Zwaan, R. A., & Radvansky, G. A. (1998). Situation models in language comprehension and memory. *Psychological Bulletin, 123*, 62–185.

Zwaan, R. A., Magliano, J. P., & Graesser, A. C. (1995). Dimensions of situation model construction in narrative comprehension. *Journal of Experimental Psychology: Learning, Memory, and Cognition, 21*, 386–397.

Name Index

Subject Index

藤井樹